# NTC's COMPACT ENGLISH DICTIONARY

## THE CORE VOCABULARY FOR LEARNERS

EDITOR-IN-CHIEF

RICHARD A. SPEARS, PH.D.

*NTC Publishing Group*

**Library of Congress Cataloging-in-Publication Data**

Spears, Richard A.
NTC's compact English dictionary / Richard A. Spears.
p. cm.
ISBN 0-8442-0107-3
1. English language—Dictionaries. I. Title: Compact English dictionary. II. Title.

PE1628 .S58263 2000
423—dc21 00-21655

## Editorial Staff

*Editor-in-Chief*
Richard A. Spears

*Associate Editors*
Nancy L. Dray
Michelle Davidson

*Copy Editor*
Karen Schenkenfelder

Cover design by Nick Panos
Interior design by Terry Stone

Published by NTC Publishing Group
A division of NTC/Contemporary Publishing Group, Inc.
4255 West Touhy Avenue, Lincolnwood (Chicago), Illinois 60712-1975 U.S.A.

Printed in the United States of America
International Standard Book Number: 0-8442-0107-3
01 02 03 04 05 LB 18 17 16 15 14 13 12 11 10 9 8 7 6 5 4 3 2

# Contents

# Introduction

*NTC's Compact English Dictionary* is for persons who are seeking to improve their ability to speak, read, write, and understand American English. It is a simplified dictionary in that it focuses on basic vocabulary presented in a clear and uncomplicated format and uses a minimum of codes, abbreviations, and typographical devices.

Learners at all skill levels approach dictionaries with a wide variety of needs. This dictionary defines words using the smallest possible vocabulary, but when it is necessary, additional words are used to define difficult concepts. In many cases, more than one definition is given, so the learner has additional help in figuring out the meaning of a word or expression. In a few instances, these definitions use words that are not defined in the dictionary.

Every full entry contains at least one full-sentence example that demonstrates the typical use of the entry word in context. Users will often rely on the examples more than the definitions to figure out the precise meaning of a specific sense of a word. By using the dictionary in this way, learners will develop the ability to acquire vocabulary from its use in everyday English, which is a vital skill if one is to advance in language learning and develop a vocabulary equal to that of a native speaker.

Special attention has been paid to those elements of English that learners find most difficult, including pronunciation, the use of the plural, and irregular forms. Irregular forms appear as main entries, with pronunciation guides and a cross-reference to the full noun, verb, adjective, or adverb entry.

# How to Use This Dictionary

Many of the entry words in the dictionary have more than one sense. *Please study all the relevant senses* to make sure you have found the right one.

Nouns that do not follow the regular spelling rules in the formation of the plural are marked *irreg.*, and the form of the plural is given in the entry. Verbs that do not follow the regular rules for the formation of the past tense and past participle are marked *irreg.*, and the proper forms are given in the entry. The comparative and superlative forms of adjectives and adverbs are listed when there are forms—as with *red, redder, reddest*—that replace, or that exist in addition to, the comparatives and superlatives formed with *more* and *most.* After many of the definitions, you will find comments—enclosed in parentheses—containing further information about the entry word.

You will often find it informative to consult the examples before reading the definitions. In many instances, the linguistic context available in the example sentences will provide valuable clues to the understanding of the word or sense that you are consulting. Keep in mind that the goal in using a monolingual learner's dictionary is not only to find the meanings of specific words, but also to develop the skills needed to acquire new words and senses of words from their actual use in context.

# About This Dictionary

There are essentially six parts to an entry: entry word, pronunciation guide, part of speech, definition, comments, and the example. When a main entry has more than one sense, the pronunciation guide is not repeated for each numbered sense unless one or more of the senses is pronounced differently. In that case, every numbered sense is provided with a pronunciation guide. Where a word has one or more irregular forms, such as an irregular past tense or past participle for a verb, those forms are listed as a comment for the first or only sense of the word and are not repeated for each of the senses. Each sense with irregular forms is marked *irreg.*, however.

Main entries and words or expressions that are the equivalent of main entries are in **boldface sans-serif type**. Entry words that are cited or referred to in the text are in lighter sans-serif type. Putting a word in lighter sans-serif type carries with it the suggestion that the user would benefit from consulting the word that is printed in this way. Other words or phrases that are cited are placed in *italic type*. Putting a word in italic type does not carry with it the suggestion that the user consult the word. Examples are preceded by the symbol □ and are in *italic type*. Examples showing nouns that are *plural only when referring to different kinds, types, instances, or varieties* begin with 🄲. Examples showing the transposed adverb in phrasal verbs begin with 🅃.

The parts of speech used here are *transitive verb*, *intransitive verb*, *adjectival*, *nominal*, *adverb*, *conjunction*, *preposition*, *article*, and *pronoun*. Other labels are also used: *idiom*, *phrase*, *interrogative*, *interjection*, *prefix*, *suffix*, *infinitive*, *auxiliary verb*, and *contraction*. Phrasal verbs are labeled as transitive or intransitive verbs plus adverbs, e.g., *iv. + adv.* Verbs that take a prepositional phrase are labeled as transitive or intransitive verbs plus prepositional phrases, e.g., *iv. + prep. phr.* Patterns of this type are listed as separate senses of the verb.

The word *something* is used in entry phrases and definitions to refer to any thing or object. The word *someone* is used to refer to any person. Sometimes *some creature* is used to emphasize that a thing can include a living creature other than a human. Great care has been taken to indicate which English transitive verbs take *someone* or *something* or both as an object. *One* is used in entries, definitions, and examples to refer to a hypothetical person or hypothetical persons whose sex is irrelevant. Generic expressions such as *someone or something* are found in a different typeface (someone or something) when they are part of an entry head. The pronouns *they*, *them*, and *their* are used only with plural antecedents.

Material enclosed in square brackets, [like this], is often included to clarify or limit a definition. This material is not part of the definition, but it is essential to understanding it. Some definitions are enclosed in angled brackets, <like this>. These brackets are used to enclose definitions that describe the entry word instead of providing an equivalent for it.

A numeral enclosed in a circle, like ① or ②, is a sense number. When a number in a circle follows a word in lighter sans-serif type, as in word ③, it refers to the specific numbered sense of the word in lighter sans-serif type. That is, word ③ means the third sense of the entry **word**. A number in a circle with no word in lighter sans-serif type preceding it refers to a numbered sense within the same entry.

Comments about a word or sense are contained in parentheses and follow the definition of the word or sense. Parentheses are also used to enclose material that is optional. In ['kæb (ə) nət], the [ə] is optional—that is, the word can be pronounced ['kæb ə nət] or ['kæb nət].

# Useful Spelling Rules

The following basic spelling rules equip the learner to create and identify the most important derived and inflected forms of regular English nouns and verbs. Words that have important irregular forms that do not follow these rules are identified in the dictionary.

## Regular verb forms

*Note:* Many verbs that have irregular past-tense forms or irregular past participles nevertheless form the present tense and the present participle regularly.

**For the third-person singular (the form used with *he*, *she*, *it*, and singular nouns) in the present tense:**

- Add *-s* to the bare verb. (If the bare verb ends in *y* preceded by a consonant, change *y* to *ie* and then add *-s*. If the bare verb ends in *s*, *z*, *x*, *ch*, or *sh*, add *-es*.)

  *like > Bill likes*
  *cry > the baby cries*
  *walk > Anne walks*
  *buy > the man buys*
  *carry > a truck carries*
  *fix > she fixes*
  *pass > it passes*
  *notify > he notifies*
  *catch > she catches*

**For the past tense and the past participle:**

- Add *-ed* to the bare verb. (If the bare verb ends in *y* preceded by a consonant, change *y* to *i* before adding *-ed*. If the bare verb ends in *e*, just add *-d*.)

  *walk > walked*
  *like > liked*
  *judge > judged*
  *try > tried*
  *carry > carried*
  *measure > measured*

**For the present participle:**

- Add *-ing* to the bare verb. (If the bare verb ends in a single *e* preceded either by a consonant or by *u*, drop the *e* before adding *-ing*. If the bare verb ends in *ie*, change *ie* to *y* before adding *-ing*.)

  *judge > judging*
  *take > taking*
  *ask > asking*
  *carry > carrying*
  *pay > paying*
  *pursue > pursuing*
  *hoe > hoeing*
  *see > seeing*
  *go > going*
  *lie > lying*

**Doubling of consonants in participles and past-tense forms:**

- When *-ed* or *-ing* is added to a word that ends in a consonant (other than *h*, *w*, *x*, or *y*) preceded by a single vowel and the final syllable is stressed, then the consonant is normally doubled. Thus *commit* and *control*, which are accented on the last syllable, become *committed* and *controlling*, but *limit* and *cancel*, which are accented on the first syllable, become *limited* and *canceling*. Similarly, *stop* becomes *stopping*, but *look*, in which the consonant is preceded by two vowels, becomes *looking*.

- Within the dictionary, forms that do not follow these doubling rules are noted or illustrated in individual entries. The most typical exceptions to the doubling rules are words with a final *c* that becomes *ck* rather than doubling, e.g., *picnicking*, verbs that are compounds, and verbs with closely related noun senses or more than one pronunciation. Outside the dictionary, learners will encounter other exceptions, as well as some variation, because sometimes another option, although less familiar in American English, is also correct.

## Regular noun plurals

**To form the plural of a regular noun:**

- If the singular ends in *s*, *z*, *x*, *ch*, or *sh*, add *-es*.

  *kiss > kisses*
  *box > boxes*
  *match > matches*
  *dish > dishes*
  *bus > buses*

- If the singular ends in *y* preceded by a consonant, change *y* to *ie* and then add *-s*.

  *baby > babies*
  *library > libraries*
  *university > universities*
  *butterfly > butterflies*

- For nouns ending in *o*, the regular plural may be formed by adding *-es* or by adding *-s*. For some words, both spellings are possible. In this dictionary, each entry for a noun ending in *o* specifies the correct plural form or forms for that word.

  *radio > radios*
  *potato > potatoes*
  *tornado > tornados* or *tornadoes*

- For all other regular nouns, add *-s* to the singular to form the plural.

  *table > tables*
  *boy > boys*
  *television > televisions*
  *valley > valleys*

## *An Important Note on the English Plural*

The English plural is something that makes English very difficult for adults to learn. English nouns often cannot be made plural, unlike their counterparts in other languages. There is nothing that sounds more "non-English" than *advice*, *information*, or *baggage* with the plural *s* on the end. There are many American English nouns in this dictionary that the learner should not attempt to make plural—ever! See a list of these nouns in List A on page xii. In addition, there are many nouns in English that can be followed by the plural *s* that seem to be plural, but really refer to kinds or types of the noun in question. In the following entry, when the word *margarine* has an *s* on the end, it refers to different kinds, types, or varieties of margarine. The example with the *C* in the box marks this special kind of plural.

> **margarine** ['mɑr dʒə rɪn] *n.* a food made from animal or vegetable fats, used in place of butter; a spread for bread. (Plural only when referring to different kinds, types, instances, or varieties.) □ *I spread margarine on my toast.* 🄲 *Margarines vary greatly in taste and fat content.*

There are many American English nouns that can take the plural *s* when referring to different kinds, types, instances, or varieties of the noun. See them in List B on page xv.

# Important Lists of Words

These are important lists of words that can be consulted quickly. For further information, definitions, and examples, each word should be looked up in this dictionary.

## List A

Nouns defined in this dictionary that never take the plural *s*. See the entry heads listed for details.

admiration
advice
anybody
anyone
anything
applause
appreciation
arctic
arrogance
assistance
attendance
aviation
awe
baggage
bathwater
blackness
bliss
bloodshed
bookkeeping
bowling
bulk
carelessness
cash
Catholicism
cattle
Centigrade
chaos
chatter
chess
citizenship
clothing
common sense
confusion
consent
conservation
contempt
courage
cowardice
cream cheese
dark
darkness
daybreak
daylight
decay
destruction
devout
digestion
diplomacy
dirt
disgust
dishwater
distress
distrust
drainage
dust
ease
east
electricity
elegance
employment
endurance
equipment
esteem
estimation
evidence
excellence
Fahrenheit
fame
few
filth
flesh
former
freight
frostbite
fun
furniture
fuzz
glamour
gloom
golf
gratitude
greed
grief
grime
ground beef
guilt
happiness
health
hockey
homework
housework
hypnotism

ill will
importance
independence
indigestion
information
insurance
intelligence
interference
isolation
jazz
jet propulsion
jewelry
knowledge
laughter
law of gravity
leakage
left
legislation
leisure
lighting
lightning
likelihood
lint
literacy
livestock
logic
loot
luck
luggage
machinery
magic
magnetism
maintenance
malice
mankind
math
mayonnaise
menstruation
merchandise

Midwest
might
mirth
misconduct
mistrust
moderation
moisture
molasses
moonlight
morale
morality
more
most
motherhood
much
mucus
nausea
needlework
neglect
nightlife
nonsense
north
northeast
northwest
nothing
now
nutrition
obedience
occult
offspring
old age
ooze
opposition
outer space
overkill
overtime
ownership
oxygen
ozone

pantyhose
paradise
parcel post
parsley
participation
patience
peace
pep
perfection
perjury
personnel
persuasion
petroleum
photography
pity
plenty
plumbing
poetry
police
poor
pork
postage
poultry
poverty
precision
preservation
prevention
prey
produce
progress
propaganda
prose
prosperity
prudence
psychiatry
psychology
publicity
punctuation
quickness

quiet
racism
ransom
rapidity
readiness
real estate
realism
reasoning
recklessness
recognition
recreation
redness
refuse
rejoicing
relief
research
revenge
ridicule
rot
rubbish
rudeness
running
rust
sadness
safekeeping
safety
salt water
sameness
sanitation
sanity
sarcasm
say
scenery
schoolwork
science
scrutiny
scuba
seafood
seaside

seclusion
secrecy
segregation
self-confidence
self-control
self-discipline
self-esteem
self-respect
self-service
selfishness
senility
seniority
serenity
seriousness
several
severity
sewage
sewing
sexual intercourse
shame
shelving
shipping
shopping
shrewdness
shrubbery
shyness
sightseeing
significance
silence
silver
silverware
simplicity
sincerity
sizzle
skepticism
skiing
slander
slavery
sleep
sleet
slime
slow motion
slush
small talk
smuggling
soccer
social security
software
some
something
sorcery
south
southeast
southwest
spaghetti
spinach
starvation
static
stationery
storage
strife
stuff
stupidity
sunlight
sunshine
supervision
surf
suspense
tact
teamwork
tennis
terrorism
thunder
tourism
traction
traffic
transportation
trash
twilight
underclothing
underwear
undoing
unrest
upkeep
uranium
valor
vanilla
veal
vegetation
vigor
violence
vomit
warmth
wastepaper
wealth
wealthy
wear
weather
welfare
west
wetness
wilderness
willpower
wisdom
woodwork
worship
worth
wrath
wreckage
young
zeal
zest
zinc

## List B

Nouns defined in this dictionary that can take the plural *s* resulting in the meaning "kinds, types, instances, or varieties of." See the entry heads listed for details.

action
addition
adhesive
adhesive tape
adoption
adventure
agony
alcohol
amputation
appointment
architecture
ash
bacon
bait
ballet
bark
beer
behavior
bleach
blue
brass
bronze
broth
brown
butter
buzz
cake
cancer
candy
canvas
caramel
cardboard
cargo
cement
cereal
chalk
champagne
change
charcoal
charm
cheese
cherry
chocolate
choice
cider
clay
cleaner
cloth
coal
coffee
combination
comparison
concern
confession
conflict
conquest
contraction
conversation
copulation
cord
cork
cost
cotton
court
crime
cruelty
crystal
debt
defense
denial
depth
destiny
detention
dew
difference
difficulty
dip
disagreement
discipline
discomfort
disgrace
division
divorce
dough
duck
dynamite
elm
enjoyment
escape
evaluation
evil
examination
explanation
exposure
fabric
failure
fantasy
fashion
fat
fate
fear
feed
felt
fiber
fiction
film
fire
flight
flour
flu
foam
foil
food
force
friendship
frost
frosting
fruit
fur
future
gas
gasoline
gauze
glass
glue
gold
grain
grammar
grass
gravel
gravy
gray
green
gum
ham
harmony

honey
horror
hurt
identification
immersion
increase
indentation
infection
influence
injection
ink
inspection
intensity
irritation
ivy
jam
jelly
juice
ketchup
landscape
language
leather
length
liquor
lotion
loyalty
lubrication
luxury
marble
margarine
meal
meat
meatloaf
medicine
membership
mesh
metal
meter
mileage
misfortune
mold
mortar
moss
motion
mousse
movement
mulch
mustard
mystery
mythology
noise
notepaper
novelty
number
oak
oil
opinion
orange
pain
paint
pardon
passion
pasta
paste
pastry
payment
pecan
pepper
performance
perfume
philosophy
pick
pie
pigment
pine
pink
pitch
pizza
plaster
plastic
pleasure
poison
polish
pollen
popcorn
poplar
posture
powder
power
prejudice
primer
privilege
prohibition
promotion
pronunciation
prophecy
protection
pudding
purple
quarantine
race
reality
rebellion
red
redwood
regularity
regulation
religion
repetition
resignation
responsibility
rhythm
rice
rope
routine
sacrifice
salt
sand
sandpaper
satin
satisfaction
sauce
scripture
seaweed
separation
shampoo
sherbet
shortening
silk
sin
skin
smell
soap
soil
soup
speculation
speed
stain
starch
stew
stock
stone
stool
stress
substitution
subtraction
success
sugar
sunblock
sunburn
sunscreen
syrup
tape
taste
tea
technology

tension
terror
theft
theology
theory
thread
tile
tissue
tobacco
toil
toothpaste
torment
tradition
translation
triumph
twine
use
utterance
vacation
vaccination
variation
variety
varnish
velocity
velvet
victory
volume
walnut
war
wax
whiskey
white
wine
wood
wool
worry
yeast
yellow

## List C

Nouns defined in this dictionary that have irregular or variable plurals. Plural variants are separated by "/". The asterisk "*" means there is a unique feature of pronunciation. See the entry heads listed for details.

aircraft, aircraft
antenna, antennas/antennae
aquarium, aquaria/aquariums
basis, bases
bath*
beaver
bookshelf, bookshelves
booth*
buffalo
cactus, cactuses/cacti
calf, calves
chairman, chairmen
child, children
cloth*
cod
courthouse*
craftsman, craftsmen
crisis, crises
deer
die, dice
doghouse*
dwarf, dwarves
elf, elves
elk
emphasis, emphases
fish
fisherman, fishermen
focus, focuses/foci
foot, feet
footpath*
formula, formulae/formulas
fowl
fungus, funguses/fungi
gentleman, gentlemen
goldfish*
goose, geese
grandchild, grandchildren
greenhouse*
half, halves
hippopotamus, hippopotamuses/hippopotami
hoof, hooves
house*
index, indexes/indices
knife, knives
leaf, leaves
life, lives
lighthouse*
loaf, loaves
man, men
medium, mediums/media
mink
moose
moth*
mouse, mice
mouth*
nucleus, nuclei
oasis, oases
oath*

octopus, octopuses/ octopi
ox, oxen
parenthesis, parentheses
path*
penthouse*
perch
policeman, policemen
policewoman, policewomen
radius, radiuses/ radii
rhinoceros, rhinoceros/ rhinoceroses
salesman, salesmen
salesperson, salespeople/ salespersons
saleswoman, saleswomen
salmon
scarf, scarves
schoolchild, schoolchildren
sheath*
sheep
shelf, shelves
shellfish
shrimp
sister-in-law, sisters-in-law
snowman, snowmen
sole
sportsman, sportsmen
thief, thieves
tooth, teeth
tree
house*
trout
tuna, tuna/tunas
warehouse*
washcloth*
wharf, wharves
wife, wives
wolf, wolves
woman, women
wreath*
yen
zebra, zebra/zebras

## List D

Transitive verbs defined in this dictionary that can take a clause beginning with *that* as an object. [As with *I know that you can do it!*] These verbs can also take other forms of direct object. See the entry heads listed for details.

accept
admit
advertise
advise
announce
answer
anticipate
appreciate
argue
ask
assume
believe
calculate
claim
confess
confirm
consider
decide
declare
demand
deny
determine
detest
discover
dream
establish
estimate
expect
explain
feel
find
foresee
forget
guarantee
guess
hear
imagine
indicate
know
learn
legislate
maintain
mention
murmur
note
notice
observe
ordain
parrot
petition
plead
pledge
preach
predict
prefer
prescribe
proclaim
profess
prophesy
propose

| | | | |
|---|---|---|---|
| protest | report | sense | think |
| prove | request | shout | threaten |
| realize | require | show | urge |
| recognize | resent | signal | vow |
| recommend | reveal | signify | wail |
| regret | say | state | whimper |
| relate | scream | stress | whine |
| remark | scribble | suggest | whisper |
| remember | see | suspect | wire |

## List E

Transitive verbs defined in this dictionary that have a clause beginning with *that* as an object. [As with *I agree that you should go.*] See the entry heads listed for details.

| | | | |
|---|---|---|---|
| agree | figure | judge | reply |
| believe | grant | move | respond |
| bet | guess | note | rule |
| brag | hint | observe | suppose |
| comment | hope | pray | trust |
| conclude | imagine | pretend | understand |
| exclaim | imply | promise | wager |
| fear | indicate | provide | wish |
| feel | joke | reason | worry |

## List F

Verbs (transitive or intransitive) defined in this dictionary that have one or more senses where the verb is followed by an infinitive. [As with *I agreed to do it.* and *I advised her to do it.*] See the entry heads listed for details.

advise *tv.*
afford *iv.*
agree *iv.*
aim *iv.*
allow *tv.*
attempt *iv.*
begin *iv.*
continue *iv.*
dare *iv./tv.*
desire *iv.*
expect *iv./tv.*
forget *iv.*
get *iv./tv.*
happen *iv.*
hate *iv.*
have *iv.*
instruct *tv.*
love *iv.*
manage *iv.*
mean *iv./tv.*
need *iv./tv.*
neglect *iv.*
oblige *tv.*
offer *iv.*
ought *iv.*
plan *iv.*
pledge *iv.*
plot *iv.*
prefer *iv.*
prepare *iv./tv.*
pretend *iv.*
promise *iv./tv.*
refuse *iv.*
seek *iv./tv.*
swear *iv.*
tend *iv.*
think *iv.*
threaten *iv.*
try *iv.*
urge *tv.*
want *iv./tv.*
wish *iv./tv.*

## List G

Verbs defined in this dictionary that have irregular past tenses or past participles. These are the principal parts of the verb. Commas separate the principal parts of the verbs. The present tense comes first, then the past, and then the past participle. Variants are separated by "/".

arise, arose, arisen
awake, awaked/awoke, awaked/awoke/awoken
babysit, babysat, babysat
bear, bore, borne/born
beat, beat, beat/beaten
become, became, become
begin, began, begun
bend, bent, bent
bet, bet, bet
bid, bid, bid
bind, bound, bound
bite, bit, bitten
bleed, bled, bled
blow, blew, blown
break, broke, broken
breed, bred, bred
bring, brought, brought
build, built, built
burn, burned/burnt, burned/burnt
burst, burst, burst
buy, bought, bought
catch, caught, caught
cut, cut, cut
deal, dealt, dealt
dig, dug, dug
dive, dived/dove, dived
do, did, done
draw, drew, drawn
dream, dreamed/dreamt, dreamed/dreamt
drink, drank, drunk
drive, drove, driven
dwell, dwelled/dwelt, dwelled/dwelt
eat, ate, eaten
fall, fell, fallen
feed, fed, fed
feel, felt, felt

fight, fought, fought
find, found, found
fit, fit/fitted, fit/fitted
flee, fled, fled
fly, flew, flown
forbid, forbad/forbade, forbidden
foresee, foresaw, foreseen
forget, forgot, forgotten
forgive, forgave, forgiven
freeze, froze, frozen
get, got, got/gotten
give, gave, given
go, went, gone
grind, ground, ground
grow, grew, grown
hang, hung, hung (hang, hanged, hanged)
have, had, had
hear, heard, heard
hide, hid, hidden
hit, hit, hit
hold, held, held
housebreak, housebroke, housebroken
hurt, hurt, hurt
input, input/inputted, input/inputted
keep, kept, kept
kneel, knelt/kneeled, knelt/kneeled
know, knew, known
lay, laid, laid
lead, led, led
leap, leaped/leapt, leaped/leapt
leave, left, left
lend, lent, lent
let, let, let
lie, lay, lain
lie, lied, lied
light, lighted/lit, lighted/lit
lose, lost, lost
make, made, made
mean, meant, meant
meet, met, met
mislay, mislaid, mislaid
mistake, mistook, mistaken
misunderstand, misunderstood, misunderstood
mow, mowed, mown
outgrow, outgrew, outgrown
overcome, overcame, overcome
overeat, overate, overeaten
oversee, oversaw, overseen
oversleep, overslept, overslept
overthrow, overthrew, overthrown
panic, panicked, panicked
pay, paid, paid
picnic, picnicked, picnicked
plead, pleaded/pled, pleaded/pled
prepay, prepaid, prepaid
proofread, proofread, proofread
prove, proved, proved/proven
put, put, put
quit, quit, quit
read, read, read
rebuild, rebuilt, rebuilt
redo, redid, redone
repay, repaid, repaid
retake, retook, retaken
rewind, rewound, rewound
rewrite, rewrote, rewritten
ride, rode, ridden
rid, rid, rid
ring, rang, rung
rise, rose, risen
run, ran, run
saw, sawed, sawed/sawn
say, said, said
see, saw, seen
seek, sought, sought
sell, sold, sold
send, sent, sent
set, set, set
sew, sewed, sewed/sewn
shake, shook, shaken
shave, shaved, shaved/shaven
shear, sheared, sheared/shorn
shed, shed, shed

shine, shined/shone, shined/shone
shoot, shot, shot
show, showed, showed/shown
shrink, shrank/shrunk, shrunk/shrunken
shut, shut, shut
sing, sang, sung
sink, sank, sunk
sit, sat, sat
slay, slew, slain
sleep, slept, slept
slide, slid, slid
sling, slung, slung
slit, slit, slit
sneak, sneaked/snuck, sneaked/snuck
sow, sowed, sowed/sown
speak, spoke, spoken
speed, sped, sped
spell, spelled/spelt, spelled/spelt
spend, spent, spent
spill, spilled/spilt, spilled/spilt
spin, spun, spun
spit, spit/spat, spit/spat
split, split, split
spread, spread, spread
spring, sprang/sprung, sprung
stand, stood, stood
steal, stole, stolen
stick, stuck, stuck
sting, stung, stung
stink, stank, stunk
strike, struck, struck
string, strung, strung
swear, swore, sworn
sweat, sweat/sweated, sweat/sweated
sweep, swept, swept
swell, swelled, swelled/swollen
swim, swam, swum
swing, swung, swung
take, took, taken
teach, taught, taught
tear, tore, torn (tear, teared, teared)
tell, told, told
think, thought, thought
thrive, thrived/throve, thrived/thriven
throw, threw, thrown
thrust, thrust, thrust
undergo, underwent, undergone
understand, understood, understood
undo, undid, undone
unwind, unwound, unwound
upset, upset, upset
wake, waked/woke, waked/woken
wear, wore, worn
weave, wove, woven
wed, wedded/wed, wedded/wed
weep, wept, wept
wet, wetted/wet, wetted/wet
wind, wound, wound
wind, winded, winded
win, won, won
withhold, withheld, withheld
withstand, withstood, withstood
write, wrote, written

## List H

Words defined in this dictionary having pronunciations that vary from sense to sense.

a
address
approximate
arithmetic
associate
bases
bow
close
combat
complex
concrete
conduct
conflict
construct
consummate
content
contest
contract
contrary
contrast
decrease
defect
desert
detail
digest
discharge
dove
entrance
estimate
excess
excuse
export
graduate
grease
house
impact
import
incline
increase
inside
lead
live
midday
minute
misuse
mobile
moderate
mouth
object
offense
offensive
overhead
overlap
overlook
overnight
perfect
perfume
permit
present
proceed
produce
progress
project
protest
read
rebel
rebound
recess
record
recount
refund
refuse
reject
replay
research
retake
rewrite
row
separate
sewer
sow
survey
suspect
tear
torment
upset
upstairs
use
used
why
wind
wound

# Pronunciation

The symbols of the International Phonetic Alphabet are used to show the pronunciation of the words in this dictionary. The speech represented here is that of educated people, but it is not formal or overly precise. It is more representative of the West and the middle of the country than of the East, South, or upper Midwest.

Pronunciation of American English is variable in different regions of the country, but most native speakers of American English can understand one another quite well.

The goal of the pronunciation scheme is to provide the student with one acceptable model of pronunciation for each entry. Where the numbered senses of an entry are all pronounced the same way, the phonetic representation follows the main entry word. In entries where *even one* of the numbered senses is pronounced differently from the rest, all the senses are provided with a phonetic representation.

Sounds represented here as [or] are often pronounced as [ɔr] in some parts of the East. Similarly, the sequence [ɛr] is often pronounced [ær] in parts of the East. One heavy stress is marked for each word. The dictionary user should expect to hear variation in the pronunciation of most of the words listed in this or any dictionary, but should remain confident that the model provided here is understood and accepted in all parts of the country.

The chart on the next page shows the symbols used here and what they correspond to in some simple English words.

| | | | |
|---|---|---|---|
| [ɑ] | st**o**p, t**o**p | [ʌ] | n**u**t, sh**u**t |
| [æ] | s**a**t, tr**a**ck | [ɝ] | b**ir**d, t**ur**tle |
| [ɑʊ] | c**ow**, n**ow** | [f] | **f**eel, i**f** |
| [ɑɪ] | b**i**te, m**y** | [g] | **g**et, fro**g** |
| [b] | **b**eet, **b**u**bb**le | [h] | **h**at, **wh**o |
| [d] | **d**ea**d**, bo**d**y | [i] | f**ee**t, l**ea**k |
| [ð] | **th**at, **th**ose | [ɪ] | b**i**t, h**i**ss |
| [dʒ] | **j**ail, **j**u**dg**e | [j] | **y**ellow, **y**ou |
| [e] | d**a**te, s**ai**l | [k] | **c**an, **k**eep |
| [ɛ] | g**e**t, s**e**t | [l] | **l**awn, ye**ll**ow |
| [ə] | **a**bove, **a**round | [m] | fa**m**ily, sla**m** |

| | | | |
|---|---|---|---|
| [n] | **n**ew, fu**nn**y | [θ] | **th**in, fai**th** |
| [ŋ] | bri**ng**, thi**ng** | [u] | f**oo**d, bl**ue** |
| [o] | c**oa**t, wr**o**te | [ʊ] | p**u**t, l**oo**k |
| [oɪ] | sp**oi**l, b**oy** | [v] | sa**v**e, **v**an |
| [ɔ] | c**au**ght, y**aw**n | [w] | **w**ell, **w**ind |
| [p] | ti**p**, **p**at | [ʍ] | **wh**eel, **wh**ile |
| [r] | **r**at, be**rr**y | [z] | fu**zz**y, **z**oo |
| [s] | **s**un, fa**s**t | [ʒ] | plea**s**ure, trea**s**ure |
| [ʃ] | fi**sh**, **s**ure | [ˈ] | ˈwater, hoˈtel |
| [t] | **t**op, po**t** | | |
| [tʃ] | **ch**eese, pi**tch**er | | |

# Terms and Abbreviations

①②③, etc., are sense numbers. When they follow a word in special type that looks like **this**, they refer to an entry word outside the entry in which they are used. When there is no word in special type, they refer to senses within the entry in which they are used. See page vii.

< >, [ ] See page vii.

☐ marks the beginning of a normal example.

[T] marks the beginning of an example that shows the alternative word order of a phrasal verb, i.e., the difference between **call something off** and **call off something.**

[C] marks the beginning of an example that shows a countable variety of a noun that can be both count and noncount, as indicated by the comment: *Plural only when referring to different kinds, types, instances, or varieties.*

**adj.** adjectival.

**adv.** adverb.

AND follows an entry word and introduces a related or variant form of the entry word.

**article** a small word, such as *a*, *an*, or *the*, that comes before a noun.

**aux.** auxiliary verb.

**colloquial** means that the word or phrase is primarily spoken or is used more often in a spoken style than in a written style.

**comp** comparative.

**conj.** conjunction.

**cont.** contraction.

**derogatory** refers to words that are insulting or disparaging to someone or something.

**euphemism** is a word or expression that seems to be more polite or less offensive than another possible word choice.

**fig. on** indicates which numbered sense a figurative word or expression is based on.

**formal** refers to vocabulary that appears most often in writing or in polite use among educated people.

**idiom** is a phrase or expression that must be interpreted in a special, nonliteral way.

**inf.** infinitive.

**interj.** interjection.

**interrog.** interrogative.

**irreg.** irregular; refers to nouns that have plural forms that do not follow the regular rules of plural formation or to verbs whose past tense and/or past participle forms do not follow the regular rules.

**iv.** intransitive verb.

**n.** nominal or noun.

**No plural form.** means that the noun in this sense is not normally counted when it has this meaning. Usually when it is possible to make such a noun plural, it has a different meaning; for example, it might mean a number of types of things rather than a number of things.

**not prenominal** refers to an adjective that does not occur before a noun.

**obj.** object.

**phr.** phrase.

**pl** plural.

**pp** past participle.

**prefix** is a form that has meaning and is attached to the beginnings of certain words.

**prenominal** refers to a word that comes before a noun.

**prenominal only** refers to an adjective that can only occur before a noun.

**prep.** preposition.

**prep. phr.** prepositional phrase.

**pron.** pronoun.

**pt** past tense.

**pt/pp** past tense and past participle.

**reflexive** refers to a verb that has the same subject and object, as in *Bob shaved himself every day.* where *Bob* and *himself* are the same person.

**see** means go to the entry word or numbered sense that follows the word see.

**see also** means to consider the meaning or form of the entry word that follows **see also**.

**short for** indicates a shortened or abbreviated form of a word or phrase.

**slang** refers to very informal vocabulary that is not normally used in writing except for special effects.

**suffix** is a form that has meaning and is attached to the ends of certain words.

**sup** superlative.

**taboo** to be avoided; not used in polite or decent discussions or writing.

**term of address** refers to a word or phrase that can be used as if it were someone's name.

**Treated as plural.** refers to a word that is treated as if it were plural even if its form is singular.

**Treated as singular.** refers to a word that is treated as if it were singular even if its form is plural.

**Treated as singular or plural.** refers to a word that can be treated as if it were singular or as if it were plural.

**tv.** transitive verb.

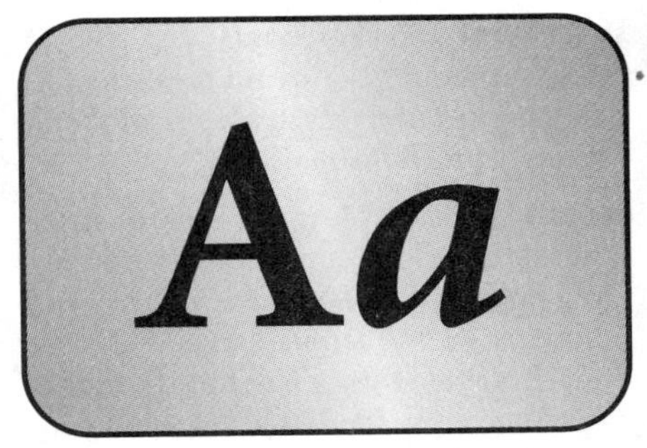

**a** **1. A** ['e] *n.* the first in a series; the highest grade. □ *John earned an A in each of his courses.* **2.** ['e, ə] *article* one; any. (See the note at **an**.) □ *Please give me a dollar.* **3.** ['e, ə] *prep.* each; every; per. (See the note at **an**.) □ *This apartment costs nine hundred dollars a month.*

**abandon** [ə 'bæn dən] *tv.* to leave someone or something and not return; to desert someone or something. □ *The cat abandoned its kittens.*

**abbreviation** [ə bri vi 'e ʃən] *n.* a shortened word or phrase that takes the place of a longer word or phrase. □ *The abbreviation of* North Dakota *is* N.D.

**ability** [ə 'bɪl ə ti] *n.* the power, capacity, or skill to do something. □ *Bob has the ability to swim across the lake.*

**able** ['e bəl] **1.** *adj.* skilled; well qualified; capable. (Adv: *ably.*) □ *Your able assistant can complete the project while you are on vacation.* **2. able to** do something *adj.* + *inf.* having the power or skill to do something. □ *Are you able to carry those bags by yourself?*

**about** [ə 'bɑʊt] **1.** *prep.* regarding someone or something; concerning someone or something; having to do with someone or something. □ *Did you hear the news about Jane?* **2.** *prep.* back and forth and here and there in a certain place. □ *Bill drove about town, looking for Jane's house.* **3.** *adv.* approximately; nearly. □ *Our dog is about 12 years old.* **4.** *adv.* almost; not quite. □ *Are you about done?* **5. about to** do something *phr.* almost ready to do something. □ *Bill was about to leave when the phone rang.*

**above** [ə 'bʌv] **1.** *prep.* over—but not touching—someone or something. □ *Put this painting above the other picture.* **2.** *prep.* greater than something; higher than something; more than something. □ *If the price is above $20, I don't want to buy it.* **3.** *adv.* [written about or presented] previously [in the same written work or on the same page]. □ *As shown above in Table 3, annual costs have been increasing.* **4.** *adv.* in or at a higher place; over. □ *Above, the sun was covered with dark clouds.* **5.** *adv.* of a greater amount or quantity. □ *If your score is 75 or above, you passed the test.*

**abroad** [ə 'brɔd] *adv.* in another country; overseas. □ *In her junior year, Jane studied abroad.*

**absence** ['æb səns] **1.** *n.* the quality of [someone's] not being present. (No plural form.) □ *Absence from the ones you love causes sadness.* **2.** *n.* a period of time when someone is not present; an instance of not being there. □ *How many absences does John have this month?* **3.** *n.* a lack; a deficiency. (No plural form.) □ *In the absence of evidence, the defendant will go free.*

**absent** ['æb sənt] **1.** *adj.* not present at a place; away from a place. □ *The president was absent, so the vice president ran the meeting.* **2.** *adj.* not in existence; not evident; not present or visible. □ *A motive for the crime was absent.* **3.** *adj.* [appearing] vague or not interested. (Adv: *absently.*) □ *Bob, tired from the trip, had an absent look in his eyes.*

**absorb** [əb 'zorb] **1.** *tv.* to soak up a liquid. □ *My napkin absorbed the coffee I spilled in my lap.* **2.** *tv.* to learn something; to take in new information; to learn something easily. (Fig. on ①.) □ *I cannot absorb all the rules of English grammar in one day!*

A

**absorbent** [əb 'zor bənt] *adj.* able to soak up liquids. (Adv: *absorbently.*) ☐ *The paper towel was so absorbent that it cleaned up all the moisture.*

**accent** ['æk sɛnt] **1.** *n.* the force or stress put on a word or a part of a word during speech. ☐ *The accent in the word* hotel *is on the second syllable.* **2.** *n.* a mark written over a letter of the alphabet that gives the letter a special pronunciation or stress. ☐ *French, Italian, and Spanish use accents.* **3.** *n.* a way of speaking a language, and especially of pronouncing a language, that is characteristic of a particular country or region where that language is spoken. ☐ *Mary used to speak with a Southern accent.* **4.** *tv.* to emphasize something, especially to put ① on a word or a part of a word during speech. ☐ *Not "HOtel"! You have accented the wrong syllable.* **5.** *tv.* to make something have more visual interest. ☐ *The yellow curtains accented an otherwise dull room.*

**accept** [æk 'sɛpt] *tv.* to take something that is offered. (Compare this with except. The object can be a clause with that ⑦.) ☐ *I accept your apology.*

**acceptable** [æk 'sɛp tə bəl] *adj.* worth accepting; satisfactory; good enough. (Adv: *acceptably.*) ☐ *John's excuse is acceptable.*

**accident** ['æk sɪ dənt] *n.* an unexpected event, usually involving harm to someone or something. ☐ *I didn't mean to bump into you. It was an accident.*

**accidental** [æk sɪ 'dɛn təl] *adj.* not on purpose; done or happening by mistake. (Adv: *accidentally.*) ☐ *The police investigated the accidental death.*

**accomplish** [ə 'kɑm plɪʃ] *tv.* to finish something; to successfully complete something. ☐ *I was not able to accomplish all that I set out to do.*

**accomplishment** [ə 'kɑm plɪʃ mənt] *n.* something that has been completed or achieved; a success. ☐ *Getting a good mortgage for our new house was quite an accomplishment.*

**according** [ə 'kord ɪŋ] **1. according to** someone or something *phr.* as stated by someone; as indicated by something. ☐ *The guests will arrive at noon, according to Mary.* **2. according to** something *phr.* in proportion to something; in relation to something. ☐ *She gets paid according to the number of hours she works.*

**account** [ə 'kɑʊnt] **1.** *n.* a report; a description; one's version of what happened in an event. ☐ *John's account of the accident differed from mine.* **2.** *n.* a record of income [or money received] and expenses [or money paid out] assigned to a particular person, business, or class of transactions; a record of money kept—or credit given—for a particular person or business, showing how much is added or taken away. ☐ *My checking account had several errors.* **3. account for** something *iv. + prep. phr.* to give an explanation for something. ☐ *How do you account for what happened today?*

**accountant** [ə 'kɑʊnt nt] *n.* someone who is responsible for maintaining financial records or accounts; someone who prepares tax records. ☐ *My accountant will prepare my taxes.*

**accuracy** ['æk jə rə si] *n.* correctness; the degree of freedom from errors. (No plural form.) ☐ *She always hits the target with complete accuracy.*

**accurate** ['æk jə rət] *adj.* correct; exact; without error. (Adv: *accurately.*) ☐ *Your statements about the cost of the house were not accurate.*

**accuse** [ə 'kjuz] *tv.* to claim or charge that someone has done something, usually something wrong or illegal. ☐ *I accused John of hitting my dog.*

**ache** ['ek] **1.** *n.* a pain; a soreness. ☐ *I have aches in both legs from running.*

**2.** *iv.* to hurt; to be sore. □ *My head aches when I read too much.*

**acknowledgment** [æk 'nɑl ɪdʒ mənt] **1.** *n.* admission; stating that something is so. (No plural form in this sense.) □ *Acknowledgment of Sue's part in the plot came only after much questioning.* **2.** *n.* the recognition given to someone for doing something well. □ *We all appreciated the committee's acknowledgment of our work.* **3.** *n.* a report of having received something. □ *I received an acknowledgment of the gift I sent Susan.*

**across** [ə 'krɔs] **1.** *prep.* from one side of something to the other side. □ *Bill jumped across the stream.* **2.** *prep.* on the other side of something. □ *The bank is across the river, just over that bridge.* **3.** *adv.* to the other side of something. □ *I could row across.*

**act** ['ækt] **1.** *n.* a division of a play or musical. □ *In the first act of the play, the young lovers meet.* **2.** *n.* one of many short performances within a longer program. □ *The first act was a funny skit, and the second was a song.* **3.** *n.* a deed; something that is done; an instance of doing something. □ *Susan's act of kindness was very comforting.* □ *Angry people sometimes commit violent acts.* **4.** *n.* a law. □ *The senator supported the act that made selling alcohol illegal.* **5.** *iv.* to perform in a play, film, TV program, or similar performance. □ *The famous actor has acted in more than 25 movies.* **6.** *iv.* to do [something]; to start [doing something]. □ *The county officials will not act on a request unless it is presented in writing.* **7.** *iv.* to behave in a certain way; to behave as if one is or feels a certain way; to show through one's actions that one is or feels a certain way; to behave like someone or something. □ *If Bill acts happy, then he is happy. He doesn't pretend.* □ *Tom acts as if he hates Anne, but I know he really likes her.*

**action** ['æk ʃən] **1.** *n.* activity; movement. (Plural only when referring to different kinds, types, instances, or varieties.) □ *We saw no action in the office. Everyone was at lunch.* Ⓒ *Their actions were well planned.* **2.** *n.* the plot of a story; the events that happen in a story. (No plural form.) □ *The action was hard to follow toward the end of the movie.* **3.** *n.* fighting or battles during a war or conflict. (No plural form.) □ *There was military action on the beach during the invasion.*

**active** ['æk tɪv] **1.** *adj.* moving; functioning; operating. (Adv: *actively.*) □ *I keep active, and that keeps me healthy.* **2.** *adj.* lively; moving at a rapid, steady pace; busy. (Adv: *actively.*) □ *Susan's personal life is very active.* **3.** *adj.* of or about sentences in which the subject does the action that is expressed in the verb. (The opposite of **passive** ②. Adv: *actively.*) □ *"The girl cut the flower" is an active sentence.* □ *"The flower was cut by the girl" is a passive sentence, not an active one.*

**actor** ['æk tɚ] *n.* a performer, male or female, in a play, musical, or movie. (See also **actress**.) □ *The director told the actors what to do.*

**actress** ['æk trəs] *n.* a female performer in a play, musical, or movie. (See also **actor**.) □ *The actress performed her part very well.*

**actual** ['æk tʃu əl] *adj.* real; existing. (Adv: *actually.*) □ *I have seen pictures of whales, but I have never seen an actual whale in the ocean.*

**actually** ['æk tʃ(u )ə li] *adv.* in fact; really. □ *Actually, Anne is the person you need to see.*

**ad** ['æd] *n.* an **advertisement**. □ *I saw an ad for computers on sale.*

**add** ['æd] **1.** *tv.* to join something to something else; to include something with something else. □ *Please add some*

A

*water to the vase of flowers.* **2. add something (up)** *tv. + obj. (+ adv.)* to figure the total of two or more numbers. □ *The waiter added up the bill correctly.*

**addition** [ə 'dɪ ʃən] **1.** *n.* the adding together of two or more numbers. (Plural only when referring to different kinds, types, instances, or varieties as in.) □ *There is an error in your addition.* Ⓒ *I have a few more additions to perform.* **2.** *n.* putting someone or something into something else. (Plural only when referring to different kinds, types, instances, or varieties.) □ *The addition of yeast made the bread dough rise.* Ⓒ *The newest additions to our family are the twins.*

**additional** [ə 'dɪʃ ə nəl] *adj.* extra; [something] further; more; added. (Adv: *additionally.*) □ *There is room for an additional person on this bus.*

**address 1.** ['æ drɛs, ə 'drɛs] *n.* the street name and number, city, state, and other information telling the location of something, such as a building or house. □ *Please print your address on the envelope.* **2.** [ə 'drɛs] *n.* a formal speech. □ *I am going to give an address to the English teachers.* **3.** [ə 'drɛs] *tv.* to write the street name, number, city, state, and other information on an envelope or package. □ *I have to address all these envelopes.* **4.** [ə 'drɛs] *tv.* to speak directly to a person. □ *I was addressing Susan, not you.* **5.** [ə 'drɛs] *tv.* to speak formally before a crowd of people. □ *John addressed the English teachers for an hour.* **6.** [ə 'drɛs] *tv.* to respond to a question; to say something about an issue or problem. □ *In her speech, the manager addressed the matter of pay increases.*

**adequate** ['æd ə kwɪt] *adj.* just enough but not more than enough; good enough. (Adv: *adequately.*) □ *I had an adequate amount of food for dinner.*

**adhesive** [æd 'hi sɪv] **1.** *adj.* sticky; designed to stick to things. (Adv: *adhesively.*) □ *I used an adhesive bandage to cover the cut on my finger.* **2.** *n.* glue; paste. (Plural only when referring to different kinds, types, instances, or varieties.) □ *The adhesive was difficult to clean from my hands.* Ⓒ *Different adhesives dry at different speeds.*

**adhesive tape** [æd 'hi sɪv tep] *n.* a fabric or plastic tape with a sticky side. (Plural only when referring to different kinds, types, instances, or varieties.) □ *Adhesive tape will keep the bandage in place.* Ⓒ *Some adhesive tapes do not stick well when they are wet.*

**adj.** an abbreviation of **adjectival**.

**adjectival** [æ dʒɛk 'tɑɪ vəl] *adj.* serving as an adjective. (Abbreviated *adj.* Adv: *adjectivally.* **Adjectival** forms include adjectives, such as *red*, and adjectives made from other parts of speech, such as *running* in *running dog.*) □ *Many nouns have an adjectival use.* □ *The adjectival form of* center *is* central.

**adjective** ['æ dʒɛk tɪv] *n.* a word that describes or modifies a noun or nominal. □ *In the phrase "the red barn,"* red *is an adjective.* □ *Adjectives usually come before nouns in English.*

**adjust** [ə 'dʒʌst] **1.** *tv.* to change something in a small way in order to try to make it work or fit better. □ *Mary adjusted the TV to get a better picture.* **2.** *iv.* to become used to someone or something; to adapt to someone or something. □ *The new student adjusted to his surroundings.*

**adjustable** [ə 'dʒʌst ə bəl] *adj.* changeable; able to be changed in small amounts. (Adv: *adjustably.*) □ *The height of my desk chair is not adjustable.*

**administration** [æd mɪn ɪ 'stre ʃən] **1.** *n.* the work of managing and directing. (No plural form.) □ *Bob enjoyed administration, but he liked teaching* *better.* **2.** *n.* the office and staff of a high-ranking elected official, such as a president, governor, or mayor. □ *The president's administration had little experience in foreign affairs.* **3.** *n.* a group of people who manage something. □ *The university's administration tried to keep costs low.*

**admiration** [æd mə 're ʃən] *n.* a feeling of pride, pleasure, and respect for someone or something. (No plural form.) □ *Mr. Jones has a lot of admiration for his coworkers.*

**admire** [æd 'mɑɪɚ] *tv.* to regard someone or something with pride, pleasure, and respect. □ *I have always admired my mother's charm.*

**admit** [æd 'mɪt] **1.** *tv.* to allow someone to enter into some place. □ *They would not admit us because we arrived late.* **2.** *tv.* to allow someone to become a member of a club or organization. □ *The club refused to admit people from other states.* **3.** *tv.* to say that one has done something one is accused of; to say that something is true. (The object can be a clause with **that** ⑦.) □ *I admit that I did it.*

**adolescence** [æd ə 'lɛs əns] *n.* the period of time between being a child and being an adult; the teenage years. □ *Adolescence can be a confusing time.*

**adolescent** [æd ə 'lɛs ənt] **1.** *n.* a teenager; someone who is older than a child but not yet an adult. □ *Many of the camp counselors were adolescents.* **2.** *adj.* <the adj. use of ①.> □ *Adolescent emotions are hard for teenagers to deal with.*

**adopt** [ə 'dɑpt] **1.** *iv.* to become the parent or parents of a child through legal proceedings. □ *The decision to adopt should be thought about carefully.* **2.** *tv.* to gain possession of and become responsible for the child of someone else, through the legal system. □ *The Browns adopted the baby when she was just three months old.* **3.** *tv.* to acquire a new practice, belief, or habit. □ *The company adopted new policies regarding absences.*

**adoption** [ə 'dɑp ʃən] **1.** *n.* acquiring and becoming responsible for the child of someone else, through the legal system. (Plural only when referring to different kinds, types, instances, or varieties.) □ *Adoption can provide homes for many children who are without parents.* Ⓒ *The Johnsons managed two adoptions last year, but they were expensive.* **2.** *n.* acquiring a new practice, belief, or habit. (No plural form.) □ *Mary's adoption of a strange lifestyle made her parents unhappy.*

**adorable** [ə 'dor ə bəl] *adj.* very cute; worthy of being adored. (Adv: *adorably.*) □ *The adorable puppy rolled around on the lawn.*

**adore** [ə 'dor] *tv.* to admire and be fond of someone or something. □ *Grandpa adored Grandma from the day they first met.*

**adult** [ə 'dʌlt] **1.** *adj.* mature; fully grown; fully developed. □ *Adult cats are not as playful as kittens.* **2.** *adj.* showing the behavior of a mature person. □ *Max has an adult outlook on life.* **3.** *adj.* intended for persons who are mature. (Often used referring to sex and violence in entertainment.) □ *Sometimes I think that adult movies are intended for childish people.* **4.** *n.* someone or something that is fully grown. □ *An adult has more responsibility than a child.*

**adv.** an abbreviation of **adverb**.

**advance** [æd 'væns] **1.** *n.* a forward motion. □ *The invading army made an advance inland from the coast.* **2.** *n.* money that is given to someone ahead of schedule or before it is earned; a loan taken against money that is to be paid at a later time. □ *Dad will never give me an advance on my allowance!* **3.** *iv.* to

A

progress or move forward; to move to a higher or better level. □ *The sun advanced across the sky slowly.* **4.** *tv.* to move someone or something forward or to a higher level. □ *He advanced the chess piece one space.* **5.** *tv.* to give someone money ahead of schedule or before it is earned. □ *Mom advanced me $2. I will pay her back from my allowance.* **6.** *adj.* prior; before the event. (Prenominal only.) □ *The workers received no advance warning of the factory's closing.*

**advantage** [æd 'væn tɪdʒ] **1.** *n.* something good or useful that will help someone with something; a benefit. □ *Not everyone has the advantage of a good education.* **2. take advantage of** someone *phr.* to use someone unfairly for one's own benefit. □ *You took advantage of Tom by bringing a stranger to his party.* **3. take advantage of** something *phr.* to make good use of something; to benefit from something; to benefit from an opportunity. □ *I took advantage of Max's offer of free tickets to the opera.*

**adventure** [æd 'vɛn tʃɚ] *n.* excitement; challenge. (Plural only when referring to different kinds, types, instances, or varieties.) □ *I love adventure, but I enjoy reading about it best of all.* ⓒ *Hiking in the mountains is an adventure.*

**adverb** ['æd vɚb] *n.* a word that modifies or describes a verb, a verb phrase, an adjective, a sentence, or another adverb. (Abbreviated "adv:" or *adv.* here.) □ *Many adverbs end in* -ly. □ *In the sentence "The dog slowly walked away,"* slowly *and* away *are adverbs.*

**advertise** ['æd vɚ tɑɪz] **1.** *iv.* to make [something] known to the public, especially through signs, television, radio, newspapers, or magazines. □ *The company has advertised on television for thirty years.* **2.** *tv.* to make something known to the public through signs, television, radio, newspapers, magazines, or other means; to publicize something. (The object can be a clause with **that** ⑦.) □ *We advertised our sale in the local paper.*

**advertisement** [æd vɚ 'tɑɪz mənt] *n.* a commercial; a notice about something, displayed to the public. □ *The store's advertisement about its grand opening drew customers.*

**advice** [æd 'vɑɪs] *n.* recommendations or suggestions provided to help someone. (Compare this with **advise**. No plural form. Number is expressed with *piece(s)* or *bit(s) of advice.*) □ *In times of trouble, people ask friends for advice.*

**advise** [æd 'vɑɪz] **1.** *tv.* to give [someone] a particular kind of advice; to suggest doing something. (The object can be a clause with **that** ⑦.) □ *I advise caution in this matter.* **2. advise** someone **to** do something *tv. + obj. + inf.* to supply someone with a suggestion of something to do. □ *I advise you to be cautious.*

**affect** [ə 'fɛkt] **1.** *tv.* to influence someone or something; to have an effect on someone or something. (Compare this with **effect**.) □ *How did John's bad news affect Mary?* **2.** *tv.* to display or exhibit a kind of behavior, especially by pretending or imitating. □ *Bill affected a silly accent to entertain us.*

**affection** [ə 'fɛk ʃən] *n.* love, caring, or fondness. (No plural form. Other senses may use plural, as with *his affections.*) □ *John has difficulty showing affection.*

**affirmative** [ə 'fɚ mə tɪv] *adj.* meaning *yes.* □ *She gave an affirmative answer, which pleased all of us.*

**afford** [ə 'ford] **1.** *tv.* to have enough money to buy something; to be able to buy something. (With *able to* or *can.*) □ *Can we afford a new car this year?* **2.** *tv.* to endure the results of something. (With *able to* or *can.*) □ *I don't think I can afford another of my mother's lec-*

*tures.* **3. afford to** do something *iv. + inf.* to have enough money to do something. (With *able to* or *can.*) □ *Bob rides his bicycle to work because he can't afford to buy a car.* **4. afford to** do something *iv. + inf.* to endure the results of doing something. (With *able to* or *can.*) □ *I don't think I can afford to get another low grade.*

**afraid** [ə 'fred] **1.** *adj.* fearful of someone or something; scared of someone or something. (Not prenominal.) □ *Don't worry. I am not afraid.* **2. afraid to** do something *adj. + inf.* fearful of doing something. □ *I am afraid to drive in the rain.*

**after** ['æf tɚ] **1.** *conj.* at a later time than when someone or something does something; later in time than when something happens; when something has finished happening. □ *After he came, we left.* **2.** *prep.* at a later time than something; later in time than something. □ *It's 20 minutes after three o'clock.* **3.** *prep.* further along in a sequence or series than someone or something. □ *The letter* p *comes after the letter* o. **4.** *prep.* in spite of something. □ *After all the plans we made for a party in his honor, Bill decided to stay home.* **5.** *prep.* in the name of someone; in honor of someone; for someone. □ *The company is named after my father, who founded it.* **6.** *adv.* behind; to the rear; following. □ *Jane walked in the door, and John came after.*

**afternoon** [æf tɚ 'nun] **1.** *n.* the time of day from noon until the evening. □ *I took a nap on Saturday afternoon.* **2.** *adj.* <the adj. use of ①.> □ *The baby has an afternoon nap each day.* **3. afternoons** *adv.* every afternoon ①. □ *Dad sleeps afternoons and works during the night.*

**again** [ə 'gɛn] **1.** *adv.* once more; another time. □ *Please don't say that again!* **2.** *adv.* as [something was] before. □ *Bill lost his job, but now he is working again.*

**against** [ə 'gɛnst] **1.** *prep.* in opposition to someone or something; as an opponent of someone or something. □ *John was against Bob in the lawsuit.* **2.** *prep.* in a direction opposite to something. □ *Don't sand the wood against the grain.* **3.** *prep.* coming toward and meeting someone or something. □ *The rain splattered against the windowpanes.* **4.** *prep.* [leaning or tilting and] in contact with someone or something. □ *Place the rake against the side of the house.*

**age** ['edʒ] **1.** *n.* the amount of time that someone or something has been alive or in existence; the passage of time while something is in existence. (No plural form.) □ *Many things become better with age.* **2.** *n.* advanced ①; evidence of much ①; oldness. (No plural form.) □ *Age showed on the old man's wrinkled face.* **3.** *n.* the specific ① of a person, usually given as a number of years; the specific ① of something. □ *What are the ages of your children?* **4.** *n.* [for a person] the condition of having a certain ③; the time when a person has a certain ③. (The number comes after *age* and refers to years, unless some other measure is given, such as months, weeks, or days.) □ *Age 2 was very difficult for Jimmy and his parents.* **5.** *n.* a period or stage of life. □ *Adolescence can be a difficult age.* **6.** *n.* a period of history; a generation; an era. □ *In this modern age, speed is important.* **7.** *iv.* to become old; to show increasing ①. □ *As people age, their looks change.* **8.** *iv.* [for cheese, wine, whiskey, beef, etc.] to mature; to reach a peak of quality, taste, and strength. □ *The cheese aged in the cave during the winter.* **9.** *tv.* to cause someone or something to grow old or appear old. □ *Wearing your new shoes every day will quickly age them.*

A

**agent** ['e dʒənt] **1.** *n.* someone who represents someone else; someone who has the power to act for someone else; someone who sells certain things such as insurance, travel, tickets, land, buildings, etc. ☐ *David worked as a travel agent.* **2.** *n.* something that causes someone or something else to do something; something that causes some result to happen. ☐ *Fear is often an agent of change.* **3.** *n.* a spy. ☐ *The enemy arrested all of our secret agents.*

**ago** [ə 'go] **1.** *adj.* in the past; [time] already gone by. (After a noun that expresses a length of time.) ☐ *I came here four days ago.* **2. long ago** *phr.* long before this time; much earlier than now. ☐ *Our dog died long ago.*

**agony** ['æg ə ni] *n.* an intense, deep pain in the mind or the body; a deep suffering. (Plural only when referring to different kinds, types, instances, or varieties.) ☐ *Bill was in agony with a bad headache.* Ⓒ *Oh, the agonies of being a teenager in love!*

**agree** [ə 'gri] **1.** *iv.* [for people] to be in harmony or have the same opinion; [for people] to have no conflict of opinion or desire. ☐ *I am glad that we agree.* **2.** *iv.* [for facts or things] to be consistent or to harmonize. ☐ *These colors just do not agree!* **3. agree (with** someone**)** *iv. (+ prep. phr.)* to concur with someone; to accept someone's opinion and be in harmony with someone as in ①. ☐ *Do you agree with me on this matter?* **4. agree (to** do something**)** *iv. (+ inf.)* to consent to do something; to say that one will do something. ☐ *I agreed to clean the house.* **5.** *iv.* [for a form of a word] to match the form of another word grammatically. ☐ *The subject and verb of a sentence must agree.* **6.** *tv.* to decide together that something is true or should happen; to accept someone's opinion that something is true or should happen; to decide or accept that something is the case. (The object is a clause with **that** ⑦.) ☐ *We agreed that we would meet again in a week.*

**ahead** [ə 'hɛd] **1.** *adv.* into the future; [preparing] for the future. ☐ *John smiled, thinking ahead to his vacation.* **2.** *adv.* forward; continuing in the same direction. ☐ *Move ahead, please.* **3.** *adv.* into an advanced position; into a better position. ☐ *It is not easy to get ahead these days.* **4. ahead of** someone or something *phr.* to or at a place in front of or in advance of someone or something; at an earlier time than someone or something. ☐ *The black car is ahead of the green car.*

**aid** ['ed] **1.** *n.* help; assistance; support. (No plural form.) ☐ *The politician offered aid to poor people.* **2.** *n.* something that helps someone or something else. ☐ *Uncle Bill used a cane as an aid in walking.* **3.** *tv.* to provide someone or something with ①. ☐ *The politicians promised to aid the poor people.*

**aim** ['em] **1. aim** something **at** someone or something *tv. + obj. + prep. phr.* to point something toward a target or a goal. ☐ *The firefighter aimed the hose at the fire.* **2. aim to** do something *iv. + inf.* to intend to do something; to mean to do something. ☐ *John aimed to be home for dinner but was late.* **3.** *n.* a goal; a purpose; an intention. ☐ *John's aim was to give an interesting talk.* **4.** *n.* the pointing of something accurately. (No plural form.) ☐ *The archer has good aim.*

**air** ['er] **1.** *n.* the mixture of gases that surrounds the earth; the mixture of gases that people normally breathe. (No plural form.) ☐ *Jane took a deep breath of fresh air.* **2.** *n.* a mood or atmosphere. (No plural form.) ☐ *The balloons gave the room a festive air.* **3. air** something **out** *tv. + obj. + adv.* to ventilate something; to freshen something by exposing it to fresh **air** ①. ☐ *Mary opened all the windows to air the room out.* Ⓣ *She* *aired out the room.* **4.** *tv.* to express a view or an opinion in public; to make something known. □ *I try to air my opinions, but no one listens.*

**aircraft** ['er kræft] *n., irreg.* a machine, such as an airplane or a helicopter, that flies in the air. (Pl: *aircraft.*) □ *Several aircraft were waiting to take off.*

**airline** ['er laɪn] *n.* a company that operates a number of aircraft for passengers or cargo. □ *The airline provides meals on some flights.*

**airmail** ['er mel] **1.** *n.* a system for sending international mail by airplane. (No plural form.) □ *A package arrived by airmail from France.* **2.** *adv.* [sending mail] by ①. □ *Grandma sent her letter to England airmail.* **3.** *tv.* to send something by ①. □ *Did Grandma airmail her letter to Japan?*

**airplane** ['er plen] *n.* a heavier-than-air vehicle that flies through the air. □ *John owns an airplane, but he doesn't fly it.*

**airport** ['er port] *n.* a place where airplanes land and take off. □ *John's uncle watched the planes land at the airport.*

**alarm** [ə 'lɑrm] **1.** *n.* a warning sound or signal. □ *When we heard the alarm, we left the house quickly.* **2.** *n.* a device that makes a warning sound or signal. □ *The fire alarm made a loud noise when the house began to fill with smoke.* **3.** *n.* excitement, anxiety, or shock. (No plural form.) □ *The bright student's failure was cause for alarm.* **4.** *n.* a clock that has a bell or other signal that is sounded to wake someone up. □ *I set the alarm before I went to bed.* **5.** *tv.* to frighten or scare someone; to make someone afraid or fearful of danger. □ *Jane's test results alarmed her doctors.*

**alcohol** ['æl kə hɔl] **1.** *n.* a liquid chemical used to make wounds and skin very clean or sterile or to dissolve substances. (Plural only when referring to different kinds, types, instances, or varieties.) □ *Jane cleaned the scratch on her arm with alcohol.* 🄲 *Which of these alcohols is likely to kill all the germs?* **2.** *n.* the substance found in beer, wine, and hard liquors that causes someone to be drunk. (Plural only when referring to different kinds, types, instances, or varieties.) □ *Beer contains a small amount of alcohol.* 🄲 *Alcohols from different sources all bring about the same results.* **3.** *n.* beer, wine, whiskey, spirits; drinks that contain ②. (No plural form.) □ *You can bring your own alcohol if you wish.*

**alert** [ə 'lɚt] **1.** *adj.* wary; aware; watchful. (Adv: *alertly.*) □ *Mary was awake but not very alert when the alarm rang.* **2.** *tv.* to warn someone about something, especially danger. □ *We alerted the police to watch for the missing child.*

**algebra** ['æl dʒə brə] *n.* a branch of mathematics using letters and other symbols to represent numbers or sets of numbers in equations. (No plural form.) □ *High-school students must take a course in algebra.*

**alike** [ə 'laɪk] **1.** *adj.* similar; the same or almost the same. (Not prenominal.) □ *The habits of John and his father are alike.* **2.** *adv.* in the same way. □ *John and his dad walk very much alike.* **3.** *adv.* equally; in the same amount or degree. □ *The dean is respected by teachers and students alike.*

**alive** [ə 'laɪv] **1.** *adj.* living; not dead. (Not prenominal.) □ *The dog is not dead. It is alive, but it is sleeping.* **2.** *adj.* active, lively, or full of energy. (Fig. on ①. Not prenominal.) □ *Fresh air makes me feel so alive!*

**all** ['ɔl] **1.** *adj.* each and every one [of the people or things]; the full amount [of something]; the whole extent of [something]. □ *Why did you drink all the milk?* **2.** *adj.* the greatest amount possible [of something]. □ *In all sincerity, I don't like your pie.* **3.** *pron.* everything

A

or everyone mentioned earlier in the conversation or writing. (Treated as singular or plural.) □ *My dog just had five puppies, and all are healthy.* **4.** *pron.* everything. (Treated as singular.) □ *We have all we need right here on this island.* **5.** *adv.* completely. □ *Tom left, and I am all alone.* **6. at all** *phr.* [not] to any extent or degree; [not] in any way. (Always in the negative or questions.) □ *I do not like cats at all.* □ *It was so dark, we could hardly see at all.*

**alley** ['æl i] **1.** *n.* a narrow road or pathway behind or between buildings. □ *John parked his car in the alley.* **2.** *n.* a bowling alley. □ *When I bowl, I try to keep the ball in the middle of the alley as much as possible.*

**alligator** ['æl ə get ɚ] *n.* a large reptile of the crocodile family. □ *A huge alligator crawled out of the water onto the riverbank.*

**allow** [ə 'lɑʊ] **1. allow** someone **to** do something *tv.* + *obj.* + *inf.* to permit someone to do something; to let someone do something. □ *Allow me to introduce myself.* **2.** *tv.* to make sure that there is a certain amount of time for something to be done. □ *Traffic is very heavy, so allow enough time.*

**allowance** [ə 'lɑʊ əns] **1.** *n.* an amount of something, such as money, given to someone. □ *Bill's allowance is twenty dollars a week.* **2. make allowances for** something *phr.* to keep something in mind when making a decision or policy. □ *The company made no allowances for bad weather in its attendance policy.*

**almost** ['ɔl most] *adv.* nearly, but not quite. □ *We are almost home now.*

**alone** [ə 'lon] **1.** *adj.* by oneself; having no one else nearby. (Not prenominal.) □ *Mary was alone for an hour in the small room.* **2.** *adv.* by oneself; with no help. □ *I can't lift this piano alone.*

**along** [ə 'lɔŋ] **1.** *prep.* next to something for a distance; in a path next to something. □ *Tom and Jane walked along the bank of the river each morning.* **2. along with** someone or something *phr.* in addition to someone or something; together with someone or something. □ *I ate some chocolates along with some fruit.*

**aloof** [ə 'luf] *adj.* unfriendly; reserved; unsympathetic. (Adv: *aloofly.*) □ *Jane is aloof and businesslike at the office.*

**aloud** [ə 'lɑʊd] *adv.* audibly; [of speech] spoken so that it can be heard. □ *Bill never has the courage to say aloud what he's thinking.*

**alphabet** ['æl fə bɛt] *n.* the list of letters—in proper order—used to write a language. □ *Children learn the alphabet in kindergarten.*

**alphabetical** [æl fə 'bɛt ɪ kəl] *adj.* arranged in the order of the letters in the alphabet. (Adv: *alphabetically* [...ɪk li].) □ *Dictionaries list words in alphabetical order.*

**alphabetize** ['æl fə bə tɑɪz] *tv.* to place words in the same order as the letters of the alphabet. □ *The students learned to alphabetize a list of words.*

**already** [ɔl 'rɛd i] *adv.* by now; by this point in time; previously. (This is different from *all ready.*) □ *John has eaten dinner already.*

**also** ['ɔl so] *adv.* as well; too; in addition. □ *I must buy some bread also.*

**although** [ɔl 'ðo] *conj.* even though; despite; in spite of. □ *Although it rained, we stayed outdoors.*

**altogether** ['ɔl tə gɛð ɚ] *adv.* completely. (Different from *all together.*) □ *Tom was altogether unprepared for college.*

**aluminum** [ə 'lum ə nəm] **1.** *n.* a metal that is lightweight and does not rust easily. (No plural form.) □ *Aluminum cans can be melted and reused.* **2.** *adj.*

made of ①. □ *Most soft drinks come in aluminum cans.*

**always** ['ɔl wez] **1.** *adv.* every time; each time. □ *The phone always rings while we are eating dinner.* **2.** *adv.* forever; without end. □ *I will always love you.*

**am** ['æm] *iv., irreg.* <the first-person present singular form of **be**.> (Reduced to *'m* in the contraction **I'm**.) □ *I am eager to learn English.*

**amaze** [ə 'mez] *tv.* to cause wonder in someone; to astound or astonish someone. □ *My neighbor's flowers never cease to amaze me.*

**ambulance** ['æm bjə ləns] *n.* a vehicle for taking sick or injured people to the hospital. □ *The ambulance raced through the city streets.*

**amend** [ə 'mɛnd] **1.** *tv.* to change something; to modify something (especially laws). □ *Did Grandma amend her will before her death?* **2. make amends (for something)** *phr.* to do something to show that one is sorry for some error, injury, or loss that one has caused, especially by giving something or by doing something good for the person who suffered from the error. □ *After amends had been made, Jane took her friend to dinner.*

**amendment** [ə 'mɛnd mənt] *n.* a change made by correcting or adding to something. □ *After much debate, several amendments were made to the law.*

**among** [ə 'mʌŋ] **1.** *prep.* in the midst of things or people; surrounded by things or people. □ *There was one pink flower among the red ones.* **2.** *prep.* within a group; within a set of choices. (Use **between** with two. Use **among** with more than two.) □ *Please choose among these four.*

**amount** [ə 'mɑʊnt] **1.** *n.* how much there is of something; the quantity. □ *What is the total amount of money in the account?* **2. amount to something** *iv. + prep. phr.* to be equal to a numerical figure; to total up to something. □ *The damage after the fire amounted to $50,000.* **3. amount to something** *iv. + prep. phr.* to have the same effect, value, or meaning as something; to constitute something; to develop into something. □ *You had better go to school if you want to amount to something.*

**amphibian** [æm 'fɪb i ən] *n.* a kind of animal, such as the frog, that lives in water and on land. □ *Toads, newts, and salamanders are amphibians.*

**ample** ['æm pəl] *adj.* large enough; sufficient and adequate. (Adv: *amply.* Comp: *ampler;* sup: *amplest.*) □ *We have an ample supply of food for three days.*

**amputation** [æm pjə 'te ʃən] *n.* the removal of all or part of an arm, a leg, a finger, or a toe. (Plural only when referring to different kinds, types, instances, or varieties.) □ *Amputation was the only way to keep the cancer from spreading.* Ⓒ *The surgeon performed three amputations this morning.*

**amuse** [ə 'mjuz] *tv.* to make someone laugh or smile; to give someone pleasure. □ *This cartoon amuses me.*

**amusement** [ə 'mjuz mənt] **1.** *n.* happiness; pleasure; enjoyment. (No plural form.) □ *To our amusement, the kittens tried to climb onto the chair.* **2.** *n.* something that makes someone happy; entertainment. □ *The guest entertained herself with some small amusements.*

**an** ['æn] **1.** *article* one; any. (Note: Use **a** before words that begin with a consonant sound; use **an** before words that begin with a vowel sound.) □ *I will be there in an hour.* **2.** *prep.* each; per. (See note at ①.) □ *At the market, corn was twenty-five cents an ear.*

**analyze** ['æn ə lɑɪz] *tv.* to examine the details of something. □ *Dr. Jones analyzed the blood samples.*

A

**ancestor** ['æn sɛs tɚ] *n.* a person, usually no longer living, from whom a person descends. ☐ *Mr. Macdonald's ancestors came from Scotland.*

**anchor** ['æŋ kɚ] **1.** *n.* a heavy object, attached to a ship or boat, that catches on the sea bottom to keep the ship or boat from drifting away. ☐ *A heavy anchor prevented our boat from drifting.* **2.** *n.* something that holds something else in place. ☐ *The campers used a rock as an anchor to keep the tent flap in place.* **3.** *n.* a newscaster; a central newscaster who introduces news reports from other people. (From *anchorman.*) ☐ *The anchor on the nine o'clock news wears glasses.* **4.** *tv.* to keep a ship in place by lowering ① into the water. ☐ *The sailors anchored the ship near the island.* **5.** *tv.* to secure something; to hold something in place. ☐ *Anne anchored the bracket to the wall with a long bolt.* **6.** *iv.* [for a ship] to remain in a place by dropping ①. ☐ *The huge ship anchored out in the bay.*

**ancient** ['en tʃənt] **1.** *adj.* from long ago in history. ☐ *Jane found an ancient manuscript in the cave.* **2.** *adj.* very old. ☐ *I would never drive that ancient car anywhere!* **3.** *n.* someone who lived long ago. ☐ *The drawings were done by the ancients of North America.*

**and** ['ænd] **1.** *conj.* in addition to; plus; also. ☐ *Be on time, and don't forget to dress nicely.* ☐ *Remember to buy both apples and oranges.* **2.** *conj.* then; as a result. ☐ *Bill got dressed and drove to work.*

**angel** ['en dʒəl] **1.** *n.* a heavenly being; a messenger of God. ☐ *There are many mentions of angels in the Bible.* **2.** *n.* a very kind, sweet person. (Fig. on ①.) ☐ *You're such an angel for baking a cake for my birthday!*

**anger** ['æŋ gɚ] **1.** *n.* a state of being upset and **mad** ②; strong feelings of annoyance. (No plural form.) ☐ *John's anger erupted when he learned that his car had been stolen.* **2.** *tv.* to upset someone; to annoy someone very much. ☐ *The stain on the carpet angered Mom.*

**angle** ['æŋ gəl] **1.** *n.* a figure formed where two lines or surfaces come together. ☐ *John used a compass to draw a right angle.* **2.** *n.* a point of view; a way of looking at an issue or idea. (Informal.) ☐ *I have a good angle for a story on the high cost of housing.* **3.** *tv.* to place two surfaces or lines so that they intersect. ☐ *Mary angled the books so they would stand up by themselves.* **4.** *iv.* to turn, perhaps sharply. ☐ *The street angles to the right just past the post office.*

**angry** ['æŋ gri] *adj.* irate; upset; annoyed. (Adv: *angrily.* Comp: *angrier;* sup: *angriest.*) ☐ *Susan was so angry with me that she yelled quite loudly.*

**anguish** ['æŋ gwɪʃ] *n.* mental pain or suffering; grief. (No plural form.) ☐ *John experienced anguish over his brother's death.*

**animal** ['æn ə məl] **1.** *n.* a living creature that is not a plant. ☐ *Many types of animals can be seen at the zoo.* **2.** *adj.* from or containing ①. ☐ *Eating animal fat is bad for your health.* **3.** *adj.* relating to functions of the body instead of the mind. ☐ *John was not able to control his more violent animal instincts.*

**ankle** ['æŋ kəl] *n.* the joint that connects the foot with the leg. ☐ *John stepped in a hole and twisted his ankle.*

**anklebone** ['æŋ kəl bon] *n.* the main bone of the ankle. ☐ *Something in Bill's boot rubbed against his anklebone.*

**announce** [ə 'nɑʊns] **1.** *tv.* to make something known to people. (The object can be a clause with **that** ⑦.) ☐ *Mike announced that dinner was served.* **2.** *tv.* to speak out the name of someone or something that is arriving. ☐ *Mary announced the guests one by one as they arrived.*

**announcement** [ə 'nɑʊns mənt] *n.* a declaration; a public statement. □ *The Smiths sent out an announcement of their baby's birth.*

**annoy** [ə 'nɔɪ] *tv.* to bother or pester someone. □ *Jimmy annoyed his sister by stealing her diary.*

**anonymous** [ə 'nɑn ə məs] *adj.* unnamed; from an unknown source; created or done without revealing the name or identity of the creator or doer. (Adv: *anonymously.*) □ *This was written by an anonymous author.*

**another** [ə 'nʌð ɚ] **1.** *pron.* an additional one; a different one. □ *If you don't like that dress, get another.* **2.** *adj.* consisting of one more of the same kind; [an] additional [one]. (Prenominal only.) □ *I asked the hostess for another glass of water.*

**answer** ['æn sɚ] **1.** *n.* a reply; a response to a question; a solution to a problem on a test. □ *I asked Tom what he'd like for supper, but he gave no answer.* **2.** *n.* a response to a situation; a way of solving a problem. □ *Hiring more police was the mayor's answer to the crime problem.* **3.** *tv.* to give a response to something, such as a test question or a letter. □ *The president of the company answered all his mail personally.* **4.** *tv.* to reply to someone. (The object can be a clause with **that** ⑦.) □ *Please answer me!* **5.** *iv.* to give a reply. □ *I called out Bill's name, but he didn't answer.*

**ant** ['ænt] *n.* a small insect that lives in a colony. □ *Jimmy looked at the ants on the sidewalk.*

**antenna** [æn 'tɛn ə] **1.** *n.* a device that collects or receives electromagnetic signals that have been broadcast, such as for radio or television. (Pl: *antennas.*) □ *Our television antenna needs to be adjusted.* **2.** *n., irreg.* one of the sensitive feelers found in pairs on the heads of insects and some sea creatures. (Pl: **antennae** or *antennas.*) □ *The moth had a feathery antenna on each side of its head.*

**antennae** [æn 'tɛn i] a pl of **antenna** ②.

**antic** ['æn tɪk] **1.** *n.* a playful or silly act. (Often plural.) □ *Jimmy's antics in class bothered the teacher.* **2.** *adj.* silly; playful. (Adv: *anticly* or *antically* [...ɪk li].) □ *The antic expressions of the clown made the children laugh.*

**anticipate** [æn 'tɪs ə pet] *tv.* to expect something to happen; to prepare for something that is expected to happen. (The object can be a clause with **that** ⑦.) □ *We anticipated the storm and brought raincoats.*

**antique** [æn 'tik] **1.** *adj.* old, especially if valuable; belonging to a time long ago. □ *I collect antique china.* **2.** *n.* an object that was made long ago. □ *Be careful with that bowl. It's an antique.*

**antonym** ['æn tə nɪm] *n.* a word that means the opposite of another word. □ Fast *is the antonym of* slow.

**anxiety** [æŋ 'zɑɪ ə ti] *n.* nervousness; worry. (Singular or plural with the same meaning. Not countable.) □ *Anxiety about the test almost made me sick.* □ *Mary helped Bill reduce his anxieties.*

**anxious** ['æŋk ʃəs] **1.** *adj.* nervous; worried; troubled, especially with a feeling of dread or concern. (Adv: *anxiously.*) □ *The host was anxious about the party.* **2. anxious to do something** *adj. + inf.* eager to do something; excited about doing something. □ *The children were anxious to open their gifts as soon as possible.*

**any** ['ɛn i] **1.** *pron.* whichever one or ones. (To point out one from a group of two, use **either**.) □ *I need three of them. Any will do.* **2.** *pron.* even the smallest amount or number. (Always in the negative or questions. Use **some** in affirmative statements or commands.) □ *Would you like any of this ice cream?*

**3.** *adj.* whichever [one or ones]. (To point out one from a group of two, use **either**.) □ *Just hand me any book from that shelf.* **4.** *adj.* even the smallest amount or number [of something]. (Always in the negative or questions. Use **some** in affirmative statements or commands.) □ *"Did any letters come for me in the mail?" Tom asked.* **5.** *adv.* even the smallest amount. □ *I can't run any farther.*

**anybody** ['ɛn i bɑd i] **1.** *pron.* some person; any person; anyone; even one person. (Always in the negative or questions. Use **somebody** in affirmative statements or commands. No plural form.) □ *"Is anybody home?" the visitor asked.* **2.** *n.* an important person. (Used in the negative or questions; use **somebody** in affirmative statements or commands. No plural form.) □ *You're not anybody! Why are you acting so important?* **3.** *n.* any random person; whoever; no matter who. (No plural form.) □ *I don't date just anybody, you realize.*

**anyhow** ['ɛn i hɑʊ] *adv.* in any case; anyway; at any rate. □ *Anyhow, let's get back to the point.*

**anymore** [æn i 'mor] **1.** *adv.* at the present time in contrast to an earlier time. (This is different from *any more.* Usually in negative sentences.) □ *Bill doesn't live here anymore.* **2.** *adv.* nowadays; recently. (This is different from *any more.* Colloquial. Common but not standard English when used in affirmative sentences.) □ *Anymore, my back hurts all the time.*

**anyone** ['ɛn i wən] **1.** *pron.* some person; any person; anybody. (Always in the negative or questions. Use **someone** in the affirmative. No plural form.) □ *"Is anyone home?" the visitor asked.* **2.** *n.* just any person; whoever; no matter who. (No plural form.) □ *I don't date just anyone, you realize.*

**anyplace** ['ɛn i ples] **1.** *adv.* no matter where; in, at, or to any place; wherever. (See also **anywhere**.) □ *Set that box down anyplace. I don't care where you put it.* **2.** *adv.* [not] in, at, or to any place; [not] in, at, or to even one place. (Always in the negative or questions. Use **someplace** in the affirmative. See also **anywhere**.) □ *I can't find John anyplace.*

**anything** ['ɛn i θɪŋ] **1.** *n.* any thing, object, or event. (No plural form.) □ *The famous singer can sing anything.* **2.** *n.* [not] a single thing; [not] even one thing, object, or event. (Always in the negative or questions. Use **something** in the affirmative. No plural form.) □ *I didn't get anything done today.* **3.** *adv.* in any way. (Always in the negative or questions.) □ *Bob and John are twins, but they don't look anything alike.*

**anytime** ['ɛn i tɑɪm] *adv.* whenever; at any time; no matter when. □ *John goes on vacation anytime he wants.*

**anyway** ['ɛn i we] *adv.* in any case; anyhow; nevertheless; at any rate. □ *Mary was not hungry, but she ate anyway.*

**anywhere** ['ɛn i ʍɛr] **1.** *adv.* anyplace; wherever; in, at, or to any place; in, at, or to an unnamed place; in, at, or to whatever place. □ *I can't find it anywhere.* **2.** *adv.* [not] somewhere; [not] in, at, or to even one place. (Always in the negative or questions. Use **somewhere** in affirmative statements and commands.) □ *Why don't you want to go anywhere for dinner?*

**apart** [ə 'pɑrt] **1.** *adv.* not together; separately. □ *Dave was feeling sad and stood apart from the crowd.* **2.** *adv.* in pieces; into pieces. □ *Bob pulled the radio apart to see how it worked.*

**apartment** [ə 'pɑrt mənt] *n.* a place to live within a large building; living quarters. □ *I have rented an apartment for three years.*

A

**ape** ['ep] **1.** *n.* a large monkey-like mammal without a tail. □ *We love to watch the apes at the zoo.* **2.** *tv.* to copy or mock someone or something; to imitate someone or something. □ *John aped his little sister until she cried.*

**apologize** [ə 'pɑl ə dʒɑɪz] *iv.* to make an apology; to say that one is sorry. □ *I apologized for breaking the vase.*

**apology** [ə 'pɑl ə dʒi] *n.* a statement of regret for having done something. □ *Bill's apology did not make Jane feel better.*

**apostrophe** [ə 'pɑs trə fi] **1.** *n.* the mark of punctuation (') showing where one or more letters have been omitted. □ *Words that are contractions are written with apostrophes in English, as with* can't *and* I'm. **2.** *n.* the mark of punctuation (') used to show possession in nouns. (In regular singular nouns, add the apostrophe plus an *s.* In regular plural nouns, add the apostrophe after the plural *s.*) □ *You have to add an apostrophe and the letter* s *to a singular noun to indicate possession.* □ *The apostrophe in* Bob's *indicates possession.*

**appeal** [ə 'pil] **1.** *n.* a plea for help; a request. □ *My appeal for justice was ignored.* **2.** *n.* a legal request that a court decision be examined by a higher judge or court. □ *The lawyer made an appeal to the Supreme Court.* **3.** *n.* attraction; something that draws someone or something closer. (No plural form.) □ *I never understood the appeal of living in the city.* **4.** *tv.* to request that a court decision be examined by a higher judge or court. □ *The lawyer appealed the case to a higher court.* **5. appeal to someone or something** *iv.* + *prep. phr.* to ask someone or some organization for something; to make a plea for something. □ *The charity appealed to everyone in town for money.* **6. appeal to someone** *iv.* + *prep. phr.* to be attractive to someone. □ *Fast cars appeal to John, but he can't afford one.*

**appear** [ə 'pɪr] **1.** *iv.* to become visible; to come into sight. □ *The sun appeared on the horizon at five o'clock this morning.* **2.** *iv.* to seem to be a certain way; to look a certain way. □ *Bill appears tired this morning.*

**applaud** [ə 'plɔd] **1.** *iv.* to clap the hands together to show appreciation or approval. □ *At the end of the performance, the audience applauded loudly.* **2.** *tv.* to show appreciation for someone or something by clapping one's hands together. □ *The other athletes applauded Jane's amazing performance.*

**applause** [ə 'plɔz] *n.* a show of approval by clapping one's hands together. (No plural form.) □ *There should be no applause until the symphony is over.*

**apple** ['æp əl] *n.* a firm, round fruit that has red, green, or yellow skin and is white inside. □ *Mary bought some apples to use in a pie.*

**appliance** [ə 'plɑɪ əns] *n.* a machine, usually found in the home, with a specific function. □ *None of the kitchen appliances worked when the power went out.*

**apply** [ə 'plɑɪ] **1.** *tv.* to put or spread something on something else. □ *I applied some soap to the stain.* **2.** *tv.* to use something; to make use of something. □ *You have to apply all the strength you have to lift this box.* **3.** *tv.* to cause oneself to work or study hard. (Takes a reflexive object.) □ *If you apply yourself, you'll get good grades.* **4. apply for something** *iv.* + *prep. phr.* to request something that requires approval—such as a loan, a job, or admission to a school—usually in writing or through some other formal process. □ *How many jobs did Bob apply for?* **5. apply to someone or something** *iv.* + *prep. phr.* to be appropriate or relevant to some-

A

one or something. □ *The rules don't apply to this situation.*

**appoint** [ə 'poɪnt] **1.** *tv.* to choose someone for a job or position; to assign someone to a position. □ *I appointed Bill to be my assistant.* **2.** *tv.* to fill a vacant office, position, or job; to determine who will serve in an office, position, or job. □ *Max will appoint the new manager tomorrow.* **3.** *tv.* to set a time. □ *The committee appointed a time for the next meeting.*

**appointment** [ə 'poɪnt mənt] **1.** *n.* choosing someone to fill a position or to take a job. (Plural only when referring to different kinds, types, instances, or varieties.) □ *The appointment of a replacement is very important.* Ⓒ *Several new appointments were announced today.* **2.** *n.* an arranged meeting; an agreement to meet at a specific time and place. □ *I have an appointment with the dentist at four o'clock.*

**appreciate** [ə 'pri ʃi et] **1.** *tv.* to be grateful for someone or something; to value someone or something. (The object can be a clause with **that** ⑦.) □ *We appreciated the help of our friends.* □ *John appreciates fine art.* **2.** *iv.* to increase in value. □ *Unfortunately, new cars do not appreciate after you buy them.*

**appreciation** [ə pri ʃi 'e ʃən] **1.** *n.* a feeling of being grateful for someone or something. (No plural form.) □ *Mary showed her appreciation for the gift by writing a thank-you note.* □ *A box of candy is often given to someone to show appreciation.* **2.** *n.* the recognition of the value of something. (No plural form.) □ *John does not have an appreciation of good literature.* **3.** *n.* a rise in value; an increase in value. (No plural form.) □ *Do not expect any appreciation on a new automobile.*

**approach** [ə 'protʃ] **1.** *tv.* to go near someone or something; to get closer to someone or something in time or space. □ *We were quickly approaching the end of our vacation, but we didn't want to go home.* **2.** *iv.* [for someone or something] to come closer in time or space. □ *We stood still as the deer approached.* **3.** *n.* a way of solving a problem. □ *What is your approach to solving this problem?* **4.** *n.* an entrance; a path to something. □ *A tree-lined driveway formed the approach to the old house.* **5.** *n.* an instance of [someone or something] coming closer. □ *We could hear the approach of the train.*

**approve** [ə 'pruv] **1. approve (of someone or something)** *iv. (+ prep. phr.)* to judge someone or something to be satisfactory or agreeable. □ *I simply do not approve of the torn shirt you are wearing.* **2.** *tv.* to grant approval of someone or something. □ *The school's principal approved the new curriculum.*

**approximate 1.** [ə 'prɑk sə mət] *adj.* estimated; not exact. (Adv: *approximately.*) □ *The clerk told us the approximate cost of the new radio.* **2.** [ə 'prɑk sə met] *tv.* to estimate something; to guess the amount of something. □ *Can you approximate the distance from here to New York City?* **3.** [ə 'prɑk sə met] *tv.* to be similar to someone or something; to appear to be almost the same as someone or something. □ *This costume approximates authentic seventeenth-century dress.*

**apricot** ['e prə kɑt] **1.** *n.* a soft, fuzzy, yellowish fruit that is smaller than a peach and has a large pit. □ *Tom just loves to eat canned apricots for dessert.* **2.** *adj.* made with ①. □ *This apricot jam is delicious!*

**April** ['e prəl] Go to **month**.

**apron** ['e prən] **1.** *n.* a protective skirt worn over one's clothing; a protective covering for the front of one's clothing. □ *Bob loves to cook, so we gave him an apron for his birthday.* **2.** *n.* the part of a theater stage that is in front of where the curtain hangs. □ *When the main curtain closed, a chair remained out on the apron.*

**apt** ['æpt] **1. apt to** do something *adj. + inf.* likely to do something; prone to doing something. □ *Bill is apt to forget half of the groceries if he doesn't make a list.* **2.** *adj.* clever; easily taught. □ *John is an apt pupil and learns his lessons quickly.* **3.** *adj.* suitable; appropriate; fitting. (Adv: *aptly.*) □ *The professor made an apt analogy to explain his point.*

**aquaria** [ə 'kwɛr i ə] a pl of aquarium.

**aquarium** [ə 'kwɛr i əm] **1.** *n., irreg.* a container for plants and animals that live in the water. (Pl: *aquariums* or aquaria.) □ *There is a leak in my aquarium.* **2.** *n., irreg.* a public building containing ① for public viewing. □ *Feeding time at the aquarium is popular with the children.*

**Arabic numeral** ['ɛr ə bɪk 'num ə rəl] *n.* the most usual form of number, such as 1, 2, 3, 4, 5. (These forms come from Arabic script.) □ *Arabic numerals have been used in the European languages for centuries.*

**arc** ['ɑrk] **1.** *n.* a curve; a portion of a circle. □ *The stream twisted through the forest in a series of arcs.* **2.** *iv.* to form a curve; to take the shape of a curve. (Past tense: ['ɑrkt].) □ *The rocket's path arced gracefully over the sea.*

**arch** ['ɑrtʃ] **1.** *n.* a curved structure over an opening, usually holding the weight of the wall above it. □ *We huddled under the arch of the bridge during the storm.* **2.** *n.* the curved part of the bottom of the foot. □ *The dancer had high arches.* **3.** *iv.* to bend in the shape of ①; to curve like ①. □ *The trees arched over the road.*

**archery** ['ɑrtʃ ə ri] *n.* the sport or skill of shooting with a bow and arrow. (No plural form.) □ *Archery is a sport requiring good aim.*

**architect** ['ɑrk ə tɛkt] *n.* someone who designs buildings. □ *The architect has won awards for his designs.*

**architecture** ['ɑrk ɪ tɛk tʃɚ] **1.** *n.* the designing of buildings; the study of building design. (Plural only when referring to different kinds, types, instances, or varieties.) □ *The field of architecture offers many opportunities.* Ⓒ *The architectures of different European periods are shown in this expensive book.* **2.** *n.* the particular design of a building. (No plural form.) □ *We admire the architecture of the old homes.*

**arctic** ['ɑrk tɪk] **1. the Arctic** *n.* the area around the Arctic Ocean, near the North Pole. (No plural form. Treated as singular.) □ *I would hate to be lost in the Arctic.* **2.** *adj.* relating to ①. (Sometimes capitalized.) □ *The Arctic explorers wore special clothing to keep warm.* **3.** *adj.* very cold; freezing. (Adv: *arctically* [...ɪk li].) □ *I wore very warm sweaters because of the arctic weather we were having.*

**are** ['ɑr] *iv., irreg.* <a form of the verb be used in the second-person singular present and in all three persons in the present-tense plural.> (Reduced to *'re* in contractions.) □ *Jane, you are the only person who can help me.*

**area** ['ɛr i ə] **1.** *n.* a space; a section. □ *Please keep out of this restricted area.* **2.** *n.* a measure of a section of a flat surface, determined for instance by multiplying the length of the surface by its width. □ *The surveyor determined the area of the yard.* **3.** *n.* a subject; a field of interest or study. □ *What is your main area of study?*

**area code** ['ɛr i ə kod] *n.* a series of numbers, used especially when making a long-distance phone call, that identifies the general location of the person being called. □ *Please give me your telephone number, area code first.*

A

**aren't** ['ɑrnt] **1.** *cont.* "are not." □ *Aren't you going to introduce me to your friend?* **2. aren't I** *cont.* "am I not." (Used in the asking of certain questions.) □ *Aren't I the best cook in town?*

**argue** ['ɑr gju] **1.** *iv.* to disagree [with someone] verbally; to quarrel [with someone] verbally. □ *"Don't argue!" Dad warned Bob.* **2.** *tv.* to debate a point or issue by means of an argument. (The object can be a clause with **that** ⑦.) □ *Jane argued her point well.*

**argument** ['ɑr gjə mənt] **1.** *n.* a quarrel, especially if spoken; a dispute. □ *The children had an argument about who should close the door.* **2.** *n.* a debate or discussion of an issue on which people disagree. □ *Your argument contains several flaws.*

**arise** [ə 'rɑɪz] **1.** *iv., irreg.* to get up; to rise; to stand up. (Pt: **arose**; pp: **arisen**.) □ *I will arise and greet him when he arrives.* **2.** *iv., irreg.* to develop; to happen. □ *If something unexpected arises at the office, I will be home late.*

**arisen** [ə 'rɪz ən] pp of **arise**.

**arithmetic 1.** [ə 'rɪθ mə tɪk] *n.* the part of mathematics using numbers to add, subtract, multiply, and divide. □ *Arithmetic is a basic school subject.* **2.** [ɛr ɪθ 'mɛt ɪk] *adj.* <the adj. use of ①.> (Adv: *arithmetically* [...ɪk li].) □ *This arithmetic formula is very complex.*

**arm** ['ɑrm] **1.** *n.* one of the upper limbs of a human being. □ *My arms ached after I moved the heavy boxes.* **2. arms** *n.* guns; weapons. □ *The troops were ordered to drop their arms.* **3.** *n.* the parts of a chair that support the **arms** ① of someone who sits in the chair. □ *One of the arms of the chair broke off as I leaned on it.* **4.** *tv.* to equip someone or something with weapons. □ *The soldiers armed themselves for battle.*

**armchair** ['ɑrm tʃɛr] *n.* a seat, usually cushioned, with raised **arms** ③. □ *My favorite armchair is in the living room.*

**armed** ['ɑrmd] **1.** *adj.* carrying a gun or other weapons. □ *The armed police officer stopped the robbery.* **2.** *adj.* ready for war; prepared for battle. □ *The armed soldiers marched toward the battlefield.*

**armpit** ['ɑrm pɪt] *n.* the hollow underneath the place where the arm joins the shoulder. □ *Mary applied deodorant to her armpits.*

**armrest** ['ɑrm rɛst] *n.* the part of a chair or seat that supports someone's arm. □ *One of the armrests on this chair is loose.*

**army** ['ɑrm i] *n.* a large group of land-based soldiers. □ *Have you served in the army?*

**aroma** [ə 'rom ə] *n.* an odor, especially one that is pleasant or agreeable. □ *The roses give the room a pleasant aroma.*

**arose** [ə 'roz] pt of **arise**.

**around** [ə 'rɑʊnd] **1.** *prep.* enclosing someone or something all about; surrounding someone or something. □ *A ring of flowers grew around the base of the tree.* **2.** *prep.* close to a certain time or location. □ *The meeting will start around three o'clock.* **3.** *prep.* [traveling or touring] in various places in something; at different locations within something. (With verbs such as *run, walk, go, crawl, travel,* and *drive.*) □ *I spent last summer driving around Europe.* **4.** *prep.* moving in a circular pathway with relation to someone or something. □ *They like to walk around the lake.* **5.** *prep.* in a direction that changes or turns at a corner. □ *The bathroom is around the corner to your left.* **6.** *adv.* on every side; on all sides. □ *After the accident, people gathered around.* **7.** *adv.* following a circle or a curve. □ *The tree trunk measured six inches around.* **8.** *adv.* in a circular manner; in circles. □ *The hands of the clock turn around slowly.*

**arrange** [ə 'rendʒ] **1.** *tv.* to put things in a particular order; to put things in specific locations. □ *The florist arranged the roses in the vase.* **2.** *tv.* to prepare plans for something; to plan details for something. □ *Bob arranged a party for Mary's birthday.* **3.** *tv.* to adapt a piece of music in a particular way. □ *The conductor arranged the song for two singers.*

**arrangement** [ə 'rendʒ mənt] **1.** *n.* the order or positions in which things have been put or placed. □ *Max carefully planned the arrangement of food on the serving table.* **2.** *n.* a group of flowers arranged in a pleasing way. □ *There is a lovely arrangement on the table.* **3. make arrangements** *phr.* to prepare a plan or plans; to create a scheme in advance. □ *John made arrangements to meet Mary at eight o'clock.*

**arrest** [ə 'rɛst] **1.** *n.* the taking and holding of someone in the name of the law. □ *How many arrests do the police make each month?* **2.** *tv.* to take someone to the police station for breaking a law. □ *The police arrested the robber.* **3.** *tv.* to stop something from moving or working; to bring something to an end. □ *A sudden loss of income arrested my plans for buying a house.*

**arrival** [ə 'rɑɪ vəl] *n.* the reaching of the place that one is going to; coming to a place. □ *Our flight's arrival is scheduled for eight o'clock.*

**arrive** [ə 'rɑɪv] *iv.* to reach the place that one is going to. □ *Our guests arrived late in the evening.*

**arrogance** ['ɛr ə gəns] *n.* an unpleasant attitude of superiority; excessive pride. (No plural form.) □ *We didn't tip the waiter very much because of his arrogance toward us.*

**arrogant** ['ɛr ə gənt] *adj.* with an unpleasant attitude of superiority; showing arrogance. (Adv: *arrogantly.*) □ *The waiter's arrogant manner made the customers angry.*

**arrow** ['ɛr o] **1.** *n.* a thin, sharply pointed stick that is shot from a bow. □ *The hunter put an arrow in his bow.* **2.** *n.* a pointed symbol, indicating direction or position. □ *An arrow pointed the way to the door.*

**art** ['ɑrt] **1.** *n.* the skilled creation of things of beauty or significant interest. (No plural form. Typically painting, drawing, sculpture, fiction, poetry, theater, dance, music, film, and photography.) □ *John got a degree in art and made his living as a sculptor.* **2.** *n.* the product of ①, such as a painting, drawing, or sculpture. (No plural form. Number is expressed with *work(s) of art.*) □ *I love to see the art on display at the museum.* **3.** *n.* the skill required to do or to make something creative; a creative craft. □ *The art of arranging flowers is difficult to learn.* **4. the arts** *n.* areas of activity associated with ①. (Treated as plural.) □ *Many of the arts are supported by charitable donations.*

**article** ['ɑr tɪ kəl] **1.** *n.* a small part or section of a written document, especially an official document such as a contract. □ *The last article in the publisher's contract explains the author's rights.* **2.** *n.* a specific item; a piece of something. □ *Jane has several articles of clothing that need to be washed.* **3.** *n.* <a word like **a**, **an**, and **the** in English.> □ *If a noun begins with a vowel sound, it takes the article* an *rather than* a. **4.** *n.* a small section of writing in a larger work, as in a newspaper or an encyclopedia. □ *Mary often writes short articles for the local newspaper.*

**artificial** [ɑr tə 'fɪʃ əl] *adj.* not authentic; not occurring in nature. (Adv: *artificially.*) □ *The soldier who lost a leg in battle now has an artificial limb.*

A

**artist** ['ɑr tɪst] *n.* someone who creates **art** ② or practices **art** ①. □ *The artist's works were exhibited at the museum.*

**artistic** [ɑr 'tɪs tɪk] *adj.* creatively pleasing; showing creativity. (Adv: *artistically* [...ɪk li].) □ *The ugly painting had no artistic merit.*

**artwork** ['ɑrt wɚk] **1.** *n.* one or more pieces of art, such as a painting or a sculpture. (No plural form.) □ *I own only one piece of original artwork.* **2.** *n.* the pictures or illustrations that appear with written text. (No plural form.) □ *Max's book has lots of color artwork in it.*

**as** ['æz] **1. as...as** *conj.* to the same amount or degree; equally; in the same way. □ *Mary is as busy as ever.* **2.** *conj.* while; during; at the same time. □ *Sally sang as she worked.* **3.** *conj.* in the way that. □ *Do your work as I told you to do it.* **4.** *conj.* because; since. □ *Mary left the movie early as she felt ill.* **5. as if** *conj.* in the same way that it would be if [something were to happen]. □ *The pale man looked as if he had seen a ghost.* **6. as though** *conj.* in the same way that it would be if [something were to happen]. □ *The cat, sleeping in the sunlight, lay motionless as though it were dead.* **7. as for** someone or something *phr.* in regard to someone or something; concerning someone or something. □ *As for the window you broke, you'll have to pay for it!* **8. as to** someone or something *phr.* regarding someone or something; concerning someone or something; about someone or something. □ *What can you tell us as to the whereabouts of Jimmy's runaway cat?* **9.** *prep.* in the role or function of something. □ *She used her table as a desk.*

**ash** ['æʃ] **1.** *n.* what remains after matter has burned or exploded. (The plural form is used when referring to the individual particles and pieces.) □ *Ash from the volcano's eruption drifted down into the village.* **2.** *n.* a tree of the olive family. □ *The ash in front of our house was hit by lightning.* **3.** *n.* the wood of ②. (Plural only when referring to different kinds, types, instances, or varieties.) □ *Don't waste good ash by burning it in the fireplace.* Ⓒ *The carpenter used a variety of different ashes in the construction project.*

**ashamed** [ə 'ʃemd] *adj.* having shame [about something]. (Adv: *ashamedly* [ə 'ʃem əd li].) □ *Aren't you ashamed to wear those old clothes?*

**aside** [ə 'sɑɪd] **1.** *n.* something said that is not meant to be heard by all present; a remark made by an actor to the audience. □ *The actor's aside made the audience laugh.* **2.** *adv.* to the side; to one side; apart from someone or something. □ *Susan moved aside so the cart could pass.* **3.** *adv.* away from oneself; to the side of oneself. □ *The baby pushed its bottle aside.*

**ask** ['æsk] **1.** *tv.* to put a question to someone. □ *I asked the visitor her name.* **2.** *tv.* to request information by stating a question. (The object can be a clause with **that** ⑦.) □ *Mary asked, "What time is it?"* **3. ask** someone **for** something *tv. + obj. + prep. phr.* to request that someone do something or give one something. □ *Mary asked me for a ride to work.* **4. ask** someone **about** someone or something *tv. + obj. + prep. phr.* to question someone about someone or something. □ *I asked Mary about her vacation in Florida.* **5.** *tv.* to invite someone to do something; to suggest that someone do something. □ *We asked some friends to come over for a barbecue.*

**asleep** [ə 'slip] **1.** *adj.* sleeping; not awake. (Not prenominal.) □ *Be quiet. Anne is asleep on the couch.* **2.** *adj.* [of arms, legs, hands, feet] temporarily not feeling anything. (Not prenominal.) □ *When my foot is asleep, I cannot walk on it.*

**aspirin** ['æs prɪn] **1.** *n.* a medication for relieving pain, used especially for headaches. (No plural form.) □ *The nurse gave me aspirin for my headache.* **2.** a tablet of ①. (Singular or plural with the same meaning.) □ *Take two aspirins and call the doctor tomorrow.*

**assail** [ə 'sel] **1.** *tv.* to attack someone or something. □ *A police officer assailed the crook with a club.* **2.** *tv.* to criticize someone or something strongly. □ *Angry citizens assailed the mayor for her lack of honesty.*

**asset** ['æ sɛt] **1.** *n.* an item of value; an item of someone's property. □ *The bank manager wanted to know about my assets.* **2.** *n.* a useful skill; a useful quality. (Fig. on ①.) □ *My sense of direction was an asset when I got lost.*

**assist** [ə 'sɪst] **1.** *tv.* to help someone or something; to help someone with something. □ *A nurse assisted the surgeon during the operation.* **2.** *n.* an act of assistance. □ *Thanks to his teammate's assist, the athlete was able to score the winning goal.*

**assistance** [ə 'sɪs təns] *n.* help; aid; cooperation. (No plural form.) □ *The university offers financial assistance to good students.*

**assistant** [ə 'sɪs tənt] *n.* someone who helps someone; someone whose job is to help someone. □ *The editor hired an assistant to work on the manuscripts.*

**associate** **1.** [ə 'so si ət] *n.* a colleague; someone who works with someone else. □ *Anne ate lunch with a business associate.* **2.** [ə 'so si ət] *adj.* [of a job or position] not at the highest level, but typically at a higher level than an assistant. □ *The associate sales manager left the meeting early.* **3.** [ə 'so si et] *iv.* to make social contact with someone. □ *John and his coworkers do not associate on weekends.*

**association** [ə so si 'e ʃən] **1.** *n.* a connection or link between two things, people, or thoughts. □ *What is your association with the organization?* **2.** *n.* a club, society, or organization; an alliance. □ *This book lists all the medical associations in the country.* **3.** *n.* a friendship; a relationship. □ *Business relationships often lead to close personal associations.*

**assume** [ə 'sum] **1.** *tv.* to believe that something really is as one thinks it is; to suppose something is true. (The object can be a clause with **that** ⑦.) □ *Fred always assumes that the worst will happen.* **2.** *tv.* to take control of something; to move into a role of leadership or responsibility for something. □ *The prince assumed the throne after the king's death.*

**assure** [ə 'ʃʊr] *tv.* to promise someone something; to say something encouraging and positive to someone. □ *Bob assured me that he would pay back the loan.*

**at** ['æt] **1.** *prep.* located on a point or in a place. (Used to show location in time or space.) □ *The children waited at the corner for the bus.* **2.** *prep.* in the direction of someone or something; toward someone or something. □ *Bill threw a rock at the window.* **3.** *prep.* engaged in something; being in a certain state or process. □ *The yellow sign warns that there are men at work.* **4.** *prep.* toward someone or something. (Used to show the object of an emotion.) □ *Yesterday, my teacher was angry at me.*

**ate** ['et] pt of **eat**.

**athlete** ['æθ lit] *n.* someone who participates in sports actively, especially a team member. □ *An athlete must eat well and exercise often.*

**athletic** [æθ 'lɛt ɪk] **1.** *adj.* strong; active; in good physical condition. (Adv: *athletically* [...ɪk li].) □ *The athletic old* *man ran five miles each day.* **2.** *adj.* relating to athletes; in or for ③. (Adv: *athletically* [...ɪk li].) □ *The university's athletic facilities attracted many students.* **3. athletics** *n.* active sports; exercise and training for sports. (Treated as singular or plural, but not countable.) □ *The quiet scholar never cared for athletics.*

**atlas** ['æt ləs] *n.* a book of maps. □ *The Smiths took a road atlas on their trip in case they got lost.*

**atmosphere** ['æt məs fɪr] **1.** *n.* the mixture of gases that surrounds a planet, especially the air that surrounds Earth. □ *The earth's atmosphere is many miles thick.* **2.** *n.* the air that is nearby; the air that one is breathing. (No plural form.) □ *The atmosphere was thick with smoke and dust.* **3.** *n.* the mood or feeling in a particular place. (No plural form.) □ *The atmosphere at the conference was very formal.*

**atom** ['æt əm] *n.* the smallest part of an element that has all the chemical properties of the element. □ *All matter is made of atoms.*

**attach** [ə 'tætʃ] **1.** *tv.* to fasten something to something else. □ *Bill attached a big bow to the birthday present.* **2.** *tv.* to associate a quality with someone or something; to think of a quality as belonging to someone or something. □ *I attach no significance to this matter.*

**attack** [ə 'tæk] **1.** *tv.* to try to harm someone or something, physically or verbally. □ *Our dog attacked the neighbor's cat.* **2.** *tv.* to begin work on a problem. (Fig. on ①.) □ *Bob attacked the puzzle eagerly.* **3.** *n.* an act of physical or verbal violence against someone or something. □ *Did the cat survive the attack by the neighbor's dog?* **4.** *n.* a sudden period of sickness or disease. □ *Bob had an attack of coughing.*

**attempt** [ə 'tɛmpt] **1.** *n.* an effort to do something; a try at doing something. □ *My attempt to bake a cake failed miserably.* **2.** *tv.* to make an effort at doing something. □ *I attempted it again, being more careful.* **3. attempt to do something** *iv.* + *inf.* to try to do something. □ *We will attempt to do it better this time.*

**attend** [ə 'tɛnd] **1.** *tv.* to be present at a place or event; to be present somewhere over a period of time. □ *Bob attended school until he was 17.* **2. attend to someone or something** *iv.* + *prep. phr.* to deal with someone or something; to manage something. □ *Please attend to the customers waiting in line.*

**attendance** [ə 'tɛn dəns] **1.** *n.* someone's presence at a location or event. (No plural form.) □ *Attendance at the meeting is mandatory.* **2.** *n.* the number of people present; the identity of the people attending something. (No plural form.) □ *Was there a large attendance at the baseball game?*

**attention** [ə 'tɛn ʃən] **1.** *n.* care in doing something; careful and watchful awareness. (No plural form.) □ *Special attention was given to the elderly at the church.* **2. attentions** *n.* ① that indicates a romantic interest. □ *John's attentions were not welcomed by his neighbor.*

**attic** ['æt ɪk] *n.* the room at the top of a house, just under the roof. □ *The attic of our house is a large room with slanted walls.*

**attitude** ['æt ə tud] **1.** *n.* a way of thinking, behaving, and feeling. □ *The clerk had a bad attitude and treated customers poorly.* **2.** *n.* a particular position or angle, especially of an aircraft. □ *A computer controls the attitude of the aircraft.*

**attractive** [ə 'træk tɪv] *adj.* pretty; pleasing to the eye; handsome; creating interest. (Adv: *attractively.*) □ *The flowers looked attractive on the kitchen table.*

**auction** ['ɔk ʃən] **1.** *n.* a sale where each item is sold to the person offering to pay the highest price. ☐ *The charity held an auction to raise money.* **2. auction something (off)** *tv.* + *obj.* *(+ adv.)* to sell something to the person who will pay the most money for it, as with ①. ☐ *The artist auctioned off his works shortly before he died.*

**audience** ['ɔ di əns] **1.** *n.* a group of spectators who watch and listen to someone or something. ☐ *The audience loved the opera and applauded loudly.* **2.** *n.* the group of people who see a particular film, TV show, etc. ☐ *The newspaper owners hoped for a large audience for their ads.* **3.** *n.* a formal interview or meeting with a very important person. (Usually with someone of very high rank.) ☐ *William sought an audience with the king.*

**audio** ['ɔ di o] **1.** *n.* broadcast or recorded sound, not video; the part of television that can be heard. (No plural form.) ☐ *Who did the audio for the commercial?* **2.** *adj.* <the adj. use of ①.> ☐ *The audio control on the television set broke.*

**auditorium** [ɔ dɪ 'tor i əm] **1.** *n.* the part of a performance hall where the audience sits. ☐ *The new auditorium had velvet seats.* **2.** *n.* a large room or building used for public meetings, lectures, and similar things. ☐ *The students came to the auditorium to hear the principal speak.*

**August** ['ɔg əst] Go to **month**.

**aunt** ['ænt] *n.* the sister of one's mother or father; the wife of the brother of one's mother or father; the wife of one's uncle. (Also a term of address.) ☐ *Aunt Mary sent me a birthday card last week.*

**authentic** [ɔ 'θɛn tɪk] *adj.* real; genuine; known to be real or true. (Adv: *authentically* [...ɪk li].) ☐ *Is your diamond ring authentic?*

**author** ['ɔ θɚ] **1.** *n.* someone who writes books, poems, plays, articles, or similar compositions. ☐ *Who is the author of the play we saw last night?* **2.** *tv.* to write something; to compose something. ☐ *Mary has authored three books about plants.*

**authority** [ə 'θor ə ti] **1.** *n.* the power and right to do something; control and managing in general. (No plural form.) ☐ *The teacher gave her assistant the authority to grade papers.* **2.** *n.* an expert. ☐ *Jane is an authority on French art.* **3. authorities** *n.* members of a group who have the **authority** ① to do something, such as to make rules; the police; the government. ☐ *We reported the car accident to the local authorities.*

**auto** ['ɔt o] *n.* a car; an **automobile**. ☐ *My auto was in the shop, so I took the bus to work.*

**autograph** ['ɔt ə græf] **1.** *n.* someone's signature, especially the signature of a famous person. ☐ *I have more than 100 autographs of famous people.* **2.** *adj.* <the adj. use of ①.> ☐ *My autograph collection numbers more than 100.* **3.** *tv.* to sign one's name on something. ☐ *The child held up a book for the singer to autograph.*

**automatic** [ɔt ə 'mæt ɪk] **1.** *adj.* [of a machine] acting by itself; not needing outside help to perform a process. (Adv: *automatically* [...ɪk li].) ☐ *The Smiths bought an automatic dishwasher.* **2.** *adj.* done without thinking; done out of habit or by instinct. (Adv: *automatically* [...ɪk li].) ☐ *Fear is an automatic reaction to a threat.*

**automobile** [ɔt ə mo 'bil] *n.* a car; a vehicle that can carry a small number of passengers. ☐ *Mary is learning to repair automobiles.*

**autumn** ['ɔt əm] *n.* fall; the season after summer and before winter. ☐ *In the* *autumn, the leaves turn colors and fall off the trees.*

**aux.** an abbreviation of **auxiliary verb.**

**auxiliary** [ɔg 'zɪl jə ri] **1.** *adj.* secondary; supplementary; substitute. □ *The auxiliary power unit turned on during the storm.* **2.** *n.* an **auxiliary verb.** □ *Some auxiliaries, such as* do *and* have, *are also regular verbs.*

**auxiliary verb** AND **verbal auxiliary** [ɔg 'zɪl jə ri vɚb, 'vɚb əl ɔg 'zɪl jə ri] *n.* a word that is used before a verb to affect its tense, aspect, or mood. (Also called a *helping verb* or **auxiliary**. Abbreviated *aux.* here. Examples: *can, could, did, do, does, had, has, have, may, might, must, ought, shall, should, will, would.*) □ *Some auxiliary verbs, such as* do *and* have, *are also regular verbs.* □ *In the sentence "I have done it,"* have *is an auxiliary verb.*

**avail** [ə 'vel] **1. avail** oneself **of** something *phr.* to help oneself by making use of something that is available. (Reflexive.) □ *We availed ourselves of Tom's kind offer and let him repair the fence.* **2. to no avail** *phr.* of no benefit or help; without having the desired result. □ *We struggled to no avail and lost the battle.*

**available** [ə 'vel ə bəl] *adj.* ready; accessible and not assigned or committed to something else. □ *Are you available to serve on the committee?*

**avenue** ['æv ə nu] **1.** *n.* a wide street in a city, sometimes lined with trees. □ *The city planted trees along Washington Avenue.* **2.** *n.* a pathway. (Often figurative, such as the way a problem is approached.) □ *We explored all the avenues, but this is the only solution that is reasonable.*

**average** ['æv (ə) rɪdʒ] **1.** *n.* an amount obtained by adding several numbers together and then dividing that total by the quantity of numbers that were added. □ *The average of 10, 22, and 34 is 22.* **2.** *n.* something that is usual, typical, or normal. (No plural form.) □ *There is nothing unique about this. This is just the average.* **3. average** something **(up)** *tv.* + *obj.* (+ *adv.*) to add several figures and then divide that total by the number of figures that were added. □ *I have to average up these numbers for the boss.* **4.** *adj.* usual; typical; normal; ordinary. (Adv: *averagely.*) □ *John is an average, hardworking businessman.* **5. on the average** *phr.* generally; usually. □ *I eat meat three times a week, on the average.* **6. above average** *phr.* higher or better than the general level of quality. □ *His intelligence is above average.* **7. below average** *phr.* lower or worse than the general level of quality. □ *Dad asked why my grades are below average.*

**aviation** [ev i 'e ʃən] *n.* the flying of aircraft; the management of flying aircraft. (No plural form.) □ *We bought a book on the history of aviation.*

**avocado** [ɑv ə 'kɑd o] **1.** *n.* a tropical fruit with rough green, black, or purple skin, soft green flesh, and a large pit. (Pl ends in *-s.*) □ *The dip was made from avocados and lemon juice.* **2.** *n.* the edible part of ①. (No plural form.) □ *I put some avocado in the salad.* **3.** *adj.* made from ②. □ *Your avocado salad is delicious.*

**avoid** [ə 'vɔɪd] **1.** *tv.* to elude contact with someone or something; to manage not to make contact with someone or something. □ *To avoid the huge dog, I turned around and ran away.* **2.** *tv.* to prevent something from occurring. □ *Try to avoid getting soap in your eyes.*

**await** [ə 'wet] *tv.* to expect someone or something to arrive; to wait for the arrival of someone or something. □ *Jane awaited the mail each day, expecting a letter.*

**awake** [ə 'wek] **1.** *adj.* not asleep; alert. (Not prenominal.) □ *The playful kitten* *was wide awake and wouldn't let me fall asleep.* **2.** *iv., irreg.* to stop sleeping; to wake. (Pt: **awoke;** pp: **awoken.** See also **awaken.**) □ *Tom awoke early and finished studying for the exam.* **3.** *tv., irreg.* to make someone or something stop sleeping; to wake someone or something up. (See also **awaken.**) □ *Tom awoke his roommate at dawn.* **4.** *tv., irreg.* to bring back memories of someone or something into one's thoughts. (Fig. on ③. See also **awaken.**) □ *The sound of the thunder awoke terrors in those who had survived the war.*

**awaken** [ə 'wek ən] **1.** *iv.* to stop sleeping; to wake. (See also **awake.**) □ *Tom awakened and got ready for work.* **2.** *tv.* to make someone or something stop sleeping; to wake someone or something up. (See also **awake.**) □ *The kittens awakened their mother because they were hungry.* **3.** *tv.* to bring back memories of someone or something into one's thoughts; to arouse in someone a new or hidden feeling, interest, talent, awareness, or emotion. (Fig. on ②. See also **awake.**) □ *The teacher hoped that visiting the laboratory would awaken the children's interest in science.*

**award** [ə 'word] **1.** *n.* something given to someone as repayment; something given to someone as a prize. □ *The committee gave Mary an award for her hard work.* **2.** *tv.* to give something to someone as the result of an official legal decision; to order the payment of money in a court of law. □ *The judge awarded $10,000 to the plaintiff.* **3.** *tv.* to give a prize to someone; to give someone something as the result of an official decision. □ *The judges awarded the runner a medal for first place.*

**aware** [ə 'wɛr] **1.** *adj.* alert; conscious; having control of one's senses. (Not usually prenominal.) □ *The cat is half asleep, but she is more aware than you might think.* **2.** *adj.* knowledgeable; in a state of knowing something. (Takes a clause with *that.*) □ *John was aware that he was being rude, but he didn't care.* **3. aware of** someone or something *adj. + prep. phr.* conscious of someone or something. □ *Are you aware of the problems that you have caused?*

**away** [ə 'we] **1.** *adj.* at some distance; apart in distance. (Not prenominal.) □ *The ship on the horizon was actually more than 60 miles away.* **2.** *adj.* [of a game] not played on the home team's court or field. □ *The team traveled for an hour to get to the final away game.* **3.** *adv.* from one position or direction to another; from one state or position to another. □ *I turned my head away from the accident.* **4.** *adv.* without stopping; continuously. □ *Bob banged away at the piano.*

**awe** ['ɔ] **1.** *n.* a strong feeling of wonder and respect. (No plural form.) □ *I am always in awe of people who can cook well.* **2.** *tv.* to fill someone with wonder and respect. □ *The campers were always awed by a beautiful sunset.*

**awful** ['ɔ fʊl] *adj.* horrible; terrible; very bad. (Adv: **awfully.**) □ *Monday was an awful day. Everything went wrong.*

**awfully** ['ɔf (ə) li] **1.** *adv.* terribly; horribly; badly. □ *Bob scored awfully on his test.* **2.** *adv.* very; really. □ *This coffee is awfully strong.*

**awhile** [ə 'ʍɑɪl] *adv.* for a short length of time; for a little bit of time. □ *Let's rest awhile before finishing our hike.*

**awkward** ['ɔk wɚd] **1.** *adj.* clumsy; not graceful. (Adv: *awkwardly.*) □ *The growing teenager went through an awkward stage.* **2.** *adj.* hard to manage; hard to control; not easily used. (Adv: *awkwardly.*) □ *These are awkward shoes, and I know I will trip when I wear them.* **3.** *adj.* embarrassing; embarrassed. (Adv: *awkwardly.*) □ *Tom was always a bit awkward when meeting new people.*

A

**awning** ['ɔ nɪŋ] *n.* a covering, extending over a walkway, door, or window. □ *When the storm started, we ran under the awning.*

**awoke** [ə 'wok] pt of **awake.**

**awoken** [ə 'wok ən] pp of **awake.**

**ax(e)** ['æks] *n.* a tool that consists of a heavy metal wedge attached to a handle, used to chop wood. (Pl: **axes.**) □ *The axe had been left in the rain and was rusted.*

**axes 1.** ['æk siz] pl of **axis. 2.** ['æk sɪz] pl of **axe** and **ax.**

**axis** ['æks ɪs] *n., irreg.* an imaginary line that goes through the center point of a sphere or a ball. (Pl: **axes.**) □ *The earth spins on its axis.* □ *A rod runs along the axis of my globe and is attached to the stand that supports the globe.*

**axle** ['æk səl] *n.* the rod that connects a pair of wheels. □ *Trucks often have more than two axles.*

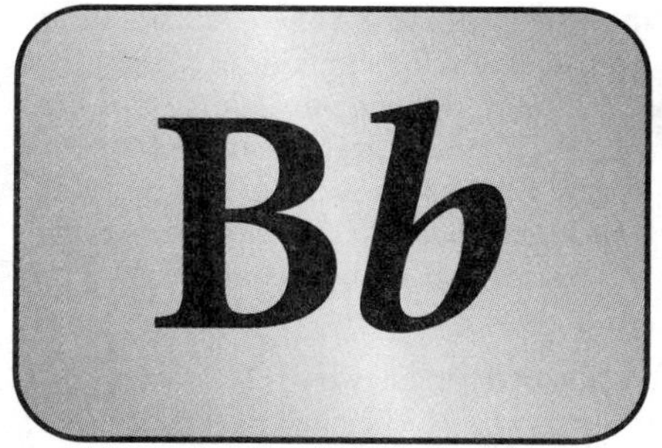


**baby** ['be bi] **1.** *n.* an infant; a newly born child. □ *The Smiths named their new baby Anne.* **2.** *tv.* to treat someone or something like ①. □ *Jane babies her children, and they love her very much.* **3.** *adj.* <the adj. use of ①>; specially made for ①. □ *Please buy some baby soap.*

**babysat** ['beb i sæt] pt/pp of **babysit.**

**babysit** ['be bi sɪt] **1.** *iv., irreg.* to care for someone else's children. (Pt/pp: **babysat.**) □ *Can Mary babysit for Jimmy Saturday night?* **2.** *tv., irreg.* to take care of children whose parents are away. □ *Jane babysat her nephew last night.*

**babysitter** ['be bi sɪt ɚ] *n.* someone who takes care of children whose parents are away. □ *The babysitter put the children to bed at nine o'clock.*

**back** ['bæk] **1.** *n.* the part of a body along the spine. □ *The children stood with their backs pressed to the wall.* **2.** *n.* the rear part of something. □ *The back of your shirt has a tear in it.* **3.** *n.* the part of a chair that supports ①. □ *The back of the chair was broken, and I fell off.* **4. in back of** someone or something *phr.* behind someone or something. □ *Jane hid in back of the shed.* **5. back out (of** something**)** *iv. + adv. (+ prep. phr.)* to move backward out of something. □ *Please back out of the garage carefully.* **6. back** something **up** *tv. + obj. + adv.* to make a copy of one's computer work for safekeeping. □ *Does the secretary back the computers up each night?* [T] *Nobody backs up the computers.* **7. back** something **out** *tv. + obj. + adv.* to make something move **back** ⑪ and go out of something. □ *Susan backed the car out of the garage.* [T] *She backed out the car.* **8.** *tv.* to support someone or something; to agree with someone or something. □ *I always back my boss on department policy.* **9.** *tv.* to support someone or something with money. □ *The wealthy banker backed the entire opera season.* **10.** *adj.* rear; opposite the front. (Prenominal only.) □ *There was a pool table in the bar's back room.* **11.** *adv.* to or toward the rear; backward. □ *I moved back to let the busy clerk pass me.* **12.** *adv.* in or to the original place. □ *Please put the cookie jar back where it belongs.* **13.** *adv.* earlier; in or to the past. □ *Sue suddenly realized that she should have gotten off the bus three stops back.* **14.** *adv.* in reply; in repayment of something. □ *Six months after I borrowed the money, I paid back the loan.*

**back and forth** ['bæk ən 'forθ] *adv.* moving in one direction and then the other, over and over; moving from one to the other, again and again. □ *We tossed the ball back and forth between us.*

**backbone** ['bæk bon] *n.* the spine. □ *The hiker's backbone broke in the fall.*

**background** ['bæk graʊnd] **1.** *n.* [in a picture] the scene behind the main subject. □ *The Rocky Mountains formed the background of the photo.* **2.** *n.* the events leading up to something. (No plural form.) □ *We arrived late for the movie and didn't know the background of the story.* **3.** *n.* the past training, education, and experience of someone. □ *Jane told the foster parents about the child's background.*

**backrest** ['bæk rɛst] *n.* the vertical part of a chair that supports someone's back. □ *Don't sit on that chair. The backrest is broken.*

B

**backup** ['bæk əp] **1.** *n.* a substitute or replacement for someone or something. ☐ *Is there a backup for John? He is sick.* **2.** *n.* [in computers] a copy of a computer file or document. ☐ *Did you make backups of your files?* **3.** *adj.* spare; extra. ☐ *Susan had some backup film for the camera.*

**backward** ['bæk wɚd] **1.** *adv.* toward the rear; with the back part going first. (Also **backwards**.) ☐ *The kitten inched backwards when it saw the dog.* **2.** *adv.* in a way that is the opposite of the normal way; in a way that reverses the order or direction of something. (Also **backwards**.) ☐ *The appliance didn't work because it was assembled backwards.* **3.** *adj.* directed toward the back or the starting point. ☐ *I didn't feel the backward motion of the car until we hit the car behind us.* **4.** *adj.* in a worse or earlier state; not modern. (Adv: *backwardly.*) ☐ *The senator's backward views made us laugh.* **5.** *adj.* hesitant or shy. (Adv: *backwardly.*) ☐ *Tom was a little backward around the other students.*

**backyard** ['bæk 'jɑrd] *n.* the lawn or area behind a house. ☐ *The children were playing in the backyard.*

**bacon** ['bek ən] *n.* meat from the back and sides of a hog. (Plural only when referring to different kinds, types, or varieties.) ☐ *I love crisp bacon, but it is not good for me.* Ⓒ *I tried different bacons, but none is as good as the kind I grew up with.*

**bacteria** [bæk 'tɪr i ə] *n.* a group of tiny, one-celled organisms. (**Bacteria** is plural. The singular is *bacterium.*) ☐ *Some bacteria cause harmful diseases.*

**bad** ['bæd] **1.** *adj., irreg.* wicked; evil; not good. (Adv: *badly.* Comp: **worse**; sup: **worst**.) ☐ *The children found the house of a very bad witch.* **2.** *adj., irreg.* of poor quality; inferior; worthless; defective; not good. (Adv: *badly.* Comp: **worse**; sup: **worst**.) ☐ *Driving while drunk is a bad idea.* **3.** *adj., irreg.* serious; severe. (Adv: *badly.* Comp: **worse**; sup: **worst**.) ☐ *Tom has a bad cold.* **4.** *adj., irreg.* harmful; not healthful. (Adv: *badly.* Comp: **worse**; sup: **worst**.) ☐ *Fatty foods are bad for your health.* **5.** *adj., irreg.* [of a person, a creature, or a part of one's body feeling or appearing] sick, hurt, or unwell. ☐ *After Mary sprained her ankle, it felt bad for several weeks.* **6.** *adj., irreg.* unpleasant; disagreeable; not nice. (Adv: *badly.* Comp: **worse**; sup: **worst**.) ☐ *I was upset because I had a bad day.* **7.** *adj.* [of food] decayed or spoiled. ☐ *The milk turned bad overnight.* **8.** *adv.* very much. (Colloquial.) ☐ *This cut really hurts bad!*

**badge** ['bædʒ] *n.* a pin or medal worn to show membership in an organization. ☐ *The officer handed out badges to the new members.*

**bag** ['bæg] **1.** *n.* a sack; a pouch-like container. ☐ *I carried the groceries in a plastic bag.* **2.** *n.* the contents of ①. ☐ *Put a whole bag of nuts in the recipe.* **3.** *tv.* to put items into ①. ☐ *The clerk broke the eggs when she bagged my groceries.* **4.** *tv.* to kill wild game. ☐ *The hunter bagged a large duck.*

**baggage** ['bæg ɪdʒ] *n.* luggage or suitcases. (No plural form. Treated as singular. Number is expressed with *piece(s) of baggage.*) ☐ *The airline lost our baggage!*

**baggy** ['bæg i] *adj.* puffy; having extra material that hangs in loose folds. (Adv: *baggily.* Comp: *baggier;* sup: *baggiest.*) ☐ *I don't like how those baggy pants look on you.*

**bait** ['bet] **1.** *n.* someone or something used as a lure or temptation. (Plural only when referring to different kinds, types, instances, or varieties.) ☐ *The store offered free candy as bait to lure customers inside.* Ⓒ *Different species of fish respond to different baits.* **2.** *tv.* to put a worm or some kind of food on a hook in order to attract fish. □ *Dad didn't catch any fish because he forgot to bait his hook.* **3.** *tv.* to put a lure into a trap. □ *The hunters baited their traps carefully.*

**bake** ['bek] **1.** *tv.* to cook something using dry heat, usually in an oven. □ *The recipe says to bake the casserole for an hour.* **2.** *tv.* [for the sun or hot, dry weather] to make someone or something very hot. (Fig. on ①.) □ *The hot sun baked the dry land, and the farmers hoped for rain.* **3.** *iv.* to cook food by placing it in a hot oven. □ *Bill is at home baking for the coming week.*

**baker** ['bek ɚ] *n.* someone who bakes foods, usually breads or pastries. □ *Tom went to cooking school to become a baker.*

**bakery** ['bek ri] *n.* a store or place where bread products and pastries are prepared and sold. □ *I bought a fancy cake at the local bakery.*

**balance** ['bæl əns] **1.** *n.* an even placement of weight; a stable position with weight placed evenly; the ability to stay in such a position; equilibrium. (No plural form.) □ *I lost my balance and fell.* **2.** *n.* a device that compares the weights of two objects. □ *The merchant weighed the goods on an old balance.* **3.** *n.* an equality in weight, proportion, or value; harmony. (No plural form.) □ *Bill arranged the pictures carefully to achieve a nice balance on the wall.* **4.** *n.* the amount of money remaining on a bill after part of the bill has been paid; the amount of money remaining in an account after a transaction. □ *The balance in my checking account is low.* **5.** *tv.* to place something in such a way that it is stable. □ *I balanced the book on top of the stack.* **6.** *tv.* to apply credits and debits to an account to determine the correct amount of money in the account. □ *Jane balances her checking account each month.* **7.** *tv.* to make something have symmetry in appearance or character. □ *Mary balanced the planting in her garden carefully.*

**balcony** ['bæl kə ni] **1.** *n.* a platform that extends outward from a room that is higher than ground level. □ *The bedrooms on the second floor of the house have balconies.* **2.** *n.* [in a hall or auditorium] an upper level of seats that extends over the main floor. □ *Our seats at the opera were in the balcony.*

**bald** ['bɔld] *adj.* having no hair on the head; without hair. (Comp: *balder;* sup: *baldest.*) □ *Many new babies are bald.*

**ball** ['bɔl] **1.** *n.* a round object; a sphere. □ *The yarn was wound into a ball.* **2.** *n.* a toy that is a round object. □ *The children threw the ball back and forth.* **3.** *n.* an elegant dance or party. □ *Mary danced at the ball for several hours.*

**ballet** [bæ 'le] *n.* a form of graceful and precise dance that tells a story without using speech or singing. (Plural only when referring to the works of different composers or performers.) □ *The dancer began studying ballet when she was only five years old.* Ⓒ *We went to a ballet where the star kept falling down.*

**balloon** [bə 'lun] *n.* a container of rubber, fabric, or some other material that can be filled with air or gas. □ *The party room was decorated with colorful balloons.*

**ballot** ['bæl ət] **1.** *n.* a method of voting involving pieces of paper or machines. □ *The club's president is elected by ballot.* **2.** *n.* a piece of paper on which one's vote is marked. □ *Who will count the ballots?*

**bamboo** [bæm 'bu] **1.** *n.* a type of very tall, woody grass typically found in warm countries. (No plural form.) □ *Bamboo is sometimes used to make furniture.* **2.** *adj.* made from the stems or wood of ①. □ *This room has bamboo chairs and tables and numerous tropical plants in pots.*

B

**banana** [bə 'næn ə] **1.** *n.* a long, tropical fruit with a yellow skin around a soft, white edible pulp. □ *The gorillas at the zoo love bananas.* **2.** *adj.* made of or flavored with ①. □ *Max loves banana ice cream.*

**band** ['bænd] **1.** *n.* a group of musicians, often including singers. □ *The couple hired a band to play at their wedding reception.* **2.** *n.* a tribe; a group of people. □ *The band of hunters took shelter in a cave.* **3.** *n.* a flat, thin strip of some material that is used to hold objects together. □ *I sealed the box with a band of tape.* **4.** *n.* a stripe. □ *A band of red accented the design.*

**bandage** ['bæn dɪdʒ] **1.** *n.* a wrapping used to cover and protect a wound against dirt, germs, and infection. □ *Jane put a bandage on the cut on her finger.* **2.** *tv.* to place ① on someone or something. □ *I had to bandage my own sprained ankle.*

**bandit** ['bæn dɪt] *n.* a robber, especially one belonging to a band of outlaws. □ *The bandit tried to hide from the sheriff.*

**bang** ['bæŋ] **1.** *n.* a sudden, loud noise; the sound of an explosion. □ *I heard a bang and went to see what had fallen.* **2. bangs** *n.* hair that hangs down over the forehead or eyes rather than being combed back. (Treated as plural, but not countable.) □ *Jane asked her mother to cut her bangs.* **3.** *tv.* to hit something against something else, making a loud noise. □ *Bob banged the TV with his fist, and the picture cleared.* **4.** *iv.* to hit [something]; to make loud noises by striking something. □ *Who is banging around in the kitchen?*

**bank** ['bæŋk] **1.** *n.* a corporation that lends, saves, and protects money. □ *We got a personal loan from the bank.* **2.** *n.* the building where money is loaned, saved, and protected. □ *The post office is across the street from the bank.* **3.** *n.* a place where certain objects are stored. □ *Bill made a contribution to the food bank.* **4.** *n.* the land along the side of a river, stream, or canal. □ *The lovers sat on the bank of the river and had a picnic.* **5.** *n.* a row or set of objects. □ *We installed a bank of lights in the ceiling of our basement.* **6.** *iv.* to do business with ①. □ *John banks where there are no service charges.* **7.** *tv.* to cause an airplane to tilt to one side in order to turn right or left. □ *The pilot banked the plane as we made a turn.*

**banker** ['bæŋ kɚ] *n.* someone who is an owner of or an important officer in a bank. □ *The firm hired a retired banker to manage its money.*

**banquet** ['bæŋ kwɪt] **1.** *n.* a dinner and speeches, usually connected with a celebration or an event. □ *The banquet is held at the same hotel each year.* **2.** *n.* a special dinner with a large menu; a feast. □ *Mary served us a banquet that was fit for a king.*

**bar** ['bɑr] **1.** *n.* a counter or flat surface that someone stands behind to prepare and serve drinks or food to people. □ *John walked up to the bar and asked for another drink.* **2.** *n.* a counter or flat surface where different kinds of food items are kept, from which people choose whatever they would like to eat. □ *The salad bar included spinach, carrots, and tomatoes.* **3.** *n.* a place where people can buy alcoholic drinks. □ *They went to the bar and had a few drinks.* **4.** *n.* a rigid rod of metal, wood, or some other material. □ *A bar of iron fell off the truck and struck a car.* **5.** *n.* a rectangular object made of certain kinds of material, such as soap or various metals. □ *The treasure chest contained a few bars of gold.* **6. the bar** *n.* the legal profession. (No plural form. Treated as singular.) □ *Dave consulted a member of the bar for legal advice.* **7.** *n.* a measure in a piece of music. □ *There was a mistake in the third bar of the music.* **8.** *tv.* to secure a door or window by placing ④ across it. □ *The frightened family barred the door against the intruder.*

**barbecue** AND **barbeque** ['bɑr bə kju] **1.** *n.* an outdoor grill used to cook food. □ *Meat is cooking on the barbecue.* **2.** *n.* a party or meal where people eat food cooked on a grill. □ *Let's have our friends over for a barbecue Saturday!* **3.** *n.* the food that is prepared on an outdoor grill, especially food cooked with a spicy tomato sauce. □ *John's barbecue tastes bad because it's too salty.* **4.** *tv.* to cook food on a grill, often with a spicy tomato sauce. □ *David barbecued dinner on the grill.* **5.** *iv.* [for food] to cook on an outdoor grill, often with a spicy tomato sauce. □ *The hot dogs were barbecuing while we played volleyball.*

**barbeque** ['bɑr bə kju] Go to **barbecue**.

**barber** ['bɑr bɚ] *n.* someone who cuts or styles hair, especially men's hair. □ *The barber had a shop on Main Street for thirty years.*

**bare** ['bɛr] **1.** *tv.* to uncover. □ *The dog bared its teeth and growled.* **2.** *adj.* naked; exposed. (Adv: *barely.* Comp: *barer;* sup: *barest.*) □ *The edge of the bathtub is cold on my bare bottom.* **3.** *adj.* empty. (Adv: *barely.* Comp: *barer;* sup: *barest.*) □ *The shelves were bare, so I went to the grocery store.*

**barefoot(ed)** ['bɛr fʊt(əd)] **1.** *adv.* without shoes or socks; with nothing on the feet. □ *The children ran barefoot in the grass.* **2.** *adj.* not wearing shoes or socks; having nothing on the feet. □ *The barefoot child stepped on a piece of glass.*

**barely** ['bɛr li] *adv.* hardly; only just; not quite. □ *There was barely enough food to go around.*

**bargain** ['bɑr gən] **1.** *n.* something that was bought for less money than it would normally cost. □ *The new car I bought on sale was quite a bargain.* **2.** *n.* an agreement. □ *Mother made a bargain with Jimmy about bedtime.* **3. bargain (with** someone**)** *iv.* (+ *prep. phr.*) to set the terms of an agreement or a sale with someone. □ *John bargained with the salesman over the price of the used car.* **4. bargain on** something**; bargain for** something *iv.* + *prep. phr.* to expect something; to be prepared for something happening. □ *I hadn't bargained on the party ending by midnight.*

**bark** ['bɑrk] **1.** *n.* the outer surface of a tree. (Plural only when referring to different kinds, types, instances, or varieties.) □ *A message was etched into the bark of the tree.* Ⓒ *The barks of various trees can be burned for heating purposes.* **2.** *n.* the sound that is made by a dog. □ *Sue's little dog has an annoying bark.* **3.** *iv.* to make the noise of a dog. □ *Why does that dog bark all the time?*

**barn** ['bɑrn] **1.** *n.* a large farm building for keeping livestock and storing supplies and equipment. □ *Farm animals are kept in barns.* **2.** *n.* a large building where trucks and buses are kept and serviced. □ *The train was sent to the barn for repairs.*

**barnyard** ['bɑrn jɑrd] *n.* the fenced area surrounding a barn; a farmyard. □ *Dozens of chickens ran around the barnyard.*

**barometer** [bə 'rɑm ə tɚ] **1.** *n.* a device that measures the air pressure that is all around us. □ *The barometer indicated that the air pressure was dropping.* **2.** *n.* something that indicates possible changes. (Fig. on ①.) □ *The stock market is a barometer for the state of the economy.*

**barrel** ['bɛr əl] **1.** *n.* a large, rounded wooden container with a flat top and bottom. □ *The barrels are full of oil.* **2.** *n.* the contents of ①. (The exact amount depends on the size of the barrel.) □ *The pigs were fed an entire barrel of feed each week.* **3.** *n.* the standard measurement of oil, equal to 42 U.S. gallons. □ *The small country consumed about 10,000 barrels of oil per day.* **4.** *n.* the part of a gun through which the bullets travel. □ *Susan has a special tool to clean the barrel of her gun.*

**barricade** ['bɛr ə ked] **1.** *n.* something that blocks the way. □ *The police barricade kept thieves away from the crime scene.* **2.** *tv.* to block off a passageway or a pathway. □ *The workers barricaded the sidewalk after they poured the cement.*

**barrier** ['bɛr i ɚ] **1.** *n.* something that physically separates people or things. □ *The police officers kept us behind the concrete barrier.* **2.** *n.* something that emotionally or spiritually separates people or things. (Fig. on ①.) □ *Tom's and Anne's political beliefs are a barrier to their friendship.*

**base** ['bes] **1.** *n.* the bottom, supporting part of something. □ *The base of the lamp is made of wood.* **2.** *n.* a starting point; the foundation from which other things develop. □ *This theory forms the base of the argument.* **3.** *n.* a center of operations; the main site of a business or organization. □ *The steel company's base was in Pittsburgh.* **4.** *n.* the center of operations and living quarters of a military unit. □ *Most of the soldiers live on the base.* **5.** *n.* a chemical that is the opposite of an acid. □ *All alkalis are bases.* **6.** *n.* [in baseball] one of the four points of the baseball diamond. □ *The player stood on the base and waited for the pitch.* **7.** *adj.* forming or serving as ① or ②; acting as a foundation. □ *The base price for this car is $20,000.*

**baseball** ['bes bɔl] **1.** *n.* a team sport played with two teams of nine members each. (No plural form.) □ *Baseball is a very popular sport in America.* **2.** *n.* the white, leather-covered ball used in ①. □ *The catcher caught the baseball in his glove.*

**basement** ['bes mənt] *n.* a space within the foundations of a building, tall enough to permit a person to stand. □ *We stored all our old things in the basement.*

**bases** **1.** ['be siz] pl of **basis.** **2.** ['be sɪz] pl of **base.**

**basic** ['bes ɪk] **1.** *adj.* fundamental; simple and required. (Adv: *basically* [...ɪk li].) □ *Freedom of speech is a basic right in the United States.* **2.** *adj.* simple. (Adv: *basically* [...ɪk li].) □ *I signed up for a basic German class, but it was too easy.* **3. the basics** *n.* the first principles of something on which other principles are built. (Treated as plural, but not countable.) □ *Where did you learn the basics of business?*

**basin** ['be sən] **1.** *n.* a large, shallow bowl or similar structure. □ *The basin was filled with water.* **2.** *n.* the contents of ①. □ *Pour another basin of water onto the plants.* **3.** *n.* the area of land that is drained by a river or a system of rivers. □ *The soil along the river basin was very good for farming.*

**basis** ['be sɪs] **1.** *n., irreg.* the foundation of something; the part of something from which other things develop. (Pl: **bases** ['be siz].) □ *The professor's new theory formed the basis for her lecture.* **2.** *n., irreg.* an agreed-upon standard or status. □ *The skilled worker was hired on a permanent basis.*

**basket** ['bæs kɪt] **1.** *n.* a container woven of strips of wood, twigs, or similar material. □ *I filled my basket with vegetables from the garden.* **2.** *n.* the contents of ①. □ *We bought a basket of flowers.* **3.** *n.* [in basketball] the net, and the hoop to which it is attached, that are part of a basketball goal. □ *The basketball dropped through the basket.* **4.** *n.* a goal or score in the game of basketball. □ *The referee didn't see the basket.*

B

**basketball** ['bæs kɪt bɔl] **1.** *n.* a team sport where a goal is made by sending a ball through a **basket** ③. (No plural form.) □ *The movie was about the sport of basketball.* **2.** *n.* a ball used in ①. □ *The basketball missed the hoop and fell to the ground.*

**bat** ['bæt] **1.** *n.* a mouse-like mammal that has large wings and usually flies at night. □ *There are bats in the old house's attic.* **2.** *n.* a wooden or metal club used in the game of baseball. □ *The baseball player threw down the bat and ran for first base.* **3.** *tv.* to hit a ball with ②. □ *Everyone laughed at the way Bill batted the ball.* **4.** *tv.* to hit something; to slap at something. □ *Tom batted the flies away from him.*

**batch** ['bætʃ] **1.** *n.* a group of things processed at the same time. □ *This batch of cookies is burned.* **2.** *tv.* to group things together. □ *We batched the photographs by year.*

**bath** ['bæθ] **1.** *n., irreg.* the washing of someone or something. (Pl: ['bæðz] or ['bæθs].) □ *Jimmy really needs a bath.* **2.** *n., irreg.* water for bathing. □ *Mary sprinkled some fragrant oil into her bath.* **3.** *n., irreg.* a bathtub; a tub used for bathing. □ *This bath really needs scrubbing.* **4.** *n., irreg.* a bathroom; a room with a bathtub or shower. □ *My parents' house has five bedrooms and two baths.*

**bathe** ['beð] **1.** *iv.* to take a bath; to wash. (The present participle is *bathing* for all senses.) □ *Max wanted to ask his coworker to bathe more frequently.* **2.** *tv.* to clean or wash someone; to give someone a bath. □ *I bathed the children and put them into bed.* **3.** *tv.* to put water on something; to make something wet or moist. □ *Grandpa bathes his feet in hot water each night.*

**bathrobe** ['bæθ rob] *n.* a loose, coat-like garment worn before or after bathing or over pajamas. (See also **robe**.) □ *Jane got out of the shower and reached for her bathrobe.*

**bathroom** ['bæθ rum] **1.** *n.* a room having at least a toilet and a sink, and usually also a bathtub or a shower. □ *How many bathrooms does the new house have?* **2. go to the bathroom** *phr.* to use the toilet; to urinate; to defecate. □ *Jimmy has to go to the bathroom right now.*

**bathtub** ['bæθ təb] *n.* a large tub for bathing. □ *Jimmy loves to play with his boats in the bathtub.*

**bathwater** ['bæθ wɑt ɚ] *n.* water for bathing; the water contained in a bathtub. (No plural form.) □ *I relaxed while soaking in the bathwater.*

**battery** ['bæt ə ri] **1.** *n.* a cylinder-shaped or square object inserted into flashlights, portable radios, cameras, etc., to provide electrical power. □ *The batteries in my camera were dead.* **2.** *n.* beating someone; striking and harming someone. (No plural form.) □ *The criminal was arrested for battery.* **3.** *n.* a group of many large guns or other weapons. □ *A battery of cannons was installed on the wall of the fortress.* **4.** *n.* a series of tests or examinations. □ *The doctor ordered a battery of tests.*

**battle** ['bæt əl] **1.** *n.* a fight between two opposing forces during a war. □ *The troops met in an open field for a battle.* **2.** *n.* a fight or crusade against someone or something. (Fig. on ①.) □ *Mike and Jane led a battle against drunk drivers.* **3.** *tv.* to fight someone or something. □ *Bill had to battle his competition to get a promotion.*

**bay** ['be] **1.** *n.* an opening in the shoreline of an ocean, sea, or lake, capable of sheltering ships. □ *Our favorite fishing spot is in the bay.* **2.** *iv.* to make a long, deep howl like a dog, wolf, etc. □ *The wolves bayed at the moon all night long.*

B

**be** ['bi] **1.** *iv., irreg.* to exist in a certain way or as a certain thing; to exist in a certain state or condition. (Present tense: *I am, you are, he is, she is, it is, we are, you are, they are.* Past tense: *I was, you were, he was, she was, it was, we were, you were, they were.* Past participle: **been**. Present participle: *being.*) □ *Jimmy is a young boy.* □ *The sunrise was beautiful.* **2.** *iv., irreg.* to occur; to happen. □ *Our vacation will be next week.* **3.** *iv., irreg.* to have a location; to exist at a specific place. □ *The magazine is on the coffee table.* **4.** *iv., irreg.* to exist. (Usually with **there** ③.) □ *Do you believe there is a heaven?* **5.** *iv., irreg.* to **be** ① in the process of doing something. (The progressive tenses are formed when a form of **be** comes before a verb ending in *-ing.*) □ *The trees were swaying in the breeze.*

**beach** ['bitʃ] **1.** *n.* a shore covered with sand, pebbles, or stones. □ *The children collected shells at the beach.* **2.** *tv.* to run or drive something onto the shore. □ *Dave beached the boat and ran ashore.*

**bead** ['bid] **1.** *n.* a small piece of wood, metal, glass, plastic, stone, gemstone, or other material, usually with a hole through it for a string or a thread. □ *The necklace was made of beads strung together.* **2.** *n.* a droplet of a liquid. □ *Beads of sweat clung to the Bob's forehead.*

**beak** ['bik] *n.* the bill of a bird; the hard mouth structure of a bird or a turtle. □ *The bird held a worm in its beak.*

**beam** ['bim] **1.** *n.* a long, flat piece of wood, concrete, or metal. □ *The worker examined the beams in the ceiling.* **2.** *n.* a ray of light; a stream of light; a stream of laser energy. □ *A beam of sunlight came into the room through the partially open door.* **3.** *iv.* to radiate light; to make or give light. □ *The sun was beaming while we played on the beach.* **4.** *iv.* to smile brightly; to look very happy. □ *Susan beamed when she heard the good news.*

**bean** ['bin] *n.* a seed of certain kinds of plants, and sometimes also the pod, used as food. □ *The coffee beans smelled wonderful.*

**bear** ['bɛr] **1.** *n.* a powerful, furry animal with a short tail and claws. □ *The bear pulled a fish out of the stream with its paw.* **2.** *n.* someone who believes that prices on stocks or bonds will fall. □ *Bob is a bear on the stock market and will not risk his money.* **3.** *tv., irreg.* to carry or transport something. (Pt: **bore**; pp: **borne**.) □ *The camels bore their cargo across the desert without complaint.* **4.** *tv., irreg.* to accept or endure the consequences of something; to take responsibility for something. □ *We bore the consequences of the young employees' mistakes.* **5.** *tv., irreg.* to manage to support someone or something; to carry the weight of someone or something. □ *Can this old chair bear my weight?* **6.** *tv., irreg.* to undergo something; to suffer and endure something. □ *Can the patient bear the pain of further tests?* **7.** *tv., irreg.* to produce offspring; to give birth to a child. (When this sense is used in the passive and focuses on the child, as in *Jimmy was born in 1996*, the past participle is **born**; otherwise, the past participle is **borne**.) □ *Mary has borne three healthy children.* □ *All of her children have been born in this hospital.* **8.** *tv., irreg.* [for a plant] to produce or yield something, such as fruit, flowers, or leaves. □ *Despite daily care, the tree never bore any fruit.* **9.** *iv., irreg.* to turn; to go in a certain direction. □ *Bear right at the second stoplight.*

**beard** ['bɪrd] *n.* hair that grows on the side of the face, the chin, and the neck, usually of a male. □ *Bill trims his beard each day.*

**beast** ['bist] **1.** *n.* a monster; a scary creature. □ *The beast arose and roared at the* *hunters.* **2.** *n.* an animal, especially one with four feet. □ *The hunter would shoot at any beast along the path.*

**beat** ['bit] **1.** *n.* the rhythm of poetry or music. □ *The untalented dancer couldn't find the beat of the music.* **2.** *n.* one unit of a musical measure. □ *The conductor indicated each beat with his baton.* **3.** *n.* the area or route that someone, especially a police officer, walks on a regular basis. □ *Officer Brown walked the same beat for thirty years.* **4.** *tv., irreg.* to hit someone or something, especially repeatedly. (Pt: *beat;* pp: **beaten**.) □ *The musician uses special sticks to beat the drum.* **5.** *tv., irreg.* to mix food ingredients with a kitchen tool. □ *Tom beat the eggs with a fork.* **6.** *tv., irreg.* to win a game against someone or something; to triumph over someone or something in a competition. □ *Did the rival team beat your team again?* **7. beat** someone **up** *tv., irreg. + obj. + adv.* to strike someone as in ④; to hit someone repeatedly, typically with the fists. □ *Two bullies tried to beat Max up.* 🅃 *Who would want to beat up poor old Max?* **8.** *iv., irreg.* to hit against someone or something again and again. □ *The rain is beating on the roof.* **9.** *iv., irreg.* [for a heart] to throb; [for a heart] to pulse over and over. □ *My heart is beating very fast.*

**beaten** ['bit n] pp of **beat**.

**beautiful** ['bju tə fʊl] **1.** *adj.* having great beauty; very pretty. (Adv: *beautifully* ['bju tə fli].) □ *The flowers in the garden are beautiful.* **2.** *adj.* excellent; wonderful. (Informal. Adv: *beautifully* ['bju tə fli].) □ *That's a beautiful plan, but what if it rains?*

**beauty** ['bju ti] **1.** *n.* the quality that makes someone or something very pleasing to look at; the quality that makes something very pleasing to hear or to think about. (No plural form.) □ *We enjoyed the beauty of the scenery.* **2.** *n.* someone or something that is beautiful or excellent. □ *That horse is a beauty!* **3.** *n.* excellence; suitability; cleverness. (No plural form.) □ *The beauty of the plan is its simplicity.*

**beaver** ['bi vɚ] *n., irreg.* a furry, plant-eating animal that dams up streams to form a pond in which it builds its dwelling or lodge. (Pl: *beaver* or *beavers.*) □ *Beavers chewed at the tree until it fell.*

**became** [bɪ 'kem] pt of **become**.

**because** [bɪ 'kɔz] **1.** *conj.* for the reason that. □ *Jane was late for work because her car broke down.* **2. because of** someone or something *phr.* due to someone or something; on account of someone or something. □ *Because of the rain, the hike was canceled.*

**become** [bɪ 'kʌm] **1.** *iv., irreg.* to come to be something; to grow to be something. (Pt: **became**; pp: *become.*) □ *The student became a very good musician.* □ *Mary became ill and had to go home.* **2.** *iv., irreg.* to turn into something; to change into something. □ *In the story, the frog suddenly became a prince.* **3.** *tv., irreg.* [for clothing, a haircut, etc.] to look good on someone; to make someone look attractive. □ *These ugly clothes do not become you.*

**bed** ['bɛd] **1.** *n.* a piece of furniture used to sleep on, usually raised and with a mattress, sheets, and blankets. □ *The large bed barely fit in the small room.* **2.** *n.* a flat base; a foundation; a bottom layer of support. □ *We loaded the lumber onto the bed of the truck.* **3.** *n.* the earth on the bottom of a body of water. □ *Divers examined the bed of the sea.* **4.** *n.* an area of soil where flowers and other plants grow. □ *The kids ran right through the bed of flowers.*

**bedclothes** ['bɛd klo(ð)z] *n.* sheets and a blanket; the cloth coverings for a bed. (Treated as plural, but not countable.)

□ *The maid changed the bedclothes every morning.*

B

**bedding** ['bɛd ɪŋ] *n.* the mattress coverings, sheets, and blankets used on a bed. (No plural form.) □ *Bedding is kept in the linen closet.*

**bedroom** ['bɛd rum] *n.* a room in a dwelling place where someone sleeps. □ *Bill was asleep in the bedroom when the fire started.*

**bedside** ['bɛd saɪd] *n.* the side of a bed; the area beside a bed. □ *Bob sat by his wife's bedside until she was well.*

**bedtime** ['bɛd taɪm] *n.* the time when someone usually goes to bed. □ *Jimmy's bedtime is eight o'clock.*

**bee** ['bi] *n.* a small insect that can sting and that makes honey. □ *Jimmy got stung by a bee.*

**beef** ['bif] *n.* the meat of a cow, steer, or bull. (No plural form.) □ *Hamburgers are generally made from beef.*

**beefsteak** ['bif stek] *n.* a slice of the flesh of a cow, steer, or bull, eaten as food. (Usually **steak**.) □ *Bill craved a good beefsteak about once a week.*

**beehive** ['bi haɪv] *n.* a place where bees live, reproduce, and make honey. □ *The beehive is full of honey.*

**been** [bɪn] pp of **be**.

**beer** ['bɪr] **1.** *n.* a beverage (containing alcohol) made from grain and flavored with hops. (Plural only when referring to different kinds, types, instances, or varieties.) □ *Americans like beer to be cold.* Ⓒ *Different beers have different amounts of alcohol.* **2.** *n.* a glass or can of ①; a serving of ①. □ *I would like a beer, please.*

**beet** ['bit] *n.* a plant with a large red root that is eaten as a vegetable. □ *The farmer's main crop was beets.*

**beetle** ['bit əl] *n.* a small insect whose wings are hard and protect its body. □ *The cat chased the beetle around on the sidewalk.*

**before** [bɪ 'for] **1.** *conj.* at an earlier time than; previous to the time when [something happens]. □ *I will be ready before you arrive.* **2.** *prep.* earlier than something; previous to something. □ *Before noon, we washed the laundry.* **3.** *prep.* in front of someone or something. □ *I stood before the judge and said again that I was innocent.* **4.** *adv.* earlier; previously. □ *The party starts at 9:00, and not a moment before.* **5.** *adv.* until this moment in time; in the past. □ *I had never sailed before, but I loved it immediately.*

**beg** ['bɛg] *iv.* to plead for something; to ask for something very humbly. □ *The hungry man begged for some food.*

**began** [bɪ 'gæn] pt of **begin**.

**beggar** ['bɛg ɚ] *n.* someone who asks for charity, especially money or food; a panhandler. □ *The beggar stood on the sidewalk and asked people for money as they walked by.*

**begin** [bɪ 'gɪn] **1.** *iv., irreg.* [for something] to start [happening]; for someone or something to start [doing something]. (Pt: **began**; pp: **begun**.) □ *When does the concert begin?* **2. begin to do something** *iv., irreg. + inf.* to start to do something. □ *It is beginning to rain.* **3.** *tv., irreg.* to start something; to commence something. □ *Mary began her studies when she was a child.*

**beginner** [bɪ 'gɪn ɚ] *n.* someone just learning to do something; an amateur. □ *My German class is full of beginners.*

**begun** [bɪ 'gʌn] pp of **begin**.

**behavior** [bɪ 'hev jɚ] *n.* the manner in which someone acts or behaves; conduct; manners. (Plural only when referring to different kinds, types, instances, or varieties.) □ *The chairman's behavior was embarrassing.* Ⓒ *Unpleasant* *behaviors are often due to poor social conditions.*

**behind** [bɪ 'haɪnd] **1.** *prep.* in or to a place farther back than someone or something else; at the rear of someone or something. □ *Put the plant behind the table.* **2.** *prep.* later than someone or something; coming after someone or something; not current with something. □ *This project is behind schedule.* **3.** *prep.* serving as the reason for something. □ *What is behind these practical jokes?* **4.** *prep.* in support of someone or something. □ *The fans stood behind the losing baseball team.* **5.** *adv.* toward the back; further back in place or time. □ *I am falling behind in my work.*

**being** ['bi ɪŋ] *n.* a living thing; a living creature. □ *Every being should have the same basic right to life.*

**belief** [bɪ 'lif] **1.** *n.* something that is thought to be true; an opinion. □ *John held the belief that people are basically good.* **2.** *n.* a rule or principle of a religion or faith. (Often plural.) □ *Different religions have different beliefs.*

**believe** [bɪ 'liv] **1.** *tv.* to accept that someone or something is true or real. (The object can be a clause with **that** ⑦.) □ *The judge did not believe our story.* **2.** *tv.* to have an opinion about something; to suppose something. (The object is a clause with **that** ⑦.) □ *I believe that you are correct.* **3. believe in** someone or something *iv. + prep. phr.* to accept that someone or something exists or is real. □ *Do you believe in ghosts?* **4. believe in** someone or something *iv. + prep. phr.* to have faith in someone or something; to trust someone or something. □ *Jane believes in the fairness of the legal system.*

**bell** ['bɛl] **1.** *n.* a cupped metal shell that makes a ringing sound when struck. □ *Mother rang a bell to call the children home.* **2.** *n.* the sound made by ① to mark the start or the finish of a period of time. □ *When we heard the bell, we left.*

**belly** ['bɛl i] **1.** *n.* the stomach area of the body; a large and sometimes rounded front part of the body. (Informal.) □ *I tickled the baby's belly, and he laughed.* **2.** *n.* the inside of certain things. □ *Gold was hidden in the belly of the ship.* **3.** *n.* the underside of certain things. □ *The belly of the plane scraped the trees before the crash.*

**belong** [bɪ 'lɔŋ] **1.** *iv.* [for someone or something] to have a proper or appropriate place or typical location. □ *Clothes belong in the closet.* **2. belong to** someone or something *iv. + prep. phr.* to be the property of someone or something. □ *Does this book belong to you?* **3. belong to** something *iv. + prep. phr.* to be a member of something. □ *John and I belong to the same club.*

**belongings** [bɪ 'lɔŋ ɪŋz] *n.* the things that one owns; one's possessions. (Treated as plural, but not countable.) □ *Mary told Bill to gather his belongings and leave.*

**below** [bɪ 'lo] **1.** *prep.* beneath someone or something; under someone or something; lower than someone or something. □ *Below each painting was a plaque showing its name.* **2.** *prep.* lower in status or rank than someone or something. □ *Detroit ranks below New York in population.* **3.** *adv.* to a lower deck on a ship. □ *All the officers went below to eat supper.* **4.** *adv.* later [in a book or other written work]; after or following [on the same page or within the same written work]. □ *The complete story is told below, starting on page 12.*

**belt** ['bɛlt] **1.** *n.* a strip of leather or similar material fastened around the waist, to hold up trousers. □ *After I lost thirty pounds, my belt was too big.* **2.** *n.* a region; an area with a common characteristic. (In compounds.) □ *The southern states are sometimes referred to as the*

B

*Bible Belt.* **3.** *n.* a long, continuous loop of strong, flexible material used in machinery to transfer power. □ *One of the engine's belts broke, causing the car to stall.* **4.** *n.* a **seat belt**; a strap in a car that holds people securely in the seat. □ *Anne asked us to latch our belts before she started the car.*

**bench** ['bɛntʃ] **1.** *n.* a seat—often unpadded—for two or more people. □ *Bob sat on the bench at the bus stop.* **2.** *n.* a place where players on a sports team sit when they are not playing. □ *The players waited on the bench to be put in the game.* **3.** *n.* the seat a judge sits on. □ *Judge Brown sat down on the bench and called the court to order.* **4.** *n.* a judge or a group of judges in a court of law. □ *The bench ruled against the motion.*

**bend** ['bɛnd] **1.** *n.* a curve; a turn. □ *The car raced around the bend in the road.* **2.** *iv., irreg.* to become curved or crooked; to go in a direction away from a straight line. (Pt/pp: **bent**.) □ *The road bends a lot in the mountains.* **3.** *iv., irreg.* to change one's mind; to yield. (Fig. on ②.) □ *Dad bent a little on the issue of bedtime.* **4.** *tv., irreg.* to cause an object to curve; to change the shape of a flexible object. □ *We bent the pipe so that it would fit against the wall.*

**beneath** [bɪ 'niθ] **1.** *prep.* under someone or something; below someone or something; lower than someone or something. □ *Hide the letter beneath the newspaper.* **2.** *prep.* inferior to someone or something; worse than someone or something. □ *Bob felt labor was beneath him.*

**benefit** ['bɛn ə fɪt] **1.** *n.* an advantage; something that is helpful or has a good effect. □ *What are the benefits of doing it your way?* **2.** *n.* the sum of money paid to someone under the terms of an insurance or retirement contract. (Often plural.) □ *The insurance policy listed no benefits for illnesses related to smoking.* **3.** *n.* something that one receives—in addition to a salary—for working, such as health insurance, life insurance, etc. □ *Health insurance is a benefit that all workers expect to receive.* **4.** *n.* an event with special entertainment, given to raise money for a worthy cause. □ *Where will the church benefit be held this year?* **5.** *tv.* to serve to the good of someone or something. □ *Volunteer work benefits society.* **6.** *iv.* to improve or to profit from something; to be better because of something. □ *The students would benefit from better instruction.*

**bent** ['bɛnt] **1.** pt/pp of **bend**. **2.** *adj.* crooked or curved; not straight. □ *The bent antenna ruined the television's reception.*

**berry** ['bɛr i] *n.* the small, juicy fruit of a bush or shrub. □ *We picked berries in the garden all afternoon.*

**beside** [bɪ 'sɑɪd] *prep.* at, by, or to the side of someone or something; next to someone or something. □ *Put the bookcase beside the piano.*

**besides** [bɪ 'sɑɪdz] **1.** *prep.* in addition to someone or something; as well as someone or something. □ *What games should we play besides baseball?* **2.** *adv.* also; furthermore; in any case; at any rate. □ *Besides, nothing bad is going to happen.*

**best** ['bɛst] **1.** *adj.* the most excellent [thing]. (The superlative form of **good**. See also **better**.) □ *Mario's serves the best pizza in town.* **2.** *adv.* most excellently. (The superlative form of **well**. See also **better**.) □ *This one best suits your purposes.* **3.** *tv.* to defeat someone; to do [something] much better than someone; to outwit someone. □ *Your cooking bests that of any fancy restaurant.* **4. the best** *n.* someone or something that is better than anything else. (Stands for singular or plural nominals.) □ *These are all great, but this one is the best.*

**bet** ['bɛt] **1.** *n.* an amount of money gambled on something; a wager. □ *The bet was only twenty dollars.* **2.** *tv., irreg.* to make a wager. (Pt/pp: *bet.*) □ *What will you bet that Bill is late?* **3.** *tv., irreg.* to predict something; to make a guess that something will happen. (The object is a clause with **that** ⑦.) □ *I bet that John and Anne will leave the party together.* **4. bet on** someone or something *iv., irreg.* + *prep. phr.* to gamble on the success of a participant in a contest. □ *Tom bet on the black horse.*

**betray** [bɪ 'tre] **1.** *tv.* to do something that shows that one is not loyal to a person; to be unfaithful to someone or something. □ *John betrayed my trust when he told my secret.* **2.** *tv.* to show a sign of something; to reveal something. □ *Susan's facial expression betrayed her feelings.*

**better** ['bɛt ɚ] **1.** *adj.* of more goodness; of greater benefit. (The comparative form of **good**. See also **best**.) □ *I have a better idea than that.* **2.** *adj.* healthier than before; improved in health; having recovered from an illness; in good health again. (Not prenominal.) □ *I felt better after the operation.* □ *I was sick for two weeks, but now I'm better.* **3.** *adv.* with more quality; with greater benefit. (The comparative form of **well**. See also **best**.) □ *After being in France for a year, Mary speaks French much better than she did when she first arrived.* **4.** *tv.* to improve oneself; [for something] to improve itself. (Reflexive.) □ *Mary tried to better herself by taking a class.* **5. the better** *n.* [of a choice of two things] the one that is superior or more excellent. (No plural form. Treated as singular.) □ *Of the two cakes, this one is the better.* **6. had better** *phr.* is obliged to; should. (Often *-'d better.*) □ *He had better be here on time!*

**between** [bɪ 'twin] **1.** *prep.* in the middle of two things or people; with something on both sides. (See the note at **among**.) □ *The couch is between the end tables.* **2.** *prep.* both together; in combination with the two. □ *Between Anne and me, we ate the whole pizza.* **3.** *prep.* in comparing two things or people. □ *Do you know the difference between right and left?*

**beverage** ['bɛv rɪdʒ] *n.* a drink other than water. □ *Can I get you a beverage?*

**beware** [bɪ 'wɛr] **beware of** someone or something *iv., irreg.* + *prep. phr.* to use caution with someone or something. (Almost always a command.) □ *Beware of the ice on the sidewalk.*

**bewildered** [bɪ 'wɪl dɚd] *adj.* confused; puzzled; perplexed. (Adv: *bewilderedly.*) □ *The bewildered doctor could not diagnose his patient's illness.*

**beyond** [bi 'jɑnd] **1.** *prep.* farther than someone or something; on the other side of someone or something. □ *Beyond the stream, the deer frolicked.* **2.** *prep.* past someone's ability to understand or comprehend. □ *Why John traveled to Greenland is beyond me.* **3.** *adv.* past; further; on the other side of someone or something. □ *The children are allowed to walk to the school, but not beyond.*

**bias** ['bɑɪ əs] **1.** *n.* a prejudice. □ *A political bias was evident in the newspaper article.* **2.** *tv.* to prejudice someone. □ *The journalist tried to bias the readers with his article.*

**bib** ['bɪb] *n.* a napkin or piece of cloth worn around the neck. □ *Babies wear bibs to catch stray bits of food.*

**bible** ['bɑɪb əl] **1. Bible** *n.* the holy writings of the Jewish religion; the Hebrew Scriptures. □ *In Judaism, the Bible is what Christians call the Old Testament.* **2. Bible** *n.* the holy writings of the Christian religion. □ *In Christianity, the*

B

*Bible consists of the Old and New Testaments.* **3.** *n.* a manual; a guidebook; a book of authority. □ *That cookbook is the chef's bible.*

**biblical** ['bɪb lɪ kəl] *adj.* relating to the Bible. (Adv: *biblically* [...ɪk li].) □ *The paintings in the pastor's office had a biblical theme.*

**bicycle** ['bɑɪ sɪ kəl] **1.** *n.* a vehicle with a metal frame and two wheels, operated by foot pedals. □ *Jimmy got his first bicycle on his fifth birthday.* **2.** *iv.* to travel by ①. □ *The kids bicycled to school every day.*

**bid** ['bɪd] **1.** *n.* an offer of an amount of money for something for sale, especially at an auction. □ *I made a small bid on the antique dresser.* **2.** *n.* the presentation of the price for one's services, especially in a competition joined by others to do the same work. □ *John's bid for the job indicated how long the work would take.* **3.** *n.* an attempt to seek or take power or control of something. □ *Bill's bid for the open position at his company went unnoticed.* **4.** *tv., irreg.* to offer an amount of money for something, especially at an auction. (Pt/pp: *bid.*) □ *We just couldn't bid more money at the auction.*

**big** ['bɪg] **1.** *adj.* large; great in amount or size. (Comp: *bigger;* sup: *biggest.*) □ *A big ship entered the harbor.* **2.** *adj.* important. (Comp: *bigger;* sup: *biggest.*) □ *The big executives all ate lunch together.* **3.** *adj.* adult; grown-up. (Comp: *bigger;* sup: *biggest.*) □ *The big people ate at a separate table from the children.*

**bike** ['bɑɪk] **1.** *n.* a bicycle. □ *Susie rode her bike to school.* **2.** *n.* a motorcycle. □ *The gang members got on their bikes and drove off.* **3.** *iv.* to ride a bicycle or motorcycle. □ *Anne bikes to work, rain or shine.*

**bilingual** [bɑɪ 'lɪŋ gwəl] **1.** *adj.* [of a person] able to speak two languages. (Adv: *bilingually.*) □ *The bilingual child spoke both English and Spanish.* **2.** *adj.* referring to two languages. (Adv: *bilingually.*) □ *The teachers promoted bilingual education.*

**bill** ['bɪl] **1.** *n.* a written notice of money owed. □ *My mailbox was full of bills.* **2.** *n.* a legal draft of a proposed law. □ *The senator introduced a bill that would limit government officials' terms.* **3.** *n.* a piece of printed money, which is different from a coin. □ *I only had bills in my wallet.* **4.** *n.* the hard part of a bird's mouth. □ *The bird had a bright yellow bill.* **5.** *n.* the visor of a cap; the part of a cap that extends from the head and shields the eyes from the sun. □ *The cap had the team's name on its bill.* **6.** *tv.* to present a notice of charges to someone or something. □ *The doctor billed me for the medical tests.*

**billion** ['bɪl jən] **1.** *n.* 1,000,000,000; a thousand million of something, usually units of money. (A British billion is a million million. Additional numbers formed as with *two billion, three billion, four billion,* etc.) □ *The country is more than two billion in debt.* **2.** *adj.* amounting to or equal to 1,000,000,000 of something. □ *The government's debt was over a billion dollars.*

**bin** ['bɪn] *n.* a container or enclosed space used for storage. □ *The farmer's bins were full of grain after the harvest.*

**bind** ['bɑɪnd] **1.** *tv., irreg.* to secure something to something else with a tie or band; to tie something together with something else. (Pt/pp: **bound.**) □ *Bind the newspapers in a stack so we can carry them out.* **2. bind** someone or something **to** something *tv., irreg. + obj. + prep. phr.* to hold someone or something by force; to tie someone or something to something. □ *The guards bound the prisoner to his bed.* **3. bind** someone **to** something *tv., irreg. + obj. + prep. phr.* [for a contract] to oblige someone to obey or abide by something. □ *The contract binds me to our agreement.* **4.** *iv., irreg.* to be stuck and thus fail to move. □ *The window binds against the window frame.*

**binocular** [bə 'nɑk jə lɚ] **1.** *adj.* relating to both eyes; involving both eyes. □ *Most animals have binocular vision.* **2. binoculars** *n.* a viewing device made of two small telescopes, side by side. (Treated as a plural. Number is expressed with *pair(s) of binoculars.*) □ *The binoculars were so strong, we could see craters on the moon!*

**biology** [bɑɪ 'ɑl ə dʒi] *n.* the scientific study of living animals and plants. (No plural form.) □ *Biology deals with the study of animal life including humans.*

**bird** ['bɚd] *n.* an animal that has feathers and wings. □ *A bird perched on the telephone wire.* □ *Birds have warm blood.*

**bird of prey** ['bɚd əv 'pre] *n.* a bird that lives by killing and eating other animals. (Pl: *birds of prey.*) □ *Many birds of prey eat other birds.*

**birth** ['bɚθ] **1.** *n.* the process of being born. □ *The difficult birth took twenty hours.* **2.** *n.* the origin of something; the way something has come into being. (Fig. on ①.) □ *The birth of jazz took place in the southern part of the U.S.*

**birthday** ['bɚθ de] *n.* the date on which someone was born; a date of birth. □ *I plan to celebrate my birthday tomorrow with my family.*

**birthmark** ['bɚθ mɑrk] *n.* a pigmented mark on the skin, usually red, brown, black, or purple, present from birth. □ *The baby had a tiny birthmark on its arm.*

**birthplace** ['bɚθ ples] *n.* the city and country where someone was born; the place of someone's birth. □ *Dave visited his birthplace overseas last year.*

**biscuit** ['bɪs kɪt] *n.* a round, flat cake of bread, made with baking powder. □ *This restaurant is well known for its biscuits and roast beef.*

**bit** ['bɪt] **1.** pt of **bite**. **2.** *n.* a small amount of something; a tiny piece of something. □ *I spilled a bit of the rice on the floor.* **3.** *n.* the mouthpiece on a bridle, used to control a horse. □ *Mary put the bit into the horse's mouth.* **4.** *n.* the basic unit of information in a computer; a binary digit. □ *There are usually 8 bits in a computer character.* **5.** *n.* the end of a drilling tool that bores or cuts holes. □ *Jane used a large bit to drill the hole in the wall.*

**bite** ['bɑɪt] **1.** *n.* a mouthful of food; the amount of food taken in at one time. □ *The baby shoved a huge bite of food into his mouth.* **2.** *n.* a light meal; a snack; a small amount of food. □ *Let's get a bite to eat before the movie.* **3.** *n.* the mark or wound made on the skin when someone is **bitten** as in ⑤ by an animal or stung by an insect. □ *The camper woke up with a spider bite.* **4.** *tv., irreg.* to grip or tear something with the teeth; to close the teeth around an object. (Pt: **bit**; pp: **bitten.**) □ *Dave bites his fingernails.* **5.** *iv., irreg.* [for a creature] to be able to pierce skin with its teeth; [for a creature] to have a habit of attacking people or other creatures with its teeth. □ *Our dog bites, so be careful.* **6.** *iv., irreg.* [for a fish] to take a lure. □ *I hope the fish are biting tonight!*

**bitten** ['bɪt n] pp of **bite**.

**bitter** ['bɪt ɚ] **1.** *adj.* very sharp or harsh in taste. (Adv: *bitterly.* As one of the four basic tastes, not sweet, salty, or sour.) □ *This lettuce is old and bitter.* **2.** *adj.* [of wind or weather] extremely cold. (Adv: *bitterly.*) □ *I hate this bitter weather!* **3.** *adj.* emotionally painful; distressful. (Adv: *bitterly.*) □ *Not getting the promotion was a bitter experience for Anne.* **4.** *adj.* resentful; hateful. (Adv:

*bitterly.*) □ *The opponents flung bitter words at each other.*

**bizarre** [bɪ 'zɑr] *adj.* very strange; eccentric; weird. (Adv: *bizarrely.*) □ *A bizarre series of events preceded the murder.*

**black** ['blæk] **1.** *adj.* the color of coal; the color of the darkest night; the opposite of white. (Comp: *blacker;* sup: *blackest.*) □ *It was very black outside last night.* **2.** *adj.* [of coffee served] without cream or milk. □ *I asked for a cup of black coffee.* **3.** *adj.* evil; wicked. (Adv: *blackly.* Comp: *blacker;* sup: *blackest.*) □ *The black plan unfolded as the evil king had planned.* **4.** *adj.* [of people, usually of African decent] having dark-colored skin. (Occasionally capitalized.) □ *Tom is studying Black culture in school.* **5.** *adv.* [of coffee served] without cream or milk. □ *John drinks his coffee black.* **6.** *n.* someone who is of African descent having dark-colored skin. (Sometimes capitalized.) □ *Both blacks and whites are among Tom's friends.*

**blacken** ['blæk ən] **1.** *tv.* to make something black; to cause something to become black. □ *Smoke from the fire blackened the wallpaper.* **2.** *iv.* to become very dark or black; to turn black. □ *The wood blackened in the fire.*

**blackness** ['blæk nəs] *n.* the state of being black. (No plural form.) □ *I was surprised by the blackness of the sky.*

**blackout** ['blæk ɑʊt] **1.** *n.* a complete loss of all electricity or power; a situation of complete darkness, especially caused by a loss of electrical power. □ *Luckily, we had candles ready in case of a blackout.* **2.** *n.* a state of not being conscious. □ *Jane had a short blackout after she fell and hit her head.*

**blade** ['bled] **1.** *n.* the flat, sharpened edge of a knife or tool. □ *The rusty saw blade would not cut the wood.* **2.** *n.* the flat, wide part of an oar or propeller. □ *The blade of the oar made gentle ripples in the water.* **3.** *n.* a long, flat leaf of grass or other plant. □ *A small beetle crawled up the blade of grass.* **4.** *n.* the metal part of an ice skate that makes contact with the ice. □ *The skater's blades glided across the ice.*

**blame** ['blem] **1.** *n.* the responsibility for causing something that is bad or wrong. (No plural form.) □ *Who took the blame for the unsuccessful project?* **2.** *tv.* to place the responsibility for doing something wrong on a person. □ *Mother blamed Jimmy for tracking mud on the carpet.*

**blank** ['blæŋk] **1.** *n.* an empty line or a space on a form. □ *The applicant filled in the blanks on the form.* **2.** *adj.* without marks; having no writing. (Comp: *blanker;* sup: *blankest.*) □ *The writer just sat and stared at the blank sheets of paper.* **3.** *adj.* [of a facial expression] not showing recognition or response. (Adv: *blankly.* Comp: *blanker;* sup: *blankest.*) □ *The teacher's scolding got only a blank look from the student.*

**blanket** ['blæŋ kɪt] **1.** *n.* a piece of thick fabric, used to keep someone warm. □ *During the winter, Jane keeps three blankets on her bed.* **2.** *n.* a layer of something that covers something else. (Fig. on ①.) □ *The ground was covered with a blanket of snow.* **3.** *tv.* [for something as in ②] to cover something. □ *Presents blanketed the table at the wedding.*

**blare** ['blɛr] **1.** *n.* a loud, harsh noise. □ *The blare of a car horn startled Mary.* **2.** *iv.* to make a loud, harsh noise. □ *Your radio is blaring! Turn it down!*

**blast** ['blæst] **1.** *n.* a strong, sudden gust of air; a sudden, heavy wind. □ *The leaves were lifted into the air by a sudden blast of wind.* **2.** *n.* the noise and violent gust of air created by an explosion. □ *The loud blast from the truck's tailpipe startled the other drivers.* **3.** *n.* an explosion. □ *The building was torn apart by the blast.* **4.** *tv.* to blow something up;

B

to explode something. □ *The robbers blasted the bank vault open.*

**blaze** ['blez] **1.** *n.* a fire; a flame. □ *The blaze had been set by an angry criminal.* **2.** *iv.* to burn brightly; to burn with bright flames. □ *The logs blazed in the fireplace.*

**bleach** ['blitʃ] **1.** *n.* a substance that removes color or stains. (Plural only when referring to different kinds, types, instances, or varieties.) □ *You can remove some stains from white shirts with a little bleach.* Ⓒ *Bleaches are different even though they are made from the same chemicals.* **2.** *iv.* to become white or lighter; to turn white or lighter. □ *The dark pants bleached in the wash.* **3.** *tv.* to turn something white or lighter; to cause something to become white or lighter. □ *The hair stylist bleached my hair.*

**bled** ['blɛd] pt/pp of **bleed**.

**bleed** ['blid] **1.** *iv., irreg.* to lose blood, as from a wound. (Pt/pp: **bled**.) □ *Your cut will bleed if you pick the scab.* **2.** *iv., irreg.* [for color, ink, or dye] to seep or soak into other colors or dyes. □ *The dyes in that shirt will bleed if you wash the shirt in hot water.*

**blend** ['blɛnd] **1.** *n.* a mixture. □ *This blend of spices tastes delicious.* **2.** *tv.* to combine something with something else. □ *The decor blends traditional furniture with modern pieces.* **3.** *iv.* to mix well or attractively with people or things. □ *The draperies blend well with the rest of the room.*

**bless** ['blɛs] **1.** *tv.* to make someone or something holy through a religious ritual. □ *We asked the minister to bless our new house.* **2.** *tv.* to ask God to place favor on the food that is to be eaten. □ *Dad blessed the food at the dinner table.*

**blessing** ['blɛs ɪŋ] **1.** *n.* a prayer calling for God's favor or protection. □ *Mary gave a blessing before dinner.* **2.** *n.* God's favor or good fortune given to someone or something. □ *The family enjoyed the blessing of good health and a comfortable house.* **3.** *n.* approval. □ *Anne would not get married without her parents' blessing.*

**blew** ['blu] pt of **blow**.

**blind** ['bluɪnd] **1.** *adj.* unable to see; sightless. (Adv: *blindly.* Comp: *blinder;* sup: *blindest.*) □ *The blind man had a dog that led him around.* **2.** *adj.* [of anger] irrational. (Adv: *blindly.* Comp: *blinder;* sup: *blindest.*) □ *Tom flew out of the house in a blind fury.* **3.** *tv.* to take away someone's or something's sight permanently or temporarily. □ *Dave was blinded by a childhood illness.* **4. blinds** *n.* a kind of window shade made of horizontal, or sometimes vertical, slats that can be tilted to block vision or shut out light. (Treated as plural.) □ *I adjusted the blinds so the carpet would not fade from the sunlight.*

**blink** ['blɪŋk] **1.** *n.* [for an eye] to close and open quickly. (Compare this with **wink**.) □ *We were rubbing our eyes and blinking because the wind blew dust in our eyes.* **2.** *iv.* [for a light] to flash on and off quickly. □ *The lights in the theater blinked at the end of intermission.* **3.** *tv.* to close and open one's eyes quickly. □ *"Blink your eyes if you can hear me," the doctor said.* **4.** *tv.* to turn a light on and off quickly; to flash a light. □ *Blink the lights in the backyard to tell the children it's time to come in and go to bed.*

**bliss** ['blɪs] *n.* complete happiness; joy. (No plural form.) □ *Jane was in a state of bliss after graduating.*

**blister** ['blɪs tɚ] **1.** *n.* a bubble of fluid under the skin, formed by a burn or irritation. □ *The rowboat's oars gave my hands blisters.* **2.** *iv.* [for a part of the skin] to raise up and fill with fluid in response to a burn or irritation. □ *My skin blistered from my sunburn.* **3.** *tv.* to cause ① to form on someone

B

or something. □ *The sun blistered the swimmer's skin.*

**blizzard** ['blɪz ɚd] *n.* a snowstorm with strong winds, heavy snow, and possible thunder and lightning. □ *Wow! There's a blizzard outside!*

**block** ['blɑk] **1.** *n.* a solid piece of something, such as wood, stone, or ice. □ *A heavy block of wood props the door open.* **2.** *n.* a large, flat piece of stone or wood on which items are cut, chopped, or split. □ *The baked turkey glistened on the carving block.* **3.** *n.* the distance along a street from one intersection to the next. □ *Jane lives three blocks from my house.* **4.** *n.* a group of seats or tickets for seats that are next to each other, as with the theater, an airline flight, or a sporting event. □ *We reserved the best block of seats in the theater.* **5.** *tv.* to be or get in the way of something. □ *The gate blocked the entrance to the driveway.*

**blond** ['blɑnd] **1.** *adj.* [of hair] fair or light in color. (Comp: *blonder;* sup: *blondest.*) □ *I have always admired Tom's blond hair.* **2.** *n.* someone with light-colored hair. (**Blonde** is sometimes used for females.) □ *My brothers are all blonds with blue eyes.*

**blonde** ['blɑnd] *n.* a woman or a girl with light-colored hair. □ *Bill's sisters are all blondes.*

**blood** ['blʌd] *n.* a red fluid moving through the bodies of animals. (No plural form.) □ *Blood from the wound dripped onto the floor.*

**bloodshed** ['blʌd ʃɛd] *n.* injury or death caused by violence. (No plural form.) □ *The fight between the boys ended in bloodshed.*

**blood vessel** ['blʌd vɛs əl] *n.* a tube that carries blood through the bodies of living things. □ *Something is blocking an important blood vessel in her heart.*

**bloom** ['blum] **1.** *iv.* [for a plant] to produce flowers or blossoms. □ *My roses bloomed early this year.* **2.** *iv.* [for a flower bud] to open. □ *The buds bloomed into huge flowers.*

**blossom** ['blɑs əm] **1.** *n.* a flower. □ *I wore a hat decorated with ribbons and blossoms.* **2.** *iv.* to produce flowers; to bloom. □ *When does this type of plant blossom?* **3.** *iv.* [for a flower bud] to open. □ *We picked the flowers after they blossomed.*

**blouse** ['blɑʊs] *n.* a woman's shirt. □ *Mary bought a white blouse and a red skirt on sale.*

**blow** ['blo] **1.** *iv., irreg.* [for wind or air] to be in motion. (Pt: **blew;** pp: **blown.**) □ *Fresh air blew through the open windows.* **2.** *iv., irreg.* [for something] to be lifted by or carried in the air or wind. □ *The flag blew in the breeze.* **3.** *iv., irreg.* [for a sound-producing device, such as a horn] to make sound. □ *A whistle blows at the factory at the end of the day.* **4.** *iv., irreg.* [for a fuse] to burn out. □ *This is the second fuse that has blown today.* **5. blow up** *iv., irreg. + adv.* to break suddenly and violently into pieces, with a loud noise; to explode. □ *A bomb blew up and injured four people.* **6. blow** something **up** *tv., irreg. + obj. + adv.* to cause something to explode. □ *Tom blew a whole box of firecrackers up.* 🅃 *He blew up the whole box.* **7. blow** something **up** *tv., irreg. + obj. + adv.* to inflate something; to push air into something so that it becomes full of air. □ *I am so tired that I can't blow Jimmy's balloon up.* 🅃 *I'll blow up his balloon.* **8.** *tv., irreg.* to exhale air or smoke. □ *The rude smoker blew smoke into our faces.* **9.** *tv., irreg.* to sound a whistle or a horn, trumpet, or similar instrument. □ *The children merrily blew their whistles.* **10.** *n.* a hard hit or knock. □ *A few blows with the hammer, and the nail was in the wall.*

**blown** ['blon] pp of **blow.**

**blue** ['blu] **1.** *n.* the color of a clear sky on a bright day; the color of a deep, clear ocean. (Plural only when referring to different kinds, types, instances, or varieties.) ☐ *The living room was painted a beautiful pale blue.* Ⓒ *I cannot tell the difference between blues and greens.* **2. (the) blues** *n.* a type of music, similar to slow jazz. (Sometimes treated as singular. See also ③.) ☐ *Bill's musical taste includes the blues.* **3. the blues** *n.* sadness; depression. (Sometimes treated as singular.) ☐ *Many people get the blues on Sunday night.* **4.** *adj.* <the adj. use of ①.> (Comp: *bluer;* sup: *bluest.*) ☐ *We bought the blue car.* **5.** *adj.* sad. (Adv: *bluely.* Comp: *bluer;* sup: *bluest.*) ☐ *The children were blue when their vacation was canceled.*

**bluff** ['blʌf] **1.** *n.* a steep hill or cliff with a wide front. ☐ *The hikers descended the bluff and walked into the valley.* **2.** *n.* a harmless deception; a trick that will not result in harm. ☐ *I ignored the card player's bluff.* **3.** *tv.* to deceive someone or some creature; to mislead someone or some creature into doing something. ☐ *Dave bluffed us and took a shortcut to school.*

**blunder** ['blʌn dɚ] **1.** *n.* a stupid mistake; a clumsy error. ☐ *I made several serious blunders on my taxes.* **2.** *iv.* to make a stupid mistake. ☐ *The accountant blundered when adding up this column.*

**blunt** ['blʌnt] **1.** *adj.* without a sharp edge or point. (Adv: *bluntly.* Comp: *blunter;* sup: *bluntest.*) ☐ *The knife was too blunt to cut through the tough meat.* **2.** *adj.* to the point; frank; not subtle. (Adv: *bluntly.* Comp: *blunter;* sup: *bluntest.*) ☐ *The politician's blunt statements offended many people.* **3.** *tv.* to make something dull; to make something less sharp. ☐ *Years of use blunted the blade of the knife.*

**board** ['bord] **1.** *n.* a flat, thin piece of wood; a plank. ☐ *Boards were nailed over the windows of the old house.* **2.** *n.* a flat piece of wood or other rigid material, used for a specific purpose. ☐ *The children's artwork was pinned to the bulletin board.* **3.** *n.* daily meals. (No plural form. Treated as singular.) ☐ *Bob offered to work for his board.* **4.** *n.* a group of people who manage a company or other organization. ☐ *The board of directors voted to expand the business.* **5.** *n.* a flat, sturdy piece of material on which a game is played. ☐ *John accidentally lifted the board, and all the chess pieces fell off.* **6.** *tv.* to get on a ship, bus, train, or plane. ☐ *The passengers stood in line to board the bus.* **7.** *iv.* to receive meals and living space in exchange for money or work. ☐ *Bill boards in town while he goes to college.*

**boast** ['bost] **1.** *n.* a bragging statement. ☐ *Tom's boast was that he could beat anyone at cards.* **2.** *iv.* to brag or exaggerate. ☐ *Jimmy boasted about his grades often.* **3.** *tv.* to offer or have a particular characteristic. ☐ *The car boasted leather seats.*

**boat** ['bot] *n.* a floating means of transportation, smaller than a ship, that carries people and cargo. ☐ *We rowed across the lake in a boat.*

**bob** ['bɑb] **1.** *n.* a quick up-and-down movement. ☐ *I made a quick bob of the head in agreement.* **2.** *iv.* to move up and down quickly, as with something floating on water. ☐ *The ball bobbed in the pool of water.* **3.** *tv.* to cut something, especially hair, short. ☐ *Have you considered bobbing your hair?*

**body** ['bɑd i] **1.** *n.* the whole physical structure of a living creature or plant. ☐ *The athlete makes her body work very hard.* **2.** *n.* a dead human or animal; a corpse. ☐ *The funeral home received a body last night.* **3.** *n.* the main part of something. ☐ *The body of the text needs*

B

*to be rewritten.* **4.** *n.* a collection of people or things taken as a group; a group; a collection. □ *They arrived as a body.* **5.** *n.* a large mass of something; an object. □ *We looked through the telescope at the heavenly bodies.*

**boil** ['bɔɪl] **1.** *n.* a painful, sore place surrounding an infection. □ *The doctor examined the boil on my foot.* **2.** *n.* the condition of something that is **boiling** as in ⑤. (No plural form.) □ *I let the water reach a rapid boil and then added the pasta.* **3.** *tv.* to make a liquid so hot that it bubbles and turns into vapor. □ *"Bill can barely boil water without burning it!" his wife exclaimed.* **4.** *tv.* to cook something by putting it in a liquid that is **boiling** as in ⑤. □ *I boiled the pasta for our dinner.* **5.** *iv.* [for a liquid] to become so hot that it bubbles and turns into vapor. □ *I waited 10 minutes for the pot of soup to boil.* **6.** *iv.* [for something] to cook in a liquid that is **boiling** as in ⑤. □ *The eggs boiled for fifteen minutes.*

**bold** ['bold] **1.** *adj.* confident; sure of oneself; courageous. (Adv: *boldly.* Comp: *bolder;* sup: *boldest.*) □ *It was very bold of you to support Jane in front of the boss.* **2.** *adj.* without shame; rude; not shy. (Adv: *boldly.* Comp: *bolder;* sup: *boldest.*) □ *The employee paid for his bold remark by getting extra work.* **3.** *adj.* [of printing] darker and thicker. (Comp: *bolder;* sup: *boldest.*) □ *The word "poison" appeared in bold letters on the label.*

**bolt** ['bolt] **1.** *n.* a metal pin or rod, with **threads,** used to connect or attach things. □ *The carpenter connected the boards with three bolts.* **2.** *n.* a rod that fastens a door, window, or gate. □ *The door was secured with a strong bolt.* **3.** *n.* a flash or streak of lightning. □ *A bolt of lightning lit up the sky.* **4.** *n.* a sudden, quick movement; an unexpected, quick movement. □ *The cat made a bolt for the door.* **5.** *n.* a roll of cloth. □ *The tailor bought a whole bolt of cloth.* **6.** *tv.* to fasten two or more objects together with ①. □ *Anne bolted the shelves to the wall.* **7.** *tv.* to lock a door, gate, or window by sliding a metal rod into place. □ *Please bolt the door before you go to bed.* **8.** *iv.* to run away from someone or something; to move away from someone or something quickly and suddenly. □ *The cat bolted when it saw the dog coming.*

**bomb** ['bɑm] **1.** *n.* an explosive weapon or device. □ *The army dropped bombs on the enemy country.* **2.** *tv.* to attack an area by dropping ① on it from planes. □ *The air force bombed the country until the citizens surrendered.* **3.** *tv.* to use ① to cause damage or injury to someone or something. □ *The terrorists bombed the building.*

**bond** ['bɑnd] **1.** *n.* a link or something in common that brings together two people or two groups of people. □ *The common experience forged a bond between Bill and Tom.* **2.** *n.* something that causes two objects to stick together. □ *The glue made a strong bond between the layers of wood.* **3.** *n.* an agreement in which someone or a company promises, as an investment, to pay back a certain sum of money by a particular date. □ *Grandma bought all her grandchildren bonds when they were born.* **4.** *iv.* [for an adhesive or paint] to become firmly attached. □ *This paint will bond to the wall very well.*

**bone** ['bon] **1.** *n.* the hard substance of which ② is made. (No plural form.) □ *The old flute was made of bone.* **2.** *n.* any one of the many parts of an animal's skeleton. □ *The skier broke several bones in the skiing accident.* **3.** *tv.* to remove ② from meat before cooking it. □ *You must bone the chicken before it can be added to the soup.*

**bonfire** ['bɑn faɪɚ] *n.* a large, controlled outdoor fire. □ *The campers sat around the bonfire.*

**bonus** ['bon əs] **1.** *n.* something extra. □ *At the end of the year, the employees all received cash bonuses.* **2.** *adj.* extra; offering more than expected. □ *The huge store offered many bonus deals with a large purchase.*

**book** ['bʊk] **1.** *n.* a stack of pages, held within a cover. □ *The children read their favorite books on the days that it rained.* **2.** *n.* a subdivision of a longer written work contained within ①. □ *The first volume contained books one and two.* **3.** *n.* a set of objects that are held together under a cover. □ *Please stop by the post office and buy a book of stamps.* **4. books** *n.* the records of the money spent and earned by a company or organization. (Treated as plural, but not countable.) □ *The government sent someone to audit the company's books.* **5.** *tv.* to process a charge against someone who has been arrested for committing a crime. □ *The police officer booked the criminal.* **6.** *tv.* to reserve space in advance for something, such as a play, an airplane flight, a room in a hotel, or a table in a restaurant. □ *The Smiths booked their flight to Europe three months before their trip.* **7.** *tv.* to reserve the services of a performer in advance. □ *The party organizer wanted to book an entire orchestra for the dance.*

**bookcase** ['bʊk kes] *n.* a set of shelves for books. □ *The bookcase held all sorts of interesting books.*

**bookkeeper** ['bʊk kip ɚ] *n.* someone who keeps track of the accounts of a company or an organization; someone who takes care of the **books** ④. □ *One of the bookkeepers where I work taught me how to make a budget.*

**bookkeeping** ['bʊk kip ɪŋ] *n.* the job of keeping track of the accounts of a company or an organization. (No plural form.) □ *Mary does the bookkeeping for her family.*

**booklet** ['bʊk lət] *n.* a thin book; a pamphlet. □ *The dentist gave me a booklet about teeth.*

**bookmark** ['bʊk mɑrk] *n.* something placed between the pages of a book to keep the reader's place. □ *The bookmark fell out of Jane's book, and she lost her place.*

**bookshelf** ['bʊk ʃɛlf] *n., irreg.* a horizontal board for holding and displaying books. (Often one of several such shelves, positioned one over the other in a **bookcase**. Pl: **bookshelves**.) □ *The bookshelf only had a few books on it.*

**bookshelves** ['bʊk ʃɛlvz] pl of **bookshelf**.

**bookshop** ['bʊk ʃɑp] *n.* a store where books are sold. □ *I went to a bookshop to buy a book about dogs.*

**bookstore** ['bʊk stor] *n.* a store where books are sold. □ *I called the bookstore to order a book.*

**boom** ['bum] **1.** *n.* a large, echoing noise made when something explodes or crashes. □ *The crash of the airplane made a loud boom.* **2.** *n.* a time of strong economic growth. □ *During the boom, many companies hired lots of people.* **3.** *iv.* to make a large, echoing noise like an explosion or a crash. □ *Bob's deep voice boomed over the radio.*

**boost** ['bust] **1.** *n.* an upward push; an upward movement. □ *Could you give me a boost? I can't reach the top shelf.* **2.** *tv.* to push someone or something upward from beneath. □ *Boost the baby into the chair, please.* **3.** *tv.* to increase something; to raise something. □ *The landlord boosted our rent.*

**boot** ['but] **1.** *n.* a heavy shoe, often waterproof. □ *One of my boots has a hole in the sole.* **2.** *tv.* to kick someone or something. □ *The cruel man booted the cat across the room.* **3.** *tv.* to start a computer, causing it to make a series of checks and set up its operating system.

B

☐ *I boot my computer each day in the morning.*

**booth** ['buθ] **1.** *n., irreg.* a seating area in a restaurant having bench seats with backs, placed on two sides of the table or around the table. (Pl: ['buðz] or ['buθs].) ☐ *The hostess asked if we would prefer a table or a booth.* **2.** *n., irreg.* a small, enclosed space, such as the enclosure containing a public telephone. ☐ *The voting booth had a curtain for privacy.* **3.** *n., irreg.* a display table or area—possibly enclosed—at a fair or a market. ☐ *Jane sold her work in a booth at the fair.*

**border** ['bor dɚ] **1.** *n.* a decorated area at the edge of something, and the edge itself. ☐ *The wallpaper had a dark border at the top.* **2.** *n.* the dividing line between two countries, states, or other political units. ☐ *The government securely guards its borders.* **3.** *tv.* to adjoin or be next to a particular area. ☐ *The shrubs border our yard on the east side.*

**bore** ['bor] **1.** pt of **bear**. **2.** *tv.* to drill a hole in something. ☐ *The carpenter bored a hole in the tabletop.* **3.** *tv.* to make someone tired by being dull. ☐ *That professor's voice would bore anyone.* **4.** *iv.* to drill; to make a hole. ☐ *This special drill can bore through solid rock.* **5.** *n.* someone or something that is boring; someone or something that is dull. ☐ *My guest was such a bore that I began to yawn.*

**boring** ['bor ɪŋ] *adj.* dull; not entertaining; causing people to lose interest and perhaps become sleepy. (Adv: *boringly.*) ☐ *Dave found the lecture on art history to be very boring.*

**born** ['born] **1.** a pp of **bear** ⑦. **2.** *adj.* possessing a certain quality or character since birth; by birth; natural. (Prenominal only.) ☐ *Jane announced that her child was a born pianist.* **3.** *adj.* having a particular place of birth or national heritage. (Usually in hyphenated combinations.) ☐ *Their children were all American-born.*

**borne** ['born] a pp of **bear**.

**borrow** ['bɑr o] **1.** *tv.* to ask for, accept, and use something from someone with the intention of returning or replacing it. ☐ *Sue borrowed my dress to wear to the party.* **2.** *tv.* to take something, such as a custom, trait, or idea, and use it as one's own. ☐ *The melody in this piece of music was borrowed from a folk song.*

**boss** ['bɔs] *n.* someone who is in charge of other people's work or of other workers. ☐ *Bill has a meeting with his boss each week to go over his work.*

**both** ['boθ] **1.** *adj.* one and one other; the two [things or people]. (See also **each** and **every**.) ☐ *I spoke to both Anne and David about the problem.* **2.** *pron.* one thing or person and another thing or person; the two things or people. ☐ *When offered pizza or a hamburger, I chose both.*

**bother** ['bɑð ɚ] **1.** *n.* something that is time-consuming or annoying to do. ☐ *We'll do it even though it is a real bother.* **2.** *tv.* to annoy someone or something; to upset someone or something. ☐ *What's bothering you?* **3.** *tv.* to interrupt or disturb someone. ☐ *Don't bother your dad. He's sleeping.*

**bottle** ['bɑt əl] **1.** *n.* a container, usually glass or plastic, with an opening at the end of a short or long neck. ☐ *The shelf is full of bottles of pop.* **2.** *n.* the contents of ①. ☐ *I drank two bottles of orange juice.* **3.** *tv.* to put something in ①, usually for future use or sale. ☐ *The company bottles all sorts of juices.*

**bottleneck** ['bɑt l nɛk] *n.* a narrow or crowded passage, like the neck of a bottle. ☐ *Anne squeezed through the bottleneck at the doorway.*

**bottom** ['bɑt əm] **1.** *n.* the lowest level of something; the deepest point of something. □ *I got some water from the bottom of the well.* **2.** *n.* the underside of something; the lowest surface of something. □ *My aquarium has a glass bottom.* **3.** *n.* land underneath water; the ground under a body of water. □ *The river had a muddy bottom.* **4.** *n.* the part of the body on which one sits; the buttocks. □ *Jane spanked her unruly child on his bottom.* **5.** *adj.* relating to the lowest part of something; relating to the underneath part of something. □ *The socks are in the bottom drawer of the dresser.*

**bought** ['bɔt] pt/pp of **buy**.

**boulder** ['bol dɚ] *n.* a huge stone. □ *During the storm, huge boulders rolled down the side of the mountain.*

**boulevard** ['bʊl ə vɑrd] *n.* a wide city street, usually lined with trees. □ *Anne lives on Maple Boulevard near the park.*

**bounce** ['bɑʊns] **1.** *n.* the return movement of an object when it hits a surface. □ *The basketball made a quick bounce off the wall.* **2.** *iv.* to spring up or away after hitting a surface. □ *Susie bounced on her bed so much that it broke.* **3.** *tv.* to toss someone upward gently, causing an upward movement as in ②. □ *Dad bounced Jimmy on his knee.* **4.** *tv.* to cause something to hit against a surface and spring back. □ *Stop bouncing that ball!*

**bound** ['bɑʊnd] **1.** pt/pp of **bind**. **2.** *adj.* tied up; fastened; glued into covers. □ *John put the bound copies of the magazines onto the reading table.* **3.** *iv.* to jump; to leap forward; to bounce up. □ *As soon as the lecture was over, the students bounded out the door.* **4.** *n.* an upward jump; a forward jump. □ *In one bound, Bill jumped across the stream.*

**boundary** ['bɑʊn dri] *n.* a border; a line that marks the edge of a thing or a place. □ *Where is the boundary of your property?*

**bouquet** [bo 'ke] **1.** *n.* an arrangement of cut flowers; a grouping of cut flowers that can be held in one hand. (From French.) □ *John sent me a bouquet of flowers for my birthday.* **2.** *n.* the characteristic aroma of a type of wine. □ *David tested the wine's bouquet by sniffing the wine in his glass.*

**bout** ['bɑʊt] **1.** *n.* an attack of a disease. □ *Mary is still weak after her bout with the flu.* **2.** *n.* a specific contest or event, especially a boxing match. □ *The best fighter won the bout.*

**bow 1.** ['bo] *n.* a pretty knot, usually with two or more large loops. □ *The ribbon holding the little girl's hair was tied in a bow.* **2.** ['bo] *n.* a weapon that shoots arrows. □ *The arrow flew from the bow as Jim released the string.* **3.** ['bo] *n.* a stick with strings of hair stretched from end to end, used to play a stringed instrument, such as a violin. □ *The musician drew his bow across the strings of his cello.* **4.** ['bɑʊ] *n.* an act of bending the body to show respect or in response to applause. □ *When I was in Japan, I greeted my host with a deep bow.* **5.** ['bɑʊ] *n.* the front part of a ship or a boat. □ *Mary sat in the bow of the rowboat.* **6.** ['bo] *iv.* to bend into a curve, similar to ②; to form a curve. □ *The old man's legs bowed slightly.* **7.** ['bɑʊ] *iv.* to bend the body when greeting or honoring someone. □ *The servant bowed before the king.* **8.** ['bo] *tv.* to cause something to bend into a curve, like the curve of ②; to cause something straight to form a curve. □ *The weight of the books bowed the shelf.*

**bowel** ['bɑʊ əl] **1.** *n.* the upper or lower intestine; the upper and lower intestine. □ *The spicy meal gave Bill trouble with his bowels.* **2. bowels** *n.* the inner part of something; the inner workings of something. (Fig. on ①.) □ *The supplies were stored deep in the bowels of the building.*

**bowel movement** ['bɑʊl muv mənt] *n.* an act of expelling or getting rid of feces. □ *I usually have a bowel movement once a day.*

**bowl** ['bol] **1.** *n.* a deep, rounded dish; a deep, rounded container. □ *We made small bowls in ceramics class.* **2.** *n.* the contents of ①. □ *Every morning, Bill eats a bowl of cereal for breakfast.* **3.** *n.* the part of a pipe that holds the tobacco. □ *David packed some tobacco into the bowl of his pipe.* **4.** *n.* a special football game; an important football game where the best teams play against one another. □ *Which teams are playing in the Rose Bowl this year?* **5.** *iv.* to play the game of bowling. □ *John bowls every Wednesday night.*

**bowling** ['bo lɪŋ] *n.* a game where a player rolls a large, hard ball along a narrow wooden floor in order to knock down as many as possible of the ten pins at the other end. (No plural form.) □ *I have never been very good at bowling.*

**bowling alley** [bo lɪŋ 'æl i] **1.** *n.* the path down which one rolls a large, hard ball in the game of bowling. □ *Bowling alleys are usually made of wood.* **2.** *n.* the building that houses a number of ①. □ *We went to the bowling alley for the evening.*

**box** ['bɑks] **1.** *n.* a rigid, cube-shaped container, used for storage or delivery. □ *The books were stored in boxes in the basement.* **2.** *n.* the contents of ①. □ *I used a whole box of nails repairing the fence.* **3.** *n.* a private seating area in a sports stadium, theater, etc. □ *We sat in a box at the baseball field.* **4.** *n.* an empty square printed on a piece of paper or on a form. □ *Check the box when you complete the task.* **5.** *n.* a square or rectangular container or receptacle designed for any of a number of special functions. □ *The employee dropped an angry note in the suggestion box.*

**boy** ['boɪ] **1.** *n.* a male human, not yet fully matured. □ *The boy often plays with toy trucks.* **2.** *n.* one of a group of male friends; one of a group of men. (Not necessarily a young male.) □ *The boys are coming to play cards tonight.*

**brace** ['bres] **1.** *n.* a support; something that holds something else in place. □ *The rope acted as a brace to hold the tree upright.* **2. braces** *n.* metal wires or bands attached to teeth to straighten them. (Treated as plural, but not countable.) □ *Jane has worn braces for three years.* **3.** *tv.* to prepare oneself for an impact or some other strong force. (Takes a reflexive object.) □ *Brace yourself. We are going around a curve.* **4.** *tv.* to prepare oneself for bad news. (Takes a reflexive object.) □ *I braced myself when the test scores were announced.*

**bracelet** ['bres lɪt] *n.* a piece of jewelry worn around the wrist. □ *The gold bracelet fell off Anne's wrist, and she never found it.*

**bracket** ['bræk ɪt] **1.** *n.* an L-shaped object attached to a wall to support a shelf. □ *The shelf rested on the brackets.* **2.** *n.* a printed character used to set off items or to enclose a set of words; [ and ]. □ *The extra information is in brackets.* **3.** *tv.* to enclose something in **brackets** ② [such as these words]. □ *The editor bracketed the unimportant words.*

**brag** ['bræg] **1.** *iv.* to boast; to say too many good things about oneself. □ *The boss bragged about himself all the time.* **2.** *tv.* to claim something in a boastful manner. (The object is a clause with **that** ⑦.) □ *Everyone was tired of hearing John brag that he was wealthy.*

**braggart** ['bræg ɚt] *n.* someone who brags; someone who boasts. □ *Mary is a braggart who talks about her successes constantly.*

**braid** ['bred] **1.** *tv.* to interweave three or more strands of rope or bundles of hair, string, etc., into one rope-like band. □ *Bob braided the grass to make a basket.* **2.** *n.* a rope-like band made of woven strands. □ *The basket was made from braids of grass.*

**brain** ['bren] *n.* the part of the body inside the head that is the center of thinking and feeling and that controls the movement and operation of the body. □ *The surgeons removed a tumor from the patient's brain.*

**brake** ['brek] **1.** *n.* a device that slows or stops a machine or vehicle. (Often plural. Compare this with **break**.) □ *Mary's car needs new brakes.* **2.** *tv.* to cause something to stop or slow down. (Pt/pp: *braked.*) □ *Brake the car to slow down.* **3.** *iv.* to stop or slow down. □ *The bicyclists braked at the stop sign.*

**branch** ['bræntʃ] **1.** *n.* a part of a tree that grows out of the trunk; an arm-like part of a tree. □ *The branches had ripe apples on them.* **2.** *n.* a small stream or river that joins to a larger river. □ *The map showed all of the river's branches.* **3.** *n.* a division of a company; a smaller part of a larger organization or structure. □ *Susan moved from one branch of her company to another.*

**brand** ['brænd] **1.** *n.* a trade name; the name of a product by which the product is widely recognized. □ *I always buy the cheapest brand.* **2.** *n.* a special kind or type of something. □ *The king's brand of democracy is not really democracy at all.* **3.** *n.* a mark burned into the skin of cattle. □ *The cattle bore the brand of the Triple D ranch.* **4.** *tv.* to mark cattle by burning a unique mark into their skin. □ *The ranchers branded their calves each spring.*

**brass** ['bræs] **1.** *n.* a metal made from copper and zinc. (Plural only when referring to different kinds, types, instances, or varieties.) □ *The door hinges were made of brass.* Ⓒ *Some brasses are shinier than others.* **2.** *n.* the family of wind instruments made of ① or some other metal, including the trumpet, trombone, and tuba. (Plural only when referring to different kinds, types, instances, or varieties.) □ *Bill especially likes the sound of brass.* Ⓒ *The brasses were too loud.* **3.** *adj.* made out of ①. □ *Mary fastened a brass knocker to the front door.* **4.** *adj.* <the adj. use of ②.> □ *Jane played the trombone in a brass band.*

**brave** ['brev] **1.** *adj.* showing courage; willing to face danger. (Adv: *bravely.* Comp: *braver;* sup: *bravest.*) □ *The brave little boy stood up to the bully.* **2.** *tv.* to withstand something; to face something without fear. □ *Anne braved the storm in order to make it to the wedding.*

**bread** ['brɛd] **1.** *n.* a type of food made by baking a mixture of flour, water, and other ingredients, often including yeast. (No plural form. Treated as singular. Number is expressed with *piece(s)* or *slice(s)* or *loaves of bread.*) □ *I eat bread with every meal.* **2.** *tv.* to cover food with crumbs or meal before cooking it. □ *The fish were breaded before they were fried.*

**breadth** ['brɛdθ] **1.** *n.* width; the measurement of something from side to side. □ *The shelf has a breadth of two feet.* **2.** *n.* extent. □ *Bill has a wide breadth of experience from his travels.*

**break** ['brek] **1.** *n.* a fracture; a place where something—especially a bone—has been **broken** as in **break** ⑩. (Compare this with **brake**.) □ *The doctor suspected a break when the boy came in limping badly.* **2.** *n.* a short period of rest from work. □ *The workers took a coffee break at 2:30.* **3.** *n.* the period of time between school terms. □ *My friends and I went to Florida during the break.* **4.** *n.* an escape from jail or prison. □ *Only one break occurred*

B

*at the prison in ten years.* **5.** *n.* the ending of a relationship with someone or something; the ending of an association with someone or something. □ *Bill made a clean break with his business partner.* **6.** *n.* a stop in a continuous action; an interruption. □ *The electricity failed and caused a break in our routine.* **7.** *n.* a chance to do something; an opportunity to do something. □ *All Jane needed was a break, and her career would be a success.* **8.** *tv., irreg.* to cause something to fall apart; to crush something. (Pt: **broke**; pp: **broken**.) □ *Please don't break the glass.* **9.** *tv., irreg.* to damage something; to make something not work correctly; to make something unusable. □ *Jane accidentally broke her sister's camera.* **10.** *tv., irreg.* to crack something; to fracture something, especially a bone. □ *Jane broke her leg in three places.* **11.** *tv., irreg.* to violate an agreement or promise by failing to do what was promised. □ *That company is known for breaking its promises.* **12.** *tv., irreg.* to exchange a large unit of money for the same amount of money in smaller units. □ *Bill asked the cashier to break a hundred-dollar bill.* **13.** *iv., irreg.* to shatter; to smash; to fall apart. □ *The glass broke when it hit the tile floor.* **14.** *iv., irreg.* to fail to operate; to stop functioning properly. □ *The refrigerator broke, and all the food in it spoiled.* **15.** *iv., irreg.* to crack; to fracture. □ *His leg broke when he fell.* **16. break into some place** *phr.* to enter a closed area by force. □ *I forgot my key and had to break into my own house!* **17. break a habit; break the habit; break one's habit** *phr.* to end a habit. □ *It's hard to break a habit that you have had for a long time.*

**breakfast** ['brɛk fəst] **1.** *n.* the first meal of the day. □ *My breakfast is usually just coffee and toast.* **2.** *iv.* to eat ① [somewhere or at some time]. □ *We breakfasted at the local restaurant.*

**breast** ['brɛst] **1.** *n.* the chest; the part of the body between the neck and the stomach. (Formal.) □ *The baby lay on its mother's breast.* **2.** *n.* the edible upper body of a fowl. □ *We cooked the chicken breasts on the barbecue.* **3.** *n.* one of the two milk-producing parts on the chest of the human female; a mammary gland. □ *The baby fed at its mother's breast.*

**breath** ['brɛθ] **1.** *n.* the air that moves in and out of the body when someone or something **breathes**. □ *When Bob took a breath of the stale air, he almost choked.* **2.** *n.* someone's exhaled air, especially if felt or smelled. □ *Jane could feel the baby's breath on her neck.*

**breathe** ['brið] **1.** *iv.* to suck air into the lungs and push air out of the lungs. □ *The athlete breathed heavily after the strenuous workout.* **2.** *tv.* to inhale or exhale something; to take something into the lungs or expel something from the lungs or throat. □ *The hikers breathed the fresh mountain air.*

**bred** ['brɛd] pt/pp of **breed**.

**breed** ['brid] **1.** *n.* a group of creatures representing a unique or different kind or type; a subgroup of a certain species. □ *Anne only likes certain breeds of dogs.* **2.** *n.* a kind of something; a class of something. □ *This decade has produced a new breed of politician.* **3.** *iv., irreg.* to reproduce; to mate. (Pt/pp: **bred**.) □ *How does that type of insect breed?* **4.** *tv., irreg.* to cause selected members of some kind of animal to reproduce, often for specific characteristics. □ *The Smiths tried to breed their dog with the neighbor's.*

**breeze** ['briz] **1.** *n.* a light wind; a gentle wind. □ *A gentle breeze swept over the porch and cooled us.* **2. a breeze** *n.* something that is very easy; something that is easily done. (Informal. No plural form.) □ *Cooking might be a breeze for you, but it's not for me.*

**brew** ['bru] **1.** *n.* a liquid drink made by heating various ingredients in water. □ *The wizard made a special brew to cure the sick man.* **2.** *tv.* to make a liquid drink by mixing and heating various ingredients in water. □ *Can I brew a cup of tea for you?* **3.** *tv.* to make beer or ale. □ *John brews his own beer at home.* **4.** *iv.* to develop; to gather; to form. □ *We could tell by the clouds that a storm was brewing.* **5.** *iv.* [for a liquid drink] to develop into its final form. □ *Some sort of special tea is brewing in the kitchen.*

**brick** ['brɪk] **1.** *n.* a rectangular block—used in building things—made of cement or baked clay. □ *The front of my house is faced with bricks.* **2.** *adj.* built of ①. □ *Anne laid a brick patio in her backyard.*

**bride** ['brɑɪd] *n.* a woman who is about to be married or has just been married. □ *Everyone congratulated the bride and groom after the ceremony.*

**bridge** ['brɪdʒ] **1.** *n.* a raised way over a river, street, train tracks, etc. □ *San Francisco is known for its Golden Gate Bridge.* **2.** *n.* something that links people or things. (Fig. on ①.) □ *The marriage created a bridge between the two families.* **3.** *n.* the navigation and control center of a ship. □ *The captain stood on the bridge of the ship.* **4.** *n.* the upper part of the nose; the part of the nose between the eyes. □ *The ball hit Bill on the bridge of his nose.* **5.** *n.* the part of a pair of eyeglasses that rests on the nose. □ *I don't like the bridge on that style of glasses.* **6.** *n.* a type of card game for four people. (No plural form.) □ *Bill, Tom, Jane, and Mary played bridge all day.*

**brief** ['brif] **1.** *adj.* short in time; to the point. (Adv: *briefly.* Comp: *briefer;* sup: *briefest.*) □ *The police chief gave a brief statement on the status of the case.* **2.** *n.* [in law] a document that describes certain facts or information about a legal case. □ *The law students wrote many briefs during the semester.* **3. briefs** *n.* short and close-fitting underpants. (Treated as plural. Number is expressed with *pair(s) of briefs.* Also countable.) □ *Tom prefers white cotton briefs.* Ⓒ *Tom packed seven briefs and seven undershirts.* **4.** *tv.* to acquaint someone with certain facts or information. □ *Our manager briefed us on company sales for the year.*

**bright** ['brɑɪt] **1.** *adj.* shiny; full of light; reflecting much light. (Adv: *brightly.* Comp: *brighter;* sup: *brightest.*) □ *I wore dark glasses because the sun was so bright.* **2.** *adj.* smart; intelligent. (Adv: *brightly.* Comp: *brighter;* sup: *brightest.*) □ *It was not very bright to leave the tools out in the rain.* **3.** *adj.* vivid; brilliant. (Adv: *brightly.* Comp: *brighter;* sup: *brightest.*) □ *Tom is wearing a bright green shirt.*

**brim** ['brɪm] **1.** *n.* the top edge of something, such as a cup. □ *I filled my coffee cup to the brim.* **2.** *n.* the circular, flat edge of a hat. □ *The wind caught the brim of my hat, and it blew off my head.*

**bring** ['brɪŋ] **1.** *tv., irreg.* to carry or escort someone or something from a more distant place to a closer place. (Pt/pp: **brought.**) □ *Please bring that package to me.* **2.** *tv., irreg.* to cause something to happen; to result in something. □ *April showers bring May flowers.* **3. bring** someone or something **with** one *tv., irreg. + obj. + prep. phr.* to carry or convey someone or something as one comes to a place; to escort someone as one comes to a place. □ *Don't worry. I will bring it with me.* **4.** *tv., irreg.* to cause something to enter into a different state. □ *Let's bring this matter to an end.*

**brisk** ['brɪsk] **1.** *adj.* [of movement, actions, activity, or rhythm] quick, rapid, or swift; [of rhythm, music, or activity] lively. (Adv: *briskly.* Comp:

B

*brisker;* sup: *briskest.*) □ *A brisk walk before breakfast is a good way to start the day.* **2.** *adj.* stimulating; chilly. (Adv: *briskly.* Comp: *brisker;* sup: *briskest.*) □ *We hiked through the forest on a brisk fall day.*

**bristle** ['brɪs əl] *n.* a short, stiff hair, as on a brush or on the back of a hog. □ *The bristles on the brush scratched Mary's scalp.*

**broad** ['brɔd] **1.** *adj.* wide; vast; extensive; far-reaching. (Adv: *broadly.* Comp: *broader;* sup: *broadest.*) □ *The plains are broad and flat.* **2.** *adj.* main; general. (Adv: *broadly.* Comp: *broader;* sup: *broadest.*) □ *The professor explained the theory in very broad terms.*

**broccoli** ['brɑk ə li] *n.* a green vegetable that grows in branched stalks ending in clumps of buds. (From Italian. No plural form.) □ *The grocery store has lots of fresh broccoli.*

**broil** ['broɪl] **1.** *tv.* to cook something by placing it over or under an open flame. □ *Mary broiled steaks for her dinner party.* **2.** *iv.* [for food] to cook over or under an open flame. □ *The meat is broiling on the grill.*

**broke** ['brok] **1.** pt of break. **2.** *adj.* having no money; completely without money; penniless. □ *I was broke after buying a new car.*

**broken** ['brok ən] **1.** pp of break. **2.** *adj.* not working; not functioning; not operating; out of order. □ *I took the broken television set to the repair shop.*

**bronze** ['brɑnz] **1.** *n.* a brownish metal made from copper and tin. (Plural only when referring to different kinds, types, instances, or varieties.) □ *Bronze carries electricity well.* Ⓒ *The duller of the bronzes is called antique bronze.* **2.** *n.* a third-place medal; an award for coming in third place in a competition. □ *The skater took the bronze three years in a row.* **3.** *adj.* made from ①. □ *The bronze statue stood in the courtyard.*

**brook** ['brʊk] *n.* a stream; a creek; a small river. □ *The kids discovered a brook in the woods.*

**broom** ['brum] *n.* a long-handled brush that is used to sweep floors. □ *Sue swept the patio with a broom.*

**broth** ['brɔθ] *n.* the liquid part of soup. (Plural only when referring to different kinds, types, instances, or varieties.) □ *I ate only broth when I had the flu.* Ⓒ *The different broths they used in their cooking provided subtle flavor differences.*

**brother** ['brʌð ɚ] *n.* a male sibling. □ *My brother has three children.*

**brought** ['brɔt] pt/pp of bring.

**brown** ['brɑʊn] **1.** *n.* a deep, reddish tan color similar to the color of dirt or wood. (Plural only when referring to different kinds, types, instances, or varieties.) □ *The walls were painted a dark brown.* Ⓒ *All browns look the same to me.* **2.** *adj.* of the color of ①. (Comp: *browner;* sup: *brownest.*) □ *My brown shoes matched my brown belt.* **3.** *tv.* to cook something until it turns dark or gets crisp. □ *Brown the ground beef in the pan before adding it to the sauce.* **4.** *iv.* [for food] to cook until it becomes ②. □ *The potatoes are browning in the oven.*

**browse** ['brɑʊz] **browse through something** *iv. + prep. phr.* to look through goods casually when shopping; to search through books or collections of documents. □ *Mary browsed through the clothes that were on sale, but she didn't buy anything.*

**bruise** ['bruz] **1.** *n.* a colored mark on the skin caused by being struck. □ *Mary got a bruise where she bumped against the table.* **2.** *tv.* to cause ① by striking the body. □ *The ball bruised Bill's arm when it struck him.*

**brush** ['brʌʃ] **1.** *n.* a device used for cleaning, combing, or painting—made of hard bristles attached to a handle. □ *I removed the rust from the car with a steel brush.* **2.** *tv.* to clean something, such as one's teeth, with ①. □ *Jane brushed her dog's coat.* **3.** *tv.* to arrange or groom hair with ①. □ *Go back upstairs and brush your hair!*

**bubble** ['bʌb əl] **1.** *n.* a thin, spherical film of liquid that encloses a pocket of gas or air. □ *The soap made bubbles in the water.* **2.** *n.* a sphere of air within a solid or a liquid. □ *There were lots of tiny bubbles in the soft drink.* **3.** *iv.* [for moving liquid] to make a sound that includes the popping or collapsing of ① or ②. □ *The brook bubbled merrily along its way.* **4.** *iv.* to show much happiness, especially in one's speech. □ *Sue bubbled with excitement when she received her final grade.*

**buck** ['bʌk] **1.** *n.* the male of certain kinds of animals, such as deer and rabbits. □ *A large buck stood in the clearing in the forest.* **2.** *n.* one American dollar bill; a dollar. (Slang.) □ *Jane found a couple of bucks under the sofa.* **3.** *iv.* [for an animal that is being ridden] to jump in an attempt to throw its rider. □ *The horse bucked when I rode it.*

**bucket** ['bʌk ɪt] **1.** *n.* a pail; an open-topped container with a curved wire handle. □ *The farmer poured the cow's milk into a bucket.* **2.** *n.* the contents of ①. □ *I mixed a small amount of soap with a bucket of water.*

**buckle** ['bʌk əl] **1.** *n.* a fastener for securing a belt or strap. □ *The buckle on my belt broke.* **2.** *tv.* to fasten a shoe, belt, etc., by using ①. □ *Sue buckled the belt around her waist.* **3.** *tv.* to cause pavement to bend and rise up. □ *The summer heat buckled the roads.* **4.** *iv.* [for pavement] to rise, fold, or break due to a force such as an earthquake or because of excessive heat. □ *The hot sun made the sidewalk buckle.* **5.** *iv.* [for someone's knees] to fold or collapse. □ *Anne's knees buckled when she fainted.*

**bud** ['bʌd] **1.** *n.* the part of a plant that becomes a leaf or a flower. □ *In the spring, tiny buds appeared on all the trees.* **2.** *n.* a flower that has not opened all the way; a flower whose petals are still wrapped together. □ *The bud of the flower never opened.* **3.** *iv.* [for a plant] to develop and open the parts that become leaves or flowers. □ *The trees budded in early April.*

**budget** ['bʌdʒ ət] **1.** *n.* a financial plan; an estimate of how much money will be earned and spent during a period of time. □ *Sue was careful about keeping within her budget.* **2.** *n.* an amount of money allocated for a particular purpose. □ *The budget for groceries is two hundred dollars a month.* **3.** *tv.* to provide or reserve an amount of money for a particular purpose. □ *We've budgeted $1,000 for advertising.* **4.** *adj.* cheap; economical. □ *The department store always has lots of budget clothing.*

**buffalo** ['bʌf ə lo] *n., irreg.* a type of wild ox native to Asia, Africa, and the Americas. (Pl: *buffalo, buffalos,* or *buffaloes.*) □ *Cave drawings sometimes show buffalos and other animals.*

**buffet** [bə 'fe] **1.** *n.* a large cabinet for holding utensils for serving and eating and tablecloths and napkins. (From French.) □ *Grandma keeps the good china in the buffet.* **2.** *n.* a table or counter having bowls of food that diners can serve themselves. □ *The buffet featured all of our favorite foods.* **3.** *adj.* <the adj. use of ②.> □ *The church has a buffet supper each week.*

**bug** ['bʌg] **1.** *n.* any small insect or creature like an insect; any annoying insect. □ *Bugs crawled all over the plant.* **2.** *n.* the flu; any minor sickness. (Informal.) □ *This particular bug gives its victims diarrhea.* **3.** *n.* an electronic device that

B

permits someone to listen to someone's private conversation in secret. □ *The police planted a bug in the criminal's apartment.* **4.** *n.* a problem; something that is wrong with a system, especially in a computer program. □ *Every time a bug appeared, the program crashed.* **5.** *tv.* to equip a room, telephone, etc. with ③. □ *The suspect knew that her room had been bugged.* **6.** *iv.* [for someone's eyes] to open up and become very apparent. □ *Anne's eyes bugged when she heard the news.*

**build** ['bɪld] **1.** *tv., irreg.* to make something from separate pieces; to construct something. (Pt/pp: **built**.) □ *Anne helped Dad build a fence with old boards.* **2.** *tv., irreg.* to develop something; to establish something a little bit at a time. □ *Max built the business slowly over many years.* **3.** *iv., irreg.* [for something] to increase. □ *The volume of the music kept building until it was very loud.* **4.** *n.* the form of the body; the shape of the body; the muscle structure of the body. □ *The police say the robber has a large build.*

**building** ['bɪl dɪŋ] **1.** *n.* a structure where people live, work, or play. □ *The apartment building housed fifty people.* **2.** *n.* the business of constructing ①. (No plural form.) □ *After I quit my office job, I went into building.* **3.** *adj.* <the adj. use of ②.> □ *The building trade is booming these days.*

**built** ['bɪlt] pt/pp of **build**.

**bulb** ['bʌlb] **1.** *n.* any rounded or globular-shaped object. □ *The vase had a narrow neck and a bulb as a base.* **2.** *n.* a glass globe, with a special wire inside, that is used to create light from electricity. □ *The lamp needs a new bulb. The old one is burned out.* **3.** *n.* a swelling between the stem and roots of some plants, used for storing food for the plant. □ *Jane planted tulip bulbs in the garden.* **4.** *n.* a species of flower that is grown from ③. □ *I've never had good luck growing bulbs.*

**bulk** ['bʌlk] **1.** *n.* a great amount; a large amount of something. (No plural form.) □ *Dave placed his great bulk on the tiny chair, and it broke.* **2.** *n.* the major portion of something; the largest and most important part. (No plural form.) □ *John did the bulk of the cooking for the party.* **3.** *adj.* [containing] large [quantities or amounts]. □ *Jane made a bulk purchase of office supplies for her company.*

**bull** ['bʊl] **1.** *n.* the male animal corresponding to a **cow**, if it is able to breed. □ *The bull stayed on the land around the farm.* **2.** *n.* someone who believes that prices on stocks or bonds will rise. □ *Bill is a bull on the technology stocks.* **3.** *adj.* [of certain animals] male. □ *The bull elephants tramped through the tall grass.*

**bulldozer** ['bʊl doz ɚ] *n.* a powerful tractor equipped with a strong blade that can push dirt and rocks. □ *A huge bulldozer was parked near the unfinished building.*

**bullet** ['bʊl ɪt] *n.* a small piece of lead fired from a gun. □ *This pistol holds six bullets.*

**bulletin** ['bʊl ə tən] **1.** *n.* a special news report; a piece of news; official information. □ *The bulletin announced a change in the date of the rocket launch.* **2.** *n.* a journal or newsletter published by a specific group. □ *The medical association publishes a bulletin each month.*

**bulletin board** ['bʊl ə tən bord] *n.* a board where notices and signs can be posted. □ *No advertisements can be posted on the company bulletin board.*

**bully** ['bʊl i] **1.** *n.* someone, usually a male, who is mean or threatening. □ *The students were threatened by a bully who took their money.* **2.** *tv.* to threaten someone; to be mean to someone. □ *The older students bullied the younger.*

**bumblebee** ['bʌm bəl bi] *n.* a large, hairy, black and yellow bee. □ *The bumblebee frightened me.*

**bump** ['bʌmp] **1.** *n.* a lump or swelling in an otherwise flat area. □ *Our car ran over a big bump in the road.* **2.** *n.* a knock; a blow; a hit; a forceful contact. □ *Suddenly, I felt a bump and knew that someone had hit my car.* **3.** *tv.* to make forceful contact with someone or something. □ *I bumped the wall and got wet paint on my shirt.* **4.** *tv.* [for an airline] to cancel someone's airplane reservation without warning. □ *Our vacation was ruined when the airline bumped us.* **5. bump into** someone or something *iv.* + *prep. phr.* to make contact with someone or something; to run into someone or something. □ *My car bumped into the car in front of me.* **6. bump into** someone *iv.* + *prep. phr.* to have a surprise meeting with someone. □ *Sue bumped into Bob at the supermarket.*

**bumper** ['bʌm pɚ] **1.** *n.* a strong, protective metal or fiberglass bar on the front and back of vehicle. □ *The accident caused the car's bumper to fall off.* **2.** *n.* any device designed to protect someone or something from an impact. □ *The baby's crib had a soft bumper around the inside.* **3.** *adj.* large; abundant; plentiful. □ *We had a bumper harvest this year.*

**bun** ['bʌn] **1.** *n.* a bread product, such as that used to hold cooked hamburger meat or a wiener. □ *The guests ate their hamburgers on bread instead of buns.* **2.** *n.* a sweetened bread roll, sometimes with fruit or other fillings. □ *Jelly buns are our favorite.*

**bunch** ['bʌntʃ] **1.** *n.* a group of things that grow together or are placed together. □ *Jane arranged a bunch of flowers in the vase.* **2.** *n.* a group of things or people; a large number of things or people. □ *I saved a bunch of boxes for our next move.*

**bundle** ['bʌn dəl] **1.** *n.* a group of things gathered together. □ *Mary gave a bundle of clothes to charity.* **2. bundle** someone or something **up** *tv.* + *obj.* + *adv.* to wrap someone or something up; to wrap someone or something tightly. □ *Bundle the children up well—it's bitterly cold today.* 🅃 *I'll bundle up the children.* **3.** *tv.* to include a selection of software with the sale of computer hardware. □ *The marketing department likes to bundle the computer products.*

**bunny** ['bʌn i] *n.* a rabbit; a hare. □ *The Easter basket contained a chocolate bunny.*

**buoy** ['bɔɪ, 'bu i] **1.** *n.* a floating aid to navigation, used to display warnings or directions. □ *Buoys marked off the swimming area at the beach.* **2.** *n.* a floating ring that can support a person in the water. □ *The ship's deck held buoys in case of an emergency.* **3. buoy** someone or something **(up)** *tv.* + *obj.* (+ *adv.*) to prevent someone or something from sinking; to keep someone or something floating. □ *A floating board buoyed the swimmer up.* **4. buoy** someone **(up)** *tv.* + *obj.* (+ *adv.*) to make someone happy; to cheer someone up. (Fig. on ③.) □ *The good news buoyed Jane through another day.*

**burden** ['bɚd n] **1.** *n.* a heavy load. □ *The burden of five grocery bags slowed me down.* **2.** *n.* a heavy responsibility that strains a person. (Fig. on ①.) □ *At sixteen, Jane was not ready for the burden of college.* **3.** *tv.* to give someone or something a heavy load. □ *We burdened each of the campers with loads of the same weight.*

**burglar** ['bɚg lɚ] *n.* a criminal who enters someplace illegally to steal things. □ *Anne caught the burglar stealing her jewelry.*

B

**burial** ['bɛr i əl] *n.* the burying of something, especially a dead body. □ *The sailor had a burial at sea.*

**burn** ['bɚn] **1.** *n.* the mark caused by a flame or something that is very hot. □ *How did this burn get on the table?* **2.** *n.* an injury caused to someone who has been harmed by high heat. □ *Tom has a burn on his hand from the hot stove.* **3.** *tv., irreg.* to set fire to something; to destroy something by fire. (Pt/pp: usually *burned*, but sometimes **burnt**.) □ *The criminal burned the building to the ground.* **4.** *tv., irreg.* to damage someone or something with too much heat. □ *The faulty oven burned my dinner.* **5.** *tv., irreg.* to consume a fuel or an energy source. □ *During the last winter we burned lots of oil.* **6.** *tv., irreg.* to sting something; to cause something to have a sharp feeling of heat. □ *The hot pepper sauce burned Mary's mouth.* **7.** *iv., irreg.* to provide light; to give off light. □ *Lights were burning in every room of the house.* **8.** *iv., irreg.* to sting. □ *The medicine burned when I put it on the wound.* **9.** *iv., irreg.* to be on fire. □ *The wood burned brightly.* **10.** *iv., irreg.* [for food] to become scorched from overcooking. □ *What is burning in the kitchen?*

**burner** ['bɚ nɚ] *n.* a device that makes a controlled flame for cooking or heating. □ *The cook had something cooking on every burner.*

**burnt** ['bɚnt] a pt/pp of **burn**.

**burrow** ['bɚ o] **1.** *n.* a hole that an animal digs in the ground for a place to live. □ *The animal's burrow is under the bush.* **2.** *iv.* [for a small animal] to work its way, digging, into soil, leaves, snow, etc. □ *The animal burrowed in the soil, looking for worms.*

**burst** ['bɚst] **1.** *tv., irreg.* to break something open; to cause something to explode. (Pt/pp: *burst.*) □ *The flood of water burst the dam.* **2.** *iv., irreg.* to explode; to suddenly break open. □ *The pipes burst from the cold.* **3.** *n.* a sudden, powerful happening. □ *The children were surprised by a burst of shouting.*

**bury** ['bɛr i] **1.** *tv.* to put something in the ground, to cover something with dirt or soil. □ *The dog buried its bone in the yard.* **2.** *tv.* to place a dead person or other creature in the ground. □ *The family buried their father in the cemetery.* **3.** *tv.* to conceal someone or something; to hide someone or something. □ *The kids buried themselves under the covers to hide from their parents.*

**bus** ['bʌs] **1.** *n.* an enclosed motor vehicle that carries many passengers. □ *Mary rides the bus to work every day.* □ *Buses are not as fast as trains.* **2.** *n.* [in a computer] a circuit that allows new devices and equipment to be connected to the main computer. □ *This board plugs directly into the bus.* **3.** *tv.* to transport someone using ①. □ *The school district bussed the children across town to school.* **4.** *tv.* to remove dirty dishes from a table after a meal in a restaurant or cafeteria. □ *The waitress bussed the table so new customers could be seated.*

**bush** ['bʊʃ] *n.* a plant with several woody branches. □ *The bush had beautiful yellow blossoms on it.*

**bushel** ['bʊʃ əl] **1.** *n.* a unit of measurement of dry goods, especially crops, equal to 64 pints or 32 quarts. □ *We were given a bushel of apples as a gift.* **2.** *adj.* holding or containing ①. □ *The bushel basket was full of apples.*

**business** ['bɪz nəs] **1.** *n.* a profession; an occupation. □ *Bill's business is cooking.* **2.** *n.* buying, selling, or trading. (No plural form.) □ *Anne's gift shop has a lot of business during the holidays.* **3.** *n.* a corporation; a company. □ *Our family business was founded in 1901.* **4.** *n.* affair; concern; a matter of interest. (No plural form.) □ *Okay, I'll mind my own business.*

B

**busy** ['bɪz i] **1.** *adj.* working; at work; having things to do. (Adv: *busily.* Comp: *busier;* sup: *busiest.*) ☐ *The busy clerk waited on customers all day.* **2.** *adj.* [of a telephone connection] in use. (Comp: *busier;* sup: *busiest.*) ☐ *The busy phone really annoyed me.* **3.** *adj.* occupied with something else at the time. (Comp: *busier;* sup: *busiest.*) ☐ *I can't do it tomorrow because I'm busy all day.* **4.** *adj.* distracting to look at because of clashing patterns; having too much detail. (Adv: *busily.* Comp: *busier;* sup: *busiest.*) ☐ *The flowered wallpaper is too busy.* **5.** *tv.* to make work for oneself; to occupy oneself with something. (Takes a reflexive object.) ☐ *Anne busied herself preparing for the test.*

**but** ['bʌt, bət] **1.** *conj.* on the contrary; however. ☐ *John ordered peas, but he was served carrots.* **2.** *conj.* except. ☐ *I have done nothing but think about you since you left.* **3.** *prep.* except someone or something; except for someone or something; other than someone or something; besides someone or something. ☐ *No one but the best student passed the exam.* **4.** *adv.* only; merely; just. ☐ *That nonsense is but the product of your imagination.*

**butcher** ['bʊtʃ ɚ] **1.** *n.* someone who kills animals that will be used for meat. ☐ *The butcher plans to slaughter the hogs today.* **2.** *n.* someone who cuts up and sells the meat of animals. ☐ *The butcher cut a thick slice of beef for me.* **3.** *tv.* to kill and cut up an animal for food. ☐ *The farmer butchered several hogs.* **4.** *tv.* to kill someone or something with great cruelty. ☐ *Many innocent people were butchered during the war.*

**butt** ['bʌt] **1.** *n.* the end or base of something. ☐ *John placed the butt of his rifle against his shoulder.* **2.** *n.* the leftover end of a cigar or cigarette. ☐ *Please take your stale cigar butt out of this house!* **3.** *n.* part of the body on which one sits; the buttocks. (Informal.) ☐ *Tom tripped and fell on his butt.* **4.** *n.* someone who is the victim of ridicule or the object of jokes or rudeness. ☐ *Bill was always the butt of Tom's ridicule.* **5.** *tv.* to strike or push hard against someone or something with the head. (Said especially of animals with horns.) ☐ *The goat butted the dog and forced it out of the barnyard.* **6. butt in (on someone or something)** *iv. + adv. (+ prep. phr.)* to interrupt someone or something. ☐ *Excuse me for butting in on you, but I need an answer now.*

**butter** ['bʌt ɚ] **1.** *n.* the fatty part of milk left after it has been stirred and mixed over and over. (Plural only when referring to different kinds, types, instances, or varieties.) ☐ *Bread and butter will be served with dinner.* Ⓒ *Some butters are too salty, others taste bland.* **2.** *n.* certain foods mashed into a spreadable substance. (Plural only when referring to different kinds, types, instances, or varieties.) ☐ *Peanut butter is made from crushed peanuts.* Ⓒ *Who would think that peanut butters could differ so much.* **3.** *tv.* to put ① on something, usually bread. ☐ *Please butter the bread for the sandwiches.*

**butterfly** ['bʌt ɚ flaɪ] *n.* an insect with large, brightly colored wings. ☐ *A butterfly lighted on the picnic table.*

**buttermilk** ['bʌt ɚ mɪlk] *n.* a drink made from milk to which certain kinds of bacteria have been added. (No plural form.) ☐ *The recipe calls for buttermilk, rather than regular milk.*

**button** ['bʌt n] **1.** *n.* a small, hard disc, used to fasten clothes or fabric. ☐ *The buttons on my sweater are black and white.* **2.** *n.* a small disc or similar device that is pressed to close an electrical circuit. ☐ *I had to push in the button in order to use my hair dryer.* **3.** *n.* a badge bearing a message, worn on the clothing. ☐ *The voter's jacket was* *covered with political buttons.* **4.** *tv.* to fasten or close two pieces of fabric together with ①. □ *Jane buttoned her jacket against the wind.*

**buy** ['bɑɪ] **1.** *tv., irreg.* to purchase something; to pay money in exchange for something. (Pt/pp: **bought**.) □ *I bought groceries today.* **2.** *tv., irreg.* to acquire something, such as time. (Fig. on ①.) □ *The boss's absence bought us another day to finish the project.* **3.** *tv., irreg.* to believe something. (Informal.) □ *The teacher didn't buy the student's poor excuse.* **4.** *n.* something that is offered for sale at a very good price. □ *This outfit was a great buy.*

**buzz** ['bʌz] **1.** *n.* the sound that bees make; a rapid humming sound. (Plural only when referring to different kinds, types, instances, or varieties.) □ *The buzz of the alarm clock woke me from my sleep.* [C] *I hear two different buzzes and I think one is the door, but I don't recognize the other one.* **2.** *iv.* to make a loud humming sound like bees do. □ *The swarm of insects buzzed all night.*

**by** ['bɑɪ] **1.** *prep.* near someone or something; next to someone or something; alongside someone or something; beside someone or something. □ *I sat in the chair by the window.* **2.** *prep.* [passing] near someone or something. □ *Tom and Jane walked by the fountain.* **3.** *prep.* through the use of someone or something. □ *Tom traveled through Europe by train.* **4.** *prep.* through the cause of someone or something. (Indicating who or what did something in a passive sentence.) □ *The party was hosted by Bob.* **5.** *prep.* [done] through the process of doing something. □ *John amused his class by telling funny stories.* **6.** *prep.* <a form used in indicating the dimensions of something, especially the dimensions of a square area.> (See also **multiply** ①.) □ *This office measures 12 feet by 8 feet.* **7.** *prep.* before some time; not later than some time. □ *You must read the next chapter by tomorrow.* **8.** *prep.* [surpassing someone or something] according to a specific amount. □ *This path is longer than that one by a mile.* **9.** *prep.* allotted according to something; in units of something. □ *Eggs are usually sold by the dozen.* **10.** *prep.* with the aid of a particular light source. □ *The detective searched the garden by moonlight.* **11.** *adv.* past; beyond. □ *An ambulance rushed by.*

**Bye(-bye)** ['bɑɪ ('bɑɪ)] *interj.* Good-bye; Farewell. □ *Bill said "Bye" and hung up the phone.*

**byte** ['bɑɪt] *n.* a unit of computer data, made up of eight bits. □ *How many bytes of memory does your computer have?*

**cab** ['kæb] *n.* a **taxi,** a **taxicab.** (Short for **taxicab.**) ☐ *I missed my bus, so I took a cab.*

**cabbage** ['kæb ɪdʒ] *n.* a large, round vegetable with green or purple leaves. (Not usually plural unless referring to different kinds, types, or varieties. Number is expressed with *head(s) of cabbage.*) ☐ *The grocery store had a sale on cabbage.*

**cabin** ['kæb ən] **1.** *n.* a small house made of wood, especially in a faraway area. ☐ *The cabin had one room with a small fireplace.* **2.** *n.* a private room on a ship. ☐ *The ship's cabin had a sink and bunks.* **3.** *n.* the part of an airplane where the passengers sit. ☐ *It was noisy in the cabin, so no one heard what the pilot said.*

**cabinet** ['kæb (ə) nət] **1.** *n.* a piece of furniture with shelves, used for storing or displaying something; a small storage unit with a door, as found in a kitchen. ☐ *The pots and pans are in the cabinet.* **2.** *n.* the group of people who advise a president, prime minister, etc. ☐ *The president consulted his cabinet on the issue.*

**cacti** ['kæk tɑɪ] a pl of **cactus.**

**cactus** ['kæk təs] *n., irreg.* a desert plant with pulp on the inside and needles on the outside. (Pl: **cacti** or *cactuses.*) ☐ *Cacti do not need much water.*

**café** [kæ 'fe] *n.* a place to buy simple meals; a small restaurant. ☐ *There is a small café near our apartment.*

**cafeteria** [kæf ə 'tɪr i ə] *n.* a restaurant where one can choose from many selections, usually by passing by the items and placing one's choice of food on a tray. ☐ *Bill and Bob had lunch in the school cafeteria.*

**cage** ['kedʒ] **1.** *n.* an enclosure with bars or wires, where living creatures are kept. ☐ *Animals live in large cages at the zoo.* **2.** *tv.* to put someone or something in ①. ☐ *Jane cages her bird at night, but during the day it flies free.*

**caged** ['kedʒd] *adj.* enclosed; not free. ☐ *The caged animals grew weak and helpless.*

**cake** ['kek] **1.** *n.* a sweet, baked, bread-like food. (Plural only when referring to different kinds, types, instances, or varieties. Number is expressed with *slice(s)* or *piece(s) of cake.*) ☐ *Should we have cake or pie for dessert?* 🄲 *I prefer the cakes they bake using real butter.* **2.** *n.* a single, complete unit of ①. ☐ *We cut the cake into eight equal pieces.*

**calculate** ['kæl kjə let] **1.** *iv.* to estimate; to figure out values. ☐ *Please be quiet. I'm calculating.* **2.** *tv.* to add, subtract, multiply, or divide numbers; to figure out the value of something. (The object can be a clause with **that** ⑦.) ☐ *Mary calculated her monthly expenses.*

**calculator** ['kæl kjə let ɚ] *n.* a machine that adds, subtracts, multiplies, and divides figures and performs other mathematical functions. ☐ *Accountants keep calculators on their desks.*

**calculus** ['kæl kjə ləs] *n.* a branch of higher mathematics using special symbols and operations. (No plural form.) ☐ *I failed my course in calculus three times.*

**calendar** ['kæl ən dɚ] **1.** *n.* a system for keeping track of years and the divisions of years. ☐ *Our modern calendar is only a few centuries old.* **2.** *n.* a chart or table showing days, weeks, and months. □ *A calendar hangs on the kitchen wall.* **3.** *n.* a schedule of events; a list of events. □ *The busy manager's calendar is full this month.*

**calf** ['kæf] **1.** *n., irreg.* a young cow or bull. (Pl: **calves.**) □ *The new calf stood up on shaking legs.* **2.** *n., irreg.* the back of the leg from the knee to the ankle. □ *Tom had a bruise on his calf where the horse kicked him.*

**call** ['kɔl] **1.** *n.* a shout; a cry. □ *The injured man made a loud call for help.* **2.** *n.* an instance of someone contacting someone by telephone; a message or a conversation using the telephone; a **telephone call**; a **phone call**. □ *May I use your phone to make a quick call?* **3.** *n.* a decision; a choice. □ *It's your call—do you want Chinese or Italian food for dinner?* **4.** *tv.* to try to contact someone by telephone; to telephone someone. □ *David calls his mother every day.* **5.** *tv.* to demand someone's presence. □ *Anne called the children, and they came immediately.* **6.** *tv.* to name someone or something; to refer to or address someone or something as something. □ *The boy's name is Randolph, but he's called Randy.* **7.** *tv.* [for an umpire] to make a decision in a ball game. □ *The umpire called a strike.* **8. call something off** *tv.* + *obj.* + *adv.* to cancel something, especially an event that has been planned for a certain date. □ *The nervous groom called the wedding off.* 🆃 *No, the bride called off the wedding!*

**caller** ['kɔ lɚ] **1.** *n.* someone who makes a telephone call. □ *The caller left a message on the answering machine.* **2.** *n.* a visitor. □ *A caller appeared at the front door.*

**calm** ['kɑm] **1.** *adj.* quiet; serene; at peace. (Adv: *calmly.* Comp: *calmer;* sup: *calmest.*) □ *The canoe moved across the calm water.* **2.** *n.* a time or feeling of peace and quiet. (No plural form.) □ *At sunset, a calm came over the lake.* **3. calm someone or some creature (down)** *tv.* + *obj.* (+ *adv.*) to soothe someone or some creature; to cause someone or some creature to relax. □ *The trainer calmed the dog after gaining its trust.* **4. calm down** *iv.* + *adv.* to relax; to become ①. □ *The children calmed down as soon as I told them to be quiet.*

**calorie** ['kæl ə ri] *n.* a unit of energy supplied by food. □ *I always eat meals low in calories.*

**calves** ['kævz] pl of **calf**.

**came** ['kem] pt of **come**.

**camel** ['kæm əl] *n.* a large desert animal with one or two fatty humps on its back. □ *While on vacation in the Middle East, Mary rode a camel.*

**camera** ['kæm (ə) rə] **1.** *n.* a device that takes pictures; a device that makes photographs. □ *We forgot the camera when we went to the park.* **2.** *n.* a device that records live action for television or movies. □ *Mike took his video camera on vacation.*

**camp** ['kæmp] **1.** *n.* a remote or rural temporary residence, such as for soldiers, pioneers, refugees, people on vacation, etc. □ *We made our camp on the bank of the river.* **2.** *n.* a remote or rural place where children are sent in the summer. □ *The camp provided horseback riding and archery lessons.* **3.** *n.* a permanent training and living area for training and retraining members of various military organizations. □ *The buildings at the camp were painted every year.* **4.** *iv.* to take a vacation in a natural setting; to stay outside in a remote or rural area, sleeping in a tent or a camper instead of a hotel. □ *We camped at a large national park for a week.*

**campaign** [kæm 'pen] **1.** *n.* the period of time before an election when the candidates try to persuade people to vote for them. □ *The presidential campaign lasted for months.* **2.** *n.* a coordinated series of events with a specific goal or purpose. □ *The mayor started a campaign against crime.*

**camper** ['kæm pɚ] **1.** *n.* someone who **camps** ④; someone who takes a vacation in a rural or remote area. □ *The Smiths aren't campers—they prefer nice hotels.* **2.** *n.* a special vehicle, designed for camping. □ *My neighbors did not want me to park my camper in my front yard.*

**campfire** ['kæmp fɑɪɚ] *n.* a fire that campers cook on and sit around at night to keep warm while telling stories and enjoying the outdoors. □ *The campers huddled near the campfire to keep warm.*

**campsite** ['kæmp sɑɪt] *n.* the area where campers set up their tents. □ *The campsite had a public shower and bathroom in a nearby building.*

**campus** ['kæmp əs] **1.** *n.* the buildings, lawns, and other areas of a school, college, or university. □ *My brother and I walked around the college campus.* **2.** *n.* the buildings and surrounding areas of a large company. □ *The company's campus has benches surrounding a little fountain.* **3.** *adj.* <the adj. use of ①.> □ *The campus buildings had been built decades ago.* **4. off campus** *phr.* not located within ① of a college or university. □ *Tom has an apartment off campus.* **5. on campus** *phr.* located within ① of a college or university. □ *Do you live on campus or off campus?*

**can** ['kæn, kən] **1.** *aux.* <a word indicating ability to do something.> (See also **could**.) □ *Mary can ski really well.* **2.** *aux.* <a form indicating permission to do something.> (In general use but considered informal. In more formal English, **may** is used for this function. See also **could**.) □ *Mother says we can go to the movies.* **3.** *tv.* to preserve food by sealing it in an airtight container. (Pt/pp: *canned.*) □ *We ate some carrots from our garden and canned the rest.* **4.** *n.* a container shaped like a tube with a top and a bottom, usually made of metal. □ *We always buy coffee in a can.* **5.** *n.* the contents of ④. □ *Add one can of tomatoes to the stew.*

**canal** [kə 'næl] *n.* a long waterway—usually man-made—that is not a river. □ *A canal linked the two bodies of water.*

**canary** [kə 'nɛr i] *n.* a small, yellow bird that sings. □ *In the living room was a small cage with a canary in it.*

**cancel** ['kæn səl] **1.** *tv.* to end or stop something that is occurring or planned. □ *The boss canceled the meeting.* **2.** *tv.* to place a mark on a postage stamp, check, ticket, etc., so that it cannot be used again. □ *The post office cancels the postage on each letter.*

**cancer** ['kæn sɚ] **1.** *n.* a disease characterized by a tumor or tumors growing and spreading throughout the body. (Plural only when referring to different kinds, types, instances, or varieties.) □ *The doctor suspected that the patient had cancer.* Ⓒ *Different cancers grow at different rates.* **2.** *n.* something evil or horrible that spreads out over an area. (Fig. on ①.) □ *Crime is an evil cancer in many cities.*

**candidate** ['kæn dɪ det] **1.** *n.* someone who is seeking a public office or other job. □ *The reporter asked the candidate some hard questions.* **2.** *n.* a recommended or possible choice of a thing or person. □ *My car is a good candidate for the rubbish heap!*

**candle** ['kæn dəl] *n.* an object made of wax molded around a string or wick. (The wick burns and gives off light.) □ *The dining room was lit with candles.*

**candy** ['kæn di] **1.** *n.* a sweet food made with sugar and additional flavors. (Plural only when referring to different kinds, types, instances, or varieties. Number is expressed with *piece(s) of candy.*) □ *Jane took a box of candy to her friend as a gift.* Ⓒ *I prefer chocolate candies, although they're all heavenly.* **2.** *n.* a piece or a serving of ①. □ *There was a bowl of little candies on the table.*

**cane** ['ken] *n.* a stick used as an aid in walking. □ *Grandfather's cane is carved from strong wood.*

**cannot** [kə 'nɑt] *aux.* the negative form of **can**. (See also **can't**.) □ *I cannot remember which street Bill lives on.*

**canoe** [kə 'nu] **1.** *n.* a small boat that is moved by paddling. □ *The campers learned to paddle a canoe.* **2.** *iv.* to travel by ①. □ *The children canoed to the island for a picnic.*

**can't** [kænt] *cont.* "cannot." □ *Jimmy can't go out and play today because he's sick.*

**canvas** ['kæn vəs] **1.** *n.* a heavy, sturdy fabric made from cotton or another strong fiber. (Plural only when referring to different kinds, types, instances, or varieties.) □ *The tent was made of waterproof canvas.* Ⓒ *Different canvases repel water differently.* **2.** *n.* a panel of fabric—usually stretched on a frame—that painters paint on. □ *My art instructor likes to paint on large canvases.* **3.** *n.* a painting that has been painted on ②. □ *The decorator placed many small canvases on the walls.*

**canyon** ['kæn jən] *n.* a deep, narrow valley, often with a river running through it. □ *This photo shows a beautiful canyon in the wilderness.*

**cap** ['kæp] **1.** *n.* a (round) cover for the head, often with a shade for the eyes. □ *Bill took his cap off when he entered the house.* **2.** *n.* the cover or the top of a bottle or small jar; a small lid. □ *Remember to put the cap back on the jar of paste, or the paste will dry out.* **3.** *tv.* to close something with ②; to put ② on something. □ *I capped the water bottle and put it back into the refrigerator.* **4.** *tv.* to limit something at a specific point. □ *We need to cap spending in every department.*

**capable** ['ke pə bəl] **1.** *adj.* able; having the power or ability to do something. (Adv: *capably.*) □ *Jane and Tom hired a capable babysitter to watch their children.* **2. capable of** something *adj.* + *prep. phr.* having the ability to do something or for doing something. (Can take a verb ending in *-ing.*) □ *No one I know is capable of such a crime!* □ *I'm not capable of lifting that box.*

**capacity** [kə 'pæs ə ti] **1.** *n.* the amount of something that a space or container will hold. □ *The bottle's capacity is one liter.* **2.** *n.* the ability to accommodate someone or something. (No plural form.) □ *The hotel has the capacity to hold large banquets.* **3.** *n.* a job, role, or function; a set of responsibilities. □ *John and I both serve on the committee, but in different capacities.*

**cape** ['kep] **1.** *n.* a long, sleeveless garment worn over clothes. □ *The magician's cape was lined with red cloth.* **2.** *n.* a piece of land that sticks out into a body of water. □ *The explorer sailed around the Cape of Good Hope.*

**capital** ['kæp ɪ təl] **1.** *n.* a city that is the center of a government. (Compare this with **capitol**.) □ *Des Moines is the capital of Iowa.* **2.** *n.* any special or central city, with reference to a certain feature or attribute. □ *Nashville, Tennessee, is the country-music capital of the world.* **3.** *n.* an uppercase letter of the alphabet. □ *A sentence begins with a capital.* **4.** *n.* money that is invested with the hope that it will earn more money. (No plural form.) □ *The banker lost a lot of capital in the bad investment.* **5.** *adj.* [of a crime] punishable by death. □ *Murder is a capital crime in this state.*

**capitol** ['kæp ɪ təl] *n.* the building where legislators do their work. (Compare this with **capital**.) □ *The capitol is a large government building.*

**captain** ['kæp tən] **1.** *n.* someone in charge of a ship, boat, or airplane. □ *During our cruise, we never saw the ship's captain.* **2.** *n.* an officer in the military or the police. □ *The mayor hired a new police captain to help fight crime.* **3.** *n.* the leader of a team. □ *The football captain asked the team to do better.*

**capture** ['kæp tʃɚ] **1.** *tv.* to catch someone or something; to make someone or something a captive. □ *The war was ended when we captured the enemy's major city.* **2.** *tv.* to take something by force; to take control of something. □ *The hunters captured the tiger.* **3.** *tv.* to accurately show a feeling or atmosphere through artistic expression. □ *This painting captures the joy of swimming at the lake.*

**car** ['kɑr] **1.** *n.* an automobile; a vehicle that can carry a small number of passengers. □ *I don't drive a car to work because parking is expensive downtown.* **2.** *n.* one unit of a train. □ *The last car of a train is where the crew sleeps.* **3.** *n.* any of a number of different structures used to carry goods or people. □ *You should move to the rear of an elevator car.*

**caramel** ['kær ə məl, 'kɑr məl] **1.** *n.* a kind of candy made by heating sugar. (Plural only when referring to different kinds, types, instances, or varieties.) □ *The piece of caramel had a chocolate coating.* Ⓒ *We like the caramels that are made with real butter.* **2.** *adj.* made with or flavored with ①. □ *I love caramel candy, but it sticks to my teeth.*

**carbon** ['kɑr bən] **1.** *n.* a chemical element occurring in nature as coal, graphite, and diamonds. (No plural form.) □ *There is one atom of carbon in a molecule of carbon dioxide.* □ *Carbon's atomic symbol is C, and its atomic number is 6.* **2.** *n.* a **carbon copy**. □ *Please make two carbons when you type this report.*

**carbon copy** ['kɑr bən 'kɑp i] **1.** *n.* a copy of a document made by placing a special kind of carbon-coated paper between two other sheets of paper while one types the document on a typewriter. □ *How many carbon copies do you want of this letter?* **2.** *n.* someone or something that is almost identical to someone or something else. (Fig. on ①.) □ *Anne is a carbon copy of her mother.*

**card** ['kɑrd] **1.** *n.* a stiff, rectangular piece of paper. □ *I wrote the recipe on a note card.* **2.** *n.* a rectangle of stiff paper used in games, such as bridge or poker. □ *Mary dealt the cards, and the game began.*

**cardboard** ['kɑrd bord] **1.** *n.* a kind of heavy, thick, stiff paper. (Plural only when referring to different kinds, types, instances, or varieties.) □ *The gift came in a box made of cardboard.* Ⓒ *It's amazing how many different cardboards are used in making the boxes that software comes in.* **2.** *adj.* made of ①. □ *He put all his books into a cardboard box.*

**cardinal** ['kɑrd nəl] **1.** *n.* a bird—the males of which are bright red—with a crest on its head. □ *A cardinal perched on the bird feeder.* **2.** *n.* a high-ranking official of the Roman Catholic Church. □ *The cardinals wear red robes.* **3.** See **cardinal numeral**.

**cardinal numeral** AND **cardinal number** ['kɑrd (ə) nəl 'num ə rəl, 'kɑrd (ə) nəl 'nʌm bɚ] *n.* a number used in counting, such as one, two, three. (Can be shortened to **cardinal**. See also **ordinal number**.) □ Three *is a cardinal numeral, and the corresponding ordinal numeral is* (the) third. □ *Cardinal numbers are used when adding figures.*

**care** ['kɛr] **1.** *n.* serious attention; focused thought; caution. (No plural form.) □ *The architects put a lot of care into their designs.* **2.** *n.* the responsibility of providing for, protecting, or medically treating someone. (No plural form.) □ *Mary and John gave loving care to their grandmother.* **3.** *n.* a worry; a source of anxiety; a concern. □ *I am happy, and I don't have a care in the world.* **4. care (about** someone or something**)** *iv.* (+ *prep. phr.*) to have concern for someone or something; to show serious interest in the welfare of someone or something. □ *My teacher really cares about each student.* **5. care for** someone or something *iv.* + *prep. phr.* to be responsible for someone or something; to watch over someone or something. □ *Will you care for my cat while I'm on vacation?* **6. care for** someone or something *iv.* + *prep. phr.* to like someone or something; to want something. (Usually in the negative or in questions.) □ *Would you care for a second helping?*

**career** [kə 'rɪr] **1.** *n.* one's chosen work; what one does to earn money. □ *Mary's career is in computers.* **2.** *adj.* <the adj. use of ①>; done or chosen as ① for one's whole life. □ *I made the wrong career choice, and I am unhappy with my work.*

**careful** ['kɛr fʊl] **1.** *adj.* cautious; avoiding danger or damage. (Adv: *carefully.*) □ *Mary was very careful as she handled the antique vase.* **2.** *adj.* detailed; thorough. (Adv: *carefully.*) □ *Bill did a careful job preparing the statistics for his report.*

**careless** ['kɛr ləs] *adj.* without care; clumsy; done without thought. (Adv: *carelessly.*) □ *It was careless of you to forget to invite Bob to the party.*

**carelessness** ['kɛr ləs nəs] *n.* a lack of concern; a lack of care. (No plural form.) □ *Carelessness with matches may cause a fire.*

**cargo** ['kɑr go] *n.* goods being carried by a vehicle; freight. (Plural only when referring to different kinds, types, instances, or varieties. Treated as singular.) □ *The truck had no cargo—it was empty.* Ⓒ *This truck is designed to carry dry cargoes as well as wet substances.*

**carnival** ['kɑr nə vəl] *n.* a circus; a traveling amusement show having **rides** ④. □ *Each summer the town holds a carnival.*

**carol** ['kɛr əl] *n.* a song of joy, especially a Christmas song. □ *The choir sang well-known carols.*

**carpenter** ['kɑr pən tɚ] *n.* someone who builds things with wood. □ *I hired a carpenter to build my bookshelves.*

**carpet** ['kɑr pɪt] **1.** *n.* a rug; a thick floor covering made out of fabric. □ *David spilled grape juice on the carpet.* **2.** *tv.* to cover a floor with ①. □ *Not many people carpet their kitchen floors.*

**carriage** ['kɛr ɪdʒ] *n.* a car or vehicle pulled by horses. □ *The carriage was drawn by two white ponies.*

**carrot** ['kɛr ət] *n.* a vegetable with a long, thin, edible orange root. □ *A rabbit ate some carrots from our garden.*

**carry** ['kɛr i] **1.** *tv.* to pick up and take someone or something somewhere. □ *Mary carried one suitcase onto the plane.* **2.** *tv.* to support the weight of something. □ *This beam will carry over three tons.* **3.** *tv.* to spread a disease or sickness. □ *The dog carried a serious disease.* **4.** *tv.* to win the vote of a state or district. □ *Polls showed that the dishonest politician carried the entire city.* **5.** *tv.* [when adding a column of numbers, if the result is greater than 9] to transfer units of ten to the next column to the left as units of one. □ *Your answer is wrong because you forgot to carry the 2.* **6.** *tv.* [for a store] to have an item available for sale. □ *The clothing store carries* *only small sizes.* **7. carry** something **out** *tv. + obj. + adv.* to complete, accomplish, or execute a task, order, or assignment. □ *I was not able to carry the orders out.* 🅃 *I couldn't carry out the orders.* **8.** *iv.* [for a voice or sound] to travel far. □ *You have a peculiar laugh that carries a long way.*

**cart** ['kɑrt] **1.** *n.* a vehicle pulled by a horse, mule, dog, etc. □ *A small boy snuck a ride on the back of the cart.* **2.** *n.* a large basket on wheels, such as those found in grocery stores and other shops. □ *I filled my cart with groceries.*

**carton** ['kɑrt n] **1.** *n.* a cardboard or plastic container or package. □ *In the refrigerator, the milk was leaking from its carton.* **2.** *n.* ① considered as a measurement of something. □ *I bought a carton of eggs at the market.*

**cartoon** [kɑr 'tun] **1.** *n.* a drawing or series of drawings that is usually intended to be funny. □ *The newspaper has a large section of cartoons.* **2.** *n.* a film in which each frame is a drawing. (Also an *animated cartoon.*) □ *Many children's movies are cartoons.*

**carve** ['kɑrv] **1.** *tv.* to cut or sculpt wood, ivory, soap, or some other substance into a shape. □ *The figure on the mantel was carved by hand.* **2.** *tv.* to slice or cut up cooked meat for serving at a meal. □ *Bill carved the Thanksgiving turkey.*

**case** ['kes] **1.** *n.* a crate; a box. □ *We unloaded five cases of canned vegetables from the truck.* **2.** *n.* an instance; an occurrence. □ *This is a simple case of failure to complete an agreement.* **3.** *n.* a legal action or lawsuit. □ *The jurors could not discuss the case with anyone.* **4. in case** *phr.* in the event [that] something happens; preparing for something that may happen. □ *We should close the windows just in case it rains.*

**cash** ['kæʃ] **1.** *n.* money; currency, but not a check or a credit card. (No plural form.) □ *That store accepts cash and credit cards—no checks.* **2.** *tv.* to exchange a check for currency. □ *Where can I cash this check?* **3.** *tv.* to give money in exchange for a check. □ *The restaurant would not cash our check.*

**cashier** [kæ 'ʃɪr] *n.* someone who handles the paying out and taking in of money, especially at a store or bank. □ *The cashier took the money and put my purchase in a box.*

**cassette** [kə 'sɛt] *n.* a plastic case containing a pair of reels of magnetic audiotape or videotape. □ *John put his favorite cassette into the tape player.*

**cassette player** [kə 'sɛt ple ɚ] *n.* a device that plays back sound recorded on a cassette. □ *Our neighbors played their cassette player loudly all night.*

**cassette recorder** [kə 'sɛt rɪ 'kor dɚ] *n.* a device that records sound onto a cassette and plays it back. □ *The cassette recorder played back the recorded message.*

**cast** ['kæst] **1.** *n.* all of the performers in a play, musical, opera, TV show, or movie. □ *After the play, the audience applauded the cast.* **2.** *n.* a protective support for a broken bone, often made from plaster. □ *John's broken arm was in a cast for two months.* **3.** *tv., irreg.* to throw something. (Pt/pp: *cast.*) □ *Anne cast a stone into the water.* **4.** *tv., irreg.* to throw a fishing lure into the water; to drop a fishing net into the water. □ *Bill cast his line into the lake, hoping to catch a fish for dinner.* **5.** *tv., irreg.* to create a shadow on something. □ *The tree cast a long shadow on the lawn.* **6.** *tv., irreg.* to move and aim one's eyes or line of sight at someone or something. □ *The teacher cast a look at Jimmy that stopped him from talking.* **7.** *tv., irreg.* to select the performers for a play, film, opera, etc. □ *Tom hoped to be cast in the play.* **8.** *tv.,* *irreg.* to create an object by pouring a soft substance into a mold and letting it harden into the shape of the mold. □ *The bell was cast from molten bronze.*



**castle** ['kæs əl] **1.** *n.* a large fortress where a country's king and queen live. □ *The castle was surrounded by a large moat.* **2.** *n.* a game piece in chess, usually shaped like ①. □ *Bill lost both castles early in the chess game.*

**casual** ['kæʒ ju əl] **1.** *adj.* [of someone] relaxed and free; [of an event] not formal. (Adv: *casually.*) □ *Tom is a happy, casual guy who always has a smile.* **2.** *adj.* done without thought or planning. (Adv: *casually.*) □ *The Smiths dropped in yesterday for a casual visit.*

**cat** ['kæt] **1.** *n.* the family of mammals that includes ②, lions, leopards, tigers, jaguars, and lynxes. □ *The documentary was about the cats of Africa.* **2.** *n.* a small animal (as in ①) often kept as a pet. □ *Jane got a cat for her birthday.*

**catch** ['kætʃ] **1.** *tv., irreg.* to seize and hold someone or something. (Pt/pp: **caught.**) □ *I caught the ball that Mary threw toward me.* **2.** *tv., irreg.* to find someone in the act of doing something. □ *The teacher caught Jimmy lying.* **3.** *tv., irreg.* to get a disease caused by bacteria or viruses. □ *I hope I don't catch the flu this winter.* **4.** *tv., irreg.* to reach or make contact with someone or something just in time. □ *Can you catch Mary before she leaves the office?* **5.** *tv., irreg.* to experience something through one of the senses; to understand someone or something. □ *I never quite catch what the professor is saying.* **6.** *tv., irreg.* [for something] to snare or entangle someone or something. □ *The drawer handle caught the edge of my pants pocket.* **7.** *n.* a game or pastime where people throw and receive a ball back and forth. □ *Susie and Jimmy played catch all afternoon.* **8.** *n.* an act of grasping or receiving something as in ①. □ *Bob wanted to make the catch, but Bill beat him to it.* **9.** *n.* a fastener; a locking or latching device. □ *The cat got out because the catch on the door wasn't hooked.*

**catcher** ['kætʃ ɚ] *n.* [in baseball] the player who is behind the batter. □ *The catcher wears a protective mask.*

**caterpillar** ['kæt ə pɪl ɚ] *n.* the creature, somewhat like a worm, that is the young form of a butterfly or a moth. □ *The caterpillar rested on a leaf of the bush.*

**cathedral** [kə 'θi drəl] *n.* a large, important church, especially a major, ancient church. □ *The tourists admired the beautiful windows in the cathedral.*

**catholic** ['kæθ (ə) lɪk] **1.** *adj.* universal; wide ranging. (Adv: *catholically* [...ɪk li].) □ *Her musical tastes were catholic and ranged from classical to jazz.* **2. Catholic** *adj.* <the adj. use of ③>; of or about Catholicism. □ *There is a Catholic church at the end of our block.* **3. Catholic** *n.* a member of the Roman Catholic Church. □ *Although Mary is a devout Catholic, she married a Jewish man.*

**Catholicism** [kə 'θɑl ə sɪz əm] *n.* the religion and teachings of the Roman Catholic Church. (No plural form.) □ *The teacher spent a week discussing Catholicism.*

**catsup** ['kæt səp] Go to **ketchup**.

**cattle** ['kæt əl] *n.* <the general name for cows and bulls.> (No plural form. Treated as plural, but not countable. Number is expressed with *head of cattle*, as in *10 head of cattle.*) □ *The farmer raised cattle as well as crops.*

**Caucasian** [kɔ 'ke ʒən] **1.** *adj.* [of a person, usually of European descent] having light-colored skin; **white** ③. (In common, but not technical, use.) □ *The suspect was described as being tall and Caucasian.* **2.** *n.* a **Caucasian** ① person; a person having **white** ③ skin. □ *The* *murder suspect is a male Caucasian about thirty years old.*

**caught** ['kɔt] pt/pp of catch.

**cause** ['kɔz] **1.** *tv.* to make something happen. □ *Jane's angry words caused a fight.* **2.** *n.* someone or something that makes something happen; someone or something that produces an effect. □ *What was the cause of the accident?* **3.** *n.* a philosophy or a charity; a political or social movement. □ *David donated money to his favorite cause.*

**cave** ['kev] *n.* a natural chamber or tunnel inside a mountain or under the earth. □ *The hikers stayed in the cave until the rain stopped.*

**cavern** ['kæv ɚn] *n.* a large cave; a large chamber in a cave. □ *The tunnel led to a cavern deep within the earth.*

**cavity** ['kæv ɪ ti] **1.** *n.* a hole; a hollow, enclosed space. □ *A rabbit nestled in a cavity of the old tree trunk.* **2.** *n.* a rotten place on a tooth. □ *The dentist repaired the cavity in my tooth.*

**cease** ['sis] **1.** *tv.* to stop doing something; to quit doing something. □ *Jimmy ceased tormenting Susie as he became more mature.* **2.** *iv.* to stop; to finish. □ *When the rain ceased, the kids went out to play.*

**ceiling** ['si lɪŋ] **1.** *n.* the underside of a roof; a surface that forms the overhead part of a room. □ *The ceiling in the living room was leaking water.* **2.** *n.* the upper limit of something, especially of costs. (Fig. on ①.) □ *The president ordered a ceiling on prices to hold down inflation.*

**celebrate** ['sɛl ə bret] **1.** *tv.* to have a festive event or a party on a special day or for a special reason. □ *Bill doesn't celebrate his birthday now that he's over fifty.* **2.** *tv.* to perform a specific procedure or a ritual. □ *Yom Kippur is a Jewish holiday celebrated by fasting and praying.* **3.** *tv.* to praise someone or something. □ *A museum exhibit celebrated the invention of electricity.* **4.** *iv.* to be festive for a certain reason. □ *It was a beautiful sunny day, so we celebrated by having a picnic.*

**celebration** [sɛl ə 'bre ʃən] *n.* a festival; a festive event. □ *A celebration honoring the graduates was held Friday night.*

**celery** ['sɛl (ə) ri] *n.* a light-green vegetable with long, crisp stalks and leafy ends. (No plural form. Number is expressed with *stick(s)* or *stalk(s) of celery.*) □ *I added chopped celery to the soup.*

**cell** ['sɛl] **1.** *n.* the basic biological unit of living tissue. □ *The biology class studied the structure of a cell.* **2.** *n.* a subdivision of certain things, such as in a beehive or as with zones for portable wireless telephones. □ *The queen lays one egg in each cell of the hive.* □ *When using my cellular telephone, I can drive through various cells and still continue a telephone conversation.* **3.** *n.* a cage-like room for keeping prisoners. □ *The cell had a metal door rather than bars.* **4.** *n.* a battery; one of the sections of a battery. □ *One of the cells of the battery is dead.*

**cellar** ['sɛl ɚ] *n.* a basement; an underground room. □ *We stored canned vegetables in the cellar beneath the house.*

**cello** ['tʃɛl o] *n.* a stringed instrument, similar to a violin but larger. (It stands on the floor between the player's knees.) (Pl ends in *-s.*) □ *The cello makes beautiful, low tones.*

**cellular** ['sɛl jə lɚ] *adj.* <the adj. form of cell ①.> (Adv: *cellularly.*) □ *In my science class, we studied cellular biology.*

**cell(ular) telephone** ['sɛl (jə lɚ) 'tɛl ə fon] *n.* a portable telephone using radio-wave transmission within a large area that is divided into smaller cells, allowing the same radio frequency to be used in different cells by different users. (Often shortened to *cell phone.*) □ *My* *new cellular telephone is small enough to fit in my pocket.*

**cement** [sɪ 'mɛnt] **1.** *n.* something like glue, that joins things together. (Plural only when referring to different kinds, types, instances, or varieties.) □ *Wallpaper paste is a kind of cement that attaches paper to walls.* Ⓒ *We tried a number of cements before we found one that would work.* **2.** *n.* a gray powder made of clay and limestone that hardens when mixed with water. (No plural form.) □ *The construction workers mixed cement for the foundation.* **3.** *tv.* to join two things together. □ *The wallpaper paste cemented the paper to the wall.*

**cemetery** ['sɛm ə tɛr i] *n.* a graveyard; a place where dead people are buried. □ *My relatives are buried in the town cemetery.*

**censor** ['sɛn sɚ] **1.** *n.* someone who seeks to remove offensive words and pictures from material seen by the public. □ *The censor sought to change the TV script.* **2.** *tv.* to suppress the publication or performance of offensive material. □ *The obscene outburst was censored from the TV show.*

**census** ['sɛn səs] **1.** *n.* the process of counting the number of people who live in an area. □ *As a part of each census, the ages and occupations of the people in the town are recorded.* **2.** *n.* the official number of people who live in an area; a report of what was found in collecting information for ①. □ *According to the last census, the population of Smithville is 5,000.*

**cent** ['sɛnt] *n.* a penny; one one-hundredth of a dollar. □ *I'm not lending you another cent until you pay me what you owe me.*

**center** ['sɛn tɚ] **1.** *n.* the point in the middle of a circle or sphere which is the same distance from all points on the circle or on the surface of the sphere; a place that is in the middle of something. □ *Please place a dot in the center of the circle.* **2.** *n.* a major site or focus of an activity. □ *The university is a center of learning.* **3.** *adj.* middle. (Prenominal only.) □ *The magician turned the center card over.* **4.** *tv.* to place someone or something in the middle of something. □ *The decorator centered the picture on the wall.*

**Centigrade** ['sɛnt ə gred] *n.* the metric system of measuring temperature. (No plural form. The same as *Celsius.* Abbreviated *C.*) □ *Centigrade is used in most countries, but not in the U.S.*

**centimeter** ['sɛnt ə mit ɚ] *n.* a measure of length, equal to one one-hundredth of a meter. (An inch is 2.54 centimeters.) □ *There are a hundred centimeters in one meter.*

**central** ['sɛn trəl] **1.** *adj.* near the center. (Adv: *centrally.*) □ *City hall is in a central area of the city.* **2.** *adj.* primary; essential. (Adv: *centrally.*) □ *Honor is the central theme of the book.*

**century** ['sɛn tʃə ri] **1.** *n.* one hundred years. □ *This antique vase is a century old.* **2.** *n.* a block of time that begins every one hundred years, starting sometime close to the birth of Jesus Christ or some other specific event. □ *The 21st century begins on January 1, 2001, and ends on December 31, 2100.* □ *Some people think the 21st century begins in the year 2000.*

**ceramic** [sə 'ræm ɪk] **1.** *adj.* made of hard, baked clay, able to withstand great heat. □ *The ceramic pot can be used in a hot oven.* **2. ceramics** *n.* the making of pottery by shaping clay and baking it until it hardens. (Treated as singular.) □ *Bill took a class in ceramics and made all sorts of pottery.*

**cereal** ['sɪr i əl] **1.** *n.* one of a number of plants that provide grain. (Plural only when referring to different kinds, types, or varieties.) □ *Cereal is grown in most of the Midwest.* Ⓒ *A number of important cereals are grown in my state.* **2.** *n.* a food product made from grains, usually served at breakfast with milk. (Plural only when referring to different kinds, types, instances, or varieties.) □ *Hurry up and eat your cereal!* Ⓒ *My favorite cereals already have sugar on them.*

**ceremony** ['sɛr ə mon i] **1.** *n.* a tradition or ritual associated with a particular event. □ *The wedding ceremony took place in a garden.* **2.** *n.* the formal behavior seen in certain religious, social, or political events. (No plural form.) □ *Sue is uncomfortable with too much formal ceremony.*

**certain** ['sɚt n] **1. certain to** do something *adj.* + *inf.* sure to do something. □ *Jane is certain to be late because traffic is so bad.* **2.** *adj.* definite or known, but not stated; particular and specific, but not identified. (Prenominal only.) □ *Certain students do not turn in their homework on time.* **3.** *adj.* sure; confident; having no doubt (about something). □ *I heard what you said, but are you certain?*

**certainly** ['sɚt n li] **1.** *adv.* definitely; surely; positively. □ *That is certainly a beautiful dress.* **2.** *adv.* yes, by all means. (An answer to a question.) □ *Certainly. Help yourself.*

**certainty** ['sɚt n ti] **1.** *n.* the state of being sure or certain. (No plural form.) □ *I can say with certainty that we like your work.* **2.** *n.* something that is known to be true. □ *It is a certainty that the sun will rise each day.*

**chain** ['tʃen] **1.** *n.* links or rings, especially made of metal, that are joined together in a row. □ *Mary is wearing a gold chain around her neck.* **2.** *n.* one of a group of stores or businesses with the same name, owned by the same company or person. (A *chain store.*) □ *Is that restaurant part of a chain?* **3.** *tv.* to bind someone or something with **chains** ①. □ *The sheriff chained the criminal to keep him from escaping.*

**chair** ['tʃɛr] **1.** *n.* a piece of furniture for sitting, sometimes with arms; a piece of furniture for one person to sit on. (See also **armchair**.) □ *Five chairs surround the dining-room table.* **2.** *n.* a person who presides over a committee or a meeting. □ *Please direct your questions to the chair.* **3.** *n.* the head of a department, especially in a university. □ *Who is the chair of the English Department?* **4.** *tv.* to lead or preside over a meeting, department, or committee. □ *Mary chairs the finance committee.*

**chairman** ['tʃɛr mən] *n., irreg.* the head of a department or committee; the person in charge of a meeting. (Either male or female. See also **chair**. Pl: **chairmen**.) □ *The committee elects a new chairman each year.*

**chairmen** ['tʃɛr mən] pl of **chairman**.

**chalk** ['tʃɔk] **1.** *n.* a soft, white limestone. (Plural only when referring to different kinds, types, instances, or varieties.) □ *They discovered deposits of chalk near the coast.* Ⓒ *The best chalks can be made into chalk for writing.* **2.** *n.* a stick of ① used for writing, as on a chalkboard. (No plural form. Number is expressed with *piece(s)* or *stick(s) of chalk.*) □ *I dropped the chalk and it broke all over the floor.*

**challenge** ['tʃæl ɪndʒ] **1.** *n.* a dare; an invitation to a competition. □ *Bill issued a challenge to Mary to solve the puzzle before he did.* **2.** *n.* a difficult task. □ *It was a challenge to convince Dave to take a vacation.* **3.** *tv.* [for a difficult task] to test someone or something. □ *The homework assignment challenged Bill.*

C

**chamber** ['tʃem bɚ] **1.** *n.* a room. □ *The sparsely furnished chamber has only a bed and a dresser.* **2.** *n.* a division of government, such as the House of Representatives or the Senate of the United States Congress, separately; certain organizations, such as the chamber of commerce of an area. □ *The entire chamber voted on the proposed law.* **3.** *n.* a compartment within something; an enclosed space inside the body. □ *The human heart consists of four chambers.*

**chameleon** [kə 'mil (i )jən] **1.** *n.* a lizard that changes the color of its skin to match its surroundings. □ *The chameleon turned green when it rested on the leaf.* **2.** *n.* someone who is very changeable. (Fig. on ①.) □ *Jane is such a chameleon. Her reactions are changeable and not predictable.*

**champ** ['tʃæmp] *n.* a champion; a winner. □ *Bill has been wrestling champ for the last three years.*

**champagne** [ʃæm 'pen] *n.* a sparkling white wine made in the Champagne area of France, or similar wines made elsewhere. (Plural only when referring to different kinds, types, instances, or varieties.) □ *We opened a bottle of champagne to celebrate.* Ⓒ *Champagnes from France are said to be the best.*

**champion** ['tʃæmp i ən] **1.** *n.* a winner; someone who has won a contest or competition. □ *Do you think there will be a new champion after the contest?* **2.** *n.* someone who supports or argues in favor of someone or something; someone who advocates something. □ *The lawyer was a champion of tax reform.* **3.** *tv.* to support someone or something; to speak in favor of someone or something. □ *One popular candidate champions tax reform.*

**chance** ['tʃæns] **1.** *n.* fate; fortune. (No plural form.) □ *Chance will determine who will win the lottery.* **2.** *n.* the probability that something might happen. (No plural form.) □ *Is there much chance that the train will be late?* **3.** *n.* an opportunity. □ *This job is the chance of a lifetime.* **4.** *tv.* to risk something. □ *Let's leave the umbrella at home and chance it. It won't rain.* **5. by chance** *phr.* accidentally; randomly; without planning. □ *We met by chance in a class in college.* **6. take a chance** *phr.* to take a gamble or a risk. □ *Don't take a chance. Look before you cross the street.*

**change** ['tʃendʒ] **1.** *n.* the process of becoming something different. (Plural only when referring to different kinds, types, instances, or varieties.) □ *There has been very little change in the weather for several weeks.* Ⓒ *We have been experiencing a lot of changes in the past few years.* **2.** *n.* something new or different; something that replaces something else. □ *A vacation would be a good change right now.* **3.** *n.* bills or coins of lower value given in exchange for bills or coins of a higher value; the money returned to someone who had paid a sum higher than the price. (No plural form. Treated as singular.) □ *Dave handed the clerk a $5 bill when he bought the newspaper, and his change was $4.50.* **4.** *n.* loose coins. (No plural form. Treated as singular.) □ *I always have some change at the bottom of my purse.* **5.** *tv.* to replace something. □ *The maid changes the sheets on the bed every day.* **6.** *tv.* to cause something to become different. □ *The dye changed the color of the fabric.* **7.** *tv.* to remove clothing and put on different clothing. □ *Bill changed his clothes for the party.* **8.** *tv.* to replace a baby's dirty diaper with a clean one. □ *No one wanted to change the baby's diapers.* **9.** *iv.* to become different. □ *While she was away at school, Jane changed a lot.* **10.** *iv.* to take off one set of clothes and put on another. □ *I have to change before I can go out.*

**channel** ['tʃæn l] **1.** *n.* a deeper passage through a harbor, where vessels can sail safely; the deepest part of a river or stream. □ *The boat moved through the channel to the open sea.* **2.** *n.* the frequencies assigned to a particular television station. □ *What channel is the football game on?*

**chaos** ['ke ɑs] *n.* complete confusion; complete disorder; anarchy. (No plural form.) □ *There was chaos in the crowded theater after the fire alarm went off.*

**chapel** ['tʃæp əl] *n.* a place of worship that is smaller than a sanctuary. □ *The service was held in the chapel of the church.*

**chapter** ['tʃæp tɚ] **1.** *n.* a division within a book; a section of a book. □ *The book was divided into five chapters.* **2.** *n.* a division of an organization or society. □ *Bill joined the local chapter of the club.*

**character** ['kɛr ɪk tɚ] **1.** *n.* a person in a book, movie, play, television show, etc. □ *Readers identified with the main character of the book.* **2.** *n.* the nature of someone or something; the essential qualities of someone or something, especially someone's moral qualities. □ *If you observe John's actions, you will learn something about his character.* **3.** *n.* high personal quality; integrity; moral goodness. (No plural form.) □ *People of character are honest about their mistakes and do not tell lies.* **4.** *n.* an unusual or eccentric person. □ *Mary is such a character. She's always making odd jokes.* **5.** *n.* a symbol used in writing, such as a letter, number, or other symbol. □ *The characters on the threatening letter were cut from magazines.*

**characteristic** [kɛr ɪk tə 'rɪs tɪk] **1.** *n.* a single feature; a special quality of someone or something. □ *Heavy snow is a characteristic of winter around here.* **2.** *adj.* relating to the features or qualities of something. (Adv: *characteristically* […ɪk li].) □ *Bill has the characteristic symptoms of the flu.*

**charcoal** ['tʃɑr kol] *n.* a carbon-based fuel made by burning wood partially. (Plural only when referring to different kinds, types, instances, or varieties.) □ *Tom bought a bag of charcoal to use in the barbecue.* Ⓒ *I've tried a lot of charcoals, but this brand is the best.*

**charge** ['tʃɑɚdʒ] **1.** *n.* the cost of something; the amount of money needed to pay for something. (Often plural.) □ *The charge to repair your shoes is ten dollars.* **2.** *n.* control [of someone or something]. (No plural form.) □ *After the sudden death of the sheriff, the deputy took charge.* **3.** *n.* someone or something that must be watched over. □ *The babysitter's young charges ran around the house in their diapers.* **4.** *n.* an accusation; a statement that someone has done something criminal. □ *The charge placed against the man was murder.* **5.** *n.* a sudden, moving attack. □ *The dog made a charge at the cat.* **6.** *n.* the amount of electrical energy stored in a battery or a particle of matter. □ *This battery has no charge left in it.* **7.** *n.* the explosive material used in one explosion. □ *When the charge exploded, it nearly deafened us.* **8.** *tv.* to present a claim of a sum of money for goods or services. □ *The hotel charged us for the extra bed.* **9.** *tv.* to place ① on an account instead of paying cash. □ *Mary charged the meal on her credit card.* **10.** *tv.* to rush toward someone or something in attack. □ *The dog charged the intruder and bit him.* **11.** *tv.* to provide a battery with energy; to send electricity through something, such as a circuit. □ *The car charges its own battery while the engine is running.* **12.** *tv.* to ask for pay at a certain rate. □ *The designer charges $50 an hour.*

**charity** ['tʃɛr ɪ ti] **1.** *n.* love, kindness, and generosity shown toward other people. (No plural form.) □ *The quality of charity is always welcome.* **2.** *n.* an organization that helps people in need.

C

□ *The charity's goal is to help people help themselves.*

**charm** ['tʃɑrm] **1.** *n.* a pleasing, attractive personality trait. (Plural only when referring to different kinds, types, instances, or varieties.) □ *My mother had lots of personal charm.* 🄲 *I used all of my charms to impress Bill.* **2.** *n.* a small toy or trinket worn on a necklace or bracelet. □ *The girls collected charms for their bracelets.* **3.** *n.* something that has magical powers. □ *The superstitious man carried a charm to ward off evil.* **4.** *tv.* to influence someone by using ①. □ *The speaker charmed the audience.*

**chase** ['tʃes] **1.** *n.* an act of running after someone or something. □ *The dog seems to enjoy the chase more than catching rabbits.* **2.** *tv.* to run after someone or something. □ *Jane chased Jimmy until she caught him.*

**chat** ['tʃæt] **1.** *iv.* to talk; to have a friendly talk. □ *Dave chatted on the telephone all evening.* **2.** *n.* a pleasant conversation; a friendly talk. □ *The two friends sat on the porch and had a chat.*

**chatter** ['tʃæt ɚ] **1.** *iv.* to talk about unimportant things. □ *The children chattered endlessly as they played.* **2.** *iv.* [for one's teeth] to click together because of fear or coldness. □ *Mary's teeth chattered with the cold.* **3.** *n.* unimportant talk. (No plural form.) □ *Mary was tired of Bill's chatter by the end of the evening.*

**cheap** ['tʃip] **1.** *adj.* inexpensive; not costing a lot of money. (Adv: *cheaply.* Comp: *cheaper;* sup: *cheapest.*) □ *Mary bought some cheap curtains for her apartment.* **2.** *adj.* poorly made; of poor quality; of poor value. (Adv: *cheaply.* Comp: *cheaper;* sup: *cheapest.*) □ *Those cheap clothes look really terrible.*

**cheat** ['tʃit] **1.** *tv.* to deceive someone in a game or in commerce, as a means of gaining money. □ *Anne cheated her friends while playing cards.* **2.** *iv.* to succeed by doing something that is not fair or dishonest. □ *The students cheated on the test but were soon caught.* **3.** *n.* someone who **cheats** as in ① or ②; someone who does not play fairly. □ *No one will play cards with Mike because he is a cheat.*

**check** ['tʃɛk] **1.** *n.* a written order to a bank to pay an amount of money to someone or something. □ *Bill wrote a check to pay for the groceries.* **2.** *n.* the mark "✓." □ *I put a check on the list by each chore that I had completed.* **3.** *n.* the bill for a meal in a restaurant. □ *The waitress put our check on the table.* **4.** *n.* something that stops or restrains someone or something. □ *The store's security officer is a check against shoplifters.* **5.** *n.* a brief look at someone or something; an inspection of someone or something. □ *Could you give my work a quick check?* **6. check** something **off** *tv.* + *obj.* + *adv.* to place a "✓" by an item on a list after it has been looked at, examined, or accounted for. □ *Bill checked their names off.* 🅃 *He checked off all the names, one by one.* **7.** *tv.* to examine something; to look at something closely but quickly. □ *The boss said she would check Mike's work.* **8.** *tv.* to put one's belongings into the care of someone and receive a receipt for the property. □ *We checked our coats at the restaurant.* **9.** *tv.* to restrain someone or something; to stop someone or something. □ *A pull on the rope checked the dog as it wandered about.* **10. check on** someone or something *iv.* + *prep. phr.* to investigate concerning someone or something; to seek out the facts about someone or something. □ *The babysitter checked on the sleeping children.*

**cheek** ['tʃik] *n.* the part of the face below the eye. □ *The baby laid its cheek on the pillow.*

**cheekbone** ['tʃik bon] *n.* the bone just below the eye. □ *Sue's haircut flattered her cheekbones.*

**cheer** ['tʃɪr] **1.** *n.* an encouraging yell; some applause and shouting meant to encourage someone. □ *The crowd gave a cheer when the team scored.* **2.** *n.* happiness; a good state of mind. (No plural form.) □ *The office was in need of some cheer.* **3.** *iv.* to yell and shout in support of someone or something; to yell in encouragement. □ *The crowd cheered for the team.* **4.** *tv.* to encourage someone by shouts of support. □ *The crowd cheered the team.* **5. cheer someone (up)** *tv. + obj. (+ adv.)* to improve someone's mood or morale; to make someone happy. □ *Chocolate always cheers Bob up when he is sad.*

**cheerful** ['tʃɪr fʊl] **1.** *adj.* in good spirits; full of cheer; happy. (Adv: *cheerfully.*) □ *The friendly nurse had a cheerful manner.* **2.** *adj.* pleasant; [of something] bright and pleasing. (Adv: *cheerfully.*) □ *The cheerful sitting room was sunny.*

**cheery** ['tʃɪr i] **1.** *adj.* full of cheer; showing cheer. (Adv: *cheerily.* Comp: *cheerier;* sup: *cheeriest.*) □ *The nurse always has a cheery smile.* **2.** *adj.* bright and cheerful; causing cheer. (Adv: *cheerily.* Comp: *cheerier;* sup: *cheeriest.*) □ *The restaurant had a cheery atmosphere.*

**cheese** ['tʃiz] **1.** *n.* a food made from the solid parts of processed milk. (Plural only when referring to different kinds, types, instances, or varieties.) □ *The hostess served cheese and crackers for an appetizer.* Ⓒ *My favorite cheeses are the soft ones from France.* **2.** *adj.* <the adj. use of ①.> □ *Could I please have a cheese sandwich?*

**chef** ['ʃɛf] **1.** *n.* a professional cook. □ *The chef had trained in France.* **2.** *n.* any cook; whoever is doing the cooking. □ *Who's the chef around your house?*

**chemical** ['kɛm ɪ kəl] **1.** *n.* an element or a mixture of basic elements. □ *All the chemicals were stored in large jars in the storeroom.* **2.** *adj.* of or about ①. (Adv: *chemically* [...ɪk li].) □ *What is the chemical composition of this substance?*

**chemist** ['kɛm ɪst] *n.* a scientist whose specialty is the theory and use of substances. □ *The chemist produced a new type of plastic in the lab.*

**cherish** ['tʃɛr ɪʃ] **1.** *tv.* to treat someone or something very lovingly; to have great fondness for someone or something. □ *The new parents cherished their baby.* **2.** *tv.* to keep the idea of someone or something in one's mind. □ *Bill cherished the thought of owning his own boat.*

**cherry** ['tʃɛr i] **1.** *n.* a tree that produces small, round, bright red fruits with one pit. □ *We planted cherries and oaks along the fence.* **2.** *n.* wood from ①. (Plural only when referring to different kinds, types, instances, or varieties.) □ *The cabinet was made of cherry.* Ⓒ *Some cherries have a richer color and better grain than others.* **3.** *n.* the fruit of ①. □ *I prepared the cherries for the pie.* **4.** *adj.* made with or flavored with ③. □ *We all ate cherry pie for dessert.* **5.** *adj.* made from ②. □ *Tom placed the cherry cabinet next to the window.*

**chess** ['tʃɛs] *n.* a game played by two people on a special board, with 32 pieces. (No plural form.) □ *I taught Bill how to play chess.*

**chest** ['tʃɛst] **1.** *n.* the upper front part of the body. □ *The ball hit John right in the chest.* **2.** *n.* a piece of furniture with drawers, used to store clothes, linen, and other items. (Often *chest of drawers.*) □ *An old chest of drawers stood in the attic gathering dust.* **3.** *n.* a large, wooden storage box. □ *Grandma's wedding dress is stored in a chest.*

C

**chew** ['tʃu] **1.** *tv.* to crush food with the teeth before swallowing it. □ *It was difficult to chew the tough meat.* **2.** *iv.* to bite down with the teeth. □ *The meat was tough and difficult to chew.*

**chick** ['tʃɪk] *n.* a baby chicken or other baby bird. □ *The barnyard was filled with chicks last spring.*

**chicken** ['tʃɪk ən] **1.** *n.* a bird raised on a farm for meat and eggs; a hen or a rooster. □ *The farmer raised chickens.* **2.** *n.* the meat of ①. (No plural form.) □ *This recipe can be made with either chicken or beef.* **3.** *adj.* made with or flavored with ②. □ *Susan ordered a chicken sandwich for lunch.*

**chief** ['tʃif] **1.** *n.* the head of an organization or group; the leader. □ *Bill is the chief of this committee.* **2.** *adj.* most important; principal; main. (Adv: *chiefly.*) □ *Mike is chief chef at the hotel.*

**child** ['tʃaɪld] *n., irreg.* a young person; a boy or a girl; someone's son or daughter. (Pl: **children.**) □ *The children took the bus to school.*

**children** ['tʃɪl drɪn] pl of **child.**

**chill** ['tʃɪl] **1.** *n.* a coldness, especially a damp coldness. □ *Mary felt a chill in the air.* **2.** *n.* a cold feeling; a lasting cold feeling caused by being in the cold too long. □ *The child got a chill while playing in the snow.* **3.** *n.* a coldness of manner; an unpleasant attitude; an unfriendly attitude. (Fig. on ①. No plural form.) □ *Mary and Bill had been arguing, and we could all feel the chill between them at dinner.* **4.** *n.* a sense of severe fright, possibly accompanied by the feeling of ②. □ *The thought of falling off the cliff gave me a chill.* **5.** *tv.* to cool something. □ *I chilled the champagne before serving it.* **6.** *iv.* to become cool or cold. □ *The salad is chilling in the refrigerator.*

**chimney** ['tʃɪm ni] *n.* the structure that carries smoke to the outside and above a building. □ *Smoke billowed out of the chimney.*

**chimpanzee** [tʃɪm 'pæn zi] *n.* an African ape, closely related to humans. □ *A chimpanzee swung from branch to branch in the forest.*

**chin** ['tʃɪn] *n.* the part of the face below the lower lip. □ *Milk ran down Jimmy's chin.*

**china** ['tʃaɪn ə] *n.* high-quality dishes, cups, and saucers made of fine, thin ceramic material. (No plural form.) □ *On holidays, we use the good china.*

**chip** ['tʃɪp] **1.** *n.* a small piece that has broken off a larger object. □ *I stepped on a chip of stone and bruised my heel.* **2.** *n.* the dent that is left where a small piece of something has broken off. □ *I noticed a chip in the cup after I dropped it.* **3.** *n.* a flat, crunchy, fried or baked snack made of starch. (Usually made from potatoes or corn. Also short for **potato chip.**) □ *I needed a snack so I bought a bag of chips.* **4.** *tv.* to break off a small piece of something. □ *I chipped some ice off the block.* **5.** *tv.* to shape something by picking away or cutting away at it piece by piece. □ *The sculptor chipped the marble with tiny blows.* **6.** *iv.* [for something] to lose a small bit, through **chipping** ④. □ *The pitcher chipped when I knocked it off the counter.*

**chocolate** ['tʃɑk (ə) lət] **1.** *n.* a tasty, candy-like food made from roasted cacao beans, usually in the form of candy, syrup, a brewed beverage, or a flavor in cooking. (Plural only when referring to different kinds, types, instances, or varieties.) □ *Chocolate is a popular candy.* Ⓒ *Some of the best chocolates come from Belgium.* **2.** *n.* a piece of ①. □ *Someone gave me a box of chocolates for my birthday.* **3.** *adj.* made with or flavored with ①. □ *Would you like some chocolate cake?*

**choice** ['tʃoɪs] **1.** *n.* a selection from which one can choose. (Plural only when referring to different kinds, types, instances, or varieties.) □ *There is very little choice on this menu.* Ⓒ *There are very few choices on this menu.* **2.** *n.* the actual selection; someone or something chosen or selected. □ *My choice for club president was Anne.* **3.** *adj.* of very high quality; excellent; best; optimal. (Adv: *choicely.*) □ *We had a choice table at the restaurant.*

**choir** ['kwɑɪɚ] *n.* a singing group, especially one in a church. □ *The choir sang Grandma's favorite song at her funeral.*

**choke** ['tʃok] **1.** *n.* the part of an engine that controls the amount of air that goes into the engine. □ *I have to adjust the choke on my lawnmower when I start it.* **2.** *tv.* to cut off someone's or some creature's air supply. □ *The tight collar choked the dog.* **3.** *iv.* to react to having one's air supply cut off. □ *Bill choked on the apple.*

**choose** ['tʃuz] **1.** *tv., irreg.* to pick or select someone or something from a group. (Pt: chose; pp: chosen.) □ *You can choose the classes you want to take.* **2.** *iv., irreg.* to do the process of selection. □ *Please choose carefully, so you will get the best one.*

**choosy** ['tʃu zi] *adj.* hard to please; hard to make happy; particular. (Adv: *choosily.* Comp: *choosier;* sup: *choosiest.*) □ *Anne is very choosy about the fruit she buys.*

**chop** ['tʃɑp] **1.** *n.* a movement with an axe or blade that cuts into something; a blow that cuts into something. □ *The log split with the third chop of Bill's axe.* **2.** *n.* a slice of meat, including some bone, especially lamb or pork. □ *We ate lamb chops for dinner.* **3.** *tv.* to cut someone or something by hitting it with something sharp. □ *Anne chopped the logs in two with an axe.*

**chore** ['tʃor] *n.* a regular task; a duty. □ *After doing their chores, the kids went outside to play.*

**chorus** ['kor əs] **1.** *n.* a group of people who sing together; a choir. □ *Jane and Bill are members of the high-school chorus.* **2.** *n.* the part of a song that is repeated after each verse. □ *The chorus of this song is the part that everyone knows.* **3.** *n.* words or noises that are said together or at the same time. □ *The mayor's idea was met with a chorus of complaints.*

**chose** ['tʃoz] pt of choose.

**chosen** ['tʃo zən] pp of choose.

**Christian** ['krɪs tʃən] *n.* a member of the Christian religion. □ *Mary became a Christian when she was thirty.*

**Christianity** [krɪs tʃi 'æn ə ti] Go to Christian religion.

**Christian religion** AND **Christianity** ['krɪs tʃən rɪ 'lɪdʒ ən, krɪs tʃi 'æn ə ti] *n.* a religion whose basis is in the teachings of Jesus Christ. □ *The lecture contrasted the Christian religion with Jewish beliefs.*

**Christmas** ['krɪs məs] *n.* December 25; the day on which the birth of Christ is celebrated by many Christians. □ *Every Christmas, we decorate a pine tree.*

**chromosome** ['krom ə som] *n.* one of many very tiny cellular structures containing genes. □ *Humans have 23 pairs of chromosomes.*

**chum** ['tʃʌm] *n.* a good friend; a buddy. □ *Max played chess with his chums after school.*

**chunk** ['tʃʌŋk] *n.* a thick, irregularly shaped piece of something. □ *Bill cut himself a huge chunk of chocolate cake.*

**church** ['tʃɚtʃ] **1.** *n.* a building where Christians gather to worship. □ *The church was adorned with stained-glass windows.* **2.** *n.* the worship service celebrated within ①. (No plural form.) □

C

*Mary's parents took her to church when she was young.* **3.** *n.* the members of a particular religious organization. ☐ *The church held a benefit to earn money.* **4.** *n.* the institutional organization of a religious body, its policies, and its practices. (No plural form.) ☐ *We believe in the separation of church and state.*

C

**cider** ['sɑɪ dɚ] *n.* apple juice; juice pressed from apples. (Plural only when referring to different kinds, types, instances, or varieties.) ☐ *I served cider and cookies to my guests.* 🄲 *The ciders made early in the season are the tangiest.*

**cigar** [sɪ 'gɑr] *n.* a carefully packed roll of dried tobacco leaves, used for smoking. ☐ *Bill puffed on a cigar as he watched the sun set.*

**cigarette** [sɪg ə 'rɛt] *n.* a small roll of cut tobacco wrapped in paper, used for smoking. ☐ *Mary smoked a cigarette while she waited for the bus.*

**circle** ['sɚ kəl] **1.** *n.* a curved line where every point on the line is the same distance from a center point. ☐ *The geometry students drew circles with compasses.* **2.** *n.* anything shaped like ①; a ring. ☐ *The children sat in a circle around Jane, who told them stories.* **3.** *n.* a group of people with related interests. ☐ *Mary had a large circle of friends when she was in college.* **4.** *tv.* to form a ring around someone or something. ☐ *Huge rings of rocks circle the planet Saturn.* **5.** *tv.* to draw a ring around something that is written or printed. ☐ *The instructions said to circle the correct answer.*

**circuit** ['sɚ kɪt] **1.** *n.* a complete trip around something. ☐ *The bus driver makes three circuits around the city each day.* **2.** *n.* the path that the flow of electricity follows. ☐ *There was a problem in one of the power circuits in my computer.*

**circular** ['sɚ kjə lɚ] **1.** *n.* a printed sheet that is sent to many people. ☐ *The circular announced the store's upcoming sale.* **2.** *adj.* in the shape of a circle; round; ring-like. (Adv: *circularly.*) ☐ *The carpenter used a special saw to cut a circular hole.*

**circus** ['sɚ kəs] *n.* a traveling show featuring clowns, acrobats, animals, magicians, and other similar acts. ☐ *The circus is coming to town this summer!*

**cite** ['sɑɪt] **1.** *tv.* to use someone or something as a reference to support a fact. ☐ *The boss cited Bill's excessive absences when he fired him.* **2.** *tv.* to refer to or list a citation. ☐ *Mary could cite five incidents of Bill being late.* **3.** *tv.* to recognize someone for having done an exceptional deed. ☐ *The commanding officer cited the troops for their extreme bravery.* **4.** *tv.* to give someone an order to appear in court. ☐ *The driver was cited for speeding.*

**citizen** ['sɪt ə zən] *n.* someone who is a legal resident of a specific political region; someone who has full rights of membership in a state or country. ☐ *Citizens protested loudly against the tax increase.*

**citizenship** ['sɪt ə zən ʃɪp] **1.** *n.* the state of being an official citizen. (No plural form.) ☐ *The immigrant's goal was to achieve citizenship.* **2.** *n.* the behavior expected of a citizen. (No plural form.) ☐ *The teacher promoted good citizenship among the students.*

**citrus** ['sɪ trəs] **1.** *n.* a family of fruit including oranges, tangerines, grapefruit, limes, lemons, etc. (No plural form.) ☐ *I like apples, but not citrus.* **2.** *adj.* <the adj. use of ①.> ☐ *Bob prefers citrus fruit to apples.*

**city** ['sɪt i] **1.** *n.* a large town; a large residential and business center. ☐ *Bill grew up in the city but moved to the country later in life.* **2.** *adj.* <the adj. use of ①.> ☐ *Bill just prefers city life.*

**city hall** ['sɪt i 'hɔl] **1.** *n.* the administrative building for a city government. (Sometimes capitalized.) □ *City hall is located downtown, next to the library.* **2.** *n.* a city government or administration; the offices in ① and the government leaders working in ①. (Sometimes capitalized.) □ *City hall raised our local taxes again this year.*

**civil** ['sɪv əl] **1.** *adj.* of or about citizens and their government, activities, rights, and responsibilities. □ *Following the court decision, there was a lot of civil unhappiness.* **2.** *adj.* polite; courteous; behaving properly. (Adv: *civilly.*) □ *Bill spoke in a civil tone, but his words were insulting.* **3.** *adj.* relating to a legal action that does not deal with criminal law. □ *The judge dealt with about a dozen civil cases a week.*

**civilian** [sɪ 'vɪl jən] *n.* a citizen who is not in the military. □ *After thirty years in the military, Bob retired and became a civilian.*

**civilize** ['sɪv ə lɑɪz] *tv.* to make someone or a culture more organized and less primitive. □ *It may take decades to fully civilize the remote peoples.*

**claim** ['klem] **1.** *n.* a document or statement requesting that a payment be made. □ *Mary made a claim for her hospital bills with the insurance company.* **2.** *n.* a statement presented as fact; a statement that something is true. □ *The detective investigated the victim's claims.* **3.** *tv.* to assert one's right to own something. □ *Bill claimed the last cookie for himself.* **4.** *tv.* to say a statement as fact; to state that something is true. (The object can be a clause with **that** ⑦.) □ *The job applicant claimed he had a college degree.*

**clam** ['klæm] **1.** *n.* an edible marine animal having a pair of shells that open like a book. □ *The cook put a lot of clams in the cooking pot.* **2.** *adj.* <the adj. use of ①.> □ *Jimmy found lots of clam shells on the beach.*

**clamp** ['klæmp] **1.** *n.* a device that holds things together with pressure. □ *A clamp held the board firmly while Jane sawed it.* **2.** *tv.* to hold things together with pressure. □ *The carpenter clamped the board to the bench.*

**clap** ['klæp] **1.** *n.* the sound made when one brings one's palms together, as in applause. □ *The guard gave a clap to get my attention.* **2.** *n.* a loud burst of thunder. □ *Lightning followed the clap of thunder.* **3.** *iv.* to make applause. □ *The actors bowed, and the audience clapped.*

**clarinet** [klɛr ə 'nɛt] *n.* a tube-shaped musical instrument of the woodwind family. □ *A lot of music is written for the jazz clarinet.*

**class** ['klæs] **1.** *n.* a group of similar things. □ *This particular class of antique furniture is very valuable.* **2.** *n.* someone's social and economic ranking. □ *Most people marry within their own class.* **3.** *n.* a course that is taught; a subject that is taught. □ *I think my history class is the most interesting one this term.* **4.** *n.* a specific session of learning; a period of time spent in instruction. □ *After an hour of the class, Bob began to fall asleep.* **5.** *n.* all the people in a certain grade or year of schooling. □ *The sophomore class sponsored a dance after the basketball game.* **6.** *n.* <a term of address for a group of students in a classroom.> (No plural form.) □ *Now, class, let's turn to page twelve.* **7.** *n.* the ability to behave properly, politely, or elegantly. (No plural form.) □ *Ignoring rude people shows a lot of class.*

**classic** ['klæs ɪk] **1.** *n.* something, especially art, music, or writing, that is of very high quality and will be or is remembered through history. □ *Bill wanted to read the classics of English literature.* **2.** *adj.* of high quality; the best; of great and lasting importance; serving

C

as a standard for others of its kind. □ Gone with the Wind *is a classic historical story.* **3.** *adj.* typical; just as one would anticipate. □ *Running out of gas is the classic excuse for getting home late.*

**classical** ['klæs ɪ kəl] **1.** *adj.* of or about ancient Greece and Rome. (Adv: *classically* [...ɪk li].) □ *Jane majored in classical studies.* **2.** *adj.* [of music, such as symphonies, operas, or dance and other art forms] serious and requiring a high degree of training and skill. □ *Bill likes all classical music, especially symphonies.*

**classmate** ['klæs met] *n.* someone in the same class at school. □ *Jimmy played with his classmates after school.*

**classroom** ['klæs rum] *n.* a room in a school or building where classes are held. □ *The classroom held twenty desks.*

**clause** ['klɔz] **1.** *n.* a phrase that has a subject and a verb. (See also **relative clause**.) □ *A clause can be introduced with* that *or* which. □ *The sentence had too many clauses in it.* **2.** *n.* a single provision in a legal document. □ *The author agreed to all but one clause in the contract.*

**claw** ['klɔ] **1.** *n.* a sharp, hard, curved nail on the foot of an animal or a bird. □ *The cat's claw snagged my sweater.* **2.** *n.* the pinchers of a lobster, crab, or other shellfish. □ *The restaurant served lobster claws.* **3.** *n.* the part of the hammer that is used for removing nails. □ *Anne used the claw of the hammer to remove the old, rusty nail.* **4.** *tv.* to scratch or tear someone or something with ①. □ *The cat clawed the carpet.*

**clay** ['kle] **1.** *n.* a kind of sticky soil, used for pottery. (Plural only when referring to different kinds, types, instances, or varieties.) □ *The children liked any craft that involved clay.* Ⓒ *Jed prefers the clays he digs up himself.* **2.** *adj.* made of or concerning ①. □ *The clay sculpture hardened when I placed it in the oven.*

**clean** ['klin] **1.** *adj.* tidy; not dirty. (Adv: *cleanly.*) □ *Bill washed his hands until they were clean.* **2.** *adj.* new; fresh; unused. □ *The maid put clean sheets on the bed.* **3.** *adj.* morally pure; not **dirty** ②. (Adv: *cleanly.*) □ *Their parents allow them to watch only clean movies.* **4.** *adj.* smooth; even; not rough. (Adv: *cleanly.*) □ *The saw made a clean cut through the wood.* **5.** *tv.* to make something ①. □ *I cleaned the kitchen after dinner.* **6.** *tv.* to prepare an animal for cooking and eating by removing the parts that cannot be eaten. □ *The hunters cleaned their kill.*

**cleaner** ['kli nɚ] **1.** *n.* soap, bleach, or some other product that cleans. (Plural only when referring to different kinds, types, instances, or varieties.) □ *The cleaner removed the stains in the kitchen sink.* Ⓒ *We tried a lot of cleaners before we found the one we like.* **2.** *n.* someone who cleans clothing and fabric for a living. □ *The cleaner got the spot out of my blouse.* **3. cleaners** *n.* a business that launders or cleans clothing and other items. (Treated as singular or plural.) □ *I took my wool suit to the cleaners.*

**cleanse** ['klɛnz] *tv.* to clean something well; to make something more pure. □ *The nurse cleansed the wound before sewing it up.*

**clear** ['klɪr] **1.** *adj.* transparent; allowing light through. (Adv: *clearly.* Comp: *clearer;* sup: *clearest.*) □ *The shower curtain is made of clear plastic.* **2.** *adj.* bright; free from clouds or fog. (Adv: *clearly.* Comp: *clearer;* sup: *clearest.*) □ *On a clear day you can see the mountains from here.* **3.** *adj.* without marks or blemishes; without defects. (Comp: *clearer;* sup: *clearest.*) □ *The teenager wished for a clear face.* **4.** *adj.* easy to understand; making perfect sense. (Adv: *clearly.* Comp: *clearer;* sup: *clearest.*) □ *The instructions were clear, but we still couldn't put the toy together.*

**5.** *adj.* easy to hear or see. (Adv: *clearly.* Comp: *clearer;* sup: *clearest.*) ☐ *The careless thief left clear fingerprints all over the house.* **6.** *adj.* certain; easy to understand. (Adv: *clearly.* Comp: *clearer;* sup: *clearest.*) ☐ *The reason for the accident may never be clear.* **7.** *adj.* without anything in the way. (Comp: *clearer;* sup: *clearest.*) ☐ *The cat had a clear path to the open door.* **8.** *adv.* completely; all the way. ☐ *The dog jumped clear over the sleeping cats.* **9.** *tv.* to move someone or something so that the way is open. ☐ *Please clear all that stuff out of here!* **10.** *tv.* to make an area empty by removing things or people. ☐ *Would you please clear the table?* **11.** *tv.* to chop down trees and remove stones from the land. ☐ *The land had been cleared to make a pasture.* **12.** *tv.* to remove blame or guilt from someone. ☐ *The court cleared the suspect of all the charges.* **13.** *tv.* [for a bank] to send a check successfully through procedures necessary to have the check paid. ☐ *The bank cleared your check yesterday.* **14.** *iv.* [for a check] to successfully travel through the procedures necessary to assure payment. ☐ *You cannot have the cash until the check clears.* **15.** *iv.* [for the sky] to become free of clouds. ☐ *The sky cleared, and the sun came out.*

**clergy** ['klɚ dʒi] *n.* ministers; priests; pastors. (No plural form. Number is expressed by the phrase *member(s) of the clergy.*) ☐ *Bill and his wife are both members of the clergy.*

**clerk** ['klɚk] **1.** *n.* an office worker, especially one who keeps track of records, files, and information. ☐ *The clerk spent the afternoon filing documents.* **2.** *n.* someone who helps customers with goods and sales; someone who works behind a counter and helps customers. ☐ *The clerk at the post office sold me some stamps.*

**clever** ['klɛv ɚ] *adj.* [of someone or a creature] capable of interesting, creative activities. (Adv: *cleverly.* Comp: *cleverer;* sup: *cleverest.*) ☐ *Our dog is clever enough to open the door.*

**cliché** [kli 'she] *n.* an expression that is trite and tiresome and is used too often. ☐ *"A fine time was had by one and all" is a good example of a cliché.*

**click** ['klɪk] **1.** *n.* a short, quick noise; a snapping sound. ☐ *The lock closed with a loud click.* **2.** *tv.* to make a noise by snapping things together. ☐ *Tom clicked his keys on the window to get my attention.* **3.** *iv.* to snap; to make a snapping noise. ☐ *The camera clicked as the button was pushed.*

**client** ['klɑɪ ənt] *n.* someone served by a company or by a professional such as a lawyer. ☐ *The client was pleased with the advertising company's service.*

**cliff** ['klɪf] *n.* a high, steep wall of rock or earth. ☐ *The dangerous road ran along the edge of the cliff.*

**climate** ['klɑɪ mət] **1.** *n.* the typical weather conditions of a certain area. ☐ *The climate in this part of the country is very mild.* **2.** *n.* the general atmosphere, mood, attitude, or feeling. ☐ *The climate at the party became joyous when the presents were opened.*

**climax** ['klɑɪ mæks] **1.** *n.* the most exciting point in an event; the most intense part of an event; the most dramatic point of a story. ☐ *The climax of the week is when I get paid.* **2.** *iv.* to reach the most exciting point in an event. ☐ *The novel climaxed on the next to the last page.*

**climb** ['klɑɪm] **1.** *n.* the process of going up something, especially through much effort or using the hands and feet. ☐ *The long climb up the ladder to the roof was scary.* **2.** *tv.* to go up something, especially through much effort or using the hands and feet. ☐ *The hikers slowly* *climbed the mountain.* **3.** *iv.* to go to a higher level. □ *The temperature climbed and climbed until it was almost too hot to breathe.*

C

**climber** ['klaɪm ɚ] **1.** *n.* someone who hikes or climbs up mountains, cliffs, slopes, etc. □ *The climber bought special ropes and other equipment.* **2.** *n.* a plant that grows up something. □ *The gardener planted a climber along the side of the house.*

**clinic** ['klɪn ɪk] *n.* a medical office where minor medical problems are treated. □ *Mary took her sick child to the clinic.*

**clip** ['klɪp] **1.** *n.* a device that holds sheets of paper together; a small device for gripping or holding things together. □ *The papers were held together with a metal clip.* **2.** *n.* a brief part of a film, book, magazine, or newspaper. □ *My father mailed me a clip from the local newspaper.* **3.** *tv.* to hold things together with ①. □ *I clipped the memo to the book and placed it on the shelf.*

**cloak** ['klok] **1.** *n.* a long coat without sleeves; an outer garment like a cape. □ *The princess wore a long velvet cloak.* **2.** *tv.* to cover something up; to obscure something. □ *Mary cloaked her true feelings and smiled bravely.*

**clock** ['klɑk] **1.** *n.* a machine that keeps track of the time of day; a timepiece. □ *The Smiths have a clock in every room of their house.* **2.** *tv.* to measure the length of time it takes for someone or something to do something; to measure a rate of speed. □ *Mike clocked his run at ten minutes.*

**close 1.** ['klos] *adj.* near in space or time. (Adv: *closely.* Comp: *closer;* sup: *closest.*) □ *The closest store was only two blocks from our house.* **2.** ['klos] *adj.* near in spirit; dear; intimate; confidential. (Adv: *closely.* Comp: *closer;* sup: *closest.*) □ *Bill and Mary have become very close friends.* **3.** ['klos] *adj.* careful; strict. (Adv: *closely.* Comp: *closer;* sup: *closest.*) □ *I paid close attention to my boss's instructions.* **4.** ['klos] *adj.* almost equal; almost the same. (Adv: *closely.* Comp: *closer;* sup: *closest.*) □ *There is a close resemblance between Mary and her daughter.* **5.** ['klos] *adv.* near in space or time. □ *Don't stand so close to me!* **6.** ['kloz] *tv.* to shut something. □ *Please close the door when you leave.* **7.** ['kloz] *tv.* to bring something to an end; to conclude something. □ *The professor closed the lecture with a funny story.* **8.** ['kloz] *tv.* to complete an electrical circuit. □ *The lights went on when the circuit was closed.* **9.** ['kloz] *iv.* to shut. □ *The curtain closed after the last act of the play.* **10.** ['kloz] *iv.* to end; to finish; to bring to an end; to conclude. □ *The play closed with a happy ending.* **11.** ['kloz] *n.* the end; the finish; the conclusion. □ *At the close of his life, Grandpa had no regrets.*

**closed** ['klozd] *adj.* not open; shut. □ *The closed door signaled that a meeting was taking place.*

**closet** ['klɔz ɪt] **1.** *n.* a small room where clothing and personal objects are kept. □ *Mary hung her coat in the closet.* **2.** *adj.* secret; hiding; covert. □ *Susan was a closet poet who never shared her work.*

**cloth** ['klɔθ] **1.** *n.* woven material; woven fabric. (Plural only when referring to different kinds, types, instances, or varieties.) □ *The dress was made from imported cotton cloth.* Ⓒ *We use only the finest cloths in our garments.* **2.** *n., irreg.* a piece of woven material or fabric. (Pl: [klɔðz].) □ *John wiped up the spill with a cloth.*

**clothe** ['kloð] *tv.* to put garments on someone or something; to dress someone or something. □ *Susie clothed the doll in a fancy dress.*

**clothes** ['klo(ð)z] *n.* clothing; garments; something to wear, such as a shirt, a sweater, pants, or socks. (Treated as plural, but not countable.) □ *Bill bought new clothes when he got his new job.*

**clothesline** ['kloz lɑɪn] *n.* a length of rope on which clothes and other laundry can be hung to dry. □ *I will hang the sheets on the clothesline to dry.*

**clothespin** ['kloz pɪn] *n.* a wooden or plastic clip used to attach damp clothes to a clothesline. □ *The clothes were hung on the line with clothespins.*

**clothing** ['klo ðɪŋ] *n.* clothes; garments. (No plural form. Treated as singular.) □ *The children were instructed to keep their clothing clean.*

**cloud** ['klɑʊd] **1.** *n.* a large white or gray mass in the sky, made of water vapor. □ *The sky filled with clouds, and it began to rain.* **2.** *n.* a large puff of smoke or dust; a visible mass of gas or particles that is still or moves in the air. □ *The burning building was enveloped in a cloud of smoke.* **3.** *tv.* to obscure something; to hide something. □ *Moisture clouded the windows.*

**cloudy** ['klɑʊ di] **1.** *adj.* [of sky] having clouds. (Adv: *cloudily.* Comp: *cloudier;* sup: *cloudiest.*) □ *We lay on our backs in the field and gazed at the cloudy sky.* **2.** *adj.* not able to be seen through clearly. (Fig. on ①. Adv: *cloudily.* Comp: *cloudier;* sup: *cloudiest.*) □ *The water was a bit cloudy, and no one would drink it.*

**clown** ['klɑʊn] **1.** *n.* a performer who wears a funny costume and makeup and tries to make people laugh. □ *A clown entertained the kids at the birthday party.* **2.** *n.* someone who is always making jokes and trying to make other people laugh. □ *My office is full of clowns who are always making jokes.*

**club** ['klʌb] **1.** *n.* a large, thick, blunt wooden stick. □ *The police officer carried a club for protection.* **2.** *n.* a nightclub; a place where liquor is served or where people can dance. □ *Let's go to the club and dance.* **3.** *n.* an organization or group of people who meet to pursue a specific activity. □ *The club began its meeting at eight o'clock.* **4.** *n.* one of four different symbols found in a deck of playing cards; the symbol "♣." □ *The club looks somewhat like a plant with three leaves.* **5.** *n.* the stick with a metal end used to hit a golf ball. (Short for **golf club**.) □ *I keep my clubs in the car so I can play golf whenever I have a chance.* **6.** *tv.* to beat someone or something with ①. □ *The police officers clubbed the thief.*

**clue** ['klu] *n.* a hint; some information that will help to solve a problem. □ *Bill gave his friend a clue to the secret.*

**clump** ['klʌmp] **1.** *n.* a group of something; a mass of something. □ *The plow turned up huge clumps of earth.* **2.** *tv.* to group things together; to gather something into **clumps** ①. □ *Susan clumped the soil around the roots of the plant.*

**clumsy** ['klʌm zi] *adj.* awkward; likely to trip or stumble on something. (Adv: *clumsily.* Comp: *clumsier;* sup: *clumsiest.*) □ *The clumsy waiter dropped the plates on the floor.*

**coach** ['kotʃ] **1.** *n.* someone who is in charge of a team; someone who trains players on a team. □ *The coach made the team practice for three hours every day.* **2.** *n.* someone who trains someone else. □ *Jane's voice coach helped her learn how to sing better.* **3.** *n.* an enclosed carriage, typically pulled by horses. □ *The coach stopped in front of the theater, and the passengers got out.* **4.** *n.* a railway car where passengers ride in seats. (As opposed to railway cars where people can eat or can lie down to sleep.) □ *We rode in the coach all night because we had not paid for a place in the sleeping car.* **5.** *n.* a cross-country bus; a bus used for touring or carrying people over a long distance. □ *Susan traveled by coach*

C

*from Detroit to Miami.* **6.** *n.* the tourist section of an airplane; the cheapest kind of air travel. (No plural form.) □ *I always fly in coach.* **7.** *adv.* [traveling] in or by ⑥. □ *Dave couldn't imagine traveling coach all the way to Europe!* **8.** *tv.* to instruct someone in a sport, skill, or craft. □ *Anne coached Mary on her public-speaking skills.*

**coal** ['kol] **1.** *n.* a black mineral made of carbon, used as fuel. (Plural only when referring to different kinds, types, instances, or varieties.) □ *The furnace was fueled with coal.* © *Some coals are harder than others and burn longer and hotter.* **2.** *n.* a hot, glowing chunk of burning ① or charcoal. □ *After the barbecue, we poured water over the hot coals to cool them.*

**coarse** ['kors] **1.** *adj.* having a rough texture; not smooth. (Adv: *coarsely.* Comp: *coarser;* sup: *coarsest.*) □ *I put some lotion on my coarse skin.* **2.** *adj.* vulgar; crude. (Adv: *coarsely.* Comp: *coarser;* sup: *coarsest.*) □ *Bill's coarse manners were becoming quite offensive.*

**coast** ['kost] **1.** *n.* land along and beside the sea. □ *The coast along the ocean was lined with houses.* **2.** *iv.* to glide without using energy. □ *The kids coasted down the hill on their bicycles.*

**coastal** ['kos təl] *adj.* along the coast; on the coast. (Adv: *coastally.*) □ *San Francisco is a coastal city on the Pacific Ocean.*

**coat** ['kot] **1.** *n.* a heavy item of clothing, worn over one's other clothes during cold weather. □ *Each winter I buy a new wool coat.* **2.** *n.* the fur of an animal; the pelt of an animal. □ *The dog's coat is dirty.* **3.** *n.* a layer of something, such as paint, that covers a surface. □ *Mary put a coat of paint on the fence.* **4.** *tv.* to cover the surface of something with a layer of something. □ *The workers coated the roof with tar.*

**cob** ['kɑb] *n.* the central core of an ear of corn. (Short for **corncob**.) □ *We eat corn fresh—while it is still on the cob.*

**cocoon** [kə 'kun] *n.* the protective shell in which a caterpillar wraps itself while it transforms into a butterfly or a moth. □ *The butterfly emerged from its cocoon and flew away.*

**cod** ['kɑd] **1.** *n., irreg.* a kind of edible fish that lives in cold water. (Pl: *cod.*) □ *The fishermen went out on their boats to fish for cod.* **2.** *n.* the flesh of ①, eaten as food. (No plural form.) □ *The restaurant offered a special on fried cod.*

**code** ['kod] **1.** *n.* a secret writing system; a system of symbols used for communication. □ *The spy sent his message in a secret code.* **2.** *n.* a set of laws; a set of rules. □ *The apartment building violated the city's safety code.* **3.** *tv.* to translate a message into ①. □ *The army general coded the message in case the enemy intercepted it.* **4.** *tv.* to mark an object with a special number or symbol. □ *The electrical wires were coded by color.*

**coffee** ['kɔf i] **1.** *n.* the roasted beans of a kind of tree. (Either whole or ground. Plural only when referring to different kinds, types, instances, or varieties.) □ *The coffee in the canister smelled fresh.* © *Coffees from Brazil are very popular.* **2.** *n.* a drink made from roasted, ground ①. (No plural form.) □ *Bill needs a cup of coffee each morning before he can work.*

**coffee break** ['kɔf i brek] *n.* a rest period during which coffee or some other refreshment is enjoyed. □ *The workers took a coffee break each morning.*

**coffeepot** ['kɔf i pɑt] *n.* a pot used to brew and serve coffee. □ *Lisa brewed the coffee in a new coffeepot.*

**coffin** ['kɔf ən] *n.* a box in which the body of a dead person is placed for burial. □ *The funeral ended as the coffin was lowered into the ground.*

**coil** ['kɔɪl] **1.** *n.* a length of something, such as rope, wound into a stack of circular loops. □ *Bob set the coil of wire on the counter.* **2.** *n.* a circular loop. □ *Place a coil over the post and tie it tight.* **3.** *tv.* to wrap something around and around into a circle. □ *Bob coiled the wires before he placed them in the box.* **4.** *iv.* to form into a circular loop. □ *The colorful flowers coiled around the post.*

**coin** ['kɔɪn] **1.** *n.* a piece of money made from metal. □ *Bill's pocket was full of coins.* **2.** *tv.* to press metal into ①; to make money from metal. □ *The huge machine was designed to coin money.* **3.** *tv.* to invent a new word; to make up a new word. □ *Many new words are coined each year.*

**cold** ['kold] **1.** *n.* a physical state or property of something having relatively less heat. (No plural form.) □ *Cold is really the absence of heat.* **2.** *n.* weather that is characterized by ①; a lack of warmth in the outside temperature. (No plural form.) □ *When I came in from the cold, I sat near the fireplace.* **3.** *n.* a common illness that causes sneezing, a runny nose, a sore throat, etc. □ *I caught a cold from one of my coworkers.* **4.** *adj.* not hot; not having heat. (Comp: *colder;* sup: *coldest.*) □ *The cold vegetables had to be heated for dinner.* **5.** *adj.* [of a living creature] uncomfortable from not having heat. (Adv: *coldly.* Comp: *colder;* sup: *coldest.*) □ *I got very cold swimming in the lake.* **6.** *adj.* mean; unfriendly; unpleasant. (Adv: *coldly.* Comp: *colder;* sup: *coldest.*) □ *Jane can be very cold to people she does not know.*

**collapse** [kə 'læps] **1.** *n.* an instance of falling down; a loss of the air contained in something. (No plural form.) □ *An earthquake hastened the ultimate collapse of the ancient house.* **2.** *n.* the total ruin of something. □ *People were penniless after the bank's collapse.* **3.** *iv.* to fall down; to become ruined. □ *The building collapsed during the earthquake.* **4.** *iv.* to fail; to break down completely. □ *When negotiations collapsed, the union called a strike.*

**collar** ['kɑl ɚ] **1.** *n.* the part of a piece of clothing that wraps around the neck. □ *Jane buttoned the top button of her collar.* **2.** *n.* a band around the neck of an animal. □ *I attached a bell to my cat's collar so I could hear her move about.*

**collect** [kə 'lɛkt] **1.** *tv.* to ask for or to receive money that is owed. □ *The landlord collects the rent every month.* **2.** *tv.* to gather items together; to bring items together. □ *The old newspapers were collected and recycled.* **3.** *tv.* to find and take, get, or buy something or a class of things as a hobby. □ *Anne collects stamps.* **4.** *adj.* [of a telephone call] charged to the person or number called. □ *Mary did not accept the collect call.* **5.** *adv.* charging a telephone call to the person or telephone number called. □ *Bill called his parents collect.*

**college** ['kɑl ɪdʒ] *n.* a school of higher education; an undergraduate division within a university. □ *Bill's counselor helped him apply to colleges.*

**colonial** [kə 'lon i əl] **1.** *adj.* of or about a colony. (Adv: *colonially.*) □ *Britain had colonial holdings in Africa until the 1960s.* **2.** *adj.* of or about the original thirteen colonies of the United States. (Adv: *colonially.*) □ *In colonial days, men often wore fancy wigs.* **3.** *n.* a person who lives or lived in a colony. □ *Some towns in New England are named for famous colonials.*

**colony** ['kɑl ə ni] **1.** *n.* an area that is settled and ruled by a country but is located apart from it. □ *Algeria was once a colony of France.* **2.** *n.* the place where a social group of ants or termites lives and breeds. □ *A colony of ants lives under our driveway.*

**color** ['kʌl ɚ] **1.** *n.* the quality of light that causes people to see the differences among red, orange, yellow, blue, green, purple, etc.; a hue; a tint. □ *Mary decorated the room with bright colors.* **2.** *tv.* to give something ①; to paint or draw with something that has ①. □ *John colored the drawing of the horse green.* **3.** *tv.* to affect something; to influence something. (Fig. on ②.) □ *The day's events were colored by the loud argument.* **4.** *iv.* to draw with crayons or markers. □ *The children colored all afternoon.* **5.** *adj.* [of film or video recording] using all the colors, not just black and white. □ *The color photographs turned out better than the black-and-white ones.*

**colt** ['kolt] *n.* a young male horse. □ *The colt was afraid of its owner.*

**column** ['kɑl əm] **1.** *n.* a supporting pillar or a thick post. □ *The columns supporting the house were in decay.* **2.** *n.* a series of words or symbols arranged in a line from top to bottom. □ *The computer aligned the columns of text.* **3.** *n.* a newspaper article, especially one written by a columnist. □ *The column was about proper treatment of children.*

**comb** ['kom] **1.** *n.* a toothed strip of plastic or something similar, used for arranging hair. □ *Run a comb through your hair before you leave.* **2.** *n.* the red growth on top of the heads of chickens and turkeys. □ *The rooster has a bright red comb.* **3.** *tv.* to arrange one's hair with ①. □ *Comb your hair before dinner.* **4.** *tv.* to thoroughly look through an area for something; to search a place for something. □ *We combed the house for the missing key.*

**combat 1.** ['kɑm bæt] *n.* war; conflict; battle. (No plural form.) □ *The soldiers were trained for combat.* **2.** ['kɑm bæt] *adj.* <the adj. use of ①.> □ *Bill wore combat boots to the rock concert.* **3.** [kəm 'bæt] *tv.* to fight someone or something; to battle someone or something. (Pt/pp: *combated.*) □ *The doctor used a new medicine to combat the disease.*

**combination** [kɑm bɪ 'ne ʃən] **1.** *n.* the process of combining. (Plural only when referring to different kinds, types, instances, or varieties.) □ *The combination of blue and yellow makes green.* Ⓒ *I want to be able to select from a variety of combinations.* **2.** *n.* something that is made by an act of combining. □ *This is a combination of two powerful chemicals.* **3.** *n.* the sequence of numbers needed to open a **combination lock**. □ *Bill couldn't remember the combination to the lock on the shed.*

**combination lock** [kɑm bɪ 'ne ʃən lɑk] *n.* a lock that is opened by turning a dial to a secret **combination** ③ of numbers or by pressing numbered buttons in the proper sequence, instead of with a key. □ *I have a combination lock on the door of my shed.*

**combine** [kəm 'bɑɪn] **1.** *tv.* to join two or more things together. □ *I combined the eggs with the flour mixture.* **2.** *iv.* to unite; to join. □ *Mary's and Bob's businesses combined to form a new company.*

**come** ['kʌm] **1.** *iv., irreg.* to move toward someone or something; to move toward the location of the person who is speaking. (Pt: **came**; pp: *come.*) □ *Please come over to my house at three o'clock.* **2.** *iv., irreg.* to arrive; to get somewhere. □ *We came to the theater early to get a good seat.* **3.** *iv., irreg.* [for goods that have been purchased] to arrive or be available equipped in a certain way. □ *This vacuum cleaner comes fully equipped.*

**comedy** ['kɑm ə di] **1.** *n.* a funny play or movie; the opposite of a tragedy. □ *Bill likes to see plays if they are comedies.* **2.** *n.* the element of movies or plays that makes people laugh; the opposite of tragedy. (No plural form.) □ *Timing is very important in comedy.*

**comic** ['kɑm ɪk] **1.** *adj.* funny; humorous. (Adv: *comically* [...ɪk li].) □ *The comic movie lifted our spirits.* **2.** *n.* a pamphlet printed in color on cheap paper where stories are told in **comic strips.** (From *comic book.*) □ *Bill has a big stack of old comics in his attic.* **3.** *n.* someone who tells jokes and funny stories. □ *No one enjoyed the comic's old jokes.* **4. comics** *n.* the newspaper pages containing cartoons and **comic strips.** (Treated as plural.) □ *The comics weren't very funny today.*

**comic strip** ['kɑm ɪk strɪp] *n.* a series of several cartoons printed in a row; a cartoon series that appears daily or weekly, usually in newspapers. □ *The newspaper prints comic strips every day.*

**command** [kə 'mænd] **1.** *n.* an order; a statement that tells someone what to do; a direction; an instruction. □ *Mike's young dog learned many verbal commands.* **2.** *tv.* to give an order to someone. □ *Bob commanded his dog to sit.* **3.** *tv.* to control someone or something. □ *The ship's captain commands the crew.* **4.** *tv.* [for someone or someone's character] to deserve and receive respect and attention. □ *The famous scholar commanded respect.*

**comment** ['kɑm ɛnt] **1.** *n.* a remark about something; a statement about something. □ *Mary whispered her comments about the movie, but everyone heard her.* **2. comment on** something *iv.* + *prep. phr.* to make a statement about something; to remark about something. □ *I asked the professor to comment on my writing style.* **3.** *tv.* to state an opinion; to make a remark. (The object is a clause with **that** ⑦.) □ *Anne commented that she wanted to eat pizza for dinner.*

**commit** [kə 'mɪt] **1.** *tv.* to do a crime; to do something illegal. □ *The police do not know who committed the robberies.* **2. commit** someone **to** something *tv.* + *obj.* + *prep. phr.* to place someone under the control or authority of a hospital, institution, or prison. □ *John committed his sick father to the hospital.* **3. commit** someone **to** something *tv.* + *obj.* + *prep. phr.* to pledge oneself to do something. (Usually reflexive.) □ *Dave committed himself to working for the good of all people.* **4.** *tv.* to place someone [in a mental institution]. □ *The court committed the sick man to protect him.*

**committee** [kə 'mɪt i] *n.* a group of people who meet to perform a specific duty, usually as part of a larger organization. □ *How many members are on the finance committee?*

**common** ['kɑm ən] **1.** *adj.* usual; typical; frequently encountered; widespread. (Adv: *commonly.* Comp: *commoner;* sup: *commonest.*) □ *Colds and flu are common in the winter months.* **2.** *adj.* shared or used by two or more people. (Adv: *commonly.*) □ *These two bedrooms share a common bathroom.* **3.** *adj.* without distinction; ordinary. (Adv: *commonly.* Comp: *commoner;* sup: *commonest.*) □ *This is the common variety of daisy.*

**common sense** ['kɑm ən 'sɛns] *n.* basic reasonable and practical thinking. (No plural form.) □ *He has a lot of common sense and doesn't panic in a bad situation.*

**communication** [kə mjun ɪ 'ke ʃən] **1.** *n.* sending and receiving information. (No plural form.) □ *Bill has had no communication with his brother for 10 years.* **2. communications** *n.* the means or media for communication. □ *During the storm, all communications were out of service.* **3.** *n.* an announcement or statement in written or spoken form. □ *A communication from the office outlined the new policy.*

**community** [kə 'mjun ə ti] **1.** *n.* an area or region where people live and communicate with each other; a neighborhood or town. □ *There are seven churches in our community.* **2.** *n.* a group of people who have a common interest, occupation, or background. □ *A church is sometimes called a community of believers.* **3.** *adj.* <the adj. use of ①.> □ *The convicted criminal was forced to do community service.*

**companion** [kəm 'pæn jən] **1.** *n.* someone with whom time is spent. □ *My companions and I went to the museum.* **2.** *n.* something that matches something else; something that is part of a set. □ *I cannot find the companion to this black sock.*

**company** ['kʌm pə ni] **1.** *n.* a business organization; a business. □ *Mary works for a computer software company.* **2.** *n.* guests; visitors. (No plural form. Treated as singular.) □ *We are having company tonight, so we must clean the house.*

**comparative** [kəm 'pɛr ə tɪv] **1.** *adj.* of or about studies based on comparison. (Adv: *comparatively.*) □ *Susan took a course in comparative literature.* **2.** *adj.* of or about a form of an adverb or adjective that typically has an *-er* suffix or is a combination of the adverb or adjective and the word *more.* (Some adverbs and adjectives have irregular **comparatives** ④, however.) □ Better *is the comparative form of* good. □ *In grammar class we learned about comparative adjectives.* **3.** *adj.* as compared with others. (Adv: *comparatively.*) □ *Bill is a comparative stranger in town. He just moved here.* **4.** *n.* the **comparative** ② form of an adjective or adverb. □ Better *is the comparative of* good. □ *In grammar class we learned about comparatives and superlatives.*

**compare** [kəm 'pɛr] **1.** *tv.* to determine or show how two things are the same or different. □ *The teacher compared the two historical events.* **2. compare** someone or something **with** someone or something *tv. + obj. + prep. phr.* to determine or show how a person or thing resembles, or differs from, another person or thing. □ *Tom compared Bill with Bob to see who was taller.* **3. compare** someone or something **to** someone or something *tv. + obj. + prep. phr.* to point out the similarities between a person or thing and another person or thing. □ *Bob compared Mary's messy hair to a bird's nest.*

**comparison** [kəm 'pɛr ə sən] *n.* showing how things are the same or different. (Plural only when referring to different kinds, types, instances, or varieties.) □ *Your comparison of the two ideas is very insightful.* Ⓒ *A series of comparisons of the two stories revealed that one was based on the other.*

**compass** ['kʌm pəs] **1.** *n.* a device that points to the north and indicates direction for the purposes of travel or finding out where one is located. □ *Mary used a compass when she became lost in the strange town.* **2.** *n.* a simple device used to draw circles or parts of circles. □ *The architect made an arc on the blueprint with the compass.*

**compete** [kəm 'pit] *iv.* to participate in a game, contest, or rivalry, with the hope of winning; to take part in a game or contest. □ *Children sometimes compete for their parents' attention.*

**competition** [kɑm pɪ 'tɪ ʃən] **1.** *n.* a contest. □ *The wrestling competition was held in the gymnasium.* **2.** *n.* the state that exists between rivals. (No plural form.) □ *The best students were in competition with each other at school.* **3.** *n.* a rival or a group of rivals. (No plural form.) □ *The gymnast checked out his competition at the championship meet.*

**competitive** [kəm 'pɛt ɪ tɪv] **1.** *adj.* eager to compete; aggressive in competition. (*Adv: competitively.*) □ *Susan is quite competitive when she plays baseball.* **2.** *adj.* low in price; [of a low price] able to compete. (*Adv: competitively.*) □ *The advertising firm's fees are competitive.* **3.** *adj.* involving competition. (*Adv: competitively.*) □ *Advertising is a very competitive business.*

**complain** [kəm 'plen] *iv.* to say that one is unhappy, angry, or annoyed. □ *We complained a lot about our cold food.*

**complaint** [kəm 'plent] **1.** *n.* a statement expressing annoyance or anger about something. □ *Mary made a strong complaint at the department store.* **2.** *n.* a statement that a crime has been committed. □ *An old complaint against Bob stayed in his records permanently.* **3.** *n.* a sickness; an illness. □ *The doctor could not diagnose Bill's complaint.*

**complete** [kəm 'plit] **1.** *adj.* entire; whole; with all the necessary parts. (Adv: *completely.*) □ *Bill told us the complete story over coffee.* **2.** *tv.* to finish something; to end something; to do something until it is done. □ *I will complete my project next year.* **3.** *tv.* to make something whole; to fill in all the parts of something. □ *Please complete the application form for the job.*

**complex** **1.** ['kɑm plɛks] *n.* a set of related buildings. □ *The complex will be complete when two more buildings are finished.* **2.** ['kɑm plɛks] *n.* a psychological condition. □ *Mary has a complex about being late.* **3.** [kəm 'plɛks, 'kɑm plɛks] *adj.* difficult; complicated; hard to understand. (Adv: *complexly.*) □ *Poverty is a complex problem in many of the world's cities.*

**composition** [kɑm pə 'zɪ ʃən] **1.** *n.* the process of putting things together to form one whole thing. (No plural form.) □ *The composition of this essay took weeks.* **2.** *n.* the arrangement of the parts of something. (No plural form.) □ *The composition of the photograph was perfectly balanced.* **3.** *n.* a piece of music, a symphony; a piece of writing, an essay, a poem. □ *The orchestra played compositions by classical composers.* **4.** *n.* creating a piece of properly written writing. (No plural form.) □ *All first-year students must take a course in composition.* **5.** *n.* the things that make up something; the ingredients of something; the parts of something. (No plural form.) □ *What is the composition of this sticky substance?*

**comprehend** [kɑm prɪ 'hɛnd] *tv.* to understand something. □ *The test determined if the students comprehended the material.*

**computer** [kəm 'pjut ɚ] **1.** *n.* an electronic machine that processes data at high speeds. □ *I installed some new software on my computer.* **2.** *adj.* <the adj. use of ①.> □ *My computer keyboard needs cleaning.*

**computer file** [kəm 'pjut ɚ 'fɑɪl] *n.* a unit of data or information in digital form, stored on a floppy disk or hard drive. □ *Could I have a copy of the computer file that has my letter in it?*

**comrade** ['kɑm ræd] *n.* a friend; a companion. □ *Jane went golfing with her comrades from work.*

**conceal** [kən 'sil] *tv.* to hide someone or something. □ *The criminal concealed a knife in his boot.*

**concept** ['kɑn sɛpt] *n.* a thought; an idea; a notion. □ *Our teacher explained the concept of gravity.*

**concern** [kən 'sɚn] **1.** *tv.* to matter to someone; to be important to someone; to worry someone. □ *Crime concerns the mayor very much.* **2.** *tv.* to be about something; to have to do with something; to deal with something. □ *This book concerns wildflowers.* **3.** *n.* a matter of interest; a matter of importance; something that is of interest. □ *This matter is not a concern of yours.* **4.** *n.* care; worry; anxiety. (Plural only when referring to different kinds, types, instances, or varieties.) □ *Do you think* *this new policy is a cause for concern?* Ⓒ *Our concerns are not addressed by your statement.*

C

**concert** ['kɑn sɚt] **1.** *n.* a musical performance by one or more musicians. □ *The pianist will give a concert at the high school.* **2.** *adj.* <the adj. use of ①.> □ *Mary is a concert violinist.*

**conclude** [kən 'klud] **1.** *tv.* to finish something; to come to the end of something. □ *They concluded the dance at midnight.* **2.** *tv.* to reach an opinion by thinking about something. (The object is a clause with **that** ⑦.) □ *Mary concluded that Bill was going to be late.* **3.** *iv.* [for a process or activity] to finish or end. □ *The movie concludes at ten o'clock.*

**conclusion** [kən 'klu ʒən] **1.** *n.* the end of something. □ *At the conclusion of my story, everyone laughed.* **2.** *n.* the final decision reached by thinking about something. □ *The scientist's conclusions were based on the experiment's results.*

**concrete 1.** ['kɑn krit] *n.* a stone-like material made from cement, sand, gravel, and water, used in construction and paving. (No plural form.) □ *Jimmy hit his head on the concrete when he fell off his tricycle.* **2.** ['kɑn krit] *adj.* made from ①. □ *Jimmy banged his head on the concrete sidewalk when he fell.* **3.** [kɑn 'krit] *adj.* actual; existing; real; definite; not abstract. (Adv: *concretely.*) □ *Bill prefers concrete facts to abstract ideas.*

**condition** [kən 'dɪ ʃən] **1.** *n.* a state of being; a situation that someone or something is in. (No plural form.) □ *My shoes are in bad condition and need to be replaced.* **2. conditions** *n.* a group of related states or situations, as with the weather or the state of the economy. □ *When conditions were right for take off, the plane left for Honolulu.* **3.** *n.* the state of someone's health. (No plural form.) □ *The physician said Bill was in great condition.* **4.** *n.* something that is necessary before something else can happen. □ *Passing a drug test was a condition of employment at the company.* **5.** *tv.* to shape someone's or something's behavior; to train someone or something. □ *We conditioned our dog to bring in the newspaper.* **6.** *tv.* to cause someone to become more physically fit. □ *The trainer designed exercises to condition the athlete.*

**conduct 1.** ['kɑn dəkt] *n.* behavior; the way someone behaves. (No plural form.) □ *My uncle's conduct was always very polite.* **2.** [kən 'dʌkt] *tv.* to lead someone or something; to guide someone or something. □ *The mountaineer conducted the hikers along the trail.* **3.** [kən 'dʌkt] *tv.* to behave [oneself] in a particular manner. (Takes a reflexive object.) □ *Please conduct yourself properly.* **4.** [kən 'dʌkt] *tv.* to provide a path for electricity or heat to travel. □ *Metal conducts heat very well.*

**conductor** [kən 'dʌk tɚ] **1.** *n.* someone who directs an orchestra, band, choir, or other musical group. □ *The conductor stopped the rehearsal and corrected the woodwinds.* **2.** *n.* someone who checks tickets and collects fares on a train. □ *A conductor announced the name of each station.* **3.** *n.* a substance electricity or heat can travel through. □ *Copper is an excellent conductor of electricity.*

**cone** ['kon] **1.** *n.* a solid form that changes from a circle at one end to a point at the other end. □ *The top of a cone comes to a sharp point.* **2.** *n.* a crisp, thin, ①-shaped pastry, used for holding ice cream. □ *The child crunched the cone after the ice cream was gone.* **3.** *n.* the seed-bearing fruit of a pine tree. □ *The forest floor was covered with pine cones.*

**conference** ['kɑn frəns] *n.* a meeting to discuss a specific topic. □ *Anne had a* *conference with her son's teacher to discuss his progress.*

**confess** [kən 'fɛs] **1.** *tv.* to admit something; to state that one has done something wrong. (The object can be a clause with **that** ⑦.) □ *The suspect never confessed the crime.* **2. confess to** **something** *iv.* + *prep. phr.* to admit doing something; to state that one has done something wrong. □ *Jimmy confessed to breaking the window.*

**confession** [kən 'fɛ ʃən] *n.* the process or activity of confessing or admitting something. (Plural only when referring to different kinds, types, instances, or varieties.) □ *Only confession will stop the guilt that you feel.* Ⓒ *The newspaper printed the robbers' confessions.*

**confidence** ['kɑn fɪ dəns] **1.** *n.* a strong trust in someone or something; a strong belief in someone or something. (No plural form.) □ *I have confidence that you will pass the test.* **2.** *n.* a feeling of assurance; a belief in oneself and one's abilities. (No plural form.) □ *A series of failures undermined the child's confidence.*

**confidential** [kɑn fɪ 'dɛn ʃəl] **1.** *adj.* secret; kept as secret. (Adv: *confidentially.*) □ *The government files are confidential.* **2.** *adj.* [of someone] trusted with secrets. □ *Jane's confidential advisor handled her financial matters.*

**confine** [kən 'fɑɪn] **1.** *tv.* to keep someone or a creature in a small space; to enclose someone or some creature in a small space. □ *Bill confined his dog to the house all day.* **2.** *tv.* to restrict or limit conversation or statements to a particular subject. □ *Please confine your remarks to the subject we are discussing.*

**confirm** [kən 'fɚm] **1.** *tv.* to check something to make certain it is true, accurate, complete, or still in effect. (The object can be a clause with **that** ⑦.) □ *Please confirm our reservations at the restaurant.* **2.** *tv.* to approve and agree that someone should be officially chosen for office. (The object can be a clause with **that** ⑦.) □ *The Senate confirmed the president's choice for the job.*

C

**confirmed** [kən 'fɚmd] **1.** *adj.* shown to be true, accurate, complete, or still in effect. □ *Two passengers held confirmed reservations for the same seat.* **2.** *adj.* determined to remain in a particular state. □ *Susan is a confirmed believer in eating fat-free food.*

**conflict** **1.** ['kɑn flɪkt] *n.* disagreement; fighting. (Plural only when referring to different kinds, types, instances, or varieties.) □ *We try to avoid conflict when it is possible to do so.* Ⓒ *The conflicts lasted until the town was destroyed in battle.* **2.** [kən 'flɪkt] *iv.* [for things] to differ or disagree. □ *The ideas in these two statements conflict.*

**confuse** [kən 'fjuz] **1.** *tv.* to puzzle someone; to make someone wonder about something. □ *Algebra just confused many of the students.* **2. confuse** **someone or something with someone or something** *tv.* + *obj.* + *prep. phr.* to mistake someone or something for someone or something else. □ *I often confused the twins with each other because they looked alike.*

**confusion** [kən 'fju ʒən] **1.** *n.* a feeling of being confused or puzzled. (No plural form.) □ *I experience confusion whenever I look at a map.* **2.** *n.* a noisy lack of order. (No plural form.) □ *The teacher yelled for quiet in the confusion.*

**congratulate** [kən 'græt∫ ə let] *tv.* to extend one's good wishes to someone. □ *I congratulated Jane on her engagement.*

**congregation** [kɑŋ grə 'ge ʃən] *n.* a group of people, especially in a church service. □ *The congregation sang the final hymn.*

C

**congress** ['kɑŋ grəs] **1.** *n.* the group of people elected to make laws. □ *Congress will vote on the law in the next session.* **2.** *n.* a meeting of representatives to or members of an organization. □ *I went to a congress of book sellers.* **3. Congress** *n.* the House of Representatives and the Senate of the United States. (No plural form.) □ *The lobbyists spoke to each member of Congress.*

**conj.** an abbreviation of **conjunction**.

**conjugate** ['kɑn dʒə get] *tv.* to tell the forms of a verb in a language. □ *I don't know how to conjugate that verb because it is irregular.*

**conjunction** [kən 'dʒʌŋk ʃən] *n.* a part of speech that connects words, phrases, and clauses. (Abbreviated *conj.* here.) □ *Conjunctions—including* and, but, for, or, nor, *and* yet*—connect words, phrases, and clauses to each other.* □ *Use a comma before a conjunction when it joins two clauses.*

**connect** [kə 'nɛkt] **1.** *tv.* to serve as a link between two things. □ *A bridge connects the two sides of the river.* **2.** *tv.* to join or attach certain electronic devices. □ *Please connect the keyboard to the computer.* **3.** *tv.* to link someone to someone or something through an electronic means. □ *What commands will connect me to your Web site?* **4.** *tv.* to relate something to something else; to associate one thought with another. □ *I couldn't connect the points the professor was making.* **5.** *iv.* to link with something; to link to something. □ *This road connects with the main road to town.*

**connection** [kə 'nɛk ʃən] **1.** *n.* the physical link among or between things. □ *A short rope was the only connection between the boat and the dock.* **2.** *n.* the relationship among or between thoughts. □ *I easily made the connection between the two ideas.* **3.** *n.* the electronic link that connects two people by telephone. □ *There is noise on this connection. I can hardly hear you.* **4.** *n.* an airplane flight that one boards at an intermediate stop. □ *The agent announced gate numbers for passengers making connections.* **5.** *n.* someone who is a social or business contact. □ *After twenty years in the industry, David had many connections.*

**conquer** ['kɑŋ kɚ] **1.** *tv.* to defeat someone in war; to subdue a people, army, or land. □ *The Romans conquered many lands.* **2.** *tv.* to overcome a difficulty. □ *Bill finally conquered his bad habit of laughing during sad movies.*

**conquest** ['kɑŋ kwɛst] **1.** *n.* the attempt to subdue, defeat, or conquer a people or a country. (Plural only when referring to different kinds, types, instances, or varieties.) □ *Conquest is exciting for some, bad for others.* Ⓒ *The country's hostile conquests made all of its neighbors nervous.* **2.** *n.* the object or target of ①. (Fig. on ①.) □ *The city of Rome was the conquest that tempted the mad adventurer.* **3.** *n.* someone who is the target of a romantic or sexual quest. □ *Susan didn't mind being someone's conquest, as long he was her conquest, too.*

**conscious** ['kɑn ʃəs] **1.** *adj.* awake, alert, and aware of immediate surroundings. (Adv: *consciously.*) □ *I fainted briefly but was conscious again in a few seconds.* **2. conscious of** something *adj.* + *prep. phr.* aware of or knowledgeable about something. □ *Tom is conscious of a small problem with his finances.* **3.** *adj.* intentional; intended. (Adv: *consciously.*) □ *I made a conscious effort to get to work on time.*

**consent** [kən 'sɛnt] **1. consent (to** something**)** *iv.* (+ *prep. phr.*) to agree to something; to permit something. □ *I refuse to consent to your demand!* **2.** *n.* permission; approval. (No plural form.) □ *The manager happily gave his consent to my request.*

**conservation** [kɑn sɚ 've ʃən] *n.* the practice of conserving, protecting, or preserving something, such as water, the state of the land, or other resources. (No plural form.) □ *The government encourages the conservation of natural gas.*

**consider** [kən 'sɪd ɚ] **1.** *tv.* to think carefully about something. (The object can be a clause with **that** ⑦.) □ *I considered taking a trip to the coast.* **2.** *tv.* to think of someone or something in a certain way. (The object can be a clause with **that** ⑦.) □ *Bill considers chocolate cake to be the best dessert.* **3.** *tv.* to take something into account. (The object can be a clause with **that** ⑦.) □ *Before you take a trip, consider your budget.*

**consist** [kən 'sɪst] **consist of** something *iv.* + *prep. phr.* to be made of something. □ *My dinner consists of roast beef, potatoes, and broccoli.*

**consonant** ['kɑn sə nənt] **1.** *n.* a speech sound that is made by restricting the flow of sound or air in the vocal tract; a speech sound that is not a vowel. (The word has different meanings depending on whether one is talking about sounds or spelling letters.) □ *The consonants among the sounds used in English are* p, t, k, b, d, g, f, h, s, m, n, ŋ, v, z, ʒ, ʃ, θ, ð, l, r, w, j. □ *There are two consonants in the word* thin. **2.** *n.* a letter of an alphabet that represents ①. □ *The consonants included in English spelling are* b, c, d, f, g, h, j, k, l, m, n, p, q, r, s, t, v, w, x, y, z. □ *There are three consonants in the word* sweet.

**constant** ['kɑn stənt] **1.** *adj.* continuous; continuing without stopping. (Adv: *constantly.*) □ *Please stop tormenting me with your constant questions.* **2.** *adj.* loyal; faithful; unchanging. (Adv: *constantly.*) □ *Bill's constant companion was his dog.* **3.** *n.* a figure, quality, or measurement that stays the same. □ *The temperature was always a constant in the experiment.*

**constellation** [kɑn stə 'le ʃən] *n.* a particular group of stars. □ *The astronomer described the different constellations to us.*

**constrict** [kən 'strɪkt] *tv.* to tighten something; to make something narrower; to make something contract. □ *Bill complained that a tie would constrict his breathing.*

**construct 1.** [kən 'strʌkt] *tv.* to build something; to put something together. □ *A famous architect constructed a model of a new cathedral.* **2.** ['kɑn strʌkt] *n.* a theory; a made-up idea. □ *My idea for a story is only a imaginary construct.*

**construction** [kən 'strʌk ʃən] **1.** *n.* the process of building. (No plural form.) □ *Construction of the building stopped during the winter months.* **2.** *n.* the business of building buildings; the business of constructing buildings. (No plural form.) □ *Mike has been in construction for twenty years.*

**consult** [kən 'sʌlt] **1.** *tv.* to seek advice or information from someone or something. □ *I consulted a weather report before planning the picnic.* **2.** *iv.* to offer and supply technical business advice as a profession. □ *I have been consulting for more than three years.* **3. consult with** someone *iv.* + *prep. phr.* to discuss something with someone, seeking advice. □ *I consulted with a lawyer about what to do.*

**consultant** [kən 'sʌl tənt] *n.* someone who consults; someone who is hired by a company to give advice. □ *The company hired a consultant to develop a new computer system.*

**consume** [kən 'sum] **1.** *tv.* to eat or drink something. □ *At our Thanksgiving dinner, we consumed an entire turkey.* **2.** *tv.* to use something; to use all of something. □ *The Smiths consume a lot of goods each year.*

C

**consumer** [kən 'su mɚ] *n.* someone who buys a product or a service. □ *A marketing company surveyed consumers.*

**consummate 1.** ['kɑn sə mət] *adj.* perfect; total and ideal. (Adv: *consummately.*) □ *After years of training, Mary is a consummate violinist.* **2.** ['kɑn sə met] *tv.* to fulfill something; to complete something; to make something complete. □ *Signing the contract consummated the deal.*

**cont.** an abbreviation of **contraction** ③.

**contact** ['kɑn tækt] **1.** *tv.* to communicate with someone; to get in touch with someone. □ *I contacted Bill to see how he was doing.* **2.** *tv.* to touch someone or something. □ *The copper wire must contact the brass screw to complete the circuit.* **3.** *n.* touching; coming together. (No plural form.) □ *When the fly came into contact with the sticky substance, it got stuck.* **4.** *n.* a person inside an organization through whom one can get needed information or favors. □ *Bill has contacts at the governor's office.* **5.** *n.* a metal part that touches another metal part, closing an electrical circuit. □ *When the contacts closed, the lights went on.*

**contagious** [kən 'te dʒəs] *adj.* [of a disease] easily passed from person to person. (Adv: *contagiously.*) □ *The flu is a highly contagious disease.*

**contain** [kən 'ten] **1.** *tv.* to hold someone or something; to have, hold, or include someone or something as a part of a larger thing. □ *Maple syrup contains a great deal of sugar.* **2.** *tv.* to hold back something; to restrain something; to keep something in control. □ *The spilled oil was contained in a small area along the coast.*

**container** [kən 'te nɚ] *n.* something that contains something. □ *The perfume was in a beautiful glass container.*

**contamination** [kən tæm ə 'ne ʃən] **1.** *n.* making something impure; polluting something. (No plural form.) □ *The contamination of the lake was caused by improper waste management.* **2.** *n.* a substance that causes ①. (No plural form.) □ *Laboratory tests showed a lot of contamination in the water.*

**contemplation** [kɑn təm 'ple ʃən] *n.* serious thought. (No plural form.) □ *Mike found relaxed contemplation almost impossible.*

**contempt** [kən 'tempt] *n.* hatred; loathing. (No plural form.) □ *Jane's voice was filled with contempt as she described her family.*

**content 1.** [kən 'tɛnt] *adj.* satisfied; pleased. (Adv: *contently.*) □ *Tom looked quite content as he lay sleeping.* **2.** ['kɑn tɛnt] *n.* something that is contained within something, such as the text of a book or the ingredients of food. (No plural form.) □ *This dessert has a high fat content.* **3. contents** ['kɑn tɛnts] *n.* the ingredients that make up something; everything that is contained within something. (Treated as plural. Sometimes singular. See also **table of contents.**) □ *Food producers must list the product's contents on its container.*

**contest 1.** ['kɑn tɛst] *n.* a competition that will determine a winner. □ *A pie-eating contest was held at the county fair.* **2.** [kən 'tɛst] *tv.* to challenge something, especially in a court of law. □ *The lawyer contested the judge's ruling.*

**contestant** [kən 'tɛs tənt] *n.* someone who competes in a contest; a competitor. □ *The contestants stretched their muscles before the race.*

**context** ['kɑn tɛkst] *n.* the words before and after another word that help determine its meaning. □ *I guessed the mean-*

*ing of the word from its context in the paragraph.*

**continent** ['kɑn tə nənt] *n.* one of the large landmasses of Earth: Africa, Australia, North America, South America, Antarctica, Europe, and Asia. ☐ *Explorers have traveled on every continent on Earth.*

**continental** [kɑn tə 'nɛn təl] **1.** *adj.* of or about a continent; contained within a continent. (Adv: *continentally.*) ☐ *Hawaii is not located in the continental United States.* **2.** *adj.* of or about the continent of Europe and the cultures and people found there. (England is sometimes included.) ☐ *I really enjoy continental cooking styles, and Spanish cooking in particular.*

**continual** [kən 'tɪn ju əl] *adj.* happening again and again; repeated; over and over. (Compare this with **continuous**. Adv: *continually.*) ☐ *I have grown tired of Jane's continual complaining about her job.*

**continue** [kən 'tɪn ju] **1.** *tv.* to make something keep on happening. (Takes a gerund as an object.) ☐ *Jane continued taking piano lessons until she was twenty.* **2.** *tv.* to resume something after an interruption. ☐ *The speaker continued speaking after the interruption.* **3.** *tv.* to postpone a trial until a later time. ☐ *The trial was continued until next month.* **4. continue to** do something *iv. + inf.* to do something again and again. ☐ *Jane continued to take piano lessons until she was twenty.* **5.** *iv.* to go on happening; to remain the same way. ☐ *The rain continued all afternoon.* **6.** *iv.* to resume after being stopped. ☐ *The television show continued after the announcement.*

**continuous** [kən 'tɪn ju əs] *adj.* without stopping; without an interruption; ongoing. (See also **continual**. Adv: *continuously.*) ☐ *I grew tired of Bill's continuous complaining about work.*

**contract 1.** ['kɑn trækt] *n.* a legal document that describes an agreement between two or more people or companies. ☐ *The contract outlined the carpenter's fees.* **2.** [kən 'trækt] *tv.* to hire someone under a contract for a specific project. ☐ *Bill contracted an artist to paint his portrait.* **3.** [kən 'trækt] *tv.* to catch a disease. ☐ *The child contracted chickenpox from a classmate.* **4.** [kən 'trækt] *iv.* to enter into an agreement with someone; to agree to do something by contract. ☐ *The author contracted to write a book.* **5.** [kən 'trækt] *iv.* to shrink; to shorten; to come together; to become narrow. ☐ *The metal lid contracted when it got cold, and I couldn't open the jar.*

**contraction** [kən 'træk ʃən] **1.** *n.* an amount of shrinking. (Plural only when referring to different kinds, types, instances, or varieties.) ☐ *The contraction of spending led to a recession.* Ⓒ *A series of budget contractions reduced spending to an unacceptable level.* **2.** *n.* the tensing of a muscle, especially of the uterus during childbirth. ☐ *When contractions were 3 minutes apart, the doctor was notified.* **3.** *n.* a shortened word, made by replacing a letter or letters with an apostrophe ('); the shortening of one or more spoken words by removing a sound or sounds. (Shortened to **cont.**) ☐ Wouldn't *is a contraction of* would not. ☐ Can't *is a contraction.*

**contrary 1.** ['kɑn trɛr i] *adj.* completely opposite; opposed. (Adv: *contrarily* [kɑn 'trɛr ə li].) ☐ *The results were contrary to what we expected.* **2.** [kən 'trɛr i, 'kɑn trɛr i] *adj.* stubborn; refusing to do what is wanted. (Adv: *contrarily* [kɑn 'trɛr ə li].) ☐ *The contrary student angered the teacher.*

**contrast 1.** ['kɑn træst] *n.* a noticeable difference; an obvious difference. ☐ *Mary's modern apartment is a real contrast to her old one.* **2.** ['kɑn træst] *n.*

noticeable differences between the light and dark parts of an image. (No plural form.) □ *My computer monitor has no contrast left. I will have to get a new one.* **3.** [kən 'træst] *tv.* to compare the differences found in two or more things. □ *The essay contrasts two characters in the book.* **4.** [kən 'træst] *iv.* to be noticeably different. □ *The mansion contrasted with the small houses that surrounded it.*

**control** [kən 'trol] **1.** *n.* authority; the power to direct someone or something. □ *We have no control over the weather.* **2.** *n.* a lever or other device used to operate machinery or something like a radio or television set. (Often plural.) □ *The front of the radio was covered with mysterious controls.* **3.** *tv.* to have power over something; to have authority over something; to direct someone or something; to rule someone or something. □ *No one can control the weather.* **4.** *tv.* to exercise the power to restrain, regulate, steer, guide, or command someone or something. □ *I could not control the car on the icy road.* **5. out of control** *phr.* not manageable; not restrained; disorderly. □ *We called the police when things got out of control.* **6. under control** *phr.* manageable; restrained and controlled; not ⑤. □ *We finally got things under control and functioning smoothly.*

**convenient** [kən 'vin jənt] **1.** *adj.* suitable. (Adv: *conveniently.*) □ *Tom picked a convenient time to come for a visit.* **2.** *adj.* available; within reach. (Adv: *conveniently.*) □ *The extra bedroom was convenient when guests stayed overnight.*

**convention** [kən 'vɛn ʃən] **1.** *n.* a large meeting; a group of people gathered together for a specific purpose. □ *The convention was held to discuss new things in medicine.* **2.** *n.* a formal agreement between countries. □ *The Geneva Convention addresses the treatment of prisoners of war.* **3.** *n.* the way things are typically done; the way things are expected to be done. □ *The rude guest paid no attention to manners or convention.*

**conventional** [kən 'vɛn ʃə nəl] *adj.* usual and typical; basic and standard. (Adv: *conventionally.*) □ *"Don't count your chickens before they hatch" is a piece of conventional wisdom.*

**conversation** [kɑn vɚ 'se ʃən] *n.* discussion; talk between people. (Plural only when referring to different kinds, types, instances, or varieties.) □ *The art of conversation is acquired through practice.* Ⓒ *Mary and Bill had long conversations on the telephone every night.*

**convey** [kən 've] **1.** *tv.* to take someone or something from one place to another. □ *Trucks conveyed the goods from New York to Chicago.* **2.** *tv.* to express something; to communicate something. (Fig. on ①.) □ *The expression on Bill's face conveyed his thoughts.*

**convince** [kən 'vɪns] *tv.* to persuade someone about something; to persuade someone that something is true. □ *What can I do to convince you of the truth?*

**convincing** [kən 'vɪn sɪŋ] **1.** *adj.* acting to persuade someone of something. (Adv: *convincingly.*) □ *Mary always has convincing arguments to justify her political views.* **2.** *adj.* realistic; like the real thing. (Adv: *convincingly.*) □ *The movie gave a convincing portrayal of medieval life.*

**convulsion** [kən 'vʌl ʃən] *n.* an uncontrollable, violent jerking of muscles. □ *The children collapsed on the floor in convulsions of laughter.*

**cook** ['kʊk] **1.** *n.* someone who prepares food to be eaten. □ *The cook prepared a three-course dinner.* **2.** *tv.* to prepare food for eating by heating it. □ *I cooked the chicken for an hour in the oven.* **3.** *iv.*

to prepare food; to work as ①. ☐ *I hate to cook!*

**cookbook** ['kʊk bʊk] *n.* a book that gives detailed instructions on how to prepare different kinds of food; a book of recipes. ☐ *The cookbook contained hundreds of recipes.*

**cookie** ['kʊk i] *n.* a small, hard, sweet cake made of flour, sugar, eggs, and other ingredients. ☐ *The jar was full of cookies for the children.*

**cool** ['kul] **1.** *adj.* between warm and cold; somewhat cold but not very cold. (Adv: *coolly.* Comp: *cooler;* sup: *coolest.*) ☐ *If it is not too cool, we'll go swimming this afternoon.* **2.** *adj.* calm, not excited; relaxed. (Informal. Adv: *coolly.* Comp: *cooler;* sup: *coolest.*) ☐ *Bill tried to remain cool after winning the contest.* **3.** *adj.* less than friendly; unfriendly; reserved. (Adv: *coolly.* Comp: *cooler;* sup: *coolest.*) ☐ *Lisa was cool toward Bob because she was mad at him.* **4.** *adj.* admirable; very good. (Informal. Comp: *cooler;* sup: *coolest.*) ☐ *It's so cool that Bill won the contest.* **5.** *tv.* to make something less warm. ☐ *The breeze from the window cooled the room.* **6.** *iv.* to become less warm. ☐ *The air cooled as evening approached.*

**cooperate** [ko 'ɑp ə ret] *iv.* to work together with someone to get something done; to unite in order to get something done more easily. ☐ *The children learned to cooperate and did the project together.*

**cop** ['kɑp] *n.* a police officer. (Informal.) ☐ *I called the cops when I saw a thief break into a car.*

**copier** ['kɑp i ɚ] *n.* a machine that makes copies of documents. ☐ *I went to the copier to make a copy of a letter I had just typed.*

**copper** ['kɑp ɚ] *n.* a soft, reddish-tan metal element. (No plural form.) ☐ *Pennies are made from copper.*

**copulate** ['kɑp jə let] *iv.* [for two creatures] to join together sexually, usually in order to breed. ☐ *Soon after the birds copulated, the female laid six eggs.*

**copulation** [kɑp jə 'le ʃən] *n.* sexual intercourse; joining together sexually. (Plural only when referring to different kinds, types, instances, or varieties. Number is expressed with *act(s) of copulation.*) ☐ *The copulation of frogs occurs early in the spring, near the water.* Ⓒ *Repeated copulations assured that the lioness would become pregnant.*

**copy** ['kɑp i] **1.** *n.* one item made to look like or work like another item; a duplicate; a replica. ☐ *This work of art is a copy of a well-known painting.* **2.** *n.* a single issue of a newspaper, book, or magazine. ☐ *Can I borrow your copy of the book?* **3.** *n.* written material that is ready to be edited or rewritten. (No plural form.) ☐ *The copy was so bad it had to be rewritten.* **4.** *tv.* to make a duplicate of something. ☐ *Bill copied the original article for his personal use.* **5.** *tv.* to imitate someone's actions. ☐ *Jimmy copied everything his older sister said.* **6.** *tv.* to reproduce written material by writing it by hand. ☐ *The teacher told the children to copy the word into their notebooks.* **7.** *tv.* to cheat on a test by writing the answers from someone else's paper. ☐ *The teacher saw the student copy the answers.*

**copyright** ['kɑp i rɑɪt] **1.** *n.* the legal right to produce, publish, or sell a book, play, song, movie, or other work of music or literature. ☐ *The composer owns the copyright to this music.* ☐ *A copyright is indicated by the symbol "©."* **2.** *tv.* to protect one's exclusive right to publish a work of music or literature by registering one's ownership with the government copyright office. ☐ *The publishing company copyrighted the novel.*

**cord** ['kord] **1.** *n.* a thick string; a thin rope. (Plural only when referring to different kinds, types, instances, or varieties.) □ *The package was tied with some strong cord.* Ⓒ *Nylon cords are usually stronger than cords made from natural fibers.* **2.** *n.* a wire with a protective covering, especially those that connect an electrical appliance to an electrical outlet. □ *I tripped over the cord of the television set.*

**cordless** ['kord ləs] *adj.* not having or needing an electrical power cord; operated by battery. (Adv: *cordlessly.*) □ *Mike takes a cordless razor with him when he travels.*

**core** ['kor] **1.** *n.* the center of something; the heart of something; the important part. □ *The core of the issue is money.* **2.** *n.* the hard part of the inside of a fruit, especially of an apple or a pear. □ *John accidentally ate the core of the apple.* **3.** *tv.* to cut ② from a piece of fruit. □ *The cook peeled and cored twelve apples.*

**cork** ['kork] **1.** *n.* the light, soft bark of the cork oak tree, used in many products. (Plural only when referring to different kinds, types, instances, or varieties.) □ *The bulletin board is made of cork.* Ⓒ *Not all corks are suitable for being made into seals for bottles.* **2.** *n.* the piece of shaped ① that fits in the neck of a bottle. □ *The wine bottle has a cork in it.* **3.** *adj.* made of ①. □ *I sealed the bottle with a cork plug.* **4.** *tv.* to seal a bottle by putting ② into the neck of the bottle. □ *Please cork the bottle after you have poured your drink.*

**corn** ['korn] **1.** *n.* a tall cereal plant producing large grains on corncobs, sometimes called *maize.* (No plural form. Number is expressed with *corn stalk(s).*) □ *The corn was harvested at the end of the summer.* **2.** *n.* the soft and tender young grains of corn eaten by humans as a vegetable. (No plural form. Number is expressed with *kernel(s) of corn* for the individual grains. *Ear(s) of corn* refers to grains of ① still attached to the **corncob** it grows on.) □ *John sprinkled some salt on his corn.* **3.** *n.* hard grains of ①, eaten by livestock or processed into other foods. (No plural form. Number is expressed with *ear(s) of corn* or *kernel(s) of corn* as in ②.) □ *A huge machine ground the corn into meal.* **4.** *n.* a hard, painful patch of skin on the foot or toe. □ *The corn was caused by shoes that didn't fit properly.* **5.** *adj.* made from ③; having ③ as an ingredient. □ *Corn syrup is used to sweeten many food products.*

**corncob** AND **cob** ['korn kɑb, 'kɑb] *n.* the cylinder of fiber that corn grows on. □ *We pick corn fresh in the field and then roast it while it is still on the cob.*

**corner** ['kor nɚ] **1.** *n.* the point where two lines meet; the line formed where two surfaces meet. □ *This piece of paper has four corners.* **2.** *n.* the space where two walls meet. □ *The cat lay curled in one corner of the room.* **3.** *n.* one of the four squared areas nearest to the intersection of two streets. □ *The school is located at the corner of Main Street and 4th Street.* □ *I waited on the corner for the bus.* **4.** *tv.* to trap someone or some creature in a place or situation from which it is difficult or impossible to escape. □ *The mouse was cornered by the cat.*

**cornfield** ['korn fild] *n.* a field where corn is grown; a field of corn plants. □ *The cows are in the cornfield, eating the corn.*

**cornflakes** ['korn fleks] *n.* a breakfast cereal of toasted flakes of corn. (Treated as singular or plural.) □ *I poured some milk over a bowl of cornflakes for breakfast.*

**corporation** [kor pə 're ʃən] *n.* a business, firm, or company. □ *Mary* *works for a corporation that produces computers.*

**corpse** ['korps] *n.* a dead body. □ *A corpse was found in the park.*

**corral** [kə 'ræl] **1.** *n.* a fenced area where horses and cattle are kept. □ *The corral behind the barn has three horses in it.* **2.** *tv.* to put livestock into ①. □ *The cowboys corralled the cattle to brand them.*

**correct** [kə 'rɛkt] **1.** *adj.* right; without error; true. (Adv: *correctly.*) □ *The correct answers are given at the back of the book.* **2.** *adj.* proper; acceptable. (Adv: *correctly.*) □ *I learned the correct way to wrap a gift.* **3.** *tv.* to mark answers on a test as right or wrong; to point out the mistakes. □ *Mary likes teaching but hates to correct papers.* **4.** *tv.* to fix a mistake; to change a wrong answer to the right answer; to make something right. □ *I corrected my mistake in the report.*

**correction** [kə 'rɛkt ʃən] *n.* a change that is made when something wrong is replaced with something right. □ *My teacher's corrections on my paper were written in red ink.*

**correspond** [kor ə 'spɑnd] **1. correspond (to something)** *iv.* (+ *prep. phr.*) to match (with something else); to follow the pattern (of something). □ *The peak on this graph corresponds to an increase in sales last year.* **2. correspond (with someone)** *iv.* (+ *prep. phr.*) to exchange letters (with someone). □ *The two poets corresponded for many years without ever meeting.*

**corrupt** [kə 'rʌpt] **1.** *adj.* not honest; [of politicians] easily influenced by the payment of money. (Adv: *corruptly.*) □ *The reporter exposed the corrupt politician.* **2.** *tv.* to make someone become bad; to make a good person become bad; to make a moral person become immoral. □ *Bill corrupted his younger brother by teaching him to smoke.* **3.** *tv.* to ruin something in the execution of a process. □ *The computer file was corrupted during the transfer.*

**cost** ['kɔst] **1.** *n.* the price of something; the amount of money that one must pay to buy something. (Plural only when referring to different kinds, types, instances, or varieties.) □ *The cost of seeing a movie is seven dollars.* Ⓒ *We have to control costs carefully, or we will not make a profit.* **2.** *n.* a sacrifice; the loss of something in order to achieve something. □ *Catching a cold was the cost of not wearing a coat.* **3.** *tv., irreg.* to require a specific amount of money for purchase. (Pt/pp: *cost.*) □ *The groceries cost two hundred dollars.* **4.** *tv., irreg.* to cause the loss of something; to sacrifice something. □ *The mistake cost Jane her job.* **5.** *tv., irreg.* to require the expenditure of time, work, or energy. □ *This silly project is going to cost me a full day's work.*

**costly** ['kɔst li] **1.** *adj.* costing a lot of money; expensive. (Comp: *costlier;* sup: *costliest.*) □ *The car needs some costly repairs.* **2.** *adj.* serious; troublesome; unfortunate. (Comp: *costlier;* sup: *costliest.*) □ *Driving drunk can be a costly mistake.*

**costume** ['kɑs tum] *n.* clothes that are worn when someone is pretending to be someone else or from another time or place; clothes that represent another culture, time period, or person, as used in the theater. □ *The actors in the play had beautiful costumes.*

**cot** ['kɑt] *n.* a narrow bed made of a piece of canvas stretched over a frame, used especially for camping. □ *The hotel sent an extra cot to our room for our daughter.*

**cottage** ['kɑt ɪdʒ] *n.* a small house, especially a small home in the country; a vacation house. □ *Sue and Bill bought a cottage near the lake.*

**cotton** ['kɑt n] **1.** *n.* a soft white fiber used to make yarn, thread, and fabric. (No plural form. Number is expressed with *bale(s) of cotton.*) □ *Bales of cotton were loaded onto the truck.* **2.** *n.* cloth woven of ①. (Plural only when referring to different kinds, types, instances, or varieties.) □ *The summer dress was made of cotton.* 🄲 *Not all cottons will provide long wear.* **3.** *n.* the plant that produces ①. (Plural only when referring to different kinds, types, instances, or varieties.) □ *Cotton is a major crop of the southern United States.* 🄲 *We planted a number of different cottons until we found one that would do well in our soils.* **4.** *adj.* made out of ① or ②. □ *A cotton dress kept me cool on the hot day.*

**couch** ['kɑʊtʃ] *n.* a long piece of furniture that two or more people can sit on or that someone can lie down on; a sofa. □ *The children sat on the couch while watching TV.*

**cougar** ['ku gɚ] *n.* a large, tan, wild cat; a mountain lion. □ *Cougars can be found in the mountains in some states.*

**cough** ['kɔf] **1.** *n.* the act or sound of forcing air from the lungs quickly and with force, making a dry, rough noise through the throat. □ *The doctor heard Bill's cough and prescribed some medicine.* **2.** *iv.* to force air out of the lungs as in ①. □ *The smoke-filled room made us cough.*

**cough drop** ['kɔf drɑp] *n.* a piece of medicated material—often like candy—that is held in the mouth to soothe a sore throat and prevent coughing. □ *A cough drop helped me to stop coughing.*

**could** ['kʊd] **1.** *aux.* <the past form of **can** ①, expressing ability.> □ *I thought I could do it, but I was not strong enough.* **2.** *aux.* <the past form of **can** ②, expressing permission.> □ *Yesterday, Aunt Mary said I could go to the park.* **3.** *aux.* <a form of **can** ②, used in making polite requests.> □ *Could you please speak more clearly?* **4.** *aux.* <a form of **can** ① expressing possibility, or an explanation.> □ *Where is Bill? Do you think he could be waiting in the other office?*

**couldn't** ['kʊd nt] **1.** *cont.* "could not"; was not able [to do something]. □ *Mike couldn't remember where he had parked his car.* **2.** *cont.* "could not"; wouldn't you please? □ *Couldn't you hurry up a little bit?*

**could've** ['kʊd əv] *cont.* "could have." (Where **have** is an auxiliary.) □ *Tom could've won the race if he had tried harder.*

**council** ['kɑʊn səl] *n.* a group of people who are appointed or elected to make laws for a city, school, church, or other organization. (Compare this with **counsel.**) □ *The town council meets twice a month.*

**counsel** ['kɑʊn səl] **1.** *tv.* to advise someone; to give someone advice. (Compare this with **council.**) □ *Mary counseled her daughter about good study habits.* **2.** *n.* advice; a piece of advice. (No plural form.) □ *Bill always received good counsel from his parents.*

**counselor** ['kɑʊn sə lɚ] **1.** *n.* someone who advises people; someone who gives advice. □ *A counselor at our school helps students find jobs.* **2.** *n.* someone who is in charge of children at a camp. □ *The camp counselor taught the children to swim.* **3.** *n.* a lawyer. (Also a term of address for a lawyer.) □ *"Approach the bench, counselor," the judge instructed.*

**count** ['kɑʊnt] **1.** *n.* the total of people or things obtained after one has figured out how many there are. □ *I took a count of the people at the meeting.* **2.** *tv.* to figure out how many; to determine how many. □ *The child counted the blocks.* **3. can count** *iv.* to be considered as part of something; to be included. □ *Those points don't count because you were cheating!* **4. count on someone or something** *phr.* to rely on someone or something; to depend on someone or something. □ *I can count on Bill to get the job done.*

**countable** ['kaʊnt ə bəl] *adj.* able to be counted or enumerated; subject to being counted. □ *The noun* cattle *is plural and is not countable.*

**counter** ['kaʊn tɚ] **1.** *n.* a flat surface at which customers sit or stand to be served in a fast-food store, bank, or other establishment. □ *The clerk put all my purchases on the counter.* **2.** *n.* [in a kitchen] a flat surface where food is prepared. □ *I placed the cake on the counter and sliced it into eight pieces.* **3.** *n.* a device that is used to count objects or people; a device that keeps track of the number of objects or people. □ *The bank teller used a mechanical counter to count the pennies.*

**counterfeit** ['kaʊn tɚ fɪt] **1.** *adj.* fake; imitation; not genuine. □ *This counterfeit money is obviously an imitation.* **2.** *n.* an illegal copy; a fake. □ *The art collector did not know that the painting was a counterfeit.* **3.** *tv.* to make an illegal copy of something, especially money. □ *The criminals were arrested for counterfeiting bonds.*

**country** ['kʌn tri] **1.** *n.* a nation, including its land and its people; a political subdivision. □ *The tiny country declared its independence.* **2.** *n.* land without many people or buildings; the opposite of *city.* (No plural form in this sense.) □ *We could see nothing but miles and miles of country.* **3.** *adj.* <the adj. use of ②.> □ *When we drive on country roads, we see a lot of trees and farms along the way.*

**county** ['kaʊn ti] *n.* a political division of most U.S. states. □ *Chicago is one of several cities in Cook County, Illinois.*

**couple** ['kʌp əl] **1.** *n.* two people, usually male and female, usually sharing a romantic interest. (Treated as singular when referring to a unit and plural when referring to the individuals.) □ *The young couple got engaged before they finished college.* **2. a couple of people or things** *phr.* two; two or three; a few; some; not many. (**Couple** is treated as plural, but not countable.) □ *Bill grabbed a couple of beers from the refrigerator.*

**coupon** ['ku pɑn, 'kju pɑn] *n.* a printed form that offers a discount for a product or service. □ *The manufacturer mailed out coupons for its products.*

**courage** ['kɚ ɪdʒ] *n.* bravery; a lack of fear. (No plural form.) □ *The young soldiers showed a lot of courage in battle.*

**courageous** [kə 're dʒəs] *adj.* fearless; facing danger in spite of fear. (Adv: *courageously.*) □ *The courageous firefighter saved the child's life.*

**courier** ['kɚ i ɚ] *n.* a messenger; someone who transports documents or other valuable items. □ *A courier delivered the package to our office.*

**course** ['kors] **1.** *n.* the pathway or route of someone or something. □ *The balloon took an upward course.* **2.** *n.* a sequence of actions. □ *The university requires a certain course of study for each major.* **3.** *n.* a class offered by a school or an instructor. □ *Mary took a biology course at the local university.* **4.** *n.* one of the parts of a meal in which parts are served separately. □ *Dessert was the final course of the meal.* **5.** *n.* the land where certain sporting events take place, such as golfing and racing. □ *The golf course was green and lush.* **6.** *iv.* [for water] to flow in a river; [for tears] to run down one's face. □ *Tears of joy coursed down my face when I heard the good news.*

C

**court** ['kort] **1.** *n.* the place where legal matters are decided and the people who are present there, such as a judge and other officials. (Plural only when referring to different kinds, types, instances, or varieties.) □ *I have to go to court today to give evidence in a trial.* Ⓒ *There are a number of different courts in the federal courthouse.* **2. the court** *n.* the judge, often speaking for the entire **court** ①. (No plural form. Treated as singular.) □ *The court will now hear the prosecutor's evidence.* **3.** *n.* the space where certain games such as basketball and tennis are played. □ *We had seats right near the court and saw everything that happened in the basketball game.*

**courteous** ['kɚ ti əs] *adj.* showing courtesy; polite; well mannered. (Adv: *courteously.*) □ *The courteous child always said "please" and "thank you."*

**courtesy** ['kɚ tɪs i] **1.** *n.* a state of being polite and showing good manners. (No plural form.) □ *The rude man was not known for his courtesy.* **2.** *n.* an act of kindness; a favor; a thoughtful act. □ *Mary extends many courtesies to her houseguests.*

**courthouse** ['kort hɑʊs] **1.** *n., irreg.* a building containing the rooms where court is held. (Pl: [...hɑʊ zəz].) □ *The case was heard in the town's courthouse.* **2.** *n., irreg.* the building that houses the government offices—including the county court—of a particular county. □ *Bill and Lisa got their marriage license at the courthouse.*

**courtroom** ['kort rum] *n.* a room where a session of court is held. □ *When the judge enters the courtroom, everyone stands up.*

**cousin** ['kʌz ən] *n.* the child of one's aunt or uncle; the nephew or niece of one's parent. □ *When I visited my aunt, I ate dinner with my cousins.*

**cove** ['kov] *n.* a small bay along the coast. □ *Our boat drifted into the tiny cove.*

**cover** ['kʌv ɚ] **1.** *n.* the protective top—like a lid—for something. □ *The cover for the garbage can is missing.* **2.** *n.* the front and back of a book or magazine. □ *The book had a beautifully designed cover.* **3.** *n.* a blanket. □ *Tom put another cover on his bed because it was cold.* **4.** *n.* something that is hiding a secret; a legal business that is operating as a disguise for an illegal business. □ *This shop is just a cover for the smugglers.* **5.** *tv.* to place something on top of something else to protect or hide it; to spread something on top of something else to protect or hide it. □ *I covered the leftovers and put them in the refrigerator.* **6.** *tv.* to coat the surface of something; to spread over something. □ *I covered the wall with a coat of paint.* **7.** *tv.* to amount to enough money to pay for something. □ *The insurance check did not cover all the car repairs.* **8.** *tv.* to include something; to discuss or reveal something. □ *The professor covered one chapter with each lecture.* **9.** *tv.* to travel a certain distance. □ *The travelers covered about two hundred miles a day.* **10.** *tv.* to occupy a certain area; to extend over a certain area. □ *Our farm covers 640 acres.* **11.** *tv.* to shelter someone or something; to provide shelter for someone or something. □ *The tent covered us during the rain.*

**cow** ['kɑʊ] **1.** *n.* an adult female of a kind of very large animal that provides milk and is eaten for meat. (See also **bull**.) □ *The farmer milked the cows every morning.* □ *Cows eat grass and provide us with beef and leather when they are slaughtered.* **2.** *n.* the female of certain animals, including the elephant. □ *The mature cow looked small next to the large bull elephant.*

**coward** ['kɑʊ ɚd] *n.* someone who has no courage; someone who runs away from danger. □ *The coward was frightened by shadows on the wall.*

**cowardice** ['kaʊ ɚ dɪs] *n.* lack of courage. (No plural form.) □ *Cowardice prevented Bill from accepting the challenge.*

**cowboy** ['kaʊ bɔɪ] *n.* someone, usually a male, who works on a cattle ranch. □ *The cattle were rounded up by cowboys at the end of the day.*

**coworker** ['ko wɚ kɚ] *n.* a fellow worker; someone with whom one works. □ *On his first day of work, Mike met all his coworkers.*

**coyote** [kaɪ 'ot (i)] *n.* an animal, similar to a large, skinny dog, that lives in western North America. □ *We heard the coyotes howling in the desert.*

**cozy** ['ko zi] *adj.* snug; warm and comfortable. (Adv: *cozily.* Comp: *cozier;* sup: *coziest.*) □ *The Smiths own a cozy little cabin by a lake.*

**crab** ['kræb] **1.** *n.* an edible sea creature with a hard shell, four pairs of legs, and one pair of claws. □ *Along the beach, we saw many crabs.* **2.** *n.* the meat of ① eaten as food. (No plural form.) □ *I love to eat fresh crab.* **3.** *n.* an unhappy person who complains a lot. □ *After he lost the race, Mike was a real crab.*

**crabby** ['kræb i] *adj.* unhappy and making complaints. (Adv: *crabbily.* Comp: *crabbier;* sup: *crabbiest.*) □ *Anne is always crabby in the morning.*

**crack** ['kræk] **1.** *n.* the line that is made in something when it splits or breaks; a narrow opening in something or between two things. □ *The old wall had many cracks in it.* **2.** *n.* a short, sharp noise like the noise of a powerful slap. □ *The whip made a crack as it hit the horse's back.* **3.** *n.* a remark that is intended to hurt or make someone feel bad. □ *Anne made a crack about my cooking.* **4.** *tv.* to break something without separating it into pieces; to fracture something. □ *The movers cracked the pitcher when they moved it.* **5.** *tv.* to strike someone; to hit someone somewhere. □ *I cracked the robber over the head with an empty bottle.* **6.** *iv.* [for something] to break without separating into pieces. □ *The vase fell and cracked.*

**cracker** ['kræk ɚ] *n.* a flat, thin, square, unsweetened biscuit, often salted. □ *For a snack, we had cheese and crackers.*

**cradle** ['kred l] **1.** *n.* a small, rocking bed for a baby or a doll. □ *I placed the baby in her cradle and rocked her to sleep.* **2.** *n.* the place where something begins; the origin of something. □ *Greece is called the cradle of civilization.* **3.** *tv.* to hold a baby in one's arms while rocking it back and forth; to hold something carefully. □ *The new father gently cradled the infant in his arms.*

**craft** ['kræft] **1.** *n.* a special skill for creating something; a special talent. □ *After she retired, Sue learned the craft of making pottery.* **2.** *n., irreg.* a boat, especially a small one. (Pl: *craft.*) □ *Dave rowed the craft away from the pier.* **3.** *tv.* to build or create something that requires skill or talent. □ *The early explorers crafted canoes from huge trees.*

**craftsman** ['kræfts mən] *n., irreg.* someone who builds something by hand. (Pl: **craftsmen.**) □ *We bought an unusual wooden table from a craftsman at the art show.*

**craftsmen** ['kræfts mən] pl of **craftsman.**

**cram** ['kræm] **1.** *tv.* to force someone or something into a small space. □ *I crammed as many clothes as I could into the suitcase.* **2.** *tv.* to fill a space too full; to put too many things or people into a space. □ *The decorator crammed the room with antique furniture.*

**crane** ['kren] **1.** *n.* a bird with long legs and a long neck—usually feeding on fish, frogs, etc. □ *I saw a flock of cranes* *near the bay.* **2.** *n.* a large machine with a movable arm that lifts and moves very heavy things. □ *The construction worker operated the crane skillfully.*

**crank** ['kræŋk] **1.** *n.* an arm or lever that transfers rotating motion to a shaft or axle. □ *The first automobiles were started by turning a crank.* **2.** *tv.* to make something work by turning ①. □ *John cranked the hand mixer to beat the eggs.*

**crash** ['kræʃ] **1.** *n.* the loud sound of something hitting something else. □ *When we heard a crash, we ran to see what had fallen.* **2.** *n.* a sudden economic disaster; a time when the stock market falls rapidly. □ *Bob predicted that a market crash was overdue.* **3.** *n.* a vehicle accident; a loud collision of vehicles. □ *The crash involved five cars.* **4.** *tv.* to cause a loud collision of a vehicle and something else. □ *John lost control of the car and crashed it against a tree.* **5.** *iv.* to make a sudden, loud noise. □ *Something crashed in the middle of the night and woke me up.* **6.** *iv.* [for a computer] to stop working. □ *Suddenly, my computer crashed and would not work.*

**crate** ['kret] **1.** *n.* a rough wooden or plastic shipping box. □ *The goods were shipped overseas in a crate.* **2. crate something (up)** *tv. + obj. (+ adv.)* to pack something in ①. □ *The goods were crated up in the warehouse.*

**crave** ['krev] *tv.* to have a very strong desire for something; to want something very badly. □ *Anne craved unusual foods when she was pregnant.*

**crawl** ['krɔl] **1.** *iv.* to move on one's hands and knees; to move forward in a horizontal position. □ *Most babies learn to crawl before they walk.* **2.** *iv.* [for something] to move very slowly. (Fig. on ①.) □ *Traffic was crawling on the highway this morning.*

**crayon** ['kre ɑn] *n.* a colored stick of wax, used for drawing on paper or making pictures. □ *The child used crayons to draw a picture of a house.*

**crazy** ['krez i] **1.** *adj.* insane; mentally ill. (Adv: *crazily.* Comp: *crazier;* sup: *craziest.*) □ *Because the man behaved so strangely, Mary thought he was crazy.* **2.** *adj.* stupid; foolish. (Adv: *crazily.* Comp: *crazier;* sup: *craziest.*) □ *Driving while drunk is crazy.* **3.** *adj.* wild; bizarre. (Adv: *crazily.* Comp: *crazier;* sup: *craziest.*) □ *I won't listen to any more of your crazy talk.*

**cream** ['krim] **1.** *n.* the fatty part of cow's milk that rises to the top. (No plural form.) □ *Sue always drinks her coffee with cream in it.* **2.** *n.* a soft, thick substance used to benefit or carry medicine to the skin. □ *This cream will relieve dry skin.* **3.** *tv.* to mash something to a creamy texture. □ *The first step in making cake is to cream the butter and sugar together.*

**cream cheese** ['krim tʃiz] *n.* a soft, thick, white cheese made from cream and milk. (No plural form.) □ *I spread cream cheese on my bread.*

**creamy** ['krim i] *adj.* containing a lot of cream; as smooth as cream. (Adv: *creamily.* Comp: *creamier;* sup: *creamiest.*) □ *The cake had a creamy frosting.*

**crease** ['kris] **1.** *n.* a deep fold; a line made in something by folding it and pressing down along the fold. □ *I ironed my trousers along the crease.* **2.** *tv.* to make a line in something, such as paper or fabric, by folding it and pressing down. □ *I creased the paper when I folded it in half.*

**create** [kri 'et] **1.** *tv.* to bring something new into being; to invent something. □ *The inventor created a new time-saving device.* **2.** *tv.* to cause something to happen; to bring about something. □ *Music creates a relaxing atmosphere.*

**creation** [kri 'e ʃən] **1.** *n.* bringing something new into being. (No plural form.)

☐ *The artist explained the creation of his work in detail.* **2.** *n.* the process of bringing the universe into being. (No plural form.) ☐ *The substances that make up the earth have been around since creation.* **3.** *n.* the universe; everything created by God. (No plural form.) ☐ *All the creatures of creation are part of the life on this planet.* **4.** *n.* something that is invented; something that is produced or made for the first time. ☐ *The chef was proud of his new creation.*

**creative** [kri 'e tɪv] *adj.* able to think of new ideas or new ways to solve problems; able to develop works of art. (Adv: *creatively.*) ☐ *Susie is very creative and likes to draw and paint.*

**creature** ['kri tʃɚ] *n.* a living animal; a living being. ☐ *A little creature ran across the yard.*

**credible** ['krɛd ə bəl] *adj.* believable; worthy of belief; worthy of trust. (Adv: *credibly.*) ☐ *Is the man's story credible, or do you think he is lying?*

**credit** ['krɛd ɪt] **1.** *n.* an arrangement allowing a person to purchase goods or services now and pay later, or to borrow money now and pay it back later. (No plural form.) ☐ *If you can prove that you have a job and always pay your bills on time, the store might give you credit.* **2.** *n.* the amount of money in an account; an account balance greater than zero. ☐ *My records show a credit of $120.00 reflecting your recent payment.* **3.** *n.* an amount of money that is added to an account. ☐ *The bank teller recorded a credit to my account after I made a payment.* **4.** *n.* recognition given to someone for having done something. (No plural form.) ☐ *The author was not given proper credit for writing the book.* **5.** *n.* mention of someone's work on a book, movie, or performance appearing in a list of similar writers, artists, or technicians. ☐ *I got a credit in the movie for saying just one word on camera.*

**credit card** ['krɛd ɪt 'kɑrd] *n.* a plastic card that allows someone to use **credit** ① extended by a bank. ☐ *I bought a new refrigerator using my credit card.*

C

**creek** ['krik] *n.* a small, narrow river; a small stream. ☐ *The children threw rocks into the creek.*

**creep** ['krip] **1.** *iv., irreg.* to move slowly, with the body close to the ground. (Pt/pp: *creeped* or **crept**.) ☐ *The cat slowly crept along the floor.* **2.** *iv., irreg.* to grow along a surface; to grow up a wall. ☐ *Over the years, the ivy slowly crept up the side of the house.* **3.** *n.* a very slow movement. (No plural form.) ☐ *The quiet creep of the cat brought it very close to the mouse.*

**crept** ['krɛpt] a pt/pp of **creep**.

**crew** ['kru] **1.** *n.* a group of people who work together, especially on a ship, on a plane, at a theater, etc. ☐ *The crew worked very hard to anchor the ship.* **2.** *n.* the people on the team that competes in boat races. ☐ *The crew rowed the boat up and down the river.*

**crib** ['krɪb] **1.** *n.* a baby's bed that has sides so the baby can't fall out. ☐ *The infant slept in the crib.* **2.** *n.* a storage shed for grain. ☐ *The farmer found a dead mouse in the crib where the corn is stored.*

**cricket** ['krɪk ɪt] **1.** *n.* a small, long-legged insect, the male of which makes a chirping noise by rubbing his front wings together. ☐ *From the porch we could hear the crickets chirping.* **2.** *n.* an outdoor sport played in England with a (flat) bat and a ball. (No plural form.) ☐ *When visiting London, I watched games of cricket on television.*

**crime** ['krɑɪm] *n.* the breaking of laws in general. (Plural only when referring to different kinds, types, instances, or varieties.) ☐ *The president announced a program to fight crime.* Ⓒ *Murder and arson are two of the most serious crimes.*

C

**criminal** ['krɪm ə nəl] *n.* someone who commits a crime; someone who breaks a law. □ *The clever criminal was never caught by the police.*

**crises** ['kraɪ siz] pl of crisis.

**crisis** ['kraɪ sɪs] *n., irreg.* a serious and threatening situation, the resolution of which will determine the future. (Pl: crises.) □ *The theft became an international crisis.*

**crisp** ['krɪsp] **1.** *adj.* easily broken; easily snapped into parts. (Adv: *crisply.* Comp: *crisper;* sup: *crispest.*) □ *I spread butter on a crisp piece of toast.* **2.** *adj.* fresh; firm. (Adv: *crisply.* Comp: *crisper;* sup: *crispest.*) □ *The bank teller gave me two crisp, new ten-dollar bills.* **3.** *adj.* [of air] cool and refreshing. (Adv: *crisply.* Comp: *crisper;* sup: *crispest.*) □ *We walked in the park on a crisp autumn day.*

**critic** ['krɪt ɪk] **1.** *n.* someone who writes evaluations of artistic works or performances. □ *Art critics praised the young artist's work.* **2.** *n.* someone who finds fault with people or things. □ *Most of the students were critics of the poorly run school system.*

**criticism** ['krɪt ə sɪz əm] **1.** *n.* the process of evaluating and presenting statements that analyze and make judgements about something or someone's performance. (No plural form.) □ *Criticism is an important part of the study of literature.* **2.** *n.* a critical remark or statement. (Usually negative unless specifically positive.) □ *Billy was upset by his parents' constant criticism.*

**criticize** ['krɪt ə saɪz] **1.** *tv.* to find fault with someone or something. □ *A long newspaper article criticized the mayor's actions.* **2.** *iv.* to judge the good and bad points of something. (Usually negative unless specifically positive.) □ *Please don't criticize all the time!*

**croak** ['krok] **1.** *n.* the noise that a frog makes. □ *The frog made a loud croak.* **2.** *iv.* to make the characteristic sound of a frog. □ *We could hear the frogs croaking down by the swamp.* **3.** *iv.* to make a noise like ①. □ *The choking man croaked and gasped.*

**crocodile** ['krɑk ə daɪl] **1.** *n.* a large, dangerous reptile with many teeth and a powerful tail. □ *Crocodiles live in the rivers of many parts of the world.* **2.** *adj.* made from the skin of ①. □ *Crocodile shoes are very expensive.*

**crook** ['krʊk] **1.** *n.* a criminal; a thief. □ *The police caught the crook who stole my car.* **2.** *n.* a bent part of something; a hooked part of something. □ *Dave held my baby in the crook of his arm.* **3.** *tv.* to bend something; to make a bend or a hook in something. □ *The glove won't go on because you've crooked your fingers.* **4.** *iv.* to bend. □ *The top of the tree crooks a bit toward the house.*

**crooked** ['krʊk əd] **1.** *adj.* bent; not straight; twisted. (Adv: *crookedly.*) □ *The picture on the wall is crooked.* **2.** *adj.* not honest; thieving; criminal. (Adv: *crookedly.*) □ *The crooked employee was caught stealing money from the company.*

**crop** ['krɑp] **1.** *n.* a plant or food product grown and harvested by a farmer. □ *What types of crops are grown in this state?* **2.** *tv.* to cut or trim something. □ *The photographer cropped the photo to fit in the frame.*

**cross** ['krɔs] **1.** *n.* a sign or structure in a form similar to an X. □ *Tom drew a cross on the wall exactly where he planned to drill the hole.* **2.** *n.* a vertical post with a horizontal post attached to it near the top that people were hung on as a punishment in ancient times. □ *In biblical times, criminals were often executed on a cross.* **3.** *n.* the shape of the Christian symbol, representing ② on which Jesus died. □ *The cross is the* *main symbol of Christianity.* **4.** *n.* a combination or blend; a hybrid. □ *Anne's expression was a cross between wonder and disbelief.* **5.** *tv.* to move from one side of something to the other; to go across something. □ *We need to cross the street because the restaurant is on the other side.* **6.** *tv.* to form an intersection with something else. □ *Main Street crosses First Avenue downtown.* **7.** *tv.* to anger someone; to upset someone. □ *Don't cross Dave when he is in a bad mood.* **8.** *tv.* to breed species or varieties of animals in such a way as to give yet a different creature. □ *A mule is the result of crossing a horse and a donkey.* **9.** *iv.* to make an intersection; to form the shape of ②. □ *State Street and Madison Street cross in downtown Chicago.*

**crow** ['kro] **1.** *n.* a large, black bird. □ *The yard was filled with crows.* **2.** *iv.* [for a rooster] to make its loud noise. □ *The rooster crowed at sunrise.*

**crowd** ['krɑʊd] **1.** *n.* a large group of people; a gathering of people. □ *A crowd waited to enter the museum for the special exhibit.* **2.** *iv.* [for many people or creatures] to gather closely together. □ *The fans crowded around the famous singer.*

**crown** ['krɑʊn] **1.** *n.* the circular metal object worn on the heads of royal persons. □ *The queen's crown was decorated with jewels.* **2.** *n.* something that is worn around the head like ①. □ *The actress wore a crown of flowers in her hair.* **3.** *n.* the office or authority of a monarch. (No plural form.) □ *In a modern monarchy, the crown has little authority.* **4.** *n.* the top part of something, especially a tooth, a hat, or a mountain. □ *A wide ribbon circled the crown of the hat.* **5.** *tv.* to make someone king or queen. □ *The prince was crowned king when he reached eighteen.*

**crude** ['krud] **1.** *adj.* in a natural state; not refined; raw. (Adv: *crudely.* Comp: *cruder;* sup: *crudest.*) □ *Crude oil has to be refined before it can be used.* **2.** *adj.* vulgar; without manners. (Adv: *crudely.* Comp: *cruder;* sup: *crudest.*) □ *Bill's crude behavior embarrassed everyone at the table.* **3.** *adj.* not expertly done; rough; awkward. (Adv: *crudely.* Comp: *cruder;* sup: *crudest.*) □ *I could only make a crude translation of the document.*

**cruel** ['kru əl] **1.** *adj.* evil; wicked; fond of causing pain. (Adv: *cruelly.* Comp: *crueler;* sup: *cruelest.*) □ *The cruel man kicked his dog.* **2.** *adj.* causing pain; causing suffering. (Adv: *cruelly.* Comp: *crueler;* sup: *cruelest.*) □ *The student never forgot the teacher's cruel words.*

**cruelty** ['kru əl ti] *n.* harshness; the qualities of causing pain and distress. (Plural only when referring to different kinds, types, instances, or varieties.) □ *This organization seeks to prevent cruelty to animals.* Ⓒ *The war criminal was tried for cruelties committed during the war.*

**cruise** ['kruz] **1.** *n.* a trip on a boat for pleasure; a vacation on a boat or ship. □ *The Smiths took a cruise to Alaska.* **2.** *iv.* to travel at a constant speed. □ *My car can cruise along at 70 miles per hour on the highway.*

**crumb** ['krʌm] *n.* a particle of bread or cake. □ *I brushed crumbs from the cake off the kitchen counter.*

**crunch** ['krʌntʃ] **1.** *n.* the sound of something snapping and breaking, especially of something being chewed. □ *The hard cookie made a loud crunch as the child bit into it.* **2.** *n.* the pressure felt when many deadlines happen at the same time. □ *There is always a crunch at work toward the end of the year.*

**crunchy** ['krʌn tʃi] *adj.* making a breaking noise when chewed. (Adv: *crunchily.*

Comp: *crunchier;* sup: *crunchiest.*) □ *Bill likes his cookies crunchy rather than soft.*

C

**crusade** [kru 'sed] **1. the Crusades** *n.* the religious expeditions of the Christians against the Muslims in the twelfth and thirteenth centuries. (Treated as plural.) □ *Soldiers and knights fought in the Crusades.* **2.** *n.* a fight against something bad; a fight for something good. □ *Lisa's organization led a crusade against cruelty to animals.* **3.** *iv.* to fight against something bad; to fight for something good. □ *The researcher crusaded against cancer.*

**crush** ['krʌʃ] **1.** *tv.* to squeeze or press on something with great force and collapse it. □ *The box was crushed under the heavier crates.* **2.** *tv.* to break something into small pieces by pressing or pounding. □ *The huge machine crushed the rocks into small stones.* **3.** *tv.* to force juice out of fruit by squeezing it. □ *They used their bare feet to crush the grapes.* **4.** *n.* a strong desire for someone; an infatuation with someone. □ *John had a crush on one of his classmates.*

**crust** ['krʌst] *n.* the hard outside layer of something, including the earth, a pie, a loaf of bread, etc. □ *The crust of the pie was delicious.*

**crutch** ['krʌtʃ] *n.* a support under the arms that helps a lame person walk. □ *After I broke my leg, I used crutches for a long time.*

**cry** ['krɑɪ] **1.** *n.* an expression of pain or anger; a loud expression of emotion. □ *The baby gave a cry as her mother walked away.* **2.** *n.* a shout; a call. □ *Bill did not hear my cry to him from across the street.* **3.** *n.* a period of weeping. □ *During the sad movie, I had a good cry.* **4.** *iv.* to weep; to sob; to shed tears. □ *Jane cried because she was very sad.*

**crystal** ['krɪs təl] **1.** *n.* a solid chemical compound occurring in a regular shape, such as a square or rectangle. □ *Salt crystals can be found in every home.* **2.** *n.* a hard, clear substance like glass that contains a lot of lead. (Plural only when referring to different kinds, types, instances, or varieties.) □ *Crystal is made into many beautiful objects.* Ⓒ *The best crystals were to be found in Germany.* **3.** *n.* clear, expensive drinking vessels made of ②. (No plural form.) □ *Mary received her crystal as a wedding gift.* **4.** *n.* the clear cover over the face of a watch. □ *The jeweler put a new crystal on my watch.* **5.** *adj.* made from ②. □ *The room was lit by crystal lamps.* **6.** *adj.* clear; transparent. □ *I gazed into the crystal depths of the pool.*

**cub** ['kʌb] *n.* one of the young of certain animals, including bears, lions, and foxes. □ *The bear cubs wrestled with each other.*

**cube** ['kjub] **1.** *n.* a solid object having six square sides all the same size. □ *I put some ice cubes in my drink.* **2.** *n.* the number that is the result of multiplying some other number by itself two times. □ *The cube of 5 is 125.* **3.** *tv.* to multiply a number by itself two times, that is, number × number × number. □ *Do you get 125 when you cube 5?* **4.** *tv.* to cut up food into little **cubes** ①. □ *Anne cubed the fruit for the dessert recipe.*

**cucumber** ['kju kəm bɚ] *n.* a long, green vegetable, eaten raw in salads or pickled. □ *My salad was made from sliced cucumbers.*

**cud** ['kʌd] *n.* a lump of chewed food that an animal, such as a cow, brings back into its mouth from its stomach in order to chew on it some more. □ *Cows spend many hours chewing their cud.*

**cuddle** ['kʌd l] *tv.* to hold someone with love and affection; to hug someone for a while. □ *Susie cuddled the baby kitten.*

**cue** ['kju] **1.** *n.* a long, narrow stick used to hit balls in pool and similar games. □ *The pool cues were in a rack mounted on the wall.* **2.** *n.* something that is a signal for someone to do or say something; a line that prompts an actor to say the next line or do the next action. □ *The actor got his cue from the director.* **3.** *tv.* to signal something to do or say something; to give someone ②. □ *The producer cued the orchestra conductor to begin.*

**cuff** ['kʌf] **1.** *n.* the turned-up edge of cloth near the ankles on trousers; the thicker material near the wrists on shirts. □ *Lint gets caught in the cuffs of my pants.* **2.** *tv.* to hit someone with one's hand. □ *The boxer cuffed his opponent.*

**cuisine** [kwɪ 'zin] **1.** *n.* a particular way—usually national or cultural—of preparing food. □ *Some cuisines use hot spices.* **2.** *n.* food, especially the food of a particular country or region. □ *I really love Mexican cuisine.*

**cult** ['kʌlt] **1.** *n.* members of a strange or radical system of worship or admiration. □ *The cult leader believed he was the king of the world.* **2.** *adj.* attracting a small number of fans, who seem like ①. □ *The famous singer has a cult following.*

**culture** ['kʌl tʃɚ] **1.** *n.* the social patterns of the people in a particular domain. □ *Weddings and funerals are a part of most cultures.* **2.** *n.* the artistic and social tastes of a society. (No plural form.) □ *Folk songs are part of American culture.* **3.** *n.* a growth of bacteria in a container in a laboratory. □ *The scientist studied the culture under a microscope.*

**cup** ['kʌp] **1.** *n.* a drinking container having a loop-shaped handle. □ *I filled my cup with coffee.* **2.** *n.* the contents of ①. □ *The whole cup of juice splashed onto the floor.* **3.** *n.* a standard unit of measurement equal to eight ounces. □ *Can I borrow a cup of sugar?* **4.** *n.* an award; a trophy. (Often shaped like ① or a larger vessel.) □ *The hockey team won the most treasured cup of all.*

**cupboard** ['kʌb ɚd] *n.* a cabinet lined with shelves, used to store plates, cups, food, or kitchen supplies. □ *The plates are in the cupboard above the stove.*

**cupcake** ['kʌp kek] *n.* a small cake, shaped as if it had been cooked in a cup. □ *The children ate cupcakes at the birthday party.*

**curb** ['kɚb] **1.** *n.* the raised edge or rim of a road. □ *The grass extends all the way to the curb.* **2.** *n.* a restraint; a control. □ *The drug acts as a curb on hunger.* **3.** *tv.* to restrain something; to control something; to keep something back. □ *Bill tried to curb his anger.*

**cure** ['kjʊr] **1.** *n.* a medicine that will make a sick person better; a remedy. □ *Sleep is a cure for exhaustion.* **2.** *tv.* to make someone well again; to get rid of a disease or a bad habit. □ *The medicine cured Mary.* **3.** *tv.* to preserve meat by salting, smoking, or drying it. □ *The hunter cured the salmon over a smoking fire.*

**curious** ['kjʊr i əs] **1.** *adj.* inquisitive; wanting to learn about something. (Adv: *curiously.*) □ *The book was about a curious monkey.* **2.** *adj.* weird; odd; strange; unusual. (Adv: *curiously.*) □ *The family had a few curious traditions that other people found strange.*

**curl** ['kɚl] **1.** *n.* a group of hairs that are looped or twisted. □ *The baby had a head full of curls.* **2.** *n.* twist; an amount of twisting. (No plural form.) □ *Bill does not like the curl of his hair.* **3.** *n.* something that is shaped like a loop or a spiral. □ *Curls of wood on the floor showed that the carpenter was at work.* **4.** *tv.* to cause a bunch of hairs to twist into loops or coils. □ *It's hard to curl my straight hair.* **5.** *tv.* to cause something to wind around an object; to wind something around an object. □ *The cat curled itself around my ankle.* **6.** *iv.* to twist into loops or coils. □ *The snake curled and twisted around the poor mouse.*

**currency** ['kɚ ən si] **1.** *n.* the kind of money that is used in a particular country. □ *We exchanged our currency at a bank in the airport.* **2.** *n.* the quality of being in general use. (No plural form.) □ *Your old theories have no currency in modern science.*

**current** ['kɚ ənt] **1.** *adj.* up-to-date; recent; of or about the present time. (Adv: *currently.*) □ *At the current moment, I'm running late for work. Excuse me.* **2.** *n.* a moving stream of air or water; a flow. □ *This river is dangerous because of its strong current.* **3.** *n.* the flow of electricity; the rate of the flow of electricity. □ *How much current does this light bulb use?*

**curse** ['kɚs] **1.** *n.* a word or statement asking a powerful being to bring evil or to harm someone or something. □ *This radio won't work. Is there a curse on it?* **2.** *n.* a word used when saying ①. □ *Jane uttered a curse when she stubbed her toe.* **3.** *tv.* to utter ② against someone or something. (Pt/pp: ['kɚst].) □ *Tom cursed his pen when it ran out of ink.* **4.** *iv.* to utter ②. □ *Please stop cursing!*

**curt** ['kɚt] *adj.* rudely brief; short (with someone or something) in a rude way. (Adv: *curtly.*) □ *The rude customer gave the salesclerk a curt response.*

**curtain** ['kɚt n] *n.* a piece of fabric hung as a barrier to sight. □ *Heavy curtains hang in each window.*

**curve** ['kɚv] **1.** *n.* a smooth bend; a continuously bending line. □ *The mountain road is full of curves.* **2.** *tv.* to make something bend; to bend something into ①. □ *The dancer curved her arms above her head.* **3.** *iv.* to bend in the shape of ①. □ *The road curves gently to the right just before the lake.*

**cushion** ['kʊʃ ən] **1.** *n.* a padded pillow for sitting. □ *My rocking chair has a soft cushion.* **2.** *tv.* to soften something from shock or impact. □ *The carpet cushioned the fall of the vase.*

**custodian** [kə 'stod i ən] **1.** *n.* someone who has custody over someone else; someone who is in charge of someone or something. □ *Mike is the custodian of his company's art collection.* **2.** *n.* a janitor; someone who keeps someplace clean and makes small repairs. □ *I called the custodian when the refrigerator in my apartment broke down.*

**custom** ['kʌs təm] **1.** *n.* a tradition; a social tradition; a socially expected practice. □ *Eating roast turkey is a Thanksgiving custom.* **2.** *n.* a habit; a regular practice; a usual event. □ *Bill is never on time. He has made a custom of being late.* **3.** *adj.* made to order; specially made for a customer. □ *Bill wears only custom suits.*

**customer** ['kʌs tə mɚ] *n.* someone who buys a product or a service from a person or a business. □ *The clerk packed the customer's groceries.*

**cut** ['kʌt] **1.** *n.* an opening made in the skin accidentally. □ *My cut hurts me very much.* **2.** *n.* a reduction in an amount of money; the taking away of funds for something. □ *The baseball players all took a cut in pay.* **3.** *n.* a piece of something that has been **cut** ④ from something; a piece [of meat]. □ *The butcher held a sale on some cuts of meat.* **4.** *tv., irreg.* to separate something from something else with a sharp object; to sever something from something else. (Pt/pp: *cut.*) □ *The butcher cut the fat from the steak.* **5.** *tv., irreg.* to make an opening in something with a sharp object. □ *Max cut a hole in the wall with a knife.* **6.** *tv., irreg.* to shorten something with a sharp object; to trim something with a sharp object. □ *I cut the grass with my mower.* **7.** *tv., irreg.* to reduce something; to decrease something. □ *Congress voted to cut the budget.* **8.** *tv., irreg.* to dissolve something; to dilute something. □ *It took a strong soap to cut the grease.* **9. cut** something **out** *tv., irreg. + obj. + adv.* to cut something, such as a piece of paper, loose so it can be removed. □ *The children cut dolls out of paper.* 🅃 *They cut out paper dolls.* **10.** *iv., irreg.* to slice into something. □ *I sharpened my knife and was ready to cut.*

**cut-and-dried** ['kʌt æn 'draɪd] *adj.* routine; not requiring much thought or effort. □ *This is a simple question that requires only a cut-and-dried answer.*

**cute** ['kjut] *adj.* clever and pretty; simple and attractive. (Adv: *cutely.* Comp: *cuter;* sup: *cutest.*) □ *The flowers on your hat are really cute.*

**cycle** ['saɪ kəl] **1.** *n.* one instance of a process that repeats over and over. □ *The washing machine's rinse cycle takes fifteen minutes.* **2.** *iv.* to ride a bicycle. □ *The kids cycled along the lake.*

**cyclist** ['saɪ klɪst] *n.* someone who rides a bicycle or motorcycle, especially as a regular activity. □ *Cyclists sometimes wear special clothing.*

**cyclone** ['saɪ klon] *n.* a tornado; a strong, violent wind that moves in a circle. □ *The cyclone destroyed all the farms in its path.*

**cylinder** ['sɪl ən dɚ] **1.** *n.* a tube; a solid or hollow object with a circular top and bottom and long, curved sides. □ *A vase in the shape of a simple cylinder held a single rose.* **2.** *n.* the part of a car engine in which a piston moves back and forth. □ *One cylinder cracked, and the engine was ruined.*

**cymbal** ['sɪm bəl] *n.* one of a pair of brass discs that are struck together to make a loud, ringing noise in orchestras and bands. □ *William plays the cymbals in the orchestra.*

**cynic** ['sɪn ɪk] *n.* someone who believes the worst about everything and everybody. □ *A cynic does not find much joy in life.*

**cynical** ['sɪn ɪ kəl] *adj.* believing the worst about everything and everybody. (Adv: *cynically* [...ɪk li].) □ *The manager's cynical attitude depressed everyone at work.*

**czar** ['zɑr] **1.** *n.* the male leader of Russia; a Russian king. (Until 1917. Also spelled *tsar.*) □ *The museum has a photo of the czar and his family.* **2.** *n.* a leader; someone who is in charge of something. (Fig. on ①.) □ *The U.S. drug czar tried to lead a war on illegal drugs.*

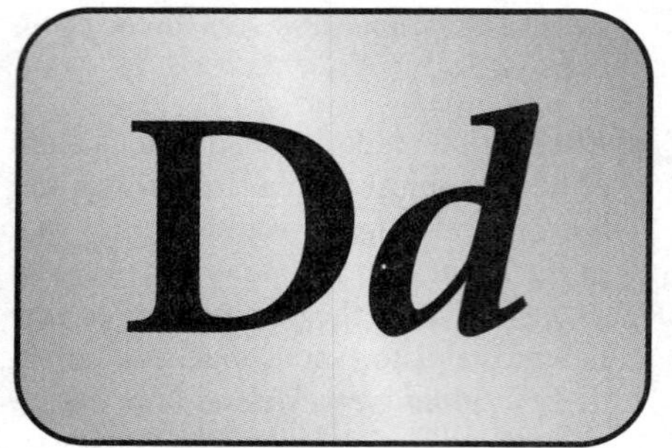


**dad** ['dæd] *n.* a father. (Also a term of address.) □ *My dad is taller than yours.*

**daddy** ['dæd i] *n.* <a form used as a familiar nickname for a father>. □ *Is your daddy at home, little boy?*

**daily** ['de li] **1.** *adj.* done or occurring every day. □ *Jimmy's grandmother enjoys his daily visits.* **2.** *adj.* suitable for a single day. □ *David ate his daily ration of chocolate quickly.* **3.** *adv.* on every day. □ *Anne goes for a walk daily through the park.*

**dairy** ['dɛr i] **1.** *n.* a company that processes milk products. □ *The dairy produces safe, clean milk.* **2.** *adj.* <the adj. use of ①.> □ *Bob is unable to eat or drink any dairy products.*

**daisy** ['de zi] *n.* a long-stemmed plant bearing circular flowers, typically white with yellow centers. □ *We saw a whole field of daisies in the valley.*

**dam** ['dæm] **1.** *n.* a solid barrier in a river or stream that holds back the flow of water. □ *Beavers built a dam in the stream.* **2. dam** something **(up)** *tv. + obj. (+ adv.)* to build a solid barrier in a river or a stream to hold back the flow of water. □ *Beavers dammed the creek up.*

**damage** ['dæm ɪdʒ] **1.** *n.* harm; an act that causes loss or pain. (No plural form.) □ *The vandals caused much damage in the building.* **2. damages** *n.* charges or costs for harm or loss, usually considered to be a punishment. □ *The damages as determined by the jury were very high.* **3.** *tv.* to harm something. □ *Someone damaged my book by spilling milk on it.*

**damn** ['dæm] **1.** *adj.* cursed; declared to be bad as in ③. (Prenominal only. A curse word. Use only with caution.) □ *That damn dog bit me!* **2. Damn!** *interj.* I am angry!; I am frustrated! (A curse word. Use only with caution.) □ *I just missed the last train. Damn!* **3.** *tv.* to declare something to be bad. □ *Lisa damned the rain that had ruined her new haircut.*

**damp** ['dæmp] *adj.* moist; slightly wet. (Adv: *damply.* Comp: *damper;* sup: *dampest.*) □ *Tony wiped the counter with a damp rag.*

**dance** ['dæns] **1.** *tv.* to perform a type of movement of the body, usually with music. □ *We danced the waltz in the moonlight.* **2.** *iv.* to move one's body in a rhythm, usually to music, usually with another person. □ *Everyone at the nightclub danced until dawn.* **3.** *n.* the art and study of the movement of the body, in rhythm, especially to music. (No plural form.) □ *The director was looking for actors who had studied dance.* **4.** *n.* a set series of body movements done to music. □ *I learned a new dance last night at the party.* **5.** *n.* an act or session of ②. □ *Excuse me. May I have this dance?* □ *She did her little dance and then sat down.* **6.** *n.* a social event where music is played and people **dance** ②. □ *The dance was enjoyed by everyone who attended.*

**danger** ['den dʒɚ] **1.** *n.* the possibility of harm. (No plural form.) □ *Danger is everywhere in a war.* **2.** *n.* someone or something that could cause harm, injury, or death. □ *The vicious dog was a danger to visitors.*

**dangerous** ['den dʒɚ əs] *adj.* risky; having the potential for causing harm. (Adv: *dangerously.*) □ *This small toy is dangerous for little babies.*

**dare** ['dɛr] **1.** *n.* a challenge; a statement that challenges someone to take a risk. ☐ *Anne climbed the mountain on a dare.* **2. dare** someone **to** do something *tv.* + *obj.* + *inf.* to challenge someone to do something risky. ☐ *Anne dared me to jump into the pool.* **3.** *aux.* to have enough courage or boldness [to do something]. (Usually used in negative sentences and questions.) ☐ *Do you dare swim in the lake at night alone?*

**dark** ['dɑrk] **1.** *adj.* without light. (Adv: *darkly.* Comp: *darker;* sup: *darkest.*) ☐ *Lisa took a flashlight into the dark cave.* **2.** *adj.* not light in color; having little brightness or color. (Adv: *darkly.* Comp: *darker;* sup: *darkest.*) ☐ *John wore a dark suit to the funeral.* **3.** *n.* the absence of light; darkness; nighttime. (No plural form.) ☐ *I prefer daylight to dark.*

**darken** ['dɑr kən] **1.** *tv.* to make something darker. ☐ *Clouds darkened the sky.* **2.** *iv.* to become darker. ☐ *When the sun sets, the sky darkens.*

**darkness** ['dɑrk nəs] *n.* the quality of having no light. (No plural form.) ☐ *In the darkness of the theater, Anne fell asleep.*

**data** ['det ə, 'dæt ə] *n.* information; pieces of information; facts; a set of facts. (The Latin plural of *datum.* Treated as singular or plural in English.) ☐ *The data were already loaded into the computer when I started working.* ☐ *The data was already loaded into the computer when I started working.*

**date** ['det] **1.** *n.* the number of the day of a month, often including the name of the month or the name of the month and the year; the name of a month and the year; the year. (① refers to the number of the day of a month; the day of the week is called the **day**.) ☐ *I know the day is Thursday, but what's the date of the meeting?* **2.** *n.* a brown, fleshy fruit with a long pit, grown on certain palm trees. ☐ *The bread was filled with dates and nuts.* **3.** *n.* a social meeting between two people who have planned to go somewhere or do something together. (Typically male and female.) ☐ *Bob was afraid to ask anyone for a date.* **4.** *tv.* to mark something with ①; to show the **date** ① of something. ☐ *Please date your checks when you write them.* **5.** *tv.* to show or signal that someone or something is out-of-date or old-fashioned. ☐ *The style of cars dated the movie.* **6.** *tv.* to have **dates** ③ with a particular person. ☐ *How long have you been dating Anne?* **7.** *iv.* to go out on **dates** ③ frequently or habitually. ☐ *My parents dated for two years before they got married.*

**daughter** ['dɔ tɚ] *n.* a female child. ☐ *The couple had five daughters and no sons.*

**dawn** ['dɔn] **1.** *n.* the period of morning when light is first seen in the eastern sky; sunrise. ☐ *The light of dawn was obscured by the clouds.* **2.** *n.* the beginning of something. (Fig. on ①.) ☐ *The dawn of a new age began with the invention of the automobile.* **3.** *iv.* [for the day] to become bright or light. ☐ *The day dawned with a beautiful sunrise.*

**day** ['de] **1.** *n.* a period of 24 hours, especially from midnight to midnight; one of the seven divisions of the week. (The days of the week, in order, are **Monday, Tuesday, Wednesday, Thursday, Friday, Saturday, Sunday.**) ☐ *The day after Wednesday is Thursday.* **2.** *n.* the period of time between sunrise and sunset; the opposite of night. ☐ *Some animals sleep during the day.* **3.** *n.* the time spent at work; the hours of work. ☐ *At work, my day begins at 7 each morning.* **4.** *n.* a time; a period. ☐ *There was a day when women weren't allowed to vote.* **5. days** *adv.* during the daytime; during each day. ☐ *I sleep days and work nights.*

D

**daybreak** ['de brek] *n.* dawn; the first light of day. (No plural form.) □ *The farmer awoke before daybreak.*

**daylight** ['de lɑɪt] *n.* the light of day. (No plural form.) □ *As daylight approached, the rooster began to crow.*

**day-to-day** ['de tə 'de] *adj.* daily; happening every day. □ *My day-to-day expenses are small, except when I buy food.*

**dead** ['dɛd] **1.** *adj.* no longer living. □ *Susan threw the dead flowers away.* **2.** *adj.* not having the electrical energy to work. (Fig. on ①.) □ *This circuit is dead. Try another.* **3.** *adj.* not active; dull. (Fig. on ①. Comp: *deader;* sup: *deadest.*) □ *Things are really dead around here. Let's go.* **4.** *adv.* completely; exactly; absolutely. □ *The arrow hit the target dead center.* **5. the dead** *n.* dead ① people; people who have died. (No plural form. Treated as plural, but not countable.) □ *We remember the dead on Memorial Day.* **6.** *n.* the time when it is the darkest, coldest, etc. (No plural form.) □ *Everything is so bleak in the dead of winter.*

**deadline** ['dɛd lɑɪn] *n.* the date when something is due; the time by which something must be finished. □ *When is the deadline for the research report?*

**deaf** ['dɛf] **1.** *adj.* not able to hear. (Adv: *deafly.* Comp: *deafer;* sup: *deafest.*) □ *The partially deaf child wore a hearing aid.* **2.** *adj.* unwilling to hear; heedless. (Fig. on ①. Adv: *deafly.* Comp: *deafer;* sup: *deafest.*) □ *My advice fell on deaf ears.* **3. the deaf** *n.* people who are ①. (No plural form. Treated as plural, but not countable.) □ *Mary is a teacher of the deaf.*

**deal** ['dil] **1.** *tv., irreg.* to pass out cards in a card game. (Pt/pp: **dealt.**) □ *It's your turn to deal the cards.* **2.** *tv., irreg.* to deliver something, such as a blow. □ *I dealt a forceful blow to the robber's chin.* **3.** *iv., irreg.* to pass out cards in a card game. □ *It is Mary's turn to deal.* **4. deal with something** *iv., irreg. + prep. phr.* [for something, such as a book, essay, article, explanation, etc.] to tell about, discuss, or concern something. □ *The poem deals with death.* **5. deal with something** *iv., irreg. + prep. phr.* to cope with something; to manage to handle something; to have control of something. □ *I cannot deal with having ants in the kitchen.* **6. deal with someone or something** *iv., irreg. + prep. phr.* to do business with someone or some entity. □ *I don't deal with that store, because the clerks there are very rude.* **7.** *n.* a bargain; an agreement for the purchase of goods or services, especially if at a cost lower than expected. □ *I got a really good deal on a new car!*

**dealer** ['di lɚ] **1.** *n.* someone who passes out cards in a card game. □ *The dealer collected the discarded cards.* **2.** *n.* someone who is in the business of trade; someone who buys and sells certain products. (Usually a **retail** merchant.) □ *A new car dealer is opening a store in the middle of town.*

**dealt** ['dɛlt] pt/pp of **deal.**

**dean** ['din] *n.* the head of a teaching division within a university, a college, or a private school. □ *Only the dean can cancel classes.*

**dear** ['dɪr] **1.** *adj.* loved very much. (Adv: *dearly.* Comp: *dearer;* sup: *dearest.*) □ *My dear friend baked me a cake for my birthday.* **2.** *adj.* <a form of address used at the beginning of a letter.> □ *"Dear Max," the letter began.* **3.** *n.* a treasured person; a person who is loved very much. (Also a term of address.) □ *Oh, Mary! You are such a dear to help!*

**death** ['dɛθ] **1.** *n.* the state of being dead. (No plural form.) □ *In death, the troubled man finally found peace.* **2.** *n.* the act of dying; the end of life. □ *The death of the beautiful swan saddened the children.*

**debate** [dɪ 'bet] **1.** *n.* an event where two or more people with different points of view talk about an issue. □ *There's a debate in the meeting room about next year's budget.* **2.** *n.* a formal, structured argument where the two sides of an issue are presented in an orderly fashion by opposing speakers. □ *The candidates agreed to the rules for the debate.* **3.** *n.* formal, structured arguing done as a school activity. (No plural form.) □ *I participated in debate throughout high school.* **4.** *tv.* to discuss and argue something with someone. □ *My grandfather will debate politics with anyone.* **5.** *iv.* [for two people or groups] to speak for the opposite sides of an issue. □ *We debated for hours, but neither of us could convince the other.*

**debit** ['dɛb ɪt] **1.** *n.* a record of an amount that is owed or must be subtracted from the balance in an account. (Compare this with **debt.**) □ *My mortgage payment is a debit in my accounts.* **2.** *tv.* to charge an amount of money against someone's account. □ *My bank debited $20 for service charges last month!* **3.** *tv.* to charge someone's account for a sum of money. □ *The bank debited Sue's account for the amount of the check she had written.*

**debt** ['dɛt] *n.* the condition of owing something to someone. (Plural only when referring to different kinds, types, instances, or varieties.) □ *Bill is working very hard to get out of debt.* Ⓒ *John ran up many debts when he was unemployed.*

**decade** ['dɛk ed] **1.** *n.* a period of ten years. □ *I moved here a decade ago.* **2.** *n.* one of the ten equal divisions of a century, such as 1950–1959. □ *The Great Depression occurred in the decade of the 1930s.*

**decay** [dɪ 'ke] **1.** *n.* rot; the rotting of something. (No plural form.) □ *The wooden bridge was unsafe because of decay.* **2.** *iv.* to rot. □ *The fallen tree branch will soon decay.* **3.** *tv.* to cause something to rot. □ *Too much candy decayed the child's teeth.*

**deceive** [dɪ 'siv] *tv.* to make someone believe something that is not true. □ *Mary deceived her boss about her work experience.*

**December** [dɪ 'sɛm bɚ] Go to **month.**

**decide** [dɪ 'sɑɪd] **1.** *tv.* to determine the outcome of something. □ *One vote decided the election.* **2.** *tv.* to make a choice; to reach a decision about something. (The object can be a clause with **that** ⑦.) □ *I could not decide where to go on vacation.* **3. decide on** *iv. + prep. phr.* to choose something; to pick something out. □ *I could not decide on what to order from the menu.*

**decimal point** ['dɛs (ə) məl pɔɪnt] *n.* a period (.) that separates whole numbers from fractions. □ *Your numbers are right, but the decimal point is in the wrong place.*

**decision** [dɪ 'sɪ ʒən] *n.* a choice; a selection; a judgment; a resolution. □ *The judge's decision is final.*

**deck** ['dɛk] **1.** *n.* a set of cards; a pack of cards. □ *A full deck has fifty-two cards.* **2.** *n.* the floor of a ship. □ *The sailors cleaned the deck every day.* **3.** *n.* a raised wooden patio, attached to the back door of a house. □ *Tom built a deck in his backyard for parties.*

**declare** [dɪ 'klɛr] *tv.* to proclaim something; to make something known; to say something publicly. (The object can be a clause with **that** ⑦.) □ *Five politicians declared that they wanted to be elected mayor.*

**decline** [dɪ 'klɑɪn] **1.** *iv.* to move from good to bad; to move from high to low; to go from better to worse. □ *As the dog grew older, its health declined.* **2.** *iv.* to turn [something] down; to refuse [something]. □ *When asked to accept an* *overseas position, Mary declined.* **3.** *tv.* to list the different case endings of a noun or adjective. (Compare this with **conjugate.**) □ *I learned to decline several Latin nouns today!* **4.** *tv.* to turn something down; to refuse an offer. □ *Susan declined my offer of help.* **5.** *n.* the gradual change from high to low; the loss of power, strength, or health. □ *Jane suffered a decline in health.*

D

**decorate** ['dɛk ə ret] **1.** *tv.* to put up decorations. □ *Bill decorated his office with his trophies and awards.* **2.** *tv.* to honor a soldier with a medal. □ *At the ceremony, the major was decorated for his brave acts.* **3.** *iv.* to paint a room, put up wallpaper, hang drapes, lay carpet, or add furniture to a room. □ *Before we decorate, we must fix the roof.*

**decoration** [dɛk ə 're ʃən] **1.** *n.* an object or things used to make something or a place look pretty. □ *A large wreath hung on the door as a decoration.* **2.** *n.* an award or honor given to a soldier. □ *A decoration was awarded to Max for bravery.*

**decorative** ['dɛk ə rə tɪv] *adj.* pretty; used for decorating. (Adv: *decoratively.*) □ *Lisa makes decorative pottery.*

**decrease 1.** ['di kris] *n.* a drop; a fall; a lessening; a reduction. □ *The church experienced a decrease in attendance.* **2.** ['di kris] *n.* the amount that something has been reduced or lessened. □ *The decrease in Mary's pay was greater than she expected.* **3.** [dɪ 'kris] *iv.* to become less; to become smaller in size or strength. □ *The pain decreased after I took an aspirin.* **4.** [dɪ 'kris] *tv.* to cause something to become less; to cause something to become smaller in size or strength. □ *The manager decreased the size of the order.*

**deed** ['did] **1.** *n.* something that is performed; an act; an action. □ *"Who has done this terrible deed?" shouted Max.* **2.** *n.* a legal document that officially transfers the ownership of land or buildings to someone. (Compare this with **title** ④.) □ *The deed shows that you are legally the owner of the property.*

**deep** ['dip] **1.** *adj.* extending far down from the top or far back from the front. (Adv: *deeply.* Comp: *deeper;* sup: *deepest.*) □ *I'm afraid to swim in deep water.* **2.** *adj.* reaching a certain depth; extending a certain distance down, in, or back. (Follows a measure of depth. Comp: *deeper.*) □ *These shelves are ten inches deep.* **3.** *adj.* [of a sound] low-pitched and strong. (Adv: *deeply.* Comp: *deeper;* sup: *deepest.*) □ *The men who sing bass in the choir have deep voices.* **4.** *adj.* [of a color] intense or strong. (Adv: *deeply.* Comp: *deeper;* sup: *deepest.*) □ *The clear mountain stream was a deep blue.* **5.** *adj.* intense; strong; extreme. (Adv: *deeply.* Comp: *deeper;* sup: *deepest.*) □ *Jane has deep respect for her teachers.* **6.** *adj.* difficult to understand; past one's understanding. (Comp: *deeper;* sup: *deepest.*) □ *Many people think philosophy is a deep subject.*

**deer** ['dɪr] *n., irreg.* a fast, hoofed animal, the males of which have antlers. (Pl: *deer.*) □ *Deer foraged through the forest for food.*

**defeat** [dɪ 'fit] **1.** *tv.* to cause someone to lose; to beat someone in a contest. □ *The debate team defeated its rival.* **2.** *n.* loss [of a contest]; failure to win. (No plural form.) □ *Lisa found defeat hard to accept.* **3.** *n.* an instance of winning as in ①. □ *The army's defeat of the enemy was quick, but many lives were lost.* **4.** *n.* a loss of a contest. □ *The candidate's defeat in the last election ended his career as a politician.*

**defect 1.** ['di fɛkt, dɪ 'fɛkt] *n.* a flaw. □ *The manufacturer recalled the car due to a defect in the engine.* **2.** [dɪ 'fɛkt] *iv.* to go over to the other side of a conflict; to join up with one's enemies. □ *The traitor decided to defect during the night.*

**defend** [dɪ 'fɛnd] *tv.* to stick up for someone or something; to fight for someone or something physically or verbally; to protect someone or something. □ *Bill defended his little brother from the larger boys.*

**defendant** [dɪ 'fɛn dənt] *n.* someone who is the target of legal action in a court of law. □ *The defendant whispered to his lawyer frequently during the trial.*

**defense** [dɪ 'fɛns] **1.** *n.* protection against someone or something; defending someone or something; preparation to defend against someone or something. (Plural only when referring to different kinds, types, instances, or varieties.) □ *The small boy relied on his quick thinking for defense.* 🄲 *The town's defenses are weak and it may fall to the enemy.* **2.** *n.* the skill of a sports team in protecting its goal or in preventing the other team from scoring points. (Plural only when referring to different kinds, types, instances, or varieties.) □ *The soccer team's defense was excellent. The opposing team never scored.* 🄲 *The team's defenses include strong, fast players.* **3.** *n.* the lawyer or lawyers who defend someone in court. (No plural form.) □ *The defense was shocked by the judge's ruling.* **4.** *n.* the way that a lawyer argues a case in favor of a defendant; an argument used to defend oneself. (No plural form.) □ *The jury did not agree with the lawyer's defense.*

**define** [dɪ 'fɑɪn] *tv.* to explain the meaning of a word or expression. □ *The dictionary defines thousands of words.*

**defy** [dɪ 'fɑɪ] *tv.* to resist authority; to go against a rule or a regulation. □ *Bill defied his boss and left work early.*

**degree** [dɪ 'gri] **1.** *n.* a unit of measurement, as used for measuring temperature or angles. □ *There are ninety degrees in a right angle.* **2.** *n.* the extent of something; the level of something. □ *The nurse treated the firefighter for first-degree burns.* **3.** *n.* a title awarded by a university or college to a student who has met certain requirements. □ *The local college offers two-year and four-year degrees.* **4.** *n.* a level in the comparison of adjectives and adverbs. □ *The superlative degree of* slow *is* slowest.

D

**delete** [dɪ 'lit] *tv.* to remove something from something, especially from a list or a piece of writing. □ *The editor deleted the incorrect sentence from the manuscript.*

**delicate** ['dɛl ə kɪt] **1.** *adj.* fragile; easily damaged. (Adv: *delicately.*) □ *The playful dog broke the delicate lamp.* **2.** *adj.* subtly flavored. (Adv: *delicately.*) □ *Tom prefers strong spices over more delicate flavors.*

**delicious** [dɪ 'lɪʃ əs] *adj.* pleasing to the senses, especially taste and smell. (Adv: *deliciously.*) □ *The food at the banquet was delicious.*

**deliver** [dɪ 'lɪv ɚ] **1.** *tv.* to take something [to someone or some place]. □ *Bill delivers pizzas for a living.* **2.** *tv.* [for a woman] to give birth to a baby. □ *Anne delivered a healthy set of twins.* **3.** *tv.* [for a doctor or someone else] to assist a baby in being born. □ *The doctor who delivered me also delivered my sister.* **4.** *tv.* to give a speech; to read something out loud. □ *Bob delivered his report to the class.*

**delivery** [dɪ 'lɪv ə ri] **1.** *n.* the act of taking something to someone. □ *The worker finally completed the delivery of the package.* **2.** *n.* something that is taken to someone. □ *The delivery arrived an hour late.* **3.** *n.* the process of giving birth. □ *Anne's first delivery took ten hours.* **4.** *n.* the style or manner of speaking; the style used when giving a speech. (No plural form.) □ *The story's humor was in its delivery.*

**deluxe** [də 'lʌks] *adj.* of very good quality; of great luxury. (Adv: *deluxely.*) □ *We bought the deluxe model of the car.*

**demand** [dɪ 'mænd] **1.** *n.* an urgent request; a strong order. □ *His demand for help could not be refused.* **2.** *n.* [buyers'] strength of desire for a product or service. (No plural form.) □ *Consumer demand will determine the success of a product.* **3.** *tv.* to ask urgently for something; [for an authority] to request something firmly. (The object can be a clause with **that** ⑦.) □ *The injured student demanded help.* **4.** *tv.* to require something; to need something. (The object can be a clause with **that** ⑦.) □ *His injuries demanded surgery.*

**democracy** [dɪ 'mɑ krə si] **1.** *n.* the system of government ultimately controlled by the people who are governed. (No plural form.) □ *Democracy is spreading around the world in various forms.* **2.** *n.* a country whose system of government is ①. □ *The United States is a democracy.*

**demon** ['di mən] *n.* an evil spirit; a devil. □ *The ancient culture had a ceremony to chase away demons.*

**denial** [dɪ 'nɑɪ əl] *n.* insisting that something does not exist or is not true; denying that something exists or is true. (Plural only when referring to different kinds, types, instances, or varieties.) □ *Denial of the problem will keep it from being solved.* Ⓒ *The police would not believe Max's repeated denials.*

**dense** ['dɛns] *adj.* thick; tightly packed together. (Adv: *densely.* Comp: *denser;* sup: *densest.*) □ *It was hard to see the path in the dense forest.*

**dent** ['dɛnt] **1.** *n.* a shallow hollow in a surface; an indentation; a place where a small part of a surface has been pressed down or pressed inward. □ *There was a dent in the kitchen counter where Mary had dropped a can of beans.* **2.** *tv.* to make a small hollow in something. □ *A stone falling from the back of a truck dented the hood of my car.*

**dental** ['dɛn təl] *adj.* of or about the teeth or their care. (Adv: *dentally.*) □ *My dentist follows proper dental procedures.*

**dentist** ['dɛn tɪst] *n.* a health-care professional who specializes in the care of the teeth. □ *My dentist was as gentle as possible while cleaning my teeth.*

**deny** [dɪ 'nɑɪ] **1.** *tv.* to declare that something is not true. (The object can be a clause with **that** ⑦.) □ *The students all denied cheating on the test.* **2.** *tv.* to refuse to grant someone or something permission to do something; to refuse to allow someone or something to have something. □ *The state denied the elderly man a driver's license.*

**depart** [dɪ 'pɑrt] **1.** *iv.* to go away; to start a journey by leaving a place. □ *I said good-bye and departed.* **2.** *tv.* to go away from a place; to leave a state or status. □ *When we depart this life, we die.*

**department** [dɪ 'pɑrt mənt] **1.** *n.* a unit within an organization. □ *The Department of History is a part of the College of Arts.* **2.** *adj.* <the adj. use of ①.> □ *Do you know the department policy regarding use of the fax machine?*

**department store** [dɪ 'pɑrt mənt stor] *n.* a large store where all sorts of merchandise is sold in various departments. □ *I bought shoes, a hat, and a new television at the department store.*

**dependent** [dɪ 'pɛn dənt] **1.** *adj.* relying on someone else for support or care. (Adv: *dependently.*) □ *I wish you were not so dependent! Learn to take care of yourself!* **2.** *n.* someone who relies on someone else for support. □ *Mary is her parents' only dependent.* **3.** *n.* someone who can be listed on a wage earner's income-tax form as ② and thereby reduce the wage earner's taxes. □ *Tom has four dependents, counting his ailing mother, whom he supports.*

**deposit** [dɪ 'pɑz ɪt] **1.** *n.* an amount of money paid toward a product or service. □ *The couple made a deposit on the new furniture.* **2.** *n.* an amount of money paid as security on a rented dwelling. □ *Susan had to pay one month's rent as a deposit.* **3.** *n.* something that is put down; something that is laid down. □ *Thick mud deposits lay at the mouth of the river.* **4.** *n.* money that is put in a monetary account. □ *The deposit was sent electronically from my employer to the bank.* **5.** *tv.* to place money in a monetary account. □ *You need to deposit some cash before you can write checks.* **6.** *tv.* to put something down in a specific place. □ *The tornado deposited the car in the middle of the park.*

**depository** [dɪ 'pɑz ɪ tor i] **1.** *n.* a place where things are kept safe; a place where things are deposited and kept safe. □ *A safety-deposit box is a type of depository.* **2.** *n.* a warehouse. □ *Most of the goods are stored in a local depository.*

**depth** ['dɛpθ] *n.* distance from top to bottom or front to back. (Plural only when referring to different kinds, types, instances, or varieties.) □ *The depth of the cabinets allowed for extra storage.* 🄲 *I measured the depths of all four pieces of land.*

**derogatory** [dɪ 'rɑg ə tor i] *adj.* showing contempt; rude; very negative and critical. (Adv: *derogatorily* [dɪ rɑg ə 'tor ə li].) □ *Anne's anger erupted when she heard the derogatory comment about her work.*

**descend** [dɪ 'sɛnd] **1.** *tv.* to move from a higher part to a lower part on or along something; to climb down something. □ *Bill descended the stairs to the basement.* **2.** *iv.* to go down; to go from a high place to a lower place; to move downward. □ *As evening came, the sun descended.* **3.** *iv.* to come from an earlier time. □ *Your philosophy descends from the Dark Ages.*

**describe** [dɪ 'skrɑɪb] *tv.* to tell about someone or something in written or spoken words. □ *The poem describes moonlight on the lake.*

**description** [dɪ 'skrɪp ʃən] *n.* a statement that describes someone or something. □ *The advertisement's description was very misleading.*

**desert 1.** ['dɛz ɚt] *n.* an area of land with little rainfall and little or no human population. □ *The hot, dry sand of the desert burned our feet.* **2.** ['dɛz ɚt] *adj.* <the adj. use of ①.> □ *The desert climate is good for your health.* **3.** [dɪ 'zɚt] *tv.* to abandon someone or something; to go away and leave someone or something behind. □ *Jimmy quickly deserted his friends when he was called to dinner.* **4.** [dɪ 'zɚt] *tv.* to leave a place and make it empty. □ *When the rains came, the people deserted the park.* **5.** [dɪ 'zɚt] *iv.* to be absent from military duty without permission. □ *The frightened soldier deserted.*

**desert island** ['dɛz ɚt 'ɑɪ lənd] *n.* a remote island, usually small and uninhabited, and typically having the features of a desert. □ *How could anyone live on a desert island with no food or water?*

**deserve** [dɪ 'zɚv] *tv.* to be worthy of something; to merit something. □ *After six years in college, I think I deserve a good job.*

**design** [dɪ 'zɑɪn] **1.** *n.* a plan showing how something will be made; the way something is arranged; the layout of something. □ *The design of the golf course includes a lake.* **2.** *n.* a (visual) pattern; drawings or markings. □ *The expensive sweater had an intricate design.* **3.** *tv.* to make the plans for building or decorating something. □ *We designed our house ourselves.* **4.** *tv.* to plan and execute an arrangement of pictures, images, diagrams, lines, circles, etc. □ *Lisa designed the book cover for her new novel.*

**designer** [dɪ 'zɑɪ nɚ] *n.* someone who makes designs; someone who plans how buildings, clothing, rooms, or works of graphic art will look. □ *The designer was proud of her fall fashions.*

D

**desire** [dɪ 'zɑɪɚ] **1.** *n.* a strong wish for something; a request for something. □ *Bill has a desire to be a lawyer.* **2.** *n.* someone or something that is wished for. □ *Success is Bill's desire.* **3.** *tv.* to want something very much. □ *Bill desires a good job above everything else.* **4. desire to** do something *iv.* + *inf.* to want to do something very much. □ *She desires to leave as soon as possible.*

**desk** ['dɛsk] *n.* a piece of furniture with a flat top—often with drawers on the lower part. □ *My desk is filled with important papers.*

**dessert** [dɪ 'zɚt] *n.* a special, often sweet, food served at the end of a meal. □ *For dessert, we had ice cream.*

**destiny** ['dɛs tə ni] *n.* the force that determines future events. (Plural only when referring to different kinds, types, instances, or varieties.) □ *Focus on today, and leave tomorrow to destiny.* Ⓒ *We cannot know our destinies.*

**destroy** [dɪ 'strɔɪ] *tv.* to make someone or something completely useless; to do away with someone or something. □ *The accident destroyed the car.*

**destruction** [dɪ 'strʌk ʃən] **1.** *n.* ruining or destroying something. (No plural form.) □ *The tornado caused the destruction of the town.* **2.** *n.* ruins; the result of destroying. (No plural form.) □ *The destruction caused by the tornado lay all around.*

**detail 1.** ['di tel, dɪ 'tel] *n.* a small fact about something. □ *Mary shortened the story by omitting a few details.* **2.** ['di tel] *n.* a drawing that shows all of the fine or small parts of something. □ *The picture is a detail of a larger painting.* **3.** [dɪ 'tel] *tv.* to give all the facts of a story or issue. □ *The victim detailed the crime for the police officer.*

**detain** [dɪ 'ten] **1.** *tv.* to delay someone or something; to keep someone or something from leaving. □ *Please do not detain me. I am in a hurry.* **2.** *tv.* [for the police] to keep or hold someone. □ *The police detained the suspect for questioning.*

**detective** [dɪ 'tɛk tɪv] *n.* a police officer or other licensed person who searches for information about crimes. □ *The detective specialized in investigating murder.*

**detention** [dɪ 'tɛn ʃən] *n.* keeping someone from leaving; holding someone in a place such as a jail or a classroom. (Plural only when referring to different kinds, types, instances, or varieties.) □ *The prisoner was starved during his detention.* Ⓒ *After a series of short detentions, John was finally put in prison.*

**determine** [dɪ 'tɚ mɪn] *tv.* to figure something out. (The object can be a clause with **that** ⑦.) □ *Anne has determined that she will win the election.*

**deterrent** [dɪ 'tɚ ənt] *n.* something that keeps someone or something from doing something; something that encourages someone or something not to do something. □ *The forecast of rain was a deterrent to our attending the outdoor concert.*

**detest** [dɪ 'tɛst] *tv.* to hate someone or something very much. (The object can be a clause with **that** ⑦.) □ *My children detest onions.*

**detour** ['di tu ɚ] **1.** *n.* a route that turns away from the regular route and is taken to avoid someone or something. □ *Bill took a detour through the office to avoid his boss.* **2.** *iv.* to use ①; to travel the long way around something. □ *The* *construction was minor and did not require anyone to detour.*

**develop** [dɪ ˈvɛl əp] **1.** *tv.* to create something and attempt to cause it to flourish. □ *The committee developed a plan for a new product.* **2.** *tv.* [in photography] to cause images to appear on film through chemical processes. □ *Special chemicals are needed to develop film.* **3.** *tv.* [for someone or some creature] to begin to show signs of something or experience something. □ *Mary developed an allergy to dogs.* **4.** *tv.* to build houses, buildings, and stores on empty land. □ *An investor is developing a mall near my house.* **5.** *iv.* to grow and mature. □ *Bob was kind as a child and developed into a thoughtful teenager.* **6.** *iv.* to grow and prosper; to strengthen; to mature. □ *My creativity developed in art class.*

**device** [dɪ ˈvɑɪs] *n.* a tool or machine meant to be used for a specific purpose. □ *Dave bought a special device to peel potatoes.*

**devil** [ˈdɛv əl] **1.** *n.* an evil spirit; a demon. □ *The chant was supposed to rid the room of devils.* **2.** *n.* Satan; the supreme spirit of evil. (Sometimes capitalized.) □ *The cult claims to worship the devil.* **3.** *n.* someone who is mischievous. □ *Our youngest son is a little devil and always in trouble.*

**devote** [dɪ ˈvot] **devote** something **to** something *tv. + obj. + prep. phr.* to give or allot something to something. (Often passive.) □ *Mike devotes his time to fixing up his house.*

**devout** [dɪ ˈvɑʊt] **1.** *adj.* actively religious. (Adv: *devoutly.*) □ *The devout worshiper attended church each week.* **2.** *adj.* sincere; deeply committed to someone or something. (Fig. on ①. Adv: *devoutly.*) □ *Bill is a devout believer in exercise.* **3. the devout** *n.* religious people. (No plural form. Treated as plural, but not countable.) □ *The really devout always attend church.*

**dew** [ˈdu] *n.* tiny drops of water that have fallen from cooling, moist air. (Plural only when referring to different kinds, types, instances, or varieties.) □ *We went out early in the morning, when the grass was still covered with dew.* Ⓒ *The dews in the east seem heavier than those in the west.*

D

**diabetes** [dɑɪ ə ˈbit ɪs] *n.* a disease where there is too much sugar in the blood and urine. (Treated as singular.) □ *Lisa had to take medicine for her diabetes.*

**diagram** [ˈdɑɪ ə græm] **1.** *n.* a drawing that helps explain something. □ *A good diagram helped me assemble the bike.* **2.** *tv.* to make a drawing to help explain something. □ *Fred diagramed the inside of the clock, including tiny pictures of the springs and gears.* **3.** *tv.* to make a drawing that shows the relationships between the parts of a sentence. □ *To diagram a sentence, you must first understand grammar.*

**dial** [ˈdɑɪl] **1.** *n.* on an older telephone, the wheel—with holes for one's finger—that is turned in order to make a telephone call. □ *Telephones with dials are very old-fashioned.* **2.** *n.* the part of a watch or a clock that has the numbers on it; the face of a watch or clock. □ *The dial of the watch has Roman numerals on it.* **3.** *tv.* to place a telephone call to someone or to some number, either by rotating the **dial** ① of a telephone or by pushing the buttons of a telephone. □ *The lonely college student dialed his parents.* **4.** *iv.* to operate a telephone by turning ① or pushing buttons. □ *I put money into the pay phone before I dialed.*

**dialect** [ˈdɑɪ ə lɛkt] *n.* a variety of a language. □ *My grandfather spoke a rural Greek dialect.*

**dialogue** AND **dialog** [ˈdɑɪ ə lɔg] **1.** *n.* speech between two or more people. (No plural form.) □ *The entire play* *consisted of dialogue and no movement.* **2.** *n.* a discussion between two or more people who express differences of opinion. □ *The political dialogue between the candidates has grown unpleasant.*

D

**dial tone** ['dɑɪl ton] *n.* the sound heard when one picks up a telephone receiver, indicating that a telephone call can be made. □ *This phone must be out of order, because there is no dial tone.*

**diameter** [dɑɪ 'æm ɪ tɚ] *n.* the length of a straight line within a circle and going through the center of the circle. □ *The diameter of the pipe is three inches.*

**diamond** ['dɑɪ (ə) mənd] **1.** *n.* a figure with four sides of equal length that is viewed as standing on one of its points. □ *The small window in the front door of our house is a diamond.* **2.** *n.* a playing card that has one or more shapes like ♦ on it. □ *If the card is printed in red, it must be a heart or a diamond.* **3.** *n.* a clear gem formed from carbon. □ *A diamond can cut glass.* **4.** *n.* [in baseball] the space defined by the three bases and home plate. □ *The pitcher stands in the middle of the baseball diamond.*

**diaper** ['dɑɪ (ə) pɚ] **1.** *n.* a piece of cloth or other fiber that a baby wears between its legs before the baby has learned to use a toilet. □ *The baby's diaper needed to be changed.* **2.** *tv.* to put ① on a baby. □ *The babysitter diapered the infant.*

**diary** ['dɑɪ (ə) ri] *n.* a journal; a book in which one records the events in one's life. □ *A diary is a very personal book.*

**dice** ['dɑɪs] **1.** pl of die ④. **2.** *tv.* to chop a food up into tiny cubes. □ *I diced the onions and added them to the salad.*

**dictionary** ['dɪk ʃə nɛr i] *n.* a book that explains the meanings of words. □ *The dictionary gives the pronunciation for each word.*

**did** [dɪd] pt of do.

**didn't** ['dɪd nt] *cont.* "did not." □ *You washed the dishes last night, didn't you?*

**die** ['dɑɪ] **1.** *iv.* to stop living; to become dead. (Present participle: **dying**.) □ *Every living thing eventually dies.* **2.** *iv.* [for a machine] to stop working. (Fig. on ①.) □ *One day, our old car just died.* **3. die out; die down** *iv.* + *adv.* to fade away. □ *As the train pulled away, the shouts of farewell died out.* **4.** *n., irreg.* a small cube that has a different number of spots on each side. (Usually has from 1 to 6 spots on each side and is used in games of chance. Pl: **dice**. Usually plural.) □ *Who throws the dice next?*

**diet** ['dɑɪ ɪt] **1.** *n.* the food that a person or an animal usually and typically eats. □ *A rabbit's diet includes grass and leaves.* **2.** *n.* a controlled or prescribed selection of foods. □ *John cheated on his diet by eating ice cream.* **3.** *iv.* to control one's choice of foods for the purpose of losing weight. □ *Anne dieted by restricting her fat intake.*

**difference** ['dɪf rəns] **1.** *n.* a way that two things or people are not alike. (Plural only when referring to different kinds, types, instances, or varieties.) □ *There is not much difference in the new version.* Ⓒ *There are only minor differences in the shades of the color.* **2.** *n.* the amount remaining when one amount is subtracted from another. (No plural form.) □ *The difference between ten and eight is two.*

**different** ['dɪf rənt] **1.** *adj.* not the same. (Adv: *differently*.) □ *Could I please have a different book? I've read this one already.* **2. different from someone or something** *adj.* + *prep. phr.* not like someone or something; not the same as someone or something. (Also with **than**. Adv: *differently*.) □ *Bill's account of the party was different from Bob's account.*

**difficult** ['dɪf ə kəlt] *adj.* hard to do; hard to understand. (Adv: *difficultly*.) □ *Juggling objects is difficult for many people.*

**difficulty** ['dɪf ə kəl ti] *n.* the quality of being hard to do or understand. (Plural only when referring to different kinds, types, instances, or varieties.) ☐ *Sue walked with difficulty after the accident.* Ⓒ *Some difficulties are more serious than others.*

**dig** ['dɪg] *tv., irreg.* to make a hole in something by removing part of it, as with removing soil with a shovel. (Pt/pp: **dug.**) ☐ *The gardener dug a hole for the new tree.*

**digest 1.** ['dɑɪ dʒɛst] *n.* a short version of a long piece of writing; a summary or a collection of summaries. ☐ *The movie digest told about new films.* **2.** [dɪ 'dʒɛst] *tv.* to dissolve food in the stomach so that it can be changed into a form that the body can use. ☐ *Bill felt better after his food had been digested.* **3.** [dɪ 'dʒɛst] *tv.* to take thoughts into the mind; to think about something very deeply and make it part of one's thinking. (Fig. on ②.) ☐ *Bob digested the difficult article slowly.*

**digestion** [dɪ 'dʒɛs tʃən] *n.* the process of breaking down food in the stomach so that it can be changed into a form that will give nourishment to the rest of the body. (No plural form.) ☐ *We studied digestion in our biology class.*

**digit** ['dɪdʒ ɪt] **1.** *n.* a number from 0 through 9. ☐ *The number 567 has three digits.* **2.** *n.* a finger or a toe. ☐ *Humans have five digits on each hand.*

**digital** ['dɪdʒ ɪ təl] **1.** *adj.* [of a clock or watch] using numbers rather than hands. (Adv: *digitally.*) ☐ *I prefer real hands to the symbols on a digital watch.* **2.** *adj.* of or about storing, retrieving, and working with information that is stored electronically using the digits 0 and 1. (Adv: *digitally.*) ☐ *The digital computer revolutionized the way information is processed.*

**dignity** ['dɪg nə ti] *n.* self-respect; personal worth. (No plural form.) ☐ *The black robes of a judge give a look of dignity.*

**dilute** [dɪ 'lut] **1.** *tv.* to weaken something by the addition of a fluid. ☐ *As the ice melted, it diluted my drink.* **2.** *tv.* to make something weaker; to make something less severe. (Fig. on ①.) ☐ *John's smile and pleasant manner diluted his criticism.*

**dim** ['dɪm] **1.** *adj.* barely lit; not bright. (Adv: *dimly.* Comp: *dimmer;* sup: *dimmest.*) ☐ *Mike's eyes adjusted slowly to the dim room.* **2.** *adj.* vague; unclear in the mind; hard to remember. (Adv: *dimly.* Comp: *dimmer;* sup: *dimmest.*) ☐ *I have a dim memory of my grandfather who died many years ago.*

**dime** ['dɑɪm] *n.* a coin worth 10 U.S. cents. ☐ *Ten dimes equal one dollar.*

**dimension** [dɪ 'mɛn ʃən] *n.* the measurement of something in one direction; the length, the width, or the depth of something. ☐ *What are the dimensions of the painting?*

**diminish** [dɪ 'mɪn ɪʃ] **1.** *tv.* to cause something to become smaller; to cause something to become less important; to reduce something. ☐ *Adding a patio to your house will diminish the size of your lawn.* **2.** *iv.* to become smaller; to become less important; to decrease. ☐ *The food supply diminished gradually.*

**dine** ['dɑɪn] *iv.* to eat a meal, especially to eat dinner. ☐ *I usually dine late in the evening.*

**dining room** ['dɑɪn ɪŋ rum] *n.* in a house, building, or apartment, the room where meals are served. ☐ *Our apartment does not have a dining room, so we eat in the kitchen.*

**dinner** ['dɪn ɚ] **1.** *n.* the main meal of the day; either a large midday meal or a large evening meal. ☐ *Since Mike works in the evenings, he eats his dinner at noon.* **2.** *n.* a formal event where an evening meal is served. ☐ *Many rich* *donors attended the museum's annual dinner.*

**dinosaur** ['daɪ nə sor] *n.* a large, prehistoric reptile that is now extinct. □ *The young students were fascinated by dinosaurs.*

**dip** ['dɪp] **1.** *n.* a sharp slope downward. □ *The ball gained speed as it rolled down the dip in the driveway.* **2.** *n.* a quick plunge into water or other liquid; a quick swim in water. □ *The dog took a dip in the pool.* **3.** *n.* a creamy mixture of foods or a thick sauce that is eaten with crackers, potato chips, or vegetables. (Plural only when referring to different kinds, types, instances, or varieties.) □ *We served vegetables and dip at the party.* 🄲 *I chose this one from a variety of dips.* **4.** *tv.* to lower and raise something quickly. □ *The plane dipped its wing as it flew over.*

**diplomacy** [dɪ 'plo mə si] **1.** *n.* tact; skill used in dealing with people. (No plural form.) □ *Bill's diplomacy keeps him on good behavior with everybody.* **2.** *n.* the business of maintaining good relationships between countries. (No plural form.) □ *Diplomacy between the two countries is strained.*

**direct** [dɪ 'rɛkt] **1.** *adj.* going from one place to another place without leaving the path; going the straightest or shortest way. (Adv: *directly.*) □ *I would like to fly to Chicago by the most direct route.* **2.** *adj.* exact; to the point; forthright. (Adv: *directly.*) □ *The students appreciated the professor's direct comments.* **3.** *tv.* to guide someone or something; to be in charge of someone or something. □ *The camp counselors direct programs for the children.* **4.** *tv.* to establish and oversee the design and execution of a play or a film, particularly overseeing the actors' performances; to instruct actors how to perform in a particular play, opera, film, etc. □ *John directed the play in which Mary Smith played a major role.*

**direction** [dɪ 'rɛk ʃən] **1.** *n.* the guidance or control of something. (No plural form.) □ *I work under the direction of a manager.* **2.** *n.* the path taken by something that moves; movement. □ *The birds all flew in the same direction.* **3.** *n.* the way that someone or something faces, such as to the north, south, east, or west. □ *The compass will show you the right direction.* **4. directions** *n.* instructions. □ *The directions for assembling the desk were printed on the box.* **5. directions** *n.* a statement of how to get to a place. □ *The man stopped to ask for directions to the beach.*

**direct object** [də 'rɛkt 'ɑb dʒɛkt] *n.* a noun, pronoun, or phrase that receives the action of a **transitive verb**; a noun, pronoun, or phrase on which the verb operates. (In the examples, *flower* is the **direct object**, and *Mary* is the **indirect object**.) □ *I gave Mary a flower.* □ *I gave a flower to Mary.*

**director** [dɪ 'rɛk tɚ] **1.** *n.* someone who leads a group of musicians as they perform; a conductor; someone who **directs** ④ actors, films, plays, etc. □ *Who is the director of this year's student play?* **2.** *n.* someone who is in charge of an institution, company, school, or department. □ *The company director ordered all of the employees to go home.*

**directory** [dɪ 'rɛk tə ri] **1.** *n.* a list of names arranged in the order of the alphabet, usually including addresses and telephone numbers. □ *Anne's telephone number was not in the directory.* **2.** *n.* any list that shows where to find someone or something. □ *I looked at the store directory to find where shoes were located.*

**dirt** ['dɚt] **1.** *n.* soil; earth. (No plural form.) □ *My children love to dig in dirt and get covered with grime.* **2.** *n.* dust, grime, mud; filth. (No plural form.) □

*The air was filled with dirt raised by the construction crew.*

**dirty** ['dɚ ti] **1.** *adj.* not clean. (Adv: *dirtily.* Comp: *dirtier;* sup: *dirtiest.*) □ *Bill washed the dirty floor.* **2.** *adj.* of or about sex or excrement in a crude way. (Adv: *dirtily.* Comp: *dirtier;* sup: *dirtiest.*) □ *The boys laughed as they told dirty stories.* **3.** *tv.* to cause something to become unclean. □ *Driving through the puddle dirtied the car.*

**disagree** [dɪs ə 'gri] **1.** *iv.* not to agree with someone; to have an opinion different from someone else's opinion. □ *I gave my answer to the question, but Mark disagreed.* **2. disagree with someone** *iv. + prep. phr.* [for food] to cause someone to have an upset stomach. □ *Onions disagree with me.*

**disagreeable** [dɪs ə 'gri ə bəl] *adj.* not pleasant; unpleasant. (Adv: *disagreeably.*) □ *The children avoided their disagreeable neighbor.*

**disagreement** [dɪs ə 'gri mənt] *n.* a difference in opinion; a failure to agree. (Plural only when referring to different kinds, types, instances, or varieties.) □ *Bill and Jane were in disagreement over who would prepare dinner.* Ⓒ *After a series of disagreements, the boys began to fight.*

**disappear** [dɪs ə 'piɚ] **1.** *iv.* to vanish; to cease to appear; to go out of sight. □ *I was so embarrassed, I wished I could disappear.* **2.** *iv.* to cease to exist in a place; to be no longer in a place. □ *The food disappeared quickly from the hungry man's plate.*

**disappoint** [dɪs ə 'pɔɪnt] *tv.* to fail to please someone; to make someone unhappy by not doing something that was expected or desired; to make someone unhappy by not being or happening as expected or desired. □ *Sue was disappointed by the cheap gift.*

**disapproval** [dɪs ə 'pruv əl] *n.* rejection; the failure to give approval to someone or something; unfavorable opinion. (No plural form.) □ *Tom could not hide his disapproval of the new manager.*

**disapprove** [dɪs ə 'pruv] **disapprove (of someone or something)** *iv. (+ prep. phr.)* not to approve of someone or something; to have a bad opinion of someone or something. □ *It is fine with me, but Bill disapproves.*

**disc** ['dɪsk] Go to **disk**.

**discharge 1.** ['dɪs tʃɑrdʒ] *n.* the sound of setting off of an explosion; the firing of a gun. □ *A child was wounded by the accidental discharge of the gun.* **2.** ['dɪs tʃɑrdʒ] *n.* the release of someone or something, especially when this requires official approval. □ *The soldier received a discharge from the army.* **3.** ['dɪs tʃɑrdʒ] *n.* the carrying out of one's duties; the performance of one's duties. (No plural form.) □ *In the military, the proper discharge of one's duties is essential.* **4.** ['dɪs tʃɑrdʒ] *n.* giving something off; releasing something. □ *Press the bandage against the wound to stop the discharge of blood.* **5.** ['dɪs tʃɑrdʒ] *n.* something that is given off; something that is let out. □ *Tears are just a normal discharge from the eye.* **6.** [dɪs 'tʃɑrdʒ] *tv.* to fire a gun; to cause an explosion. □ *The hunter accidentally discharged his gun while cleaning it.* **7.** [dɪs 'tʃɑrdʒ] *tv.* to dismiss someone from employment. □ *The company discharged 200 employees to cut costs.* **8.** [dɪs 'tʃɑrdʒ] *tv.* to let something out; to pour something out. □ *The engine discharged a stream of oil onto the floor.* **9.** [dɪs 'tʃɑrdʒ] *tv.* to do one's duty; to keep a promise; to repay a debt. □ *The judge ordered Mike to discharge his debts.*

**discipline** ['dɪs ə plɪn] **1.** *n.* controlled behavior achieved as the result of training; order. (Plural only when referring to different kinds, types, instances, or varieties.) □ *The soldier lived a life of discipline.* Ⓒ *John attempted to follow a number of disciplines in his daily life, but he always fell back on his own kind of chaos.* **2.** *n.* a field or branch of learning. □ *The student chose the discipline of mathematics.* **3.** *tv.* to punish someone. □ *The child was disciplined for telling a lie.* **4.** *tv.* to train someone or something to behave; to train someone or something to be obedient. □ *We disciplined our children well, and they are very well behaved.*

**discomfort** [dɪs 'kʌm fɚt] **1.** *n.* an uncomfortable feeling. (Plural only when referring to different kinds, types, instances, or varieties.) □ *Bill's discomfort was evident from the look on his face.* Ⓒ *You would never believe the discomforts I have suffered!* **2.** *n.* something that causes an uncomfortable feeling. *Damp clothing is just one of the discomforts of camping in the rain.*

**discover** [dɪ 'skʌv ɚ] *tv.* to find something for the first time; to become aware of something for the first time; to find out for the first time how something functions or happens. (The object can be a clause with **that** ⑦.) □ *We discovered a new restaurant in the city.*

**discovery** [dɪ 'skʌv ə ri] **1.** *n.* an instance of discovering something. □ *The discovery of the star made the young man famous.* **2.** *n.* someone or something that has been discovered; something not known of before. □ *The young man's discovery was a new star.*

**discreet** [dɪ 'skrit] *adj.* very cautious, so as not to draw anyone's attention; keeping something a secret; able to keep a secret. (Adv: *discreetly.*) □ *You can tell Jane anything. She is very discreet.*

**discuss** [dɪ 'skʌs] *tv.* to talk about something; to have a conversation about something. □ *The employees like to discuss their work at lunch.*

**disease** [dɪ 'ziz] *n.* an illness; a sickness. □ *There are no cures for many diseases.*

**disgrace** [dɪs 'gres] **1.** *n.* shame; the loss of honor. (Plural only when referring to different kinds, types, instances, or varieties.) □ *The disgrace caused by the shooting incident affected the soldier for many years.* Ⓒ *After a series of public disgraces, the mayor resigned.* **2.** *tv.* to bring shame upon someone. □ *The scandal disgraced the government.*

**disguise** [dɪs 'gaɪz] **1.** *n.* something that conceals who someone really is; something that conceals what something really is. □ *A clever disguise concealed the burglar's identity.* **2.** *tv.* to change the appearance of a thing or a person to make identification difficult. □ *Bill disguised himself as a soldier for the party.*

**disgust** [dɪs 'gʌst] **1.** *n.* a strong feeling of dislike; a loathing for someone or something. (No plural form.) □ *The horror film filled Mike with disgust.* **2.** *tv.* to revolt someone; to offend someone. □ *The raw fish disgusted me, so I left the table.*

**dish** ['dɪʃ] **1.** *n.* a plate; a flat, circular object used to serve food or to eat from. □ *The dishes are in the bottom cupboard.* **2.** *n.* a particular food that is served at a meal. □ *Meatloaf is my favorite dish.* **3. do the dishes** *phr.* to wash and dry **dishes** ①, as well as other items used at the table, after a meal. □ *Why am I always the one who has to do the dishes?*

**dishonest** [dɪs 'ɑn ɪst] *adj.* not honest. (Adv: *dishonestly.*) □ *The dishonest student lied to the teacher.*

**dishwater** ['dɪʃ wɑt ɚ] *n.* the water that dishes are to be washed in; water that dishes have been washed in. (No plural form.) □ *The dishwater was warm and soapy.*

**disillusioned** [dɪs ə 'lu ʒənd] *adj.* freed from illusion. □ *The disillusioned student was very unhappy about life.*

**disk** AND **disc** ['dɪsk] *n.* a thin, flat, and circular object. (See also **diskette, floppy disk.**) ☐ *Each of the table legs rested on a thin metal disk.*

**disk drive** ['dɪsk drɑɪv] *n.* a device inside a computer, used for reading and storing digital information on a spinning disk. (Can be shortened to **drive.**) ☐ *My disk drive is too full to hold any more software.*

**diskette** [dɪ 'skɛt] *n.* a device—usually held in a square of plastic—for storing digital computer information. (Can be shortened to **disk.**) ☐ *Bob loaded the program onto his computer from the diskette.*

**dismal** ['dɪz məl] *adj.* dull and filled with gloom. (Adv: *dismally.*) ☐ *The dismal, cold day made Bill unhappy.*

**dismiss** [dɪs 'mɪs] **1.** *tv.* to allow people to leave; to send people away. ☐ *At the end of the lecture, the professor dismissed the students.* **2.** *tv.* to end someone's employment. ☐ *Mary dismissed one of her employees today.* **3.** *tv.* to refuse to consider something; to refuse to listen to someone or something. ☐ *The parent dismissed the child's constant requests.*

**display** [dɪ 'sple] **1.** *tv.* to show something; to exhibit something. ☐ *Five artists will display their work at the gallery.* **2.** *n.* something that is shown; something that is exhibited. ☐ *The display of antique cars drew a large crowd.*

**dispose** [dɪ 'spoz] **dispose of** something *iv. + prep. phr.* to get rid of something; to throw something away. ☐ *The murderer disposed of the murder weapon.*

**dissolve** [dɪ 'zɑlv] **1.** *tv.* to melt a solid, such as sugar, into a liquid. ☐ *The recipe says to dissolve the sugar in the melted butter.* **2.** *tv.* to break up a union or a bond; to end an association. ☐ *The president dissolved the committee when there was no longer a need for it.* **3.** *iv.* [for a solid] to become mixed in a liquid. ☐ *The sugar dissolved in the boiling water.*

**distance** ['dɪs təns] *n.* the length of the space between two things. ☐ *The distance between my house and my office is 5 miles.*

**distant** ['dɪs tənt] **1.** *adj.* far away; not near in space or time. (Adv: *distantly.*) ☐ *The distant star was almost not visible.* **2.** *adj.* not very friendly; aloof. (Adv: *distantly.*) ☐ *John seems distant because he is upset.*

**distinct** [dɪ 'stɪŋkt] **1.** *adj.* different; separate; able to be seen as unique. (Adv: *distinctly.*) ☐ *The twins may look alike, but they have quite distinct personalities.* **2.** *adj.* obvious; easy to notice. (Adv: *distinctly.*) ☐ *There was a distinct smell of gas in the room before the explosion.*

**distress** [dɪ 'strɛs] **1.** *n.* grief; anxiety. (No plural form.) ☐ *In her distress, Jane called her best friend.* **2.** *tv.* to trouble someone; to cause someone to feel anxiety, discomfort, or suffering. ☐ *The unpleasant rumor distressed the celebrity.*

**district** ['dɪs trɪkt] *n.* an area; a region; a part of a country, state, county, or city. ☐ *What district does Max represent?*

**distrust** [dɪs 'trʌst] **1.** *n.* a lack of trust. (No plural form.) ☐ *The child had a distrust of strangers.* **2.** *tv.* not to trust someone or something; not to put one's trust in someone or something. ☐ *The dog distrusts John and won't go near him.*

**disturb** [dɪ 'stɚb] **1.** *tv.* to bother or annoy someone or something; to interrupt someone or something. ☐ *Every morning the birds disturb my sleep.* **2.** *tv.* to change, handle, or move something. ☐ *Every time Anne visits, she disturbs my furniture arrangement.*

**ditch** ['dɪtʃ] **1.** *n.* a long, low, narrow deep place in the ground, where water can flow. ☐ *The two fields were separated by a ditch.* **2.** *tv.* to land an airplane in the water and abandon it. ☐ *The pilot* *missed the runway and ditched the plane in the lake.*

**dive** ['dɑɪv] **1.** *n.* a jump into something, especially water, usually with one's hands or head first. □ *The athlete performed a fancy dive.* **2.** *n.* an underwater swim, as with scuba diving; time spent underwater. □ *John went on a dive in the Caribbean.* **3.** *n.* a plunge; a quick movement down. □ *The kite took a small dive when Anne pulled on the string.* **4.** *iv., irreg.* to jump into deep water, entering smoothly, leading with the feet or with the hands raised above the head. (Pt: *dived* or **dove**; pp: *dived.*) □ *Anne dove from the highest diving board.* **5.** *iv., irreg.* to spend time underwater, as with scuba diving. □ *Bill dives for coral.* **6.** *iv., irreg.* to go down quickly; to plunge down. □ *The submarine dived toward the sea bottom.* **7.** *iv., irreg.* to move away and hide quickly. □ *The frightened kitten dived under the couch.*

**diver** ['dɑɪ vɚ] **1.** *n.* someone who dives into water, especially in a contest with other divers. □ *The diver did a complicated dive and entered the water almost silently.* **2.** *n.* someone who swims underwater, as with scuba diving. □ *I watched the bubbles that followed the diver's path.*

**divide** [dɪ 'vɑɪd] **1. divide** a number **into** a number *tv. + obj. + prep. phr.* to determine what a number must be multiplied by to result in a given number; to determine how many times a number goes into a given number. □ *Divide 10 into 70 and you'll get 7.* **2. divide** a number **by** a number *tv. + obj. + prep. phr.* to split an amount into a stated number of equal parts; to determine how many times a number can be **divided into** ① by another number. (The symbol "÷" means *divided by.*) □ *If you divide 70 by 10, you'll get 7.* **3.** *tv.* to split something into smaller portions. □ *The woman's estate was divided into four parts, one for each of her children.* **4.** *iv.* to separate; to split up. □ *Here is where the path divides, with one trail leading to the left and the other to the right.* **5. divide by** a number *iv. + prep. phr.* to split [the amount represented by a number] into a given number of equal parts; to **divide** ② [a number] by another number. □ *To get a monthly average, Bob added up the column of numbers and then divided by 12.*

**divine** [dɪ 'vɑɪn] **1.** *adj.* of or about God; holy; sacred. (Adv: *divinely.*) □ *Every Sunday the minister preached about the divine word.* **2.** *adj.* fabulous; excellent; wonderful. (Fig. on ①. Adv: *divinely.*) □ *You make such divine fudge!*

**division** [dɪ 'vɪ ʒən] **1.** *n.* the process of dividing one number by another number. (No plural form.) □ *The teacher taught the children division.* **2.** *n.* a split; a dividing line. □ *The fence marked the division between the neighbors' yards.* **3.** *n.* a major part of a very large company. □ *The large corporation had divisions in various states.* **4.** *n.* dividing into portions. (Plural only when referring to different kinds, types, instances, or varieties.) □ *Tom's will ordered the division of his estate among his favorite charities.* Ⓒ *In our filing system, a red card marks the divisions between the different letters of the alphabet.*

**divorce** [dɪ 'vors] **1.** *n.* the legal ending of a marriage. (Plural only when referring to different kinds, types, instances, or varieties.) □ *Divorce is unpleasant for everyone involved.* Ⓒ *Tom had had two divorces in the last three years.* **2.** *tv.* to end one's marriage to someone. □ *Bill and Jane divorced each other.* **3.** *tv.* to grant ① to a husband and wife. □ *The judge divorced the couple.*

**dizzy** ['dɪz i] **1.** *adj.* feeling like everything is spinning around; not steady. (Adv: *dizzily.* Comp: *dizzier;* sup: *dizziest.*) □ *Watching the spinning wheel* *makes me dizzy.* **2.** *adj.* confusing; hectic. (Informal. Adv: *dizzily.* Comp: *dizzier;* sup: *dizziest.*) □ *After a few dizzy days, things calmed down at the office.*

**do** ['du] **1.** *tv.* to perform an action; to finish an action; to end an action. (Pt: **did**; pp: **done**. See also **does**, the third-person singular present.) □ *I did the report last night.* **2.** *tv.* to solve something; to find an answer. □ *Jimmy did the puzzle very quickly.* **3.** *tv.* to cover a distance; to go at a certain speed. □ *This car does over 100 miles per hour.* **4.** *iv.* to be OK; to suit one's needs. □ *Any color of paint will do.* **5.** *iv.* to get along; to function or exist. (Used to ask if someone is feeling all right, to inquire of someone's health.) □ *Sally was doing fine with her new job.* **6.** *aux.* <a question word in the present and past tenses.> (In the future tense, *will* is used.) □ *Did you go to New York or Boston last year?* **7.** *aux.* <a form used to make negative constructions.> □ *I don't want any peas, thank you.* **8.** *aux.* <a form used to emphasize a verb.> □ *I do want carrots tonight!* **9.** *aux.* <a particle used to repeat a verb that has already been said or written.> □ *My brother loves pizza, and so do I.* □ *He eats more than I do.* **10. have to do with someone or something** *phr.* to concern or affect someone or something; to be associated with or related to someone or something. □ *The new law has to do with lowering taxes.*

**dock** ['dɑk] **1.** *n.* a pier; a platform built for moving things and people on and off boats and ships. □ *Several people were fishing off the dock early in the morning.* **2.** *n.* a platform for loading and unloading goods. □ *The dock for loading trucks is at the back of the factory.* **3.** *tv.* to bring a ship or boat up to ①. □ *The captain gently docked the boat.* **4.** *iv.* [for a boat or ship] to arrive at ①; [for a boat or ship] to tie up to ①. □ *The ship from Europe docks tonight.*

**doctor** ['dɑk tɚ] **1.** *n.* someone who has received the highest degree from a university. (Abbreviated *Dr.*) □ *Most professors are doctors of philosophy.* **2.** *n.* someone who is licensed to practice medicine; a medical doctor. (Abbreviated *Dr.* when used as a title.) □ *Only doctors can write prescriptions.*

**document** ['dɑk jə mənt] **1.** *n.* a piece of paper or an electronic file with information (usually writing or printing) on it; a text. □ *The computer printed my document.* **2.** *tv.* to make and keep written records about something. □ *The manager documented the employee's errors.* **3.** *tv.* to list the evidence that will support what one has written. □ *I documented all the dates of birth in the family tree.* **4.** *tv.* to record something in detail over time. □ *Grandma's diary documented her entire life.*

**doe** ['do] *n.* a female of certain animals, such as the deer. □ *A doe and her baby lived in the woods.*

**does** ['dʌz] *aux.* <the third-person present singular of **do**.> □ *What does she do at the office all day?*

**doesn't** ['dʌz ənt] *cont.* "does not." □ *Jimmy doesn't like to go to school.*

**dog** ['dɔg] **1.** *n.* the common pet found in many homes, and used in hunting. □ *Please make your dog stop barking.* □ *The dog and its puppies ran outside to play with the children.* **2.** *tv.* to follow someone closely; to pursue someone eagerly. □ *Reporters dogged the candidate, trying to make him answer their questions.*

**doghouse** ['dɔg hɑʊs] *n., irreg.* a small outdoor shelter for a dog to sleep in. (Pl: [...hɑʊ zəz].) □ *Bob built a doghouse for his dog.*

**doll** ['dɑl] **1.** *n.* a figure of a human or animal, often a baby, used as a toy. □ *The child gently laid the doll in the crib.* **2.** *n.* an attractive or cute male or female

D

of any age. (Informal.) □ *Bob's girlfriend is quite a doll.*

**dollar** ['dɑl ɚ] *n.* the main unit of money in the United States; 100 cents; $1. (The dollar is also the name of the main unit of money in several other countries, but each is worth a value different from that of the U.S. dollar.) □ *The prices were rounded to the nearest dollar.*

**domain** [do 'men] **1.** *n.* the area where someone or something is typically found. □ *The library is my domain during the school year.* **2.** *n.* the area under the control of a ruler. □ *The chief marked the bounds of his domain with special symbols.*

**dome** ['dom] *n.* a rounded roof; the top of a building shaped like an upside-down bowl. □ *The church's dome could be seen for miles.*

**domestic** [də 'mɛs tɪk] **1.** *adj.* of or about the home; of, about, or within the family. (Adv: *domestically* [...ɪk li].) □ *When I arrive home from work, I must attend to my domestic chores.* **2.** *adj.* not imported; not foreign. (Adv: *domestically* [...ɪk li].) □ *Jane bought a domestic car.* **3.** *adj.* tame; not wild. (Adv: *domestically* [...ɪk li].) □ *Dogs are domestic animals.*

**dominate** ['dɑm ə net] *tv.* to control someone or something; to be the most important person or thing among certain other people or things. □ *The older brother dominated his younger brothers and sisters.*

**donate** ['do net] *tv.* to give something to a charity or other organization. □ *Mary donates money to several charities regularly.*

**done** ['dʌn] **1.** pp of **do**. **2.** *adj.* completed; finished. (Not compared. Not prenominal.) □ *Tell me when you are done.* **3.** *adj.* [of food] having been cooked fully or enough. (Can be compared.) □ *Your steak is more done than mine.*

**donkey** ['dɔŋ ki] *n.* an animal that has four feet and hooves, is smaller than a horse, and is used to carry things or people. □ *A donkey carried the heavy load.*

**don't** ['dont] *cont.* "do not." □ *Don't move!*

**doom** ['dum] **1.** *n.* a horrible fate; a death that cannot be avoided. (No plural form.) □ *The hero saved the city from doom.* **2.** *tv.* to cause someone or something to fail; to cause something to be ruined or destroyed. □ *The factory closings doomed the city.* **3.** *tv.* [for something] to condemn someone to an unpleasant future. □ *The prison sentence doomed the thief to many years in jail.*

**door** ['dor] **1.** *n.* a movable panel of wood, glass, or metal that fits into an opening through which someone or something may pass. □ *The door swung open when I pushed the handle.* **2.** *n.* the opening into which ① fits. □ *Bob walked through the door carrying some packages.* **3.** *n.* the (figurative) route or pathway to something, such as opportunity. (Fig. on ②.) □ *College is the door to greater success in life.*

**dorm** ['dorm] *n.* a **dormitory;** a building in which students live on a college campus. □ *Jane was assigned to a brand-new dorm at college.*

**dormitory** ['dorm ɪ tor i] **1.** *n.* a building or room containing beds for a number of people, especially on a college campus. (Abbreviated as **dorm.**) □ *The dormitory is not occupied during the summer.* **2.** *n.* a room housing sleeping facilities for a number of people. □ *There is a dormitory on the second floor and a large kitchen on the first floor.*

**dose** ['dos] **1.** *n.* the amount of medicine that is to be taken at one time. □ *Jane* *took a dose of medicine every four hours.* **2.** *tv.* to give someone or something a specific amount of medicine. □ *The sick man dosed himself with medicine.*

**dot** ['dɑt] *n.* a small spot; a small, round mark. □ *The leaky pen left dots of ink on the tablecloth.*

**double** ['dʌb əl] **1.** *adj.* having twice the amount as something else. (Adv: *doubly.*) □ *I made a double batch of cookies.* **2.** *tv.* to cause something to become twice the amount that it previously was. □ *Adding six new chapters doubled the size of the textbook.* **3.** *iv.* to become twice the amount that something was previously. □ *As the bread dough rises, it will double in size.*

**doubt** ['dɑʊt] **1.** *n.* lack of belief; a state of not being certain. (No plural form.) □ *There is little doubt that it will rain today.* **2.** *n.* a feeling of disbelief about something; a feeling of not being certain about something. (Often plural.) □ *The confident boxer had no doubts about his chances of winning.* **3.** *tv.* not to believe or trust something; to be uncertain about something; to consider something unlikely. □ *No one doubts Mary's abilities at the office.*

**dough** ['do] *n.* a soft mixture of flour, water, and possibly other ingredients. (Plural only when referring to different kinds, types, instances, or varieties.) □ *I added chocolate chips to the cookie dough.* Ⓒ *I prefer homemade cookie doughs to the store-bought doughs.*

**dove 1.** ['dov] a pt of **dive**. **2.** ['dʌv] *n.* a gray or white bird, a little smaller than a pigeon. (Often thought of as a symbol of peace.) □ *A white dove is a symbol of peace.*

**down** ['dɑʊn] **1.** *adj.* aimed toward a lower place or level; associated with a place or area that is lower than where one is at the moment. □ *Please do not go up the down staircase.* **2.** *adj.* sad; unhappy. □ *John really looks down. Let's go try to cheer him up!* **3.** *adj.* finished; completed. (Not prenominal.) □ *One chore down, three to be completed.* **4.** *adv.* from a higher place to a lower place; in a direction from a higher place to a lower place. □ *Please put that book down!* **5.** *adv.* from an earlier time to a later time. □ *The watch was handed down from father to son over the years.* **6.** *adv.* [moving] toward the south; [moving] to a place that corresponds to south on a map. □ *Every winter my parents leave the snow behind and go down to Florida.* **7.** *adv.* onto paper; into writing. □ *Anne writes her appointments down on her calendar.* **8.** *adv.* as an advance payment against the purchase price. □ *The Smiths put a deposit down on a new house.* **9.** *adv.* toward having less energy, strength, production, volume, or intensity. □ *Production at the factory went down after the accident.* **10.** *adv.* over [to some place]; in a specific direction. (Informal.) □ *If you go down to the corner, you can buy a newspaper there.* **11.** *prep.* on or along something to a lower place. □ *The path led down the hill.* **12.** *prep.* to the end of something; along the length of something. □ *Lost in thought, Mary walked down the empty beach.* **13.** *tv.* to make someone fall to the ground; to knock someone over. (Informal.) □ *Not looking where he was running, Billy downed the smaller child.* **14.** *tv.* to eat or swallow something very quickly and without much chewing. □ *The coyote downed the chicken and then quickly fled.* **15.** *n.* soft feathers, used inside pillows, quilts, etc. (No plural form.) □ *Blankets filled with down are warm and cozy on cold winter nights.*

**downpour** ['dɑʊn por] *n.* a very heavy rainfall. □ *The streets were flooded by the downpour.*

**downtown** ['dɑʊn 'tɑʊn] **1.** *adv.* [moving] toward the center of a town or city; [moving] into the center of a town or city. □ *We went downtown after work.* **2.** *adv.* at the center of a town or city. □ *We ate lunch downtown.* **3.** *adj.* in the center of a town or city; in the business district of a town or city. □ *I live 14 miles away from my downtown office.* **4.** *n.* the center of a town or city; the business district of a town or city. (No plural form.) □ *There's a huge statue in the center of downtown.*

**downward** ['dɑʊn wɚd] **1. downward(s)** *adv.* toward a lower position; toward a lower level. □ *The feather floated slowly downward.* **2.** *adj.* moving or directed toward a lower position; moving toward a lower level. (Adv: *downwardly.*) □ *The downward movement of the stock averages worried the investors.*

**doze** ['doz] **1.** *n.* a nap; a small amount of sleep. □ *Jane felt refreshed after a short doze.* **2.** *iv.* to take a nap; to sleep for a short period of time. □ *The student dozed during the lecture.*

**dozen** ['dʌz ən] **1.** *n.* a set of 12 things. □ *These napkins are sold by the dozen.* **2.** *adj.* twelve; a set or total of twelve. □ *The baker sold me a dozen rolls.*

**drab** ['dræb] *adj.* dull; gray; boring; not exciting. (Adv: *drably.* Comp: *drabber;* sup: *drabbest.*) □ *The detective wore a drab old coat.*

**draft** ['dræft] **1.** *n.* a current of air—usually cold—inside an enclosed space. □ *It is warm by the fire, but there is a draft by the door.* **2.** *n.* a roughly drawn plan; an early version of a document before the final copy is written. □ *Bill wrote the first draft of his paper.* **3.** *tv.* to force someone to serve in the military. □ *The military used to draft young men over the age of 18.* **4.** *tv.* to choose someone to do a job or a task. (Fig. on ③.) □ *The teacher drafted Tom and Sue to pass out papers.*

**drag** ['dræg] **1.** *tv.* to pull someone or something along on the ground. □ *I dragged Mary across the snow on the sled.* **2.** *tv.* to force someone or something to come along. □ *I had to drag my sister to the beach with me.* **3.** *iv.* [for someone or something] to touch the ground while being moved. □ *The curtains were too long and dragged on the floor.*

**drain** ['dren] **1.** *n.* a pipe or ditch that takes liquids away from an area. □ *The developer planned to build a drain so that the house would not flood.* **2.** *n.* something that takes away something else a little bit at a time; something that slowly takes something else away. □ *John's physical illness was a drain on his mental health, too.* **3.** *tv.* to draw liquid away from a place. □ *The doctor drained fluid from the wound.* **4.** *tv.* to empty a container of a liquid. □ *To drain the bathtub, just pull the plug.* **5.** *tv.* to take something away slowly, a bit at a time. (Fig. on ④.) □ *The heat drained our energy.* **6.** *tv.* to drink all the contents of a glass or container. □ *Anne drained the juice from her glass at breakfast.* **7.** *tv.* to empty something by drinking all the liquid from it. (Informal.) □ *The thirsty traveler drained the cup quickly.* **8.** *tv.* to remove someone's energy, endurance, or other quality. □ *The race drained me of all my strength.* **9.** *iv.* [for something] to lose liquid slowly. □ *The dishes drained on the counter.*

**drainage** ['dren ɪdʒ] **1.** *n.* removing liquid from something or some place. (No plural form.) □ *Drainage of the wound will promote healing.* **2.** *n.* the ability of an area to drain properly. (No plural form.) □ *The drainage on the golf course is excellent.*

**drama** ['drɑm ə] **1.** *n.* the study of plays and the theater. (No plural form.) □ *The famous director had studied drama in college.* **2.** *n.* a serious play or movie; a play or movie that is not a comedy. □ *The drama was so depressing that the whole audience was crying.* **3.** *n.* emotional, exciting, or thrilling events. (No plural form. Treated as singular.) □ *Sue related the drama of getting lost in the foreign city.*

**drank** ['dræŋk] pt of **drink**.

**drape** ['drep] **1.** *n.* a heavy curtain. (Often plural.) □ *Mary opened the drapes to let the sunlight in.* **2.** *n.* the particular way that fabric hangs. (No plural form.) □ *The silk had an elegant drape to it.* **3.** *tv.* to cover someone or something with fabric that hangs down in a decorative way. □ *An American flag draped the casket.*

**draw** ['drɔ] **1. a draw** *n.* a tie; a game where both teams have the same score. □ *If a football game ends in a draw, it goes into overtime.* **2.** *n.* an attraction; a reason people go to a particular place. □ *Florida's warm climate is one of its draws.* **3.** *iv., irreg.* to make pictures using pen, pencil, crayon, etc. (Pt: **drew**; pp: **drawn**.) □ *The artist draws very well.* **4.** *iv., irreg.* to approach someone or something; to get closer to someone or something. □ *As the car drew closer, I honked my horn.* **5.** *tv., irreg.* to make a picture of something with a pen, pencil, crayon, marker, etc. □ *The artist likes to draw cats.* **6.** *tv., irreg.* to attract someone or something. □ *The sound of music drew people to the park.* **7. draw** something **out (of** someone**)** *tv., irreg. + obj. + adv. (+ prep. phr.)* to encourage someone to say or tell something; to get some information from someone, with difficulty. □ *Mary drew the truth out of her son.* 🅃 *She drew out the truth.* **8.** *tv., irreg.* to take a breath; to take in air. □ *Lisa drew a large breath of fresh air.*

**drawer** ['drɔr] *n.* a storage box or compartment that slides in and out of a desk, dresser, etc. □ *When the desk drawer stuck, Mike forced it open with a knife.*

**drawn** ['drɔn] pp of **draw**.

**dread** ['drɛd] **1.** *n.* strong fear that something [bad] might happen or fear of something that is going to happen. (No plural form in this sense.) □ *The defendant faced the judge with much dread.* **2.** *tv.* to approach something in the future with fear, wishing that it would not happen. □ *Sally dreads appointments with her dentist.*

**dream** ['drim] **1.** *iv., irreg.* to have thoughts and images while one sleeps. (Pt/pp: *dreamed* or **dreamt**.) □ *Mary was dreaming when the alarm clock woke her up.* **2. dream of** something *iv., irreg. + prep. phr.* to think happily about something nice happening. □ *Anne dreams of owning her own business.* **3.** *tv., irreg.* to see something in one's **dreams** ④. (The object can be a clause with **that** ⑦.) □ *Mary dreamed that she saw her dead parents.* **4.** *n.* the thoughts and images one has while sleeping. □ *Tom told his best friend about his dreams.* **5.** *n.* a desire; a wish. □ *Owning a pony is Susie's dream.* **6. a dream** *n.* a very beautiful person or thing; something excellent; something that is of high quality. (No plural form.) □ *In the beautiful dress, Jane looked like a dream.*

**dreamt** ['drɛmt] a pt/pp of **dream**.

**drench** ['drɛntʃ] *tv.* to cover someone or something with liquid—water unless some other liquid is mentioned. □ *Jane drenched her french fries with ketchup.*

**dress** ['drɛs] **1.** *n.* an item of women's clothing covering an area from the shoulders to somewhere along the legs. □ *Anne's dress had a belt at the waist.* **2.** *n.* clothing in general. (No plural form.) □ *What is the proper dress for the party?* **3.** *adj.* [of clothing, shoes, etc.] formal. (Prenominal only.) □ *Tom hated wearing his dress clothes.* **4.** *tv.* to put clothes on someone. □ *Susie carefully dressed her doll.* **5.** *tv.* to bandage a wound or cut. □ *The nurse dressed the* *patient's cut.* **6.** *tv.* to prepare an animal's body for cooking or for market. ☐ *The butcher dressed the chicken quickly.* **7.** *iv.* to put clothes on oneself or someone else as in ④. ☐ *Mary dressed and got ready to leave the house.*

D

**dresser** ['drɛs ɚ] *n.* a piece of furniture with several drawers that clothes are kept in; a chest of drawers. ☐ *The dresser has five drawers.*

**drew** ['dru] pt of **draw**.

**drift** ['drɪft] **1.** *n.* a mass of snow or sand that is moved by the wind. ☐ *The strong wind made the desert sand form drifts.* **2.** *n.* a gradual movement toward someone or something, especially in air or water. (No plural form.) ☐ *I pulled on the string, trying to stop the kite's drift toward the tree.* **3.** *iv.* to move toward something or away from something gradually; to move gradually in some direction. ☐ *The sailboat drifted toward shore.* **4.** *iv.* [for someone] to move from place to place without a purpose or established plan. ☐ *Bill drifted from one job to another.*

**drill** ['drɪl] **1.** *n.* a machine that is used to make a hole in something. ☐ *Dave made a small hole in the wall with a drill.* **2.** *n.* a classroom practice exercise. ☐ *Every morning the students did a math drill.* **3.** *n.* an event where people practice what they would do in a real emergency. ☐ *An alarm sounded on the ship, but it was just a drill.* **4.** *tv.* to make a hole in something with ①. ☐ *The carpenter drilled a hole in the wall.* **5.** *tv.* to train people by having them practice. ☐ *The teacher drilled the students in math.* **6.** *iv.* to make holes with ①. ☐ *The carpenter drilled through the thick board.*

**drink** ['drɪŋk] **1.** *tv., irreg.* to swallow a liquid. (Pt: **drank**; pp: **drunk**.) ☐ *The thirsty guests drank a lot of water.* **2.** *iv., irreg.* to use or consume [alcohol]. ☐ *Mary doesn't drink because of her health.* **3.** *n.* a liquid meant to be swallowed. ☐ *I really need a drink. I am thirsty.* **4.** *n.* a container filled with a liquid that is meant to be swallowed. ☐ *I packed a drink in my lunch box.* **5.** *n.* a kind of drink that contains alcohol. ☐ *Bill needed a drink after his stressful day.*

**drip** ['drɪp] **1.** *n.* the action of liquid falling one drop at a time. ☐ *Jane could see a steady drip of fluid under her car.* **2.** *n.* the sound of a liquid falling one drop at a time. ☐ *The drip isn't very loud, but it still keeps me awake.* **3.** *tv.* to cause something to fall one drop at a time. ☐ *Please don't drip coffee on the tablecloth.* **4.** *iv.* to fall one drop at a time; to leak; to release one drop at a time. ☐ *The ice cream dripped onto the table as it melted.*

**drive** ['draɪv] **1.** *tv., irreg.* to cause a car or other vehicle to move, and to direct its movement. (Pt: **drove**; pp: **driven**.) ☐ *The driver drove the bus along the crowded street.* **2.** *tv., irreg.* to take someone in a vehicle to some place. ☐ *Jane drove her children to school.* **3.** *tv., irreg.* to ram or force something into or through something else. ☐ *The force of the wind drove a branch through the window.* **4.** *iv., irreg.* to ride in and steer or direct [a vehicle]. ☐ *The farmer drove to town on his tractor.* **5.** *n.* a trip in a car or other vehicle; the act of traveling as in ④. ☐ *Young children can make a long drive unpleasant.* **6.** *n.* the energy and desire to do something. (No plural form.) ☐ *Mike has the drive to work hard and succeed.* **7.** *n.* a place to **drive** ① a car between a road and a house or garage. ☐ *The drive leading to the garage is concrete.* **8.** *n.* an electronic device inside a computer, used for storing and reading computer files and programs. (Short for **disk drive**.) ☐ *I can't hear my disk drive spinning, and the stupid computer won't work! I guess it crashed.*

**driven** ['drɪv ən] pp of **drive**.

**driver** ['drɑɪ vɚ] *n.* someone who drives a car or other vehicle. □ *The police officer gave the driver a ticket for speeding.*

**drop** ['drɑp] **1.** *n.* a small ball of liquid; a small amount of liquid. □ *Drops of water ran down the side of the wall.* **2.** *n.* a sudden fall; a sudden downward movement. □ *The drop in the price of the company's stock was bad news.* **3.** *n.* the length of a fall; the distance between something and the ground. □ *There is a 50-foot drop from the cliff to the beach below.* **4.** *tv.* to let someone or something fall, either by accident or on purpose. □ *The tree dropped leaves onto the patio.* **5.** *tv.* to leave something out; to omit something. □ *The editor dropped the quotation from the article.* **6.** *tv.* to stop something; to end something; to stop talking about something. □ *Sally agreed to drop the lawsuit against her neighbor.* **7.** *iv.* to fall; to go lower; to sink. □ *Dead leaves dropped from the tree.*

**drove** ['drov] pt of **drive**.

**drown** ['drɑʊn] **1.** *tv.* to kill someone or something by suffocating the person or thing underwater. □ *The farmer drowned the unwanted kittens.* **2.** *tv.* to flood an area with a liquid. □ *Heavy rains drowned the newly planted fields.* **3.** *iv.* to die underwater as in ①. □ *The exhausted swimmer drowned.*

**drowsy** ['drɑʊ zi] *adj.* tired; sleepy. (Adv: *drowsily.* Comp: *drowsier;* sup: *drowsiest.*) □ *The heat made us all drowsy.*

**drug** ['drʌg] **1.** *n.* a medicine. □ *The drug made the patient feel better.* **2.** *n.* a substance used illegally for the pleasure it creates. □ *The drug was brought into the country illegally.* **3.** *tv.* to give someone ①. □ *The patient was drugged before surgery.*

**druggist** ['drʌg ɪst] *n.* someone who is licensed to package and sell medicine. □ *Ask the druggist to fill your prescription.*

**drugstore** ['drʌg stor] *n.* a place where medicine is sold, along with makeup, toothpaste, and many other items. □ *I bought some aspirin at the drugstore on the corner.*

**drum** ['drʌm] **1.** *n.* a musical instrument, usually shaped like a cylinder, with a flexible cover stretched over one or both ends. □ *Jane played drums in a local rock band.* **2.** *n.* a container shaped like ①. □ *The oil is stored in metal drums.*

**drunk** ['drʌŋk] **1.** pp of **drink**. **2.** *n.* a person who has taken too much alcohol. □ *Some drunk nearly hit our car.* **3.** *adj.* concerning a person who has taken too much alcohol. (Also **drunken**. Comp: *drunker;* sup: *drunkest.*) □ *A drunk driver nearly hit our car.*

**drunken** ['drʌŋk ən] Go to **drunk** ③.

**dry** ['drɑɪ] **1.** *adj.* not wet; not moist; without water. (Adv: *dryly.* Comp: *drier;* sup: *driest.*) □ *The wood is very dry and will burn well.* **2.** *adj.* not allowing alcohol to be sold; without alcohol. □ *The mayor wants to have a dry town.* **3.** *adj.* boring; not interesting. (Adv: *dryly.* Comp: *drier;* sup: *driest.*) □ *The very dry lecture caused me to yawn.* **4.** *tv.* to cause something to be ①; to remove all the moisture from something. □ *The heat of the fire will dry the pottery.* **5.** *iv.* to become ①; to completely lose moisture. □ *The shirts should dry in the clothes dryer.*

**dryer** ['drɑɪ ɚ] *n.* a machine that dries clothes. □ *Bill moved the clothes from the washing machine into the dryer.*

**dual** ['du əl] *adj.* having two parts; having two purposes. (Adv: *dually.*) □ *The television program had a dual purpose—to entertain and to educate.*

**duck** ['dʌk] **1.** *n.* a kind of fowl that lives near water, has a bill, and has webbed feet for swimming. □ *The ducks flew south for the winter.* **2.** *n.* the meat of ①.

(No plural form.) ☐ *I prefer duck to chicken, because it is juicier.* **3.** *n.* a sturdy kind of cotton cloth. (Plural only when referring to different kinds, types, instances, or varieties.) ☐ *Duck is a very strong fabric, once used for tents and awnings.* Ⓒ *The ducks that we normally stock come in a variety of weights and colors.* **4.** *iv.* to stoop down so that one doesn't get hit by something; to dip one's head so one doesn't bump it into something. ☐ *The children ducked as the ball flew over their heads.* **5.** *iv.* to avoid being seen by moving quickly somewhere. ☐ *Billy ducked behind the couch, trying to hide from his parents.* **6.** *tv.* to dip one's head down so that it is not hit against something. ☐ *The basketball player ducked his head as he walked down the stairs.*

**due** ['du] **1. dues** *n.* a sum of money owed by each member of an organization. (Treated as plural. Rarely countable.) ☐ *Each member must pay dues in order to attend meetings.* **2.** *adj.* owing; having to be paid. (Not prenominal.) ☐ *A payment is due now.* **3.** *adv.* directly; in the exact direction; straight. ☐ *The troops marched due south.* **4. due to someone or something** *phr.* owing to someone or something; because of someone or something. (This use is objected to by some.) ☐ *The play was canceled due to a fire in the theater.*

**duet** [du 'ɛt] *n.* music to be performed by two people. ☐ *The conductor chose two musicians to play the duet.*

**dug** ['dʌg] pt/pp of **dig**.

**dull** ['dʌl] **1.** *adj.* not sharp; blunt. (Adv: *dully.* Comp: *duller;* sup: *dullest.*) ☐ *The butcher sharpened the dull knife.* **2.** *adj.* not exciting; boring. (Adv: *dully.* Comp: *duller;* sup: *dullest.*) ☐ *I fell asleep during the dull movie.* **3.** *adj.* not shiny. (Adv: *dully.* Comp: *duller;* sup: *dullest.*) ☐ *Dull silverware should be polished.* **4.** *adj.* not smart; somewhat stupid. (Adv: *dully.* Comp: *duller;* sup: *dullest.*) ☐ *Our dog is very dull and is hard to train.* **5.** *tv.* to make something less sharp. ☐ *Cutting the heavy paper dulled the scissors.* **6.** *tv.* to lessen physical or emotional pain. ☐ *The soft music dulled Mary's sorrow.*

**dumb** ['dʌm] **1.** *adj.* stupid; foolish; not smart. (Adv: *dumbly.* Comp: *dumber;* sup: *dumbest.*) ☐ *Sometimes you seem so dumb!* **2.** *adj.* [of animals] not able to speak. (Can be offensive when applied to humans. Adv: *dumbly.* Comp: *dumber;* sup: *dumbest.*) ☐ *Animals—except for humans, of course—are dumb.*

**dump** ['dʌmp] **1.** *n.* a place where trash is taken. ☐ *The dump caught fire.* **2.** *tv.* to unload something into a pile; to empty something into a pile. ☐ *A big truck dumped the sand into the backyard.*

**dunce** ['dʌns] *n.* a stupid-acting person; someone who learns things slowly. ☐ *Mike feels like a dunce in math class.*

**dung** ['dʌŋ] *n.* feces, especially from animals. (No plural form.) ☐ *The pasture was littered with cow dung.*

**dunk** ['dʌŋk] *tv.* to push someone underwater for a few moments. ☐ *Laughing, the children tried to dunk their father.*

**during** ['dɚ ɪŋ] **1.** *prep.* throughout an event that lasts a period of time; all through a period of time. ☐ *During class, the students sit at their desks.* **2.** *prep.* at some point in a period of time; at some time within a period of time. ☐ *The alarm rang twice during history class.*

**dusk** ['dʌsk] *n.* the period of the day after the sun sets but before it is completely dark; twilight. ☐ *The stars begin to appear at dusk.*

**dust** ['dʌst] **1.** *n.* a fine powder of dried earth. (No plural form.) ☐ *Dust blew into my eyes and stung them.* **2.** *n.* a fine powder, especially particles that settle from the air and coat indoor surfaces. (No plural form.) □ *The dust on the antique table was thick.* **3.** *tv.* to clean a surface or a place by removing ②. □ *The maid dusted the room until it was spotless.* **4.** *tv.* to cover something with ① or ②. □ *The wind will dust the patio furniture with dirt.* **5.** *tv.* to spray crops with an insect killer or a weed-killer. (Referred originally to powdered chemicals.) □ *The plane will dust the crops from the sky.* **6.** *iv.* to remove ② from something or from a place as a part of cleaning. □ *I have to dust before the guests arrive.*

**dusty** ['dʌs ti] **1.** *adj.* covered with dust; full of dust. (Adv: *dustily.* Comp: *dustier;* sup: *dustiest.*) □ *It was hard to recognize the dusty old painting.* **2.** *adj.* like dust; [of a color] somewhat gray, as if mixed with dust. (Comp: *dustier;* sup: *dustiest.*) □ *The decorator painted the walls a dusty rose.*

**duty** ['du ti] **1.** *n.* a task; an obligation; a responsibility. □ *The officer's first duty was to balance the company's budget.* **2.** *n.* a tax placed on products from another country. □ *Congress voted to raise the duty on imported cars.*

**dwarf** ['dworf] **1.** *n., irreg.* someone or something that is smaller than normal or typical. (Pl: **dwarves** or *dwarfs.*) □ *Mike is a dwarf, but he prefers to be called a little person.* **2.** *adj.* smaller than expected; smaller than normally found. (Prenominal only.) □ *A dwarf tree is smaller than a regular tree.* **3.** *tv.* [for someone or something large] to make someone or something appear even smaller in a comparison. □ *The giant oak dwarfed the tiny young tree.*

**dwarves** ['dworvz] a pl of **dwarf.**

**dwell** ['dwɛl] **1.** *iv., irreg.* to live some place; to live in a place. (Pt/pp: *dwelled* or **dwelt.**) □ *Many people dwell in the mountains and love it.* **2. dwell on** something *iv., irreg. + prep. phr.* to linger on something; to keep thinking about an idea. □ *The candidate dwelled on his opponent's flaws.*

**dwelling** ['dwɛl ɪŋ] *n.* a residence; a place where someone lives. □ *A dormitory is the typical dwelling for a college student.*

**dwelt** ['dwɛlt] a pt/pp of **dwell.**

**dye** ['dɑɪ] **1.** *n.* a liquid that is used to color fabric or hair. (See also **stain.**) □ *We asked for a green dye, but they sent yellow.* **2.** *tv.* to color something by placing it in ①; to color something with ①. (Present participle: *dyeing.*) □ *I asked the hairdresser to dye my hair blond.*

**dying** ['dɑɪ ɪŋ] **1.** the present participle of **die. 2.** *adj.* in the process of becoming dead. □ *The dying man reached for the nurse's hand.*

**dynamite** ['dɑɪ nə mɑɪt] **1.** *n.* a chemical that is meant to explode, usually ammonium nitrate. (Plural only when referring to different kinds, types, instances, or varieties.) □ *The engineers used dynamite to destroy the old warehouse.* Ⓒ *We tested dynamites of different ages and found them all equally good.* **2.** *n.* someone or something that causes a great shock or surprise; someone or something exciting that attracts a lot of attention or interest. (Fig. on ①. Informal.) □ *These clothes would be dynamite on you!* **3.** *tv.* to destroy something by an explosion with ①. □ *The demolition crew dynamited the old warehouse.*

D

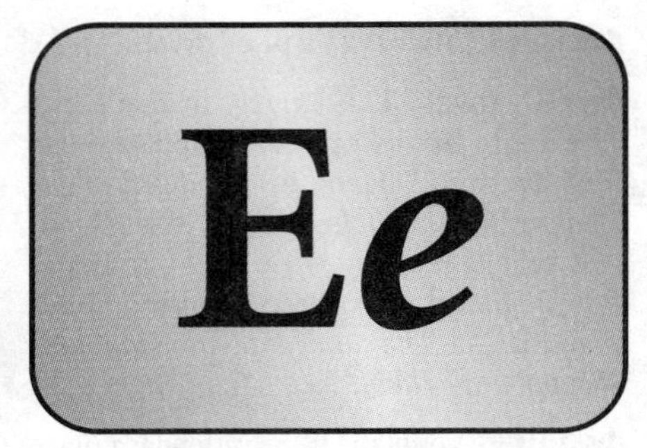

E

**each** ['itʃ] **1.** *adj.* every [one]. □ *Each egg in the carton was broken.* **2.** *pron.* every one [of those mentioned before]; every individual person or thing [of those mentioned before]. □ *I have two little puppies. Each is soft and warm.* **3.** *adv.* for every one. □ *The children were given one cookie each.*

**eager** ['i gɚ] **1.** *adj.* acting very willing and ready to do something. (Adv: *eagerly.*) □ *The eager puppy jumped around at our feet.* **2. eager to** do something *adj.* + *inf.* having a strong desire to do something and being very willing to do it. □ *I am eager to dance because they are playing my favorite music.*

**eagle** ['i gəl] *n.* a strong bird of prey of the hawk family, having excellent vision. □ *An eagle soared above our heads.*

**ear** ['ɪr] **1.** *n.* the organ of hearing, one of which is located on either side of the head. □ *I have some hearing loss in my right ear.* **2.** *n.* the external, visible part of the organ of hearing. □ *The girl brushed her hair behind her ears.* **3.** *n.* a corncob and the corn growing on it. (Short for ear of corn.) □ *I think I'll have another ear of that corn. It's delicious.*

**eardrum** ['ɪr drəm] *n.* a very thin bit of tissue inside the ear that vibrates when struck by sound waves. □ *Anne's right eardrum was operated on by an ear surgeon.*

**early** ['ɚ li] **1.** *adj.* happening toward the first part of something; happening toward the beginning of something. (Comp: *earlier;* sup: *earliest.*) □ *Some of the early reports about the plane crash were not correct.* **2.** *adj.* arriving before the expected time. (Comp: *earlier;* sup: *earliest.*) □ *The train is never early. It is always on time.* **3.** *adj.* ancient; happening long ago in time. (Comp: *earlier;* sup: *earliest.*) □ *Bob wants to study early people when he goes to college.* **4.** *adv.* during or toward the first part of something. (Comp: *earlier;* sup: *earliest.*) □ *The mail carrier comes early in the day.* **5.** *adv.* before the expected time. (Comp: *earlier;* sup: *earliest.*) □ *Let's leave early for the beach.*

**earn** ['ɚn] **1.** *tv.* to gain a sum of money or something else of value, especially by working. □ *Jane earns $40,000 a year.* **2.** *tv.* to merit something; to deserve something. (Fig. on ①.) □ *Mary earned a promotion at work.*

**earnest** ['ɚ nəst] **1.** *adj.* very serious; wishing to do [something] very well. (Adv: *earnestly.*) □ *The earnest student studied constantly.* **2. in earnest** *phr.* [done] with good and honest intentions. □ *Mary's comments were made in earnest. She really meant them.*

**ear of corn** ['ɪr əv 'korn] *n.* the rod-like, fiber core on which grains of corn grow. (Pl: *ears of corn.*) □ *I just love to eat freshly picked ears of corn.*

**earth** ['ɚθ] **1.** *n.* the planet we live on; the third planet from the sun. (Often capitalized. No plural form.) □ *More than two-thirds of the earth is covered with water.* **2.** *n.* soil; land. (No plural form.) □ *Blades of grass emerged from the damp earth.* **3.** *n.* the surface of ①. (No plural form.) □ *The plane fell to earth.*

**earthly** ['ɚθ li] *adj.* of or on the earth; of a part of life on earth rather than in heaven. □ *This earthly life will soon come to an end.*

**earthquake** AND **quake** ['ɚθ kwek, 'kwek] *n.* a violent shaking of the ground by natural forces. □ *An earthquake struck a large city on the coast.*

**earthworm** ['ɚθ wɚm] *n.* a worm that lives in the soil. □ *Earthworms burrow through the soil.*

**ease** ['iz] **1.** *tv.* to make something less hard to do; to make something easier. □ *A burst of energy eased Bill's task.* **2.** *tv.* to make something become less strong or have less pain. □ *The drugs eased my pain.* **3.** *tv.* to move something [somewhere] gently and carefully. □ *Bill eased the gift into the box.* **4.** *iv.* to become less hard or less difficult. □ *Toward the end of the year, Jane's work finally eased.* **5.** *n.* freedom from problems or bother; peaceful rest. (No plural form.) □ *If I had enough money, I would live a life of ease.*

**east** ['ist] **1.** *n.* the direction to the right of someone or something facing north; the direction where the sun appears to rise. (No plural form.) □ *We watched the sun rise in the east.* **2.** *n.* the eastern region of a country. (Capitalized when referring to a region of the U.S.) □ *Bob came from the East and never felt comfortable in the West.* **3.** *adj.* in ①; from ①; toward ①; of or about ①. (Prenominal only.) □ *Susan lived on the east side of town.* **4.** *adv.* at, facing, or toward ①. □ *When you get to the corner, turn east.*

**easy** ['i zi] **1.** *adj.* simple; not hard; not difficult. (Adv: *easily.* Comp: *easier;* sup: *easiest.*) □ *Math is not easy for many people.* **2.** *adv.* without stress; without worry; relaxed. (Comp: *easier.*) □ *Let's just take it easy today and go to the beach.*

**eat** ['it] **1.** *tv., irreg.* to put food in one's mouth, chew, and swallow it. (Pt: **ate**; pp: **eaten**.) □ *We ate lunch in a restaurant.* **2.** *tv., irreg.* to create a hole by chewing or wearing something away. □ *A mouse ate a hole in the cereal box.* **3.** *iv., irreg.* to take food into the body. □ *When are we going to eat? I'm hungry.*

**eaten** ['it n] pp of eat.

**echo** ['ɛk o] **1.** *n.* a sound that is heard twice because the sound waves have bounced off a surface and returned. (Pl ends in *-es.*) □ *An echo bounced off the bluff.* **2.** *iv.* [for a sound] to reflect back. □ *The hiker's voice echoed clearly.* **3.** *tv.* to reflect sound; to repeat a sound. □ *The mountains echoed the thunder.* **4.** *tv.* to repeat something that someone has said. □ *Susan echoed everything her mother said.*

**economic** [ɛk ə 'nɑm ɪk] **1.** *adj.* of or about ③. (Adv: *economically* [...ɪk li].) □ *Our city suffered economic problems when the factory closed.* **2.** *adj.* saving money; using money wisely. (Also **economical**. Adv: *economically* [...ɪk li].) □ *Buying in large quantities is an economic way to shop.* **3. economics** *n.* financial matters or issues. (Usually treated as singular.) □ *A committee was formed to study the economics of closing some military bases.* **4. economics** *n.* the study of the production and use of goods and services in a society. (Treated as singular.) □ *Mary has a college degree in economics.*

**edge** ['ɛdʒ] **1.** *n.* the rim of something; the outer border of something. □ *The children stood at the edge of the pond.* **2.** *n.* the cutting part of a cutting tool or instrument. □ *The butter knife has a dull edge.* **3.** *n.* an advantage. (No plural form.) □ *A good education will give you an edge in the job market.* **4.** *tv.* to provide something with a border. □ *I edged the curtains with lace.*

**edible** ['ɛd ə bəl] *adj.* able to be eaten. (Adv: *edibly.*) □ *The food you cook is simply not edible.*

**edit** ['ɛd ɪt] *tv.* to prepare text, video, or audio for publication or production. □

E

*You must edit this video before it goes on television.*

**edition** [ɪ 'dɪ ʃən] *n.* the copies of one book made in one printing or series of printings until the text is changed or revised. □ *A new edition of the dictionary is coming out soon.*

E

**editor** ['ɛd ɪ tɚ] **1.** *n.* someone who prepares text for publication; someone who prepares film, video, or audio for production. □ *Bill is an editor for a book publishing company.* **2.** *n.* someone who works for a newspaper, a magazine, or a book publisher, arranging for new material, editing, and production. □ *The editor is responsible for getting new manuscripts.*

**educate** ['ɛdʒ ə ket] *tv.* to teach someone something; to instruct someone how to do something. □ *Please educate Bill in the rules of good manners.*

**education** [ɛdʒ ə 'ke ʃən] **1.** *n.* the teaching of knowledge and skills; a system for teaching knowledge and skills. (No plural form.) □ *What could be more important than the education of our children?* **2.** *n.* the learning or knowledge that is obtained by studying or being taught. (No plural form.) □ *I lacked enough education to get a good job.*

**eel** ['il] **1.** *n.* a long, snake-like fish not having fins. □ *Eels have smooth skin and can be eaten.* **2.** *n.* the edible flesh of ①. (No plural form.) □ *Pickled eel is a tasty kind of food.*

**effect** [ɪ 'fɛkt] **1.** *n.* a result; something that happens because of something else. (Compare this with **affect**.) □ *Noise from airplanes has a bad effect on people who live near the airport.* **2.** *tv.* to cause a result; to produce a result. □ *The countries that had been at war effected a peace treaty.*

**effective** [ɪ 'fɛk tɪv] *adj.* good at producing or causing results. (Adv: *effectively.*) □ *Anne is an effective lecturer.*

**efficient** [ɪ 'fɪ ʃənt] *adj.* organized; using time, energy, and money without waste. (Adv: *efficiently.*) □ *Anne is an efficient worker.*

**effort** ['ɛf ɚt] *n.* the use of physical or mental energy to do hard work. □ *Please make an effort to improve your grades at school.*

**egg** ['ɛg] **1.** *n.* the female reproductive cell. □ *A fertilized egg usually grows into a baby.* **2.** *n.* a round object, containing ①, covered with a shell, produced by a female bird or reptile and often used for food. □ *A yellow chick came out of the egg.* **3.** *n.* the edible part of an **egg** ②. □ *You should put an egg in the cake batter.* **4.** *n.* some of an **egg** ②. (No plural form. Treated as singular.) □ *There is some egg on the counter.*

**eggshell** ['ɛg ʃɛl] *n.* the hard, protective outside layer of a bird's egg. □ *The eggshell was cracked, so I did not use the egg.*

**ego** ['i go] **1.** *n.* one's sense of oneself and one's value. (Pl ends in *-s.*) □ *Bill's ego is very fragile today. Be nice to him.* **2.** *n.* an overly large sense of self-esteem; a view of oneself that makes one seem far more important than one really is. (Pl ends in *-s.*) □ *The actor's huge ego is ruining the play.*

**eight** ['et] 8. Go to **four** for senses and examples.

**eighteen** ['et tin] 18. Go to **four** for senses and examples.

**eighteenth** [et 'tinθ] 18th. Go to **fourth** for senses and examples.

**eighth** ['etθ] 8th. Go to **fourth** for senses and examples.

**eightieth** ['ɛt i əθ] 80th. Go to **fourth** for senses and examples.

**eighty** ['et i] 80. Go to **forty** for senses and examples.

**either** ['i ðɚ] **1.** *adj.* one or the other [choosing between two people or things]; no matter which [of two]. □ *You can enter the building through either door.* **2.** *adj.* both; each of two; one and the other. □ *There is a door at either end of the hall.* **3.** *pron.* one person or thing, or the other person or thing; one person or thing from a choice of two people or things. (Treated as singular.) □ *Either will work fine, but if given a choice, I prefer the red one.* **4.** *conj.* one or the other from a choice of two things. (With *or.*) □ *Either finish the project by 5:00, or you will be fired.* □ *I need to talk to either Bob or Anne about the problem.* **5.** *adv.* as well; in addition; also. (Only in negative constructions. Use **too** in the affirmative.) □ *I don't like the zoo, and I don't like the museum, either.*

**elastic** [ə 'læs tɪk] **1.** *adj.* [of something that is] able to return to its original shape after being stretched. (Adv: *elastically* [...ɪk li].) □ *The skirt has an elastic band around its waist.* **2.** *n.* [in clothing] a band of fabric and rubber that can stretch. □ *I broke the elastic in my skirt and now it won't stay up.*

**elbow** ['ɛl bo] **1.** *n.* the joint where the arm bends in the middle. □ *I could not bend my elbow when my arm was in a cast.* **2.** *n.* a pipe that is bent, curved, or shaped like the angle of ①. □ *The plumber replaced the broken elbow under the sink.*

**elect** [ɪ 'lɛkt] *tv.* [for a group of voters] to choose someone by voting. □ *The students elected David as junior class president.*

**election** [ɪ 'lɛk ʃən] *n.* the process of voting to choose between two or more options. □ *How many people voted in the last election?*

**electric** [ɪ 'lɛk trɪk] **1.** *adj.* carrying electricity; of or about electricity. (Also *electrical.* Adv: *electrically* [...ɪk li].) □ *Many electric cables run underneath the office building.* **2.** *adj.* producing electricity. □ *The electric utility company increased its rates.* **3.** *adj.* powered by electricity. (Adv: *electrically* [...ɪk li].) □ *Our apartment has electric heat.* **4.** *adj.* exciting; full of excitement; thrilling. (Adv: *electrically* [...ɪk li].) □ *Mary's brief, electric speech stunned the audience.*

**electricity** [ɪ lɛk 'trɪs ə ti] *n.* a source of power that comes from batteries, electric companies, and natural occurrences like friction and lightning. (No plural form.) □ *The dam produced electricity for the whole valley.*

**electric plug** [ɪ 'lɛk trɪk 'plʌg] **1.** *n.* a device used to attach a lamp or appliance to an electrical outlet. (Can be shortened to **plug.**) □ *John damaged the lamp's electric plug when he stepped on it.* **2.** *n.* an electrical outlet or receptacle. (Informal. Can be shortened to **plug.**) □ *I moved my computer so that it would be closer to the electric plug.*

**electric receptacle** [ɪ 'lɛk trɪk rɪ 'sɛp tɪ kəl] *n.* an electric outlet; a connection, usually in the wall, to which lamps and appliances can be attached. (Can be shortened to **receptacle.**) □ *There is no electric receptacle in the entire room!*

**electromagnetic** [ɛ lɛk tro mæg 'nɛt ɪk] *adj.* concerning electric and magnetic waves, especially as used in broadcasting. (Adv: *electromagnetically* [...ɪk li].) □ *Electromagnetic waves carry information to radios, television sets, and cellular telephones.*

**electron** [ɪ 'lɛk trɑn] *n.* a negatively charged particle, smaller than an atom. □ *Electrons orbit around an atom's nucleus.*

**electronic** [ɪ lɛk 'trɑn ɪk] **1.** *adj.* of or about modern electrical circuits as found in radios and television sets. (Adv: *electronically* [...ɪk li].) □ *I took a course in electronic technology.* **2. electronics** *n.* the study and design of the electrical circuits used in computers, radios, televisions, etc. (Treated as singular.) ☐ *Susan took a basic course in electronics at the university.*

**elegance** ['ɛl ə gəns] *n.* fine style, grace, and beauty. (No plural form.) ☐ *Bill is known for his charm and quiet elegance.*

**elegant** ['ɛl ə gənt] *adj.* beautiful; having or showing good taste. (Adv: *elegantly.*) ☐ *Anne wore an elegant gown to the party.*

**element** ['ɛl ə mənt] **1.** *n.* one of several kinds of basic matter that cannot be broken down further into other kinds of basic matter. ☐ *All matter is made of the different elements.* **2.** *n.* a piece of a larger theme. ☐ *The film lacked some of the elements of a good mystery.* **3. the elements** *n.* the weather; air, wind, rain, and sunlight. (Treated as plural, but not countable.) ☐ *Exposure to the elements will cause the car to rust.*

**elementary** [ɛl ə 'mɛn tri] *adj.* basic; introductory. ☐ *I am taking a course in elementary math.*

**elephant** ['ɛl ə fənt] *n.* a large land mammal of Africa and Asia, with tough gray skin, large ears, and a long trunk. ☐ *The baby elephant performed tricks at the circus.*

**elevator** ['ɛl ə ve tɚ] *n.* a moving cage or chamber that carries people and things from floor to floor in a building with more than one story. ☐ *Does this elevator go to the 32nd floor?*

**eleven** [ɪ 'lɛv ən] 11. Go to **four** for senses and examples.

**eleventh** [ɪ 'lɛv ənθ] 11th. Go to **fourth** for senses and examples.

**elf** ['ɛlf] *n., irreg.* a small human-like creature—full of mischief—of fairy tales and myths. (Pl: **elves.**) ☐ *Susie read a story about elves and fairies.*

**elk** ['ɛlk] **1.** *n., irreg.* [in North America] a large deer, the males of which have large, spreading horns. (Pl: *elk* or *elks.*) ☐ *Tom hunts elk each fall.* **2.** *n., irreg.* [in Europe] a moose. ☐ *There are many elk in Sweden and Russia.*

**elm** ['ɛlm] **1.** *n.* a large tree that loses its leaves each fall and is planted to make shade. ☐ *We sat in the shade under an elm.* **2.** *n.* wood from ①. (Plural only when referring to different kinds, types, instances, or varieties.) ☐ *This bench is made of elm.* Ⓒ *The elms used in fine furniture usually have finer grains.* **3.** *adj.* made of ②. ☐ *We sat on a strong elm bench and ate lunch.*

**else** ['ɛls] **1.** *adj.* otherwise; apart from someone or something; instead. ☐ *Bill wasn't invited to the party, but everybody else at the office was.* **2.** *adj.* in addition to someone or something; as well. ☐ *What else do you want for your birthday?*

**elsewhere** ['ɛls ʍɛr] *adv.* in some other place. ☐ *My house keys are not where I thought I left them last night. I will have to search elsewhere to find them.*

**elude** [ɪ 'lud] **1.** *tv.* to evade or avoid capture, often by being clever. ☐ *The robber's goal was to elude the police.* **2.** *tv.* [for a concept] to be hard to remember or understand. ☐ *The correct answer eludes me.*

**elusive** [ɪ 'lu sɪv] *adj.* [of someone or something that is] hard to find or hard to catch. (Adv: *elusively.*) ☐ *The elusive butterfly could not be caught.*

**elves** ['ɛlvz] pl of **elf.**

**embarrass** [ɛm 'bɛr əs] *tv.* to make someone feel ashamed or uncomfortable by making something visible or known in public. ☐ *Please don't embarrass me in public again!*

**emergency** [ɪ 'mɚ dʒən si] **1.** *n.* a time when urgent action is needed; a dangerous situation that must be taken care of at once. ☐ *The earthquake created an emergency.* **2.** *adj.* <the adj. use of ①.> ☐ *We keep an emergency food supply in the basement.*

**emergency room** [ɪ 'mɚ dʒən si rum] *n.* the place in a hospital where injuries and sudden illnesses are cared for. □ *We took Bill to the emergency room because he had pains in his chest.*

**emotion** [ɪ 'mo ʃən] **1.** *n.* feeling—other than with the physical senses—or a show of feeling. (No plural form.) □ *Jane's poems usually have a lot of emotion.* **2.** *n.* a feeling, such as sadness, joy, anxiety, etc. □ *I suddenly felt emotions I had not felt in years.*

**emperor** ['ɛmp ɚ rɚ] *n.* someone, especially a male, who rules an **empire**. □ *When the emperor died, his son took his place.*

**emphases** ['ɛm fə siz] pl of **emphasis**.

**emphasis** ['ɛm fə sɪs] **1.** *n.* importance that is placed on or given to something. (No plural form.) □ *I want you to give this idea extra emphasis in your letter.* **2.** *n., irreg.* something that has received or should receive ①. (Pl: **emphases**.) □ *Money is too much of an emphasis in his life.* **3.** *n.* increased loudness or (voice) stress given to particular syllables, words, or phrases. (No plural form.) □ *Place more emphasis on the first syllable.*

**emphasize** ['ɛm fə saɪz] **1.** *tv.* to place special importance on something. □ *I tried to emphasize the importance of good grades to Tom.* **2.** *tv.* to stress something, especially a syllable, word, or phrase. □ *You need not emphasize the last syllable so much.*

**empire** ['ɛm paɪr] *n.* a group of countries ruled by an **emperor** or **empress**. □ *When the emperor died, his son began to rule the empire.*

**employ** [ɛm 'plɔɪ] **1.** *tv.* to hire someone to do work for pay. □ *Do you have the authority to employ these people?* **2.** *tv.* to use something for a particular purpose. □ *Susan employed all the resources available to her.*

**employable** [ɛm 'plɔɪ ə bəl] *adj.* suitable for employment. (Adv: *employably.*) □ *Jane is certainly employable in any executive position.*

**employee** [ɛm 'plɔɪ i] *n.* someone who works for a company or a person for pay. □ *There are over 100 employees at this company.*

**employer** [ɛm 'plɔɪ ɚ] *n.* a person or company that employs people. □ *I asked my employer for a raise.*

**employment** [ɛm 'plɔɪ mənt] **1.** *n.* the condition of holding a job. (No plural form.) □ *I searched for employment in the classified ads of the newspaper.* **2.** *n.* the work that one does; one's job. (No plural form.) □ *John enjoys his employment as a photographer.*

**empress** ['ɛm prəs] *n.* a woman who rules an **empire**. □ *When the empress died, her daughter began to rule the empire.*

**empty** ['ɛmp ti] **1.** *adj.* having nothing or no one within; vacant. (Comp: *emptier;* sup: *emptiest.*) □ *Put the empty boxes in the garage.* **2.** *adj.* without meaning; without purpose; senseless. (Fig. on ①. Adv: *emptily.* Comp: *emptier;* sup: *emptiest.*) □ *If your life is empty, you should develop a hobby.* **3.** *tv.* to cause something to be ① by removing all the contents. □ *Bill emptied the fish bucket into the sink.* **4.** *iv.* [for something] to become ①. □ *The stadium emptied quickly after the game.*

**enact** [ɛn 'ækt] **1.** *tv.* to make a bill into a law; to pass a law. □ *Congress enacted the new crime bill.* **2.** *tv.* to perform a part in a play or a movie; to act something out. □ *The cast enacted the entire play in a church.*

**enclose** [ɛn 'kloz] **1.** *tv.* to put something in an envelope, box, etc. □ *I enclosed a check with my letter.* **2.** *tv.* to close something in on all sides; to put

E

walls up around something. □ *A tall, concrete wall encloses the prison.*

**enclosed** [ɛn 'klozd] **1.** *adj.* included in an envelope or a package. □ *Please look at the enclosed list.* **2.** *adj.* shut in on all sides; surrounded; having walls around on all sides. □ *The dog runs around in the enclosed yard.*

E

**encore** ['ɑŋ kor] **1.** *n.* the performance of an additional piece of music, or a repeat of a piece of music, after the end of a concert, at the demand of the audience. □ *The singer returned to the stage for an encore.* **2.** *adj.* repeated. □ *Bill did an encore performance of his best jokes.*

**encounter** [ɛn 'kɑʊn tɚ] **1.** *tv.* to meet someone or something by chance. □ *I encountered a lot of difficulty when I tried to take the test.* **2.** *n.* a meeting, especially by chance. □ *Our encounter at the train station caught me by surprise.*

**encourage** [ɛn 'kɚ ɪdʒ] *tv.* to give someone the courage or confidence to do something. □ *Jane encouraged me to work hard in school.*

**encouragement** [ɛn 'kɚ ɪdʒ mənt] *n.* words or actions that encourage someone. (No plural form.) □ *The athlete acknowledged our cries of encouragement by waving at us.*

**end** ['ɛnd] **1.** *n.* the final stopping point of a continuing process. (No plural form.) □ *I will love you until the end of time.* **2.** *n.* the last part of something. □ *The end of the movie was actually quite boring.* **3.** *n.* death. (A euphemism.) □ *The old man's end came just before dawn.* **4.** *n.* a purpose; an intended outcome; a result. □ *Your actions are not a means to an end.* **5.** *iv.* to stop; to finish; to exist no longer. □ *With death, his pain finally ended.* **6.** *tv.* to stop something; to finish something. □ *Let's end this discussion right now.*

**endless** ['ɛnd ləs] *adj.* without end; continuous; without stopping. (Adv: *endlessly.*) □ *The long and boring drive seemed endless.*

**endurance** [ɛn 'dur əns] *n.* the ability to keep going; the ability to endure. (No plural form.) □ *Do you have the endurance needed to run this race?*

**endure** [ɛn 'dur] **1.** *tv.* to withstand something; to put up with something; to tolerate something. □ *I can't endure your tasteless humor.* **2.** *iv.* to last; to keep going. □ *This old car won't endure forever.*

**enemy** ['ɛn ə mi] **1.** *n.* an opponent of someone or something; someone who fights against someone or something. □ *The popular president didn't have an enemy in the world.* **2.** *n.* a country that another country fights against during a war; an army that another army fights against during a war. □ *The enemy forced the troops to retreat.*

**energy** ['ɛn ɚ dʒi] *n.* the power needed to do something; the force that powers people or machines. (No plural form.) □ *The energy used to power most cars comes from gasoline.*

**engage** [ɛn 'gedʒ] **1.** *tv.* to take up someone's time; to keep someone busy. □ *The matter engaged a considerable amount of our time.* **2.** *tv.* to obtain the services of someone. □ *We engaged a trio of trumpeters for the ceremony.* **3.** *tv.* to rent something or a place. □ *Anne engaged the largest hall in town for the party.* **4.** *iv.* [for mechanical parts] to move into operating position with one another. □ *The car's gears engaged just in time.*

**engine** ['ɛn dʒən] **1.** *n.* a machine that uses power from gas, electricity, water pressure, steam, etc., to create power or motion. □ *The airplane has a jet engine.* **2.** *n.* a powered train car that pulls or pushes the other train cars; a locomotive. □ *The train engine blew its whistle as it roared through town.*

**engineer** [ɛn dʒə 'nɪr] **1.** *n.* someone who drives a locomotive engine. □ *The engineer drove the train through the tunnel.* **2.** *n.* someone who has training in a branch of engineering. □ *The car company employed dozens of engineers.* **3.** *tv.* [for ②] to do the designing and planning of something, such as a building, bridge, computer, automobile, etc. □ *Bob helped engineer the complex new bridge.*

**enjoy** [ɛn 'dʒoɪ] *tv.* to have something that is good; to feel fortunate to have something. □ *I have enjoyed my fulfilling career in law.*

**enjoyment** [ɛn 'dʒoɪ mənt] *n.* joy; pleasure; happiness. (Plural only when referring to different kinds, types, instances, or varieties.) □ *I take great enjoyment in climbing mountains.* Ⓒ *Eating is one of my few enjoyments.*

**enormous** [ɪ 'nor məs] *adj.* huge; large; very big. (Adv: *enormously.*) □ *The truck hauled an enormous load from the warehouse.*

**enough** [ɪ 'nʌf] **1.** *adj.* as much as is needed; as much as is necessary; adequate. □ *Do you have enough change to pay the bill?* **2.** *pron.* a necessary amount; an adequate amount. □ *I have enough. I don't need more.* **3.** *adv.* to an adequate degree. (Follows an adjective or a verb.) □ *I am hungry enough to eat a horse.*

**enroll** AND **enrol** [ɛn 'rol] **1. enrol(l) (in something)** *iv.* (+ *prep. phr.*) to become a member of a club, school, or other group. □ *I enrolled early, long before school actually started.* **2.** *tv.* to sign someone up for a club, school, or other group. □ *Twenty students have enrolled themselves in the art class.*

**ensure** [ɛn 'ʃʊr] *tv.* to make sure that something happens; to make something certain to happen. (Compare this with insure.) □ *I will do what is necessary to ensure that things go well.*

**enter** ['ɛn tɚ] **1.** *tv.* to go into a place; to come into a place. □ *We entered the building through the front door.* **2.** *tv.* to join something; to begin a career or course of study. □ *John entered the field of music.* **3.** *tv.* to write down something in a journal, log, or record book. □ *I entered my thoughts in a diary.* **4.** *tv.* to type data or other information into a computer. □ *Dave entered all the data in only a few hours.* **5.** *n.* the key labeled "enter" on a computer keyboard. □ *I hit "enter" to save the information.*

**entertain** [ɛn tɚ 'ten] **1.** *tv.* to amuse someone; to provide an audience with amusement. □ *The clown entertained the children.* **2.** *tv.* to provide guests or associates with food, amusement, and hospitality. □ *We entertained a group of students from Sweden.* **3.** *tv.* to consider something; to think about something. □ *How could you even entertain such an idea?*

**entertainment** [ɛn tɚ 'ten mənt] *n.* amusement; an entertaining performance. (A plural form is rare.) □ *Who will provide the entertainment for the child's party?*

**entire** [ɛn 'tɑɪɚ] *adj.* whole; including everyone or everything. (Adv: *entirely.*) □ *The entire class passed the exam.*

**entrance 1.** ['ɛn trəns] *n.* the right to go into a place; the right to enter a place. (No plural form.) □ *We gained entrance to the concert with special passes.* **2.** ['ɛn trəns] *n.* an instance of entering. □ *The singer's entrance was greeted with applause.* **3.** ['ɛn trəns] *n.* the way into a room or place; the door to a room or other place. □ *The school's front entrance is locked after three o'clock.* **4.** [ɛn 'træns] *tv.* to charm someone. □ *Anne was entranced by the charming stranger on the train.*

**entrust** [ɛn 'trʌst] **1. entrust** someone or something **with** someone or something *tv. + obj. + prep. phr.* to charge someone or some group with the care of someone or something. ☐ *We entrusted the babysitter with our children.* **2. entrust** someone or something **to** someone or something *tv. + obj. + prep. phr.* to place someone or something in the care of someone or something. ☐ *Mary and Bill entrusted their children to the babysitter.*

**entry** ['ɛn tri] **1.** *n.* going into a place or a room. ☐ *The actor's grand entry caused the audience to applaud.* **2.** *n.* an entrance; the way into a room or a place. ☐ *The entry is blocked by furniture.* **3.** *n.* a piece of information or data that is put into a computer, journal, database, dictionary, encyclopedia, or record book, or is put on a list. ☐ *The bookkeeper checked that all the entries in the record books were correct.*

**envelop** [ɛn 'vɛl əp] *tv.* to wrap around someone or something; to completely cover someone or something. ☐ *Snow completely enveloped the hikers.*

**envelope** ['ɛn və lop] *n.* a paper cover that letters and documents are placed in for mailing. ☐ *I put a stamp on the envelope and mailed it.*

**environment** [ɛn 'vɑɪ ɚn mənt] **1.** *n.* the state and nature of the immediate area. ☐ *The work environment at this factory is not healthy.* **2. the environment** *n.* nature, including the atmosphere, oceans, lands, and all creatures. (No plural form. Treated as singular.) ☐ *The environment is getting less healthy every year.*

**envy** ['ɛn vi] **1.** *n.* a negative, greedy feeling toward someone who has someone or something that one wants. (No plural form.) ☐ *Tom tried to ignore his feelings of envy when Bill bought a new car.* **2.** *tv.* to have a negative feeling toward someone who has someone or something that one wants. ☐ *I envy people who drive expensive cars.*

**equal** ['i kwəl] **1.** *adj.* the same as someone or something; in the same amount or degree. (Adv: *equally.*) ☐ *Both children got equal amounts of cake.* **2.** *tv.* to be the same as someone or something else; to have the same amount or degree of something as someone or something else. ☐ *Two plus three equals five.* **3.** *n.* a person who is on the same level as someone else—in social standing, ability, rank, etc. ☐ *When it comes to getting work done quickly and efficiently, my secretary has no equal.*

**equality** [ɪ 'kwɑl ə ti] *n.* the condition of having the same amount or degree of something as someone or something else. (No plural form.) ☐ *I believe in equality of opportunity for all people.*

**equalize** ['i kwə lɑɪz] *tv.* to cause something to equal something else. ☐ *It is difficult to equalize the amount of time I spend with each of my students.*

**equation** [ɪ 'kwe ʒən] *n.* a statement showing that two amounts are equal. ☐ *In an equation, the "=" symbol is used to mean "is equal to."* ☐ 5 + 4 = 9 is a simple equation.

**equator** [ɪ 'kwet ɚ] *n.* the imaginary line around the middle of the earth (or any planet); halfway between the north and south poles. ☐ *The ship sailed across the equator.*

**equip** [ɪ 'kwɪp] **1. equip** someone **with** something *tv. + obj. + prep. phr.* to provide someone with the necessary supplies. ☐ *The campers equipped themselves with sleeping bags and tents.* **2. equip** something **with** something *tv. + obj. + prep. phr.* to provide something with additional or needed parts or devices. ☐ *The manufacturer had equipped our car with seat belts.*

**equipment** [ɪ 'kwɪp mənt] *n.* things that are furnished or supplied, especially the tools and supplies needed to do a job. (No plural form. Number is expressed with *piece(s) of equipment.*) □ *Do you have the equipment you need to repair the car?*

**equivalent** [ɪ 'kwɪv ə lənt] *adj.* same; equal in level or degree. (Adv: *equivalently.*) □ *My donations to both charities were equivalent.*

**erase** [ɪ 'res] **1.** *tv.* to remove something written or drawn in pencil, ink, or chalk by rubbing it with an eraser. □ *Please erase that word from the chalkboard.* **2.** *tv.* to wipe something clean by removing the writing—especially chalk or pencil writing—on it. □ *Please erase the paper carefully, so you don't tear it.* **3.** *tv.* to remove something completely. (Fig. on ①.) □ *Bob couldn't erase the memory of his nightmare.*

**eraser** [ɪ 'res ɚ] *n.* a small rubber object that erases pencil markings; a rectangular block of felt that rubs out chalk markings. □ *Jane borrowed my pencil eraser.*

**erect** [ɪ 'rɛkt] **1.** *adj.* standing straight up in a vertical position. (Adv: *erectly.*) □ *The erect model had excellent posture.* **2.** *adj.* upright; straight up. □ *Please stand erect.* **3.** *tv.* to build something. □ *Jimmy and his friends erected a tree house.* **4.** *tv.* to cause something to stand in a vertical position. □ *The citizens erected a flagpole in the park.*

**err** [ɛr, ɚ] *iv.* to make a mistake; to be wrong. □ *I erred when adding the numbers.*

**error** ['ɛr ɚ] **1.** *n.* a mistake; something that is wrong. □ *Jane made an error in her addition.* **2.** *n.* a bad play by someone on a baseball team. □ *The player made an error that made our team lose.*

**erupt** [ɪ 'rʌpt] **1.** *iv.* [for a volcano] to explode. □ *The volcano erupted violently.* **2.** *iv.* [for anger, violence, arguments, etc.] to be released suddenly. □ *We were afraid that violence would erupt again, so we left.* **3. erupt in** something; **erupt with** something *iv. + prep. phr.* to develop a rash on the skin. □ *My body erupts with hives if I eat chocolate.*

**eruption** [ɪ 'rʌp ʃən] **1.** *n.* an explosion of a volcano; a flowing out of material form a volcano. □ *An eruption of the volcano threw the citizens into a panic.* **2.** *n.* a bursting forth of anger, violence, fighting, etc. □ *Lisa's eruption of anger shocked all of us.*

**escalator** ['ɛs kə le tɚ] *n.* a moving staircase that carries people to a higher or lower floor of a building. □ *I rode up the escalator in the department store.*

**escape** [ɛ 'skep] **1.** *n.* fleeing a dangerous place, an enclosed place, or a bad situation. (Plural only when referring to different kinds, types, instances, or varieties.) □ *The hostage knew that escape was impossible.* Ⓒ *There have been no escapes from this prison since it was built.* **2.** *iv.* to become free; to get away. □ *The prisoners escaped when it was very dark.* **3.** *iv.* to leak from a container. □ *A little bit of milk escaped from the damaged carton.* **4.** *iv.* to elude being caught; to avoid being caught. □ *The robbers escaped during the chaos after the robbery.* **5.** *tv.* to (seem to) avoid being seen, heard, remembered, etc. □ *Tom's address has escaped my memory.*

**especially** [ɛ 'spɛʃ ə li] *adv.* mainly; primarily; particularly. □ *John is especially pleased with the wine you chose.*

**essay** ['ɛs e] *n.* a written work about a specific topic. □ *Your essay contains far too many mistakes.*

**essence** ['ɛs əns] **1.** *n.* the most important part of something; the important features that make up someone or something. □ *Do you understand the essence of this novel?* **2.** *n.* a perfume or similar substance. □ *This essence reminds me of wildflowers.*

**establish** [ɛ 'stæb lɪʃ] **1.** *tv.* to start an organization; to found an organization. □ *The college established a scholarship for poor students.* **2.** *tv.* to start something, such as a policy or plan. □ *It is time to establish a new system for dealing with mail delivery.* **3.** *tv.* to place oneself or itself as something or in a specific role. (Takes a reflexive object.) □ *Bill established himself as head of the new division.* **4.** *tv.* to prove something; to determine the truth of something. (The object can be a clause with **that** ⑦.) □ *He could not establish the truth of his statement.*

E

**establishment** [ɛ 'stæb lɪʃ mənt] **1.** *n.* establishing something. (No plural form.) □ *I believe in the establishment of better housing policies for everyone.* **2.** *n.* a company or organization. □ *How long have you worked at this establishment?*

**estate** [ɛ 'stet] **1.** *n.* everything that someone owns; the property of someone who has just died. □ *I can only estimate the value of my estate.* **2.** *n.* a house and related buildings set on a large piece of property. □ *The rich woman lives at an estate in the country.*

**esteem** [ɛ 'stim] *n.* opinion or regard, favorable unless indicated otherwise. (No plural form.) □ *I have a great deal of esteem for my parents.*

**estimate 1.** ['ɛst ə mət] *n.* a statement that shows about how much someone will charge to do a certain amount of work; an approximate calculation of an amount of money, intended to represent the final cost fairly closely. □ *The clerk gave Jane an estimate of the cost to fix her toaster.* **2.** ['ɛst ə met] *tv.* to calculate how much something will cost; to determine an approximate amount of money. (The object can be a clause with **that** ⑦.) □ *I estimate the cost at $4,000.*

**estimation** [est ə 'me ʃən] *n.* one's opinion or judgment. (No plural form.) □ *What is your estimation of the seriousness of the problem we are facing?*

**etc.** an abbreviation of **et cetera**.

**et cetera** ['ɛt 'sɛt ə rə] and other similar things; and so forth; and other things like those just named. (Abbreviated as etc.) □ *He says he will eat almost anything: pizza, hamburgers, French fries, etc.*

**eternal** [ɪ 'tɚ nəl] *adj.* without ending; existing forever. (Adv: *eternally.*) □ *Parents share an eternal bond with their children.*

**eternity** [ɪ 'tɚ nə ti] *n.* time without beginning or end. (No plural form.) □ *I felt that the lecture would last for all eternity.*

**ethic** ['ɛθ ɪk] **1.** *n.* the body of morals governing a person or a group. (No plural form.) □ *Dishonesty is not part of Mary's personal ethic.* **2. ethics** *n.* standards of right and wrong within a society. (Treated as plural, but not countable.) □ *Lisa has very strong ethics.* **3. ethics** *n.* the study of the standards of right and wrong; the study of morals. (Treated as singular.) □ *I wrote an essay on morality for my class in ethics.*

**ethnic** ['ɛθ nɪk] *adj.* of or about a particular variety, group, or subgroup of people, such as divisions according to race, language, country, etc. (Adv: *ethnically* [...ɪk li].) □ *The chef prepared many ethnic dishes.*

**euphemism** ['ju fə mɪz əm] *n.* a word or phrase that replaces a less polite or more harsh word or expression. □ Large *is a word often used as a euphemism for the word* fat.

**evade** [ɪ 'ved] *tv.* to avoid doing something; to avoid the consequences of something. □ *Bill evaded answering the questions I asked him.*

**evaluate** [ɪ 'væl ju et] *tv.* to study and make a judgment about the value of someone or something. □ *I want to evaluate my options thoroughly before making a decision.*

**evaluation** [ɪ væl ju 'e ʃən] **1.** *n.* studying the worth, value, or status of something. (Plural only when referring to different kinds, types, instances, or varieties.) □ *Evaluation of something complex will take a lot of time.* Ⓒ *Careful evaluations take a long time.* **2.** *n.* a judgment or statement about the status or quality of someone or something. □ *The manager gave the lazy employees negative job evaluations.*

**eve** ['iv] *n.* the night or day before an important day. □ *Jimmy could hardly sleep on the eve of his birthday.*

**even** ['i vən] **1.** *adj.* smooth; not rough; level; on the same level; uniform. (Adv: *evenly.*) □ *The surface of the wall was very even, so it was easy to apply wallpaper.* **2.** *adj.* [of a number] able to be divided by 2 with nothing left over. (Adv: *evenly.*) □ *2, 4, 6, and 8 are examples of even numbers.* □ *If you add two even numbers together, the result will be an even number as well.* **3.** *adj.* equal. (Adv: *evenly.*) □ *Jane's salary is even with mine.* **4.** *adv.* still more; yet more. (Used to make a comparison stronger.) □ *Jane is tall, Mary is taller, and Susan is even taller.* **5.** *adv.* more than expected; in a way that would not be expected. □ *Even a candle seems bright after one has been in total darkness.* **6.** *tv.* to smooth something out; to make something smooth; to make something level. □ *The gardener evened the hedge by trimming it.*

**evening** ['iv nɪŋ] **1.** *n.* the last part of the day; the period of the day after the afternoon and before the night. □ *I have invited the neighbors to come over tomorrow evening.* **2.** *adj.* <the adj. use of ①.> □ *We are going to an evening performance of the opera today.* **3. evenings** *adv.* every ①; happening every ①. □ *I work evenings, five days a week.*

**event** [ə 'vɛnt] *n.* something that happens; an occurrence. □ *The happy event will be celebrated by friends and family.*

**eventual** [ə 'vɛn tʃu əl] *adj.* at some time in the future. (Adv: *eventually.*) □ *Owning a restaurant is Bill's eventual goal, but now he is just a cook.*

**ever** ['ɛv ɚ] **1.** *adv.* at any time. (Used especially in negative sentences, questions, and sentences with *if*, and after comparatives with *than*, after superlatives, or after *as.*) □ *Have you ever heard of any such thing?* □ *I can't ever seem to find my keys in the morning.* □ *After the surgery, John felt better than ever.* **2.** *adv.* always; forever. □ *I will love you forever and ever.*

**every** ['ɛv ri] **1.** *adj.* all; each. (For two things or people, use **both**.) □ *I gave every child at the party a small toy.* **2.** *adj.* per; once during each unit. □ *I take one vitamin every day.* **3.** *adj.* all possible. □ *I tried every option, but none would work.*

**everybody** ['ɛv ri bɑd i] *pron.* every person; everyone. □ *Everybody likes to walk barefoot on the beach.*

**everyday** ['ɛv ri de] **1.** *adj.* happening every day. (Prenominal only.) □ *Taking her pills is an everyday event for Jane.* **2.** *adj.* common; ordinary; not special. (Compare this with *every day* (adv.), meaning "each day.") □ *I usually wear my everyday clothes to the gym.*

**everyone** ['ɛv ri wən] *pron.* every person; all; everybody. (Treated as singular.) □ *Everyone likes to walk on the beach.*

**everything** ['ɛv ri θɪŋ] **1.** *pron.* each thing. □ *The lawyer questioned everything that I said.* **2.** *pron.* the only thing that is important; the only goal or value. □ *"Winning isn't everything," the coach told the losing team.*

**everywhere** ['ɛv ri ʍɛr] *adv.* in all places; in every location; at every point. ☐ *Mosquitos are everywhere this summer!*

**evidence** ['ɛv ə dəns] *n.* something that proves a claim or statement. (No plural form.) ☐ *This evidence does not prove the man's guilt.*

E

**evil** ['i vəl] **1.** *adj.* very bad; capable of doing very bad things. (Adv: *evilly.*) ☐ *Mike was known for his evil temper and for yelling at people.* **2.** *n.* badness. (Plural only when referring to different kinds, types, instances, or varieties.) ☐ *Good and evil exist in this world.* © *Greed and laziness are evils that harm many people.*

**evolution** [ɛv ə 'lu ʃən] **1.** *n.* the changes of something from an early stage to a more advanced stage. (No plural form.) ☐ *The evolution of computer technology in this decade has been very fast.* **2.** *n.* the scientific theory that all living creatures developed from simpler forms of life over millions of years. (No plural form.) ☐ *We studied the process of evolution in our science class.*

**exact** [ɪg 'zækt] *adj.* without mistakes; precise; completely correct. (Adv: *exactly.*) ☐ *You need exact change for the bus.*

**exactly** [ɪg 'zækt li] **1.** *adv.* precisely; accurately; only as requested or ordered. ☐ *Meet me at exactly noon in front of the building.* **2. Exactly!** *interj.* "That is quite right!" ☐ *Exactly! That is just the way to do it.*

**exam** [ɪg 'zæm] *n.* an examination. ☐ *Do you think you passed the math exam?*

**examination** [ɪg zæm ɪ 'ne ʃən] **1.** *n.* examining, studying, or observing someone or something. (Plural only when referring to different kinds, types, instances, or varieties.) ☐ *Examination of your documents will take only a few minutes.* © *Careful examinations take a long time.* **2.** *n.* a test; a series of questions given to test someone's knowledge of a certain topic. ☐ *Bill passed his calculus examination easily.*

**examine** [ɪg 'zæm ɪn] **1.** *tv.* to look at someone or something very closely. ☐ *Jane examined every clause in the contract before she signed it.* **2.** *tv.* to made a medical study of the state of someone's body. ☐ *The doctor examined the pregnant woman.*

**example** [ɪg 'zæm pəl] **1.** *n.* something that clarifies what one is talking about; a sample of what is being talked about. ☐ *Can you give me an example of the type of music you like?* **2.** *n.* someone or something that should be imitated; a model. ☐ *Mary's years of excellent teaching are an example to new teachers everywhere.*

**exceed** [ɛk 'sid] **1.** *tv.* to go beyond the limits of something; to surpass the upper boundary of something. ☐ *I never exceed the speed limit on the highway.* **2.** *tv.* to surpass something. ☐ *Mary exceeded Susan's speed record in the track event.*

**excel** [ɛk 'sɛl] *iv.* to do very well at something; to be outstanding at something. ☐ *Anne is in good physical condition and excels at many sports.*

**excellence** ['ɛk sə ləns] *n.* a superior quality; the best quality possible; an extremely good quality. (No plural form.) ☐ *Excellence is our goal in all our work.*

**excellent** ['ɛk sə lənt] *adj.* superior; extremely good; outstanding; of very high quality. (Adv: *excellently.*) ☐ *My grades this semester were excellent.*

**except** [ɛk 'sɛpt] **1.** AND **except for** someone or something *prep.* other than someone or something; besides someone or something; not including someone or something. ☐ *I like all green vegetables except spinach.* **2. except for** someone or something *phr.* were it not for someone or something; if someone or something were different. □ *I would go bowling with you, except for the fact that I have other plans.* **3.** *tv.* to exclude someone or something; to omit someone or something. (Compare this with **accept**.) □ *The company's rules except no one, not even the owner.*

**excess 1.** ['ɛk sɛs] *n.* the amount that is over a certain limit or boundary; the part of something that is too much. (No plural form.) □ *This meat has an excess of fat.* **2. excesses** [ɛk 'sɛs əs] *n.* spending for expensive things; wasting money by spending it on things that cost a lot of money. □ *Your many excesses have caused you to go into debt.* **3.** ['ɛk sɛs] *adj.* extra; beyond the proper limit; beyond what is needed. □ *Don't bring any excess baggage on this trip.*

**excessive** [ɛk 'sɛs ɪv] *adj.* extra; beyond the proper limit; beyond what is needed; too much. (Adv: *excessively.*) □ *I will not buy the meat if there is excessive fat on it.*

**exchange** [ɛks 'tʃendʒ] **1.** *tv.* to trade something for something else; to trade someone for someone else. □ *I exchanged belts with Bill because mine wasn't large enough.* **2.** *n.* an instance of giving someone something for something else; an instance of trading something for something else. □ *Bill and I were satisfied with the exchange of belts.* **3.** *n.* a conversation; a short dialogue. □ *I came away from the exchange with a deeper understanding of Dave's problems.* **4.** *n.* a place where things, such as stocks, are bought and sold. □ *Every major country has a stock exchange.* **5.** *n.* a particular part of the telephone switching system, represented by the first three digits of a local telephone number in the United States. □ *Our number is 555-2345. We are in the 555 exchange.*

**excite** [ɛk 'saɪt] *tv.* to interest or stimulate someone or something. □ *Rumors of the musician's surprise appearance excited the crowd.*

**excitement** [ɛk 'saɪt mənt] *n.* the feeling of great interest, eagerness, and stimulation. (A plural form is rare and is not countable.) □ *The children's excitement grew as they opened their presents.*

**exciting** [ɛk 'saɪ tɪŋ] *adj.* causing excitement; very interesting; stimulating. (Adv: *excitingly.*) □ *The critic praised the exciting movie.*

**exclaim** [ɛk 'sklem] *tv.* to shout something; to say something with strong feeling. (The object is a clause with **that** ⑦.) □ *Mary exclaimed that someone forgot to turn the water off in the bathroom.*

**exclamation** [ɛk sklə 'me ʃən] *n.* a loud statement; a statement made with strong feeling or emotion. □ *The lifeguard's exclamation about seeing a shark startled the swimmers.*

**exclamation point** [ɛk sklə 'me ʃən pɔɪnt] *n.* a punctuation mark "!" written at the end of a word, phrase, or sentence that is an exclamation. □ *Commands and warnings such as "Stop!" and "Look out!" and interjections such as "Eureka!" are often written with exclamation points.*

**excrement** ['ɛk skrə mənt] *n.* feces; solid waste from the bowels. (No plural form.) □ *David found dog excrement on his lawn every morning.*

**excuse 1.** [ɛk 'skjus] *n.* a reason that attempts to explain or justify something that is wrong. □ *Anne had a good excuse for missing work yesterday.* **2.** [ɛk 'skjuz] *tv.* to forgive someone for bad manners; to pardon someone. □ *Please excuse me for interrupting you.* **3.** [ɛk 'skjuz] *tv.* to give someone permission to leave. □ *Please excuse me. I must go.*

**execute** ['ɛks ə kjut] **1.** *tv.* to do something as ordered; to carry out something; to perform an act. □ *The soldier executed the general's order.* **2.** *tv.* to kill someone as a punishment; to punish someone with death. □ *The state executed the murderer.* **3.** *tv.* to make a document effective as of a certain date by signing it. □ *Bill executed the agreement in front of two witnesses.*

E

**execution** [ɛks ə 'kju ʃən] **1.** *n.* the doing of something; the carrying out of an order. (No plural form.) □ *The execution of the dancer's routine was flawless.* **2.** *n.* the killing of someone as a punishment. □ *Members of the press were allowed to view the criminal's execution.*

**executive** [ɛg 'zɛk jə tɪv] **1.** *n.* someone who manages an organization in business or government. □ *The chief executive called a meeting of the company's board of directors.* **2.** *adj.* in the manner of ①; firm and authoritative. □ *The bank's vice president could not make an executive decision and was fired.* **3.** *adj.* of or about the branch of government that manages, but not the branches that make laws and run the courts. □ *The president issued an executive order.*

**exempt** [ɛg 'zɛmpt] **1.** *tv.* to free someone from a duty or obligation. □ *The doctor's note exempted Mary from gym class.* **2.** *adj.* free from a duty or obligation. □ *You are not exempt from the rules!*

**exhale** [ɛks 'hel] **1.** *iv.* to breathe out; to push air out from the lungs. □ *Mary sighed and exhaled slowly.* **2.** *tv.* to breathe air or smoke out of the body. □ *Bill exhaled the cigar smoke.*

**exhaust** [ɛg 'zɔst] **1.** *n.* steam, gas, or vapor that is the waste product of burning. (No plural form.) □ *Buses produce lots of black exhaust.* **2.** *tv.* to use up all of someone's or something's resources or energy. □ *I give up. I've exhausted every idea I have.* **3.** *tv.* to cause someone to become very tired. □ *The hard work exhausted the employee.*

**exist** [ɛg 'zɪst] **1.** *iv.* to be; to be in reality. □ *Everyone knows that ghosts do not exist.* **2.** *iv.* to last through time; to continue to be. □ *Memories exist forever in our hearts.* **3.** *iv.* to manage to live with only the minimum of physical needs met. □ *The prisoners existed on bread and water.*

**existence** [ɛg 'zɪs təns] **1.** *n.* being; the condition of actually being or existing. (No plural form.) □ *Do you believe in the existence of ghosts?* **2.** *n.* living; continuing to be; a way of living. (No plural form.) □ *Susan's very existence now depends on the surgeon's skills.*

**exit** ['ɛg zɪt] **1.** *n.* the way out, especially from a place or room. □ *The theater's exits were marked with lighted signs.* **2.** *n.* the roadway leading off a highway. □ *The exit from the highway onto Route 28 was blocked.* **3.** *n.* leaving someplace, especially a stage. □ *Bill's angry exit from the meeting shocked everyone.* **4.** *iv.* to leave [a place, such as a stage or a highway]. □ *The cars exited from the highway.* **5.** *tv.* to leave a place. □ *The actor exited the stage gracefully.*

**expect** [ɛk 'spɛkt] **1. expect to** do something *iv. + inf.* to think that one will do something. □ *I expect to promote Bill in the Spring.* **2.** *tv.* to anticipate the arrival of something; to anticipate the birth of a baby; to anticipate that something will happen. (The object can be a clause with **that** ⑦.) □ *We expect the train at 2:30.*

**expedition** [ɛk spɪ 'dɪ ʃən] *n.* a trip; a journey; a specific course of travel to a certain place. □ *The explorers started on a month-long expedition down the river.*

**expel** [ɛk 'spɛl] **1.** *tv.* to force someone or something out of a place. □ *When you sneeze, you expel air from your lungs.*

**2.** *tv.* to order that someone not attend a school, usually because of bad behavior or bad grades; to end someone's membership in an organization. ☐ *The school board voted to expel John for setting fire to the school.*

**expense** [ɛk 'spɛns] *n.* the amount of money that a product or service costs; an item of cost, as in a budget. ☐ *Which expenses in the budget can be reduced?*

**expensive** [ɛk 'spɛn sɪv] *adj.* costing a lot of money; high-priced; costly. (Adv: *expensively.*) ☐ *All of the meals at the fancy restaurant were quite expensive.*

**experience** [ɛk 'spɪr i əns] **1.** *n.* knowledge gained from remembering past events and the results of one's actions during those events; skills gained from living one's life. (No plural form.) ☐ *To apply for this job, you must have five years of experience in sales.* **2.** *n.* something that happens to someone; an event that gives someone ①. ☐ *I had a frightening experience while I was in the city today.* **3.** *tv.* to learn about something by being involved in it when it happens; to feel or encounter something. ☐ *When Mary's dog died, she experienced great sorrow.*

**experiment** [ɛk 'spɛr ə mənt] **1.** *n.* a test that is carried out to prove an idea or theory or show that it is wrong. ☐ *An experiment proved that the new medicine worked well.* **2.** *iv.* to try something in order to find out about it. ☐ *I experimented with different recipes before I made a batch of cookies I really liked.*

**expert** ['ɛk spɚt] **1.** *n.* someone who is an authority on something; someone who knows a lot about a certain topic. ☐ *Bob is an expert on cats.* **2.** *adj.* having a lot of knowledge or skill. (Adv: *expertly.*) ☐ *The museum has many works done by expert sculptors.*

**explain** [ɛk 'splen] **1.** *tv.* to make something easier to understand; to talk in detail about something; to make something clear. ☐ *Please explain your answer so that we can understand it.* **2.** *tv.* to give an excuse for something. (The object can be a clause with **that** ⑦.) ☐ *Can you explain why your grades are so low at school?*

**explanation** [ɛk splə 'ne ʃən] *n.* information that makes something easier to understand; description. (Plural only when referring to different kinds, types, instances, or varieties.) ☐ *The instructions are not clear. I need more explanation.* 🄲 *Your explanations are almost impossible to understand.*

**explode** [ɛk 'splod] **1.** *iv.* to blow up, as with a bomb; to burst. ☐ *The red balloon exploded when I stuck it with a pin.* **2.** *iv.* to get very angry. (Fig. on ①.) ☐ *I exploded when I found another parking ticket on my car.* **3.** *tv.* to cause something to **explode** ①. ☐ *Jimmy exploded a firecracker at school.*

**explore** [ɛk 'splor] **1.** *tv.* to study and examine a place that has not been examined before. ☐ *The survivors from the shipwreck explored the deserted island.* **2.** *tv.* to examine or consider a plan or idea carefully. (Fig. on ①.) ☐ *The physician explored all the new theories of cancer treatment.*

**explosion** [ɛk 'splo ʒən] *n.* a loud, violent burst; an act of exploding; the blowing up of something. ☐ *An explosion destroyed the house.*

**export** **1.** ['ɛk sport] *n.* a product that is shipped to another country; a product that is sold to another country. ☐ *Grain and cotton are exports from the United States.* **2.** ['ɛk sport] *adj.* <the adj. use of ①.> ☐ *We will not meet our export goals for the coming year.* **3.** [ɛk 'sport] *tv.* to ship a product to another country for sale; to sell a product in another country. ☐ *The United States used to export wheat to Russia.*

**exposure** [ɛk ˈspo ʒɚ] **1.** *n.* showing something to the public; showing something that was hidden. (Plural only when referring to different kinds, types, instances, or varieties.) □ *Because of the reporter's exposure of the crime, the mayor was arrested.* Ⓒ *Repeated exposures of the mayor's dishonesty angered the citizens.* **2.** *n.* attention given to someone or something by newspapers, television, magazines, etc. (No plural form.) □ *Lots of advertising gave the new product lots of exposure.* **3.** *n.* a section of film [used in photography] that will produce a single image. □ *There are 24 exposures on this roll of film.*

**express** [ɛk ˈsprɛs] **1.** *tv.* [for someone] to put a thought or idea into words; to speak about an idea. □ *Mary expressed her complex thoughts eloquently.* **2.** *tv.* [for someone] to convey a feeling or emotion through words, signs, gestures, or writing. □ *He expressed his love for flowers through poetry.* **3.** *tv.* [for something] to indicate something; to show something. □ *Jimmy's sad face expressed his disappointment.* **4.** *adj.* [of transportation] traveling without stopping or with fewer stops. □ *We took the express bus downtown.* **5.** *adj.* of or about a rapid means of shipment or delivery. □ *We sent the box by express delivery.*

**expression** [ɛk ˈsprɛ ʃən] **1.** *n.* the look on one's face that indicates how one feels. □ *The expression on Mary's face indicated that she was shocked.* **2.** *n.* the process of expressing oneself in some way. □ *Jane needed an outlet for her artistic expression.* **3.** *n.* a phrase or clause that is used to express an idea; an idiom. □ *What does the expression "in seventh heaven" mean?*

**extend** [ɛk ˈstɛnd] **1.** *tv.* to stretch something, making it longer. □ *Tom extended the telescope to its full length.* **2.** *tv.* to make something last longer in time. (Fig. on ①.) □ *The judge extended the prisoner's sentence.* **3.** *tv.* to present an offer; to utter an offer or a wish. □ *Let me extend an offer of help to you.* **4.** *iv.* to increase in length. □ *The rubber band extended as it was stretched.* **5.** *iv.* to spread out in all directions. □ *Cornfields extend over the entire landscape.* **6.** *iv.* to continue in space or time. □ *My cousin's visit extended longer than expected.*

**extension** [ɛk ˈstɛn ʃən] **1.** *n.* something that is added to something to make it longer or larger; an additional part. □ *The handle isn't long enough. I need an extension.* **2.** *n.* extra time given beyond a deadline. □ *I requested an extension from the government for paying my taxes.* **3.** *n.* an electric cord that acts to extend the distance between an electric receptacle and the device that needs to be plugged in. (Short for **extension cord**.) □ *This lamp is too far from the electric receptacle. Do you have an extension?*

**extension cord** [ɛk ˈstɛn ʃən ˈkord] *n.* a length of electrical cord with a plug on one end and a receptacle on the other. (Can be shortened to **extension**.) □ *Where is the extension cord? It is never where it should be.*

**extent** [ɛk ˈstɛnt] *n.* the distance or degree to which something extends or reaches; the degree to which something is covered or accounted for. □ *What is the extent of your interest in this matter?*

**exterior** [ɛk ˈstɪr i ɚ] **1.** *n.* the outside of something. □ *There's a dent on the exterior of the box.* **2.** *adj.* <the adj. use of ①.> □ *There are scratches on the exterior surface of the box.*

**external** [ɛk ˈstɚ nəl] **1.** *adj.* outside; outer. (Adv: *externally.*) □ *The electric wires are sealed in an external plastic covering.* **2.** *adj.* coming from the outside; being affected by someone or something on the outside. (Adv: *exter-*

*nally.*) □ *An accountant was hired to conduct an external review of the company's finances.*

**extinct** [ɛk 'stɪŋkt] **1.** *adj.* [of a plant or animal species that is] no longer in existence. □ *It is natural for some species to become extinct every few years.* **2.** *adj.* [of a volcano] no longer capable of erupting. □ *Some islands are the tips of extinct volcanoes rising up from the ocean floor.*

**extra** ['ɛk strə] **1.** *adj.* more or greater than is expected; more or greater than usual; additional. □ *Did you eat an extra bowl of cereal this morning?* **2.** *adv.* more than usual; additionally. □ *I am extra hungry tonight!* **3.** *n.* an actor who is hired to be part of the background or part of a crowd. □ *Mary was an extra in the restaurant scene on the soap opera.*

**extreme** [ɛk 'strim] **1.** *adj.* to the greatest degree; to the furthest point possible in any direction; furthest. (Adv: *extremely.*) □ *I felt extreme grief when my brother died.* **2.** *n.* one of two things that are as far apart from each other as possible. □ *Good and evil are two extremes that coexist in this world.*

**eye** ['ɑɪ] **1.** *n.* one of the two organs of sight; an **eyeball**. □ *I covered my eyes to protect them from blowing dust.* **2.** *n.* the ring of color on someone's eye; the iris. □ *The color of your sweater matches your eyes.* **3.** *tv.* to glance at or look at someone or something; to watch someone or something. (The present participle is *eying* or *eyeing.*) □ *Bill eyed the door, waiting for Mary to arrive.*

**eyeball** ['ɑɪ bɔl] *n.* the round part of the eye that sits in the socket. (The same as **eye** ①.) □ *John placed the contact lens on his eyeball.*

**eyebrow** ['ɑɪ brɑʊ] *n.* the curved ridge of hair on one's forehead, just above the eye. □ *Mary dyed her eyebrows a lighter color.*

**eyeglasses** ['ɑɪ glæs əz] *n.* two lenses held together by a frame and worn in front of the eyes to improve vision. (Treated as plural. Usually shortened to **glasses**.) □ *Mary needs to wear eyeglasses when she drives.*

**eyelash** ['ɑɪ læʃ] *n.* one of the many small, thin hairs that grow on the edge of the eyelid. □ *When an eyelash fell into my eye, my eye began to hurt.*

**eyelid** ['ɑɪ lɪd] *n.* the fold of skin that moves over the eye. □ *The accident victim's eyelids were swollen shut.*

**eyewitness** ['ɑɪ 'wɪt nəs] *n.* someone who sees an event happen; someone who sees an accident or crime take place. □ *Eyewitnesses reported the accident to the police.*

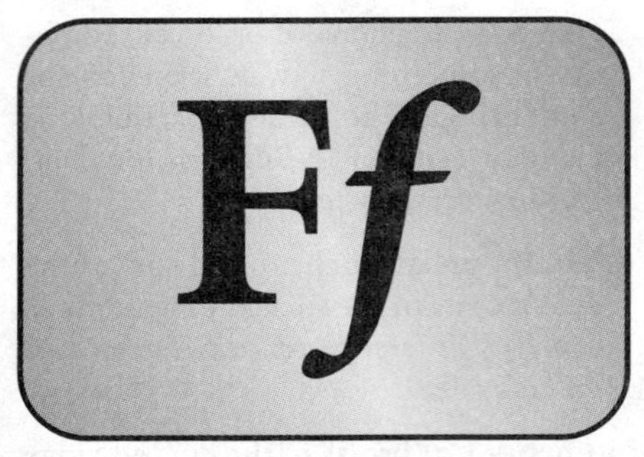

F

**F.** Go to **Fahrenheit**.

**fable** ['fe bəl] **1.** *n.* a story that teaches a lesson, often using animals as the characters of the story. □ *I read an ancient fable about the importance of telling the truth.* **2.** *n.* a lie; a story about an event that did not really happen. □ *The teacher did not believe John's fable that the dog ate his homework.*

**fabric** ['fæb rɪk] *n.* material or cloth made by weaving threads together. (Plural only when referring to different kinds, types, instances, or varieties.) □ *My shirt is made of cotton fabric.* Ⓒ *Different fabrics require different kinds of care.*

**fabricate** ['fæb rɪ ket] **1.** *tv.* to build something. □ *The factory fabricated one hundred cars every day.* **2.** *tv.* to make up a story or a lie; to invent an excuse. (Fig. on ①.) □ *John fabricated an excuse for missing the meeting.*

**face** ['fes] **1.** *n.* the front part of the head from the hair to the chin. □ *The baseball struck John's face, just to the left of his nose.* **2.** *n.* a look; an expression; the way someone's **face** ① looks. □ *What a sad face! Is something bothering you?* **3.** *n.* the front part or surface of something. □ *The face of the building was decorated with red bricks.* **4. face toward** someone or something *iv.* + *prep. phr.* to look toward someone or something or toward a particular direction; to be directed toward a particular direction. □ *The same side of the moon always faces toward the earth.* **5.** *tv.* to look at someone or something or toward a particular direction. □ *Tom faced Mary while they ate dinner.* **6.** *tv.* to deal with someone or something. □ *The senator faced his drinking problem and sought professional help.* **7.** *tv.* to cover the front part of something or the edges of something with a decoration. □ *The designer faced the side wall with marble tile.* **8. make a face** *phr.* to twist one's **face** ① into a strange expression to show one's emotion or to make someone laugh. (Also plural: *make faces.*) □ *The clown made faces to amuse the children.*

**facility** [fə 'sɪl ə ti] **1.** *n.* something—especially buildings or equipment—built, provided, or established for a specific purpose; a building or site used by a company for its business, especially for a factory or offices. (Often plural.) □ *The company's president inspected the new facility.* **2. facilities** *n.* a bathroom; a restroom. (Euphemistic. Treated as plural, but not countable.) □ *I'm sorry, we have no facilities for public use in the store.*

**fact** ['fækt] **1.** *n.* something that is true; something that really happened. □ *She told me a few facts about the city.* **2. in fact** *phr.* truthfully; actually. □ *I wasn't in California last week. In fact, I've never been there.*

**factor** ['fæk tɚ] *n.* one of a number of elements that contribute to a result. □ *Lack of clean water is an important factor in the spread of many diseases.*

**factory** ['fæk tə ri] *n.* a building where products are made, usually with machines. □ *My dad works in a factory that produces cars.*

**faculty** ['fæk əl ti] **1.** *n.* the teachers at a school, college, or university, as a group. □ *Jane is a member of the faculty at the local university.* **2.** *n.* a skill; an ability, especially a mental ability. □ *Mary has* *a remarkable faculty for adding large numbers in her head.* **3.** *adj.* <the adj. use of ①.> □ *Jane is a faculty member at the local university.*

**fad** ['fæd] *n.* a very popular thing that everyone does or has for a short period of time. □ *Wearing pants with wide cuffs was a fad of the 1970s.*

**fade** ['fed] **1.** *iv.* to lose color; to become pale; to become less bright. □ *Over the years, the bright red carpet faded to pink.* **2.** *iv.* to become weak; to lose energy. (Fig. on ①.) □ *Our hopes of winning the game faded when two of our players were injured.* **3.** *tv.* to cause something to lose color or become pale as in ①. □ *The sunlight faded the red carpet.*

**Fahrenheit** ['fɛr ən hɑɪt] **1.** *n.* a system of measuring temperature that is not metric. (No plural form. From Gabriel Fahrenheit, a German physicist who invented the Fahrenheit scale.) □ *Is this temperature measured in Fahrenheit or centigrade?* **2.** *adj.* <the adj. use of ①.> (② follows **degree(s)**. Abbreviated *F.*) □ *Water boils at 212 degrees Fahrenheit and freezes at 32 degrees Fahrenheit.*

**fail** ['fel] **1.** *tv.* not to succeed at something, especially a course or an examination in school. □ *I never bothered to study, so I failed my math test.* **2.** *tv.* to give a student a grade that means failure. □ *Mr. Smith failed the students who did not come to class.* **3.** *tv.* not to help someone; to let someone down. □ *Grandpa's eyes failed him at about the age of 90.* **4.** *iv.* [for part of a person's body] to become weak; [for something] to stop working; [for something] not to succeed. □ *When Grandma turned 85, her eyes began to fail.* **5.** *iv.* [for a business] not to succeed. □ *Bill's business failed because he didn't advertise enough.* **6.** *iv.* not to succeed in a task that one has tried to do; not to pass a school course. □ *I took the course three times, and I failed each time.*

**failure** ['fel jɚ] **1.** *n.* failing; not succeeding. (Plural only when referring to different kinds, types, instances, or varieties.) □ *Failure is common to all humans. No one is perfect.* 🄲 *Tom's many failures at work were caused by his lack of skill.* **2.** *n.* someone whose life has had almost no success. □ *Even though Sue was wealthy, she felt like a failure.*



**faint** ['fent] **1.** *adj.* barely noticeable; dim; not clear. (Adv: *faintly.* Comp: *fainter;* sup: *faintest.*) □ *This soup has a faint taste of chicken.* **2.** *adj.* [of someone] temporarily weak or dizzy; [of someone] about to pass out. (Adv: *faintly.* Comp: *fainter;* sup: *faintest.*) □ *I need to sit down. I'm a little faint.* **3.** *iv.* to pass out; to lose consciousness. □ *After seeing the terrible accident, Tom fainted on the street.*

**fair** ['fɛr] **1.** *n.* a yearly event held in a town, state, or county. □ *We went to the fair to look at the farm animals.* **2.** *adj.* just; honest; giving good judgments; not favoring one thing or person over another. (Adv: *fairly.* Comp: *fairer;* sup: *fairest.*) □ *It's not fair! Why does Jimmy get more ice cream than I do?* **3.** *adj.* [of skin or hair] very light in color. (Adv: *fairly.* Comp: *fairer;* sup: *fairest.*) □ *My hair is brown now, but when I was younger it was very fair.* **4.** *adj.* [of someone] having **fair** ③ skin or hair. (Comp: *fairer;* sup: *fairest.*) □ *Since the baby is so fair, we keep him out of the sun.* **5.** *adj.* considerable; ample. (Adv: *fairly.*) □ *I have a fair amount of work to do before I leave the office.* **6.** *adj.* not too bad; pretty good; adequate. (Adv: *fairly.* Comp: *fairer;* sup: *fairest.*) □ *Is the new mayor doing a good, fair, or poor job?*

**fairy** ['fɛr i] *n.* a small mythical being that looks human, does magic, and sometimes has wings. □ *The fairy used its magic to make the wind stop blowing.*

**faith** ['feθ] **1.** *n.* a strong belief in something that cannot be proved; a strong belief in someone or in a god. (No plural form.) □ *Faith is the basis of many of the large religions.* **2.** *n.* a particular religion. □ *I changed faiths when I married.* **3.** *n.* loyalty; trust. (No plural form.) □ *I have lost faith in my landlord's repeated promises to make repairs to my apartment.*

**faithful** ['feθ fʊl] *adj.* loyal. □ *Tom's faithful dog was killed by a car.*

F

**fake** ['fek] **1.** *tv.* to make a copy of something with the purpose of deceiving someone. □ *Anne faked her parents' signatures on her application.* **2.** *tv.* to pretend to do something or have something in order to deceive someone. □ *I faked interest in the boring lecture because I didn't want to offend the speaker.* **3.** *n.* something that is made to take the place of an original in order to deceive someone. □ *Mary owns a lot of jewelry, but she wears glass fakes when traveling.* **4.** *n.* someone who is a fraud. □ *You are not a real doctor! You're a fake.* **5.** *adj.* false; not genuine; made in order to deceive someone. □ *Bill tried to buy a hamburger with a fake $2 bill.*

**fall** ['fɔl] **1.** *iv., irreg.* to drop to a lower level from a higher level. (Pt: **fell**; pp: **fallen**.) □ *I tripped and fell down the stairs.* **2.** *iv., irreg.* to lose power; to be defeated. (Fig. on ①.) □ *After the king fell from power, he left the country.* **3.** *iv., irreg.* [for vision] to aim downward. □ *Bill's eyes fell because he was too ashamed to look at me.* **4.** *iv., irreg.* to go from a standing position to a lying position in one quick movement; to collapse. □ *Don't run in the house. You'll fall and hurt yourself.* **5.** *iv., irreg.* [for an event] to happen on a particular day of the week or in a particular month of the year. □ *Last year, my birthday fell on a Saturday.* **6.** *n.* the autumn; the season between summer and winter. □ *I began kindergarten in the fall of 1971.* **7.** *n.* suddenly going from a standing position to a lying position. □ *The football player's fall caused a broken leg.* **8.** *n.* a decrease; a drop; a lowering. □ *I lost a lot of money because of a fall in the value of silver.* **9.** *n.* the collapse of a political unit; a defeat, especially when at war. □ *No one is sure what caused the fall of the empire.* **10. falls** *n.* a waterfall. (Treated as plural.) □ *Thousands of tourists visit Niagara Falls each day.* **11. fall in love** *phr.* to begin to experience romantic love for someone. □ *Anne has fallen in love many times.*

**fallen** ['fɔl ən] pp of **fall**.

**false** ['fɔls] **1.** *adj.* not true; wrong; incorrect. (Adv: *falsely.* Comp: *falser;* sup: *falsest.*) □ *The theory that Max committed the crime turned out to be false.* **2.** *adj.* not loyal; not faithful. (Adv: *falsely.* Comp: *falser;* sup: *falsest.*) □ *A false friend will repeat things that are told secretly.* **3.** *adj.* not real; artificial; fake. (Comp: *falser;* sup: *falsest.*) □ *Even though it was a false alarm, the firefighters wouldn't let us return to the building.*

**fame** ['fem] *n.* the quality of being very well known. (No plural form.) □ *Because of the president's fame, everyone recognized him.*

**familiar** [fə 'mɪl jɚ] **1.** *adj.* known; well known; common. (Adv: *familiarly.*) □ *I think I am lost, because nothing here looks familiar.* **2.** *adj.* friendly; overly friendly. (Adv: *familiarly.*) □ *Anne's familiar manner made it easy to get to know her.*

**family** ['fæm (ə) li] **1.** *n.* a group of people related to each other. □ *Brown hair and green eyes are common in my family.* **2.** *n.* a mother, father, and one child or more; a parent and one child or more. □ *My company provides special services for families.* **3.** *n.* a group of things that are related in some way or share common features, such as animals, plants, languages, etc. □ *The*

*Romance language family includes Italian, French, and Spanish.* **4.** *adj.* <the adj. use of ① or ②.> □ *Every three years we pose for a new family portrait.*

**famine** ['fæm ən] *n.* a period of time when there is little or no food. □ *A long famine was caused by a terrible flood.*

**famous** ['fe məs] *adj.* very well known. □ *Abraham Lincoln is a very famous U.S. president.*

**fan** ['fæn] **1.** *n.* someone who admires someone or something very much. (A shortening of **fanatic**.) □ *The movie star gladly signed autographs for the excited fans.* **2.** *n.* a device or machine used to move air in order to cool someone or something. □ *The fan blew all the papers off my desk.* **3.** *tv.* to move air onto something. □ *The fire was dying, so I fanned it.*

**fanatic** [fə 'næt ɪk] *n.* someone who is too eager about and devoted to someone or something. □ *Bob is a fanatic about keeping his desk clean.*

**fancy** ['fæn si] **1.** *adj.* elegant; stylish; nicely decorated. (Adv: *fancily.* Comp: *fancier;* sup: *fanciest.*) □ *This dress is too fancy. Do you have anything simpler?* **2.** *n.* the imagination; the ability to create imaginative ideas or images. □ *Lisa let her fancy take hold and wrote an excellent story.* **3.** *n.* something that is imagined; a notion. □ *It was my fancy that we'd go on a vacation.*

**fang** ['fæŋ] *n.* a long, sharp tooth. □ *The snake sank its fangs into the mouse.*

**fantasy** ['fæn tə si] *n.* interesting thoughts and visions in the mind, somewhat like a dream. (Plural only when referring to different kinds, types, instances, or varieties.) □ *Bill had no friends, so he developed his own world of fantasy.* Ⓒ *In my wildest fantasies, I never thought I'd go skiing in Europe.*

**far** ['fɑr] **1.** *adj., irreg.* more distant; not as close as something else. (Comp: **farther** or **further**; sup: **farthest** or **furthest**.) □ *Could you get me the paint? It's on the far side of the garage.* **2.** *adv., irreg.* at or to a distant time or place; a long way away in time or space. (Comp: **farther** or **further**; sup: **farthest** or **furthest**.) □ *John traveled far away from the country where he was born.* **3.** *adv.* much; many; a lot. (Used before a comparative such as *more, less,* or *longer.*) □ *I like baseball far more than I like football.*

**fare** ['fɛr] **1.** *n.* the amount of money required to ride a bus, train, plane, subway, taxi, etc. □ *Mary and I took a taxi home from the party and split the fare.* **2.** *n.* the food that is served at a meal. (No plural form.) □ *I could offer my guests only modest fare.*

**farewell** [fɛr 'wɛl] **1.** *n.* an act of leaving and saying good-bye. □ *Anne's farewell at the bus terminal was quite sad.* **2.** *adj.* <the adj. use of ①.> □ *His farewell speech took too long.* **3.** *interj.* "good-bye." □ *Farewell. I will see you next week.*

**farm** ['fɑrm] **1.** *n.* a parcel of land used to grow crops or to raise animals. □ *There used to be a farm where these houses are today.* **2.** *tv.* to work on the land to make it grow plants, especially food; to plow land. □ *Our food comes from thousands of Americans who farm the land.* **3. farm** something **out** *tv.* + *obj.* + *adv.* to assign work among people; to distribute work among people. □ *While I was on vacation, my work was farmed out.* Ⓣ *They farmed out my work.* **4.** *iv.* to grow crops and raise animals as a living. □ *My grandparents farmed for fifty years before they retired.* **5.** *adj.* <the adj. use of ①.> □ *We sold all of our farm machinery at an auction.*

**farmer** ['fɑr mɚ] *n.* someone who grows crops and raises animals on a farm. □ *The farmer harvested the corn crop in September.*

**fart** ['fɑrt] **1.** *iv.* to release gas from the bowels through the anus. (Potentially offensive. The topic and the word are not heard in polite company. Use with caution.) □ *Okay, who farted?* **2.** *n.* the sound or odor of the release of gas from the bowels. □ *Who made that smelly fart?* **3.** *n.* a stupid and annoying person. □ *The guy's nothing but a fart. Just forget him.*

F

**farther** ['fɑr ðɚ] **1.** *adj.* more far; more distant in space or time. (One of the comparative forms of **far**, along with **further**.) □ *We sailed past the nearer island and stopped at the farther one.* **2.** *adv.* more far; more distant in space or time. (One of the comparative forms of **far**, along with **further**.) □ *How much farther must we walk? I'm getting tired.*

**farthest** ['fɑr ðəst] *adj.* the most far; the most distant in space or time. (One of the superlative forms of **far**, along with **furthest**.) □ *Paying attention to traffic was the farthest thing from my mind when I got into the accident.*

**fashion** ['fæ ʃən] **1.** *n.* the current, typical styles of dress or behavior within a society. (Plural only when referring to different kinds, types, instances, or varieties.) □ *Fashion has never interested me. I want comfort.* Ⓒ *This store sells expensive clothing in the latest fashions.* **2.** *n.* the manner or way in which something is done; a method. (No plural form.) □ *The criminal was executed in a cruel fashion.* **3.** *tv.* to form or shape something; to form something by hand. □ *I can fashion a swan by folding paper in a certain way.*

**fast** ['fæst] **1.** *adv.* quickly; rapidly. (Comp: *faster;* sup: *fastest.*) □ *Move fast. We're already 20 minutes late.* **2.** *adv.* tight(ly); without moving; securely. □ *The ropes held the mattress fast to the roof of the car.* **3.** *adj.* quick; rapid; speedy; not slow. (Comp: *faster;* sup: *fastest.*) □ *My boss likes my fast typing.* **4.** *adj.* [of a clock or watch] showing a time that is later than the real time. (Comp: *faster;* sup: *fastest.*) □ *The clock in the kitchen is five minutes fast.* **5.** *iv.* to go without food. □ *Bob is fasting in order to lose weight.* **6.** *n.* a period of time when someone does not eat, for religious, health, or political reasons. □ *I ended my fast by eating a small piece of chicken.*

**fasten** ['fæs ən] **1.** *tv.* to tie, lock, or hook something closed. □ *We fastened the gate after we went through it.* **2.** *tv.* to attach something to someone or something. □ *Please fasten this label to your book.*

**fastener** ['fæs ən ɚ] *n.* a device that secures or fastens something shut. □ *I pressed the fastener until it was securely shut.*

**fastidious** [fæ 'stɪd i əs] **1.** *adj.* hard to please; choosing carefully. (Adv: *fastidiously.*) □ *Max is a fastidious eater, choosing only the best food.* **2.** *adj.* preferring cleanliness and orderliness. (Adv: *fastidiously.*) □ *I'm so fastidious that you could eat off my kitchen floor.*

**fat** ['fæt] **1.** *n.* animal tissue filled with oil. (Plural only when referring to different kinds, types, instances, or varieties.) □ *I always cut the fat from pork chops before I cook them.* Ⓒ *Eating animal fats is probably harmful to your health.* **2.** *n.* loose flesh filled with ①. (No plural form.) □ *I decided to exercise because my fat shook when I walked.* **3.** *adj.* overweight; having too much ②. (Adv: *fatly.* Comp: *fatter;* sup: *fattest.*) □ *These narrow chairs are uncomfortable for fat people.*

**fate** ['fet] **1.** *n.* a force that is said to control what happens. (Plural only when referring to different kinds, types, instances, or varieties.) □ *When I lost control of my car, my life was placed in the hands of fate.* Ⓒ *The fates decided who was to marry the prince and live* *happily ever after.* **2.** *n.* the destiny of someone or something; what will happen to someone or something. □ *I don't know what the fate of my lost dog was, but I miss her a lot.* **3.** *tv.* [for **fate** ①] to determine what happens to someone or something. (Usually passive.) □ *The airplane was fated to crash into the sea.*

**father** ['fɑ ðɚ] **1.** *n.* the male parent of a child. (Also a term of address.) □ *I bought my father a tie for his birthday.* **2.** *n.* the inventor of something; the founder of something; the leader of something. (Fig. on ①.) □ *George Washington is the father of the United States.* **3.** *tv.* [for a male creature] to fertilize an egg, which will lead to the development of a child. □ *Tom fathered his first child when he was 23.*

**fatigue** [fə 'tig] **1.** *n.* a state of being very tired from too much mental or physical work. (No plural form.) □ *I suffered from mental fatigue because of stress in my job.* **2.** *tv.* to tire someone or something; to make someone or something tired. □ *Playing baseball fatigued all the kids.*

**fatten** ['fæt n] **1.** *tv.* to cause someone or something to grow larger. □ *We fattened the chickens by feeding them corn.* **2.** *tv.* to increase the size or value of an offer. (Fig. on ①.) □ *The company fattened the deal by increasing my salary.*

**fatty** ['fæt i] *adj.* full of or containing fat. (Comp: *fattier;* sup: *fattiest.*) □ *My doctor warned me to avoid fatty foods.*

**faucet** ['fɔs ɪt] *n.* a device that controls the flow of water or some other liquid from a pipe or container; a tap. □ *Hot water comes from the left faucet.*

**fault** ['fɔlt] **1.** *n.* a personal shortcoming; a flaw in someone's personality. □ *I'm willing to overlook your faults as long as you try to improve.* **2.** *n.* the responsibility for causing something bad to happen. (No plural form.) □ *Whose fault is it that the door was left unlocked?* **3.** *n.* a crack in the surface of the earth. □ *Our house insurance costs a lot because we live near a fault.*

**faulty** ['fɔl ti] *adj.* flawed; incorrect; having an error or mistake. (Adv: *faultily.* Comp: *faultier;* sup: *faultiest.*) □ *I don't understand your faulty logic.*

F

**favor** ['fe vɚ] **1.** *n.* a state of being valuable or worthy in someone else's view. (No plural form.) □ *Anne was in the boss's favor and got easy tasks.* **2.** *n.* an act of kindness; something nice that is done for someone else. □ *Please do me a favor and shut the window.* **3.** *tv.* to prefer someone or something; to like someone or something at the expense of someone or something else. □ *I favor chocolate ice cream, but I will eat any flavor happily.* **4.** *tv.* to support someone or something; to support an issue, a plan, a theory, an option, etc. □ *Bob favored going home early.* **5.** *tv.* to expect someone or something to win. □ *I favor our current senator to win the election.*

**favorite** ['fev (ə) rɪt] **1.** *adj.* preferred over every other choice; liked better than everything or everyone else. □ *Mr. Smith's favorite pupil always got good grades.* **2.** *n.* someone or something that is preferred over every other choice; someone or something that is liked better than everyone or everything else. □ *The students were all jealous of Dave, who was their teacher's favorite.*

**fax** ['fæks] **1.** *n.* a machine that sends an exact copy of a piece of paper to another machine, over telephone lines. □ *My fax places the current time on the top of each page it prints.* **2.** *n.* something that has been sent or received by way of ①. □ *It was hard to read the fax because the print was too light.* **3.** *adj.* <the adj. use of ①>; of or about sending and receiving ②. □ *The fax manual describes how to use the machine.*

**4.** *tv.* to send a document to someone by using ①. □ *I faxed it to you last night.*

**fear** ['fɪr] **1.** *n.* the feeling of being afraid; the feeling of being in danger. (Plural only when referring to different kinds, types, instances, or varieties.) □ *Dogs can sense whether you have fear for them or not.* Ⓒ *She suffers from many fears, most of them imaginary.* **2.** *n.* a specific source of ① and the feeling caused by that source. □ *I have a constant fear that I will have a car accident.* **3.** *tv.* to be afraid of someone or something. □ *I want to ask for a raise, but I fear my boss's temper.* **4.** *tv.* to feel that something unpleasant is the case or may happen. (Often used as a polite way of expressing regret that one must say something unpleasant. The object is a clause with **that** ⑦.) □ *I fear that you're mistaken in this matter.*

F

**feast** ['fist] **1.** *n.* a large meal, especially one for a special occasion; a banquet. □ *Every Sunday, I cook a huge feast.* **2.** *iv.* to eat a lot of food, often in the company of others, especially as part of a celebration. □ *My friends and I feasted well after we learned that we passed our final exams.*

**feat** ['fit] *n.* a remarkable accomplishment; an act or deed that shows skill or talent. □ *It was quite a feat, but the bridge was repaired within two months after the earthquake.*

**feather** ['fɛð ɚ] *n.* one of many hard stems bearing soft fibers that cover the body of a bird. □ *My pillow is filled with feathers.*

**feature** ['fi tʃɚ] **1.** *n.* an important aspect of something; a quality of something that stands out. □ *The business plan's most important feature is that it will save $100,000.* **2.** *n.* a part of the face. □ *My features cannot be seen clearly in this photograph.* **3.** *n.* a special article in a newspaper; an important news story. □ *The editor put Bill's feature on the front page.* **4.** *tv.* to present or focus on an important element of something. □ *The instruction manual features clear instructions on how to operate the computer.* **5.** *tv.* to present someone special as an actor in a movie, play, or television show. □ *This movie version of* Hamlet *features Sir Laurence Olivier.*

**February** ['fɛb ru ɛr ɪ] Go to **month**.

**feces** ['fi siz] *n.* excrement; animal waste. (From Latin. Treated as plural, but not countable.) □ *I had to clean my shoes because I stepped in some animal feces.*

**fed** ['fɛd] pt/pp of **feed**.

**federal** ['fɛd (ə) rəl] **1.** *adj.* of or about the organization of a group of states. (Adv: *federally.*) □ *The United States is a federal organization of states.* **2.** *adj.* of or about the U.S. government. (Adv: *federally.*) □ *The FDIC is the Federal Deposit Insurance Corporation.*

**fee** ['fi] *n.* money that is paid in exchange for a service or privilege. □ *My lawyer's fee is $130 for every hour.*

**feeble** ['fi bəl] *adj.* weak; frail; lacking force; lacking strength. (Adv: *feebly.* Comp: *feebler;* sup: *feeblest.*) □ *The feeble old man stumbled as he walked.*

**feed** ['fid] **1.** *tv., irreg.* to nourish someone or something with food; to give food to someone or something. (Pt/pp: **fed**.) □ *What time should I feed the dog tonight?* **2.** *tv., irreg.* to supply something without stopping; to provide something without stopping. (Fig. on ①.) □ *The sewing machine feeds thread through the eye of the needle.* **3.** *n.* food that is given to animals, especially on a farm. (Plural only when referring to different kinds, types, instances, or varieties.) □ *We grow corn for use in our cattle's feed.* Ⓒ *We tried any number of feeds, but the chickens still do not grow fast enough.*

**feel** ['fil] **1.** *tv., irreg.* to touch someone or something. (Pt/pp: **felt.**) □ *Susan felt the soft blanket with the tips of her fingers.* **2.** *tv., irreg.* to experience or sense being touched by someone or something. □ *Do you feel a little pressure on your arm? I am touching you there.* **3.** *tv., irreg.* to receive information by touching. □ *I felt the wet spot the drinking glass had left on the table.* **4.** *tv., irreg.* to experience an emotion; to experience something in one's mind. (The object can be a clause with **that** ⑦.) □ *Tom felt discomfort when he read the disturbing account of the fire.* **5.** *tv., irreg.* to consider something; to have an opinion about something. (The object is a clause with **that** ⑦.) □ *Jane felt that I had made a mistake.* **6.** *iv., irreg.* to experience [an emotion]; to experience [something in one's mind]. □ *Bill feels unhappy every year on the anniversary of his father's death.* **7.** *n.* a kind of shape or texture that is sensed by touching. (No plural form.) □ *The wood has a rough feel that makes it a poor choice for furniture.*

**feeler** ['fi lɚ] **1.** *n.* an antenna; a part of the body of an insect or shellfish that is used for touching or sensing. □ *Some insects use their feelers to find food.* **2.** *n.* an inquiry or suggestion that is made to determine what other people are thinking or feeling. □ *Send out a feeler and see if the staff wants to go bowling.*

**feeling** ['fi lɪŋ] **1.** *n.* sensation produced by touching something or by being touched by something; the ability to feel things. (No plural form.) □ *After the accident, Bob could not walk and had no feeling in his legs.* **2.** *n.* a sensation that is a response to touch, pressure, heat, cold, or pain. □ *The pain of a headache is an unpleasant feeling.* **3.** *n.* an emotion. □ *Seeing my grandchildren always gives me a feeling of joy.* **4.** *n.* an idea based on what one feels or suspects. □ *I have a feeling that it's going to rain soon.*

**feet** ['fit] pl of **foot.**

**fell** ['fɛl] pt of **fall.**

**fellow** ['fɛl o] **1.** *n.* a man; a male. □ *I spoke to some fellow from Boston during lunch.* **2.** *n.* a position of rank or status at a school or university, usually without teaching responsibilities. (For either sex.) □ *Anne is a fellow in the English department at the university.* **3.** *adj.* similar; alike; sharing a common interest or occupation. (For either sex. Prenominal only.) □ *I'd like to thank my fellow students for their help.*

**fellowship** ['fɛl o ʃɪp] **1.** *n.* a group; a social organization. (Not restricted to males.) □ *At church, Sue belongs to a fellowship of devout worshipers.* **2.** *n.* friendly discussion and activity with other people; friendship. (No plural form.) □ *After the meeting, we had refreshments and enjoyed the fellowship of the group.* **3.** *n.* money that is given to an advanced student to pay for schooling. □ *I couldn't afford to continue my studies without a fellowship.*

**felt** ['fɛlt] **1.** pt/pp of **feel. 2.** *n.* a thick cloth made of pressed fibers. (Plural only when referring to different kinds, types, instances, or varieties.) □ *Black felt seems to attract lint.* Ⓒ *The lighter felts cannot be used to make hats.* **3.** *adj.* made of ②. □ *Bob usually wears an old felt hat.*

**female** ['fi mel] **1.** *adj.* of or about women or girls; of or about animals of the sex that can bear young or lay eggs. □ *The female employees played softball together after work.* **2.** *n.* a woman; a girl; an animal of the sex that bears young or lays eggs. □ *Breast cancer is more common in females than in males.*

**feminine** ['fɛm ə nɪn] **1.** *adj.* of or about the characteristics of women; of or about the qualities of women. (Adv:

F

*femininely.*) □ *Jim asked Mary for a feminine viewpoint on the issue.* **2.** *adj.* of or about the one of the three grammatical genders that is neither masculine nor neuter. □ *In Spanish, many feminine nouns end in* a. □ *The word for "work" in German is feminine in gender.*

**fence** ['fɛns] *n.* a barrier that encloses a space to keep things or people from coming into or leaving that space. □ *The horses are safe behind the tall fence.*

F

**fender** ['fɛn dɚ] *n.* a part of a vehicle's body that forms a protective shield over a wheel. □ *I polish the fenders every time I clean my car.*

**ferryboat** ['fɛr i 'bot] *n.* a boat that takes cars and people across a river or a lake. □ *The ferryboat is just now leaving the opposite shore.*

**fertile** ['fɚt əl] **1.** *adj.* able to reproduce or develop new life easily. (Adv: *fertilely.*) □ *The very fertile couple had six children in eight years.* **2.** *adj.* [of soil] rich in (plant) food that helps reproduction and growth. (Adv: *fertilely.*) □ *The fertile land yields many crops.* **3.** *adj.* creative; able to produce good ideas. (Fig. on ①. Adv: *fertilely.*) □ *The meeting was quite fertile, with a number of fine ideas being discussed.*

**fertilize** ['fɚ tə lɑɪz] **1.** *tv.* to provide nutrients to the land so that crops will grow well. □ *The farmer fertilized the farmland every year.* **2.** *tv.* [for a male reproductive cell] to join with a female reproductive cell; [for a male's sperm] to join with a female's ovum (egg). □ *The first sperm that reaches the ovum fertilizes it.* **3.** *tv.* to cause a male reproductive cell to join with a female reproductive cell, as in ②. □ *A scientist fertilized the frog ova in the laboratory.*

**fervor** ['fɚ vɚ] *n.* passion; excitement; strong emotion. (No plural form.) □ *The newspapers generated a huge amount of fervor for the election.*

**festive** ['fɛs tɪv] *adj.* merry; exciting; like a celebration; joyous. (Adv: *festively.*) □ *The winning team was in a festive mood after the game.*

**fetch** ['fɛtʃ] **1.** *tv.* to bring something to someone; to go somewhere and get something for someone. □ *Would you please fetch me my shoes?* **2.** *tv.* [for something] to bring in a certain amount of money when sold. □ *My antique car fetched $75,000 at the auction.*

**fever** ['fi vɚ] *n.* a state of sickness where the temperature of the body rises above normal. □ *Your forehead feels very hot. I think you have a fever.*

**feverish** ['fi vɚ ɪʃ] **1.** *adj.* having a higher body temperature than normal. (Adv: *feverishly.*) □ *Your forehead feels very hot. Are you feverish?* **2.** *adj.* excited and fast; restless. (Fig. on ①. Adv: *feverishly.*) □ *I walked at a feverish pace to get to my meeting on time.*

**few** ['fju] **1.** *adj.* not many; a smaller number than expected. (Used with items that can be counted. Compare this with **little**. Without *a*. Comp: *fewer;* sup: *fewest.*) □ *Few people showed up for the party—not nearly the number we had expected.* □ *John is fortunate because he has very few problems.* **2.** *adj.* a small number; some. (With *a*. Comp: *fewer;* sup: *fewest.*) □ *Dave has a few problems, but then, who doesn't?* **3.** *n.* only some, not many [of those previously mentioned]; a smaller number than expected. (No plural form. Treated as plural.) □ *I invited lots of people to the party, but few came.* **4. a few** *n.* a small number [of those items previously mentioned]. (Treated as plural. Use *a little* for quantities.) □ *I invited lots of people to the party, but only a few came.*

**fiber** ['fɑɪ bɚ] **1.** *n.* one of many threads, strands, or rigid cellular structures that form many plant, animal, and artificial substances. □ *I picked up loose fibers* *from my sweater.* **2.** *n.* edible plant **fibers** ①. (Plural only when referring to different kinds, types, instances, or varieties. Treated as singular.) □ *Beans have lots of fiber.* 🄲 *Different fibers have different uses, such as with clothing and food.*

**fiction** ['fɪk ʃən] **1.** *n.* literature that is written about imagined events and not about real events. (No plural form.) □ *The school library keeps fiction on the second floor.* **2.** *n.* information that is not true but instead has been created by someone. (Plural only when referring to different kinds, types, instances, or varieties.) □ *Dave's account of why he was late for work was fiction.* 🄲 *Bob's testimony was a series of fictions that fooled no one.*

**fiddle** ['fɪd l] **1.** *n.* a violin. (Informal.) □ *We sat around the campfire and sang while Bill played the fiddle.* **2.** *iv.* to play ①. □ *Do you know how to fiddle well enough to play in our band?*

**field** ['fild] **1.** *n.* a large area of land used for a specific purpose, such as growing crops, raising cattle, playing certain sports, fighting a battle, landing airplanes, etc. □ *The baseball field was covered with mud after two weeks of rain.* **2.** *n.* an area of knowledge; an area of study. □ *John does research in the field of computer science.*

**fierce** ['fɪrs] *adj.* violent; cruel; untamed; wild. (Adv: *fiercely.* Comp: *fiercer;* sup: *fiercest.*) □ *We saw fierce tigers in the zoo.*

**fifteen** ['fɪf 'tin] 15. Go to **four** for senses and examples.

**fifteenth** ['fɪf 'tinθ] 15th. Go to **fourth** for senses and examples.

**fifth** ['fɪfθ] **1.** 5th. Go to **fourth** for senses and examples. **2.** *n.* a **fifth** ① of a gallon of liquor. □ *How much tax is there on a fifth of liquor?*

**fiftieth** ['fɪf ti əθ] 50th. Go to **fourth** for senses and examples.

**fifty** ['fɪf ti] 50. Go to **forty** for senses and examples.

**fig** ['fɪg] *n.* a soft, sweet fruit with many seeds. □ *This dessert is made with figs and dates.*

**fight** ['fɑɪt] **1.** *n.* a struggle; a battle. □ *I broke my nose in a fight.* **2.** *tv., irreg.* to battle someone; to make combat against someone. (Pt/pp: **fought.**) □ *Bob fought Bill and got hit in the face.* **3.** *iv., irreg.* to do battle; to argue. □ *I don't enjoy fighting with my parents.*

**fig. on** an abbreviation of **figurative on.**

**figurative on** [of a word or phrase] based on some other, more literal, word or phrase.

**figure** ['fɪg jɚ] **1.** *n.* a human body; the form of a human body. □ *My sister and I are the same height, but we have very different figures. She is much thinner than I am.* **2.** *n.* a person, usually well known or important. □ *For class, Tom wrote an essay about a famous figure in American history.* **3.** *n.* a digit; one of the numbers from 0 to 9. □ *Please write each figure neatly on the paper.* **4.** *n.* a total; a sum; an amount. □ *Add your wages together and place that figure on line 5 of the tax form.* **5.** *n.* a chart or diagram in a book that explains information in the text. □ *Please refer to Figure 2.8 for a graph of the data discussed here.* **6. figure** someone or something **out** *tv.* + *obj.* + *adv.* to come to understand someone or something; to solve something such as a puzzle, a riddle, or a mystery. □ *The police could not figure Max out.* 🅃 *I can't figure out poor old Max either.* **7. figure** something **(up)** *tv.* + *obj.* + *(adv.)* to add, subtract, multiply, or divide numbers to create a new number; to calculate something. □ *Max figured the totals in his head.* **8.** *tv.* to consider something; to believe something. (The object is a clause with **that** ⑦.) □ *I figure that there were 25,000 people at the parade.*

**file** ['fɑɪl] **1.** *n.* a metal tool that is scraped over rough surfaces to make them smooth and even. □ *Use a file to smooth the rough places on the railing.* **2.** *n.* a folder or other container used for holding and storing papers in an organized way. □ *I accidentally dropped a stack of files, and all the papers fell out.* **3.** *n.* the papers within ②; the information contained in ②. □ *I can talk to you after I have read this file.* **4.** *n.* a **computer file**; a unit of data or information in digital form, such as is stored on a floppy disk or disk drive. □ *I pressed the wrong key and accidentally deleted an important file.* **5.** *tv.* to smooth something with ①. □ *I filed my fingernails after I cut them.* **6.** *tv.* to organize papers by putting them into the appropriate **file** ②; to put a piece of paper in the appropriate **file** ②. □ *I filed the reports in the drawer.* **7.** *iv.* to move in a line, going into or out of a place. □ *The students calmly filed out of the room during the emergency.*

**fill** ['fɪl] **1. fill something (up)** *tv. + obj. (+ adv.)* to put something into a container or a place until there is no more room to put anything else in. □ *John filled the glass up with water.* **2. fill something (up)** *tv. + obj. (+ adv.)* to take up all available space or time; to occupy all available space or time. □ *The speech filled up two hours exactly.* **3.** *tv.* to provide what is requested; to supply a product when it is requested; to meet someone's demand for something. □ *I am sorry, but we are unable to fill your order.* **4. fill something in** *tv. + obj. + adv.* to put words in blank spaces on a form. □ *Please fill this blank in with your name.* 🅃 *Fill in all the blanks.* **5. fill something out** *tv. + obj. + adv.* to complete a form. □ *Please fill all these forms out.* 🅃 *I won't fill out a single form!* **6.** *iv.* to become full. □ *The kitchen filled with thick, black smoke.*

**film** ['fɪlm] **1.** *n.* the material that photographs or movies are recorded on. (Plural only when referring to different kinds, types, instances, or varieties.) □ *I bought some new film for my camera.* 🄲 *Older films were subject to decay and damage from heat.* **2.** *n.* a movie; a motion picture. □ *Last night we went to dinner and then watched a film.* **3.** *n.* a thin layer of something; a coating. □ *The throat is covered with a thin film of mucus.* **4.** *tv.* to record someone or something on **film** ① in a particular place or manner. □ *Most television shows are filmed in Los Angeles.*

**filter** ['fɪl tɚ] **1.** *n.* a device that strains fluids or gases to separate solids from them; a device that cleans a fluid or gas that passes through it. □ *The filter of a cigarette helps prevent some of the harmful substances from entering the body.* **2.** *tv.* to pass a substance through ①. □ *The scientist filtered the liquid to make it pure.*

**filth** ['fɪlθ] *n.* grime; dirt that is difficult to clean off. (No plural form.) □ *Wash that filth off your hands before you come to dinner!*

**fin** ['fɪn] **1.** *n.* a flat organ—like a small fan—on a fish that allows it to control its movement in the water. □ *The biologist studied how fish use their fins in strong currents of water.* **2.** *n.* one of a pair of rubber or plastic shoes with flat projections, used by divers to move themselves through the water. □ *It's hard to walk on land while wearing fins.*

**final** ['fɑɪ nəl] **1.** *adj.* last; at the end; ultimate. (Adv: *finally.*) □ *After the final contestant has performed, the judges will decide who won.* **2.** *n.* the last examination in a school course. (Often plural, referring to the last examinations in all of one's courses for the term or semester.) □ *I can't go on vacation that week because I've got finals then.*

**find** ['fɑɪnd] **1.** *tv., irreg.* to discover or locate someone or something that one was looking for. (Pt/pp: **found**.) □ *I found just what I needed at the small shop in town.* **2.** *tv., irreg.* to recover something; to discover something. □ *The dog found an old bone in the ditch.* **3. find** something **out** *tv., irreg. + obj. + adv.* to learn something; to learn information. □ *Did you find the truth out?* 🅃 *I finally found out the truth.* **4.** *tv., irreg.* to decide that someone or something has a certain quality; to consider someone or something to be a certain way. (The object can be a clause with **that** ⑦.) □ *Everyone found the movie entertaining.*

**fine** ['fɑɪn] **1.** *n.* an amount of money that must be paid as a punishment; a penalty. □ *I had to pay a large fine for speeding, but I was innocent!* **2.** *adj.* acceptable or suitable; very good; excellent. (Adv: *finely.* Comp: *finer;* sup: *finest.*) □ *The weather is fine for outdoor games.* **3.** *adj.* of high quality; very delicate and of high quality. (Adv: *finely.* Comp: *finer;* sup: *finest.*) □ *We carefully packed the fine dishes in a special box.* **4.** *adj.* not coarse; consisting of small particles; in the form of a powder. (Adv: *finely.* Comp: *finer;* sup: *finest.*) □ *We went to the beach and walked barefoot on the fine sand.* **5.** *adj.* very thin; very small. (Adv: *finely.* Comp: *finer;* sup: *finest.*) □ *That thread isn't fine enough to fit through the eye of this needle.* **6.** *adv.* well; nicely; excellently. □ *I don't need a more expensive watch. This one works fine.* **7.** *tv.* to charge someone or something an amount of money as a punishment or penalty. □ *The judge found the defendant guilty and fined him $100.*

**finger** ['fɪŋ gɚ] *n.* one of the five extensions or **digits** at the end of the hand. □ *I accidentally hit my finger with a hammer.*

**fingernail** ['fɪŋ gɚ nel] *n.* the hard, flat covering at the end of each finger. □ *Bob cleaned the dirt from under his fingernails with a file.*

**fingerprint** ['fɪŋ gɚ prɪnt] *n.* the light, oily mark left by the ridges on the skin of one's fingers. □ *The thief left his fingerprints on the table.*

F

**fingertip** ['fɪŋ gɚ tɪp] *n.* the end of a finger. □ *Anne cut her fingertip with a knife while slicing bread.*

**finish** ['fɪn ɪʃ] **1.** *tv.* to bring something to an end; to complete or conclude something. □ *Has he finished his work yet?* **2.** *tv.* to use all of something; to eat or drink all of something. □ *Finish your vegetables, or you won't get any dessert.* **3.** *tv.* to cover something made out of wood with a protective coat of varnish, paint, or something similar. □ *I finished the bookshelf with a light stain.* **4.** *iv.* [for someone] to reach the end of doing something. □ *As soon as I finished, I went home.* **5.** *n.* the end; the conclusion; the final part of something. □ *Have you reached the finish of the novel yet? It's really good.* **6.** *n.* a protective coating of paint, varnish, lacquer, or stain on a wooden surface; a protective coating on any surface. □ *A strong finish protected the wood from rain damage.*

**fire** ['fɑɪɚ] **1.** *n.* heat, flames, and light made by burning something. (Plural only when referring to different kinds, types, instances, or varieties.) □ *Fire destroyed the building quickly.* 🄲 *The fires produced by lightning destroy many forest trees each year.* **2.** *n.* an area of burning with ①. □ *There is a terrible fire on Maple Street.* **3.** *n.* passion; strong emotion; fervor. (Fig. on ①. No plural form.) □ *I was impressed by Jimmy's fire for learning.* **4.** *n.* the shooting of weapons; the noise made by shooting guns. (No plural form.) □ *The* *leader commanded the troops to hold their fire.* **5.** *tv.* to get rid of an employee; to end someone's employment. ☐ *If your work does not improve, we will have to fire you.* **6. on fire** *phr.* burning; being burned with flames. ☐ *That house on the corner is on fire!*

**firecracker** ['fɑɪɚ kræk ɚ] *n.* a small device that explodes when set afire, making a lot of noise. ☐ *I was punished for exploding a firecracker at school.*

F

**fire engine** ['fɑɪɚ ɛn dʒɪn] *n.* a truck that carries water and hoses to put out fires. ☐ *A fire engine arrived at the fire shortly after I made an emergency call.*

**fire escape** ['fɑɪɚ ə skep] **1.** *n.* a special exit from a building in case the building catches fire. ☐ *In case of fire, use the fire escape instead of the elevators.* **2.** *n.* a special metal staircase attached to the outside of the building, used as an escape route in case of **fire** ①. ☐ *Our fire escape is inspected each year to make sure it is safe.*

**firefighter** ['fɑɪɚ fɑɪt ɚ] *n.* someone who is trained to put out fires and rescue people. ☐ *The firefighter entered the burning building to save the children inside.*

**fireplace** ['fɑɪɚ ples] *n.* a place in a house or building where a fire can be built to provide heat. ☐ *I warmed my feet in front of the fireplace.*

**fireproof** ['fɑɪɚ pruf] **1.** *adj.* not able to catch fire; hard to burn. ☐ *We keep our important documents in a fireproof metal box.* **2.** *tv.* to make something so it is able to resist to fire. ☐ *They used a special paint to fireproof the wood.*

**firm** ['fɚm] **1.** *adj.* solid; hard. (Adv: *firmly.* Comp: *firmer;* sup: *firmest.*) ☐ *Keep a firm grip on the steering wheel when you are driving.* **2.** *adj.* not easily moved; steady. (Adv: *firmly.* Comp: *firmer;* sup: *firmest.*) ☐ *Sue never gets emotional in an argument. She always remains firm and calm.* **3.** *adj.* final and not to be changed. (Adv: *firmly.* Comp: *firmer;* sup: *firmest.*) ☐ *No, you cannot go to the movie. My answer is firm.* **4.** *n.* a company; a business. ☐ *After ten years of hard work, Anne became a partner in the law firm.*

**first** ['fɚst] **1.** *adj.* before everything or everyone else; at the beginning. (The ordinal number for **one**. Adv: *firstly.*) ☐ *The first letter of the alphabet is* A. ☐ *Here's a picture of my first haircut—when I was two years old.* **2.** *adv.* before anything else; before another event. ☐ *First, pour a cup of milk into a bowl, and then add the flour.* **3.** *adv.* for the **first** ① time; never having happened before. ☐ *Sue first studied piano when she was 5.* **4.** *n.* someone or something that is the **first** ① thing or person. (No plural form.) ☐ *The first to arrive at parties is usually the last to leave.*

**first-aid kit** ['fɚst 'ed kɪt] *n.* a box that holds medicine, bandages, and other useful things to take care of someone in an emergency. ☐ *Mary keeps a first-aid kit in her car in case of emergencies.*

**firsthand** ['fɚst 'hænd] **1.** *adj.* direct; coming from the source directly; witnessed. ☐ *I have firsthand knowledge of what it's like to live in the mountains.* **2.** *adv.* directly; from the source. ☐ *I learned it firsthand. It isn't gossip.*

**first name** ['fɚst 'nem] *n.* one's name, given at birth and—in English—placed before one's surname. ☐ *John Smith's first name is John.*

**fish** ['fɪʃ] **1.** *n., irreg.* any of various animals without legs that live underwater and typically have fins and scales. (Pl: *fish* unless referring to a number of species.) ☐ *Bob caught two large fish in this stream.* **2.** *n.* the meat of ① used as food. (No plural form.) ☐ *My brother, a vegetarian, doesn't eat fish.* **3.** *iv.* to try to catch ①. ☐ *Every Saturday I go to the lake to fish.*

**fishbowl** ['fɪʃ bol] *n.* a container that fish are kept in; a small aquarium. (See also **fishtank.**) □ *I placed the fish in the sink while I cleaned the fishbowl.*

**fisherman** ['fɪʃ ɚ mən] *n., irreg.* someone who catches fish for a living; a man who fishes. (Pl: **fishermen.**) □ *The fishermen left early in the morning in their boats.*

**fishermen** ['fɪʃ ɚ mən] pl of **fisherman.**

**fishhook** ['fɪʃ hʊk] *n.* a sharp hook used to catch fish. □ *I cut my finger on the fishhook.*

**fishtank** ['fɪʃ tæŋk] *n.* an aquarium; a container for holding fish or other creatures, usually with water. □ *My fishtank contains two frogs and a variety of plants.*

**fist** ['fɪst] *n.* the hand with the fingers closed tightly. □ *Nervously, I held my house keys in my fist.*

**fit** ['fɪt] **1.** *iv., irreg.* to be the right size for something. (Pt/pp: *fit* or *fitted.*) □ *Does this pair of shoes fit?* **2.** *tv., irreg.* to suit someone or something; to be matched to someone or something. □ *The antique furniture does not fit the style of the room.* **3.** *tv., irreg.* [for something] to be the right size for someone or something. □ *This belt fits my waist perfectly.* **4.** *tv., irreg.* to make something match something else in some way. □ *The judge tried to make the punishment fit the crime.* **5.** *adj.* suitable; having the things that are needed. (Adv: *fitly.* Comp: *fitter;* sup: *fittest.*) □ *This violent movie is not fit for children.* **6.** *adj.* healthy; in good condition. (Comp: *fitter;* sup: *fittest.*) □ *Grandpa is quite fit for a man of his age.* **7.** *n.* the way that something **fits** ①. □ *I had gained weight, so the pants were a tight fit.*

**five** ['fɑɪv] **1.** 5. Go to **four** for senses and examples. **2.** *n.* a **bill** ③ or **note** ③ worth **five** ① dollars. □ *Can I borrow a five until next week?*

**fix** ['fɪks] **1.** *tv.* to repair something; to make something work again. □ *Do you know how to fix a car engine?* **2.** *tv.* to make something firm; to place something firmly into something. □ *The bench had been fixed in place, and I could not move it.* **3.** *tv.* to prepare food or drink. □ *Can I fix you something to eat?* **4.** *tv.* to choose a date and time; to determine a date, time, or place. □ *Max fixed the time of the meeting at noon.*

**flag** ['flæg] **1.** *n.* a piece of cloth of a certain color pattern that represents a country, state, city, school, or organization, or is used as a signal. □ *The ship flew a flag meaning that it was anchored.* **2. flag** someone or something **down** *tv. + obj. + adv.* to signal someone to stop. □ *The police officer flagged the speeding car down.* Ⓣ *He flagged down the wrong car.* **3.** *iv.* to become tired; to weaken. □ *After a week in the woods, the lost hiker's spirits began to flag.*

**flagpole** ['flæg pol] *n.* a pole on which a flag is mounted or attached. □ *Once a year, we hired someone to paint the tall flagpole.*

**flake** ['flek] **1.** *n.* a loose piece of something; a bit of something; a thin, light piece of something. □ *The children caught flakes of snow on their tongues.* **2. flake off** *iv. + adv.* to fall off in thin, loose pieces. □ *The edges of the step flaked off when I rubbed my dirty shoes against them.*

**flame** ['flem] **1.** *n.* a tongue of fire; a segment of yellow, white, blue, or red light that shoots out from a fire. □ *Flames roared out of the burning house.* **2.** *n.* an angry e-mail message. □ *Someone sent me a nasty flame because I expressed my opinion.* **3.** *tv.* to criticize someone sharply in a message on the Internet. (Slang.) □ *Dave was flamed for posting an insulting message on the Internet.*

**flammable** ['flæm ə bəl] *adj.* **inflammable;** likely to catch fire; easily set on fire.

F

(Adv: *flammably.*) □ *Gasoline is an extremely flammable liquid.*

**flap** ['flæp] **1.** *n.* a cover, placed over an opening, that is hinged or attached at one end. □ *I tied the tent flap closed to keep out the rain.* **2.** *iv.* to move back and forth, as with the movement of birds' wings. □ *Bill's mouth flaps a lot, but he never says anything important.* **3.** *tv.* to move something back and forth, as with the movement of birds' wings. □ *The bird flapped its wings very fast.*

**flare** ['flɛr] **1.** *n.* a bright flame. □ *A flare of light hurt my eyes.* **2.** *n.* something that provides a bright light, used as a signal or as a warning of danger. □ *We lit flares on the island's shore in hopes of being rescued.*

**flash** ['flæʃ] **1.** *n.* a quick, strong burst of light. □ *I was temporarily blinded by a flash of light.* **2.** *n.* an important news report, especially one that interrupts regular programs. □ *The latest news flash reported that the police had caught the dangerous criminal.* **3.** *iv.* to give off a burst of light for a brief moment. □ *Lightning flashed across the sky.* **4.** *tv.* to make something give off a burst of light for a brief moment. □ *The driver flashed the blinker to indicate a left turn.*

**flashlight** ['flæʃ lɑɪt] *n.* a small, portable light that uses batteries for power. □ *The only light in the cave came from my flashlight.*

**flat** ['flæt] **1.** *adj.* [of a surface] level, even, and smooth. (Adv: *flatly.* Comp: *flatter;* sup: *flattest.*) □ *This region is very flat. There are no hills or mountains.* **2.** *adj.* having lost air; not filled with air. (Adv: *flatly.* Comp: *flatter;* sup: *flattest.*) □ *I pumped air into the tire because it was flat.* **3.** *adj.* stable; not moving higher or lower. (Comp: *flatter;* sup: *flattest.*) □ *Interest rates are flat right now, but they're expected to climb.* **4.** *adj.* dull; not exciting. (Adv: *flatly.* Comp: *flatter;* sup: *flattest.*) □ *Your writing is flat and not interesting.* **5.** *adj.* [sounding a musical sound] lower in pitch than what something is supposed to be. (Adv: *flatly.* Comp: *flatter;* sup: *flattest.*) □ *Your piano is flat. You should have it tuned.* **6.** *n.* an apartment. □ *I live in a flat in New York City.* **7.** *n.* a note that is one-half step lower in pitch than a natural note. □ *You are singing D, and it should be D-flat.* **8.** *n.* a tire with no air in it. (Short for **flat tire**.) □ *My car has a flat, and I don't know how to change it.*

**flat tire** ['flæt 'tɑɪɚ] *n.* a tire that does not have enough air. (Can be shortened to **flat**.) □ *I'm late because I had to change a flat tire on the way here.*

**flavor** ['fle vɚ] **1.** *n.* a specific taste; the way something tastes. □ *The stew has a strong tomato flavor.* **2.** *n.* something that is added to a food to give it a specific taste. □ *This ice cream has natural vanilla flavor.* **3.** *n.* a special quality or characteristic. □ *Bands of colored paper gave the party a flavor of the holiday season.*

**flaw** ['flɔ] *n.* a fault; a defect; an indication of damage. □ *A flaw in the design of the airplane caused it to crash.*

**flea** ['fli] *n.* a tiny insect that lives on an animal's skin, sucking blood and eating dead skin. □ *It's difficult to find fleas on a furry animal because they are so small.*

**fled** ['flɛd] pt/pp of **flee**.

**flee** ['fli] **1.** *tv., irreg.* to escape from danger. (Pt/pp: **fled**.) □ *My grandmother fled the civil war in her country.* **2.** *iv., irreg.* to run quickly away from something or toward something. □ *The thief fled from the police.*

**flesh** ['flɛʃ] **1.** *n.* the soft part of the body covered by skin; meat. (No plural form.) □ *The cook removed the chicken's flesh from its bones.* **2.** *n.* the soft part of a fruit or vegetable that can be eaten.

(No plural form.) □ *The worms had eaten the flesh of the ripe tomatoes.*

**flew** ['flu] pt of fly.

**flexible** ['flɛk sə bəl] **1.** *adj.* able to bend easily; not rigid. (Adv: *flexibly.*) □ *Jane easily bent the flexible wire into a loop.* **2.** *adj.* able to be changed; able to serve a number of purposes. (Fig. on ①. Adv: *flexibly.*) □ *My schedule is flexible. I can meet you anytime.*

**flight** ['flɑɪt] **1.** *n.* flying; flying through the air. (Plural only when referring to different kinds, types, instances, or varieties.) □ *Humans have been interested in flight for thousands of years.* Ⓒ *The early flights are full. I can put you on the 4:30 plane.* **2.** *n.* running away from someone or something; an escape from danger. (No plural form.) □ *The soldier talked about his flight from the enemy's prison.* **3.** *n.* a set of stairs. □ *Tom fell down a flight of stairs and broke his arm.*

**flip** ['flɪp] **1.** *n.* a throw that tosses something into the air; a tossing action that moves something. □ *I turned on the lights with a flip of the switch.* **2.** *n.* a kind of jump where one turns one's body in the air. □ *The swimmer did a flip from the diving board.* **3.** *tv.* to cause something to turn about or spin through the air. □ *Tom flipped the car upside down when he ran it off the road.*

**flirt** ['flɚt] **1. flirt (with someone)** *iv.* (+ *prep. phr.*) to behave in a way that gets someone's attention—with romance in mind. □ *After Anne had flirted with John for a few weeks, she was embarrassed to learn that he was married.* **2.** *n.* someone who tries to attract someone's attention romantically or sexually. □ *That little flirt asked me for my phone number.*

**float** ['flot] **1.** *iv.* to remain on top of water or a liquid; to stay above water. □ *A small boat floated on the surface of the pond.* **2.** *iv.* to hover; to remain in the air. (Fig. on ①.) □ *The balloons floated in the breeze.* **3.** *tv.* to release something so it can move as in ①. □ *We floated the raft down the river.*

**flood** ['flʌd] **1.** *n.* a large amount of water lying on land that is normally dry. □ *The flood left behind tons of mud and dead fish.* **2.** *n.* a powerful surge of water moving over the land. □ *The flood spilled over onto the land and into the town.* **3.** *n.* a large amount of something. (Fig. on ②.) □ *I can't leave the office now because I have a flood of paperwork on my desk.* **4.** *tv.* to cover an area with water; to cover something with water. □ *The heavy rains flooded the land around the river.* **5.** *iv.* to spill or overflow with great volumes of water; to become covered with a great amount of water. □ *We had to leave the town when it flooded.*

**floor** ['flor] **1.** *n.* the surface of a room that is walked on; the inside bottom surface of a room. □ *I knocked the plate off the table and onto the floor.* **2.** *n.* one level of a building; a story. □ *My apartment is on the third floor.*

**floppy disk** ['flɑp i 'dɪsk] *n.* a round, flat, magnetic computer storage device that can be moved from computer to computer. □ *I saved my homework on a floppy disk and printed it out on a computer at school.*

**florist** ['flor ɪst] *n.* someone who arranges and sells flowers for a living. □ *I asked the florist to put together a $30 flower arrangement.*

**flour** ['flɑʊ ɚ] *n.* a powder made from grinding wheat, corn, or other grain, used in cooking. (Compare this with **flower**. Plural only when referring to different kinds, types, instances, or varieties.) □ *I bought five pounds of flour at the grocery store.* Ⓒ *Cheaper flours have to be sifted one or more times.*

**flow** ['flo] **1.** *n.* the movement of running water; the movement of a fluid. (No plural form.) □ *Sue applied pressure to the cut to stop the flow of blood.* **2.** *n.* the even and ordered movement of things in a series. (No plural form. Fig. on ①.) □ *This lever controls the flow of parts that come down the assembly line.* **3.** *iv.* to move like running water; to move smoothly along a route. □ *Hot water flowed from the open pipe.* **4.** *iv.* to move easily and in an orderly fashion. □ *The students flowed in and out of the cafeteria during lunch.*

**flower** ['flaʊ ɚ] **1.** *n.* a plant that produces blossoms. (Compare this with **flour**.) □ *Mary bought many pots of flowers and brought them home to plant them.* **2.** *n.* a blossom; the brightly colored petals of a plant. □ *Anne pressed the pretty flower between the pages of a book.* **3.** *iv.* to bloom; [for a plant] to produce ②. □ *The roses flowered early this year.*

**flown** ['flon] pp of **fly**.

**flu** ['flu] **the flu** *n.* influenza; a disease like a very bad cold. (Plural only when referring to different kinds, types, or varieties. Treated as singular.) □ *My whole family has influenza. I thought I had a common cold, but I have the flu, just like the others.* Ⓒ *This year's flus seem to be from three separate and different sources.*

**fluent** ['flu ənt] *adj.* able to speak, read, write, or understand a language as well as a native speaker of that language. (Adv: *fluently.*) □ *This job requires you to be fluent in English and Spanish.*

**fluid** ['flu ɪd] **1.** *n.* a liquid or a gas; a substance that can flow. (Technically, a gas is a fluid.) □ *The engineer measured the pressure of the fluid flowing in the pipes.* □ *I am dizzy because I have fluid in my ears.* **2.** *adj.* moving freely; flowing freely as with a liquid or a gas. (Adv: *fluidly.*) □ *Sand in the desert seems quite fluid when you walk through it.*

**flush** ['flʌʃ] **1.** *n.* an act of releasing water to cleanse a toilet bowl. □ *The toilet is still running after the last flush.* **2.** *tv.* to clean something, especially a toilet bowl, with a stream of water. □ *Please make sure that Jimmy flushes the toilet.*

**flute** ['flut] *n.* a musical instrument that is shaped like a long, thin pipe. □ *I played the flute in my high school's marching band.*

**fly** ['flɑɪ] **1.** *tv., irreg.* to drive an airplane; to guide something that moves through the air. (Pt: **flew**; pp: **flown**.) □ *I flew the kite in the park.* **2.** *tv., irreg.* to raise or otherwise display a flag. □ *All the ships in the harbor are flying the flags of different nations.* **3.** *iv., irreg.* to move through the air; to move in the air. □ *The bird flew from its nest to the river.* **4.** *iv., irreg.* to travel by airplane. □ *Max prefers to fly except on short trips.* **5.** *iv., irreg.* [for time] to pass quickly. (Fig. on ③.) □ *I was so busy at work that the time flew by.* **6.** *n.* a small insect; a bug; a mosquito. □ *I swatted the fly sitting on the table.* **7.** *n.* the flap of material that covers a zipper in trousers. □ *Bob's shirt became caught in his fly when he zipped up his pants.*

**foam** ['fom] *n.* a mass of small bubbles; froth. (Plural only when referring to different kinds, types, instances, or varieties.) □ *The dirty dishes sat in the sink under the soapy foam.* Ⓒ *He used to shave with one of the leading foams, but now he uses a gel.*

**foci** ['fo sɑɪ] a pl of **focus**.

**focus** ['fok əs] **1.** *n.* the position or setting of a lens that provides the clearest image. (No plural form.) □ *Please adjust the focus before I look through the telescope.* **2.** *n., irreg.* the center of attention; the center of interest. (Fig. on ①. Pl: *focuses* or **foci**.) □ *Jimmy always* *wants to be the focus of attention.* **3. focus on** someone or something *iv.* + *prep. phr.* [for a lens] to cause light rays or lines of sight to converge on a particular point or person. □ *My eyes focused on the candle.* **4.** *tv.* to adjust a lens, or the eyes, so that the image that passes through them is sharp and clear. □ *The photographer focused the lens and then took the picture.*

**foe** ['fo] *n.* the enemy in general; an enemy. □ *The guard asked if the traveler was one of the king's foes.*

**fog** ['fɔg] **1.** *n.* water vapor suspended in the air; a heavy mist. (No plural form.) □ *The thick morning fog slowly went away.* **2. fog** something **up** *tv.* + *obj.* + *adv.* to make something, especially glass, partially opaque with water vapor. □ *Breathing on the cold car windows will fog them up.* Ⓣ *Stop fogging up my windows.*

**foggy** ['fɔg i] *adj.* covered or filled with fog; [of weather] having much fog. (Adv: *foggily.* Comp: *foggier;* sup: *foggiest.*) □ *When I landed at the airport, it was very foggy.*

**foil** ['fɔɪl] **1.** *n.* a very thin, light sheet of metal, usually aluminum, used to wrap food or as a decoration. (Plural only when referring to different kinds, types, instances, or varieties.) □ *Each piece of candy is wrapped in a separate piece of foil.* Ⓒ *There are a number of useful foils on the market, and most of these are made of aluminum.* **2.** *tv.* to spoil someone's plans; to prevent something from happening. □ *The bank teller foiled the robbery by tricking the robber.*

**fold** ['fold] **1.** *tv.* to bend something so that part of it lies on top of the rest of it; to double something over onto itself. □ *I took the laundry from the dryer and then folded it.* **2. fold** one's **arms** *phr.* to cross one's arms and bring them close to one's body. □ *Jane stood in the doorway, folded her arms, and refused to let me leave.*

**folder** ['fol dɚ] *n.* a holder made of heavy paper used for filing, organizing, or storing papers. □ *The office manager put Mary's letter in her folder.*

**folk** ['fok] **1.** *n.* a group of people. (No plural form. Treated as plural.) □ *The thief pleaded to the village folk for mercy.* **2. folks** *n.* people in general. (Treated as plural. Informal.) □ *The president talked to folks on the street to get their opinions.* **3.** one's **folks** *n.* relatives, especially one's own parents. (Treated as plural, but not countable.) □ *Where do your folks live?* **4.** *adj.* of or about the common people; traditional. □ *Folk medicine can help cure some diseases.*

**folklore** ['fok lor] *n.* traditions, stories, customs, and beliefs that are passed down from generation to generation within a culture. (No plural form.) □ *Many of our fairy tales come from European folklore.*

**folk song** ['fok sɔŋ] *n.* a song that is in the traditional style of a country or group of people. □ *At the dance, the band played German folk songs.*

**fond** ['fɑnd] **1.** *adj.* loving; tender. (Adv: *fondly.* Comp: *fonder;* sup: *fondest.*) □ *I gave my aunt a fond hug as I entered her house.* **2. fond of** someone or something *adj.* + *prep. phr.* liking someone or something; having a desire for someone or something. (Comp: *fonder;* sup: *fondest.*) □ *John is fond of Mary, so he sent her some flowers.*

**food** ['fud] *n.* something that is eaten by animals and plants. (Plural only when referring to different kinds, types, instances, or varieties.) □ *I must give my dog some food and water each day.* Ⓒ *This grocery store sells all my favorite foods.*

**fool** ['ful] **1.** *n.* an idiot; a stupid person; someone who has no common sense.

F

□ *Stop acting like a fool, or I'll send you to your room.* **2.** *tv.* to trick someone; to play a joke on someone. □ *I fooled Bill by putting sugar in the salt shaker.* **3. fool around** *iv.* + *adv.* to play around; to waste time playing or doing something. □ *Bob accidentally broke a vase when we were fooling around in the house.*

F

**foolish** ['ful ɪʃ] *adj.* silly; lacking sense; stupid; ridiculous. (Adv: *foolishly.*) □ *The foolish student tried to cheat while the teacher was watching.*

**foolproof** ['ful pruf] *adj.* not capable of failing; so simple that a fool could use it without problems. □ *I had a foolproof plan to keep Mary away while we prepared for her surprise party.*

**foot** ['fʊt] **1.** *n., irreg.* the end of a leg; the part of a human or animal body that touches the ground and supports the body. (Pl: **feet.**) □ *I removed the thorn from my dog's foot.* **2.** *n.* the bottom or lower end of a bed, mountain, cliff, ladder, hill, page, etc. (No plural form.) □ *Mary stood at the foot of the mountain.* **3.** *n., irreg.* a unit of measurement equal to 12 inches or just over 30 centimeters. □ *The first step is one foot high.* **4. on foot** *phr.* [running or walking] using the **feet** ①. □ *We go everywhere on foot.*

**football** ['fʊt bɔl] **1.** *n.* a sport played between two teams of eleven players each, on a field having a goal on each end, using ②. (No plural form. Compare this with **soccer.**) □ *Dave played football in college.* **2.** *n.* the leather, oval ball used in ①. □ *Bill threw the football to another player.* **3.** *adj.* <the adj. use of ①.> □ *Our football team never wins.*

**footnote** ['fʊt not] **1.** *n.* a note at the bottom of a page that clarifies or provides a source for something that appears higher on the page. □ *Footnotes are usually printed in a smaller type than the rest of the words on the page.* **2.** *tv.* to provide ① for a piece of information. □ *I footnoted the foreign phrase and provided an English translation.*

**footpath** ['fʊt pæθ] *n., irreg.* a path that is made for walking. (Pl: ['fʊt pæðz].) □ *Bicycles are not allowed on the footpath.*

**footprint** ['fʊt prɪnt] **1.** *n.* the mark made by pressing a foot in soft earth or snow. □ *The detective examined the footprint underneath the kitchen window.* **2.** *n.* the mark made by tracking dirt from a muddy area onto a clean floor. □ *I see someone's footprints on the kitchen floor.*

**for** [for] **1.** *prep.* meant to be used by someone or something; meant to belong to someone; meant to be given to someone. (Indicates who or what will benefit.) □ *I cooked dinner for Mary.* **2.** *prep.* meant to be used in doing something; with a function or purpose connected with something. □ *Ink pens are used for writing.* **3.** *prep.* instead of someone or something; in place of someone or something. □ *I answered the telephone for Anne when she was on vacation.* **4.** *prep.* in favor of someone or something; in support of someone or something. □ *The president is for the new tax cut.* **5.** *prep.* in search of someone or something. (Indicates the target of the search.) □ *The doctor checked my body for diseases.* **6.** *prep.* in a certain amount; by the exchange of a certain amount. □ *I will sell it to you for thirty dollars.* **7.** *prep.* during something; throughout a period of time. □ *I will be your substitute teacher for the next week.* **8.** *conj.* because; since; as. (Formal.) □ *Bill usually ate too much, for he was always hungry.*

**forbade** AND **forbad** [for 'bed, for 'bæd] pt of **forbid.**

**forbid** [for 'bɪd] **1.** *tv., irreg.* to prohibit something. (Pt: **forbad** or **forbade;** pp: **forbidden.**) □ *The teacher forbade eating in class.* **2.** *tv., irreg.* to state that someone must not do something; to prohibit someone from doing something. □ *Company rules forbid me to smoke in the factory.*

**forbidden** [for 'bɪd n] **1.** pp of **forbid**. **2.** *adj.* prohibited; banned; not allowed. □ *Military police kept the soldiers away from the forbidden area.*

**force** ['fors] **1.** *n.* power; physical strength. (Plural only when referring to different kinds, types, instances, or varieties.) □ *The force of the crash destroyed both cars.* Ⓒ *All of these sensors measure the various forces experienced by the pilot during the flight.* **2.** *n.* military strength. (No plural form.) □ *The army used force to overthrow the government.* **3.** *n.* an influence; someone or something that is an influence. □ *My English professor was a major force in my life.* **4.** *n.* a group of soldiers, police officers, etc. □ *A well-armed force was called in to stop the riot.* **5.** *tv.* to push or move something using ①. □ *Sue forced the square peg into the round hole.* **6.** *tv.* to make someone do something, especially by the use of ①. □ *The police forced us to leave the building.*

**forehead** ['for hɛd] *n.* the part of the face between the eyebrows and the hair. □ *Mary's thick hair completely covers her forehead.*

**foreign** ['for ɪn] *adj.* not native to one's country; of or about a country other than one's own. (Adv: *foreignly.*) □ *Do you speak any foreign languages?*

**foreigner** ['for ən ɚ] *n.* someone who comes from another country; someone who was born in another country. □ *The foreigner asked the police officer for directions.*

**foresaw** [for 'sɔ] pt of **foresee**.

**foresee** [for 'si] *tv., irreg.* to be aware of something before it happens; to imagine or predict that something will happen. (Pt: **foresaw**; pp: **foreseen**. The object can be a clause with **that** ⑦.) □ *I foresaw that there would be trouble with my neighbors shortly after they moved in.*

**foreseen** [for 'sin] pp of **foresee**.

**forest** ['for əst] *n.* a large area of land covered with trees. □ *We own a cabin in the forest next to a lake.*

**forever** [for 'ɛv ɚ] *adv.* always; with no beginning and no end; throughout all time. □ *The movie was so long, it seemed to go on forever.*

**forfeit** ['for fɪt] *tv.* to give up something; to lose something as a punishment. □ *Anne's driver's license was forfeited when she was arrested for drunk driving.*

**forgave** [for 'gev] pt of **forgive**.

**forget** [for 'gɛt] **1.** *tv., irreg.* to lose a piece of information from one's memory. (Pt: **forgot**; pp: **forgot** or **forgotten**. The object can be a clause with **that** ⑦.) □ *I forgot what her name is.* **2.** *tv., irreg.* to leave someone or something behind; not to take someone or something with oneself. □ *Bob forgot his umbrella, and of course, it rained.* **3. forget to** do something *iv., irreg. + inf.* to fail to remember to do something. □ *Bob forgot to water his plants this week.*

**forgive** [for 'gɪv] **1.** *tv., irreg.* to pardon someone for an error or wrongdoing. (Pt: **forgave**; pp: **forgiven**.) □ *Can you ever forgive me for insulting you?* **2.** *tv., irreg.* to cancel payment of a debt; to relieve someone of a debt before it is paid back. □ *The United States aided the small nation by forgiving its debt.*

**forgiven** [for 'gɪv ən] pp of **forgive**.

**forgot** [for 'gɑt] pt of **forget**; a pp of **forget**.

**forgotten** [for 'gɑt n] a pp of **forget**.

**fork** ['fork] **1.** *n.* an eating tool with a handle and two, three, or four spikes, used to gather and hold food when eating. □ *At the picnic, we ate with plastic forks.* **2.** *n.* the place where something splits into two branches. □ *When you reach the fork in the path, go left.* **3.** *n.* one of the two branches that something splits into. □ *I took the wrong fork and got completely lost.* **4.** *iv.* to split into two branches. □ *Where the path forks, you should go to the left.*

**form** ['form] **1.** *n.* a shape; the shape of someone or something; the way someone or something is shaped. □ *Mike exercised to get a more muscular form.* **2.** *n.* a kind; a sort; a type. □ *Torture is a cruel form of punishment.* **3.** *n.* a document that has blank spaces on it that need to be filled with information. □ *Anne mailed the contest entry form before the deadline.* **4.** *n.* a word or part of a word. □ Exam *is a shortened form of the word* examination. □ *In Spanish, the feminine form of* amigo, *which means "friend," is* amiga. **5.** *iv.* to come into being; to be created. □ *A crowd formed on the street corner.* **6.** *tv.* to develop something; to develop into something; to cause something to come into being. □ *The council formed new policies at the meeting last night.* **7.** *tv.* to make up something; to be a part of something. □ *A triangle is formed with three lines.*

**formal** ['form əl] **1.** *adj.* according to custom; according to rules. (Adv: *formally.*) □ *The two candidates agreed to participate in a formal debate.* **2.** *adj.* [of behavior, language use, clothes, etc.] serious and proper; [of a person or situation] having serious and proper behavior, dress, etc. (Adv: formally. See also **informal.**) □ *Sometimes Bob uses formal words when informal words would be better.* **3.** *adj.* [of clothing] of the highest level or style prescribed by the rules of manners. (Adv: *formally.*) □ *We were asked to wear formal clothing to the dinner.* **4.** *adj.* [of an event] where **formal** ③ clothing is expected or required. (Adv: *formally.*) □ *Mary wore a beautiful gown to the formal dance.* **5.** *n.* a woman's (usually long) gown suitable for a **formal** ④ event. □ *Sue wore a blue formal to her brother's wedding.*

**format** ['for mæt] **1.** *n.* the way events are ordered or arranged; the way things are placed on a page. □ *The format of the class will consist of a short speech followed by a discussion.* **2.** *tv.* to arrange something to look a certain way, as with the order and arrangement in the pages of a book or other document. (Pt/pp: *formatted.* Present participle: *formatting.*) □ *Format your report so that the page number appears at the top of each page.* **3.** *tv.* to make a computer disk ready to accept information. (Pt/pp: *formatted.* Present participle: *formatting.*) □ *Have you formatted this disk for this computer?*

**former** ['for mɚ] **1. the former** *n.* the first of two things mentioned. (No plural form. Treated as singular or plural, but not countable.) □ *Roses and daisies are both beautiful, but I prefer the former because they smell so good.* **2.** *adj.* past; previous. (Prenominal only. Adv: *formerly.*) □ *John's former wife receives $650 a month to live on.* **3. the former** *adj.* of or about the first of the two things mentioned. (Prenominal only.) □ *We visited both London and Paris, and I prefer the former city.*

**formula** ['form jə lə] **1.** *n., irreg.* a series of symbols that show the chemical ingredients of a substance. (Pl: *formulas* or **formulae.**) □ *The chemical formula of salt is NaCl.* **2.** *n., irreg.* a mathematical rule that is expressed with numbers or symbols. (Pl: *formulas* or **formulae.**) □ *The formula for the area of a circle is* $\pi r^2$. □ *Because the formula for the volume of a cube is* $s^3$, *the volume of a cube 5 inches tall is 125 cubic inches.* **3.** *n.* a pattern or a standard set of parts or actions. (Fig. on ②.) □ *Following the successful formula she used in her first* *year of teaching, Anne patterned all her courses in the same way.* **4.** *n.* animal milk or another milk substitute for feeding babies. (No plural form.) □ *The baby finished all of the formula and cried for more.*

**formulae** ['form jə lɑɪ] a pl of **formula.**

**fort** ['fort] **1.** *n.* a structure or building used for defense that can withstand enemy attack; a number of strong buildings behind a barrier. □ *The soldiers stayed inside the fort until more troops arrived.* **2.** *n.* a permanent military base. □ *They built a fort near the harbor to protect the ships.*

**forth** ['forθ] *adv.* forward; onward; outward. (See also **back and forth.**) □ *Go forth among the people and tell them the good news.*

**fortieth** ['for ti əθ] 40th. Go to **fourth** for senses and examples.

**fortress** ['for trɪs] *n.* a very strong building built to resist attacks. □ *Soldiers attacked the enemy fortress.*

**fortunate** ['for tʃə nɪt] **1.** *adj.* lucky; bringing good results; representing good fortune. (Adv: *fortunately.*) □ *We celebrated the fortunate occurrence with a bottle of champagne.* **2.** *adj.* having had good luck. (Adv: *fortunately.*) □ *One fortunate player won the lottery last week.*

**fortune** ['for tʃən] **1.** *n.* good luck; success. (No plural form.) □ *I had the fortune of going to a good college.* **2.** *n.* everything that will happen to someone in the future. □ *My fortune consists of working every day until I retire.* **3.** *n.* a lot of money and property that someone owns. □ *The millionaire made her fortune in the computer industry.*

**forty** ['for ti] **1.** *n.* the cardinal number 40; the number between 39 and 41. (No plural form. Similar definitions and examples for **twenty, thirty, fifty, sixty, seventy, eighty, ninety.**) □ *Here are forty of them.* **2. forties** *n.* the decade beginning in 1940; the 1940s. (Similar definitions and examples for *twenties, thirties, fifties, sixties, seventies, eighties, nineties.*) □ *Tom was born in the forties and got married in the sixties.* **3.** *adj.* 40; consisting of 40 things; having 40 things. (Similar definitions and examples for **twenty, thirty, fifty, sixty, seventy, eighty, ninety.**) □ *This shirt costs forty dollars.* **4.** *pron.* 40 things or people already mentioned or able to be determined by context. (Similar definitions and examples for **twenty, thirty, fifty, sixty, seventy, eighty, ninety.**) □ *Of every million parts produced by our factory, only forty are damaged.*

**forum** ['for əm] *n.* a meeting where someone can discuss something; a place where someone can talk about something, especially items of public interest. □ *The angry citizens demanded a forum in which their criticism could be heard.*

**forward** ['for wɚd] **1.** *adv.* ahead; toward the front; into the future. (Also **forwards.**) □ *Each student in line faced forward.* **2.** *adj.* [moving] toward the front; [looking] into the future. □ *I fell down when the bus made a sudden forward movement.* **3.** *tv.* to have mail sent onward to a new address when one moves. □ *The post office is forwarding my mail to my new address.*

**forwards** ['for wɚdz] Go to **forward** ①.

**fought** ['fɔt] pt/pp of **fight.**

**foul** ['fɑʊl] **1.** *adj.* dirty; nasty and rotten. (Adv: *foully.* Comp: *fouler;* sup: *foulest.*) □ *The meat turned foul because I didn't put it in the refrigerator.* **2.** *adj.* nasty; rude and unpleasant. (Adv: *foully.* Comp: *fouler;* sup: *foulest.*) □ *I was punished for telling a foul joke.* **3.** *adj.* evil; really bad. (Fig. on ①. Adv: *foully.* Comp: *fouler;* sup: *foulest.*) □ *Everyone hated the foul ruler.* **4.** *adj.* [of a ball] going outside the proper playing area.

F

(Sports.) □ *The batter hit another foul ball.* **5.** *adj.* [of weather] bad. (Adv: *foully.* Comp: *fouler;* sup: *foulest.*) □ *Foul weather caused several traffic accidents.* **6.** *tv.* to make something dirty. □ *Bill fouled the food by touching it with his dirty hands.* **7. foul** someone or something **up** *tv.* + *obj.* + *adv.* to make errors with someone or something; to mess someone or something up. (Informal.) □ *Who fouled the plans up for the picnic?* 🅃 *I didn't foul up anybody's plans!* **8. foul up** *iv.* to make an error. (Informal.) □ *If you keep fouling up, you will be fired.* **9.** *n.* an action in a game that is against the rules. □ *The referee called a foul on the basketball player.* **10.** *n.* [in baseball] a ball that is hit outside the proper playing area. □ *A foul counts as a strike unless it would be the third strike.*

F

**found** ['fɑʊnd] **1.** pt/pp of **find**. **2.** *tv.* to establish an organization; to provide money or support to help start an organization. (Pt/pp: *founded.*) □ *This firm was founded in 1909.*

**foundation** [fɑʊn 'de ʃən] **1.** *n.* the base of a building. (Rarely plural.) □ *The foundation for the new factory covered many acres.* **2.** *n.* the base of a custom or tradition; a basis. (Fig. on ①.) □ *The judge told the lawyer to lay a foundation for the question being asked.* **3.** *n.* an institution that gives out money or grants to special causes. □ *I researched the kinds of grants available from various foundations.*

**fountain** ['fɑʊnt n] **1.** *n.* a stream of water that sprays up into the air. □ *A small fountain of water squirted from the crack in the water pipe.* **2.** *n.* a structure—designed and built by humans—that sprays a stream of water into the air. □ *The fountain is lit with colored lights at night.*

**four** ['for] **1.** *n.* the cardinal number 4; the number between 3 and 5. (No plural form. The ordinal form is **fourth**. Similar definitions and examples for **one, two, three, five, six, seven, eight, nine, ten, eleven, twelve, thirteen, fourteen, fifteen, sixteen, seventeen, eighteen, nineteen.**) □ *One plus three is four.* **2.** *adj.* 4; consisting of 4 things; having 4 things. (The ordinal form is **fourth**. This covers other terms as in ①.) □ *Four musicians played for the wedding.* **3.** *pron.* 4 people or things already mentioned or able to be determined by context. (The ordinal form is **fourth**. This covers other terms as in ①.) □ *Four can easily be seated in this room.*

**fourteen** ['fort 'tin] 14. Go to **four** for senses and examples.

**fourteenth** ['fort 'tinθ] **1.** *n.* one of 14 equal parts. □ *One fourteenth of a week is 12 hours.* **2.** *adj.* of the 14th item in a series of things; of the item in a series between the 13th and 15th. □ *Vermont was the fourteenth state to join the Union.* **3.** *pron.* the 14th item in a series of things or people already mentioned or able to be determined by context. □ *Flag Day is on the fourteenth of June.*

**fourth** ['forθ] **1.** *n.* 4th; one of 4 equal parts; a quarter; a half of a half. (Similar definitions for **third, fifth, sixth, seventh, eighth, ninth, tenth, eleventh, twelfth, thirteenth, fourteenth, fifteenth, sixteenth, seventeenth, eighteenth, nineteenth, twentieth, thirtieth, fortieth, fiftieth, sixtieth, seventieth, eightieth, ninetieth, [one] hundredth, [one] thousandth, [one] millionth, [one] billionth,** and **[one] trillionth.** See also **first, second.**) □ *Fold a sheet of paper into fourths.* **2.** *n.* the 4th item in a series of things or people already mentioned or able to be determined by context. (This covers other terms as in ①. See also **first, second.**) □ *I have a reply from everyone except the fourth on the list.* **3.** *adj.* of the 4th item in a series of things; of the item in a series between the 3rd and 5th. (This covers other terms as in ①. See also **first, second.**) □ *This is the fourth book I have checked out of the library.* **4.** *adv.* in the 4th position or rank. (This covers other terms as in ①. See also **first, second.**) □ *We all got a chance to state our views. I spoke fourth in the long list of complainers.*

**Fourth of July** [forθ əv dʒə 'lɑɪ] *n.* an American holiday celebrating independence from Great Britain on July 4, 1776. □ *Our city has a fireworks display every Fourth of July.*

**fowl** ['fɑʊl] **1.** *n., irreg.* one of a number of kinds of birds of limited flight, kept for their eggs or meat, such as the chicken, duck, turkey, etc. (Pl: *fowl* or *fowls.*) □ *Should I put the geese in the yard with the rest of the fowl?* **2.** *n.* the meat of ①. (No plural form.) □ *My sister eats fowl, but only the flesh without the skin.*

**fox** ['fɑks] **1.** *n.* a wild animal related to the dog, having a bushy tail. □ *I saw a fox running through the woods.* **2.** *n.* the fur or pelt of ①. (No plural form.) □ *The collar of my coat is silver fox.* **3.** *adj.* made of ②. □ *Fox coats are no longer popular.*

**fraction** ['fræk ʃən] **1.** *n.* a part of a whole number. □ *If you convert .25 into a fraction, you get ¼.* **2.** *n.* a small piece or portion of something. (No plural form.) □ *Each month I can pay only a small fraction of my bills.*

**fracture** ['fræk tʃɚ] **1.** *n.* a break or crack, especially a break in a bone. □ *I turned the vase around so that its fracture faced the wall.* **2.** *tv.* to break something by creating a crack in it. □ *I fractured the ice with a heavy ice pick.* **3.** *iv.* to break; to crack. □ *The vase fractured into a hundred pieces.*

**fragile** ['frædʒ əl] *adj.* easily broken; delicate. (Adv: *fragilely.*) □ *You must cushion fragile objects carefully when you pack them.*

**fragment** ['fræg mənt] **1.** *n.* a small piece of something. □ *The dog is choking on a fragment of bone.* **2.** *iv.* to break into pieces or sections. □ *My mirror fragmented when I dropped it.* **3.** *tv.* to break something into pieces or sections. □ *A rock thrown by a child has fragmented my kitchen window.*

**fragrance** ['fre grəns] *n.* a smell or scent that is pleasant. □ *The fragrance of chocolate lured me into the kitchen.*

**fragrant** ['fre grənt] *adj.* smelling good; having a nice smell. (Adv: *fragrantly.*) □ *The flowers are very fragrant. Unfortunately, they make me sneeze.*

**frail** ['frel] *adj.* thin and weak; not strong; easily hurt. (Adv: *frailly.*) □ *My grandmother is frail, but she's still very alert.*

**frame** ['frem] **1.** *n.* a structure that provides support for something. □ *The frame of the building was weakened by the earthquake.* **2.** *n.* a firm border that something, such as a door, a window, or a picture, is set into. □ *I live in the old white house with brown window frames.* **3.** *n.* the shape or form of a human body; the structure of the body. □ *Because of my small frame, I cannot carry anything heavy.* **4.** *tv.* to place something in ②; to build ② for something. □ *The carpenter framed the window skillfully.* **5.** *tv.* to cause someone to appear guilty of a crime by manipulating evidence or lying. □ *Max said he was innocent and that the cops had framed him.*

**frantic** ['fræn tɪk] *adj.* very excited; wild with emotion. (Adv: *frantically* [...ɪk li].) □ *I had a frantic conversation with my bank after they said I had no money left.*

**fraud** ['frɔd] **1.** *n.* cheating; something done to deceive someone. (No plural form.) □ *A committee was formed to fight fraud in the workplace.* **2.** *n.* a false or deceiving thing or act. □ *The contract* *the company gave me was a fraud.* **3.** *n.* someone who pretends to be someone or something else. □ *The man claiming to be a doctor turned out to be a fraud.*

**freak** ['frik] **1.** *n.* someone or something that is not normally developed. (Not polite for humans.) □ *A purple pumpkin would be a real freak.* **2.** *adj.* very unusual. (Prenominal only.) □ *Mary was hurt in a freak accident involving a glass of milk.*

**freckle** ['frɛk əl] **1.** *n.* one of many small dark dots on the skin. □ *I kissed the freckle on my baby sister's nose.* **2.** *iv.* to become covered with ①, usually because of exposure to the sun. □ *Sue wore a big hat so her face wouldn't freckle.*

**free** ['fri] **1.** *adj.* independent; not someone's slave; not ruled by a bad ruler. (Adv: *freely.* Comp: *freer;* sup: *freest.*) □ *As a result of the Civil War, the slaves became free.* **2.** *adj.* costing no money; without cost. □ *Some restaurants offer free coffee with meals.* **3.** *adj.* not limited; not restricted; not bound by rules. (Adv: *freely.* Comp: *freer;* sup: *freest.*) □ *A free press can print almost anything, even if the government doesn't like it.* **4.** *adj.* not busy; available. (Comp: *freer;* sup: *freest.*) □ *I'd like to speak to you when you're free.* **5.** *adj.* generous; lavish; giving. (Adv: *freely.* Comp: *freer;* sup: *freest.*) □ *If you continue to be so free with your money, you'll soon be in debt.* **6.** *adj.* having an open path; having nothing in one's way. □ *After the storm, we cleared the road so that it was free of branches.* **7.** *adv.* without cost; without having to pay money. □ *This lamp came free with the living-room furniture.* **8.** *tv.* to release someone or something. □ *The army freed the prisoners of war.*

**freedom** ['fri dəm] **1.** *n.* liberty; a state where one is free from constraint. (No plural form.) □ *On the Fourth of July, Americans celebrate their freedom from England.* **2.** *n.* a right. □ *Freedom of speech is one of our precious freedoms.*

**freeze** ['friz] **1.** *iv., irreg.* to become solid as the temperature gets colder. (Pt: **froze**; pp: **frozen.**) □ *When water freezes, it is called ice.* **2.** *iv., irreg.* [for someone or some creature] to become very cold in cold weather. □ *Close the window, or I will freeze to death.* **3.** *iv., irreg.* to become completely still; to stop all movement. (Fig. on ①.) □ *The robber ordered me to freeze.* **4.** *tv., irreg.* to turn something into ice; to cause something to harden as the temperature gets colder. □ *A blast of very cold air froze the pond.* **5.** *tv., irreg.* to place food in a freezer so that it stays fresh; to preserve something at an extremely low temperature. □ *You should freeze the leftover hamburger so that it doesn't spoil.* **6.** *tv., irreg.* to cause someone or something to become completely still. □ *The accident froze traffic in all directions.* **7.** *tv., irreg.* to keep the price of something at a certain level; not to allow an amount to change. □ *My company froze the rate of pay increases at the rate of inflation.* **8.** *n.* a time when the temperature is 32 degrees Fahrenheit, 0 degrees centigrade, or below. □ *A sudden freeze trapped many boats in the harbor.*

**freezer** ['friz ɚ] *n.* an appliance that remains at a temperature below 32 degrees Fahrenheit in order to store and preserve food and other things. □ *When our freezer broke, all of our ice melted.*

**freight** ['fret] **1.** *n.* cargo; products that are carried by truck, plane, train, etc. (No plural form.) □ *Freight is carried by truck across the country.* **2.** *n.* the cost of shipping something as ①. □ *Who will pay the freight on this order?* **3.** *adj.* <the adj. use of ①.> □ *The freight yard is filled with freight cars.*

**french fry** ['frɛntʃ frɑɪ] *n.* a long, narrow piece of potato that has been fried in deep fat. (Usually plural. Can be shortened to **fries**.) □ *Would you like french fries with your hamburger?*

**frenzy** ['frɛn zi] *n.* a wild fury; an excited state. □ *The frenzy of the emergency room shocked the young doctor.*

**frequency** ['fri kwən si] **1.** *n.* the rate of [something] happening; how often an event occurs. (No plural form.) □ *With increasing frequency, people are volunteering to help with today's social problems.* **2.** *n.* the number of times that something occurs within a given period of time. □ *Middle A on the piano has a frequency of 440 cycles per second.*

**frequent** ['fri kwənt] **1.** *adj.* happening often; occurring often; common. (Adv: *frequently.*) □ *The couple's frequent arguments led to a divorce.* **2.** *tv.* to go to a certain place often. □ *The restaurant was frequented by local residents.*

**fresh** ['frɛʃ] **1.** *adj.* new; newly or recently made, done, obtained, etc., especially if not yet used or changed. (Adv: *freshly.* Comp: *fresher;* sup: *freshest.*) □ *Be careful! That's a fresh coat of paint on the door.* **2.** *adj.* not stale; not spoiled; [of foods] not canned, frozen, dried, or preserved in another way; [of fruits or vegetables] recently picked or harvested. (Adv: *freshly.* Comp: *fresher;* sup: *freshest.*) □ *I need some fresh air.*

**fret** ['frɛt] *iv.* to worry about something; to be upset. □ *Don't fret. Everything will be OK.*

**friction** ['frɪk ʃən] **1.** *n.* rubbing against something that resists the rubbing. (No plural form.) □ *The friction between the carpet and my arm reddened my skin.* **2.** *n.* the resistance that keeps one object from sliding over another object. (No plural form.) □ *There is very little friction between ice and the blade of an ice skate.* **3.** *n.* a disagreement because of differences in opinions. □ *I left home because of the friction between my parents and me.*

**Friday** [frɑɪ de] Go to **day**.

**friend** ['frɛnd] **1.** *n.* someone whom someone else knows well and likes. □ *I drove my friend to the airport.* **2.** *n.* someone or something that supports or helps someone or something. □ *The caller asked if I wanted to become a friend of the museum.*

**friendly** ['frɛnd li] *adj.* like a friend; nice, kind, or pleasant. (Comp: *friendlier;* sup: *friendliest.*) □ *I held open the door for Tom as a friendly gesture.*

**friendship** ['frɛnd ʃɪp] *n.* being friends with someone. (Plural only when referring to different kinds, types, instances, or varieties.) □ *Without friendship and the warmth of human kindness, life would be very unpleasant.* Ⓒ *Many of my friendships came to an end as I lived longer than my friends.*

**fries** ['frɑɪz] Go to **french fry; fry**.

**fright** ['frɑɪt] *n.* fear; terror; the condition of being scared. (No plural form.) □ *The fright of seeing the accident made Lisa terrified of driving.*

**frill** ['frɪl] **1.** *n.* a decorative edge on cloth. □ *The tablecloth had a colorful frill on each edge.* **2.** *n.* something that is an added bonus but is not necessary. (Usually plural.) □ *Passengers in the front of the plane receive many frills, such as free drinks.*

**frisk** ['frɪsk] *tv.* to pat and press on the body in a search for weapons, drugs, evidence, or stolen property. □ *The police frisked the students as they entered the school.*

**frog** ['frɔg] *n.* a small creature, living in water and on land, that hops and has special feet for swimming. □ *I was kept awake by the sound of the frogs in our backyard.*

**from** ['frʌm] **1.** *prep.* starting at a particular time or place; originating at a particular time or place. □ *The office is* *open from noon to 6.* **2.** *prep.* <a word indicating separation or difference.> □ *Susan and Mary are identical twins, and I can't tell one from the other.* **3.** *prep.* out of someone or something. □ *The speeding car came from a side street and passed me.* **4.** *prep.* sent by someone or something; given by someone or something. □ *This present is from your aunt.* **5.** *prep.* because of something; owing to something. □ *The baby was crying from hunger.*

F

**front** ['frʌnt] **1.** *n.* the part of something that faces forward. □ *The bullet struck Tom in the front of his chest.* **2.** *n.* a border between two masses of air of a different temperature or pressure. □ *A warm front moved over the region, breaking the cold spell.* **3.** *n.* the way one appears to other people; the way one seems to be when around other people; an outward appearance. □ *Bob claims to be happy, but I know his smile is just a front.* **4.** *iv.* to face in a certain direction. □ *My apartment fronts directly onto the street.* **5.** *adj.* closest to ①. (Prenominal only.) □ *Sue sat in the front seat next to the driver.*

**frost** ['frɔst] **1.** *n.* frozen moisture on the surface of something, especially on the ground; small ice crystals on the surface of something. (Plural only when referring to separate instances of ①.) □ *We covered the tomato plants to protect them from frost.* Ⓒ *The frosts we had this fall seemed much more severe than usual.* **2.** *iv.* to be covered with small ice crystals; to be covered with frozen moisture. □ *Did it frost last night?* **3.** *tv.* to put frosting on a cake or dessert. □ *You have to let the cake cool before you frost it.*

**frostbite** ['frɔst bɑɪt] *n.* an injury caused by exposing skin to extremely cold weather without protection. (No plural form.) □ *The mountain climber's fingers were purple with frostbite.*

**frosting** ['frɔs tɪŋ] *n.* a mixture of sugar and other things that is spread on top of a cake or pastry. (Plural only when referring to different kinds, types, instances, or varieties.) □ *Mary tasted the frosting with her finger.* Ⓒ *I like the rich frostings that are made with butter better.*

**froth** ['frɔθ] *n.* foam; a mass of white bubbles that forms on top of liquids or around the mouth. (No plural form.) □ *Tom served some sort of fruit drink with a sweet froth on top.*

**frown** ['frɑʊn] **1.** *n.* the opposite of a smile; the look on one's face made by pulling the eyebrows together and squinting the eyes. □ *Jimmy's frown went away when the clown gave him a balloon.* **2.** *iv.* to pull one's eyebrows together and squint the eyes; to scowl; to look angry. □ *Sue frowned because she was stuck in traffic.*

**froze** ['froz] pt of **freeze**.

**frozen** ['froz ən] pp of **freeze**.

**fruit** ['frut] *n.* the part of a plant that contains seeds and can be eaten as food. (Plural only when referring to different kinds, types, instances, or varieties. Number is expressed with *piece(s) of fruit.*) □ *This drink is made from fruit.* Ⓒ *It is important to eat a variety of fruits and vegetables.*

**fruitcake** ['frut kek] *n.* a cake that has dried fruit and spices in it. □ *This fruitcake is difficult to slice because it's too hard.*

**fry** ['frɑɪ] **1.** *tv.* to cook something in hot fat. □ *Mary fried the fish that she caught.* **2. fries** *n.* thin pieces of potato fried in hot fat. (Treated as plural. Short for **french fries**.) □ *The fries made my hands greasy.*

**fuck** ['fʌk] **1.** *tv.* to copulate [with] someone or some creature. (Taboo. Potentially offensive. Use only with discretion. A highly offensive word to many people. There are many additional meanings and constructions with the word.) ☐ *He actually said in public that one dog—you know—fucked the other one.* **2.** *iv.* to copulate. (Comments as with ①.) ☐ *He said they were fucking because that was the only word he knew.*

**fudge** ['fʌdʒ] **1.** *n.* a thick, rich chocolate candy. (No plural form.) ☐ *I ignored my diet and ate a piece of rich fudge.* **2.** *iv.* to attempt to lie to or deceive someone. (Informal.) ☐ *The politician fudged when he answered the question.*

**fuel** ['fjul] **1.** *n.* material that is burned to make heat or energy. ☐ *The scientist predicted America would run out of fuel within 20 years.* **2.** *tv.* to supply something with ①. ☐ *It's your turn to fuel the car.* **3.** *tv.* to provide someone or something with energy or encouragement. (Fig. on ②.) ☐ *Quit arguing with John! You'll only fuel his anger.*

**full** ['fʊl] **1.** *adj.* completely filled; having no empty space. (Adv: *fully.* Comp: *fuller;* sup: *fullest.*) ☐ *The full bucket was very heavy, and some water spilled out of it as I walked.* **2.** *adj.* entire; complete; whole. (Adv: *fully.*) ☐ *I placed the full amount of detergent into the washing machine.* **3.** *adj.* at the highest or greatest extent or amount possible. ☐ *We traveled down the highway at full speed.*

**fun** ['fʌn] **1.** *n.* enjoyment, especially from play or amusement. (No plural form.) ☐ *Did you have any fun at the beach today?* **2.** *adj.* entertaining; playful. (Colloquial.) ☐ *We had a fun day at the beach.*

**function** ['fʌŋk ʃən] **1.** *n.* the proper use of something; the purpose of something. ☐ *What is the function of this lever?* **2.** *n.* a social gathering; an event where people get together and do things such as talk, drink, or celebrate. ☐ *I was asked to bring some bread to the annual social function.* **3.** *iv.* to work properly; to operate; to be in proper use. ☐ *Your toaster won't function unless you plug it in.*

**fund** ['fʌnd] **1.** *n.* an amount of money that is reserved for a specific reason. ☐ *Jane donated money to her university's scholarship fund.* **2. funds** *n.* money; an amount or supply of money. (Treated as plural, but not countable.) ☐ *Max lacks the funds needed to continue his education.* **3.** *n.* an investment that is really a combination of other investments, such as stocks and bonds. (Short for **mutual fund**.) ☐ *I own some stocks, but most of my money is in funds.* **4.** *tv.* to provide someone or something with money; to provide money for something. ☐ *My parents funded my college education.*

**funeral** ['fjun (ə) rəl] **1.** *n.* a ceremony performed when someone is buried. ☐ *Hundreds of people attended the senator's funeral.* **2.** *adj.* <the adj. use of ①.> ☐ *The funeral ceremony was very sad.*

**funeral home** ['fjun (ə) rəl 'hom] the place where a funeral is held; the place of business of an undertaker. ☐ *Will the funeral be held at the funeral home or at the church?*

**fungi** ['fʌn dʒɑɪ] a pl of **fungus**.

**fungus** ['fʌŋ gəs] *n., irreg.* a plant that does not have leaves and is not green, such as the mushroom. (Pl: **fungi** or *funguses.*) ☐ *Humans sometimes get a fungus that grows on the skin.*

**funnel** ['fʌn əl] *n.* a cone-shaped device with a wide mouth and a narrow spout on the bottom, used when pouring liquids from one container into another. ☐ *I used a funnel to fill the bottles with water.*

**funny** ['fʌn i] **1.** *adj.* amusing; causing laughter. (Comp: *funnier;* sup: *funniest.*) ☐ *We all laughed at the funny story.* **2.** *adj.* strange; weird; unusual; odd. (Comp: *funnier;* sup: *funniest.*) ☐ *Bill* *was embarrassed when he realized what a funny thing he had said about your mother.*

**fur** ['fɚ] **1.** *n.* the short, soft hair that grows on many mammals. (Plural only when referring to different kinds, types, instances, or varieties.) □ *The rabbit's fur is very soft.* 🄲 *Some furs are coarse and others are fine and silky.* **2.** *n.* a coat or other garment made from animal skin covered with ①. □ *I wear a fur in the winter because it's very warm.* **3.** *adj.* made from animal skin covered with ①. □ *Mary took her fur coat to the cleaners.*

**furnace** ['fɚ nəs] *n.* an oven that can be heated at very high temperatures to melt metal, heat a building, etc. □ *This furnace is used to melt the iron that will be made into steel.*

**furnish** ['fɚ nɪʃ] to provide something; to supply something. □ *The hotel furnished towels and sheets.*

**furniture** ['fɚ nɪ tʃɚ] *n.* the objects in a house, apartment, or office that can be moved, such as tables, chairs, desks, etc. (No plural form. Number is expressed with *piece(s) of furniture.*) □ *We received several pieces of furniture as wedding gifts.*

**furry** ['fɚ i] *adj.* covered with fur; having fur. (Adv: *furrily.* Comp: *furrier;* sup: *furriest.*) □ *A bear rubbed its furry back against the tree.*

**further** ['fɚ ðɚ] **1.** *adj.* more far; more distant in space or time. (One of the comparative forms of **far**, along with **farther.**) □ *Which town is further from here, Adamsville or Millsville?* **2.** *adv.* more far; more distant in space or time. (One of the comparative forms of **far**, along with **farther.**) □ *We talked further into the night than I had expected.* **3.** *adv.* to a greater degree or extent; to a more advanced level. (One of the comparative forms of **far**, along with **farther.**) □ *The advanced student has progressed further in his studies than the beginner has.* **4.** *tv.* to advance or promote someone or something. □ *Please do what you can to further this project.*

**furthermore** ['fɚ ðɚ mor] *adv.* also; in addition to what has been said or stated. □ *I demand that you be quiet! Furthermore, I think you should apologize for waking me up.*

**furthest** ['fɚ ðəst] *adj.* the most far; the most distant in space or time. (One of the superlative forms of **far**, along with **farthest.**) □ *Paying attention to traffic was the furthest thing from my mind when I got into the accident.*

**fury** ['fjɚ i] **1.** *n.* violent anger; rage. (No plural form.) □ *Bill hid in the closet to protect himself from his roommate's fury.* **2.** *n.* power or force. □ *The fury of the storm broke our windows.*

**fuse** ['fjuz] **1.** *tv.* to melt something together with something else; to melt two things together. □ *The plumber fused the pipes with a hot flame.* **2.** *iv.* [for two or more things] to melt together. □ *The plastic cups fused into a solid block in the heat.* **3.** *n.* a part of an electrical circuit that melts and stops the flow of electricity when there is a dangerous amount of electricity flowing through the circuit. □ *I had to change the fuse in the dark because the flashlight didn't work.*

**fuss** ['fʌs] **1.** *iv.* to whine and cry. □ *Jimmy fusses whenever he is tired.* **2.** *n.* argument; complaints. (Informal.) □ *What is all the fuss about?*

**fussy** ['fʌs i] *adj.* hard to please; likely to complain about everything. (Adv: *fussily.* Comp: *fussier;* sup: *fussiest.*) □ *If you weren't so fussy, we could have finished shopping an hour ago.*

**futile** ['fjut əl] *adj.* hopeless; useless; worthless. (Adv: *futilely.*) □ *The mayor's futile efforts only angered us more.*

**future** ['fju tʃɚ] **1.** *adj.* coming; yet to come; later. (Prenominal only.) □ *My future plans include starting my own restaurant.* **2.** *n.* the time that is to come; events that will happen. (No plural form.) □ *Jane claimed that she could see into the future.* **3.** *n.* the things that are planned for one's life. (Plural only when referring to different kinds, types, instances, or varieties.) □ *I planned for my future by saving a lot of money.* 🄲 *The prisoners could only look forward to dismal futures and low incomes for life.* **4.** *n.* <the tense of verbs that describe actions that are to happen or actions that will happen.> □ *The future and the past are found in most languages.*

**fuzz** ['fʌz] *n.* short, soft, light hairs. (No plural form.) □ *Peaches are covered with fuzz.*

**fuzzy** ['fʌz i] *adj.* having fuzz; covered with fuzz. (Adv: *fuzzily.* Comp: *fuzzier;* sup: *fuzziest.*) □ *The fuzzy skin of a peach can be eaten.*

G

**gadget** ['gædʒ ɪt] *n.* any small, practical device, tool, or appliance. □ *I bought some sort of a gadget to help open jars.*

**gain** ['gen] **1.** *tv.* to get something; to obtain something; to acquire something. □ *I gained 10 pounds during my first year in college.* **2.** *tv.* [for a clock or watch] to reach a later time than it should have. □ *My watch gains five minutes every week.* **3.** *tv.* to earn or save time. □ *We gained an hour by taking the expressway instead of country roads.* **4.** *iv.* to earn, get, or acquire something of value. □ *The company would gain by merging with its competitor.* **5.** *n.* a profit. (Often plural.) □ *The thief spent his gains from the robbery on a new car.* **6.** *n.* an increase in something. □ *Her recent weight gain made her look fat.*

**galaxy** ['gæl ək si] *n.* a large mass or cluster of stars and their solar systems in space. □ *Our galaxy contains many stars.*

**gale** ['gel] **1.** *n.* a very strong wind. □ *The hurricane caused strong gales in its path.* **2.** *n.* an outburst, especially of laughter. (Often plural.) □ *My friends responded to my joke with gales of laughter.*

**gallant** ['gæl ənt] *adj.* honorable and brave; very polite. (Refers especially to men who are very polite toward women. Adv: *gallantly.*) □ *A gallant gentleman offered Anne his seat on the bus.*

**gallery** ['gæl ə ri] **1.** *n.* a balcony, often running along a wall or outside a window. □ *We stood on the gallery and enjoyed the view.* **2.** *n.* a room or building where art is displayed. □ *My paintings are on display in a gallery in New York City.*

**gallon** ['gæl ən] *n.* a unit of liquid measure, equal to 4 quarts, 8 pints, or almost 3.8 liters. □ *My gas tank holds 15 gallons of gasoline.*

**gallop** ['gæl əp] **1.** *n.* a fast way that a horse runs. (In a **gallop**, all four of the horse's feet are off the ground once during each stride.) □ *The horse went into a gallop when it saw the barn.* **2.** *iv.* to move quickly; [for a horse] to run fast. □ *The horse galloped away from the fire.*

**game** ['gem] **1.** *n.* a kind of contest, sporting event, or pastime played according to a set of rules. □ *Baseball is a very popular game.* **2.** *n.* an instance of playing ①. □ *When the game is over, please come right home.* **3.** *n.* wild animals that are hunted for sport or food. (No plural form. Treated as a singular.) □ *Every November, I hunt for wild game, especially deer.*

**game warden** ['gem 'word n] *n.* someone who enforces laws of or about hunting and fishing. □ *The game warden asked to see our fishing permits.*

**gang** ['gæŋ] **1.** *n.* a group of people who work, play, or do things together. □ *After work, John went bowling with a gang of friends.* **2.** *n.* a group of young criminals. □ *The Smiths moved from the inner city to the suburbs because they were afraid of gangs.*

**gap** ['gæp] **1.** *n.* an opening created by a crack; an opening created where two objects or structures do not meet. □ *I filled the gap around the window frame with wood.* **2.** *n.* an interruption in time; a period of time between two events or the parts of an event. □ *There was a ten-*

*minute gap between acts while the set was changed.* **3.** *n.* an easily seen difference between two things or groups of people. □ *The gap between the rich and the poor is widening.*

**garage** [gə 'rɑʒ] *n.* a building used to store a car or other motor vehicle. □ *Mr. Smith parked his car in the garage.*

**garbage** ['gɑr bɪdʒ] **1.** *n.* trash; rubbish; useless things that are thrown away. (No plural form.) □ *Please throw this garbage away now!* **2. the garbage** *n.* the container that holds ① and the ① that it holds. (No plural form in this sense.) □ *I threw the leftover food into the garbage.*

**garden** ['gɑrd n] **1.** *n.* a piece of land where plants, flowers, or vegetables are grown. □ *These tomatoes are fresh from the garden.* **2.** *iv.* to raise and take care of plants grown in ①. □ *My dad loves to garden.*

**gardener** ['gɑrd nɚ] *n.* someone who takes care of a garden; someone who plants and nourishes plants in a garden. □ *The gardener pulled the weeds out of the garden.*

**garment** ['gɑr mənt] *n.* an article of clothing; a piece of clothing. □ *David's garments were torn in the accident.*

**gas** ['gæs] **1.** *n.* vapor; a substance that is not in a liquid or solid state at a temperature that is comfortable for people. (Plural only when referring to different kinds, types, instances, or varieties. Plural is usually *gases.*) □ *The earth is surrounded with gas.* 🄲 *Three major gases—oxygen, nitrogen, and carbon dioxide—make up the atmosphere of earth.* **2.** *n.* a naturally occurring vapor that will burn and is used for cooking and heating. (No plural form.) □ *I prefer cooking on stoves that use gas instead of electricity.* **3.** *n.* **gasoline,** the liquid made from petroleum that is used to operate motors and engines. (Plural only when referring to different kinds, types, instances, or varieties.) □ *My car's tank holds 12 gallons of gas.* 🄲 *Most of today's gases are custom blended for different areas of the country.*

**gash** ['gæʃ] **1.** *n.* a large or deep cut or wound; a slash. □ *The doctor stitched up the gash on Anne's arm.* **2.** *tv.* to slash or cut something. □ *Mary gashed her forehead on the low ceiling above the stairs.*

**gasoline** [gæs ə 'lin] *n.* a liquid that is made from oil and is used to operate motors and engines. (Plural only when referring to different kinds, types, instances, or varieties. See also **gas.**) □ *My lawn mower is powered by gasoline.* 🄲 *Different gasolines provide different amounts of power.*

**gasp** ['gæsp] **1.** *n.* a quick, short inward breath; a quick breathing in of air. □ *There was a loud gasp from the audience when the actor fell.* **2.** *iv.* to breathe in suddenly as in surprise, shock, fear, etc. □ *After being saved from drowning, the swimmer gasped and gasped.*

**gate** ['get] **1.** *n.* a barrier that can be opened or closed at an opening in a fence or wall. □ *Bill closed the gate behind him to keep the dog inside the yard.* **2.** *n.* a decorative structure, including ①, serving as a formal entrance to a park, cemetery, street, etc. □ *I'll meet you at the gate in front of the park at three o'clock.* **3.** *n.* the place where people enter a stadium, arena, etc. □ *Mary stood at the gate, taking tickets as people entered the stadium.* **4.** *n.* the entrance to the passage to an airplane in an airport. □ *When Bob flew into town, Susan went to the airport and met him at the gate.*

**gather** ['gæð ɚ] **1.** *tv.* to bring something together; to collect something together; to bring people together. □ *Anne gathered her thoughts before answering the question.* **2.** *tv.* to gain or increase in something, especially speed or intensity.

G

□ *The ball gathered speed as it rolled downhill.* **3.** *iv.* to come together into a big group. □ *People gathered in the town square to hear the mayor speak.*

**gathering** ['gæð ɚ ɪŋ] *n.* a group of people; a group of people who have come together for a specific purpose. □ *The senator spoke to the gathering about taxes.*

**gauze** ['gɔz] *n.* a thin, loosely woven cloth. (Plural only when referring to different kinds, types, instances, or varieties.) □ *The nurse covered the wound with clean gauze.* Ⓒ *The more expensive gauzes are more absorbent and last longer.*

G

**gave** ['gev] pt of **give.**

**gay** ['ge] **1.** *adj.* happy; cheerful; brightly colored. (Adv: *gaily.* Comp: *gayer;* sup: *gayest.*) □ *The party room was decorated with gay balloons and ribbons.* **2.** *adj.* [of someone, usually a male] attracted to people of the same sex. (Comp: *gayer;* sup: *gayest.*) □ *Mary's son recently told her that he is gay.* **3.** *n.* a **gay** ② person, usually a male. □ *A group of gays sued the company for discrimination.*

**gear** ['gɪr] **1.** *n.* a wheel, with teeth along its edge, that moves similar wheels of differing diameters. □ *Gears serve to transfer power and change the direction of rotation.* **2.** *n.* equipment; tools; the things required to do a certain activity. (No plural form. Treated as singular.) □ *The hiker bought new gear for a two-week camping trip in Vermont.*

**geese** ['gis] pl of **goose.**

**gem** ['dʒɛm] **1.** *n.* a jewel; a precious stone, especially one used in jewelry. □ *The gem fell out when my ring fell to the floor.* **2.** *n.* someone or something that is very beautiful or wonderful; a perfect example of someone or something. (Fig. on ①.) □ *My secretary is a real gem!*

**gender** ['dʒɛn dɚ] **1.** *n.* [in grammar] a subdivision of nouns into masculine, feminine, and, sometimes, neuter categories. □ *In languages that have gender, all nouns have gender even if they represent things that do not have sexual distinctions.* □ *In German, the gender of the word* Hund, *meaning "dog," is masculine.* **2.** *n.* **sex** ③; the condition of being male or female. □ *I couldn't determine the gender of the baby dressed in green.*

**gene** ['dʒin] *n.* a part of a chromosome within every living cell that determines the characteristics of a plant or animal. □ *The scientists searched for the human gene that causes senility.*

**general** ['dʒɛn ə rəl] **1.** *adj.* widespread; commonly known, understood, believed, or experienced. (Adv: *generally.*) □ *Contrary to the general belief, the tomato is actually a fruit.* **2.** *adj.* not specific; not specialized. (Adv: *generally.*) □ *Bill took general courses until he chose history as a major.* **3.** *adj.* usual; regular; appropriate to most situations. (Adv: *generally.*) □ *As a general rule, you should brush your teeth after you eat.* **4.** *n.* a high-ranking army or air force officer. □ *The president honored the general for his bravery during the war.* **5. in general** *phr.* referring to the entire class being discussed, without being specific; speaking broadly of the entire range of possibilities; in most cases or situations. □ *I like vegetables in general, but not beets.*

**generation** [dʒɛn ə 're ʃən] **1.** *n.* producing or creating something. (No plural form.) □ *The generation of energy from solar power creates little pollution.* **2.** *n.* one stage in the history of a family. □ *My sisters, brothers, and cousins belong to the same generation as I do.* **3.** *n.* all the people of the same culture who were born around the same time, taken as a group. □ *Jane, like* *many other members of her generation, grew up with TV.*

**generous** ['dʒɛn ə rəs] **1.** *adj.* not selfish; giving freely. (Adv: *generously.*) □ *I thanked my aunt for her generous offer to help me go to college.* **2.** *adj.* [of an amount] more than is needed; [of an amount] large. (Adv: *generously.*) □ *My mashed potatoes were covered with a generous amount of gravy.*

**gentle** ['dʒɛn təl] *adj.* pleasantly mild; not rough; tame; kind. (Adv: **gently** ['dʒɛnt li]. Comp: *gentler;* sup: *gentlest.*) □ *A gentle wind blew through the valley.*

**gentleman** ['dʒɛn tl mən] **1.** *n., irreg.* a man who is refined, polite, and well mannered. (The male counterpart of **lady**. Pl: **gentlemen.**) □ *A gentleman holds the door open for the person behind him.* **2.** *n., irreg.* a polite term for **man** ①. □ *Ladies and gentlemen, please be seated.*

**gentlemen** ['dʒɛn tl mən] pl of **gentleman.**

**gently** ['dʒɛnt li] **1.** *adv.* in a kind way; in a way that does not cause pain or worry. □ *The doctor told Jane the bad news very gently.* **2.** *adv.* smoothly; mildly; not roughly. □ *The wind blew gently across the plains.*

**genuine** ['dʒɛn ju ɪn] **1.** *adj.* real; actual; not fake; not artificial. (Adv: *genuinely.*) □ *My necklace is made with genuine pearls.* **2.** *adj.* sincere. (Adv: *genuinely.*) □ *My friends expressed genuine sorrow when my dog died.*

**geography** [dʒi 'ɑ grə fi] *n.* the study of the features of the surface of Earth, including the land and climate, countries, and the people and cultures of the countries. (No plural form.) □ *Mary took a course on geography and learned all about the countries of Asia.*

**geology** [dʒi 'ɑl ə dʒi] *n.* the study of the origin and the structure of Earth. (No plural form.) □ *The study of the composition of the earth's crust is a part of geology.*

**geometry** [dʒi 'ɑm ɪ tri] **1.** *n.* the part of mathematics that deals with the relationships and properties of points, lines, curves, angles, surfaces, and solids. (No plural form.) □ *Geometry demands lots of reasoning.* **2.** *adj.* <the adj. use of ①.> □ *The geometry student figured out the radius of the circle.*

**germ** ['dʒɝm] *n.* a very small organism that causes disease. □ *Germs collect on surfaces that people have touched.*

G

**gesture** ['dʒɛs tʃɚ] **1.** *n.* a movement made with a part of the body to communicate or to emphasize a statement, emotion, or feeling. □ *With a gesture of his hand, the waiter indicated where I should sit.* **2.** *n.* an act of kindness or courtesy; an act that demonstrates friendship. □ *Please accept this gift as a gesture of my thanks.* **3.** *iv.* to use hand motions and facial movements when communicating; to make ①. □ *The waiter gestured toward the table where he wanted us to sit.*

**get** ['gɛt] **1.** *tv., irreg.* to obtain something; to receive something. (Pt: **got**; pp: **got** or **gotten.**) □ *I got a sprained ankle when I fell.* **2.** *tv., irreg.* to bring something; to fetch something. □ *Could you go to the store and get a gallon of milk?* **3.** *tv., irreg.* to understand something; to comprehend something. □ *I don't get what you're trying to say.* **4. get** someone **to** do something *tv., irreg. + obj. + inf.* to persuade someone to do something; to convince someone to do something. □ *Could I get you to do me a small favor?* **5.** *tv., irreg.* to cause something to happen to someone or something; to cause someone or something to be a certain way. □ *I need a strong cup of coffee in the morning to get me going.* **6.** *iv., irreg.* to become. □ *This book gets more boring page after page.* **7.** *iv., irreg.* to arrive somewhere; to reach a certain point or place. (Followed by an adverb such as **home, there,** or **somewhere** or by a prepositional phrase.) □ *When did you get to the party?* **8. get to** do something *iv., irreg. + inf.* to be allowed to do something; to be permitted to do something. □ *Mary got to sing the national anthem before the game.* **9. have got to** do something *phr.* to be obliged to do something; must do something. (Used only with the present tense of **have**, as with *have got to* or *has got to,* and often reduced in contractions to *'ve got to* and *'s got to.* It means the same as **have to do something**—at **have** ⑤—which is never made into a contraction.) □ *I've got to finish this book by tomorrow.* **10. have got** something *phr.* to have something; to possess something. (Used only with the present tense of **have** ⑥, as with *have got* or *has got,* and usually reduced in contractions to *'ve got* and *'s got.* It means the same as **have** ①, which is never made into a contraction.) □ *I've got a brand-new coat.*

**ghost** ['gost] *n.* an apparent image of a dead person, moving among the living. □ *Some people say that the old mansion is haunted by ghosts.*

**giant** ['dʒɑɪ ənt] **1.** *n.* a fictional or mythical human-like creature who is very large. □ *In the story, the hero fought against a powerful giant.* **2.** *n.* an unusually large person or animal. □ *The boy grew into a giant and was always bumping his head.* **3.** *n.* a person who is very important or known to be excellent at something. □ *Alfred Hitchcock was a giant in the film industry.* **4.** *adj.* very large; enormous. (Prenominal only.) □ *Four giant oak trees stood near the courthouse.*

**gift** ['gɪft] **1.** *n.* a present; something that is given to someone without expecting anything in return. □ *My bicycle was a birthday gift from my parents.* **2.** *n.* a special skill or talent. □ *Susie enjoys her piano lessons and seems to have a gift for music.*

**giraffe** [dʒə 'ræf] *n.* an African animal that has long legs and a very long neck. □ *The lecture explained the evolution of the giraffe's neck.*

**girl** ['gɚl] **1.** *n.* a female child. □ *My sister gave birth to a baby girl last night.* **2.** *n.* a woman. (Informal. Considered derogatory by some.) □ *The secretaries referred to each other as girls.* **3.** *n.* a man's girlfriend. (Informal.) □ *John took his girl out dancing every Friday.*

**girlfriend** ['gɚl frɛnd] **1.** *n.* a woman with whom someone is romantically involved. □ *Michael introduced his girlfriend to his parents.* **2.** *n.* a female friend. □ *Anne helped her girlfriend pick out a wedding dress.*

**give** ['gɪv] **1.** *tv., irreg.* to cause someone or something to have or receive something; to cause something to become owned by someone. (Pt: **gave**; pp: **given.**) □ *Susan gave David the news.* □ *Please give this book to Sue.* **2.** *tv., irreg.* to supply something; to provide something. □ *The sun gives heat and light.* **3.** *tv., irreg.* to make some sort of a sound with the mouth. □ *Bill gave a sigh of relief when the test was over.* **4. give** something **off** *tv., irreg. + obj. + adv.* to release or send out something; to emit or exude something. □ *The stove gives a lot of heat off.* Ⓣ *It gives off heat.* **5. give** something **up** *tv., irreg. + obj. + adv.* to yield something or someone. □ *Lisa refuses to give her bad habits up.* Ⓣ *She won't give up her bad habits.* **6.** *iv., irreg.* to be flexible; to be elastic; not to break when pushed or pulled. □ *The branch gave a little when I sat on it, then suddenly it broke.* **7. give up; give in** *iv., irreg. + adv.* to yield; to quit. □ *The weak team finally gave up and quit playing.*

**given** ['gɪv ən] pp of **give**.

**glad** ['glæd] **1.** *adj.* happy; content; pleased; joyful. (Adv: *gladly.* Comp: *gladder;* sup: *gladdest.*) □ *I'm glad for your good fortune.* **2.** *adj.* causing happiness, pleasure, or joy. (Adv: *gladly.* Comp: *gladder;* sup: *gladdest.*) □ *The team celebrated the glad event of winning first place.*

**glamour** ['glæm ɚ] *n.* charm and beauty. (No plural form.) □ *Mary was fascinated by the glamour of Hollywood.*

**glance** ['glæns] **1.** *n.* a brief look toward someone or something. □ *With a quick glance in each direction, Bill checked for traffic.* **2. glance at** something**; glance through** something**; glance over** something *iv.* + *prep. phr.* to quickly look at or over someone or something; to read something quickly. □ *I glanced at the headlines in the newspaper.*

**glare** ['glɛɚ] **1.** *n.* a harsh, angry stare. □ *Jane's icy glare indicated that she was very mad.* **2.** *n.* strong, bright light. (No plural form.) □ *I shielded my eyes from the glare of the sun.* **3.** *iv.* to stare angrily. □ *Jane glared at Dave after he spilled his coffee.*

**glass** ['glæs] **1.** *n.* a hard, stiff, easily broken, usually clear substance, used to make windows, drinking **glasses** ②, eyeglasses as in ④, etc. (Plural only when referring to different kinds, types, instances, or varieties.) □ *Glass breaks easily.* Ⓒ *The harder glasses are more brittle and break more easily.* **2.** *n.* a container that is used to drink from, usually made of ①. (The **glass** for drinking does not have a handle.) □ *Susan filled her glass with milk.* **3.** *n.* the contents of ②. □ *Susan drank an entire glass of milk.* **4. glasses** *n.* eyeglasses. (Treated as plural. Short for **eyeglasses**. Number is expressed with *pair(s) of glasses.*) □ *I can't see very well without my glasses.*

**glee** ['gli] *n.* great happiness. (No plural form.) □ *The glee we felt after we won the game made us want to jump and yell.*

**gleeful** ['gli fʊl] *adj.* very happy; joyful. (Adv: *gleefully.*) □ *The citizens were gleeful when the war finally ended.*

**glide** ['glaɪd] **1.** *iv.* to move smoothly. □ *The tip of the pen glided across the sheet of paper.* **2.** *iv.* to move through the air without engine power. □ *The plane glided to a safe landing after its engines failed.*

**global** ['glob əl] *adj.* of or about the whole world; worldwide. (Adv: *globally.*) □ *The war started small but soon became a global crisis.*

**globe** ['glob] **1.** *n.* a ball; a sphere. □ *Oranges have the shape of a globe.* **2.** *n.* a ball or sphere with a map of the world on it. □ *I bought a new globe to show all the changes in the countries of the world.* **3.** *n.* the earth; the world. □ *I had traveled around the globe before I was 21.*

**gloom** ['glum] *n.* the feeling of sadness and dullness. (No plural form.) □ *I was unable to ignore the gloom caused by the bad news.*

**glorify** ['glor ə faɪ] **1.** *tv.* to honor or worship someone; to praise someone or something. □ *They sang a lovely song that glorified love and nature.* **2.** *tv.* to exaggerate the importance of someone or something. □ *The writer tried to glorify his book with his own praise.*

**glorious** ['glor i əs] *adj.* beautiful; splendid; wonderful. (Adv: *gloriously.*) □ *Since it's such a glorious day, let's go to the beach.*

**glory** ['glor i] **1.** *n.* praise and honor. (No plural form.) □ *The worshipers gave glory to God.* **2.** *n.* something of great beauty or wonder. □ *The sunset was a glory to behold.*

**glossary** ['glɔs ə ri] *n.* a list of words and their definitions, as used within a particular book or article. □ *My editor suggested I list the hard words in a glossary.*

**glove** ['glʌv] *n.* one of a pair of fitted coverings for the hand, typically made of fabric or leather and having individual "pockets" for each finger and thumb. □ *The thief who wore gloves left no trace of fingerprints.*

**glow** ['glo] **1.** *iv.* to shine; to give off a weak light. □ *A small light glowed in the hallway outside the bedrooms.* **2.** *iv.* to be very hot; to be so hot as to be red, yellow, or white with heat. □ *The molten iron glowed with the heat.* **3.** *iv.* to be very excited with emotion or energy. □ *Susan's face glowed with excitement during the party.* **4.** *iv.* to show a healthy appearance; to have bright red cheeks. □ *Mary's skin glowed as she jogged through the park.* **5.** *n.* a weak light. □ *In the distance, I saw the glow of the city.* **6.** *n.* a healthy appearance; a reddened face. (No plural form.) □ *After she exercised, her skin had a healthy glow.*

**glue** ['glu] **1.** *n.* a thick, sticky liquid that is used to make something stick to something else; an adhesive. (Plural only when referring to different kinds, types, instances, or varieties.) □ *Jimmy pulled off the dried glue that was stuck to his fingers.* Ⓒ *Glues made from animal products are usually meant for wood and leather.* **2.** *tv.* to stick something to something else using ①. □ *Anne glued the pieces of the broken vase back together.*

**glum** ['glʌm] *adj.* sad; disappointed. (Adv: *glumly.* Comp: *glummer;* sup: *glummest.*) □ *I tried to cheer up my glum friend.*

**glut** ['glʌt] **1.** *n.* too much of something. □ *I dislike the glut of violence in the movies.* **2.** *tv.* to supply someone or something with too much of something. □ *Last year, the farms produced too much grain and glutted the market.*

**gnat** ['næt] *n.* a small fly that bites. □ *We were all bitten by gnats at the picnic.*

**go** ['go] **1.** *tv., irreg.* to practice or perform certain sports activities, such as running, swimming, canoeing, fencing, jogging, skiing, walking, or others expressed with words ending in *-ing.* (Pt: **went;** pp: **gone.** The third-person singular present tense is **goes.**) □ *Tom went skiing last week.* **2.** *iv., irreg.* to move from one place to another; [for time] to progress or pass. □ *I went downtown after school.* **3.** *iv., irreg.* to leave. □ *When you go, please turn out the lights.* **4.** *iv., irreg.* to reach a certain time or place; to extend to a certain time or place. □ *This movie goes until 11:00.* **5.** *iv., irreg.* to work; to function. □ *Mary assures me that her computer is still going, even though it is six years old.* **6.** *iv., irreg.* to become. □ *Some diseases can make you go blind.* **7. go for an amount** *iv., irreg. + prep. phr.* [for something] to sell for or be sold at a certain price. □ *What does this radio go for? The price tag is missing.* **8.** *iv., irreg.* to become worn out; to weaken. □ *The actor's voice started going during the second act.* **9.** *iv., irreg.* to belong in a certain place. □ *The number 12 goes after the number 11.* **10.** *iv., irreg.* [for the activities in a period of time] to unfold in some way, good or bad. □ *How did your trip to Florida go? Last time you went, things didn't go so well.* **11.** *iv., irreg.* to progress though a series of words or musical notes. □ *How does the melody of "Moon River" go?* **12. go with something** *iv., irreg. + prep. phr.* to match something; to look good with something. □ *Your shoes don't go with your purse.* **13. go into a number** *iv., irreg. + prep. phr.* [for a number] to divide into another number. □ *How many times does 5 go into 20?* **14. going to do something** *phr.* planning to do something; intending or meaning to do something. (A form of the future tense in English.) □ *I am going to do it tomorrow.* □ *She thinks she is going to win the game.*

**goal** ['gol] **1.** *n.* an aim; a purpose; a result that one would like to achieve from doing something. □ *Anne's goal was to become a lawyer.* **2.** *n.* [in sports] a place where players try to send a ball in order to score points. □ *The goalie kicked the soccer ball away from the goal.* **3.** *n.* [in sports] an instance of sending a ball through or past ②, and the points earned by doing this. □ *A goal in soccer is worth one point.* **4.** *n.* the finish line; the end point of a race. □ *The winner broke through the tape that stretched across the goal.*

**goalie** ['go li] *n.* a **goalkeeper**. (A shortening of **goalkeeper**.) □ *The ball hit the goalie in the chest.*

**goalkeeper** ['gol kip ɚ] *n.* [in sports] the player whose position is in front of the team's goal and who tries to prevent players on the other team from scoring. □ *The goalkeeper blocked the ball with his leg.*

**goat** ['got] *n.* an animal with horns, similar to a sheep. □ *Uncle John raised a goat for its milk.*

**god** ['gɑd] **1.** *n.* a male spiritual being who is worshiped. (Compare this with **goddess**.) □ *The ancient Greeks worshiped several gods.* **2.** *n.* someone or something admired as ①. □ *The famous singer was a god to his obsessed fans.* **3. God** *n.* [in religions such as Christianity, Islam, and Judaism] the one spiritual being that is worshiped as the creator and ruler of everything. (No plural form.) □ *I prayed to God that my mother's operation would be successful.*

**goddess** ['gɑd əs] *n.* a female spiritual being who is worshiped. □ *The farmer offered a prayer to the goddess of the harvest.*

**goes** ['goz] the third-person singular, present tense of **go**.

**goggles** ['gɔg əlz] *n.* a pair of protective lenses that are worn during swimming, skiing, biking, and other activities. (Treated as plural. Number is expressed with *pair(s) of goggles*.) □ *I won't open my eyes underwater unless I'm wearing goggles.*

**gold** ['gold] **1.** *n.* a chemical element that is a soft, yellow metal, is very valuable, and is the standard for money in many countries. (No plural form.) □ *The pages of many valuable old books are edged with gold.* **2.** *n.* coins or jewelry made of ①. (No plural form.) □ *Should I wear silver or gold with this dress?* **3.** *n.* a deep yellow color. (Plural only when referring to different kinds, types, instances, or varieties.) □ *Our kitchen is decorated in green and gold.* © *The reds and golds of the forest glowed brightly in the autumn sunlight.* **4.** *adj.* made of ①. □ *Should I wear silver or gold earrings with this dress?* **5.** *adj.* deep yellow in color. (Comp: *golder;* sup: *goldest*.) □ *The field was full of gold sunflowers.*

**golden** ['gol dən] **1.** *adj.* made from gold; yellowish as if made from gold. □ *Anne often wears a large golden bracelet.* **2.** *adj.* [of anniversaries] the fiftieth. □ *My parents went to Las Vegas for their golden anniversary.*

**golden rule** ['gol dən 'rul] *n.* the principle that one should treat other people the way one would like to be treated. (From the Bible.) □ *I use the golden rule as my philosophy of life.*

**goldfish** ['gold fɪʃ] *n., irreg.* a kind of small fish, typically orange or gold, commonly kept as a pet. (Pl: *goldfish*.) □ *A dead goldfish floated upside down in the tank.*

**golf** ['gɔlf] **1.** *n.* a game played on a large area of land, where players use a club to hit a small ball into a hole, using as few strokes as possible. (No plural form.) □ *After work, I played nine holes of golf.* **2.** *iv.* to play ①. □ *The board members discussed business while they golfed.*

G

**golf club** ['gɔlf kləb] *n.* a long, metal mallet used in the game of golf. (Can be shortened to **club**.) □ *Bill left his golf clubs at the golf course.*

**gone** ['gɔn] pp of go.

**good** ['gʊd] **1.** *adj., irreg.* having positive qualities; satisfactory; suitable; not negative. (Adv: **well**. Comp: **better**; sup: **best**.) □ *My dog has a good sense of smell.* **2.** *adj., irreg.* having proper morals; moral; not evil. □ *My brother is forgetful, but he's really a good person.* **3.** *adj., irreg.* enjoyable; pleasant; satisfying. (Adv: *well.*) □ *We had a good time at the beach.* **4.** *adj., irreg.* complete; thorough; full. (Adv: *well.*) □ *Give your room a good cleaning before you leave tonight.* **5.** *adj.* [of a total of] at least. (Prenominal only.) □ *We drove a good 500 miles today.* **6.** *adj., irreg.* (Adv: *well.*) skillful; talented; able to do something right. □ *Mary's a good golfer.* **7.** *adj., irreg.* properly behaved; obedient. □ *"Good dog," Mary said as she patted it on the head.* **8.** *adj.* ripe; edible; not spoiled; not rotten. □ *Is the milk in the refrigerator still good?* **9.** *adj.* of high quality; best available. (See also **best**.) □ *Bob wore his good clothes to the interview.* **10.** *n.* excellence; virtue; goodness. (No plural form.) □ *In the end, the forces of good will win over the forces of evil.* **11. goods** *n.* items for sale; products that are made to be sold. (Treated as plural, but not countable.) □ *What aisle are the paper goods located in?*

**good-bye** [gʊd 'bɑɪ] **1.** *interj.* "farewell," as said when someone leaves. □ *"Good-bye," I said to my guests as they left.* **2.** *adj.* of or about leaving; of or about a departure. □ *We threw our boss a good-bye party when he retired.*

**goose** ['gus] *n., irreg.* a bird having a long neck and similar to a large duck. (Pl: **geese**.) □ *The baby goose fell as it walked behind its mother.*

**gorilla** [gə 'rɪl ə] *n.* the largest kind of ape. □ *The gorilla at the zoo was kept in a cage that was too small.*

**gospel** ['gɑs pəl] **1. Gospel** *n.* one of the first four books of the New Testament of the Bible. □ *The minister read from the Gospel during the service.* **2.** *n.* the absolute truth; something that is absolutely true. (Fig. on the assumption of truth in the four **Gospels** ①. No plural form.) □ *The defendant swore that her testimony was gospel.*

**gossip** ['gɑs əp] **1.** *n.* talk about other people, which may or may not be true; rumors about other people. (No plural form.) □ *I demanded to know who had been spreading vicious gossip about me.* **2.** *n.* someone who often talks about other people and other people's private lives. □ *I told the annoying gossip to mind his own business.* **3.** *iv.* to talk about other people and their private lives; to spread rumors about other people. □ *You shouldn't gossip, because you could hurt someone's feelings.*

**got** ['gɑt] **1.** pt and a pp of **get**. **2. have got to** do something Go to **get** ⑨.

**gotten** ['gɑt n] a pp of **get**.

**gourmet** [gor 'me] **1.** *n.* someone who enjoys fine foods and wine. □ *The waiter asked the gourmet if the wine was suitable.* **2.** *adj.* [of food and drink] produced according to the highest cooking standards. □ *The gourmet meal cost $50 per person.*

**govern** ['gʌv ɚn] **1.** *iv.* to rule [over someone or something]; to be the leader of a group of people. □ *The evil king governed unfairly.* **2.** *tv.* to rule or lead a group of people. □ *The president governed the nation for 8 years.* **3.** *tv.* to guide, control, or regulate something. □ *The committee governed the firm's day-to-day operations.*

**government** ['gʌv ɚn mənt] **1.** *n.* the system of rule over a country and its people. (No plural form.) □ *Democracy is one form of government.* **2.** *n.* the political organization ruling in a particular area. □ *The country's current government is honest and efficient.* **3.** *adj.* <the adj. use of ① or ②.> (Also *governmental.*) □ *Everyone hates government bureaucracy.*

**governor** ['gʌv ɚ nɚ] **1.** *n.* the title of the executive officer of each state of the United States. □ *Detroit's mayor met with the governor of Michigan to discuss crime.* **2.** *n.* someone who governs or rules certain organizations. □ *Mr. Smith is a member of the bank's board of governors.* **3.** *n.* a device that controls the speed of a car or other vehicle, either keeping it at a constant speed or not allowing it to go over a certain speed. □ *The car's governor prevented speeds over 55 miles per hour.*

**gown** ['gɑʊn] **1.** *n.* a formal dress for a woman. □ *Susan's wedding gown was made of white satin.* **2.** *n.* a **nightgown.** □ *She wore a sleeveless gown to bed in the summer.* **3.** *n.* a type of loose ceremonial covering or robe such as is worn at graduation ceremonies. □ *Jane's graduation gown completely covered her dress.*

**grab** ['græb] **1.** *tv.* to seize and hold someone or something; to snatch someone or something; to take something rudely. □ *Mary kicked the assailant who had grabbed her from behind.* **2.** *tv.* to get and bring something; to fetch something. (Informal.) □ *Could you grab my slippers when you go upstairs?* **3.** *n.* an act of seizing as in ①. □ *I thwarted the thief's quick grab for my purse.*

**grace** ['gres] **1.** *n.* elegance, smoothness, or attractiveness of form or motion. (No plural form.) □ *We all admired the athletes' grace as they ran.* **2.** *n.* calm and tolerant elegance. (No plural form.) □ *The king was well known for the grace he showed in settling disputes between his subjects.* **3.** *n.* favor; mercy; favorable regard. (No plural form.) □ *Only through the grace of God did I survive the accident.* **4.** *n.* a prayer said before eating. (No plural form.) □ *I said grace quickly because I was rather hungry.* **5.** *tv.* to make something more beautiful or elegant; to add beauty or elegance to something. □ *Flowers graced the tables in the lovely room.*

**grade** ['gred] **1.** *n.* a level in school corresponding to a year of study. □ *Students in the 10th grade are called sophomores.* **2.** *n.* a mark, given to a student for a class, test, paper, or assignment, that shows how well or how poorly the student did. □ *All of my grades this term were A's, except for a B in History.* **3.** *n.* a degree of quality. □ *Hundreds of grade B movies were filmed in the 1950s.* **4.** *n.* the slope of a road, roof, terrace, etc. □ *The sign warned drivers about the steep grade of the upcoming hill.* **5.** *tv.* to give ② for the work of a student. □ *Mr. Davis graded the students' essays for grammar and creativity.*

**graduate 1.** ['græ dʒu ət] *n.* someone who has completed high school, college, or university. □ *It's harder to get a good job if you're not a graduate.* **2. graduate (from** some place**)** ['græ dʒu et...] *iv.* *(+ prep. phr.)* to depart from a school, college, or university with a degree. □ *When did you graduate from high school?* **3.** ['græ dʒu et] *tv.* to depart from a school, college, or university with a degree. □ *I graduated college when I was 21.*

**graduation** [græ dʒu 'e ʃən] **1.** *n.* the ceremony where students become **graduates** ①. □ *I began working at a new job a week after graduation.* **2.** *n.* one of a series of marks on something showing the units of measurement. □ *Are the graduations on this ruler in inches or centimeters?*

**grain** ['gren] **1.** *n.* grass or cereal plants grown for their edible seeds. (Plural only when referring to different kinds, types, instances, or varieties.) □ *This is a good year for growing grain.* Ⓒ *The grains we planted each produced good crops, but the potatoes were a failure.* **2.** *n.* seeds of ①. (Plural only when referring to different kinds, types, instances, or varieties.) □ *We bought enough grain to feed the cattle for a month.* Ⓒ *We tried a variety of cheaper grains on the old cow, but she really likes corn the best.* **3.** *n.* an individual seed of ①. □ *The farmer planted two grains in each hole.* **4.** *n.* a tiny particle of something, such as sand or salt. □ *I removed a grain of sand from my eye.* **5.** *n.* a very small unit of weight, equal to about 64.8 milligrams. □ *One ounce is equal to 480 grains.* **6.** *n.* the pattern or direction of the fibers of wood. (Plural only when referring to different kinds, types, instances, or varieties.) □ *The grain of this wood makes a very pretty pattern.* Ⓒ *Oak grows with many different grains, and each one is suitable for a different purpose.*

**gram** ['græm] *n.* the basic unit for measuring weight in the metric system, equal to 1/1,000 of a kilogram or about 1/28 of an ounce. □ *This coin weighs about 5 grams.*

**grammar** ['græm ɚ] **1.** *n.* a system of rules and principles in a language that determine how sentences are formed; the study of sentence structure and the relationships between words within sentences. (Plural only when referring to different kinds, types, instances, or varieties. Adj: *grammar; grammatical.*) □ *I hope to be able to master English grammar and pronunciation.* Ⓒ *The grammars of Swedish and Danish are somewhat alike.* **2.** *n.* a statement of the rules of a language that account for how sentences are formed, especially the description of what the standard form of the language is like. □ *The linguist wrote a new grammar for English, but it was difficult to understand.* **3.** *n.* following the rules of ② in the use of written and spoken language. (No plural form.) □ *Jane received an A for good grammar and punctuation in her essay.*

**grammar school** ['græm ɚ 'skul] *n.* a school at the elementary level. □ *I went to grammar school in Florida and high school in California.*

**grand** ['grænd] **1.** *adj.* impressive; magnificent. (Adv: *grandly.* Comp: *grander;* sup: *grandest.*) □ *The cathedral in our town is a very grand building.* **2.** *n.* a thousand dollars. (Slang. No plural form.) □ *Mary won five grand in last week's lottery!*

**grandchild** ['græn(d) tʃɑɪld] *n., irreg.* a child of one's child. (Pl: **grandchildren.**) □ *John helped pay for his grandchild's education.*

**grandchildren** ['græn(d) tʃɪl drən] pl of grandchild.

**granddad** ['græn dæd] *n.* grandfather; the father of one's mother or father. (Also a term of address.) □ *Jimmy often went fishing with his granddad.*

**granddaughter** ['græn dɔt ɚ] *n.* the daughter of one's son or daughter. □ *John moved in with his granddaughter when he couldn't live alone anymore.*

**grandfather** ['græn(d) fɑ ðɚ] *n.* the father of one's mother or father. (Also a term of address.) □ *My grandfather came to this country when he was twelve.*

**grandma** ['græm mɑ] *n.* grandmother; the mother of one's mother or father. (Also a term of address.) □ *My grandma makes the best apple pie in the world.*

**grandmother** ['græn(d) məð ɚ] *n.* the mother of one's mother or father. (Also a term of address.) □ *My grandmother went back to school when she was 65.*

**grandpa** ['græm pɑ] *n.* grandfather; the father of one's mother or father. (Also a term of address.) □ *My grandpa parked his tractor in the barn.*

**grandparent** ['græn(d) pɛr ənt] *n.* a grandmother or a grandfather; the parent of one's parent. (The plural usually refers to one or more pairs consisting of a **grandmother** and a **grandfather**.) □ *I lived with my grandparents during the summer.*

**grandson** ['græn(d) sən] *n.* the son of one's child. □ *Bill and his grandson went hunting for deer.*

**grand total** ['grænd 'tot əl] *n.* the complete total; the final total. □ *The computer added the columns and displayed the grand total.*

**grant** ['grænt] **1.** *n.* money that is given by a government or a private agency for a worthy purpose. □ *Mary's research is funded by a grant from a foundation.* **2.** *tv.* to give something formally to someone. □ *The foundation granted $10,000 to the art project.* **3.** *tv.* to give permission for something to someone; to give someone permission for something. □ *The famous celebrity refused to grant the reporter an interview.* **4.** *tv.* to concede that something is true; to admit to someone that something is true. (The object is a clause with **that** ⑦.) □ *I'll grant that your point is correct, but I think it's irrelevant.*

**grape** ['grep] **1.** *n.* a red, green, or purple fruit that grows in bunches on vines. □ *I picked a bunch of grapes straight off the vine.* **2.** *adj.* made of or flavored with ①. □ *I spread some grape jam on a slice of bread.*

**graph** ['græf] **1.** *n.* a drawing that shows the difference between two or more amounts or the changes in amounts through time. □ *The graph showed the annual temperatures in New York City since 1980.* **2.** *tv.* to place information on ①; to make ①. □ *I graphed the increase in the temperature during the past 20 years.*

**grass** ['græs] *n.* a plant with thin blades instead of leaves. (Plural only when referring to different kinds, types, instances, or varieties.) □ *I love the scent of freshly cut grass.* Ⓒ *Some of the grasses of the field died in the hot, dry weather.*

**gratitude** ['græt ə tud] *n.* the quality of being thankful; a feeling or expression of thanks. (No plural form.) □ *My grandparents will always have my gratitude for sending me money while I was in college.*

**grave** ['grev] **1.** *n.* the place where someone is buried; a burial site. □ *The cemetery is filled with row after row of graves.* **2.** *n.* the actual hole that someone is buried in. □ *The workers placed the coffin into the grave.* **3. the grave** *n.* death. (No plural form. Treated as singular.) □ *After living 90 years, Susan didn't fear the grave.* **4.** *adj.* very serious; dire. (Adv: *gravely.*) □ *The grave situation demanded my immediate attention.*

**gravel** ['græv əl] *n.* crushed rock; pebbles about the size of peas. (Plural only when referring to different kinds, types, instances, or varieties. Treated as singular.) □ *The workers mined gravel from the quarry.* Ⓒ *The river bed provides one of the best gravels available for concrete.*

**graveyard** ['grev jɑrd] *n.* a cemetery; a place where dead people are buried. □ *The coffin was carried from the church to the graveyard.*

**gravity** ['græv ə ti] **1.** *n.* the force that pulls things toward the center of planets, suns, moons, etc.; the force that pulls things toward the center of Earth. (No plural form.) □ *Things fall to the ground because of the effects of gravity.* **2.** *n.* seriousness; importance. (No plural form.) □ *I don't think you understand the gravity of the situation.*

**gravy** ['gre vi] **1.** *n.* the juice that drips from meat when it cooks. (Plural only when referring to different kinds, types, instances, or varieties.) □ *There was a lot of gravy in the pan from cooking the turkey.* 🄲 *I have to avoid fatty gravies and rich sauces.* **2.** *n.* a sauce made from ①, often thickened with flour or something similar. (Plural only when referring to different kinds, types, instances, or varieties.) □ *The cook thickened the gravy with flour.* 🄲 *The buffet had two different gravies, one made from pork juices and the other from chicken stock.*

**gray** ['gre] **1.** *n.* the color made when white is mixed with black. (Plural only when referring to different kinds, types, instances, or varieties.) □ *The picture on a black-and-white television actually contains several shades of gray.* 🄲 *The different grays in the photographs showed they were printed on different photographic paper.* **2.** *n.* **gray** ① found in the hair. (No plural form.) □ *John is only 25, but he already has some gray.* **3.** *adj.* <the adj. use of ①.> (Adv: *grayly.*) □ *The gray rain clouds blocked the sun.* **4.** *iv.* [for hair] to become ③; [for someone] to develop ②. □ *I'm going to dye my hair when it starts to gray.*

**grease 1.** ['gris] *n.* melted animal fat or any similarly oily substance. (No plural form.) □ *Bob tried to remove some of the grease with a paper towel.* **2.** ['gris, 'griz] *tv.* to coat something with ①. □ *The mechanic greased the hinges on my car doors.*

**great** ['gret] **1.** *adj.* large in size or importance. (Adv: *greatly.* Comp: *greater;* sup: *greatest.*) □ *The shadow of the great building darkened the entire street.* **2.** *adj.* good; very good. (Adv: *greatly.* Comp: *greater;* sup: *greatest.*) □ *I thanked Bob for the great dinner that he had cooked.* **3. Great!** *interj.* "Super!"; "Wonderful!" (Sometimes used sarcastically.) □ *Great! It's stopped raining!*

**greed** ['grid] *n.* a strong desire for money, possessions, or power. (No plural form.) □ *Bill has gotten into trouble because of his greed for power.*

**greedy** ['gri di] *adj.* showing greed; desiring money, possessions, or power too strongly. (Adv: *greedily.* Comp: *greedier;* sup: *greediest.*) □ *The greedy man would not donate any money to the poor.*

**green** ['grin] **1.** *n.* the color of grass or of the leaves of trees in the summer; the color made when blue and yellow are mixed together. (Plural only when referring to different kinds, types, instances, or varieties.) □ *I added some green to the painting by including more trees.* 🄲 *The first greens we looked at were too blue, and these are too yellow.* **2.** *n.* a grassy area. □ *A jazz band played on the village green.* **3. greens** *n.* the leaves of certain plants eaten as food. (Treated as plural.) □ *I cooked the turnip greens with ham for extra flavor.* **4.** *adj.* <the adj. use of ①.> (Comp: *greener;* sup: *greenest.*) □ *The grass is very green after a rain.* **5.** *adj.* unripe; not yet ripe or mature. (Comp: *greener;* sup: *greenest.*) □ *The peaches are still green, but in a week or two they will be ready to eat.* **6.** *adj.* without experience; young. (Fig. on ⑤. Comp: *greener;* sup: *greenest.*) □ *You did a very good job for someone who's still green.*

**greenhouse** ['grin hɑʊs] *n., irreg.* a building with a glass roof and glass walls where the temperature is controlled so that plants can grow inside all year round. (Pl: [...hɑʊ zəz].) □ *Since I have a greenhouse, I can have fresh tomatoes all year.*

**greet** ['grit] *tv.* to welcome someone; to address someone, especially upon meeting or arrival. □ *The mayor greeted the governor and invited him to sit down.*

**greeting** ['gri tɪŋ] *n.* a word, phrase, or action—such as *Hello*—said or done when meeting someone or when answering the telephone. □ *The greeting on your answering machine is too long.*

**grew** ['gru] pt of **grow**.

**grid** ['grɪd] **1.** *n.* a series of lines arranged vertically and horizontally forming squares, especially as found on maps or graphs. □ *It is easy to draw a chart on a grid.* **2.** *n.* a series of rods, bars, or wires arranged as in ①. □ *A grid of iron bars covered each ground-floor window.* **3.** *n.* a network of electrical lines spread over a large area; a network of roads. □ *When lightning disabled the electrical grid near Adamsville, all the lights went out.*

**grief** ['grif] *n.* sorrow; distress. (No plural form.) □ *I comforted Bob in his grief following his mother's death.*

**grill** ['grɪl] **1.** *n.* a grid of metal rods set over a fire, on which food is placed to cook. □ *Don't touch the grill! It's still hot!* **2.** *n.* an outdoor stove that cooks food placed on a framework of rows of metal bars. □ *Dave placed six hamburgers on the grill.* **3.** *tv.* to cook food on ① or ②. □ *We grilled pieces of chicken for dinner.* **4.** *tv.* to question someone forcefully and thoroughly. □ *A lawyer grilled the witness in the courtroom.* **5.** *iv.* [for food] to be cooked on ① or ②. □ *The hot dogs swelled up as they grilled.*

**grille** ['grɪl] **1.** *n.* a grate above the front bumper of a car in front of the radiator. (Compare this with **grill**.) □ *The grille was covered with hundreds of dead insects.* **2.** *n.* a grid of metal bars placed in a door or window. □ *Five people died in the fire because their exit was blocked by a grille over the window.*

**grim** ['grɪm] **1.** *adj.* not likely to turn out well. (Adv: *grimly.* Comp: *grimmer;* sup: *grimmest.*) □ *Your job prospects will be grim if you don't finish school.* **2.** *adj.* [looking] stern and harsh. (Adv: *grimly.* Comp: *grimmer;* sup: *grimmest.*) □ *The students disliked their teacher's grim attitude.*

**grime** ['graɪm] *n.* thick, oily dirt. (No plural form.) □ *While fixing the engine, I got black grime all over my hands.*

**grin** ['grɪn] **1.** *n.* a big smile. □ *David's sly grin indicated that he knew about the surprise.* **2.** *iv.* to smile widely so that one's teeth show. □ *Everyone grinned when Bob told the funny joke.*

**grind** ['graɪnd] **1.** *tv., irreg.* to make something into a powder or tiny chunks, by crushing or pounding it. (Pt/pp: **ground**.) □ *The waiter ground some pepper onto my salad.* **2.** *tv., irreg.* to rub things together with force. □ *Anne grinds her teeth in her sleep.* **3. grind** something **(down)** *tv., irreg. + obj. (+ adv.)* to wear something down through friction or grinding; to smooth a rough object by using friction. □ *Mary ground down the pencil in the electric sharpener.*

**grindstone** ['graɪnd ston] **1.** *n.* a thick, round wheel of stone that is used to sharpen knives. □ *I sharpened the knives against the spinning grindstone.* **2. keep** one's **nose to the grindstone** *phr.* to work hard at one's job or task. □ *Keep your nose to the grindstone, and you will succeed.*

**grip** ['grɪp] **1.** *tv.* to hold someone or something tightly with one's hands. □ *I gripped the railing as I walked down the stairs.* **2.** *n.* a tight hold on someone or something. □ *My brother broke from my grip and ran into the street.*

**gripe** ['graɪp] **1.** *n.* a complaint. □ *What do you expect me to do about your gripes?* **2. gripe (about** someone or something**)** *iv. (+ prep. phr.)* to complain about someone or something; to whine about someone or something. □ *Mary gripes about everything. She loves to complain.*

**groan** ['gron] **1.** *n.* a loud, deep noise of pain, disappointment, or disapproval.

G

☐ *My friend responded to my bad joke with a loud groan.* **2.** *iv.* to make a loud, deep noise of pain, disappointment, or disapproval. ☐ *The audience groaned when Tom told a bad joke.* **3.** *iv.* [for an enormous bulk] to make a deep noise or creak. ☐ *The building swayed and groaned during the earthquake.*

**grocer** ['gro sɚ] *n.* someone who owns or runs a grocery store; someone who sells food and basic supplies. ☐ *The grocer placed my purchases in a plastic bag.*

G

**grocery** ['gros ri] **1. grocery (store)** *n.* a store where food can be bought. ☐ *I'm going to the grocery now. Do you need anything?* **2. groceries** *n.* items bought at ①. (Treated as plural, but not countable.) ☐ *I paid for my groceries with a credit card.* **3.** *adj.* <the adj. use of ①.> ☐ *She paid for her grocery items and left the store.*

**groom** ['grum] **1.** *n.* a man who is getting married. ☐ *The groom wore a tuxedo and a red tie.* **2.** *tv.* to clean and comb a horse. ☐ *John has to groom his horse before the parade.* **3.** *tv.* to make someone's hair neat. ☐ *Sally spends a lot of time grooming her long hair.* **4.** *tv.* to prepare someone for a specific duty. ☐ *The Browns groomed their children to take over the store after they retired.*

**ground** ['graʊnd] **1.** pt/pp of **grind**. **2.** *adj.* broken or chopped into powder or into tiny chunks by grinding. ☐ *Please buy 3 pounds of ground beef at the store.* **3.** *n.* the surface of the earth. (No plural form.) ☐ *I tripped and fell to the ground.* **4. grounds** *n.* powdered coffee beans after coffee has been made. (Treated as plural, but not countable.) ☐ *I dumped the coffee grounds into the garbage.* **5.** *tv.* to cause a pilot, airplane, or bird to stay on the surface of the earth. (Pt/pp: *grounded.*) ☐ *The geese were grounded by the ice storm.* **6.** *tv.* to make someone stay in a certain place as punishment. (Fig. on ⑤. Pt/pp: *grounded.*) ☐ *The Smiths grounded their son in his bedroom for swearing at them.* **7.** *tv.* to make an electrical device safer by extending a wire into ③. (Pt/pp: *grounded.*) ☐ *The electrician grounded the wiring around our patio.*

**ground beef** ['graʊnd 'bif] *n.* beef that has been chopped or ground fine; hamburger. (No plural form.) ☐ *I use ground beef to make hamburgers and meatloaf.*

**group** ['grup] **1.** *n.* a number of things or people considered as a unit; a category. ☐ *I went with a group of friends to the zoo.* **2.** *tv.* to arrange things or people into categories; to place things or people together in ①. ☐ *The librarian grouped all the dictionaries on one shelf.*

**grow** ['gro] **1.** *tv., irreg.* to care for plants, causing them to mature. (Pt: **grew**; pp: **grown**.) ☐ *The farmer grows wheat and soybeans.* **2.** *iv., irreg.* to become bigger, larger, or more powerful; to increase. ☐ *The tall oak tree had grown from a tiny acorn.* **3. grow into** something *iv., irreg.* + *prep. phr.* to develop into something. ☐ *The local singer grew into an international celebrity.* **4.** *iv., irreg.* to become a certain way. ☐ *I grew tired and went to bed.*

**growl** ['graʊl] **1.** *n.* a deep, threatening sound, especially that made in anger. ☐ *The dog's growl scared the burglar away.* **2.** *iv.* to make a deep, threatening sound; to say something in a deep, threatening way, especially when angry or irritated. ☐ *My father growled at me to be quieter.*

**grown** ['gron] **1.** pp of **grow**. **2.** *adj.* fully developed; adult; mature; ripe. ☐ *You don't often see grown men cry in public.*

**growth** ['groθ] **1.** *n.* development; the amount someone or something develops in a certain period of time. (No plural form.) ☐ *The biologist studied the growth of embryos.* **2.** *n.* an increase; the process of becoming bigger, larger, or more powerful. (No plural form.) □ *What has caused the growth in the number of words in the English language?* **3.** *n.* an unnatural or unhealthy lump of tissue; a tumor. □ *My doctor removed two cancerous growths from my spine.*

**guarantee** [gɛr ən 'ti] **1.** *n.* a written document that promises that a certain product will operate properly for a certain amount of time. □ *I bought a computer with a one-year guarantee.* **2.** *n.* a written or verbal promise that one will be responsible for something, especially for certain debts or actions. □ *You have my guarantee that your daughter will be home by midnight.* **3.** *tv.* to promise that something will be done. (The object can be a clause with **that** ⑦.) □ *Max guaranteed that he would fix the computer if it ever broke.* **4.** *tv.* to promise to be responsible for certain debts, actions, or results. □ *The carpenter guaranteed completion of the job in six months.* **5.** *tv.* to provide ① promising that a product will work properly for a period of time. □ *They guaranteed the car for two years.*

**guard** ['gɑrd] **1.** *n.* someone or some creature that watches and protects someone or something. □ *The guard locked the prisoner in the cell.* **2.** *adj.* <the adj. use of ①.> □ *Our guard dog is trained to attack burglars.* **3.** *tv.* to protect someone or something; to keep someone or something from escaping. □ *Security officers guarded the bank vault.*

**guess** ['gɛs] **1.** *n.* an opinion or statement that is given without really knowing what is true. □ *What's your guess as to why the problem failed?* **2. guess at something** *iv. + prep. phr.* to make a try at getting the right answer to a question. □ *Max could only guess at the number of pages in the book.* **3.** *tv.* to make a successful try at figuring out the right answer to a question. (The object can be a clause with **that** ⑦.) □ *Max correctly guessed the number of pages in the book.* **4.** *tv.* to think that something will probably happen; to suppose that something will happen. (The object is a clause with **that** ⑦.) □ *I guess that it could rain tonight.*

**guest** ['gɛst] **1.** *n.* someone who visits another person's home because of an invitation. □ *I invited Bill to be my guest whenever he came to town.* **2.** *n.* someone who is taken to dinner or to a place of entertainment by someone else, who is paying for it. □ *Please be my guest for dinner.* **3.** *n.* someone who is invited by an organization or government to make a visit. □ *The guest spoke to the government committee about banks.* **4.** *n.* a customer of a hotel, motel, etc. □ *We hope that all our guests will be comfortable in our hotel.*

**guide** ['gɑɪd] **1.** *n.* someone who shows someone else the way. □ *Bill was our guide as we walked through the woods.* **2.** *n.* someone who leads tours. □ *A guide led the tourists around the castle.* **3.** *n.* a book or chart of information about a thing or a place. □ *I stayed in hotels that the travel guide recommended.* **4.** *tv.* to lead someone to the right place. □ *I guided the lost tourist toward the subway.* **5.** *tv.* to lead a tour. □ *Max guides tours for a living.* **6.** *tv.* to direct the business of something; to control something. □ *The manager will guide the growth of the new department.* **7.** *tv.* to advise someone. □ *I hope I can guide you to make the right decision.*

**guilt** ['gɪlt] **1.** *n.* the feeling that one has done something wrong or bad. (No plural form.) □ *A lot of guilt came over me after I lied to my parents.* **2.** *n.* the burden or responsibility of having done something wrong or bad. (No plural form.) □ *I am free from guilt in this crime!*

**gulf** ['gʌlf] **1.** *n.* an area of sea, larger than a bay, surrounded by land on two

G

or three sides. □ *John and Bill went fishing in the gulf.* **2.** *n.* a large or wide separation. (Fig. on ①.) □ *A friend helped bridge the gulf between the warring armies.*

**gum** ['gʌm] **1.** *n.* a soft, sticky, flavored substance that people chew. (Plural only when referring to different kinds, types, instances, or varieties. Number is expressed with *stick(s) of gum.*) □ *I stepped on some gum that someone had dropped.* Ⓒ *The sugared gums are too sweet for me. I prefer sugar-free.* **2.** *n.* the upper or lower ridge of flesh that covers the jaw bones and surrounds the bases of the teeth. □ *The dentist says my gums are pink and healthy.*

**gun** ['gʌn] **1.** *n.* a weapon that shoots bullets. □ *I held the gun in my hand and pulled the trigger.* **2.** *n.* a device or tool that has a handle and trigger like ①, used for applying or installing something. □ *Bill used a staple gun to staple the shingles onto the roof.*

**gush** ['gʌʃ] **1.** *n.* a large flow of a fluid. □ *When I turned on the faucet, water came out in a gush.* **2.** *iv.* to flow out rapidly and in large amounts. □ *Oil gushed out of the well.* **3.** *tv.* to allow a fluid to flow; to make a flow of fluid. □ *The cut on my wrist gushed blood.*

**gust** ['gʌst] **1.** *n.* a strong rush of wind or smoke. □ *The truck sent a gust of smoke from its exhaust pipe.* **2.** *iv.* [for the wind] to move in short, strong bursts. □ *The wind gusted and howled all through the night.*

**gut** ['gʌt] **1.** *n.* the area of the intestine or stomach. (No plural form.) □ *The horse has some sort of disorder in the gut.* **2. guts** *n.* the intestines. (Treated as plural, but not countable. Colloquial.) □ *The bully slugged Bob in the guts.* **3. guts** *n.* courage. (Treated as plural, but not countable. Colloquial.) □ *I wish I had the guts to challenge the corrupt mayor.* **4.** *tv.* to take the intestines and organs out of an animal. □ *I cleaned and gutted the fish before I fried it.*

**gutter** ['gʌt ɚ] **1.** *n.* a metal channel hanging on the edge of a roof to carry away water when it rains. □ *The violent storm ripped the gutters away from the roof.* **2.** *n.* the wide, wooden channel on either side of a bowling lane. □ *The bowling ball slowly rolled down the gutter.* **3.** *n.* on a street, a lower, formed channel that leads water and other waste to the entrance of a sewer. □ *My wallet is wet because I dropped it in the gutter.*

**guy** ['gɑɪ] **1.** *n.* a man; a boy. (Informal.) □ *Bill went drinking with the guys after work.* **2.** *n.* a person, male or female, usually in a group. (Informal.) □ *What do you guys want to do for dinner tonight?*

**gym** ['dʒɪm] **1.** *n.* a gymnasium. □ *I worked very hard at the gym today.* **2.** *adj.* <the adj. use of ①.> □ *I carried my gym clothes in my gym bag.*

**gymnasium** [dʒɪm 'nez i əm] *n.* a large room or building for physical education, physical training, or certain sports events such as basketball and wrestling. (Can be shortened to **gym.**) □ *The school dance was held in the gymnasium.*

**habit** ['hæb ɪt] **1.** *n.* an action that is done over and over, usually without thinking about it. □ *Anne made a habit of locking her door, even when she was at home.* **2.** *n.* an addiction; a strong need for drugs, tobacco, alcohol, etc. □ *Because of her smoking habit, Jane is often short of breath.* **3.** *n.* the uniform worn by a monk or a nun. □ *The man's habit indicated that he was a monk.*

**had** ['hæd] **1.** pt/pp of **have. 2.** *aux.* <the past-tense form of **have** ⑥, used in forming the past **perfect** verb form.> (Used before the past participle of a verb. Reduced to *'d* in contractions. See also **has.**) □ *Bill had put the toys away.*

**hadn't** ['hæd nt] *cont.* "had not." □ *Because John hadn't eaten breakfast, he was hungry.*

**hag** ['hæg] *n.* an ugly old woman; a witch. □ *Mary dressed up as a hag for Halloween.*

**hail** ['hel] **1.** *n.* round pellets of ice that fall from the sky like rain. (No plural form. Number is expressed with **hailstone(s).**) □ *Hail dented the roof of Lisa's car.* **2.** *n.* a group of things that come in small, sharp units. □ *The car was dented by a hail of pebbles falling from the truck ahead.* **3.** *n.* a continual series of demands, objections, questions, etc. □ *Bill refused to answer the hail of questions about the scandal.* **4.** *tv.* to greet or welcome someone with cheers, joy, and approval. □ *The city hailed the winning team with a parade.* **5.** *tv.* to honor and praise someone or something; to praise and approve something eagerly. □ *The president hailed the work of the legislature but vetoed the law.* **6.** *iv.* [for ①] to fall from the sky. □ *The sidewalks were dangerous after it hailed.*

**hailstone** ['hel ston] *n.* a small, round ball of ice that falls from the sky like rain. □ *After the storm, the street was covered with hailstones.*

**hailstorm** ['hel storm] *n.* a storm that produces or includes hail. □ *A hailstorm delayed the game.*

**hair** ['hɛr] **1.** *n.* the strands or fibers that grow on the body of an animal, especially the ones that grow on top of the heads of humans. (No plural form. Treated as singular.) □ *Mary dyed her hair black.* **2.** *n.* one of the strands or fibers that grow on the body of an animal as in ①. □ *Mary became angry when she found a hair in her soup.*

**hairbrush** ['hɛr brəʃ] *n.* a brush used for smoothing hair and making it look orderly. □ *Mary ran a hairbrush through her hair.*

**haircut** ['hɛr kət] **1.** *n.* an act or instance of cutting hair, especially the hair on top of someone's head. □ *I needed a haircut before going for my job interview.* **2.** *n.* the particular way that one's hair has been cut; a hair style. □ *Bob's short haircut makes him look like he's in the army.*

**hairy** ['hɛr i] *adj.* covered with hair; having a lot of hair. (Comp: *hairier;* sup: *hairiest.*) □ *The hairy dog left its fur all over the house.*

**half** ['hæf] **1.** *n., irreg.* either of two equal parts that form a complete thing. (Pl: **halves.**) □ *Which half of the sandwich do you want?* **2.** *n.* one **half** ① of the amount of things or people already mentioned or referred to. (Treated as singular or plural.) □ *Of all the people in the audience, only half really seemed* *to enjoy the movie.* **3.** *adj.* being ① of an amount; being one of two equal parts. □ *We walked a half mile to the bank.* **4.** *adv.* part of the way; not completely. □ *The potatoes were only half cooked.*

**hall** ['hɔl] **1.** *n.* a passage that connects rooms and stairways inside a house or building. □ *The bathroom is at the end of the hall and on the right.* **2.** *n.* a large room for big meetings, lectures, dances, etc. □ *The city council meets in the meeting hall every month.* **3.** *n.* a building where college students live, sleep, study, or have classes. □ *What hall are you living in?*

**hallway** ['hɔl we] *n.* a hall; a passage that connects rooms and stairways inside a house or building. □ *A hallway led through the house and out to the garage.*

**halt** ['hɔlt] **1.** *iv.* to stop. □ *The police ordered the thief to halt.* **2.** *tv.* to cause someone or something to stop. □ *The police officers in the street halted the thief.*

**halves** ['hævz] pl of **half**.

**ham** ['hæm] **1.** *n.* the upper part of a hog's rear hip and thigh, preserved by salt and a special kind of wood smoke. □ *I bought half a ham for the party.* **2.** *n.* ① eaten as food. (Plural only when referring to different kinds, types, instances, or varieties.) □ *I don't care for ham. It's too salty.* 🄲 *I've tried different hams, but I always long for the old country ham my mother used to serve.*

**hamburger** ['hæm bɚ gɚ] **1.** *n.* beef that has been ground into tiny bits. (No plural form.) □ *I browned some hamburger in a skillet.* **2.** *n.* a sandwich made of cooked ground beef and a specially shaped bun. □ *I put pickles, onion, and mustard on my hamburger.*

**hammer** ['hæm ɚ] **1.** *n.* a tool with a heavy metal head that is used to pound nails or to break things. □ *I used the claw on one side of the hammer to remove a nail.* **2.** *tv.* to hit something with ①. □ *Bob missed the nail and accidentally hammered his thumb.*

**hand** ['hænd] **1.** *n.* the structure at the end of the arm used for grasping; the most distant part of the arm, below the wrist. □ *Jane writes with her left hand.* **2.** *n.* the cards given or dealt to someone in a card game; one session in a game of cards. □ *I won the last hand.* **3.** *n.* side; direction. (No plural form.) □ *At Bob's right hand stood his brother and his father.* **4.** *n.* one of the pointers on a clock or watch. □ *The second hand no longer works on my watch.* **5.** *tv.* to give something to someone by using one's **hands** ①. □ *Please hand that dish to me.* **6.** *adj.* <the adj. use of ①>. □ *Anne keeps a hand mirror in her purse.*

**handkerchief** ['hæŋ kɚ tʃɪf] *n.* a square of soft fabric used to wipe one's nose or face. □ *Bob blew his nose into his handkerchief.*

**handle** ['hæn dəl] **1.** *n.* the part of an object that is held onto so that the object can be used, moved, picked up, pushed, pulled, opened, or closed. □ *I gripped the handle tightly and lifted the pot.* **2.** *tv.* to feel someone or something with one's hands; to use one's hands on someone or something. □ *The book was damaged by readers who had handled it with dirty hands.* **3.** *iv.* [for something] to work in a certain way while being used; [for a vehicle or boat] to be guided, driven, or steered. □ *My little car does not handle well in the snow.*

**handsome** ['hæn səm] **1.** *adj.* very attractive; [of a male] very good-looking. (Adv: *handsomely.* Comp: *handsomer;* sup: *handsomest.*) □ *The handsome actor got lots of attention from the audience.* **2.** *adj.* ample; generous; more than enough. (Adv: *handsomely.* Comp: *handsomer;* sup: *handsomest.*) □ *The antique chair brought a handsome price at the auction.*

**hang** ['hæŋ] **1.** *tv., irreg.* to suspend something from a higher place, using a rope, chain, etc. (Pt/pp: **hung**.) □ *Mary plans to hang the flower pot from a hook in the ceiling.* **2.** *tv., irreg.* to attach something to a wall. □ *Tom hung a mirror over the mantel.* **3.** *tv.* to execute a person by suspending the person by the neck. (Pt/pp: *hanged* for this sense.) □ *The prisoner was hanged at midnight.* **4.** *iv., irreg.* to be suspended over something; to remain above some place or thing. □ *A light bulb hangs over my desk.* **5. hang (around); hang (out)** *iv., irreg. (+ adv.)* to waste time somewhere; to do nothing for a period of time. □ *The kids hung around and did nothing during the summer.*

**hangar** ['hæŋ ɚ] *n.* a large building where airplanes are stored and serviced. □ *The plane taxied toward the hangar.*

**hanger** ['hæŋ ɚ] *n.* a wooden, metal, or plastic frame for suspending clothing inside a closet. □ *Bob put his suit on the hanger and hung it in the closet.*

**happen** ['hæp ən] **1.** *iv.* to occur; to take place. □ *We know what happens when you drop an egg. Yes, it makes a mess.* **2. happen to** do something *iv. + inf.* to do something by chance, without planning to do it; to have the good or bad fortune to do something. □ *Did you happen to see Mary today?* **3. happen to** someone or something *iv. + prep. phr.* to be done to someone or something; to be experienced by someone or something. □ *You won't believe what happened to me at the parade!*

**happiness** ['hæp i nəs] *n.* being happy; being glad or joyful. (No plural form.) □ *The lovely wedding ceremony filled the guests with happiness.*

**happy** ['hæp i] **1.** *adj.* [of someone or some creature] feeling or showing joy or being in a good mood; [of someone] glad, pleased, or willing. (Adv: *happily.* Comp: *happier;* sup: *happiest.*) □ *I am happy to accept your kind invitation.* **2.** *adj.* causing joy; joyful. (Adv: *happily.* Comp: *happier;* sup: *happiest.*) □ *An anniversary is a happy occasion.*

**harbor** ['hɑr bɚ] **1.** *n.* a sheltered port where ships and boats can anchor safely. □ *A tugboat will guide the ship into the harbor.* **2.** *tv.* to keep something in one's mind, especially bad feelings toward someone. □ *The bully harbored a plan for revenge against the teacher who had punished him.*

**hard** ['hɑrd] **1.** *adj.* firm; solid; not soft. (Comp: *harder;* sup: *hardest.*) □ *The plants wouldn't grow in the hard ground.* **2.** *adj.* difficult; not easy to do. (Comp: *harder;* sup: *hardest.*) □ *Few students were able to solve the hardest math problem.* **3.** *adj.* severe; harsh; demanding. (Comp: *harder;* sup: *hardest.*) □ *Losing both parents was a hard experience for Jimmy.* **4.** *adj.* forceful; violent; not gentle. (Comp: *harder;* sup: *hardest.*) □ *We could hear the hard rain pounding on the roof.* **5.** *adj.* [of water] having a high mineral content. (Comp: *harder;* sup: *hardest.*) □ *The hard water had a bitter taste.* **6.** *adv.* with great force or energy. (Comp: *harder;* sup: *hardest.*) □ *The wind blows hard during a blizzard.*

**hardly** ['hɑrd li] *adv.* barely; almost not at all. □ *With her sore throat, Mary could hardly talk.*

**harm** ['hɑrm] **1.** *n.* mental or physical damage to someone or something. (No plural form.) □ *The storm caused great harm to the house.* **2.** *tv.* to damage someone or something. □ *The accident harmed five people and damaged two cars.*

**harmful** ['hɑrm fʊl] *adj.* causing damage or harm to someone or something. (Adv: *harmfully.*) □ *Eating too much fat can be harmful to your health.*

**harmony** ['hɑr mə ni] **1.** *n.* the effect of different musical notes that are played or sung together with a pleasant sound.

(Plural only when referring to different kinds, types, instances, or varieties.) □ *Members of the choir blended their voices in perfect harmony.* Ⓒ *Modern composers seem to use different harmonies from those I am used to.* **2.** *n.* agreement; peace. (No plural form. Fig. on ①.) □ *I lived in harmony with six friends in a large house.*

**harp** ['hɑrp] **1.** *n.* a musical instrument having strings attached to a frame of wood. □ *The musician's hands moved swiftly over the harp's strings.* **2. harp on** something *iv. + prep. phr.* to keep talking about something until everyone is tired of hearing about it. (Informal.) □ *Please stop harping on this subject!*

**harsh** ['hɑrʃ] **1.** *adj.* rough; unpleasant to look at or listen to; unpleasant to touch, taste, or smell. (Adv: *harshly.* Comp: *harsher;* sup: *harshest.*) □ *The harsh towel irritated my skin.* **2.** *adj.* mean; cruel; severe. (Adv: *harshly.* Comp: *harsher;* sup: *harshest.*) □ *The judge gave the criminal a harsh sentence.*

**harvest** ['hɑr vəst] **1.** *n.* the gathering of a crop of grain, fiber, fruit, vegetables, or other foods. □ *The harvest was difficult because we had bad weather.* **2.** *n.* the total amount of grain, fiber, fruit, or vegetables produced in an area. □ *The entire corn harvest was lost because of the heavy rain.* **3.** *tv.* to collect a crop of grain, fiber, fruit, or vegetables when it is ready. □ *The workers harvested the apples.*

**has** ['hæz] **1.** *tv.* <the present-tense form of **have** used for the third-person singular, that is, with *he, she, it,* and singular nouns.> □ *Bill has a new car.* **2.** *aux.* <the present-tense form of **have** ⑥ used for the third-person singular, that is, with *he, she, it,* and singular nouns, in forming the present **perfect** verb form.> (Used before the past participle of a verb. Reduced to *'s* in contractions.) □ *Where has Mary gone?*

**hat** ['hæt] *n.* an article of clothing shaped to cover the head. □ *Please take your hat off when you're indoors.*

**hatch** ['hætʃ] **1.** *n.* an opening in a wall, ceiling, or floor. □ *The pilot closed and locked the airplane hatch.* **2.** *iv.* [for a baby bird or reptile] to break an eggshell from the inside and come out. □ *The children watched in awe as the baby robin hatched.*

**hate** ['het] **1.** *n.* intense dislike. (No plural form.) □ *Driven by hate, the mob attacked the foreigner.* **2.** *tv.* to dislike someone or something intensely. □ *Sue hates cats and will not go near them.* **3. hate to** do something *iv. + inf.* to strongly dislike doing something. □ *I hate to drive in heavy traffic.*

**haul** ['hɔl] **1.** *tv.* to carry something, using force; to drag something heavy. □ *We hauled the boxes to the basement.* **2.** *tv.* to carry or bring someone or something by truck or other vehicle. □ *The moving truck hauled our furniture to the new house.* **3.** *n.* an instance of traveling from one place to another, and the distance, time, or effort involved. □ *Covering the entire distance in one day will be quite a haul.*

**have** ['hæv] **1.** *tv., irreg.* to own something; to possess something; to possess a quality. (Pt/pp: **had;** in the present tense, the third-person singular form is **has.**) □ *Bob has a wonderful sense of humor.* **2.** *tv., irreg.* to undergo something; [for something] to happen to oneself; to experience something. □ *Bill and Jane had an argument.* **3.** *tv., irreg.* to eat or drink something; to consume something. □ *Make sure you have a glass of milk before you go to bed.* **4.** *tv., irreg.* to cause something to be done; to cause someone or something to do something. □ *Mary will have the car cleaned today.* **5. have to** do something *iv., irreg. + inf.* to be obligated to do something; must do something. □ *Bill has to do* *homework tonight.* **6.** *aux.* <an auxiliary verb that is used to form the **perfect** verb forms, which show that an action is completed.> (Used before the past participle of a verb. The form **have**, which is used with *I, we, you, they,* and plural nouns to form the present **perfect** is reduced to *'ve* in contractions. See also **had, has.**) □ *We have visited the zoo twice since June.*

**have-nots** ['hæv 'nɑts] *n.* people who do not have enough money to live comfortably. □ *Bob says that there are too few haves and too many have-nots in the world.*

**haves** ['hævz] *n.* people who have enough money to live comfortably; people who are rich and privileged. □ *There are fewer haves than have-nots in the world.*

**hawk** ['hɔk] **1.** *n.* a bird of prey, similar to a falcon, with a strong beak and claws, a long tail, and good eyesight. □ *The hawk caught the mouse in its claws.* **2.** *tv.* to sell something, especially in the street. □ *The children hawked lemonade from a table on the sidewalk.*

**hay** ['he] *n.* grass or plants cut, dried, and used as food for cattle. (No plural form.) □ *Horses and cows eat hay.*

**he** ['hi] **1.** *pron.* <a third-person singular masculine pronoun.> (Refers to male creatures. Used as a subject of a sentence or a clause. See also **him, himself,** and **his.**) □ *My puppy is hungry. He wants to eat.* □ *Tom is sad because he lost his dog.* **2.** *pron.* <a third-person singular pronoun.> (Used when the sex of a grammatical subject is not important, indeterminate, undetermined, or irrelevant. Objected to by some as actually referring only to males in this sense. Compare this with ⑤. See also **they** ②.) □ *Each runner should get to the finish line as fast as he can.* **3.** *n.* a male person or creature. □ *Is your new baby a she or a he?* **4. he or she** *phr.* [where there is known to be a choice between male and female] either **he** ① or **she** ①. □ *John and Mary arrived at noon, and either he or she left the door open.* **5. he or she** *phr.* <a third-person singular pronoun.> (Used when the sex of a grammatical subject is not important, indeterminate, undetermined, or irrelevant. Also used to establish that both sexes are involved.) □ *Each runner should get to the finish line as fast as he or she can.*

**head** ['hɛd] **1.** *n.* the part of the body of humans and animals above the neck, including the face, eyes, nose, mouth, ears, brain, and skull. □ *Sue laid her head on her pillow and fell asleep.* **2.** *n.* the brain; the mind. □ *You can solve the problem if you will just use your head.* **3.** *n.* an individual animal, used especially in counting cows, horses, and sheep. (No plural form. Always a singular form preceded by words that tell how many.) □ *Fourteen head of cattle were led into the barn.* **4. head of cabbage; head of lettuce** *n.* the edible top part of a cabbage or a lettuce plant. □ *Please buy a couple of heads of lettuce at the market.* **5.** *n.* the leader of a company, country, organization, group, etc.; a chief; someone who is in charge. □ *Only the head of the organization can make the important decisions.* **6.** *n.* the top, front, or upper part of something, such as a table, a page, a sheet of paper, a line [of people], or a [school] class. □ *The host sat at the head of the table.* **7.** *adj.* primary; chief; foremost. (Prenominal only.) □ *I am an assistant to the head teacher.* **8.** *tv.* to lead a group of people; to be in charge of a group of people or part of a company. □ *Jane was chosen to head the committee after Bill retired.* **9.** *iv.* to move in a certain direction. □ *At closing time, the shoppers headed out of the store.*

**headache** ['hɛd ek] **1.** *n.* a pain in the head, especially one that lasts a long time. □ *A severe headache made it hard for Mike to think.* **2.** *n.* a problem; a bother; a worry. (Fig. on ①.) □ *Driving in the city is a headache because there are too many cars.*

**health** ['hɛlθ] **1.** *n.* freedom from diseases of the mind or the body. (No plural form.) □ *Sue is in good health because she exercises and eats properly.* **2.** *n.* vigor; general condition. (No plural form. Fig. on ①.) □ *The general health of the nation's economy was not good.* **3.** *adj.* <the adj. use of ①>; promoting ①. □ *The company offered its employees health insurance.*

**heap** ['hip] *n.* a large pile of things; a stack of things piled together. □ *Don't leave your dirty laundry in a heap in the middle of the floor!*

**hear** ['hɪr] **1.** *iv., irreg.* to be able to sense or experience sounds by means of the ears. (Pt/pp: **heard.**) □ *I could hear better when I was younger.* **2.** *tv., irreg.* to sense or receive a certain sound or a certain utterance. □ *Did you hear that noise?* **3.** *tv., irreg.* to learn that something has happened. (The object can be a clause with **that** ⑦.) □ *We heard that Sam had an accident.* **4.** *tv., irreg.* [for a court of law] to listen to the two sides of a court case. □ *The judge agreed to hear the case next week.* **5.** *tv., irreg.* to pay attention to someone or something; to listen to someone or something. (The object can be a clause with **that** ⑦.) □ *You are not hearing what I am telling you!*

**heard** ['hɝd] pt/pp of **hear**.

**heart** ['hɑrt] **1.** *n.* a large, four-chambered muscle that pumps blood throughout the body. □ *When I place my hand over my chest, I can feel my heart beating.* **2.** *n.* ① considered as a symbol of the center of a person's emotions, thoughts, and love. (Fig. on ①.) □ *John loves Lisa with all his heart.* **3.** *n.* the shape ♥. □ *Jane's skirt had a pattern of tiny hearts all over it.* **4.** *n.* [in a deck of playing cards] one card of a group of cards that bears a red ♥. □ *Susan has four hearts in her hand.* **5. the heart** *n.* the most central, essential, or vital part of something; the core of something. (No plural form. Treated as singular. Fig. on ①.) □ *At the heart of the problem is the need for education.* **6. hearts** *n.* the playing cards that have the symbol ♥. (Treated as singular or plural.) □ *The king of hearts captured the ten of diamonds.*

**heat** ['hit] **1.** *n.* hotness; the quality that is felt as a higher temperature. (No plural form.) □ *The heat of the fire warmed the room.* **2.** *n.* hot weather. (No plural form.) □ *The summer heat was unbearable.* **3.** *n.* a grouping of contestants in a sporting event. (The winners of different **heats** compete in later **heats** or the final event.) □ *The winners of the five heats advanced to the final game.* **4.** *tv.* to cause something to become hotter. □ *The sun heated the water in the lake.* **5.** *iv.* to become hotter or warmer. □ *Dinner is heating in the oven.*

**heaven** ['hɛv ən] **1.** *n.* [in certain religions] the place where God resides and where the souls of good people go after death. (Usually associated with the sky. No plural form.) □ *The minister asked me if I felt that I would go to heaven.* **2. the heavens** *n.* the sky; space. (Treated as plural.) □ *The heavens opened up, and the rain came pouring down.*

**heavy** ['hɛv i] **1.** *adj.* weighing a lot; of great weight. (Adv: *heavily.* Comp: *heavier;* sup: *heaviest.*) □ *The heavy sled had to be pulled by six dogs.* **2.** *adj.* [of sound] strong, deep, and ponderous. (Adv: *heavily.* Comp: *heavier;* sup: *heaviest.*) □ *The music was too heavy in the low notes.* **3.** *adj.* great in amount; dense; intense; thick. (Adv: *heavily.* Comp: *heavier;* sup: *heaviest.*) □ *A* *heavy snowfall blanketed the town.* **4.** *adj.* serious; requiring a lot of thought to understand. (Adv: *heavily.* Comp: *heavier;* sup: *heaviest.*) □ *On the weekend, I do not want to listen to a heavy lecture about economics.*

**hectic** ['hɛk tɪk] *adj.* very active; very excited; very busy. (Adv: *hectically* [...ɪk li].) □ *After a hectic day, Jane was exhausted.*

**heed** ['hid] *tv.* to pay close attention to something, such as advice. (See also **take heed.**) □ *Children should heed their parents' instructions.*

**heel** ['hil] **1.** *n.* the back part of the foot; the part of the foot that bears the weight of the body. □ *Bob stopped running when he injured his heel.* **2.** *n.* the part of a shoe or sock that covers the back part of the foot. □ *The heel of Dave's sock had a hole in it.* **3.** *n.* the part of a shoe that supports the back part of the foot. □ *I like shoes with rubber heels.* **4. heels** *n.* shoes with tall **heels** ③, worn by women, usually on formal occasions. (Short for **high heels.** Treated as plural, but not countable. Number is expressed with *pair(s) of heels.*) □ *Wearing heels makes my feet hurt!*

**height** ['hɑɪt] **1.** *n.* the amount that someone or something is tall; vertical length [of a person or of a vertical object]. (No plural form.) □ *The men in our family are of average height.* **2.** *n.* the length of something from bottom to top; the distance to a higher point from a lower level. □ *The height of this flagpole is 15 feet.*

**heighten** ['hɑɪt n] **1.** *tv.* to cause something to become more intense or exciting. □ *The music heightened the suspense of the movie.* **2.** *iv.* to become more intense or exciting. □ *Our anxiety heightened as the day for the test grew nearer.*

**held** ['hɛld] pt/pp of **hold.**

**helicopter** ['hɛl ə kɑp tɚ] *n.* an aircraft with large, rotating blades. □ *The president's helicopter landed on the White House lawn.*

**he'll** ['hil] *cont.* "he will." □ *Bill says he'll paint the room next week.*

**hell** ['hɛl] **1.** *n.* [in certain religions] the place where the devil resides and where the souls of wicked people go after death. (No plural form. Sometimes capitalized.) □ *My brother says that hell sounds dull and painful, whereas heaven just sounds dull.* **2.** *n.* suffering, misery, and despair. (Fig. on ①. No plural form.) □ *A painful disease caused my aunt to live a life of hell.* **3.** *interj.* <a word used to indicate anger or surprise.> (Colloquial.) □ *Hell, I didn't know you were here!*

**hello** [hɛ 'lo] **1.** *n.* an act of greeting someone; an act of saying ②. (Pl ends in *-s.*) □ *The arriving passengers called their hellos to those on the dock.* **2.** *interj.* <a word used in greeting someone or in answering the telephone.> □ *Hello, my name is Lisa.*

**help** ['hɛlp] **1.** *n.* aid; assistance. (No plural form. Treated as singular.) □ *The lost child asked the police officer for help.* **2.** *n.* someone or a group hired to do a job, usually a service job. (No plural form. Treated as singular or plural, but not counted.) □ *After the party, the help cleaned up.* **3.** *iv.* to give assistance. □ *I need some assistance. Please help if you can.* **4.** *tv.* to give assistance to someone or something; to aid someone or something. □ *The pay raise helped me with my bills.* **5.** *tv.* to relieve an illness or condition; to ease the discomfort caused by something; to make a sickness or discomfort less severe. □ *This medicine will help your headache.* **6. Help!** *interj.* <a cry used when one needs aid or assistance.> □ *Help! I've been robbed!* **7. help (someone) do something** *phr.* to assist someone [to] do something. ☐ *I am too tired to help mow the grass.* ☐ *Mary helped her mother carry the groceries.*

**hem** ['hɛm] **1.** *n.* the folded and sewn edge of a piece of cloth. ☐ *The seamstress measured and sewed the hem of the dress.* **2.** *tv.* to make a nice, even edge on a piece of cloth by folding and sewing. ☐ *I will hem your skirt tomorrow.*

**hemisphere** ['hɛm əs fɪr] **1.** *n.* half of a sphere; half of a ball. ☐ *A plane that passes through a sphere's center forms two hemispheres.* **2.** *n.* one of two halves of the earth. ☐ *The Northern Hemisphere is north of the equator.*



**hen** ['hɛn] *n.* a female bird, especially a female chicken. ☐ *A hen and her chicks wandered across the barnyard.*

**her** ['hɚ] **1.** *pron.* <an objective form of **she**, referring to females.> (Used after prepositions and as the object of verbs.) ☐ *Anne asked me to help her paint the kitchen.* **2.** *pron.* <an objective form of **she**, referring to ships and certain countries.> (Also other informal uses.) ☐ *England is a great country, and we welcome her friendship.* **3.** *pron.* <a possessive form of **she**, referring to females.> (Used as a modifier before a noun. Compare this with **hers**.) ☐ *Why did Anne leave before eating her dinner?*

**herb** ['ɚb] *n.* a plant whose seeds or leaves are used for flavoring food or for medicines. ☐ *I put of lot of tasty herbs in the sauce.*

**herd** ['hɚd] **1.** *n.* a large group of cattle or other similar large animals such as elk, buffalo, zebra, elephants, etc. ☐ *A single cow strayed from the herd.* **2.** *tv.* to cause a large group of people or animals to move together. ☐ *The cowboys herded the cows toward the corrals.* **3.** *tv.* to take care of cattle, sheep, or other groups of animals. ☐ *The farmer's daughter herds the sheep in the meadow.* **4.** *iv.* to form into a group; to move as a group. ☐ *As the people left the movie, they herded into the street.*

**here** ['hɪr] **1.** *adv.* in, at, to, or from the location of the speaker or writer who uses this word. ☐ *Come here.* **2.** *adv.* now; at this point in time or in a process. ☐ *The director said "Pause here!" in the middle of the actor's speech.* **3.** *adv.* <a form that begins a sentence and is followed by a verb, which then is followed by the subject of the sentence.> (Often used to point out or offer something. Takes *be, go, stand, rest,* or a similar verb.) ☐ *Here are the tickets I promised you.* **4.** *n.* this place. ☐ *Why did you bring that dog in here?*

**heritage** ['hɛr ɪ tɪdʒ] *n.* the cultural background of a group of people. (No plural form.) ☐ *Italians have a heritage rich in music.*

**hermit** ['hɚ mɪt] *n.* someone who moves away from society and who lives alone in isolation. ☐ *The hermit lived in a tiny cottage in the woods.*

**hero** ['hɪr o] **1.** *n.* someone who is honored and respected for bravery or courage. (Compare this with **heroine**. Pl ends in *-es*.) ☐ *After rescuing the child, the firefighter was hailed as a hero.* **2.** *n.* the main male character in a story, movie, or play. (See also **heroine**. Pl ends in *-es*.) ☐ *The hero in the movie solved the mystery.*

**heroic** [hɪ 'ro ɪk] *adj.* courageous; brave; valiant. (Adv: *heroically* [...ɪk li].) ☐ *David was awarded a medal for his heroic rescue of the child.*

**heroine** ['hɛr o ɪn] **1.** *n.* a brave and courageous woman; a woman who does heroic actions. (Compare this with **hero**.) ☐ *The heroine saved the children from the fire.* **2.** *n.* the main female character in a story, movie, or play. (See also **hero**.) ☐ *The heroine in this musical sings five songs.*

**hers** ['hɚz] *pron.* <a possessive form of **she**.> (Used in place of a noun. Compare this with **her**.) □ *I asked my friends for a pencil, and Anne gave me one of hers.*

**herself** [hɚ 'sɛlf] **1.** *pron.* <the reflexive form of **she**.> (Used after a verb or a preposition when the subject of the sentence is the same female to which the pronoun refers.) □ *Did Sue hurt herself when she fell down?* **2.** *pron.* <an emphatic form of **she**.> (Follows the nominal that is being emphasized.) □ *Susan herself greeted us at the door.* **3. by herself** *phr.* with the help of no one else. □ *Susan is unable to get there by herself.* **4. by herself** *phr.* with no one else present; alone. □ *She sat by herself at a table big enough for six people.*

**he's** ['hiz] **1.** *cont.* "he is." □ *Bill said that he's going on vacation next week.* **2.** *cont.* "he has." (Where **has** is an auxiliary.) □ *I spoke to John. He's already purchased the tickets.*

**hid** ['hɪd] pt of **hide**.

**hidden** ['hɪd n] pp of **hide**.

**hide** ['hɑɪd] **1.** *tv., irreg.* to place something out of view; to place something so that it cannot be seen; to conceal something. (Pt: **hid**; pp: **hidden**.) □ *The dog hides his bones in the garden.* **2.** *iv., irreg.* to place oneself so that one cannot be seen; to conceal oneself. □ *You can't see John in this picture. He's hiding behind that tree.* **3.** *n.* the skin of an animal, especially when used to make leather. □ *The hide was large enough to make two pairs of shoes.*

**high** ['hɑɪ] **1.** *adj.* far above the ground; further above than the average; not low. (Comp: *higher;* sup: *highest.*) □ *Put the candy on a high shelf where the children can't reach it.* **2.** *adj.* extending a certain distance upward; at or reaching a particular distance above the ground or above sea level. (Follows the measure of height. Comp: *higher.*) □ *That tall building is 50 stories high.* **3.** *adj.* great in power, rank, or importance. (Adv: *highly.* Comp: *higher;* sup: *highest.*) □ *The information was given to the reporter by a high official in the government.* **4.** *adj.* [of heat, number, pitch, price, velocity, intelligence, standards, etc.] great or strong, or greater or stronger than what is normal or average. (Adv: *highly.* Comp: *higher;* sup: *highest.*) □ *Slow down! Don't drive at such a high speed.* **5.** *n.* the top point; a peak. □ *Our sales are at a high for the year.* **6.** *adv.* to or at a place that is far up. (Comp: *higher;* sup: *highest.*) □ *Jimmy climbed high in the tree and then was afraid to come down.*

**high heels** ['hɑɪ 'hilz] *n.* women's shoes having long or tall heels. (Treated as plural, but not countable. Can be shortened to **heels**.) □ *High heels will make you look much taller.*

**highly** ['hɑɪ li] *adv.* <the adv. form of **high** ③>; very much. (Comp: *higher;* sup: *highest.*) □ *This paper is highly important. Please take care of it.*

**high school** ['hɑɪ skul] **1.** *n.* a school for students who have finished the lower grades of school. □ *After high school, you can go to college.* **2. high-school** *adj.* <the adj. use of ①.> □ *I remember my high-school days very well.*

**highway** ['hɑɪ we] *n.* a main road—especially one designed for high speed—used to get from one city to another. □ *Several major highways go right through the city.*

**hike** ['hɑɪk] **1.** *n.* a long walk, especially in the woods, mountains, etc. □ *I like to take a hike to get exercise.* **2.** *iv.* to travel or walk as in ①. □ *We hiked through the woods until we reached the lake.*

**hiker** ['hɑɪk ɚ] *n.* someone who hikes. □ *The hiker traveled four miles before noon.*

**hill** ['hɪl] **1.** *n.* a raised part of the earth's surface smaller than a mountain. □ *We* *climbed to the top of the smallest hill.* **2.** *n.* a heap or mound of earth, especially one made by an animal. □ *The dog made a little hill where he buried his bone.*

**hilltop** ['hɪl tɑp] *n.* the top of a hill. □ *The view from the hilltop was breathtaking.*

**him** ['hɪm] **1.** *pron.* <an objective form of **he** ①.> (The pronoun used to refer to males. Used after prepositions and as the object of verbs.) □ *I will call him tomorrow.* □ *I did it for him.* **2.** *pron.* <an objective form of **he** ②.> (Used when the sex of a grammatical object of a verb or preposition is not important, indeterminate, undetermined, or irrelevant. Objected to by some as actually referring only to males in this sense. Compare this with ④. See also **them** ②.) □ *Everyone there will get what is coming to him.* **3. him or her** *phr.* [where there is known to be a choice between male and female] either **him** ① or **her** ①. □ *Both John and Mary are expecting phone calls, so when the telephone rings, it will probably be for him or her.* **4. him or her** *phr.* <a third-person plural objective pronoun.> (Used when the sex of a grammatical object of a verb or preposition is not important, indeterminate, undetermined, or irrelevant. Also used to establish that both sexes are involved.) □ *If someone calls, please tell him or her to call back later.*

**himself** [hɪm 'sɛlf] **1.** *pron.* <the reflexive form of **he** ①.> (Used after a verb or a preposition when the subject of the sentence is the same male to which the pronoun refers.) □ *John took himself out of the contest.* **2.** *pron.* <the reflexive form of **he** ②.> (Used after a verb or a preposition when the sex of the subject of the sentence is not important, indeterminate, undetermined, or irrelevant. This sense is objected to by some as actually referring only to males. Compare this with ⑥.) □ *Each candidate was asked to remove himself from the room.* **3.** *pron.* <an emphatic form of **him**.> (Follows the nominal being emphasized.) □ *The mayor himself will come to the reception.* **4. by himself** *phr.* with the help of no one else. (Refers only to a male.) □ *The two-year-old boy can get dressed by himself.* **5. by himself** *phr.* alone; with no one else present. (Refers only to a male.) □ *He is home by himself tonight.* **6. himself or herself** *phr.* <the reflexive form of **he** or **she**.> (Used after a verb or a preposition when the sex of the subject of the sentence is not important, indeterminate, undetermined, or irrelevant.) □ *Each citizen was invited to introduce himself or herself to the mayor.*

**hind** ['hɑɪnd] *adj.* positioned at the rear or back of something. (Prenominal only.) □ *The dog's hind leg was broken.*

**hinge** ['hɪndʒ] *n.* a jointed device that fits two things together so that one of the things, such as a door or gate, can move. □ *The garden gate swung open on its hinges.*

**hint** ['hɪnt] **1.** *n.* a clue; a suggestion that helps solve a puzzle or answer a question. □ *Mary gave Bill a hint about his birthday present.* **2.** *n.* a small trace; a little bit of something; a small amount. □ *There was a hint of pepper in the tomato sauce.* **3.** *tv.* to suggest ①; to provide ①. (The object is a clause with **that** ⑦.) □ *John hinted that he wanted a new shirt for his birthday.*

**hip** ['hɪp] **1.** *n.* the joint that connects the leg with the body; the area on each side of the body, below the waist, where the leg joins the trunk of the body. □ *The teacher stood with his hand on his hip and frowned.* **2.** *adj.* in style; fashionable. (Older slang. Comp: *hipper;* sup: *hippest.*) □ *Teenagers can tell you all the hip new words.*

**hippopotami** [hɪp ə 'pɑt ə mɑɪ] a pl of **hippopotamus**.

**hippopotamus** [hɪp ə 'pɑt ə məs] *n., irreg.* a large, roundish African animal that lives in and near rivers, having thick skin and no hair. (Pl: *hippopotamuses* or **hippopotami.**) □ *The hippopotamus has a large head and mouth.*

**hire** ['hɑɪɚ] *tv.* to employ someone at a job; to pay someone to do work. □ *I want to hire Bill, but he wants too much money.*

**his** ['hɪz] **1.** *pron.* <the possessive form of **he**, referring to a male who has already been mentioned.> (Comes before a noun.) □ *Mike said that it was his idea.* **2.** *pron.* <the possessive form of **he**, referring to a male who has already been mentioned.> (Used in place of a noun.) □ *Mike said that the idea was his.* **3.** *pron.* <the possessive form of **he**, referring to a person who has already been mentioned.> (Used when the sex of the person referred to is not important, indeterminate, undetermined, or irrelevant. Objected to by some as referring only to males in this sense. See also **their** ②.) □ *Everyone was told to take his seat.* **4.** *pron.* <the possessive form of **he**, referring to a person who has already been mentioned.> (Used in place of a noun. Used when the sex of the person referred to is not important, indeterminate, undetermined, or irrelevant. Objected to by some as actually referring only to males in this sense. Compare this with ⑥.) □ *None were left. Each student had taken his.* **5. his or her** *phr.* [where there is known to be a choice between male and female] either **his** ① or **her** ③. □ *Both John and Mary are expecting phone calls, so when the telephone rings, it will probably be his or her call.* **6. his or her** *phr.* <a third-person singular possessive pronoun.> (Used when the sex of the person referred to is not important, indeterminate, undetermined, or irrelevant. Also used to establish that both sexes are involved.) □ *Each student should hang his or her coat in the closet.*

**hiss** ['hɪs] **1.** *n.* the sound that a snake makes, a long [s] sound. □ *We heard the hiss before we saw the snake.* **2.** *iv.* to make ①. □ *The steam hissed as it escaped from the leaky pipe.*

**history** ['hɪs tə ri] **1.** *n.* the study of events that have happened. (No plural form.) □ *History fascinates Jane, especially life during the Middle Ages.* **2.** *n.* a record of events that have happened. □ *We have written a book showing the history of our family.* **3.** *n.* background; facts about the past of someone or something. □ *The history of this ship is interesting.*

**hit** ['hɪt] **1.** *tv., irreg.* to strike someone or something; to contact someone or something violently or with force. (Pt/pp: *hit.*) □ *The batter hit the ball.* **2.** *tv., irreg.* to reach something. □ *Our sales hit a record low for the year.* **3.** *n.* someone or something that is very successful. □ *The song quickly became a hit.* **4.** *n.* [in baseball] a play where the batter **hits** ① the ball with a bat and is able to get to a base safely. □ *The batter only had two hits in the game.* **5.** *adj.* [of music or performances] popular. (Prenominal only.) □ *Everyone was singing the hit song.*

**hive** ['hɑɪv] **1.** *n.* the box, container, or structure that bees live in. (See also **beehive.**) □ *The hive was full of honey.* **2. hives** *n.* any one of various skin diseases characterized by a rash. (Treated as singular or plural, but not countable.) □ *Bob's hives hurt and required constant care.*

**hobby** ['hɑb i] *n.* an activity that is done in one's spare time; an activity that one likes to do. □ *My hobby is reading books.*

**hobo** ['ho bo] *n.* a tramp; someone who travels from city to city looking for food or work. (Usually male. Pl ends in *-s* or

-*es*.) □ *The hobo asked the farmer if he could work in exchange for a meal.*

**hockey** ['hɑk i] *n.* a game, played on ice, where skaters try to hit a rubber disk into a goal area. (No plural form.) □ *During the winter, my friends and I play hockey.*

**hoe** ['ho] **1.** *n.* a garden tool consisting of a small blade attached to a long handle, used to remove weeds or to break up soil. □ *My hoe has a wooden handle and a metal blade.* **2.** *tv.* to use ① on something; to remove weeds or break up soil with ①. □ *David hated hoeing the garden in the hot sun.*

**hog** ['hɔg] **1.** *n.* a full-grown pig, especially one raised for food or to produce young. □ *Most hogs weigh more than a hundred pounds.* **2.** *n.* someone who is very greedy or messy. (Fig. on ①.) □ *Our house is so messy, people will think we are hogs.* **3.** *tv.* to take more than one's fair share of something. (Informal.) □ *My roommate hogs the TV on Sunday afternoons to watch sports.*

**hoist** ['hɔɪst] **1.** *n.* a device for lifting heavy things. □ *We will need a hoist to get the car out of the ditch.* **2.** *tv.* to raise something using ropes or chains. □ *We hoisted the car out of the ditch.*

**hold** ['hold] **1.** *tv., irreg.* to keep someone or something in one's arms or hands. (Pt/pp: **held**.) □ *Mary held her baby in her arms.* **2.** *tv., irreg.* to support the weight of someone or something; to bear the weight of someone or something. □ *Be careful! That old table can't hold such a heavy box.* **3.** *tv., irreg.* to grasp something so it remains in a certain position. □ *Hold the mirror in the light so I can see.* **4.** *tv., irreg.* to reserve something; to set something aside, waiting for further action. □ *Please hold a table for two for dinner.* **5.** *tv., irreg.* to contain something; to have enough room for something. □ *I've eaten enough. I can't hold any more food.* **6.** *tv., irreg.* to cause an event to take place. □ *Let's hold the party next week.* **7.** *tv., irreg.* to retain a certain position or condition. □ *Hold that position while I get my camera.* **8.** *tv., irreg.* to restrain someone or something; to keep someone or something in control. □ *The leash couldn't hold the strong and active dog.* **9.** *iv., irreg.* to withstand a strain; not to break under pressure. □ *When we pull hard on the rope, will this knot hold?* **10.** *iv., irreg.* to remain connected to a telephone line while one's call has been temporarily suspended—so the caller or the person who was called can talk on another telephone line. □ *Please hold. I've got another call coming in.* **11. hold out** *iv., irreg. + adv.* to endure; to last. □ *I cannot hold out much longer. Please help me.* **12.** *n.* a grasp; a grip. □ *When I released my hold on the puppy, it ran away.* **13.** *n.* a good or secure grasp of something. □ *The climber took a good hold on the rock.* **14.** *n.* the place in a ship or plane where cargo is stored. □ *The hold was full when the ship left port.*

**holder** ['hold ɚ] *n.* something that holds something; something that keeps something in a certain position. □ *Where is the holder for the postage stamps?*

**holdup** ['hold əp] **1.** *n.* a robbery, especially one committed with a gun; a stickup. □ *My neighbor was the victim of a holdup at the train station.* **2.** *n.* a delay; the reason that something is not moving properly. □ *The traffic holdup made Jane miss her plane.*

**hole** ['hol] *n.* an opening made in or through a solid object; an opening in the surface of something. □ *The carpenter cut a hole in the wall for a window.*

**holiday** ['hɑl ə de] **1.** *n.* a period of time when most businesses and schools are closed in honor of someone or something. □ *Thanksgiving is a national holiday, and most businesses are closed.* **2.** *n.*

a holy day; a religious celebration. □ *Important Jewish holidays are Yom Kippur and Rosh Hashanah.*

**hollow** ['hɑl o] **1.** *n.* an open space inside an object; a cavity. □ *The fox lived in a hollow in the rocks.* **2.** *n.* a small valley; a sunken area of land. □ *There was a stream at the bottom of the hollow.* **3.** *adj.* having an open space inside; not solid. (Adv: *hollowly.* Comp: *hollower;* sup: *hollowest.*) □ *A basketball is hollow, but a baseball is not.* **4.** *adj.* sunken. (Adv: *hollowly.* Comp: *hollower;* sup: *hollowest.*) □ *The sick child had sad eyes and hollow cheeks.*

**holster** ['hol stɚ] *n.* a fabric or leather case for a gun, worn on the body or attached to a saddle. □ *The sheriff's leather holster held a heavy gun.*

**holy** ['hol i] *adj.* sacred; associated with divine matters. (Comp: *holier;* sup: *holiest.*) □ *The Bible is a holy book.*

**home** ['hom] **1.** *n.* the place where one lives; one's house or apartment. □ *Mary invited me to dinner at her home.* **2.** *n.* the place where someone was born; the place that someone comes from; the place where someone grew up. □ *Tom's home is Los Angeles, and his parents still live there in the same house where he was born.* **3.** *n.* an institution or building where people who need special care live. □ *A new home for retired people is being built in town.* **4.** *n.* a place where something is found, based, or located; a place where something originated or was invented. □ *Detroit, Michigan, is the home of the U.S. auto industry.* **5.** *adj.* <the adj. use of ①.> □ *Anne's home city is Boston.* **6.** *adj.* <the adj. use of ④.> □ *The basketball team won most of its games on its home court.* **7.** *adv.* at ① or ②; to ① or ②. □ *Mary phoned home once a week.*

**homemaker** ['hom mek ɚ] *n.* a person who manages a home, especially a married woman who manages her home and, possibly, children. □ *The homemaker picked up her children after school at three o'clock.*

**home office** ['hom 'ɔf ɪs] **1.** *n.* the central office of a company. □ *The company's home office is in New York.* **2.** *n.* an office in one's home. □ *Tom is a salesman and does his paperwork in his home office.*

**homeowner** ['hom o nɚ] *n.* someone who owns a home. □ *Homeowners spend a lot of money on repairs.*

**homesick** ['hom sɪk] *adj.* sad and depressed because one is away from one's home. □ *The homesick college student left school and went home.*

**homework** ['hom wɚk] **1.** *n.* schoolwork that is to be completed at home or elsewhere outside the school building. (No plural form.) □ *Anne does her homework at the library.* **2.** *n.* preparation that should be done before a meeting or discussion. (Fig. on ①. No plural form.) □ *Before a job interview, it is good to do your homework and learn about the company.*

**honest** ['ɑn əst] **1.** *adj.* always telling the truth; not lying; able to be trusted. (Adv: *honestly.*) □ *The honest person returned the lost wallet to its owner.* **2.** *adj.* obtained fairly and legally; not stolen. (Adv: *honestly.*) □ *Every dollar that Tom earned was an honest dollar.* **3.** *adj.* sincere; appearing fair and ①. (Adv: *honestly.*) □ *With her honest face, Mary is trusted by everyone.*

**honesty** ['ɑn ɪs ti] *n.* the quality of being honest; truthfulness. (No plural form.) □ *You can trust Bob, because he is well known for his honesty.*

**honey** ['hʌn i] *n.* a sweet, sticky substance made by bees. (Plural only when referring to different kinds, types, instances, or varieties.) □ *The beehive is full of honey.* Ⓒ *We were able to sample* *a few different local honeys at the county fair.*

**honk** ['hɔŋk] **1.** *n.* the sound made by a horn or a goose. □ *I heard the honk of the car behind me.* **2.** *iv.* to make the sound of a horn or a goose. □ *As it pulled up in the drive, the taxi honked.* **3.** *tv.* to sound a horn; to cause a horn to make a noise. □ *The angry driver honked her horn at the truck.*

**honor** ['ɑn ɚ] **1.** *n.* the respect or regard shown to someone or something. (No plural form.) □ *Honor is due to those who died in battle.* **2.** *n.* character and integrity; honesty and fairness; a way of being that earns trust. (No plural form.) □ *Anne is a woman of honor.* **3.** *n.* a pleasure; a privilege. □ *David felt that it was a great honor to meet the president.* **4.** *tv.* to hold someone in high regard; to respect someone. □ *We honor those soldiers who died in wars.* **5.** *tv.* to make a payment as agreed; for a bank to accept a check and pay out the money that the check was written for. □ *The bank refuses to honor the check that I wrote.*

H

**hood** ['hʊd] **1.** *n.* a covering for the head and neck, sometimes attached to a coat and sometimes also covering the face. □ *The child hung up his coat by its hood.* **2.** *n.* the metal panel that covers the top of the front of a car. □ *The mechanic lifted the hood to look at the engine.*

**hoof** ['hʊf, 'huf] *n., irreg.* the hard part on the bottom of the foot of a horse, deer, and certain other animals. (Pl: **hooves**.) □ *I need to have a new shoe put on my horse's left front hoof.*

**hook** ['hʊk] **1.** *n.* a bent or curved piece of plastic, wood, wire, or metal, used to catch, pull, or hold something. □ *I hung my coat up on a hook in the closet.* **2.** *n.* [in boxing] a short blow given while one's elbow is bent. □ *The boxer was known for repeated right-hand hooks.* **3.** *tv.* to catch and pull something with ①. □ *The unlucky fisherman hooked a sunken log.*

**hoot** ['hut] **1.** *n.* the noise that an owl makes. □ *The owl's hoot echoed through the canyon.* **2.** *iv.* to make ①; to make a noise like ①. □ *When the owl hooted, it scared me very much!*

**hooves** ['huvz] pl of **hoof**.

**hop** ['hɑp] **1.** *n.* a small movement upward, like a jump. □ *Mary did a little hop when she stepped on the hot sand.* **2.** *n.* an airplane flight, especially a short one. □ *My flight is just a hop, so I'll be there in about an hour.* **3.** *iv.* to jump up and down; to jump forward a small distance. □ *The excited child hopped up and down with glee.* **4.** *iv.* [for frogs, rabbits, kangaroos, etc.] to move by jumping. □ *The frog hopped away as we approached.* **5. hop in** something *iv. + prep. phr.* to get into a car, truck, van, or taxi quickly to make a quick or short trip. □ *Anne hopped in her car and drove to the store.* **6. hop on** something *iv. + prep. phr.* to board a plane, train, bus, or bicycle to make a quick trip. □ *Anne hopped on a plane to go to New York.*

**hope** ['hop] **1.** *n.* the happy feeling that something one wants to happen will actually happen. (No plural form.) □ *The negotiations provided the hostages' families with hope.* **2.** *n.* something that is desired; something that one wants to happen; an expectation. □ *Jane said her hope is to buy a new car next month.* **3.** *tv.* to feel happy about and wish for something that one wants to happen in the future. (The object is a clause with **that** ⑦.) □ *I hope that the train will arrive when it is supposed to.* **4. hope to do something** *phr.* to feel happy about and wish to do something in the future. □ *I hope to go to Europe in the future.*

**horizon** [hə 'rɑɪ zən] **1.** *n.* the line in the distance where the sky seems to meet the earth. □ *At daybreak, the sun rose up over the horizon.* **2. on the horizon**

*phr.* soon to happen. □ *Do you know what's on the horizon?*

**horizontal** [hor ə 'zɑn təl] *adj.* flat; parallel to flat ground; not up and down. (Adv: *horizontally.*) □ *We built the tree house on a large, horizontal branch.*

**horn** ['horn] **1.** *n.* the hard substance that an animal's **horn** ② or hoof is made of. (No plural form.) □ *A letter opener, made of horn, lay on Anne's desk.* **2.** *n.* a hard, usually pointed growth on the heads of cattle, goats, antelope, sheep, etc. □ *The bull lowered its horns and ran toward us.* **3.** *n.* a device that makes noise, as in a car or other vehicle. □ *Jimmy has a horn on his bike.* **4.** *n.* one of the brass musical instruments, such as the trumpet, the cornet, the tuba, the French horn, and the trombone, played by blowing air through a shaped tube. (Often in compounds.) □ *The French horn is a difficult instrument to learn to play.*

**hornet** ['hor nɪt] *n.* a large kind of stinging wasp. □ *Hornets built a nest at the corner of our house.*

**horrible** ['hor ə bəl] **1.** *adj.* causing horror or terror. (Adv: *horribly.*) □ *I ran to my window when I heard the horrible scream.* **2.** *adj.* awful; bad. (Adv: *horribly.*) □ *No one would eat the horrible cake.*

**horrify** ['hor ə fɑɪ] *tv.* to frighten someone very badly; to terrify someone. □ *The ghost story horrified the children.*

**horror** ['hor ɚ] **1.** *n.* intense dread or fear; fright. (Plural only when referring to different kinds, types, instances, or varieties.) □ *I never felt such horror as when my house caught fire.* Ⓒ *The horrors we had as we went through the flood seem just unimaginable!* **2.** *n.* someone or something that causes fear or fright; an experience of ①. □ *War is a horror that people hope to avoid.*

**horse** ['hors] *n.* an animal, larger than a donkey, that is used for carrying people and pulling heavy things, especially on farms. (See also **donkey** and **mule**.) □ *Anne rode a horse across the meadow.*

**hose** ['hoz] **1.** *n.* a flexible tube used to direct water or some other liquid. (Treated as singular. Pl: *hoses.*) □ *The children sprayed each other with the garden hose.* **2.** *n.* men's socks, especially to go with formal clothing. (No plural form. Treated as plural, but not countable. Number is expressed with *pair(s) of hose.*) □ *John's nylon hose make his feet sweat.* **3.** *n.* women's long, sheer stockings, made of silk or nylon. (No plural form. Treated as plural, but not countable. Number is expressed with *pair(s) of hose.*) □ *Mary wore black hose with her gown.* **4.** *n.* **pantyhose**. (No plural form. Treated as plural, but not countable. Number is expressed with *pair(s) of hose.*) □ *Many women wear hose with skirts and dresses.*

**hospital** ['hɑs pɪt əl] *n.* a building where medical care for serious diseases and illnesses is provided. □ *After the surgery, Jane stayed in the hospital for two weeks.*

**host** ['host] **1.** *n.* someone who receives and welcomes guests. (Male or female. Sometimes *hostess* is also used for a female.) □ *There was no host at the door, so we just walked in.* **2.** *n.* the person arranging a party or gathering, especially where food is served. (Male or female. Sometimes *hostess* is also used for a female.) □ *The host asked his guests to come to the table for dinner.* **3.** *n.* someone who introduces people on a television show; someone who has a talk show on television. □ *Many hosts start their shows with a series of jokes.* **4.** *n.* a large number of people or things. □ *Our picnic drew a host of insects.* **5.** *tv.* to be ③ on a television show. □ *A well-known actress is hosting the TV program that we plan to watch.* **6.** *tv.* to be ① or

H

② at a party. □ *Frank hosted the poker party last Saturday.*

**hostage** ['hɑs tɪdʒ] **1.** *n.* someone or something held by force, to be released only when stated demands are met. □ *The hostage was tied up and given nothing to eat.* **2.** *adj.* <the adj. use of ①.> □ *The reporter covered the hostage situation at the local bank.*

**hot** ['hɑt] **1.** *adj.* having a high temperature; not cold or warm. (Adv: *hotly.* Comp: *hotter;* sup: *hottest.*) □ *The cat sat in the hot sunlight.* **2.** *adj.* [of food] very spicy, causing a burning feeling in the mouth. (Adv: *hotly.* Comp: *hotter;* sup: *hottest.*) □ *Bob gulped water after eating the hot pepper.* **3.** *adj.* very intense; excited or angry. (Fig. on ①. Adv: *hotly.* Comp: *hotter;* sup: *hottest.*) □ *John has a hot temper and gets angry a lot.* **4.** *adj.* currently popular. (Informal. Comp: *hotter;* sup: *hottest.*) □ *What kind of music is hot right now?*

**hotel** [ho 'tɛl] *n.* a building where people can rent a place to stay while away from home on business or vacation. □ *The large hotel had a pool and two restaurants.*

**hour** ['aʊ ɚ] **1.** *n.* a unit of time measurement equal to 60 minutes or 1⁄24 of a day. □ *How many hours until we arrive?* **2.** *n.* a period of time set aside for some activity. □ *We do not like to be disturbed during our dinner hour.* **3.** *n.* the distance that can be traveled in ①. □ *My parents live an hour south of the city by car.*

**hourly** ['aʊ ɚ li] **1.** *adj.* happening every hour; happening once an hour. □ *Checking my e-mail has become an hourly event.* **2.** *adv.* every hour; once an hour. □ *I have to take this medicine hourly.*

**house 1.** ['hɑʊs] *n., irreg.* a building where a person or a family lives; a home. (Pl: ['hɑʊ zəz] or ['hɑʊ səz].) □ *Our house is located in the center of the city.* **2.** ['hɑʊs] *n.* a household; all the people who live in ①. (No plural form.) □ *The crying baby woke the entire house.* **3.** ['hɑʊs] *n., irreg.* a legislature; a legislative body. □ *The U.S. Senate is sometimes called a house.* **4.** ['hɑʊs] *n., irreg.* the part of a theater where the audience sits. □ *We have a full house tonight, so we will do our best.* **5.** ['hɑʊz] *tv.* to provide shelter to someone or some creature. □ *The barn housed the farm animals.*

**housebreak** ['hɑʊs brek] *tv., irreg.* to train a pet not to defecate or urinate in the house, or in the case of a cat, outside its special place. (Pt: **housebroke**; pp: **housebroken**.) □ *I managed to housebreak the cat in just a few days.*

**housebroke** ['hɑʊs brok] pt of **housebreak**.

**housebroken** ['hɑʊs brok ən] pp of **housebreak**.

**household** ['hɑʊs hold] **1.** *n.* the group of people who live in a house or apartment. □ *Someone in our household is always sick.* **2.** *adj.* found in ①; associated with ①. □ *Spot, a small, white dog, is our household pet.*

**housekeeper** ['hɑʊs kip ɚ] **1.** *n.* someone who is paid to manage household chores. □ *Our housekeeper has the weekend off, and the cook is sick. We'll starve!* **2.** *n.* someone who manages the cleaning in a hotel, resort, hospital, or large building. □ *The housekeeper inspects each hotel room and approves it before a guest is assigned to it.* **3.** *n.* a person who is paid to clean someone's house. (Euphemistic.) □ *Lisa told her housekeeper to clean every room.*

**house pet** ['hɑʊs pɛt] *n.* a dog, cat, bird, fish, or other animal kept in a house as a pet. □ *The landlord does not allow house pets.*

**houseplant** ['haʊs plænt] *n.* a plant usually grown indoors. □ *The houseplant added a touch of color to the room.*

**housework** ['haʊs wɚk] *n.* cooking, cleaning, washing, and other household tasks. (No plural form.) □ *The only part of housework I don't like is vacuuming.*

**how** [haʊ] **1.** *interrog.* in what way?; by what means? □ *How does he manage to do it?* **2.** *interrog.* to what extent?; to what degree? □ *How tall are you?* **3.** *interrog.* in what condition? □ *How are you?* **4.** *conj.* the way in which; the manner in which. □ *I know how to tie my shoes.*

**however** [haʊ 'ɛv ɚ] **1.** *adv.* but; nevertheless; in spite of something. □ *It is raining; however, I think the game will be played.* **2.** *adv.* no matter how. (Followed by an adjective or adverb.) □ *However far away you go, I will always find you.* **3.** *conj.* in whatever way; by whatever means. □ *You can do it however you want.*

**howl** ['haʊl] **1.** *n.* a long wail, as with the cry of a wolf or the sound of a high wind. □ *The howls of the wolves kept me awake last night.* **2.** *iv.* to make ①. □ *The wolf howled all night long.*

**how many** [haʊ 'mɛn i] *interrog.* in what number(s)? □ *How many puppies did your dog have?*

**how much** [haʊ 'mʌtʃ] *interrog.* in what amount? □ *I can bring potato salad to the picnic. How much?*

**huddle** ['hʌd l] **1.** *n.* a group of people crowded together. □ *There was a huddle of cold campers around the campfire.* **2.** *n.* [in football] a group of players close together, planning the next play. □ *The quarterback calls the plays in the huddle.* **3.** *iv.* [for a number of people] to stand closely together in a small space, especially to keep warm. □ *The cold campers huddled around the campfire.* **4.** *iv.* [for a creature] to curl up somewhere; to bring one's arms and legs close to the body, as if to keep warm. □ *I huddled by the wood stove to keep warm.*

**hue** ['hju] *n.* color; a variety, shade, or intensity of a color. □ *The room was decorated in different hues of blue.*

**hug** ['hʌg] **1.** *n.* an act of holding someone or something in one's arms in a friendly or loving way. □ *Bob gave Sue a hug when he came home from work.* **2.** *tv.* to hold someone as in ①. □ *The couple hugged each other at the airport.* **3.** *tv.* to stay close to a curb, railing, wall, or some other object as one moves along. □ *The bicycle rider hugged the curb to stay out of the way of cars.*

**huge** ['hjudʒ] **1.** *adj.* [of size] very large or enormous. (Adv: *hugely.* Comp: *huger;* sup: *hugest.*) □ *The huge bear frightened the campers.* **2.** *adj.* of a notable extent; [of extent, degree, or amount] notably large. (Adv: *hugely.* Comp: *huger;* sup: *hugest.*) □ *The party was a huge success.*

**hum** ['hʌm] **1.** *n.* a long, vibrating sound, like a long "mmmmmmm"; a low murmur; a quiet buzzing sound. (No plural form.) □ *We could hear the hum of the busy bees.* **2.** *iv.* to make a long, vibrating sound, like a long "mmmmmmmmm"; to sing with one's mouth closed. □ *I hummed with the orchestra and hoped no one could hear me.* **3.** *tv.* to sing musical notes with one's mouth closed, as in ②. □ *I hummed the melody that I had heard on the radio.*

**human** ['hju mən] **1.** *n.* a person; a human being. □ *Humans are supposed to be the most intelligent beings.* **2.** *adj.* <the adj. use of ①.> (Adv: *humanly.*) □ *Human love is a very powerful emotion.* **3.** *adj.* showing feelings that people normally show. (Adv: *humanly.*) □ *Being angry at something that is unfair is very human.*

H

**human being** ['hju mən 'bi ɪŋ] *n.* a person; a human creature, especially considering special human characteristics, such as intelligence, kindness, sympathy, etc. (The same as a **human.**) ☐ *Where do you suppose that the first human being lived?*

**humble** ['hʌm bəl] **1.** *adj.* aware of one's faults; modest. (Adv: *humbly.* Comp: *humbler;* sup: *humblest.*) ☐ *Jane is too humble to boast about her successes.* **2.** *adj.* simple; lowly; not elegant. (Adv: *humbly.* Comp: *humbler;* sup: *humblest.*) ☐ *The poor family lived in a humble dwelling.* **3.** *tv.* to lower the position of someone; to cause someone to become ①. ☐ *The arrogant athlete was humbled by the defeat.*

**humid** ['hju mɪd] *adj.* [of weather] damp; [of air] containing much moisture. (Adv: *humidly.*) ☐ *My laundry took a long time to dry in the humid weather.*

**humor** ['hju mɚ] **1.** *n.* the quality of being funny. (No plural form.) ☐ *There wasn't much humor in Jane's story about the accident.* **2.** *tv.* to tolerate someone who behaves oddly; to accept someone who has strange whims or desires. ☐ *Anne humored her son, who liked to dress up like his father.*

**humorous** ['hju mə rəs] *adj.* funny; amusing; having humor. (Adv: *humorously.*) ☐ *Bill is a humorous guy and tells jokes well.*

**hump** ['hʌmp] *n.* a large, rounded bump or swelling. ☐ *A hump in the carpet showed where Jimmy had lost his toy car.*

**hunch** ['hʌntʃ] *n.* a guess based on how one feels. ☐ *The detective had a hunch about the case.*

**hundred** ['hʌn drəd] **1.** *n.* the number 100; the number between 99 and 101. (Additional forms as with *two hundred, three hundred, four hundred,* etc.) ☐ *Ten times twenty is two hundred.* **2.** *n.* 100 things or people. ☐ *I ordered a hundred of the colorful calendars for gifts.*

**hung** ['hʌŋ] **1.** a pt/pp of **hang. 2.** *adj.* [of a jury] unable to reach a decision; [of a jury] not having a majority. ☐ *The hung jury could not reach a verdict and was excused.*

**hunger** ['hʌŋ gɚ] **1.** *n.* a general lack of food. (No plural form.) ☐ *Hunger is a problem in many of the world's countries.* **2.** *n.* the feeling of a need for something. (Fig. on ①. No plural form.) ☐ *Their cries and protests showed their great hunger for justice.*

**hungry** ['hʌŋ gri] *adj.* wanting food; lacking food; having an empty stomach. (Adv: *hungrily.* Comp: *hungrier;* sup: *hungriest.*) ☐ *The hungry dog sat by its bowl and whined.*

**hunk** ['hʌŋk] *n.* a large, solid amount of something. ☐ *The only food in my refrigerator right now is a large hunk of cheese.*

**hunt** ['hʌnt] **1.** *tv.* to search for and kill animals for food or for sport. ☐ *The cat hunts mice.* **2.** *iv.* to search for and kill animals as in ①. ☐ *I couldn't hunt unless I absolutely needed food.* **3. hunt for someone or something** *iv. + prep. phr.* to search for someone or something. ☐ *Everyone in town hunted for the lost child.*

**hunter** ['hʌn tɚ] *n.* someone who hunts; someone who searches for and kills animals for food or sport. ☐ *As a hunter, I kill only what I can eat.*

**hurl** ['hɚl] **1.** *tv.* to throw someone or something with force. ☐ *The sheriff hurled the robber out of the bank into the dusty road.* **2.** *tv.* to shout something negative, such as an insult or bad words. ☐ *Someone hurled insults at the president.*

**hurry** ['hɚ i] **1.** *iv.* to move quickly or briskly. ☐ *The store was closing, so the* *shopper hurried.* **2.** *tv.* to cause someone or something to move quickly or briskly. □ *The teacher hurried the students through their lessons.*

**hurt** ['hɚt] **1.** *n.* pain of the body or emotions; an ache. (Plural only when referring to different kinds, types, instances, or varieties.) □ *The hurt of losing his job made Tom depressed.* Ⓒ *He has lots of little hurts, but nothing really major or dangerous.* **2.** *tv., irreg.* to injure a part of the body; to harm one's mental processes or emotional well-being. (Pt/pp: *hurt.*) □ *Anne hurt her arm when she fell.* □ *Tom's jealousy hurt his ability to reason.* **3.** *tv., irreg.* to have a bad effect on someone or something; to be bad for someone or something. □ *Losing today hurt our chances for winning the championship.* **4.** *tv., irreg.* to cause pain in something; to give someone pain. □ *The tight shoes hurt my feet.* **5.** *iv., irreg.* to feel pain. □ *After the accident, the driver hurt all over.*

**husband** ['hʌz bənd] *n.* a married man; the man that a woman is married to. □ *Sue introduced Dave as her husband.*

**hush** ['hʌʃ] **1.** *n.* silence; quiet; calm. (No plural form.) □ *There was a strange hush before the tornado struck.* **2.** *tv.* to cause someone or something to be calm and quiet. □ *The teacher's angry look hushed the noisy students.* **3.** *iv.* to become calm and quiet. □ *As the actors walked onstage, the audience hushed.*

**husky** ['hʌs ki] **1.** *adj.* [of a voice] low, sounding as if the speaker has a sore throat. (Adv: *huskily.* Comp: *huskier;* sup: *huskiest.*) □ *Anne's cold made her voice husky.* **2.** *adj.* big and strong; muscular. (Adv: *huskily.* Comp: *huskier;* sup: *huskiest.*) □ *The husky boy worked as hard as an adult.* **3.** *n.* a kind of dog that pulls sleds in the far north. □ *Huskies have thick coats to keep them warm in the bitter cold.*

**hut** ['hʌt] *n.* a small shelter; a humble dwelling. □ *You can warm yourself in the huts along the ski trail.*

**hutch** ['hʌtʃ] **1.** *n.* a cage for rabbits or other small animals. □ *We kept the rabbit hutch outside.* **2.** *n.* a cupboard or cabinet with shelves. □ *The hutch had four shelves for plates and cups and a glass door.*

**hyena** [hɑɪ 'i nə] *n.* a wild, dog-like animal that eats meat and has a loud cry that sounds like laughter. □ *The hyena hunts at night.*

H

**hymn** ['hɪm] *n.* a religious song of praise meant to be sung by worshipers. □ *The church service included two hymns praising God's works.*

**hype** ['hɑɪp] **1.** *n.* an extreme amount of publicity; exaggerated praise used for publicity. (No plural form.) □ *There is always lots of hype around major sports events.* **2.** *tv.* to provide ① for someone or something. □ *The White House hyped the president's upcoming speech on taxes.*

**hyphen** ['hɑɪ fən] *n.* the mark of punctuation "-". (It is placed between the parts of some compound words, between the words in certain phrases, or between syllables where a word has been split between two lines of print.) □ *There is a hyphen in the word "twenty-two."*

**hypnotism** ['hɪp nə tɪz əm] **1.** *n.* hypnotizing people as a method of exploring and influencing the mind. (No plural form.) □ *Doctors are not in agreement on the benefits of hypnotism.* **2.** *n.* the process of hypnotizing someone. (No plural form.) □ *Hypnotism cannot be done against a person's will.*

**hypnotize** ['hɪp nə tɑɪz] *tv.* to place someone in a sleep-like condition. □ *It is difficult to hypnotize some people.*

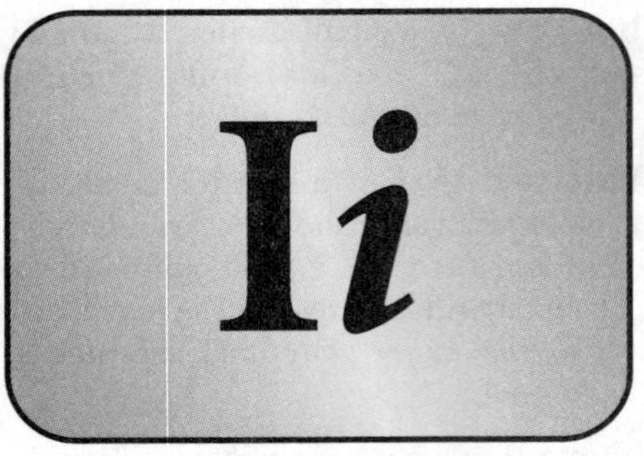

**I** ['ɑɪ] *pron.* <the first-person singular pronoun—in writing, it refers to the writer, and in speaking, it refers to the speaker.> (Used as the subject of a sentence or a clause. Compare this with **me**.) □ *Bill and I had lunch together yesterday.*

**ice** ['ɑɪs] **1.** *n.* frozen water. (No plural form. Number is expressed with *piece(s)* or *cube(s) of ice.*) □ *Susan put a piece of ice in her coffee to cool it.* **2.** *tv.* to cover a cake with icing or frosting. □ *Jane iced the cake with chocolate frosting.*

**iceberg** ['ɑɪs bɚg] *n.* an enormous piece of ice floating in the sea. □ *The huge ship sank after running into an iceberg.*

**ice cream** ['ɑɪs 'krim] **1.** *n.* a frozen dessert or snack food made from cream or milk and some kind of fruit or other flavoring. (No plural form.) □ *After dinner, John ate a bowl of strawberry ice cream for dessert.* **2. ice-cream** *adj.* <the adj. use of ①.> □ *Where is the ice-cream scoop?*

**ice cube** ['ɑɪs kjub] *n.* a small cube of ice, used to make drinks and liquids cold. □ *Susan put an ice cube in her soup to cool it.*

**ice skate** ['ɑɪ(s) sket] **1.** *n.* a boot with a thin blade on the bottom that allows one to glide on top of ice. □ *Bill put on his ice skates and walked carefully toward the frozen pond.* **2. ice-skate** *iv.* to glide across ice while wearing a pair of ①. (Can be shortened to **skate**.) □ *John ice-skates every day as part of his hockey training.*

**icicle** ['ɑɪs sɪ kəl] *n.* a pointed spike of ice that hangs from something such as a tree branch. □ *Icicles form when dripping water freezes.*

**icing** ['ɑɪ sɪŋ] *n.* cake frosting; a sweet coating for cakes, cookies, and other desserts. (No plural form.) □ *Anne's birthday cake has lemon icing.*

**icy** ['ɑɪ si] **1.** *adj.* covered with or made of ice. (Adv: *icily.* Comp: *icier;* sup: *iciest.*) □ *Bob slipped and fell on the icy sidewalk.* **2.** *adj.* very cold; freezing cold. (Adv: *icily.* Comp: *icier;* sup: *iciest.*) □ *Susan was glad to be home after walking against the icy wind.*

**I'd** ['ɑɪd] **1.** *cont.* "I would." □ *I'd like to go to the store now.* **2.** *cont.* "I had." (Where **had** is an auxiliary.) □ *I returned home because I'd forgotten my schoolwork.*

**idea** [ɑɪ 'di ə] **1.** *n.* a thought produced by the mind; an opinion. □ *My mind was full of new ideas after I listened to the lecture.* **2.** *n.* a picture of something produced by the mind; a mental picture. □ *My idea of the perfect house is one with a white fence.* **3.** *n.* a suggestion; a plan. □ *Your idea was a good one.*

**ideal** [ɑɪ 'dil] **1. the ideal** *n.* the best example of something; the perfect type. (No plural form. Treated as singular.) □ *A job that both pays well and is enjoyable is the ideal.* **2. ideals** *n.* high moral standards; strong moral beliefs. □ *Max didn't understand his parents' ideals.* **3.** *adj.* perfect; perfectly suitable. (Adv: *ideally.*) □ *My ideal car would be one that uses very little gasoline.*

**identical** [ɑɪ 'dɛn tɪ kəl] **1.** *adj.* equal; exactly alike. (Adv: *identically* [...ɪk li].) □ *The first and second printings of this book are identical.* **2. identical to someone or something** *adj.* + *prep. phr.* exactly the same as someone or something. □ *The amount of milk in your glass is identical to the amount in mine.*

**identification** [ɑɪ dɛn tə fə 'ke ʃən] **1.** *n.* identifying someone or something; the condition of being identified. (Plural only when referring to different kinds, types, instances, or varieties.) □ *Identification of the poison will require many tests.* Ⓒ *It will take another hour to complete all these identifications.* **2.** *n.* some kind of document that identifies someone; something that proves who someone is. (No plural form.) □ *The guard will ask for identification before you enter.*

**identify** [ɑɪ 'dɛn tə fɑɪ] **1.** *tv.* to state who or what someone or something is; to allow the identification of someone or something. □ *The doctor identified the disease that made me sick.* □ *I identified Max as the thief who stole my bicycle.* **2.** *tv.* to reveal someone's identity. □ *His passport identified him as John Smith.*

**idiom** ['ɪd i əm] **1.** *n.* a phrase whose meaning is different from the combined literal meanings of the separate words that make up the phrase. □ *Idioms occur in every language and make languages hard to learn.* □ Hit the hay *is an idiom that means "go to bed."* **2.** *n.* a mode of expression or design. □ *Susan's clothing designs reflect a modern idiom.*

**idiot** ['ɪd i ət] *n.* a foolish person; a stupid person. □ *Anyone who crosses the street without checking for traffic is an idiot.*

**if** ['ɪf] **1.** *conj.* in the event [that something is the case]; on the condition [that something is the case]. □ *If you lend me $10, I'll pay you back on Friday.* **2.** *conj.* whether. (Often introduces an indirect question.) □ *Go ask Bill if he is ready to leave.* **3.** *conj.* although; even though. □ *The helpful, if scared, witness talked to the police willingly.* **4. if not** *phr.* otherwise; if that does not happen; if that is not the case; if that is not so. □ *I must leave here by 5:15. If not, I will miss my bus.* **5. if so** *phr.* if that is the case; if that is so; if that happens. □ *She might be late. If so, we will eat dinner without her.*

**ignore** [ɪg 'nor] *tv.* to pay no attention to someone or something. □ *Max threw rocks at me, but I continued to ignore him.*

**I'll** ['ɑɪl] *cont.* "I will." □ *I'll be back in a few minutes.*

**ill** ['ɪl] **1.** *adj.* sick; not well; not healthy. □ *The bad food made Mary ill.* **2.** *adv.* badly. (Before a participle or certain adjectives. Usually hyphenated.) □ *You would be ill-advised to turn in your homework without checking it for spelling mistakes.* □ *Bob is an ill-mannered young man.* **3. ills** *n.* troubles. □ *John's list of ills was long and included many problems with his family.* **4.** *n.* harm. (No plural form.) □ *The new law did very little good and much ill.*

**illegal** [ɪ 'li gəl] *adj.* not legal; against the law. (Adv: *illegally.*) □ *In some states, it is illegal to carry a gun.*

**illness** ['ɪl nəs] **1.** *n.* a sickness; a disease. □ *Bill developed a serious illness and died a few weeks later.* **2.** *n.* a period of being sick. □ *During Mary's long illness, she slept almost all day.*

**illusion** [ɪ 'lu ʒən] **1.** *n.* a vision of something that is not really there; a false image. □ *The artist created an illusion of a dog in the complex design.* **2.** *n.* a false belief; something that seems to be true but is not true. □ *Your belief that you control your fate is only an illusion.*

**ill will** ['ɪl 'wɪl] *n.* angry feelings or bad intentions. (No plural form. Treated as singular.) □ *Dave felt such ill will toward his children that he left his money to his best friend.*

**I'm** ['ɑɪm] *cont.* "I am." □ *I'm flying to Hawaii this summer.*

**image** ['ɪm ɪdʒ] **1.** *n.* that which is seen in a mirror or similar surface. ☐ *Jane stared at her image in the mirror.* **2.** *n.* a sculpture, painting, or other form of art that represents someone or something; a picture or photograph of someone or something. ☐ *Several of my paintings are images of the Revolutionary War.* **3.** *n.* a picture of something in one's mind; a mental picture. ☐ *The police officer had a clear image of what had happened during the crime.* **4.** *n.* the opinion that people have about a certain person or thing; someone's or something's reputation. ☐ *The senator damaged his image by accepting the bribe.*

I

**imagery** ['ɪm ɪdʒ ri] *n.* words, music, or pictures that represent or create images, often also making one think about situations or feelings; pictures that are created in a person's mind, especially in response to poetry, music, art, etc. (No plural form. Treated as singular.) ☐ *The imagery of death and decay in the artist's paintings made them very sad.*

**imaginary** [ɪ 'mædʒ ə nɛr i] *adj.* existing only in the mind; not real. (Adv: *imaginarily* [ɪ mædʒ ə 'nɛr ə li].) ☐ *The doctor believed that all of Bill's problems were imaginary.*

**imagination** [ɪ mædʒ ə 'ne ʃən] **1.** *n.* the part of the mind that produces thoughts and images that are not real or not experienced; the part of the mind that imagines things. (No plural form.) ☐ *Most of Bill's health problems were in his imagination.* **2.** *n.* the ability to think of new and interesting ideas; the ability to imagine something. (No plural form.) ☐ *Susan shows imagination in her writing style.*

**imagine** [ɪ 'mædʒ ɪn] **1.** *tv.* to think of someone or something; to form an image of someone or something in one's mind. (The object can be a clause with **that** ⑦.) ☐ *The soldier imagined what it would be like to be a general.* **2.** *tv.* to think something; to believe something; to suppose something; to guess something. (The object is a clause with **that** ⑦.) ☐ *I imagine that your parents are quite concerned about your low grades.*

**imitate** ['ɪm ə tet] **1.** *tv.* to attempt to copy the style, behavior, or success of someone whom one admires or wants to be like. ☐ *Anne imitated the famous artist's style in her own paintings.* **2.** *tv.* to copy the behavior, speech, and movement of someone for amusement. ☐ *The students laughed when I imitated our teacher.*

**imitation** [ɪm ə 'te ʃən] **1.** *n.* copying someone's actions or deeds; copying something. (No plural form.) ☐ *Imitation is a compliment to the person who is being imitated.* **2.** *n.* a copy; a duplicate. ☐ *This dress is an imitation of an expensive gown worn by the queen.* **3.** *n.* an act of imitating someone or something. ☐ *The audience laughed at Bob's imitation of the president.* **4.** *adj.* fake; artificial; resembling something. ☐ *These gloves are made of imitation leather.*

**immaculate** [ɪ 'mæk jə lɪt] *adj.* pure; absolutely clean; spotless. (Adv: *immaculately.*) ☐ *I cleaned for hours until the kitchen was immaculate.*

**immaterial** [ɪm ə 'tɪr i əl] *adj.* not relevant; having nothing to do with something. (Adv: *immaterially.*) ☐ *The judge ordered that the lawyer's immaterial comments be removed from the record.*

**immediate** [ɪ 'mid i ɪt] **1.** *adj.* happening now; happening at once. (Adv: *immediately.*) ☐ *The drowning swimmer required the lifeguard's immediate attention.* **2.** *adj.* closest to someone or something in space or time; next to someone or something. (Adv: *immediately.*) ☐ *We took shelter because there was a tornado in the immediate vicinity.*

**immense** [ɪ 'mɛns] *adj.* very large; huge; enormous. (Adv: *immensely.*) ☐ *The amount of money stolen from the treasury was immense.*

**immerse** [ɪ 'mɚs] **1. immerse** someone or something **in** something *tv.* + *obj.* + *prep. phr.* to put someone or something into a liquid; to put someone or something underwater. ☐ *Sally immersed the potatoes in boiling water.* **2. immerse** oneself **in** something *tv.* + *obj.* + *prep. phr.* to become deeply involved with something; to become absorbed in something. (Fig. on ①. Reflexive object.) ☐ *Anne immerses herself in her job, often working late into the evening.*

**immersion** [ɪ 'mɚ ʒən] **1.** *n.* placing something under water or in a liquid. (Plural only when referring to different kinds, types, instances, or varieties.) ☐ *Immersion of a burn in cold water will ease the pain.* Ⓒ *Repeated immersions in clear water will clean fresh vegetables of most of their sand and soil.* **2.** *n.* being completely involved in something. (Fig. on ①. No plural form.) ☐ *Bill's immersion in his work caused him to neglect his family.*

**immigrate** ['ɪm ə gret] *iv.* to come into a new country to live. ☐ *My grandparents immigrated to this country when they were very young.*

**immodest** [ɪ 'mɑd əst] **1.** *adj.* not modest; revealing; shameless. (Adv: *immodestly.*) ☐ *Mary wore a very immodest outfit to the party.* **2.** *adj.* not modest about oneself; often bragging. (Adv: *immodestly.*) ☐ *Dave is very immodest and constantly talks about how well he can sing.*

**immoral** [ɪ 'mor əl] *adj.* without morals; not moral; breaking moral rules. (Adv: *immorally.*) ☐ *Killing people is immoral and illegal.*

**immortal** [ɪ 'mor təl] **1.** *adj.* everlasting; lasting forever; never dying; living forever. (Adv: *immortally.*) ☐ *The Greek gods were considered immortal.* **2.** *adj.* continuing to be remembered forever; never forgotten. (Adv: *immortally.*) ☐ *William Shakespeare is famous for his immortal plays.*

**immune** [ɪ 'mjun] **1. immune (to** something**)** *adj.* (+ *prep. phr.*) protected against a certain disease, either naturally or through medication. (Adv: *immunely.*) ☐ *I had the disease when I was six, so now I am immune.* **2. immune (to** something**)** *adj.* (+ *prep. phr.*) not in danger of being affected by something; secure from the danger of something. (Fig. on ①. Adv: *immunely.*) ☐ *No one is immune to new ideas.*

I

**impact 1.** ['ɪm pækt] *n.* the crash of objects striking one another with force. ☐ *The car crumpled when it made a hard impact against the solid brick wall.* **2.** ['ɪm pækt] *n.* the influence or effect of someone or something. (Fig. on ①.) ☐ *The impact of the tax cut will not be felt for five years.* **3.** [ɪm 'pækt] *tv.* to crash into something. ☐ *The meteor impacted the surface of the moon and left a large hole.*

**impatient** [ɪm 'pe ʃənt] *adj.* not patient; not able to wait for someone or something. (Adv: *impatiently.*) ☐ *My impatient brother paced back and forth, waiting for Mary to arrive.*

**imply** [ɪm 'plɑɪ] *tv.* to suggest something; to indicate something without actually saying it. (The object is a clause with **that** ⑦.) ☐ *When my wife said she felt tired, I think she was implying that we should go home soon.*

**impolite** [ɪm pə 'lɑɪt] *adj.* rude; not polite; not courteous. (Adv: *impolitely.*) ☐ *I must apologize for my impolite behavior earlier today.*

**import 1.** [ɪm 'port] *tv.* to bring in (to one country) a product from a foreign country. □ *This cheese was imported from Switzerland.* **2.** ['ɪm port] *n.* a product that is brought into one country from another country. □ *Dave decided to buy an American car instead of a Japanese import.*

**importance** [ɪm 'port ns] **1.** *n.* the condition of being important. (No plural form.) □ *I have always taught my children the importance of manners.* **2.** *n.* the relative position or rank of someone or something. (No plural form.) □ *Prince John's importance could be seen from the way people treated him.*

**important** [ɪm 'port nt] *adj.* having a great effect, value, or influence. (Adv: *importantly.*) □ *I missed the most important part of the lecture.*

**impure** [ɪm 'pjʊr] **1.** *adj.* not pure; dirty; mixed with other things. (Adv: *impurely.*) □ *Anne coughed when she breathed the impure air.* **2.** *adj.* not morally pure. (Adv: *impurely.*) □ *Almost everyone has thoughts that could be regarded as impure.*

**in** [ɪn] **1.** *prep.* inside something; within something; surrounded by something else. □ *Detroit is in Michigan.* **2.** *prep.* into something; entering into a space; going through a boundary and to a position that is surrounded by something else. □ *Put the letter in the envelope.* **3.** *prep.* at some point during a certain time period. □ *I started college in 1984.* **4.** *prep.* after a certain period of time. □ *I will go to the store in two minutes.* **5.** *prep.* with something or using something, especially a language or a way of writing or expressing something. □ *John communicated in French.* **6.** *adv.* inward; indoors; going into something; in a way that someone or something will be in a position that is surrounded by something else. □ *I went up to the door, opened it, and ran in.* **7.** *adv.* at home; at one's office; available. □ *Dr. Fields won't be in until this afternoon.*

**inaccurate** [ɪn 'æk jə rɪt] *adj.* not accurate; incorrect. (Adv: *inaccurately.*) □ *The book I bought contained many inaccurate statements.*

**inactive** [ɪn 'æk tɪv] **1.** *adj.* not active; not moving. (Adv: *inactively.*) □ *John works nights, so he's usually inactive during the day.* **2.** *adj.* [of someone] not or no longer working actively or actively involved. (Adv: *inactively.*) □ *Sally has become inactive in our club and no longer pays her dues.* **3.** *adj.* having no effect; [of a chemical] not reacting. (Adv: *inactively.*) □ *This substance is inactive until it is heated.*

**inadequate** [ɪn 'æd ə kwɪt] *adj.* not adequate; not enough; not good enough. (Adv: *inadequately.*) □ *The plant died because it received an inadequate amount of water.*

**inch** ['ɪntʃ] **1.** *n.* a unit of measurement of distance, equal to 1/12 of a foot or 2.54 centimeters. □ *Jimmy grew three inches taller during the summer.* **2.** *iv.* to move very slowly; to move an **inch** ① at a time. (Especially with *by* or *along.*) □ *The hours inched by while I waited for the plane to arrive.*

**incline 1.** ['ɪn klɑɪn] *n.* a slant; a slope; a surface that is on an angle to flat ground. □ *The farmer placed the board at an incline against the barn.* **2.** [ɪn 'klɑɪn] *iv.* to slant; to slope. □ *The path up the hill inclines at about 25 degrees.*

**include** [ɪn 'klud] **1.** *tv.* [for something] to contain something or to have something among its parts. □ *The meal will include bread, soup, and a salad.* **2.** *tv.* [for someone] to cause someone or something to be a part of something; to add something to something else. □ *Mary included an index at the end of her report.*

**income** ['ɪn kəm] *n.* the amount of money received as wages, interest, or similar payments; money received in exchange for goods. □ *Most of Bill's income comes from stocks and bonds.*

**income tax** ['ɪn kəm tæks] *n.* a federal, state, or local tax on income that has been earned. □ *I always pay my income tax on April 14.*

**incorrect** [ɪn kə 'rɛkt] *adj.* not correct; wrong; false. (Adv: *incorrectly.*) □ *Your answer to my question is incorrect.*

**increase 1.** ['ɪn kris] *n.* growth; becoming larger. (Plural only when referring to different kinds, types, instances, or varieties.) □ *The puppy's increase in size was quite noticeable.* Ⓒ *Susan received two pay increases last year.* **2.** [ɪn 'kris] *iv.* to become larger, faster, or more powerful; to become larger in number or amount. □ *As you drive out of town, the speed limit increases to 45 miles per hour.* **3.** [ɪn 'kris] *tv.* to cause something to become larger, faster, or more powerful; to cause something to become larger in number or amount. □ *Congress increased the speed limit to 65 miles per hour.*

**incubator** ['ɪŋ kjə bet ɚ] **1.** *n.* a container that keeps eggs warm until they hatch. □ *The baby chicken hatched in an incubator.* **2.** *n.* a special container or device in which babies that are born too early are kept for warmth and care. □ *The nurse fed the baby and then returned it to the incubator.*

**indeed** [ɪn 'did] **1.** *adv.* very much so; quite. □ *This morning was cold indeed.* **2.** *adv.* in fact; actually. □ *Mary said she would win the race, and indeed she did win it.* **3.** *interj.* "Amazing!" □ *"It snowed 8 inches last night." "Indeed!"*

**indent** [ɪn 'dɛnt] *tv.* [in writing or typing] to begin a line a few spaces farther from the edge than the other lines, as at the beginning of a paragraph. □ *Mary indented the first line of each paragraph.*

**indentation** [ɪn dɛn 'te ʃən] **1.** *n.* a notch; a dent; a cut. □ *The hail made deep indentations in the hood of the car.* **2.** *n.* indenting lines of type or writing. (Plural only when referring to different kinds, types, instances, or varieties.) □ *Indentation helps readers find their way on the page.* Ⓒ *You need an indentation at the beginning of this paragraph.*

**independence** [ɪn dɪ 'pɛn dəns] *n.* freedom from someone or some government; liberty. (No plural form.) □ *John proved his independence by moving out of his parents' house.*

**independent** [ɪn dɪ 'pɛn dənt] **1.** *adj.* not dependent on someone or something; not controlled by others; not ruled by other people or countries. (Adv: *independently.*) □ *Many African countries became independent in the 1960s.* **2.** *adj.* not needing the support of others; self-supporting. (Adv: *independently.*) □ *Independent television stations are not part of a network.* **3.** *adj.* separate; distinct from other things. (Adv: *independently.*) □ *Lisa runs two independent businesses.* **4.** *n.* a politician or a voter who does not belong to a political party. □ *The governor of that state is an independent.*

**index** ['ɪn dɛks] **1.** *n., irreg.* an alphabetical list of topics showing where each topic can be found in the main part of a book, report, magazine, journal, etc. (Pl: *indexes* or **indices.**) □ *Mary checked the index to see if the book had any information on Russia.* **2.** *n., irreg.* a scale where prices or amounts of certain things are compared with the prices or amounts of those same things at an earlier date. □ *According to the consumer price index, the price of food doubled between 1960 and 1975.* **3.** *tv.* to locate important topics and list them and their locations, as in ①. □ *My computer program indexes topics automatically.*

**indicate** ['ɪn də ket] **1.** *tv.* to point something out verbally; to state a fact. (The object is a clause with **that** ⑦.) □ *John indicated that he was feeling well.* **2.** *tv.* to make something known; to draw someone's attention to something. (The object can be a clause with **that** ⑦.) □ *I indicated that I wanted to leave.* **3.** *tv.* [for a meter, chart, signal] to show specific information. (The object can be a clause with **that** ⑦.) □ *The meter indicated that we were nearly out of gas.*

**indices** ['ɪn dɪ siz] a pl of **index**.

**indigestion** [ɪn də 'dʒɛs tʃən] *n.* an upset stomach; the digestion of food that causes pain. (No plural form.) □ *I get indigestion from spicy food.*

**individual** [ɪn də 'vɪ dʒu əl] **1.** *n.* a person; one person. □ *An individual was seen leaving the library late in the afternoon.* **2.** *adj.* separate; single. (Adv: *individually.*) □ *Each individual slice of cheese was wrapped in plastic.*

**indoor** ['ɪn dor] *adj.* inside a building; kept within walls and under a roof. (Prenominal only.) □ *This is indoor carpeting and should not be placed outdoors.*

**indoors** [ɪn 'dorz] *adv.* in or into a building. □ *When it started raining, the children went indoors.*

**industry** ['ɪn də stri] **1.** *n.* the production of goods; the manufacture of products. (No plural form.) □ *During the early 1940s, most industry centered on the war.* **2.** *n.* the business activity concerning a specific kind of product or service. □ *The fast-food industry has grown rapidly.* **3.** *n.* hard work or labor. □ *John is lazy and lacks the industry necessary to do the job.*

**inedible** [ɪn 'ɛd ə bəl] *adj.* not able to be eaten; not good for eating. (Adv: *inedibly.*) □ *The child choked on an inedible piece of meat.*

**inf.** an abbreviation of **infinitive form**.

**infant** ['ɪn fənt] **1.** *n.* a baby; a young child. □ *Susan laid the infant down for a nap.* **2.** *adj.* <the adj. use of ①.> □ *Infant clothing is sold on the third floor.*

**infection** [ɪn 'fɛk ʃən] **1.** *n.* the entrance and growth of disease organisms in the body. (Plural only when referring to different kinds, types, instances, or varieties.) □ *Keep the wound clean to avoid infection.* Ⓒ *She experienced two separate infections of this disease only a month apart.* **2.** *n.* a disease caused by ①. □ *Billy has an ear infection and cannot go to school today.*

**inferior** [ɪn 'fɪr i ɚ] **1.** *adj.* lower in amount, rank, power, quality, or strength than someone or something else. (Adv: *inferiorly.*) □ *My old television is a cheap, inferior brand.* **2.** *n.* someone who has a lower-ranking job than someone else. □ *The boss is rude to his inferiors.*

**inferno** [ɪn 'fɚ no] **1.** *n.* a large, fierce fire. (Pl ends in *-s.*) □ *Thousands of acres of land were burned in the deadly inferno.* **2.** *n.* a place that is very hot. (Fig. on ①. Pl ends in *-s.*) □ *The kitchen was an inferno because the ovens were so hot.*

**infinitive form** [ɪn 'fɪn ə tɪv 'form] *n.* a form of a verb—preceded by *to*—that does not show tense, number, or person. (Abbreviated *inf.* here. Can be shortened to *infinitive.*) □ *The infinitive form of "am" and "are" is "to be."* □ *Infinitives can be used after some verbs, such as "want," as in "I want to go." The basic form of the verb—the infinitive without "to"—is used after auxiliary verbs such as "will," as in "I will go."*

**inflammable** [ɪn 'flæm ə bəl] *adj.* able to catch fire; **flammable**; not fireproof. (The opposite is **nonflammable**. Adv: *inflammably.* This *in* shows emphasis, not negativeness.) □ *Inflammable material should not be used in children's clothing.*

**inflation** [ɪn 'fle ʃən] **1.** *n.* the process of putting air or gas into something; blowing something up. (No plural form.) □ *After inflation, press on the ball to make sure it is not too full of air.* **2.** *n.* an economic condition in which too much money is available for purchasing too few goods. (No plural form.) □ *When inflation is a problem, manufacturing costs rise constantly.*

**influence** ['ɪn flu əns] **1.** *n.* the power or ability to cause certain results or to affect what happens. (Plural only when referring to different kinds, types, instances, or varieties.) □ *The judge was appointed because of the mayor's influence.* Ⓒ *Not hampered by the negative influences of both poverty and disease, she achieved success.* **2.** *n.* a cause of some behavior. □ *John drove into a tree when he was under the influence of alcohol.* **3.** *tv.* to affect someone or something. □ *My decision was influenced by my parents' advice.*

**influenza** [ɪn flu 'ɛn zə] *n.* the flu; an easily spread sickness caused by a virus. (No plural form.) Compare this with **flu** and **cold** ③.) □ *Between 1918 and 1920, influenza killed 20 million people.*

**informal** [ɪn 'form əl] **1.** *adj.* not formal, official, or final. (Adv: *informally.*) □ *Anne received an informal job offer, but she wouldn't accept it until she was shown a contract.* **2.** *adj.* [of words, language, or speech] used every day but a little more relaxed than more formal speech. (Adv: *informally.*) □ *People often end sentences with prepositions in informal speech.* **3.** *adj.* [of dress] not formal; casual. (Adv: *informally.*) □ *Dress at our party is informal, so please don't wear a suit.*

**information** [ɪn fɚ 'me ʃən] *n.* news; knowledge about something; facts. (No plural form. Number is expressed by *piece(s)* or *bit(s) of information.*) □ *I asked the librarian for information on photography.*

**ingredient** [ɪn 'grid i ənt] *n.* something that is part of a mixture; a part of something. □ *The ingredients in the cake included sugar, flour, eggs, and milk.*

**inhale** [ɪn 'hel] **1.** *iv.* to breathe in. □ *Mary inhaled deeply, enjoying the fresh air.* **2.** *tv.* to breathe something in. □ *Mary inhaled the fresh morning air.*

**inherit** [ɪn 'hɛr ɪt] **1.** *tv.* to receive the assets of a person when the person dies. □ *I inherited 64 acres of farmland from my grandfather.* **2.** *tv.* to receive a characteristic or feature from the genes of one's parents or ancestors. □ *Mary inherited her brown eyes from her mother.*

**inject** [ɪn 'dʒɛkt] **1.** *tv.* to put a liquid into a living body through a hollow needle. □ *A nurse injected a painkiller.* **2.** *tv.* to introduce a fluid into something under pressure. □ *I used a small hose to inject cement into the crack in the wall.*

**injection** [ɪn 'dʒɛk ʃən] *n.* injecting something. (Plural only when referring to different kinds, types, instances, or varieties.) □ *Injection is the best way to administer some medicines.* Ⓒ *Repeated injections of the drug cured the disease.*

**injure** ['ɪn dʒɚ] *tv.* to harm someone or something; to damage someone or something. □ *John injured Bob's feelings in the argument.*

**injury** ['ɪn dʒə ri] *n.* physical or mental damage or harm; a specific instance of damage or harm. □ *The injury to Bill's leg will heal in a few months.*

**ink** ['ɪŋk] **1.** *n.* a colored liquid used for writing or printing. (Plural only when referring to different kinds, types, instances, or varieties.) □ *Please sign your name in black ink.* Ⓒ *Some inks are easier to remove from paper when it is recycled.* **2.** *n.* a liquid that is injected into the water by an octopus—and by some other sea animals—to confuse pursuers. (No plural form.) □ *The octopus released a cloud of ink and fled.*

**inn** ['ɪn] *n.* a small hotel; a place that offers rooms to rent for travelers. □ *While skiing in Switzerland, we stayed in a cozy mountain inn.*

**inner** ['ɪn ɚ] *adj.* on the inside; nearer to the center; further inside. □ *The outside of a melon is hard, but the inner part is soft and full of juice and seeds.*

**inning** ['ɪn ɪŋ] *n.* [in baseball] a period of playing time that ends after the two teams have received three outs each during their turns batting. □ *Players from one team bat in the first half of each inning, and players from the other team bat in the second half.*

**innocent** ['ɪn ə sənt] **1.** *adj.* free from guilt or sin; not guilty. (Adv: *innocently.*) □ *Anne was found innocent of the crime.* **2.** *adj.* harmless; not meant to cause harm. (Adv: *innocently.*) □ *John gave Bill's arm an innocent, playful punch.* **3.** *adj.* too trusting; not recognizing things that are evil; inexperienced. (Adv: *innocently.*) □ *The crooks took advantage of the innocent tourists.*

**input** ['ɪn pʊt] **1.** *n.* addition; the act of putting something into something. (No plural form.) □ *The input of opinions at the meeting was very limited.* **2.** *n.* advice; opinions; ideas or suggestions. (Informal. No plural form.) □ *Jane felt that John was ignoring her input.* **3.** *n.* information; data; information that is put into a computer. (No plural form.) □ *Your input is in the wrong format.* **4.** *n.* an electronic signal that is fed into a circuit. □ *The input was cut off when the wire snapped.* **5.** *tv., irreg.* (Pt/pp: *inputted* or *input.*) to put data into a computer. □ *The data were inputted without any mistakes.*

**inquire** [ɪn 'kwɑɪɚ] *iv.* to ask someone about something. (Also spelled *enquire.*) □ *Susan inquired about Bob's success.*

**inquiry** [ɪn 'kwɑɪɚ i] **1.** *n.* a question. (Also spelled *enquiry.*) □ *Please direct your inquiry to the information desk.* **2.** *n.* an investigation; a search for truth; a search for an answer. □ *The police organized an inquiry into the man's death.*

**insane** [ɪn 'sen] **1.** *adj.* crazy; not sane. (Adv: *insanely.*) □ *The murderer was judged to be insane.* **2.** *adj.* owing to insanity; done because of insanity. (Adv: *insanely.*) □ *The patient's insane comments were hard to understand.* **3.** *adj.* very stupid; very foolish; very idiotic. (Informal. Adv: *insanely.*) □ *If you think I'd quit school now, you're insane!*

**insanity** [ɪn 'sæn ə ti] *n.* the state or condition of being insane. (No plural form.) □ *The criminal's insanity was not in question. He was clearly insane.*

**insect** ['ɪn sɛkt] **1.** *n.* a small creature with wings and six legs. □ *The tiny insect carried a deadly virus.* **2.** *n.* a bug; any creature similar to ①. □ *This special collar protects my dog from insects, including fleas and ticks.*

**inside 1.** ['ɪn 'sɑɪd] *n.* the interior of a building or an object; the part of an object that is within something. □ *The inside of the fruit was rotten.* **2.** [ɪn 'sɑɪd, 'ɪn sɑɪd] *adj.* interior; in, of, or about ①. □ *The painter painted the inside walls light brown.* **3.** [ɪn 'sɑɪd] *adv.* in or into a room or building; in or into an object. □ *I came inside because it started to rain.* **4.** [ɪn 'sɑɪd, 'ɪn sɑɪd] *prep.* within a room or building; within an object; within the interior; in an interior position. □ *Inside a pumpkin there are hundreds of seeds.*

**insight** ['ɪn sɑɪt] **1.** *n.* wisdom; the ability to observe and identify things that are important. (No plural form.) □ *I* *never questioned my teacher's insight.* **2.** *n.* a statement showing that one has observed and identified something important. □ *I agree with Anne's insights into the author's motivation.*

**inspect** [ɪn 'spɛkt] *tv.* to examine someone or something carefully. □ *The general inspected the soldiers.*

**inspection** [ɪn 'spɛk ʃən] *n.* study; inspecting and reviewing. (Plural only when referring to different kinds, types, instances, or varieties.) □ *Without frequent inspection, airplane engines would not be safe.* Ⓒ *The restaurant passed its last four health inspections.*

**instance** ['ɪn stəns] **1.** *n.* an example; a case; an occurrence. □ *How many instances of tornadoes were there in 1958?* □ *This is another instance of the same problem.* **2. for instance** *phr.* for example. □ *I've lived in many cities, for instance, Boston, Chicago, and Detroit.*

**instant** ['ɪn stənt] **1.** *n.* one moment in time; a very short amount of time. □ *The computer calculated the figures in an instant.* **2.** *adj.* immediate; without delay. (Adv: *instantly.*) □ *My boss demanded an instant response to her question.* **3.** *adj.* [of food or drink] easily and quickly prepared. □ *I drank instant coffee for breakfast.*

**instead** [ɪn 'stɛd] **1.** *adv.* in place of something; as another choice. □ *I don't want to go home. Let's go to a movie instead.* **2. instead of** someone or something *phr.* in place of someone or something; as a substitute for someone or something. □ *Instead of Florida, let's go to Mexico this winter.*

**instinct** ['ɪn stɪŋkt] *n.* an ability someone or some creature is born with to act or respond in a particular way. □ *Birds migrate because of instinct.*

**institution** [ɪn stɪ 'tu ʃən] **1.** *n.* an organization that serves a special purpose. □ *The museum is an important institution in our city.* **2.** *n.* an established tradition; a habit; a custom. □ *The institution of marriage has existed for centuries.*

**instruct** [ɪn 'strʌkt] **1.** *tv.* to teach someone something; to educate someone about something. □ *Ms. Smith instructed the children in history.* **2. instruct** someone **to** do something *tv. + obj. + inf.* to order or request someone to do something. □ *Bill was instructed to leave the room.*

**instruction** [ɪn 'strʌk ʃən] **1.** *n.* education; teaching. (No plural form.) □ *The principal doubted the new teacher's methods of instruction.* **2.** *n.* an order or set of orders, a direction or set of directions. (Usually plural.) □ *The class followed the teacher's instructions.*

**instructor** [ɪn 'strʌk tɚ] *n.* a teacher; someone who instructs people about something. □ *My Spanish instructor was born in Mexico.*

**instrument** ['ɪn strə mənt] **1.** *n.* a thing that is used to help someone do something; a tool; a device. □ *A ruler is an instrument used for measuring things.* **2.** *n.* something that shows a measurement. □ *The pilots watched the instruments on the panel in front of them.* **3.** *n.* an object that produces musical notes when played. □ *An orchestra includes many different musical instruments.*

**insult** [ɪn 'sʌlt] **1.** *n.* an offensive remark; a rude statement that offends someone. □ *What Anne said to Bob was a terrible insult.* **2.** *tv.* to offend someone; to say something rude or offensive to someone. □ *I got angry when John insulted me.*

**insurance** [ɪn 'ʃɚ əns] **1.** *n.* a contract that pays a sum of money in the case of a loss or injury. (No plural form. Number is expressed with **insurance policy** or **insurance policies**.) □ *Car insurance is required by law in most* *states.* **2.** *n.* something that protects against a loss or an injury. (No plural form.) □ *Locking your car doors is insurance against theft.* **3.** *n.* the business of writing and selling ①. (No plural form.) □ *My cousin has worked in insurance for a number of years.* **4.** *adj.* <the adj. use of ③.> □ *My cousin works in the insurance industry.*

**insurance policy** [ɪn 'ʃɚ əns 'pɑl ə si] *n.* the document or contract that states the protections offered by insurance. □ *I have an insurance policy that protects my house.*

**insure** [ɪn 'ʃɚ] **1.** *tv.* to purchase insurance for someone or something. (Compare this with **ensure**.) □ *John insured the package that he sent by mail.* **2.** *tv.* [for an insurance company] to sell insurance on someone or something. □ *The airline insured its passengers' luggage against loss.*

**intelligence** [ɪn 'tɛl ɪ dʒəns] **1.** *n.* the level of someone's ability to learn and understand. (No plural form.) □ *Sometimes Bob acts as if he has the intelligence of a two-year-old.* **2.** *n.* information about an enemy and the enemy's plans. (No plural form.) □ *The agent tricked the government by providing false intelligence.* **3.** *n.* a department within a military service that gathers ②. (No plural form.) □ *Intelligence trained the best soldiers to spy on the enemy.*

**intelligent** [ɪn 'tɛl ə dʒənt] *adj.* smart; able to learn and understand things well. (Adv: *intelligently.*) □ *You're intelligent enough to solve your own problems.*

**intensity** [ɪn 'tɛn sə ti] *n.* the degree or amount of power or strength. (Plural only when referring to different kinds, types, instances, or varieties.) □ *The intensity of the light was so low that I could not see what I was reading.* Ⓒ *Radiation of two different intensities was detected outside the factory.*

**intention** [ɪn 'tɛn ʃən] *n.* a purpose; a plan. □ *The intention behind my screaming was to warn you of the truck that was coming toward you.*

**intercourse** ['ɪn tɚ kors] *n.* copulation, usually human copulation. (Short for **sexual intercourse.**) □ *They chose to avoid intercourse until they were married.*

**interest** ['ɪn trəst] **1.** *n.* the attention or concern shown toward someone or something. (No plural form.) □ *Jane studied biology with interest.* **2.** *n.* something that causes ①; something that attracts one's curiosity or attention as in ⑤. □ *Literature is a great interest of mine.* **3.** *n.* the money—usually a percentage of the amount borrowed—that a lender charges to someone who borrows money. (No plural form.) □ *The bank charged 8% interest on my loan.* **4.** *n.* the money—usually a percentage of the amount held—that a bank or other financial institution pays for holding someone's money for a period of time. (No plural form.) □ *My checking account earns 3% interest.* **5.** *tv.* to capture the attention or curiosity of someone or something. □ *Biology interests Jane greatly.*

**interesting** ['ɪn trəs tɪŋ] *adj.* causing interest or curiosity; worthy of interest; keeping someone's interest. (Adv: *interestingly.*) □ *My grandmother has had a very interesting life.*

**interestingly** ['ɪn trəs tɪŋ li] **1.** *adv.* in a way that causes or keeps someone's interest. □ *The design was interestingly complex.* **2.** *adv.* strangely; curiously. □ *Interestingly enough, I, too, have a grandfather named William.*

**interfere** [ɪn tɚ 'fɪr] **1.** *iv.* to get involved [with something that is private or restricted]. □ *Please stop interfering. This is none of your business.* **2. interfere with** someone or something *iv. + prep. phr.* to create an interruption; to disturb someone; to disturb the operation of something. □ *Our neighbor's microwave oven interferes with our television reception.*

**interference** [ɪn tɚ ˈfɪr əns] **1.** *n.* interfering; serving as a problem; getting involved and making oneself a bother. (No plural form.) □ *Dave's interference in our problem only made the matter worse.* **2.** *n.* an electronic disturbance that prevents the clear reception of a radio or television signal. (No plural form.) □ *I couldn't hear the radio announcer because there was too much interference.*

**interior** [ɪn ˈtɪr i ɚ] **1.** *n.* a part or surface that is within something; a part or surface that is inside of something. □ *The building's interior needed to be repaired.* **2.** *n.* the area within something; the space that is inside something. □ *The bear ran deep into the interior of the cave.* **3.** *adj.* <the adj. use of ① or ②.> □ *The interior dimensions of the frame are 18 inches by 24 inches.*

**interj.** an abbreviation of **interjection**.

**interjection** [ɪn tɚ ˈdʒɛk ʃən] *n.* a word, expression, or phrase that is used to express something with force or emotion. (Abbreviated *interj.* here.) □ Help! *is an interjection.*

**intermediate** [ɪn tɚ ˈmid i ɪt] *adj.* between two stages, levels, sizes, weights, etc. (Adv: *intermediately.*) □ *We only have very small and very large sizes in stock. We've sold all the intermediate sizes.*

**intermission** [ɪn tɚ ˈmɪ ʃən] *n.* a pause between the parts of a play, movie, opera, or other performance. □ *Do I have time to get to the restroom before the intermission ends?*

**international** [ɪn tɚ ˈnæʃ ə nəl] **1.** *adj.* of or about two or more countries; between two countries; among three or more countries. (Adv: *internationally.*) □ *Mexico, Canada, and the United States signed an international trade agreement.* **2.** *adj.* global; in all nations. (Adv: *internationally.*) □ *Poverty is an international problem.*

**Internet** [ˈɪn tɚ nɛt] *n.* a digital system of high-speed global communication and data transfer. (No plural form. Not a proper noun, but usually capitalized. Can be shortened to **Net**.) □ *I receive many e-mail messages every day over the Internet.*

**interrog.** an abbreviation of **interrogative**.

**interrogative** [ɪn tə ˈrɑg ə tɪv] *n.* a word or expression used to ask a question. (**Who, what, when, where, why,** and **how** are the most common **interrogatives**. Abbreviated *interrog.* here.) □ *Many of the interrogatives in English are also pronouns.*

**interrupt** [ɪn tə ˈrʌpt] **1.** *iv.* to break into a conversation; to start talking while someone else is talking. □ *Would you stop interrupting and let me finish my sentence?* **2.** *tv.* to stop the flow or movement of something; to stop something temporarily. □ *A three-car accident interrupted the flow of traffic.*

**interruption** [ɪn tə ˈrʌp ʃən] **1.** *n.* interrupting; stopping and interfering in a conversation or an activity. □ *Please excuse my interruption, but we have to leave in five minutes.* **2.** *n.* a break in the flow of something. □ *We forgot to pay our phone bill, so there was an interruption in our service.*

**intersection** [ɪn tɚ ˈsɛk ʃən] **1.** *n.* a junction of two or more roads, streets, highways, etc.; a place where roads or streets come together or cross. □ *Turn left at the next intersection.* **2.** *n.* the point at which two or more things join. □ *The leak is at the intersection of the two pipes.*

**interval** [ˈɪn tɚ vəl] **1.** *n.* a period of time between two events. ☐ *Anne coughed during the short interval between scenes.* **2.** *n.* the distance between two points in a series of points. ☐ *The interval between trees in the orchard is 20 feet.* **3.** *n.* the name of the distance between two musical tones. ☐ *Common musical intervals are thirds, fifths, and sixths.*

**interview** [ˈɪn tɚ vju] **1.** *n.* a meeting between an employer and a job seeker, where the employer asks questions of the job seeker. ☐ *I bought a new suit to wear to my job interview.* **2.** *n.* a meeting where a reporter asks questions of someone. ☐ *Did you watch the president's interview last night?* **3.** *tv.* to ask questions of someone, possibly about employment; to make direct inquiries of someone. ☐ *The researcher interviewed people about their drinking habits.* **4.** *tv.* to ask questions of someone for a television or radio program, a newspaper or magazine article, etc. ☐ *The newspaper reporter interviewed the mayor, and the photographer took a lot of pictures.*

**intestine** [ɪn ˈtɛs tɪn] *n.* the tube or channel between the stomach and the rectum. (Often plural with the same meaning.) ☐ *Susan needed surgery because her intestines were blocked.*

**into** [ˈɪn tu] **1.** *prep.* to the inner part of something; to the interior of something. ☐ *I went into the living room to watch TV.* **2.** *prep.* up against someone or something. ☐ *Mary ran into the wall.* **3.** *prep.* interested in something. (Informal.) ☐ *Mary was into mysteries, especially ones with detectives.*

**intransitive verb** [ɪn ˈtræn sə tɪv ˈvɚb] *n.* a verb not taking a direct object. (Abbreviated *iv.* here.) ☐ *"Go" is an intransitive verb.* ☐ *"John eats often" is a short sentence containing an intransitive verb.*

**introduce** [ɪn trə ˈdus] **1. introduce** someone **(to** someone**)** *tv.* + *obj.* (+ *prep. phr.*) to present someone to someone else when they meet for the first time. ☐ *We have not been introduced.* **2. introduce** someone **to** something *tv.* + *obj.* + *prep. phr.* to show someone something for the first time. ☐ *We introduced the baby to ice cream.* **3.** *tv.* to establish something; to bring something into use; to make something known or familiar to someone. ☐ *A new model of the car was introduced in Los Angeles last week.*

**introduction** [ɪn trə ˈdʌk ʃən] **1.** *n.* an instance of presenting one person to another person. ☐ *Introductions can be awkward if you don't remember someone's name.* **2.** *n.* making the availability of something known to people. ☐ *The introduction of the new book was delayed.* **3.** *n.* the part of a book, chapter, or lecture that comes at the beginning and explains its purpose. ☐ *The introduction to the book is only a few pages long.* **4.** *n.* the basic and important information about a subject. ☐ *This class is meant to be an introduction to logic.*

**invasion** [ɪn ˈve ʒən] **1.** *n.* a military attack. ☐ *The invasion of Pearl Harbor occurred on December 7, 1941.* **2.** *n.* the attack and spread of something bad or dangerous. (Fig. on ①.) ☐ *An invasion of locusts ate our crops.*

**invent** [ɪn ˈvɛnt] **1.** *tv.* to create something that has never been made before. ☐ *Thomas Edison invented the light bulb.* **2.** *tv.* to make up a story, an excuse, or a lie. (Fig. on ①.) ☐ *John invented an excuse to explain his absence.*

**invention** [ɪn ˈvɛn ʃən] **1.** *n.* the creation of a new device; the production of a new machine or a new process. (No plural form.) ☐ *The invention of the airplane made travel faster and easier.* **2.** *n.* a new device; something that has been created for the first time. □ *My new invention is a battery powered spoon for stirring soup.*

**inventor** [ɪn 'vɛn tɚ] *n.* someone who invents ① something; someone who has invented something. □ *The inventor of the telephone was Alexander Graham Bell.*

**investment** [ɪn 'vɛst mənt] *n.* money that is assigned to a project, stocks, a bank account, etc., with the hope and expectation of profit. □ *John's $2,500 investment yielded a profit when he sold the stock two years later.*

**investor** [ɪn 'vɛs tɚ] *n.* someone who puts money into an investment. □ *The investor lost all of his money in the stock-market crash.*

**invitation** [ɪn vɪ 'te ʃən] *n.* a written, printed, or spoken request to attend something. □ *I received an invitation to Mary's party in the mail today.*

**invoice** ['ɪn vɔɪs] **1.** *n.* a bill; a document showing how much money is owed for goods or services. □ *John mailed his invoice directly to the accounting department.* **2.** *tv.* to present someone or a business firm with ①. □ *The lawyer invoiced the company for 30 hours of work.*

**irk** ['ɚk] *tv.* to annoy, upset, or irritate someone. □ *It really irks me when you bite your nails.*

**iron** ['ɑɪɚn] **1.** *n.* an element that is a common metal, used to make steel. (No plural form.) □ *The iron was cast into huge blocks.* **2.** *n.* a small device with a flat metal bottom, used heated to press the wrinkles out of cloth. □ *Don't forget to unplug the iron before you leave.* **3.** *adj.* made from ①. □ *The rusted iron gate needed repair.* **4.** *tv.* to smooth the wrinkles out of clothes with ②. □ *I ironed the heavily wrinkled tablecloth.*

**irony** ['ɑɪ rə ni] **1.** *n.* using words to have a meaning opposite from their literal meaning in a funny or sarcastic way. (No plural form.) □ *Did you mean what you wrote, or were you using irony?* **2.** *n.* an event that has the opposite result of what was planned or expected. □ *The irony was that it rained the entire time we were on vacation.*

**irradiate** [ɪ 'red i et] *tv.* to treat something with radiation; to treat food with radiation to keep it from spoiling. □ *Very few grocery stores irradiate their produce.*

**irreg.** an abbreviation of **irregular** ④.

**irregular** [ɪr 'rɛg jə lɚ] **1.** *adj.* not regular; oddly shaped; uneven. (Adv: *irregularly.*) □ *The fluffy cloud has an irregular shape.* **2.** *adj.* happening at differing intervals of time; not happening regularly. (Adv: *irregularly.*) □ *I made irregular business trips to New York throughout the year.* **3.** *adj.* different from what is normal, and therefore unacceptable. (Euphemistic.) □ *Your request to leave early is highly irregular.* **4.** *adj.* [of the form of a noun, verb, adjective, or adverb] not regular in the way it takes suffixes, such as the plural, past tense, comparative, or superlative. (Abbreviated *irreg.* here. Adv: *irregularly.*) □ *The verb* take *has an irregular past-tense form:* took. □ Geese *is the irregular plural form of* goose.

**irritate** ['ɪr ɪ tet] **1.** *tv.* to cause a part of the body to become red or swollen. □ *The smoke irritates my eyes.* **2.** *tv.* to bother or annoy someone or something. □ *My little sister irritates me when I try to study.*

**irritation** [ɪr ɪ 'te ʃən] **1.** *n.* a bother; something that irritates. □ *Cigarette smoke is an irritation that I cannot endure.* **2.** *n.* the condition of being sore or itchy; soreness or tenderness of skin or other body tissues. (Plural only when referring to different kinds, types, instances, or varieties.) □ *Applying the lotion has helped, but there is still some* *irritation on my left arm.* 🄲 *You should put medicine on those irritations.*

**is** [ɪz] *iv.* <a form of **be**, used in the present tense of the third-person singular, that is, with *he*, *she*, *it*, and singular nouns.> (Reduced to *'s* in contractions.) □ *It is raining.*

**island** ['ɑɪ lənd] **1.** *n.* a piece of land surrounded by water and smaller than a continent. □ *Staten Island is part of New York City.* **2.** *n.* something that is completely surrounded by something else. (Fig. on ①.) □ *An island of ice cream arose from a pool of hot fudge.*

**isle** ['ɑɪl] *n.* an island. □ *The tiny isle is surrounded by deep blue water.*

**isn't** ['ɪz ənt] *cont.* "is not." □ *John isn't here yet.*

**isolate** ['ɑɪ sə let] *tv.* to keep someone or something separate from other things or people; to separate someone or something from other things or people. □ *John isolated himself and spoke to no one.*

**isolation** [ɑɪ sə 'le ʃən] *n.* the state of being isolated; someone or something in which someone or something is kept away from other things or people. (No plural form.) □ *Isolation from other human beings can cause mental illness.*

**issue** ['ɪ ʃu] **1.** *n.* one of a set of publications that are available regularly. □ *The March issue of the magazine included a story about the president.* **2.** *n.* the number of stamps or magazines printed at one time. □ *In July, we printed an issue of 40,000 copies.* **3.** *n.* a topic; the topic being discussed; a concern. □ *Crime will be an important issue in the next election.* **4.** *tv.* to assign something to someone; to supply something to someone. □ *They issued one textbook to each student.* **5.** *tv.* to speak or utter a command; to deliver or publish a written command or order. □ *When the boss issues a command, everyone obeys it.* **6.** *tv.* to publish a magazine, bulletin, newsletter, or newspaper. □ *The next edition of the newsletter will be issued in the fall.*

**it** [ɪt] **1.** *pron.* <a form referring to something that is not human; a form referring to a plant, an animal, or something that is not living.> (However, **it** is sometimes used to refer to a baby or a small child. See also **its** and **itself**. The plural is **they**.) □ *The plant does not need water now, but it will later.* **2.** *pron.* <a form used as the subject of a sentence where there is no real actor or doer.> (Usually with the verb **be**, but with others also.) □ *It rains every weekend.* □ *It looks like rain.* □ *How's it going?* **3.** *n.* the player who must find or chase everyone else in various children's games. □ *I touched Jane, and now she's it.*

**itch** ['ɪtʃ] **1.** *n.* a feeling on the skin that makes one want to scratch. □ *I felt an itch and knew I'd gotten a rash.* **2.** *iv.* [for the skin] to have ①. □ *My skin itches where the spider bit me.*

**itchy** ['ɪtʃ i] *adj.* with the feeling of itching; constantly itching. (Comp: *itchier;* sup: *itchiest.*) □ *Bill has an itchy rash.*

**it'd** ['ɪt ɪd] **1.** *cont.* "it would." □ *If I had a dog, it'd be named Fido.* **2.** *cont.* "it had," where **had** is an auxiliary. □ *By midnight, it'd stopped snowing.*

**item** ['ɑɪ təm] *n.* one thing that is part of a list or a series; a unit; a piece of information; a piece of news. □ *The first item on the shopping list is bread.*

**it'll** ['ɪt əl] *cont.* "it will." □ *The forecast says it'll rain tomorrow.*

**it's** ['ɪts] **1.** *cont.* "it is." (Compare this with **its**.) □ *It's 2:00 in the morning.* **2.** *cont.* "it has," where **has** is an auxiliary. (Compare this with **its**.) □ *Please polish the table. It's lost its shine.*

**its** ['ɪts] *pron.* <the possessive form of **it**>; belonging to it. (Compare this with **it's**.) □ *I own a car, but its engine needs repair.*

**itself** [ɪt 'sɛlf] **1.** *pron.* <the reflexive form of **it**.> □ *The streetlight shuts itself off automatically.* **2.** *pron.* <an emphatic form of **it**.> (Follows the nominal that is being emphasized.) □ *Please place the report itself on the table, but give the copy to me.* **3. by itself** *phr.* with the help of nothing else; without the addition of anything else. □ *Will this be enough by itself?*

**iv.** an abbreviation of **intransitive verb**.

**I've** ['ɑɪv] *cont.* "I have." (Where **have** is an auxiliary.) □ *I've got to be leaving soon.*

**ivory** ['ɑɪ vri] **1.** *n.* the hard, white substance of which an elephant's tusk is made. (No plural form.) □ *White piano keys used to be made of ivory.* **2.** *n.* the color of ①. □ *We prefer ivory walls to pure white walls.* **3.** *adj.* made of ①. □ *The valuable ivory necklace was stolen.* **4.** *adj.* <the adj. use of ②>; a shade of white that contains a small amount of yellow. □ *I wore my ivory shirt to the party.*

**ivy** ['ɑɪv i] *n.* a plant that holds onto walls, trees, etc., and climbs as it grows. (Plural only when referring to different kinds, types, instances, or varieties.) □ *I removed the ivy that covered the windows.* 🄲 *We planted four different ivies and only one grew well.*

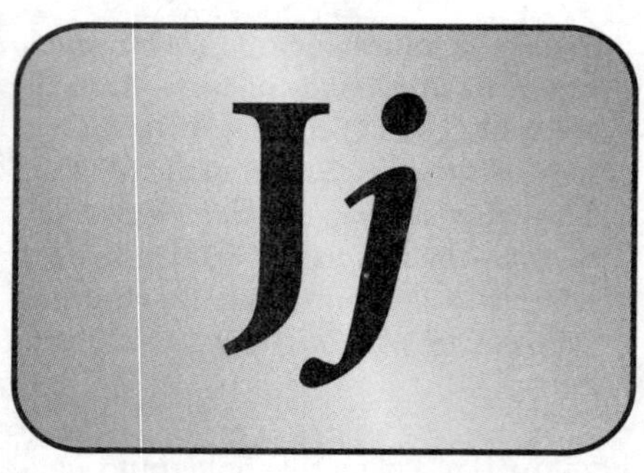

**jack** ['dʒæk] **1.** *n.* a device used to lift heavy things off the ground, especially to push up a car wheel in order to change a tire. □ *Anne used a jack to help fix her flat tire.* **2.** *n.* [in a deck of playing cards] a card that has a picture of a young man on it and is signified by the letter *J.* □ *The jack comes after the ten and before the queen in a deck of cards.* **3. jack** something **up** *tv. + obj. + adv.* to push something up with ①. □ *Please help me jack the car up.* 🅃 *Help me jack up the car.*

J

**jacket** ['dʒæk ɪt] **1.** *n.* a light coat; the light coat that is part of a suit. □ *Put on a jacket, it's cool outside.* **2.** *n.* a covering for a book or a sound recording. □ *The book's plot is summarized on the inside of the book jacket.*

**jail** ['dʒel] **1.** *n.* a building where criminals are locked up or where people are locked up while waiting for a trial. □ *The thief was sent to jail.* **2.** *tv.* to put someone in ①; to order someone to spend time in ①. □ *The judge decided to jail the thief for a full year.*

**jam** ['dʒæm] **1.** *n.* a sweet food made by boiling fruit and sugar until it is thick. (Plural only when referring to different kinds, types, instances, or varieties.) □ *Mike bought two jars of jam at the store.* 🄲 *These are the best jams on the market.* **2.** *tv.* to cause something to become stuck; to force something to fit someplace. □ *I jammed the book into the bookcase.* **3.** *iv.* to become stuck; to be unable to work properly because something is stuck; to be unable to move because something is stuck. □ *When the tape recorder jammed, Anne had to pick out pieces of the tape.*

**janitor** ['dʒæn ɪ tɚ] *n.* someone who cleans and takes care of a building. □ *You can find the janitor's office near the basement stairs.*

**January** ['dʒæn ju ɛr ɪ] Go to **month**.

**jar** ['dʒɑr] **1.** *n.* a container with a wide, circular top, usually made of glass or clay, and usually without handles. □ *Do the jars have lids that fit?* **2.** *n.* the contents of ①. □ *We finished half a jar of jam.* **3.** *tv.* to hit (lightly) or shake someone or something. □ *Don't jar the table, or you will spill my coffee.*

**jaw** ['dʒɔ] **1.** *n.* the upper or lower bone that forms the mouth and supports the teeth. □ *John broke his jaw in the car accident.* **2.** *n.* one of the two parts of a device that holds something tight, such as a vise or pliers. □ *The jaws of the machine held the part tightly while it was being smoothed.*

**jawbone** ['dʒɔ bon] *n.* the upper or lower bone that forms the mouth and supports the teeth. □ *Bill's jawbone was shattered in the car crash.*

**jazz** ['dʒæz] **1.** *n.* a style of music characterized by its rhythms, harmony, and the creative ways its players work together while it is being played. (No plural form.) □ *I love to listen to New Orleans jazz.* **2.** *adj.* <the adj. use of ①.> □ *My cousin plays the trumpet in a jazz band.*

**jealous** ['dʒɛl əs] *adj.* not liking anyone who might try to take away one's things or the people one loves. (Adv: *jealously.*) □ *Tom is jealous of anyone who talks to his girlfriend.*

**jealousy** ['dʒɛl ə si] *n.* the condition of being jealous; not liking someone who has something one wants. (No plural form.) □ *I try to hide my feelings of jealousy.*

**jeans** ['dʒinz] *n.* a pair of cloth pants, often dark blue, made of sturdy material. (Treated as plural. Number is expressed by *pair(s) of jeans.*) □ *I always put on my jeans as soon as I get home from the office.*

**jelly** ['dʒɛl i] **1.** *n.* a soft food that is made by boiling fruit juice and sugar together and is often spread on bread. (Plural only when referring to different kinds, types, instances, or varieties.) □ *When you go to the store, please buy some grape jelly.* 🄲 *I've tried all the jellies that this company makes. They're all good.* **2.** *adj.* made with ①. □ *Jim loves to eat jelly sandwiches.*

**jerk** ['dʒɚk] **1.** *n.* a sudden push or pull of the muscles; a movement made when something starts or stops quickly. □ *The driver stopped the bus too quickly, and the sudden jerk threw me out of my seat.* **2.** *tv.* to push or pull someone or something suddenly as the result of a sudden movement. □ *When Billy reached for the toy, his sister jerked it away.* **3.** *iv.* to move with ①; make a movement like ①. □ *Bill's arm jerked involuntarily.*

**jet** ['dʒɛt] **1.** *n.* a stream of air, water, steam, or another fluid that is shot out from a small opening at high pressure. □ *A jet of hot gases rushed out of the plane's engine.* **2.** *n.* an airplane that moves at high speed using engines similar to a rocket. (Short for **jet plane**.) □ *There is no jet going to Springfield, so we decided to drive rather than fly.* **3.** *iv.* [for water, steam, or another fluid] to form a stream by being forced out of a small opening under pressure. □ *Water jetted from the broken pipe.* **4.** *iv.* to travel by ②. □ *We jetted to the Bahamas on the company plane.* **5.** *tv.* to cause water, steam, or another fluid to form a stream by forcing it out of a small opening under pressure. □ *The firefighters' hoses jetted powerful streams of water into the burning building.*

**jet-black** ['dʒɛt 'blæk] *adj.* deep, shiny black in color. □ *Mary has jet-black hair.*

**jet engine** ['dʒɛt 'ɛn dʒən] *n.* an engine powered by **jet propulsion**. □ *The plane has four jet engines and is fast and powerful.*

**jet plane** ['dʒɛt 'plen] *n.* a high-speed plane; a plane that has one or more jet engines. (Can be shortened to **jet**.) □ *We flew to Europe on a jet plane.*

**jet propulsion** ['dʒɛt prə 'pʌl ʃən] *n.* a means of pushing something forward by forcing a jet out of the back. (No plural form.) □ *Jet propulsion is noisy but very efficient.*

**jewel** ['dʒu əl] *n.* a gem; a valuable stone; a piece of jewelry. □ *I bought a necklace having several precious jewels.*

**jeweler** ['dʒu (ə) lɚ] *n.* someone who deals in watches, valuable gems, and precious metals. □ *I had my watch repaired by the local jeweler.*

**jewelry** ['dʒu (ə)l ri] *n.* objects usually made of valuable metals or stones, such as rings, earrings, necklaces, bracelets, and pins. (No plural form. Treated as singular. Number is expressed with *piece(s) of jewelry.*) □ *I only wear 24-karat gold jewelry.*

**jiggle** ['dʒɪg əl] **1.** *tv.* to move someone or something up and down or from side to side. □ *Tom jiggled the key in the lock to try to open the door.* **2.** *iv.* to move up and down or from side to side. □ *Stop jiggling!*

**jingle** ['dʒɪŋ gəl] **1.** *n.* the ringing noise of metal objects gently hitting together; the noise of a small bell being struck. □ *I heard the jingle of Mary's keys as she pulled them out of her purse.* **2.** *n.* a tune or song used in advertising. □ *The shampoo ad has a catchy jingle.* **3.** *tv.* to make ringing noises by hitting metal objects together. □ *Anne jingled her bracelets as she put them on her arm.* **4.** *iv.* [for metal objects] to make noises when struck together; [for a small bell] to make a noise when shaken. □ *The bells on the door jingled as the door was opened.*

**job** ['dʒɑb] **1.** *n.* a career; an occupation; regular employment. □ *Bill got a job as a painter.* **2.** *n.* a task; a duty; a responsibility; a piece of work. □ *It is your job to feed the cats daily.* **3.** *n.* the performance or result of one's work. □ *Mary did a good job of painting the kitchen.*

**jog** ['dʒɔg] **1.** *n.* a slow, gentle run usually done for exercise; a [human] trot. □ *I felt really great after a jog around the neighborhood.* **2.** *n.* a bend to the right or the left; something that causes a line not to be straight. □ *Mary failed to see the jog in the road, and her car crashed into the fence.* **3.** *iv.* to exercise by running slowly. □ *Sue likes to jog in cool weather.*

**jogger** ['dʒɔg ɚ] *n.* someone who exercises by jogging. □ *The joggers run each morning, no matter how bad the weather is.*

**join** ['dʒɔɪn] **1.** *iv.* to come together; to connect; to unite. □ *Can you see where the two sections of the wall join?* **2.** *tv.* to connect someone or something to someone or something else; to unite people or things into a single unit. □ *A local judge joined the couple in marriage.* **3.** *tv.* to enroll in a club, class, the military, or some organization; to become a member of an organization. □ *Tom joined the army when he graduated from high school.*

**joint** ['dʒɔɪnt] **1.** *n.* a place where two things, especially bones, join. □ *The boards fit together in a tight joint.* **2.** *adj.* (Adv: *jointly.*) done or owned together; joined; united. □ *Mary and Jane shared joint ownership of the house.*

**joke** ['dʒok] **1.** *n.* something said or done to make people laugh, especially a short story told to make people laugh. □ *Jimmy told his sister a silly joke.* **2.** *tv.* to say something in a teasing or playful manner; to say something that is meant to be funny. (The object is a clause with **that** ⑦.) □ *When Mary wore a bright yellow dress, Bob joked that he needed sunglasses to look at her.* **3.** *iv.* to tell ①; to kid or tease [someone]; to say or do things that are meant to be funny. □ *Dave jokes and laughs because he is happy and friendly.*

**journal** ['dʒɚ nl] **1.** *n.* a diary; a book where one writes down one's feelings, thoughts, or activities. □ *Mary writes in her journal every night.* **2.** *n.* a magazine, periodical, or scholarly publication. □ *I subscribe to three scholarly journals in the field of medicine.*

**journey** ['dʒɚn i] **1.** *n.* a trip; a voyage. □ *Let's take a journey around the world.* **2.** *iv.* to travel. □ *We journeyed to another state over the weekend.*

**joy** ['dʒoɪ] **1.** *n.* extreme pleasure or happiness. (No plural form.) □ *My heart is filled with joy.* **2.** *n.* someone or something that causes extreme pleasure or happiness. □ *My child's birth was a joy.*

**joyous** ['dʒoɪ əs] *adj.* full of joy; extremely happy; very glad. (Adv: *joyously.*) □ *Our wedding day will be a joyous experience.*

**judge** ['dʒʌdʒ] **1.** *n.* an official who hears and settles cases in a court of law and who presides over trials. □ *The lawyer regarded the judge as a fair woman who had a good sense of professional ethics.* **2.** *n.* someone who helps decide the winner of a contest or competition. □ *I am a judge for the high-school science fair.* **3.** *tv.* to hear and settle a case in a court of law; to preside over a trial in a court of law. □ *Bob disagreed with the way the case was judged.* **4.** *tv.* to help decide the winner of a contest or competition. □ *Tom will judge the annual piano competition.* **5.** *tv.* to state an opinion about someone or something; to evaluate someone or something. □ *I will not judge Sue's behavior.* **6.** *tv.* to estimate something; to make a guess that something will happen. (The object is a clause with **that** ⑦.) □ *Bob judged that the car trip would take about five hours.*

**judgment** ['dʒʌdʒ mənt] **1.** *n.* the ability to make the proper decisions; the ability to judge. (No plural form.) □ *You made the error because your judgment is faulty.* **2.** *n.* the result of judging; the decision made by a judge or a jury. □ *It is the judgment of this court that you are guilty of murder.* **3.** *n.* an opinion. (No plural form.) □ *In Bob's judgment, we are all wrong.*

**juggle** ['dʒʌg əl] **1.** *tv.* to keep three or more objects moving through the air by catching and throwing them in a circle. □ *Tom juggled the oranges in the air.* **2.** *iv.* to toss objects in the air as in ①. □ *That clown juggles very well.* **3.** *tv.* to deal with several things at the same time. (Fig. on ②.) □ *John had a problem juggling his numerous responsibilities at work.*

**juice** ['dʒus] *n.* the liquid part of fruit, vegetables, or meat. (Plural only when referring to different kinds, types, instances, or varieties.) □ *Would you like a glass of orange juice?* Ⓒ *Which juices would you like to serve at the brunch?*

**July** [dʒə 'laɪ] Go to **month**.

**jumbo** ['dʒʌm bo] *adj.* extra large; larger than regular. □ *I ordered jumbo shrimp at the seafood restaurant.*

**jump** ['dʒʌmp] **1.** *iv.* to leap up; to spring up; to push off the ground with one's legs. □ *My cat jumped into my lap.* **2.** *iv.* to move suddenly, as if surprised or scared. □ *Sue jumped when I touched her shoulder.* **3.** *iv.* to go up sharply; to increase sharply; to rise sharply. (Fig. on ①.) □ *Have you noticed how much the price of food has jumped in the past year?* **4.** *tv.* to start a car by connecting its battery to another car's battery. □ *You need cables to jump your battery.* **5.** *n.* a leap off the ground; a leap off the ground and over, through, or across something. □ *The horse did not want to make the jump.* **6.** *n.* a sudden rise; an increase. (Fig. on ⑤.) □ *The jump in gas prices meant we could not afford to travel very much.*

**junction** ['dʒʌŋk ʃən] *n.* a place where two or more things come together, especially the place where roads or train tracks come together or cross. □ *I'll meet you at the junction of Main Street and Lincoln Road.*

**June** ['dʒun] Go to **month**.

**jungle** ['dʒʌŋ gəl] *n.* a tropical forest of thick, lush plant growth, usually near the equator. □ *The monkeys jumped from tree to tree in the jungle.*

**junior** ['dʒun jɚ] **1.** *adj.* of or about the third year of high school or college. (Prenominal only.) □ *Tom and Anne went to the junior prom.* **2.** *n.* a student in the third year of high school (11th grade) or the third year of college. □ *I am a junior this year at college.*

**junk** ['dʒʌŋk] **1.** *n.* things that are worthless; things that should be thrown away. (No plural form.) □ *Throw that junk out! It's been sitting in the attic for years.* **2.** *tv.* to throw something away. □ *I'm going to junk that old car. It hasn't worked right since I bought it.*

**jury** ['dʒɚ i] **1.** *n.* a group of people who listen to evidence at a trial in a court of law and make a decision about the truth of the facts of the case. □ *The jury could not reach agreement on the criminal's guilt.* **2.** *adj.* <the adj. use of ①.> □ *The lawyer requested a jury trial.*

**just** ['dʒʌst] **1.** *adj.* fair; not biased; honest; right; in accordance with the law. (Adv: *justly.*) □ *I feel I made a just decision on the matter.* **2.** *adj.* as someone deserves; appropriate. (Adv: *justly.*) □ *The criminal received a just punishment.* **3.** *adv.* only. □ *There is just one cookie left in the package.* **4.** *adv.* barely; by a small amount. □ *Bob ran quickly, but he still just missed the train.* **5.** *adv.* exactly [the right amount and no more]. □ *I had just enough paint to cover the whole wall.*

**justice** ['dʒʌs tɪs] **1.** *n.* the quality or condition of being just; fairness, especially in a court of law. (No plural form.) □ *I felt that there was justice in the punishment that the criminal received.* **2.** *n.* the administration of law; the practice of law within the court system. (No plural form.) □ *The lawyer took a job with the Department of Justice.* **3.** *n.* a judge. (Also a title and term of address.) □ *Justice Smith presided over the municipal court.*

**justify** ['dʒʌs tɪ fɑɪ] *tv.* to explain why one did something; to give a good reason for something. □ *How can you justify what you did yesterday?*

**juvenile** ['dʒu və nɑɪl] **1.** *n.* a child [from a legal point of view]. □ *Each year, many juveniles are arrested for shoplifting.* **2.** *n.* a young animal. □ *The juveniles will be able to fly as soon as their feathers grow.* **3.** *adj.* youthful; for young people. □ *I found a book for my grandson in the juvenile section of the library.*

J

**kangaroo** [kæŋ gə 'ru] *n.* a large animal of Australia that hops on its hind legs. (Pl ends in -*s*.) □ *The female kangaroo has a pouch in which she carries her babies.*

**keel** ['kil] *n.* the main beam along the bottom of a boat or ship on which the frame is built. □ *The boat's keel scraped the rocky bottom of the harbor.*

**keen** ['kin] **1.** *adj.* [of a cutting edge] sharp. (Adv: *keenly.* Comp: *keener;* sup: *keenest.*) □ *The keen edge of the razor blade was made of special steel.* **2.** *adj.* [of a sense of taste, vision, hearing, touch, or smell] very sensitive or sharp. (Fig. on ①. Adv: *keenly.* Comp: *keener;* sup: *keenest.*) □ *The dog had a keen sense of smell.*

**keep** ['kip] **1.** *tv., irreg.* to cause someone or something to remain somewhere. □ *Please keep the children in the backyard.* **2.** *tv., irreg.* to have something for a period of time; to continue to have something. □ *I kept my car for four years, and then I sold it.* **3. keep doing something** *phr.* to continue doing something. (Pt/pp: **kept**.) □ *Someone kept knocking on my door for a long time.* **4. keep something up** *tv., irreg. + obj. + adv.* to maintain something; to manage or run something; to tend or take care of something. □ *You must keep your appearance up.* Ⓣ *I keep up my appearance.*

**keeper** ['kip ɚ] *n.* someone who keeps someone or something; a protector; a guard; someone who cares for animals in a zoo. □ *I don't know where Tom is. I am not his keeper.*

**keepsake** ['kip sek] *n.* something that is kept to remind the owner of someone or something; a memento. □ *Uncle John left a small keepsake to Anne in his will.*

**kennel** ['kɛn əl] *n.* a place where dogs are kept. □ *We placed our two dogs in the local kennel when we went on vacation.*

**kept** ['kɛpt] pt/pp of **keep**.

**ketchup** ['kɛtʃ əp] *n.* a thick liquid, made from tomatoes, that is put on food for flavoring. (The same as **catsup**. Plural only when referring to different kinds, types, instances, or varieties.) □ *John loves ketchup on his fries.* Ⓒ *Most ketchups taste the same.*

K

**kettle** ['kɛt əl] *n.* a large cooking pot; a pot for heating liquids. □ *Mary stirred the soup in the kettle slowly.*

**key** ['ki] **1.** *n.* a device that unlocks or locks a lock; something that unlocks something that is locked. (**Keys** are typically flat, metal, and notched along one edge.) □ *I used my key to unlock the car door.* **2.** *n.* something that gives access to an answer or a solution; something that provides the answers or solutions for something. (Fig. on ①.) □ *The answer key is in the back of the book.* **3.** *n.* a part of a machine or instrument that is pressed down to make something happen, as on a computer keyboard, a typewriter, or a piano. □ *I pressed the "Enter" key on the computer keyboard.* **4.** *n.* a musical scale that begins on a particular note; a set of related musical notes. □ *You must sing the song in a higher key.* **5.** *adj.* important; essential; basic. □ *The key point is missing from your speech.*

**keyboard** ['ki bord] **1.** *n.* a row of keys that make a certain musical sound when pressed. □ *Keyboards are found on accordions, organs, pianos, harpsichords,* *and other similar instruments.* **2.** *n.* an electronic device that creates music. ☐ *The electric keyboard can make all sorts of sounds.* **3.** *n.* the rows of keys standing for letters, symbols, and numbers as found on typewriters, computers, etc. ☐ *Don't pound on the keyboard so hard. You'll damage it.*

**keynote** ['ki not] *adj.* [of a speech or a speaker] primary or main. (Prenominal only.) ☐ *The keynote speaker was given a standing ovation.*

**keypad** ['ki pæd] **1.** *n.* [on a computer] a special, separate set of number keys arranged as on a calculator. ☐ *Dave typed his account number on the keypad.* **2.** *n.* any small control panel having an arrangement of push buttons, as found on a telephone or a calculator. ☐ *The calculator has an oversized keypad.*

K

**kick** ['kɪk] **1.** *tv.* to strike someone or something with the foot, usually the toe of a shoe or boot. ☐ *Please don't kick the cat!* **2.** *iv.* to move one's legs back and forth as if **kicking** something as in ①. ☐ *The baby lay on its back in the crib and kicked.* **3.** *n.* an act of striking someone or something with the foot, as in ①. ☐ *The kick from the mule was painful.*

**kid** ['kɪd] **1.** *n.* a child; a youngster. ☐ *My kid loves to play with toys.* **2.** *n.* a baby goat. ☐ *The hungry kid cried for food.* **3.** *n.* the skin of ②. (No plural form.) ☐ *The gloves were made of brown kid.* **4.** *tv.* to tease someone; to joke with someone; to trick someone. ☐ *We kidded Tom about his new short haircut.* **5.** *adj.* [of a brother or sister] younger. (Informal. Prenominal only.) ☐ *Dave's kid brother is a real pest.*

**kidney** ['kɪd ni] **1.** *n.* one of the two organs that separate waste and water from the bloodstream. ☐ *The kidneys filter waste from the bloodstream.* **2.** *adj.* <the adj. use of ①.> ☐ *The kidney operation was a success.*

**kill** ['kɪl] **1.** *tv.* to cause the death of someone or something directly. ☐ *The cat killed a mouse and brought it into the house.* **2.** *tv.* to end something; to cause something to end. (Fig. on ①.) ☐ *Kill the project. We've run out of money.* **3.** *iv.* to cause death. ☐ *The police are worried that the crazy murderer will kill again.* **4.** *n.* an animal that is hunted and **killed** ①. (No plural form.) ☐ *The hunters took their kill to their truck.*

**killer** ['kɪl ɚ] *n.* someone or something that kills; someone or something that causes death. ☐ *The criminal became a dangerous killer when he was provoked.*

**kilogram** ['kɪl ə græm] *n.* a metric unit of weight, equal to 1,000 grams or about 2.2 pounds. ☐ *The flour was measured in kilograms.*

**kilometer** [kɪ 'lɑm ə tɚ] *n.* a metric unit of distance, equal to 1,000 meters or about 5/8 of a mile. ☐ *The town was located 30 kilometers from our home.*

**kilowatt** ['kɪl ə wɑt] *n.* a metric unit of electrical power, equal to 1,000 watts per hour. ☐ *Our toaster uses 2 kilowatts.*

**kind** ['kɑɪnd] **1.** *n.* a sort; a type; a variety. ☐ *I don't want that kind. I think it's ugly.* **2.** *adj.* thoughtful; helpful. (Adv: *kindly.* Comp: *kinder;* sup: *kindest.*) ☐ *Would you be kind enough to lend me your handkerchief?*

**kindergarten** ['kɪn dɚ gɑrd n] *n.* the grade before first grade, usually for children between the ages of 4 and 6. ☐ *Anne learned to count to 25 when she was in kindergarten.*

**king** ['kɪŋ] **1.** *n.* the male ruler of a nation where the head of the country inherits his office from a previous ruler. ☐ *The prince will someday become king of England.* **2.** *n.* a playing card with a picture of ① on it. ☐ *Mary laid down the king of spades.* **3.** *n.* a playing piece in chess that can move one space in any direction. □ *It's your turn to move your king.*

**kingdom** ['kɪŋ dəm] **1.** *n.* a country ruled by a king or queen. □ *King Edward ruled over a vast kingdom.* **2.** *n.* one of three divisions of nature—animal, vegetable, and mineral. □ *Humans are members of the animal kingdom.*

**kiss** ['kɪs] **1.** *n.* a touching of one's lips to someone or something, especially someone else's lips. □ *Jane gave her boyfriend a good-bye kiss.* **2.** *tv.* to touch one's lips to someone or something, especially someone else's lips. □ *Bob kissed Jane before he went to work.* **3.** *iv.* [for two people] to **kiss** each other on the lips, as in ②. □ *Lovers were kissing in the park.*

**kit** ['kɪt] **1.** *n.* a container or carrying device that holds tools, equipment, or supplies for a specific purpose. □ *The kit in the trunk holds many tools.* **2.** *n.* the parts and instructions needed to build a particular thing, such as a model airplane. □ *I bought Tom a model-car kit for his birthday.*

**kitchen** ['kɪtʃ ən] **1.** *n.* a room where food is stored and cooked. □ *Sue loves to cook, so she spends a lot of time in the kitchen.* **2.** *adj.* <the adj. use of ①.> □ *Move the kitchen chair away from the oven.*

**kite** ['kɑɪt] *n.* a small wooden frame covered with cloth, paper, or plastic and attached to a long string—flown in the wind for amusement. □ *Jane flew her paper kite in the park.*

**kitten** ['kɪt n] *n.* a baby cat; a young cat. □ *My kitten is only two months old.*

**knee** ['ni] **1.** *n.* the front part of the joint in the middle of the leg. □ *I bruised my knee when I ran into the table.* **2.** *n.* the part of a pants leg that covers ①. □ *Sue ripped a hole in the knee of her pants.*

**kneecap** ['ni kæp] *n.* the flat bone at the front of the knee. □ *Mike kicked John in the kneecap.*

**kneel** ['nil] *iv., irreg.* to put the weight of one's body on one or both knees. (Pt/pp: *kneeled* or **knelt**.) □ *The worshipers knelt in church during the service.*

**knelt** ['nɛlt] a pt/pp of **kneel**.

**knew** ['nu] pt of **know**.

**knife** ['nɑɪf] **1.** *n., irreg.* a long, flat utensil or tool that has a handle and a sharp edge used for cutting. (Pl: **knives**.) □ *Anne cuts her steak with a sharp knife.* **2.** *tv.* to stab someone or something. □ *The criminal was arrested for knifing his victims.*

**knit** ['nɪt] *tv.* to make a fabric or clothing by using long needles to loop yarn or thread together. □ *Mary likes to knit scarves in the winter.*

**knives** ['nɑɪvz] pl of **knife**.

**knock** ['nɑk] **1.** *n.* the noise made by rapping or tapping as with ④. □ *Did you hear that knock? I think someone is at the door.* **2.** *n.* a sharp hit; a rap; a thump. □ *Bill received a knock on the head.* **3.** *tv.* to hit or bump something and make it move or fall; to hit something against someone or something. □ *I knocked the vase off the coffee table.* **4.** *iv.* to hit one's knuckles against something. □ *Sue knocked so hard that her knuckles hurt.*

**knot** ['nɑt] **1.** *n.* a tight lump made where pieces of rope, cord, hair, string, etc., are tied together. □ *Anne tied a knot in her scarf.* **2.** *n.* a hard circle of wood in a board, where a small branch was joined. □ *I pounded the knot out of the board with a hammer.* **3.** *n.* a unit of speed equal to 1.15 miles traveled per hour, used to measure the movement of ships and wind at sea. □ *The ship was traveling at 10 knots.* **4.** *tv.* to tie something in ①; to fasten something with ①. □ *Can you knot the ends of the cord* *together?* **5.** *iv.* to become tied or twisted into ①. □ *As the rope twisted, it knotted.*

**know** ['no] **1.** *tv., irreg.* to have met and become familiar with someone. (Pt: **knew**; pp: **known**.) □ *I know your family well.* **2.** *tv., irreg.* to understand something; to have had experience with something. □ *I know what you mean.* **3.** *tv., irreg.* to recognize someone or something. □ *I know trouble when I see it.* **4.** *tv., irreg.* to have knowledge about someone or something; to have information about someone or something. (The object can be a clause with **that** ⑦.) □ *Did you know that we will be leaving tomorrow?*

**knowledge** ['nɑl ɪdʒ] *n.* the information that is known about someone or something. (No plural form.) □ *It takes special knowledge to program a computer.*

**known** ['non] pp of **know**.

**knuckle** ['nʌk əl] *n.* the joint between the bones of a finger or the joint between the finger and the hand. □ *I scraped my knuckles on the concrete wall.*

K

**lab** ['læb] *n.* **laboratory.** □ *The scientist took the specimen back to the lab.*

**label** ['leb əl] **1.** *n.* a small notice bearing important information. □ *I tore the label loose from my shirt collar.* **2.** *tv.* to attach ① to something. □ *Bill labeled the children's presents with their names.*

**labor** ['leb ɚ] **1.** *n.* a kind of work, especially hard, physical work. (No plural form.) □ *Building a house requires a lot of labor.* **2. one's labor(s)** *n.* one's work or the product of one's work; effort. (Singular or plural with the same meaning, but not countable.) □ *Her labors were rewarded with a good salary increase.* **3.** *n.* workers, especially in contrast to people in management. (No plural form. Treated as singular.) □ *There is a shortage of skilled labor in this area.* **4.** *n.* the work a woman's body does to bring about birth; the contractions of the womb in the process of giving birth. (No plural form.) □ *Labor started 12 hours before the baby was born.* **5.** *adj.* <the adj. use of ③.> □ *The economics professor specialized in labor issues.* **6.** *iv.* to work hard. □ *The crew labored for days on the difficult project.*

**laboratory** ['læb rə tor i] **1.** *n.* a room or building that contains scientific equipment for experiments, tests, manufacture, or instruction. (Often shortened to **lab**.) □ *The nurse took the blood samples to the laboratory.* **2.** *adj.* <the adj. use of ①.> □ *I spilled some chemicals on my laboratory coat.*

**labor pains** ['leb ɚ 'penz] *n.* the (mother's) pains that accompany the birth of a child. □ *When Susan's labor pains were two minutes apart, she left home for the hospital.*

**lace** ['les] **1.** *n.* a delicate web of cotton or other thread woven into a design or pattern. (No plural form.) □ *Her elegant blouse was made of fine lace.* **2.** *n.* a string used for tying something closed, especially for tying one's shoes

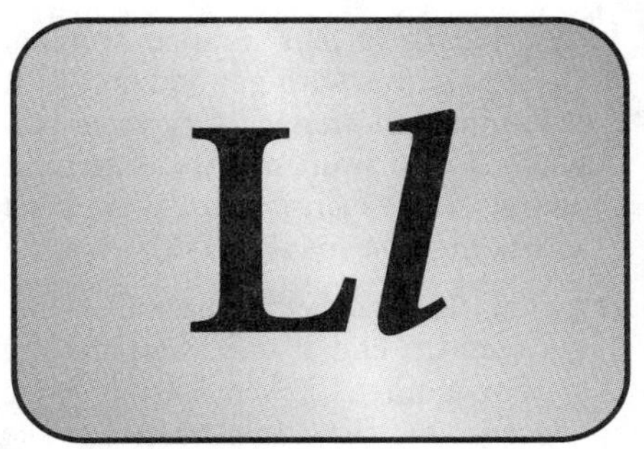

closed; a **shoelace.** □ *Your laces are untied.* **3. lace** something **(up)** *tv. + obj. (+ adv.)* to tie something, especially one's shoes, closed using a string that goes through a series of holes or loops. □ *I laced up my shoes tightly.* **4.** *adj.* made of ①. □ *I washed the delicate lace tablecloth carefully.*



**lack** ['læk] **1.** *n.* a shortage of something; the condition of not having any of something. □ *The frightened soldier suffered from a lack of courage.* **2.** *tv.* to need something; not to have enough of something; to be without something. □ *Because the soldier lacked courage, he ran from the battle.*

**lacy** ['les i] **1.** *adj.* made of lace. (Adv: *lacily.* Comp: *lacier;* sup: *laciest.*) □ *The lacy shawl tore easily when I caught it on a twig.* **2.** *adj.* delicate and complex like lace; having a delicate pattern. (Fig. on ①. Adv: *lacily.* Comp: *lacier;* sup: *laciest.*) □ *The spider's lacy web caught many flies.*

**ladder** ['læd ɚ] *n.* a set of steps attached to two side pieces, used for climbing up to reach something or climbing down from something. □ *Be careful. The bottom rung of that ladder is broken.*

**ladle** ['led l] **1.** *n.* a large, deep spoon with a long handle, used for serving a liquid from a bowl. □ *I used the ladle to put some soup in each person's bowl.* **2.** *tv.* to serve a liquid using ①. □ *I ladled some punch into my cup.*

**lady** ['led i] **1.** *n.* a refined woman. (Compare this with **gentleman.**) □ *A polite and well-dressed lady greeted each guest.* **2.** *n.* a woman. (Also a term of address.) □ *A short lady asked me to get a book from the top shelf.*

**lag** ['læg] **1.** *n.* a delay; the period of time between the end of one event and the start of another. □ *There was a brief lag when we switched from one telephone system to another.* **2. lag behind someone or something** *iv.* + *prep. phr.* to travel behind someone or something, especially because of moving more slowly. □ *My horse was slow and lagged behind all the others.*

**laid** ['led] pt/pp of **lay.**

**lain** ['len] a pp of **lie.**

**lair** ['lɛr] *n.* an animal's shelter; the place where an animal sleeps. □ *The hunter followed the bear back to its lair.*

**lake** ['lek] *n.* a large body of water surrounded by land. □ *Most lakes contain fresh water.*

**lamb** ['læm] **1.** *n.* a young sheep. □ *The farmer found the lost lamb in the pasture.* **2.** *n.* the meat of ① used as food. (No plural form.) □ *The butcher sold me a pound of lamb.*

**lame** ['lem] *adj.* not able to walk properly; limping; crippled. (Adv: *lamely.* Comp: *lamer;* sup: *lamest.*) □ *My horse was lame and couldn't carry me.*

**lamp** ['læmp] **1.** *n.* a device that makes light; an electric light bulb. □ *The glass part that holds the glowing wire is the lamp. We call it a bulb, but the box says it's a lamp.* **2.** *n.* a stand—often ornamental—that holds an electric light bulb. □ *I sat next to the lamp and read my book.*

**lamppost** ['læmp post] *n.* a post that supports a street light. □ *The workers replaced the light at the top of the lamppost.*

**lampshade** ['læmp ʃed] *n.* a cover that fits over the electric light bulb in a lamp to soften the glare of the light. □ *The light of the lamp was too strong without the lampshade.*

**land** ['lænd] **1.** *n.* the dry, solid part of the earth's surface; the part of the earth's surface that is not covered with water. (No plural form.) □ *Amphibians live both in water and on land.* **2.** *n.* ground; dirt; soil. (No plural form.) □ *Few plants grow here because the land is very dry.* **3.** *n.* a portion of ①; an area of ground. (No plural form.) □ *The land west of the river is not part of this county.* **4.** *n.* a country. □ *I enjoy visiting foreign lands.* **5.** *iv.* [for someone or something that is moving or falling through the air] to stop and come to rest somewhere, especially on the ground. □ *I dropped the hammer, and it landed on my foot.* **6.** *iv.* [for an airplane] to return to the ground safely. □ *The plane landed five minutes late.* **7.** *tv.* [for a pilot] to return an airplane to the ground safely. □ *Bob landed the jet in the thick fog.*

**landlady** ['lænd led i] *n.* a woman who owns and rents out space where people can live, such as houses and apartments; a woman who manages residential rental property. □ *I asked my landlady if I could pay the rent a few days late.*

**landlord** ['lænd lord] *n.* a person or a company that manages and collects rent for houses, apartments, and offices. □ *I asked my landlord to fix the broken refrigerator.*

**landscape** ['lænd skep] **1.** *n.* the land and the things visible on it, such as trees, bodies of water, rocks, hills, etc. (Plural only when referring to different kinds, types, instances, or varieties.) □ *Anne sat on a hill and gazed at the landscape around her.* Ⓒ *Iceland and Arizona have remarkably different landscapes.* **2.** *n.* a painting of land or outdoor scenes. □ *The landscape above my sofa was painted by my mother.* **3.** *tv.* to arrange flowers, trees, bushes, hills, rocks, and other objects to make a yard or park look beautiful. □ *The park was landscaped with a wide variety of bushes.*

**lane** ['len] **1.** *n.* a road, path, or route. □ *I live on Cherry Lane.* **2.** *n.* a section of a road wide enough for one line of traffic; a section of a running track wide enough for one person to run; a division of a swimming pool wide enough for one person to swim. □ *The swimmer in the fifth lane won the race.*

**language** ['læŋ gwɪdʒ] **1.** *n.* the system of spoken and written symbols used by people to express thoughts, meaning, and emotions. (Plural only when referring to different kinds, types, instances, or varieties.) □ *The study of language is called linguistics.* Ⓒ *German is the language spoken by most people in Germany.* **2.** *n.* any system of symbols used in a computer program. □ *Our new programmer only knows an older version of the language our computers use.* **3.** *n.* a specific style of expression. (No plural form.) □ *Please do not use dirty language.*

**lantern** ['læn tɚn] *n.* a protective case with clear sides, containing a source of light. □ *A dim candle flame flickered inside the lantern.*

**lap** ['læp] **1.** *n.* the flat surface formed by the tops of the upper legs when someone is sitting. □ *I put the dinner plate on my lap since there was no table.* **2.** *n.* one trip around a track; two lengths of a swimming pool. □ *The swimming team members swim 20 laps each day.* **3. lap something (up)** *tv. + obj. (+ adv.)* to drink a liquid by taking it in with the tongue, as a cat or dog does. □ *The cat lapped up the milk in its bowl.* **4.** *iv.* [for water] to move in small waves, making a gently splashing noise. □ *The water lapped against the side of the pool.*

**lapel** [lə 'pɛl] *n.* on a coat or jacket, one of the flaps that is folded back toward the shoulders, just below the collar. □ *I brushed some lint from my lapel.*

**large** ['lɑrdʒ] **1.** *adj.* greater in size than average; more than average; big. (Comp: *larger;* sup: *largest.*) □ *The large building towered over the other ones.* **2.** *n.* an object, especially one for sale, that is **large** ① in size. □ *I think I need to buy a large, because the medium doesn't fit.*

**largely** ['lɑrdʒ li] *adv.* primarily; mainly. □ *I left there largely because I wanted to live in a warmer climate.*

**lash** ['læʃ] **1.** *n.* a blow from a whip. □ *The mules felt the lash from the driver's whip.* **2.** *n.* an **eyelash**. □ *The pretty model had long, black lashes.* **3.** *tv.* to hit someone or something with a whip. □ *The victim was lashed three times.* **4.** *tv.* to tie someone or something [to something]; to bind someone or something. □ *To carry the new mattress home from the store, we lashed it to the top of our car.*

**last** ['læst] **1.** *adj.* final; at the end; after all other things or people. (Adv: *lastly.*) □ *The last month of the year is December.* **2.** *adj.* the most recent; nearest in the past; latest. □ *Who was the last president?* **3.** *adj.* least likely; least appropriate. □ *My selfish brother is the last person I'd ask for help.* **4.** *iv.* to continue for a length of time; to remain; to endure. □ *I hope my luck lasts a little longer.* **5. at last** *phr.* finally; after a long wait. □ *At last, we have gotten something to eat.*

**latch** ['lætʃ] **1.** *n.* a device for holding a door or window closed; a lock for a door or window that can be locked and unlocked with a key. □ *I shut the window and slid the latch into place.* **2.** *tv.* to close a door or window so that the **latch** ① seizes and holds the door or window closed firmly. □ *I latched the front door before I went to bed.* **3.** *iv.* [for ①] to seize and hold [something]; [for something] to close firmly with ①. □ *The cabinet door won't latch!*

**late** ['let] **1.** *adj.* not on time; past the time that something is supposed to happen; past the time that someone or something is to be in a place. (Comp: *later;* sup: *latest.*) □ *The teacher scolded the student for being late.* **2.** *adj.* far into a certain period of time; toward the end of a certain period of time. □ *The Spanish-American War was in the late 19th century.* **3.** *adj.* no longer living; dead, especially having died recently; now dead. (Prenominal only.) □ *Her late husband was a very famous man.* **4.** *adv.* after the time that something is supposed to happen. □ *I came to class five minutes late.*

**lately** ['let li] *adv.* recently. □ *Lately, I've been working more hours than usual.*

L

**later** ['let ɚ] *adv.* at a time after the present time; at a future time. □ *Bob will be here later.*

**lather** ['læð ɚ] **1.** *n.* white foam that is made by mixing soap with water. (No plural form.) □ *I rinsed the lather from my body in the shower.* **2.** *tv.* to cover something with ①. □ *I have to lather the dog with a special soap that kills fleas.*

**laugh** ['læf] **1.** *iv.* to express pleasure or amusement by making short, happy sounds with the voice. □ *The children laughed when the clown fell down.* **2.** *n.* the noise that someone makes when amused, as in ①. □ *When I heard his laugh, I knew he liked my joke.*

**laughter** ['læf tɚ] *n.* the sound(s) made when people laugh. (No plural form. Treated as singular.) □ *The movie theater echoed with the audience's laughter.*

**launch** ['lɔntʃ] **1.** *tv.* to set a new boat or ship into the water for the first time. □ *We officially named the new boat when we launched it.* **2.** *tv.* to send a rocket or its cargo into the air. □ *The government launched a huge spaceship.* **3.** *tv.* to begin a project; to start carrying out a plan. (Fig. on ①.) □ *The government launched a new program to help the poor.* **4.** *n.* an instance of sending something as in ① or ②. □ *The launch of the ship was postponed because of the hurricane.*

**launching pad** ['lɔn tʃɪŋ pæd] *n.* the platform from which rockets are launched. □ *The reporters gathered near the launching pad to view the rocket.*

**launder** ['lɔn dɚ] *tv.* to wash clothes or fabric; to wash and iron clothes or fabric. □ *The housekeeper laundered my dirty clothes.*

**laundry** ['lɔn dri] **1.** *n.* clothes that need to be washed; clothes that have just been washed and dried. (No plural form.) □ *I placed the clean laundry on the table and started folding it.* **2.** *n.* a business where clothes can be taken to be washed. □ *How much will the laundry charge for cleaning 10 shirts?* **3.** *n.* a location in a house or apartment building where clothes are washed. □ *Our laundry is in the basement.*

**lavatory** ['læv ə tor i] **1.** *n.* a sink used for washing one's hands; a wash basin with running water available. □ *I used the lavatory to wash my hands before dinner.* **2.** *n.* a bathroom; a room with a toilet. (Euphemistic.) □ *Can you tell me where the lavatory is?*

**lavish** ['læv ɪʃ] *adj.* in or involving large amounts; grand and excessive. (Adv: *lavishly.*) □ *Lisa's wealthy parents throw lavish parties.*

**law** ['lɔ] **1.** *n.* a rule; a statement of obligation within a legal system. □ *When the president signed the bill, it became a law.* **2. the law** *n.* the police force; police officers. (No plural form. Treated as singular.) □ *The criminal was eventually caught by the law.* **3.** *n.* a principle that describes something that happens as a regularity in mathematics or the natural world. ☐ *Everything in the universe obeys natural laws.* **4.** *n.* the study of the system of **laws** ①. (No plural form.) ☐ *My lawyer studied law at Columbia University.*

**lawn** ['lɔn] *n.* an area of ground with cut grass; a yard. ☐ *The front lawn needs to be mowed.*

**lawn mower** ['lɔn mo ɚ] *n.* a machine with blades that is used for cutting grass. (Can be shortened to **mower**.) ☐ *John pushed the lawn mower into a row of flowers accidentally.*

**law of gravity** ['lɔ əv 'græv ə ti] *n.* the fact that gravity pulls things toward the center of the earth. (No plural form. Also *law of gravitation*.) ☐ *When I let go of this book, it will fall. This demonstrates the law of gravity.*

**lawsuit** ['lɔ sut] *n.* a claim or complaint brought into a court of law. (Can be shortened to **suit**.) ☐ *The judge dismissed the man's groundless lawsuit.*

**lawyer** ['lɔ jɚ] *n.* someone who is trained in law and is a member of the bar. ☐ *Lisa got advice from a lawyer before she went to court.*

**lax** ['læks] *adj.* loose; not strict; not demanding. (Adv: *laxly.* Comp: *laxer;* sup: *laxest.*) ☐ *The rules about what people should wear to work at my office are very lax.*

**lay** ['le] **1.** a pt of **lie**. **2.** *adj.* not trained in a profession, such as law or medicine; not ordained as a religious leader. ☐ *This book explains cancer in language that a lay reader can understand.* **3.** *tv., irreg.* to place something on a surface or in a flat position. (Compare this with ④ and **lie**. Pt/pp: **laid**.) ☐ *I laid the car keys on the kitchen table.* **4.** *tv., irreg.* [for a hen] to produce and deposit an egg. ☐ *The bird laid her eggs in the nest.*

**layer** ['le ɚ] *n.* a level; one level of thickness that is placed on a surface. ☐ *A layer of dust covered the old desk.*

**layer cake** ['le ɚ kek] *n.* a cake made of sections of cake placed on top of each other and separated by frosting. ☐ *For my birthday, we had a chocolate layer cake with chocolate frosting.*

**lazy** ['lez i] **1.** *adj.* doing almost no work; avoiding work. (Adv: *lazily.* Comp: *lazier;* sup: *laziest.*) ☐ *The lazy student rarely did his homework.* **2.** *adj.* moving slowly. (Fig. on ①. Adv: *lazily.* Comp: *lazier;* sup: *laziest.*) ☐ *The raft moved slowly down the lazy river.*

**lead 1.** ['lɛd] *n.* a heavy, soft, grayish metal element. (No plural form.) ☐ *The pipes in the old building were made of lead.* **2.** ['lid] *n.* a clue; a hint; information that can be used to help solve a crime. ☐ *The detective followed every lead until he solved the crime.* **3. the lead** [...'lid] *n.* the front position; the first place. ☐ *The runner from Mexico held the lead throughout the entire race.* **4.** ['lid] *n.* the distance or amount by which someone or something is ahead of someone or something else, especially in a race or contest. ☐ *The team had a big lead during the whole game.* **5.** ['lid] *n.* the main role in a movie or play. ☐ *She has played the female lead in many musicals.* **6.** ['lid] *tv., irreg.* to guide someone or something; to show someone or something the way. (Pt/pp: **led**.) ☐ *The guide led the tourists through the castle.* **7.** ['lid] *tv., irreg.* to be the leader of someone or something; to be in charge of someone or something. ☐ *The researchers were led by the project director.* **8.** ['lid] *tv., irreg.* to be ahead of another team or other players in a competition. ☐ *Our team led Bill's team by five points.* **9.** ['lid] *iv., irreg.* to guide; to show the way. ☐ *Because no one else knew the way, John led.*

**leader** ['lid ɚ] *n.* a ruler; someone who leads or is in charge of a group of people. ☐ *The project leader gave me a new work assignment.*

L

**leaf** ['lif] **1.** *n., irreg.* the flat, usually green, part of a tree or plant that is attached to a branch or stem. (Pl: **leaves.**) □ *Leaves turn energy from the sun into food for the plant.* **2.** *n., irreg.* an extra section that can be placed in the top of a table to make it larger. □ *I removed the extra leaves so that the table would fit in the small room.*

**leafy** ['lif i] *adj.* having a lot of leaves; covered with leaves. (Comp: *leafier;* sup: *leafiest.*) □ *We had a picnic in the shade of a leafy tree.*

**league** ['lig] **1.** *n.* a group of people, organizations, or countries that work together because they have a common interest or goal. □ *The sculptor belonged to the local league of artists.* **2.** *n.* a group of sports teams that play against each other. □ *John wants to play baseball in the major leagues.*

**L**

**leak** ['lik] **1.** *n.* an opening in a channel, pipe, tire, container, etc., that allows something to escape. □ *I patched the leak in the tire.* **2.** *n.* an instance of something escaping from an opening as in ①. □ *A leak of gas from a pipe caused the fire.* **3.** *n.* an instance of secret information being revealed secretly. (Fig. on ②.) □ *Who is responsible for the leak of secret information?* **4.** *iv.* [for a container] to have an opening as in ① that allows water, air, or something else to escape. □ *If your tires leak, you should have them replaced.* **5.** *tv.* [for a container with an opening as in ①] to allow water, air, or something else to escape or enter as in ①. □ *The bag leaked sand all over the floor.* **6.** *tv.* to secretly reveal secret information. (Fig. on ⑤.) □ *The agent leaked state secrets to the enemy.*

**leakage** ['lik ɪdʒ] **1.** *n.* the process of leaking. (No plural form.) □ *Close the jar tightly to prevent leakage.* **2.** *n.* something that is leaked. (No plural form.) □ *Leakage from the broken pipe made the floor slippery.*

**leaky** ['lik i] *adj.* tending to leak; likely to leak. (Comp: *leakier;* sup: *leakiest.*) □ *The leaky water faucet dripped all night long.*

**lean** ['lin] **1.** *iv.* to be slanting; to be sloped. □ *The old tree leaned to one side.* **2.** *adj.* [of someone or something] very thin or skinny. (Adv: *leanly.* Comp: *leaner;* sup: *leanest.*) □ *The lean and frowning model showed us the latest fashions.* **3.** *adj.* [of meat] having almost no fat. (Adv: *leanly.* Comp: *leaner;* sup: *leanest.*) □ *I grilled some lean chicken for dinner.*

**leap** ['lip] **1.** *iv., irreg.* to jump from one place to another. (Pt/pp: *leaped* or **leapt.**) □ *The frog leapt from stone to stone.* **2.** *tv., irreg.* to jump over something. □ *The runner leaped every hurdle.* **3.** *n.* a jump; an instance of leaping. □ *A quick leap got the frog into the water.*

**leapt** ['lɛpt] a pt/pp of **leap.**

**learn** ['lɚn] **1.** *tv.* to receive knowledge; to gain a particular piece of knowledge. (The object can be a clause with **that** ⑦.) □ *Today in science class we learned the names of the planets.* **2. learn about someone or something; learn of someone or something** *iv. + prep. phr.* to be told about something; to receive news or information about someone or something. □ *I learned of the bank robbery from the radio.*

**lease** ['lis] **1.** *n.* a rental contract. □ *I signed a lease to rent the apartment for a year.* **2. lease something (from someone or some group)** *tv. + obj. (+ prep. phr.)* to rent something from someone. □ *I leased a car from the dealership instead of buying one.* **3. lease something (to someone)** *tv. + obj. (+ prep. phr.)* to rent something to someone. □ *Bob leased a car to Mary for a year.*

**least** ['list] **1.** *adj.* <a superlative form of **little**>; the smallest [amount]. □ *Even the least amount of pepper in my food burns my throat.* **2.** *adv.* in the smallest amount; to the smallest degree; the opposite of **most**. □ *I watched the least offensive of the three movies that were available.* **3.** *pron.* the smallest amount. □ *Give Mary the most, give Bill a little less, and give me the least.*

**leather** ['lɛð ɚ] **1.** *n.* a material made from the skin of an animal, used to make shoes, coats, belts, gloves, etc. (Plural only when referring to different kinds, types, instances, or varieties.) □ *My purse and my shoes are both made of brown leather.* Ⓒ *Leathers from different animals are suitable for widely differing products.* **2.** *adj.* made of ①. □ *The police officer wore leather gloves in the winter.*

**leave** ['liv] **1.** *iv., irreg.* to go away; to exit from a place. (Pt/pp: **left**.) □ *The police ordered the loud teenagers to leave.* **2.** *tv., irreg.* to depart from a place. □ *I left the hospital last Friday.* **3.** *tv., irreg.* to depart [from a place], letting someone or something remain in the place. □ *Mary left her books in the library.* **4.** *tv., irreg.* to depart from and abandon someone, such as a husband or wife. □ *Bill left Mary for another woman.* **5.** *tv., irreg.* to cause someone or something to be in a certain condition. □ *The sad movie left me crying.* **6.** *tv., irreg.* to will something to someone or something; to give something to someone or something after one dies. □ *My grandfather left me his gold watch.* **7.** *n.* an extended period of time away from one's duties. □ *The sailor spent his leave at his sister's house.*

**leaves** ['livz] pl of **leaf**.

**lecture** ['lɛk tʃɚ] **1.** *n.* a long talk about a certain subject; a speech. □ *Today's history lecture was about the War of 1812.* **2.** *n.* a speech that warns or scolds. □ *The police officer gave me a lecture about obeying the speed limit.* **3.** *iv.* to give a **lecture** ①; to talk about a certain subject. □ *The professor lectured for hours, it seemed.* **4.** *tv.* to talk to people about a certain subject, especially to talk to an audience or a class. □ *The professor lectured the class about Asian history.* **5.** *tv.* to scold someone about something; to give a **lecture** ② to someone. □ *The Smiths lectured their son about driving safely.*

**lecturer** ['lɛk tʃɚ ɚ] **1.** *n.* someone who gives a lecture. □ *The lecturer talked about Russian literature.* **2.** *n.* someone who gives lectures; especially someone below the rank of professor or instructor who teaches at a university or college. □ *Bob got promoted from lecturer to instructor.*

**led** ['lɛd] pt/pp of **lead**.

**ledge** ['lɛdʒ] *n.* a narrow surface that sticks out along a wall or under a window; a shelf. □ *I jumped from a third-story ledge to escape the burning building.*

**leer** ['lɪr] **1.** *n.* a look of sexual desire or interest. □ *Susan returned Bill's leer with a cold stare.* **2. leer at** someone *iv.* + *prep. phr.* to stare at someone with sexual desire or lust. □ *Mary fled from the strange man who leered at her.*

**left** ['lɛft] **1.** pt/pp of **leave**. **2.** *n.* the direction to the west when you are facing north. (No plural form.) □ *I chose to travel on the path on my left.* □ *Left is the opposite of right.* **3. the Left** *n.* politicians or citizens whose political views are liberal or radical rather than conservative; politicians or citizens who favor social and economic progress, change, and reform, often through government control and management. (No plural form. Treated as singular.) □ *The Left attacked the conservative senator's views.* **4.** *adj.* on the **left** ②; located at ②. □ *About 10 percent of all people write* *with the left hand.* **5.** *adv.* toward ②. □ *Turn left at the next light.*

**left-hand** ['lɛft hænd] *adj.* left; on, to, or at one's left side. (Prenominal only.) □ *Make a left-hand turn at the next intersection.*

**left-handed** ['lɛft hæn dɪd] **1.** *adj.* favoring the use of the left hand. (Adv: *left-handed* or *left-handedly.*) □ *The left-handed batter hit the ball into right field.* **2.** *adj.* designed for people who are ①. □ *I bought a set of left-handed golf clubs.* **3.** *adv.* [of writing] done with the left hand. □ *The teacher can write both left-handed and right-handed.*

**leftover** ['lɛft ov ɚ] *adj.* remaining; unused and therefore extra. (Prenominal only.) □ *I put the leftover salad in the refrigerator.*

**leftovers** ['lɛft ov ɚz] *n.* portions of food left over from a meal; portions of food remaining after a meal. (Treated as plural. Rarely countable.) □ *I put the leftovers in the refrigerator.*

**leg** ['lɛg] **1.** *n.* one of the two body parts that support a human; one of the four body parts that support most other mammals, or similar parts that support certain other animals, such as insects. □ *The fox's leg was caught in a trap.* **2.** *n.* the part of a piece of clothing that wraps around ①. □ *You've got mud on the left leg of your pants.* **3.** *n.* [in furniture or other structures] a vertical piece that supports weight. □ *One of the chair legs broke when I tipped the chair over.* **4.** *n.* a part of a trip; a part of a distance to be covered. □ *We stopped in the Bahamas on the first leg of the cruise.*

**legal** ['lig əl] **1.** *adj.* lawful; according to the law. (Adv: *legally.*) □ *It's legal to turn right at a red light in most states.* **2.** *adj.* of or about law. (Adv: *legally.*) □ *I consulted the company's legal department before firing my assistant.*

**legal tender** ['lig əl 'tɛn dɚ] *n.* legal money; money that must be accepted as payment. □ *I exchanged the huge check at the bank for a mountain of legal tender.*

**legend** ['lɛdʒ ənd] **1.** *n.* an old and often repeated story; a fable; a myth. □ *According to the legend, the ghost of the murdered man still walks around the old house at night.* **2.** *n.* an explanation of symbols used on a map, plan, chart, etc. □ *I referred to the map's legend to see how toll roads were drawn.*

**legislate** ['lɛdʒ ɪ slet] **1.** *tv.* to make laws. □ *Congress legislates federal laws.* **2.** *tv.* to pass a law about something. (The object can be a clause with **that** ⑦.) □ *Congress legislated new income-tax rates.*

**legislation** [lɛdʒ ɪ 'sle ʃən] **1.** *n.* writing and making laws. (No plural form.) □ *Legislation is the job of the legislative branch of government.* **2.** *n.* laws that have been made; a set of laws. (No plural form. Number is expressed with *piece(s) of legislation.*) □ *The lawyer studied the legislation concerning fraud.*

**legislative** ['lɛdʒ ɪ sle tɪv] *adj.* of or about making laws or the people who make laws. (Adv: *legislatively.*) □ *We learned about the legislative process in government class.*

**legislator** ['lɛdʒ ɪ sle tɚ] *n.* someone who makes laws; a member of a legislature. □ *I questioned my state legislator about his voting record.*

**legislature** ['lɛdʒ ɪ sle tʃɚ] *n.* the group of people who are elected or appointed to make laws. □ *The state legislature lowered the speed limit.*

**leisure** ['li ʒɚ] **1.** *n.* free time; time that is not spent at work or sleeping; time when one can do what one wants. (No plural form.) □ *In my leisure, I like to read novels.* **2.** *adj.* <the adj. use of ①.> □ *In my leisure time, I like to read romance novels.*

**lemon** ['lɛm ən] **1.** *n.* a sour, yellow citrus fruit. □ *We squeezed the fresh lemons and used the juice to make lemonade.* **2.** *n.* a product, such as a car, that does not work properly and cannot be repaired. (Informal.) □ *This new TV doesn't work at all. It must be a lemon.* **3.** *adj.* made or flavored with ①. □ *I put some lemon juice in my tea.*

**lemonade** [lɛm ən 'ed] *n.* a drink made from the juice of lemons, sugar, and water. (No plural form.) □ *The kids sold lemonade for a quarter a cup.*

**lend** ['lɛnd] **1.** *tv., irreg.* to grant someone permission to use or borrow something for a period of time. (Pt/pp: **lent**.) □ *I lent Anne my book.* □ *I lent my book to Anne.* **2.** *tv., irreg.* to contribute an effect to something; to add a quality to something. (Fig. on ①.) □ *The tablecloth lent an air of style to dinner.*

**length** ['lɛŋkθ] **1.** *n.* the measurement of something from end to end; the amount of time that has passed. (The opposite of **width**. Plural only when referring to different kinds, types, instances, or varieties.) □ *Yardsticks are 36 inches in length.* 🄲 *We both measured the board and came up with two different lengths!* **2.** *n.* a piece of something of a certain or known ①. □ *The plumber bought a length of pipe four inches long.*

**lengthen** ['lɛŋk θən] **1.** *tv.* to make something longer. □ *The author lengthened her novel by adding more chapters.* **2.** *iv.* to become longer. □ *The voting lines lengthened after people left work.*

**lens** ['lɛnz] **1.** *n.* a piece of curved glass, or some other clear material, that bends rays of light. □ *I wear special, strong lenses to correct my bad vision.* **2.** *n.* the clear, curved part of the eye—located behind the pupil—that focuses light rays on the retina. □ *Squinting distorts the shape of the lenses.*

**lent** ['lɛnt] pt/pp of **lend**.

**leopard** ['lɛp ɚd] *n.* a large animal in the cat family, typically having yellowish fur with black spots. □ *Leopards run very swiftly.*

**less** ['lɛs] **1.** *adj.* <the comparative form of **little**>; a smaller amount. (Used with things that are measured in quantities. Compare this with *fewer*, at **few**, which is used with things that can be counted.) □ *You gave me less rice than you gave to Jimmy.* **2.** *adv.* to a smaller extent or degree; not as much. □ *I weigh myself less frequently than you do.* **3. -less** *suffix* <a form meaning *without* that can be added to nouns and to adjectives that have come from verbs.> (The resulting adjectives can be made into nouns with the *-ness* suffix and into adverbs with the suffix *-ly*.) □ *I prefer seedless oranges.*

**lessen** ['lɛs ən] **1.** *iv.* to become less; to decrease in size, amount, or power. □ *The amount of sunlight lessens as night approaches.* **2.** *tv.* to cause something to become less. □ *Seat belts lessen the impact of an accident on the people in the car.*

**lesson** ['lɛs ən] **1.** *n.* a session of instruction with a teacher; the material to be covered in one session of instruction; something, such as a school assignment, that is to be learned, studied, or prepared. □ *The first lesson gives the students some very basic information.* **2.** *n.* something that one learns from an experience; an experience that one learns something from. □ *John learned a valuable lesson from the argument.*

**let** ['lɛt] **1.** *tv., irreg.* to allow someone or something to do something; to allow something to happen. (Pt/pp: *let*.) □ *Mary let the reporters ask her questions.* □ *Let me do it.* **2.** *tv., irreg.* to rent an apartment or room (to someone). □ *We finally let the studio apartment on the first floor.*

**let's** ['lɛts] *cont.* "let us"; we will [do something]. (A gentle command or request. A response is usually expected.) ☐ *Let's order pizza for dinner.*

**letter** ['lɛt ɚ] **1.** *n.* a written or printed symbol in an alphabet. ☐ *There are six letters in the word* picnic. **2.** *n.* a written message sent to a person or a company. ☐ *I just received a long letter from Aunt Jane.*

**letter carrier** ['lɛt ɚ kɛr i ɚ] Go to mail carrier.

**lettuce** ['lɛt ɪs] *n.* a leafy, green vegetable, often used in salads. (No plural form. Number is expressed with *leaf* or *leaves of lettuce* and *head(s) of lettuce.*) ☐ *I placed a leaf of lettuce on my sandwich.*

**level** ['lɛv əl] **1.** *n.* a flat surface; a horizontal plane. ☐ *It is easier to build a house on the level than on the side of a hill.* **2.** *n.* one of the floors of a building or other structure. ☐ *I parked on the sixth level of the parking garage.* **3.** *n.* a layer; a step or a stage. ☐ *The tunnel ran through several levels of rock and sand.* **4.** *n.* the amount of a measurement; a position on a scale of measurement. ☐ *The level of security at the airport is more than adequate.* **5.** *n.* a tool or device that shows when a surface is exactly horizontal or vertical. ☐ *The carpenter placed the level on the shelf.* **6.** *adj.* [of a surface] exactly horizontal, so every point is the same height. ☐ *The carpenter fixed the shelf so that it was level.* **7.** *adj.* [of a measurement] steady; not changing. (Fig. on ⑥.) ☐ *The inflation rate remained level for several months.* **8.** *tv.* to knock down trees, buildings, or other objects until the land is flat; to clear land by knocking down trees or buildings. ☐ *An earthquake leveled most of the town.*

**lever** ['lɛv ɚ] **1.** *n.* a bar of metal or wood, positioned so that it increases one's power in lifting or moving heavy objects. ☐ *I snapped the lever in half while trying to lift the heavy box.* **2.** *n.* a bar or handle that serves as a control device. ☐ *The emergency brake is operated with that lever next to your foot.*

**liar** ['lɑɪ ɚ] *n.* someone who tells lies; someone who does not tell the truth. ☐ *You can never believe what Bob tells you. He's such a liar.*

**liberty** ['lɪb ɚ ti] **1.** *n.* the freedom from control; the freedom to think or act for oneself. (No plural form.) ☐ *The prisoners prayed for liberty.* **2.** *n.* the permission to do something; a right or a privilege that one has been given. ☐ *The students were given liberty to leave campus on weekends.*

**librarian** [lɑɪ 'brɛr i ən] *n.* someone who manages or helps operate a library. ☐ *The librarian decides which new books to buy for the library.*

**library** ['lɑɪ brɛr i] **1.** *n.* a building or room that has a supply of books or similar materials available for use by a number of people. ☐ *The city's public library is open to every city resident.* **2.** *n.* a collection of books, records, videotapes, etc. ☐ *John has a large video library of early American films.*

**license** ['lɑɪ səns] **1.** *n.* a document that proves that someone has official permission to do or own something. ☐ *I went downtown to renew my driver's license.* **2.** *n.* a freedom to do something. (No plural form.) ☐ *The bad grammar in the poem was due to the author's poetic license.* **3.** *tv.* to give someone a license ① for something; to authorize someone or something; to permit someone or something. ☐ *The city licensed me to open a restaurant.*

**license plate** ['lɑɪ səns 'plet] *n.* a rectangular panel, showing a car's license number, that is put on the rear and, in some states, the front of a car. (Can be shortened to plate.) ☐ *The new license plate is aluminum.*

**lick** ['lɪk] **1.** *tv.* to move the tongue along someone or something; to taste something by moving one's tongue along it; to make something wet by moving one's tongue along it. ☐ *I licked the edge of the envelope so it would stay sealed.* **2.** *n.* the movement of the tongue along the surface of something as in ①. ☐ *The dog's lick was wet and smelly.* **3.** *n.* a small amount of something that one gets by moving the tongue as in ①. ☐ *You took more than one lick of my ice cream!*

**lid** ['lɪd] **1.** *n.* a cover for a container, surface, hole, or other object. ☐ *Who didn't put the lid back on the juice bottle?* **2.** *n.* the fold of skin over the eye; an **eyelid**. ☐ *Anne put some makeup on her lids.*

**lie** ['lɑɪ] **1.** *n.* a statement that is not true and that the speaker knows is not true; a false statement. ☐ *Don't tell me lies!* **2.** *iv.* to say something that is not true; to tell a **lie** ①. (Pt/pp: **lied**. Present participle: **lying**.) ☐ *The judge charged John with perjury for lying under oath.* **3.** *iv., irreg.* to be in a flat position; to place oneself in a flat position. (Pt: **lay**; pp: **lain**. See also **lay**. Present participle: **lying**.) ☐ *The baby was lying in her crib.* **4.** *iv., irreg.* to be located; to be in a certain place. ☐ *Nevada lies west of Utah.* **5.** *iv., irreg.* to remain in a place or condition; to stay in a certain condition or position. ☐ *Please lie still and don't make any noise.*

**lied** ['lɑɪd] pt/pp of **lie** ②.

**life** ['lɑɪf] **1.** *n.* the power that causes plants and animals to exist, in general. (No plural form.) ☐ *We must have food and water in order to have life.* **2.** *n., irreg.* an individual instance of ① that can be lived, lost, saved, spent, wasted, etc.; the period of time between the time of one's birth and one's death or between the time of one's birth and the present. (Pl: **lives**.) ☐ *The lifeguard saved my life!* **3.** *n., irreg.* the activities, experiences, and habits of a person. ☐ *The traveler led an exciting, adventurous life.* **4.** *n.* excitement; vigor. (No plural form.) ☐ *My sweet old grandmother is still full of life.* **5.** *n.* a kind of living; a quality of living. (No plural form.) ☐ *Country life is the best for me.*

**lifeboat** ['lɑɪf bot] *n.* a boat used to carry people away from a sinking ship; a boat used to save people in danger of drowning. ☐ *The survivors crowded onto the only lifeboat.*

**lifeguard** ['lɑɪf gɑrd] *n.* someone who works at a beach or swimming pool to encourage water safety and rescue people from danger in the water. ☐ *The lifeguard saved the drowning swimmer.*

**life jacket** AND **life preserver; life vest** ['lɑɪf dʒæk ət, ... prə 'zɚv ɚ, ... vɛst] *n.* a thick jacket without sleeves that floats and will keep the person who wears it from sinking in the water. (See also **lifesaver**.) ☐ *You must wear a life jacket if you take this boat ride.*

**lifesaver** ['lɑɪf sev ɚ] **1.** *n.* someone or something that saves someone's life. ☐ *My dog's a real lifesaver. He woke me up when my house was on fire.* **2.** *n.* something that serves well in an emergency. (Fig. on ①.) ☐ *Thanks for lending me the money. You're a lifesaver!*

**lifetime** ['lɑɪf tɑɪm] **1.** *n.* the time that a person or animal is living. ☐ *My dog has only been lost once in his entire lifetime.* **2.** *n.* the period of time that something works or can be used. (Fig. on ①.) ☐ *Most batteries have a lifetime of only a few years.*

**lift** ['lɪft] **1.** *tv.* to pick someone or something up from the ground; to raise someone or something to a higher level. ☐ *I lifted the baby from his crib.* **2.** *iv.* [for clouds, fog, smoke, smog] to rise or go away. ☐ *I stayed indoors until the smog lifted.* **3.** *n.* a free ride in a car or truck. (Informal.) ☐ *Can you give me a lift, please?* **4.** *n.* something that makes someone feel happier, stronger, or more awake. □ *The song gave my emotions a lift.*

**light** ['laɪt] **1.** *n.* a form of radiation or energy that makes things visible. (No plural form.) □ *It is easier to see objects in the light than in the dark.* **2.** *n.* something that produces ①, such as a lamp or a flame. □ *It's too dark in here. How do I turn on the light?* **3.** *n.* something, such as a match, that produces fire. (No plural form.) □ *Do you have a light? I forgot my matches.* **4.** *n.* the period of time when the sun is in the sky; daytime. (No plural form.) □ *I stayed at the party until the light of dawn.* **5.** *n.* a traffic signal that uses red, yellow, and green **lights** ② to control people and vehicles. (Short for **traffic light**.) □ *The light changed just as I came to a stop.* **6.** *n.* a view; the way that something is seen or thought of. (No plural form.) □ *In this light, your actions seem reasonable.* **7.** *adj.* pale in color; not dark or deep; mixed with white. (Adv: *lightly.*) □ *The sky is a light blue.* **8.** *adj.* not heavy; not weighing much; easy to carry. (Adv: *lightly.*) □ *I took two light suitcases onto the airplane.* **9.** *adj.* not having much force; gentle. (Fig. on ⑧. Adv: *lightly.*) □ *A light breeze blew from the west.* **10.** *iv., irreg.* [for a creature] to land on a surface after flight. (Pt/pp: *lighted* or **lit**.) □ *The insect lighted on the wall.* **11.** *tv., irreg.* to set something on fire; to cause something to begin to burn. □ *I will light the candles.*

**lighter** ['laɪt ɚ] *n.* a device that makes a flame to light cigarettes or cigars. □ *I lit Anne's cigarette with my lighter.*

**lighthouse** ['laɪt haʊs] *n., irreg.* a tall structure near the sea with a bright light near the top that warns ships away from danger. (Pl: [...haʊ zəz].) □ *The Coast Guard operated the lighthouse out on the island.*

**lighting** ['laɪt ɪŋ] **1.** *n.* light that makes things and people visible; illumination; the type or quality of light in a room or other place. (No plural form.) □ *I bumped into the walls because the lighting was very dim.* **2.** *n.* the equipment that directs light, especially for effect in a television or movie studio or on a stage. (No plural form.) □ *A technician controlled the lighting with the help of a computer.*

**lightning** ['laɪt nɪŋ] *n.* a flash or streak of light in the sky, especially during a thunderstorm. (No plural form. Number is expressed with *bolt(s)* or *flash(es) of lightning.*) □ *Loud thunder followed the bolt of lightning.*

**lightning bug** ['laɪt nɪŋ bəg] *n.* a type of beetle that is able to fly and to illuminate its body in the dark. (Also called *firefly.*) □ *The lightning bugs flashed in the night sky.*

**like** ['laɪk] **1.** *n.* a desire; something that one **likes** ② to have or do. □ *My likes include walking in the park and dancing.* **2.** *tv.* to enjoy someone or something; to find someone or something pleasant. □ *John likes chocolate ice cream.* **3.** *adj.* similar; same. (Prenominal only.) □ *I gave John $20, and he wrote me a check for the like amount.* **4.** *prep.* similar to someone or something; in the same way as someone or something. □ *This song sounds like the one you wrote.* **5.** *prep.* for instance, the following things or people; such as the following things or people. □ *Many elements, like oxygen and carbon, are needed to sustain life.* **6.** *conj.* in the same way as someone or something does; similar to the way someone or something is. (Viewed as incorrect by some people.) □ *I solved the math problem like my teacher showed us.* **7.** *conj.* as though; as if. (Viewed as incorrect by some people.) □ *This dog is barking like it wants to bite me.*

**likelihood** ['laɪk li hʊd] *n.* the chance of being likely; the state of something being probable. (No plural form.) □ *What's the likelihood of rain tomorrow?*

**likely** ['laɪk li] **1.** *adj.* probable. □ *It's not likely to snow in August.* **2.** *adj.* suitable; apt. □ *John is a likely candidate for the job.* **3. likely to** do something *adj.* + *inf.* apt to do something; tending to do something. □ *It's likely to rain tomorrow.*

**lily** ['lɪl i] *n.* a flower with large petals that grows from a bulb. □ *I sent my mother a lily for Easter.*

**limb** ['lɪm] **1.** *n.* a large tree branch. □ *The bird built its nest on a strong limb.* **2.** *n.* an arm, leg, or wing. □ *The driver lost a limb in the car accident.*

**lime** ['laɪm] **1.** *n.* a small, green citrus fruit. □ *I cut the lime into small wedges.* **2.** *n.* a white substance, made by burning a kind of rock, which is used to make plaster, cement, and mortar. (No plural form.) □ *They added lime to the plaster to make it white.* **3.** *adj.* made or flavored with ①. □ *Would you care for some lime sherbet?*

**limit** ['lɪm ɪt] **1.** *n.* a boundary; the edge; the farthest point of something; the greatest amount allowed or possible. □ *My teacher encouraged me to follow my dreams to the limit.* **2.** *tv.* to prevent someone or something from passing a certain point or amount; to restrict something to a certain amount of space or time. □ *Please limit your acceptance speech to one minute.*

**limp** ['lɪmp] **1.** *n.* an uneven walk; a way of walking where one foot drags or moves as if it is injured. □ *My grandfather had a limp because he had injured his leg in the war.* **2.** *iv.* to walk to somewhere showing ①. □ *I limped to the clinic after I cut my foot.* **3.** *adj.* not stiff; having no resistance. (Adv: *limply.* Comp: *limper;* sup: *limpest.*) □ *I tried unsuccessfully to curl my limp hair.*

**line** ['laɪn] **1.** *n.* a thin mark, straight or curved, made on the surface of something. □ *The artist used a ruler to draw a straight line.* **2.** *n.* a border; a mark that shows the limit, border, or end of something. □ *The referee placed the football on the fifty-yard line.* **3.** *n.* a wide band; a stripe. □ *A bright white line was painted along the edge of the road.* **4.** *n.* a string, rope, or cord. (On boats and ships, ropes are called **lines**.) □ *My fishing line broke, and the fish got away.* **5.** *n.* a wire, pipe, or cable that carries a public utility company's product, such as electricity, water, gas, telephone, etc. □ *The city installed a new sewer line under the street.* **6.** *n.* a telephone connection. □ *This line is noisy, and I can't hear the caller.* **7.** *n.* a row or series of people standing and waiting for a turn to do something. □ *There is often a long line at the post office at noon.* **8.** *n.* a row of words in printing or writing. □ *The last line is too long to fit on the page.* **9.** *n.* something that is said by an actor onstage or in a film. □ *The director told me to say the line with more emotion.* **10.** *tv.* to put a lining in something; to cover the inside of something with something else. □ *The tailor lined the jacket with silk.* **11. line up** *iv.* + *adv.* to get into ⑦; to join or form ⑦. □ *Please line up in a straight line.*

**lining** ['laɪn ɪŋ] *n.* a fabric or other material put on the inside surface of something for protection, warmth, etc. □ *My gloves have a furry lining.*

**link** ['lɪŋk] **1.** *n.* one of the loops or circles that make up a chain. □ *The chain snapped when one of the links broke.* **2.** *n.* someone or something that connects someone or something to someone or something else. (Fig. on ①.) □ *I keep my grandmother's wedding dress as a link with the past.* **3.** *tv.* to connect

L

someone or something to someone or something else. □ *I linked the two ends of the chain together.*

**lint** ['lɪnt] *n.* a tiny piece of thread; a small cluster of threads, dirt, hair, etc. (No plural form.) □ *I removed a piece of red lint from my yellow shirt.*

**lion** ['lɑɪ ən] *n.* a large, tan-colored wild animal in the cat family, native to Africa. □ *The lion in the zoo ate all the meat in one bite.*

**lip** ['lɪp] **1.** *n.* one of the two ridges of flesh on the outside of the mouth. □ *I bit my lip accidentally while eating.* **2.** *n.* a rim; an edge, especially a part of an edge of a container. □ *The lip of the glass jar was chipped.*

**liquid** ['lɪk wɪd] **1.** *n.* a flowing substance, such as water, that is not a gas or a solid. □ *I poured the hot liquid into a glass container.* **2.** *n.* the sounds [l] and [r]. □ *Some people have trouble pronouncing the liquids* [l] *and* [r]. **3.** *adj.* in the form of ①. □ *I washed my hands with liquid soap.* **4.** *adj.* [of an asset that can be] easily converted to cash. □ *He owns a house and two cars, but none of his assets are liquid.*

**liquor** ['lɪk ɚ] **1.** *n.* broth or juices from cooking. (No plural form.) □ *I cooked the rice with some of the liquor from the stewed chicken.* **2.** *n.* alcohol for drinking. (Plural only when referring to different kinds, types, instances, or varieties.) □ *I can smell liquor on your breath.* Ⓒ *They offered a choice of liquors—scotch, bourbon, or gin.*

**list** ['lɪst] **1.** *n.* a printed or written series of words, names, or items. □ *The teacher checked off every name on the class list.* **2.** *n.* a slant or tilt to one side, as with a ship. □ *The ship's list was caused by shifting cargo.* **3.** *tv.* to write things on ①. □ *List five states that border the Atlantic Ocean.* **4.** *iv.* to lean to one side. □ *The sinking ship listed to its left.*

**listen** ['lɪs ən] *iv.* to pay attention to a source of sound. □ *I listened to the radio for the weather report.*

**lit** ['lɪt] a pt/pp of **light**.

**liter** ['lit ɚ] *n.* a metric unit of liquid measurement equal to 1.06 quarts. □ *I brought two liters of pop to the party.*

**literacy** ['lɪt ə rə si] *n.* the ability to read and write. (No plural form.) □ *The factory offered classes to improve the literacy of its workers.*

**literal** ['lɪt ə rəl] **1.** *adj.* [of the meaning of a word or phrase] basic instead of secondary or figurative. (Adv: *literally.*) □ *The literal meaning of* hot air *is "air that is hot." The figurative sense means "nonsense."* **2.** *adj.* exact, especially pertaining to translations; translating or interpreting one word at a time. (Adv: *literally.*) □ *The literal interpretation of idioms is often funny.*

**literature** ['lɪt ə rə tʃɚ] **1.** *n.* writing considered as art, such as fiction, plays, and poetry. (No plural form.) □ *What kind of literature do you like to read?* **2.** *n.* all the written material of a specific subject or region. (No plural form.) □ *This library has a vast collection of literature about farming.* **3.** *n.* information; a brochure or small book that has information about something. (No plural form.) □ *According to the literature, this city was founded in 1840.*

**little** ['lɪt əl] **1.** *adj.* small in size. (Comp: *littler;* sup: *littlest.*) □ *Jimmy is little for his age.* **2.** *adj., irreg.* not much. (Without *a.* Comp: **less**; sup: **least**. Used with items that cannot be counted. Compare this with **few** ①.) □ *Mary has little musical ability and sings terribly.* **3.** *adj., irreg.* some; a small amount. (With *a.* Comp: **less**; sup: **least**. Used with items that cannot be counted. Compare this with **few** ②.) □ *I can speak a little*

*French.* **4.** *adv., irreg.* not much; not a lot. (Comp: **less**; sup: **least**.) ☐ *Mary sleeps very little and spends most of her time working.* **5. a little** *adv.* somewhat; to some degree or in some amount. (Comp: **less**; sup: **least**.) ☐ *I was a little tired after the long walk.* ☐ *Sue slept a little after dinner.* **6. a little** *n.* a small amount [of something mentioned before or known from the context]; some. (No plural form. Treated as singular. Use *a few* for items that are counted.) ☐ *I bought a pizza and gave my brother a little.*

**livable** ['lɪv ə bəl] *adj.* suitable to be lived in or with. (Adv: *livably.*) ☐ *The mayor promised livable housing for everyone in the city.*

**live 1.** ['lɑɪv] *adj.* not dead; having life. ☐ *The live fish squirmed out of my hands.* **2.** ['lɑɪv] *adj.* carrying electricity; electrically charged. (Fig. on ①.) ☐ *The live wire gave me a shock.* **3.** ['lɑɪv] *adj.* on the air; not taped; broadcast at the same time something is happening. ☐ *The performer promised to be polite on the live broadcast.* **4.** ['lɑɪv] *adv.* while something is really happening; broadcast at the moment that something is happening. ☐ *The concert was broadcast live.* **5.** ['lɪv] *iv.* to be; to exist; to be alive; to survive. ☐ *My grandfather lived until he was 80.* **6.** ['lɪv] *iv.* to reside at a certain address; to reside in or at a certain place. ☐ *I live at 123 Main Street.* **7.** ['lɪv] *iv.* to exist in a certain way. ☐ *Someday, all nations will live in peace.*

**lively** ['lɑɪv li] *adj.* showing energy or excitement; cheerful; active. (Comp: *livelier;* sup: *liveliest.*) ☐ *The lively teenagers danced until dawn.*

**liver** ['lɪv ɚ] **1.** *n.* an organ, in the body of an animal, that produces fluids used in digestion and performs other important functions. ☐ *John's liver was damaged by alcohol.* **2.** *n.* a whole **liver** ①, eaten as food. ☐ *The recipe called for a calf's liver.* **3.** *n.* ①, eaten as food. (No plural form.) ☐ *The children just hate liver.*

**lives 1.** ['lɑɪvz] pl of **life**. **2.** ['lɪvz] the third-person singular of **live**.

**livestock** ['lɑɪv stɑk] *n.* animals that are kept on a farm or ranch, usually for the production of food. (No plural form. Treated as singular or plural, but not countable.) ☐ *Most of the livestock live in the barn in the winter.*

**living room** ['lɪv ɪŋ rum] *n.* the main room of a house or apartment, large enough to hold a number of people. ☐ *Our living room has two sofas and a chair.*

**lizard** ['lɪz ɚd] *n.* a reptile with legs, scaly skin, and a tail. ☐ *The green lizard blended in with the tall grass.*

**load** ['lod] **1.** *n.* something that is carried; a burden; a weight. ☐ *I cannot walk very far with this heavy load.* **2.** *n.* the amount of something that can be carried; one large portion of something for carrying. ☐ *I carried a load of bricks over to the wall.* **3.** *n.* the amount of electricity used by an electrical device. ☐ *The refrigerator's heavy load blew a fuse.* **4.** *tv.* to put bullets into a gun; to put film or videotape into a camera; to install computer software into a computer. ☐ *Can you help me load the software into the computer?* **5.** *tv.* to fill something with something. ☐ *The workers loaded the truck with boxes of fruit.*

**loaf** ['lof] **1.** *n., irreg.* a mass of bread dough baked in one piece. (Pl: **loaves**.) ☐ *I cut a slice of bread from the loaf.* **2.** *n., irreg.* a mass of food cooked in a shape like ①. (Often part of a compound.) ☐ *We love meatloaf and mashed potatoes.* **3.** *iv.* to waste time. ☐ *I loafed all day Saturday.*

**loan** ['lon] **1.** *n.* something, especially money, that is lent to someone. ☐ *Mary*

L

*got a loan from the bank so she could buy a car.* **2.** *tv.* to lend something to someone; to let someone borrow something. (Some people object to the use of **loan** in this sense rather than **lend**, reserving **loan** for the lending of money.) □ *Can you loan me a pencil? I've forgotten mine.*

**loathe** ['loð] *tv.* to hate someone or something very much. □ *I quit my job because I loathed it.*

**loaves** ['lovz] pl of **loaf**.

**lobby** ['lɑb i] **1.** *n.* the entrance room of a building. □ *There's an information desk in the lobby of the museum.* **2.** *tv.* to try to influence someone who makes laws or regulations to vote a certain way. □ *The tobacco company lobbied the senators for support.*

**lobster** ['lɑb stɚ] **1.** *n.* an edible sea animal with six legs and (possibly) two large claws. □ *Lobsters are usually caught in traps in the sea.* **2.** *n.* the meat of ① used as food. (No plural form.) □ *I had lobster and potatoes for dinner.* **3.** *adj.* made or flavored with ②. □ *I ordered pasta with lobster sauce.*

L

**local** ['lok əl] **1.** *adj.* of or about the nearby area. (Adv: *locally.*) □ *The local newspaper focuses on neighborhood news.* **2.** *n.* a bus or train that stops at every station. □ *The locals run more often than the express trains.* **3.** *n.* a person who lives in the area that something is in. (Often plural.) □ *While vacationing, I asked some locals where I should eat.*

**locate** ['lo ket] **1.** *tv.* to find someone or something; to learn where someone or something is. □ *The student located Brazil on the map.* **2.** *tv.* to place someone or something in a particular place. □ *The company located its offices near its customers.*

**location** [lo 'ke ʃən] *n.* the place where someone or something is; the place where someone or something is found. □ *I found my wallet in the exact location where I had left it.*

**lock** ['lɑk] **1.** *n.* a device on a door opening that prevents the door from being opened without a key. □ *The thief broke the lock with a hammer.* **2.** *n.* a device similar to a ① that controls access to something. □ *All our windows have levers that serve as locks.* **3.** *n.* a part of a canal or river between two heavy, watertight gates where the level of the water can be raised or lowered, allowing boats to move from one level of water to another. □ *The ship entered the lock, and a heavy gate closed behind it.* **4.** *n.* a small bundle of [head] hair; a strand or curl of hair. □ *Mary kept a lock of her baby's hair in an envelope.* **5. lock** something **(up)** *tv. + obj. (+ adv.)* to secure something by using ①, so it cannot be opened without a key. □ *I always lock up my car when I go shopping.* **6. lock** someone or something **up** *tv. + obj. + adv.* to put someone or something into a place that can be secured with ①; to put someone in jail. □ *The sheriff locked the criminal up.* [T] *The sheriff locked up the criminal.* **7.** *iv.* not to be able to move. □ *The steering wheel locked when I tried to turn it.*

**locker** ['lɑk ɚ] *n.* a cabinet like a tiny closet that can be locked, where clothes and valuables are kept. □ *My tennis shoes are in my locker at the gymnasium.*

**locomotive** [lok ə 'mot ɪv] **1.** *n.* a train engine. □ *A speeding locomotive crashed into a stalled car.* **2.** *adj.* <the adj. use of ①.> □ *My uncle is a locomotive engineer.*

**locust** ['lok əst] *n.* a kind of insect that travels in large swarms and destroys crops. □ *Locusts came into the valley and ate every plant.*

**lodge** ['lɑdʒ] **1.** *n.* a small, privately owned cabin for campers, hunters, skiers, and others who like to stay in the country. □ *We stayed in the lodge* *because there was a blizzard outside.* **2.** *n.* the place where a men's organization meets. □ *On Thursdays, my dad bowls with friends from his lodge.* **3.** *n.* the structure that beavers build to live in. □ *Beavers spend the winter in their lodge.* **4.** *iv.* to become stuck somewhere; to become wedged in something. □ *The bullet lodged in the wall behind me.*

**log** ['lɔg] **1.** *n.* a length of the trunk or main branch of a tree with all of the branches removed. □ *I put some logs in the fireplace so I could build a fire.* **2.** *n.* a detailed record of a trip written by the captain of a ship, plane, train, etc. □ *A record of every change of direction is made in the log.* **3.** *tv.* to note something in ②. □ *The last entry was logged an hour before the ship sank.*

**logic** ['lɑdʒ ɪk] **1.** *n.* the science of reasoning; the part of philosophy that deals with reason. (No plural form.) □ *Logic is an important part of sound reasoning.* **2.** *n.* a method of argument or reasoning. (No plural form.) □ *According to John's logic, no one should pay taxes.* **3.** *n.* sense; rational thought; the ability to reason. (No plural form.) □ *The mediator's logic helped settle the dispute.*

**logical** ['lɑdʒ ɪ kəl] *adj.* making sense; according to the rules of logic. (Adv: *logically* [...ɪk li].) □ *I demand a logical explanation for your behavior.*

**lollipop** ['lɑl i pɑp] *n.* a piece of hard candy on the end of a stick. □ *This lollipop is cherry-flavored.*

**lone** ['lon] *adj.* only; alone; without others. (Prenominal only. See also **alone**. No comparative or superlative.) □ *A lone robin sat in the tree and sang.*

**lonely** ['lon li] **1.** *adj.* sad because one is alone; lonesome. (Comp: *lonelier;* sup: *loneliest.*) □ *Mary was lonely after she graduated from school.* **2.** *adj.* isolated; away from other people. (Comp: *lonelier;* sup: *loneliest.*) □ *You couldn't reach the lonely town during the winter.*

**lonesome** ['lon səm] *adj.* lonely; sad because one is alone. (Adv: *lonesomely.*) □ *Susan was lonesome without her friends.*

**long** ['lɔŋ] **1.** *adj.* great in length or in amount of time. (Comp: *longer;* sup: *longest.*) □ *I fell asleep during the long lecture.* **2.** *adj.* having a certain length; lasting a certain amount of time. (Follows the measure of length or time. Comp: *longer.*) □ *The snake was five feet long.* **3. all day long; all night long; all month long; all year long; all summer long; etc.** *adv.* throughout an entire period of time. □ *The concert lasted all night long.* **4.** *adv.* for a great extent of time before or after the time indicated. □ *John stayed up long past his bedtime.* **5.** *adj.* seeming to take more time than normal; seeming to be farther than normal. (Comp: *longer;* sup: *longest.*) □ *I spent one long week in jail.* **6. as long as; so long as** *phr.* provided that...; on the condition that.... □ *As long as you do what you are told, everything will be fine.* **7. as long as; so long as** *phr.* since; given the fact that.... □ *As long as I have to take this check to the bank, I can also take my sister to the dentist.* **8. as long as** *phr.* during or throughout the period of time that.... □ *As long as we have lived here, the basement has never flooded.*

**long ago** ['lɔŋ ə 'go] Go to **ago**.

**long distance** ['lɔŋ 'dɪs təns] **1.** *n.* telephone service between points that are far apart. (No plural form.) □ *How much do you pay for long distance?* **2. long-distance** *adj.* covering a great distance; linking people or things that are far apart. □ *John and Mary's long-distance relationship lasted only a year.* **3. long-distance** *adv.* in a way that covers a great distance; not locally. □

L

*The salesman conducted his business long-distance over the phone.*

**look** ['lʊk] **1.** *n.* an act of seeing [someone or something] as in ④; an act of trying to see someone or something. □ *Do you want to have a look at my photos?* **2.** *n.* a manner or style of appearing. □ *The models wore the latest look in fashion.* **3.** *n.* an expression on the face. □ *Wipe that angry look off your face and eat your peas.* **4. look at someone or something** *iv.* + *prep. phr.* to move the eyes to see or examine someone or something. □ *I looked at the stars in the sky.* **5.** *iv.* to seem; to appear [to be]. □ *Tonight's homework assignment looks difficult.* **6.** *iv.* to face a certain direction; to be positioned in a certain direction. □ *The bedroom window looked toward the sea.*

L

**loom** ['lum] **1.** *n.* a machine used for weaving cloth, blankets, or rugs. □ *Mary threaded the loom with brightly colored yarn.* **2.** *iv.* to appear somewhere in a threatening or unfriendly way. □ *Signs of a recession loomed in the distance.*

**loop** ['lup] *n.* anything that looks like a circular figure formed by a line that curves and possibly crosses itself. □ *Our cat pawed at a loop of yarn.*

**loose** ['lus] **1.** *adj.* not tight; having room to move. (Adv: *loosely.* Comp: *looser;* sup: *loosest.*) □ *I wiggled my loose tooth.* **2.** *adj.* free; escaped and not confined. □ *The dog is loose. You'd better go find him.* **3.** *adj.* not exact. (Fig. on ①. Adv: *loosely.* Comp: *looser;* sup: *loosest.*) □ *This movie is a very loose version of the book.* **4.** *adj.* [of morals] lax or not restrained. (Adv: *loosely.* Comp: *looser;* sup: *loosest.*) □ *Bob was well known for his loose morals.* **5.** *adv.* freely. □ *Can I let my dog run loose in this park?*

**loot** ['lut] **1.** *n.* stolen money and objects. (No plural form.) □ *The pirates buried the loot on a remote island.* **2.** *tv.* to rob things or places, especially during a war or a riot. □ *The teenagers looted the department store during the excitement.* **3.** *iv.* to steal [something], especially during a war or riot. □ *The police stopped the teenagers from looting.*

**lose** ['luz] **1.** *tv., irreg.* [for someone or something] to "escape" from one's care, ownership, or possession; to fail to keep someone or something in one's possession. (Pt/pp: **lost.**) □ *Mary lost her child in the department store.* **2.** *tv., irreg.* to have less of something after doing something or after something happens. □ *I lost a lot of money playing poker last night.* **3.** *tv., irreg.* not to win something; not to gain or receive something. □ *Our team lost the tournament.* **4.** *iv., irreg.* not to win; to be defeated. □ *I made a bet that the team would lose.*

**loss** ['lɔs] **1.** *n.* an instance of losing something. □ *The loss of my wallet was a major problem.* **2.** *n.* the value of something that was lost; how much something lost costs; money that is lost or never earned. □ *I suffered a terrible loss when the storm wrecked my house.* **3.** *n.* the death of someone; the death of a loved one. □ *At John's funeral, I spoke with his family about their loss.* **4.** *n.* a defeat; the failure to win. □ *Our coach said our loss was due to not practicing enough.*

**lost** ['lɔst] **1.** pt/pp of **lose. 2.** *adj.* unable to be found. □ *The library charged me a fine for the lost book.* **3.** *adj.* no longer owned; no longer in one's possession. □ *The lost computer data had never been copied onto other disks.* **4.** *adj.* not knowing where one is; not knowing how to get to where one wants to be. □ *A lost tourist asked me for directions.*

**lot** ['lɑt] **1.** *n.* a part of the available goods; a group of goods. □ *We received a huge shipment of goods yesterday, but two lots had to be sent back because they were damaged.* **2.** *n.* fate; destiny; the kind of life that one has been granted. □ *I accepted my lot as a lonely taxi driver.* **3.** *n.* an area of land; a share of land; a piece of property. □ *The Browns built their new house on a wide lot.* **4. a lot; lots** *n.* many of the people or things already mentioned; much of something already mentioned. (Treated as singular or plural, but not countable.) □ *Some of the children went to school during the storm, but a lot stayed home.* **5. a lot** *adv.* much; often. □ *Bob works a lot during the week and sleeps a lot on weekends.* □ *I don't go to movies a lot—only about twice a year.* **6. a lot of** someone or something; **lots of** someone or something *phr.* many people or things; much of someone or something. □ *I got a lot of presents for my birthday.* □ *Please put lots of ketchup on my hamburger.*

**lotion** ['lo ʃən] *n.* a creamy liquid that is rubbed on the body to soothe, add moisture, or clean the skin. (Plural only when referring to different kinds, types, instances, or varieties.) □ *Your skin will feel softer and smoother if you put some lotion on it.* Ⓒ *I sampled the different lotions, but they all smelled too strong.*

**loud** ['lɑʊd] **1.** *adj.* [of sound] having much volume or intensity; not quiet. (Adv: *loudly.* See also **loud** ③. Comp: *louder;* sup: *loudest.*) □ *My neighbors' loud argument woke me up.* **2.** *adj.* too bright; showy. (Fig. on ①. Adv: *loudly.* Comp: *louder;* sup: *loudest.*) □ *The painting's loud colors contrasted with the ivory walls.* **3.** *adv.* in a **loud** ① manner. (Comp: *louder;* sup: *loudest.*) □ *Why do you talk so loud when I am right beside you?*

**love** ['lʌv] **1.** *n.* a strong emotion of attraction, care, romance, or desire toward someone. (No plural form.) □ *John promised his love to Mary for as long as he lived.* **2.** *n.* a strong interest in something. (No plural form.) □ *Anne donated money to the museum because of her love of art.* **3.** *n.* [in tennis] a score of zero. □ *After the first serve, the score was 15–love.* **4.** *tv.* to care deeply for someone romantically. □ *The young couple loved each other deeply.* **5.** *tv.* to care deeply for someone; to care very much about someone. □ *John loved his closest friends.* **6.** *tv.* to care about or like something very much. □ *I love chocolate!* **7. love to** do something *iv.* + *inf.* to enjoy something; to enjoy doing something; to have an interest in doing something. □ *I love to swim, and so does Bob.*

**lovely** ['lʌv li] *adj.* beautiful; pretty; attractive. (Comp: *lovelier;* sup: *loveliest.*) □ *Anne wore a lovely dress to the party.*

**lover** ['lʌv ɚ] **1.** *n.* one of two people who love each other in a romantic way. □ *The lovers walked slowly along the beach, hand in hand.* **2.** *n.* someone whom one loves in a romantic way; a mate to whom one may or may not be married. □ *The newspaper printed a picture of the senator's lover.* **3.** *n.* someone who enjoys something; someone who enjoys doing something. □ *The chef prepared a special meal for the lover of fine food.*

**low** ['lo] **1.** *adj.* only a little way above the ground or sea level; not high. (Comp: *lower;* sup: *lowest.*) □ *The low area near the river floods often.* **2.** *adj.* near the bottom of something. (Comp: *lower;* sup: *lowest.*) □ *Put the book on the low shelf.* **3.** *adj.* less than average in amount, power, volume, height, intensity, cost, etc. (Comp: *lower;* sup: *lowest.*) □ *I have a low opinion of the mayor.* **4.** *adj.* [feeling] weak or unhappy. (Comp: *lower;* sup: *lowest.*) □ *I eat ice cream when I'm feeling low.* **5.** *adj.* mean; unkind; cruel. (Comp: *lower;* sup: *lowest.*) □ *The villain was a low and mean character.* **6.** *adj.* [of a supply or of strength] inadequate or not enough.

(Comp: *lower;* sup: *lowest.*) ☐ *The charge in the battery is low.* **7.** *adv.* to or at a position below or near the bottom of something. ☐ *We crouched low behind the bush to keep from being seen.*

**lower** ['lo ɚ] **1.** *iv.* [for something] to go from a high level to a low level. ☐ *His eyelids lowered as he grew more and more sleepy.* **2.** *tv.* to cause something to go from a high level to a low level; to move something down. ☐ *I lowered the shade to make the room dark.*

**lowercase** ['lo ɚ 'kes] *adj.* [of a letter or letters] in the smaller size as with *i* in *Bill*; not capitalized. (Compare this with **uppercase**.) ☐ *Do not use a lowercase letter at the beginning of a sentence.*

**lowly** ['lo li] *adj.* humble; low in rank; simple; meek. (Comp: *lowlier;* sup: *lowliest.*) ☐ *The manager ordered the lowly clerk to clean the floors.*

L

**loyal** ['lɔɪ əl] *adj.* true to one's friends, country, or promises. (Adv: *loyally.*) ☐ *My parents have always been loyal to each other.*

**loyalty** ['lɔɪ əl ti] *n.* the quality of being loyal. (Plural only when referring to different kinds, types, instances, or varieties.) ☐ *Anne never questioned her brother's loyalty.* Ⓒ *Our loyalties lie with the colleges we went to years ago.*

**lubrication** [lu brə 'ke ʃən] **1.** *n.* applying something that will make things slippery; applying oil or grease. (No plural form.) ☐ *Proper lubrication will keep your engine running longer.* **2.** *n.* something like oil or grease that makes things slippery. (Plural only when referring to different kinds, types, or varieties.) ☐ *Grease makes good lubrication for the wheels.* Ⓒ *Different lubrications will begin to break down at different temperatures.*

**luck** ['lʌk] **1.** *n.* random chance; fortune; chance. (No plural form.) ☐ *With any luck, it'll stop raining before the picnic.* **2.** *n.* good or bad fortune; success or failure. (No plural form.) ☐ *The number 13 is thought to be a sign of bad luck.*

**lucky** ['lʌk i] **1.** *adj.* [of someone] having good luck; fortunate. (Comp: *luckier;* sup: *luckiest.*) ☐ *Bob must be really lucky, because he found a hundred dollars.* **2.** *adj.* causing good luck; bringing good fortune. (Comp: *luckier;* sup: *luckiest.*) ☐ *Anne brought her lucky charm to the casino.* **3.** *adj.* showing, having, or being good luck. (Adv: *luckily.* Comp: *luckier;* sup: *luckiest.*) ☐ *I found a hundred dollars! I guess it's my lucky day.*

**lug** ['lʌg] **1.** *n.* a small piece that sticks out of something. ☐ *This nut attaches to a lug on the side of the axle.* **2.** *tv.* to carry or move someone or something heavy. ☐ *I lugged the bowling ball upstairs to the attic.*

**luggage** ['lʌg ɪdʒ] *n.* baggage; suitcases. (No plural form. Number is expressed with *piece(s) of luggage.*) ☐ *My luggage was stolen at the bus station.*

**lukewarm** ['luk 'worm] **1.** *adj.* slightly warm. ☐ *The lukewarm pop did not quench my thirst.* **2.** *adj.* without excitement; without enthusiasm. (Fig. on ①. Adv: *lukewarmly.*) ☐ *The critic gave the bad movie a lukewarm review.*

**lull** ['lʌl] *n.* a quiet moment between long periods of noise or activity; a temporary calm. ☐ *During a lull in the storm, we quickly got back to the shore.*

**lullaby** ['lʌl ə baɪ] *n.* a quiet song that is sung to help someone fall asleep. ☐ *The mother sang a lullaby to quiet her crying baby.*

**lumber** ['lʌm bɚ] **1.** *n.* timber, logs, and boards used for building. (No plural form.) ☐ *Bob bought some lumber and built a new porch for his house.* **2.** *iv.* to move in a heavy or clumsy way. ☐ *The tired man lumbered toward his nice warm home.*

**lump** ['lʌmp] **1.** *n.* a hard mass of some substance having no specific shape. ☐ *There was a lump of gum stuck to the bottom of my desk.* **2. lump** things or people **together** *tv.* + *obj.* + *adv.* to think of or treat several things or people as a single group; to think of several things or people as being the same or as being in the same category. ☐ *The economic report lumped the former Soviet republics together into a single unit.* 🅃 *This report lumps together the new and the old methods.*

**lump sum** ['lʌmp 'sʌm] *n.* money paid in a single, general payment. ☐ *You must repay this loan in one lump sum.*

**lunch** ['lʌntʃ] **1.** *n.* a meal eaten around noon; a meal eaten in the middle of the day. ☐ *I brought my lunch to work in a paper bag.* **2.** *iv.* to eat a meal around noon; to eat ①. ☐ *Anne lunched with her friends from work.*

**luncheon** ['lʌn tʃən] *n.* a formal meal in the middle of the day. (Fancier than a lunch, and usually involving a number of people.) ☐ *I accepted an invitation for luncheon at the private club.*

**lunchroom** ['lʌntʃ rum] *n.* a room where people in a school, office, or factory eat lunch. ☐ *I will meet you in the lunchroom for lunch.*

**lung** ['lʌŋ] *n.* one of a pair of organs in the body that are used when breathing. ☐ *The lungs expel carbon dioxide when we exhale.*

**lunge** ['lʌndʒ] **1.** *iv.* to move forward suddenly with force. ☐ *The cat lunged at the bird.* **2.** *n.* a sudden forward movement with force. ☐ *The lion made a lunge and grabbed the zebra in its claws.*

**lurch** ['lɚtʃ] **1.** *n.* a sudden movement like a jerk or a jump. ☐ *A sudden lurch of the bus caused me to fall out of my seat.* **2.** *iv.* to move in a way that is out of control; to move without control. ☐ *The heavy winds caused the airplane to lurch.*

**lure** ['lʊr] **1.** *tv.* to try to attract or catch a person or an animal by offering something the person or animal wants; to tempt someone or something. ☐ *The prospect of fame lures actors to Hollywood.* **2.** *n.* someone or something that attracts; something that is used to attract a person or animal. ☐ *The trout bit the brightly colored fishing lure.*

**lurk** ['lɚk] **1.** *iv.* to hang out someplace without being noticed; to be someplace without being noticed. ☐ *Someone is lurking near my back door, and I am frightened.* **2.** *iv.* to connect to an Internet discussion and just read messages without ever sending any. ☐ *There must be thousands who lurk and only a few who ever really communicate.*

**lush** ['lʌʃ] **1.** *adj.* [of a place] very comfortable; [of a place] richly comfortable. (Adv: *lushly.* Comp: *lusher;* sup: *lushest.*) ☐ *I couldn't afford to stay at the lush hotel a second night.* **2.** *adj.* covered with plants and thick vegetation. (Adv: *lushly.* Comp: *lusher;* sup: *lushest.*) ☐ *I grew many kinds of vegetables in my lush garden.*

**luxury** ['lʌg ʒə ri] **1.** *n.* expensive comfort; elegance; the very best of things. (Plural only when referring to different kinds, types, instances, or varieties.) ☐ *The king and queen were accustomed to luxury and the best of care.* 🄲 *I occasionally enjoy small luxuries, such as a meal in a restaurant.* **2.** *n.* something that is not necessary but is desired. ☐ *A telephone was considered a luxury in the 1920s.*

**lying** ['laɪ ɪŋ] present participle of lie.

**lynch** ['lɪntʃ] *tv.* to capture and hang someone who is thought to have committed a crime. (Outside the legal system.) ☐ *The prisoner was taken from the sheriff and lynched by an angry mob.*

**lynx** ['lɪŋks] *n.* a type of wild cat with a short tail, long legs, and ears that have fluffy fur at the tips. □ *I mistook the lynx for a baby cougar.*

**lyric** ['lɪr ɪk] **1.** *adj.* of or about poetry that expresses the feelings of the poet. (Adv: *lyrically* [...ɪk li].) □ *Susan expressed her anger by writing lyric poetry.* **2.** *n.* a short poem. □ *My first lyric was published in a magazine.* **3. lyrics** *n.* the words of a song. (Treated as plural.) □ *Our band needs someone to write lyrics for our music.*

**ma'am** ['mæm] *cont.* <a polite form of address for a woman.> (A contraction of *madam.*) ☐ *Can I help you with anything, ma'am?*

**macaroni** [mæk ə 'ron i] *n.* pasta in the shape of curved tubes. (No plural form.) ☐ *They are serving macaroni and cheese today.*

**machine** [mə 'ʃin] *n.* a device created to do some kind of work. ☐ *The restaurant has a machine that slices potatoes.*

**machinery** [mə 'ʃin (ə) ri] *n.* machines and parts of machines, in general. (No plural form.) ☐ *Be careful, or your sleeve will get caught in the machinery.*

**mad** ['mæd] **1.** *adj.* crazy; insane; mentally ill. (Adv: *madly.* Comp: *madder;* sup: *maddest.*) ☐ *The mad scientist wanted to rule the world.* **2.** *adj.* angry; upset. (Comp: *madder;* sup: *maddest.* Not prenominal.) ☐ *The teacher became very mad and yelled at the unruly students.*

**made** ['med] pt/pp of **make**.

**magazine** [mæg ə 'zin] *n.* a booklet that is published at regular intervals of time. ☐ *I read several current magazines on my flight to New York.*

**magic** ['mædʒ ɪk] **1.** *n.* sorcery or the use of special, unnatural, or evil powers. (No plural form.) ☐ *The villagers were afraid of the wizard's magic.* **2.** *n.* the art of performing tricks that use illusion to fool an audience. (No plural form.) ☐ *I learned some magic when I worked at the circus.* **3.** *n.* a special quality or power that lures or interests people. (Fig. on ①. No plural form.) ☐ *The tourist was entranced by the magic of Niagara Falls.* **4.** *adj.* <the adj. use of ①.> (Adv: *magically* [...ɪk li].) ☐ *The sorcerer spoke the magic words and disappeared.*

**magical** ['mædʒ ɪ kəl] **1.** *adj.* having or using **magic** ①. (Adv: *magically* [...ɪk li].) ☐ *The wizard in the story has magical powers.* **2.** *adj.* exciting and interesting; romantic. (Adv: *magically* [...ɪk li].) ☐ *Bill and Mary stared into each other's eyes for a few magical moments.*

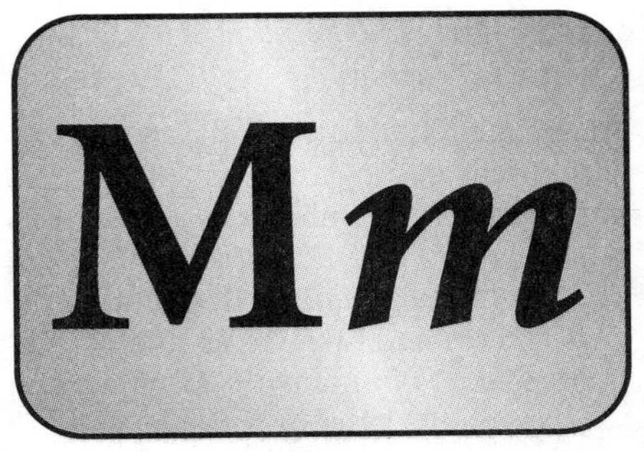

**magician** [mə 'dʒɪ ʃən] **1.** *n.* someone who practices magic or sorcery. ☐ *The magician cast a spell on the evil king.* **2.** *n.* a performer who entertains by creating illusions. ☐ *We saw a magician at the birthday party.*

**magnet** ['mæg nət] **1.** *n.* an iron or steel object that draws other iron or steel objects toward it. ☐ *I picked up the paper clips with a magnet.* **2.** *n.* someone or something that things or people are attracted toward. (Informal. Fig. on ①.) ☐ *An unlocked car is a crime magnet.*

**magnetic** [mæg 'nɛt ɪk] **1.** *adj.* able to draw or attract iron or steel in the way that a magnet does. (Adv: *magnetically* [...ɪk li].) ☐ *The pieces of iron were stuck together by magnetic force.* **2.** *adj.* able to be affected or harmed by magnetism. (Adv: *magnetically* [...ɪk li].) ☐ *I stored the data on magnetic tape.*

**magnetism** ['mæg nə tɪz əm] **1.** *n.* the physical laws of how magnets attract metal. (No plural form.) ☐ *The physics exam will cover principles of magnetism.* **2.** *n.* a charm or attraction that attracts people toward someone. (Fig. on ①. No plural form.) ☐ *The senator's magnetism helped him win the election.*

**maid** ['med] *n.* a woman who is paid to cook, clean, and do other work around the house. □ *The maid does laundry every Wednesday.*

**mail** ['mel] **1.** *n.* letters and packages that are delivered by the post office. (No plural form. Number is expressed with *piece(s) of mail.*) □ *There's nothing but bills in today's mail.* **2. the mail** *n.* the postal system. (Treated as singular.) □ *My check is in the mail.* **3.** *tv.* to send (someone) a letter or package by ②. □ *I mailed a check to you last week.*

**mailbox** ['mel bɑks] **1.** *n.* a place where mail is put so it can be picked up and taken to the post office and then delivered. □ *This mailbox is emptied every day at noon.* **2.** *n.* a container into which a mail carrier delivers mail. □ *My mailbox is full of bills!* **3.** *n.* the electronic version of ②, where e-mail is received. □ *I erased all the e-mail in my mailbox.*

**mail carrier** AND **letter carrier** ['mel kɛr ɪ ɚ, 'lɛt ɚ kɛr ɪ ɚ] *n.* someone who works for the postal system and picks up and delivers mail. □ *My dog always barks at mail carriers.*

M

**main** ['men] **1.** *adj.* most important; primary; chief. (Prenominal only. Adv: *mainly.*) □ *What is the main reason that you want to leave home?* **2.** *n.* an important pipe that carries water, sewage, gas, etc. □ *When the water main burst, our street flooded.*

**maintain** [men 'ten] **1.** *tv.* to continue something as before; to keep doing something. □ *At the intersection, maintain a straight course until you come to the end of the road.* **2.** *tv.* to take care of something; to make sure that something works properly. □ *If you maintain an automobile properly, it will last longer.* **3.** *tv.* to support someone or something, especially with money. □ *The art museum was maintained by a large government grant.* **4.** *tv.* to assert an opinion; to defend one's opinion and continue to assert it when someone argues against it. (The object can be a clause with **that** ⑦.) □ *The professor maintained that the theory had many flaws.* □ *Bob maintained his innocence.*

**maintenance** ['men tə nəns] *n.* keeping equipment and supplies in good condition. (No plural form.) □ *Proper car maintenance includes checking the oil regularly.*

**majesty** ['mædʒ ə sti] *n.* dignity; greatness and importance, especially of royalty. (No plural form.) □ *I bowed before the majesty of the king and queen.*

**major** ['me dʒɚ] **1.** *adj.* large in size or amount; great; important; serious. □ *A major fire threatened hundreds of homes.* **2.** *adj.* primary; more important. (Prenominal only.) □ *My major field of study is European history.* **3.** *n.* an officer in the army, air force, or marines above a captain and below a lieutenant colonel. (Sometimes a term of address.) □ *The captain received his orders from the major.* **4.** *n.* a student's primary area of study. □ *Sue knows a lot about history because that's her major.* **5.** *n.* someone whose **major** ④ is in a certain subject. □ *My roommate is dating a chemistry major.* **6. major in** something *iv.* + *prep. phr.* to specialize in a certain subject in school. □ *Anne is majoring in chemistry.*

**majority** [mə 'dʒor ə ti] **1.** *n.* those people who are part of the largest group or division of people, considered as a single group. (No plural form. Treated as singular.) □ *In voting, the majority rules.* **2.** *n.* [in a group] a number of people or things equal to more than half of the whole group, considered as individuals. (No plural form.) □ *The majority of the people in my neighborhood are Italian.* **3.** *n.* the largest number of votes; a number of votes equal to a specific proportion of all the votes. (No plural form.) □ *No one had a majority. It was a tie.*

**make** ['mek] **1.** *tv., irreg.* to bring something into being; to put something together from other parts; to form something; to build something; to produce something. (Pt/pp: **made.**) ☐ *John made a table out of oak.* **2.** *tv., irreg.* to cause someone or something to be in a certain condition. ☐ *Fishing makes Grandpa happy.* **3.** *tv., irreg.* to cause someone or something [to] do something; to force someone or something [to] do something. ☐ *Anne made me tell her the truth.* ☐ *We made them do it.* **4.** *tv., irreg.* to assign someone to a job; to appoint someone to a position. ☐ *The company made Sue manager of the warehouse.* **5.** *tv., irreg.* to earn money; to acquire something. ☐ *How much money do you think I make?* **6.** *tv., irreg.* to arrive at a place; to arrive at a place in time for something; to reach something; to manage to get to something. ☐ *I didn't make the 9:00 train, so I took a taxi instead.* **7. make** someone **up** *tv., irreg. + obj. + adv.* to put makeup on someone, usually oneself. (Often takes a reflexive object.) ☐ *I have to make myself up before the party.* 🅃 *The teacher made up the children before the play.* **8. make** something **up** *tv., irreg. + obj. + adv.* to invent something; to imagine something. ☐ *Jimmy made a very scary story up.* 🅃 *He made up a ghost story.* **9. make up something** *tv., irreg. + obj. + adv.* to form or constitute something; to be a part of something. ☐ *How many players make up a team in baseball?* **10.** *tv., irreg.* to become something; to assume a certain status or job. ☐ *Tom makes a good chef.* **11.** *n.* a brand; a certain style or kind. ☐ *The car dealer had many foreign makes.* **12. make a friend; make friends** *phr.* to establish a link of friendship with someone. ☐ *I have never found it difficult to make friends.*

**makeup** ['mek əp] **1.** *n.* substances applied to the face to improve its appearance. (No plural form. Treated as singular.) ☐ *Sally put on makeup before she left for the party.* **2.** *n.* the contents of something; the parts or substances that form something. (No plural form. Treated as singular.) ☐ *The makeup of the faculty by sex is 40 percent female and 60 percent male.* **3.** *adj.* <the adj. use of ①.> ☐ *I keep a small makeup mirror in my purse.*

**male** ['mel] **1.** *adj.* of or about men or boys; of or about animals of the sex that is, at maturity, capable of causing a female to become pregnant. ☐ *A male sheep is called a ram.* **2.** *adj.* [of an electrical or electronic connector] having short metal rods to be inserted into or between electrical contacts. ☐ *You can't connect two male connectors!* **3.** *n.* a **male** ① human or animal. ☐ *So far, all American presidents have been males.*

**malice** ['mæl ɪs] *n.* the desire to harm someone or something; the desire to do something evil. (No plural form.) ☐ *The thief was filled with malice for the police.*

**mall** ['mɔl] **1.** *n.* a large building with many stores inside; a shopping center. ☐ *After school, I met my friends at the mall.* **2.** *n.* a wide, formal walkway, usually lined with trees. ☐ *The mall led to the front entrance of the courthouse.*

**mallet** ['mæl ət] *n.* a tool shaped like a hammer with a large head. ☐ *I drove the peg into the board with a mallet.*

**mammal** ['mæm əl] *n.* one of a large class of warm-blooded animals whose females are able to produce milk to feed their young. ☐ *A few kinds of mammals are humans, apes, dogs, cats, rodents, cattle, sheep, horses, and bats.*

**man** ['mæn] **1.** *n., irreg.* an adult male person. (Pl: **men.**) ☐ *My history professor is a 60-year-old man.* **2.** *n.* the human race; all people. (No plural form. Treated as singular.) ☐ *Man is a warm-blooded animal.* **3.** *n., irreg.* a strong and brave human male. ☐ *Are*

M

you a man, or do you let everyone boss you around? **4.** *tv.* to provide a business or organization with one's services or labor. □ *The café was manned by college students.*

**manage** ['mæn ɪdʒ] **1.** *tv.* to be in charge of someone or something; to guide someone or something. □ *The football team was managed by a former player.* **2. manage to** do something *iv.* + *inf.* to be able to do something, even though there are problems. □ *I managed to finish the project on time.*

**manager** ['mæn ɪ dʒɚ] *n.* someone who manages or controls someone or something. □ *I asked the theater manager to refund my ticket.*

**maniac** ['men i æk] **1.** *n.* someone who has a dangerous, sometimes violent, mental illness. □ *The dangerous maniac was jailed in a hospital for the criminally insane.* **2.** *n.* someone who is wild, foolish, and too eager. (Fig. on ①.) □ *Did you see that maniac ignore the stop sign?*

**mankind** ['mæn 'kɑɪnd] *n.* the human race; all people. (No plural form. Treated as singular.) □ *The scientist looked for cures that would benefit mankind.*

**manner** ['mæn ɚ] **1.** *n.* a method; a style; a way of doing something; a way of being. □ *Anne always did her work in a careful manner.* **2. manners** *n.* the elements of proper and polite behavior. □ *My parents taught me very good manners.*

**mannerism** ['mæn ə rɪz əm] *n.* a gesture or movement of a certain person; a habit or trait of a certain person. □ *Mr. Smith's strange mannerisms frightened me.*

**mansion** ['mæn ʃən] *n.* a very large house; a large, elegant house. □ *The mansion was set back half a mile from the road.*

**mantel** ['mæn təl] *n.* the frame around a fireplace, and especially the shelf above the fireplace. □ *I keep my antique clock on the mantel.*

**mantle** ['mæn təl] *n.* something that completely covers or weighs down someone or something, as if covering someone or something with a heavy coat. □ *A mantle of snow covered the countryside.*

**manual** ['mæn j(u )əl] **1.** *n.* a book that explains how to do or use something; an instruction book; a book of information about something. □ *The car manual is in the back seat.* **2.** *adj.* of or about the hand or hands. (Adv: *manually.*) □ *Bob seems to lack any manual skills.*

**manufacture** [mæn jə 'fæk tʃɚ] **1.** *n.* the science and business of making products in factories or industry. (No plural form.) □ *Michigan's economy is linked with the manufacture of cars.* **2.** *tv.* to make something in large amounts in a factory or by using machines. □ *The United States manufactures many kinds of automobiles.*

**manufacturer** [mæn jə 'fæk tʃɚ ɚ] *n.* a person, business, or company that manufactures products. □ *Anne sued the manufacturer when her television set exploded.*

**manuscript** ['mæn jə skrɪpt] **1.** *n.* a book or text that is written by hand. □ *The author's manuscript was destroyed in a fire.* **2.** *n.* the original copy of a book or article that is sent to a publisher. □ *Her manuscript is due in the publisher's office on Friday.*

**many** ['mɛn i] **1.** *adj., irreg.* numerous; of a large number. (See also **more** and **most** for the comparative and superlative. **Many** is used with things that can be counted. Compare this with **much.**) □ *The financial report had many flaws.* **2.** *pron.* a large number of people; a large number of people or things already referred to. ☐ *During the famine, many died.*

**map** ['mæp] **1.** *n.* a drawing that shows certain features of the earth's surface; a sketch or drawing that shows locations or relations between things or places. ☐ *Interesting places were marked on the city map.* **2.** *tv.* to draw ①. ☐ *We mapped our route to the cabin so we could find our way back.*

**marble** ['mɑr bəl] **1.** *n.* a kind of stone that can be cut, shaped, and polished. (Plural only when referring to different kinds, types, instances, or varieties.) ☐ *John carved a small statue out of marble.* Ⓒ *We compared different marbles and chose a light-colored one.* **2.** *n.* a small, solid ball of colored glass, used in ③. ☐ *I had a fine collection of marbles when I was a child.* **3. marbles** *n.* a game involving directing one ② into a group of ②. ☐ *The students played marbles during recess.* **4.** *adj.* made of ①. ☐ *The elegant palace has marble floors.*

**march** ['mɑrtʃ] **1.** *iv.* to walk in rigid steps, in the manner of a soldier. ☐ *The children marched in a single line.* **2.** *iv.* to walk someplace with a certain goal in mind; to walk someplace for a certain reason. ☐ *I marched to the manager's office with a complaint.* **3.** *tv.* to force someone to move or walk. ☐ *The army marched the villagers into the center of town.* **4.** *n.* an act of walking in a line, like soldiers. ☐ *The refugees' grueling march to the border took six hours.* **5.** *n.* a demonstration or protest where people are walking with signs or chanting. ☐ *Dozens of protesters were arrested at the march.* **6.** *n.* music that has a strong beat and is used in parades or while soldiers march ①. ☐ *Many marches are patriotic.* **7. March** Go to month.

**margarine** ['mɑr dʒə rɪn] *n.* a food made from animal or vegetable fats, used in place of butter; a spread for bread. (Plural only when referring to different kinds, types, instances, or varieties.) ☐ *I spread margarine on my toast.* Ⓒ *Margarines vary greatly in taste and fat content.*

**margin** ['mɑr dʒɪn] **1.** *n.* the space between the edge of a text and the edge of the page. ☐ *My professor wrote comments in the margins of my essay.* **2.** *n.* an extra amount; the amount that is more than what is needed. ☐ *When it comes to safety, there can be no margin for error.*

**marine** [mə 'rin] **1.** *adj.* of or about salt water and the creatures that live in salt water. ☐ *Lobsters and whales are kinds of marine animals.* **2.** *adj.* of, about, from, or concerning the sea. ☐ *A marine assault led to the capture of the port city.* **3.** *adj.* of or about ships and shipping on salt water. ☐ *A cruise ship is a form of marine travel.* **4.** *n.* someone who is a member of the U.S. Marine Corps, a branch of the United States military services that serves on land and sea and in the air. ☐ *The young marine was homesick.*

**mark** ['mɑrk] **1.** *n.* a spot; a stain; a dent; something that spoils a clear or clean surface; a line or figure made by a pencil, crayon, pen, or other writing device. ☐ *There are marks on the wall where someone hit it.* **2.** *n.* something that is a sign of something; something that stands for something else. ☐ *Bill wears an earring as a mark of rebellion.* **3.** *iv.* to be able to draw or make ①. ☐ *This felt pen marks with permanent ink.* **4.** *tv.* to put a spot on something; to stain something; to spoil an otherwise clear or clean surface with ①. ☐ *The young child marked the wall with crayons.* **5.** *tv.* to indicate something; to show something; to symbolize or represent something; to stand for something. ☐ *We left a pile of rocks near a tree to mark the place where we turned.*

**market** ['mɑr kɪt] **1.** *n.* a place or building where people gather to buy and sell things. □ *Can you pick up some milk at the market?* **2.** *n.* the business, building, or system through which company shares are traded. (Short for **stock market.**) □ *I watch reports of action on the market every hour.* **3.** *n.* an area or a country where a product is needed or used; a certain group of people for which a product is needed or by which a product is used. □ *Our profits doubled when we expanded into overseas markets.* **4.** *n.* the demand for a certain product. □ *Is there a market for a better mousetrap?* **5.** *tv.* to advertise a product; to promote a product; to make a plan for selling a product. □ *We can make a lot of money from this invention if we market it correctly.*

**marketplace** ['mɑr kɪt ples] **1.** *n.* a place, usually outside, where things are bought and sold. □ *We bought some fruit and flowers in the marketplace.* **2.** *n.* trade; buying and selling. (No plural form.) □ *The business student studied the global marketplace.*

**markup** ['mɑrk əp] *n.* a price increase; the amount a price is raised. □ *The oil shortage caused a markup in the price of gasoline.*

**marriage** ['mɛr ɪdʒ] **1.** *n.* the religious or legal union of a husband and a wife. □ *Bill and Mary's marriage ended in divorce.* **2.** *n.* the ceremony that joins a man and a woman in ①; a wedding. □ *Our marriage took place in a small church in the country.*

**marry** ['mɛr i] **1.** *iv.* to unite with someone in a marriage. □ *I don't plan to marry until I'm 30.* **2.** *tv.* to unite two people in a marriage; to perform a wedding ceremony. □ *The young couple was married by a judge.* **3.** *tv.* to take someone as a husband or a wife. □ *Bill married a famous actress.*

**marsh** ['mɑrʃ] *n.* a low area of land sometimes covered with water. □ *I paddled my canoe through the marsh.*

**marshmallow** ['mɑrʃ mɛl o] *n.* a soft, spongy candy made from sugar. (Originally made from the roots of a flower called the *marsh mallow.*) □ *I put some small marshmallows on top of the cake.*

**marvel** ['mɑr vəl] *n.* someone or something that is amazing or surprising. □ *Anne's expensive new car is a real marvel!*

**masculine** ['mæs kjə lɪn] **1.** *adj.* having features usually associated with a male; manly. (Adv: *masculinely.*) □ *Anne has a very masculine handshake.* **2.** *adj.* <a grammar term describing a certain class of nouns, some of which refer to males.> (See also **gender.**) □ Gato, *the Spanish word for "cat," is masculine.*

**mash** ['mæʃ] *tv.* to crush something until it is a soft paste; to beat something into a pulp or paste. □ *I mashed the boiled potatoes with my fork.*

**mask** ['mæsk] **1.** *n.* a covering that disguises the face. □ *All the guests at the Halloween party wore masks.* **2.** *n.* a covering that protects the face, eyes, nose, or mouth. □ *The smog was so bad that I wore a gas mask.* **3.** *tv.* to conceal something; to hide something; to put ② on someone or something. □ *The spy masked the message in a secret code.*

**mass** ['mæs] **1.** *n.* an amount of something with no specific shape; a lump; a heap. □ *The chemist analyzed the sticky mass taken from the murder site.* **2.** *n.* the scientific term for the amount of matter that makes up an object. (No plural form.) □ *The students measured the mass of the object in kilograms.* **3. Mass** *n.* a Christian church service with Communion. □ *I sing in the choir at Mass.* **4.** *adj.* suitable for many people or things; involving many people or things. (Prenominal only.) □ *The government funded mass education.*

**massive** ['mæs ɪv] *adj.* very large; enormous; powerful. (Adv: *massively.*) □ *A massive stone blocked the entrance to the cave.*

**mast** ['mæst] *n.* [on a ship] an upright beam or pole to which sails are attached. □ *I saw the mast of an enemy ship on the horizon.*

**master** ['mæst ɚ] **1.** *n.* a person who has authority over people, animals, or things; a man who has authority over people, animals, or things. □ *The dog returned the stick to its master.* **2.** *n.* someone who is very skilled at something. □ *Bob is a master at teaching math.* **3.** *n.* an original page or document that copies are made from. □ *Be sure to copy the master and not one of the copies.* **4.** *adj.* <the adj. use of ③.> (Prenominal only.) □ *The master document was protected by a plastic pouch.* **5.** *adj.* primary; main; chief; controlling everything else. (Prenominal only.) □ *The mayor described his master plan for the city's revival.* **6.** *adj.* of professional standing or quality. (Prenominal only.) □ *A master plumber was needed for the complicated job.* **7.** *tv.* to become skilled in something; to learn how to do something well; to gain control of an ability. □ *David finally mastered German after living in Germany for many years.*

**mat** ['mæt] **1.** *n.* a piece of material for covering part of a floor, especially in front of a door. □ *My cat is sleeping on the mat.* **2.** *n.* a piece of thick, padded material used to cushion falls in certain sports. □ *The athlete was knocked down to the mat.* **3.** *n.* a tangled mass of hair, weeds, strings, or other things. □ *Mats of dead weeds ruined the vegetable garden.*

**match** ['mætʃ] **1.** *n.* a sporting event; a competition. □ *Do you want to go to a tennis match today?* **2.** *n.* someone or something that is the equal of or just like someone or something else; two people or things that are equal or alike. □ *These two guys are a perfect match in a basketball game.* **3.** *n.* a thin stick with a chemical substance on one end, which, when struck against a hard surface, creates fire. □ *I lit the candle with a match.* **4.** *tv.* [for something] to be exactly like something else; to fit something exactly; to go with something well. □ *Your opinions match mine very closely.* **5.** *iv.* to be exactly alike; to go together well; to fit together well. □ *I can't find any socks that match.*

**mate** ['met] **1.** *n.* the sexual partner of a living creature. □ *A male goose has only one mate until he or the female goose dies.* **2.** *n.* a spouse; a husband or a wife. □ *I taught my mate how to bowl.* **3.** *n.* one of a pair. □ *Can you help me find this red sock's mate?* **4.** *n.* a friend or colleague; a person who shares some place or activity with someone. (In compounds.) □ *I drove my roommate to the airport.* **5.** *iv.* to have sex; to breed. (Used primarily of animals.) □ *Birds typically mate in the spring.* **6.** *tv.* to bring a male and female animal together so that breeding will result. □ *The breeder mated the prize-winning dogs.*

**material** [mə 'tɪr i əl] **1.** *n.* a substance that an object is made of; a substance that can be used to make things. □ *What material is the exterior of your car made of?* **2.** *n.* cloth; fabric. (No plural form.) □ *I made a dress from five yards of material.* **3.** *n.* information, knowledge, experience, or imagination used to develop a story, movie, book, program, etc. (No plural form.) □ *Many writers get their material from their own lives.* **4.** *adj.* of or about the physical world. (Adv: *materially.*) □ *The rich celebrity surrounded himself with material comforts.* **5.** *adj.* of importance or relevance. (Adv: *materially.*) □ *The material witness's testimony damaged the defendant's case.*

**maternal** [mə 'tɚ nəl] **1.** *adj.* of or about mothers or motherhood. (Adv: *maternally.*) □ *Jane's maternal instinct led her to check on her baby.* **2.** *adj.* related through the mother's side of the family. (Adv: *maternally.*) □ *My maternal grandfather immigrated to this country from Sweden.*

**math** ['mæθ] **1.** *n.* mathematics. (No plural form. Treated as singular.) □ *Mary teaches math at the local high school.* **2.** *adj.* <the adj. use of ①.> □ *I left my math book at school.*

**mathematic** [mæθ ə 'mæt ɪk] *adj.* having the exactness or precision of mathematics. (See also **mathematics.**) □ *With mathematic precision, he measured the wood before he cut it.*

**mathematics** [mæθ ə 'mæt ɪks] *n.* the science that studies the properties and relationships of numbers and shapes. (Treated as singular.) □ *Engineers have a thorough understanding of mathematics.*

M

**matter** ['mæt ɚ] **1.** *n.* anything that takes up space. (No plural form.) □ *Water, gas, gold, lead, tar, and bananas are all different kinds of matter.* **2.** *n.* a certain kind of substance. (No plural form.) □ *The detective examined the bloody matter on the knife.* **3.** *n.* a concern; an issue; an affair. □ *The candidates discussed important matters at the debate.* **4.** *iv.* to be important; to have meaning. □ *It doesn't matter if it's raining. Let's go.*

**mattress** ['mæ trɪs] *n.* a large, rectangular pad that is used to sleep on. □ *I prefer a large mattress since I am so tall.*

**mature** [mə 'tʃʊr] **1.** *adj.* [of someone] adult or fully grown; [of fruit or vegetables] ripe or ready to eat. (Adv: *maturely.*) □ *I picked the mature grapes from the vine.* **2.** *adj.* characteristic of an adult; sensible; responsible. (Adv: *maturely.*) □ *My children act very mature for their age.* **3.** *tv.* to cause someone or something to become ① or ②. □ *John's new job helped mature him a little more.* **4.** *iv.* to become ①. □ *The girl matured into a young woman.* **5.** *iv.* [for a bond] to reach full value; [for a payment] to be due. □ *These bonds will mature in 10 years.*

**maturity** [mə 'tʃʊr ə ti] **1.** *n.* the state of being mature or developed; the degree to which someone or something is mature. (No plural form.) □ *Mike has the maturity of a 10-year-old.* **2.** *n.* human wisdom; adult thinking. (No plural form.) □ *I rely on the maturity of my uncle, who always gives good advice.* **3.** *n.* the date when an amount of money becomes due and must be paid. □ *Some banks charge a penalty if you repay a loan before maturity.*

**maximum** ['mæk sə məm] **1.** *n.* the highest amount or degree possible; the upper limit or boundary. □ *John turned the volume on his stereo up to the maximum.* **2.** *adj.* greatest; highest; most. □ *John turned the oven to the maximum temperature.*

**may** ['me] **1.** *aux.* be allowed to do something; have permission to do something. (Often **can** is used in place of **may**, even though, in standard English, **can** refers to ability, and **may** refers to permission. See also **might.**) □ *May I leave early today?* **2.** *aux.* be possible. (See also **might.**) □ *We may go bowling tomorrow.* **3.** *aux.* <a form used to extend a wish or express a hope>; let it be that.... □ *May all your wishes come true.* **4. May** Go to **month.**

**maybe** ['me bi] *adv.* perhaps; possibly yes, possibly no. □ *Maybe I'll go to the store this afternoon. I'm not sure.*

**mayonnaise** [me ə 'nez] *n.* a creamy sauce for salads and sandwiches; a sauce made from eggs, oil, and vinegar. (No plural form.) □ *I spread some mayonnaise on some bread for a sandwich.*

**mayor** ['me ɚ] *n.* the elected leader of a city, town, or village. □ *The city council voted against the mayor's proposed budget.*

**maze** ['mez] **1.** *n.* a network of connected passages, arranged so that it is hard to get from one place to another because most of the paths are blocked. □ *The garden included a maze of tall shrubbery.* **2.** *n.* something that is as confusing as ①. (Fig. on ①.) □ *Each year, the maze of tax forms gets more confusing.*

**me** ['mi] **1.** *pron.* <the objective form of **I**, the first-person singular pronoun.> (Used after prepositions and transitive verbs and as an indirect object. □ *This package is for David and me.* **2.** *pron.* <a first-person singular form.> (Used after a shortened form of **be** to refer to the speaker or writer. Usually, either "It's me" or the more formal "It is I." Rarely, if ever, "It's I" or "It is me.") □ *"Who's calling?" "It's me."*

**meadow** ['mɛd o] *n.* an area of grass-covered land; an area of land where cows, sheep, or goats can eat. □ *The sheep moved into the meadow, where the grass was plentiful.*

**meal** ['mil] **1.** *n.* a regular occasion where food is eaten, especially breakfast, lunch, or dinner. □ *I'm on a diet, so I don't snack between meals.* **2.** *n.* the food that is eaten at ①. □ *I made a meal of the leftover turkey.* **3.** *n.* crushed grain; flour. (Plural only when referring to different kinds, types, instances, or varieties.) □ *I coated the fish in meal before frying it.* 🄲 *Some meals are too coarse for the kind of bread I like to bake.*

**mean** ['min] **1.** *adj.* cruel; not kind; selfish. (Adv: *meanly.* Comp: *meaner;* sup: *meanest.*) □ *The other children were very mean to Jimmy and made him cry.* **2.** *adj.* average. (Prenominal only.) □ *The mean age of the people I work with is 28.* **3.** *n.* an average; the average of a group of numbers. □ *The mean of 2, 5, and 11 is 6.* **4.** *tv., irreg.* [for language] to represent, indicate, or express something; [for someone] to indicate, express, or intend something by words or actions. (Pt/pp: **meant.**) □ *The words* jump *and* leap *mean almost the same thing.* □ *What did you mean by that rude remark?* **5.** *tv., irreg.* [for something] to indicate or signal something. □ *Bob is yawning. I guess that means we should go now.* **6. mean to do something** *iv., irreg.* + *inf.* to intend to do something. □ *Did you mean to give so many cookies to Billy?*

**meaning** ['min ɪŋ] *n.* the sense of a word, statement, or symbol; what a word, statement, or symbol means. □ *The artist explained the meaning of her abstract painting.*

**meant** ['mɛnt] pt/pp of **mean.**

**measles** ['mi zəlz] *n.* an easily spread disease common in children. (Treated as singular or plural, but not countable. Often preceded by *the.*) □ *The measles cause a high fever and a skin rash of small red dots.*

**measure** ['mɛ ʒɚ] **1.** *n.* a unit in a system that determines the amount of something. □ *The hour is a measure of time.* **2.** *n.* one of the series of groups of musical notes that makes up a piece of music. □ *The last measure in a piece of music contains the final note.* **3.** *n.* the extent, amount, or quantity of something. □ *I won the race by a considerable measure.* **4.** *n.* a course of action; a plan. □ *I wore a life jacket as a safety measure.* **5.** *n.* a law; a proposed law; a resolution. □ *The president vetoed the taxation measure.* **6.** *tv.* to determine the size, extent, amount, degree, etc., of something. □ *The nurse measured the child's height.* **7.** *iv.* to be a certain size, extent, amount, degree, etc. □ *Billy measures precisely 4 feet tall.*

**measurement** ['mɛ ʒɚ mənt] **1.** *n.* a system of measuring. (No plural form.) □ *Canada has switched to metric measurement.* **2.** *n.* the process of measuring. (No plural form.) □ *A ruler is used for the measurement of length.* **3.** *n.* the size, length, weight, or amount of something, as determined by measuring. □ *I made a list of the measurements of everyone I wanted to buy gifts for.*

**meat** ['mit] **1.** *n.* the flesh of animals used as food. (Plural only when referring to different kinds, types, instances, or varieties. See also **fish, fowl, poultry.**) □ *Does Mary eat meat, or is she a vegetarian?* 🄲 *All of the different meats are kept in the refrigerated section of the store.* **2.** *n.* the main idea or content of something. (Fig. on ①. No plural form.) □ *You can skip the introduction. The meat of the report begins on page 6.*



**meatloaf** ['mit lof] **1.** *n.* a dish of chopped meat shaped like a loaf of bread and baked. (Plural only when referring to different kinds, types, instances, or varieties.) □ *Mike ate two slices of meatloaf for dinner.* 🄲 *We sampled many different meatloaves at the county fair, but mine is still the best.* **2.** *n.* a unit or loaf of ①. □ *Please get a meatloaf out of the freezer for dinner.*

**medal** ['mɛd l] *n.* a small piece of metal—usually flat and having a design or words on it—that is given to someone as an honor. □ *The brave soldier was awarded several medals after the war.*

**medallion** [mə 'dæl jən] **1.** *n.* a large medal. □ *The brave soldier was awarded a bronze medallion.* **2.** *n.* a large design or decorative element; a decorative element resembling a large coin or medal. □ *The model's earrings were silver medallions.*

**meddle** ['mɛd l] **1. meddle in** something *iv.* + *prep. phr.* to interfere in someone's business; to involve oneself in someone's business when one is not wanted. □ *Don't meddle in other people's business.* **2. meddle with** something *iv.* + *prep. phr.* to play with and interfere with something. □ *Jimmy is meddling with the television set.*

**media** ['mid i ə] **1.** *n.* <the Latin plural of **medium** ①.> (Although it is a Latin plural, **media** can be treated as singular or plural in English. Not countable.) □ *The media are interested in focusing on controversial matters.* **2.** *n.* <the (Latin) plural of **medium** ②.> (Often treated as singular. Not countable.) □ *Which media is best for growing bacteria?* □ *I spilled some media on the table.* **3.** *n.* <the Latin plural of **medium** ③.> (Often treated as singular. Not countable.) □ *The painter frequently worked in other media also.*

**mediator** ['mid i et ɚ] *n.* someone who helps negotiate the settlement of a disagreement. □ *The heads of the two armies agreed to meet with a mediator.*

**medical** ['mɛd ə kəl] *adj.* of or about medicine and the study and practice of medicine. (Adv: *medically* [...ɪk li].) □ *I need to see a medical doctor, not a doctor of philosophy!*

**medicate** ['mɛd ə ket] *tv.* to put medicine on or in someone or something; to treat someone or something with medicine or drugs. □ *The doctor did not medicate the patient but instead gave her some special exercises to do.*

**medication** [mɛd ə 'ke ʃən] **1.** *n.* the use or application of medicine. (No plural form.) □ *Medication and rest are the best way to treat your disease.* **2.** *n.* a kind of medicine; a dose of medicine. □ *What medications are you taking for your infection?*

**medicine** ['mɛd ə sən] **1.** *n.* the science and study of preventing, identifying, and curing diseases in the body. (No plural form.) □ *Each year many important advances are made in medicine.*

**2.** *n.* something that is used to treat a disease, especially something that is taken by the mouth or injected into the body. (Plural only when referring to different kinds, types, instances, or varieties.) □ *The doctor gave me some medicine and sent me home.* Ⓒ *Which of these medicines is the most effective?*

**medieval** [mid i 'i vəl] *adj.* of or about the Middle Ages in Europe, from about *A.D.* 500 to 1450. (Adv: *medievally.*) □ *We would be very uncomfortable living in medieval Europe.*

**mediocre** [mi di 'o kɚ] *adj.* only average; halfway between good and bad; just acceptable. □ *I got mediocre grades last semester.*

**medium** ['mid i əm] **1.** *n., irreg.* a channel or pathway for sending information—such as newspapers, radio, television, print advertising, etc. (The Latin plural is **media**, and the English plural is *mediums.*) □ *The largest medium in the U.S. is television.* **2.** *n., irreg.* a substance in which organisms such as bacteria can be grown and kept alive. (Rarely used in the singular. Pl: **media**.) □ *Some bacteria can be grown only in a specially prepared medium.* **3.** *n., irreg.* the [different kinds of] materials used by an artist. (The Latin plural is **media**, and the English plural is *mediums.*) □ *The painter usually worked in only one medium—paints.* **4.** *n.* the middle size of an object for sale that comes in different sizes. (Pl: *mediums.*) □ *Do you want a medium or a large?*

**meek** ['mik] *adj.* letting others do as they want; not protesting. (Adv: *meekly.* Comp: *meeker;* sup: *meekest.*) □ *The meek old man waited quietly in line.*

**meet** ['mit] **1.** *tv., irreg.* to come together with someone either by chance or on purpose; to encounter someone. (Pt/pp: **met**.) □ *Tom hoped to meet Mary at the library.* **2.** *tv., irreg.* [for something] to touch someone or something; to come into contact with someone or something. □ *The carpet meets the wall on all sides.* **3.** *tv., irreg.* to be introduced to someone. □ *I'd like you to meet an old friend of mine.* **4.** *iv., irreg.* to come together; to join; to connect; to make contact; to touch. □ *The two electrical wires met, giving off dangerous sparks.*

**meeting** ['mit ɪŋ] **1.** *n.* a group of people who have come together for a specific reason. □ *Every Monday morning we have a sales meeting.* **2.** *n.* an instance of people coming together, perhaps by accident. □ *My last meeting with Susan was two days ago, when I saw her in the supermarket.*

**megabyte** ['mɛg ə bɑɪt] *n.* a unit consisting of about one million bytes. (The abbreviation is *MB,* and the word can be shortened to *meg.*) □ *I used all the available memory on my 24-megabyte hard drive.*

**mellow** ['mɛl o] **1.** *adj.* [of colors, sounds, textures, or tastes that are] soft, deep, relaxing, or muted. (Adv: *mellowly.* Comp: *mellower;* sup: *mellowest.*) □ *This expensive tea has a soothing, mellow flavor.* **2.** *adj.* relaxed and quiet. (Informal. Fig. on ①. Adv: *mellowly.* Comp: *mellower;* sup: *mellowest.*) □ *Taking a long, warm bath puts me in a mellow mood.* **3.** *tv.* to cause someone or a group to become ②. □ *The wine mellowed all of the party guests.* **4.** *iv.* to become ②. □ *My father was always nervous, but he mellowed as he got older.*

**melody** ['mɛl ə di] *n.* the series of notes that make up the tune of a song; a song; a tune. □ *I whistled a happy melody as I walked down the street.*

**melon** ['mɛl ən] **1.** *n.* one of a family of large round or oval fruits with thick rinds and juicy, edible insides. □ *I knocked on the melon to see if it was ripe.* **2.** *n.* the edible part of ①; ① used as food. (No plural form. Number is

M

expressed with *piece(s)* or *slice(s) of melon.*) □ *Give Jimmy a slice of melon.*

**melt** ['mɛlt] **1.** *iv.* [for a solid] to become liquid; to turn into a liquid. □ *Steel melts at very high temperatures.* **2.** *tv.* to cause something solid to become liquid; to cause something solid to turn into a liquid. □ *The hot water melted the ice.* **3.** *tv.* to cause something to disappear or fade. (Fig. on ②.) □ *Kind words melted my fears away.* **4.** *n.* an instance of turning into a liquid as in ①. □ *The rapid snow melt caused the rivers to flood.*

**member** ['mɛm bɚ] *n.* someone who belongs to a group or an organization. □ *Most health clubs are only open to members and their guests.*

**membership** ['mɛm bɚ ʃɪp] **1.** *n.* the connection between one person and an organization to which the person belongs. (Plural only when referring to different kinds, types, instances, or varieties.) □ *I signed up for membership at the local health club.* Ⓒ *I hold memberships at four different clubs.* **2.** *n.* all of the members of a group or organization. (No plural form.) □ *The president of the group spoke to the entire membership.*

**memento** AND **momento** [mə 'mɛn to] *n.* a souvenir; something that reminds one of someone else or of a place that one has been. □ *I keep this small lock of hair as a memento of a dear friend.*

**memo** ['mɛm o] *n.* a note or announcement, especially in an office. (A shortened form of the word *memorandum.* Pl ends in *-s.*) □ *Tom read the brief memo and then threw it in the trash.*

**memorable** ['mɛm ə rə bəl] *adj.* worth remembering; easy to remember. (Adv: *memorably.*) □ *I spent a memorable weekend in Palm Beach.*

**memorial** [mə 'mor i əl] **1.** *adj.* [of something] used to remind someone of a person, thing, place, or event. (Prenominal only.) □ *The memorial ceremony marked the anniversary of the end of the war.* **2.** *n.* something that is a reminder of an event in the past or of a person no longer living. □ *Millions of tourists have visited the Lincoln Memorial in Washington, D.C.*

**memory** ['mɛm ə ri] **1.** *n.* the brain or mind, thought of as a place where ideas, words, images, and past events reside. (No plural form.) □ *Tom recited the story from memory.* **2.** *n.* the functioning or quality of ①; the ability of ① to function. □ *Mary has a very good memory for people's names.* **3.** *n.* an instance of remembering a past event, experience, person, or sensation; someone or something that is remembered. □ *I have many happy memories of my childhood.* **4.** *n.* the part of a computer where information is kept until it is needed or stored. (No plural form.) □ *My new computer has more memory than my old one.*

**men** ['mɛn] pl of **man**.

**menace** ['mɛn ɪs] **1.** *n.* a threat; someone or something that threatens harm, violence, or danger. □ *The enemy's huge army is a menace to peace.* **2.** *tv.* to threaten someone or something with harm, violence, or danger. □ *The terrorist menaced the hostages.*

**mend** ['mɛnd] **1.** *tv.* to fix something; to repair something. □ *I mended the hole in my sock.* **2.** *iv.* to become healthy; to become well. □ *Grandma mended slowly after a serious illness.*

**menstrual** ['mɛn str(u )əl] *adj.* associated with menstruation. (Adv: *menstrually.*) □ *Anne told her doctor about her menstrual pains.*

**menstrual period** ['mɛn str(u )əl 'pɪr i əd] *n.* the time during the month when a woman menstruates. (Can be shortened to **period**.) □ *Anne felt very bad just before her menstrual period started.*

**menstruate** ['mɛn stru et] *iv.* to experience menstruation; to have a menstrual period. □ *My daughter first menstruated when she was 11 years old.*

**menstruation** [mɛn stru 'e ʃən] *n.* the monthly process in sexually mature women who are not pregnant in which the lining of the uterus is shed. (No plural form.) □ *The teacher explained menstruation to the health class.*

**mental** ['mɛn təl] **1.** *adj.* of or about the mind; done by the mind. (Adv: *mentally.*) □ *I am very slow at mental work.* **2.** *adj.* of or about **mental** ① illness. □ *Tom visited a friend in a mental hospital.*

**mention** ['mɛn ʃən] **1.** *tv.* to say or write something; to tell about something briefly. (The object can be a clause with **that** ⑦.) □ *Mary mentioned that she wanted to leave soon.* **2.** *tv.* to refer to someone or something. □ *Just mention money, and Bill gets excited.* **3.** *n.* an instance of saying or writing something as in ②; a brief statement; a reference. □ *The mayor made only a brief mention of the crime problem.*

**menu** ['mɛn ju] **1.** *n.* a list of food and drink available at a restaurant. □ *Waiter, could I see a menu please?* **2.** *n.* a list of options or functions available in a computer program. (Fig. on ①.) □ *To see what options are available, click on "Menu."*

**meow** [mi 'aʊ] **1.** *n.* the sound a cat makes. □ *I heard a cat's meow and looked everywhere for the animal.* **2.** *iv.* [for a cat] to make its characteristic sound. □ *The cat stood on the porch and meowed.*

**merchandise** ['mɚ tʃən daɪs] *n.* products for sale or trade; things that are for sale. (No plural form. Treated as singular.) □ *Please don't touch the merchandise. If you break it, you will pay for it.*

**merchant** ['mɚ tʃənt] *n.* someone who buys and sells products in order to make money; a retailer. □ *The merchant helped me choose a good camera.*

**mercury** ['mɚ kjə ri] **1.** *n.* a silver-gray element that is liquid at room temperature. (No plural form.) □ *Mercury is an element, and its symbol is Hg.* **2. Mercury** *n.* the closest planet to the sun in our solar system. □ *Mercury revolves around the sun once every 88 days.*

**mercy** ['mɚ si] *n.* kindness; pity; compassion. (No plural form in this sense except when referring to *God's mercies.*) □ *The sinner prayed to God for mercy.*

**mere** ['mɪr] *adj.* only; nothing more than. (Prenominal only. Adv: **merely**. Comp: none; sup: *merest.*) □ *It was a mere ten degrees above zero last night.*

**merely** ['mɪr li] *adv.* this only; only this and nothing else; just. □ *John and Mary are merely friends, not lovers.*

M

**merge** ['mɚdʒ] **1.** *iv.* to join with something else. □ *The two small companies merged into one large one.* **2.** *iv.* to enter the flow of traffic. □ *The right lane ends up ahead, so merge left.* **3.** *tv.* to cause two or more things to come together and become one. □ *The corporation merged two of its divisions together.*

**merger** ['mɚdʒ ɚ] *n.* an act or process of joining two organizations into one. □ *The business merger resulted in the loss of many jobs.*

**merit** ['mɛr ɪt] **1.** *n.* worth; value. (No plural form.) □ *Your ideas lack merit, and I will ignore them.* **2.** *n.* a good point; a virtue. (Usually plural.) □ *The judge reviewed the merits of the case.* **3.** *tv.* to deserve something; to be worthy of something. □ *Your brave action merits a reward.*

**merry** ['mɛr i] *adj.* happy; cheerful; joyful. (Adv: *merrily.* Comp: *merrier;* sup:

*merriest.*) □ *The merry children opened their presents.*

**mesh** ['mɛʃ] *n.* material that is woven in such a way that there are holes between the threads or wires. (Plural only when referring to different kinds, types, instances, or varieties.) □ *The metal mesh of the window screen was starting to rust.* Ⓒ *We tried meshes of different sizes, but the horrible little bugs got through them all.*

**mess** ['mɛs] **1.** *n.* something or some place that is dirty or untidy. □ *Our son's bedroom is always a mess.* **2.** *n.* a group of things that are not in order; a situation that is not organized; confusion. □ *At 5 P.M.*, traffic in the city is a mess. **3.** *n.* [in the military services] a meal, eaten by a group. □ *I'm hungry. What time is mess?* **4. mess something up** *tv. + obj. + adv.* to make something dirty; to cause something not to work right. □ *How could you mess things up so badly in one day?* Ⓣ *I messed up everything badly.*

M

**message** ['mɛs ɪdʒ] **1.** *n.* a communication between two or more people; a piece of written or spoken information for someone. □ *I listened to my answering machine for messages.* **2.** *n.* the moral of a story; a lesson that is to be learned from a story. □ *I couldn't figure out the message of the confusing movie.*

**messenger** ['mɛs ən dʒɚ] *n.* someone who delivers messages, documents, parcels, or flowers. □ *Have the messenger deliver these documents to our lawyer.*

**messy** ['mɛs i] *adj.* dirty or not organized; not clean and tidy. (Adv: *messily.* Comp: *messier;* sup: *messiest.*) □ *My desk is so messy that I can't see its surface.*

**met** ['mɛt] pt/pp of **meet**.

**metal** ['mɛt əl] **1.** *n.* a solid mineral substance that can be cast or beaten into different shapes. (Plural only when referring to different kinds, types, instances, or varieties.) □ *Is this railing made of wood or metal?* Ⓒ *Most metals are mined from the earth.* **2.** *adj.* made from ①. □ *I collect old metal buttons.*

**meter** ['mit ɚ] **1.** *n.* the basic unit of the measurement of length in the metric system, equal to 39.37 inches. □ *My sister is 1.5 meters tall.* **2.** *n.* a device that measures and displays the amount of something that is used. □ *Someone from the gas company stopped by to read my gas meter.* **3.** *n.* the rhythms caused by accents in poetry and music. (Plural only when referring to different kinds, types, instances, or varieties. Treated as singular.) □ *Free verse lacks rhyme and meter.* Ⓒ *The poem was written is several different meters. We cannot agree on how many.* **4.** *tv.* to measure the flow of something with ②. □ *The air flow was metered in order to maintain a steady rate.*

**method** ['mɛθ əd] *n.* a way of doing something; a system; a procedure. □ *The principal disagreed with the teacher's methods.*

**metric** ['mɛ trɪk] *adj.* of or about the system of measurement based on the meter. (Adv: *metrically* [...ɪk li].) □ *A yard is about 1 meter in the metric system.*

**mice** ['mɑɪs] a pl of **mouse**.

**microphone** ['mɑɪ krə fon] *n.* a device that changes sound waves into electrical waves so that the sound can be broadcast, recorded, or made louder. (Can be shortened to **mike**.) □ *Speak into the microphone! We can't hear you!*

**microscope** ['mɑɪ krə skop] *n.* a device that makes very small objects appear much larger. □ *I looked through the microscope and saw bacteria for the first time.*

**midair** ['mɪd 'ɛr] *adj.* in the air; not touching the ground. □ *The pilot avoided a midair crash.*

**midday 1.** ['mɪd 'de] *n.* noon; the middle of the day. (No plural form.) □ *It started to rain at midday.* **2.** ['mɪd de] *adj.* happening in the middle of the day; happening at noon. (Prenominal only.) □ *We ordered food to eat during the midday meeting.*

**middle** ['mɪd l] **1.** *n.* a place or time halfway between two ends or sides; the center. □ *I placed the vase in the middle of the table.* **2.** *n.* the area of the waist; halfway along the body of a human or other creature. □ *These pants are too tight around my middle.* **3.** *adj.* central; at the same distance from either end; halfway between the beginning and the end. (Prenominal only.) □ *John Joseph Smith's middle name is Joseph.*

**midnight** ['mɪd nɑɪt] **1.** *n.* 12:00 at night; twelve o'clock at night. □ *The bar closes at midnight.* **2.** *adj.* happening at ①; beginning at ①. (Prenominal only.) □ *I fell asleep during the midnight movie.*

**Midwest** ['mɪd 'wɛst] **1.** *n.* the middle part of the United States. (No plural form.) □ *The Midwest is primarily very flat and has many farms.* **2.** *adj.* <the adj. use of ①.> □ *I grew up in a Midwest farm town.*

**might** ['mɑɪt] **1.** *n.* power; strength. (No plural form.) □ *Dave pushed the car with all of his might.* **2.** *aux.* <a form that expresses possibility.> (See also **may**.) □ *It might rain tonight.* **3.** *aux.* <a form expressing permission.> (See also **may** and **could**.) □ *Anne asked if she might be excused from the dinner table.*

**mighty** ['mɑɪt i] *adj.* powerful; strong; very great. (Adv: *mightily.* Comp: *mightier;* sup: *mightiest.*) □ *A mighty torrent of water rushed down the river.*

**mike** ['mɑɪk] *n.* a device for converting sounds to electronic audio signals. (Short for **microphone**.) □ *Please speak directly into the mike.*

**mild** ['mɑɪld] **1.** *adj.* gentle or calm; not extreme, powerful, or severe. (Adv: *mildly.* Comp: *milder;* sup: *mildest.*) □ *A mild breeze blew inland from the lake.* **2.** *adj.* [of food] plain and not spicy. (Adv: *mildly.* Comp: *milder;* sup: *mildest.*) □ *I have to eat mild food because my stomach is easily upset.* **3.** *adj.* light; not severe or harsh. (Adv: *mildly.* Comp: *milder;* sup: *mildest.*) □ *I responded to the mild insult by walking away.*

**mile** ['mɑɪl] *n.* a unit of measurement of length, equal to 5,280 feet or about 1.6 kilometers. □ *I live five miles from the highway.*

**mileage** ['mɑɪl ɪdʒ] **1.** *n.* a distance expressed in miles. (Plural only when referring to different kinds, types, instances, or varieties.) □ *The road atlas listed the mileage between major cities.* Ⓒ *The mileages listed may not be exactly right, since they were made some years ago.* **2.** *n.* the total number of miles that can be traveled using one gallon of gasoline. (No plural form.) □ *This brand of gasoline will improve your mileage.*

M

**military** ['mɪl ə tɛr i] **1. the military** *n.* the armed forces; the army. (Treated as singular.) □ *A large percentage of the nation's budget goes to the military.* **2.** *adj.* <the adj. use of ①.> (Adv: *militarily* [mɪl ə 'tɛr ə li].) □ *Military service for young men was required during the war.*

**militia** [mə 'lɪʃ ə] *n.* a group of citizens who are not part of the professional army but who are trained as soldiers. □ *A local militia was blamed for the terrorist attack.*

**milk** ['mɪlk] **1.** *n.* the white liquid made by female mammals to feed their young. (Usually refers to cows' milk used as food. No plural form.) □ *I ordered a glass of milk and a slice of cherry pie.* **2.** *n.* a white liquid from certain plants.

(No plural form.) □ *A sticky milk seeped from the weeds' cut stems.* **3.** *tv.* to take ① from an animal. □ *How often do cows have to be milked?*

**mill** ['mɪl] **1.** *n.* a building containing the machinery needed to turn grain into meal. □ *The restaurant bought its flour directly from the mill.* **2.** *n.* a machine or device that crushes grains, seeds, or coffee beans. □ *This coffee mill grinds beans very finely.*

**milligram** ['mɪl ə græm] *n.* a unit of measurement of weight; one one-thousandth (1/1,000) of a gram. □ *There are 200 milligrams of sodium in one serving of these potato chips.*

**millimeter** ['mɪl ə mit ɚ] *n.* a unit of measurement of length; one one-thousandth (1/1,000) of a meter. □ *One inch is about 25.4 millimeters.*



**million** ['mɪl jən] **1.** *n.* the number 1,000,000. (Additional numbers are formed as with *two million, three million, four million,* etc.) □ *The population in this city is now up to a million.* **2.** *adj.* 1,000,000; consisting of 1,000,000 things; having 1,000,000 things. □ *This TV show is being watched by ten million people.*

**millionaire** [mɪl jə 'nɛr] *n.* someone who has $1,000,000 in assets after debt is subtracted. □ *Bob can afford a new car. He's a millionaire.*

**mind** ['maɪnd] **1.** *n.* the part of humans that thinks and has feelings. □ *The drugs affected Bill's mind.* **2.** *n.* the center of intelligence and memory; the imagination; the creative part of humans. □ *The young student had the mind of a genius.* **3.** *tv.* to care for someone or something; to tend to someone or something. □ *Can you mind my cat when I'm on vacation?* **4.** *tv.* to be opposed to something; to care if someone does something. □ *Do you mind pizza for dinner?* **5.** *iv.* to be opposed [to something]; to object. □ *I need to smoke. Do you mind?*

**mine** ['maɪn] **1.** *n.* an opening into the earth from which precious metals, minerals, or gems are recovered. □ *Working in a coal mine is a dangerous profession.* **2.** *n.* a source of something in large amounts; someone, something, or some place that supplies large amounts of something. (Fig. on ①.) □ *The town's librarian is a mine of information about the history of this area.* **3.** *n.* a bomb that is placed under the surface of the soil or water and explodes when it is touched. □ *Many children were killed when a mine exploded near the school.* **4.** *tv.* to fetch precious metals, minerals, or gems from the earth. □ *The old prospector mined gold.* **5.** *tv.* to place bombs under the surface of the soil or water of a particular location. □ *The enemy army mined the field, making it dangerous for anyone to go across it.* **6.** *pron.* <the first-person singular possessive pronoun.> (Used in place of a noun.) □ *Your shirt is brown, and mine is black.*

**mineral** ['mɪn (ə) rəl] **1.** *n.* one of many kinds of crystal-like substances dug from the earth; a substance that is gotten by mining. □ *Coal is a widely used mineral.* **2.** *n.* an element that plants and animals need in order to function properly. □ *People need both vitamins and minerals to be healthy.* **3.** *adj.* <the adj. use of ①.> □ *Bill discovered a vast mineral deposit in his back yard.*

**minimal** ['mɪn ə məl] *adj.* smallest possible [amount]. (Adv: *minimally.*) □ *The lazy student did only a minimal amount of studying.*

**minimum** ['mɪn ə məm] **1.** *n.* the least amount or degree possible; the smallest amount or degree possible. □ *You have to buy a minimum of two chickens to get the sale price.* **2.** *adj.* minimal; smallest; lowest; least. □ *The minimum* *speed on that highway is 45 miles per hour.*

**minister** ['mɪn ɪ stɚ] **1.** *n.* a pastor; a preacher; the leader of a Christian church. □ *Anne and Bill were married by a minister.* **2.** *n.* [in many countries] someone who is head of a government department. □ *The defense minister urged the prime minister to declare war.*

**mink** ['mɪŋk] **1.** *n., irreg.* a small, long, furry animal similar to the weasel or ferret. (Pl: *mink* or *minks.*) □ *The fur of the mink is beautiful and valuable.* □ *The trapper caught several minks in one day.* **2.** *n.* the fur of ①. (No plural form.) □ *Mink is soft, warm, and expensive.* **3.** *n.* a coat made from ②. □ *The actress wore a mink to the award ceremony.* **4.** *adj.* made from ②. □ *The actress wore a short mink coat.*

**minnow** ['mɪn o] *n.* a kind of very small, thin fish that lives in fresh water. □ *The minnows could swim through my fishing net.*

**minor** ['maɪn ɚ] **1.** *adj.* small in size or amount; not serious; not very important. □ *My editor made a few minor changes to my article.* **2.** *adj.* <the adj. use of ③.> □ *My minor field is closely related to my major field of study.* **3.** *n.* a student's secondary area of study. □ *I haven't decided on a minor yet, but my major is biology.* **4.** *n.* someone who is younger than the legal age of responsibility. □ *The store was fined for selling liquor to minors.*

**mint** ['mɪnt] **1.** *n.* a small plant with leaves that have a fresh, strong flavor, and the leaves themselves. (No plural form.) □ *The cook added some mint to the recipe.* **2.** *n.* a candy that is flavored with ①. □ *The restaurant gives each customer a mint after dinner.* **3.** *n.* a building where the government makes paper money and coins. □ *The location of the mint where paper money is printed is named on each bill.* **4.** *adj.* tasting like ①; flavored with ①. □ *I'd like a scoop of mint ice cream.* **5.** *adj.* perfect; in excellent condition. □ *I paid $1,000 for a mint first edition of the book.* **6.** *tv.* to make something, especially coins, from metal. □ *Only 200,000 copies of the special coin were minted.*

**minus** ['maɪn əs] **1.** *prep.* reduced by some amount; decreased by some amount; made less by some amount; with something omitted or subtracted. (Symbolized by "−".) □ *Five minus three is two.* **2.** *adj.* below zero; less than zero; [of a number] negative. (Precedes the amount. Symbolized by "−".) □ *Ten subtracted from three is minus seven.* **3.** *adj.* [of a school letter grade] less than the full grade. (Follows the letter. Symbolized by "−".) □ *I need an average of at least B minus to keep my scholarship.* □ *I barely passed the test. I got a D minus.* **4.** *n.* a negative factor; a lack. □ *Your lack of experience is a serious minus.*

M

**minute 1.** ['mɪn ɪt] *n.* a unit of the measurement of time, equal to 60 seconds or 1/60 hour. □ *The victim was unconscious for two minutes.* **2. minutes** ['mɪn ɪts] *n.* a written account of what happened at a meeting. (Treated as plural, but not countable.) □ *Lisa gave a copy of the minutes to the board members.* **3.** [maɪ 'nut] *adj.* very small. (Adv: *minutely.*) □ *There was a minute hair floating in my soup.*

**miracle** ['mɪr ə kəl] **1.** *n.* a remarkable event that cannot be explained by the laws of nature. □ *The magician claims to work miracles, but really he just does tricks.* **2.** *n.* an unexpected, lucky event. (Fig. on ①.) □ *It will be a miracle if our unlucky team wins the game.*

**miraculous** [mɪ 'ræk jə ləs] **1.** *adj.* not able to be explained by the laws of science or nature. (Adv: *miraculously.*) □ *God spoke to me in a miraculous vision.* **2.** *adj.* unexpectedly excellent. (Fig. on

①. Adv: *miraculously.*) □ *I get miraculous results from my new detergent.*

**mirage** [mɪ 'rɑʒ] *n.* an image of something that does not really exist, especially an image of water in the desert; something that fools one's vision. □ *The way pavement seems to shimmer when it's hot is a mirage.*

**mirror** ['mɪr ɚ] **1.** *n.* a piece of polished glass, treated in a way that makes it reflect images perfectly. □ *I looked at my gray hair in the mirror.* **2.** *n.* someone or something that shows what someone or something thinks, looks like, acts like, or is. (Fig. on ①.) □ *The author's novels are a mirror of his life.* **3.** *tv.* to show something as though it were seen in ①; to represent something. □ *My thoughts don't mirror the opinions of my company.*

**mirth** ['mɚθ] *n.* fun and laughter. (No plural form.) □ *There's no place for mirth here. I'm trying to be serious.*

M

**mischief** ['mɪs tʃɪf] **1.** *n.* playful trouble; slightly bad tricks or deeds. (No plural form.) □ *Don't get into any mischief while I'm gone!* **2.** *n.* someone—usually a child—who is a source of trouble or problems. □ *The annoying little mischief was sent to the principal's office.*

**misconduct** [mɪs 'kɑn dəkt] *n.* bad behavior; behavior that is not good or moral. (No plural form.) □ *The officers were punished for their misconduct.*

**miser** ['mɑɪz ɚ] *n.* someone who is very selfish and has a lot of money. □ *The head of the charity couldn't convince the miser to give the charity any money.*

**misfit** ['mɪs fɪt] *n.* someone who does not fit in with other people or a situation. □ *I never go to parties, because I feel like such a misfit.*

**misfortune** [mɪs 'for tʃən] *n.* bad luck; bad fortune. (Plural only when referring to different kinds, types, instances, or varieties.) □ *Misfortune and grief affected everyone in the unlucky town.* Ⓒ *Bill suffered two different misfortunes this week.*

**mishap** ['mɪs hæp] *n.* an unlucky event or accident; bad luck; an unfortunate accident. □ *The blizzard caused many mishaps on the highway.*

**misjudge** [mɪs 'dʒʌdʒ] *tv.* to make the wrong judgment about someone or something. □ *The abilities of young people are often misjudged.*

**mislaid** [mɪs 'led] pt/pp of **mislay**.

**mislay** [mɪs 'le] *tv., irreg.* to put something in a location that is later forgotten. (Pt/pp: **mislaid**.) □ *David was late because he'd mislaid his wallet.*

**mismanage** [mɪs 'mæn ɪdʒ] *tv.* to manage someone or something badly; to deal with someone or something badly. □ *The coach mismanaged the baseball team.*

**misplace** [mɪs 'ples] *tv.* to put something someplace and then forget where it is. □ *My roommate misplaced the rent check.*

**miss** ['mɪs] **1.** *tv.* to fail to hit, catch, meet, do, or reach someone or something. □ *I missed my appointment because traffic was so bad.* **2.** *tv.* to fail to locate or observe people or things that are where they are meant to be. □ *I missed the fine print at the bottom of the contract.* **3.** *tv.* to notice the absence of someone or something. □ *We missed you at the meeting this morning. Did you forget to come?* **4.** *tv.* to feel sad about the loss, departure, or absence of someone or something. □ *I missed my favorite teacher after she retired.* **5.** *tv.* to avoid or escape something; to avoid doing something. □ *Bill ran across the street and barely missed being hit by a car.* **6.** *tv.* to lack something; to fail to acquire or experience something that is available. □ *I missed the circus when it was in town.* **7.** *n.* a failure to hit, reach, catch, or do something. □ *The plane almost hit another plane, and the near miss frightened the passengers.* **8.** *n.* <a polite form of address for girls and young women.> □ *Excuse me, miss, you dropped your ticket.* **9. Miss** *n.* <a title for a girl or unmarried woman.> (Compare this with **Ms.**) □ *Miss Johnson lives in that apartment.*

**mission** ['mɪ ʃən] **1.** *n.* a journey to a place to do an important task. □ *The technicians were sent on a mission into space.* **2.** *n.* a specific task or duty; a specific aim or objective. □ *The mayor was successful in his mission to reduce crime.*

**misspell** [mɪs 'spɛl] *tv.* to spell something wrongly. □ *The word* misspell *is often misspelled with only one* s.

**mist** ['mɪst] **1.** *n.* a light spray of water or other liquid; a small cloud formed by spraying water or other liquid. □ *The gardener sprayed the plants with mist.* **2.** *tv.* to spray someone or something with water or other liquid; to cover something with ① or water vapor. □ *I misted my hair with hair spray to hold it in place.* **3. mist up; mist over** *iv.* + *adv.* [for something] to acquire a coating of ①. □ *The mirror in the bathroom misted over.*

**mistake** [mɪ 'stek] **1.** *n.* an error; something that is wrong; something that is not correct. □ *Fix the mistakes in your report before you submit it.* **2.** *tv., irreg.* to have the wrong idea about something. (Pt: **mistook**; pp: **mistaken.**) □ *You've mistaken what I said. My birthday isn't until tomorrow.* **3. mistake** someone or something **for** someone or something *tv., irreg.* + *obj.* + *prep. phr.* to think that one thing or person is another; to confuse one thing or person with another. □ *I mistook Anne for her twin sister.*

**mistaken** [mɪ 'stek ən] pp of **mistake.**

**mister** ['mɪs tɚ] *n.* <a title for an adult male; a form of address for men.> (The abbreviation, **Mr.**, is used in writing.) □ *After he turned 18, John wanted to be called "Mr. Johnson."*

**mistook** [mɪs 'tʊk] pt of **mistake.**

**mistreat** [mɪs 'trit] *tv.* to treat someone or something badly; to abuse someone or something. □ *No animals were mistreated in the making of this movie.*

**mistrust** [mɪs 'trʌst] **1.** *tv.* not to trust someone or something; to doubt someone or something. □ *I mistrusted the car salesman's claims.* **2.** *n.* lack of trust; doubts about someone or something; distrust. (No plural form.) □ *My mistrust of salespeople is based on many bad experiences.*

**misty** ['mɪs ti] *adj.* [of a surface] covered with mist; [of air] filled with mist. (Adv: *mistily.* Comp: *mistier;* sup: *mistiest.*) □ *I wiped the misty windows with a rag.*

**misunderstand** [mɪs ən dɚ 'stænd] *tv., irreg.* to understand someone or something incorrectly. (Pt/pp: **misunderstood.**) □ *I misunderstood you because you didn't speak loudly enough.*

**misunderstood** [mɪs ən dɚ 'stʊd] pt/pp of **misunderstand.**

**misuse 1.** [mɪs 'jus] *n.* incorrect use; improper use; using something wrongly. (No plural form.) □ *My editor scolded me for my misuse of the words* sit *and* set. □ *The misuse of this equipment could cause an electrical shock.* **2.** [mɪs 'juz] *tv.* to use something the wrong way; to use something for a purpose for which it was not meant to be used. □ *Bill started a fire when he misused the lighter.*

**mitten** ['mɪt n] *n.* a piece of clothing for one's hand, without separate parts for each finger but with a separate area for the thumb. □ *Woolen mittens really keep your hands warm.*

**mix** ['mɪks] **1.** *n.* a mixture; a combination of different things or people. □ *My neighborhood is a mix of many ethnic groups.* **2.** *n.* a combination of different foods that is ready to be cooked or used in cooking. □ *Lisa makes pancakes from a mix that she buys at the store.* **3.** *tv.* to combine or blend different things so that they form one thing. □ *If you mix red and blue, you get purple.* **4.** *tv.* to do two things at the same time. □ *At the convention, I mixed business with pleasure.* **5.** *iv.* to be friendly and comfortable with other people; to be with other people. □ *My shy guests didn't mix, so we all watched TV in silence.*

**mixed** ['mɪkst] **1.** *adj.* combined; blended. □ *The vinegar and oil in the mixed dressing began to separate.* **2.** *adj.* [of the thoughts or feelings that someone has about someone or something] combining very different things, such as liking and disliking. □ *My feelings about the candidate were mixed.* **3.** *adj.* having both males and females; for both sexes. □ *The local school offers mixed swimming classes.*

M

**mixture** ['mɪks tʃɚ] *n.* a combination or blend of different things or people. □ *This city has an interesting mixture of many cultures.*

**moan** ['mon] **1.** *n.* a deep, long cry of sadness, suffering, pain, or grief. □ *The firefighters could hear the moans of the victims trapped in the building.* **2.** *iv.* to make a deep, long cry of sadness, suffering, pain, or grief. □ *The mourners moaned in grief at the funeral.*

**mob** ['mɑb] **1.** *n.* a large group of people crowded around someone or something. □ *The opera singer was surrounded by a mob of fans.* **2.** *tv.* [for a large group of people] to crowd around someone or something. □ *The reporters mobbed the mayor after the press conference.*

**mobile 1.** ['mob əl] *adj.* able to move easily; able to be moved easily; movable. □ *I carry a mobile phone and use it often.* **2.** ['mo bil] *n.* a hanging arrangement of balanced objects that move with air currents. (Refers to decorations, works of art, or devices to entertain infants.) □ *The baby watched the mobile hanging above her crib.*

**mock** ['mɑk] **1.** *tv.* to make fun of someone; to laugh at or ridicule someone, especially by copying how that person speaks or acts. □ *Don't mock me just because I am different!* **2.** *tv.* to copy or imitate someone or something. □ *The children loved to mock their teacher's way of walking, until they got in trouble for it.* **3.** *adj.* not real. □ *The students voted in a mock presidential election.*

**mockery** ['mɑk ə ri] *n.* something that is a poor substitute for the real thing or person. □ *That noise is a cheap mockery of music!*

**mockingbird** ['mɑk ɪŋ bɚd] *n.* a bird native to the Americas, so called because it imitates the calls or songs of other birds. □ *The mockingbird flew from tree to tree.*

**mode** ['mod] **1.** *n.* a way of doing something; a method; a manner. □ *Our mode of doing business is to treat the customer royally.* **2.** *n.* a feature of a verb that shows whether it is a statement, command, or wish; **mood** ②. □ *The imperative mode is used to form commands.*

**model** ['mɑd l] **1.** *n.* a copy of an object, usually made smaller than the original. □ *I made a model of a volcano out of clay.* **2.** *n.* someone or something that is the perfect example of something; someone or something that is to be copied or imitated; a standard. □ *The new factory soon became a model of efficiency.* **3.** *n.* someone who is paid to wear and show off clothing that is available for sale. □ *I want to buy the red dress that this model is wearing.* **4.** *n.*

someone who poses for artists and photographers. □ *The famous model appeared on the cover of many magazines.* **5.** *n.* one style of a certain product in a series of styles. □ *The newer model of this television set has more features than the old one.* **6.** *adj.* perfect; worthy of imitation; regarded as the perfect example. (Prenominal only.) □ *The model politician refused to ridicule his opponents.* **7.** *adj.* built to a smaller scale than normal. (Prenominal only.) □ *Bob has a collection of model cars in his room.* **8.** *iv.* to work as ③ or ④. □ *Dave has to stay fit because he models for a living.* **9.** *tv.* [for a **model** ③] to wear and show off clothing. □ *John modeled the tuxedo.*

**modem** ['mod əm] *n.* a device that connects a computer with a telephone line so that information can be sent or received over telephone lines. □ *My modem transmits data at 28,800 bits per second.*

**moderate 1.** ['mɑd ə rɪt] *adj.* not extreme; in the center; average or medium. (Adv: *moderately.*) □ *I wore only a light jacket because the temperature was moderate.* **2.** ['mɑd ə rɪt] *n.* someone whose political or social views are not extreme. □ *The moderate helped the extreme sides reach an agreement.* **3.** ['mɑd ə ret] *tv.* to reduce something; to cause something to be less strong. □ *Cool breezes will moderate the high temperatures of the last two days.* **4.** ['mɑd ə ret] *tv.* to lead a discussion; to lead a meeting. □ *Sue moderates the sales meeting because she's the sales manager.*

**moderation** [mɑd ə 're ʃən] *n.* being moderate; [doing things] within reasonable limits. (No plural form.) □ *This diet allows you to eat most foods in moderation.*

**modern** ['mɑd ɚn] *adj.* up-to-date; new; of or about the present or very recent time. (Adv: *modernly.*) □ *The designer gave the old building a more modern look.*

**modest** ['mɑd ɪst] **1.** *adj.* shy; humble; not bragging about oneself. (Adv: *modestly.*) □ *The modest painter avoided the press at the gallery opening.* **2.** *adj.* not excessive; moderate; not large. (Adv: *modestly.*) □ *My family survives on a modest income.* **3.** *adj.* decent; not revealing too much of one's body. (Adv: *modestly.*) □ *The prudish man wore extremely modest clothing at the beach.*

**moist** ['moɪst] *adj.* damp; a little bit wet. (Adv: *moistly.* Comp: *moister;* sup: *moistest.*) □ *The delicious cake was moist and rich.*

**moisten** ['moɪ sən] *tv.* to make something moist; to make something damp. □ *I moistened the stamp and placed it on the envelope.*

**moisture** ['moɪs tʃɚ] *n.* wetness; water in the air; vapor. (No plural form.) □ *I could feel the moisture in the air on the muggy day.*

**molasses** [mə 'læs ɪz] *n.* a sweet, dark, sticky liquid made in the process of making sugar. (This is singular. No plural form.) □ *I mixed some molasses into the cookie batter.*

**mold** ['mold] **1.** *n.* a fuzzy or slimy growth that forms on animal or plant matter. (Plural only when referring to different kinds, types, instances, or varieties.) □ *Some smelly mold coated the plants' leaves.* Ⓒ *We counted four different molds growing on our pumpkins.* **2.** *n.* a hollow object that has a certain shape. (Certain liquids—such as clay, resin, cement, rubber, etc.—are poured into it, and when the liquid hardens, it will have the same shape.) □ *These plaster statues were made from the same mold.* **3.** *n.* something that was shaped by or made in ②. □ *The mold of potato salad was shaped like a dome.* **4.** *tv.* to shape something; to form something

M

into a certain shape; to shape something using ②. □ *The potato salad was molded in the shape of a dome.* **5.** *iv.* to be covered with ①. □ *The cheese molded when I left it on the counter.*

**mole** ['mol] *n.* a small, furry mammal that lives underground, eats worms and bugs, and cannot see well. □ *The mole burrowed deep into the soil.*

**molecule** ['mɑl ə kjul] *n.* the smallest part into which something can be divided without changing its chemical composition. □ *A water molecule contains two hydrogen atoms and one oxygen atom.*

**molt** ['molt] **1.** *tv.* [for an animal] to shed feathers, skin, fur, or horns. □ *A snake molts its skin at least once a year.* **2.** *iv.* [for animals] to shed [something], as with ①. □ *When the parrot molted, I kept its feathers.*

M

**molten** ['molt n] *adj.* melted; made into liquid. (Adv: *moltenly.*) □ *Molten lava flowed down the mountain from the volcano.*

**mom** ['mɑm] *n.* mother. (Informal. Also a term of address.) □ *Dad, do you know where Mom is?*

**moment** ['mo mənt] **1.** *n.* an instant in time; a brief period of time. □ *If you can wait, I'll be with you in just a moment.* **2.** *n.* a certain point in time. □ *Call me the moment you get home.*

**momento** [mə 'mɛn to] Go to **memento.**

**momentum** [mo 'mɛn təm] *n.* the force and speed of movement or progress. (No plural form.) □ *The momentum of the car increased as the car slid down the icy hill.*

**monarch** ['mɑn ɑrk] *n.* a king or a queen. □ *An image of the country's monarch appeared on its currency.*

**Monday** ['mʌn de] Go to **day.**

**monetary** ['mɑn ə tɛr i] *adj.* of or about money. (Adv: *monetarily* [mɑn ə 'tɛr ə li].) □ *The economist criticized the nation's monetary policy.*

**money** ['mʌn i] **1.** *n.* currency; coins and bills issued by a government. (No plural form.) □ *In Paris, I exchanged American money for French money.* **2.** *n.* wealth; riches. (No plural form.) □ *Even though he had a lot of money, John did not own a car.*

**monitor** ['mɑn ə tɚ] **1.** *n.* a device that looks somewhat like a television set and is used to display computer information. □ *My eyes get tired from looking at the monitor all day.* **2.** *n.* a measuring device that keeps a record of something. □ *The heart monitor displayed my heart rate on the screen.* **3.** *tv.* to watch, listen to, or keep a record of something. □ *My boss monitors my phone conversations.*

**monk** ['mʌŋk] *n.* a man who devotes his life to religion as part of an all-male religious organization. □ *The monks said grace before eating dinner.*

**monkey** ['mʌŋ ki] **1.** *n.* a small, hairy primate with a long tail. (The monkeys in the Americas can use their tails as a fifth limb.) □ *Some monkeys—when they stand up straight—look like small people.* □ *It is fun to watch the monkeys at the zoo.* **2. monkey around** *phr.* to fool around; to behave badly. □ *John monkeyed around while he was supposed to be working.*

**monopoly** [mə 'nɑp ə li] **1.** *n.* the condition existing when someone or something has complete control over something. □ *The government tries to make sure that no company develops a monopoly without its permission.* **2.** *n.* a business that is the only provider of a service or product. □ *The breakup of the monopoly resulted in lower prices.* **3.** *n.* the right to be the only provider of a service or product, as authorized by a government. □ *The court ended the telephone company's monopoly.*

**monster** ['man stɚ] *n.* a large creature that scares people. ☐ *The audience screamed when the monster appeared on the movie screen.*

**monstrosity** [man 'stras ə ti] *n.* someone or something that is huge and very ugly. ☐ *The run-down building is a terrible monstrosity.*

**month** ['mʌnθ] **1.** *n.* one of the 12 divisions of a year. (The months of the year, in order, are **January, February, March, April, May, June, July, August, September, October, November, December.**) ☐ *January is the first month of the year.* **2.** *n.* a period of about 30 or 31 days; a period of four weeks. ☐ *Our baby is just six months old.*

**monthly** ['mʌnθ li] **1.** *adj.* happening every month; happening once a month. ☐ *The workers can discuss their problems at the monthly meeting.* **2.** *adv.* every month; once a month. ☐ *I visit my parents monthly.*

**monument** ['man jə mənt] **1.** *n.* a structure that is built in memory of a person or event. ☐ *The city built a monument to the war hero.* **2.** *n.* something that preserves the memory of a person, culture, or event. (Fig. on ①.) ☐ *We started a scholarship fund as a monument to the founder of the college.*

**mood** ['mud] **1.** *n.* a state of mind; the way one is feeling. ☐ *John's in a bad mood, so I wouldn't talk to him now.* **2.** *n.* a feature of a verb that shows whether it is a statement, a command, or a wish; **mode** ②. ☐ *In Greek class, I learned the various moods of the verb.*

**moon** ['mun] **1.** *n.* a large natural satellite that orbits around a planet. ☐ *The space probe discovered a new moon that circles Jupiter.* **2.** *n.* the natural satellite that orbits around the earth. ☐ *I can't see the moon tonight because of the clouds.*

**moonlight** ['mun lɑɪt] **1.** *n.* the light from a moon. (No plural form.) ☐ *In the moonlight, I saw a skunk in my backyard.* **2.** *adj.* done at night, while the moon is shining; happening while the moon is shining. (Prenominal only.) ☐ *The young boy took a moonlight swim in the neighbors' pool.* **3.** *iv.* to have a second job in the evening or at night in addition to the job one has during the day. (Pt/pp: *moonlighted.*) ☐ *The underpaid office manager had to moonlight to earn enough to live.*

**moose** ['mus] *n., irreg.* a northern animal—similar to a large deer—the males of which have wide, flat horns on their heads. (Pl: *moose.* See also **elk** ②.) ☐ *A large moose stood in the middle of the road, blocking my path.*

**mop** ['map] **1.** *n.* a group of thick, heavy strings or a sponge, attached to a pole, used wet or dry for cleaning floors. ☐ *I put the mop in the bucket after I cleaned the floors.* **2. mop something up** *tv. + obj. + adv.* to clean something with ①, a towel, a sponge, etc. ☐ *I mopped the puddle up with a sponge.* 🅃 *I mopped up the puddle.* **3. mop up** *iv. + adv.* to clean up [liquid or dirt] with ①, a towel, a sponge, etc. ☐ *We had to spend hours mopping up after the flood.*

**moral** ['mor əl] **1.** *adj.* of or about good and bad, according to society's standards of right and wrong. (Adv: *morally.*) ☐ *One needs moral strength to avoid temptation.* **2.** *adj.* showing or representing good behavior and values. (Adv: *morally.*) ☐ *Jimmy was taught basic, moral behavior.* **3.** *n.* the lesson that can be learned from a story. ☐ *The moral of the story is that you should be yourself.* **4. morals** *n.* a person's **moral** ① principles of behavior, especially concerning sex. (Treated as plural, but not countable.) ☐ *The senator's morals were beyond question.*

M

**morale** [mə 'ræl] *n.* confidence; the amount of confidence felt by a person or group of people. (No plural form.) □ *The soldiers sang songs to boost their morale.*

**morality** [mə 'ræl ə ti] *n.* the goodness or rightness of someone's behavior; good behavior measured by society's standards of right and wrong. (No plural form.) □ *Max felt that the best way to improve society's morality was to improve his own.*

**moral support** ['mor əl sə 'port] *n.* help that is mental or psychological rather than physical or monetary. □ *My friends gave me moral support during my period of grief.*

**more** ['mor] **1.** *adj.* <the comparative form of **much** or **many**>; a greater amount or number. (Prenominal only.) □ *I don't have much money. John has more money than I do.* **2.** *pron.* <the comparative form of **much** or **many**>; a greater amount or number. □ *I don't have much money. Anne has more than I do.* **3.** *n.* an additional amount or number. (No plural form.) □ *Don't take more. You have too much already.* **4.** *adv.* <a word used to form the comparative form of some adjectives and adverbs>; to a greater extent. □ *If I drive to work and you walk, I will get there more quickly than you will.* **5.** *adv.* of a greater amount. □ *Bob sleeps more than I do.*

**morning** ['mor nɪŋ] **1.** *n.* the period of the day from midnight to noon. □ *I spent the morning writing letters.* **2.** *n.* dawn; sunrise. □ *When I left the party, I saw the light of morning.* **3.** *adj.* happening during ①. (Prenominal only.) □ *I missed my morning class because I overslept.* **4. mornings** *adv.* every ①. □ *I can't make a 10:00 A.M. appointment because I work mornings.* □ *Mornings, I work downtown. At night I work at home.*

**morsel** ['mor səl] *n.* a small piece of something, especially food. □ *The dog ate some morsels that had fallen to the floor.*

**mortal** ['mor təl] **1.** *n.* a human being; someone or something that must die; someone or something that will not live forever. □ *I know I am only a mortal, but I want to live forever.* **2.** *adj.* unable to live forever; having to die at some time. (Adv: *mortally.*) □ *Because humans are mortal, we all must die.*

**mortar** ['mor tɚ] **1.** *n.* a kind of cement that binds bricks or stones to each other, especially when a wall is being built. (Plural only when referring to different kinds, types, instances, or varieties.) □ *Don't touch that wall until the mortar has dried.* 🄲 *Mortars of different colors were used on different parts of the building.* **2.** *n.* a short, wide cannon that shoots shells in a high arc. □ *The shell from the mortar damaged an apartment building.* **3.** *n.* a hard bowl used to hold substances being ground into powder. □ *The cook ground the spices in a mortar.*

**mortgage** ['mor gɪdʒ] **1.** *n.* an agreement by which a borrower grants a lender the ownership of an asset in exchange for a loan of money, thus protecting the loan with the asset. (When the loan is repaid, the ownership of the property is returned to the borrower. If the borrower is unable to pay the loan, the asset then belongs to the lender.) □ *We had a party when we made the last payment on our home mortgage.* **2.** *tv.* to use an asset to secure a loan. □ *The mall was mortgaged by its owner so she could buy more property.*

**mosquito** [mə 'skit o] *n.* a small insect, the female of which sucks blood from warm-blooded creatures. (Pl ends in *-s* or *-es.*) □ *I became sick after I was bitten by a mosquito.*

**moss** ['mɔs] *n.* a small, soft green plant without flowers that grows in masses on rocks and other surfaces. (Plural only when referring to different kinds, types, instances, or varieties.) □ *I sat on the moss that surrounded the base of the tree.* Ⓒ *The forest floor was covered with mosses and fallen leaves.*

**most** ['most] **1.** *adj.* <the superlative form of **much** or **many**>; the greatest amount or number. (Prenominal only.) □ *I know a lot of songs. Susan knows more songs than I do. Anne knows the most songs of all.* **2.** *adj.* over half; almost all. (Prenominal only. Adv: *mostly.*) □ *Most mornings, I'd rather stay in bed.* **3.** *n.* over half or almost all of a certain group of things or people; over half or almost all of something. (No plural form. Treated as singular or plural, but not countable.) □ *The bananas are cheap, but most aren't ripe yet.* **4.** *adv.* <a word used to form the superlative form of some adjectives and adverbs>; to the greatest extent. (Usually with *the.*) □ *Mary's car starts the most quickly.* **5.** *adv.* very. (Used for emphasis.) □ *I had a most difficult day at work today.*

**mostly** ['most li] **1.** *adv.* more than half; for the most part. □ *I might be sick, but I am mostly tired.* **2.** *adv.* most of the time; usually. □ *Mostly, I read and take naps on the weekend.*

**motel** [mo 'tɛl] *n.* a hotel for people traveling by car; a hotel alongside a highway. (From *MOtor* + *hoTEL.*) □ *There aren't any vacancies at the motels near the beach.*

**moth** ['mɔθ] *n., irreg.* a small insect with large, broad wings and antennae, similar to a butterfly, but usually not as colorful. (Pl: ['mɔðz].) □ *I swatted the moth that was flying around my head.*

**mothball** ['mɔθ bɔl] *n.* a small ball of a substance that keeps moths away from clothes. □ *Mothballs have an unpleasant odor that keeps moths away.*

**mother** ['mʌð ɚ] **1.** *n.* a female who has given birth to a child or offspring. □ *Sally is soon to become a mother.* **2. Mother** *n.* <a term of address used with one's own ①.> □ *Mother, can I borrow the car tonight?* **3.** *adj.* [of one's language or country] native. (Prenominal only.) □ *My aunt returned to her mother country when she was 80.* **4.** *tv.* to take care of someone in the manner of ①. □ *My older sister mothered all the young ones when our mother died.*

**motherhood** ['mʌð ɚ hʊd] *n.* the state of being a mother. (No plural form.) □ *Anne enjoyed motherhood and looked forward to having more children.*

**motion** ['mo ʃən] **1.** *n.* movement; moving. (Plural only when referring to different kinds, types, instances, or varieties.) □ *The apparent motion of the sun across the sky is from east to west.* Ⓒ *Bob made a few small hand motions to get the speaker's attention.* **2.** *n.* a formal proposal that something be done, made during a meeting. □ *The council voted on the motion to reduce taxes.* **3.** *tv.* to direct someone by moving a part of one's body, usually the hands. □ *The clerk motioned me over to the counter.* **4.** *iv.* to point or indicate by moving a part of one's body, usually the hands. □ *I motioned to Anne, indicating that I wanted to leave the party.*

**motion picture** ['mo ʃən 'pɪk tʃɚ] *n.* a movie; a film; a story on film. □ *The studio released four motion pictures during the summer.*

**motive** ['mot ɪv] *n.* a reason for doing something; something—such as an idea, a need, or a way of thinking—that causes a person to do something. □ *The motive for the robbery was greed.*

**motor** ['mot ɚ] *n.* an engine; a machine that changes some kind of fuel into power that can lift, turn, or move things. □ *I had to replace my washing machine's motor when it burned out.*

M

**motorboat** ['mot ɚ bot] *n.* a boat that is powered by a motor or engine. □ *The motorboat pulled the water-skier behind it.*

**motorcycle** ['mot ɚ saɪ kəl] *n.* a vehicle that has two wheels and a larger, heavier frame than a bicycle, and that is powered by a motor. □ *A motorcycle goes much faster than a bicycle.*

**motorist** ['mot ə rɪst] *n.* someone who drives a car. □ *Two motorists were hurt in the accident.*

**motto** ['mɑt o] *n.* a short statement that expresses a belief or a rule of behavior. (Pl ends in *-s* or *-es.*) □ *The motto "In God We Trust" appears on American currency.*

**mound** ['mɑʊnd] *n.* a small hill or pile. □ *I put a mound of mashed potatoes on my plate.*

M

**mount** ['mɑʊnt] **1.** *n.* a support; an object that something is attached to or hung from. □ *The mirror was fixed to the wall with a sturdy mount.* **2.** *n.* a (particular) mountain. (Abbreviated *Mt.*) □ *The eruption of Mount St. Helens covered thousands of square miles with ash.* **3.** *tv.* to get on an animal or vehicle that one must ride with one leg on either side of the animal or vehicle. □ *The children mounted their bikes and pedaled to the river.* **4.** *tv.* to climb something; to go up something. □ *I mounted the stairs too quickly and had to rest at the top.* **5.** *tv.* to hang something to a fixed support; to attach something to a fixed support. □ *Bob mounted the heavy painting on the wall using strong nails.*

**mountain** ['mɑʊnt n] **1.** *n.* a very tall mass of land that pushes up from the surface of the earth; a very tall hill. □ *The climber reached the top of the mountain.* **2.** *n.* a very tall pile of something; a very large amount of something. (Fig. on ①.) □ *I have a mountain of dirty laundry that I have to wash.*

**mountain lion** ['mɑʊnt n 'lɑɪ ən] *n.* a large, American wild animal in the cat family, also called the panther and the cougar. □ *A mountain lion killed one of our cows.*

**mountain range** ['mɑʊnt n 'rendʒ] *n.* a row or line of mountains. □ *The map showed the world's major mountain ranges.*

**mourn** ['morn] **1.** *tv.* to feel sorrow or sadness about the death or loss of someone or something. □ *The workers mourned the death of the company president.* **2.** *tv.* to feel sorrow or sadness about someone who has died. □ *We all mourned the company president who had died suddenly while golfing.* **3.** *iv.* to feel sorrow or sadness especially about someone's death. □ *The nation mourned when the president died.*

**mourner** ['mor nɚ] *n.* someone who mourns; someone who attends a funeral. □ *The minister comforted the mourners at the funeral.*

**mouse** ['mɑʊs] **1.** *n., irreg.* a small, furry rodent with tiny eyes and a long tail, like a rat but smaller. (Pl: **mice.**) □ *The scientist tested the new drug on mice.* **2.** *n., irreg.* a computer device that can be moved around by one hand to control the movements of a pointer on the screen. (Pl: **mice** or *mouses.*) □ *It is hard to find a place to use my mouse on my messy desk.*

**mousetrap** ['mɑʊs træp] *n.* a simple device that is used to trap mice that are indoor pests. □ *I baited the mousetrap with a piece of cheese.*

**mousse** ['mus] *n.* a rich, creamy dessert made from cream, eggs, and fruit or chocolate. (Plural only when referring to different kinds, types, instances, or varieties.) □ *I served the mousse with* *some whipped cream.* 🄲 *Mousses are not as hard to prepare as you might think.*

**mouth 1.** ['mauθ] *n., irreg.* the opening on the faces of animals where food and air enter the body. (Pl: ['mauðz].) □ *Please cover your mouth when you cough.* **2.** ['mauθ] *n., irreg.* an opening of something; the entrance to something. (Fig. on ①.) □ *An ice cube blocked the mouth of the pitcher.* **3.** ['mauθ] *n., irreg.* the place where a river joins a lake, sea, or ocean. □ *The mouth of the river was clogged with garbage.* **4.** ['mauð] *tv.* to move ① as if one were speaking but without producing actual speech. □ *On the other side of the window, Anne mouthed, "Come out here."*

**mouthpiece** ['mauθ pis] **1.** *n.* the part of a musical instrument that is blown into; the part of a musical instrument that is put on or between one's lips. □ *To play the flute, you must blow air over the opening in the mouthpiece.* **2.** *n.* the part of a machine or device that is placed on or next to someone or something's mouth. □ *I spoke into the mouthpiece of the telephone.*

**mouthwash** ['mauθ wɑʃ] *n.* a liquid that is used to rinse one's mouth in order to make the breath smell better or to kill germs in the mouth. □ *My mint-flavored mouthwash freshens my breath and kills germs.*

**move** ['muv] **1.** *iv.* to go to a different time or space; to change position in time or space. □ *I moved to the front row of the theater for a better view.* **2.** *iv.* to be in motion. □ *A wheel moves in a circular motion.* **3.** *iv.* to change where one lives or works. □ *The accounting department moved to another location.* **4.** *tv.* to transport to a different time or space; to cause someone or something to change position. □ *The network moved the popular show from Sunday to Thursday.* **5.** *tv.* to cause someone or something to remain in motion. □ *The wind moved the dust across the land.* **6.** *tv.* to affect someone's emotions or feelings. □ *The sad story moved the audience.* **7.** *tv.* to formally make a suggestion at a meeting; to formally propose something. (The object is a clause with **that** ⑦.) □ *John moved that we pass the motion.* **8.** *n.* an instance of changing position as in ①; a **movement.** □ *The robber made his move toward the cash register.* **9.** *n.* the act of going to a new house to live. □ *The move away from her friends was hard for Anne.* **10.** *n.* one step in a plan; an action that has a specific result. □ *Your first move should be to ask for a written statement of the company's policy.* **11.** *n.* a player's turn in a game. □ *I just played, so now it's John's move.*

**movement** ['muv mənt] **1.** *n.* moving; changing position in time or space. (Plural only when referring to different kinds, types, instances, or varieties.) □ *This electronic device is designed to detect movement of any kind.* 🄲 *The chef chopped the onions with a few quick movements of his wrist.* **2.** *n.* a division of a symphony or other classical music work. □ *The symphony's second movement is quite long and dull.* **3.** *n.* a common social or political goal and the people who work together to promote it. □ *The safe-neighborhood movement demanded the mayor's resignation.*

**movie** ['muv i] **1.** *n.* a film; a motion picture; a story on film. □ *I don't like watching scary movies.* **2.** *adj.* <the adj. use of ①.> □ *The newspaper publishes movie reviews each Friday.*

**mow** ['mo] *tv., irreg.* to cut grass. (Pp: *mowed* or **mown.**) □ *The tall grass hadn't been mowed in weeks.*

**mower** ['mo ɚ] *n.* a machine used to cut grass evenly. (Short for **lawn mower.**) □ *The mower is in the garage with the rake and the other outdoor tools.*

**mown** ['mon] a pp of mow.

**Mr.** ['mɪst ɚ] *n.* <a title for an adult male.> (The abbreviation of mister.) ☐ *I gave my homework to Mr. Brown after class.*

**Mrs.** ['mɪs əz] *n.* <a title for a married woman.> ☐ *John, this is my mother, Mrs. Smith.*

**Ms.** ['mɪz] *n.* <a title for an adult female.> ☐ *Is Ms. Smith married?*

**much** ['mʌtʃ] **1.** *adv., irreg.* to a great extent; to a great degree; a lot. (Comp: more; sup: most.) ☐ *I work too much and don't get enough sleep.* **2.** *adj., irreg.* a lot; quite an extent or degree. (Comp: more; sup: most.) ☐ *The butcher gave me too much meat.* **3.** *n.* a large extent; a large degree; a large amount. (No plural form.) ☐ *Much of my work is still unfinished.*

M

**mucus** ['mju kəs] *n.* the slimy substance secreted by the body to protect and moisten certain tissues. (No plural form.) ☐ *I wiped the mucus from my nose with a handkerchief.*

**mud** ['mʌd] *n.* a mixture of dirt and water; very wet soil. (No plural form.) ☐ *My car got stuck in the mud.*

**muddy** ['mʌd i] **1.** *adj.* covered with mud. (Adv: *muddily.* Comp: *muddier;* sup: *muddiest.*) ☐ *Billy wiped his muddy hands on the clean towels.* **2.** *adj.* not clear; cloudy. (Said especially of colors or liquids. Fig. on ①. Adv: *muddily.* Comp: *muddier;* sup: *muddiest.*) ☐ *The art teacher said my colors were too muddy.*

**muffler** ['mʌf lɚ] **1.** *n.* part of the exhaust system of a car that softens the noises of the engine. ☐ *The noise from the car without a muffler woke up the whole neighborhood.* **2.** *n.* a scarf that can be wrapped around the neck for warmth. ☐ *Wear your gloves and muffler. It's cold outside!*

**mug** ['mʌg] **1.** *n.* a drinking cup with a handle. ☐ *I want to drink water from a glass, not a heavy mug!* **2.** *n.* the contents of ①. ☐ *Could I have another mug of coffee, please?* **3.** *tv.* to attack and rob someone. ☐ *The police caught the guy who mugged me.*

**mugger** ['mʌg ɚ] *n.* someone who attacks and robs people on the street. ☐ *Muggers roam the city during the night.*

**muggy** ['mʌg i] *adj.* hot and humid. (Adv: *muggily.* Comp: *muggier;* sup: *muggiest.*) ☐ *I turn on my air conditioner when it's muggy outside.*

**mulch** ['mʌltʃ] **1.** *n.* plant matter or other covering spread on plants to protect them and to retain the moisture in the soil. (Plural only when referring to different kinds, types, instances, or varieties.) ☐ *The gardener covered the seedlings with mulch.* Ⓒ *We use different mulches on different parts of the garden, depending on the plants planted there.* **2.** *tv.* to spread ① around plants in a garden. ☐ *I mulched the seedling to protect it from frost.*

**mule** ['mjul] *n.* the offspring of one horse and one donkey. ☐ *The mules pulled the plow behind them.*

**multiple** ['mʌl tə pəl] **1.** *adj.* involving many parts; consisting of many parts. (Adv: *multiply* ['mʌl tə pli].) ☐ *Each question on the test seemed to have multiple answers.* **2.** *n.* a number that can be divided by another number without a remainder; a number that can be divided evenly by another number. ☐ *The least common multiple of 4, 5, and 6 is 60.*

**multiply** ['mʌl tə plɑɪ] **1. multiply a number by a number** *tv. + obj. + prep. phr.* to add an amount to itself the number of times shown by another number; to perform multiplication. (The symbol × means *multiplied by.*) ☐ *You have to multiply the length by the width to get the* *right answer.* **2.** *tv.* to increase something. □ *The new law has multiplied the number of forms we have to fill out.* **3.** *iv.* to reproduce; to have offspring; to breed. □ *Mosquitoes seem to multiply quickly.* **4.** *iv.* to increase. □ *Voter disgust multiplied during the election campaign period.*

**munch** ['mʌntʃ] **1.** *tv.* to eat a crisp food that makes a noise; to eat something noisily. □ *I munched a piece of cheese for lunch.* **2. munch on** something *iv.* + *prep. phr.* to eat something; to chew on something. □ *We munched on pizza while watching TV.*

**municipal** [mju 'nɪs ə pəl] *adj.* of, for, or serving a city, town, or village. (Adv: *municipally.*) □ *All municipal offices are closed on state holidays.*

**mural** ['mjʊr əl] *n.* a picture or scene that is painted on the surface of a wall. □ *This mural shows the first moon landing.*

**murder** ['mɚ dɚ] **1.** *n.* the killing of a human, done on purpose and against the law. □ *The police charged the teenager with the murder of his parents.* **2.** *tv.* to kill someone on purpose and against the law. □ *The gangster murdered the witness before the trial.*

**murderer** ['mɚ dɚ ɚ] *n.* someone who kills someone else; someone who is found guilty of murder. □ *The detective slowly learned the murderer's identity.*

**murmur** ['mɚ mɚ] **1.** *n.* a low, quiet sound. □ *The crowd's murmur of disapproval soon grew into angry cries.* **2.** *n.* an irregular sound made by the heart, caused by defects in the heart. □ *John had surgery to correct his heart murmur.* **3.** *iv.* to make low, quiet sounds; to speak very quietly. □ *Stop murmuring and speak so I can hear you!* **4.** *tv.* to say something very quietly. (The object can be a clause with **that** ⑦.) □ *Mary hugged Bill and murmured that she had missed him very much.*

**muscle** ['mʌs əl] **1.** *n.* a group of long tissues in the body that can be shortened to make parts of the body move. □ *John exercised and developed enormous muscles.* **2.** *n.* strength; power. (No plural form. Fig. on ①.) □ *The army used its muscle to overthrow the government.*

**muscular** ['mʌs kjə lɚ] **1.** *adj.* in or of the muscles. □ *I felt muscular soreness after running five miles.* **2.** *adj.* having muscles that are strong and well developed. (Adv: *muscularly.*) □ *The muscular man lifted the heavy weight over his head.*

**museum** [mju 'zi əm] *n.* a building where art or things of or about science, history, or some other subject are placed on display for the public to see and learn about. □ *The natural-science museum had a dinosaur exhibit.*

**mushroom** ['mʌʃ rum] **1.** *n.* a kind of fungus that is often used as food. □ *Thousands of mushrooms covered the dark forest floor.* **2.** *iv.* to grow very quickly or suddenly. □ *The number of people lost in the storm mushroomed as the snow continued.*

**mushy** ['mʌʃ i] *adj.* soft and pulpy. (Adv: *mushily.* Comp: *mushier;* sup: *mushiest.*) □ *I ate only mushy food after I had dental surgery.*

**music** ['mju zɪk] **1.** *n.* the sounds of the voice or of instruments making pleasant tones in a series or a series of groups. (No plural form in standard English. Number is expressed with *piece(s) of music.*) □ *I listen to music all day, even at work.* **2.** *n.* a piece of paper that shows the notes of a particular song or melody. (No plural form.) □ *Do you know how to read music?*

**musical** ['mju zɪ kəl] **1.** *adj.* causing music to be made; producing notes or tones. (Adv: *musically* [...ɪk li].) □ *The musical clock plays a short tune every hour.* **2.** *adj.* of or about music. (Adv:

M

*musically* [...ɪk li].) □ *Playing in an orchestra requires musical skill.* **3.** *n.* a play or movie in which the actors sing songs, usually as a way of moving the story forward. □ *In that musical, all of the dialogue is sung instead of spoken.*

**musician** [mju 'zɪ ʃən] *n.* someone who plays a musical instrument; someone who writes music; someone who is in a band or an orchestra. □ *I'm a musician in a local rock band.*

**muss** ['mʌs] **muss** something **(up)** *tv. + obj. (+ adv.)* to make something messy, especially one's hair; to move someone's hair out of place. □ *The wind mussed my hairdo.*

**mussel** ['mʌs əl] *n.* a kind of shellfish, usually having very dark shells, that can be eaten as food. □ *The cook put clams and mussels in the seafood stew.*



**must** ['mʌst] **1.** *aux.* <a form showing a requirement to do something>; [to] have to [do something]. (Uses *had to* for a past tense.) □ *Must I eat my peas?* **2.** *aux.* <a form indicating probability or likelihood.> (Uses the form *has to have* plus the past participle or *must have* plus the past participle for a past tense.) □ *You said it had to have been there, so I know it must be there.* **3. must not** *aux.* <a form that indicates what one is not allowed to do.> □ *We must not be late.* □ *You must not cry!* **4.** *n.* something that is necessary or essential. □ *Seeing the Statue of Liberty is a must when you visit New York.*

**mustache** ['mʌs tæʃ] *n.* hair that grows on the upper lip. □ *Bob's hair is brown, but his mustache is red.*

**mustard** ['mʌs tɚd] **1.** *n.* a plant with a bright yellow flower. (No plural form.) □ *Mustard is harvested for its seed.* **2.** *n.* a seasoning or sauce made from the powdered seeds of ①, water or vinegar, and spices. (Plural only when referring to different kinds, types, instances, or varieties.) □ *I'd like my sandwich with mustard, please.* 🄲 *We really don't care for those fancy French mustards.*

**mustn't** ['mʌs ənt] *cont.* "must not." (Indicates what one is not allowed to do or what one may not do.) □ *We mustn't be late.*

**musty** ['mʌs ti] *adj.* smelling old and stale; smelling like mold. (Adv: *mustily.* Comp: *mustier;* sup: *mustiest.*) □ *I pulled the musty suit out of the trunk.*

**mutual** ['mju tʃu əl] **1.** *adj.* shared by two or more people; equally felt or done by each person toward the other. (Adv: *mutually.*) □ *My enemy and I felt a mutual hatred toward each other.* **2.** *adj.* common to two or more people; known to two or more people. (Adv: *mutually.*) □ *Bill and I share a lot of mutual interests, so we are together often.*

**mutual fund** ['mju tʃu əl 'fʌnd] *n.* an investment in which a large number of people own shares of investments in many assets. (Can be shortened to **fund**.) □ *Most of my savings are in mutual funds.*

**muzzle** ['mʌz əl] **1.** *n.* [in certain animals] the part of the face that sticks out. □ *The wolf rubbed its muzzle against its mate.* **2.** *n.* a cover put over the mouth of an animal so that it will not bite someone or something. □ *The angry dog growled through the muzzle.* **3.** *n.* the front end of a gun; the barrel of a gun. □ *The thief placed the muzzle of his gun against my neck.* **4.** *tv.* to put ② on an animal. □ *I muzzle my dog when I take him for a walk.*

**my** ['maɪ] **1.** *pron.* <the first-person singular possessive pronoun.> (Describes people or things belonging to the speaker or writer. Used as a modifier before a noun. Compare this with **mine** ⑥.) □ *John is my best friend.* **2.** *interj.* <a word used to show surprise.> □ *My, what a beautiful baby!*

**myself** [mɑɪ 'sɛlf] **1.** *pron.* <the first-person singular reflexive pronoun.> □ *I cut myself while shaving.* **2.** *pron.* <① used to emphasize the speaker or the writer as subject of the sentence.> □ *As for myself, I'm going to bed now.* **3. by myself** *phr.* without the help of anyone else. □ *I can eat that whole pie by myself.* **4. by myself** *phr.* with no one else present; alone. □ *I will not be at the party. I will be at home by myself tonight.*

**mystery** ['mɪs tə ri] **1.** *n.* the quality of not being explained, known, or understood; the quality of being hidden or secret. (Plural only when referring to different kinds, types, instances, or varieties.) □ *The identity of the murderer is veiled in mystery.* 🄲 *The identity of the dead body remained a mystery.* **2.** *n.* a book that involves a crime or murder that is solved in the story. □ *I read a mystery almost every week.* **3.** *adj.* <the adj. use of ③.> □ *I always look in the mystery section of the bookstore.*

**myth** ['mɪθ] **1.** *n.* a fable; a story that explains a mystery of nature or tells how something came into existence. □ *The scholar studied the myths found in Asian cultures.* **2.** *n.* someone or something that is imaginary or invented; something that is not based in fact. (Fig. on ①.) □ *The story about a monster that is supposed to be at the bottom of the lake is just a myth.*

**mythical** ['mɪθ ə kəl] *adj.* imaginary; [of a character, story, or situation] invented. (Adv: *mythically* [...ɪk li].) □ *The witness provided the police with a mythical tale that included visitors from outer space.*

**mythology** [mɪθ 'ɑl ə dʒi] **1.** *n.* the study of myths. (Plural only when referring to different kinds, types, instances, or varieties.) □ *Bill is a scholar who specializes in Greek mythology.* 🄲 *We compared the mythologies of the Greeks with those found in the New World.* **2.** *n.* a collection of myths about someone, something, or some culture. □ *Mars was the god of war in Roman mythology.*

M

**n.** an abbreviation of **nominal**.

**nag** ['næg] **1.** *tv.* to continue to bother someone; to demand, by complaining all the time, that someone do something. □ *I nagged my roommate until she paid her share of the rent.* **2.** *iv.* to continue to be a bother and a pest by making demands. □ *Stop nagging! I'll clean my room later.*

**nail** ['nel] **1.** *n.* a thin rod of metal, pointed on one end. □ *Be careful. There are nails sticking out of that board.* **2.** *n.* one of the hard, flat tips at the ends of fingers and toes. □ *Jane painted her nails red.* **3.** *tv.* to attach or secure something with ①. □ *The carpenter nailed the frame into place.*

**naked** ['nek əd] **1.** *adj.* nude; wearing no clothes. □ *The police arrested the naked man who ran through the park.* **2. with the naked eye** *phr.* with eyes that are not aided by lenses as found in glasses or a microscope. □ *Bacteria are too small to be seen with the naked eye.*

**name** ['nem] **1.** *n.* the word that indicates someone, something, or some place. □ *The name of Germany's capital city is Berlin.* **2.** *n.* [someone's] fame or reputation. □ *The actress made a name for herself in the movies.* **3.** *n.* someone who is famous or important. □ *Many important names in business attended the charity concert.* **4.** *tv.* to give or apply a **name** ① to someone, something, or some place. □ *The artist named her painting* Summertime Dance. **5.** *tv.* to state or recite the ① of someone or something. □ *The witness named all the people involved in the crime.* **6.** *tv.* to appoint someone; to choose someone or something. □ *Bill was named as the chairman's successor.*

**nap** ['næp] **1.** *iv.* to sleep for a short period of time, especially during the day. □ *I napped before going out to see the long movie.* **2.** *n.* a short amount of sleep, especially during the day. □ *Jane put her child in the bed for an afternoon nap.* **3.** *n.* the upright threads of a carpet or of a piece of material, such as velvet. (No plural form.) □ *The nap of the old velvet dress was crushed.* **4. take a nap** *phr.* to sleep as in ①. □ *The baby takes a long nap each afternoon.*

**nape** ['nep] *n.* the back [of the neck]. □ *I grabbed the puppy by the nape of the neck.*

**napkin** ['næp kɪn] *n.* a square of fabric or paper used for protecting one's clothes and keeping tidy at meals. □ *I wiped my mouth with my napkin.*

**narrate** ['nɛr et] **1.** *tv.* to tell a story. □ *The story was narrated by the high-school speech teacher.* **2.** *iv.* to tell about events that are being shown in a film, a slide show, on television, or in some other performance setting. □ *John showed me pictures of his vacation while Anne narrated.*

**narrow** ['nɛr o] **1.** *adj.* not wide; short from side to side in comparison with the length from one end to the other. (Adv: *narrowly.* Comp: *narrower;* sup: *narrowest.*) □ *It was difficult moving the piano through the narrow hallway.* **2.** *adj.* limited; not broad. (Fig. on ①. Adv: *narrowly.* Comp: *narrower;* sup: *narrowest.*) □ *This brochure shows a narrow sampling of this company's product.* **3.** *tv.* to cause something to become ①. □ *Construction crews narrowed the four-lane road to two lanes.* **4.** *iv.* to become ①. □ *This river narrows just* *before the waterfall.* **5.** *iv.* to become ②. □ *Our travel options narrowed because of the storm.*

**nasal** ['nez əl] **1.** *adj.* of or about the nose. (Adv: *nasally.*) □ *My nasal passages are clogged, and I can hardly breathe.* **2.** *adj.* of the quality of sound heard when making the speech sounds [m], [n], or [ŋ]. (Adv: *nasally.*) □ *The salesclerk has a very nasal voice.* **3.** *n.* a **nasal** ② speech sound, such as [m] or [n], made by opening the passage to the nose at the back of the throat. □ *In English, the nasals are represented by* m, n, *and* ng. □ *The word* nun *begins and ends with a nasal.*

**nasty** ['næs ti] **1.** *adj.* mean; angry; unpleasant. (Adv: *nastily.* Comp: *nastier;* sup: *nastiest.*) □ *My boss is in a nasty mood today.* **2.** *adj.* dirty-minded; offensive to one's morals. (Adv: *nastily.* Comp: *nastier;* sup: *nastiest.*) □ *The bookstore kept the nasty magazines on the top shelf.* **3.** *adj.* very serious; bad; dangerous. (Adv: *nastily.* Comp: *nastier;* sup: *nastiest.*) □ *David had a nasty fall and broke his hip.* **4.** *adj.* not pleasant to see, hear, smell, taste, or touch. (Adv: *nastily.* Comp: *nastier;* sup: *nastiest.*) □ *There's a nasty smell coming from the garbage.*

**nation** ['ne ʃən] **1.** *n.* a country; a country that governs itself. □ *Our government must cooperate with other nations.* **2.** *n.* the people of a country; a group of people who are ruled by the same government. □ *The nation voted to reelect the president.*

**national** ['næʃ ə nəl] **1.** *adj.* of or about a nation; belonging to a nation; throughout a nation. (Adv: *nationally.*) □ *Baseball is one of America's national pastimes.* **2.** *n.* a citizen of a specific nation or a particular group of nations. □ *The bombing suspect was a foreign national.*

**nationality** [næʃ ə 'næl ə ti] *n.* the status that arises from having citizenship in a particular country or being born in a particular country. □ *The application asked for my nationality and place of birth.*

**native** ['ne tɪv] **1.** *n.* something that comes from a certain country or region. □ *The kangaroo is a native of Australia.* **2.** *n.* someone born in a particular place. □ *My teacher is a Texas native.* **3.** *adj.* born or raised in a certain country or region; belonging to a certain country or region. (Adv: *natively.*) □ *My teacher is a native Texan.* **4. native to some place** *phr.* originating in or existing naturally in a certain country or region. □ *The kangaroo is native to Australia.*

**Native American** ['ne tɪv ə 'mɛr ə kən] **1.** *n.* a person belonging to one of the groups of people that lived in North America when the Europeans arrived; an American Indian. (Often capitalized, but sometimes seen as *native American.*) □ *Many Native Americans live on reservations.* **2.** *adj.* <the adj. use of ①.> □ *The museum contains weapons and items of Native American clothing.*

**natural** ['nætʃ ə rəl] **1.** *adj.* made by nature; existing in nature; not artificial; not made by people; not affected by people. (Adv: *naturally.*) □ *Earthquakes and tornadoes are natural disasters.* **2.** *adj.* existing since birth; not learned. (Adv: *naturally.*) □ *John exhibits a natural skill for playing tennis.* **3.** *n.* someone who is thought of as perfect for a certain job; someone who does something very well, especially through inborn ability. □ *The talented actor was a natural for the role of the villain.* **4.** *n.* a musical note that is not a sharp or a flat; one of the white keys on the piano. □ *C and E are naturals, while F sharp is not.*

**nature** ['ne tʃɚ] **1.** *n.* everything in the world except the material products of human work and thought: people, animals, plants, rocks, land, water, the weather, etc. (No plural form.) □ *Both beauty and suffering are part of nature.* **2.** *n.* land that has not been affected by humans. (No plural form.) □ *Developers have turned vast areas of nature into suburbs.* **3.** *n.* [someone's or something's] character; the essential qualities of someone or something; what someone or something really is. □ *It is Bill's nature to be shy and quiet.*

**nausea** ['nɔ zi ə] *n.* a feeling of sickness; the feeling that one has to vomit. (No plural form.) □ *I was overcome with nausea when I smelled the rotten food.*

**nauseous** ['nɔ ʃəs, 'nɔ zi əs] **1.** *adj.* causing nausea; sickening; causing someone to feel sick. (Adv: *nauseously.*) □ *I left the movie because of the nauseous violence.* **2.** *adj.* experiencing nausea; sickened. (Adv: *nauseously.*) □ *The violence in the movie is making me nauseous.*

N

**nautical** ['nɔt ɪ kəl] *adj.* of or about ships, shipping, or sailors. (Adv: *nautically* [...ɪk li].) □ *Sailors use a lot of special nautical terms.*

**nautical mile** ['nɔt ɪ kəl 'mɑɪl] *n.* a measurement of distance at sea equal to about 1.15 miles on land. □ *The island we are visiting is about 350 nautical miles from here.*

**naval** ['ne vəl] *adj.* of or about a navy. □ *The port city was under enemy naval attack.*

**navel** ['ne vəl] *n.* the depression in the center of the belly where a baby is attached to its mother until shortly after birth. □ *Navels seem to serve no useful purpose in adults.*

**navigate** ['næv ə get] **1.** *tv.* to steer a ship, airplane, or other vehicle in some direction. □ *The captain navigated the ship around the reef.* **2.** *tv.* to travel or follow a route on the water, over land, or in the air. □ *The pilot navigated the skies in one of the world's largest airplanes.* **3.** *iv.* to determine the proper direction or route. □ *The detailed map helped me navigate through Boston.*

**navigation** [næv ə 'ge ʃən] **1.** *n.* the rules, skills, and science of navigating. (No plural form.) □ *The rules of navigation must be learned before you launch your boat.* **2.** *n.* navigating; the practice of ①. (No plural form.) □ *Tom's poor navigation got us lost.*

**navy** ['nev i] *n.* the branch of the military that deals with protecting the sea or fighting at sea. □ *The enemy navy attacked the port city.*

**near** ['nɪr] **1.** *prep.* at a place that is not far away from someone or something; at a time that is not far away from something. □ *I sat near Jane on the bus.* **2.** *adj.* close in distance, time, relationship, or effect. (Comp: *nearer;* sup: *nearest.*) □ *I expect an apology in the near future.* **3.** *adv.* at or to a place that is not far away; at or to a time that is not too distant. (Comp: *nearer;* sup: *nearest.*) □ *I swam near to the shore.* **4.** *tv.* to come closer to someone or something; to approach someone or something. □ *As the train neared the station, it slowed down.* **5.** *iv.* to come closer in time or space; to approach. □ *As the ambulance neared, I slowed down to let it pass.*

**nearby** ['nɪr 'bɑɪ] **1.** *adv.* near; close; not far away. □ *Nearby, the children were playing.* **2.** *adj.* near; close; not far away. □ *We went swimming at a nearby lake.*

**nearly** ['nɪr li] *adv.* almost; not quite. □ *John walked so close to the river that he nearly fell in.*

**neat** ['nit] *adj.* clean; tidy; orderly. (Adv: *neatly.* Comp: *neater;* sup: *neatest.*) □ *My room is neat because I clean it every day.*

**necessary** ['nɛs ə sɛr i] *adj.* required; needed. (Adv: *necessarily* [nɛs ə 'sɛr ə li].) □ *The nurse gave the child all the necessary shots.*

**necessity** [nə 'sɛs ə ti] **1.** *n.* the quality of being necessary or needed. (No plural form.) □ *The council discussed the necessity of the new law that prevents smoking in restaurants.* **2.** *n.* something that is required; something that is needed or necessary. □ *Literacy is a necessity for many kinds of employment.*

**neck** ['nɛk] **1.** *n.* the narrow part of the body that connects the head to the rest of the body; the outside of the throat. □ *The mugger held a knife to my neck.* **2.** *n.* the narrow part of something; something narrow that connects two things. (Fig. on ①.) □ *Bob held his bottle of beer by the neck.*

**necklace** ['nɛk ləs] *n.* a decorative band, chain, or similar object that is worn around the neck. □ *I helped Susan fasten the necklace around her neck.*

**necktie** ['nɛk tɑɪ] *n.* a specially made strip of decorative cloth, typically worn under the collar of a man's shirt. (Also a **tie**. Originally served the purpose of keeping the collar closed.) □ *John wore a red necktie to the party.*

**need** ['nid] **1.** *n.* something that is required or necessary; something that must be done or had; a requirement. □ *There's no need for shouting during class!* **2.** *tv.* to require something; to have to have something; to want something for a certain reason. □ *These walls need a new coat of paint.* **3. need to** do something *iv. + inf.* to have to do something. □ *I need to leave work fifteen minutes early today.*

**needle** ['nid l] **1.** *n.* a thin, pointed spike of metal having a narrow slit that thread fits through, used for sewing. □ *I accidentally stuck my thumb with a needle while I was sewing.* **2.** *n.* a thin, hollow, pointed spike of metal used for injecting and removing body fluids. □ *The doctor gave each child an injection using a clean needle.* **3.** *n.* a thin, pointed spike used to show a position on a scale or meter. □ *If the needle goes into the red zone, you're running low on oil.* **4.** *n.* the part of a record player that "rides" on a (vinyl) record as it is played. □ *The needle skipped when I bumped the record player.* **5.** *n.* a long, thin, sharply pointed leaf of a pine tree. □ *Thousands of pine needles fell into our gutters.* **6.** *n.* a long, thin, sharp thorn as found on a cactus. □ *I bumped into a cactus and got my arm full of needles.* **7.** *tv.* to annoy someone. □ *Bill needled me until I agreed to go to the store with him.*

**needlework** ['nid l wɚk] *n.* crafts that are done with a needle, such as sewing. (No plural form.) □ *Needlework is a quiet, relaxing hobby.*

**needy** ['nid i] **1.** *adj.* [of someone] very poor; [of someone] needing the basic things in life. (Adv: *needily.* Comp: *needier;* sup: *neediest.*) □ *The needy child begged for a dollar.* **2. the needy** *n.* people who are ①. (No plural form. Treated as plural, but not countable.) □ *The charity distributes food and clothing to the needy.*

N

**negative** ['nɛg ə tɪv] **1.** *adj.* meaning "not" or "no"; expressing "not" or "no"; showing refusal or denial. (Adv: *negatively.*) □ *Anne's negative response to my question surprised me.* **2.** *adj.* not positive; the opposite of positive; lacking something that makes a thing positive; not good. (Adv: *negatively.*) □ *The critic's negative review of the movie caused people to avoid seeing it.* **3.** *adj.* less than zero; minus; below the number zero. □ *The temperature outdoors is a negative number!* **4.** *adj.* cynical; not having hope; having a sad or gloomy outlook. (Adv: *negatively.*) □ *Your negative approach to your problems keeps you from solving them.* **5.** *adj.* showing that a certain disease or condition is not present. (Adv: *negatively.*) □ *The results of Jane's diabetes test were negative.* **6.** *adj.* [of some part of an electrical circuit] lower in electrical charge than other points in the same circuit, allowing electrical energy to flow from other parts of the circuit. (Adv: *negatively.*) □ *There is a negative charge right here at this point in the circuit.* **7.** *n.* a word or statement that means "not" or "no." □ *The answer to my question was always a negative—no matter whom I asked.* **8.** *n.* a piece of film (for photography) having dark and light reversed or colors reversed. □ *Please handle the negatives by their edges.* **9.** *n.* a **negative** ② quality or factor. □ *I have a nice apartment, but the lack of parking is a big negative.*

**neglect** [nɪ 'glɛkt] **1.** *tv.* not to take care of someone or something; not to pay attention to someone or something; to ignore someone or something. □ *Please do not neglect your schoolwork.* **2. neglect to** do something *iv. + inf.* to forget to do something; to fail to do something. □ *My plants died because I neglected to water them.* **3.** *n.* the lack of taking care of someone or something; a lack of paying attention to someone or something. (No plural form.) □ *Your neglect of your schoolwork will cause you to fail in school.*

**negotiate** [nə 'go ʃi et] **1.** *iv.* to discuss the matters that need to be settled before reaching an agreement. □ *The striking union agreed to negotiate with management.* **2.** *tv.* to make an agreement through discussions as in ①. □ *The company and the workers negotiated a new contract.* **3.** *tv.* to move around or through a difficult route successfully. □ *The huge ship negotiated the curve around the dock and headed out to sea.*

**neighbor** ['ne bɚ] **1.** *n.* someone who lives very close by. □ *I borrowed a cup of sugar from my neighbor.* **2.** *n.* someone who is sitting or standing next to oneself. □ *The airplane passenger talked with her neighbor during the flight.*

**neighborhood** ['ne bɚ hʊd] **1.** *n.* a specific area within a larger city or town where people live. □ *I live in a quiet, safe neighborhood.* **2.** *n.* the people who live in a certain area of the city. □ *The entire neighborhood complained about the lack of parking.*

**neither** ['ni ðɚ] **1.** *adj.* not **either**; not one person or thing nor the other; not either of two things or people. □ *Our two dogs played in the park, and neither dog wanted to go home.* **2.** *pron.* not **either**; not either one (of two people or things). (Treated as singular.) □ *John and Bill saw a new movie. Neither of them liked it.* **3.** *conj.* not. (Used before a sequence of two words or phrases connected by **nor**.) □ *Neither snow nor rain will prevent me from coming to visit you.*

**nephew** ['nɛf ju] *n.* the son of one's brother or sister; the son of one's spouse's brother or sister. □ *I raised my nephew after my brother and sister-in-law died.*

**nerve** ['nɚv] **1.** *n.* a fiber in the body that carries messages to and from the brain. □ *The optic nerve transmits images from the eye to the brain.* **2.** *n.* courage; bravery. (No plural form.) □ *The soldiers were congratulated for their nerve in battle.*

**ness** [nəs] *suffix* <a form that can be added freely to adjectives to create a noun with a parallel meaning.> □ *All of us here are very happy, so there is a lot of happiness in the room.*

**nest** ['nɛst] **1.** *n.* a structure made of twigs that is built by a bird as a shelter for its eggs and that is typically rounded and bowl-shaped. □ *I saw three blue eggs in the robin's small nest.* **2.** *n.* a place where certain animals live with their young. □ *Wasps have built a nest on our front porch.* **3.** *iv.* to build or live in ① or ②. □ *Birds nest in the trees in our yard.*

**nestle** ['nɛs əl] **nestle (down)** *iv. (+ adv.)* to snuggle; to rest somewhere while holding someone or something closely. □ *I nestled in my chair and got ready to watch television.*

**net** ['nɛt] **1.** *n.* a piece of mesh fabric—made of string, wire, or cord and sometimes attached to something—that is typically used to catch, trap, or block something. □ *The net on a tennis court separates the two players.* **2. Net** *n.* a system for fast electronic communication connecting people, businesses, and institutions. (Short for **Internet**.) □ *I do most of my shopping on the Net.* **3.** *adj.* remaining after all factors have been considered, deducted, or added, as with weight, income, cost, effect, results, outcome, etc. □ *A product's net weight doesn't include the package it comes in.*

**network** ['nɛt wɚk] **1.** *n.* a pattern of crossing lines, paths, or similar structures; a system of lines, paths, or similar structures that are connected together. □ *The technician fixed the network of wires in the control panel.* **2.** *n.* a group of computers connected to each other and the systems that connect them. □ *Anne sent a piece of e-mail to everyone on the network.* **3.** *n.* a group of radio or television stations that broadcast the same programs. □ *Which network is that show on?* **4.** *n.* a collection of friends or business contacts. □ *Jane's network of business contacts helped her find a new job.* **5.** *iv.* to make social and business contacts; to talk with people in one's area of business or interest. □ *At the conference, I networked with important people in my field.*

**neurotic** [nʊ 'rɑt ɪk] **1.** *adj.* of or about a mild psychological problem or illness such as having obsessions or irrational fears; affected by such a problem or illness. (Adv: *neurotically* [...ɪk li].) □ *Bill is hard to live with because of his neurotic behavior.* **2.** *n.* someone who has irrational fears or obsessions or some other mild psychological problem or illness. □ *The neurotic washed her hands over and over.*

**neuter** ['nut ɚ] **1.** *adj.* neither masculine nor feminine; not having a **sex** ③. □ *Our dog was a male before his operation. Now he is neuter.* **2.** *adj.* [of a class of words] not masculine or feminine. □ *The German word for "room" is neuter:* das Zimmer. □ *German has three genders, masculine, feminine, and neuter.*

**neutral** ['nu trəl] **1.** *adj.* not joining with either side in a war, conflict, or argument. (Adv: *neutrally.*) □ *The conflict was resolved with the help of a neutral mediator.* **2.** *adj.* at neither extreme; in the middle of a scale. (Adv: *neutrally.*) □ *A neutral political viewpoint is neither conservative nor liberal.*

**never** ['nɛv ɚ] *adv.* not ever; at no time. □ *I will never tell anyone your secret.*

**new** ['nu] **1.** *adj.* recently done, made, bought, acquired, discovered, or built; not existing or known of before. (Adv: *newly.* Comp: *newer;* sup: *newest.* See also **news**.) □ *The scientist discovered a new medicine.* **2.** *adj.* the more recent of two or more things. (Comp: *newer;* sup: *newest.*) □ *Make sure you're using the new manual, not the old one.* **3.** *adj.* not familiar; strange; unknown. (Adv: *newly.* Comp: *newer;* sup: *newest.*) □ *The rocket traveled to new worlds.* **4.** *adj.* different; changed. (Adv: *newly.* Comp: *newer;* sup: *newest.*) □ *The company developed a new way of doing things and made more money.* **5.** *adj.* beginning again; starting over. (Adv: *newly.* Comp: *newer;* sup: *newest.*) □ *The new semester begins next Monday.*

**newcomer** ['nu kəm ɚ] *n.* someone who recently arrived at a certain place. □ *I welcomed the newcomers to the neighborhood.*

N

**newly** ['nu li] *adv.* recently; as of late; just. □ *Our newly built house was destroyed by a tornado.*

**newlywed** ['nu li wɛd] *n.* someone who has recently married. □ *The newlyweds danced together at the reception.*

**news** ['nuz] **1.** *n.* information, particularly current information about a person or relating to a recent event. (Treated as singular. No other singular form in this sense.) □ *What's the latest news about the injured workers?* **2.** *n.* a television or radio program where information about recent events is broadcast. (Treated as singular. No other singular form in this sense.) □ *They said on the news that it's supposed to rain tomorrow.*

**newspaper** ['nuz pe pɚ] *n.* a daily or weekly publication consisting of news, articles, and advertisements printed on large sheets of paper. □ *Did you see that article in yesterday's newspaper?*

N

**newt** ['nut] *n.* a small amphibian with four legs and a tail. □ *The children bought a newt to put in their aquarium.*

**next** ['nɛkst] **1.** *adj.* following; nearest in sequence after; soonest after. □ *The next day after Monday is Tuesday.* **2.** *adj.* located in the nearest position to something; [of someone or something] beside someone or something [else]. □ *The people who live in the next house are very friendly.* **3. next to** someone or something *phr.* very near to someone or something; beside someone or something. □ *Please sit next to me.* **4.** *adv.* at the soonest time after now; in the nearest place or position after this one. □ *The math books are here. The physics books come next on the shelf.*

**next door** ['nɛks 'dor] *phr.* in or at the house or apartment next to one's own. (Hyphenated before a nominal.) □ *I went next door to borrow a shovel.*

**next-door neighbor** ['nɛks dor 'ne bɚ] *n.* the person living in the house or apartment closest to one's own. □ *I will be visiting our next-door neighbor, so if you need me, you can find me there.*

**nice** ['nɑɪs] **1.** *adj.* pleasant; agreeable; enjoyable. (Adv: *nicely.* Comp: *nicer;* sup: *nicest.*) □ *My friends and I had a nice time at the park.* **2.** *adj.* kind; friendly. (Adv: *nicely.* Comp: *nicer;* sup: *nicest.*) □ *It was nice of you to care for my dog when I was on vacation.* **3.** *adj.* good; clever; well done. (Informal. Adv: *nicely.* Comp: *nicer;* sup: *nicest.*) □ *That was a nice dive!*

**nick** ['nɪk] **1.** *n.* a small dent or chip on the surface of something. □ *I painted over the nicks in the wall.* **2.** *tv.* to put or cause a small dent or chip on the surface of something. □ *The telephone fell onto the table and nicked it.*

**nickel** ['nɪk əl] **1.** *n.* a metal element that does not rust easily. (No plural form.) □ *The faucet is made of nickel and copper.* **2.** *n.* a U.S. coin worth five cents. □ *I used eleven nickels to buy candy from a machine.*

**nickname** ['nɪk nem] **1.** *n.* a secondary, familiar, or intimate name for someone or something. □ *There are five Johns in my class, so each of them uses a nickname.* □ Bob *is the standard nickname for* Robert. **2.** *tv.* to give someone, something, or some place a **nickname** ①. □ *I was nicknamed Red, because of the color of my hair.*

**niece** ['nis] *n.* the daughter of one's brother or sister; the daughter of one's spouse's brother or sister. □ *Since I have many brothers and sisters, I also have many nieces and nephews.*

**night** ['nɑɪt] **1.** *n.* the time between sunset and sunrise; the darkness between sunset and sunrise; nighttime. (No plural form.) □ *Night is very dark in the forest.* **2.** *n.* within any 24 hours, the period of time between sunset and sunrise. □ *I sleep at least eight hours every night.* **3.** *n.* within any 24 hours, the period of time between sunset and midnight. □ *This night is over at midnight, the time when morning starts.* **4.** *n.* a specific ② or ③ when something happens or is planned. □ *This is my night to work late.* **5.** *n.* a unit of measure based on the number of **nights** ② but also including the period of time between **nights** ②. □ *The newlyweds stayed in Paris for six nights.* **6. nights** *adv.* every night; during every night; only at night. □ *Bill works nights, so he sleeps during the day.* **7.** *adj.* happening during ② or ③. □ *I took a night flight to London and arrived in time for breakfast.*

**nightclub** ['nɑɪt kləb] *n.* a bar or club open at night where there is entertainment, dancing, performance, etc. □ *You have to be 21 to get into this nightclub.*

**nightgown** ['nɑɪt gɑʊn] *n.* an item of clothing like a dress, usually for women, that is worn in bed. □ *Susan put on a nightgown after her evening bath.*

**nightlife** ['nɑɪt lɑɪf] *n.* entertainment and social activities that take place during the night. (No plural form.) □ *The nightlife in New York City can be very exciting.*

**nightmare** ['nɑɪt mɛr] **1.** *n.* a frightening dream. □ *I didn't sleep well last night because I kept having nightmares.* **2.** *n.* a real event that is frightening or awful. (Fig. on ①.) □ *Getting information from the federal government can be a nightmare.*

**night owl** ['nɑɪt ɑʊl] *n.* someone who stays up late at night; someone who works at night. □ *My roommate is a night owl and usually reads until 5:00 A.M.*

**nighttime** ['nɑɪt tɑɪm] **1.** *n.* the time during the night; the time from after sunset until sunrise. (No plural form.) □ *Bats are most active in the nighttime.* **2.** *adj.* <the adj. use of ①>; happening during the night. □ *Nighttime strolls through city parks can be dangerous.*

**nine** ['nɑɪn] 9. Go to **four** for senses and examples.

**nineteen** ['nɑɪn 'tin] 19. Go to **four** for senses and examples.

**nineteenth** ['nɑɪn 'tinθ] 19th. Go to **fourth** for senses and examples.

**ninetieth** ['nɑɪn ti əθ] 90th. Go to **fourth** for senses and examples.

**ninety** ['nɑɪn ti] 90. Go to **forty** for senses and examples.

**ninth** ['nɑɪnθ] 9th. Go to **fourth** for senses and examples.

**nip** ['nɪp] **1.** *tv.* to pinch or bite someone or something. □ *The small dog nipped my ankle.* **2.** *tv.* to remove something by pinching or biting. □ *The gardener nipped the dead leaves from the plants.*

**nitwit** ['nɪt wɪt] *n.* an idiot; someone who is foolish or stupid. □ *Stop being such a nitwit, and start being serious!*

**nix** ['nɪks] *tv.* to put a stop to something; to end something; to reject something. □ *The producer nixed the screenwriter's script.*

**no** ['no] **1.** *adj.* not any; not a; not one; not any amount of. □ *There's no milk in the refrigerator.* **2.** *adv.* <a word that is used as an answer to show that one does not agree.> □ *"It's Friday today, right?" "No. It's Thursday."* **3.** *adv.* <a word that is used to stress a negative statement.> □ *No, the capital of Michigan is not Detroit. It's Lansing.* **4.** *n.* a negative answer. (Pl ends in *-s* or *-es.*) □ *The final vote was 60 nos and 40 yeses.*

**nobility** [no 'bɪl ə ti] *n.* dignity; the quality of being noble. (No plural form.) □ *Because of his nobility, the diplomat was very much respected.*

**noble** ['nob əl] **1.** *adj.* refined; moral; showing dignity. (Adv: *nobly.* Comp: *nobler;* sup: *noblest.*) □ *Jane's offer to pay*

N

*for everything was a very noble gesture.* **2.** *adj.* <the adj. use of ④.> (Adv: *nobly.* Comp: *nobler;* sup: *noblest.*) □ *Noble ladies and gentlemen entered the great hall for the banquet.* **3.** *adj.* [of a chemical element] not able to mix with other elements; [of a chemical element] not able to react with other elements. □ *Gold is a noble metal.* **4.** *n.* a member of the nobility. □ *The event at the palace was attended mostly by nobles.*

**nobody** ['no bɑd i] **1.** *pron.* no person; no one; not anybody. (No plural form.) □ *Nobody likes cheese more than I do!* **2.** *n.* someone who is not important; someone who has no power. □ *The reporter left the party because only nobodies were there.*

**nod** ['nɑd] **1.** *n.* a quick downward or up-and-down movement of the head, usually to show agreement. □ *My mouth was full, so I replied "yes" with a nod.* **2.** *tv.* to express something by moving one's head as in ③. □ *Bill nodded his agreement.* **3.** *tv.* to move one's head in agreement as in ④. □ *Jane nodded her head in agreement.* **4.** *iv.* to move one's head down, or up and down, quickly, especially to show agreement or approval, or as a greeting. □ *Bill nodded to indicate that he wanted to go along.* **5.** *iv.* to let one's head jerk down as one begins to fall asleep. □ *During the boring movie, I began to nod.* **6.** *iv.* [for one's head] to jerk down as one begins to fall asleep while sitting or standing. □ *My head kept nodding as I sat waiting in the doctor's office.*

**noise** ['nɔɪz] *n.* annoying or unwanted sound. (Plural only when referring to different kinds, types, instances, or varieties.) □ *Tom finds that the noise at the office keeps him from working fast enough.* Ⓒ *What are those noises coming from your car's engine?*

**noisy** ['nɔɪz i] *adj.* [of a sound or of someone or something making sounds] loud; [of someone or something] making much noise. (Adv: *noisily.* Comp: *noisier;* sup: *noisiest.*) □ *The police told everyone at the noisy party to go home.*

**nominal** ['nɑm ə nəl] **1.** *n.* a noun or expression that can serve as the subject of a sentence, the direct or indirect object of a verb, or the object of a preposition. (Abbreviated *n.* here.) □ *Objects of prepositions are nominals.* **2.** *adj.* functioning as ①. (Adv: *nominally.*) □ *"Mary's big, blue hat" is a nominal phrase.* **3.** *adj.* in name only; in theory, but not in reality. (Adv: *nominally.*) □ *Max is only the nominal head of the company. His father, the owner, tells him what to do.* **4.** *adj.* [of a fee or charge] very small, especially as compared with what something is worth. (Adv: *nominally.*) □ *I paid a nominal fee for extra insurance when renting the car.*

**none** ['nʌn] **1.** *pron.* not one; not any; no person; no thing. □ *I bought some potatoes because there were none in the pantry.* **2.** *pron.* not one part; no part. □ *None of the stew was eaten.*

**nonflammable** [nɑn 'flæm ə bəl] *adj.* difficult to burn; impossible to burn; not flammable. (Adv: *nonflammably.*) □ *This tank is for hauling nonflammable liquids, such as milk.*

**nonprofit** [nɑn 'prɑf ɪt] *adj.* not making a profit; not organized or established for the purpose of making money. □ *Susan directed a play for a nonprofit theater company.*

**nonsense** ['nɑn sɛns] *n.* something that does not make sense; something that is foolish. (No plural form.) □ *The crazy man stood on the sidewalk screaming nonsense.*

**nonstop** ['nɑn 'stɑp] **1.** *adj.* without stopping or pausing; continuous. □ *My neighbor's nonstop chatter became annoying.* **2.** *adv.* without stopping; continuously. □ *At the disco, I danced nonstop until 3 A.M.*

**noodle** ['nud l] *n.* a strip or piece of pasta. □ *I covered the noodles with spicy tomato sauce.*

**noon** ['nun] *n.* the time in the middle of the day between morning and afternoon; 12:00 in the daytime; midday. (No plural form.) □ *People usually eat lunch around noon.*

**noonday** ['nun de] *adj.* happening at noon; happening in the middle of the day. (Prenominal only.) □ *I listened to the noonday news broadcast.*

**noontime** ['nun tɑɪm] **1.** *n.* noon; the middle of the day. (No plural form.) □ *Our office closes at noontime for an hour.* **2.** *adj.* happening at noon; happening in the middle of the day. (Prenominal only.) □ *I ate my noontime meal in an inexpensive restaurant.*

**noose** ['nus] *n.* a loop tied at the end of a rope, used to trap or hang someone or something. □ *The cowboy threw the noose around the bull's neck.*

**nor** ['nor] *conj.* <a word used to connect a series of persons or things that are not options or possibilities.> □ *Neither Illinois nor Kansas borders an ocean.*

**norm** ['norm] **1. the norm** *n.* the normal or expected amount, quality, or way. (No plural form.) □ *Eating three meals a day is considered the norm.* **2.** *n.* a standard of behavior according to a society or other group. □ *The political candidate accepted all of the norms of the community.*

**normal** ['nor məl] **1.** *adj.* regular; typical; usual; expected. (Adv: *normally.*) □ *Bob's weight is normal for his height.* **2.** *adj.* sane; not sick in the mind. (Adv: *normally.*) □ *Whoever committed this terrible crime is not normal!*

**north** ['norθ] **1.** *n.* the direction to the left of someone or something facing the rising sun. (No plural form.) □ *On most maps, north is toward the top.* **2.** *n.* the northern part of a region, country, or planet. (No plural form. Capitalized when referring to a region of the U.S.) □ *The refugees fled to the mountains in the north.* **3.** *adj.* at ①; on the side toward ①; facing toward ①. □ *John lives on the north side of town.* **4.** *adj.* from ①. (Used especially to describe wind.) □ *The snowstorm was accompanied by a cold north wind.* **5.** *adv.* toward ①; into the northern part of something. □ *Walk north to Main Street, and then go west.*

**northeast** [norθ 'ist] **1.** *n.* a direction halfway between north and east. (No plural form.) □ *Northeast is the opposite direction from southwest.* **2.** *n.* an area in the northeastern part of a city, region, or country. (No plural form. Capitalized when referring to a region of the U.S.) □ *The general sent more troops to the northeast.* **3.** *adj.* in ②; toward ①; facing ①. □ *I moved to the northeast side of town.* **4.** *adj.* [of wind] blowing from ①. □ *Currently, there's a strong northeast wind.* **5.** *adv.* toward ①. □ *The plane flew northeast from Phoenix to Chicago.*

**northeastern** [norθ 'ist ɚn] *adj.* in the northeast; toward the northeast; facing northeast. □ *From the northeastern window in the kitchen, you can see the lake.*

**northern** ['nor ðɚn] **1.** *adj.* in the north; toward the north; facing the north. □ *A room with a northern view has windows on its north side.* **2.** *adj.* [of wind] blowing from the north. □ *The snowstorm was accompanied by a cold northern wind.*

**northwest** [norθ 'wɛst] **1.** *n.* a direction halfway between north and west. (No plural form.) □ *San Francisco is located to the northwest of Los Angeles.* **2.** *n.* an area in the northwestern part of a country. (No plural form. Capitalized when referring to a region of the United States.) □ *The storms came in from the northwest every April.* **3.** *adj.* in ②;

toward ①; facing ①. ☐ *Morocco is in the northwest part of Africa.* **4.** *adj.* [of wind] blowing from ①. ☐ *I ran southeast with the northwest wind at my back.* **5.** *adv.* toward ①. ☐ *Turn northwest when you get to the six-way intersection.*

**northwestern** [norθ 'wɛs tɚn] *adj.* in the northwest; toward the northwest; facing northwest. ☐ *Portland is in the northwestern part of Oregon.*

**nose** ['noz] **1.** *n.* the structure between the mouth and the eyes in humans, being the organ used for smelling and breathing, and a similar structure in animals. ☐ *I asked for a tissue so I could blow my nose.* **2.** *n.* the sense of smell; ① used for smelling something. ☐ *The dog's nose led her to her puppies, which had crawled away.* **3.** *n.* the front end of an airplane, a rocket, a ship, or some other thing. (Fig. on ①.) ☐ *There was a propeller on the nose of the small airplane.*

**nosedive** ['noz dɑɪv] **1.** *n.* a sudden drop or decline, especially the sudden fall of an airplane with the nose pointing downward. ☐ *The airplane took a nosedive after its engines failed.* **2.** *iv.* to plunge with the nose pointing downward. ☐ *The puppy nosedived off the edge of the couch.* **3.** *iv.* [for a measurement] to decline or drop suddenly. (Fig. on ②.) ☐ *The employment rate nosedived when the economy was weak.*

**nostril** ['nɑs trəl] *n.* one of the two outside holes of the nose. ☐ *We can breathe in and out through our nostrils or through our mouths.*

**nosy** ['noz i] *adj.* snooping; prying. (Adv: *nosily.* Comp: *nosier;* sup: *nosiest.*) ☐ *My brother is very nosy and always wants to know what I'm doing.*

**not** ['nɑt] **1.** *adv.* <a negative particle used with verbs, adverbs, participles, prepositions, nominals, and adjectives.> (Contracted to *n't.*) ☐ *My dress is not blue. It is red.* **2.** *adv.* <a negative particle that stands for a part of a sentence that is being refused, denied, or negated.> ☐ *Do you agree with me? No, I do not [agree with you].*

**notation** [no 'te ʃən] *n.* a set of signs or symbols that is used to represent something. ☐ *Can you read musical notation?*

**notch** ['nɑtʃ] **1.** *n.* a V-shaped cut in a surface, made for a specific reason. ☐ *The cowboy cut a notch in his gun for every wolf he killed.* **2.** *n.* a degree of quality or quantity. (Fig. on ①.) ☐ *The service here is a notch below that of the restaurant across the street.* **3.** *tv.* to make a V-shaped cut for a specific reason. ☐ *The cowboy shot another wolf and notched his gun barrel one more time.*

**note** ['not] **1.** *n.* a short written message. ☐ *I wrote my aunt a thank-you note for her gift.* **2.** *n.* a comment on the bottom of a page or at the end of a book that explains, clarifies, or provides the source of something in the text. (See also **footnote**.) ☐ *A note at the bottom of the page gave the source of the quote that the author used.* **3.** *n.* a piece of paper money; a bill. ☐ *I have no change, only notes.* **4.** *n.* the written symbol for a specific musical tone. ☐ *John wrote down the notes while I sang the tune that I had made up.* **5.** *n.* a specific musical tone; one sound made by singing or playing a musical instrument. ☐ *The highest note sung by the soprano was almost too soft to hear.* **6.** *n.* a sign of something; a hint of something. ☐ *There was a note of anger in the manager's voice.* **7. notes** *n.* information that is written down by someone while listening to a lecture or reading a book. ☐ *Can I borrow your notes? I missed class yesterday.* **8.** *tv.* to write something as a short message. (The object can be a clause with **that** ⑦.) ☐ *The doctor noted her diagnosis on my medical records.* **9.** *tv.* to remark about something; to state something; to observe something.

(The object is a clause with **that** ⑦.) □ *My teacher noted that I often left class early.* **10.** *tv.* to pay attention to something; to remember something. (The object can be a clause with **that** ⑦.) □ *Note the way in which I thread the needle.*

**notebook** ['not bʊk] *n.* a book in which notes are written. □ *My notebook is full of notes from the lecture.*

**notepaper** ['not pe pɚ] *n.* paper that notes, such as thank-you notes, are written on. (Plural only when referring to different kinds, types, instances, or varieties.) □ *I found matching envelopes to go with my notepaper.* Ⓒ *This store carries all different kinds of notepapers and envelopes.*

**nothing** ['nʌθ ɪŋ] **1.** *pron.* not one thing; not a thing; not anything. (No plural form. Treated as singular.) □ *I knew nothing about chemistry until 11th grade.* **2.** *n.* [only] something that is without meaning; [only] something that is not significant or important; not anything that is significant or important. (No plural form. Treated as singular.) □ *There is nothing on TV tonight, so I am going out to see a movie.* **3.** *n.* zero; no amount. (No plural form.) □ *Our team lost the game ten to nothing.*

**notice** ['not ɪs] **1.** *tv.* to see, hear, taste, or smell someone or something; to be aware of someone or something. (The object can be a clause with **that** ⑦.) □ *The witness noticed many details about the accident.* **2.** *n.* an announcement; a sign that warns or informs; a warning. □ *The store owner put up a notice about the sale.* **3.** *n.* attention; a state of awareness [about something]. (No plural form.) □ *Your letter escaped my notice.*

**noticeable** ['not ɪs ə bəl] *adj.* able to be seen; easily seen; easily noticed. (Adv: *noticeably.*) □ *The surgery left a noticeable scar on my leg.*

**notify** ['not ə fɑɪ] *tv.* to inform someone about something; to tell someone officially about something. □ *Please notify the post office when you change your address.*

**notion** ['no ʃən] **1.** *n.* an opinion; a belief. □ *Where did you get the notion that the earth was flat?* **2.** *n.* a whim; an intention. □ *Whose silly notion was it to paint the porch floor?*

**noun** ['nɑʊn] *n.* a word that refers to a person, place, thing, or idea. (See also **nominal.**) □ *The word* child *is a noun that has an irregular plural form:* children. □ *In the sentence "The cat is on the mat," the words* cat *and* mat *are nouns.*

**nourish** ['nɚ ɪʃ] **1.** *tv.* to feed someone or something; to give someone or something the things necessary for life and health. □ *The rain nourished the crops.* **2.** *tv.* to encourage something; to support something as it develops. (Fig. on ①. Used especially with feelings and emotions.) □ *My grandparents nourished my respect for nature.*

**novel** ['nɑv əl] **1.** *n.* a written story; a book of fiction. □ *I read a complete novel during the airplane flight.* **2.** *adj.* new; original; not known before. □ *The architect won an award for his novel designs.*

**novelty** ['nɑv əl ti] **1.** *n.* the quality of being novel; the quality of being new or original. (Plural only when referring to different kinds, types, instances, or varieties.) □ *The novelty of your poetry is very refreshing!* Ⓒ *Bill likes popular music as a novelty, but he doesn't want to listen to it every day.* **2.** *n.* a small item, often inexpensive and usually interesting or amusing. □ *Anne kept a variety of novelties in a box to amuse the children.* **3.** *adj.* <the adj. use of ②>; [of something] interesting and entertaining. (Prenominal only.) □ *The shop carried some unusual novelty items.*

**November** [no 'vɛm bɚ] Go to **month.**

N

**novice** ['nɑv ɪs] **1.** *n.* someone who is new at a job or responsibility. ☐ *Although I've played golf for years, I still play like a novice.* **2.** *n.* someone who has just joined a religious order and will become a monk or a nun. ☐ *The head of the convent welcomed the novices.* **3.** *adj.* [of someone] new to a task or activity. (Prenominal only.) ☐ *Surprisingly, the novice chess player beat the expert.*

**now** ['nɑʊ] **1.** *adv.* at this moment; at this point in time; immediately. ☐ *The pizza should be ready now.* **2.** *adv.* in these days; in modern times; in present times. ☐ *It's easier to operate a computer now than it was in the 1970s.* **3.** *adv.* <a word used for emphasis, to get someone's attention, with commands, and to move on to the next topic.> ☐ *Now, where did I put my keys?* **4.** *n.* the present; this time. (No plural form.) ☐ *For now, I'd just like a cup of coffee.* **5. now and then** *phr.* sometimes; occasionally. ☐ *We visit my parents now and then, but we never have a real vacation.*

N

**nowhere** ['no ʍɛr] *adv.* at no place; to or toward no place; not to or at any place. ☐ *I gave up because all of my hard work was getting me nowhere.*

**nuclear** ['nu kli ɚ] *adj.* of or about the nucleus of an atom or the energy created by splitting or fusing the nuclei of atoms. ☐ *Nuclear energy creates radioactive waste.*

**nuclei** ['nu kli ɑɪ] pl of **nucleus**.

**nucleus** ['nu kli əs] **1.** *n., irreg.* the center of something; the core of something. (Pl: **nuclei**.) ☐ *The vice presidents of the company form the nucleus of the management committee.* **2.** *n., irreg.* the core of an atom, consisting of protons and neutrons. ☐ *Energy is created by splitting an atom's nucleus.* **3.** *n., irreg.* the control center of a living cell. ☐ *This virus attacks the nucleus of the cell.*

**nude** ['nud] **1.** *adj.* naked; not wearing any clothes. ☐ *Bathing suits are required here, so you won't see any nude swimmers.* **2.** *n.* someone who is not wearing any clothes; a statue or a painting of someone who is not wearing any clothes. ☐ *This wing of the sculpture museum features nudes from the 17th century.*

**nuisance** ['nu səns] *n.* a bother; someone or something that is annoying. ☐ *My nosy neighbor is quite a nuisance.*

**numb** ['nʌm] **1.** *adj.* unable to feel anything; unable to sense anything. (Adv: *numbly* ['nʌm li]. Comp: *number* ['nʌm ɚ]; sup: *numbest* ['nʌm əst].) ☐ *An injection made my mouth numb so the dentist could work on my tooth.* **2.** *tv.* to cause someone or something to be unable to feel anything. ☐ *The cold weather numbed my fingers and toes.*

**number** ['nʌm bɚ] **1.** *n.* a symbol or a word that expresses an amount; a symbol or a word that shows how many; a digit or series of digits that has an assigned significance. ☐ *Write the number that is the correct answer in the blank space.* **2.** *n.* a specific ① that identifies someone or something in a series. (Also appears as the symbol "#".) ☐ *I was number three in line to buy tickets for the concert.* **3.** *n.* a song; a piece of music. ☐ *The singers ended the concert with a very lovely number.* **4.** *n.* a grammatical category showing whether one or more than one person or thing is being referred to. (Plural only when referring to different kinds, types, instances, or varieties.) ☐ *In many languages, number consists of singular and plural forms.* Ⓒ *Some languages have three numbers—singular, plural, and dual.* **5. the number of** people or things *phr.* the total amount of people or things; a sum; a total. (**Number** is treated as singular.) ☐ *The number of people at the meeting was seven.* **6. a number of** people or things *phr.* some people or things, in an indefinite amount. (**Number** is treated as plural, but not countable.) ☐ *A number of people are here now.* **7.** *tv.* to assign something a ①. (Refers especially to things in a series.) ☐ *The worker numbered the parts as they came down the assembly line.* **8.** *tv.* to reach a total of a certain amount; to be a certain amount. ☐ *When the audience numbered 200, we began the show.*

**numeral** ['num ə rəl] *n.* the symbol or figure that represents a number. ☐ *The numerals at the bottom of the page were written in red ink.*

**numerous** ['num ə rəs] *adj.* many; several; a lot. (Adv: *numerously.*) ☐ *I have numerous friends from New York City.*

**nun** ['nʌn] *n.* a woman who is a member of a religious order. ☐ *Every morning, the nuns sing and pray.*

**nurse** ['nɚs] **1.** *n.* someone, usually a woman, trained to provide medical care, often under the supervision of a physician. ☐ *The nurse took my temperature.* **2.** *n.* a woman who raises other people's children; a woman who helps a family raise its children. ☐ *The children became very attached to their nurse.* **3.** *tv.* to feed a baby milk from one's breast. ☐ *My mother nursed all of her children.* **4.** *tv.* [for anyone] to treat a disease or a sick person. ☐ *I think I can nurse this cold without seeing a doctor.* **5.** *iv.* [for a female mammal] to feed a baby mammal as in ③. ☐ *She nurses while sitting in a rocking chair.* **6.** *iv.* [for a baby mammal] to suck or take milk from a female mammal. ☐ *The baby stopped nursing and fell asleep.*

**nursery** ['nɚs (ə) ri] **1.** *n.* a room for babies in a hospital or residence. ☐ *There were 12 new babies in the hospital's nursery.* **2.** *n.* a place where children are watched while their parents are busy at something else. ☐ *David picked up his children at the nursery after work.* **3.** *n.* a place where plants are grown and sold. ☐ *The nursery was kept at a constant temperature all year long.*

**nut** ['nʌt] **1.** *n.* a hard, woody shell containing an edible part. ☐ *The worker harvested the nuts from the trees.* **2.** *n.* the edible part of ①, used as food. ☐ *The waiter put a dish of salted nuts on our table.* **3.** *n.* someone who is crazy, insane, or foolish. (Slang.) ☐ *Some nut painted a star on the side of the building.*

**nutrition** [nu 'trɪ ʃən] *n.* the science of providing people with information about healthy food. (No plural form.) ☐ *Sue studied nutrition before studying to be a chef.*

**nutshell** ['nʌt ʃɛl] **1.** *n.* the hard, woody shell around the edible part of a nut. ☐ *I used a hammer to open the thick nutshell.* **2. in a nutshell** *phr.* [of news or information] in a (figurative) very small container like ①; stated in just a few words. ☐ *In a nutshell, what happened at work today?*

**nutty** ['nʌt i] **1.** *adj.* tasting like a nut; made from nuts. (Adv: *nuttily.* Comp: *nuttier;* sup: *nuttiest.*) ☐ *The fresh coffee had a nutty aroma.* **2.** *adj.* crazy; insane. (Slang. Adv: *nuttily.* Comp: *nuttier;* sup: *nuttiest.*) ☐ *What a nutty thing to do.*

**nylon** ['nɑɪ lɑn] **1.** *n.* a very strong but light, often flexible fiber made from chemicals, that is used especially to make clothes and fabric. (No plural form.) ☐ *Do you prefer stockings made from nylon or silk?* **2. nylons** *n.* a pair of pantyhose; stockings made of ①. (Treated as plural. Number is expressed with *pair(s) of nylons.*) ☐ *Susan wore black nylons with her black dress.* **3.** *adj.* made from ①. ☐ *The fisherman used a strong nylon thread for a fishing line.*

N

**oak** ['ok] **1.** *n.* a kind of strong tree that produces an edible nut. □ *The robin built its nest in a big old oak.* **2.** *n.* wood from ①. (Plural only when referring to different kinds, types, instances, or varieties.) □ *The carpenter used oak when making the rocking chair.* 🄲 *Some oaks are more suitable for flooring than others.* **3.** *adj.* made from ②. □ *The artist placed her painting in an oak frame.*

**oar** ['or] *n.* a long pole with one wide, flat end—similar to a paddle—used to steer and row boats. □ *The oar floated away from my boat when I accidentally dropped it in the water.*

O

**oases** [o 'e siz] pl of **oasis.**

**oasis** [o 'e sɪs] **1.** *n., irreg.* a place in a desert that has water and trees. (Pl: **oases.**) □ *The camels drank a lot of water at the oasis.* **2.** *n., irreg.* a place that is free of problems or difficulties. (Fig. on ①.) □ *The park near my house is a quiet oasis, far from traffic.*

**oat** ['ot] **1. oats** *n.* a cereal grain used as food for humans and cattle. (Treated as plural, but not countable.) □ *My breakfast cereal is made from oats.* **2.** *n.* a single grain of ①. □ *The farmer spilled a few oats on the ground.* **3.** *adj.* made of ①. □ *Mary baked some oat bread.*

**oath** ['oθ] **1.** *n., irreg.* a promise that one will speak only the truth; a promise that one will do something. (Pl: ['oðz].) □ *They broke their oaths when they lied.* **2. take an oath** *phr.* to make ①; to promise something as in ①. □ *When I was a witness in court, I had to take an oath that I would tell the truth.* **3. under oath** *phr.* bound by ①; having taken ①. □ *I was placed under oath before I gave evidence in the trial.*

**oatmeal** ['ot mil] **1.** *n.* crushed oats. (No plural form.) □ *The cookies are made with three cups of oatmeal and one cup of flour.* **2.** *n.* cooked ①, usually eaten with milk and sugar. (No plural form.) □ *John puts milk in his oatmeal.* **3.** *adj.* made with crushed oats. □ *Oatmeal cookies with raisins are my favorite.*

**obedience** [o 'bid i əns] *n.* the condition of being obedient. (No plural form.) □ *The unruly children showed no obedience to their parents.*

**obedient** [o 'bid i ənt] *adj.* obeying; following orders. (Adv: *obediently.*) □ *The obedient dog listened to its owner.*

**obey** [o 'be] **1.** *tv.* to yield to someone and do as one has been instructed; to follow instructions, commands, or rules. □ *You must obey the laws of the country that you're in.* **2.** *iv.* to do as one is told. □ *The students obeyed when the teacher told them to stand.*

**object 1.** ['ɑb dʒɛkt] *n.* a thing; something that can be seen or touched. □ *What is that dark object lying in the street?* **2.** ['ɑb dʒɛkt] *n.* a goal; an aim; someone or something that a thought or an action is directed toward. □ *Jane disliked being the object of Bill's attention.* **3.** ['ɑb dʒɛkt] *n.* a noun or nominal that is affected by the action or condition of a verb, and that, if replaced with **he, she,** or **they,** would be **him, her,** or **them;** a noun or nominal within a prepositional phrase. □ *In "I ate the cake," "the cake" is the object.* **4. object (to something)** [əb 'dʒɛkt...] *iv. (+ prep. phr.)* to oppose something; to argue against something; to make an objection about something. □ *My roommate objected to my plans for the party.*

**objection** [əb 'dʒɛk ʃən] *n.* a stated reason for not wanting to do something. □ *I see no problem. What are your objections?*

**oblige** [ə 'blɑɪdʒ] **1. oblige** someone **to** do something *tv.* + *obj.* + *inf.* to require someone to do something. □ *The law obliges us to pay taxes.* **2.** *iv.* to do something nice for someone; to do someone a favor. □ *I could not oblige because I was going to be out of town.*

**oblong** ['ɑb lɔŋ] *adj.* [especially of a rectangle] long and a little narrow. (Adv: *oblongly.*) □ *An oval is like an oblong circle.*

**obnoxious** [əb 'nɑk ʃəs] *adj.* very annoying; very irritating. (Adv: *obnoxiously.*) □ *I prefer to visit Mary when her obnoxious brother is not at home.*

**oboe** ['o bo] *n.* a musical instrument that has a long, thin wooden body and a mouthpiece holding a double reed. □ *Jane plays the oboe in the city's orchestra.*

**obscure** [əb 'skjʊr] **1.** *adj.* [of reasoning or explanation] not clearly stated or hard to understand. (Adv: *obscurely.*) □ *The teacher's obscure explanation of the homework confused me.* **2.** *adj.* not well known; not famous. (Adv: *obscurely.*) □ *The singer sang an obscure song from the 1920s at a special performance.* **3.** *adj.* hard to see; hidden, especially by darkness. (Adv: *obscurely.*) □ *The obscure shoreline was almost completely hidden by the fog.* **4.** *tv.* to make something hard to see; to keep something from view; to dim or darken something. □ *Fog obscured all of the downtown buildings.* **5.** *tv.* to make something difficult to understand; to cloud one's meaning. (Fig. on ④.) □ *The student's poor writing obscured the point that he was trying to make.*

**observe** [əb 'zɝv] **1.** *tv.* to watch something; to see something; to notice something. (The object can be a clause with **that** ⑦.) □ *I observed the soccer game from a distance.* **2.** *tv.* to obey a law or custom; to pay attention to a law or custom. □ *A good athlete should always observe the rules of the game.* **3.** *tv.* to celebrate a holiday. □ *Our neighbors observe Ramadan.* **4.** *tv.* to make a comment or a remark; to state something. (The object is a clause with **that** ⑦.) □ *Bob observed that owning a car can be very expensive.*

**obsessed** [əb 'sɛst] **1.** *adj.* thinking about someone or something too much, as if one were forced to do so. □ *The obsessed student couldn't stop talking about his grades.* **2. obsessed with** someone or something *adj.* + *prep. phr.* always thinking about a person, a thought, or an activity. □ *Anne was obsessed with pleasing her parents.*

**obstruct** [əb 'strʌkt] *tv.* to get in the way of someone or something; to block someone or something. □ *Some paper got in the sink and obstructed the drain.*

**obstruction** [əb 'strʌk ʃən] *n.* something that is in the way; something that is blocking the way. □ *The plumber removed a large obstruction from the pipes.*

**obtain** [əb 'ten] *tv.* to get something; to gain possession of something; to come to own something. □ *Jane had obtained the large oil painting from her sister.*

**obvious** ['ɑb vi əs] *adj.* easily recognized; easily seen or understood; plain; clear. (Adv: *obviously.*) □ *It's obvious that 2 + 2 = 4.* □ *Since you're late, it's obvious that you should have left earlier.*

**occasion** [ə 'ke ʒən] **1.** *n.* a time when something happens; a time when something occurs; an instance. □ *On several occasions, I've forgotten my keys.* **2.** *n.* a special event. □ *A wedding is a very happy occasion.*

**occasional** [ə 'ke ʒə nəl] *adj.* happening from time to time; happening once in a while; not happening all the time or

O

regularly. (Adv: *occasionally.*) □ *The silence was broken by an occasional shout.*

**occult** [ə 'kʌlt] **1. the occult** *n.* things that are hidden from regular knowledge or experience, including magic and secret things. (No plural form. Treated as singular.) □ *Voodoo is one of the mysteries of the occult.* **2.** *adj.* hidden from regular knowledge; filled with mystery. □ *The witch was questioned about her occult knowledge.*

**occupancy** ['ɑk jə pən si] **1.** *n.* occupying a house, building, or other piece of property. (No plural form.) □ *My uncle maintained occupancy of his apartment for 70 years.* **2.** *n.* the number of people that a room or building is allowed to hold. (No plural form.) □ *The sign in the lobby stated the legal occupancy of the theater.*

**occupant** ['ɑk jə pənt] *n.* someone who lives in a certain place; a business that occupies a certain building or space. □ *The occupants of this office building are all lawyers.*

O

**occupation** [ɑk jə 'pe ʃən] **1.** *n.* a job; a career; what one does for a living. □ *Mary's occupation requires her to travel a lot.* **2.** *n.* taking or keeping possession of a region or a country. □ *The occupation of the country by foreign troops frightened the residents.*

**occupy** ['ɑk jə pɑɪ] **1.** *tv.* to use or consume time by doing something. □ *I occupy my afternoons with reading.* **2.** *tv.* to keep someone busy doing something. □ *Find something to occupy the children while we go to the store.* **3.** *tv.* to be in a certain place; to take up the space in a certain place; to live in a certain place; to have one's business in a certain place. □ *Generally, dormitories are occupied by students.* **4.** *tv.* to move into and take control of another country. □ *The war began when Iraq tried to occupy Kuwait.*

**occur** [ə 'kɚ] **1.** *iv.* to happen; to take place. □ *The accident occurred when my car's brakes failed.* **2.** *iv.* to be; to exist; to be found. □ *That word only occurs once in the entire book.* **3. occur to** someone *iv. + prep. phr.* to come to someone's mind; [for a thought] to enter into someone's mind. □ *I just remembered something that occurred to me in the middle of the night.*

**occurrence** [ə 'kɚ əns] **1. the occurrence of** something *phr.* the existence of something; the appearance or happening of something in a particular place. □ *We have no evidence of the occurrence of water on Mars.* **2.** *n.* an event; something that happens; an incident. □ *Meeting someone famous is not an everyday occurrence for most people.*

**ocean** ['o ʃən] *n.* a large body of salt water that covers ¾ of the earth's surface, or one of that body's four divisions: the Arctic Ocean, the Atlantic Ocean, the Indian Ocean, and the Pacific Ocean. □ *I washed the salt from my body after swimming in the ocean.*

**o'clock** [ə 'klɑk] *adv.* <a word used to indicate the time of day.> (It follows a number from 1 to 12 and means that it is that time exactly, or zero minutes past the hour. Literally, *of the clock.*) □ *Two o'clock is also written as 2:00.*

**octagon** ['ɑk tə gɑn] *n.* a flat figure or shape with eight sides. □ *The geometry teacher drew a large octagon on the board.*

**octave** ['ɑk tɪv] *n.* a musical interval of two notes where the higher note is twelve half tones above the lower note; [on a piano] the first and eighth key in a row of eight white keys. □ *The soprano sang one octave higher than the rest of the choir.*

**October** [ɑk 'to bɚ] Go to **month**.

**octopi** ['ɑk tə pɑɪ] a pl of **octopus**.

**octopus** ['ɑk tə pəs] *n., irreg.* a boneless sea creature with eight legs. (Greek for "eight-footed." The English plural is *octopuses* or **octopi**.) □ *The deep-sea diver photographed the octopus.*

**odd** ['ɑd] **1.** *adj.* strange; different; unusual; out of place. (Adv: *oddly.* Comp: *odder;* sup: *oddest.*) □ *Jane told me an odd but funny story.* **2.** *adj.* not even; [of a number] not able to be divided by two without an amount (one) being left over. □ *Three and five are odd numbers.* □ *If you add two odd numbers together, the sum is even.* **3.** *adj.* not regular; random [occasions]; occasional. (Prenominal only. Comp: *odder;* sup: *oddest.*) □ *My car brakes stop working at odd moments.*

**oddity** ['ɑd ə ti] **1.** *n.* the state of being unusual or strange. (No plural form.) □ *The oddity of the man's behavior caused the police to suspect him.* **2.** *n.* something that is odd; something that is unusual or strange. □ *David looked for interesting oddities in his stamp collection.*

**odor** ['o dɚ] *n.* a smell; a scent; an aroma. □ *There was an odor of sweat and dirty socks in the locker room.*

**of** [əv] **1.** *prep.* belonging to someone; owned by someone; closely associated with someone. (Takes a nominal in the possessive form. Pronouns that can follow **of** in this sense are *mine, yours, his, hers, ours,* and *theirs.*) □ *A friend of yours phoned this afternoon.* **2.** *prep.* connected to someone or something; relating to someone or something; associated with someone or something; representing someone or something; being a portion or part from something. □ *We drove to the bottom of the hill.* □ *The artist painted a picture of Jane.* **3.** *prep.* made from something. □ *Anne wore a necklace of gold.* **4.** *prep.* containing something; including someone or something; having people or things as the members or parts. □ *A group of students entered the classroom.* **5.** *prep.* <a preposition expressing a measurement or an amount.> □ *I put eight gallons of gas into the car.* **6.** *prep.* <a preposition linking a type of location to the name of a location.> □ *Mary visited the city of Atlanta.* **7.** *prep.* referring to someone or something; about someone or something; concerning someone or something. □ *I often think of my childhood.* **8.** *prep.* having a certain quality or aspect. □ *This is an issue of great importance.* **9.** *prep.* between [two]; among [more than two]. □ *Of all the jobs I've had, this one is the best.* **10.** *prep.* before a certain hour. □ *I have a doctor's appointment at a quarter of three.* **11.** *prep.* <a preposition used to make a nominal phrase from an intransitive verb and its subject.> (For instance, *the children shout → the children's shouting → the shouting of the children.*) □ *The shouting of the children woke me up.* □ *We awaited the arrival of the king.* **12.** *prep.* <a preposition used to make a nominal phrase from a transitive verb and its object.> (For instance, *destroy the city → the city's destruction → the destruction of the city.*) □ *The washing of the dishes took an hour.* □ *The destruction of the city was a terrible tragedy.*

**off** ['ɔf] **1.** *prep.* away from someone or something; not on someone or something. (① through ④ are often *off of*, a construction objected to by some.) □ *The calendar fell off the wall.* **2.** *prep.* less than something; deducted from something. □ *The cashier took $1 off the regular price.* **3.** *prep.* leading away from a place or path; turning from a place or path; connecting to a place or path. □ *The bathroom is off the main hallway, on the right side.* **4.** *prep.* in or over the water near land. □ *The hurricane was just off the Florida coast.* **5.** *adj.* stopped; not being used; causing something not to function or operate, especially by stopping the flow of electricity. (Not prenominal.) □ *Before you leave, please make sure all the lights are off.* **6.** *adj.* wrong; not accurate. (Not prenominal.) □ *My scale is off by 10 pounds.* **7.** *adj.* canceled. (Not prenominal.) □ *The meeting is off for tonight.* **8.** *adj.* [of a time period] free of work. (Not prenominal.) □ *During the off season, the baseball player went on vacation.*

**offend** [ə 'fɛnd] *tv.* to shock someone, especially through one's actions, attitude, or behavior. □ *I was offended by Bob's lack of sympathy.*

**offense 1.** [ə 'fɛns] *n.* the breaking of a law; a crime; an illegal act. □ *Bob was arrested for a traffic offense.* **2.** [ə 'fɛns] *n.* something that is shocking or disgusting. □ *His rudeness was considered a serious offense.* **3.** ['ɔ fɛns] *n.* a way of attacking; an attack. □ *The army's offense surprised the enemy.*

**offensive 1.** [ə 'fɛn sɪv] *adj.* shocking; annoying; offending someone. (Adv: *offensively.*) □ *Bill's offensive joke made me angry.* **2.** ['ɔ fɛn sɪv] *adj.* of or about attacking. (Adv: *offensively.*) □ *The offensive team carried the ball closer to the goal.* **3.** [ə 'fɛn sɪv] *n.* an attack. □ *The team's surprise offensive won the game.*

O

**offer** ['ɔf ɚ] **1.** *tv.* to present something that can be taken or refused. □ *The worker offered his proposal for the remodeling job.* **2.** *tv.* to propose a price for something that is being sold. □ *John offered $3 for the plastic bucket.* **3. offer to do something** *iv. + inf.* to indicate that one is willing to do something. □ *My neighbor offered to help me when I was sick.* **4.** *n.* something that is **offered** as in ①. □ *I accepted my neighbor's offer of help.* **5.** *n.* a price or amount that is **offered** as in ②. □ *The saleswoman accepted my offer of $4,000 for the car.*

**offering** ['ɔf ɚ ɪŋ] *n.* something that is offered, especially to a church, to a charity, or as part of a religious ceremony. □ *The worshipers sacrificed a pig as an offering to the gods.*

**office** ['ɔf ɪs] **1.** *n.* a room—usually assigned to one person—where business is done. □ *We went to my office to discuss the business proposal.* **2.** *n.* the combined work places of a number of people. □ *Our office is closed on federal holidays.* **3.** *n.* a position of power and responsibility, especially in a government or an organization. □ *If elected to this office, I promise to put more people to work.*

**office hours** ['ɔf ɪs aʊ ɚz] *n.* the times when an office is open. (Treated as plural. Rarely singular.) □ *Our office hours are from 9 A.M. to 5 P.M.*

**officer** ['ɔ fə sɚ] *n.* someone in a position of authority, especially in the military, the government, or an organization. □ *One of the company officers was chosen for a national award.*

**official** [ə 'fɪ ʃəl] **1.** *n.* an officer; someone in a position of authority. □ *I spoke to an official about getting permission to enter the building.* **2.** *adj.* of or about the power, authority, and responsibility of an office or an officer. (Adv: *officially.*) □ *The president issued an official statement about the crisis.*

**offshore** ['ɔf 'ʃor] *adj.* located or occurring in, on, or over the water away from the shore. □ *The offshore storm quickly moved toward the coast.*

**offspring** ['ɔf sprɪŋ] *n.* [a person's] child or children; [an animal's] young. (No plural form. Treated as singular or plural.) □ *All of Mary's offspring are in Florida.*

**offstage** ['ɔf 'stedʒ] **1.** *adj.* next to the visible part of the stage of a theater, but not visible to the audience. □ *An offstage chorus sang during the first act.* **2.** *adv.* at, to, or toward the area next to the visible part of the stage. □ *The* *actors waited offstage for their cues to come onstage.*

**often** ['ɔf ən] *adv.* frequently; happening many times. □ *Anne often takes her dog for a walk after dinner.*

**oh** ['o] *interj.* <a form expressing surprise or other feelings.> □ *"Today is my birthday." "Oh, really? Happy birthday!"*

**oil** ['oɪl] **1.** *n.* a slick, greasy liquid that does not dissolve in water. (Plural only when referring to different kinds, types, instances, or varieties.) □ *Oil obtained from plants and animals is used in cooking and in medicine.* Ⓒ *Edible oils are a necessary part of our diet.* **2.** *tv.* to put lubrication on something using ①; to make something slippery by putting ① on it; to put ① on something. □ *The cook oiled the bottom of the pan.*

**oilcan** ['oɪl kæn] *n.* a can that is used to apply oil as lubrication. □ *I keep a full oilcan in the trunk of my car for emergencies.*

**oily** ['oɪl i] *adj.* made of oil; containing oil; soaked with oil. (Comp: *oilier;* sup: *oiliest.*) □ *The fire started from a pile of oily rags.*

**oink** ['oɪŋk] **1.** *n.* the sound made by a pig. □ *I hear one oink after another when I go near the pigs.* **2.** *iv.* to make the sound of a pig. □ *Jimmy oinked like a pig as he played in the mud.*

**ointment** ['oɪnt mənt] *n.* a substance that is put on the skin to heal it, soothe it, or soften it. □ *The soothing ointment felt good on my sunburned skin.*

**okay** AND **OK** [o 'ke] **1.** *adv.* all right; adequately. □ *This television works okay, considering it's so old.* **2.** *adv.* to a degree of intensity below "very good" but above "poor." □ *I felt okay after the accident, but I went to the hospital anyway.* **3.** *adj.* just good, but not excellent. □ *Bill gets okay grades, but his parents know he can do better.* **4.** *interj.* <a word used to confirm that one understands something.> □ *"This organ here is the kidney." "Okay. What's that one?"* **5.** *n.* approval. □ *The manager gave her OK to the budget proposal.* **6.** *tv.* to approve something. □ *The homeowners okayed the plans for the new garage.*

**old** ['old] **1.** *adj.* having been alive for a long time; not recently born; not young. (Comp: *older;* sup: *oldest.*) □ *The old lady walked with a cane.* **2.** *adj.* having existed for a long time; not recently made; not new. (Comp: *older;* sup: *oldest.*) □ *A row of oak trees lined the dusty old road.* **3.** *adj.* of a certain age. (Follows the age. Comp: *older.*) □ *My brother turns 17 years old today.* **4.** *adj.* previous; former. (Comp: *older;* sup: *oldest.*) □ *I sold my old car and bought a new one.*

**old age** ['old 'edʒ] **1.** *n.* the period when one is old. (No plural form.) □ *In my old age, I hope to travel.* **2. old-age** *adj.* <the adj. use of ①.> □ *I have a few old-age aches and pains.*

**old-fashioned** ['old 'fæʃ ənd] *adj.* belonging to the style, actions, behavior, or rules of the past. (Adv: *old-fashionedly.*) □ *Anne wore an old-fashioned dress to the costume party.*

**olive** ['ɑ lɪv] **1.** *n.* a tree grown in warm climates for its fruit. □ *We planted a few olives along with the poplar trees.* **2.** *n.* the fruit of ①, used for food. □ *Green olives are usually very salty.*

**omelet** ['ɑm lɪt] *n.* a dish made of beaten eggs, cooked flat and folded over, sometimes stuffed with other foods. □ *I bought some eggs so I could make an omelet.*

**omission** [o 'mɪʃ ən] **1.** *n.* not listing or not including someone or something; omitting someone or something. □ *The omission of your article from the journal was accidental.* **2.** *n.* something that has been left out; something that has been omitted. □ *A number of people should*

O

*have been on your list. Here is a list of the omissions.*

**omit** [o 'mɪt] *tv.* to leave someone or something out; to forget to list or include something. □ *The publisher omitted the third chapter of the book by mistake.*

**on** ['ɔn] **1.** *prep.* above and supported by someone or something; covering or partially covering someone or something; touching the surface of someone or something. □ *Dinner is on the table.* □ *The calendar is on the wall.* **2.** *prep.* traveling by [plane, train, boat, bus, motorcycle, bicycle, etc.] (But one travels *in* an automobile.) □ *I hate riding on the train.* **3.** *prep.* near something; at the edge of [a body of water]. □ *My parents have some land on the lake.* **4.** *prep.* about someone or something. □ *I saw a movie on the life of Queen Victoria.* **5.** *prep.* [happening] at a specific time, identified by the date or the day. □ *I left for Florida on the 29th of October.* □ *John will arrive on Tuesday.* **6.** *prep.* as a member or part of some group. □ *I spoke to each member serving on the school board.* **7.** *adj.* operating; turned on ⑨. □ *Are the lights still on in the basement?* **8.** *adj.* still happening; not canceled; continuing as scheduled. □ *We're still on for dinner tomorrow, aren't we?* **9.** *adv.* so that something operates; so that something has the power to operate. □ *Mary switched the lights on when she entered the dark room.*



**once** ['wʌns] **1.** *adv.* one time. □ *I've only been to Mexico once, but I'd like to go back again.* **2.** *adv.* at a time in the past; formerly. □ *Once, Bill had brown hair, but now his hair is gray.*

**oncoming** ['ɔn kəm ɪŋ] *adj.* coming toward [oneself]; approaching. □ *The driver drove into the left lane and crashed into an oncoming car.*

**one** ['wʌn] **1.** 1. Go to four for senses and examples. **2.** *n.* a bill ③ or note ③ worth a dollar. □ *If I give you a five-dollar bill, will you give me five ones?* **3.** *adj.* happening on or at a particular time. (Prenominal only.) □ *One morning, I locked myself out of the house.* **4.** *adj.* united; together; joined. (Not prenominal.) □ *East and West Germany became one again in 1990.* **5.** *pron.* a person or thing that is referred to. □ *Those cookies look good. May I have one?* **6.** *pron.* you; anybody; a person. □ *One should brush one's teeth twice each day.*

**oneself** [wən 'sɛlf] **1.** *pron.* <the reflexive form of the pronoun one ⑥.> (Used when *one* is the subject of the sentence.) □ *One should not shave oneself with a dull razor.* **2. by oneself** *phr.* with the help of no one else. □ *This engine is simple enough to repair by oneself.* **3. by oneself** *phr.* with no one else present; alone. □ *If one lives by oneself, one probably does not need a five-bedroom house.*

**onion** ['ʌn jən] **1.** *n.* a plant with a large, round edible bulb and thin green stalks. □ *Bill pulled an onion from the ground by its stalk.* **2.** *n.* the edible bulb of ①, sometimes sliced or chopped. □ *The chef put grilled onions on my hamburger.* **3.** *adj.* made with or flavored with ②. □ *I was served some onion soup.*

**only** ['on li] **1.** *adj.* sole; single. (Prenominal only.) □ *This is the only house I've ever lived in.* **2.** *adv.* [this and] nothing more. (Note the position of only in the examples.) □ *The cat only sat on the mat and did nothing else.* □ *The cat sat only on the mat and nowhere else.* **3.** *conj.* except that. □ *I would buy a car, only I don't have any money.*

**onset** ['ɔn sɛt] *n.* the beginning of something; the start of something. □ *I know this is the onset of a major cold, because I am sneezing and feel terrible.*

**onstage** ['ɔn 'stedʒ] **1.** *adj.* located or happening on the part of a stage that an audience can see. □ *Members of the onstage chorus were dressed in blue robes.*

**2.** *adv.* on, to, or toward a part of the stage that an audience can see. □ *The actor said his line as he ran onstage.*

**onto** ['ɔn tu] *prep.* to a position that is on something. □ *The pie fell onto the floor.*

**onward** ['ɔn wɚd] *adv.* further in space or time; forward in space or time. □ *I walked onward toward the next town.*

**ooze** ['uz] **1.** *n.* mud; slime; a thick liquid. (No plural form.) □ *I cleaned the smelly ooze from the bottom of my refrigerator.* **2.** *iv.* to flow slowly, like mud or a very thick liquid; to seep out of a hole slowly. □ *The mud oozed up through the crack in the earth.*

**opaque** [o 'pek] **1.** *adj.* not able to be seen through; not allowing light to pass through; not clear. (Adv: *opaquely.*) □ *The opaque wall blocked all sunlight from entering the room.* **2.** *adj.* hard to understand. (Fig. on ①. Adv: *opaquely.*) □ *It's very hard to read this textbook because it's so opaque.*

**open** ['o pən] **1.** *adj.* not shut; not closed; not sealed. □ *The food in the open container started to spoil.* **2.** *adj.* allowing customers to enter; ready for business. □ *The new café will be open for business next week.* **3.** *adj.* not decided. □ *The open issue was debated for hours by the committee.* **4.** *adj.* available; free and not restricted. (Adv: *openly.*) □ *The citizens demanded open access to the city parks at all times.* **5.** *adj.* sincere; honest about one's feelings. (Adv: *openly.*) □ *John is very open about his feelings for Susan.* **6.** *tv.* to cause something to become ①; to allow a place to be entered into or exited from. □ *John opened the window so the bird could fly out of the room.* **7.** *tv.* to establish the beginning of something; to cause something to start. □ *The lawyer opened the trial by describing the crime.* **8.** *iv.* to be accessible; to become ready for business or use. □ *The new airport finally opened to the public after several delays.*

**opener** ['o pə nɚ] *n.* someone or something that opens something. □ *I removed the cap from the beer with a bottle opener.*

**opening** ['o pə nɪŋ] **1.** *n.* a way into a container, compartment, or room; a way through a wall or barrier. □ *The couch barely fit through the narrow opening to the room.* **2.** *n.* something that is available; a job that is available. □ *There's an opening for a waiter at that restaurant.* **3.** *n.* an opportunity to do something or say something. (Figurative on ①.) □ *When he stopped talking, it gave me an opening to present my ideas.* **4.** *adj.* at the beginning; the first; the earliest. □ *On opening night of the play, several critics were in the audience.*

**opera** ['ɑ prə] **1.** *n.* the branch of theater or music where lengthy performances include solo and choral singing, orchestra music, and sometimes dance. (No plural form.) □ *The professor contrasted opera with other music.* **2.** *n.* a presentation or performance of a musical production as in ①. □ *My favorite opera is* Madame Butterfly. □ *All the operas I like are sung in a foreign language.*

**operate** ['ɑp ə ret] **1.** *iv.* [for a machine or device] to work or function. □ *Why isn't this elevator operating?* **2.** *iv.* to perform surgery; to perform an operation. □ *That surgeon talks very little while he operates.* **3. operate on** someone or something *iv.* + *prep. phr.* to perform surgery on a certain part of the body or on someone. □ *The surgeons operated on the patient with stomach problems.* **4.** *tv.* to cause something to work or function; to direct or manage something. □ *Can you operate this electric drill?*

**operation** [ɑ pə 're ʃən] **1.** *n.* surgery; a medical procedure where something is done to the body, usually involving cutting. □ *During the operation, the patient's injury was repaired.* **2.** *n.* the

O

way something works; the way something is used. □ *My boss trained me in the operation of the equipment.*

**operator** ['ɑp ə ret ɚ] **1.** *n.* someone who operates a machine. □ *The operator must wear safety goggles at all times.* **2.** *n.* someone who handles telephone calls; the person one talks to when one dials "0" on a telephone. □ *The operator placed a collect call for me.*

**opinion** [ə 'pɪn jən] **1.** *n.* thought, ideas, or attitudes concerning someone or something. (Plural only when referring to different kinds, types, instances, or varieties.) □ *Are you expressing fact or only opinion?* 🄲 *My opinions about taxation are very different from John's.* **2.** *n.* advice from a professional or an expert. □ *That lawyer charges too much for simple legal opinions.*

**opossum** [ə 'pɑs əm] *n.* a small, gray, furry animal with a hairless, flexible tail. □ *I braked to avoid hitting the opossum that was crossing the road.*

**opponent** [ə 'pon ənt] *n.* someone who is on the opposite side in a contest, fight, or argument. □ *The senator convinced his opponent to join him in a debate.*

**opportunity** [ɑp ɚ 'tu nə ti] *n.* a good chance for doing something; a favorable time for doing something. □ *Winning the contest gave me the opportunity to quit my job.*

**oppose** [ə 'poz] *tv.* to be against someone or something; to fight against someone or something; to argue against someone or something. (Often passive.) □ *Our candidate was opposed by another candidate from another town.*

**opposite** ['ɑp ə sɪt] **1.** *adj.* completely different in at least one major respect. (Adv: *oppositely.*) □ *Taking the opposite side is easy for Bob. He loves to argue.* **2.** *adj.* of or about a location that is the farthest point away within a defined area. (Adv: *oppositely.*) □ *The plane I need to board is at the opposite end of the airport.* **3.** *prep.* across from someone or something; facing someone or something. □ *The bakery is opposite the church.* **4.** *n.* someone or something that is **opposite** ① someone or something else. □ *Anne is my opposite when it comes to most political issues.*

**opposite sex** ['ɑp ə sət 'sɛks] *n.* [from the point of view of a female] a male; [from the point of view of a male] a female. □ *Mary says that she just hates the opposite sex and will never get married.*

**opposition** [ɑp ə 'zɪ ʃən] **1.** *n.* a state of being against someone or something; resistance. (No plural form.) □ *The tax plan was met with strong opposition.* **2.** *n.* the people who are against something. (No plural form.) □ *The mayor met with the opposition to discuss their concerns.*

**oppress** [ə 'prɛs] *tv.* to rule someone or a group of people harshly or cruelly; to keep someone from succeeding. □ *The poor nation was oppressed by an evil tyrant.*

**optic** ['ɑp tɪk] *adj.* of or about the eye or vision. (Adv: *optically* [...ɪk li].) □ *My head injury caused severe optic problems.*

**optical** ['ɑp tɪ kəl] *adj.* of or about the eye or vision. (Adv: *optically* [...ɪk li].) □ *I was given an optical exam to determine my range of vision.*

**option** ['ɑp ʃən] *n.* a choice; something [else] that is available for choosing. □ *I examined all my options before making a decision.*

**or** ['or] **1.** *conj.* <a word used in a list of items to show a choice or difference.> □ *Would you like coffee, tea, or juice?* **2.** *conj.* otherwise; if not. □ *Take your vitamins, or you will become sick.* **3.** *conj.* that is to say. □ *10 is one-half, or 50%, of 20.*

**oral** ['or əl] **1.** *adj.* of or about the mouth. (Adv: *orally.*) □ *My cracked tooth was removed by an oral surgeon.* **2.** *adj.* spoken. (Adv: *orally.*) □ *The witness gave both a written and an oral statement to the police.*

**orange** ['or ɪndʒ] **1.** *n.* a color of the rainbow between red and yellow, and the color of ②. (Plural only when referring to different kinds, types, instances, or varieties.) □ *I decorated the room in orange and black for Halloween.* Ⓒ *We looked at samples of the various oranges, but decided that they were all too shocking.* **2.** *n.* a round, juicy citrus fruit—of the color ①—that grows on a tree. □ *You must peel an orange before eating it.* **3.** *adj.* of the color ①. □ *The invitations for the Halloween party were printed on orange paper.* **4.** *adj.* made with ②; flavored with ②. □ *I had a glass of orange juice for breakfast.*

**orbit** ['or bɪt] **1.** *n.* a pathway around a planet or a star, such as that taken by a planet, a moon, or a rocket. □ *Our planet is in an orbit around the sun.* **2.** *tv.* to move in a circle around a star or planet. □ *Earth orbits the sun every 365 days.* **3.** *iv.* to move in a circle around a star or planet. □ *Is the satellite orbiting yet?*

**orchard** ['or tʃɚd] *n.* a farm of fruit or nut trees. □ *The cherry orchard contains hundreds of trees.*

**orchestra** ['or kə strə] *n.* a group of musicians and the instruments they play, usually including strings. □ *Orchestras play symphonies and the music for operas and dance.*

**orchid** ['or kɪd] *n.* a flower with unusually shaped and brightly colored petals. □ *The gardener planted a row of orchids next to the porch.*

**ordain** [or 'den] **1.** *tv.* to confer the status of being a priest or a minister on someone. □ *Our minister was ordained after he graduated.* **2.** *tv.* to order something; to make something a law. (The object can be a clause with **that** ⑦.) □ *The legislature ordained that smoking in public places be made illegal.*

**ordeal** [or 'dil] *n.* a very difficult experience. □ *The soldier faced many ordeals during the war.*

**order** ['or dɚ] **1.** *n.* the sequence in which a series of things is arranged. □ *The records were filed in the order in which they were received.* **2.** *n.* a state of everything being in its proper place. (No plural form.) □ *The new office manager brought order to the messy filing system.* **3.** *n.* a state of being able to be used; condition. (No plural form. See also **out of order**.) □ *I expect my lawn mower to be returned to me in good order.* **4.** *n.* a state wherein people are following rules and behaving properly. (No plural form.) □ *The police restored order after the riot.* **5.** *n.* a command. □ *The children ignored my order to be quiet.* **6.** *n.* a request for certain goods or services. □ *The customer placed an order for an item that wasn't in stock.* **7.** *n.* one serving of a kind of food. □ *I'd like a large order of french fries, please.* **8.** *tv.* to request goods or services. □ *Mary ordered some skis from a catalog.* **9.** *tv.* to request a serving of food or a full meal. □ *Anne ordered a large pizza.* **10.** *tv.* to arrange someone or something into a certain sequence. □ *John ordered the cards according to the alphabet.* **11. in order to do something** *phr.* for the purpose of doing something; to permit something to happen; to allow the doing of something. □ *I opened the window in order to let some fresh air in.*

**orderly** ['or dɚ li] **1.** *adj.* neat; in order. □ *Mary was praised for her orderly work.* **2.** *n.* a hospital worker who assists doctors and nurses in caring for patients. □ *The doctor asked the orderly for some assistance.*

O

**ordinal numeral** AND **ordinal number** ['or dɪ nəl 'nu mə rəl, 'or dɪ nəl 'nʌm bɚ] *n.* the number used to show rank or position in a series, such as first, second, third, etc. (See also **cardinal numeral.**) □ *The ordinal numerals are used when stating the order of people or things.* □ *When the cardinal number is* ten, *the ordinal numeral is* tenth.

**ordinary** ['ord n nɛr i] *adj.* usual; common; typical; regular. (Adv: *ordinarily* [ord n 'nɛr ə li].) □ *The magician held up an ordinary deck of playing cards.*

**organ** ['or gən] **1.** *n.* a part of an animal that performs a specific function. □ *The eye is the organ of sight.* **2.** *n.* a musical instrument with keyboards that control the air flow into many pipes of different lengths, each sounding a different note. □ *Mr. Smith plays the organ at our church.*

**organism** ['or gə nɪz əm] *n.* a plant or an animal; a living thing. □ *Thousands of tiny organisms live in and on the human body.*



**organization** [or gə nə 'ze ʃən] *n.* a group of people, such as those in a club or society; a company; a department of government. □ *Since I belong to this organization, I have the right to vote for its president.*

**organize** ['or gə naɪz] **1.** *tv.* to arrange different parts in a way so that they work properly; to arrange different parts into a system. □ *Susan organized her boss's business calendar.* **2.** *tv.* to form an organization or meeting. □ *Tom organized a stamp-collecting club.* **3.** *iv.* to form a labor union. □ *Against management's wishes, the factory workers organized.*

**origin** ['or ə dʒən] *n.* the starting point; something that other things develop from. □ *The origin of this river is a spring up in the mountains.* □ *No one could remember the origin of the conflict between the two families.*

**original** [ə 'rɪdʒ ə nəl] **1.** *adj.* not copied or based on something else. □ *The students had to write an original short story for class.* **2.** *adj.* first; earliest. (Adv: *originally.*) □ *The antique doll was still in its original package.* **3.** *n.* something that copies are made from; the first example of something that other examples are based on. □ *This statue is a poor copy of the original.*

**originate** [ə 'rɪdʒ ə net] **1.** *tv.* to cause something to exist; to found something; to establish something, such as an organization. □ *The restaurant originated a new kind of sandwich that soon became popular throughout the country.* **2.** *iv.* to start; to begin. □ *Flight 720, which originated in St. Louis, will arrive in 5 minutes.*

**orphan** ['or fən] **1.** *n.* a young child whose parents are dead or missing. □ *My brother and I were both orphans.* **2.** *tv.* to cause someone to become ①. (Typically passive.) □ *Jimmy was orphaned when his parents were killed in an accident.*

**ostrich** ['ɑs trɪtʃ] *n.* a large bird that runs very quickly but cannot fly. □ *Ostriches occur naturally in Africa.*

**other** ['ʌð ɚ] **1.** *pron.* the second of two; the remaining thing or person. □ *John helped one of the twins, and I helped the other.* **2.** *adj.* <the adj. use of ①.> □ *I'll take one of the twins in my car, and you take the other one.* **3.** *adj.* more of the same or similar kind of thing or people. □ *Put this book on the shelf next to the other ones.* □ *Would you like chocolate, or would you prefer some other flavor?*

**otherwise** ['ʌð ɚ waɪz] **1.** *conj.* or else; or it is that. □ *You'd better quit smoking. Otherwise, you might get cancer.* **2.** *adv.* in another way; in a different way; differently. □ *Bill passed time by watching TV. John passed time otherwise.* **3.** *adv.* in every regard except [this one]; in every way except [this one]. □ *Today*

*I lost my favorite hat. Otherwise, it's been a great day.*

**otter** ['ɑt ɚ] **1.** *n.* a long, thin, furry animal that lives in and near water, and eats fish. ☐ *The hunter trapped the otter for its fur.* **2.** *n.* the skin and fur of ①. (No plural form.) ☐ *Nothing looks better in otter than an otter.* **3.** *adj.* made from ②. ☐ *She owned an otter coat made from the skin of 30 otters.*

**ought** ['ɔt] **1. ought to** do something *aux.* + *inf.* have to do something; obliged to do something. ☐ *You ought to go home after school.* **2. ought to** do something *aux.* + *inf.* likely to happen; should happen. ☐ *That pumpkin ought to weigh ten pounds.*

**ounce** ['ɑʊns] **1.** *n.* a unit of measurement of weight equal to 1⁄16 of a pound or about 28 grams. ☐ *I need additional postage because the letter weighs two ounces.* **2.** *n.* a unit of measurement of liquid equal to 1⁄16 of a pint or 1⁄8 of a cup. ☐ *This container holds 32 fluid ounces.*

**our** ['ɑɚ] **1.** *pron.* <the first-person plural possessive pronoun including the speaker or writer.> (Used as a modifier before a noun.) ☐ *Our house is seventy years old.* **2. ours** *pron.* <the first-person plural possessive pronoun.> (Used in place of a noun.) ☐ *John's house is white, but ours is blue.*

**ourselves** ['ɑɚ 'sɛlvz] **1.** *pron.* <the first-person plural reflexive pronoun.> ☐ *Let's keep this secret to ourselves.* **2.** *pron.* <a form used to emphasize we.> ☐ *We ourselves are to thank for the changes that have been made.* **3. by ourselves** *phr.* with the help of no one else. ☐ *Can we lift this by ourselves, or do we need some help?* **4. by ourselves** *phr.* with no one else present; alone. ☐ *We like to eat by ourselves, so we can talk about private matters.*

**oust** ['ɑʊst] *tv.* to get rid of someone or something; to remove someone or something by force. ☐ *The landlord ousted the tenant who never paid rent.*

**out** ['ɑʊt] **1.** *adv.* away from a place; not in a place; not in the usual condition; not at the usual position; to a point beyond a limit. ☐ *Get out and stay out!* **2.** *adv.* in the open air; into the open air; outside; not inside. ☐ *Let's go out before it gets dark.* **3.** *adj.* not at the usual position; to a point beyond a limit; not at home; not at work. (Not prenominal.) ☐ *Mr. Jones is not here. He is out.* **4.** *adj.* no longer in style; old-fashioned. (Not prenominal.) ☐ *The magazine listed which fashions were in and which were out.* **5.** *adj.* not a possible choice. (Not prenominal. Informal.) ☐ *Pizza is out. Anne doesn't like it.* **6.** *adj.* no longer burning; no longer giving off light. (Not prenominal.) ☐ *The bathroom light is out. Do you have any more bulbs?* **7.** *adj.* not working; not functioning properly. (Not prenominal.) ☐ *John lay in bed because his back was out.* **8.** *adj.* [in baseball, of someone] no longer permitted to play in a particular turn. (Not prenominal.) ☐ *If you get three strikes, then you're out.* **9.** *adj.* used up; no longer having more of a substance. (Not prenominal.) ☐ *Sorry, there is no more. We're out.* **10.** *adj.* unconscious; not aware; not awake. (Not prenominal.) ☐ *After getting hit in the head, Bill was out for a few seconds.*

**outcast** ['ɑʊt kæst] *n.* someone who has been rejected, abandoned, or deserted. ☐ *When Bill insulted all of his friends, he became an outcast among them.*

**outcome** ['ɑʊt kəm] *n.* the final result; the effect of something. ☐ *The newspaper reported the outcome of the meeting.*

**outcry** ['ɑʊt krɑɪ] **1.** *n.* a strong protest; an uproar. ☐ *There was an outcry when the respected leader was arrested.* **2.** *n.* a loud cry. ☐ *I heard the outcry of the people trapped in the wreckage.*

O

**outdoor** [ɑʊt 'dor] *adj.* not inside; not in a building; used or done **outdoors.** □ *I bought some outdoor furniture for my back porch.*

**outdoors** ['ɑʊt 'dorz] *adv.* in or into the open air; not inside a building. □ *According to company policy, employees must go outdoors to smoke.*

**outer** ['ɑʊ tɚ] **1.** *adj.* farther away from the center. □ *The outer particles of an atom are called electrons.* **2.** *adj.* exterior; on the outside. □ *My house's outer walls need to be painted.*

**outer space** ['ɑʊ tɚ 'spes] *n.* the universe beyond the atmosphere of Earth. (No plural form.) □ *The strange ship came from outer space.*

**outgrew** [ɑʊt 'gru] pt of **outgrow.**

**outgrow** [ɑʊt 'gro] **1.** *tv., irreg.* to no longer fit into one's clothes because one has grown. (Pt: **outgrew;** pp: **outgrown.**) □ *Susie has outgrown last year's coat.* **2.** *tv., irreg.* to become too mature to do certain things meant for younger children. (Fig. on ①.) □ *I outgrew my interest in dolls by the time I entered high school.* **3.** *tv., irreg.* to grow to be taller or to grow faster than someone else. □ *Mary outgrew her mother by four inches.*

**outgrown** [ɑʊt 'gron] pp of **outgrow.**

**outlaw** ['ɑʊt lɔ] **1.** *tv.* to make something illegal; to declare that something is against the law. □ *Some people would like to outlaw the sale of liquor.* **2.** *n.* a criminal. □ *The sheriff put the outlaw in jail.*

**outlay** ['ɑʊt le] *n.* money spent for a certain reason; time or energy spent for a certain reason. □ *Our annual outlay for heating has grown greater and greater.*

**outlet** ['ɑʊt lɛt] **1.** *n.* the socket in a wall where something can be plugged in for electrical power. □ *I needed an extension cord to plug the lamp into the outlet.* **2.** *n.* a way out for something. □ *A chimney is a kind of an outlet for smoke from a fireplace.* **3.** *n.* a way to let one's feelings out; a way to use one's creativity. (Fig. on ②.) □ *Boxing is an outlet for Bill's aggression.*

**outline** ['ɑʊt lɑɪn] **1.** *n.* the shape of someone or something; the border of someone or something. □ *This map shows the outline of the Florida coast.* **2.** *n.* a list of the main topics of a speech or text; a plan. □ *John wrote a detailed outline before writing his paper.* **3.** *tv.* to draw the shape of someone or something; to draw the border of someone or something. □ *The police outlined the shape of the murder victim on the street with chalk.* **4.** *tv.* to list the main topics of a speech or text. □ *David outlined the major topics in his report.* **5.** *tv.* to describe a plan. □ *The tyrant outlined his plan to take over the world.*

**outlive** [ɑʊt 'lɪv] *tv.* to live longer than someone else; to work, function, or last longer than something else. □ *My car outlived Bill's car by 30,000 miles.*

**outlook** ['ɑʊt lʊk] **1.** *n.* an imagined view of the future course that something may take. (No plural form.) □ *Mary analyzed her company's outlook for the next 10 years.* **2.** *n.* the way of looking at things that happen. □ *Talking to Sue is depressing because she has a very negative outlook.*

**out of order** ['ɑʊt əv 'or dɚ] *phr.* not working; not functioning; broken. □ *I read a book last night because my television was out of order.*

**output** ['ɑʊt pʊt] **1.** *n.* the amount of something that is made; production. (No plural form.) □ *The boss recorded the workers' output in the computer.* **2.** *n.* something that is produced. (No plural form.) □ *The oil well's output was carried to a huge tank.* **3.** *n.* the energy that is produced by a machine. (No plural form.) □ *The power plant's output provided electricity for the nearby towns.* **4.** *n.* information that is produced by a computer. (No plural form.) □ *The researcher analyzed the output from the computer program.*

**outrage** ['aʊt redʒ] **1.** *n.* a very cruel or horrible deed. □ *The terrorist attack was a horrible outrage.* **2.** *n.* anger caused by a very cruel or horrible action. (No plural form.) □ *There was a lot of outrage over the terrorist attack.* **3.** *tv.* to anger someone greatly by doing a very cruel or horrible deed. □ *The terrorist attack outraged the government and the people.*

**outside** ['aʊt 'saɪd] **1.** *n.* the part of something that faces away from the center of something; the surface of something that is out. (Also plural with the same meaning, but not countable.) □ *John painted the outside of his house.* **2.** *adj.* on ①; external; not inside a building. □ *The paint on the outside walls is starting to peel.* **3.** *adj.* farther from the center than something else. □ *John's outside layers of clothing were totally wet.* **4.** *adj.* not associated with the inner group. (Prenominal only.) □ *The strict parents sheltered their children from all outside influences.* **5.** *adv.* to or toward ①; on or at ①; in or into the outdoors. □ *Why don't you go outside and play?* **6.** *prep.* past the limit of something; beyond something; on or toward the **outside** ① of something. □ *The package was left outside my front door.*

**outward** ['aʊt wɚd] **1.** *adv.* away; away from some place; toward the outside. □ *The window opened outward, allowing us to leave it open when it rained.* **2.** *adj.* of or about one's appearance instead of one's feelings or thoughts. (Adv: *outwardly.*) □ *Mary's outward expression was one of joy.*

**outweigh** [aʊt 'we] **1.** *tv.* to weigh more than someone or something else. □ *The older boxer outweighs the younger one by five pounds.* **2.** *tv.* to be more important than someone or something else. (Fig. on ①.) □ *My boss's opinion outweighs mine.*

**outwit** [aʊt 'wɪt] *tv.* to be more clever than someone and therefore win at something. □ *My brother outwitted me at a game of chess.*

**oval** ['o vəl] **1.** *adj.* shaped like an egg; almost shaped like a circle, but flatter. (Adv: *ovally.*) □ *Mary served the turkey on an oval platter.* **2.** *n.* a shape like that of an egg; the shape of a flattened circle. □ *The lenses of my glasses are shaped like ovals.*

**oven** ['ʌv ən] **1.** *n.* an appliance or enclosed space within an appliance that can be heated to cook food. □ *I heated the oven to 350 degrees before baking the cake.* **2.** *n.* an appliance that is heated to dry and harden pottery or other objects. □ *The clay pots dried in the oven and became very hard.*

**over** ['o vɚ] **1.** *prep.* above someone or something; higher than someone or something. □ *I mounted the clock on the wall over the bookshelf.* **2.** *prep.* on someone or something; covering someone or something. □ *Anne places a cloth over the bird cage at night.* **3.** *prep.* across something; from one side of something to the other; above and to the other side of something. □ *Hold your hands over the fire until they are warm, but don't burn yourself.* **4.** *prep.* off and down from something. □ *The mouse fell over the edge of the shelf.* **5.** *prep.* during something; throughout some period of time. □ *I lived in Seattle over the summer.* **6.** *prep.* more than a certain measurement; greater than something. (Some people prefer *more than* to **over** in this sense.) □ *You must be a resident for over 30 days in order to vote here.* **7.** *prep.* with something noisy in the background. □ *It's hard to hear over all the noise from the airport.* **8.** *prep.* from [the radio, the Internet, or a telephone].

O

□ *I get my news over the Internet.* **9.** *prep.* covering the surface of someone or something. □ *I sprayed red paint over the entire wall.* **10.** *adv.* at some other place; on the other side of something. □ *The crayons are over by the table.* **11.** *adv.* down; so that a surface faces down. □ *The upright book fell over onto its front.* **12.** *adv.* again. □ *After I was interrupted, I started over.* □ *I practiced the song over and over until I could sing it well.* **13.** *prefix* too; too much. (Usually in a compound.) □ *The reporter's comments on the problem were oversimplified.* **14.** *adj.* done; finished; at the end. (Not prenominal.) □ *When the game was over, the players went to the locker room.*

**overate** [o vɚ 'et] pt of **overeat.**

**overcame** [o vɚ 'kem] pt of **overcome.**

**overcharge** [o vɚ 'tʃɑrdʒ] *tv.* to charge someone more money for something than it really costs. □ *The store manager was fired for overcharging customers.*

**overcoat** ['o vɚ kot] *n.* a heavy coat that is worn over other clothes. □ *In the spring, I took my overcoat to the cleaners.*

**overcome** [o vɚ 'kʌm] **1.** *tv., irreg.* to defeat someone or something; to fight and win against someone or something. (Pt: **overcame;** pp: *overcome.*) □ *I overcame my fear of flying by taking several short flights last month.* **2.** *tv., irreg.* to cause someone to become helpless, especially because of emotion. □ *Shame overcame the accused criminal.*

**overdose** ['o vɚ dos] **1.** *n.* a large dose of a drug that causes someone to faint or die. □ *John committed suicide by taking an overdose of medicine.* **2.** *iv.* to become unconscious or die because one has taken too many drugs or too much medicine. □ *Mary accidentally overdosed and nearly died.*

**overeat** [o vɚ 'it] *iv., irreg.* to eat too much. (Pt: **overate;** pp: **overeaten.**) □ *I always overeat at Thanksgiving because there is so much food.*

**overeaten** [o vɚ 'it n] pp of **overeat.**

**overhead** **1.** ['o vɚ hɛd] *n.* the costs of running a business; business expenses. (No plural form. Treated as singular.) □ *The company reduced overhead by moving to a smaller office.* **2.** ['o vɚ hɛd] *adj.* <the adj. use of ①.> □ *The accountant included overhead costs in the budget.* **3.** ['o vɚ hɛd] *adj.* above one's head. (Prenominal only.) □ *Fluorescent overhead lighting is too harsh for an art gallery.* **4.** ['o vɚ 'hɛd] *adv.* above one's head; in the air; passing through the air. □ *As the clouds passed overhead, it started to rain.*

**overheat** [o vɚ 'hit] **1.** *iv.* to become too hot; to break or stop working because of being worked too hard. □ *The hair dryer overheated because I had it on too long.* **2.** *tv.* to cause something to become too hot. □ *I overheated the engine when I drove through the desert.*

**overkill** ['o vɚ kɪl] *n.* the condition of having or doing more than is necessary. (No plural form.) □ *Having three different bands at the wedding reception was overkill.*

**overlap** **1.** [o vɚ 'læp] *iv.* [for parts of two or more things] to happen at the same time. □ *My class and the club meeting overlap by fifteen minutes, so I will arrive at the meeting late.* **2.** [o vɚ 'læp] *iv.* [for parts of two or more things] to cover the same space. □ *The bedroom carpeting overlaps with the carpeting in the hallway.* **3.** [o vɚ 'læp] *tv.* [for something] to partially cover something [else]. □ *The bedroom carpeting overlaps the carpeting in the hallway.* **4.** [o vɚ 'læp] *tv.* [for something] to begin before something else finishes; to place the beginning of something over the end of something else. □ *My math class overlaps my English class from noon to 12:20.* **5.** ['o vɚ læp] *n.* the extra part of something that extends over something else. (No plural form.) ☐ *I had to trim off the overlap.* **6.** ['o vɚ læp] *n.* the amount by which things **overlap** ① or ②. (No plural form.) ☐ *There was a two-day overlap between the start of Mary's term and the end of mine.*

**overlook 1.** ['o vɚ lʊk] *n.* a high place that provides a good view of a lower place. ☐ *The hikers walked up to the overlook to look at the river.* **2.** [o vɚ 'lʊk] *tv.* to forget or neglect something. ☐ *When Tom was watering the plants, he overlooked the small one by the window.* **3.** [o vɚ 'lʊk] *tv.* to ignore something. ☐ *My boss overlooked my good work and focused on my mistakes.*

**overnight 1.** ['o vɚ nɑɪt] *adj.* done during the night; lasting through the night. ☐ *The overnight bus trip is half the cost of a daytime trip.* **2.** [o vɚ 'nɑɪt] *adv.* through the night; during the night. ☐ *If you travel overnight, the bus fare is cheaper.* **3.** [o vɚ 'nɑɪt] *adv.* in just one night. ☐ *The new shopping mall seemed to appear overnight.* ☐ *We finished the report overnight and were ready for the meeting the next day.*

**oversaw** [o vɚ 'sɔ] pt of **oversee**.

**overseas** [o vɚ 'siz] **1.** *adv.* across the sea; on the other side of the ocean. ☐ *Anne traveled overseas from New York to London.* **2.** *adj.* done, used, or about a place on the other side of the ocean. ☐ *I placed an overseas phone call to my friend in Paris.*

**oversee** [o vɚ 'si] *tv., irreg.* to supervise someone or something; to watch over someone or something so that something is done properly. (Pt: **oversaw**; pp: **overseen**.) ☐ *The prison workers were overseen by guards.*

**overseen** [o vɚ 'sin] pp of **oversee**.

**oversight** ['o vɚ sɑɪt] *n.* something that is not noticed or thought of. ☐ *Due to an oversight in planning, I missed two appointments.*

**oversleep** [o vɚ 'slip] *iv., irreg.* to sleep longer than one wanted to; to sleep too long. (Pt/pp: **overslept**.) ☐ *John was late for work because he had overslept.*

**overslept** [o vɚ 'slɛpt] pt/pp of **oversleep**.

**overthrew** [o vɚ 'θru] pt of **overthrow**.

**overthrow** [o vɚ 'θro] *tv., irreg.* to remove someone or something from power; to seize power from a government. (Pt: **overthrew**; pp: **overthrown**.) ☐ *The opposition sought to overthrow the government.*

**overthrown** [o vɚ 'θron] pp of **overthrow**.

**overtime** ['o vɚ tɑɪm] **1.** *n.* time at work past the time when one normally finishes. (No plural form.) ☐ *My boss asked me if I could work some overtime on Saturday.* **2.** *n.* money earned by working past the time when one normally finishes. (No plural form.) ☐ *Overtime is taxed at the same rate as other earnings.* **3.** *n.* [in a sporting event] an extra amount of playing time allowed in order to break a tie score. (No plural form.) ☐ *Because the teams were tied, the game went into overtime.* **4.** *adv.* past the hours when one normally finishes. ☐ *I'm paid double when I work overtime.* **5.** *adj.* of or about working extra as in ①. ☐ *The government does not tax overtime wages at a higher rate.*

**overture** ['o vɚ tʃɚ] **1.** *n.* the piece of music at the beginning of an opera, symphony, ballet, etc., that introduces key melodies and themes. ☐ *The overture of a musical usually includes parts of songs from the musical.* **2.** *n.* the communication of an intention to make an offer of something. ☐ *An overture of peace was sent by messenger to the president.*

**owe** ['o] **1.** *tv.* to be in debt for a sum of money; to have to pay someone for something. ☐ *John owes his sister a lot of money.* **2.** *tv.* to be obliged to give someone something. ☐ *I owe Bill a dinner, because he paid for my dinner last night.* **3. owing to** something *phr.* because of something; due to the fact of something. ☐ *We were late owing to the heavy traffic.*

**owl** ['ɑʊl] *n.* a bird that has large eyes that face the front, a short, curved beak, and is active at night. ☐ *The hoots of the owls scared the young children.*

**own** ['on] **1.** *tv.* to possess something; to have something as a belonging. ☐ *My parents own a cabin on the lake.* **2.** *adj.* belonging to oneself or itself. ☐ *I can't help Jane with her work. That's her own problem.* **3.** *adj.* <a form indicating something already mentioned as belonging to oneself or itself.> ☐ *That house is my brother's, but this one is my own.*

**owner** ['o nɚ] *n.* someone who owns something. ☐ *The police officer asked to speak to the owner of the house.*

O

**ownership** ['o nɚ ʃɪp] *n.* the state of being an owner; the right one has to own something. (No plural form.) ☐ *The ownership of the farm was disputed in court.*

**ox** ['ɑks] *n., irreg.* an adult male of a kind of cattle. (An **ox** has been made unable to breed. Pl: **oxen.**) ☐ *The farmer put a yoke on the oxen.*

**oxen** ['ɑk sən] pl of **ox.**

**oxygen** ['ɑks ɪ dʒən] *n.* a gas that makes up about 20% of the air we breathe. (No plural form.) ☐ *We cannot live without breathing oxygen.* ☐ *The atomic number for oxygen is 8, and its symbol is O.*

**oyster** ['ɔɪs tɚ] **1.** *n.* a small sea creature that lives between two hinged shells and sometimes produces pearls. ☐ *Thousands of oysters are harvested from this bay.* **2.** *n.* ① used as food. ☐ *We ordered oysters as an appetizer before our meal.*

**ozone** ['o zon] *n.* a kind of oxygen produced when an electrical spark, such as lightning, passes through the air. (No plural form.) ☐ *Sometimes you can smell ozone after lightning has struck.*

**pace** ['pes] **1.** *n.* the speed at which someone or something moves. (No plural form.) □ *The last hour of the day crept by at a slow pace.* **2.** *n.* the distance of one step when running or walking. □ *I walked two paces behind the person in front of me.* **3.** *iv.* to walk back and forth slowly and regularly. □ *The prisoner paced back and forth in his jail cell.*

**pack** ['pæk] **1.** *n.* a group of things that have been placed together—in a case, for example—so they can be carried. □ *Anne took a pack of gum from her purse.* **2.** *n.* a group of animals that live, hunt, and travel together. □ *A pack of wild dogs roamed through the park.* **3.** *tv.* to fill a container completely. □ *Bill carefully packed the box until it was full.* **4.** *tv.* to gather, assemble, and arrange things and place them in a space or container. □ *I packed the things into the box.*

**package** ['pæk ɪdʒ] **1.** *n.* a group of things that are wrapped together or boxed; a container in which goods are sold or shipped. □ *These cupcakes are sold in a package of four.* **2.** *n.* a parcel, especially one that is wrapped in paper or something similar. □ *There is a package for you on your desk.* **3.** *tv.* to place something in a container, especially to make it available for sale. □ *Most kinds of breakfast cereal are packaged in cardboard boxes.*

**pact** ['pækt] *n.* an agreement; a treaty. □ *Bill and John made a pact to help each other as much as possible.*

**pad** ['pæd] **1.** *n.* a small cushion or mass of soft material used to protect something, make something comfortable, absorb fluid, or give something a certain shape. □ *I removed the makeup from my face with a cotton pad.* **2.** *n.* a tablet of paper; a stack of pieces of paper that are glued together along one edge. □ *The investigator wrote some information on her note pad.* **3.** *iv.* to walk softly and very quietly. □ *The cat padded across the carpet to its favorite chair and went to sleep.* **4.** *tv.* to make a movie, book, program, etc., longer by adding extra words, longer pauses, extra performance material, etc. □ *John padded his term paper by writing* very *before every adjective.* □ *The movie was padded with three long dance numbers.*

**paddle** ['pæd l] **1.** *n.* a kind of oar used to steer and move a canoe or other small boat. □ *Mary splashed water on me with her paddle.* **2.** *n.* a round or long flat object used to spank someone. □ *Jimmy started to behave himself when his father brought out the paddle.* **3.** *tv.* to move a canoe with ①. □ *Bill paddled the boat against the current.* **4.** *tv.* to spank someone with ② or with the hand. □ *The principal threatened to paddle the problem student.* **5.** *iv.* to propel [something] with a paddle. □ *John paddled against the current.*

**pagan** ['pe gən] **1.** *n.* someone whose religion is not Christianity, Islam, or Judaism; someone who has no religion. □ *Some groups of pagans worshiped nature in special ceremonies.* **2.** *adj.* of, by, for, or about ①. □ *Tom claimed the ceremony was held to honor a pagan god.*

**page** ['pedʒ] **1.** *n.* one sheet of paper in a book. □ *Mary placed the bookmark between two pages.* **2.** *n.* one side of one sheet of paper in a book. □ *I wrote some notes in the margin of the page.* **3.** *n.* a sheet of paper suitable for writing or printing or having writing or printing.

P

□ *A page of music fell from my music stand.* **4.** *n.* a signal or message that someone has a message or a waiting telephone call, especially a beep from a pager. □ *John responded to the page by calling back on his cellular phone.* **5.** *tv.* to alert someone that a message or telephone call is waiting. □ *The nurse paged Dr. Jones for a phone call.*

**pager** ['pe dʒɚ] *n.* an electronic device that makes a signal to alert someone to a waiting message or telephone call. □ *My pager signaled me during the meeting.*

**paid** ['ped] **1.** pt/pp of pay. **2.** *adj.* hired; employed; receiving money. □ *There aren't any paid employees here. We're all volunteers.*

**pail** ['pel] **1.** *n.* a bucket; a container without a lid and with a curved handle that connects to opposite sides of the rim. □ *Jimmy took a plastic pail and a small shovel to the beach.* **2.** *n.* the contents of ①. □ *Jimmy emptied a pail of sand onto the beach.*

**pain** ['pen] *n.* hurt or ache caused by injury, sickness, or mental distress. (Plural only when referring to different kinds, types, instances, or varieties.) □ *How much pain should I expect after the operation, Doctor?* Ⓒ *Too much food gives me severe pains in the stomach.*

**painkiller** ['pen kɪl ɚ] *n.* a type of a medicine or drug that ends or relieves pain. □ *Do you have any painkillers? I've got a really bad headache.*

**paint** ['pent] **1.** *n.* a colored liquid that is spread on a surface to give the surface color and protection and that gets hard when it dries. (Plural only when referring to different kinds, types, instances, or varieties.) □ *Don't lean against this door. The paint is still wet.* Ⓒ *The two major paints, latex and oil based, each has its advantages.* **2.** *tv.* to cover something with ①, using a brush or something similar. □ *Jane painted the walls in her bedroom blue.* **3.** *tv.* to make a picture of someone or something using ①. □ *Mary painted flowers on the canvas.* **4.** *iv.* to cover walls or other objects with ①. □ *If the workers paint today, can I move into the apartment tomorrow?* **5.** *iv.* to make pictures with ①. □ *The successful artist painted for a living.*

**paintbrush** ['pent 'brʌʃ] *n.* a brush used to apply paint to a surface. □ *The artist used a tiny paintbrush to paint the details.*

**painting** ['pen tɪŋ] **1.** *n.* the art and study of making pictures with paint. (No plural form.) □ *The art school offered night courses in painting and sculpture.* **2.** *n.* a picture that is made with paint. □ *A painting of my family hangs in the living room.*

**pair** ['pɛr] **1.** *n.* a set of two similar or matching things; two people or two things. □ *I need a new pair of shoes.* □ *Bob and Mary are an interesting pair.* **2.** *n.* [in card games] two cards with the same number or value. □ *The card player quit because he had only one pair and the cards had a low value.* **3.** *tv.* to sort or order things or people into pairs ①. □ *The dance instructor paired the two remaining students.*

**pajamas** [pə 'dʒɑ məz] **1.** *n.* clothes worn in bed or worn at night before one goes to bed. (Treated as plural. Number is expressed by *pair(s) of pajamas.*) □ *We rushed out of the burning house in our pajamas.* **2. pajama** *adj.* of, by, for, or about ①. □ *Jimmy always leaves his pajama pants on the floor.*

**pal** ['pæl] *n.* a friend; a chum. (Informal.) □ *Would you be a pal and lend me some money until Friday?*

**palace** ['pæl ɪs] *n.* a very large, luxurious house, especially one where a king, queen, or important political leader lives or once lived. □ *The ruler's palace has more than one hundred rooms.*

**pale** ['pel] **1.** *adj.* having a lighter color than usual; faded. (Adv: *palely.* Comp: *paler;* sup: *palest.*) □ *Our kitchen is painted pale yellow.* **2.** *iv.* to become lighter in color; to whiten or weaken in color; to fade. □ *The flower was red in the center, but it paled to pink around the edges.* **3.** *iv.* [for someone] to become ① and appear faint. □ *After hearing the bad news, Anne paled and fainted.* **4.** *iv.* [for something] to appear to be weak or inadequate. □ *Bob's sloppy work pales in comparison with David's effort.*

**palm** ['pɑm] **1.** *n.* the front of the hand between the wrist and the bottom of the fingers. □ *I applauded so hard that my palms hurt.* **2.** *n.* a tree with a long trunk and long, pointed leaves at the top attached to a hard stem. (Short for **palm tree.**) □ *The beach is lined with palms, and the water is blue and inviting.* **3.** *tv.* to hide something in one's **palm** ①. □ *The shoplifter palmed an expensive watch at the jewelry store.*

**palm tree** ['pɑm tri] *n.* a tree with a long trunk that has no branches and long, pointed leaves attached to a hard stem. (Can be shortened to **palm.**) □ *Many streets in Los Angeles are shaded by palm trees.*

**pan** ['pæn] **1.** *n.* a wide, shallow vessel used for cooking. □ *When I cooked the meat, it stuck to the bottom of the pan.* **2.** *tv.* to give a bad review about a movie, book, or play; to criticize something harshly. □ *The newspapers panned the mayor's plans to raise taxes.* **3.** *iv.* [for a camera] to move while filming, traveling over a scene as one's eyes might move. □ *The camera panned slowly along the row of prisoners, showing each one's sad face.*

**pancake** ['pæn kek] *n.* a thin, round cake made of flour, eggs, and milk that is cooked on both sides. (**Pancakes** can include other ingredients.) □ *Today's breakfast special is apple pancakes.*

**pane** ['pen] *n.* a section of glass in a window or door. □ *The thief broke the pane in order to unlock the door.*

**panel** ['pæn əl] **1.** *n.* a thin, flat square or rectangular section of hard material. □ *The carpenter nailed panels of wood to the beams.* **2.** *n.* a group of people who are selected to talk about something or judge someone or something. □ *A panel of experts discussed the crisis on the news program.* **3.** *tv.* to cover the walls of a room with ①. □ *My bedroom had been paneled with solid oak years ago.*

**panic** ['pæn ɪk] **1.** *n.* a fear that is out of control; a sense of terror. (No plural form.) □ *Panic seized the entire population after the earthquake.* **2.** *iv., irreg.* to feel ①; to experience fear that is frantic and out of control. (Pt/pp: **panicked.** Present participle: *panicking.*) □ *When the airplane lost power, many passengers panicked and began screaming.* **3.** *tv., irreg.* to cause someone or some creature to experience ①. □ *The earthquake panicked the people inside the tall building.*

**panicked** ['pæn ɪkt] pt/pp of **panic.**

**pant** ['pænt] **1.** *iv.* to make quick, shallow breaths, as an overheated dog does. □ *Bill panted for several minutes after running up the stairs.* **2.** *n.* a gasp; a quick, shallow breath. □ *He was so exhausted that his breathing was only a series of quick pants.* **3. pants** *n.* trousers; clothing worn below the waist, having a separate tube, hole, or compartment for each leg. (Treated as plural. Number is expressed with *pair(s) of pants.* Also countable.) □ *Bill tried on three pairs of pants at the clothing store.* Ⓒ *He packed four pants and three shirts.*

**pantry** ['pæn tri] *n.* a small room near a kitchen, where pots, pans, dishes, silverware, tablecloths, food, and other kitchen items are kept. □ *The cook went to the pantry to get a bag of flour.*

**panty** ['pæn ti] **1. panties** *n.* a pair of women's underpants. (Treated as plural. Number is expressed with *pair(s) of panties.* Also countable.) □ *Jane likes lacy panties made of silk.* 🄲 *She packed four panties and three blouses.* **2.** *adj.* <the adj. use of ①.> □ *There was a panty sale at the department store last week, so I bought a dozen.*

**pantyhose** ['pæn ti hoz] *n.* a garment that is a combination of long, sheer stockings extending from a pair of panties. (No plural form. Treated as plural, but not countable. Number is expressed with *pair(s) of pantyhose.*) □ *Mary snagged her pantyhose on the edge of the car door.*

**paper** ['pe pɚ] **1.** *n.* processed fiber and other substances, pressed into sheets, used for writing, printing, drawing on, and other things. (No plural form. Number is usually expressed with *piece(s)* or *sheet(s) of paper.*) □ *Wood fiber is used in the making of paper.* **2. papers** *n.* documents; sheets of ① in groups or stacks, bearing information. (Treated as plural, but not countable.) □ *The papers concerning the project are supposed to be in the filing cabinet.* **3. papers** *n.* documents that prove who one is; one's passport or visa, carried while visiting a foreign country. (Treated as plural, but not countable.) □ *The police officer asked to look at the tourists' papers.* **4.** *n.* **wallpaper**; decorated paper that is glued to walls. (No plural form.) □ *Bob put the new paper up in strips, carefully matching the pattern at each edge.* **5.** *n.* a newspaper. □ *Anne read the morning paper during breakfast.* **6.** *n.* an article; an essay. □ *Mary went to the library to work on her paper for history class.* **7.** *adj.* made from ①. □ *At the picnic, we put our food on paper plates.* **8.** *tv.* to cover something with wallpaper. □ *Anne papered the kitchen walls instead of painting them.*

P

**paper clip** ['pep ɚ 'klɪp] *n.* a device made of bent wire that can hold a few sheets of paper together. □ *I keep a little bowl of paper clips on my desk.*

**paperweight** ['pe pɚ wet] *n.* a heavy object placed on a stack of papers to keep them from blowing away. □ *When I opened the window, I had to set a paperweight on my papers.*

**parachute** ['pɛr ə ʃut] **1.** *n.* a large bowl-shaped piece of fabric attached to and supporting someone who jumps from an airplane or some other very high place. □ *The soldier's parachute got tangled in some tree branches as he landed.* **2.** *iv.* to drift downward, wearing a parachute. □ *When Tom parachuted from the top of the tower, he was arrested.*

**parade** [pə 'red] **1.** *n.* a public event where people march or ride down a street with people watching from both sides. □ *The parade was canceled because it rained.* **2.** *iv.* to march somewhere in ①. □ *A few local politicians paraded down the avenue as part of a holiday parade.* **3.** *tv.* to make someone march in front of people. □ *The terrorist paraded the hostages in front of the reporters.*

**paradise** ['pɛr ə dɑɪs] **1.** *n.* heaven. (No plural form.) □ *The minister talked to his congregation about paradise.* **2.** *n.* somewhere on earth that seems as lovely and wonderful as ①. (No plural form.) □ *The beautiful Caribbean island was paradise for the happy tourists.*

**paragraph** ['pɛr ə græf] *n.* a sentence or group of sentences usually related some way in meaning. □ *The first line of a paragraph is often indented.*

**parallel** ['pɛr ə lɛl] **1.** *adj.* [lines or plane surfaces] at the same distance apart or at an equal distance apart everywhere. □ *The rails of a train track are parallel to each other.* **2.** *adj.* similar; like [situation]; analogous. □ *When I was in a parallel situation, I called the police.*

**3.** *tv.* to go or be in route or direction **parallel** ① to something else. ☐ *The sidewalk parallels the street in most of the downtown district.*

**paraphrase** ['pɛr ə frez] **1.** *n.* something that someone has said or has written in a different way. ☐ *I understood Anne's paraphrase better than her original statement.* **2.** *tv.* to restate something as in ①. ☐ *The reporter paraphrased the president's comments.*

**parasite** ['pɛr ə saɪt] **1.** *n.* a plant or animal completely dependent on another species of plant or animal for food or support. (**Parasites** on humans and animals cause diseases or health disorders.) ☐ *The sick cow was covered with parasites.* **2.** *n.* someone who depends on other people for food and shelter; a useless person who is supported by other people. (Fig. on ①.) ☐ *Susan's brother had become a real parasite and did nothing to share the cost of food or rent.*

**parcel** ['pɑr səl] **1.** *n.* a package, especially one that is mailed or delivered; something that is wrapped up. ☐ *The parcel was delivered to my office by a courier.* **2.** *n.* an amount of land that is sold as a unit. ☐ *The developer divided the former farm into smaller parcels.*

**parcel post** ['pɑr səl 'post] **1.** *n.* a class of mail in the postal system limited to small parcels. (No plural form.) ☐ *The cost of sending something by parcel post depends on its weight.* **2.** *adv.* by way of ①. ☐ *I sent the package parcel post.*

**pardon** ['pɑr dn] **1.** *n.* forgiving someone. (Plural only when referring to different kinds, types, instances, or varieties.) ☐ *Your pardon in this matter is highly appreciated.* Ⓒ *You are all so kind and understanding about my error. I am grateful for your pardons and your good wishes.* **2.** *n.* an act that keeps someone from being punished under the law. ☐ *The criminal sought a pardon from the king.* **3.** *tv.* to forgive someone; to excuse someone. ☐ *Anne pardoned Bill for bumping into her.* **4.** *tv.* to release someone from jail; to order that someone not be executed; to keep someone from being punished. ☐ *The governor pardoned the woman who had been sentenced to die.*

**parent** ['pɛr ənt] **1.** *n.* the father or the mother of a living creature. ☐ *I am one of the parents of this healthy baby boy.* **2.** *n.* a business that owns another business; the main office of one or more businesses or other organizations. ☐ *The main office of the organization—the parent of the various chapters—is located in New York.* **3.** *adj.* serving as a ②. ☐ *Our group has separated itself from the parent organization.*

**parentheses** [pə 'rɛn θə siz] pl of **parenthesis**.

**parenthesis** [pə 'rɛn θə sɪs] *n., irreg.* either of the pair of symbols "(" and ")" used to enclose information of secondary importance in writing or printing. (Pl: **parentheses**.) ☐ *I put parentheses around the translation of the foreign phrase.*

**park** ['pɑrk] **1.** *n.* a piece of land set aside by a city, state, county, or nation for use by the public, usually having trees, grass, and other natural features. ☐ *Anne jogs through Central Park every morning.* **2.** *tv.* to stop a car or other vehicle and leave it in a certain place for a period of time. ☐ *The driver parked the bus next to the stadium during the game.* **3.** *iv.* to leave a car or other vehicle in a certain place for a period of time. ☐ *You cannot park in an area that has a "No Parking" sign.*

**parking lot** ['pɑr kɪŋ lɑt] *n.* an area of paved land, used to park cars on. ☐ *I left my car somewhere in this huge parking lot!*

**parlor** ['pɑr lɚ] **1.** *n.* a living room; a place in a home where guests can sit and talk. (Old-fashioned.) ☐ *Aunt Susan* *likes to drink tea in the front parlor.* **2.** *n.* a store that sells a certain product or service, such as hair care, ice cream, or funerals. □ *I bought a chocolate sundae at the ice-cream parlor.*

**parrot** ['pɛr ət] **1.** *n.* a kind of tropical bird, often brightly colored, that can copy human speech. □ *My parrot repeats whatever I say.* **2.** *tv.* to repeat someone else's words or ideas without thinking. (Fig. on ①. The object can be a clause with **that** ⑦.) □ *On the test, Mary only parroted her professor's comments.*

**parsley** ['pɑrs li] *n.* an herb used in cooking to add flavor to food or as a decoration. (No plural form. Number is expressed with *sprig(s) of parsley.*) □ *I added fresh parsley to the chicken soup.*

**part** ['pɑrt] **1.** *n.* one piece of the whole; one section of the entire amount. □ *Which part of this is mine?* □ *Part of your responsibility is to clean up after yourself.* **2.** *n.* one of a set of equal divisions. □ *Add ten parts water to one part vinegar, and mix well.* **3.** *n.* an actor's role in a play or movie. □ *I am trying to get a part in the school play.* **4.** *n.* the line between two sections of hair on the head, established when combing it. □ *John wears his part to the side.* **5.** *tv.* to make a pathway or an opening through a group of people or things. □ *The hunters parted the bushes and plants so they could walk through the woods.* **6.** *tv.* to separate one's hair along a line, especially when combing it into two sides. □ *John parted his hair down the middle.* **7.** *iv.* to divide or separate, making an opening. □ *The crowd parted to allow the police to pass through.*

**participate** [pɑr 'tɪs ə pet] **participate (in something)** *iv. (+ prep. phr.)* to be one of a group of things or people doing or involved in something. □ *Mary participated in several school sports.*

**participation** [pɑr tɪs ə 'pe ʃən] *n.* joining in and doing something with other people. (No plural form.) □ *Parents' participation in school activities is always welcomed.*

**participle** ['pɑrt ə sɪp əl] *n.* <either the *present participle* (the -ing form) or the *past participle.*> □ *The present participle of* smile *is* smiling, *and it functions as an adjective in* the smiling man. □ *The past participle of* freeze *is* frozen, *and it functions as an adjective in* a box of frozen vegetables.

**particle** ['pɑrt ɪ kəl] **1.** *n.* a small piece of something. □ *The cat swatted at particles of dust floating in the sunlight.* **2.** *n.* a kind of short, basic word or a part of a word—such as a conjunction, article, or preposition—that affects the meaning of another word. □ *Nouns, verbs, adjectives, and adverbs are never considered particles.* **3.** *n.* a basic unit of matter, such as a proton, neutron, or electron. □ *The proton is a particle with a positive charge, the electron has a negative charge, and the neutron has no charge.*

**particular** [pɑr 'tɪk jə lɚ] **1.** *adj.* specific; distinct [from others]. (Adv: *particularly.*) □ *"Was there a particular item you wanted?" the clerk asked me.* **2.** *adj.* unusual; noticeable; worth noticing. (Adv: *particularly.*) □ *Lisa wrote the letter with particular attention to her choice of words.* **3.** *adj.* hard to please. (Adv: *particularly.*) □ *Bob is a very particular eater, and he sent his steak back to the kitchen twice.*

**partner** ['pɑrt nɚ] **1.** *n.* someone with whom one shares a business; one of the owners of a business. □ *My business partner and I discussed business during lunch.* **2.** *n.* someone who shares an activity with someone else. □ *My partner in the game lost the ball to another pair of players.*

**part of speech** ['pɑrt əv 'spitʃ] *n.* one of the classes or divisions of words that reflect grammatical usage, such as **noun, verb, adjective,** etc. ☐ *What part of speech is* house *in the sentence "He lives in the house on the corner"?* ☐ *"Adverb" and "adjective" are parts of speech.*

**part-time** ['pɑrt 'tɑɪm] **1.** *adj.* for only part of the time and not full-time. ☐ *Most part-time employees aren't eligible for benefits.* **2.** *adv.* [working] only part of the working week; not as full-time. ☐ *John paints houses part-time during the summer.*

**party** ['pɑr ti] **1.** *n.* a social gathering of people; a gathering of people who are having fun. ☐ *Bill received many gifts at his birthday party.* **2.** *n.* a group of people who are together for a specific reason. ☐ *"How many people are in your party?" asked the waiter.* **3.** *n.* a group of people united with a common goal or with common ideas, especially in politics. ☐ *The politician's party raised money for his campaign.* **4.** *n.* a person. ☐ *What is the name of the party you are looking for?* **5.** *adj.* <the adj. use of ③.> ☐ *The party leaders boasted about their candidate.* **6.** *iv.* to celebrate; to have fun with other people. (Informal.) ☐ *My friends and I partied after I got a job promotion.*

**pass** ['pæs] **1.** *tv.* to reach someone or something and go beyond. ☐ *The winner passed the finish line before the other runners.* **2.** *tv.* to succeed in a [school] course or examination; to have a medical examination where no problems are discovered. ☐ *I easily passed the history exam.* **3.** *tv.* to use up a period of time [doing something]; to occupy a period of time [doing something]. ☐ *Lisa passed time by reading the newspaper.* **4.** *tv.* to approve or agree to something, such as a motion, law, or regulation, by means of a vote. ☐ *The Senate passed the bill by a vote of 70–30.* ☐ *The president vetoed the law that Congress had passed.* **5.** *tv.* to hand something over to someone; to give something to someone. ☐ *Please pass me the salt.* **6.** *tv.* to throw a ball to someone in a game. ☐ *I passed the football to my teammate.* **7.** *iv.* to reach and go beyond. ☐ *Spectators shouted encouragement to the runners as they passed.* **8.** *iv.* to meet the requirements for successfully completing a [school] course. ☐ *If you attend every lecture, you should pass.* **9.** *iv.* [for a motion or law] to be approved by means of a vote. ☐ *The law passed despite the public opposition to it.* **10.** *iv.* [for time] to progress or proceed. ☐ *As the years passed, Bill began to regret his actions.* **11. pass out** *iv. + adv.* to faint; to become unconscious. ☐ *When I broke my foot, I passed out from the pain.* **12.** *n.* a ticket or document showing that one is allowed to go somewhere. ☐ *My bus pass is good for 20 rides, and then I have to buy a new one.* **13.** *n.* the transfer of a ball or something similar in various sports. ☐ *I caught my teammate's pass and threw the ball toward the basket.* **14.** *n.* a narrow road or pathway, especially through mountains. ☐ *A fallen tree blocked the only pass leading out of the mountain village.*

**passable** ['pæs ə bəl] **1.** *adj.* able to be crossed or passed through; able to be traveled over. ☐ *We shoveled the snow to make our sidewalk passable.* **2.** *adj.* [a motion or proposition] likely to get enough votes to pass. ☐ *The proposed law was too costly to be passable.* **3.** *adj.* only adequate; fair; okay. (Adv: *passably.*) ☐ *Although John's work is passable, it's certainly not excellent.*

**passage** ['pæs ɪdʒ] **1.** *n.* a path or hallway. ☐ *The movers moved the piano through the narrow passage very slowly.* **2.** *n.* the progress or movement of time. (No plural form.) ☐ *After the passage of three months of peace and quiet, the teacher returned to work.* **3.** *n.* the

P

approval of a law or motion, usually by a vote. (No plural form.) □ *The passage of the new tax law caused a public protest.* **4.** *n.* a short section of a piece of music, a speech, or a written work. □ *The violinist practiced the difficult passage again and again.*

**passbook** ['pæs bʊk] *n.* a book for keeping track of one's savings account in a bank. □ *I use electronic banking and therefore do not have a passbook.*

**passenger** ['pæs ən dʒɚ] *n.* someone who is riding in a vehicle but is not driving it. □ *The pilot greeted the passengers as they boarded the plane.*

**passion** ['pæʃ ən] **1.** *n.* strong romantic and sexual feeling. (Plural only when referring to different kinds, types, instances, or varieties.) □ *The movie had so much passion in it that I was embarrassed.* Ⓒ *Reggie's passions overcame him and he seized Penelope and kissed her on the cheek.* **2.** *n.* a very strong interest in something. □ *John has a passion for fishing, so he fishes as often as he can.*

**passive** ['pæs ɪv] **1.** *adj.* not resisting; not active; letting others take charge or control a situation. (The opposite of **active**. Adv: *passively.*) □ *I urged my passive friend to be more bold.* **2.** *adj.* of or about a grammatical state where the verb acts on the subject of the sentence. (The opposite of **active**. Adv: *passively.*) □ *I rewrote my demand in the passive voice.* **3.** *n.* a **passive** ② verb phrase. □ The house was painted by Mr. Smith *is a passive.* □ *You can use the passive once or twice in your article, but not in every sentence!*

**passport** ['pæs port] *n.* a document shaped like a small book, showing what country one is a citizen of. (It is needed to enter certain countries.) □ *Mary applied for a passport four months before her trip to Japan.*

**password** ['pæs wɚd] *n.* a secret word, phrase, or set of symbols that allows someone access to something. □ *John entered his password so he could open the computer files.*

**past** ['pæst] **1.** *n.* a time that has gone by; things that have happened; history. (No plural form.) □ *My grandfather entertained me with stories of the past.* **2.** *adj.* most recent; occurring in the time just before this time. □ *I spent the past hour wondering where you were.* **3.** *adj.* occurring or completed at some previous time. □ *The student's past performance in class had been excellent.* **4.** *adj.* <the adj. use of ①.> □ *The past form of many English words ends in* -ed. **5.** *adv.* by; toward or alongside someone or something and then beyond. □ *The car honked when it drove past.* **6.** *prep.* farther [in space, time, ability, or quality] than someone or something; beyond [in space, time, ability, or quality] someone or something. □ *The bank is just past the bookstore.* □ *The time is 15 minutes past noon.*

**pasta** ['pɑs tə] *n.* a food prepared by mixing flour, water, and sometimes egg to make a dough or paste, and then shaping it into different forms; noodles. (Plural only when referring to different kinds, types, instances, or varieties. Treated as singular.) □ *John put tomato sauce on top of his pasta.* Ⓒ *Some pastas look like they were designed by a madman!*

**paste** ['pest] **1.** *n.* a soft mixture that is easily spread. (Plural only when referring to different kinds, types, instances, or varieties.) □ *Peanut butter is a paste made of peanuts.* Ⓒ *Her dips are just awful! Nothing more than colored, salty pastes that absolutely ruin the taste of the food!* **2.** *n.* a soft mixture that causes objects to stick together. (Plural only when referring to different kinds, types, instances, or varieties.) □ *I smeared wallpaper paste on the wallpaper before*

*I placed it on the wall.* Ⓒ *We tried a variety of pastes, but none would hold the new paper to the wall.* **3.** *tv.* to cause something to stick to something else with ②. □ *It took me several hours to paste all the wallpaper onto the wall.*

**pastime** ['pæs tɑɪm] *n.* an activity that one enjoys; an enjoyable activity that is done to pass the time. □ *My favorite pastime is reading.*

**pastor** ['pæs tɚ] *n.* a minister in a Christian church. □ *At church, the pastor spoke about right and wrong.*

**pastry** ['pe stri] **1.** *n.* rich dough that is made with flour and butter or fat and is baked. (Plural only when referring to different kinds, types, instances, or varieties.) □ *Prepare the pastry for the piecrust before you start making the filling.* Ⓒ *I went to cooking school to learn how to make pastries and doughs.* **2.** *n.* baked foods, typically sweet, usually made with ①. (Plural only when referring to different kinds, types, instances, or varieties. Treated as singular. Number is expressed with *piece(s) of pastry.*) □ *The bakery on the corner sells wonderful pastry.* Ⓒ *I love pastries except that they make me fat!* **3.** *n.* a piece or item of ②; a sweet roll, small cake, or other sweetened, baked food, often with fruit or with a sweet coating or filling. □ *Jane served a selection of pastries for dessert.*

**past tense** ['pæst 'tɛns] *n.* the tense of a verb or **auxiliary verb** that indicates an event or a state that has existed at a previous time. (Abbreviated "pt" in this dictionary.) □ *In English, a verb ending in* -ed *is in the past tense.* □ *Since the accident happened yesterday, you must use the past tense to describe it.*

**pasture** ['pæs tʃɚ] *n.* a field of grass, especially one where animals eat. □ *The cow stood eating grass in the pasture.*

**pat** ['pæt] **1.** *n.* a gentle tap, especially with the palm of one's hand. □ *With a few pats of his hand, the baker shaped the dough for baking.* **2.** *tv.* to touch or tap someone or something gently a few times, especially with the palm of the hand. □ *Dad patted me on the back because I'd done a good job.* **3.** *adj.* perfectly, as if rehearsed or from memory. (Adv: *patly.*) □ *The witness had pat answers prepared for every question.*

**patch** ['pætʃ] **1.** *n.* a piece of cloth or other material used to repair a hole or a tear or to cover something. □ *I sewed a patch over the hole in my pants.* **2.** *n.* a small area of land. □ *Anne picked some daisies from the flower patch.* **3.** *n.* a small area on a surface that is different from the area around it. □ *The dark patch on the carpet is a permanent stain.*

**patent** ['pæt nt] **1.** *n.* the exclusive right, registered with the government, to benefit from the ownership of a process or invention. □ *Sally applied for a patent for a process she invented that makes it possible to reuse old newspapers.* **2.** *tv.* to seek and gain ① on something. □ *The inventor patented his idea before he actually mentioned it in public.*

**path** ['pæθ] **1.** *n., irreg.* a track or trail along the earth. (Pl: ['pæðz] or ['pæθs].) □ *The bicycle path was blocked by a fallen tree.* **2.** *n., irreg.* the route someone or something takes to achieve a result. (Fig. on ①.) □ *Anne has created her own path to success.*

**pathway** ['pæθ we] *n.* a **path**. □ *Mary walked down the pathway toward the lake.*

**patience** ['pe ʃəns] *n.* the quality of being patient and not becoming anxious or annoyed. (No plural form.) □ *Patience is needed when you deal with very young children.*

**patient** ['pe ʃənt] **1.** *adj.* able to wait for something to happen without complaining or becoming anxious or annoyed. (Adv: *patiently.*) □ *Be patient! I'll help you in a moment.* **2.** *n.* someone who is getting medical help from a

P

doctor, nurse, or hospital. □ *The nurse prepared the patient for surgery.*

**patio** ['pæt i o] *n.* a paved surface connected to one's house where one can relax, gather with others, barbecue food, etc. (From Spanish. Pl ends in *-s.*) □ *I moved the grill to the patio in preparation for cooking.*

**patrol** [pə 'trol] **1.** *tv.* to watch over an area by walking or driving around. □ *The police patrolled the dangerous city streets.* **2.** *iv.* to watch over [an area] by walking or driving around. □ *The police officers patrol often because of recent robberies.* **3.** *n.* people who watch over an area as in ①. □ *Members of the patrol remained in contact with their leader.*

**patronize** ['pe trə nɑɪz] **1.** *tv.* to be a regular customer of a store, restaurant, hotel, or other business. □ *Anne has patronized that restaurant for years.* **2.** *tv.* to act as if one is superior to someone else. □ *John keeps patronizing his coworkers, even though many of them have more knowledge and experience than he does.*

**patter** ['pæt ɚ] **1.** *n.* a series of quick tapping sounds. (No plural form.) □ *I heard the patter of people's feet running down the stairs.* **2.** *iv.* [for falling rain] to make quick tapping sounds as it strikes something. □ *When the rain began to patter on the roof, I fell asleep.*

**pattern** ['pæt ɚn] **1.** *n.* a design; an arrangement of shapes and colors, especially one that is repeated. □ *Bob's new shirt has a pattern made of large, colored spots.* **2.** *n.* a repeated element in a series of events. □ *There is no pattern to this illness. On some days there is a fever, and some days there is not.* **3.** *n.* a printed or drawn outline of the parts of a garment or something that is to be built. □ *Jane bought a pattern for a new shirt for Jimmy.*

**patty** ['pæt i] *n.* a thin, flat disk of ground or mashed food, especially one formed of ground meat. □ *Mix the ground meat with onions, and then use your hands to shape the mixture into patties.*

**pause** ['pɔz] **1.** *n.* a brief delay; a moment where someone or something stops talking, moving, or working. □ *There was an uncomfortable pause in the conversation after Bill insulted Anne.* **2.** *iv.* to stop for a moment; to stop moving or talking for a moment. □ *Anne paused before she responded to Bill's insult.*

**pave** ['pev] *tv.* to build or cover a road, street, driveway, highway, etc., with cement, concrete, or some other hard surface. □ *The field was paved to make a new parking lot.*

**pavement** ['pev mənt] *n.* a flat surface of concrete, cement, or some other hard surface covering an area, especially covering a street or sidewalk. (No plural form.) □ *The car drove off the pavement and into the ditch.*

**paw** ['pɔ] **1.** *n.* the foot of a clawed animal. □ *Anne's cat is black with white paws.* **2.** *tv.* to handle someone or something with hands or ①. □ *The huge bear pawed her cubs tenderly.*

**pay** ['pe] **1.** *tv., irreg.* to give money (to someone) in exchange for a product or a service or to settle a debt. (Pt/pp: **paid**.) □ *I will have to pay a lot of money for that car!* **2.** *tv., irreg.* to give someone an amount of money in exchange for a product or service or to settle a debt. □ *I will have to pay John immediately.* **3.** *tv., irreg.* to settle a bill or a debt. □ *I went to the cashier and paid the bill.* **4.** *tv., irreg.* [for something] to yield a certain amount of money or a certain benefit. □ *My bank account pays 5% interest annually.* **5. pay (for** something**)** *iv., irreg.* *(+ prep. phr.)* to transfer money in exchange for a product or service. □ *I paid for the meal and then left the restaurant.* **6.** *n.* wages; salary; the amount of money that one earns from a job. (No plural form. Treated as singular.) ☐ *On Fridays, Anne deposits her pay at the bank.* **7.** *adj.* requiring money in order to be used. ☐ *An angry shopper complained about having to use a pay toilet.*

**payday** ['pe de] *n.* the day on which a company pays its workers. ☐ *Payday at my office is the last day of each month.*

**payment** ['pe mənt] **1.** *n.* transferring money [to someone]. (Plural only when referring to different kinds, types, instances, or varieties.) ☐ *Payment must be made on time, or interest will be charged.* Ⓒ *Current payments will be reflected in next month's statement.* **2.** *n.* an amount of money paid or to be paid; something that is paid [to someone or something]. ☐ *I can barely afford my monthly mortgage payments.*

**payroll** ['pe rol] *n.* the list of a company's employees and their salaries. ☐ *Many of the mayor's friends were on the city payroll.*

**pea** ['pi] **1.** *n.* a small, round, green vegetable that grows in a pod on a vine-like plant. ☐ *My meatloaf was served with potatoes and peas.* **2.** *n.* the plant that **peas** ① grow on. (No singular in this sense. Number is expressed with *pea plant(s).*) ☐ *John planted peas in his garden.*

**peace** ['pis] **1.** *n.* a condition where there is no war or fighting; a time when there is order and harmony. (No plural form.) ☐ *The fragile peace was ended by another attack by the enemy.* **2.** *n.* silence; freedom from anxiety. (No plural form.) ☐ *The student found peace and quiet in the library.*

**peaceful** ['pis fʊl] **1.** *adj.* without war or fighting; not at war; orderly. (Adv: *peacefully.*) ☐ *The mediator found a peaceful solution to the disagreement.* **2.** *adj.* happy and calm; free from anxiety. (Adv: *peacefully.*) ☐ *The baby looked peaceful as he slept in his crib.*

**peach** ['pitʃ] **1.** *n.* a soft, sweet, juicy, round fruit with a fuzzy skin, yellowish-orange pulp, and a large pit in the middle. ☐ *The farmer sold me a bushel of peaches.* **2.** *adj.* made with ①; tasting like ①. ☐ *I had peach pie for dessert.*

**peak** ['pik] **1.** *n.* the top of something, especially a mountain; the highest point of something. ☐ *The peak of Mt. Everest is the highest place on Earth.* **2.** *n.* the maximum amount of effort or accomplishment. ☐ *As the sound reached its peak, the window broke.* **3.** *iv.* to form or rise to ①. ☐ *The witch's hat peaked about a foot over her head.* **4.** *iv.* to reach ②. ☐ *The tennis player peaked when she was 21.*

**peal** ['pil] **1.** *n.* the [loud] ringing sound that bells make. ☐ *When I heard the peal of the old-fashioned fire bell, I knew something was wrong.* **2.** *n.* a long, loud sound, such as with laughter. ☐ *The audience responded to the comedy with peals of laughter.* **3.** *iv.* to ring loudly; to sound loudly. ☐ *Laughter pealed from the auditorium as Bill told his best jokes.*

**peanut** ['pi nət] **1.** *n.* a plant with seed pods that grow underground. ☐ *They grow a lot of peanuts in the South.* **2.** *n.* the nutmeat of ①; the nutmeat and shell of ①. ☐ *I love salted, roasted peanuts.*

**peanut butter** ['pi nət bət ɚ] **1.** *n.* an edible paste made from crushed peanuts. (No plural form.) ☐ *Some kinds of peanut butter have pieces of peanuts in them.* **2. peanut-butter** *adj.* made with ①. ☐ *Jane makes the best peanut-butter cookies!*

**pear** ['per] *n.* a yellow, brown, or green fruit that is rounded at the bottom and narrower toward the top. ☐ *Anne went to the orchard and picked a bushel of pears.*

P

**pearl** ['pɚl] *n.* a hard, white, round substance formed inside an oyster, usually used in jewelry. ☐ *When we opened the oyster, we found a beautiful pearl inside.*

**pebble** ['pɛb əl] *n.* a small stone. ☐ *Pebbles are rounded and smooth, unlike rocks or sharp stones.*

**pecan** [pɪ 'kɑn] **1.** *n.* a tall tree native to the southern United States and Mexico. ☐ *We planted the huge field in pecans and oaks.* **2.** *n.* the edible part of ①; the nutmeat and shell of ①. ☐ *I sprinkled some crushed pecans on top of my ice-cream sundae.* **3.** *n.* the wood of ①. (Plural only when referring to different kinds, types, instances, or varieties.) ☐ *Pecan is not as popular as walnut for furniture and paneling.* Ⓒ *We chose this lighter wood from a large sample of pecans, all of them quite expensive.* **4.** *adj.* made with ②. ☐ *I ate some pecan brownies.* **5.** *adj.* made from ③. ☐ *We have a pecan bookcase in the living room.*

**pedal** ['pɛd l] **1.** *n.* a device that controls something and is operated with the feet. ☐ *Bicycles have two pedals, one for each foot.* **2.** *tv.* to ride a bicycle. ☐ *Jimmy can't pedal his bike very far because he is so small.* **3.** *iv.* to ride [a bicycle] somewhere. ☐ *John pedaled down the bike trail.*

**pedestal** ['pɛd ə stəl] *n.* a base that supports a statue, vase, column, etc. ☐ *The stone pedestal cracked under the statue's weight.*

**peek** ['pik] **1.** *n.* a quick, sly look; a quick look at something that one is not supposed to look at. ☐ *The nosy employee took a quick peek at the company files.* **2.** *iv.* to look quickly at something that one is not supposed to look at. ☐ *John peeked at his presents a week before Christmas.*

**peel** ['pil] **1.** *n.* the outer skin of certain fruits and vegetables. (No plural form. See also **peeling**.) ☐ *The peel of the apple is bright red.* **2.** *tv.* to remove ①. ☐ *John peeled the orange with his fingers.* **3.** *tv.* to remove an outer layer from something. (Fig. on ②.) ☐ *Bill peeled the plastic from the slice of cheese.* **4.** *iv.* [for an outer layer] to come off. ☐ *The old paint started to peel from the wall.*

**peeling** ['pi lɪŋ] *n.* a part of something, especially fruits and vegetables, that has been peeled off. (Often plural.) ☐ *Please dispose of the potato peelings.*

**peep** ['pip] **1.** *n.* a high noise, such as that made by a baby chicken or other birds. ☐ *The farmer heard the peeps of the chicks that had just hatched.* **2.** *iv.* to have a quick look at something, especially in secret; a peek. ☐ *I see a shadow at the window. I think someone is peeping.* **3.** *iv.* to make a noise, as with ①. ☐ *My smoke alarm peeps when its batteries run low.*

**peg** ['pɛg] **1.** *n.* a thick wooden or plastic pin used to hold objects together. ☐ *Three pegs held the leg onto the table.* **2.** *tv.* to attach something to something with ①. ☐ *Bill pegged the board to the floor.*

**pelican** ['pɛl ɪ kən] *n.* a bird that lives on or near the water and that has a bill with a large scoop on the lower part. ☐ *The pelican caught a fish with its bill.*

**pellet** ['pɛl ɪt] *n.* a hard, small ball of something, such as ice, wax, dirt, or metal. ☐ *Tiny pellets of ice beat against my window.*

**pen** ['pɛn] **1.** *n.* a thin writing instrument that uses ink. ☐ *The pen in my pocket leaked ink and ruined my shirt.* **2.** *n.* a confined area where certain animals are kept. ☐ *The zookeeper threw raw meat into the lizards' pen.* **3.** *tv.* to write something, usually with ①. ☐ *The author penned a new story in four months.*

**penalty** ['pɛn əl ti] *n.* a punishment for breaking a rule or law. ☐ *John's penalty for breaking the law was a one-year jail term.*

P

**pencil** ['pɛn səl] **1.** *n.* a thin writing instrument with a pointed core made of a soft black material. ☐ *You cannot sign this contract with a pencil; it must be signed in ink.* **2.** *tv.* to write something with ①. ☐ *Anne penciled her thoughts in the margins of the book.*

**pencil sharpener** ['pɛn səl 'ʃɑr pə nɚ] *n.* a machine or device that sharpens things, usually pencils. ☐ *Mary stuck a pencil in her electric pencil sharpener.*

**penny** ['pɛn i] *n.* a cent; 1/100 of a dollar in the United States and various other nations. ☐ *I gave Bill 25 pennies in exchange for a quarter.*

**pension** ['pɛn ʃən] *n.* money that is paid to a former employee, from retirement until death, or some other period of time, to replace a salary. ☐ *The city raised taxes to support its employees' pensions.*

**penthouse** ['pɛnt hɑʊs] *n., irreg.* a special apartment on the top floor of a building. (Pl: [...hɑʊ zəz].) ☐ *The rich lawyer rode the private elevator to his penthouse.*

**people** ['pip əl] **1.** *n.* persons. (No plural form. Treated as a plural. Used as a plural of **person**.) ☐ *Over 50,000 people attended the concert.* **2.** *n.* a specific group of ①; a race or ethnic group of ①. (Singular or plural with the same meaning.) ☐ *Many different peoples lived within the old Soviet Union.*

**pep** ['pɛp] *n.* energy; vigor. (No plural form.) ☐ *The tired driver hoped the coffee would give him some pep.*

**pepper** ['pɛp ɚ] **1.** *n.* a vegetable, often green or red, that is mostly hollow and often very hot and spicy. ☐ *Mary sliced up a green pepper and put the pieces in her salad.* **2.** *n.* the dried berry of various plants, usually ground, used to season food. (Usually black in the United States and white in Europe. Plural only when referring to different kinds, types, instances, or varieties.) ☐ *The waiter ground some pepper onto my salad.* Ⓒ *Black, white, pink, and green! I didn't know there were so many peppers!* **3.** *tv.* to sprinkle ② on food as a seasoning. ☐ *The cook peppered the fish while grilling it.* **4.** *tv.* [for many tiny things] to strike something lightly. ☐ *Sand, blown by the wind, peppered the sides of the little cabin on the beach.*

**peppy** ['pɛp i] *adj.* full of energy; active; excited. (Adv: *peppily.* Comp: *peppier;* sup: *peppiest.*) ☐ *The peppy young cat ran in circles, chasing its tail.*

**perceive** [pɚ 'siv] *tv.* to be aware of someone or something with one's mind; to be aware of someone or something through one's senses. ☐ *The eyes perceive color, and the ears perceive sound.*

**percent** [pɚ 'sɛnt] *n.* a one-hundredth part. (No plural form. Usually expressed with a number ranging from 0 through 100. Also expressed as "%.") ☐ *Thirty percent of the people surveyed had no opinion.*

**percentage** [pɚ 'sɛn tɪdʒ] *n.* a part that is less than the whole amount. ☐ *The salesclerks earned a percentage of the price of all the goods they sold.*

P

**perch** ['pɚtʃ] **1.** *n.* a branch or rod that a bird grasps with its feet when it is at rest. ☐ *The bird sat on its perch in its cage.* **2.** *n.* a place to sit that is high off the floor or ground; a high ledge. (Fig. on ①.) ☐ *Bob waved at everyone from his perch on the balcony.* **3.** *n., irreg.* any one of several species of edible fish. (Pl: *perch*, except when referring to a number of species.) ☐ *David cleaned the perch and fried them for dinner.* **4.** *iv.* to sit on top of something; to stand on top of something, as does a bird. ☐ *The cat perched on the top of the sofa.*

**perfect 1.** ['pɚ fɪkt] *adj.* being the best; completely correct; without flaws. (Adv: *perfectly.*) ☐ *I made sure my spelling was perfect before turning in my* *work.* **2.** ['pɚ fɪkt] *adj.* exactly suitable; exactly what is needed. (Adv: *perfectly.*) □ *A hot cup of coffee would be perfect with dessert.* **3.** ['pɚ fɪkt] *adj.* complete; total. (Adv: *perfectly.*) □ *After the party, my house was a perfect mess.* **4.** ['pɚ fɪkt] *n.* <a construction showing a completed action or condition; a form of the verb that shows that something was completed, is completed, or will be completed.> (In English, it consists of the past participle of the verb that follows a form of **have** ⑥. No plural form.) □ *"I have eaten" contains an example of the present perfect.* **5.** [pɚ 'fɛkt] *tv.* to make something **perfect** ①. □ *My boss perfected my design with a few small enhancements.*

**perfection** [pɚ 'fɛk ʃən] **1.** *n.* the condition of being perfect. (No plural form.) □ *Perfection requires care and effort.* **2.** *n.* becoming perfect; making something perfect. (No plural form.) □ *The perfection of the painter's skill is most evident in this painting.*

**perform** [pɚ 'form] **1.** *tv.* to do something; to do an action. □ *The soldier performed his duties well during the war.* **2.** *tv.* to present a play, sing a song, play a piece of music, do a dance, etc., for an audience. □ *Jimmy performed a dance for his class.* **3.** *iv.* to act, sing, dance, or play music, especially in front of people. □ *The famous singer performed for 2,000 people.* **4.** *iv.* to function; to do what is expected or has been assigned. □ *The students performed well on the test.*

**performance** [pɚ 'for məns] **1.** *n.* a presentation of a play, a piece of music, a song, a dance, etc. □ *Each performance of the play lasted three hours.* **2.** *n.* the quality of performing or functioning; how well someone or something performs. (Plural only when referring to different kinds, types, instances, or varieties.) □ *John's performance on the test was poor.* Ⓒ *The performances by the various cast members varied in quality and professionalism.*

**performer** [pɚ 'for mɚ] *n.* someone who performs, such as an actor, a singer, a musician, a dancer. □ *The audience applauded the performer after her act.*

**perfume** **1.** ['pɚ fjum, pɚ 'fjum] *n.* a mixture of pleasant-smelling natural or artificial oils and alcohol that is put on people's skin. (Plural only when referring to different kinds, types, instances, or varieties.) □ *Susan sprayed some perfume on her neck.* Ⓒ *The women at the party were all wearing different perfumes.* **2.** [pɚ 'fjum] *tv.* to place a pleasant-smelling substance on someone; to add a pleasant-smelling substance to the air in a room. □ *John perfumed the living room with a pleasant-smelling spray.*

**perhaps** [pɚ 'hæps] *adv.* maybe; possibly; maybe yes, maybe no. □ *Perhaps you would care for some coffee before dinner.*

**period** ['pɪr i əd] **1.** *n.* a punctuation mark "." used at the end of a sentence or at the end of an abbreviation. □ Etc. *is an abbreviation that ends with a period.* **2.** *n.* a certain length of time, including certain times in history. □ *The 1920s were an interesting period in American history.* **3.** *n.* a section or part of certain games, such as basketball. □ *A break occurs between the second and third periods in basketball.* **4.** *n.* a division of the school day. □ *The class in calculus is only offered during second period.* **5.** *n.* the time during the month when a woman menstruates. (Short for **menstrual period**.) □ *Sally has missed her second period. She may be pregnant.* **6.** *adj.* [of art, architecture, crafts, or literature] having to do with a certain time in history. □ *The old building was a period piece left over from the 1880s.*

**perish** ['pɛr ɪʃ] **1.** *iv.* to die. □ *The stray dog perished during the harsh winter.* **2.** *iv.* [for something] to go away or fade away. □ *Radio drama perished with the coming of television.*

**perjury** ['pɚ dʒə ri] *n.* lying in court after one has taken an oath promising not to lie. (No plural form.) □ *Committing perjury in court can result in a prison sentence.*

**permanent** ['pɚ mə nənt] **1.** *adj.* intended or designed to last forever or for a long time; not temporary. (Adv: *permanently.*) □ *The fax machine seems to be a permanent fixture in our office.* **2.** *n.* a type of hair treatment where the hair is caused to stay in a particular arrangement for a long time. (From *permanent wave.*) □ *Mary's hair used to be straight until she got a permanent.*

**permission** [pɚ 'mɪ ʃən] *n.* consent; agreement that something may be done. (No plural form.) □ *My father gave me permission to borrow his car.*

**permit 1.** ['pɚ mɪt] *n.* an official document that allows someone to do something. □ *Mary's permit allows her to fish in the river.* **2.** [pɚ 'mɪt] *tv.* to allow someone to do something; to let someone do something. □ *I permitted John to borrow my car.*

**persist** [pɚ 'sɪst] **1.** *iv.* to continue to do something; not to give up, even if it is difficult or if one faces opposition. □ *Keep persisting on this point until they agree.* **2.** *iv.* to continue to exist. □ *My cough has persisted for two months.*

**person** ['pɚ sən] **1.** *n.* a human being; a man, a woman, a boy, or a girl. (**People** is sometimes used as the plural.) □ *I asked the person standing next to me for the time.* **2.** *n.* <a grammar term, used to show the relationship of the speaker or writer to the receiver of the message.> (The first person refers to the speaker or writer, such as **I, me, my, mine, we, us, our,** and **ours**. The second person refers to the listener or reader, such as **you, your,** and **yours**. The third person refers to someone or something being spoken about, such as **he, him, his, she, her, hers, it, its, they, them, their,** and **theirs.**) □ Takes *is the third-person singular form of* take, *because it is used with third-person singular forms, such as* he. *For example:* He takes out the garbage.

**personal** ['pɚ sən əl] **1.** *adj.* of or about the private affairs of a particular person; belonging to or used by a particular person. (Adv: *personally.*) □ *I bought a computer for my own personal use.* **2.** *adj.* done by a certain person, instead of by someone else. (Adv: *personally.*) □ *The actress made a personal visit to a seriously ill fan of hers.*

**personality** [pɚ sə 'næl ə ti] **1.** *n.* aspects of one's thinking and behavior that make one different from everyone else. □ *John is very quiet and shy, but Bill has a very happy personality and loves to meet people.* **2.** *n.* someone who is well known; a famous person. □ *I collect autographs of famous sports personalities.*

**personnel** [pɚ sə 'nɛl] *n.* the people who work for a company or organization. (No plural form.) □ *The parking lot is for company personnel only.*

**perspire** [pɚ 'spaɪɚ] *iv.* to sweat. □ *I was so nervous that I began to perspire.*

**persuade** [pɚ 'swed] *tv.* to use argument or discussion to cause someone to do or think something. □ *Anne persuaded her nephew to stay in school.*

**persuasion** [pɚ 'swe ʒən] *n.* efforts to persuade someone of something. (No plural form.) □ *No amount of persuasion could get Lisa to agree to sell her paintings to me.*

**pertain** [pɚ 'ten] **pertain to** someone or something *iv. + prep. phr.* to have to do with someone or something; to be relevant to someone or something. □ *Your comments don't pertain to the topic of conversation.*

**pesky** ['pɛs ki] *adj.* being a **pest** ① or ②; irritating; annoying; troublesome. (Adv: *peskily.* Comp: *peskier;* sup: *peskiest.*) □ *Anne asked her pesky brother to leave her alone.*

**pest** ['pɛst] **1.** *n.* any animal or insect that destroys crops, spreads disease, and enters people's homes. □ *The city tried to kill the pests that carried the disease.* **2.** *n.* someone or something that causes trouble; someone or something that is a nuisance. □ *Some pest on the bus kept bothering me for money.*

**pester** ['pɛs tɚ] *tv.* to bother someone; to annoy someone. □ *Some man I didn't know pestered me for money on the bus.*

**pet** ['pɛt] **1.** *n.* an animal that is kept in one's home or yard as a companion. □ *I have a few pets, including two dogs, a cat, and a rabbit.* **2.** *adj.* [of an animal] kept as ①. (Prenominal only.) □ *Anne's pet rabbit was always eating the houseplants.* **3.** *adj.* special; particular; favorite. (Prenominal only.) □ *Lisa's pet theory is that there is life on Mars.* **4.** *tv.* to stroke or pat someone or some creature. □ *John petted his cat's soft fur.*

P

**petal** ['pɛt əl] *n.* one of the colored sections of the blossom of a flower. □ *Mary picked the petals off the daisy, one by one.*

**petite** [pə 'tit] **1.** *adj.* [of a woman] small; [of a woman] short. (From French. Adv: *petitely.*) □ *The petite librarian stood on a chair to reach the top shelf.* **2.** *adj.* [of a clothing size or range of sizes] fitting women who are ①. □ *This is a very nice skirt, but do you have it in a petite size?*

**petition** [pə 'tɪ ʃən] **1.** *n.* a document signed by many people who are demanding something from someone. □ *The workers signed a petition demanding better working conditions.* **2.** *tv.* to request something formally of a government or of an authority, often through the use of ①. (The object can be a clause with **that** ⑦.) □ *The students petitioned the university for a change in the grading policy.*

**petroleum** [pə 'tro li əm] *n.* oil that is pumped from under the ground, used to make gasoline and other substances. (No plural form.) □ *Petroleum is used for many kinds of fuel and even plastic.*

**phantom** ['fæn təm] **1.** *n.* a ghost; an image or memory that is "seen" by the mind in a dream or in a vision, but is not real. □ *Phantoms of his long-forgotten friends raced through the dying man's mind.* **2.** *adj.* like a ghost; unreal; apparent, but not real. □ *The beast is not real, of course. It's just a phantom threat.*

**phase** ['fez] **1.** *n.* a stage in the development of someone or something; a stage in a sequence of events. □ *The doctor explained the three different phases of the disease.* **2.** *n.* any of the stages of the appearance of the moon as seen from Earth. □ *A chart of the phases of the moon can be found in the daily newspaper.*

**philosophy** [fɪ 'lɑs ə fi] **1.** *n.* the science and study of the meaning of truth, knowledge, reality, and existence. (No plural form.) □ *A few of my friends decided to study philosophy in college.* **2.** *n.* the way one looks at life; the principles one uses to live one's life. (Plural only when referring to different kinds, types, instances, or varieties.) □ *I use the golden rule as my philosophy of life.* Ⓒ *This one little rule is more effective than all the philosophies mankind has dreamed of.*

**phobia** ['fob i ə] *n.* an unreasonable fear; a strong dread. (Also in combinations, such as *claustrophobia, hydrophobia.*) □ *Bill always stays at home because of his phobia for crowds.*

**phone** ['fon] **1.** *n.* a telephone. □ *John had a car accident while talking on his car phone.* **2.** *tv.* to call someone by ①; to **telephone** someone. □ *Bill phoned his boss to say that he was sick and couldn't come to work.*

**phone call** ['fon kɔl] *n.* a message or a conversation using the telephone. (Shortened from **telephone call.** Can be shortened to **call.**) □ *There were a few phone calls while you were out.*

**photo** ['fo to] *n.* a photograph; a snapshot; a picture made by a camera. □ *The tourist took some photos of the monument.*

**photograph** ['fo tə græf] **1.** *n.* a picture made by a camera; a photo; a snapshot. □ *I placed my vacation photographs in a large album.* **2.** *tv.* to take a picture, with a camera, of someone or something. □ *The tourist photographed all the famous monuments.*

**photographer** [fə 'tɑ grə fɚ] *n.* someone who takes pictures with a camera, especially for a living. □ *The photographer checked the lighting before taking the picture.*

**photography** [fə 'tɑ grə fi] *n.* the science, study, art, or act of taking a picture with a camera. (No plural form.) □ *Anne studied photography to learn how to take better pictures.*

**phr.** an abbreviation of **phrase** ① and ②.

**phrase** ['frez] **1.** *n.* a group of words that functions as a unit of grammar within a sentence. (Abbreviated *phr.* here.) □ *The phrase* in the house *consists of a preposition* in *and a nominal* the house. **2.** *n.* an expression usually including several words. (Abbreviated *phr.* here.) □ On vacation *is a common phrase.* **3.** *n.* a series of notes that is a part of a piece of music. □ *My piano teacher told me to play the first phrase again.* **4.** *tv.* to put communication into words. □ *The speaker phrased his ideas in a confusing way, and the audience didn't understand what he meant.* **5.** *tv.* to perform music, grouping into a series the notes that belong to ③. □ *Please phrase the last line just as it was written.*

**physical** ['fɪz ɪ kəl] **1.** *adj.* of or about the body; of the body. (Adv: *physically* [...ɪk li].) □ *After the accident, I had a lot of physical symptoms as well as anger.* **2.** *adj.* of or about the laws of nature; of or about the study of physics. □ *The science students memorized physical laws.* **3.** *adj.* of or about real objects; of or about matter. (Adv: *physically* [...ɪk li].) □ *What is the physical evidence of the crime?* **4.** *n.* a thorough examination by a doctor. (Short for **physical examination.**) □ *I have a physical every year before school starts.*

**physical examination** ['fɪz ɪ kəl ɪg zæm ə 'ne ʃən] *n.* an examination of someone's body and health by a doctor. (Can be shortened to **physical.**) □ *The company doctor gave me a physical examination when I was hired.*

**physician** [fɪ 'zɪ ʃən] *n.* a medical doctor. □ *I asked my physician if I needed any X-rays.*

**physics** ['fɪz ɪks] *n.* the science and study of the properties of and relationships between matter and energy. (Treated as singular.) □ *Understanding physics is easier if you know calculus.*

**piano** [pi 'æ no] *n.* a large musical instrument in which small, soft hammers connected to a keyboard strike tuned metal strings. (Pl ends in *-s.*) □ *Bill taught himself how to play the piano.*

**pick** ['pɪk] **1.** *n.* a tool that is a heavy, pointed metal bar attached to a handle, used for breaking apart ice, rocks, and other objects. □ *The mountain climber stuck a pick into the hard rock.* **2.** *n.* a choice; a selection. (Plural only when referring to different kinds, types, instances, or varieties.) □ *If you had your pick, which of these shirts would you*

P

*choose?* Ⓒ *I'll take these three. These are my picks.* **3.** *tv.* to choose a particular person or thing. □ *Jane picked John as her partner for the card game.* **4.** *tv.* to remove something from someplace, especially using one's fingers or a pointed tool. □ *Bill picked the piece of meat from between his teeth.* **5.** *tv.* to gather or harvest flowers, fruit, cotton, peas, beans, etc. □ *The workers picked cotton in the hot sun.* **6. pick** something **out** *tv. + obj. + adv.* to select or choose something, such as an item of clothing. □ *Max picked some new shoes out but didn't have enough money to pay for them.* Ⓣ *He picked out some expensive shoes.* **7. pick** someone or something **up** *tv. + obj. + adv.* to grasp and raise someone or something; to lift someone or something. □ *Tom picked the baby up and took her into the living room.* Ⓣ *He picked up the baby.* **8. pick** someone or something **up** *tv. + obj. + adv.* to collect someone or something; to stop at a place and gather, obtain, or secure someone or something. □ *I will stop by your house and pick you up at noon.* Ⓣ *You will pick up your other passengers shortly after noon.* **9. pick at** something *iv. + prep. phr.* to eat something a little bit at a time, without interest. □ *Jane usually has a good appetite, but she just picked at her dinner.*

**pickle** ['pɪk əl] **1.** *n.* a cucumber—whole, sliced, chopped, or in sections—that has been preserved in salt water or vinegar. □ *I put some sliced pickles on my hamburger.* **2.** *tv.* to preserve food, especially vegetables, in salt water or vinegar. □ *Sue's grandmother pickled the small onions she grew in her garden.*

**picnic** ['pɪk nɪk] **1.** *n.* a meal prepared to be eaten informally outdoors. □ *I brought a blanket to sit on at the picnic.* **2.** *iv., irreg.* to have ①. (Pt/pp: **picnicked**. Present participle: **picnicking**.) □ *My friends and I were picnicking when it started to rain.* **3.** *adj.* used for ①. □ *All the picnic tables were being used, so we sat on the ground.*

**picnicked** ['pɪk nɪkt] pt/pp of **picnic**.

**picnicking** ['pɪk nɪk ɪŋ] present participle of **picnic**.

**picture** ['pɪk tʃɚ] **1.** *n.* a drawing, a painting, or a photograph; an image of someone or something. □ *Bill keeps a picture of his children in his wallet.* **2.** *n.* a movie; a **motion picture**. □ *Which picture won the most awards last year?* **3.** *n.* the image on a television screen. □ *Anne made the picture sharper by adjusting the tuner.* **4.** *tv.* to think of someone or something; to make a mental image of someone or something; to imagine something. □ *Try to picture how Mary would act if she saw me now.* **5.** *tv.* to show someone or something in ①. □ *The death of the king was pictured in the painting.*

**pie** ['pɑɪ] **1.** *n.* a kind of food that has a crust of pastry or something similar and is filled with meat, fruit, or some sweet substance. (The crust can be on the bottom or both bottom and top. Plural only when referring to different kinds, types, instances, or varieties.) □ *Shall I make cake or pie for the banquet?* Ⓒ *Pies are usually made from fruit.* **2.** *n.* a single, complete, round unit of ①. □ *The pie was cut into six equal pieces.*

**piece** ['pis] **1.** *n.* a part of something; a part broken off of or removed from something; an object that is put together with other objects to make something. □ *I've lost the last piece to this puzzle.* **2.** *n.* an example of something, especially of an art or craft, such as music. □ *The pianist played a lovely piece and played it very well.* **3.** *n.* [in games such as chess or checkers that are played on a special board] an object that is placed on the board and, typically, moved to different places on the board according to the rules of the particular game. □ *The card said to move my piece back two spaces.*

**piecrust** ['paɪ krəst] *n.* a piece of pastry found on the bottom and often the top of a pie. □ *Anne made a piecrust for a cherry pie.*

**pier** ['pɪr] *n.* a dock; a structure like a bridge that extends into the water from the shore, supported by posts or columns. □ *The ship you want to board is at pier 4.*

**pierce** ['pɪrs] *tv.* to make a hole through someone or something; to cause something to go through something else. □ *I pierced the paper with my pencil.*

**pig** ['pɪg] **1.** *n.* a farm animal with short legs and a curled tail, raised for food, especially bacon, ham, and pork. (Thought of as greedy and messy.) □ *The pigs oinked loudly before they were slaughtered.* **2.** *n.* someone who eats a lot of food. (Fig. on ①.) □ *Don't be such a pig. Save some for me!* **3.** *n.* someone who is dirty or messy. (Fig. on ①.) □ *My roommates are pigs—they leave their dirty clothes and dishes everywhere.*

**pigeon** ['pɪdʒ ən] *n.* a bird, commonly found in cities, with short legs and a heavy body, whose head bobs as it walks. □ *As I walked up to the pigeons, they flew away.*

**pigment** ['pɪg mənt] *n.* a substance that causes paint, skin, dye, or plant tissue to have a certain color. (Plural only when referring to different kinds, types, instances, or varieties.) □ *White rabbits with red eyes have no pigment at all.* Ⓒ *The dye contains green and yellow pigments.*

**pile** ['paɪl] **1.** *n.* a mound, stack, or heap of something, such as clothing, leaves, or dirt. □ *There's a pile of dirty clothes in the laundry room.* **2.** *n.* a beam of wood or steel that is driven into the ground to support a building, bridge, or other structure. □ *One of the bridge's piles punctured a tunnel under the river.* **3.** *tv.* to place or form things or matter into a shape like ①. □ *Mary piled the files on top of her desk.*

**pilgrim** ['pɪl grɪm] **1.** *n.* someone who travels, especially to a holy place, as a religious act. □ *The religious site attracted many devout pilgrims.* **2. Pilgrim** *n.* one of the settlers of Plymouth Colony in 1620. □ *The Pilgrims crossed the Atlantic Ocean in a ship called the* Mayflower. □ *Many Pilgrims did not survive the first winter in the New World.*

**pill** ['pɪl] *n.* a small, formed mass containing vitamins, medicine, or some other drug that is swallowed. □ *My grandfather takes pills for his heart condition.*

**pillow** ['pɪl o] *n.* a cloth bag filled with feathers or a similar soft material, typically used to support one's head while sleeping, or for decoration. □ *My neck hurts because I slept without a pillow last night.*

**pillowcase** ['pɪl o kes] *n.* a fabric cover for a pillow. □ *I put a new feather pillow inside the pillowcase.*

**pilot** ['paɪ lət] **1.** *n.* someone who flies a plane; someone who guides a boat along a channel. □ *The pilot steered the boat through the shipping channel in the harbor.* **2.** *tv.* to fly an airplane; to guide a boat through a channel. □ *Dave piloted the ship away from the reef.* **3.** *adj.* experimental; serving as a test. □ *The researchers refined the methods used in the pilot study.*

**pimple** ['pɪm pəl] *n.* a small, round infection on the skin. □ *Makeup gives me pimples.*

**pin** ['pɪn] **1.** *n.* a thin, stiff, pointed wire occurring in a variety of forms, such as with a flat top, a plastic end, a safety cover on the end, etc. (The simple ① is also called a *straight pin.*) □ *Mary accidentally stuck her finger with a pin.*

P

**2.** *n.* a piece of jewelry that is attached to clothing with a variety of ①. ☐ *Mary wore an attractive pin on the lapel of her jacket.* **3.** *tv.* to attach something to something else with some variety of ①. ☐ *The secretary pinned an important message to the message board.* **4.** *tv.* to press someone or something against something. ☐ *The police officer pinned the thief to the wall.*

**pinch** ['pɪntʃ] **1.** *n.* an act of squeezing a fold of skin, usually causing pain. ☐ *Susie returned Jimmy's insult with a pinch on the arm.* **2.** *n.* a small amount of something, such as a spice, that can be held between one's first finger and one's thumb. ☐ *This tomato sauce needs another pinch of salt.* **3.** *tv.* to squeeze or hold something, such as a fold of flesh, between two surfaces. ☐ *Mary got a bruise when Bob pinched her arm.*

**pine** ['pɑɪn] **1.** *n.* a kind of tree that has long, thin, sharp needles for leaves. ☐ *The mountain cabin was surrounded by tall pines.* **2.** *n.* wood from ①. (Plural only when referring to different kinds, types, instances, or varieties.) ☐ *The hunter carved a figure out of pine.* 🄲 *The pines that we use for flooring are much harder than the soft pine used for woodwork.* **3.** *adj.* made from ②; composed of ②. ☐ *I stained the pine desk to protect the wood.* **4. pine for** someone or something *iv.* + *prep. phr.* to suffer because one does not have or has lost someone or something. ☐ *Bob pined for his lost dog for weeks.*

**pineapple** ['pɑɪn æp əl] **1.** *n.* a large, juicy tropical fruit that is yellow on the inside and has a very rough skin. ☐ *The cook used a sharp knife to slice through the pineapple.* **2.** *n.* the edible part of ①. (No plural form.) ☐ *The cook added some pineapple to the cake batter.* **3.** *adj.* made from ②; containing or flavored with ②. ☐ *Mary drank a glass of pineapple juice with her breakfast.*

**pink** ['pɪŋk] **1.** *n.* the color of red mixed with white; a light, pale red. (Plural only when referring to different kinds, types, instances, or varieties.) ☐ *For the Valentine's Day dance, the school gym was decorated in pink and red.* 🄲 *The pinks and reds of the sunrise were stunningly beautiful.* **2.** *adj.* <the adj. use of ①.> (Comp: *pinker;* sup: *pinkest.*) ☐ *Mary is wearing a pink blouse today.*

**pint** ['pɑɪnt] **1.** *n.* a unit of liquid measure, equal to half a quart or 1/8 of a gallon or 16 fluid ounces. ☐ *One quart equals two pints, and a pint equals two cups.* **2.** *n.* a unit of dry measure, equal to half a quart or 1/64 of a bushel. ☐ *Mary bought a pint of fresh blueberries.* **3.** *adj.* <the adj. use of ① or ②>; [of a container] holding ① or ②. ☐ *I sold the honey in plastic pint containers.*

**pioneer** [pɑɪ ə 'nɪr] **1.** *n.* someone who is one of the first of a particular group of people to settle a new area. (From the point of view of the particular group.) ☐ *Jimmy wants to be one of the first pioneers to live on the moon.* **2.** *n.* someone who is one of the first to investigate an area of science that has never been examined; someone who is one of the first people to do something, preparing the way for other people to do the same. ☐ *My grandfather was an early pioneer in science.* **3.** *tv.* to prepare the way for other people to do something; to help develop something for other people. ☐ *Alexander Graham Bell pioneered the development of the telephone.*

**pipe** ['pɑɪp] **1.** *n.* a hollow tube that is used to carry a fluid from one place to another. ☐ *Oil was transported from the well through a very long pipe.* **2.** *n.* a tube connected to a small bowl, used to smoke tobacco. ☐ *Bill gave up smoking a pipe for the sake of his health.*

**pirate** ['pɑɪ rət] **1.** *n.* someone who robs ships at sea. ☐ *The ship's cargo was stolen by pirates.* **2.** *tv.* to steal or capture something, especially while at sea. □ *The rebels pirated the ship's cargo of gold and silver.* **3.** *tv.* to take something; to use something when one does not have the right to use it. (Fig. on ②.) □ *John pirated office supplies from his workplace.* **4.** *tv.* to duplicate and sell copies of books, records, videos, and software without the permission of the original publisher. (Fig. on ②.) □ *Some countries do not punish persons who pirate videos and records.*

**piss** ['pɪs] **1.** *iv.* to urinate. (Potentially offensive. The topic and the word are not heard in polite company. Use with caution.) □ *That dog is pissing on my shoe!* **2.** *n.* urine. (Comments as with sense ①.) □ *There's piss on my shoe.*

**pissed off** ['pɪst 'ɔf] *adj.* angry. (Not often heard in polite company, but its use is increasing.) □ *I am so pissed off, I could just scream!*

**pistol** ['pɪs təl] *n.* a small gun that can be held and shot with one hand. □ *The robber pointed the pistol at the clerk.*

**piston** ['pɪs tən] *n.* a solid cylinder that is moved up and down inside a tube by some force, such as that found in an engine. □ *Does your car's engine have four pistons or six?*

**pit** ['pɪt] **1.** *n.* a large hole in the ground. □ *My dog dug a shallow pit in the backyard.* **2.** *n.* a large, hard seed at the center of some kinds of fruit. □ *Anne spit the cherry pits into the sink.* **3. pit someone or something against someone or something** *tv. + obj. + prep. phr.* to place someone or something in competition with someone or something else. □ *I pitted my wits against the computer in a game of chess.* **4.** *tv.* to remove ② from fruit. □ *Have these chocolate-covered cherries been pitted?*

**pitch** ['pɪtʃ] **1.** *tv.* to toss something toward someone or something. □ *Lisa pitched a rock into the pond.* **2.** *tv.* [in baseball] to toss or throw a ball toward the batter. □ *Don't pitch it so hard!* **3.** *tv.* to toss or throw someone or something. □ *The farmer pitched the hay into the wagon.* **4.** *iv.* [in baseball] to throw a baseball toward a batter. □ *My older brother pitches in the major leagues.* **5.** *iv.* [for a ship] to plunge up and down; [for the front of a ship] to rise and fall in rough water. □ *The heavy waves and wind caused the ship to pitch.* **6.** *n.* [in baseball] the movement of the ball from the pitcher toward the batter or the throw that moves the ball toward the batter. □ *The catcher caught the fast pitch.* **7.** *n.* slope; the amount that something is slanted. (Plural only when referring to different kinds, types, instances, or varieties.) □ *It was hard to install shingles on the roof because of its pitch.* Ⓒ *The different pitches of the roof and the many gables give the house character and an air of mystery.* **8.** *n.* the measure of highness or lowness of a sound. (Plural only when referring to different kinds, types, instances, or varieties.) □ *A note is flat if its pitch is too low.* Ⓒ *When high pitches are loud they hurt my ears.* **9.** *n.* the standard number of vibrations each second that makes a certain tone; the standard musical sound for a given note. □ *Please sing exactly on this pitch, which is middle C.*

**pitcher** ['pɪtʃ ɚ] **1.** *n.* the baseball player who pitches the baseball toward the other team's players who then may strike it with the bat. □ *The catcher threw the baseball back to the pitcher.* **2.** *n.* a tall container with a handle, used for serving liquids. □ *Bill carried water to the dinner table in a pitcher.* **3.** *n.* the contents of ②. □ *I watered the plant with a pitcher of water.*

**pity** ['pɪt i] **1.** *n.* a feeling of sorrow caused by seeing or learning about the suffering of other people; sympathy. (No plural form.) □ *The rich man was moved by pity and gave the charity a*

P

*large donation.* **2.** *tv.* to be sorry for someone or something; to feel ① for someone or something. □ *I pitied the poor children of the cruel parents.*

**pizza** ['pit sə] *n.* a food made of a baked disk of dough covered with spicy tomato sauce, cheese, and perhaps other foods. (Plural only when referring to different kinds, types, instances, or varieties. Number is expressed with *slice(s) of pizza.*) □ *Would you rather have pizza or hamburgers tonight?* 🄲 *Two of the pizzas have onions, and the other one does not.*

**pl** an abbreviation of plural ①.

**place** ['ples] **1.** *n.* a position in space; a location; a certain area. □ *Anne put the key in the place where she found it.* **2.** *n.* a house or apartment; a location where one lives. □ *Would you like to visit my new place?* **3.** *n.* a position in relation to other positions in a numbered series. □ *My horse finished in last place because it stumbled on the racetrack.* **4.** *tv.* to put something in a certain position; to put something on a certain surface. □ *Please place my drink on the table next to my salad.* **5.** *tv.* to remember when and where one has met someone or something in the past. □ *I know who you're talking about, but I can't place the face.*

**plague** ['pleg] **1. the plague** *n.* a disease that kills people and is quickly spread. (No plural form. Treated as singular.) □ *The plague was spread by rats.* **2. plague** someone **with** something *tv.* + *obj.* + *prep. phr.* to annoy someone with repeated questions, problems, etc. □ *The troublesome student plagued the teacher with questions.*

**plaid** ['plæd] **1.** *n.* a design of stripes that cross each other at right angles. □ *Mary's school uniform has a red plaid on the skirt.* **2.** *adj.* <the adj. use of ①.> □ *Anne wore a plaid skirt to the party.*

**plain** ['plen] **1.** *n.* a flat area of land; a prairie. (Often plural with the same meaning, but not countable.) □ *Buffalo used to roam across the plains.* **2.** *adj.* obvious; easy to see or understand. (Adv: *plainly.* Comp: *plainer;* sup: *plainest.*) □ *It was plain to everyone at the office that Bill would soon be fired for his bad performance.* **3.** *adj.* simple; not complex; not decorated. (Adv: *plainly.* Comp: *plainer;* sup: *plainest.*) □ *Anne's presentation was rather plain, but it was easy to understand.* **4.** *adj.* not attractive; average looking. (Adv: *plainly.* Comp: *plainer;* sup: *plainest.*) □ *My face is sort of plain, but I have a nice smile!* **5.** *adv.* simply; clearly; obviously. (Colloquial.) □ *John didn't play basketball because he was just plain too short.*

**plaintiff** ['plen tɪf] *n.* someone who sues someone else; someone who brings a lawsuit against someone else; someone who charges a defendant with doing wrong. □ *The plaintiff is suing the defendant for $100,000.*

**plan** ['plæn] **1.** *n.* the ideas for a future action or event; a detailed schedule for doing something. □ *Anne and John told me of their plans to get married.* **2. plans** *n.* a set of drawings of a house or building before it is built, used to help someone build the building. (Treated as plural.) □ *An architect drafted the plans for the new office building.* **3.** *n.* a program or structure that provides a benefit to workers. □ *The company has a retirement plan for all its workers.* **4.** *tv.* to make ① for an event. □ *Mary began planning her wedding a year in advance.* **5.** *iv.* to arrange [something] in advance. □ *Mary spent weeks planning for the party.* **6. plan to do** something *iv.* + *inf.* to make ① for doing something in the future; to mean to do something. □ *Bill doesn't plan to go to college.*

**plane** ['plen] **1.** *n.* a flat surface. □ *The intersection of two planes is a line.* **2.** *n.*

P

an airplane. □ *Mary took a plane from New York to London.* **3.** *n.* a tool equipped with a blade that is scraped over wood to make it flat or smooth. □ *I used a plane to smooth the wooden railing.* **4.** *tv.* to make something flat or smooth by using ③. □ *When I planed the board, wood shavings fell to the ground.*

**planet** ['plæn ɪt] *n.* a huge sphere of matter that circles a single star in a permanent orbit. □ *Some planets are orbited by moons.*

**plank** ['plæŋk] **1.** *n.* a board; a long, thin, narrow, flat piece of wood. □ *Tom nailed some planks to a pair of logs to make a raft to float on the lake.* **2.** *n.* an issue or policy that a political party officially supports. (A figurative **plank** ① in the party **platform** ③.) □ *Bob agreed with all the planks of his party's platform.*

**plant** ['plænt] **1.** *n.* a stationary living thing that takes its food from the soil or other substance that supports it. □ *Anne watered the plants in her yard.* **2.** *n.* a factory. □ *My father worked at the car plant for 30 years.* **3.** *tv.* to put a seed or a small ① in the ground so that it will grow; to place [the seeds or young ① of] a crop into the soil. □ *The gardener planted roses in the flower garden.* **4.** *tv.* to place someone or something firmly in position. (Fig. on ③.) □ *Plant yourself in that doorway, and don't let anyone leave.*

**plaster** ['plæs tɚ] **1.** *n.* a mixture of lime, water, and sand, which hardens when it dries. (Plural only when referring to different kinds, types, instances, or varieties.) □ *Plaster fell from the ceiling when something heavy crashed on the floor above.* 🄲 *Plasters of different characteristics are layered upon each other to make the wall.* **2.** *tv.* to apply ① to something. □ *The landlord plastered the ceiling and then painted it.*

**plastic** ['plæs tɪk] **1.** *n.* an artificial material, made from a variety of chemicals, that can be formed into different shapes. (Plural only when referring to different kinds, types, instances, or varieties.) □ *The lenses in my eyeglasses are made of plastic.* 🄲 *Most plastics are made from petroleum.* **2.** *adj.* made of ①. □ *The plastic spoon melted against the edge of the hot pan.* **3.** *adj.* [of something] easily molded or shaped. (Adv: *plastically* [...ɪk li].) □ *Shape the wax figure while it is still warm and plastic.*

**plate** ['plet] **1.** *n.* an almost flat, round dish for holding food. □ *Anne put some corn on my plate next to my potatoes.* **2.** *n.* a sheet of metal or glass. □ *The spy's car was reinforced with metal plates.* **3.** *n.* a metal plate that goes on the back of a vehicle showing the license number of the vehicle. (Short for **license plate.**) □ *I had to get new plates for my new car. My old plates were destroyed in an accident.* **4.** *tv.* to give one sort of metal a thin outer layer of a more valuable metal. □ *The worker plated each piece of silverware with a new layer of silver.*

**platform** ['plæt form] **1.** *n.* a flat structure that is higher than the area around it, especially one that people can occupy standing or sitting. □ *The guards prevented the fans from climbing onto the platform where the famous singer was performing.* **2.** *n.* the flat surface next to a railroad track where people get on and off trains. □ *I set my luggage on the platform while I was waiting for the train.* **3.** *n.* a formal statement of the ideas and policies of a political party. □ *Mary was upset with the philosophy of her party's platform.*

**platter** ['plæt ɚ] **1.** *n.* a large plate used for serving food. □ *The cook arranged the slices of baked ham on the platter.* **2.** *n.* the contents of ①. □ *Twenty platters of roast pork were served at the banquet.*

**play** ['ple] **1.** *n.* fun; recreation; something that is done for fun or amusement. (No plural form.) □ *The children's play was interrupted by dinner.* **2.** *n.* one movement or action in a game or sport. □ *The football team planned its next play in the huddle.* **3.** *n.* a piece of writing that is written as a series of lines that people say, for performance in a theater. □ *Bob is trying to get a part in the school play.* **4.** *n.* a performance of ③. □ *I have tickets to see a play tonight.* **5.** *iv.* [for a sound-making device] to operate or reproduce sounds that have been recorded. □ *The stereo played while I washed the dishes.* **6.** *iv.* to perform on the stage or in public; to perform. □ *The actors played for the senior citizens' group.* **7.** *iv.* [for a performance] to be performed; [for a movie] to be shown. □ Hamlet *will play at that theater for two weeks, beginning tomorrow.* **8.** *iv.* to take one's turn in a game; to lay down a card in a card game. □ *John thought for a long time before he played.* **9.** *iv.* to perform [on a musical instrument as in ⑮]. □ *The violinist stopped playing when the music fell off the stand.* **10.** *iv.* to have fun; to amuse oneself; to be active in a sport or game. □ *Jimmy and Susie got dirty when they played in the mud.* **11. play with** someone *iv.* + *prep. phr.* to join or spend time with someone or a group and **play** together as in ⑩. □ *I am not good enough, and they won't let me play with them.* **12.** *tv.* to perform a role in the theater or in a movie. □ *Anne played a leading role in the play.* **13.** *tv.* to take part in a certain game, sport, or activity; to participate in a certain game, sport, or activity. □ *John plays basketball every day after work.* **14.** *tv.* to make music with a musical instrument; to perform a particular piece of music on an instrument. □ *I can play "Home, Sweet Home" on the clarinet.* **15.** *tv.* to perform on a musical instrument. □ *Can you play the piano while I sing?* **16.** *tv.* [for an electronic device] to process tapes, records, or CDs in a way that produces the sounds or pictures that have been recorded. □ *My stereo will not play the record I just bought.* **17.** *tv.* [for someone] to cause an electronic device to produce sounds and pictures as in ⑯. □ *I can't play this record on my player!*

**player** ['ple ɚ] **1.** *n.* someone who plays a game or sport. □ *How many players are on each team?* **2.** *n.* someone who plays a particular musical instrument. □ *The conductor rehearsed the piece with the flute players.* **3.** *n.* something that plays a recording. (Compare this with **recorder** ③.) □ *I listened to the cassette on my portable tape player.*

**playful** ['ple fʊl] **1.** *adj.* liking to play; full of fun. (Adv: *playfully.*) □ *Playful children ran through the park, laughing and singing.* **2.** *adj.* funny; humorous; not serious. (Adv: *playfully.*) □ *Bob gave his friend a playful punch in the arm.*

**playground** ['ple graʊnd] **1.** *n.* an outdoor place for children to play. □ *Jimmy fell and hurt himself at the playground.* **2.** *adj.* <the adj. use of ①.> □ *The playground equipment needs to be painted.*

**plaything** ['ple θɪŋ] *n.* a toy; something that is played with. □ *The puppy grabbed the plaything from Susie's hand.*

**plea** ['pli] **1.** *n.* a request; an appeal. □ *The group of citizens made a plea for lower tax rates.* **2.** *n.* a statement in court in which one declares that one is guilty or innocent. □ *A plea of guilty from a defendant means that he will spend time in prison.*

**plead** ['plid] **1. plead for** something *iv., irreg.* + *prep. phr.* to beg for something; to ask for something. (Pt/pp: *pleaded* or **pled.**) □ *The criminal pled for mercy.* **2.** *tv., irreg.* to declare in court that one is guilty or not guilty before the trial actually begins. □ *Everyone expected the thief to plead guilty.* **3.** *tv., irreg.* to claim

P

something as an excuse. (The object can be a clause with **that** ⑦.) □ *Mary pled that she did not have enough time to be as careful as she should.*

**pleasant** ['plɛz ənt] **1.** *adj.* [of something] bringing or causing enjoyment and pleasure. (Adv: *pleasantly.*) □ *Jane played some pleasant music during dinner.* **2.** *adj.* [of someone] friendly and nice. (Adv: *pleasantly.*) □ *The pleasant clerk helped me find what I was looking for.*

**please** ['pliz] **1.** *adv.* <a word used to make requests or commands more polite.> □ *Could you please pass the salt?* **2.** *tv.* to cause someone to be happy or satisfied. □ *If your work pleases your boss, you may get a promotion.*

**pleasure** ['plɛʒ ɚ] *n.* a feeling of happiness because of something that one likes; enjoyment; a pleasing feeling or emotion. (Plural only when referring to different kinds, types, instances, or varieties.) □ *The happily married couple brought pleasure to each other's life.* Ⓒ *Bob thinks chocolate is one of life's small pleasures.*

**pled** ['plɛd] a pt/pp of **plead**.

**pledge** ['plɛdʒ] **1.** *n.* a promise; a vow; a statement that one will do something. □ *I made a pledge to stop smoking.* **2. pledge to** do something *iv. + inf.* to vow or promise to do something. □ *Bob pledged to stop smoking again.* **3.** *tv.* to promise something. (The object can be a clause with **that** ⑦.) □ *We pledged $10 toward the total amount.*

**plentiful** ['plɛn tɪ fʊl] *adj.* having enough or more than enough; ample. (Adv: *plentifully.*) □ *When jobs are plentiful, the unemployment rate is low.*

**plenty** ['plɛn ti] **1.** *n.* a full supply; more than enough. (No plural form.) □ *This year we had a good crop and experienced plenty as we never had before.* **2.** *adj.* enough; almost too much. (Not prenominal.) □ *I don't need any more soup. That's plenty.*

**pliers** ['plɑɪ ɚz] *n.* a tool with rough jaws, used to grasp objects. (Usually treated as plural. Number is expressed with *pair(s) of pliers.* Also countable.) □ *John looked in the garage for some pliers.* Ⓒ *I have two or three pliers in this drawer somewhere.*

**plot** ['plɑt] **1.** *n.* the story of a movie, book, opera, television show, play, etc. □ *The TV show's plot was so silly that I refused to finish watching it.* **2.** *n.* a secret plan to do something wrong or illegal. □ *The rebels' plot to kill the prince was foiled.* **3.** *n.* a small garden or part of a garden; a small area of land. □ *My house sits on a beautiful plot of land.* **4.** *iv.* to plan in secret. □ *The terrorists plotted late into the night.* **5. plot to** do something *iv. + inf.* to make plans to do something, especially secretly. □ *The terrorists plotted to destroy the building.* **6.** *tv.* to plan in secret to do something. □ *The terrorists plotted the murder of the president.* **7.** *tv.* to determine the position of something on a map, chart, or graph. □ *The driver plotted the easiest route to the village.*

**plotter** ['plɑt ɚ] *n.* a machine that marks points, lines, or curves on a graph. □ *The plotter graphed difficult equations accurately.*

**plow** ['plɑʊ] **1.** *n.* a farm tool made of a heavy metal blade used to break up and turn over soil. □ *The farmer used a tractor to pull the plow.* **2.** *n.* a large, curved blade in front of a vehicle that is used to move snow off a road or path. □ *After clearing the road, John removed the plow from the front of his truck.* **3.** *n.* a vehicle equipped with ②. □ *The plows cleared the main roads before rush hour.* **4.** *iv.* to use ①. □ *The farmer plowed all day but couldn't finish by dark.* **5.** *tv.* to cut into land, making rows for planting crops, with ①. □ *John plowed 90 acres* *today.* **6.** *tv.* to clear a road or path of snow with ②. □ *The store owner plowed the path clean.*

**pluck** ['plʌk] **1.** *tv.* to remove the feathers from a bird; to remove hairs from the body of a person or an animal. □ *John plucked the hair from his nose.* **2.** *tv.* to clean a bird of its feathers. □ *Of course, the duck is dead when you pluck it.* **3.** *tv.* to pull something from some place. □ *The father plucked the young child away from the dog.*

**plug** ['plʌg] **1.** *n.* a small device for closing a hole, drain, or other opening. □ *I put the plug in the drain to keep the water from running out of the bathtub.* **2.** *n.* the connector that is pushed into an electric receptacle. (Short for **electric plug.**) □ *The vacuum cleaner plug is broken, and I can't use it.* **3.** *n.* a statement made while speaking on television or radio that encourages people to buy something or do something. □ *The movie star made a plug for his favorite snack food.* **4.** *tv.* to mention a product and to encourage people to buy it. □ *The author plugged her new book on the talk show.*

**plum** ['plʌm] **1.** *n.* a fruit with a smooth skin and a soft, sweet, juicy pulp with a large pit. □ *Anne bit into a ripe, juicy plum.* **2.** *n.* a deep purple color. □ *The actress wore plum to the awards ceremony.* **3.** *adj.* deep purple in color. □ *The actress wore a plum dress to the awards ceremony.*

**plumber** ['plʌm ɚ] *n.* someone who is trained to install and repair sewer pipes, water pipes, and fixtures such as sinks, toilets, bathtubs, and drains. □ *I hired a professional plumber to replace my old tub.*

**plumbing** ['plʌm ɪŋ] **1.** *n.* the work that a plumber does. (No plural form.) □ *I learned plumbing from my father, who is a licensed plumber.* **2.** *n.* water and sewer pipes and fixtures. (No plural form.) □ *The rural family finally got indoor plumbing last year.*

**plume** ['plum] **1.** *n.* a feather, especially a bright, colorful one. □ *A bright red plume was attached to Anne's hat.* **2.** *n.* something that looks like a feather, especially a cloud of smoke or a jet of water. □ *A plume of water shot up from the fountain.*

**plump** ['plʌmp] *adj.* a little fat or swollen. □ *The plump turkey was juicy and delicious.*

**plunge** ['plʌndʒ] **1.** *n.* a dive; a jump into water. □ *I took a plunge off the high diving board.* **2.** *iv.* to dive into a liquid. □ *The swimmer plunged into the pool.*

**plural** ['plɚ əl] **1.** *n.* <a form of a word that refers to more than one thing or person.> (No plural form. Abbreviated "pl" here.) □ *In English,* [z], [s], *or* [əz] *is added to regular nouns to form the plural.* □ *The plural of* child *is* children. **2.** *adj.* <the adj. use of ①.> □ *In English, plural nouns often end in* -s.

**plus** ['plʌs] **1.** *prep.* in addition to someone or something; added to someone or something. (Symbolized by "+".) □ *2 + 4 = 6 is to be read, "Two plus four equals six."* □ *Any number plus zero equals that number.* **2.** *conj.* and also. □ *I'd like to order eggs and bacon, plus some toast.* **3.** *adj.* above zero; [marking a number] greater than zero. (Symbolized as "+".) □ *After the first round, Bob had scored –25, and Mary, +30.* **4.** *n.* an advantage; an extra. □ *As a plus, the baker gave me an extra doughnut for free.*

**ply** ['plɑɪ] **1.** *n.* a layer of something. (Hyphenated after a number.) □ *One-ply paper towels don't clean spills as well as the two-ply kinds.* **2.** *tv.* to work doing one's job, especially at one's trade. □ *Anne plies her skills as an independent bookkeeper.*

**plywood** ['plaɪ wʊd] *n.* a wooden panel made of several thin sheets of wood that are glued together. (No plural form.) □ *The store owner put plywood in the frame in place of the broken window.*

**pocket** ['pɑk ɪt] **1.** *n.* a small cloth bag that is sewn into clothing and is used to hold things, such as a wallet or keys. □ *The police searched my pockets for stolen property.* **2.** *n.* a small amount of something that is separated from other amounts of it; an isolated amount of something. □ *This neighborhood is a pocket of wealth in an otherwise poor city.* **3.** *adj.* small enough to fit in ①; meant to be put in ①. □ *I looked at my pocket watch to check the time.* **4.** *tv.* to put something in one's **pocket** ①. □ *Anne pocketed the note that Mary gave her in class.* **5.** *tv.* to steal something by putting it in one's **pocket** ①. □ *The clerk saw the teenager pocket a valuable watch.*

**pod** ['pɑd] *n.* a long, soft, narrow shell that holds the seeds of certain plants, such as peas and beans. □ *The large pod contained over ten peas.*

**poem** ['po əm] *n.* a piece of writing in a form that sometimes rhymes and often has a rhythm, usually expressing feelings, emotions, or imagination. □ *Mary wrote a romantic poem to her best friend.*

**poet** ['po ɪt] *n.* someone who writes poetry. □ *The poet read his poetry aloud in the café.*

**poetic** [po 'ɛt ɪk] **1.** *adj.* [of thoughts] expressed as a poem. (Adv: *poetically* [...ɪk li].) □ *The poetic wedding invitation was printed on fine paper.* **2.** *adj.* <the adj. form of **poetry**.> □ *My writing teacher explained the different poetic structures.*

**poetry** ['po ə tri] **1.** *n.* a poem; poems; a collection of poems. (No plural form. Treated as singular.) □ *We studied Emily Dickinson's poetry in English class.* **2.** *n.* the art of writing poems. (No plural form.) □ *Bob writes excellent stories, but he is not very good at poetry.*

**point** ['pɔɪnt] **1.** *n.* the sharp end of something. □ *I broke the pencil point by writing too hard.* **2.** *n.* the main idea of something; the purpose of something. □ *The lecturer repeated the important points of his speech.* **3.** *n.* one idea, argument, or statement in a series of ideas, arguments, or statements. □ *The last point the report addressed was the budget.* **4.** *n.* a certain position in space or moment in time; a certain degree or position of something. □ *From this point on, I vow to stop drinking.* **5.** *n.* [in geometry] the place where two lines cross each other. □ *Any three points not in a line define a plane.* **6.** *n.* a dot; a **decimal point**. □ *Bob had a temperature of ninety-nine point four.* **7.** *n.* a feature, trait, or ability of someone or something. □ *Anne's good points far outweigh her bad ones.* **8.** *n.* a unit of scoring in a game. □ *Anne beat David in cards by 200 points.* **9.** *n.* a helpful hint; a piece of advice. □ *I asked the author for some points on getting published.* **10.** *tv.* to aim someone at someone or something; to direct someone to someone or something. □ *The waiter pointed me toward the restroom.* **11.** *iv.* to indicate the location of someone or something by directing one's finger toward the location. □ *Mary pointed at the dog that had bitten her.* **12.** *iv.* to be facing in a certain direction. □ *If you're pointing north, east is to your right.*

**poison** ['pɔɪ zən] **1.** *n.* a substance that can injure or kill a living creature, especially if eaten, drunk, breathed in, or absorbed through the skin. (Plural only when referring to different kinds, types, instances, or varieties.) □ *Mary baited the rat trap with poison.* Ⓒ *We used a few different poisons on the ants, but nothing seems to work.* **2.** *tv.* to kill or harm someone or something with ①. □ *Anne* *was sent to jail for poisoning her husband.* **3.** *tv.* to put ① in something, especially food, in order to kill or harm someone or something. □ *The cook poisoned the rich man's breakfast.* **4.** *tv.* to have a harmful effect on someone or something; to corrupt someone or something. (Fig. on ②.) □ *The government lies poisoned the citizens' minds.*

**poke** ['pok] **1.** *n.* a push with one's finger, fist, or elbow, or with a blunt object. □ *Anne woke me up with a gentle poke.* **2.** *tv.* to push someone or something with one's finger, fist, or elbow, or with a blunt object. □ *Mary poked the logs in the fire.*

**poker** ['pok ɚ] **1.** *n.* a long, narrow metal rod that is used to move logs or coal in a fire. □ *I hung the poker in its stand next to the fireplace.* **2.** *n.* a card game where players win by having cards with the highest value. (No plural form.) □ *In poker, having four aces is very good.*

**polar** ['po lɚ] *adj.* of or about the areas near the north or south pole. □ *The polar climate is very cold.*

**pole** ['pol] **1.** *n.* a long, thin, solid tube of wood, steel, plastic, or other material. □ *My fishing pole jerked when I had caught a fish.* **2.** *n.* one of the two places where the imaginary axis on which a planet spins meets the surface of the planet—at the north and south ends of the planet. □ *I wanted to place a flag at the north pole, but someone had already done it.* **3.** *n.* either side of a magnet; either end of a magnet; one of the two strongest points of a magnet that either pulls or pushes metal objects. □ *A positively charged object sticks to the magnet's negative pole.*

**police** [pə 'lis] **1. the police** *n.* people who have the authority to maintain law and order by arresting people who break the law. (No plural form. Treated as plural, but not countable. Number is expressed with police officer(s).) □ *The police raced to the scene of the crime.* **2.** *tv.* to patrol an area; to control, regulate, or protect an area. □ *The security guard policed the building lobby.* **3.** *tv.* to regulate or control people, their behavior, or their actions. □ *The students' behavior was policed by the stern principal.*

**policeman** [pə 'lis mən] *n., irreg.* a police officer; a male member of a police force. (Pl: policemen or police officers.) □ *The witness told the policemen what she had seen.*

**policemen** [pə 'lis mən] pl of policeman.

**police officer** [pə 'lis ɔ fə sɚ] *n.* a member of a police department; a policeman; a policewoman. □ *There is a police officer in the car behind us.*

**policewoman** [pə 'lis wʊm ən] *n., irreg.* a female police officer; a female member of a police force. (Pl: policewomen or police officers.) □ *The female customer was searched by a policewoman.*

**policewomen** [pə 'lis wɪm ən] pl of policewoman.

**policy** ['pɑl ə si] *n.* a plan of action used by management or government; a regulation. □ *I can't issue a refund without a receipt. It's the store's policy.*

**polish** ['pɑl ɪʃ] **1.** *n.* a substance that is used to make something shiny. (Plural only when referring to different kinds, types, instances, or varieties.) □ *The maid rubbed the silverware with the special polish.* Ⓒ *Too many of the commercial polishes are abrasive and rub the silver off.* **2.** *tv.* to make a surface shiny or glossy, especially by rubbing it. □ *Please polish your shoes before you go to the wedding.* **3.** *tv.* to improve something; to make something better or perfect; to refine something. (Fig. on ②.) □ *The author polished her manuscript before mailing it to the editor.*

**polite** [pə 'lɑɪt] *adj.* courteous; having good behavior; having good manners;

P

doing things in a helpful and kind way. (Adv: *politely.*) □ *Tom is a polite host and always makes us feel comfortable.*

**political** [pə 'lɪ tɪ kəl] *adj.* of or about politics, politicians, or government. (Adv: *politically* [...ɪk li].) □ *In the primaries, my vote was limited to one political party.*

**politician** [pɑl ə 'tɪ ʃən] *n.* a person whose business is politics, especially someone holding or seeking a government office. □ *The politician voted to cut taxes.*

**politics** ['pɑl ə tɪks] **1.** *n.* the business or operation of government; the study of the management of government. (Treated as singular or plural, but not countable.) □ *Mary entered politics because she wanted to help people.* **2.** *n.* someone's beliefs about political issues. (Treated as singular or plural, but not countable.) □ *My mother asked me not to mention my politics during dinner.*

**poll** ['pol] **1.** *n.* a survey that determines the popular opinion about an issue. □ *A new poll of smokers indicates which brands they prefer.* **2. polls** *n.* the places where people vote. (Treated as plural.) □ *The election results were announced an hour after the polls closed.* **3.** *tv.* to ask someone questions as part of a survey. □ *The magazine polled college students about their political beliefs.*

**pollen** ['pɑl ən] *n.* a yellow powder made by flowers that is part of the process of causing flowers to make seeds. (Plural only when referring to different kinds, types, instances, or varieties.) □ *The bee transported pollen from one flower to the next.* Ⓒ *Which pollens are you allergic to?*

**pollute** [pə 'lut] **1.** *tv.* to cause something to become dirty or impure. □ *Car exhaust pollutes the city's air.* **2.** *iv.* to make something dirty or impure. □ *Anne rides a bike because cars pollute.*

**pompous** ['pɑmp əs] *adj.* arrogant; too formal; too grand. (Adv: *pompously.*) □ *The pompous judge never let anyone else talk.*

**pond** ['pɑnd] *n.* a small body of water; a body of water smaller than a lake. □ *The swans swam across the pond gracefully.*

**ponder** ['pɑn dɚ] **1.** *iv.* to think carefully; to consider. □ *The student pondered for a moment before writing her answer.* **2.** *tv.* to think about something carefully; to consider something. □ *John pondered his options before he made a decision.*

**ponderous** ['pɑn dɚ əs] *adj.* slow and awkward, especially because of being large or heavy. (Adv: *ponderously.*) □ *The man was so ponderous that he could hardly walk up the stairs.*

**pony** ['pon i] *n.* a small horse. □ *John brushed the pony's coat.*

**ponytail** ['pon i tel] *n.* a bunch of hair pulled toward the back of the head and tied. □ *Anne tied her ponytail with a red ribbon.*

**poodle** ['pud l] *n.* a kind of dog that has very curly fur. □ *The poodle snapped at my ankles when I walked by it.*

**pool** ['pul] **1.** *n.* a puddle of water or other liquid. □ *The dead body was found in a pool of blood.* **2.** *n.* a game played with a number of hard balls on a table covered with felt with raised sides and six pockets. □ *Bill lost the game of pool when he knocked the wrong ball into a pocket.* **3.** *tv.* to put money or things together for common use. □ *My roommates and I pooled our money to buy a new television.*

**poor** ['por] **1.** *adj.* not rich; having very little money; not owning many things. (Comp: *poorer;* sup: *poorest.*) □ *Although my family was poor, we were happy.* **2.** *adj.* below a certain level of quality; inferior in operation or function. (Adv: *poorly.* Comp: *poorer;* sup: *poorest.*) □ *My large car gets poor gas mileage.* **3.** *adj.* worthy of pity or sympathy. □ *Oh, you poor dear! You're all wet!* **4. the poor** *n.* people who are ①. (No plural form. Treated as plural, but not countable.) □ *Who looks out for the welfare of the poor?*

**pop** ['pɑp] **1.** *n.* a quick, loud noise, like an explosion. □ *The gun made a loud pop when it was fired.* **2.** *n.* father. (Informal. Also a term of address.) □ *Hey, Pop, can I borrow your car tonight?* **3.** *n.* popular music. (No plural form.) □ *The violinist preferred classical music to pop.* **4.** *n.* **soda pop**. (Informal. No plural form.) □ *I'm thirsty. Do we have any pop?* **5.** *adj.* popular; well liked; favored. □ *All pop music sounds the same to my dad.* **6.** *iv.* to make a sound as in ①; [for something with air in it] to burst suddenly. □ *The football popped when the truck ran over it.* **7.** *tv.* to cause something to make ①; to cause something with air in it to burst suddenly. □ *I popped the soap bubble with my finger.*

**popcorn** ['pɑp korn] **1.** *n.* seeds of various kinds of corn that explode into a soft, white, fluffy mass when heated. (Plural only when referring to different kinds, types, instances, or varieties. Treated as singular.) □ *David put the bag of popcorn in the microwave.* Ⓒ *Some popcorns explode into little tiny bits and others make huge puffs of stuff.* **2.** *n.* exploded and puffed up kernels of ① eaten as food. (No plural form. Treated as singular.) □ *I poured melted butter on my popcorn.*

**poplar** ['pɑp lɚ] **1.** *n.* a kind of tall, thin tree that grows quickly. □ *A robin built its nest in a poplar in my backyard.* **2.** *n.* wood from ①. (Plural only when referring to different kinds, types, instances, or varieties.) □ *The frame of the door is made of poplar.* Ⓒ *The poplars grown in the far north are stronger than the species grown in the south.* **3.** *adj.* made from ②. □ *The picture was hung in a poplar frame.*

**poppy** ['pɑp i] *n.* a flowering herb with large red blossoms. □ *The white sap of the poppy is used to make opium.*

**popular** ['pɑp jə lɚ] *adj.* liked by many people; favored by many people; well liked. (Adv: *popularly.*) □ *Vanilla and chocolate are popular ice-cream flavors.*

**populate** ['pɑp jə let] *tv.* [for living creatures] to occupy an area. (Usually passive.) □ *The United States is populated by numerous ethnic groups.*

**population** [pɑp jə 'le ʃən] **1.** *n.* the living creatures of one kind that live in a certain area. □ *A small population of farmers and merchants support the only store in town.* **2.** *n.* the number of people or creatures living in a certain place. (No plural form.) □ *What is the population of Adamsville?*

**porch** ['portʃ] *n.* a covered structure built in front of a house, usually at a doorway. □ *The mail carrier left a package on my front porch.*

**porcupine** ['por kjə pɑɪn] *n.* a large rodent covered with sharp needles or spines that it uses to defend itself. □ *John made the mistake of trying to pick up the frightened porcupine.*

**pore** ['por] **1.** *n.* a tiny opening in the skin of plants and animals. □ *I developed pimples because my pores were clogged with oil.* **2. pore over** something *iv.* + *prep. phr.* to study something closely; to look over something thoroughly. □ *The architect pored over the designs carefully.*

**pork** ['pork] *n.* the meat of a pig, eaten as food. (No plural form.) □ *We ate barbecued pork at the picnic.*

**porpoise** ['por pəs] *n.* a mammal that lives in the sea, swimming in groups, including the dolphin. □ *The crowd applauded when the porpoise performed tricks.*

P

**port** ['port] **1.** *n.* a city on an ocean, sea, or lake that has a harbor where ships can be loaded and unloaded. □ *John was born in Port Arthur, Texas.* **2.** *n.* a harbor. □ *The enemy bombed the important ports during the war.* **3.** *adj.* on, at, or toward the left side of a ship or aircraft when one is facing the front of the ship or aircraft. □ *The passengers boarded the ship from the port side.*

**porter** ['por tɚ] *n.* someone who carries luggage for other people, especially at a hotel, airport, or train station. □ *Mary tipped the porter for carrying her luggage.*

**portrait** ['por trɪt] *n.* a painting, especially of a person or a person's face. □ *Bill hung a portrait of his uncle in his living room.*

**pose** ['poz] **1.** *n.* a certain way that someone sits or stands, especially when one is getting one's picture taken or painted. □ *John's pose looks very natural in this picture.* **2.** *iv.* to sit or stand in a certain way when someone is taking or painting one's picture. □ *My friends posed for a picture.* **3. pose as** someone or something *iv. + prep. phr.* to pretend to be someone; to pretend to have some role. □ *My twin brother posed as me while I went on vacation.* **4.** *tv.* to place someone or something, as in ①. □ *I posed my friends in front of the fountain.*

**posh** ['pɑʃ] *adj.* very lavish; elegant; full of style. (Adv: *poshly.* Comp: *posher;* sup: *poshest.*) □ *The floor of the lobby in the posh hotel is made of white marble.*

**position** [pə 'zɪ ʃən] **1.** *n.* the place where someone or something is or where someone or something belongs. □ *Your position is at the end of the line, not at the beginning.* **2.** *n.* the way that someone or something is placed or situated. □ *John sat in a comfortable position with his legs crossed.* **3.** *n.* a point of view; an opinion; the way someone thinks about a certain subject or issue. □ *John disagreed with the mayor's position on crime.* **4.** *n.* a job. □ *Mary was promoted to an important position at the bank.* **5.** *tv.* to put someone or something in a certain place. □ *Anne positioned herself in the doorway.*

**possess** [pə 'zɛs] **1.** *tv.* to have something; to own something. □ *Anne possesses one dog and two cats.* **2.** *tv.* to influence someone or something completely; [for someone or something, especially an evil spirit or the devil] to control someone or something completely. □ *The contestant in second place was possessed with jealousy.*

**possession** [pə 'zɛ ʃən] **1.** *n.* ownership. (No plural form.) □ *Possession of certain drugs is a crime.* **2.** *n.* a belonging; something that belongs to someone; something that is owned by someone. □ *John insured his possessions against theft.*

**possessive** [pə 'zɛs ɪv] **1.** *adj.* selfish; unwilling to share. (Adv: *possessively.*) □ *John's possessive girlfriend won't let him speak to other women.* **2.** *adj.* [of a word] showing possession or belonging [to someone or something]. (Adv: *possessively.*) □ His, hers, *and* its *are possessive pronouns.* □ *Possessive nouns are usually written with apostrophes.* **3.** *n.* the form of a word that shows possession. □ *The possessive of* he *is* his. □ *The possessive of* woman *is written as* woman's.

**possible** ['pɑs ə bəl] *adj.* able to be done; able to exist; able to happen; able to be true, but not necessarily true. (Adv: *possibly.*) □ *John's name was mentioned as a possible candidate for governor.*

**post** ['post] **1.** *n.* an upright, thick length of wood, steel, or other material. □ *The fence was made of wires attached to wooden posts.* **2.** *n.* a job; a position in a company or a government. □ *My uncle held the post of mayor for eight years.* **3.** *tv.* to place a written notice where

P

people can see it. □ *The city posted information about free vaccinations.* **4.** *tv.* to mail something; to send something by mail. □ *John electronically posted a memo to all employees.*

**postage** ['pos tɪdʒ] **1.** *n.* the cost of sending something through the mail, usually paid for with stamps. (No plural form.) □ *How much will the postage be if I send this letter by airmail?* **2.** *n.* the stamp or stamps that are placed on something that is mailed. (No plural form. Number is expressed with *postage stamp(s).*) □ *Most postage is canceled by machine.*

**postal** ['pos təl] *adj.* of or about mail or the post office. □ *The postal system delivers tons of mail each day.*

**postcard** ['post kɑrd] *n.* a card that is thicker than paper, sometimes has a picture on one side of it, and is used to mail someone a short letter, especially when one is traveling. □ *The artist sent postcards announcing the opening of his gallery.*

**poster** ['pos tɚ] *n.* a large sheet of thick paper carrying a message or a picture. □ *John hung posters of his favorite bands in his bedroom.*

**postmaster** ['post mæ stɚ] *n.* someone who is in charge of a post office; the head of a post office. □ *The chief of the U.S. Postal Service is the Postmaster General.*

**post office** ['post ɔf ɪs] *n.* a government building where mail is taken, sorted, and sent to the proper addresses, and where other postal business can be taken care of. □ *Post offices are closed on federal holidays.*

**posture** ['pɑs tʃɚ] **1.** *n.* the way that one sits, stands, or moves; the position of the body. (Plural only when referring to different kinds, types, instances, or varieties.) □ *Your posture is horrible! Sit up straight!* Ⓒ *If I don't sit with a variety of postures, my back gets tired and sore.* **2.** *iv.* to sit or stand in a certain way; to strike a pose. □ *The beautiful model postured in front of a mirror.*

**pot** ['pɑt] **1.** *n.* a large, deep, round container, usually used to cook or hold food or liquid. □ *Bill washed the dirty pots after dinner.* **2.** *n.* a round container that holds soil and a flower or plant. □ *John moved the pot of flowers to a sunnier place.* **3.** *n.* the contents of ① or ②. □ *John dumped a pot of water on the small fire.* **4.** *tv.* to put a plant in soil in ②. □ *John potted the small shrub and placed it on the window sill.*

**potato** [pə 'te to] **1.** *n.* a vegetable root shaped like a large egg. (Pl ends in *-es.*) □ *French fries are made from potatoes.* **2.** *n.* the plant that produces ①. (Pl ends in *-es.*) □ *Jane went to the garden to water the potatoes.* **3.** *adj.* made of or with ①. □ *My aunt used to make us potato pancakes when we visited her.*

**potato chip** [pə 'te to tʃɪp]] *n.* a thin slice of potato, fried until it is very crisp. (Often plural. Can be shortened to **chip.**) □ *The restaurant served potato chips with each sandwich.*

**potent** ['pot nt] **1.** *adj.* powerful; having a strong effect. (Adv: *potently.*) □ *The potent odor made me sick.* **2.** *adj.* [of a male] able to copulate. (Adv: *potently.*) □ *Bill became potent after seeking help from his doctor.*

**pottery** ['pɑt ə ri] **1.** *n.* dishes, bowls, vases, and other objects that are made from baked clay. (No plural form.) □ *After baking it, I painted the pottery with bright colors.* **2.** *n.* the craft or art of making objects out of clay and baking them so that the clay hardens. (No plural form.) □ *John's hobbies include pottery and painting.*

**pouch** ['pɑʊtʃ] *n.* a small bag that is used to hold a small amount of something. □ *Anne kept her change in a small canvas pouch.*

P

**poultry** ['pol tri] *n.* chickens, ducks, geese, and other birds that are used as meat or for providing eggs for humans to eat. (No plural form.) □ *The farmer raised poultry for eggs and meat.*

**pound** ['paʊnd] **1.** *n.* a unit of measure of weight, equal to 16 ounces or 0.454 kilogram. □ *I bought five pounds of flour at the grocery store.* **2.** *n.* the basic unit of money in the United Kingdom. (Symbolized as £.) □ *I have £10 left after my trip to London.* **3.** *n.* a place where stray animals are kept. □ *I adopted a cute puppy from the local pound.* **4.** *tv.* to hit someone or something very hard again and again; to beat something into a certain shape by hitting it very hard again and again. □ *The boxer pounded his opponent's face until it bled.* **5.** *iv.* [for the heart or blood pressure] to beat very hard. □ *The scary movie made my heart pound with fear.*

**pour** ['por] **1.** *iv.* to flow from a place; to come out of a place quickly and continuously. □ *Water poured out of the open faucet.* **2.** *tv.* to cause something to pour out of a place quickly and continuously. □ *Anne poured juice into her glass from the pitcher.*

**poverty** ['pav ɚ ti] *n.* the lack of the necessities for life. (No plural form.) □ *The mayor vowed to reduce poverty among the city's residents.*

**powder** ['paʊ dɚ] **1.** *n.* a substance that consists of tiny particles. (Plural only when referring to different kinds, types, instances, or varieties.) □ *The scientist dissolved some kind of powder in water.* Ⓒ *When you mix all these different colored powders together, the result is just a lot of gray dust.* **2.** *tv.* to cover or dust something with ① or a substance that has been crushed or ground into ①. □ *The cook powdered the pastry with sugar.*

**power** ['paʊ ɚ] **1.** *n.* the ability to do something; strength. (Plural only when referring to different kinds, types, or varieties. Typically singular or plural with the same meaning.) □ *This special soap has the power to clean coffee stains.* Ⓒ *Reggie says he has magic powers, but I think he is a fake.* **2.** *n.* the authority to do something; control. (Plural only when referring to different kinds, types, or varieties. Singular or plural with the same meaning.) □ *Congress has the power to cure this problem.* Ⓒ *Congress has a number of special powers to cure this problem.* **3.** *n.* the number of times that a number is multiplied by itself. □ *The third power of 5 is 125, because $5 \times 5 \times 5 = 125$.* □ *The second power of a number is also called its square.* **4.** *tv.* to supply energy to a machine or other device that uses energy. □ *Our heating system is powered by natural gas.*

**powerful** ['paʊ ɚ fʊl] *adj.* having a lot of power, energy, or force; full of strength or influence. (Adv: *powerfully.*) □ *The powerful senator urged the others to vote for the bill.*

**practical** ['præk tɪ kəl] **1.** *adj.* useful; able to be used; of or about actions and results, as opposed to ideas or theories. (Adv: *practically* [...ɪk li].) □ *Mary's practical approach solved the problem quickly.* **2.** *adj.* sensible; having common sense. (Adv: *practically* [...ɪk li].) □ *My practical roommate sewed her name into all her clothes.*

**practice** ['præk tɪs] **1.** *n.* doing an action many times so that one will do it better and better. (No plural form.) □ *With practice, you'll be able to play the guitar as well as I do.* **2.** *n.* a custom; a tradition; the way something is usually done; a habit. □ *Trying to darken one's skin in the sun is an odd practice that may lead to cancer.* **3.** *n.* the business of a doctor or a lawyer. □ *The plastic surgeon's practice was very successful.* **4.** *iv.* to rehearse. □ *The cast will practice for the play each night this week.* **5.** *tv.* to work at a skill over and over in order to become better at it. □ *The actor practiced his monologue*

P

*in front of a mirror.* **6.** *tv.* to do something; to make a habit of something. □ *I try to practice good manners at all times.* **7.** *tv.* to work in medicine or law. □ *Bob practices medicine at the county hospital.*

**prairie** ['prɛr i] *n.* a very large area of land that is covered with different kinds of grasses and plants. □ *The coyote chased the rabbit through the tall grass of the prairie.*

**praise** ['prez] **1.** *n.* saying that someone or something is good; the use of words to express satisfaction or a favorable judgment. (Singular or plural with the same meaning, but not countable.) □ *My rude roommate offers many criticisms but rarely gives praise.* **2.** *tv.* to express satisfaction with someone or something; to talk about the good things someone or something does or how good someone or something is. □ *The parents praised their children's good behavior.* **3.** *tv.* to worship someone or God with words or songs. □ *The congregation praised God in song.*

**prank** ['præŋk] *n.* a trick or joke that is played on someone. □ *As a prank, Susie put sugar in the salt shaker.*

P

**prankster** ['præŋk stɚ] *n.* someone who plays a trick or joke on someone. □ *The prankster laughed when I found the fake worm in my soup.*

**pray** ['pre] **1.** *iv.* to give thanks to God; to say a prayer to God; to ask God or someone for something. (Compare this with **prey**.) □ *Jimmy prays every night before going to bed.* **2. pray for** something *iv.* + *prep. phr.* to ask God for something. □ *Bill prayed for good health and prosperity.* **3.** *tv.* to **pray** ①, asking that something will happen the way one wants. (The object is a clause with **that** ⑦.) □ *I prayed that Anne would have a safe trip.*

**prayer** ['prɛr] **1.** *n.* communication with God or some other religious being or figure. □ *Mary felt that the power of prayer was enormous.* **2.** *n.* the words one uses when worshiping or praying to God. □ *Mary said a small prayer during the rough plane flight.*

**preach** ['pritʃ] **1.** *iv.* to give a sermon; to talk about something religious. □ *The preacher preached for nearly an hour!* **2.** *tv.* to deliver a sermon; to deliver a particular message through **preaching** as in ①. (The object can be a clause with **that** ⑦.) □ *My minister always preaches love and harmony.*

**preacher** ['pritʃ ɚ] *n.* someone who preaches; the leader of a church; a minister. (Less formal than **minister**.) □ *Bill and Anne told their preacher that they wanted to get married.*

**precious** ['prɛʃ əs] **1.** *adj.* very valuable; worth a lot of money. (Adv: *preciously.*) □ *The precious diamond was valued at over $100,000.* **2.** *adj.* very much loved; very dear to someone; cherished. (Fig. on ①. Adv: *preciously.*) □ *I grabbed a few precious belongings and ran from the burning house.* **3.** *adj.* charming and cute. (Adv: *preciously.*) □ *Susie was a sweet and precious hostess at her birthday party.*

**precise** [prɪ 'sɑɪs] *adj.* exact; carefully and accurately detailed. (Adv: *precisely.*) □ *This ruler is precise to within a millimeter.*

**precision** [prɪ 'sɪ ʒən] *n.* accuracy; the quality of being precise; doing something precisely. (No plural form.) □ *Her measurements lacked precision and had to be done again.*

**predict** [prɪ 'dɪkt] *tv.* to say that something is going to happen before it happens; to prophesy that something will happen. (The object can be a clause with **that** ⑦.) □ *The weather reporter predicted rain.*

**prediction** [prɪ 'dɪk ʃən] *n.* a statement made about something that is going to happen in the future; a prophecy. □ *The weather reporter's predictions were generally accurate.*

**preface** ['prɛf ɪs] **1.** *n.* an introduction to a speech or to something that is written. □ *The lecturer stated her main idea in the preface of her speech.* **2.** *tv.* to begin a speech or written piece with an introduction. □ *The author prefaced the textbook with a list of acknowledgments.*

**prefer** [prɪ 'fɚ] **1.** *tv.* to like someone or something better than one likes someone or something else. (The object can be a clause with **that** ⑦.) □ *I prefer coffee to tea.* **2. prefer to** do something *iv.* + *inf.* to want to do something more than one wants to do something else; to like more to do one thing than to do another. □ *Mary prefers to ride the bus to work, even though she owns a car.*

**preferable** ['prɛf ə rə bəl] *adj.* more preferred; more desirable. (Adv: *preferably.*) □ *Jane finds living in Florida preferable to here.*

**preference** ['prɛf ə rəns] **1.** *n.* special attention that is given to certain people or things; favor. (No plural form.) □ *The first people in line were given preference in seating.* **2.** *n.* someone or something that is preferred over someone or something else. □ *Among wines, my preference is white.*

**prefix** ['pri fɪks] *n.* a letter or a group of letters at the beginning of a word that usually changes the meaning of the word. □ *Common English prefixes include* re-, in-, *and* un-.

**pregnant** ['prɛg nənt] *adj.* [of a woman or female creature] carrying developing offspring within. □ *Mary is pregnant with her second child.*

**prehistoric** [pri hɪ 'stor ɪk] *adj.* happening before history was first recorded. (Adv: *prehistorically* [...ɪk li].) □ *In prehistoric times, dinosaurs walked the earth.*

**prejudice** ['prɛdʒ ə dɪs] **1.** *n.* opinion formed about someone or something before learning all the facts. (Plural only when referring to different kinds, types, instances, or varieties.) □ *The foreigners faced much prejudice.* Ⓒ *The judge seemed to have a prejudice against the lawyer.* **2.** *tv.* to cause someone to have ①. □ *The lawyer's rudeness prejudiced the jury against him.*

**prelude** ['pre lud] *n.* an introduction, especially a short piece of music that comes before a longer work of music. □ *Having arrived late, we missed the prelude.*

**premier** [prɪ 'mɪr] **1.** *adj.* best; most respected. (Prenominal only.) □ *The premier legal firm served very rich clients.* **2.** *n.* the prime minister of a country. □ *The premier of the country had been elected by the people.*

**premiere** [prɪ 'mɪr] **1.** *n.* the first performance or presentation of a play, film, symphony, etc. □ *The network advertised the season premieres heavily.* **2.** *iv.* [for a play, film, symphony, etc.] to be performed for the first time. □ *The movie that I want to see premieres next Friday.*

**premium** ['prim i əm] **1.** *n.* a regular payment to an insurance company for some kind of protection. □ *If your premium is late, you must pay a special fee.* **2.** *n.* an additional cost in addition to the regular cost. □ *I paid a premium for travel during the busy season.* **3.** *n.* a small prize or reward that is given to someone to buy something or use a service. □ *The cable television company gave remote controls as a premium for starting service.* **4.** *adj.* of high quality; costing more; of greater value. □ *I prefer to stay at a premium hotel, but couldn't afford it.*

**prenominal** [pri 'nɑm ə nəl] *adj.* [of an adjective] occurring before the noun it modifies. (Adv: *prenominally.*) □ Late,

P

*meaning "dead," can be used only as a prenominal adjective.* □ *Adjectives that are not prenominal cannot be used before the noun or nominal they modify.*

**prep.** an abbreviation of **preposition**.

**prepaid** [pri 'ped] pt/pp of **prepay**.

**prepare** [prɪ 'pɛr] **1.** *tv.* to make something ready for someone or something; to make something ready for use. □ *The maid prepared the beds for the hotel guests.* **2. prepare to** do something *iv.* + *inf.* to make oneself ready to do something. □ *I am preparing to leave town tomorrow.*

**prepay** [pri 'pe] *tv., irreg.* to pay some amount before it is due; to pay for something in advance; to pay for something before one receives it. (Pt/pp: **prepaid**.) □ *Students prepaid the fee for their first year of instruction.*

**preposition** [prɛp ə 'zɪ ʃən] *n.* a word that is used to show the relationship of one word or phrase to another word or phrase. (Abbreviated *prep.* here.) □ In, on, under, *and* through *are all English prepositions.* □ *Pronouns following prepositions should be in the objective form: "John spoke to Jane and me."*

P

**preschool** ['pri skul] *n.* a school for small children before they are old enough to go to kindergarten. □ *Jimmy went to preschool because both of his parents worked.*

**prescribe** [prɪ 'skrɑɪb] **1.** *tv.* [for a physician] to recommend or order that a certain medication be sold to and taken by a patient. □ *The doctor prescribed a new medicine for John's heart problem.* **2.** *tv.* [for a doctor] to advise a patient to do something to become or stay healthy. (The object can be a clause with **that** ⑦.) □ *My doctor prescribed exercise for my condition.* **3.** *tv.* to state something as a law; to establish something as a law. (The object can be a clause with **that** ⑦.) □ *Congress prescribed minimum sentences for certain offenses.*

**prescription** [prɪ 'skrɪp ʃən] **1.** *n.* ordering or prescribing something, especially medicine or medical treatment. □ *I responded to my doctor's prescription of exercise with a laugh.* **2.** *n.* an order to do something or take medicine, especially a written order for medicine given to a patient by a doctor. □ *My doctor gave me a prescription for a special new medicine.* **3.** *n.* the actual medicine that is ordered by ②. □ *I have to purchase a prescription at the drugstore.*

**presence** ['prɛz əns] **1.** *n.* the state of being present; being in the same place as someone or something else. (No plural form.) □ *The presence of dark clouds indicated that it would rain.* **2.** *n.* the power or influence one has in a group of people or in an institution. □ *John became an important presence in his law firm.* **3.** *n.* something that can be felt or sensed but not seen, such as a spirit. □ *We can feel her presence in the house, even though she died years ago.*

**present 1.** ['prɛz ənt] *adj.* being in the same room or place as someone or something else; not absent. □ *Many of the actor's friends were present in the audience.* **2.** ['prɛz ənt] *adj.* now; at this time; happening now. (Adv: *presently.*) □ *The crime rate is one of the mayor's present concerns.* **3.** ['prɛz ənt] *n.* now; this time; this moment in time. (No plural form.) □ *At present, five fire trucks are at the site of the accident.* **4.** ['prɛz ənt] *n.* a gift; something that is given to someone else. □ *Anne sent a thank-you note for each present she had received.* **5.** ['prɛz ənt] *n.* the state of a verb that indicates present time. (Short for **present tense**.) □ *The verb* runs *is in the present.* **6.** [prɪ 'zɛnt] *tv.* to give something to someone, especially as part of a ceremony. □ *The company presented a watch to each retired worker.*

**7.** [prɪ 'zɛnt] *tv.* to make something available for the public to see; to bring something to someone's attention. ☐ *The designer presented many ideas to the board of directors.* **8.** [prɪ 'zɛnt] *tv.* to introduce someone to someone else. ☐ *Jane presented her date to her parents.*

**presentation** [prɛz ən 'te ʃən] **1.** *n.* the way that something is shown to other people; the manner or style in which something is shown to other people. (No plural form.) ☐ *The skater's presentation received high marks from the judges.* **2.** *n.* a session of showing or explaining something to other people. ☐ *Even though she is shy, Anne enjoyed giving her presentation in class.* **3.** *n.* the ceremony of giving something to someone else. ☐ *The presentation of the prizes will begin soon.*

**present-day** ['prɛz ənt 'de] *adj.* current; happening now; of or about the present time. ☐ *In English class, we read a lot of present-day literature.*

**presently** ['prɛz ənt li] **1.** *adv.* now; at this time. ☐ *Anne is presently busy and cannot come to the telephone. Can I take a message?* **2.** *adv.* soon. (Formal.) ☐ *Flight 401 from Cleveland will be arriving presently.*

**present tense** ['prɛz ənt 'tɛns] *n.* a verb tense showing that something is happening now, at the present time. (No plural form. Can be shortened to present.) ☐ *The author rewrote her manuscript in the present tense.*

**preservation** [prɛ zɚ 've ʃən] *n.* the process of preserving something; keeping something safe or in good condition. (No plural form.) ☐ *The prime minister supported the preservation of the rain forest.*

**preserve** [prɪ 'zɚv] **1.** *tv.* to keep someone or something alive, healthy, safe, or in good condition. ☐ *I hope to preserve my peace of mind well into my old age.* **2.** *tv.* to do something or add something to something to keep it from spoiling or decaying. ☐ *Tom preserved the frog in alcohol.* **3.** *n.* an area of land where plants and animals are protected. ☐ *A staff of volunteers helped to maintain the nature preserve.* **4. preserves** *n.* fruit cooked in sugar and sealed in a jar. (Treated as plural, but not countable.) ☐ *Grandma stores her preserves in the pantry.*

**preside** [prɪ 'zɑɪd] **1.** *iv.* to be in charge of a meeting or a business; to be in control. ☐ *As long as I preside, there will be order during meetings.* **2. preside over something** *iv. + prep. phr.* to oversee something, such as a meeting. ☐ *A judge presides over a courtroom.*

**president** ['prɛz ə dənt] **1.** *n.* the leader of the government of a republic, including the leader of the government of the United States of America. ☐ *President Reagan was in office from 1981 to 1989.* **2.** *n.* the leader or head officer of an organization, club, company, university, etc. ☐ *The company president gave each employee an extra day off.* **3.** *n.* the office and position of power occupied by ① or ②. ☐ *The talk-show host interviewed the candidates running for president.*

**presidential** [prɛz ə 'dɛn ʃəl] *adj.* of or about a president; associated with a president. (Adv: *presidentially.*) ☐ *The name of the presidential airplane is* Air Force One.

**press** ['prɛs] **1.** *n.* a machine that prints letters and pictures on paper for newspapers, magazines, books, etc. (Short for printing press.) ☐ *The presses work day and night to produce the newspapers we read.* **2. the press** *n.* newspapers and, sometimes, radio and television; the mass media. (No plural form. Treated as a singular.) ☐ *The press is interested in events that people want to hear about.* **3.** *n.* the coverage of an action or event by newspapers and other

P

media. (No plural form.) □ *The publicity director tried to get more press for the new book.* **4.** *tv.* to push something against something else; to push something with force; to weigh down heavily on something. □ *John pressed the button to keep the elevator doors open.* **5.** *tv.* to move a hot iron over wrinkled clothing or fabric in order to make it smooth. □ *I pressed my shirts because they were wrinkled.* **6.** *iv.* to push against something else; to push with force; to weigh down heavily; to push forward. □ *Bill pressed against the door to keep John from entering the room.*

**pressure** ['prɛʃ ɚ] **1.** *n.* the effect of a force or a weight that is pushed against someone or something. (No plural form.) □ *If there's pressure against this button, an alarm will sound.* **2.** *n.* strong influence; strong persuasion. (Fig. on ①.) □ *Because of the president's pressure, the senator voted for the bill.*

**pretend** [prɪ 'tɛnd] **1.** *iv.* to act [as if something were so]. □ *I hate to pretend, so I will tell the truth.* **2. pretend to** do something *iv. + inf.* to act as if one were doing something; to try to look as if one were doing something. □ *Bob pretended to sleep, but I knew he was awake.* **3.** *tv.* to act as if something were so; to play by acting as if something were so. (The object is a clause with **that** ⑦.) □ *The children pretended that they lived in a castle.* □ *John pretended that he liked the ugly gift.*

**pretty** ['prɪt i] **1.** *adj.* attractive; pleasing; beautiful. (Adv: *prettily.* Comp: *prettier;* sup: *prettiest.*) □ *Mary wore a pretty blue dress to the dance.* **2.** *adv.* rather; quite; very. □ *I think my interview went pretty smoothly.*

**pretzel** ['prɛt səl] *n.* a salted, baked stick of bread, often twisted in the shape of a loose knot. □ *My uncle eats pretzels when he drinks beer.*

**prevent** [prɪ 'vɛnt] **prevent** someone **from** doing something *tv. + obj. + prep. phr.* not to allow something to happen; not to allow someone to do something; to keep something from happening; to keep someone from doing something; to stop something before it begins. □ *John's parents prevented him from going to the party.*

**preventable** [prɪ 'vɛnt ə bəl] *adj.* able to be prevented. (Adv: *preventably.*) □ *Many house fires are preventable, but many people are careless.*

**prevention** [prɪ 'vɛn ʃən] *n.* preventing something. (No plural form.) □ *The prevention of some diseases is possible with vaccinations.*

**preview** ['pri vju] **1.** *n.* an opportunity to see something before it is available to the public. □ *Most of the people who saw the preview of the new TV show liked it.* **2.** *iv.* [for something] to be shown as ①. □ *The stage play previewed before a test audience.* **3.** *tv.* to watch or listen to something as ①. □ *The audience that previewed the new movie didn't like it.*

**previous** ['pri vi əs] *adj.* earlier; happening before something else; coming before. (Adv: *previously.*) □ *The previous owner of this house moved to Florida.*

**prey** ['pre] **1.** *n.* an animal that is hunted, killed, or eaten by another animal. (No plural form. Compare this with **pray**.) □ *The lion killed its prey by crushing its windpipe.* **2.** *n.* someone who is a victim of someone else. (No plural form. Fig. on ①.) □ *The criminal's prey sought compensation for his loss.* **3. prey on** some creature *iv. + prep. phr.* to hunt and kill certain animals for food. □ *The cat preys on birds and mice.* **4. prey on** someone *iv. + prep. phr.* to victimize someone. (Fig. on ③.) □ *The thief preyed on foreign tourists.*

**price** ['prɑɪs] **1.** *n.* the amount of money that something costs; the amount of money that something will be sold for.

☐ *The price of gasoline rose two cents per gallon last week.* **2.** *tv.* to determine how much something will cost; to set the amount of money that something will cost. ☐ *The salesman priced the used car below market value.*

**pride** ['prɑɪd] **1.** *n.* the pleasure that one feels when one does something well; the feeling one has when one does something good. (No plural form.) ☐ *When my son won the competition, I was full of pride.* **2.** *n.* someone or something for which one has ①. (No plural form.) ☐ *The math scholar was the pride of her family.* **3.** *n.* a good opinion of oneself; too high an opinion of oneself. (No plural form.) ☐ *The mayor's pride made him very arrogant.*

**priest** ['prist] *n.* someone who is trained to perform religious duties. (In the United States, especially in the Roman Catholic, Orthodox Catholic, and Episcopal churches.) ☐ *Priests, ministers, and rabbis came to the convention of religious leaders.*

**prim** ['prɪm] *adj.* very proper; very formal; very exact; very precise; easily shocked by rude or rough behavior. (Adv: *primly.* Comp: *primmer;* sup: *primmest.*) ☐ *Everything at the formal wedding was prim and proper.*

**primary** ['prɑɪ mɛr i] **1.** *adj.* the most important; chief; main; principal. (Adv: *primarily* [prɑɪ 'mɛr ə li].) ☐ *My primary reason for running for mayor is to reduce crime.* **2.** *n.* an election that is held to determine who will represent a political party in the election for a political office. ☐ *After winning the primary, Jane focused on the general election.*

**primary color** ['prɑɪ mɛr i 'kʌl ɚ] *n.* one of the basic colors: red, blue, and yellow. (Other colors can be made by mixing two or three of these together.) ☐ *The design was painted with primary colors only.*

**primary school** ['prɑɪ mɛr ɪ 'skul] *n.* a school having only the earliest grades. ☐ *Students attend primary school before high school.*

**prime** ['prɑɪm] **1.** *adj.* [of a state or condition] best or excellent; of the highest quality. ☐ *The diners ate the prime roast beef.* **2.** *adj.* most important; chief; first in time, order, or importance. (Adv: *primely.*) ☐ *The prime reason I'm moving to Florida is the weather.* **3.** *tv.* to add water or liquid to a pump to replace the air that is inside so that the pump is able to draw fluid. ☐ *I poured a gallon of water into the pump to prime it.* **4.** *tv.* to make someone or something ready for something. ☐ *We primed ourselves for the bad news at the hospital.* **5.** *tv.* to cover a surface with primer before painting it. ☐ *Mary primed the door today and will paint it tomorrow.*

**primer** ['prɑɪm ɚ] *n.* a liquid that is spread over wood before one covers the wood with paint. (Plural only when referring to different kinds, types, instances, or varieties.) ☐ *The carpenter uses only high-quality primer to seal the wood.* Ⓒ *We looked at a wide variety of primers and chose the most expensive one.*

**primitive** ['prɪm ə tɪv] **1.** *adj.* early in the development of something; early in the history of humans. (Adv: *primitively.*) ☐ *In its primitive stage, the plan was just a brief outline.* **2.** *adj.* very simple; not complicated. (Adv: *primitively.*) ☐ *John's old computer is a primitive version of the latest model.*

**primp** ['prɪmp] *iv.* to dress and get ready for a social event very carefully. ☐ *Anne primped for 30 minutes before going to the party.*

**prince** ['prɪns] **1.** *n.* the son or grandson of a king or a queen. ☐ *Prince Charles is Queen Elizabeth II's eldest son.* **2.** *n.* the husband of a woman who inherits the throne and becomes queen. ☐ *When* *the queen was crowned, she and her husband, the prince, moved to the castle.*

**princely** ['prɪns li] **1.** *adj.* like a prince who has great charm and manners. □ *Mr. Walters greeted us in a princely fashion.* **2.** *adj.* elegant; refined; noble. (Fig. on ①.) □ *The princely feast featured very fine food.*

**princess** ['prɪns ɛs] **1.** *n.* the daughter or granddaughter of a king or queen. □ *The knight rescued the princess from the enemy's castle.* **2.** *n.* the wife of a prince. □ *The princess was not allowed to retain her title after divorcing the prince.*

**principal** ['prɪns ə pəl] **1.** *n.* the head of an elementary, middle, or high school. (Compare this with **principle**.) □ *Ms. Jones spoke to Principal Davis about the truant student.* **2.** *n.* an amount of borrowed money on which the borrower must pay interest. □ *Interest owed is a percentage of outstanding principal.* **3.** *n.* the most important or major person in a group. □ *The principals in the robbery were all sent to prison.* **4.** *adj.* main; chief; primary; most important. (Adv: *principally* ['prɪns ə pli].) □ *Anne is playing the principal female role in the play.*

**principle** ['prɪns ə pəl] **1.** *n.* obedience to ② and ③; honor. (No plural form. Compare this with **principal**.) □ *Anne refused for the sake of principle.* **2.** *n.* a general or fundamental law or rule. □ *Formal proofs are based on the principles of logic.* **3.** *n.* a rule of behavior or conduct. □ *The ambitious leader sacrificed her principles to gain power.*

**print** ['prɪnt] **1.** *tv.* to make letters of the alphabet by hand so that each letter is separate. □ *Please print your name on the dotted line.* **2.** *tv.* to put words or pictures on a blank piece of paper, one page at a time, using some kind of machine. □ *This picture was printed on a color copier.* **3.** *tv.* to publish a book, magazine, or newspaper using a printing press or a computer printer. □ *The publisher printed 10,000 copies of the first edition.* **4.** *tv.* to publish something that is written in a book, newspaper, magazine, or other written material. □ *The newspaper printed my comments out of context.* **5.** *tv.* to make a photograph from film. □ *Were these copies printed from the negative?* **6.** *tv.* to cause a computer to **print** ② something. □ *Jane printed the message that was on her computer screen.* **7.** *iv.* to make letters of the alphabet so that each letter is separate. □ *I asked Jane to print because I couldn't read her writing.* **8.** *iv.* to make books, magazines, newspapers, and other written material with a printing press. □ *The newspaper presses printed throughout the night.* **9.** *iv.* [for a computer printer] to **print** ② [something]. □ *This printer prints in many different colors.* **10.** *n.* fabric that has a pattern on it. □ *Anne made a dress from a bright plaid print.* **11.** *n.* a photograph that is made from film; a photograph. □ *The police showed me a print of the suspect.* **12.** *n.* a **fingerprint**. □ *Whose prints are these on the gun?*

**printer** ['prɪn tɚ] **1.** *n.* a business or person that prints books, magazines, and other materials. □ *The printer shipped the books to its warehouse.* **2.** *n.* a machine that causes computer information to be put onto paper. □ *I sent the document to the printer.*

**printing** ['prɪn tɪŋ] **1.** *n.* letters or words that are printed by hand; letters that are put on paper so that the letters are separate and distinct. (No plural form.) □ *The printing on the poster was in a foreign language.* **2.** *n.* letters that are put on a page by a press or a computer. (No plural form.) □ *The printing in the second section is smeared.* **3.** *n.* all the copies of a book printed by machine at one time. □ *Fifty thousand copies were made of the book's fourth printing.*

**printing press** ['prɪn tɪŋ 'prɛs] *n.* a machine used to print text and pictures on paper. (Can be shortened to **press.**) □ *Newspapers are printed on enormous, very fast printing presses.*

**printout** ['prɪnt ɑʊt] *n.* a copy of information from a computer, printed on paper. □ *I made a copy of the printout for everyone at the meeting.*

**prison** ['prɪz ən] **1.** *n.* a building that criminals are kept in; a large jail. □ *The governor approved the construction of five new prisons.* **2.** *n.* a place where someone is not allowed to leave; a place where someone has no freedom. (Fig. on ①.) □ *The blind man lived in a prison of darkness.*

**prisoner** ['prɪz nɚ] **1.** *n.* someone who is kept in a prison. □ *The prisoner was kept locked in his cell for 3 years.* **2.** *n.* someone or a creature that is not free to go. (Fig. on ①.) □ *The frail old people were prisoners in their own home.*

**pristine** ['prɪs tin] *adj.* as fresh and clean as when it was new; spotless. (Adv: *pristinely.*) □ *I keep our house in pristine condition.*

**privacy** ['prɑɪv ə si] *n.* a state of being away from other people or away from the attention of the public. (No plural form.) □ *I demand that you respect my privacy.*

**private** ['prɑɪv ɪt] **1.** *adj.* not shared among everyone; meant only for a small number of people; not public. (Adv: *privately.*) □ *A locked gate blocked the private road.* **2.** *adj.* individual; concerning only one person. (Adv: *privately.*) □ *The president refused to talk about his private life.* **3.** *adj.* secluded; isolated; quiet; away from other people. (Adv: *privately.*) □ *I spent the winter in a private cabin in the woods.* **4.** *adj.* not owned, controlled, or managed by the government. (Adv: *privately.*) □ *The garbage in our town is collected by a private company.*

**privilege** ['prɪv (ə) lɪdʒ] *n.* special rights; special and honored status. (Plural only when referring to different kinds, types, instances, or varieties.) □ *Privilege and power are in the hands of only a few people.* Ⓒ *The committee took away all my special privileges.*

**prize** ['prɑɪz] **1.** *n.* an award that is given to a winner; an award that is given to someone who does well in a competition. □ *The contestant in third place received a small prize.* **2.** *tv.* to consider something to be worth very much; to place a great value on something. □ *The large diamond was prized for its beauty.*

**pro** ['pro] *n.* **professional**; having great skill or training. (Pl ends in *-s.*) □ *The baseball pro demanded a higher salary.*

**probable** ['prɑb ə bəl] *adj.* having a great chance of happening; likely to happen; likely to be true. (Adv: *probably.*) □ *The probable outcome of the election is the defeat of the president.*

**probably** ['prɑb ə bli] *adv.* very likely; likely to happen or likely to be true. □ *Mary is probably at the bowling alley.*

**probe** ['prob] **1.** *n.* a complete examination or detailed search for facts. □ *The senator demanded a probe of the president's affairs.* **2.** *n.* a thin rod with a rounded end that is used to examine the inside of a hole, wound, or cavity. □ *The doctor examined my wound with a probe.* **3.** *n.* a rocket or satellite that is sent into space to relay information about space or other planets to scientists on earth. □ *The researchers examined the data transmitted by the space probe.* **4.** *tv.* to examine a hole, wound, or cavity, using ② or a similar object. □ *The surgeon probed my wound for broken glass.* **5.** *iv.* to examine; to search. □ *The reporter probed into the president's affairs.*

**problem** ['prɑb ləm] **1.** *n.* a question that must be answered; a difficulty. □ *There are too many problems to be solved in a single day!* **2.** *n.* a question put forward for solving, as in a school exercise or test. □ *I was not able to solve the math problems before class.* **3.** *adj.* difficult to deal with; difficult to work with; causing difficulty. □ *The dentist examined my problem tooth.*

**procedure** [prə 'si dʒɚ] *n.* the way that something is done; the way that a process is done; a method. □ *Bill taught me the procedures for operating the machine.*

**proceed 1.** [prə 'sid] *iv.* to begin to do something. □ *Bill went to the kitchen and proceeded to eat a piece of cheese.* **2. proceeds** ['pro sidz] *n.* money that is collected or received from someone or something. (Treated as plural, but not countable.) □ *All proceeds from the auction will be donated to charity.*

**process** ['prɑ sɛs] **1.** *n.* a series of actions; a set of procedures used to do, make, achieve, prepare, or develop something. □ *This coffee maker brews coffee by a special process.* **2.** *tv.* to do a series of actions to something; to prepare, achieve, or develop something. □ *The clerk processed my request as soon as I placed my order.*

**proclaim** [prə 'klem] *tv.* to declare something officially; to make something public knowledge. (The object can be a clause with **that** ⑦.) □ *The senator proclaimed that he would seek reelection.*

**procure** [pro 'kjʊr] *tv.* to get something by work or effort. □ *My boss procured new computer equipment for our department.*

**produce 1.** ['pro dus] *n.* food or food products that are farmed or grown; fruits and vegetables. (No plural form.) □ *Mary canned produce for use during the winter months.* **2.** [prə 'dus] *tv.* to grow something; to create something. □ *Charles Dickens produced many well-known works of fiction.* **3.** [prə 'dus] *tv.* to cause something to be; to create a result. □ *The tornado produced a lot of property damage.* **4.** [prə 'dus] *tv.* to make something from parts or materials. □ *The terrorist produced a bomb from fertilizer.* **5.** [prə 'dus] *tv.* to coordinate and organize the details involved in making or presenting a movie, play, or other performance. □ *The film studio produced a cartoon for the holiday season.* **6.** [prə 'dus] *iv.* to do what is expected or required, especially in terms of business goals. □ *My boss fired the salespeople who couldn't produce.*

**producer** [prə 'dus ɚ] **1.** *n.* someone or something that produces something. □ *Japan is an important producer of electronic equipment.* **2.** *n.* someone who coordinates and organizes the details involved in making or presenting a movie, television show, play, or other performance. □ *The director reported problems on the set to the producer.*

**product** ['prɑ dəkt] **1.** *n.* something that is produced; something that is made, created, or grown. □ *Paintings are the product of the artist's imagination.* **2.** *n.* someone or something that is the result of certain conditions; a result. □ *Slippery roads are the product of rainy weather.* **3.** *n.* the number that is determined by multiplying two or more numbers together. □ *The product of any number and zero is zero.*

**production** [prə 'dʌk ʃən] **1.** *n.* producing something; making something. (No plural form.) □ *Many factories in Michigan are used for car production.* **2.** *n.* the amount of or rate of ①. (No plural form.) □ *The low production of the farm meant that the farm might fail.* **3.** *n.* a movie, television show, play, or other performance. □ *The famous actress had been in many productions.*

**profess** [prə 'fɛs] *tv.* to declare something; to claim something. (The object can be a clause with **that** ⑦.) □ *The politician professed his loyalty to his party.* □ *Max professed that the end of the world was near.*

**profession** [prə 'fɛ ʃən] **1.** *n.* a job or career, especially one that requires education or training. □ *Jane was satisfied with her chosen profession.* **2.** *n.* all or most of the people who work in a certain ①. □ *The legal profession refused to support either candidate.*

**professional** [prə 'fɛʃ ə nəl] **1.** *adj.* <the adj. form of **profession** ①.> (Adv: *professionally.*) □ *The injured man sought professional advice from his lawyer.* **2.** *adj.* showing the skill and standards of ③. (Adv: *professionally.*) □ *Bob wanted the wiring in his house to be perfect, so he hired a professional electrician.* **3.** *n.* someone who works in a profession. (Shortened to **pro** informally.) □ *Most health professionals agree that smoking is harmful.*

**professor** [prə 'fɛs ɚ] *n.* someone who holds a faculty position in a university or college. (Also a term of address.) □ *Professor Jones read my essay carefully.*

**profile** ['pro faɪl] **1.** *n.* a side view of someone or something, especially of someone's face. □ *I saw John's profile through the window.* **2.** *n.* a short description of someone or something. □ *Mary's profile stated that she spent four years in the Navy.* **3.** *tv.* to tell or write about someone's life or achievements. □ *This author profiles each president and outlines the nation's history.*

**profit** ['prɑf ɪt] **1.** *n.* the amount of money made by a person or business after all expenses are paid. □ *The four owners each had a share in the profits.* **2.** *tv.* to benefit someone or something. □ *The opening of the new factory profited the local economy.* **3. profit from something** *iv.* + *prep. phr.* to benefit from something. □ *The football team profited from many hours of practice.*

**program** ['pro græm] **1.** *n.* a broadcast show, such as on radio or television. □ *None of the programs on television tonight look interesting to me.* **2.** *n.* a booklet provided to members of an audience, giving information about the performance. □ *The program stated that there would be a 10-minute intermission.* **3.** *n.* a schedule of the parts of a performance. □ *The ice skaters skillfully executed each part of their program.* **4.** *n.* a set of coded instructions given to a computer. □ *I installed the new program onto my computer.*

**programmer** ['pro græm ɚ] *n.* someone who writes a computer program. □ *The company hired programmers to write a new accounting program.*

**progress 1.** ['prɑ grɛs] *n.* the movement made toward a result or goal. (No plural form.) □ *The car's progress toward the intersection was slowed by the heavy traffic.* **2.** ['prɑ grɛs] *n.* the improvement that someone or something makes when moving toward a goal. (No plural form.) □ *My progress at work improved after I was properly trained.* **3.** [prə 'grɛs] *iv.* to move forward; to advance. □ *The popular television show progressed upward in the rankings.* **4.** [prə 'grɛs] *iv.* to develop; to become better. □ *He would progress faster with more practice.*

**prohibit** [pro 'hɪb ɪt] *tv.* to forbid something. □ *The government prohibited public meetings during the crisis.*

**prohibition** [pro ə 'bɪ ʃən] **1.** *n.* forbidding or not allowing something. (Plural only when referring to different kinds, types, instances, or varieties.) □ *Prohibition and education have both been tried, but neither smoking nor drinking can be stopped.* 🄲 *The mayor supported the prohibitions against selling tobacco and alcohol to minors.* **2. Prohibition** *n.* the period of time in American history when it was illegal to make, sell, or transport alcohol. (No plural form.) □ *Prohibition began in 1920 and ended in 1933.*

**project 1.** ['prɑ dʒɛkt] *n.* an assignment or task that must be planned, researched, and executed. □ *Our project lost its funding due to budget cuts.* **2.** [prə 'dʒɛkt] *tv.* to cast a light onto something. □ *The flashlight projected a beam of light.* **3.** [prə 'dʒɛkt] *tv.* to make one's voice or words louder and carry farther. □ *The speaker did not project his voice, and I missed much of what he said.* **4.** [prə 'dʒɛkt] *tv.* to forecast something; to estimate something. □ *The report projected expenses for the next 10 years.* **5.** [prə 'dʒɛkt] *iv.* to be louder when speaking. □ *You'll have to project more! I can't hear you in the back row.* **6.** [prə 'dʒɛkt] *iv.* to stick out; to extend from a surface. □ *The broken arrow projected from the target.*

**projection** [prə 'dʒɛk ʃən] **1.** *n.* something that sticks out or projects. □ *A sharp projection on the kitchen cabinet snagged my trousers.* **2.** *n.* a prediction; an estimate of a future state. □ *The officers presented a number of projections of next year's profits.*

**projector** [prə 'dʒɛk tɚ] *n.* a machine that casts an image on a screen, wall, etc. (The image may have been recorded on film or digitally on tape.) □ *The light bulb in the projector suddenly burned out.*

**prolong** [pro 'lɔŋ] *tv.* to cause something to last longer than it normally would; to lengthen the time it takes to do something. □ *The manager prolonged the interview in order to ask me more questions.*

**prominent** ['prɑm ə nənt] **1.** *adj.* famous; well known; respected. (Adv: *prominently.*) □ *The reporter interviewed many prominent surgeons.* **2.** *adj.* noticeable; easy to see. (Adv: *prominently.*) □ *John has a very prominent nose.*

**promise** ['prɑm ɪs] **1.** *n.* a sign that someone will be successful or do good work. (No plural form.) □ *Your plans have promise, but I'll have to see the final results.* **2.** *n.* a pledge to do something. □ *John broke his promise to buy me a new watch.* **3.** *tv.* to pledge to do something; to vow that one will do something. (The object is a clause with **that** ⑦.) □ *I promised that I would be home by midnight.* **4.** *tv.* to cause someone to expect something. □ *I promise you a spanking if you don't behave.* **5. promise to** do something *iv.* + *inf.* to make a **promise** ② that one will do something. □ *You must come to my party. You promised to come!*

**promote** [prə 'mot] **1.** *tv.* to work for the acceptance of someone or something through advertising and other public contacts. □ *The inventor promoted his products in trade journals.* **2.** *tv.* to raise someone to a new and higher level in employment or schooling. □ *The owner promoted Anne to the office of senior vice president.*

**promotion** [prə 'mo ʃən] **1.** *n.* the movement of someone to a higher level of employment or schooling. (Plural only when referring to different kinds, types, instances, or varieties.) □ *Promotion is the way to get a better salary and a better-sounding job title.* Ⓒ *Anne got her first promotion after six months on the job.* **2.** *n.* advertising and other activity intended to sell something. (No plural form.) □ *The advertisers managed the promotion of their clients' goods.*

**prompt** ['prɑmpt] **1.** *adj.* doing something, such as arriving, at the right time; on time. (Adv: *promptly.*) □ *We have to start on time, so please be prompt.* **2.** *tv.* to encourage or cause someone to do something. □ *The bad weather prompted me to dress warmly.* **3.** *tv.* to give someone a quiet reminder of what is to be said next. (Especially in stage performances.) □ *Mary prompted her son to say "thank you."* **4.** *n.* a symbol on

P

a computer screen that shows that the computer is ready to receive information. □ *Enter the appropriate command at the prompt.*

**pron.** an abbreviation of **pronoun.**

**pronoun** ['pro naʊn] *n.* a word that takes the place of a noun or nominal and refers to someone or something already mentioned. (Abbreviated *pron.* here.) □ *In the sentence "I told Mary that she was next,"* she *is a pronoun that refers to* Mary. □ *After prepositions, pronouns should be in the objective case. For instance:* John gave the box to Anne and me.

**pronounce** [prə 'naʊns] **1.** *tv.* to speak the sound of a letter or a word; to make the sound of a letter or a word. □ *You don't pronounce the* gh *in* night. **2.** *tv.* to declare something about someone or something officially. □ *The judge pronounced the suspect guilty on all charges.*

**pronunciation** [prə nən si 'e ʃən] *n.* the way a letter, group of letters, or word sounds when spoken; the way someone says things. (Plural only when referring to different kinds, types, instances, or varieties.) □ *My pronunciation of French isn't very good.* Ⓒ *There are at least three different pronunciations of this word.*

**proof** ['pruf] **1.** *n.* something that shows that something is definitely true. (No plural form.) □ *John's fingerprints were proof that he had held the gun.* **2.** *n.* a printed copy of something that is checked for mistakes before the final copy is printed; a first or sample version of a photograph. □ *The photographer looked over the proofs and chose the best picture for the magazine cover.* **3.** *tv.* to proofread something. □ *I proofed my roommate's term paper.*

**proofread** ['pruf rid] **1.** *tv., irreg.* to read something very carefully to look for mistakes. (Pt/pp: *proofread* ['pruf rɛd].) □ *I proofread my paper before I gave it to my professor.* **2.** *iv., irreg.* to read very carefully to look for mistakes. □ *Even though I always proofread, I sometimes miss a couple of mistakes.*

**prop** ['prɑp] **1.** *n.* an object that is used in a play or in a movie by an actor. □ *The actor placed his prop on a shelf when he was finished with it.* **2. prop someone or something up** *tv. + obj. + adv.* to support someone or something; to prevent someone or something from falling. □ *I had to prop the injured woman up until the doctor came.* Ⓣ *I propped up her head so she could see.*

**propaganda** [prɑp ə 'gæn də] *n.* information that tries to influence or change how people think. (No plural form.) □ *This report is just propaganda designed to scare the public.*

**propeller** [pro 'pɛl ɚ] *n.* a set of blades that rotate very fast in air or water, used to push or move a boat or an airplane. □ *The boat's powerful propeller created large waves.*

**proper** ['prɑp ɚ] **1.** *adj.* right; suitable; correct; appropriate. (Adv: *properly.*) □ *The instructor showed me the proper way to hit the tennis ball.* **2.** *adj.* [in grammar] referring to a person or place. □ Bill *is a proper noun, whereas* man *is a common noun.* □ *Almost all proper names start with capital letters.* **3.** *adj.* <referring to a particular place itself, and not an area outside of that place.> (Not prenominal. Adv: *properly.*) □ *Susan's office is in San Diego proper.*

**properly** ['prɑp ɚ li] **1.** *adv.* in the right way; suitably; appropriately; according to what is expected. □ *You must do your assignment properly in order to get a good grade.* **2.** *adv.* strictly. □ *To be properly referred to as champagne, wine must come from the Champagne region of France.*

**property** ['prɑp ɚ ti] **1.** *n.* something that is owned. (No plural form.) □ *Please do not leave your property on*

P

*the counter, as someone may take it.* **2.** *n.* an amount of land and any structures that have been built on it. (No plural form.) □ *The farmer sold some property to pay for his taxes.*

**prophecy** ['prɑf ə si] *n.* the ability to foresee the future. (Plural only when referring to different kinds, types, instances, or varieties.) □ *Prophecy is not widely respected in our scientific age.* 🄲 *We read about the old man's prophecies, but we never believed they would come true.*

**prophesy** ['prɑf ə sɑɪ] *tv.* to predict what will happen in the future; to say that something is going to happen. (The object can be a clause with **that** ⑦.) □ *An old man prophesied danger for us in the coming year.*

**prophet** ['prɑf ɪt] **1.** *n.* someone who has the talent of being able to see into the future. □ *I asked the prophet for advice about my future.* **2.** *n.* [in some religions] a person chosen to speak for God. □ *The people all listened carefully to what the prophet had to tell them.*

P

**proposal** [prə 'poz əl] **1.** *n.* a suggestion; a plan. □ *I disagreed with the president's proposal to raise taxes.* **2.** *n.* an offer of marriage made to someone. □ *Mary refused John's proposal, since she was in love with Bill.*

**propose** [prə 'poz] **1.** *tv.* to suggest something; to say something so that it is considered. (The object can be a clause with **that** ⑦.) □ *John proposed that we eat pizza for dinner.* **2. propose (to someone)** *iv. (+ prep. phr.)* to ask someone to marry one. □ *Bill proposed to Susan in a very romantic way.*

**proposition** [prɑp ə 'zɪ ʃən] **1.** *n.* a proposal; something that is being considered; a suggestion. □ *Our banker presented us with a business proposition that was very attractive.* **2.** *n.* a statement; a statement that is to be proved either true or false. □ *The proposition "If* a = b, *then* b = a*" is true.*

**prose** ['proz] *n.* the usual form of written language; writing that is not in verse. (No plural form.) □ *There were long sections of prose between the poems.*

**prosper** ['prɑs pɚ] *iv.* to become successful; to earn enough money so that one can live well; to thrive. □ *The new toy store prospered at the mall.*

**prosperity** [prɑs 'pɛr ə ti] *n.* the condition of being prosperous; success; monetary success. (No plural form.) □ *The rich man thanked his rich parents for his prosperity.*

**prosperous** ['prɑs pə rəs] *adj.* thriving; earning or having enough money so that one can live well. (Adv: *prosperously.*) □ *The prosperous nation received its revenue from oil.*

**protect** [prə 'tɛkt] *tv.* to keep someone or something safe; to guard someone or something. □ *Glass containers protected the food and kept it clean.*

**protection** [prə 'tɛk ʃən] *n.* keeping someone or something safe; the quality offered by someone or something that protects. (Plural only when referring to different kinds, types, instances, or varieties.) □ *The police were responsible for the protection of the president while he was in town.* 🄲 *Passwords are a protection against illegal usage or entry.*

**protective** [prə 'tɛk tɪv] *adj.* protecting; giving protection; defending; keeping someone or something safe. (Adv: *protectively.*) □ *Anne's older brother was very protective of her.*

**protein** ['pro tin] *n.* one of many kinds of chemical substances important to the cells of all living plants and animals. (Usually thought of in terms of food.) □ *Meat, fish, and poultry are good sources of protein.*

**protest 1.** ['pro tɛst] *n.* a group of people displaying opposition or anger. □

*The workers' protest closed the factory for a week.* **2.** ['pro tɛst] *n.* a complaint. □ *After a few feeble protests, the children finally went to bed.* **3.** [prə 'tɛst] *tv.* to complain about something; to show disapproval of something. (The object can be a clause with **that** ⑦.) □ *We protested the plans for a dump in our neighborhood.* **4.** [prə 'tɛst] *iv.* to complain about something. □ *The workers protested about the reductions in their benefits.*

**proton** ['pro tɑn] *n.* a particle in the center of an atom that carries a positive electrical charge. □ *The nucleus of a hydrogen atom has one proton.*

**prototype** ['pro tə tɑɪp] *n.* the original example of something from which later examples are developed. □ *The architect's novel design was the prototype on which more buildings were based.*

**proud** ['prɑʊd] **1.** *adj.* showing or feeling pride; having a good opinion about oneself and what one has accomplished. (Adv: *proudly.* Comp: *prouder;* sup: *proudest.*) □ *The proud student showed her parents her good grades.* **2.** *adj.* causing someone to feel pride. (Adv: *proudly.* Comp: *prouder;* sup: *proudest.*) □ *Finishing college was a proud accomplishment for Mary.* **3.** *adj.* having too high an opinion about oneself; arrogant. (Adv: *proudly.* Comp: *prouder;* sup: *proudest.*) □ *I laughed at the proud man when he finally failed.*

**prove** ['pruv] *tv., irreg.* to provide proof of something; to be the proof of something. (Pp: *proved* or **proven**. The object can be a clause with **that** ⑦.) □ *The experiment proved my idea to be correct.*

**proven** ['pruv ən] a pp of **prove**.

**provide** [prə 'vɑɪd] **1.** *tv.* to furnish or supply someone or something with something. □ *The hotel clerk provided us with a comfortable room.* **2.** *tv.* to state or tell something. (The object is a clause with **that** ⑦. Used in legal documents.) □ *This paragraph provides that rent is due on the first of each month.* **3. provide for** something *iv. + prep. phr.* to allow something to occur or to be supplied. □ *This mortgage provides for a repayment without penalty.* **4. provide for** someone *iv. + prep. phr.* to support someone by earning enough money to supply the person with food, clothing, and shelter. □ *John provided for a family of six.*

**province** ['prɑ vɪns] **1.** *n.* one of the main divisions of a country, such as Canada, similar to a state. □ *The Canadian rock band toured through all of the provinces.* **2.** *n.* an area of study, knowledge, or activity. □ *In the province of psychology, Dr. Smith is very well respected.*

**provincial** [prə 'vɪn ʃəl] **1.** *adj.* of or about a province or provinces of a country. (Adv: *provincially.*) □ *I crossed the provincial boundary between Quebec and Ontario.* **2.** *adj.* of limited, local experience; rural in attitude and outlook. (Usually derogatory. Adv: *provincially.*) □ *John's prejudice is an example of his provincial thinking.*

**provision** [prə 'vɪ ʒən] **1.** *n.* a condition; a detail or statement. □ *This provision deals with your royalties after the third printing.* **2.** *n.* an arrangement that is made ahead of time. (Often plural.) □ *We made provisions for all possible problems.* **3. provisions** *n.* food and supplies needed for everyday living. (Treated as plural, but not countable.) □ *The hikers carried their provisions on their backs.*

**provoke** [prə 'vok] **1.** *tv.* to make someone angry; to irritate someone. □ *Anne provoked John by calling him ugly.* **2.** *tv.* to cause an action to start or to happen. (Usually leading to negative results.) □ *Lisa's comments provoked a lot of criticism.*

P

**prowl** ['proʊl] *iv.* to sneak around quietly, like an animal hunting for food or a thief looking for something to steal. ☐ *The thief prowled in the dark room, looking for valuables.*

**prowler** ['proʊl ɚ] *n.* a thief; a burglar who sneaks about in the night. ☐ *The police caught the prowler with a bag of stolen goods.*

**prude** ['prud] *n.* someone who is easily offended or shocked; someone who is overly modest or proper. ☐ *Call me a prude, but I won't wear such a tiny bathing suit!*

**prudence** ['prud ns] *n.* wisdom; care in thought and action; thoughtful judgment. (No plural form.) ☐ *John's prudence kept him from criticizing his boss.*

**prudent** ['prud nt] *adj.* wise; thinking carefully before one does something. (Adv: *prudently.*) ☐ *The prudent worker did not tell his boss exactly how angry he was.*

**prudish** ['prud ɪʃ] *adj.* too easily shocked or offended; too modest. (Adv: *prudishly.*) ☐ *Because Jane is too prudish to wear a bathing suit, she doesn't swim at all.*

**prune** ['prun] **1.** *n.* a dried plum, eaten as food. ☐ *As a snack between meals, Mary ate some prunes.* **2.** *iv.* to remove extra branches or leaves from a plant; to trim a tree, flower, bush, or shrub so that it has a nice, even shape. ☐ *After I mowed and raked, I spent an hour pruning.* **3.** *tv.* to make a plant look nice by removing extra branches or leaves. ☐ *The gardener pruned the bushes every month.*

**pry** ['praɪ] **1. pry** something **open; pry** something **up** *tv. + obj. + adv.* to open or raise something with a tool by using force; to force something open by using a tool. ☐ *Anne pried the lid up with a screwdriver.* [T] *She pried up the lid.* **2.** *iv.* to be too curious; to ask personal questions about things that should not concern one. ☐ *I don't mean to pry, but how much did you pay for that watch?*

**psychiatrist** [sɪ 'kaɪ ə trɪst] *n.* a doctor who treats people who have sicknesses of the mind. ☐ *My psychiatrist helped my state of unhappiness through therapy and drugs.*

**psychiatry** [sɪ 'kaɪ ə tri] *n.* the science of treating people who have sicknesses of the mind. (No plural form.) ☐ *David resorted to psychiatry to help cure his depression.*

**psychological** [saɪ kə 'lɑdʒ ɪ kəl] **1.** *adj.* <the adj. form of **psychology** ①.> (Adv: *psychologically* [...ɪk li].) ☐ *Dr. Clark designed a psychological experiment.* **2.** *adj.* <the adj. form of **psychology** ②.> (Adv: *psychologically* [...ɪk li].) ☐ *The criminal had lot of psychological problems.*

**psychologist** [saɪ 'kɑl ə dʒɪst] *n.* someone who is trained in psychology; a specialist in behavior. ☐ *Psychologists study how people behave.*

**psychology** [saɪ 'kɑl ə dʒi] **1.** *n.* the study and science of the mind and the behavior of individuals. (No plural form.) ☐ *Mental illness is only one part of psychology.* **2.** *n.* the way people behave, think, and feel; the way a person behaves, thinks, and feels. (No plural form.) ☐ *This book examines the psychology of serial killers.*

**public** ['pʌb lɪk] **1.** *adj.* available to everyone; available to people in general; not restricted; not private. (Adv: *publicly.*) ☐ *On hot days, I go to the public beach to swim.* **2. the public** *n.* people in general. (No plural form.) ☐ *The once private files were made available to the public.* **3. in public** *phr.* in such a place or way that other people can see or know about something. ☐ *John always tries to embarrass me whenever we're in public.*

**publication** [pəb lə 'ke ʃən] **1.** *n.* making information in written form, such as in a book, magazine, or newspaper, available to the public. (No plural form.) □ *You will receive payment upon the publication of your article.* **2.** *n.* any written document that is published. □ *My professors have all produced many publications.*

**publicity** [pəb 'lɪs ə ti] *n.* information that is brought to everyone's attention. (No plural form.) □ *There was a lot of publicity surrounding the sensational trial.*

**publicly** ['pʌb lɪk li] *adv.* [done] in public; [done] where people can see. □ *You can think what you want about the company, as long as you don't say it publicly.*

**public school** ['pʌb lɪk 'skul] *n.* a school that is paid for by the government through taxes and that is available to all local children. □ *Mary transferred from a public school to a private one.*

**publish** ['pʌb lɪʃ] **1.** *tv.* to assemble, print, and sell books, magazines, newspapers, or other printed materials. □ *My professor's first book was published in 1970.* **2.** *tv.* to make something well known. □ *This newspaper publishes the scores of most sporting events.*

**publisher** ['pʌb lɪ ʃɚ] *n.* someone or a company that assembles, prints, and makes written materials available for sale. □ *The publisher sends each author royalty checks twice a year.*

**pudding** ['pʊd ɪŋ] *n.* a soft, sweet, creamy food, usually eaten as a dessert. (Plural only when referring to different kinds, types, instances, or varieties.) □ *Jane put some strawberries on top of her pudding.* Ⓒ *Some puddings have to be cooked; others can be made much more simply.*

**puddle** ['pʌd l] *n.* a collection of water or other liquid on the ground or the surface of something. □ *There's a puddle of water under the leaky pipe.*

**puff** ['pʌf] **1.** *n.* a short blast of air, smoke, steam, gas, etc., that is blown out from something. □ *I felt a puff of cold wind on my neck.* **2.** *tv.* to blow air, steam, smoke, etc., out a little bit at a time. □ *The exhaust pipe puffed dark clouds of smoke.* **3.** *iv.* to pull smoke from a cigarette or a cigar with small breaths. □ *The executive puffed and puffed and finished his cigar in a short time.* **4.** *iv.* to breathe when one is out of breath; to breathe with short, quick breaths. □ *The fat man puffed as he ran for the bus.*

**pull** ['pʊl] **1.** *tv.* to move someone or something in some direction. □ *I pulled Anne away from the speeding car.* **2.** *tv.* to drag someone or something behind oneself; to move someone or something behind oneself while one is moving. □ *I pulled the wagon behind me, with the children sitting in it.* **3.** *n.* a tug. □ *Please help me give this rope another pull.*

**pulp** ['pʌlp] **1.** *n.* the soft part inside a fruit, vegetable, or plant. (No plural form.) □ *John removed the pulp from the inside of the pumpkin.* **2.** *n.* any soft, partially solid, wet substance. (No plural form.) □ *The gray pulp next to your hamburger is overcooked rice.* **3.** *tv.* to make ② from something. □ *This machine will pulp paper so it can be recycled.*

**pulpit** ['pʊl pɪt] *n.* a raised platform that a preacher, priest, minister, etc., stands on when preaching. □ *From his pulpit, the preacher talked about miracles.*

**pulse** ['pʌls] **1.** *n.* the rhythm of the flow of blood through one's body, caused by the beating of the heart. (No plural form.) □ *His pulse is getting faster. He is getting better.* **2.** *n.* a rhythm with a regular beat; a movement of something with regular stops and starts. □ *The other musicians followed the pulse of the* *drums.* **3.** *iv.* to beat regularly, like the beating of the heart; to beat in rhythm. □ *The ballroom pulsed with the beat of the dance music.* **4. take** someone's **pulse** *phr.* to measure the frequency of the beats of ①. □ *The nurse took my pulse and said I was fine.*

**pump** ['pʌmp] **1.** *n.* a device that forces air, liquid, or gas through a tube or pipe. □ *John got a pitcher of water from the pump next to the house.* **2.** *tv.* to force air, liquid, or gas through a tube or pipe. □ *John pumped gas into his car's gas tank.*

**pumpkin** ['pʌmp kɪn] **1.** *n.* a large, round, heavy orange fruit that grows on a vine. □ *Seeds from pumpkins are very tasty when they're roasted.* **2.** *adj.* made with ①. □ *Pumpkin soup is good.*

**punch** ['pʌntʃ] **1.** *n.* a sweet drink made by mixing many different things to drink, usually including some kind of fruit juice. (No plural form.) □ *We served a colorful fruit punch at the party.* **2.** *n.* a tool or machine that pierces holes through objects or that stamps designs on objects. □ *I made holes along the side of the paper with a paper punch.* **3.** *n.* a quick, powerful hit. □ *John's punch against the wall cracked the plaster.* **4.** *n.* impact; effective power; strength. (Fig. on ③.) □ *I gave the soup more punch by adding some spices.* **5.** *tv.* to hit someone or something powerfully with one's fist. □ *The boxer punched his opponent in the face.*

**punctuation** [pəŋk tʃu 'e ʃən] *n.* the use of **punctuation marks** to make writing easier to understand. (No plural form.) □ *I made sure my essay had proper punctuation before I turned it in.*

**punctuation mark** [pəŋk tʃu 'e ʃən mɑrk] *n.* a symbol used to make writing easier to understand, such as the period (.), the comma (,), the colon (:), the question mark (?), the exclamation point (!), and the hyphen (-), among others. □ *Punctuation marks usually aren't used in newspaper headlines.*

**puncture** ['pʌnk tʃɚ] **1.** *n.* a hole in the surface of something made by a sharp or pointed object. □ *A small puncture in the balloon caused it to lose its air.* **2.** *tv.* to make a hole in the surface of something by using a sharp or pointed object. □ *Mary punctured the balloon with a pin.*

**punish** ['pʌn ɪʃ] **1.** *tv.* to give someone a penalty for doing something wrong. □ *The criminal was punished for robbing the bank.* **2.** *tv.* to use or handle something roughly. (Fig. on ①.) □ *Heavy waves punished the shore.*

**punishment** ['pʌn ɪʃ mənt] **1.** *n.* punishing; the practice of giving penalties for doing something wrong. (No plural form.) □ *The clever thief escaped punishment.* **2.** *n.* rough treatment. (Fig. on ①. No plural form.) □ *The army tank was built to withstand very heavy punishment.*

**punk** ['pʌŋk] **1.** *n.* a young criminal; a young person who gets into trouble a lot. □ *The punk shoplifted some food from the store.* **2.** *n.* a loud, harsh style of music first made popular in the late 1970s by young people. (No plural form.) □ *The college radio station played punk after 10:00 P.M.* **3.** *adj.* <the adj. use of ②.> □ *Punk songs are usually very short, fast, and loud.*

**puny** ['pju ni] *adj.* smaller and weaker than average. (Adv: *punily.* Comp: *punier;* sup: *puniest.*) □ *The puny child was teased by his classmates.*

**pup** ['pʌp] *n.* a young dog; a puppy; the young of certain animals, including the seal. (See also **puppy**.) □ *The mother carried her pups to her den.*

**pupil** ['pju pəl] **1.** *n.* a student; someone who studies in school; someone who is taught by a teacher. □ *This school was designed for 1,200 pupils.* **2.** *n.* the

P

round, black opening in the middle of the colored part of the eye which allows light into the eye. □ *Pupils contract when light gets brighter.*

**puppy** ['pʌp i] *n.* a young dog. □ *Our dog gave birth to six puppies.*

**purchase** ['pɚ tʃəs] **1.** *n.* an instance of buying something. □ *Bill's purchase of a new car was done on impulse.* **2.** *n.* something that is bought. □ *Mary paid for her purchase with a credit card.* **3.** *tv.* to buy something. □ *Bob purchased groceries at the supermarket.*

**purchaser** ['pɚ tʃə sɚ] *n.* a buyer; someone who buys something. □ *The clerk returned some change to the purchaser.*

**pure** ['pjʊr] **1.** *adj.* completely made from only one thing; not mixed with anything. (Adv: *purely.* Comp: *purer;* sup: *purest.*) □ *We drank pure water from the mountain spring.* **2.** *adj.* [of a color] clear and not cloudy. (Adv: *purely.* Comp: *purer;* sup: *purest.*) □ *The summer sky was pure blue.* **3.** *adj.* mere; absolute; nothing but. (Adv: *purely.* Comp: *purer;* sup: *purest.*) □ *It was pure stupidity to throw rocks at that beehive.* **4.** *adj.* without sin; without evil. (Adv: *purely.* Comp: *purer;* sup: *purest.*) □ *The boy's intentions were completely pure.* **5.** *adj.* not having had sex. (Adv: *purely.* Comp: *purer;* sup: *purest.*) □ *A pure young woman was sacrificed to the gods.*

**purge** ['pɚdʒ] **1.** *n.* an instance of forcing unwanted people to leave a government, university, or other organization. □ *Twelve professors were fired as a result of the dean's purge.* **2.** *tv.* to make something clean by getting rid of what is dirty; to clean something out. □ *The plumber purged the tank of its messy contents.* **3.** *tv.* to destroy records or files. □ *The executive purged his files when he quit his job.*

**purity** ['pjʊr ə ti] *n.* the quality of being pure; the degree to which something is pure. (No plural form.) □ *The jeweler guaranteed the purity of the gold in my ring.*

**purple** ['pɚ pəl] **1.** *n.* the color made by mixing blue and red; the color of ripe grapes that are not green or red. (Plural only when referring to different kinds, types, instances, or varieties.) □ *Anne's dress is a dark purple.* Ⓒ *Most purples are too dark and heavy for informal clothing.* **2.** *adj.* of the color ①. □ *Grape-flavored drinks are often purple.*

**purpose** ['pɚ pəs] **1.** *n.* an intention; the reason that someone does something; a kind of goal. □ *My purpose for asking for a raise was that I needed the money.* **2. on purpose** *phr.* [doing something] in a way that is meant or planned; not an accident. □ *That was no accident! You did it on purpose!*

**purse** ['pɚs] **1.** *n.* a bag used, especially by women, to hold money and other personal items. □ *The thief grabbed Mary's purse as she walked through the mall.* **2.** *n.* an amount of money that is offered as a prize. □ *The winner of the race won a $25,000 purse.*

**pursue** [pɚ 'su] **1.** *tv.* to chase someone or something; to follow and attempt to catch someone or something. □ *The dog pursued the cat across the yard.* **2.** *tv.* to continue to work toward something; to seek something. □ *After retiring, Jane pursued her hobby of stamp collecting.* **3.** *tv.* to follow a plan of action. □ *The football team pursued the plan that the coach had outlined.*

P

**pursuit** [pɚ 'sut] **1.** *n.* pursuing someone or something; chasing after someone or something. (No plural form.) □ *In pursuit of happiness, Anne moved to California.* **2.** *n.* a hobby or job that fills one's time. □ *Bob's pursuit of coin collecting takes up all his spare time.*

**push** ['pʊʃ] **1.** *iv.* to force movement in a certain direction. □ *Just push hard, and the door will open.* **2.** *tv.* to apply pressure to something, as if to move it.

☐ *I pushed a button on the panel by the elevator door.* **3.** *tv.* to move something or someone by applying pressure. ☐ *Don't push me!* **4.** *n.* a shove; a powerful movement that causes something to move. (No plural form.) ☐ *I gave the table a little push, and over it went.* **5. push ahead** *iv. + adv.* to move forward or advance with force or effort; to move by using pressure. ☐ *Anne pushed ahead at her job until she ran the company.* **6. push through** something or some place *iv. + prep. phr.* to force [one's way] through a crowded place. ☐ *The hiker pushed through the vines to get back to the path.*

**put** ['pʊt] **1.** *tv., irreg.* to place something in a certain position; to cause something to be in a certain place or position; to move something to a certain place or position. (Pt/pp: *put.*) ☐ *John put some food in his mouth.* **2.** *tv., irreg.* to express something; to say something in a certain way. ☐ *This is not very good—or, to put it more bluntly, this is terrible.*

**puzzle** ['pʌz əl] **1.** *n.* something that confuses people; a problem that is confusing or difficult to solve. ☐ *All of the many colored wires in the radio were a real puzzle to Bill.* **2.** *n.* something similar to ① that people try to understand or solve for entertainment. ☐ *I like to work puzzles when I travel on the train.* **3.** *tv.* to confuse someone. ☐ *His strange performance puzzled the audience.*

**pyramid** ['pɪr ə mɪd] **1.** *n.* a four-sided structure with sides that are shaped like triangles and meet at one point on top. ☐ *Susie's pile of sand is shaped like a pyramid.* **2.** *n.* one of a group of large, Egyptian tombs—shaped like ①—in which Egyptian kings and queens were once buried. ☐ *Most of the pyramids were robbed of their contents many years ago.*

P

**quack** ['kwæk] **1.** *iv.* to make the characteristic noise of a duck. □ *The ducks quacked as they swam in the pond.* **2.** *n.* the noise that a duck makes. □ *Jimmy, can you make a quack like a duck?* **3.** *n.* someone who claims to be a doctor but who is not trained to be a doctor. □ *I switched doctors because I thought my old one was a quack.*

**quaint** ['kwent] *adj.* strange in an interesting or funny way; charming in an old-fashioned way. (Adv: *quaintly.* Comp: *quainter;* sup: *quaintest.*) □ *My great-aunt told about the quaint clothes she wore as a child.*

**quake** ['kwek] **1.** *n.* a shaking of the earth; an **earthquake**. (Short for **earthquake.**) □ *Did you feel the quake last night?* **2.** *iv.* to shake; to tremble. □ *I was quaking from fear before the test.*

**qualify** ['kwɑl ə fɑɪ] **1.** *tv.* to limit something; to restrict something; to narrow the meaning of something. □ *I had to qualify my remarks to make it clear that I was only talking about the results of one experiment.* **2. qualify for** something *iv. + prep. phr.* to meet the requirements for something, such as for a job, responsibility, or award, or for acceptance into a school or organization. □ *Mary qualified for the early-retirement program.*

**quality** ['kwɑl ɪ ti] **1.** *n.* a characteristic property of someone or something. □ *Bill's best quality is that he's so kind.* **2.** *n.* a degree or level of excellence. (No plural form.) □ *I will not buy anything of low quality.* **3.** *adj.* of a good **quality** ②. □ *I insisted on buying a quality car.*

**quantity** ['kwɑn tə ti] *n.* an amount; a certain number of something that can be counted or measured. □ *I bought a large quantity of snacks for the party.*

**quarantine** ['kwɑr ən tin] **1.** *tv.* to isolate a living thing that has a disease or has been around another creature with a disease. □ *Our dog was quarantined for a month when we moved to Asia.* **2.** *n.* 

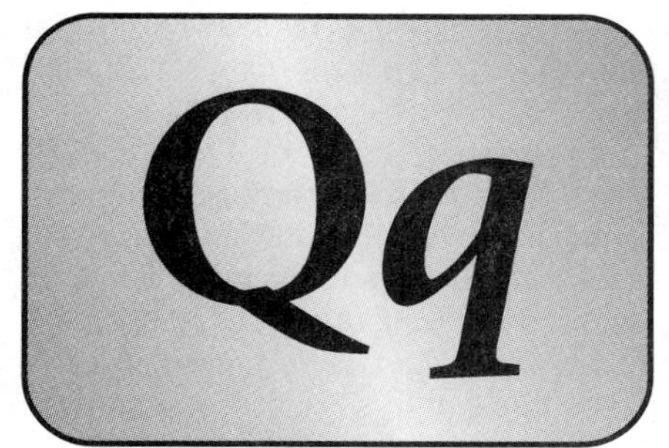

a period of isolation of living things that have an illness or have been exposed to an illness. (Plural only when referring to different kinds, types, instances, or varieties.) □ *Our dog's quarantine lasted a month after we returned from Mexico.* Ⓒ *The dog underwent two quarantines last year. We hardly saw her at all.*

**quarrel** ['kwɑr əl] **1.** *n.* an angry argument; an angry disagreement. □ *The loud quarrel ended up in a fight.* **2.** *iv.* to argue with someone angrily; for two or more people to argue angrily. □ *My brother and I quarreled over whose turn it was to wash dishes.*

**quarry** ['kwɑr i] **1.** *n.* a place where marble, granite, and other kinds of stone are removed from the earth. □ *The truck driver brought four tons of large stone from the quarry.* **2.** *n.* the object of a hunt or search. □ *The dog retrieved its quarry from the bush.* **3.** *tv.* to remove stone from ①. □ *They have been quarrying granite here for hundreds of years.*

**quart** ['kwort] *n.* a unit of measure of liquids, equal to one-fourth of a gallon, 32 ounces, or 0.95 liter. □ *My car's engine needed two quarts of oil.*

**quarter** ['kwor tɚ] **1.** *n.* one-fourth of something; one of four equal parts; one of four parts. □ *I cut the pizza into quarters.* **2.** *n.* a coin equal to 25 cents or one-fourth of a dollar. □ *This vending machine only takes quarters.* **3.** *n.* fifteen minutes; one-fourth of an hour. (Limited to *quarter to; quarter till; quarter of;*

*quarter after; quarter past.* No plural form.) □ *2:15 is a quarter after two, and also a quarter past two.* **4.** *n.* three months; one-fourth of a year. □ *The firm projected a large profit for the fourth quarter.* **5.** *n.* one of the four periods in football, basketball, and other games. □ *Our team won the game in the final minute of the fourth quarter.* **6.** *n.* a neighborhood; a section of a town; a district. □ *The mayor lived in a very fashionable quarter of town.* **7.** *n.* a period equal to one third of the school or academic year. □ *During third quarter, I took three math courses.* **8. quarters** *n.* the place where someone lives. (Treated as plural.) □ *My quarters were cramped while my house was being renovated.* **9.** *tv.* to divide something into four parts; to cut something into four parts; to split something into four parts. □ *I quartered the pizza before serving it.* **10.** *tv.* to give someone, especially soldiers, a place to stay or live. □ *During the war, the soldiers were quartered in tents near the front.*

**queasy** ['kwiz i] *adj.* feeling sick, nauseated, or uneasy. (Adv: *queasily.* Comp: *queasier;* sup: *queasiest.*) □ *The queasy passenger vomited.*

Q

**queen** ['kwin] **1.** *n.* the female ruler of a country or the wife of a king. □ *The country's currency was stamped with the queen's image.* **2.** *n.* the sole egg-laying female in a colony or hive of certain species of insects, such as bees, termites, or ants. □ *Every termite colony has a queen.* **3.** *n.* a playing card that has a picture of ① on it. □ *Mary laid down the queen of spades.* **4.** *n.* a chess piece that can move any number of spaces in a straight line in any direction. □ *I took my opponent's last rook with my queen.*

**queer** ['kwɪr] *adj.* odd; strange; unusual; weird. (Adv: *queerly.* Comp: *queerer;* sup: *queerest.*) □ *I had a queer feeling that something was wrong.*

**quell** ['kwɛl] *tv.* to calm or put an end to chaos, confusion, or some other problem. □ *The teacher quelled the chaos in the classroom.*

**quench** ['kwɛntʃ] **1.** *tv.* to put out a fire by using water. □ *Quick! Go get some water to quench the flames!* **2.** *tv.* to ease or eliminate one's thirst by drinking something. □ *Jane quenched her thirst with a cup of juice.*

**quest** ['kwɛst] *n.* a search for someone or something. □ *Bob's quest for a wife finally ended when he met Anne.*

**question** ['kwɛs tʃən] **1.** *n.* an inquiry; a speech utterance used to make an inquiry. □ *Would you please answer my question?* □ *"What time is it?" is a question.* **2.** *n.* a doubt; a concern; something that one is not sure about. (No plural form.) □ *Without question, you should do it.* **3.** *n.* a matter to be considered; a problem for solving. □ *The manager addressed the question of overtime.* **4.** *tv.* to ask ① of someone. □ *The lawyer questioned the witness.* **5.** *tv.* to doubt something; to express one's doubts or concerns about something. □ *Do what I say, and don't question my motives.*

**questionable** ['kwɛs tʃə nə bəl] **1.** *adj.* in doubt; inviting questions or scrutiny. (Adv: *questionably.*) □ *After he failed the important test, his future as a student at the college was questionable.* **2.** *adj.* possibly not honest or true. (Adv: *questionably.*) □ *The criminal had a questionable character.*

**question mark** ['kwɛs tʃən mɑrk] *n.* a punctuation mark "?" that is written at the end of a question. □ *You should put a question mark at the end of every question.*

**questionnaire** [kwɛs tʃə 'nɛr] *n.* a printed set of questions. □ *I responded to a questionnaire about my political beliefs.*

**quick** ['kwɪk] **1.** *adj.* fast; rapid; swift. (Adv: *quickly.* Comp: *quicker;* sup: *quickest.*) □ *The express train is so quick that it only takes ten minutes to get downtown.* **2.** *adj.* lasting only for a short period of time; beginning and ending in a short period of time. (Adv: *quickly.* Comp: *quicker;* sup: *quickest.*) □ *I took a quick look at the items on sale.* **3.** *adj.* able to understand or learn things in a short amount of time. (Adv: *quickly.* Comp: *quicker;* sup: *quickest.*) □ *Lisa was quick, but not as bright as Jane.* **4.** *n.* the flesh under one's fingernails or toenails. (No plural form.) □ *Bill cut his nails to the quick.* **5.** *adv.* very rapidly; with great speed. (Colloquial. Comp: *quicker;* sup: *quickest.*) □ *Come quick! I need help!*

**quicken** ['kwɪk ən] **1.** *iv.* to become faster; to move more quickly; to do something more quickly; to increase the speed of something. □ *The flow of water quickened as the hole in the pipe got larger.* **2.** *tv.* to cause something to become faster; to cause something to occur more quickly. □ *The jogger quickened his pace as he went down the hill.*

**quickness** ['kwɪk nəs] *n.* the quality of being quick. (No plural form.) □ *My friend's quickness in calling for help saved my life.*

**quicksand** ['kwɪk sænd] *n.* wet sand, often under water, into which living creatures can sink. (No plural form.) □ *The dog became trapped in the quicksand.*

**quiet** ['kwɑɪ ɪt] **1.** *adj.* not loud; making only a small amount of sound. (Adv: *quietly.* Comp: *quieter;* sup: *quietest.*) □ *The quiet music was very soothing.* **2.** *adj.* [of a person] shy and not talkative. (Adv: *quietly.* Comp: *quieter;* sup: *quietest.*) □ *My quiet cousin left the party very early.* **3.** *adj.* not active; not moving; calm; still. (Adv: *quietly.* Comp: *quieter;* sup: *quietest.*) □ *The floating raft remained motionless on the quiet water.* **4.** *adj.* peaceful; restful. (Adv: *quietly.* Comp: *quieter;* sup: *quietest.*) □ *I spent a quiet day at the beach.* **5.** *tv.* to cause someone or something to become ①. □ *Food quieted the barking dogs.* **6.** *n.* silence. (No plural form.) □ *The quiet of the forest at dawn makes me feel peaceful.*

**quilt** ['kwɪlt] **1.** *n.* a bed covering made from a soft pad between two layers of decorative cloth, stitched together. □ *I made a quilt from leftover pieces of material.* **2.** *iv.* to work at making ①. □ *My mother taught me how to quilt.*

**quip** ['kwɪp] *n.* a clever, witty, or sarcastic remark. □ *Lisa was insulted by Bob's sarcastic quip.*

**quirk** ['kwɚk] *n.* a strange habit; a strange characteristic. □ *After a while, I became used to my roommate's quirks.*

**quit** ['kwɪt] **1.** *tv., irreg.* to stop doing something. (Pt/pp: *quit.*) □ *Quit working! It's five o'clock.* **2.** *tv., irreg.* to leave a job; to resign a job. □ *Jane quit her job because she hated her boss.* **3.** *iv., irreg.* [for someone or something] to cease [doing something]. □ *I think it's time to quit now.*

**quite** ['kwɑɪt] *adv.* very; rather; completely. □ *I am quite full.*

**quiz** ['kwɪz] **1.** *n.* a small test; an informal test. (Pl: *quizzes.*) □ *There's going to be a quiz tomorrow on Chapter 5.* **2.** *tv.* to test someone on or about something; to ask someone questions about someone or something. □ *The teacher quizzed the students on the reading assignment.*

**quota** ['kwot ə] *n.* a required amount of something; a required number of things or people. □ *The auto worker completed his quota of work by three o'clock.*

**quotation** [kwo 'te ʃən] *n.* a statement that was said or written, used again by someone else; a statement that is quoted from someone or from someone's writing. □ *I consulted a book of famous quotations before writing my speech.*

**quotation marks** [kwo 'te ʃən mɑrks] *n.* <the marks " " and ' ', which are *double quotation marks* and *single quotation marks,* respectively, used to enclose actual speech in writing or printing.> □ *That sentence is a quotation and should be in quotation marks.* □ *Put this word in single quotation marks like 'this.'*

**quote** ['kwot] **1.** *tv.* to use a quotation; to repeat part of something that someone else has said or written, at the same time telling who said or wrote it. □ *I like to quote Abraham Lincoln's clever remarks.* **2.** *tv.* to cite someone or a written source as the origin of a quotation. □ *Don't quote the dictionary all the time! I know how to talk!* **3.** *n.* a quotation; a statement that was said or written by someone else. □ *I copied the quote from the newspaper, but forgot to note who said it.* **4.** *n.* an estimate of the price of something. □ *I asked the mechanic for a quote before my car was serviced.*

**rabbi** ['ræb ɑɪ] *n.* the leader of a Jewish synagogue; a Jewish religious leader. (Also a term of address.) □ *Tom spoke with the rabbi at the temple after the service.*

**rabbit** ['ræb ət] *n.* a small animal with soft fur, long ears, and a fluffy tail. □ *Sue fed carrots to her pet rabbit.*

**race** ['res] **1.** *n.* a contest that has to do with speed; a contest that has to do with how fast people, animals, or machines can move. □ *Many people bet on which horse would win the horse race.* **2.** *n.* a political election, and the time during the campaign leading up to the election. □ *Do you know who you're voting for in the presidential race?* **3.** *n.* the physical differences between humans that have to do with dividing people into different groups, especially groups based on the color of skin. (Plural only when referring to different kinds, types, instances, or varieties.) □ *The company did not consider race in its hiring.* Ⓒ *The leader wished people of all races could live together peacefully.* **4. human race** *n.* all humans as a group of people. (No plural form.) □ *As a member of the human race, the minister prayed for peace.* **5.** *iv.* to run rapidly, as if in a race; to move or operate very fast. □ *My thoughts were racing through my head as I tried to think of the answer.* **6.** *tv.* to cause someone or something to take part in ①. □ *The coach raced his best runners in the contest.* **7.** *tv.* to cause an engine to run very rapidly. □ *Bob raced his motor every time he stopped the car.* **8.** *tv.* to compete against someone to reach a specific goal. □ *Mary raced Anne to see who could get to the door first.*

**racetrack** ['res træk] *n.* the place, usually a large oval, where a race takes place, and the stadium or arena that contains it. □ *The cars sped around the racetrack.*

**racial** ['reʃ əl] *adj.* of or about **race** ③. (Adv: *racially.*) □ *Skin color, hair type, and eye shape are noticeable racial traits.*

**racism** ['res ɪz əm] *n.* prejudice, hatred, or violence shown against someone of a particular race. (No plural form.) □ *The protester accused the government of racism.*

**racist** ['res ɪst] **1.** *n.* someone who believes one race is better than another. □ *The reporter exposed the candidate as a racist.* **2.** *adj.* exhibiting racism; showing prejudice against someone's race. □ *The mayor was harshly criticized for using racist speech.*

**rack** ['ræk] *n.* a frame with shelves, rods, hooks, or pegs that is used to hang things from or put things on. □ *Racks of clothing at the store were emptied during the sale.*

**racket** ['ræk ət] **1.** AND **racquet** *n.* a device used to hit a ball or something similar back and forth, usually over a net. □ *Anne hit the tennis ball with her tennis racket.* **2.** *n.* a dishonest or illegal activity, such as fraud, done to make money. □ *The little restaurant was a front for an illegal drug racket.*

**racquet** ['ræk ət] Go to **racket**.

**radar** ['re dɑr] *n.* a device that uses radio waves to detect an object, usually a car or an aircraft, and to determine that object's location, distance, and speed. (An acronym for *radio detecting and ranging.* No plural form.) □ *The pilot's* *radar indicated there was another plane nearby.*

**radiate** ['re di et] **1.** *tv.* to cause something to spread out in all directions from a center point; to give off rays of something such as heat or light. □ *The hot stove radiated lots of heat.* **2. radiate from** something *iv. + prep. phr.* [for rays] to come from something. □ *Light radiated from the candle.* **3. radiate from** something *iv. + prep. phr.* to extend outward from a central point. □ *Thin wires radiated from the base of the antenna.*

**radiation** [re di 'e ʃən] **1.** *n.* the release of heat, light, or other energy. (No plural form.) □ *Radiation from the sun heats our planet.* **2.** *n.* radioactive particles and energy used in medical treatment. (No plural form.) □ *They treated Fred's cancer with radiation.*

**radical** ['ræd ɪ kəl] **1.** *adj.* complete and thorough; extreme. (Adv: *radically* [...ɪk li].) □ *The editor said my article needed radical revisions.* **2.** *adj.* [of someone] favoring extreme change. (Adv: *radically* [...ɪk li].) □ *The radical professor's ideas were ignored by his students.* **3.** *n.* someone who favors complete change; someone who favors extreme change. □ *The radicals demanded the release of the political prisoners.*

R

**radii** ['re di ɑɪ] a pl of **radius**.

**radio** ['re di o] **1.** *n.* the sending and receiving of sound through the air by using electromagnetic waves. (No plural form.) □ *News of the war was broadcast solely by radio.* **2.** *n.* a device that is used to receive electromagnetic waves and turn them into sound. (Pl ends in *-s*.) □ *I play the radio in my car when I'm stuck in traffic.* **3.** *adj.* <the adj. use of ① or ②.> □ *The radio announcer interrupted the music for a special bulletin.* **4.** *tv.* to send a message by ①. □ *The police officer radioed a call for help to headquarters from the police car.* **5.** *tv.* to send [a message] to someone using a radio. □ *Please radio the airport and ask if we can land.* **6.** *iv.* to use ② to send a message. □ *The policeman radioed for help.*

**radioactive** [re di o 'æk tɪv] *adj.* of or about an element or its compounds that release energy as the result of naturally occurring changes in the nuclear structure of the atoms of the element. (Adv: *radioactively*.) □ *Exposure to radioactive materials can burn or kill people and animals.*

**radius** ['re di əs] **1.** *n., irreg.* the distance from the center of a circle to any point on the circle. (Pl: **radii** or *radiuses*.) □ *A circle's diameter is twice the length of its radius.* **2.** *n., irreg.* a line that goes from the center of a circle to any point on the circle. □ *The large hand on a clock is similar to a radius.*

**raffle** ['ræf əl] **1.** *n.* a way of raising money where people buy tickets to win items or prizes that have been donated. (The winning ticket is chosen at random.) □ *The shopkeeper donated some goods for the school's raffle.* **2. raffle** something **off** *tv. + obj. + adv.* to make an item available in ①. □ *Our school raffled ten tickets off to all the football games.* 🅃 *We raffled off the tickets.*

**raft** ['ræft] **1.** *n.* boards or logs that are tied together so they will float on water; a rubber boat that is filled with air and floats on water. □ *The passengers of the sinking ship climbed into rubber rafts.* **2.** *iv.* to travel across water on ①. □ *Mary rafted down the river for a couple of miles.*

**rafter** ['ræf tɚ] *n.* one of a series of parallel boards or beams that support a roof. □ *The child's balloon soared up to the rafters.*

**rag** ['ræg] *n.* a piece of cloth, especially one that has no value or is used for cleaning. □ *The rags that I found in the trash were old torn shirts.*

**rage** ['redʒ] **1.** *n.* extreme, violent anger. □ *Susan's insults threw Jane into a wild rage.* **2.** *iv.* to show extreme, violent anger toward something. □ *The coach raged when the football team lost.*

**ragged** ['ræg əd] *adj.* torn; [of cloth] torn or damaged. (Adv: *raggedly.*) □ *I wear comfortable, ragged clothes around the house.*

**raid** ['red] **1.** *n.* a surprise attack, especially by police or soldiers. □ *During the raid, most of the village was destroyed.* **2.** *tv.* to enter someone's property or space and attack quickly, suddenly, and by surprise. □ *The soldiers raided the enemy camp at dawn.*

**rail** ['rel] **1.** *n.* a thick strip of wood or metal, usually used to support or guide someone or something. □ *There was a rail at the side of the road at the cliff's edge.* **2.** *n.* a metal **rail** ① on which a train travels. □ *At the horizon, parallel rails appear to come together.*

**railing** ['rel ɪŋ] *n.* a thick strip, rail, or tube of wood or metal that people can hold onto for support, usually found on a staircase. □ *Please hold the railing when using the stairs.*

**railroad** ['rel rod] **1.** *n.* two parallel metal rails on which a train travels. □ *Hundreds of men built the railroad that crosses the mountains.* **2.** *n.* a network or system of train tracks, train stations, and trains. □ *Most of America's railroads were built in the 19th century.* **3.** *n.* a business that operates trains. □ *The conductor had worked for the same railroad for 40 years.* **4.** *tv.* to move something quickly and forcefully; to force someone to do something quickly. □ *The salesman tried to railroad me into buying a new car.* **5.** *adj.* <the adj. use of ② or ③.> □ *We arrived at the railroad station exactly on time.*

**railway** ['rel we] **1.** *n.* a railroad; a railroad of a short length. □ *The city turned the abandoned railway into a bike path.* **2.** *adj.* <the adj. use of ①.> □ *The conductor announced the name of the next railway station.*

**rain** ['ren] **1.** *n.* water that falls down from the sky in drops. (No plural form.) □ *On the way home, I got soaked in the rain.* **2.** *n.* an instance or period of ①. (The plural usually indicates a season of **rain** that occurs annually.) □ *The rains came early this year.* □ *The rain came early this year.* **3.** *iv.* [for drops of water] to fall from the sky. (The subject must be **it**.) □ *It rained all through the night.* **4.** *tv.* to cause something to fall from the sky like ①. □ *The planes rained bombs onto the village below.*

**rainbow** ['ren bo] **1.** *n.* an arch of different colors of light that appears in the sky, caused by rays of sunlight passing through rain or mist. □ *After the storm, I saw a rainbow in the sky.* **2.** *adj.* consisting of the colors of the rainbow; from the group of colors of the rainbow. □ *The nursery's wallpaper has a rainbow pattern of colors.*

**raincoat** ['ren kot] *n.* a waterproof coat that people wear when it rains to keep their clothes dry. □ *The traffic cop's raincoat was bright orange.*

**raindrop** ['ren drɑp] *n.* one drop of rain. □ *As the raindrops started to fall heavily, I became wetter.*

**rainfall** ['ren fɔl] **1.** *n.* the drops of rain that fall when it rains; a period of falling rain. (No plural form.) □ *The rainfall washed the dirt from the street.* **2.** *n.* the amount of rain that falls in a certain place over a certain length of time. (No plural form.) □ *We had a two-inch rainfall last night.*

**rainstorm** ['ren storm] *n.* a storm that has a large amount of rain. □ *I got really wet when I was caught in the rainstorm.*

**rainy** ['re ni] *adj.* having a lot of rain. (Adv: *rainily.* Comp: *rainier;* sup: *rainiest.*) ☐ *It was a rainy day, so I stayed indoors.*

**raise** ['rez] **1.** *tv.* to lift someone or something up; to move someone or something to a higher level; to move someone or something upward; to cause someone or something to rise. (Compare this with **rise**.) ☐ *The soldier raised the flag to the top of the flagpole.* **2.** *tv.* to increase the amount of something; to increase the degree of something; to increase the force of something. ☐ *The pipe burst when the water pressure was raised.* **3.** *tv.* to cause plants to grow; to breed animals. ☐ *David raised rows of tulips next to his house.* **4.** *tv.* to bring up a child; to rear a child. ☐ *I was raised by my grandparents after my parents died.* **5.** *tv.* to collect or gather a certain amount of money. ☐ *Mary raised $1,000 to help start her new business.* **6.** *tv.* to bring up a subject or issue; to mention something; to address a subject or an issue; to begin talking about something. ☐ *The reporter raised some questions that embarrassed the mayor.* **7.** *n.* an increase in one's salary; an increase in the amount of money one earns at a job. ☐ *John asked his boss for a raise.*

R

**raisin** ['re zɪn] *n.* a dried grape, eaten as food. ☐ *Mary gave raisins to her children instead of candy.*

**rake** ['rek] **1.** *n.* a tool that has a long handle that is attached to a row of curved metal or plastic fingers, used to collect fallen leaves, loose grass, etc. ☐ *David tripped over the rake that he had left on the lawn.* **2.** *tv.* to collect something, especially leaves, hay, grass, or other objects on the ground, using ① or something similar. ☐ *The farmer raked the hay into a large pile.* **3.** *tv.* to smooth or clean something by using ①. ☐ *John raked his front yard after cutting the grass.* **4.** *iv.* to use ①; to scrape with ①. ☐ *Mary kept raking until she got a blister on her hand.*

**rally** ['ræl i] **1.** *tv.* to bring people together for a certain reason or cause. ☐ *The professor rallied his students to support his cause.* **2.** *n.* a large meeting, especially a large political meeting, held for a special reason. ☐ *After winning the election, Anne addressed the large rally.*

**ram** ['ræm] **1.** *n.* a male sheep. ☐ *The ram led the herd of sheep across the meadow.* **2.** *n.* a heavy pole or beam, the end of which is thrust against something. ☐ *The workers used a ram to knock over the metal frame.* **3.** *tv.* to hit someone or something; to crash into someone or something. ☐ *David rammed the wall with his fist.*

**rampage** ['ræm pedʒ] *n.* a period of wild, angry, or violent behavior. ☐ *The boss's rampage frightened all the staff.*

**ran** ['ræn] pt of **run**.

**ranch** ['ræntʃ] *n.* a very large farm where cattle or other animals are raised. ☐ *The cowboy rode his horse to the south part of the huge ranch.*

**rancher** ['ræntʃ ɚ] *n.* someone who works on a ranch; someone who owns a ranch. ☐ *The hunter was arrested for trespassing on the rancher's property.*

**random** ['ræn dəm] **1.** *adj.* selected by chance. (Adv: *randomly.*) ☐ *The magician chose a random volunteer from the audience.* **2. at random** *phr.* happening by chance; chosen for no special reason. ☐ *As a prank, the children dialed phone numbers at random.*

**rang** ['ræŋ] pt of **ring**.

**range** ['rendʒ] **1.** *n.* the area between two extremes; the choices, possibilities, or selections available. ☐ *The talented singer had a range of three octaves.* **2.** *n.* the distance that something can operate or be used in, especially the distance that someone can see or hear, that a weapon can fire, or that something can travel without needing more fuel. (No plural form.) ☐ *My TV doesn't get Channel 10 because we're out of its range.* **3.** *n.* a field where cattle or other animals can walk about and look for food. (No plural form.) ☐ *The cowboy felt at home on the range.* **4.** *n.* a stove with one or more ovens attached. ☐ *The cook cleans the range weekly.* **5.** *iv.* to vary between two limits or extremes; to be located between an upper limit and a lower limit. ☐ *My musical tastes range from jazz to country.*

**rank** ['ræŋk] **1.** *n.* one level in a series of levels; one level on a scale of authority, value, or importance. ☐ *Houses of the first rank are usually the most expensive.* **2.** *iv.* to occupy a certain position on a scale of authority, value, or importance; to be on a list in a certain position. ☐ *The office of president ranks above the office of vice president.* **3.** *tv.* to place someone or something on a list in its proper order or place. ☐ *The test ranked the students according to intelligence.* **4.** *adj.* smelling or tasting very bad or unpleasant. (Adv: *rankly.*) ☐ *This milk tastes rank. How old is it?* **5.** *adj.* [of vegetation] growing thickly or coarsely. ☐ *The field was covered with rank weeds.*

**rap** ['ræp] **1.** *n.* a style of music where the words of the song are spoken in a strong rhythm instead of being sung. (No plural form.) ☐ *John listened to rap on his radio all day long.* **2.** *n.* the sound made by a quick, strong knock or hit. ☐ *I hear a rap at the door. Are we expecting anyone?* **3. rap on** something *iv.* + *prep. phr.* [for someone] to hit something quickly and sharply, making a knocking sound. ☐ *I rapped hard on the door with my knuckles.* **4. rap at** something *iv.* + *prep. phr.* to hit or knock on something quickly. ☐ *The small branches rapped at my window during the storm.*

**rape** ['rep] **1.** *n.* the act and crime of forcing someone to have sex. ☐ *The instructor showed the women how to defend themselves against rape.* **2.** *tv.* to force someone to have sex. ☐ *The man who raped and killed five women was executed.*

**rapid** ['ræp ɪd] **1.** *adj.* quick; swift; moving fast; done quickly; happening quickly. (Adv: *rapidly.*) ☐ *The shoplifter made a rapid move toward the exit.* **2. rapids** *n.* the part of a river where the water moves very fast and is very active. (Treated as plural.) ☐ *Our rowboat was caught in the rapids, heading toward a waterfall.*

**rapidity** [rə 'pɪd ə ti] *n.* quickness; speed. (No plural form.) ☐ *The rapidity with which the fire spread surprised me.*

**rapture** ['ræp tʃɚ] *n.* a feeling or expression of complete joy or delight. (No plural form.) ☐ *Anne's wedding day was filled with joyous rapture as well as tension.*

**rare** ['rɛr] **1.** *adj.* not common; not often found, seen, or done. (Adv: *rarely.* Comp: *rarer;* sup: *rarest.*) ☐ *John collects rare books.* **2.** *adj.* [of meat] cooked only a little. (Comp: *rarer;* sup: *rarest.*) ☐ *The inside of the rare hamburger was pink.*

**rash** ['ræʃ] **1.** *n.* a disease or condition of the skin, making it red, itchy, and bumpy. ☐ *David put some medicine on the rash on his chest.* **2.** *adj.* not thinking about something carefully or long enough; done without careful thought. (Adv: *rashly.* Comp: *rasher;* sup: *rashest.*) ☐ *It would be rash of you to quit your job today.*

**raspberry** ['ræz bɛr i] **1.** *n.* a small, sweet, usually red or purple fruit that grows on a bush, and the bush itself. ☐ *John put some raspberries on his cereal.* **2.** *adj.* made or flavored with ①. ☐ *I made a raspberry tart for dessert.*

**rat** ['ræt] **1.** *n.* a small rodent with a long tail. ☐ *I told my landlord that I'd seen rats in the kitchen.* **2.** *n.* someone who

R

is mean, worthless, not honest, or not loyal. (Fig. on ①.) □ *Tom can be such a rat sometimes.* **3.** *iv.* to go to the police or authorities and tell them that someone is doing something wrong. □ *Jimmy was unpopular because he always ratted to the teacher.*

**rate** ['ret] **1.** *n.* an amount that is measured in relation to another amount, such as speed in relation to time. □ *At the rate we're going, we won't be finished until next week.* **2.** *n.* a price [for each unit of something]. □ *My health club's rates are cheaper than the rates at the one John goes to.* **3.** *tv.* to assign a value or rank to someone or something. □ *How would you rate this restaurant?* **4.** *tv.* to deserve something; to be worthy of something. □ *I think my letter rates a response, don't you?*

**rather** ['ræð ɚ] **1.** *adv.* instead; on the contrary. □ *No, I'm not sick; rather, I'm just tired.* **2.** *adv.* to an extent; to a degree; too; very; quite. □ *The music is rather loud, wouldn't you say?* **3. would rather** do something *phr.* would more willingly do something; would more readily do something; would prefer to do something. (Often *-'d rather.*) □ *He'd rather not eat spinach, thank you.*

R

**ratify** ['ræt ə fɑɪ] *tv.* to approve something officially; to make something be valid officially. □ *The city council ratified the mayor's proposed budget.*

**rational** ['ræʃ ə nəl] **1.** *adj.* using the mind or the brain; sensible; reasonable; logical. (Adv: *rationally.*) □ *It isn't rational to walk barefoot in the snow.* **2.** *adj.* able to use sense or reason; aware. (Adv: *rationally.*) □ *After the accident, John was no longer rational.*

**rationale** [ræʃ ə 'næl] *n.* a reason; the reason for doing something; reasoning or explanation. (No plural form.) □ *My professor disagreed with the rationale of my argument.*

**rattle** ['ræt əl] **1.** *n.* a noise-making device, usually a toy for babies, consisting of a small container with bits of hard matter inside. □ *The baby loved to shake his rattle and make lots of noise.* **2.** *n.* the noise made when a number of small things tap against something, as with ①. □ *During the earthquake, I heard the rattle of dishes and cups.* **3.** *iv.* to make a quick set of short noises. □ *The tail of the snake rattled as the snake approached its prey.* **4.** *tv.* to cause something to make a quick set of short noises. □ *The rattlesnake rattled its tail.*

**rattlesnake** ['ræt əl snek] *n.* a venomous snake with hard rings of skin on its tail that make a rattling sound when it shakes its tail. □ *The rattlesnake swallowed the rat.*

**rave** ['rev] **rave about** someone or something *iv.* + *prep. phr.* to praise or curse someone or something in a very excited or wild way; to praise someone or something. □ *The critic raved about the movie in his review.*

**raw** ['rɔ] **1.** *adj.* not cooked. (Comp: *rawer;* sup: *rawest.*) □ *I don't like raw meat.* **2.** *adj.* [of something that has been] rubbed until sore; having a layer of skin rubbed off. (Adv: *rawly.* Comp: *rawer;* sup: *rawest.*) □ *Your raw sunburn looks very painful.*

**ray** ['re] *n.* a beam of something that comes from a source, especially a beam of light, heat, or radiation. □ *The surgeon used a ray from a laser to destroy the tumor.*

**raze** ['rez] *tv.* to tear down a building completely. □ *The workers razed the old factory building.*

**razor** ['re zɚ] **1.** *n.* a tool that holds a sharp blade that is used to shave whiskers or hair. □ *Mary uses her razor in the shower.* **2.** *adj.* <the adj. use of ①.> □ *If your razor blade is dull, it won't shave you very well.*

**reach** ['ritʃ] **1.** *tv.* to arrive at some place; to get to some place. □ *The storm is supposed to reach Atlanta by noon.* **2.** *tv.* to get hold of someone by some means of communication; to contact someone. □ *I hope my letter reaches you before you move again.* **3.** *tv.* to stretch out to a certain place in space or time; to extend to a certain place in space or time. □ *The long curtains almost reach the floor.* **4.** *tv.* to affect or influence someone; to make someone else understand something. □ *The counselor was unable to reach the troubled child.* **5.** *tv.* to total a certain amount. □ *The rainfall reached 2 inches before the night was over.* **6.** *iv.* to extend all the way. □ *The storm reached from New York City to Boston.* **7. reach for someone or something** *iv. + prep. phr.* to move or stretch to touch or get something. □ *I reached for the book on the top shelf.* **8. reach out** *iv. + adv.* to attempt to make contact with someone; to seek someone who can provide help. □ *I reached out for help, but no one was there.* **9.** *n.* the distance that someone or something is able to stretch or extend; the range or capacity of someone or something. □ *The tall man had a very long reach.*

**react** [ri 'ækt] **1.** *iv.* to show a response [to something]; to make a response [to someone or something]. □ *David reacted to my comments by leaving the room.* **2.** *iv.* [for a chemical] to do something when it touches another substance; [for two chemicals] to do something when they are brought together. □ *The chemical reacted violently when water was poured into it.*

**reaction** [ri 'æk ʃən] **1.** *n.* a response to someone or something; an action that is done in response to someone or something; a feeling that is felt in response to someone or something. □ *The doctor monitored my reaction to the medicine.* **2.** *n.* the result of a chemical touching another substance; the result when two chemicals are brought together. □ *The chemist documented the changes caused by the reaction.*

**read** **1.** ['rid] *tv., irreg.* to understand what is meant by written words; to get meaning from written words. (Pt/pp: *read* ① ['rɛd].) □ *I read the sign posted on the door.* **2.** ['rid] *tv., irreg.* to say written words out loud. □ *John read his poem to the audience of students and teachers.* **3.** ['rid] *iv., irreg.* to be able to understand writing and printing. □ *Jimmy doesn't read yet. He is too young.* **4.** ['rid] *iv., irreg.* to say written words aloud. □ *The teacher reads to the class every day.*

**readily** ['rɛd ə li] **1.** *adv.* without difficulty or problems; easily. □ *The carpenter constructed a new door frame quite readily.* **2.** *adv.* without delay or doubt; eagerly. □ *I readily let my best friend borrow my car.*

**readiness** ['rɛd i nəs] *n.* the state of being ready; the state of being prepared. (No plural form.) □ *The members of the team were in a state of readiness for the game.*

**reading** ['rid ɪŋ] **1.** *n.* something written that is meant to be read. □ *I have selected a reading from Shakespeare that I am sure you will recognize.* **2.** *n.* a measurement shown on a meter or other similar device. □ *The gas-company employee came to my house to check the meter reading.* **3.** *adj.* <the adj. use of ①.> □ *Anne must wear reading glasses.*

**readjust** [ri ə 'dʒʌst] **1.** *tv.* to adjust something again; to put something back where it belongs. □ *The driver readjusted the car's mirror after I bumped it.* **2. readjust to** someone or something *iv. + prep. phr.* to get used to someone or something again. □ *I readjusted to school with great difficulty after summer vacation.*

**readjustment** [ri ə 'dʒʌst mənt] **1.** *n.* the process of getting used to something

R

again. (No plural form.) □ *My readjustment to winter takes quite some time.* **2.** *n.* an act of readjusting something; a movement or change that is made when putting something back where it belongs. □ *The photographer's readjustment of the lens resulted in a clearer picture.*

**ready** ['rɛd i] **1.** *adj.* [of something] able to be used right now. (Comp: *readier;* sup: *readiest.*) □ *The wall is ready for another coat of paint.* **2.** *tv.* to prepare something for use. □ *The maid readied the hotel room for the next guest.* **3. ready to** do something *adj. + inf.* [of someone or some creature] prepared and eager to do something. □ *If you need me, I'm ready to help.*

**real** ['ril] **1.** *adj.* existing; actual; true. (Adv: *really.*) □ *David was unsure if what he was seeing was real.* **2.** *adj.* genuine; not fake. (Adv: *really.*) □ *Is that painting real, or is it a copy?* **3.** *adv.* really; very; extremely. (Colloquial.) □ *I don't want to go to the movies, because I'm real tired.*

**real estate** ['ril ə stet] **1.** *n.* land, with all the buildings on it and all the minerals under it. (No plural form.) □ *I bought a piece of real estate in the suburbs.* **2.** *n.* the business of dealing in ①. (No plural form.) □ *I wish I had gotten into real estate when I was younger.* **3.** *adj.* <the adj. use of ②.> (Hyphenated before a nominal.) □ *Anne went to the real-estate office to sign a contract.*

**realism** ['ri ə lɪz əm] *n.* the point of view concerned with reality in life and art. (No plural form.) □ *The artist's best works were fine examples of realism.*

**realistic** [ri ə 'lɪs tɪk] **1.** *adj.* appearing or seeming to be real or authentic. (Adv: *realistically* [...ɪk li].) □ *The artist drew a realistic sketch of herself.* **2.** *adj.* accepting life as it really is; practical. (Adv: *realistically* [...ɪk li].) □ *It's not realistic to expect me to do the work of two people.*

**reality** [ri 'æl ə ti] **1.** *n.* everything that is real; something that is real; that which exists. (Plural only when referring to different kinds, types, instances, or varieties.) □ *It is time you quit dreaming and begin to face reality.* Ⓒ *The patient was living in two realities. In one she was a child and in the other an adult.* **2. in reality** *phr.* viewing things realistically; really; actually. □ *John looks happy, but in reality, he is very sad.*

**realization** [ri əl ə 'ze ʃən] *n.* an understanding that something exists or has happened. □ *Jane came to the realization that Anne was right.*

**realize** ['ri ə lɑɪz] **1.** *tv.* to understand something; to be aware of something. (The object can be a clause with **that** ⑦.) □ *Anne realized the importance of the situation.* **2.** *tv.* to make something real; to cause something to exist. □ *The thief's plans were slowly realized.*

**really** ['ri (ə) li] **1.** *adv.* actually; truly; in reality. □ *I'm serious. Jane is really an enemy spy.* **2.** *adv.* very; completely. □ *I'm really tired. Can I call you back tomorrow?*

**reappear** [ri ə 'pɪr] **1.** *iv.* to appear again. □ *The tiny mouse reappeared on the other side of the room.* **2.** *iv.* to occur again. □ *The computer problem reappeared just when I thought I had fixed it.*

**rear** ['rɪr] **1.** *n.* the part of the body one sits on. (Euphemistic.) □ *I fell right on my rear when I slipped on the ice.* **2.** *adj.* in back; hind. □ *My dog hurt one of his rear legs when he fell off the porch.* **3.** *tv.* to raise offspring. □ *The bird reared the baby birds until they left the nest.* **4.** *iv.* to rise up, especially for a horse to stand on its back legs. □ *The horse reared in fright.*

**rearrange** [ri ə 'rendʒ] *tv.* to arrange something again or in a different way, especially to place things or people in a different order or in different positions

R

with respect to each other. □ *If I rearrange my schedule of appointments, I will be able to meet you for lunch.*

**rearrangement** [ri ə 'rendʒ mənt] *n.* creating a new or different arrangement; changing the way that things or people are ordered or positioned with respect to each other. (No plural form.) □ *Your rearrangement of the furniture has really made the room look bigger.*

**reason** ['ri zən] **1.** *n.* the power or ability to think, understand, and form opinions and conclusions from facts. (No plural form.) □ *After the head injury, John lost all reason.* **2.** *n.* a cause; a motive; an explanation; a rationale. □ *The reason for the seasons is the tilt of the earth.* **3.** *iv.* to think; to be able to think; to use the power or ability to think, understand, and form opinions and conclusions. □ *I was too tired to reason very well.* **4. reason with** someone *iv.* + *prep. phr.* to persuade someone by using ①; to argue with someone by using ①. □ *John tried to reason with Fred, but Fred hit him anyway.* **5.** *tv.* to have an opinion or conclusion based on ①. (The object is a clause with **that** ⑦.) □ *The detective reasoned that David had been murdered for his money.*

**reasonable** ['ri zə nə bəl] **1.** *adj.* sensible; making sense; according to reason. (Adv: *reasonably.*) □ *Bill gave a reasonable excuse for being late.* **2.** *adj.* not expensive; having an acceptable cost. (Adv: *reasonably.*) □ *Although the neighborhood is expensive, this apartment is very reasonable.*

**reasoning** ['ri zə nɪŋ] **1.** *n.* the process or ability of thinking and forming conclusions from facts and evidence. (No plural form.) □ *My English teacher showed me why my reasoning was faulty.* **2.** *adj.* <the adj. use of ①.> □ *I had to put all my reasoning power to work on this problem.*

**reassure** [ri ə 'ʃʊr] *tv.* to restore someone's courage or confidence. □ *My boss reassured me that I would be getting a raise soon.*

**rebel 1.** ['rɛb əl] *n.* someone who fights or resists power, authority, or government. □ *The president refused to bargain with the rebels.* **2. rebel against** someone or something [rɪ 'bɛl...] *iv.* + *prep. phr.* to fight against a person, power, laws, rules, authority, or government. □ *The students rebelled against the new rules.*

**rebellion** [rɪ 'bɛl jən] *n.* rebelling; challenging authority. (Plural only when referring to different kinds, types, instances, or varieties.) □ *Rebellion is part of becoming a teenager.* Ⓒ *A series of rebellions was ended by the army.*

**rebirth** [ri 'bɝθ] *n.* seeming to be born again. (No plural form.) □ *Mary believed in the rebirth of the soul.*

**rebound 1.** ['ri baʊnd] *n.* the return movement of something that bounced off something. □ *On the second rebound, the ball hit Bill on the head.* **2.** [rɪ 'baʊnd] *iv.* to bounce back after hitting something. □ *The rubber ball rebounded off the pavement.* **3.** [rɪ 'baʊnd] *iv.* to recover. (Fig. on ②.) □ *Anne rebounded from her illness very quickly.*

R

**rebuild** [rɪ 'bɪld] *tv., irreg.* to build something again. (Pt/pp: **rebuilt.**) □ *Dave rebuilt the sand castle after John knocked it over.*

**rebuilt** [rɪ 'bɪlt] pt/pp of **rebuild.**

**receipt** [rɪ 'sit] **1.** *n.* a state of having been received. (No plural form.) □ *I expect receipt of the letter tomorrow.* **2.** *n.* a document that proves that something has been received or paid for. □ *The clerk couldn't issue a refund because I lost my receipt.* **3. receipts** *n.* money that a business receives from customers; money that is collected by a business or at a performance. (Treated as plural, but not countable.) □ *The accountant examined the records of the store's receipts.*

**receive** [rɪ 'siv] **1.** *tv.* to get something; to take something that is given. □ *John received an influenza shot from the nurse.* **2.** *tv.* to accept someone as a member of a group or organization; to welcome someone as a visitor. □ *We received four guests at our vacation home.*

**receiver** [rɪ 'siv ɚ] **1.** *n.* someone or something that receives something. □ *The receiver of the bad news called me to tell me.* **2.** *n.* the part of a telephone that one holds while one is talking. □ *After the call, Mary returned the receiver to the hook.* **3.** *n.* a radio or television set; something that receives broadcast signals. □ *My neighbor's microwave oven affects my television receiver.*

**recent** ['ri sənt] *adj.* happening only a short time ago; having existed for only a short time; not long ago. (Adv: *recently.*) □ *We were all shocked by the recent series of train crashes.*

**receptacle** [rɪ 'sɛp tə kəl] **1.** *n.* a container designed to receive something. □ *I put my used paper towel into a receptacle by the door.* **2.** *n.* a place to plug in an electric cord. (Short for **electric receptacle.**) □ *Where is a receptacle? I need to plug in my computer.*

**reception** [rɪ 'sɛp ʃən] **1.** *n.* receiving or welcoming someone. □ *John's new coworkers gave him a cold reception.* **2.** *n.* the quality of broadcast signals that are received by a television set, a radio, or other receiver. (No plural form.) □ *The radio got better reception when I moved the antenna.* **3.** *n.* a party, gathering, or celebration where people are welcomed. □ *Cheese and crackers were served at Bob's reception.*

**recess 1.** ['ri sɛs] *n.* a period of time during the school day when the children are allowed to play, usually outside. □ *Recess ended when the school bell rang.* **2.** ['ri sɛs] *n.* a period of time during the work day where someone stops working for a few minutes and takes a break; a break. □ *The judge declared a two-hour recess for lunch.* **3.** ['ri sɛs] *n.* a space cut or built into a wall; a space that is set back from a wall. □ *John put a vase of flowers in the recess in the front hallway.* **4.** [rɪ 'sɛs] *iv.* to take a break; to stop working for a short time. □ *The committee recessed while copies of the report were being made.*

**recipe** ['rɛs ə pi] **1.** *n.* a set of directions for making something to eat. □ *There are a lot of delicious recipes in this cookbook.* **2.** *n.* a set of directions for preparing or causing anything. (Fig. on ①.) □ *I asked my grandparents to tell us their recipe for a happy marriage.*

**recipient** [rɪ 'sɪp i ənt] *n.* someone who receives something. □ *John is the happy recipient of a college scholarship.*

**recital** [rɪ 'sɑɪt əl] **1.** *n.* the telling of a story; a verbal account of something. □ *I grew weary of listening to Mary's recital of all of her diseases and mental problems.* **2.** *n.* a concert or performance by students who play instruments, sing, or dance; a concert or performance, often by a single performer playing an instrument, singing, or reading poetry. □ *The young dancers were quite proud of how well they did in their dance recital.*

**recite** [rɪ 'sɑɪt] *tv.* to verbally deliver an answer in school; to repeat something, such as a poem, from memory. □ *Bob recited a poem that he had written.*

**reckless** ['rɛk ləs] *adj.* careless; not concerned with safety or danger. (Adv: *recklessly.*) □ *It is reckless to go up so high on such an old ladder.*

**recklessness** ['rɛk ləs nəs] *n.* being reckless; taking risks on purpose. (No plural form.) □ *The police were amazed at the criminal's recklessness.*

**reclaim** [rɪ 'klem] **1.** *tv.* to save or reuse something that would otherwise be thrown away. □ *The librarian reclaimed a few of the books damaged by the flood.* **2.** *tv.* to demand or claim the return of something that has been given away or taken away. □ *Bob reclaimed his watch from the woman who saw him drop it in the street.*

**recognition** [rɛk ɪg 'nɪʃ ən] **1.** *n.* realization. (No plural form.) □ *Recognition that the house badly needed painting came when the neighbors complained.* **2.** *n.* acknowledgment of the existence of someone or something. (No plural form.) □ *The country's recognition of Taiwan angered China.* **3.** *n.* acknowledgment of service or excellence. (No plural form.) □ *In recognition of their courage, the soldiers were given medals.*

**recognizable** ['rɛk ɪg nɑɪz ə bəl] *adj.* in adequate amount or degree to be noticed or identified. (Adv: *recognizably.*) □ *The burned body found by the police was not recognizable.*

**recognize** ['rɛk ɪg nɑɪz] **1.** *tv.* to identify someone or something. □ *The baby recognized her mother's face.* **2.** *tv.* to make an acknowledgment that something exists. (The object can be a clause with **that** ⑦.) □ *The university recognized the students' right to free speech.* **3.** *tv.* to give someone the right to speak, especially at a meeting. □ *When Anne was recognized, she gave her report.*

**recommend** [rɛk ə 'mɛnd] **1.** *tv.* to suggest [making] a particular choice from a range of choices. □ *The counselor recommended the easiest course of action.* **2.** *tv.* to suggest a particular course of action. (The object can be a clause with **that** ⑦.) □ *The usher recommended that I sit near the front where I could hear better.*

**recommendation** [rɛk ə mɛn 'de ʃən] *n.* a suggestion of which selection someone should choose from a range of choices; someone or something that is recommended. □ *The movie critic's recommendation turned out to be horrible.*

**reconsider** [ri kən 'sɪd ɚ] **1.** *tv.* to consider something again; to think about something again. □ *John reconsidered the things he had said to me in anger.* **2.** *iv.* to consider again; to think about again. □ *The actor reconsidered when I offered to rewrite his role.*

**record 1.** ['rɛk ɚd] *n.* a written account of facts or information about someone or something. □ *My doctor examined my medical records.* **2.** ['rɛk ɚd] *n.* a flat plastic disk that has sound **recorded** ⑤ on it, which is played on a machine that makes the recorded sounds able to be heard. □ *The record sounds bad because there are so many scratches on it.* **3.** ['rɛk ɚd] *n.* the most extreme example of something; the highest, lowest, fastest, slowest, longest, shortest, or any other extreme example of something. □ *John tried to break the world record for the long jump.* **4.** [rɪ 'kord] *tv.* to write down information about someone or something so that other people will be able to read the information. □ *Anne recorded her private thoughts in her diary.* **5.** [rɪ 'kord] *tv.* to store sound on audiotape or to store images on film or videotape; to put a sound or an image into a permanent form. □ *I recorded my daughter's wedding on videotape.*

**recorded** [rɪ 'kor dɪd] **1.** *adj.* written down; having information about someone or something written down; known. □ *Language began long before recorded history.* **2.** *adj.* stored on cassette, film, or videotape; stored in a permanent form. □ *The station broadcast a previously recorded television show.*

**recorder** [rɪ 'kor dɚ] **1.** *n.* someone who writes down and stores information. □ *The recorder of deeds keeps track of land ownership.* **2.** *n.* a musical instrument, consisting of a hollow tube of

R

wood that has holes down one side. □ *John played a folk tune on his recorder.* **3.** *n.* a machine that records sounds or images, and usually is able to play the sounds and images back. □ *Sue brought a battery-operated tape recorder to the interview.*

**recording** [rɪ 'kor dɪŋ] *n.* a record; music, speech, or other sound that has been recorded. □ *The lawyer played a recording of the testimony for the jury.*

**recount 1.** ['ri kaʊnt] *n.* another counting; a second count; another count, especially in an election when the votes are counted for a second time because the first count is thought to be faulty. □ *The election's outcome was reversed as a result of the recount.* **2.** [ri 'kaʊnt] *tv.* to tell a story; to tell the story of something that happened. □ *John recounted his day at work to me.* **3.** ['ri 'kaʊnt] *tv.* to count something again. □ *I recounted the playing cards to make sure there were 52.*

**recover** [ri 'kʌv ɚ] **1.** *iv.* to get better after a sickness or injury; to return to good health. □ *John was slow to recover from the car accident.* **2.** *tv.* to get something back that went away or was lost, stolen, or taken away. □ *Our team recovered the ball after it had been lost to the other team.* **3.** *tv.* to reclaim something; to pull out something useful from something that is not useful. □ *This process can recover valuable minerals from salt water.*

**recovery** [ri 'kʌv ə ri] **1.** *n.* the process of getting something back that went away or was lost, stolen, or taken; receiving someone or something that went away or was lost, stolen, or taken. (No plural form.) □ *I thanked the police for the recovery of my stolen car.* **2.** *n.* the return to someone's or something's regular condition, especially the return of good health after sickness or injury or the return of a good economy after a bad period of time. (No plural form.) □ *Many people found jobs during the state's economic recovery.*

**recreation** [rɛk ri 'e ʃən] *n.* amusement; play; activities that are done for pleasure, enjoyment, or fun. (No plural form.) □ *I went on vacation for rest and recreation.*

**recreational** [rɛk ri 'e ʃə nəl] *adj.* of or about **recreation**. (Adv: *recreationally.*) □ *The hotel's recreational facilities included a pool.*

**recruit** [rɪ 'krut] **1.** *tv.* to cause or persuade someone to become a new member of a group, an organization, or the military. □ *Bill and I recruited twenty other students for our chorus.* **2.** *n.* someone who has just joined a group or organization, especially the military. □ *We held a reception to welcome our club's new recruits.*

**rectangle** ['rɛk tæŋ gəl] *n.* a flat, four-sided figure with four right angles, whose opposite sides are parallel and the same length. □ *My garage is in the shape of a rectangle.*

**rectangular** [rɛk 'tæŋ gjə lɚ] *adj.* shaped like a rectangle. (Adv: *rectangularly.*) □ *Anne arranged the data in a rectangular chart.*

**rectify** ['rɛk tə faɪ] *tv.* to make something right; to correct something. □ *I rectified the situation by offering to pay for the damage I caused.*

**rectum** ['rɛk təm] *n.* the end of the lower intestine, through which human waste passes. □ *The nurse placed a thermometer in the patient's rectum.*

**recur** [ri 'kɚ] *iv.* to repeat; to happen again; to continue to happen. □ *The same dream recurred night after night.*

**recycle** [ri 'saɪk əl] **1.** *tv.* to change glass, plastic, paper, or other material into a form that can be used again; to recover a resource; to find a further use for something that might otherwise be

R

wasted. □ *The plant recycled old newspapers into a fiber that can be used in the walls of houses to hold in the heat.* **2.** *tv.* to collect or set aside used glass, plastic, paper, or other material so that it can be **recycled** ① into something useful. □ *You should recycle your newspapers.* **3.** *iv.* to collect and set aside [trash] as in ②. □ *Do you recycle?*

**recycled** [ri 'saɪk əld] *adj.* made from a substance that has already been used. □ *The shampoo bottle is made of recycled plastic.*

**red** ['rɛd] **1.** *n.* the color of blood and the traffic signal that means stop. (Plural only when referring to different kinds, types, instances, or varieties.) □ *John painted the walls of his room a dark red.* Ⓒ *The reds and golds of desert sunsets are really quite beautiful.* **2.** *adj.* <the adj. use of ①.> (Adv: *redly.* Comp: *redder;* sup: *reddest.*) □ *The dancer wore a pair of red shoes.* **3.** *adj.* [of hair] copper colored or rusty orange. (Comp: *redder;* sup: *reddest.*) □ *Red hair is actually more of a rusty orange color.* **4. in(to) the red** *phr.* in(to) debt. □ *It's easy to get into the red if you don't pay close attention to the amount of money you spend.* **5. out of the red** *phr.* out of debt. □ *If we can cut down on expenses, we can get out of the red fairly soon.*

**redbird** ['rɛd bɝd] *n.* any of various birds having red feathers. □ *A redbird flew across the yard and into a tree.*

**redden** ['rɛd n] **1.** *iv.* to become red; to turn red. □ *The apple's skin reddened as it ripened.* **2.** *tv.* to cause someone or something to become red; to cause someone or something to turn red. □ *The rash reddened my skin.*

**reddish** ['rɛd ɪʃ] *adj.* having some of the qualities of the color red. (Adv: *reddishly.*) □ *Mary's skin was reddish because of the cold.*

**redeem** [rɪ 'dim] **1.** *tv.* to get something back as the result of settling a debt. □ *Mary redeemed the car's title when she paid off the car loan.* **2.** *tv.* to convert something to cash, especially to convert a coupon, token, ticket, or other thing that is not money but represents money. □ *I redeemed the raffle ticket for the $1,500 prize.* **3.** *tv.* to do something that restores other people's good opinion of oneself. (Takes a reflexive object.) □ *If you want to redeem yourself, you can apologize to me.*

**redeeming** [rɪ 'dim ɪŋ] *adj.* making up for other faults or problems. □ *The redeeming value of the car was that it got good gas mileage.*

**redevelop** [ri dɪ 'vɛl əp] **1.** *tv.* to develop something again. □ *Bill redeveloped the ability to walk after the accident.* **2.** *tv.* to build in an area again; to construct buildings in an area again. □ *The city council voted to redevelop the public parks.*

**redhead** ['rɛd hɛd] *n.* someone who has red hair. □ *The redhead bought clothes in a color that would not look bad with her hair.*

**redid** ['ri 'dɪd] pt of **redo.**

**redirect** [ri dɪ 'rɛkt] *tv.* to direct or send someone or something to a different place; to send someone or something in a different direction. □ *The soldier redirected the large gun toward the south.*

**redness** ['rɛd nəs] *n.* being red; the condition of having the color red. (No plural form.) □ *The redness of a tomato is an indication of its ripeness.*

**redo** [ri 'du] *tv., irreg.* to do something again; to do something over. (Pt: **redid;** pp: **redone.**) □ *After I had redone the assignment, I handed it to my teacher.*

**redone** [ri 'dʌn] pp of **redo.**

**redouble** [ri 'dʌb əl] **1.** *tv.* to double the amount of something; to increase the amount of something. □ *The firefighters redoubled their efforts as the fire spread.* **2.** *iv.* to double; to increase.

R

☐ *My heavy schedule redoubled when my boss went on vacation.*

**reduce** [rɪ 'dus] **1.** *tv.* to make something smaller or less important; to decrease something. ☐ *John reduced the amount of unhealthy food that he ate.* **2.** *iv.* to lose [weight]. ☐ *My doctor ordered me to reduce.*

**reduction** [rɪ 'dʌk ʃən] **1.** *n.* making something smaller; reducing something. ☐ *I asked for a reduction in my hours at work, since I need more time at home.* **2.** *n.* the amount by which something is made smaller. ☐ *The budget was subject to a 20% reduction.*

**redundant** [rɪ 'dʌn dənt] *adj.* extra; not needed; doing the same thing as something else. (Adv: *redundantly.*) ☐ *These two words are redundant. Cross one out.*

**redwood** ['rɛd wʊd] **1.** *n.* a tall evergreen tree, found in the western United States, that lives to be very old. ☐ *The eagle soared among the redwoods.* **2.** *n.* the wood of ①. (Plural only when referring to different kinds, types, instances, or varieties.) ☐ *Redwood is a strong and long-lasting wood.* Ⓒ *The older redwoods are usually found in state and national forests.* **3.** *adj.* <the adj. use of ②.> ☐ *The redwood fence will last forever!*

R

**reed** ['rid] **1.** *n.* a tall grass-like plant with hollow stems that grows in marshes and other wet places. ☐ *The hound retrieved the wounded duck from the reeds near the marsh.* **2.** *n.* a thin piece of wood in the mouthpiece of woodwind instruments like clarinets, saxophones, and oboes or a similar metal piece in harmonicas, accordions, and pipe organs. ☐ *The reed vibrates when the player blows air over it, making the sound of the instrument.* **3.** *adj.* <the adj. use of ②.> ☐ *Saxophones, clarinets, oboes, and bassoons are reed instruments.*

**reef** ['rif] *n.* a ridge of rocks, sand, or coral that extends from the bottom of a sea or ocean to or almost to the surface of the water. ☐ *The scuba diver watched the fish swim around the reef.*

**reek** ['rik] *iv.* to smell very bad. ☐ *You should clean your refrigerator. It reeks.*

**reel** ['ril] **1.** *n.* a round frame around which string, thread, yarn, fishing line, film, audiotape, videotape, or other long materials are wound. ☐ *I couldn't catch the fish because the reel had jammed.* **2.** *iv.* to twist or turn, as when struck a by powerful blow. ☐ *I reeled after I was hit in the face.* **3. reel** something **in** *tv.* + *obj.* + *adv.* to pull something inward, toward oneself, by using ①. ☐ *Mary reeled a large fish in.* Ⓣ *She reeled in the fish.*

**reelect** ['ri ə 'lɛkt] *tv.* to elect someone again. ☐ *The voters reelected the mayor by a wide margin.*

**reelection** [ri ə 'lɛk ʃən] *n.* the election of someone to the same position for another term. ☐ *The mayor's reelection to city hall surprised no one.*

**reestablish** [ri ə 'stæb lɪʃ] *tv.* to establish something again. ☐ *Our school reestablished its annual bake sale after a two-year break.*

**refer** [rɪ 'fɚ] **1. refer to** something *iv.* + *prep. phr.* to use something for help or information; to go to someone or something for help or information. ☐ *Anne referred to the computer manual for help.* **2. refer to** something *iv.* + *prep. phr.* to have to do with something; to apply to something; to be related to something; to concern something. ☐ *My comments referred to my brother, not to you.* **3. refer** someone **to** someone or something *tv.* + *obj.* + *prep. phr.* to direct someone to use something for help or information; to direct someone to go to someone or something for help or information. ☐ *The guard referred the tourist to the museum's information desk.*

**referee** [rɛf ə 'ri] **1.** *n.* someone who judges the playing of sports events; an umpire. □ *The basketball referee blew his whistle.* **2.** *tv.* to judge the playing of a sports event. □ *My sister will referee the basketball game.* **3.** *iv.* to serve as ①. □ *Who is refereeing this evening?*

**reference** ['rɛf (ə) rəns] **1.** *n.* words that refer to something else; something that has to do with something else; something that relates to something else. □ *The movie made many references to current political events.* **2.** *n.* something, such as a book, that is used for help or information; someone or something that provides information about something. □ *The travel guide was a useful reference when I was in Europe.* **3.** *n.* a statement that someone writes about someone else for that other person's use when applying for something; a statement about someone or someone's character. □ *My new boss said that my references were full of praise.*

**refine** [rɪ 'fɑɪn] **1.** *tv.* to make something purer. □ *The factory refined sugar and packaged it for selling.* **2.** *tv.* to make something more detailed, rational, and effective. □ *The author refined the manuscript.*

**refined** [rɪ 'fɑɪnd] **1.** *adj.* made purer; pure; having impure substances removed. □ *Refined oil is used to make numerous products.* **2.** *adj.* elegant; very proper and civilized. (Adv: *refinedly.*) □ *The refined young lady spoke to us very politely.*

**refinish** [ri 'fɪn ɪʃ] *tv.* to remove an old paint or varnish finish and apply a new one. □ *John plans to refinish the woodwork around the windows.*

**reflect** [rɪ 'flɛkt] **1.** *tv.* to show an image in the manner of a mirror. □ *The mirror behind me reflected John's movements.* **2.** *tv.* to throw back heat, light, sound, or energy; to bounce back heat, light, sound, or energy. □ *Hard panels of wood reflected the music toward the audience.* **3.** *tv.* [for something] to show or reveal a personal characteristic of someone. □ *John's angry temper reflects his attitude.* **4. reflect on** something *iv.* + *prep. phr.* to think deeply or carefully; to ponder; to examine one's thoughts. □ *My father reflected on my problem before giving me advice.* **5. reflect off** something *iv.* + *prep. phr.* to be **reflected** ② away from something; [for light] to bounce off something. □ *The car lights reflected off the windows of the house.*

**reflection** [rɪ 'flɛk ʃən] **1.** *n.* a reflected glare; reflected light. □ *The shimmering reflection off the building's windows made it hard for me to see.* **2.** *n.* something, especially an image, that is reflected. □ *The reflection of my face in the mirror startled me.*

**reflexive** [rɪ 'flɛks ɪv] **1. reflexive (pronoun)** *n.* <a form used as an object of a verb or preposition that is identical to the subject.> (**Reflexive** pronouns are **myself, ourselves, yourself, yourselves, herself, himself, itself, themselves, oneself.**) □ *I gave myself some medication for my headache.* **2. reflexive (verb)** *n.* a verb or verb construction that uses ①. (Some verbs *must* have a reflexive object; others *can* have a reflexive object.) □ *"Please learn to behave yourself" contains a reflexive verb.* □ *"You need to compose yourself before answering the question" has a reflexive verb.*

**reform** [ri 'form] **1.** *tv.* to change someone or something for the better; to make someone or something better; to improve someone or something. □ *Mary gave up trying to reform John.* **2.** *iv.* to improve; to become better; to change for the better. □ *I was a mean person, but I have reformed.* **3.** *n.* a planned improvement; a change that gets rid of past flaws or errors. □ *The reform lasted for only a few years. Then things became as bad as they ever were.*

**reformer** [ri 'for mɚ] *n.* someone who reforms and improves things or people. □ *The reformers brought about changes to the welfare system.*

**refresh** [rɪ 'frɛʃ] **1.** *tv.* to make someone feel better or fresher. □ *The light meal refreshed the guests.* **2.** *tv.* to bring something into memory; to restore something to someone's memory. □ *Anne refreshed her knowledge of the material an hour before the test.*

**refreshed** [rɪ 'frɛʃt] *adj.* made to feel fresh again; made to feel better because of food, drink, sleep, or some activity. □ *After a good night's sleep, the refreshed travelers were ready to explore the city.*

**refreshing** [rɪ 'frɛʃ ɪŋ] *adj.* new and exciting; giving the feeling of being fresh. (Adv: *refreshingly.*) □ *I had a refreshing conversation with my friends at work.*

**refreshments** [rɪ 'frɛʃ mənts] *n.* food or drink that satisfies one's thirst or hunger. □ *After the conference, I had some refreshments in the lobby.*

**refrigerate** [rɪ 'frɪdʒ ə ret] *tv.* to put something in a refrigerator; to keep something cold. □ *John refrigerated the wine before serving it.*

**refrigerator** [rɪ 'frɪdʒ ə ret ɚ] *n.* an appliance into which food is placed to keep it cold. □ *There's a special shelf in my refrigerator for eggs.*

**refund 1.** ['ri fənd] *n.* the money that is given back when someone returns a product to a store. □ *Mary took the gift to the store for a refund.* **2.** [rɪ 'fʌnd] *tv.* to give someone money back when a product is returned. □ *The store refunded the money I paid for the defective product.*

**refuse 1.** [rɪ 'fjuz] *tv.* not to accept something; to reject something. □ *The union refused the contract that the owners of the company offered.* **2.** [rɪ 'fjuz] *tv.* to deny someone something; not to allow someone to have something. □ *The company refused John his annual raise.* **3. refuse (to do something)** [rɪ 'fjuz...] *iv.* (+ *inf.*) to decline to do something. □ *The clerk refused to help the unpleasant customer.* **4.** ['rɛf jus] *n.* garbage; trash; things that are thrown away. (No plural form.) □ *The sidewalks were covered with refuse.*

**regard** [rɪ 'gɑrd] **1.** *tv.* to think of someone or something in a certain way. □ *John regards his neighbor as a kind person.* **2.** *n.* respect; esteem. (No plural form.) □ *Mary's regard for her parents was great.*

**region** ['ri dʒən] **1.** *n.* an area of land that has a common social, cultural, economic, political, or natural feature; sometimes a political division of a country. □ *Anne grew up in the Southern California region.* **2.** *n.* a part; an area that has a common feature throughout it. □ *There's a region of pain around my ankle joint.*

**regional** ['ridʒ ə nəl] *adj.* of or about a region. (Adv: *regionally.*) □ *I watched the regional weather forecast on the news.*

**register** ['rɛdʒ ɪ stɚ] **1.** *n.* a machine in a store that cashiers use to keep track of money taken in or paid out. □ *The cashier couldn't open the register unless I made a purchase.* **2.** *n.* the book that a list or record of something is kept in. □ *According to the register, John was in the office until 10:00.* **3.** *tv.* to show something such as a feeling or an attitude; to express something. □ *John registered surprise when I remembered his birthday.* **4.** *iv.* to put one's name and perhaps other information on an official list. □ *Mary registered to vote.*

**registered** ['rɛdʒ ɪ stɚd] *adj.* listed as in register ④; approved by the government; enrolled. □ *Only registered voters can participate in elections.*

**registration** [rɛdʒ ɪ 'stre ʃən] **1.** *n.* the process of registering; the condition of being registered. (No plural form.) □ *You need two pieces of identification for voter registration.* **2.** *n.* the time when people choose and reserve classes at a school, college, or university. (No plural form.) □ *At registration, I got all of the classes I wanted.*

**regret** [rɪ 'grɛt] **1.** *n.* sorrow; the feeling of being sad or sorry about something that one has done. (No plural form.) □ *Overcome with regret, he sat and sobbed.* **2.** *n.* something that one is sorry about; something that causes sorrow. □ *The dying man's only regret was that he'd never flown in a plane.* **3.** *tv.* to feel sad or sorry about doing or not doing something; to feel ① about doing or not doing something. (The object can be a clause with **that** ⑦.) □ *David regretted ruining his diet by eating all of the potato chips.*

**regretful** [rɪ 'grɛt fʊl] *adj.* full of regret; feeling sad or sorry about something. (Adv: *regretfully.*) □ *The regretful student had failed to turn his homework in on time.*

**regular** ['rɛg jə lɚ] **1.** *adj.* usual; normal. (Adv: *regularly.*) □ *On a regular day, I work from 9 to 5.* **2.** *adj.* not changing; even in size, shape, or speed; uniform. (Adv: *regularly.*) □ *Each machine-made object was perfectly regular.* **3.** *adj.* following the usual pattern, especially concerning verb forms. (Adv: *regularly.*) □ To touch *is a regular verb in English.* □ *The word* tree *is regular, meaning that its plural ends in* -s.

**regularity** [rɛg jə 'lɛr ə ti] *n.* the quality of being regular. (Plural only when referring to different kinds, types, instances, or varieties.) □ *Regularity in my studies and writing will make me a better scholar.* Ⓒ *We observed regularities in the measurements every time we checked.*

**regulate** ['rɛg jə let] **1.** *tv.* to control someone or something by a rule or system; to limit someone or something by a rule or system. □ *The city council regulates the money that the city spends.* **2.** *tv.* to fix or adjust something so that it will work at a certain level or standard. □ *The temperature of the greenhouse was regulated by a computer.*

**regulation** [rɛg jə 'le ʃən] **1.** *n.* the control or order caused by rules, laws, principles, or systems. (Plural only when referring to different kinds, types, instances, or varieties.) □ *Regulation of the airline industry was ended in the 1980s.* Ⓒ *The city's regulations forbid smoking inside public buildings.* **2.** *adj.* according to a rule, law, system, or standard; suitable according to a rule, law, system, or standard; standard. □ *The baseball batter was fined for not using a regulation bat.*

**rehearsal** [rɪ 'hɚs əl] **1.** *n.* a practice performance of a play, opera, concert, etc., devoted to perfecting the final performance. □ *We need a few more rehearsals before the play is ready to open.* **2.** *adj.* <the adj. use of ①.> □ *The actors wore rehearsal clothing until the costumes were made.*

**rehearse** [rɪ 'hɚs] **1.** *tv.* to practice a part in a play, concert, dance, or performance before performing it for the public; [for performers] to practice performing. □ *The actors rehearsed their lines at home each evening.* **2.** *tv.* to cause a group of performers to practice; to cause performers to practice something that is to be performed. □ *The conductor rehearsed the orchestra during the day.* **3.** *iv.* to practice [a role, musical instrument, play, piece of music, etc.]. □ *The actors rehearsed for a month before the show was performed.*

**reign** ['ren] **1.** *iv.* to rule, especially as king, queen, emperor, or empress. □ *The monarch reigned during a time of peace.* **2.** *iv.* to be the current winner of a contest or holder of a title. □ *Tom* *reigned as the college chess champion for two years.* **3.** *n.* the period of the rule of a king, queen, emperor, or empress, as in ①. □ *Anne's reign as queen ended in 1832.*

**reinforce** [ri ɪn 'fors] *tv.* to make something stronger, more able to resist wear, or longer lasting by adding something to it. □ *I reinforced the door by nailing on boards.* □ *The mayor reinforced the police department by hiring more cops.*

**reject 1.** [rɪ 'dʒɛkt] *tv.* to refuse to take, accept, or use someone or something. □ *I rejected Bill's offer of help.* **2.** ['ri dʒɛkt] *n.* someone or something that has been refused as in ①. □ *The factory destroyed its rejects and recycled the materials.*

**rejection** [ri 'dʒɛk ʃən] *n.* refusal to accept someone or something. (No plural form.) □ *John was angered by his classmates' rejection of his ideas.*

**rejoice** [ri 'dʒoɪs] *iv.* to be very happy [about something]; to celebrate [something] joyfully. □ *John and Mary rejoiced when she gave birth to a healthy child.*

**rejoicing** [ri 'dʒoɪs ɪŋ] *n.* great joy or happiness expressed by one or more people. (No plural form.) □ *The students' rejoicing was interrupted by bad news.*

R

**relate** [rɪ 'let] **1.** *tv.* to tell a story; to tell what was heard. (The object can be a clause with **that** ⑦.) □ *The reporter related the important news of the day.* **2. relate to** someone *iv.* + *prep. phr.* to feel a bond of some type with someone because of shared experiences or a similar connection. □ *Mary related to Jane because they'd had similar experiences.*

**related** [rɪ 'let ɪd] **1.** *adj.* connected. (Adv: *relatedly.*) □ *In a related news story, the storm also closed many schools.* **2.** *adj.* part of the same family; in the same family. □ *Related employees cannot work in the same department.* **3. related to** someone *adj.* + *prep. phr.* connected to someone as a relative. □ *I am glad Anne is not related to me, because I don't like her.* **4. related to** someone or something *adj.* + *prep. phr.* linked or connected with someone or something. □ *Is your theory related to the theory originated by Albert Einstein?*

**relation** [rɪ 'le ʃən] **1.** *n.* someone who is a member of one's family; a relative. □ *John is only a distant relation.* **2.** *n.* a connection between two or more things; relationship. □ *The professor explained the relation between tides and the moon.*

**relationship** [rɪ 'le ʃən ʃɪp] **1.** *n.* a personal, romantic, business, or social connection between two people. □ *Anne has been in a romantic relationship with John for four years.* **2.** *n.* a connection between two or more things. □ *The teacher explained the relationship between thunder and lightning.*

**relative** ['rɛl ə tɪv] **1.** *n.* someone who is a member of one's family. □ *The application required me to state the names of my nearest living relatives.* **2.** *adj.* compared to something else; having meaning only as compared with something else. (Adv: *relatively.*) □ *Mary's relative inexperience makes her a poor candidate.*

**relative clause** ['rɛl ə tɪv 'klɔz] *n.* a clause that refers or is compared to someone or something. (Also called a *subordinate clause.*) □ *The sentence "My left thumb, which I hit with a hammer yesterday, is bruised" contains a relative clause.*

**relax** [rɪ 'læks] **1.** *iv.* to become less tight, less stiff, less firm, less tense, or more loose. □ *When my hand relaxed, I dropped my pen.* **2.** *iv.* to become less worried, less busy with work, or less active; to rest, be calm, or slow down. □ *Bob took a sleeping pill to help him relax.* **3.** *tv.* to cause something to become less tight, less stiff, less firm, or less tense. □ *John relaxed his tight grip on the steering wheel.* **4.** *tv.* to cause something to become less strict, less harsh, or less severe. □ *Once the riots were over, the police relaxed their control.* **5.** *tv.* to cause someone to become less worried, less busy with work, or less active; to cause someone to rest, be calm, or slow down. □ *The operator's soothing voice relaxed the panicking caller.*

**relaxation** [rɪ læk 'se ʃən] **1.** *n.* rest, especially after work or busy activity. (No plural form.) □ *I spent my vacation in Bermuda in complete relaxation.* **2.** *n.* the lessening of tightness, stiffness, tenseness, or firmness; the release of tension from something tight, stiff, tense, or firm. (No plural form.) □ *A hot bath is good for the relaxation of one's muscles.* **3.** *n.* making something less severe; the easing of strict rules. (No plural form.) □ *The relaxation of some harsh rules made work at our company more pleasant.*

**relaxing** [rɪ 'læk sɪŋ] *adj.* calming; soothing; restful; making one feel less tense, tight, stiff, or firm. (Adv: *relaxingly.*) □ *I took a long, relaxing shower.*

**relay** [rɪ 'le] *tv.* to receive something and give it to someone else; to receive something and transfer it to something else or move it further along in the process. □ *The reporter relayed the traffic information over the radio.*

**release** [rɪ 'lis] **1.** *tv.* to let someone or something free; to let someone or something go; to let someone or something loose. □ *In the park, John released his dog and let it run around.* **2.** *tv.* to make a book, movie, information, or publication available to the public. □ *The singer's agent released her touring schedule to the media.* **3.** *n.* an act of letting someone or something go; an act of setting someone or something free. □ *The release of the murderer from prison angered the citizens.*

**relevant** ['rɛl ə vənt] *adj.* connected to something; of or about the subject being discussed. (Adv: *relevantly.*) □ *The reporter provided relevant information about the blizzard.*

**relief** [rɪ 'lif] **1.** *n.* the feeling that is felt when pain, a burden, a strain, or a problem is eased. (No plural form.) □ *John felt relief when he dropped his heavy load.* **2.** *n.* something that eases pain, a burden, a strain, or a problem. (No plural form.) □ *Hiring three extra workers was quite a relief at the office.* **3.** *n.* money, clothing, food, and other aid that is made available to help poor people or to help people who are victims of a disaster. (No plural form.) □ *The flooded city requested relief from the federal government.*

**relieve** [rɪ 'liv] **1.** *tv.* to ease or get rid of pain, anxiety, or strain. □ *The good news relieved my anxiety.* **2. relieve** someone or some creature **of** something *tv. + obj. + prep. phr.* to remove someone's or some creature's burden by removing something. □ *I relieved the suffering donkey of its burden.* **3. relieve** someone **(of** something) *tv. + obj. (+ prep. phr.)* to ease someone's state of being by removing fear or anxiety. □ *The presence of the security guard relieved me of my worries.* **4.** *tv.* to begin working at a job as a replacement so that the person who was working can leave or take a break. □ *The rookie was sent in to relieve the pitcher.*

**religion** [rɪ 'lɪdʒ ən] *n.* belief in or worship of one or more gods or spirits. (Plural only when referring to different kinds, types, instances, or varieties.) □ *I am studying religion in school.* Ⓒ *Fred doesn't belong to any of the major religions.*

**religious** [rɪ 'lɪdʒ əs] **1.** *adj.* <the adj. form of **religion**.> (Adv: *religiously.*)

R

□ *Mike loves to argue about religious matters.* **2.** *adj.* believing in or worshiping one or more gods or spirits. (Adv: *religiously.*) □ *Although Anne is religious, she doesn't belong to a particular church.*

**relocate** [ri 'lo ket] **1. relocate someone or something (to some place)** *tv. + obj. (+ prep. phr.)* to move someone or something to a different place. □ *The company relocated Mary to the suburban office.* **2. relocate (to some place)** *iv. (+ prep. phr.)* to move to a different place; to move to a different house or to transfer to a different job site, especially in a different city. □ *Bob lived in Chicago before he relocated to Pittsburgh.*

**rely** [rɪ 'lɑɪ] **rely (up)on someone or something** *iv. + prep. phr.* to depend on someone or something; to trust that someone will do something; to trust that something will happen. □ *David relies on his car to get to work.*

**remain** [rɪ 'men] **1.** *iv.* to stay someplace; to continue to be in a certain place; to be left after other parts or things are taken. □ *Mary remained in the small town her whole life.* **2.** *iv.* to continue to be something; not to stop being something. □ *I remained convinced of the soundness of John's argument even after you disagreed with him.* **3. remains** *n.* things that are left behind. (Treated as plural, but not countable.) □ *The tourist walked through the remains of the old city.* **4. remains** *n.* a corpse; a dead body. (Treated as plural.) □ *The family viewed the remains before the casket was closed.*

**remainder** [rɪ 'men dɚ] **1.** *n.* the part of something that is left over after part of it is taken. (No plural form.) □ *Mary did most of the work, and Susan did the remainder.* **2.** *n.* the number that is left over after a number is divided into another one. □ *Please write the remainder as a fraction.*

**remaining** [rɪ 'men ɪŋ] *adj.* yet to happen; yet to occur; not yet done or taken care of; not yet taken away; not yet happening; not yet occurring. □ *Susan addressed my only remaining doubts.*

**remark** [rɪ 'mɑrk] **1.** *n.* a comment; a statement; something that is said or written about something. □ *Max's remarks about the meal were very kind.* **2.** *tv.* to say something; to comment about something; to state an opinion. (The object can be a clause with **that** ⑦.) □ *Jane remarked that she liked my haircut.*

**remarkable** [rɪ 'mɑrk ə bəl] *adj.* worth mentioning; worth talking about; noticeable; unusual. (Adv: *remarkably.*) □ *John's stories of working in the circus are remarkable.*

**remedy** ['rɛm ə di] **1.** *n.* a treatment; a cure; something that makes someone become healthy again. □ *The doctor's remedy was to rest and drink lots of liquid.* **2.** *n.* making bad conditions good or better; the correction of a problem. (Fig. on ①.) □ *The unemployed workers expected a remedy from the government.* **3.** *tv.* to make bad conditions good or better; to correct a problem; to fix something that is wrong or bad. □ *The mayor's plan remedied the traffic problem.*

**remember** [rɪ 'mɛm bɚ] **1.** *tv.* to bring back the thought of someone or something into one's mind, memory, or imagination; to think about someone or something again. (The object can be a clause with **that** ⑦.) □ *Do you remember the time we went fishing with John?* **2.** *tv.* not to forget someone or something; to keep someone or something in one's mind. (The object can be a clause with **that** ⑦.) □ *The soldier remembered the war throughout his life.* **3.** *iv.* to bring [someone or something] back into one's mind, memory, or imagination. □ *What is that man's name? I can't remember.*

R

**remind** [rɪ 'maɪnd] *tv.* to tell someone about something again; to cause someone to remember someone or something. ☐ *The librarian reminded the students to be quiet.*

**reminder** [rɪ 'maɪn dɚ] *n.* something that reminds someone about something. ☐ *The secretary handed Anne a reminder about her three o'clock appointment.*

**remodel** [rɪ 'mɑd l] *tv.* to decorate something in a new way; to construct something in a new way; to change a structure or room so it looks more modern. ☐ *The young couple remodeled the house before they moved in.*

**remote** [rɪ 'mot] **1.** *adj.* far away in space or time; far off; not near; distant; isolated; secluded; not near other things or places. (Adv: *remotely.* Comp: *remoter;* sup: *remotest.*) ☐ *We lived in the mountains, in a remote village, for three years.* **2.** *adj.* slight; faint. (Fig. on ①. Adv: *remotely.* Comp: *remoter;* sup: *remotest.*) ☐ *The chances of winning the lottery are very remote.* **3.** *n.* an electronic device used to control audio and video equipment. (Short for **remote control**.) ☐ *All right, Mary, where did you hide the remote this time?*

**remote control** [rɪ 'mot kən 'trol] *n.* a device that is held in the hand and used to operate a machine or appliance from a distance. (Can be shortened to **remote**.) ☐ *Mary opened the garage door with her remote control.*

**remove** [rɪ 'muv] **1.** *tv.* to take something away from a place; to get rid of something. ☐ *The plow removed the snow from the streets.* **2.** *tv.* to take off something, especially a piece of clothing. ☐ *John removed his clothes and put on a robe.*

**renew** [rɪ 'nu] **1.** *tv.* to cause someone or something to become like new again; to restore someone or something. ☐ *The medicine renewed the sick man's strength.* **2.** *tv.* to cause something that is no longer valid or effective to become useful again; to cause something to be valid for a longer period of time. ☐ *Mary renewed her driver's license.*

**renounce** [rɪ 'nɑʊns] *tv.* to give up something; to state formally that one is giving up something, especially a claim or a right. ☐ *The philosopher renounced his faith in God.*

**renovate** ['rɛn ə vet] *tv.* to fix up something so that it is in good condition; to restore something to a good condition; to repair a structure. ☐ *The landlord renovated the old building so he could charge higher rent.*

**rent** ['rɛnt] **1.** *n.* the money paid for the use of something, especially for the use of a place to live. (No plural form.) ☐ *I paid my landlady the rent on the second day of the month.* **2. rent something (from someone)** *tv. + obj. (+ prep. phr.)* to get the right to use something (from someone) by paying ①. ☐ *John rented a car so he could drive to Memphis.* **3. rent something (out) (to someone)** *tv. + obj. (+ adv.) (+ prep. phr.)* to provide something that other people pay money to use. ☐ *Sue rents studio space out to painters and photographers.* 🅃 *This company rents out cars to tourists and trucks to people who want to move.* **4.** *iv.* to live in an apartment that one does not own, but for which one pays ① to the owner. ☐ *Mary moves a lot, so she prefers to rent.*

**rental** ['rɛn təl] **1.** *adj.* [of an apartment, office space, equipment, or other thing] rented or available to be rented. ☐ *Mary is looking for a small, inexpensive rental unit.* **2.** *n.* the amount of money that is paid as rent for something. (No plural form.) ☐ *John paid the car rental in cash.*

**rented** ['rɛn təd] *adj.* occupied or used for a fee, rather than owned. ☐ *Insurance paid for the repairs when I wrecked the rented car.*

R

**reorganization** [ri or gə nə 'ze ʃən] *n.* reorganizing something; organizing something in a different way, especially so that it works or operates better; the condition of having been reorganized. □ *After three reorganizations, we are finally able to function efficiently.*

**reorganize** [ri 'or gə nɑɪz] **1.** *tv.* to organize something in a different way, especially so that it works or operates better; to arrange something in a new or different way. □ *David reorganized the messy papers on his desk for the third time.* **2.** *tv.* to reform a business, especially after it has gone bankrupt. □ *We reorganized our business in a way that saved us money.*

**repaid** [ri 'ped] pt/pp of **repay**.

**repair** [rɪ 'pɛr] **1.** *tv.* to fix something; to mend something; to cause something to work again. □ *The tailor repaired the tear in the shirt sleeve.* **2.** *n.* work that will fix or restore something. (Singular or plural with the same meaning.) □ *Without repair and maintenance, your furnace will not last another two years.*

**repairable** [rɪ 'per ə bəl] *adj.* able to be repaired; able to be fixed. (Adv: *repairably.*) □ *The mechanic said my car engine was not repairable.*

R

**repay** [rɪ 'pe] *tv., irreg.* to pay someone back for something; to pay someone for an amount that is owed. (Pt/pp: **repaid.**) □ *Anne repaid all of her debts a little bit at a time.*

**repayment** [rɪ 'pe mənt] *n.* paying back something to someone. (No plural form.) □ *My repayment was done over a 6-month period.*

**repeat** [rɪ 'pit] **1.** *tv.* to do or say something again. □ *The singer repeated the chorus three times.* **2.** *tv.* to say something that someone else has just said to find out if it has been correctly understood. □ *The clerk repeated my account number after hearing me say it.* **3.** *tv.* to say something that one has learned. □ *Mary repeated the poem from memory.*

**repeated** [rɪ 'pit ɪd] *adj.* previously done or said and being said or done again; done or said more than one time. (Adv: *repeatedly.*) □ *There was a repeated knocking at my door.*

**repetition** [rɛp ɪ 'tɪ ʃən] *n.* repeating something. (Plural only when referring to different kinds, types, instances, or varieties.) □ *Repetition is a good way to learn a language.* Ⓒ *Any more repetitions of this incident and you will be dismissed!*

**replace** [rɪ 'ples] **1.** *tv.* to take the place of someone or something else. □ *Nothing could replace my pet dog after he died.* **2.** *tv.* to exchange something for another thing that is more useful or newer. □ *Susan replaced the broken light bulb.* **3.** *tv.* to return something to the place that it belongs; to put something back where it belongs. □ *Mary replaced the hammer in the tool box after she'd used it.*

**replacement** [rɪ 'ples mənt] **1.** *n.* replacing someone or something. (No plural form.) □ *Replacement of the retiring workers would be a difficult task.* **2.** *n.* someone or something that takes the place of someone or something else. □ *The replacement lasted longer than the original part.* **3.** *adj.* used to replace someone or something else. □ *The replacement part cost $400.*

**replay 1.** ['ri ple] *n.* something that is played again; an event that is done over; a film clip that is played over, often in slow motion so one can see fast action better. □ *In the replay, you could see who won the race.* **2.** ['ri 'ple] *tv.* to play something again, especially a game or a piece of film. □ *Anne replayed the videotape of the party three times.*

**reply** [rɪ 'plɑɪ] **1.** *iv.* to answer. □ *I had to reply to the reporter's questions so she would go away.* **2.** *tv.* to say or write something as an answer. (The object is a clause with **that** ⑦.) □ *John replied that he was feeling fine.* **3.** *n.* an answer; something that is said or written when answering a question. □ *Anne's reply was a polite no.*

**report** [rɪ 'port] **1.** *n.* an account that gives information about something. □ *Jimmy presented his report on dinosaurs to the class.* **2.** *n.* the noise made when a shot is fired. □ *The rifle's report woke the neighbors.* **3.** *tv.* to describe news; to provide news. (The object can be a clause with **that** ⑦.) □ *The newspaper reported the latest events of the day.* **4. report** someone or something **to** someone or something *tv. + obj. + prep. phr.* to tell of someone's errors or something someone did wrong to someone or something. □ *Tom reported Bill to the owner of the company.* **5. report to** someone or some place *iv. + prep. phr.* to go to some place; to present oneself to someone at some place. □ *Max reported to his boss when he came in late.*

**reporter** [rɪ 'por tɚ] *n.* someone who provides a newspaper, magazine, radio station, or television station with news; someone who reports news or information. □ *The reporter finished the news article just before the deadline.*

**repossess** [ri pə 'zɛs] *tv.* [for a company] to take back something purchased on credit when the purchaser fails to make payments on time. □ *The furniture company repossessed my couch.*

**represent** [rɛp rɪ 'zɛnt] **1.** *tv.* to stand for something; to portray someone or something; to express something. □ *This painting represents the artist's view of the world.* **2.** *tv.* to act on behalf of someone else; to speak for someone else. □ *Someone who represented the company spoke at the meeting.*

**reproduce** [ri prə 'dus] **1.** *tv.* to make a copy of something. □ *I reproduced 100 copies of my résumé on the copier.* □ *The photo lab reproduced two copies of each print.* **2.** *tv.* to create something again; to do something in the way it has already been done. □ *We were able to reproduce exactly the room where Lincoln died.* **3.** *iv.* to have offspring. □ *Our rabbits reproduced often, and soon we had 30 rabbits.*

**reproduction** [ri prə 'dʌk ʃən] **1.** *n.* the process of making a copy of something. (No plural form.) □ *Reproduction of the data was impossible, so the experiment must have been flawed.* **2.** *n.* creating offspring; reproducing. (No plural form.) □ *The biology teacher explained the process of reproduction.* **3.** *n.* a copy of something, especially of a work of art or a book. □ *A reproduction of a Greek temple filled the stage.*

**reproductive** [ri prə 'dʌk tɪv] *adj.* of or about **reproduction**. (Adv: *reproductively.*) □ *The biology teacher lectured about the reproductive organs.*

**reptile** ['rɛp taɪl] *n.* a class of animals whose temperature is the same as the surrounding air, including dinosaurs, lizards, snakes, turtles, tortoises, alligators, and crocodiles. □ *Many kinds of reptiles live in the marsh behind my house.*

**republic** [rɪ 'pʌb lɪk] **1.** *n.* a nation where the people are governed by officials that they elect. □ *The capital of the Czech Republic is Prague.* **2.** *n.* a system of government where the people elect officials to represent them. □ *The cynical people had no faith in the republic.*

**reputation** [rep jə 'te ʃən] *n.* the basis for the good or bad opinion that people have about someone or something. □ *A negative newspaper story almost ruined the celebrity's good reputation.*

**request** [rɪ 'kwɛst] **1.** *tv.* to ask for something politely. (The object can be a clause with **that** ⑦.) □ *The office manager requested two new computers for the office.* **2.** *n.* a polite demand; an instance of asking for something. □ *The* *student's request to leave the room was granted.*

**require** [rɪ 'kwɑɪɚ] **1.** *tv.* to demand a particular qualification or skill. □ *Running requires a lot of energy.* **2.** *tv.* to demand that someone do something. (The object can be a clause with **that** ⑦.) □ *They required us to be home by midnight.* □ *The university required that we live on campus.*

**required** [rɪ 'kwɑɪɚd] *adj.* demanded and needed; ordered; necessary. □ *The employee wore the required uniform.*

**requirement** [rɪ 'kwɑɪɚ mənt] *n.* something that must be done; something that is required; something that is necessary. □ *The candidate met all of the requirements for the job.*

**rerun** ['ri rən] *n.* a television program that is not new; a television program that has been on television before. □ *The networks show mostly reruns during the summer.*

**rescue** ['rɛs kju] **1.** *tv.* to save someone or something that is in danger. □ *The Coast Guard rescued five people when their boat sank.* **2.** *n.* an instance of saving someone or something from danger. □ *My rescue of the cat in the tree was easy.* □ *The cat's rescue was a failure.*

R

**research 1.** ['ri sɚtʃ, rɪ 'sɚtʃ] *n.* study and examination; the collecting of information. (No plural form.) □ *The government grant paid for the biologist's research.* **2.** [rɪ 'sɚtʃ] *tv.* to collect information about something in great detail. □ *The scientist researched the matter thoroughly.*

**resemble** [rɪ 'zɛm bəl] *tv.* to look like someone or something; to be like someone or something. □ *The fancy office building resembled a pyramid.*

**resent** [rɪ 'zɛnt] *tv.* to feel bitter at someone about something; to feel insulted by someone about something. (The object can be a clause with **that** ⑦.) □ *Susan resented the work that her parents made her do.*

**resentful** [rɪ 'zɛnt fʊl] *adj.* full of anger or bitter feelings about someone or something; feeling that one has been insulted; showing anger or bitter feelings. (Adv: *resentfully.*) □ *A resentful worker damaged the office equipment.*

**reservation** [rɛz ɚ 've ʃən] **1.** *n.* a doubt about something; a concern; something that stops someone from accepting something. □ *The manager had a reservation about giving the lazy worker a raise.* **2.** *n.* a previous claim on the use of something at a specific time, such as a room in a hotel, a table at a restaurant, or a seat in a theater, airplane, or concert. □ *The fancy restaurant did not accept reservations.*

**reserve** [rɪ 'zɚv] **1.** *tv.* to schedule the use of something at a certain time; to record a claim for the future use of something at a certain time. □ *Mary reserved four seats for the opera for next Friday.* **2.** *tv.* to save something for future use. □ *John reserved the rest of the ham for a future meal.* **3.** *n.* something that is saved for future use. □ *A reserve of canned food is stored in the basement.* **4. reserves** *n.* troops or soldiers that are prepared to be called to war. (Treated as plural, but not countable.) □ *During the war, the reserves were placed on alert.*

**reserved** [rɪ 'zɚvd] **1.** *adj.* saved for a certain person or certain reason; scheduled to be used by someone at a certain time. □ *This table is reserved for someone else.* **2.** *adj.* quiet; keeping to oneself; not talking about oneself. (Adv: *reservedly* [rɪ 'zɚv əd li].) □ *The reserved student ate in the cafeteria by herself.*

**residence** ['rɛz ə dəns] **1.** *n.* the period of time that someone lives in a certain place. (No plural form. Number is expressed with *period(s) of residence.*)

☐ *Jane's residence in New York City was short.* **2.** *n.* a house or an apartment; the place where someone lives. ☐ *Bill and Mary live in a lovely brick residence on Maple Street.*

**resident** ['rɛz ə dənt] **1.** *n.* a person who lives in a certain house or apartment. ☐ *How many residents live at this address?* **2.** *n.* a person who lives in a certain city, state, or country. ☐ *The state college offered lower tuition to residents of the state.* **3.** *n.* a doctor who works full time at a hospital in order to get advanced medical training. ☐ *The resident had worked for 24 hours without sleeping.* **4.** *adj.* living in or working at a certain place. ☐ *The palace's resident poet wrote the queen a poem.*

**residential** [rɛz ə 'dɛn ʃəl] *adj.* of or about residences; of or about homes or apartments rather than offices, farms, or industry. (Adv: *residentially.*) ☐ *Mary lived in a small house on a residential street.*

**resign** [rɪ 'zaɪn] **1.** *tv.* to quit a job officially; to give up a job; to leave a job. ☐ *The office manager resigned her job last week.* **2. resign** oneself **to** something *tv. + obj. + prep. phr.* to cause oneself to accept something without complaining; to cause oneself to yield to something. (Reflexive.) ☐ *David resigned himself to losing ten pounds by summer.* **3. resign from** something *iv. + prep. phr.* to give up a job; to leave a job. ☐ *Bob resigned from his job as soon as he found a better one.*

**resignation** [rɛz ɪg 'ne ʃən] **1.** *n.* voluntarily leaving a job or an office. (Plural only when referring to different kinds, types, instances, or varieties.) ☐ *Bill chose resignation rather than submit to the demands of the company president.* Ⓒ *Two resignations left two openings on the board of directors.* **2.** *n.* a formal statement or document made by someone who is leaving a job. ☐ *Jane gave her resignation to the chairman of the board.*

**resist** [rɪ 'zɪst] **1.** *tv.* to oppose something; to refuse to accept something. ☐ *The stubborn office manager resisted new technology.* **2.** *tv.* to keep from doing something; to prevent something from happening; to stop something from happening. (Takes a verb with *-ing.*) ☐ *John resisted being sent to school every morning.* **3.** *tv.* to be undamaged by something; to be able to withstand something. ☐ *The disease resisted all forms of treatment.*

**resistance** [rɪ 'zɪs təns] *n.* resisting someone or something; the ability to resist someone or something. (No plural form.) ☐ *The old professor's resistance to new ideas was quite annoying.*

**resource** ['ri sors] *n.* someone or something that one can go to for help, information, support, or supplies. ☐ *John's computer can access the incredible resources of the Internet.*

**resourceful** [ri 'sors fʊl] *adj.* able to think of different ways to solve a problem. (Adv: *resourcefully.*) ☐ *The resourceful cook substituted molasses for brown sugar.*

**respect** [rɪ 'spɛkt] **1.** *n.* the honor, admiration, or esteem that one feels for someone or something. (No plural form.) ☐ *Anne has the utmost respect for her college professors.* **2.** *n.* the polite behavior one shows to someone whom one honors or admires. (No plural form.) ☐ *The students showed their teacher the proper respect.* **3.** *tv.* to feel or show someone or something **respect** ①. ☐ *The school respected the rights of each of the students.*

**respectable** [rɪ 'spɛk tə bəl] *adj.* worthy of respect; deserving respect; deserving honor and acceptance; admirable; decent. (Adv: *respectably.*) ☐ *Bill and Mary live in a very respectable neighborhood.*

R

**respond** [rɪ 'spɑnd] **1. respond (to** someone or something**)** *iv.* (+ *prep. phr.*) to answer someone or something; to reply to someone or something. ☐ *The judge asked the witness to respond to the question.* **2. respond (to** someone or something**)** *iv.* (+ *prep. phr.*) to react to someone or something. ☐ *David responded to the bad news by crying.* **3.** *tv.* to answer a question; to give an answer; to say something as a response. (The object is a clause with **that** ⑦.) ☐ *When the reporter asked how old I was, I responded that I was 29.*

**response** [rɪ 'spɑns] **1.** *n.* an answer; a reply; something that is said or done to answer a question. ☐ *As a response to my question, Mary said she was angry at me.* **2.** *n.* a reaction; something that is done when something happens. ☐ *I was not happy with my boss's lack of a response when I asked for an increase in salary.*

**responsibility** [rɪ spɑn sə 'bɪl ə ti] **1.** *n.* the authority for something; the duty to take care of someone or something. (Plural only when referring to different kinds, types, instances, or varieties.) ☐ *The regional sales manager has responsibility for all of the company's sales in this part of the country.* **2.** *n.* accountability for something wrong or bad; blame for causing something bad or, sometimes, credit for causing something good. (No plural form.) ☐ *The judge found that both drivers had responsibility for the accident.* **3.** *n.* the quality of being **responsible** ②. (No plural form.) ☐ *The teenager demonstrated his responsibility by taking care of the house while his parents were away.* **4.** *n.* someone or something that one is responsible for. ☐ *Typing and filing are my responsibilities at work.*

**responsible** [rɪ 'spɑn sə bəl] **1. responsible for** someone or something *adj.* + *prep. phr.* having the job of taking care of someone or something. ☐ *Susie is responsible for feeding the family dog.* **2.** *adj.* reliable; able to do something without being told what to do. (Adv: *responsibly.*) ☐ *The manager appreciated his responsible employees.*

**rest** ['rɛst] **1.** *n.* sleep. (No plural form.) ☐ *Rest was the most important thing on the weary driver's mind.* **2.** *n.* relaxation; a period of calm or quiet after work or activity. (No plural form.) ☐ *After a long day at work, I needed some rest.* **3. the rest** *n.* the remainder; the things that are left over. (Singular form. Treated like a singular or plural, but not countable.) ☐ *I cooked rice for dinner. I ate some, but you can have the rest.* **4. at rest** *phr.* not moving; not active. ☐ *Do not remove your seat belt until the plane is at rest.* **5.** *iv.* to relax after work or activity. ☐ *After playing tennis, Mary rested for an hour.* **6.** *iv.* to remain somewhere. ☐ *My computer rests on a large table by the door.* **7.** *tv.* to cause someone or an animal to relax. ☐ *The trainer rested the horses after the race.*

**restaurant** ['rɛs tə rɑnt] *n.* a place where one buys and eats a meal, which is usually served at a table. ☐ *Mary works in a fancy restaurant as a waitress.*

**restful** ['rɛst fʊl] *adj.* causing one to feel rested; peaceful; calm; quiet. (Adv: *restfully.*) ☐ *Jane sang a restful lullaby to the baby.*

**restore** [rɪ 'stor] *tv.* to return something to its original or regular condition; to put something back. ☐ *The medicine restored Anne's health.*

**restrain** [rɪ 'stren] *tv.* to prevent someone or something from moving or doing something. ☐ *The doctors restrained the patient so he wouldn't hurt himself.*

**restrict** [rɪ 'strɪkt] *tv.* to limit what someone or something can do; to make something—such as a right, movement, speech—less than it was. ☐ *This bad legislation would restrict people's rights.*

R

**restriction** [rɪ 'strɪk ʃən] *n.* a condition that limits action or movement; a rule against doing something; a regulation. ☐ *There are too many restrictions on my freedom in this job.*

**restroom** ['rɛst rum] *n.* a room with a toilet, especially in a public building. (A euphemism.) ☐ *The janitor cleans the restroom four times each day.*

**result** [rɪ 'zʌlt] **1.** *n.* the outcome of an event; something that is caused by something else. ☐ *One of the results of the new policy was a lower inflation rate.* **2.** *n.* the answer to a math problem; a solution. ☐ *Please state your result in the form of a fraction.* **3. result from** something *iv.* + *prep. phr.* to be an effect of something; to be caused by something. ☐ *Mary's promotion resulted from her hard work.* **4. result in** something *iv.* + *prep. phr.* to lead to a particular result. ☐ *Mary's hard work resulted in a promotion.*

**resulting** [rɪ 'zʌl tɪŋ] *adj.* happening because of something else; being a result. ☐ *The office caught on fire, and five people were injured in the resulting panic.*

**résumé** ['rɛz u me] *n.* a document that lists one's education, work history, and other important information. ☐ *The firm interviewed the four clients with the best résumés.* ☐ *Jane listed on her résumé that she spoke German fluently.*

**resume** [rɪ 'zum] **1.** *tv.* to do something again after having stopped for a time. ☐ *The research was resumed after its funding was increased.* **2.** *iv.* to begin again after having stopped for a time. ☐ *The television show resumed after a commercial break.*

**retail** ['ri tel] **1.** *adj.* [of a store] selling products to consumers directly. ☐ *Can I buy this in a retail shop, or is it only available to other businesses wholesale?* **2. retail for** an amount *iv.* + *prep. phr.* [for a product] to be available for purchase for a certain price in a retail ① store. ☐ *At our store, everything retails for less!*

**retailer** ['ri tel ɚ] *n.* a shopkeeper; someone or a business that sells products directly to consumers. ☐ *The retailer bought his goods from a wholesaler.*

**retain** [rɪ 'ten] **1.** *tv.* to keep something; to continue to have something. ☐ *David retained his tax records for seven years.* **2.** *tv.* to hire a lawyer. ☐ *The defendant retained the best lawyer he could afford.*

**retake 1.** ['ri tek] *n.* an act of filming a part of a movie or television show again. ☐ *The film crew spent the whole day doing retakes of the same scene.* **2.** ['ri 'tek] *tv., irreg.* to take a picture again or to film a part of a movie or television show again. (Pt: **retook**; pp: **retaken**.) ☐ *The photographer retook the picture because my eyes were closed.*

**retaken** ['ri 'tek ən] pp of **retake**.

**retire** [rɪ 'tɑɪɚ] **1.** *iv.* to stop working for a living and live on the money one has saved. ☐ *When Mary and Bob quit working, they retired and went to Florida.* **2. retire to** some place *iv.* + *prep. phr.* to quit work as in ① and move somewhere. ☐ *When Mary and Bob quit working, they retired to Florida.* **3. retire to** some place *iv.* + *prep. phr.* to go to a different place; to go to a place away from other people. ☐ *After dinner, Mary retired to the bedroom to take a nap.* **4.** *iv.* to go to bed. ☐ *Jane retired earlier than normal because she was very tired.* **5.** *tv.* to cause something to no longer be used; to remove something from use. ☐ *The Johnsons retired their broken toaster and bought a new one.* **6.** *tv.* to pay a debt; to finish paying a debt. ☐ *Mary retired her credit-card debt last month.*

**retired** [rɪ 'tɑɪɚd] *adj.* having quit working altogether, usually to enjoy one's final years. ☐ *The retired senator received a very large pension.*

R

**retirement** [rɪ 'tɑɪɚ mənt] *n.* the period of time after one has **retired** ①. (No plural form.) □ *John spent his retirement in Arizona.*

**retook** ['ri 'tʊk] pt of **retake**.

**retreat** [rɪ 'trit] **1.** *iv.* to go back, especially because one cannot fight or go forward. □ *The hikers retreated from the edge of the cliff.* **2.** *n.* an act of going back, especially during a battle, because one cannot fight or move forward. □ *The poorly trained troops made a hasty retreat from battle.* **3.** *n.* a quiet, isolated place; a place that one can go to for quiet, rest, or safety. □ *The old cathedral was a retreat for the poor and weary.*

**return** [rɪ 'tɚn] **1.** *iv.* to go back or come back to a previous time, location, position, or condition. □ *In October, we return to Standard Time.* **2.** *tv.* to give something back to the person it came from; to put something back in the place it came from. □ *I returned the book to the library.* **3.** *tv.* to cause someone or something to go back or come back to a previous time, location, position, or condition. □ *The pilot returned the plane to the gate.* **4.** *n.* an act of coming back or going back as in ①. □ *On my return from Japan, my friends met me at the airport.* **5. return(s)** *n.* profit; the amount of money that is made. □ *The manager noted that the weekend returns were low.* **6.** *n.* a set of tax forms. (Short for **tax return.**) □ *Be sure to send in your return by midnight on April 15.*

**reunion** [ri 'jun jən] *n.* a party or gathering of people who are coming together again, especially of people who have not seen each other in a long time. □ *I saw dozens of relatives at the annual family reunion.*

**reunite** [ri ju 'nɑɪt] **1.** *tv.* to bring people or things together again; to unite people or things again. □ *The police reunited the missing children with their parents.* **2.** *iv.* to bring together again; to come together again; to unite again. □ *The husband and wife reunited after a long separation.*

**reveal** [rɪ 'vil] **1.** *tv.* to allow or cause something to be seen. □ *I opened the oven door to reveal the roasted turkey.* **2.** *tv.* to make information known; to tell a piece of information. (The object can be a clause with **that** ⑦.) □ *His testimony revealed that he was guilty of the crime.*

**revealing** [rɪ 'vil ɪŋ] **1.** *adj.* allowing or causing something to be seen; showing something, especially skin. (Adv: *revealingly.*) □ *Dave forbade his daughter to wear such a revealing dress.* **2.** *adj.* giving much information; allowing concealed information to be seen or known. (Adv: *revealingly.*) □ *The revealing testimony was made known to the court.*

**revenge** [rɪ 'vɛndʒ] *n.* harm done to someone as punishment for a bad deed. (No plural form.) □ *The widower vowed revenge on those who killed his wife.*

**revenue** ['rɛv ə nu] **1.** *n.* income; money that is made from a business or an investment. (Usually singular.) □ *Companies report their revenue to the government.* **2.** *n.* money that is collected by the government from taxes. (Either singular or plural with the same meaning, but not countable.) □ *Congress determines how tax revenues are spent.*

**reverend** ['rɛv rənd] **1. (the) Reverend** *n.* <the title used for a minister.> □ *The butler announced the arrival of the Reverend Pratt.* **2. the reverend** *n.* a minister. (Informal.) □ *The reverend spoke to the congregation about sin.*

**reverse** [rɪ 'vɚs] **1.** *tv.* to cause something to go or operate backwards. □ *Jane reversed the boat's motor and stopped the boat from hitting the dock.* **2.** *tv.* to cause something to move the opposite way; to turn something the other way; to turn something upside down; to turn something inside out. □ *I reversed the socks that were inside out before washing them.* **3.** *iv.* to go or move backwards; to move in the opposite direction. □ *As the storm approached, the direction of the wind reversed.* **4.** *n.* the opposite. □ *The negative showed the reverse of the image.* **5.** *n.* the back of something; the back side. □ *The bank teller stamped something on the reverse of the check I was cashing.*

**review** [rɪ 'vju] **1.** *tv.* to examine something again. □ *I reviewed my application once before submitting it.* **2.** *tv.* to study information again, especially before a test. □ *Our teacher suggested that we review Chapter 6 tonight.* **3.** *tv.* to write or prepare ⑥ of a play, movie, book, dance, or other work of art. □ *The popular movie was reviewed in many magazines.* **4.** *iv.* to study again. □ *David reviewed for three hours before the quiz.* **5.** *n.* a formal examination or inspection. □ *In my review of the file, I found numerous errors.* **6.** *n.* an essay that evaluates a book, play, movie, dance, or other work. □ *Whoever wrote this review probably didn't even see the opera.*

**revise** [rɪ 'vɑɪz] *tv.* to make something current or up-to-date; to change something to include different information. □ *The editor revised some facts in the article before publishing it.*

**revised** [rɪ 'vɑɪzd] *adj.* updated; made current; changed to include new information. □ *The revised dictionary contained many new slang words.*

**revision** [rɪ 'vɪʒ ən] **1.** *n.* a change—usually an improvement—made to a document or a manuscript. □ *The editor's revisions were necessary for accuracy.* **2.** *n.* a document that has been revised. □ *I have included all your suggestions in the revision.*

**revival** [rɪ 'vɑɪ vəl] **1.** *n.* reviving someone or something; the process of returning life or energy to someone. □ *Her revival was made possible by modern drugs and a skilled doctor.* **2.** *n.* a new production of play or a musical that has been done before; something that has been revived. (Fig. on ①.) □ *The playwright updated the script for the revival.*

**revive** [rɪ 'vɑɪv] **1.** *tv.* to cause someone to return to a conscious state, with normal breathing and heart activity. □ *The firefighter revived the victim who was pulled from the burning building.* **2.** *tv.* to bring something back into use; to bring something back into style. □ *The discovery of a cave filled with gold revived interest in treasure hunting.* **3.** *iv.* to return to a conscious state, as in ①. □ *The woman who fainted revived a short time later.*

**revolt** [rɪ 'volt] **1.** *iv.* to fight against authority or the government. □ *The army revolted against the ruling political party.* **2.** *tv.* to cause someone to feel sick with disgust; to offend someone strongly. □ *We were revolted by the pictures in the magazine.* **3.** *n.* a rebellion; a riot; an instance of fighting as in ① against authority. □ *Hundreds of innocent people died in the revolt.*

**revolting** [rɪ 'vol tɪŋ] *adj.* sickening; very offensive. (Adv: *revoltingly.*) □ *My parents wouldn't let me see the revolting movie.*

**revolution** [rɛv ə 'lu ʃən] **1.** *n.* an act of seizing a government by force and replacing it with new rulers. □ *The government secretly aided revolutions in other countries.* **2.** *n.* a complete change. (Fig. on ①.) □ *A revolution in the methods of treating the disease cured almost all of its victims.* **3.** *n.* the circular or rotating movement made by an object going around a fixed object or position. □ *The earth makes one revolution each day.*

R

**revolve** [rɪ 'vɑlv] **1.** *iv.* [for someone or something] to rotate [around an axis]. □ *The revolving door was stuck and would not revolve.* **2. revolve around something** *iv. + prep. phr.* to move in a circle or oval around a point; to orbit around something. □ *The moon revolves around the earth.*

**reward** [rɪ 'word] **1.** *n.* something, especially money, given to someone who returns something that is lost or gives information about a crime. □ *Mary offered a reward to anyone who found her missing puppy.* **2.** *tv.* to give someone ①. □ *Mary rewarded the woman who found her bracelet.*

**rewarding** [rɪ 'wor dɪŋ] *adj.* satisfying; valuable. (Adv: *rewardingly.*) □ *My morning spent at the library was very rewarding.*

**rewind** [ri 'wɑɪnd] **1.** *tv.* to cause something, especially an audiotape, videotape, or film, to wind backward. (Pt/pp: rewound.) □ *The cassette player rewound the tape automatically.* **2.** *iv.* [for something that winds around an object, such as an audiotape, videotape, or film] to run backward. □ *The film rewound around its reel.* **3.** *n.* a button or device that causes a reverse movement as in ②. □ *Mary hit rewind in order to listen to the first song on the tape.*

R

**rewound** [ri 'wɑʊnd] pt/pp of rewind.

**rewrite 1.** [ri 'rɑɪt] *tv., irreg.* to revise something that has been written. (Pt: rewrote; pp: rewritten.) □ *The scientist rewrote the conclusion to include the new data.* **2.** ['ri rɑɪt] *n.* a copy of writing that has been revised. □ *Mary sent her rewrites to the editor for proofreading.*

**rewritten** ['ri 'rɪt n] **1.** pp of rewrite. **2.** *adj.* written in a different way; revised. □ *The rewritten textbook was clearer than the first edition.*

**rewrote** ['ri 'rot] pt of rewrite.

**rhinoceros** [rɑɪ 'nɑs ə rəs] *n., irreg.* a large animal of Africa and South Asia that has one or two large horns on its nose. (Pl: *rhinoceros* or *rhinoceroses.*) □ *Is it illegal to hunt rhinoceros?*

**rhyme** ['rɑɪm] **1.** *n.* a state existing where two or more words end in similar or identical sounds. (No plural form.) □ *Rhyme is common in poetry and the lyrics of songs.* **2.** *n.* a word showing ① with another word. □ Time *is a rhyme for* lime. □ *The poet couldn't think of a rhyme for* silver. **3.** *iv.* [for a word or phrase] to end with the same sound or sounds as another word or phrase; [for a poem] to include words or phrases ending with the same sound or sounds, especially at the ends of pairs of lines. □ Clown *and* frown *rhyme.* □ *I like your poem, even though it doesn't rhyme.*

**rhythm** ['rɪð əm] *n.* beats that occur in a pattern, such as in music. (Plural only when referring to different kinds, types, instances, or varieties.) □ *Rhythm is the basis for music and dance.* Ⓒ *I like music with Latin American rhythms.*

**rib** ['rɪb] **1.** *n.* one of the several pairs of bones that are attached to the backbone and curve around to the front of the chest. □ *I could see the starving child's ribs.* **2.** *n.* meat that contains a rib ①, eaten as food. □ *John ate ribs for dinner.*

**ribbon** ['rɪb ən] **1.** *n.* a narrow band of fabric or material, often used as a decoration. □ *David tied a ribbon around the wrapped gift.* **2.** *n.* a special kind of ①, coated with ink, used in a typewriter or computer printer; a special thin strip of plastic film used in an electric typewriter. □ *Mary installed a new ribbon in the electric typewriter.*

**rice** ['rɑɪs] **1.** *n.* a grass-like plant that produces edible seeds. (Plural only when referring to different kinds, types, instances, or varieties.) □ *Rice must be planted before the rains come.* Ⓒ *Different rices require different growing condi-*

*tions.* **2.** *n.* the edible grain of ①. (No plural form. Number is expressed with *grain(s) of rice.*) ☐ *Mary steamed some rice on the stove.*

**rich** ['rɪtʃ] **1.** *adj.* having a lot of money; wealthy; not poor. (Adv: *richly.* Comp: *richer;* sup: *richest.*) ☐ *The rich lawyer lived in an expensive apartment.* **2.** *adj.* having a lot of cream, butter, or other fats. (Adv: *richly.* Comp: *richer;* sup: *richest.*) ☐ *Rich pastry is very tasty, but will make you fat.* **3.** *adj.* [of soil] good for growing plants; fertile. (Adv: *richly.* Comp: *richer;* sup: *richest.*) ☐ *The grass grew very high in the rich earth.* **4.** *adj.* [of a color] vivid or deep. (Adv: *richly.* Comp: *richer;* sup: *richest.*) ☐ *This shag carpeting is a deep, rich red.* **5.** *adj.* plentiful; causing or yielding plenty, benefit, or value. ☐ *We found a rich store of information in the library.* **6. riches** *n.* wealth; an ample amount of anything good, especially money and property. (Treated as plural, but not countable.) ☐ *The wealthy man's riches were destroyed in the fire.* **7. the rich** *n.* people who are ①. (No plural form. Treated as plural, but not countable.) ☐ *The rich contribute a great deal of money to charity.*

**rid** ['rɪd] **1.** *tv., irreg.* to free something or a place of something. (Pt/pp: *rid.*) ☐ *I used bleach to rid my kitchen of germs.* **2.** *tv., irreg.* to make oneself free of someone or something. (Takes a reflexive object.) ☐ *John rid himself of his coat and made himself comfortable.* **3. get rid of** someone or something *phr.* to make oneself free of someone or something; to remove someone or something and be free of the person or thing. ☐ *Lisa is trying to get rid of the mice in her house.*

**ridden** ['rɪd n] **1.** pp of ride. **2.** *adj.* burdened with something; full of something. (Only in combinations.) ☐ *The flea-ridden cat needed a bath.*

**riddle** ['rɪd l] **1.** *n.* a puzzling question whose answer usually requires one to think in an unusual or clever way. ☐ *The answers to some riddles are very funny.* **2.** *n.* someone or something that is difficult to understand; someone or something that is puzzling. (Fig. on ①.) ☐ *Why Mary changed her mind is a complete riddle to me.*

**ride** ['rɑɪd] **1.** *tv., irreg.* to sit on or in something that moves; to be a passenger on or in a vehicle that moves or travels. (Pt: **rode;** pp: **ridden.** With **horse, donkey, elephant,** and other animals. With **train, bicycle, elevator, motorcycle, trolley** but *ride in* a **car, taxi, truck,** *Jeep.*) ☐ *Dave rode an elevator to the second floor.* **2.** *tv., irreg.* to travel along on something. ☐ *The swimmer rode all the way to the beach on a huge wave.* **3.** *n.* a journey using a vehicle or an animal. ☐ *I have always wanted to have a ride on a donkey.* **4.** *n.* a kind of entertainment in which people travel in some kind of vehicle to experience interesting sights and sounds, thrills, or learning. ☐ *The amusement park has dozens and dozens of interesting rides.*

**ridge** ['rɪdʒ] **1.** *n.* a long, narrow hill or mountain. ☐ *The sun set behind the rocky ridge.* **2.** *n.* a long, narrow, raised part of something. ☐ *There were marks and ridges in the lawn where the car had been driven.* **3.** *n.* the line where two surfaces slanted upward meet, as with the top edge of a roof. ☐ *A squirrel sat on the ridge of the doghouse.*

**ridicule** ['rɪd ə kjul] **1.** *tv.* to make fun of someone or something; to mock someone or something. ☐ *The bully ridiculed those who were smaller than he was.* **2.** *n.* laughter or mockery directed at someone or something, especially in a cruel way. (No plural form.) ☐ *The large child ignored the ridicule she received at school.*

**ridiculous** [rɪ 'dɪk jə ləs] *adj.* deserving to be laughed at or mocked; deserving ridicule. (Adv: *ridiculously.*) □ *John laughed at the ridiculous way in which Bill danced.*

**rifle** ['rɑɪ fʊl] **1.** *n.* a gun with a long barrel. □ *The hunter kept his rifles locked in a cabinet.* **2.** *tv.* to search an area thoroughly, stealing valuable things. □ *The spy rifled my apartment, looking for secret documents.*

**right** ['rɑɪt] **1.** *adj.* the opposite of left; to the east when someone or something faces north. (Only prenominal.) □ *The utensils are kept in the right drawer.* **2.** *adj.* correct; true; not wrong; not false. (Adv: *rightly.*) □ *Jimmy knew the right answer to the math problem.* **3.** *adj.* morally good; according to the law or social standards. (Adv: *rightly.*) □ *The jury was right to have found the criminal guilty.* **4.** *adj.* proper; suitable; being good for a situation. □ *Do you know the right way to slice turkey?* **5.** *adv.* toward the **right** ① side. □ *At the intersection, turn right.* **6.** *adv.* correctly; not wrongly. □ *Do your job right the first time, and you won't have to do it again.* **7.** *adv.* properly; suitably; in a way that is good for a situation. □ *The coach taught Bill how to throw right.* **8.** *adv.* directly; straight. (Has nothing to do with movement to the **right** ① side.) □ *John went right home after work.* **9.** *n.* that which is correct, proper, or good. (No plural form.) □ *I can tell right from wrong.* **10. right(s)** *n.* something that is due a person according to civil or moral law. (*Right* is singular; *rights* is plural.) □ *The factory was fined for violating the workers' rights.* **11.** *tv.* to cause something to be upright; to fix something that is leaning or has fallen, so that it is standing up again. □ *David righted the lamp after he knocked it over.*

**right angle** ['rɑɪt 'æŋ gəl] *n.* an angle whose sides join at 90 degrees. □ *The letter* L *is a right angle.*

**right-handed** ['rɑɪt hæn dɪd] **1.** *adj.* able to use the right hand better than the left; using the right hand to write with. (Adv: *right-handed(ly).*) □ *These scissors are designed for right-handed people.* **2.** *adj.* made to be used by the right hand. □ *Most of the desks in the classroom were right-handed.*

**rigid** ['rɪdʒ ɪd] **1.** *adj.* stiff; not bending; hard to bend; not flexible. (Adv: *rigidly.*) □ *My wet socks froze and became rigid.* **2.** *adj.* stubborn and determined. (Fig. on ①. Adv: *rigidly.*) □ *My rigid boss refused to break the company's rules.*

**rigorous** ['rɪg ə rəs] **1.** *adj.* harsh; strict; severe; demanding. (Adv: *rigorously.*) □ *The team's final practice before the big game was rigorous.* **2.** *adj.* thorough; exact; according to strict scientific standards; scientifically accurate. (Adv: *rigorously.*) □ *The rigorous accountant checked all his calculations twice.*

**rim** ['rɪm] **1.** *n.* the edge of something, especially of something that is circular. □ *The rim of the cup is cracked.* **2.** *n.* the part of a wheel that the tire is put around. □ *Dave placed the bike tire around the rim and then inflated the tire.*

**ring** ['rɪŋ] **1.** *n.* something made from a circle of material; a circular band. □ *The washer for this bolt is a simple metal ring.* **2.** *n.* a piece of jewelry made from a circle of metal that is usually worn around a person's finger. □ *Mary wore her class ring on her right hand.* **3.** *n.* a circle. □ *I drew a ring around David's face in the photograph.* **4.** *n.* a group of things or people that are in a circle. □ *A ring of mushrooms surrounded the tree.* **5.** *n.* an enclosed place where boxing and wrestling matches, circuses, and other forms of entertainment take place. □ *There were three rings under the circus tent.* **6.** *n.* sound made by a bell or a chime. (No plural form.) □ *The shrill ring of the alarm woke me up.* **7.** *n.* a

R

group of criminals, especially ones who work together as an illegal business. □ *A secret ring of thieves was exposed by the reporter.* **8.** *tv., irreg.* to cause a bell to ring. (Pt: **rang;** pp: **rung.**) □ *I rang Jane's doorbell, but she didn't answer.* **9.** *iv., irreg.* to make a noise like a bell; [for a bell] to produce a noise. □ *The alarm is set to ring at 5:30 A.M.*

**rinse** ['rɪns] **1. rinse** something **(off)** *tv. + obj. (+ adv.)* to wash something with clean water without using soap. □ *Mary rinsed her dirty shoes with the garden hose.* **2.** *n.* an act of washing with clean water, either for cleaning or to remove soap. □ *All of the dirt came out in the rinse.*

**riot** ['rɑɪ ət] **1.** *n.* a violent, uncontrolled disturbance by a crowd of angry people; a large, violent protest. □ *Four guards were injured in the riot at the prison.* **2.** *iv.* to participate in ①; to be part of ①. □ *Dozens of buildings were destroyed when the people rioted.*

**rip** ['rɪp] **1.** *n.* a tear; a gash; a ragged cut. □ *Mary taped the rip in the paper.* **2.** *tv.* to tear something apart; to tear something off; to cause something to come apart by pulling on it. □ *David ripped the wrapping from the present.* **3.** *iv.* to become torn; to be torn apart. □ *My newspaper ripped when David grabbed it from me.*

**ripe** ['rɑɪp] *adj.* ready to be eaten or used; having developed enough so that it can be eaten or used; ready. (Adv: *ripely.* Comp: *riper;* sup: *ripest.*) □ *John offered me a ripe peach.*

**ripen** ['rɑɪ pən] *iv.* to become ripe. □ *I'll pick a bushel of apples as soon as they have ripened.*

**rise** ['rɑɪz] **1.** *iv., irreg.* to go upward; to move upward; to go to a higher level. (Pt: **rose;** pp: **risen.** Compare this with **raise.**) □ *The child's balloon rose to the ceiling of the room.* **2.** *iv., irreg.* to wake up and get out of bed. □ *Bob rose when his alarm clock rang.* **3.** *iv., irreg.* [for the sun, moon, stars, and other objects in space] to appear to come up past the horizon. □ *After the full moon rose, I could see across the field.* **4.** *iv., irreg.* [of dough] to become higher and lighter. □ *After the dough rose, the baker put it in the oven.*

**risen** ['rɪz ən] pp of rise.

**rising** ['rɑɪ zɪŋ] **1.** *adj.* going higher; moving higher; going to a higher level; increasing in amount, strength, or intensity. □ *The rising tax rates angered the taxpayers.* **2.** *adj.* coming up above the horizon; moving above the horizon. □ *The dogs howled at the rising moon.*

**risk** ['rɪsk] **1.** *n.* a danger; a chance of harm or loss; a possibility of harm or loss. □ *Mary explained the risks of driving without wearing a seat belt.* **2.** *tv.* to expose someone or something to loss, harm, or death. □ *I can't risk any money on the purchase of stock.* **3. at risk** *phr.* in a situation where there is ①; in danger. □ *Your whole future is at risk if you don't stop smoking.*

**risky** ['rɪsk i] *adj.* dangerous; having a possibility of harm or loss; not safe. (Adv: *riskily.* Comp: *riskier;* sup: *riskiest.*) □ *Although it was risky, I drove on the icy roads.*

R

**rival** ['rɑɪv əl] **1.** *n.* a person or team that one works or plays against; someone against whom one competes or plays. □ *The tennis player shook hands with her rival after the game.* **2.** *adj.* <the adj. use of ①.> □ *The rival armies attacked each other on the battlefield.* **3.** *tv.* to be as good as something else; to equal something else. □ *Anne's paintings rival the ones I see in art galleries.*

**river** ['rɪv ɚ] *n.* a natural passage of fresh water that flows into a larger passage or body of water. □ *Anne crossed the river on a raft.*

**road** ['rod] **1.** *n.* a path or way that people can drive cars and other vehicles on to get from one place to another. ☐ *My family has lived on Miller Road my whole life.* **2.** *n.* a way to reach something or to achieve some result; a way of being or acting that leads to something. (Fig. on ①.) ☐ *Clean living is the road to a happy life.*

**roam** ['rom] **1.** *tv.* to travel someplace with no definite destination in mind; to wander someplace. ☐ *The tourists roamed the streets, looking at the buildings.* **2.** *iv.* to travel around with no specific goal; to wander. ☐ *John roamed across Europe when he was 18.*

**roar** ['ror] **1.** *n.* a very loud, deep noise. ☐ *The roar of the lion frightened the tourists.* **2.** *iv.* to make ①. ☐ *The engine roared when I turned the key.* **3.** *iv.* to laugh very hard and very long because someone or something is very funny. ☐ *Susan roared when I told her the funny joke.*

**roast** ['rost] **1.** *tv.* to cook something by using dry heat; to bake; to cook in an oven; to prepare something by using heat. (Most meats and vegetables are roasted. Bread and ham are baked. Potatoes are either roasted or baked.) ☐ *Jane roasted the beef at 350 degrees.* **2.** *iv.* to become cooked by using dry heat; to become cooked over fire. ☐ *I could smell the potatoes as they roasted.* **3.** *n.* meat that is suitable for cooking in dry heat; meat that has been cooked with dry heat. ☐ *Anne sliced the roast with a large knife.*

**rob** ['rɑb] *tv.* to steal something from someone; to take something from someone by force. ☐ *The thief robbed me of all my money.*

**robber** ['rɑb ɚ] *n.* someone who robs people or places; a thief. ☐ *The robber demanded all of my money.*

**robbery** ['rɑb (ə) ri] *n.* stealing something that belongs to someone else; theft. ☐ *During the robbery, the thief held a gun to my head.*

**robe** ['rob] **1.** *n.* a long, one-piece garment, especially worn to show one's rank or position. ☐ *The king and queen wore fine silk robes on the throne.* **2.** *n.* a **bathrobe**. ☐ *Anne put on a robe after her shower.*

**robin** ['rɑb ən] *n.* a songbird with orange feathers on its breast. ☐ *The cat tried to catch the robin.*

**robot** ['ro bɑt] *n.* a machine that does the work of a human and often moves like or looks like a human. ☐ *The robot was programmed to do some simple tasks.*

**rock** ['rɑk] **1.** *n.* the mineral substances of which a planet is made. (No plural form.) ☐ *I built my house on solid rock.* **2.** *n.* a stone; a hard piece of earth; a piece of mineral. ☐ *I cut my foot when I stepped on a sharp rock.* **3.** *adj.* made of ①; consisting of ① or ②. ☐ *Grass won't grow here, so I built a rock garden.* **4.** *iv.* to move back and forth; to move from side to side; to sway. ☐ *The wooden bridge rocked in the wind.* **5.** *tv.* to move something back and forth or from side to side. ☐ *The heavy waves rocked the raft.*

**rocker** ['rɑk ɚ] Go to **rocking chair**.

**rocket** ['rɑk ət] **1.** *n.* a device used to travel through space or to carry weapons. ☐ *An enemy rocket demolished the town's hospital.* **2.** *iv.* to travel by ①. ☐ *The astronauts rocketed to the moon.*

**rocking chair** AND **rocker** ['rɑk ɪŋ 'tʃɛr, 'rɑk ɚ] *n.* a chair whose legs are set into two curved pieces of wood so that it can rock back and forth. ☐ *Anne moved her rocker away from the edge of the carpet.*

**rod** ['rɑd] *n.* a long, narrow cylinder of wood, metal, plastic, or other material. ☐ *I hung the curtains from the rod over the window.*

**rode** ['rod] pt of **ride**.

**rodent** ['rod nt] *n.* a member of a group of mammals with large, strong, sharp front teeth. □ *Dozens of rodents swarmed around the pile of garbage.*

**rodeo** ['ro di o] *n.* an event including contests involving roping cattle and riding horses. (Pl ends in *-s.*) □ *The vet treated the horse that was injured at the rodeo.*

**role** ['rol] **1.** *n.* a part in a play or movie; the part that an actor plays in a play or movie. □ *The director cast me in a very difficult role.* **2.** *n.* the duty someone has in a group or organization. □ *It is the secretary's role to take minutes of official meetings.*

**roll** ['rol] **1.** *n.* a small loaf of bread made for one person; a small, round piece of bread for one person. □ *The salad was served with a warm roll.* **2.** *n.* a unit of something that has been formed into a tube. □ *I bought a roll of toilet paper at the store.* **3. class roll** *n.* a list of the names of people, especially those who are enrolled in something. □ *When the class roll is full, we will not enroll more students.* **4.** *iv.* to move forward by turning over and over; for a ball to move forward along a surface. □ *The children became dirty when they rolled down the hill.* **5.** *iv.* to move on wheels. □ *The car rolled a little bit before it stopped.* **6.** *tv.* to move something forward by turning it over and over; to move a ball forward along a surface. □ *Bill rolled the barrel on its side.* **7.** *tv.* to move something on wheels; to cause something to move on wheels. □ *I rolled the stalled car past the intersection.* **8.** *tv.* to cause something to form the shape of a tube or cylinder. □ *The sculptor rolled the clay into a rod.*

**roller skate** ['rol ɚ sket] **1.** *n.* a special shoe or boot that is fitted with wheels underneath. □ *I went to the lake on my roller skates.* **2. roller-skate** *iv.* to move on **roller skates** ①. □ *The children roller-skated around the driveway.*

**Roman Catholic** ['ro mən 'kæθ (ə) lɪk] **1.** *n.* a follower of the Christian religion that is based in Rome and governed by the Pope. □ *Roman Catholics aren't supposed to eat meat on Fridays during Lent.* **2.** *adj.* <the adj. use of ①.> □ *I play bingo at the local Roman Catholic church every week.*

**romance** [ro 'mæns] **1.** *n.* an interest in love and adventure. (No plural form.) □ *Romance inspired me to buy my date a dozen roses.* **2.** *n.* a love story. □ *This movie is a beautiful romance about two college students.* **3.** *n.* a love experience with someone. □ *Sue told me about her brief romance during her trip to Europe.* **4. Romance** *n.* a group of languages that includes French, Italian, Spanish, Portuguese, and Romanian. □ *Romance is a group of languages spoken in Europe and South America.* **5.** *tv.* to treat someone in a romantic way; to show someone love. □ *John romanced his neighbor with candy, flowers, and gifts.* **6. Romance** *adj.* <the adj. use of ④.> □ *Mike speaks French and understands all Romance languages.*

**Roman numeral** ['rom ən 'num ə rəl] *n.* the form of numbers made from letters, such as I, II, III, IV, V. □ *Large Roman numerals, such as MCMXXVI, are hard to read.*

**romantic** [ro 'mæn tɪk] **1.** *adj.* full of love and adventure; of or about a love experience; of or about love. (Adv: *romantically* [...ɪk li].) □ *My date surprised me with a very romantic kiss.* **2.** *adj.* causing romance; used to create a feeling of romance. (Adv: *romantically* [...ɪk li].) □ *We went to a ski resort for a romantic winter vacation.*

**roof** ['ruf, 'rʊf] **1.** *n.* the outside covering of the top of a building, vehicle, or other enclosed object. □ *Rain leaked through the hole in the roof.* **2.** *n.* the top part of the inside of something, such as the mouth or a cave. □ *Bats hung from the*

R

*roof of the cave.* **3.** *tv.* to put ① over something; to build ①. □ *The workers roofed the new building in the heat of the sun.*

**room** ['rum] **1.** *n.* a part of a building that is separated from other parts of the building by a wall with a door in it. □ *Anne walked into the next room and shut the door.* **2.** *n.* space that is or could be taken up by someone or something. □ *I moved my coat so there would be room for John to sit down.* **3. room with someone** *iv.* + *prep. phr.* to live with someone; to rent a room ① or an apartment with someone; to be someone's roommate. □ *Bob roomed with his cousin when he first moved to Chicago.*

**roommate** ['rum met] *n.* someone with whom one shares an apartment or room. □ *I helped my roommate wash the dishes.*

**roomy** ['rum i] *adj.* having plenty of room; having a lot of space; having a comfortable amount of space; not crowded. (Adv: *roomily.* Comp: *roomier;* sup: *roomiest.*) □ *I am looking for a roomy apartment close to the city.*

**roost** ['rust] **1.** *n.* a place, such as a nest or branch, where birds rest or sleep. □ *Small birds use my clothesline as a roost.* **2.** *iv.* to occupy ① for rest or sleep. □ *The bird wrapped its claws around the branch on which it roosted.*

R

**rooster** ['rust ɚ] *n.* an adult male chicken. □ *The rooster strutted around the barnyard.*

**root 1.** ['rut, 'rʊt] *n.* the part of a plant that is under the ground, taking water from the soil and supporting the plant. □ *Edible roots include carrots and turnips.* **2.** ['rut, 'rʊt] *n.* the part of a strand of hair that is under the surface of the skin. (Fig. on ①.) □ *This shampoo cleans down to the roots of your hair.* **3.** ['rut, 'rʊt] *n.* the origin of something; the source of something; something that causes something else. □ *I think that greed and anger are the roots of my problems.* **4.** ['rut, 'rʊt] *n.* the form of a word that other words are made from. □ *The root of the word* interestingly *is* interest. □ *The progressive is formed by adding* -ing *to verb roots.* **5.** ['rut, 'rʊt] *tv.* to cause a plant to grow roots ①. □ *You should root this plant in sandy soil.* **6.** ['rut] *iv.* to cheer for someone; to provide encouragement for someone or a team, especially for someone or a team in a contest or sports event. □ *I was rooting for the challenger to win.*

**rope** ['rop] **1.** *n.* a strong, thick cord made by twisting smaller cords together. (Plural only when referring to different kinds, types, instances, or varieties.) □ *The bank robber tied the tellers up with rope.* © *Natural ropes are as strong as synthetic ropes.* **2.** *tv.* to catch someone or something by swinging a loop of ①. □ *In the movie, the sheriff roped the bandit and tied him up.*

**rose** ['roz] **1.** pt of rise. **2.** *n.* a bright, sweet-smelling flower that grows on a plant having thorns. □ *I sent some roses to my wife on her birthday.* **3.** *n.* the bush that ② grows on. □ *John tended to the roses growing along the fence.*

**Rosh Hashanah** ['rɑʃ hə 'ʃɑ nə] *n.* a holiday in the Jewish religion marking the Jewish New Year. □ *Rosh Hashanah is celebrated on the first day of the year.*

**rosy** ['roz i] **1.** *adj.* pink; rose-colored. (Adv: *rosily.* Comp: *rosier;* sup: *rosiest.*) □ *I put some rosy polish on my nails.* **2.** *adj.* full of hope; optimistic. (Adv: *rosily.* Comp: *rosier;* sup: *rosiest.*) □ *After surgery, the doctor said that things looked rosy for the future.*

**rot** ['rɑt] **1.** *n.* decay; something that is rotten. (No plural form.) □ *I threw away the vegetable because of the rot.* **2.** *iv.* to decay; [for plant or animal material] to lose its form because of bacteria. □ *A dead squirrel rotted by the* *side of the road.* **3.** *tv.* to cause something to decay. □ *Moisture had rotted the old wooden bridge.*

**rotten** ['rɑt n] **1.** *adj.* decayed; spoiled. (Adv: *rottenly.*) □ *Rotten eggs smell just terrible.* **2.** *adj.* very bad; evil; nasty. (Adv: *rottenly.*) □ *This TV show is really rotten.*

**rough** ['rʌf] **1.** *adj.* not smooth; not even; having a surface that is uneven or bumpy. (Adv: *roughly.* Comp: *rougher;* sup: *roughest.*) □ *The wound left a rough scar on my skin.* **2.** *adj.* using force; harsh; violent. (Adv: *roughly.* Comp: *rougher;* sup: *roughest.*) □ *The young dog we adopted had undergone a lot of rough abuse.* **3.** *adj.* coarse; not delicate; not refined. (Adv: *roughly.* Comp: *rougher;* sup: *roughest.*) □ *The musicians rented a cheap apartment in a rough part of town.* **4.** *adj.* hard; difficult; severe; not easy. (Comp: *rougher;* sup: *roughest.*) □ *It was rough to drive in such a horrible snowstorm.* **5.** *adj.* not in final form; not finished; not exact; not detailed; approximate. (Adv: *roughly.* Comp: *rougher;* sup: *roughest.*) □ *My secretary made a rough outline of my schedule at the conference.*

**round** ['rɑʊnd] **1.** *adj.* shaped like a circle; circular; curved. (Adv: *roundly.* Comp: *rounder;* sup: *roundest.*) □ *The clock on the wall is round.* **2.** *adj.* shaped like a ball; spherical; curved. (Adv: *roundly.* Comp: *rounder;* sup: *roundest.*) □ *I pumped air into the basketball until it was round.* **3.** *n.* the bullet or shell for a single shot from a gun. □ *John shot two rounds before his gun jammed.* **4.** *n.* a song where people begin at different times so that the words and music of the different parts overlap. □ *When we sang the round, we were all singing different words at one time.* **5.** *prep.* **around.** (Informal. **Round** can be used informally for any of the preposition uses listed under **around.**) □ *Run round the corner and buy me a paper.* **6.** *adv.* **around.** (Informal.) □ *The detective looked round with a flashlight.*

**route** ['rut, 'rɑʊt] **1.** *n.* a road; a path; the way one travels; the way something is sent. □ *This route will take you to the factory by way of the pond.* **2.** *tv.* to send something by a particular ①. □ *The travel agent routed me through Newark to Boston.*

**routine** [ru 'tin] **1.** *n.* a regular habit; something that is done regularly. (Plural only when referring to different kinds, types, instances, or varieties.) □ *I took a vacation because I got tired of my daily routine.* Ⓒ *I have different routines on different days of the week.* **2.** *n.* a piece of entertainment; a skit; a sequence of actions in a performance. □ *The skater's routine was perfect, and she won the gold medal.* **3.** *adj.* normal; as a habit; as usually done. (Adv: *routinely.*) □ *Anne took a routine coffee break at 2:30 P.M.*

**row 1.** ['ro] *n.* a series of people or things in a line; a line of things or people. □ *A row of people stood against the wall, waiting for the bank to open.* **2.** ['ro] *n.* a line of seats in a theater, church, auditorium, classroom, or other place where people sit in a line. □ *The first six rows are reserved for important guests.* **3.** ['rɑʊ] *n.* a quarrel; an argument. □ *The bus driver ignored the loud row at the back of the bus.* **4.** ['ro] *iv.* to move through water in a boat by using oars. □ *John rowed all the way across the lake.* **5.** ['ro] *tv.* to move a boat by using oars. □ *Anne rowed the raft toward the bank.*

**rowboat** ['ro bot] *n.* a small boat that is moved by using oars. □ *During the flood, the police went through town in rowboats.*

**royal** ['rɔɪ əl] **1.** *adj.* belonging to kings and queens; of or about kings and queens. (Adv: *royally.*) □ *The gallant knight was invited to the royal castle.* **2.** *adj.* elegant; fit for royalty. (Fig. on

R

①. Adv: *royally.*) □ *Mr. Brown treated his customer to a royal evening.*

**royalty** ['rɔɪ əl ti] **1.** *n.* the rank of king or queen; the power of a king or queen. (No plural form.) □ *The young children were in awe of the queen's royalty.* **2.** *n.* people who have attained ①. (No plural form.) □ *This park is reserved for royalty.* **3.** *n.* money earned from the publication of a copyright holder's work. □ *John's contract doesn't provide for any royalties.*

**rub** ['rʌb] **1.** *tv.* to push or slide something with something else. □ *Sue rubbed the lottery ticket with the edge of a penny.* **2. rub against** something *iv.* + *prep. phr.* to push or slide against something. □ *The damaged brake rubbed against the wheel.*

**rubber** ['rʌb ɚ] **1.** *n.* a waterproof material that goes back to its original shape when stretched or pressed. (No plural form.) □ *The soles of my shoes are made of rubber.* **2.** *adj.* made from ①. □ *David's feet remained dry inside his rubber boots.*

**rubber band** ['rʌb ɚ 'bænd] *n.* a thin strip of rubber formed in a circle. □ *Lisa always keeps a rubber band around her wrist at work, in case she needs one.*

**rubbish** ['rʌb ɪʃ] *n.* trash; garbage; things that are thrown away. (No plural form.) □ *The janitor collected rubbish from the offices.*

**rudder** ['rʌd ɚ] *n.* a blade at the back of a ship or airplane that can be moved back and forth to control direction. □ *John managed the sails while David steered the boat with the rudder.*

**rude** ['rud] **1.** *adj.* not polite; not well mannered; not courteous. (Adv: *rudely.* Comp: *ruder;* sup: *rudest.*) □ *It was very rude of you to insult me in front of my friends.* **2.** *adj.* simple; not complex; primitive; coarse; rough; made without complex tools. (Adv: *rudely.* Comp: *ruder;* sup: *rudest.*) □ *Anne made a rude doghouse with some boards, a hammer, and nails.*

**rudeness** ['rud nəs] *n.* not being polite; bad manners; bad behavior. (No plural form.) □ *The student's rudeness shocked the teacher.*

**rug** ['rʌg] *n.* a carpet; a thick piece of woven fabric that is used to cover a floor. □ *John vacuumed the rug after he spilled popcorn.*

**rugged** ['rʌg əd] **1.** *adj.* [of a trail] rough and jagged. (Adv: *ruggedly.*) □ *We had to climb a rugged hill to get to the cabin.* **2.** *adj.* [of something] strong and lasting a long time; [of something] not easily broken. (Adv: *ruggedly.*) □ *The soldier drove the rugged truck across the field of rocks.* **3.** *adj.* [of someone] sturdy and strong. (Adv: *ruggedly.*) □ *The rugged campers lived in the woods for a month.*

**ruin** ['ru ɪn] **1.** *tv.* to destroy someone or something completely; to make something worthless. □ *David ruined the cake by dropping it on the floor.* **2.** *n.* the remaining part of an old building. (Often plural.) □ *The old house was a nothing but a ruin.* **3.** *n.* a great amount of destruction. (No plural form.) □ *The massive ruin caused by the tornado will be costly to repair.* **4. in ruin** *phr.* in a state of having been destroyed. □ *The crops lay in ruin after the flood.*

**ruined** ['ru ɪnd] *adj.* destroyed; completely damaged; made worthless. □ *The citizens slowly rebuilt the ruined city.*

**rule** ['rul] **1.** *n.* a statement that says what one is or is not allowed to do; a regulation. □ *The coach explained the rules of the game.* **2.** *n.* government; the control of someone in authority. (No plural form.) □ *Under the queen's rule, her word was law.* **3.** *tv.* to decide something officially. (The object is a clause with **that** ⑦.) □ *The court ruled that the law was unfair.* **4.** *tv.* to govern a country or its people. □ *A tyrant ruled the kingdom for many years.*

**ruler** ['rul ɚ] **1.** *n.* someone who rules; someone, such as a king or queen, who runs a government. □ *The ruler of the country was only 18 years old.* **2.** *n.* a straight strip of wood, plastic, metal, or other material that has marks on it that show measurement. □ *Susan drew a straight line by tracing the edge of a ruler.*

**rumble** ['rʌm bəl] **1.** *n.* a low vibrating sound, like the sound of thunder. □ *What is that rumble under the hood of your car?* **2.** *iv.* to make a low vibrating sound, like the sound of thunder. □ *My car engine rumbles loudly when I drive.*

**rumor** ['rum ɚ] *n.* news about someone or something that may or may not be true; information that is passed from person to person about someone and that may or may not be true. □ *There's a rumor going around that you're moving to Florida.*

**rump** ['rʌmp] **1.** *n.* the rear part of a person or an animal; the buttocks. □ *The baby fell down on its rump and giggled.* **2.** *n.* meat from the rear part of an animal, used as food. (No plural form. Number is expressed with *rump roast(s).*) □ *The butcher ground up some rump and sold me a pound of it.*

**run** ['rʌn] **1.** *iv., irreg.* to move quickly in such a way that both feet are off the ground during each stride. (Pt: ran; pp: *run.*) □ *Susan ran toward the finish line.* **2.** *iv., irreg.* to work; to be working; to function; to be in operation. □ *The refrigerator isn't running because you haven't plugged it in.* **3.** *iv., irreg.* to extend to a certain length or distance; to reach a certain distance or time. □ *Performances of this opera will run until May 31.* **4.** *iv., irreg.* to flow; [for liquids] to move. □ *The waiter poured the coffee into my cup until it ran over.* **5.** *iv., irreg.* [for a liquid color] to spread, flow, or bleed. □ *The actors' makeup ran under the hot stage lights.* **6.** *iv., irreg.* to move quickly as a form of exercise or as a sport. □ *David runs on the high-school track team.* **7.** *iv., irreg.* [for one's nose] to drip fluid. □ *Jimmy's nose is running, and he has a fever.* **8. run for** something *iv., irreg. + prep. phr.* to be a candidate for an office in an election. □ *Mary, John, and Susan are all running for class treasurer.* **9.** *tv., irreg.* to extend something to a certain length or distance; to cause something to reach a certain distance or time. □ *The railroad company ran the tracks all the way to the city.* **10.** *tv., irreg.* to control, own, or manage a business. □ *My uncle ran a small newspaper stand on Main Street.* **11.** *tv., irreg.* to publish something in a newspaper or magazine. □ *The magazine ran a cruel story about the movie star.* **12.** *n.* an instance of running as in ①. □ *After a short run, Max could hardly breathe.* **13.** *n.* a trip; a journey. □ *I'm making a run to the store. Do you need anything?* **14.** *n.* a point scored in baseball or softball when a player has run ① around the bases and then has safely touched home plate. □ *Jane got the first run of the softball game.* **15. run out of** something *phr.* to use up all of something and have no more. □ *I usually run out of money at the end of the month.*

**run-down** ['rʌn 'dɑʊn] **1.** *adj.* in poor health. □ *I feel tired and run-down. I think I am going to get the flu.* **2.** *adj.* [of something] in bad condition owing to neglect. □ *Who owns that run-down building?*

**rung** ['rʌŋ] **1.** pp of ring. **2.** *n.* one of the poles forming a step of a ladder. □ *Mary stood on the top rung to change the light bulb.*

**running** ['rʌn ɪŋ] **1.** *n.* the activity of someone who runs for sport, health, or pleasure. (No plural form.) □ *Bob has lost five pounds from running.* **2.** *adj.* <the adj. use of ①.> □ *The running*

R

*coach told us to buy proper shoes.* **3.** *adj.* [of talk] continuous. (Fig. on ②.) □ *The reporter provided running commentary on the football game.*

**runny** ['rʌn i] **1.** *adj.* [of eggs] not completely cooked and still somewhat liquid. (Adv: *runnily.* Comp: *runnier;* sup: *runniest.*) □ *David doesn't like to eat runny eggs.* **2. runny nose** *n.* a person's nose that is dripping due to a cold, the flu, etc. □ *My cold has given me a terribly runny nose.*

**run-of-the-mill** [rən əv ðə 'mɪl] *adj.* average; ordinary; typical; normal; regular. □ *Anne tolerated her run-of-the-mill job.*

**runway** ['rʌn we] *n.* a landing strip for an airplane; a track that an airplane takes off from and lands on. □ *The plane bounced a little when it made contact with the runway.*

**rural** ['rɚ əl] *adj.* in the country; not like the city; not urban or suburban. (Adv: *rurally.*) □ *Tired of the big city, the writer moved to a quiet rural town.*

**rush** ['rʌʃ] **1.** *n.* hurry; haste; movement in a fast and urgent manner. (No plural form.) □ *I was in a rush to get to work, but I was stuck in traffic.* **2.** *n.* a very sudden movement or flow. □ *There was a rush for the exit when someone yelled, "Fire!"*

**rust** ['rʌst] **1.** *n.* a dark red or dark orange layer that forms on iron or steel when it is exposed to air or water. (No plural form.) □ *The old metal garage door was coated with rust.* **2.** *iv.* to acquire a coating of ①. □ *John's bike rusted because he didn't take good care of it.* **3.** *tv.* to cause something to be covered with ①. □ *The rain rusted the nails holding the porch together.*

**rustle** ['rʌs əl] **1.** *n.* a soft noise, like the sound that leaves make when they are blown by the wind or the sound made when objects are rubbed together. (No plural form.) □ *I could hear the rustle of papers in the quiet library.* **2.** *iv.* [for objects] to make a soft noise when rubbed together or blown by the wind. □ *The pages of the old book rustled as Mary turned them.* **3.** *tv.* to cause objects to **rustle** ②. □ *The wind rustled the leaves in the tree.* **4.** *tv.* to steal cattle. □ *The thieves who rustled our cattle were sent to jail.*

**rusty** ['rʌs ti] **1.** *adj.* covered with rust; rusted. (Adv: *rustily.* Comp: *rustier;* sup: *rustiest.*) □ *John junked his rusty old car.* **2.** *adj.* [of a skill or knowledge] poor or lacking because it has been unused for so long a time. (Adv: *rustily.* Comp: *rustier;* sup: *rustiest.*) □ *Although I was a little rusty, I solved the calculus problem.*

**ruthless** ['ruθ ləs] *adj.* without pity; without mercy; cruel; evil. (Adv: *ruthlessly.*) □ *The ruthless judge sentenced the innocent woman to jail.*

**rye** ['rɑɪ] **1.** *n.* a tall grass that is farmed for its light brown grain. (No plural form.) □ *The barn was surrounded by acres of rye.* **2.** *n.* grain from ①. (No plural form. Number is expressed with *grain(s) of rye.*) □ *A kind of bread can be made from rye.* **3.** *adj.* made from ②. □ *Some sandwiches taste best on rye bread.*

R

**sack** ['sæk] **1.** *n.* a bag or pouch made of paper, cloth, etc. □ *The sack of potatoes is very heavy.* **2.** *n.* the contents of ①. □ *One sack was not enough to feed everyone.*

**sacred** ['se krɪd] *adj.* holy; blessed. (Adv: *sacredly.*) □ *The cemetery is a sacred burial place.*

**sacrifice** ['sæ krə fɑɪs] **1.** *n.* giving up something; not having something that is wanted or needed. (Plural only when referring to different kinds, types, instances, or varieties.) □ *We endured a lot of sacrifice to send you to college.* Ⓒ *I don't know why we made so many sacrifices to send you to college!* **2.** *n.* something that is offered to a god or spirit. □ *A goat was a sacrifice to the god.* **3.** *tv.* to take the life of a creature as in ②. □ *They sacrificed a goat to the god.* **4.** *tv.* to give up something of value [for someone else's benefit]. □ *My parents sacrificed buying a second car so that I could go to college.*

**sad** ['sæd] **1.** *adj.* not happy; feeling sorrow. (Adv: *sadly.* Comp: *sadder;* sup: *saddest.*) □ *I tried to cheer John up because he seemed so sad.* **2.** *adj.* unfortunate; [of something] not bringing pleasure. (Adv: *sadly.* Comp: *sadder;* sup: *saddest.*) □ *It was a sad day when I lost my job.*

**sadden** ['sæd n] **1.** *iv.* to become sad. □ *Mary saddened when she learned of her brother's death.* **2.** *tv.* to cause someone to become sad. □ *The horrible news of John's death saddened Bill.*

**saddle** ['sæd l] **1.** *n.* a leather seat that fits on the back of a horse or other animal that carries people. □ *Anne put the saddle on the horse's back and rode away.* **2.** *n.* a bicycle or motorcycle seat. □ *The saddle was so high that Jimmy's feet did not reach the pedals.* **3.** *tv.* to place ① on a horse or a similar animal. □ *It took an hour to saddle the horse for a 20-minute ride!*

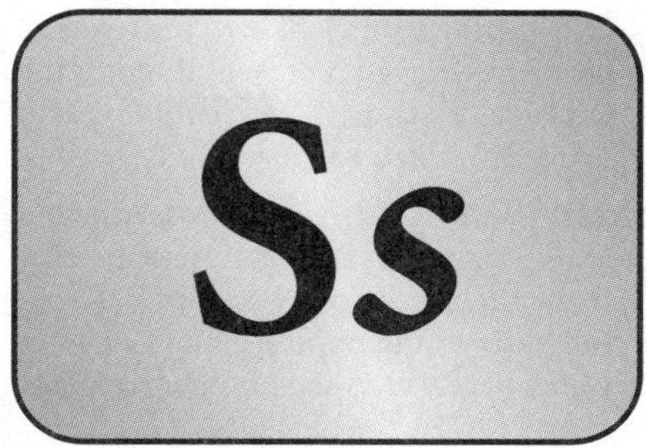


**sadness** ['sæd nəs] *n.* sorrow; having feelings of gloom or depression; a lack of happiness. (No plural form.) □ *The mayor's death caused great sadness throughout the city.*

**safe** ['sef] **1.** *n.* a solid, sturdy, steel or iron box—with a strong lock—that money, jewelry, papers, or other valuable objects are kept in for protection. □ *The cashier deposited the $20 bills in the safe.* **2.** *adj.* not dangerous; not risky; not causing or creating danger. (Adv: *safely.* Comp: *safer;* sup: *safest.*) □ *I like to ride in John's car because he's a safe driver.* **3.** *adj.* protected; secure. (Adv: *safely.* Comp: *safer;* sup: *safest.*) □ *Please put this gold ring in a safe place.* **4. safe and sound** *phr.* **safe** ③ and whole; **safe** ③ and healthy. □ *It was a rough trip, but we got there safe and sound.*

**safeguard** ['sef gɑrd] **1.** *n.* something that protects someone or something from danger. □ *The net is a safeguard for the construction workers high up on the bridge.* **2.** *tv.* to protect someone or something from danger; to keep someone or something safe. □ *Safety belts safeguard us from getting seriously injured in car accidents.*

**safekeeping** ['sef 'kip ɪŋ] *n.* keeping someone or something safe; a place or state where something is safe. (No plural form.) □ *I left my fur coat with the manager for safekeeping.*

**safety** ['sef ti] **1.** *n.* the state of being safe; freedom from harm or danger.

(No plural form.) □ *For your safety, please fasten your seat belts.* **2.** *adj.* <the adj. use of ①.> □ *You should wear a safety belt when you drive.*

**safety belt** ['sef ti bɛlt] *n.* a seat belt; a set of straps that extend across one's lap from the top of one's shoulder across the body to the opposite hip. □ *Fasten your safety belt as soon as you get in the car.*

**safe(ty)-deposit box** ['sef (ti) də 'pɑz ət 'bɑks] *n.* a metal box that is used for holding valuable items and is locked in a large safe or vault. □ *We rent a safety-deposit box at the bank.*

**sag** ['sæg] *iv.* to bend, hang, or curve downward. □ *The heavy tree branches sagged toward the ground.*

**said** ['sɛd] pt/pp of **say**.

**sail** ['sel] **1.** *n.* a sheet of cloth that is stretched on a mast of a ship to catch the energy of the wind. □ *The sails were torn by the heavy winds.* **2.** *iv.* to travel by boat or ship on the water. □ *Mary sailed across the lake to visit her grandmother.* **3.** *iv.* [for a ship or boat] to travel on the water. □ *The ship sailed toward the remote island.* **4.** *iv.* to glide through the air the way a boat moves through water. □ *The balloon sailed up to the clouds.* **5.** *tv.* to steer a boat or ship on the water. □ *I sailed my boat across the bay.* **6.** *tv.* to cause something to glide through the air. □ *Jimmy sailed his kite high above the trees.*



**sailboat** ['sel bot] *n.* a boat that has at least one sail and that moves by the power of the wind. □ *The wind pushed the sailboat across the bay.*

**sailor** ['se lɚ] **1.** *n.* someone who works on a boat or a ship. □ *The sailor notified the captain of a leak.* **2.** *n.* someone who is in the navy. □ *The sailors left the base for the evening and went into town.*

**sake** ['sek] **for** someone's or something's **sake; for the sake of** someone or something *phr.* for the purpose or benefit of someone or something; to satisfy the demands of someone or something. □ *Yes, it seems warm in here, but don't open the window for my sake. Ask the others also.*

**salad** ['sæl əd] *n.* a dish of mixed vegetables, especially lettuce, or other food mixed with vegetables, usually with a sauce called *salad dressing.* □ *Green salads contain mostly lettuce.*

**salary** ['sæl (ə) ri] *n.* the amount of money that someone is paid for working. (Compare to **wage**.) □ *When my salary increased last year, so did my taxes.*

**sale** ['sel] **1.** *n.* the exchange of a product or service for money; an act of selling. □ *The cashier rang up my sale on the cash register.* **2. sales** *n.* the amount of products or services sold during a certain period of time. (Treated as plural, but not countable.) □ *This year's sales are 10% less than last year's.* **3.** *n.* a special event where products or services are sold for less money than normal. □ *During the sale, everything at the store is reduced by 25%.* **4. for sale** *phr.* available to be sold. □ *Are the paintings on the wall for sale, or are they decorations?* **5. on sale** *phr.* available for purchase at a reduced price. □ *I bought these pants on sale for half price.*

**salesclerk** ['selz klɚk] *n.* someone who works in a store, helping customers and selling products. □ *The salesclerk showed me where the dressing room was.*

**salesman** ['selz mən] *n., irreg.* someone whose job is selling things; a man whose job is selling things. (Pl: **salesmen**.) □ *The salesman offered me a good deal on a new car.*

**salesmen** ['selz mən] pl of **salesman**.

**salespeople** ['selz pi pəl] a pl of **salesperson**.

**salesperson** ['selz pɚ sən] *n., irreg.* someone whose job is selling things. (Pl: **salespeople** or *salespersons.*) □ *Each salesperson must wear a name tag at all times.*

**saleswoman** ['selz wʊ mən] *n., irreg.* a woman whose job is selling things. (Pl: **saleswomen.**) □ *Susan bought a new car from the friendly saleswoman.*

**saleswomen** ['selz wɪ mən] pl of **saleswoman.**

**salmon** ['sæm ən] **1.** *n., irreg.* a large food fish with soft, pale pink flesh. (Pl: *salmon.*) □ *You're only allowed to catch two salmon a day at this lake.* **2.** *n.* the meat of ①. (No plural form.) □ *Could I have some more salmon, please?*

**salt** ['sɔlt] **1.** *n.* a white substance used to season or preserve food and to melt snow and ice. (No plural form.) □ *Anne sprinkled a little salt on her vegetables.* **2.** *n.* a chemical substance made by combining an acid with a metal. (Plural only when referring to different kinds, types, instances, or varieties.) □ *The shelves held bottles of acid and a jar of bright blue salt.* Ⓒ *The glass jars contained salts of many varieties.* **3.** *tv.* to season something by putting ① on it. □ *Jane salted her potatoes lightly.* **4.** *tv.* to cover something with ①. □ *The city workers salted the icy roads.*

**salted** ['sɔl tɪd] *adj.* [of food] having salt added. □ *Tom loves to eat salted nuts.*

**salt water** ['sɔlt 'wɑt ɚ] **1.** *n.* water with a high salt content, such as that found in the oceans. (No plural form.) □ *Salt water is not suitable for drinking.* **2. saltwater** *adj.* [of water] having salt; found in the ocean or the sea. □ *I prefer saltwater fish over fish from fresh water.*

**salty** ['sɔl ti] *adj.* tasting like salt; having salt. (Adv: *saltily.* Comp: *saltier;* sup: *saltiest.*) □ *These potato chips are too salty.*

**salute** [sə 'lut] **1.** *tv.* to show respect for someone by bringing the right hand to one's head. □ *The soldier saluted the general.* **2.** *n.* an act of moving the hand to the head as in ①. □ *The general returned the soldier's salute.*

**same** ['sem] **1.** *adj.* not different; being the identical person or thing. □ *Mary read the same book twice.* **2.** *adj.* being exactly like someone or something else; not different from someone or something else; alike. □ *Anne and Susan both have the same kind of car.* **3. the same as someone or something** *phr.* identical to someone or something. □ *This book is almost the same as that one except for the cover.*

**sameness** ['sem nəs] *n.* the quality of being the same; the degree of being very similar to someone or something. (No plural form.) □ *The sameness of the twins made it hard to tell them apart.*

**sample** ['sæm pəl] **1.** *n.* a small portion of something that shows what the rest of it is like. □ *The clerk offered me a small sample of perfume.* **2.** *tv.* to take, try, or taste a small portion of something. □ *I sampled the cheese spread at the display table in the store.*

**sanctuary** ['sæŋk tʃu ɛr i] **1.** *n.* a sacred or holy building; a holy place of worship. □ *The worship service is always held in the sanctuary of the church.* **2.** *n.* a place of safety or preservation, especially for birds and other wild animals. □ *You can see many unusual birds at the zoo's bird sanctuary.*

S

**sand** ['sænd] **1.** *n.* very tiny particles of rock or seashells such as are found on beaches and in deserts. (Plural only when referring to different kinds, types, instances, or varieties. Number is expressed with *grain(s) of sand.*) □ *I got sand in my shoes when I walked on the beach.* Ⓒ *The sands of Hawaiian beaches are likely to be made from lava.* **2.** *tv.* to rub something with sandpaper to make it smooth; to smooth something with sandpaper. □ *The carpenter sanded the railing to remove the splinters.* **3.** *tv.* to put or sprinkle ① on a surface, such as an icy street. □ *The city trucks sanded the icy roads.*

**sandpaper** ['sænd pe pɚ] *n.* a paper lightly coated with sand particles, used to polish or smooth a surface. (Plural only when referring to different kinds, types, instances, or varieties.) □ *Mary sanded the wooden railing with sandpaper to remove the splinters.* Ⓒ *Different sandpapers are meant to be used on different surfaces.*

**sandwich** ['sænd wɪtʃ] **1.** *n.* two pieces of bread with some kind of food in between. □ *Mary ate a jelly sandwich for lunch.* **2.** *tv.* to put someone or something tightly between or among other persons or objects. □ *The librarian sandwiched the book into a tight space on the shelf.*

**sane** ['sen] **1.** *adj.* having a healthy mind; not crazy. (Adv: *sanely.* Comp: *saner;* sup: *sanest.*) □ *Some patients at the mental hospital claimed they were sane.* **2.** *adj.* rational; sensible; having or showing common sense. (Adv: *sanely.* Comp: *saner;* sup: *sanest.*) □ *Do you have any sane reason for not wearing your seat belt?*

S

**sang** ['sæŋ] pt of **sing**.

**sanitary** ['sæn ə tɛr i] **1.** *adj.* very clean; not dangerous to one's health. (Adv: *sanitarily.*) □ *The doctor's office was extremely sanitary.* **2.** *adj.* used for the disposal of waste that is harmful to health. □ *The garbage was hauled to a sanitary landfill.*

**sanitation** [sæn ə 'te ʃən] *n.* the study and practice of preserving the health of the public, especially concerning the removal of waste. (No plural form.) □ *The city's Department of Sanitation oversees garbage removal.*

**sanity** ['sæn ə ti] *n.* sound mental health. (No plural form.) □ *The defendant's sanity was questioned during the trial.*

**sank** ['sæŋk] a pt of **sink**.

**sap** ['sæp] **1.** *n.* [in a tree] a fluid that carries important nutrients to all of its parts. (No plural form.) □ *The farmer made maple syrup by boiling sap from maple trees.* **2.** *tv.* to take away someone or something's strength or energy. □ *The continuing war sapped the strength of the nation's economy.*

**sarcasm** ['sɑr kæz əm] *n.* the use of words that have the opposite meaning from what is said. (No plural form.) □ *Jane's voice was filled with sarcasm when she said her day went well.*

**sarcastic** [sɑr 'kæs tɪk] *adj.* using sarcasm; using irony; mocking. (Adv: *sarcastically* [...ɪk li].) □ *John's sarcastic comments insulted David.*

**sat** ['sæt] pt/pp of **sit**.

**Satan** ['set n] *n.* the devil. □ *Satan rules in hell.*

**satellite** ['sæt ə lɑɪt] **1.** *n.* a natural body of rock and minerals that orbits around a planet; a moon. □ *The moon is Earth's only satellite.* **2.** *n.* a spacecraft that orbits a planet. □ *The television signal was broadcast live from a satellite.* **3.** *adj.* dependent on something else that has more power. □ *The university operates a rural satellite college where farm children can get an education.*

**satin** ['sæt n] **1.** *n.* a soft, silky, smooth cloth that is shiny on one side. (Plural only when referring to different kinds, types, instances, or varieties.) □ *The princess wore a gown of pink satin.* Ⓒ *Satins and silks are very expensive.* **2.** *adj.* made from ①. □ *The beds in this expensive hotel have satin sheets.*

**satisfaction** [sæt ɪs 'fæk ʃən] *n.* a feeling that one is content; fulfillment. (Plural only when referring to different kinds, types, instances, or varieties.) □

*The salesclerk wanted me to have complete satisfaction with my purchase.* Ⓒ *Eating fine food is one of the satisfactions I get from being a food critic.*

**satisfactory** [sæt ɪs 'fæk tə ri] *adj.* adequate; meeting certain needs or requirements. (Adv: *satisfactorily.*) □ *The plumber did a satisfactory job of fixing my leaky sink.*

**satisfy** ['sæt ɪs fɑɪ] **1.** *tv.* to make someone content; to please someone; to make someone happy with something. □ *The clerk satisfied me by helping me find what I wanted.* **2.** *tv.* to meet or fulfill certain needs or requirements. □ *I satisfied the foreign-language requirement by learning French.*

**Saturday** ['sæt ɚ de] Go to **day**.

**sauce** ['sɔs] *n.* a liquid that is put on food to add flavor to the food. (Plural only when referring to different kinds, types, instances, or varieties.) □ *I poured some tomato sauce on top of my spaghetti.* Ⓒ *There is a choice of sauces for your pasta.*

**saucer** ['sɔ sɚ] *n.* a small dish that cups are set on. □ *Anne spilled her coffee, but it landed on her saucer instead of on the tablecloth.*

**sausage** ['sɔ sɪdʒ] **1.** *n.* a food made of chopped meat mixed with spices (in the United States). (No plural form.) □ *David fried some sausage for dinner.* **2.** *n.* a food made of ① stuffed into a thin tube of animal intestine or artificial material and made into segments. □ *Please remember to buy a package of sausages.* **3.** *adj.* made with ①. □ *Would you like some sausage pizza, or would you prefer cheese?* □ *I prepared a sausage omelet for my supper.*

**savage** ['sæv ɪdʒ] **1.** *adj.* wild; not tamed; not civilized; primitive. (Adv: *savagely.*) □ *The savage child had been raised by bad parents.* **2.** *adj.* fierce; ready to fight; violent; vicious. (Adv: *savagely.*) □ *The savage dog barked at the mail carrier.* **3.** *n.* someone who is wild, not tamed, and not civilized. □ *I assure you that I am not a savage! I am highly educated.*

**save** ['sev] **1.** *tv.* to make someone or something safe from harm or danger; to rescue someone or something. □ *The crew of another boat saved the passengers from the sinking boat.* **2.** *tv.* to keep a supply of something, especially money, for future use; to place something aside, especially money, for future use. □ *Anne saved 25% of each paycheck for retirement.* **3.** *tv.* not to spend something; not to use something; to reserve something. □ *I saved gas by not making unnecessary trips.* **4.** *tv.* to cause something to be unnecessary (for someone); to prevent the need (for someone) to do something. □ *Buying the new model will save you time and money.*

**savings** ['sev ɪŋz] *n.* money that is saved for future use; money that is set aside, especially in a bank account, for future use. (Treated as plural, but not countable.) □ *John's surgery wiped out all his savings.*

**savings account** ['sev ɪŋz ə 'kɑʊnt] *n.* a bank account that is intended for saving money over a long period of time. □ *I put half of each week's pay into my savings account.*

**saw** ['sɔ] **1.** pt of **see**. **2.** *n.* a cutting tool with a thin blade that is notched with tiny, sharp teeth. □ *The carpenter replaced the blade of the saw with a sharper one.* **3.** *iv., irreg.* to cut with ②. (Pt: *sawed;* pp: *sawed* or **sawn**.) □ *The carpenter sawed until the board had been cut.* **4.** *tv., irreg.* to cut something with ②. □ *The carpenter sawed the thick beam carefully.*

**sawn** ['sɔn] a pp of **saw**.

**say** ['se] **1.** *tv., irreg.* to pronounce words; to speak words. (Pt/pp: **said**.) □ *Anne always says her words clearly and distinctly.* **2.** *tv., irreg.* to state something;

to declare something; to express something in words. (The object can be a clause with **that** ⑦.) ☐ *"This soup tastes delicious," said Jane.* ☐ *Jane said the soup tasted delicious.* **3.** *n.* a role of authority or influence [in making a decision]. (No plural form.) ☐ *I have no say in the matter.* ☐ *My boss has the final say on the department budget.*

**scale** ['skel] **1.** *n.* a series of numbers at different levels, used for measuring something. ☐ *In America, temperature is measured using the Fahrenheit scale.* **2.** *n.* the relation between a measurement on a map or design compared to the actual measurement it corresponds to. ☐ *This map's scale is one inch to every 100 miles.* **3.** *n.* a series of musical notes, from low notes to high notes or from high notes to low notes. ☐ *The musical scale in Western music is a mixture of whole steps and half steps.* **4.** *n.* the size or extent of something, especially as compared to something else or an average. (No plural form.) ☐ *The earthquake caused destruction on a very large scale.* **5.** *n.* a device that measures how much something weighs. (Singular or plural with the same meaning.) ☐ *The butcher weighed the sliced ham on a scale.* **6.** *n.* one of the small, thin pieces of hardened skin on the bodies of most fish and snakes. ☐ *John scraped the fish's scales off with a knife.* **7.** *n.* a flake of something, especially dead skin. ☐ *When Mary scratched her elbow, scales of dead skin flaked off.* **8.** *tv.* to climb something. ☐ *The climber scaled the mountain.* **9.** *tv.* to remove ⑥ from a fish. ☐ *John scaled the perch with a knife.* **10. scale** something **down** *tv.* + *obj.* + *adv.* to make something smaller by a certain amount. ☐ *They scaled Jane's salary down by 10% last year.* 🅃 *They scaled down everyone's salary.*

**scalp** ['skælp] *n.* the skin and any hair growing on it on the top and back of the head. ☐ *My scalp gets sunburned where my hair is thin.*

**scan** ['skæn] **1.** *tv.* to examine something closely and carefully, as though one were searching for something. ☐ *The detective scanned the room for clues.* **2.** *tv.* to look through something quickly and carelessly; to glance at something; to read through something quickly. ☐ *Mary only scanned the contract before signing it.* **3.** *tv.* to put a picture or a text into a computer file by placing the picture or book on a scanner. ☐ *Rather than type the article again, I scanned it into the computer.*

**scandal** ['skæn dəl] *n.* an event that causes disgrace; an instance of actions that are not legal, moral, or ethical and that become known by other people. ☐ *The tax scandal caused the company treasurer to be fired.*

**scanner** ['skæn ɚ] *n.* a machine that converts a page of a book or a picture to an image that can be stored, viewed, or changed on a computer. ☐ *Bill placed his photograph on the scanner.*

**scar** ['skɑr] **1.** *n.* a mark that is left on the surface of something, such as skin, that has been torn, cut, burned, or otherwise damaged. ☐ *John has a scar on his leg where he cut himself when he was a child.* **2.** *tv.* to cause someone or something to have ①. ☐ *Jane scarred the marble floor by dragging a desk across it.*

**scarce** ['skɛrs] *adj.* rare; hard to find. (Adv: *scarcely.* Comp: *scarcer;* sup: *scarcest.*) ☐ *Fresh water was scarce during the long, hot summer.*

**scare** ['skɛr] **1.** *tv.* to cause someone to feel fear or fright; to cause someone to be afraid. ☐ *The thunder and lightning scared the small children.* **2.** *n.* a bad fright; an instance where one is afraid; a feeling of fear. ☐ *The angry dog gave the letter carrier a bad scare.*

S

**scared** ['skɛrd] *adj.* feeling fright; filled with fear. □ *Badly scared, I walked faster toward my apartment.*

**scarf** ['skɑrf] *n., irreg.* a long strip of cloth that is wrapped around the neck or face for decoration or to keep someone warm when it is cold. (Pl: **scarves**.) □ *John covered his mouth and nose with his scarf while outside.*

**scarves** ['skɑrvz] pl of **scarf**.

**scary** ['skɛr i] *adj.* causing fear; filling one with fear; causing one to be afraid. (Adv: *scarily.* Comp: *scarier;* sup: *scariest.*) □ *Driving through the terrible blizzard was very scary.*

**scatter** ['skæt ɚ] **1.** *tv.* to cause each person or thing in a group to move in a different direction. □ *The wind scattered the leaves on the ground.* **2.** *tv.* to spread things—such as seeds, papers, ashes, etc.—over a wide area by throwing them. □ *The seeds had been scattered across the field.* **3.** *iv.* [for each person or thing in a group] to move in a different direction. □ *The papers on my desk scattered when the wind blew.*

**scene** ['sin] **1.** *n.* all that can be seen from one place. □ *The tourist surveyed the scene from the castle's window.* **2.** *n.* the place where something happens; a setting. □ *The police rushed to the scene of the crime.* **3.** *n.* a division of an act of a play; an incident in a movie or play. □ *I left the horrible play in the first scene of the first act.* **4.** *n.* a display of emotion or action, especially an angry or violent action. □ *If there is going to be a scene, I'm leaving.*

**scenery** ['sin (ə) ri] **1.** *n.* the natural surroundings, trees, mountains, etc., of an area. (No plural form.) □ *The tourism department described the country's natural scenery.* **2.** *n.* the things that are built or bought and put on a stage to represent the place where the action of a play takes place. (No plural form.) □ *Four actors were injured when the scenery collapsed on the stage.*

**scent** ['sɛnt] **1.** *n.* a smell; an aroma; an odor; the way someone or something smells. □ *The scent of certain perfumes makes me sneeze.* **2.** *tv.* to sense the smell of someone or something. □ *I scented a cigarette smoker somewhere in the room.*

**schedule** ['skɛ dʒəl] **1.** *n.* a list showing the times that events are supposed to happen. □ *According to the schedule, the plane should have landed by now.* **2.** *tv.* to put someone or something on a list or **schedule** ① for an event that happens at a particular time. □ *They scheduled me for an early flight.* **3. behind schedule** *phr.* not done by the time listed on the **schedule** ①. □ *We have to hurry and finish soon because we are behind schedule.* **4. ahead of schedule** *phr.* done before the time listed on the **schedule** ①. □ *We don't have to rush because we are ahead of schedule.*

**scheme** ['skim] **1.** *n.* a plan; a method for doing something; a way of doing something, possibly dishonestly. □ *The newspaper revealed the president's scheme to raise taxes.* **2.** *iv.* to plot; to make plans, especially dishonest ones. □ *The criminal schemed and schemed, planning a bank robbery.*

**scholar** ['skɑl ɚ] **1.** *n.* someone who studies a subject thoroughly. □ *My mother was a famous scholar in philosophy.* **2.** *n.* a student; a pupil. □ *In the library, many young scholars were studying for exams.* **3.** *n.* someone who has a scholarship. □ *Each year, the scholars were required to apply again for their scholarships.*

**scholarly** ['skɑl ɚ li] **1.** *adj.* concerning scholarship and schoolwork. □ *Her scholarly efforts earned her a fellowship at the university.* **2.** *adj.* having a lot of knowledge about a certain subject.

□ *Jane acts quite scholarly even though she has not gone to college.*

**scholarship** ['skɑl ɚ ʃɪp] **1.** *n.* knowledge that a person receives by studying; evidence of one's knowledge. (No plural form.) □ *My four books are proof of my scholarship in economics.* **2.** *n.* a sum of money given by an organization to a student for school fees or other expenses related to studying. □ *I applied for several scholarships to help pay for school.*

**school** ['skul] **1.** *n.* a building for education and instruction. □ *There are 800 students at the school where I teach.* **2.** *n.* all the people who work at and attend a school; all the people who study and teach at a school. □ *The principal spoke to the school about drug abuse.* **3.** *n.* a group of fish that swim together. □ *A school of fish swam toward the reef.* **4.** *n.* the education system; participation in the education system. (No plural form.) □ *I am glad to be free from school.*

**schoolchild** ['skul tʃɑɪld] *n., irreg.* a child of school age, especially a child in grades kindergarten through eighth grade; a child who attends school. (Pl: schoolchildren.) □ *The teacher told the schoolchild to stop running.*

**schoolchildren** ['skul tʃɪl drɪn] pl of schoolchild.

S

**schoolroom** ['skul rum] *n.* a room in a school building, especially one where students are taught. □ *The children decorated the schoolroom with their own art.*

**schoolteacher** ['skul titʃ ɚ] *n.* someone who teaches in a school. □ *The schoolteacher taught fractions to the students.*

**schoolwork** ['skul wɚk] *n.* work that a student must do for a class; the assigned projects that a student must do. (See also homework. No plural form.) □ *Susie was not allowed to watch TV until she finished her schoolwork.*

**science** ['sɑɪ əns] **1.** *n.* a system of knowledge obtained by testing and proving facts that describe the way something acts, functions, or exists. (No plural form.) □ *The researcher's conclusions were well rooted in science.* **2.** *n.* a kind of study that results in a system of knowledge obtained by testing and proving facts that describe the way something acts, functions, or exists. □ *Biology is the science of living things.*

**scientific** [sɑɪ ən 'tɪf ɪk] **1.** *adj.* using the laws or facts of a science. (Adv: *scientifically* [...ɪk li].) □ *The chemical was created through a scientific process.* **2.** *adj.* of or about science. (Adv: *scientifically* [...ɪk li].) □ *Our school purchased a lot of new scientific equipment.* □ *The library has a large number of scientific journals.*

**scientist** ['sɑɪ ən tɪst] *n.* someone who is skilled in a science; someone who works in a science. □ *The scientist explained lightning to us.*

**scissors** ['sɪz ɚz] *n.* a set of two sharp blades that have handles on one end and are connected in the middle. (Treated as singular or plural. Number is expressed with *pair(s) of scissors.*) □ *You should carry scissors with the sharp end pointed downward.*

**scold** ['skold] **1.** *tv.* to speak angrily to someone who has done something wrong. □ *The teacher scolded Jimmy for running in the classroom.* **2.** *n.* someone who scolds as in ①. □ *Tom's mother is a terrible scold.*

**scolding** ['skol dɪŋ] *n.* speaking angrily to someone as punishment. □ *The principal gave Susie a scolding for swearing in class.*

**scoop** ['skup] **1.** *n.* a shovel-like utensil or tool. □ *John removed the dead leaves from the swimming pool with a scoop.* **2.** *n.* the contents of ①. □ *Mary added a scoop of sugar to the lemonade.*

**scope** ['skop] *n.* the range of something; the limit of something; the extent of something. (No plural form.) □ *Those questions aren't within the scope of my research.*

**score** ['skor] **1.** *n.* the number of points that a person or team has received in a game or contest; the number of points that a person has received on a test. □ *The best student only got a score of 89 on the difficult test.* **2.** *n.* a written piece of music for instruments or voices. □ *The score was written for four voices.* **3.** *n.* a group of twenty things. □ *Scores of people were injured in the accident.* **4.** *tv.* to earn one or more points in a game or contest. □ *Bill scored a point for the team when he touched home plate.* **5.** *tv.* to cut lines, or grooves, into a surface; to cut a surface with a series of lines. □ *The designer scored the cardboard before splitting it in half.* **6.** *tv.* to earn a certain number of points on a test. □ *If you score a 90, you'll get an A.* **7.** *iv.* to achieve [a level of performance in academic grades]. □ *None of the students in the class scored above an 80.* **8.** *iv.* to earn [a point in a game or contest]. □ *The contestant scores for each correct answer he or she gives.*

**scowl** ['skaʊl] **1.** *n.* a frown; an angry look. □ *From Anne's scowl, I knew that she was upset.* **2.** *iv.* to look angry; to frown. □ *Mary scowled at the loud people sitting next to her.*

**scrap** ['skræp] **1.** *n.* a small piece of something, especially a small piece of something that is left over from a larger piece, especially of food or cloth. □ *John threw all the scraps into the trash.* **2.** *n.* material, such as metal, that can be reused. (No plural form.) □ *John sold his old car for scrap.* **3.** *tv.* to throw something away that is no longer wanted, needed, or able to be used. □ *Mary scrapped her broken radio.*

**scrape** ['skrep] **1.** *tv.* to damage something by rubbing a sharp or rough object against it. □ *Bob scraped the wall with a knife, damaging the wallpaper.* **2.** *tv.* to remove something by scraping and rubbing. □ *The janitor scraped the dried gum from the bottom of the chairs.* **3.** *iv.* to rub with force against something else. □ *The car scraped on the brick wall as it passed.* **4.** *n.* damage or injury to an object or skin caused by rubbing something sharp or rough against it. □ *I got a bad scrape on my knee when I fell onto the pavement.* **5.** *n.* the sound that is made when one object **scrapes** ③ against something else. □ *The scrape of fingernails against a chalkboard is terrible.*

**scratch** ['skrætʃ] **1.** *tv.* to damage an object's surface by causing a sharp object to make a cut or tear in it; to make a cut or tear in the surface of something with a sharp object. □ *The cat scratched the piano leg with its claws.* **2.** *tv.* to remove something from the surface of something using a sharp object to cut or tear into it. □ *Bill scratched the paint off the window with his fingernail.* **3.** *tv.* to rub a location of the body that itches with one's fingers, fingernails, or a sharp object. □ *Dave scratched his arm because it itched.* **4.** *iv.* to rub [a part of the body that itches]. □ *Because the puppy was scratching, I gave it a bath.* **5.** *n.* a cut, tear, or mark made by **scratching** as in ①. □ *When you moved the desk, you put a scratch in the wall.*

**scream** ['skrim] **1.** *iv.* [for someone] to make a very loud noise, especially when hurt, afraid, excited, surprised, or filled with emotion. □ *John screamed just before a truck hit our car.* **2.** *iv.* to speak very loudly; to talk in a very loud voice. □ *I can hear you fine. You don't have to scream at me.* **3.** *tv.* to say something in a very loud voice. (The object can be a clause with **that** ⑦.) □ *Mary screamed* *her response because John doesn't hear well.* **4.** *n.* a very loud noise, especially made by someone who is hurt, afraid, excited, surprised, or filled with emotion. □ *Sue let out a scream of surprise when she opened the box.*

**screen** ['skrin] **1.** *n.* a mesh made of thin wires crossing each other. □ *John put screens on the windows in April.* **2.** *n.* a piece of cloth stretched over a frame, used to block, protect, or separate someone or something from someone or something else. □ *The actress changed costumes behind a screen.* **3.** *n.* a large white surface that movies are projected onto. □ *An image of a large red rose flashed onto the screen.* **4.** *n.* the glass part of a television set or computer monitor on which images are seen. □ *Susan read the data on Mary's computer screen.* **5.** *tv.* to determine if someone will be allowed to speak or meet with someone else. □ *A butler screened the diplomat's visitors.* **6.** *tv.* to show a movie; to make a movie available to the public. □ *Hometown Theater will screen an award-winning drama tomorrow afternoon.*

**screw** ['skru] **1.** *n.* a piece of metal, similar to a nail, having a groove wrapped around its shaft. (A screw has a flat or rounded head that has a single groove or two crossed grooves.) □ *The metal chair was held together with screws.* **2.** *tv.* to fasten something to something else with ①. □ *The carpenter screwed the boards to the wall.* **3.** *tv.* to twist ① into wood or metal with a screwdriver. □ *Tom screwed the screw into the wood.* **4.** *tv.* to turn the lid, cap, or top of a container to close it tightly. □ *John screwed the cap onto the tube of toothpaste.*

**screwdriver** ['skru draɪ vɚ] *n.* a very common tool used to tighten and loosen screws. □ *A regular screwdriver fits into a narrow groove.*

**scribble** ['skrɪb əl] **1.** *tv.* to draw or write something quickly or in a messy way, especially so that it is hard to recognize or read. (The object can be a clause with that ⑦.) □ *Write carefully and don't scribble your name.* **2.** *iv.* to draw or write quickly or in a messy way so that the result is hard to recognize or read. □ *The two-year-old child scribbled with a crayon.* **3.** *n.* marks or words that are hard to recognize or read because they were drawn or written quickly or in a messy way. □ *How do you expect me to be able to read this scribble?*

**script** ['skrɪpt] **1.** *n.* a document containing the words of a play, movie, or speech. □ *The actors underlined their own lines in their scripts.* **2.** *n.* a way of writing so that the letters of a word are joined together. □ *She can read printing, but she has problems with script.*

**scripture** ['skrɪp tʃɚ] *n.* holy writings; one or more holy writings. (Plural only when referring to different kinds, types, or varieties. Singular or plural with the same meaning.) □ *The Koran is the book of Islamic scripture.* 🄲 *What do the scriptures say about this?*

**scrub** ['skrʌb] **1.** *tv.* to clean or wash the surface of someone or something by rubbing. □ *John scrubbed the carpet thoroughly.* **2.** *tv.* to remove something from something by rubbing. □ *John scrubbed the stain from the carpet.* **3.** *iv.* to clean or wash [oneself] by rubbing, usually with a stiff brush, cloth, or sponge. □ *I scrubbed and scrubbed, but I couldn't remove the ink from my fingers.* **4.** *n.* an area of small trees and low bushes; a collection of small trees and bushes. (No plural form.) □ *Nothing will grow in this poor soil except scrub.*

**scrutinize** ['skrut n aɪz] *tv.* to examine someone or something closely; to look at something very closely; to inspect someone or something. □ *My lawyer scrutinized my contract carefully.*

**scrutiny** ['skrut n i] **1.** *n.* a close examination; an inspection; looking at something closely. (No plural form.) ☐ *I gave the contract a lot of scrutiny, and it looks fine.* **2. under scrutiny** *phr.* being watched or examined closely; with close examination. ☐ *A politician's actions are always under scrutiny.*

**scuba** ['sku bə] **1. scuba (diving)** *n.* diving or exploring underwater with a tank containing air, allowing a diver to breathe, that can be carried or worn on the back. (No plural form. An acronym for *self-contained underwater breathing apparatus.*) ☐ *Scuba requires special equipment and training.* **2.** *iv.* to dive and explore underwater as in ①. (Pt: *scubaed.*) ☐ *I took lessons so I could scuba in the nearby lake.* **3.** *adj.* <the adj. use of **scuba**.> ☐ *A good scuba tank is very expensive.*

**scuba diver** ['sku bə 'dɑɪ vɚ] *n.* someone who does scuba diving. ☐ *Scuba divers wear fins and use snorkels.*

**scuff** ['skʌf] **1.** *tv.* to make scratches in the surface of something clean and smooth; to make marks on the surface of something clean and smooth. ☐ *John scuffed the clean floor with his shoes.* **2.** *iv.* to walk somewhere without picking up one's feet; to slide one's feet along as one walks. ☐ *Tired, Mary scuffed along the carpet toward the bed.*

**sculptor** ['skʌlp tɚ] *n.* an artist who makes art out of clay, stone, metal, or other solid materials. ☐ *The sculptor bent some metal rods into a work of art.*

**sculpture** ['skʌlp tʃɚ] **1.** *n.* the art of making art from clay, stone, metal, or another solid material. (No plural form.) ☐ *The art students all had to take a class in sculpture.* ☐ *Sculpture is the art of shaping solid materials.* **2.** *n.* a piece of art that is made out of clay, stone, metal, or another solid material. (Often singular with a plural meaning.) ☐ *Don't touch any of the sculptures at the museum.*

**sea** ['si] **1.** *n.* a large body of salt water that is smaller than an ocean. ☐ *The Mediterranean Sea is located south of Europe.* **2.** *n.* one of the large bodies of salt water that cover almost three-fourths of the earth's surface; an ocean. ☐ *The old sailor had spent his life on the sea.*

**seafood** ['si fud] *n.* animals from the sea, including fish, shellfish, and octopus, that are eaten as food. (No plural form.) ☐ *The restaurants in the town by the sea served a lot of seafood.*

**seal** ['sil] **1.** *n.* a large animal that has thick, coarse fur, lives in and near water, and has flat legs. ☐ *Some seals can bark like a dog.* **2.** *n.* an official mark or design of a government, business, organization, or person, which is printed or stamped on objects for identification. (A signature usually serves as a seal for an individual.) ☐ *I had to place my seal at the bottom of the document.* **3.** *n.* a piece of wax, metal, or other material that has the mark or design of a government, business, organization, or person printed or stamped on it. ☐ *Mary placed the company's seal on the confidential file.* **4.** *n.* something that causes an opening in an object to remain closed; something that prevents an opening from being opened secretly. ☐ *When I twisted open the jar, I tore the plastic seal.* **5.** *tv.* to close something tightly; to fasten something tightly, often with glue or pressure. ☐ *I put the cucumbers in a quart jar and sealed the lid tightly.* **6.** *tv.* to fill cracks in an object with a substance so that air, water, or other things cannot pass through the cracks. ☐ *Dave sealed the space between the window and the frame with glue.*

**sea level** ['si lɛv əl] *n.* the horizontal level at the surface of the oceans, which is usually close to zero. □ *Sea level is exactly between low and high tide.*

**seam** ['sim] **1.** *n.* the line of thread where two pieces of cloth have been sewn together. □ *The seam in the seat of my pants split open!* **2.** *n.* the line where two edges of anything meet. □ *A metal strip covered the seam between the carpet and the tile.*

**search** ['sɚtʃ] **1.** *iv.* to look carefully, trying to find someone or something. □ *David searched throughout the house for his lost keys.* **2.** *tv.* to examine someone or something closely to try to find something. □ *The police searched the scene of the crime for evidence.* **3.** *n.* an attempt to find someone or something. □ *John's search for his missing dog was not successful.*

**seashell** ['si ʃɛl] *n.* a shell of an animal that lives in the sea; a hard, protective covering made by an animal that lives in the sea, such as an oyster. □ *Anne walked along the beach, picking up pretty seashells.*

**seashore** ['si ʃor] *n.* the land that borders the sea; the shore that runs along a sea. □ *Anne rented a small cabin at the seashore for a relaxing week.*

**seasick** ['si sɪk] *adj.* being sick while on a boat or a ship because of the movement of the sea. □ *The seasick passenger went to the bathroom to vomit.*

S

**seaside** ['si sɑɪd] **1.** *n.* the land that borders a sea; the seashore. (No plural form.) □ *The lifeguard sat at the seaside, watching the swimmers.* **2.** *adj.* located on the seashore; at the side of the sea. □ *The seaside restaurant served fresh seafood.*

**season** ['siz ən] **1.** *n.* one of the four times of year: winter, spring, summer, and fall. □ *The seasons are caused by the tilt of the earth's axis.* **2.** *n.* a period of time marked by a certain kind of weather, an activity, or condition. □ *The theater company presented four plays last season.* **3.** *tv.* to add spices to food to make it taste better or different. □ *The cook seasoned the stew with herbs and spices.*

**seasonal** ['siz ə nəl] *adj.* <the adj. form of **season** ②.> (Adv: *seasonally.*) □ *One of the seasonal changes of spring is that the days become longer.*

**seasoning** ['siz (ə) nɪŋ] *n.* a spice; an herb; something that is added to food to make it taste better or different. □ *The seasoning in this salad is very tasty!*

**seat belt** ['sit bɛlt] *n.* a strap that buckles across one's lap, as in a car or an airplane. (See also **safety belt.**) □ *Anne told her passengers to fasten their seat belts.*

**seated** ['sit ɪd] *adj.* sitting down, in, or on something. □ *The seated audience listened to the speaker.*

**seating** ['sit ɪŋ] **1.** *n.* a particular arrangement of seats. (No plural form.) □ *The seating at the party was indicated by name cards.* **2.** *n.* the number of seats that are available in a place. (No plural form.) □ *The movie theater had seating for two hundred.*

**sea water** ['si wɔt ɚ] *n.* salt water as found in the sea. □ *You cannot drink sea water.*

**seaweed** ['si wid] *n.* a plant that grows in or at the edge of the sea. (Plural only when referring to different kinds, types, instances, or varieties.) □ *We couldn't see the bottom of the shallow part of the sea because there was too much seaweed.* Ⓒ *Some seaweeds are edible, but most are too tough.*

**seclude** [sɪ 'klud] *tv.* to keep someone away from other people; to keep something away from other things or places. □ *Mary secluded herself from her friends because she had to study.*

**secluded** [sɪ 'klud ɪd] *adj.* private; remote; set apart from other places;

kept away from other places or people. (Adv: *secludedly.*) □ *My parents live in a secluded cabin in northern Michigan.*

**seclusion** [sɪ 'klu ʒən] *n.* the condition of being private and hidden; a place away from other people. (No plural form.) □ *The remote village lay in total seclusion from the rest of the world.*

**second** ['sɛk ənd] **1.** *n.* a basic unit of the measurement of time; 1/60 of a minute; 1/3,600 of an hour. □ *One minute is equal to sixty seconds.* **2.** *n.* a moment; a very short period of time. □ *I'll be finished in a few seconds.* **3.** *n.* a unit of measurement of an angle equal to 1/60 of a minute or 1/3,600 of a degree. □ *42 degrees, 10 minutes, and 6 seconds is written:* 42°10′6″. **4.** *n.* someone or something that is **second** ⑥. □ *I will choose the second from the right.* **5. seconds** *n.* an additional serving of food. (Treated as plural.) □ *Would anyone care for seconds?* **6.** *adj.* coming, happening, or being after the first. (Adv: *secondly.*) □ *The athlete in second place received a silver medal.* **7.** *adv.* in **second** ⑥ position; in a position that is after the first position. □ *First, I will share my results; second, I will answer questions.*

**secondary** ['sɛk ən dɛr i] **1.** *adj.* second in importance; not primary. (Adv: *secondarily.*) □ *All of the mayor's concerns were secondary to fighting crime.* **2.** *adj.* [of the education of students] from the 6th to 12th or from the 9th to 12th grades, depending on the school district. □ *After graduating from a secondary school, Jane went to college.*

**secondhand** ['sɛk ənd 'hænd] **1.** *adj.* [of goods] already used by someone else; not new. □ *Jimmy wore secondhand shirts from his older brothers.* **2.** *adj.* [of stores] selling used products. □ *John buys his clothes cheaply at secondhand stores.* **3.** *adj.* not experienced directly but heard from another person. □ *Bill repeated the secondhand gossip to Mary.* **4.** *adv.* learned from someone else. □ *Anne heard the gossip secondhand from Bill.*

**secrecy** ['si krɪ si] *n.* the quality of being secret; keeping something a secret. (No plural form.) □ *The state's secrecy about the tax scandal angered the citizens.*

**secret** ['si krɪt] **1.** *n.* information known by a small number of people, especially people who have promised not to tell anyone else. □ *I'll tell you a secret, but you can't tell anyone.* **2.** *n.* a mystery; something that cannot be explained. □ *Only Tom understands the secret of getting his car to run.* **3.** *adj.* known only by a small number of people who have promised not to tell anyone else. (Adv: *secretly.*) □ *John used the secret information to blackmail the mayor.* **4.** *adj.* working at a job without others knowing what one does; doing something without others knowing what one is doing. (Adv: *secretly.*) □ *The secret agent couldn't tell me about her job.*

**secretary** ['sɛk rɪ tɛr i] **1.** *n.* someone who is employed in an office to type letters, answer telephones, organize schedules and meetings, and do other office work. □ *David's secretary opened his mail for him.* **2.** *n.* someone who keeps a written record of the things that are discussed at the official meetings of an organization. □ *The secretary asked me to speak a little louder.* **3.** *n.* someone who is in charge of a department of the United States government. □ *Henry Kissinger was the secretary of state from 1973 to 1977.* **4.** *n.* a writing desk with drawers and shelves. □ *John locked his papers inside the secretary.*

**secrete** [sɪ 'krit] **1.** *tv.* [for a part of a plant or an animal] to produce and release a fluid. □ *The eye secretes tears.* **2.** *tv.* to hide something; to put something in a place where others cannot see it or find it. □ *Mary secreted the money between the pages of a book.*

S

**secretion** [sɪ 'kri ʃən] *n.* a fluid that is produced and released by a part of a plant or an animal, such as mucus or sap. (Singular or plural with the same meaning, but not countable.) □ *John collected the tree's secretions in a wooden bucket.*

**secretive** ['si krə tɪv] *adj.* tending to do things secretly; tending not to do things publicly or openly. (Adv: *secretively.*) □ *The secretive man told his wife nothing of the trouble he was in.*

**secretly** ['si krət li] *adv.* without being known or seen by others. □ *John secretly told the reporter important political information.*

**section** ['sɛk ʃən] **1.** *n.* a separate part of a larger group, place, or thing; a division. □ *The student read the final section of each chapter.* **2.** *n.* a unit of measurement of land equal to one square mile or 640 acres. □ *The farmer owned half a section of land, or 320 acres.* **3.** *tv.* to divide something into separate parts as in ①. □ *The old warehouse had been sectioned into twelve apartments.*

**secure** [sɪ 'kjʊr] **1.** *adj.* safe from danger, harm, loss, injury, or theft. (Adv: *securely.*) □ *The jewels were secure in the hotel's vault.* **2.** *tv.* to safely fasten or close something. □ *The passengers on the plane secured their seat belts.* **3.** *tv.* to obtain something. □ *Do you know where I can secure a good hotel room for the night?*

**security** [sɪ 'kjʊr ə ti] **1.** *n.* the state of being or feeling safe from danger, harm, loss, injury, or theft. (No plural form.) □ *Anne liked the security of living in a small town.* **2.** *n.* an office or department concerned with protection of people and property. (No plural form.) □ *Jane called security when a stranger entered the office.* **3.** *n.* property that is promised to a bank or lender when money is borrowed. (If the money is not paid back, then the bank or lender will be given the property. No plural form.) □ *The bank retains ownership in your new car as security on the loan.* **4.** *n.* a monetary asset or debt agreement, such as a stock or a bond. □ *Bill sold all his securities and retired.* **5.** *adj.* <the adj. use of ②.> □ *As a security measure, the workers showed their identification at the entrance.*

**sedan** [sɪ 'dæn] *n.* a car with four doors, a front seat and a back seat, a fixed roof, and room for at least four people. □ *My friends and I rented a sedan when we drove to Texas.*

**sedate** [sɪ 'det] **1.** *adj.* quiet; calm; relaxed; not excited; not moved by excitement. (Adv: *sedately.*) □ *The sedate man quietly read his newspaper.* **2.** *tv.* to give someone or an animal a drug that causes relaxation. □ *The surgeons sedated me before the operation.*

**sedative** ['sɛd ə tɪv] **1.** *n.* a drug or medicine that causes one to sleep or relax. □ *The nurse gave the patient a sedative at bedtime.* **2.** *adj.* <the adj. use of ①.> □ *The soft music had a sedative effect on Anne.*

**sedentary** ['sɛd n tɛr i] **1.** *adj.* [of a creature] not very active and keeping still most of the time. (Adv: *sedentarily* [sɛd n 'tɛr ə li].) □ *Our old dog has become very sedentary.* **2.** *adj.* [of activity] not requiring a lot of movement. (Adv: *sedentarily* [sɛd n 'tɛr ə li].) □ *Driving a car is a sedentary activity.*

**see** ['si] **1.** *iv., irreg.* to sense or experience with the eyes. (Pt: **saw**; pp: **seen**.) □ *After the operation, I could see without my glasses.* **2.** *tv., irreg.* to observe someone or something by the use of the eyes; to sense or experience someone or something with the eyes. □ *Have you seen the new car that Jane has bought?* **3.** *tv., irreg.* to understand something; to comprehend something. (The object can be a clause with **that** ⑦.) □ *I don't see the importance of your last statement.*

**4.** *tv., irreg.* to learn something by reading or through direct observation. (The object can be a clause with **that** ⑦.) □ *In the newspaper, Mary saw how the economy was doing.* □ *She saw that it was doing well.* **5.** *tv., irreg.* to visit someone; to stop by the place where someone lives. □ *John went to the hospital to see his sick brother.* **6.** *tv., irreg.* to meet with someone for an appointment. □ *You're supposed to see the dentist at 3:00 today.* **7.** *tv., irreg.* to date someone; to have a romantic relationship with someone. □ *David was seeing someone briefly last year, but he is still single.*

**seed** ['sid] **1.** *n.* a part of a plant that a new plant will grow from if it is fertilized, similar to a fertilized egg in animals. □ *Anne spit the apple seeds from her mouth.* **2.** *tv.* to plant crops on an area of land by scattering ①. □ *This tractor can seed dozens of acres a day.*

**seedling** ['sid lɪŋ] *n.* a young plant or tree that is newly grown from a seed. □ *Anne bought some seedlings and planted them in her yard.*

**seedy** ['si di] **1.** *adj.* having a lot of seeds. (Comp: *seedier;* sup: *seediest.*) □ *This melon is very seedy.* **2.** *adj.* run-down; shabby. (Adv: *seedily.* Comp: *seedier;* sup: *seediest.*) □ *My rent is cheap, but I live in a seedy neighborhood.*

**seek** ['sik] **1.** *tv., irreg.* to try to find someone or something; to look for someone or something. (Pt/pp: **sought.**) □ *If you are seeking a new job, you should be prepared to learn new skills.* **2. seek to do something** *iv., irreg. + inf.* to try to do something; to attempt to do something; to pledge oneself to do something. □ *The detective sought to solve the crime.*

**seem** ['sim] *iv.* to appear to be a certain way; to give the impression of being a certain way. □ *The weather seems quite cold today.*

**seen** ['sin] pp of see.

**seep** ['sip] *iv.* [for a liquid] to pass through something slowly; to leak. □ *The muddy water seeped through the holes in my boots.*

**segment** ['sɛg mənt] **1.** *n.* a part of something; a part of something that can be easily separated. □ *John divided the line into one-inch segments.* **2.** *tv.* to separate something into parts; to divide something into parts. □ *The manager segmented the task and gave part to me and part to Jane.*

**segregate** ['sɛ grɪ get] **1.** *tv.* to separate someone or a group of people from other people; to isolate someone or a group of people. □ *This school segregates the slower learners from the students who learn more quickly.* **2.** *tv.* to separate people of one race from people of another race. □ *In many cities, blacks were segregated from whites.*

**segregated** ['sɛ grɪ get ɪd] *adj.* [of human races] separated by law or other forces. (Adv: *segregatedly.*) □ *The president called for an end to segregated society.*

**segregation** [sɛ grɪ 'ge ʃən] **1.** *n.* the state existing in a segregated society; the state of races being separated by law or other causes. (No plural form.) □ *Most people voted against the candidate who favored segregation.* **2.** *n.* the separation of someone or something from other things or people. (No plural form.) □ *The jail enforced the segregation of dangerous criminals.*

**seize** ['siz] **1.** *tv.* to grab, take, and hold on to someone or something. □ *The nurse seized the patient's arm as he fainted.* **2.** *tv.* to take control of something by force or by authority; to capture something by force or by authority. □ *The police seized the drug dealer's property.* **3.** *tv.* [for an emotion, idea, or feeling] to take (figurative) possession or control of someone or some creature.

S

(Fig. on ②.) □ *Panic seized John at the last minute before he was to jump.*

**seizure** ['si ʒɚ] **1.** *n.* an act of seizing someone or something. □ *The police had a court order for the seizure of the criminal's property.* **2.** *n.* a sudden attack of a sickness; a convulsion caused by a sudden attack of a sickness. □ *Soon after being poisoned, Bill began to have seizures.*

**seldom** ['sɛl dəm] *adv.* almost never; rarely. □ *It seldom rains in the desert.*

**select** [sə 'lɛkt] **1.** *tv.* to pick someone or something from a group of choices. □ *The faculty selected ten new students for the program.* **2.** *adj.* specifically chosen; exclusive; specially chosen. (Adv: *selectly.*) □ *A select few were invited to the mayor's party.*

**selection** [sə 'lɛk ʃən] **1.** *n.* a choice; someone or something that is chosen; someone or something that is selected. □ *At lunch, Jane's selection was a chicken sandwich.* **2.** *n.* a variety of things to choose from, especially in a store. □ *The local hardware store has a selection of tools.*

**selective** [sə 'lɛk tɪv] *adj.* choosing carefully; making careful choices. (Adv: *selectively.*) □ *A selective buyer compares many brands.*

S

**self** ['sɛlf] *n.* the inner being of a person. (Usually in compounds. See also **myself, yourself, herself, himself, itself, oneself, ourselves, yourselves, themselves.** No plural form.) □ *The boss likes employees who see the company as more important than one's own self.*

**self-addressed** ['sɛlf ə 'drɛst] *adj.* addressed to oneself. □ *I included a self-addressed, stamped envelope with each invitation.*

**self-centered** ['sɛlf 'sɛn tɚd] *adj.* selfish; often thinking only of oneself instead of anyone else. (Adv: *self-centeredly.*) □ *Dave is too self-centered to care about my opinion.*

**self-confidence** [sɛlf 'kɑn fɪ dəns] *n.* the belief that one is able to do something; confidence in one's own ability. (No plural form.) □ *Anne's self-confidence has improved since she left home.*

**self-conscious** [sɛlf 'kɑn ʃəs] *adj.* aware that one is being seen by other people, especially when one is shy or embarrassed around other people. (Adv: *self-consciously.*) □ *Bob feels self-conscious when he tries to talk in a group.*

**self-contained** [sɛlf kən 'tend] *adj.* containing within itself everything that is necessary. □ *All of the parts needed for correct operation are self-contained.*

**self-control** [sɛlf kən 'trol] *n.* the control of one's own actions or feelings. (No plural form.) □ *Because Anne has great self-control, she didn't respond to John's insults.*

**self-discipline** ['sɛlf 'dɪs ə plɪn] *n.* the discipline needed to control one's feelings and actions. (No plural form.) □ *It takes self-discipline to accept criticism without becoming angry.*

**self-employed** [sɛlf ɛm 'plɔɪd] *adj.* working for one's own business; not working for other people. □ *Susan is self-employed because she dislikes having a boss.*

**self-esteem** [sɛlf ə 'stim] *n.* the good opinion one has of oneself; the respect one shows for oneself. (No plural form.) □ *Anne has a great self-esteem, so she's not upset by criticism.*

**self-help** ['sɛlf 'hɛlp] **1.** *n.* helping oneself without the help of others. (No plural form.) □ *Mary doesn't like doctors, so she relies on self-help.* **2.** *adj.* [of books or techniques] showing people how to help themselves without the help of others. □ *Some self-help remedies do more harm than good.*

**selfish** ['sɛl fɪʃ] *adj.* too concerned with oneself; too concerned with what one wants instead of what other people want; showing more care for oneself than for other people. (Adv: *selfishly.*) □ *The selfish girl wouldn't share her toys with the others.*

**selfishness** ['sɛl fɪʃ nəs] *n.* the state of being too concerned with oneself and too greedy. (No plural form.) □ *Selfishness and greed can be your downfall.*

**self-reliant** [sɛlf rɪ 'lɑɪ ənt] *adj.* able to get along or do something without the help of others. (Adv: *self-reliantly.*) □ *The Smiths taught their children to be self-reliant at an early age.*

**self-respect** [sɛlf rɪ 'spɛkt] *n.* the respect and pride one has for oneself. (No plural form.) □ *Good grooming habits are a matter of self-respect.*

**self-service** ['sɛlf 'sɚ vɪs] **1.** *n.* the system by which one must serve oneself in a store or a business. (No plural form.) □ *Self-service is much cheaper than having a clerk deal with every sale.* **2.** AND **self-serve** ['sɛlf 'sɚv] *adj.* <the adj. use of ①.> □ *The customers filled their own plates at the self-serve buffet.*

**sell** ['sɛl] **1. sell for some amount** *iv., irreg. + prep. phr.* to be offered for sale for an amount of money; to be **sold** ③ for an amount of money. (Pt/pp: **sold.**) □ *The rare book will sell for hundreds of dollars.* **2.** *tv., irreg.* to transfer a product in exchange for money; to transfer a product to someone in exchange for money. □ *The clerk sold the vase to Anne.* □ *Have you sold your car yet?* **3.** *tv., irreg.* to make something available for purchase. □ *The artist sells paintings for $500 and sculptures for $750.* **4.** *tv., irreg.* to cause something to be more likely to be used or bought. □ *Often, good reporting doesn't sell news as well as sex and violence do.*

**seller** ['sɛl ɚ] *n.* someone who sells something for money. □ *The seller was asking $2,000 for the used car.*

**semester** [sɪ 'mɛs tɚ] *n.* half of a school year; a term; a 16-week to 18-week period of classes. □ *I cannot afford both semesters of college this year.*

**semicircle** ['sɛm ɪ sɚk əl] *n.* half of a circle; a shape like half of a circle. □ *The choir was arranged in a semicircle in front of the conductor.*

**semicolon** ['sɛm ɪ ko lən] *n.* a punctuation mark ";" that shows separation between two clauses, indicating more of a pause than a comma but less of a pause than a period. (It is also used to separate items in a list, if any of the items use a comma, so that the reader is not confused.) □ *John replaced the comma between the sentences with a semicolon.*

**seminar** ['sɛm ə nɑr] **1.** *n.* one of the meetings of a type of (college) course that meets regularly with a professor to discuss theories, studies, or research. □ *The students in the history seminar all presented original research.* **2.** *n.* a meeting where a speaker or panel of speakers talk, exchange information, or discuss ideas about a particular topic. □ *Many lawyers attended a seminar on legal reform.*

**senate** ['sɛn ət] **1.** *n.* the smaller of the two groups of people who are elected to make the federal laws in the United States. □ *One term in the U.S. Senate lasts six years.* **2.** *n.* the professors who are the governing body at certain schools and universities. □ *The administration asked the senate for input on the new curriculum.*

**senator** ['sɛn ə tɚ] *n.* someone who is a member of a senate. □ *President Lyndon Johnson had also been a senator from Texas.*

**send** ['sɛnd] **1.** *tv., irreg.* to cause someone or something to be transported or to go from one place to another. (Pt/pp: **sent**.) □ *Mary sent a package to John through the mail.* **2. send** someone **off** *tv., irreg. + obj. + adv.* to participate in saying good-bye to someone who is leaving. □ *We had a party to send Tom off on his vacation.* 🅃 *We sent off our visitor at the airport.* **3. send for** someone or something *iv., irreg. + prep. phr.* to request that someone come or that something be brought. □ *The executive sent for the company treasurer.*

**senile** ['si nɑɪl] *adj.* tending to forget things or be confused because of advancing age. (Adv: *senilely.*) □ *The senile woman could not remember her own name.*

**senility** [sə 'nɪl ə ti] *n.* a state of confusion and loss of memory associated with old age. (No plural form.) □ *Keeping the mind and body active may prevent senility.*

**senior** ['sin jɚ] **1.** *adj.* [of people] older; [of employees] serving an employer longer than most other employees. □ *Some senior members of the staff have worked here for more than 20 years.* **2.** *adj.* higher in rank or position. □ *A president is more senior than a vice president.* **3.** *adj.* of or for students in the fourth year of high school or college. □ *The shy boy didn't ask anyone to the senior dance.* **4.** *adj.* for very old, or elderly, people; serving elderly people. □ *The nurse gave a speech at the senior center.* **5.** *n.* an older person; a **senior citizen**. □ *When I am a senior, I hope to be able to afford medical care.* **6.** *n.* a student in the fourth year of high school (12th grade) or the fourth year of college. □ *The principal spoke to the seniors on graduation day.*

**senior citizen** ['sin jɚ 'sɪt ə zən] *n.* someone who is 65 years old or older. □ *Bob, a healthy and happy senior citizen, has no intention of retiring.*

**seniority** [sin 'jor ə ti] *n.* the quality of having been employed at one's place of work for a relatively longer period of time than someone else. (No plural form.) □ *The workers with the most seniority received the biggest bonuses.*

**sensation** [sɛn 'se ʃən] **1.** *n.* the use of the senses; the ability to see, hear, touch, taste, or smell. □ *John lost the sensation of smell after the fire.* **2.** *n.* an awareness of someone or something because of sight, sound, touch, taste, or smell. □ *The creamy dessert created a pleasant sensation on my tongue.* **3.** *n.* a vague feeling of awareness; a general feeling in the mind. (Fig. on ①.) □ *I had the eerie sensation that my best friend was in danger.* **4.** *n.* someone or something that causes people to become very excited or interested. □ *The prominent politician was quite a sensation at the banquet.*

**sensational** [sɛn 'se ʃə nəl] **1.** *adj.* very exciting or interesting; attracting a lot of attention. (Adv: *sensationally.*) □ *The singer gave a sensational performance yesterday.* **2.** *adj.* exaggerated and designed to excite and appeal to a mass audience. (Adv: *sensationally.*) □ *The newspaper's sensational coverage of the trial was criticized by the judge.*

**sense** ['sɛns] **1.** *n.* each of the abilities allowing creatures to see, hear, touch, taste, or smell. □ *A blind person has no sense of sight.* **2.** *n.* a special feeling or sensation, especially one that cannot be described. (No plural form.) □ *John had a sense that he was being followed.* **3.** *n.* the ability to understand or appreciate something. (No plural form. See also **sense of humor**.) □ *Most musicians have a good sense of rhythm.* **4.** *n.* good judgment; the ability to make good decisions. (No plural form.) □ *Sometimes Bob does not use any sense when he*

S

*is shopping.* **5.** *n.* the meaning or definition of something; a meaning. □ *A dictionary defines the various senses of its entry words.* □ *The word* bank *has at least two completely different senses.* **6.** *n.* a belief shared by a group of people. □ *The jury's sense was that the defendant was guilty.* **7.** *tv.* to be aware of something with the help of ①. (The object can be a clause with **that** ⑦.) □ *John sensed some lemon juice in his tea.* **8.** *tv.* to determine something; to have a feeling about a situation. (The object can be a clause with **that** ⑦.) □ *Anne sensed the confusion in the meeting.*

**senseless** ['sɛns ləs] **1.** *adj.* without reason; having no purpose; stupid; foolish. (Adv: *senselessly.*) □ *There was no motive for the senseless murder.* **2.** *adj.* unconscious. (Adv: *senselessly.*) □ *The senseless patient lay in the hospital for eight months.*

**sense of humor** [sɛns əv 'hju mɚ] *n.* the ability to laugh at things that are funny; the ability to see the funny aspects of a situation. (No plural form.) □ *Mike loved his wife's sense of humor.*

**sensible** ['sɛn sə bəl] **1.** *adj.* representing or showing common sense; wise. (Adv: *sensibly.*) □ *Jane is a sensible woman.* **2.** *adj.* practical instead of stylish. (Adv: *sensibly.*) □ *The furniture is sensible instead of fancy.*

**sensitive** ['sɛn sə tɪv] **1.** *adj.* able to feel the effect of something, especially light, sound, smell, taste, or texture; easily affected or harmed by something. (Adv: *sensitively.*) □ *My eyes are very sensitive to sunlight.* **2.** *adj.* easily offended; [of someone] easily affected by something. (Fig. on ①. Adv: *sensitively.*) □ *Bob is too sensitive about what people think about him.* **3.** *adj.* easily able to sense a small change in something. □ *Her eyes are very sensitive to light.*

**sensitivity** [sɛn sə 'tɪv ɪ ti] **1.** *n.* the ability to sense or perceive something. (No plural form.) □ *I wore sunglasses because of my eyes' sensitivity to bright light.* **2.** *n.* the tendency to perceive or imagine even the smallest offense. (Sometimes plural with the same meaning.) □ *Because of Bob's excessive sensitivity, he often feels insulted.*

**sensory** ['sɛn sə ri] *adj.* of the senses; of the ability to see, hear, taste, touch, or smell. □ *Some drugs reduce sensory abilities, while others increase them.*

**sensual** ['sɛn ʃu əl] *adj.* providing pleasure to the body; concerning the pleasures of eating, drinking, sex, etc. (Adv: *sensually.*) □ *He decided to enjoy all the sensual pleasures he could while he was young.*

**sensuous** [sɛn 'ʃu əs] *adj.* affecting the senses; experienced through the senses. (Adv: *sensuously.*) □ *Floating in the warm ocean water was a very sensuous experience.*

**sent** ['sɛnt] pt/pp of **send**.

**sentence** ['sɛnt ns] **1.** *n.* a group of words that forms an independent thought, usually including at least a subject and a verb. □ *"The cat is on the mat" is a sentence that is a statement.* □ *Jane's letter was only a few sentences long, but it said many important things.* **2.** *n.* the punishment given to a criminal by a judge in a court of law. □ *The judge gave the criminal the maximum sentence.* **3.** *tv.* [for a judge] to assign a punishment to a criminal. □ *The court sentenced the murderer one week after he was found guilty.*

**sentiment** ['sɛn tə mənt] **1.** *n.* a tender feeling or emotion. (No plural form.) □ *We were shocked at John's lack of sentiment at the funeral.* **2. sentiments** *n.* a written or spoken expression of ①. (Treated as plural.) □ *I wrote my sentiments on a card and gave it to the wife of the victim.*

**sentimental** [sɛn tə 'mɛn təl] *adj.* having tender feelings or emotions, often sad or romantic ones. (Adv: *sentimentally.*) □ *Everyone at the reunion had sentimental memories of high school.*

**separable** ['sɛp ɚ ə bəl] *adj.* able to be separated; able to be divided. (Adv: *separably.*) □ *The two parts of the idea are not separable.*

**separate 1.** ['sɛp rət] *adj.* not together; not joined; apart; single; individual. (Adv: *separately.*) □ *Our garage is separate from our house.* **2.** ['sɛp ə ret] *tv.* to be between two or more things or people; to keep two or more things or people apart. □ *A fence separated the sheep from the goats.* **3.** ['sɛp ə ret] *tv.* to cause two or more things or people to be apart. □ *The teacher separated the two children who kept talking in class.* **4.** ['sɛp ə ret] *iv.* to break apart; to divide; to split. □ *The legs have separated from the top of the table, and they have to be glued back on.* **5.** ['sɛp ə ret] *iv.* [for a husband and wife] to stop living together, often as a trial before beginning to divorce. □ *Bob and Jane separated a year before their divorce.*

**separated** ['sɛp ə ret ɪd] *adj.* [of a married couple] no longer living together but not divorced. □ *Well, they are still married, but they are separated.*

**separation** [sɛp ə 're ʃən] **1.** *n.* the state of having been separated. (Plural only when referring to different kinds, types, instances, or varieties.) □ *Dave's separation from his children made him sad.* Ⓒ *He experienced three such separations this year, owing to his illness.* **2.** *n.* a period of time when two people who are married no longer live together but have not yet divorced. □ *After three trial separations, they were divorced.*

**September** [sɛp 'tɛm bɚ] Go to **month**.

**sequence** ['si kwəns] **1.** *n.* the order in which a group of things or people are placed; the order in which a series of events happen. □ *The secretary placed the files in an alphabetical sequence.* **2.** *tv.* to put things or people into ①. □ *The secretary sequenced the files in alphabetical order.*

**sequester** [sɪ 'kwɛs tɚ] *tv.* to keep someone apart from other people, especially to isolate members of a jury during a trial. □ *The actress sequestered herself from others while vacationing.*

**serenade** [sɛr ə 'ned] **1.** *n.* a song sung to someone; a love song. □ *John's serenade to his girlfriend was romantic, even though he sang badly.* **2.** *tv.* to sing a romantic song to someone; to play a romantic piece of music for someone. □ *David serenaded his girlfriend with a romantic love song.*

**serene** [sə 'rin] *adj.* quiet; calm; peaceful. (Adv: *serenely.*) □ *John spent a serene week resting in a remote cabin.*

**serenity** [sə 'rɛn ɪ ti] *n.* the quality of being serene. (No plural form.) □ *Her happiness was so great it was almost serenity.*

**serial** ['sɪr i əl] **1.** *n.* a story that is presented in separate parts. □ *Each day, a new part of the serial is seen on television.* **2.** *adj.* <the adj. use of ①.> (Adv: *serially.*) □ *A new serial drama starts next week on television.*

**series** ['sɪr iz] **1.** *n.* a group of similar things that happen or appear one after the other in a certain order; a group of similar things that are arranged in a row. (Treated as singular.) □ *The reporter asked the politician a series of questions.* **2.** *n.* a set of television programs that is broadcast one at a time, usually once per week. □ *I really can't stand watching that series.*

**serious** ['sɪr i əs] **1.** *adj.* not humorous or playful. (Adv: *seriously.*) □ *Could you be serious for a minute and stop making jokes?* **2.** *adj.* important; not minor.

(Adv: *seriously.*) □ *John has a serious problem with his car.*

**seriousness** ['sɪr i əs nəs] *n.* importance; gravity; a state of being **serious.** (No plural form.) □ *The seriousness of the situation frightened the children and their parents.*

**sermon** ['sɚ mən] **1.** *n.* a speech about religion or morals, especially one given by a member of the clergy. □ *Today's sermon was based on a story from the Bible.* **2.** *n.* a long speech by someone who is giving advice or who is scolding someone else. (Fig. on ①.) □ *My roommate gave me a sermon about being too messy.*

**serpent** ['sɚ pənt] *n.* a snake. □ *The stone floor of the room was covered with serpents.*

**servant** ['sɚ vənt] *n.* someone who serves a person, the public, or God, especially someone who is paid to work for someone else in that person's house. □ *A trusted servant served dinner to the royal family.*

**serve** ['sɚv] **1.** *tv.* to provide someone with service. □ *Our old car has served us well for nearly ten years.* **2.** *tv.* to bring (previously ordered) food to someone, as in a restaurant. □ *The waitress served us our dinner.* **3.** *tv.* to provide a useful service or function. □ *The workers who no longer served a function were laid off.* **4.** *iv.* to perform military service. □ *David served for twenty years in the air force.* **5.** *iv.* to begin a play in sports like tennis by hitting the ball toward the other player. □ *John served, but the ball hit the net.*

**server** ['sɚ vɚ] **1.** *n.* a utensil used to serve certain foods. □ *Jane got a lovely silver pie server for her birthday.* **2.** *n.* a **waitress;** a **waiter.** □ *The server brought me the soup that I had ordered.*

**service** ['sɚ vɪs] **1.** *n.* the work that someone does for the benefit of someone; work done by servants, clerks, food servers, taxi drivers, etc. (No plural form. See ③.) □ *I did not like the service in that restaurant.* **2.** *n.* the repair of a machine or device; maintenance. (No plural form.) □ *I took my broken television to the repair shop for service.* **3. services** *n.* work that is done to help someone, especially the work done by a professional person. (Treated as plural, but not countable.) □ *Our company needs the services of a good accountant.* **4.** *n.* the benefit provided by a company or organization that fulfills the needs of people and that usually does not manufacture products. (This includes *electric service, natural gas service, telephone service, water service, sewer service, message service, diaper service, lawn care service,* etc.) □ *I left a message for Anne with her message service.* **5. the service** *n.* a military duty; serving [one's country in] a military organization. □ *Mike was in the service during the Persian Gulf War.* **6.** *n.* a religious meeting or ceremony. □ *The devout worshiper went to a service twice a week.* **7.** *tv.* to repair or adjust something mechanical or electronic. □ *They are servicing my car in the shop.* **8. out of service** *phr.* not working; not currently operating; not currently available to be used. □ *Both elevators are out of service, so I had to use the stairs.*

**serving** ['sɚ vɪŋ] *n.* the amount of food or drink that is usually served to one person. □ *The cafeteria worker gave me a large serving of potatoes.*

**session** ['sɛ ʃən] **1.** *n.* a period of time during which a meeting is held or an activity is pursued. □ *Mary hasn't enrolled for the fall session of classes yet.* **2. in session** *phr.* [of a court, congress, or other organization] operating or functioning. □ *Smoking is forbidden while the meeting is in session.*

**set** ['sɛt] **1.** *tv., irreg.* to put someone or something on a surface; to place

S

someone or something somewhere. (Pt/pp: **set**.) □ *Bill set a book on his desk.* **2.** *tv., irreg.* to move someone or something into a certain position. □ *Mary set the salad forks on the table.* **3.** *tv., irreg.* to join the ends of a broken bone and place them in proper position. □ *The doctor set Bill's broken arm.* **4.** *tv., irreg.* to determine or establish a value, a standard, a time, an amount, etc. □ *Have you set a time for your appointment yet?* **5.** *tv., irreg.* to adjust a machine so that it works correctly; to adjust something so that it will show the correct measurement, time, amount, etc. □ *Mary sets her clock once a week.* **6. set something up** *tv., irreg. + obj. + adv.* to arrange the time and place of a meeting, appointment, interview, etc. □ *Can I set a meeting up with you early next week?* 🅃 *Let's set up a meeting next week.* **7.** *iv., irreg.* [for a liquid] to take a certain shape; to become shaped; [for concrete or plaster] to harden. □ *The glue set as it dried.* **8.** *iv., irreg.* [for the sun] to drop below the horizon at night; to sink out of sight. □ *Tonight the sun will set at 5:39 P.M.* **9.** *n.* a collection of related things; a group of things that are found or belong together. □ *Mary's blue salt and pepper shakers are a matched set.* **10.** *n.* the location of the performing area for a play, TV show, or movie. □ *The news reporters took their places on the set.* **11.** *adj.* ready. (Not prenominal.) □ *Let me know when you're set to go.* **12.** *adj.* established; determined in advance; arranged. □ *The guests arrived at the set time.* **13. set the table** *phr.* to arrange a table with plates, glasses, knives, forks, etc., for a meal. □ *Please help me get ready for dinner by setting the table.*

**setback** ['sɛt bæk] *n.* something that causes something to change for the worse. □ *The loss of funds was a major setback to the agency.*

**settle** ['sɛt əl] **1.** *tv.* to decide something, especially an argument; to resolve something. □ *Mary settled her argument with Bob by consulting an expert.* **2.** *tv.* to pay a bill or account. □ *We settled the bill at the end of the meal.* **3.** *tv.* to place oneself in a comfortable position. (Takes a reflexive object.) □ *Anne settled herself into the hot, relaxing bathwater.* **4.** *tv.* to occupy land or a town and live there, often as a pioneer. □ *My ancestors settled this town in 1820.* **5.** *tv.* to cause something to be calm, still, or less active. □ *Some nice, hot tea will settle my nerves.* **6. settle down** *iv. + adv.* to become calm, still, or less active. □ *If you children don't settle down, I'm taking you home!* **7. settle (down)** *iv. (+ adv.)* to move into a comfortable position for resting or sleeping. □ *The dog settled down in front of the fireplace.* **8.** *iv.* to sink, especially into the earth or to the bottom of something. □ *After the heavy rains, the house creaked as it settled.*

**settlement** ['sɛt əl mənt] **1.** *n.* the establishing of towns or communities in new areas. (No plural form.) □ *The government encouraged the settlement of the West.* **2.** *n.* a town established by people who move to an area where there was no town before. □ *The mayor of the pioneer settlement was also the town's only barber.* **3.** *n.* an agreement that ends an argument, disagreement, or fight. □ *Both parties must sign the settlement in order for it to go into effect.*

**settler** ['sɛt lɚ, 'sɛt l ɚ] *n.* a pioneer; someone who is one of the first people to live in a location. □ *The settlers crossed the plains in wagons and on horses.*

**setup** ['sɛt əp] *n.* an arrangement; the way something is arranged or organized. □ *Mary thought the conference's setup was not at all organized.*

S

**seven** ['sɛv ən] 7. Go to **four** for senses and examples.

**seventeen** ['sɛv ən 'tin] 17. Go to **four** for senses and examples.

**seventeenth** [sɛv ən 'tinθ] 17th. Go to **fourth** for senses and examples.

**seventh** ['sɛv ənθ] 7th. Go to **fourth** for senses and examples.

**seventieth** ['sɛv ən ti əθ] 70th. Go to **fourth** for senses and examples.

**seventy** ['sɛv ən ti] 70. Go to **forty** for senses and examples.

**sever** ['sɛv ɚ] *tv.* to cut through something; to cut something apart. □ *I severed the dead branches from the bushes and threw them away.*

**several** ['sɛv (ə) rəl] **1.** *adj.* some; a few, but not many. □ *Anne had several things to say about my presentation.* **2.** *n.* some people or things; a few people or things. (No plural form.) □ *John had many problems with the project and mentioned several to me.*

**severe** [sə 'vɪr] **1.** *adj.* harsh; strict; not gentle. (Adv: *severely.* Comp: *severer;* sup: *severest.*) □ *The angry parents gave the child a severe punishment for her bad behavior.* **2.** *adj.* strong; violent; causing harm; not mild. (Adv: *severely.* Comp: *severer;* sup: *severest.*) □ *The cold weather is so severe that you could easily get frostbite.*

**severed** ['sɛv ɚd] *adj.* cut off; cut from; separated. □ *John threw the severed rope away.*

**severity** [sɪ 'vɛr ɪ ti] *n.* the quality of being severe. (No plural form.) □ *The severity of the crime disturbed the detective.*

**sew** ['so] **1.** *tv., irreg.* to attach two pieces of material together or to attach something to a piece of material by making stitches using a needle and thread. (Pt: *sewed;* pp: *sewed* or **sewn**.) □ *The tailor has sewn the tear in my shirt.* **2.** *iv., irreg.* to attach with stitches using needle and thread. □ *Bob learned how to sew in school.*

**sewage** ['su ɪdʒ] *n.* water and human waste that is carried away by sewers from homes and businesses. (No plural form.) □ *Because of the storm, untreated sewage was washed into the bay.*

**sewer 1.** ['su ɚ] *n.* a pipe that carries waste away from homes and businesses. □ *There was an unpleasant smell when the sewers became clogged.* **2.** ['so ɚ] *n.* someone who sews. □ *We need a few sewers to help with the project.*

**sewing** ['so ɪŋ] **1.** *n.* the work that is done with needle and thread; the stitches made in material with needle and thread. (No plural form.) □ *I ripped out the thread because Bob's sewing was uneven.* **2.** *n.* a piece of clothing or material that is being sewed. (No plural form.) □ *Where did I put the sewing I was working on?* **3.** *adj.* <the adj. use of ① or ②.> □ *The tailor used only high-quality sewing needles.*

**sewn** ['son] a pp of **sew**.

**sex** ['sɛks] **1.** *n.* human sexual responses and sexual activity. (No plural form.) □ *Bob thought about sex often.* **2.** *n.* copulation; sexual arousal leading to copulation; the urge to copulate; the subject of copulation. (No plural form.) □ *The movie showed them engaged in sex.* **3.** *n.* the state of being male or female. □ *The doctor announced the sex of the newborn infant.* **4.** *adj.* <the adj. use of ①.> □ *It was suggested that Dave buy a sex manual.*

**sexism** ['sɛks ɪz əm] *n.* the belief that men are better than women; discrimination against women because they are women. (No plural form.) □ *Tom denied the charges of sexism placed against him.*

**sexist** ['sɛk sɪst] **1.** *n.* someone, usually a male, who practices **sexism**. □ *The*

S

*female candidate claimed her opponent was a sexist.* **2.** *adj.* <the adj. use of ①.> (Adv: *sexistly.*) □ *Mary called Tom sexist because he held a door open for her.*

**sexual** ['sɛk ʃu əl] **1.** *adj.* of or about copulation or reproduction and the associated feelings and urges. (Adv: *sexually.*) □ *The students studied the sexual life of the earthworm in biology.* **2.** *adj.* requiring two creatures or organisms for reproduction. □ *Unlike some plants, most animals practice sexual reproduction.*

**sexual intercourse** ['sɛk ʃu əl 'ɪn tɚ kors] *n.* copulation; an act involving the genitals of two people for the purpose of creating pleasure or the production of offspring. (No plural form. Can be shortened to **intercourse**.) □ *Anne uses birth control every time she has sexual intercourse.*

**sexuality** [sɛk ʃu 'æl ə ti] *n.* human sexual matters and feelings; the involvement or interest a person has in sex. (No plural form.) □ *The artist had almost no interest in human sexuality.*

**sexually** ['sɛk ʃu (ə) li] *adv.* in a sexual manner; in a way that concerns sex. □ *Anne believed that her date was sexually interested in her.*

**sexy** ['sɛk si] *adj.* of or about sex appeal; causing an interest in sex; sexually exciting. (Comp: *sexier;* sup: *sexiest.*) □ *I was attracted to John's sexy smile.*

**shabby** ['ʃæb i] *adj.* having a messy appearance; looking run-down or worn out. (Adv: *shabbily.* Comp: *shabbier;* sup: *shabbiest.*) □ *The shabby buildings made the neighborhood a bad place to live.*

**shack** ['ʃæk] *n.* a small house, hut, or shed that has been built quickly or poorly. □ *The mountain community consists of hundreds of wooden shacks.*

**shade** ['ʃed] **1.** *n.* a place that is not directly exposed to sunlight because an object between that place and the sun blocks the sunlight. (No plural form.) □ *Mary sat in the shade in the park and read.* **2.** *n.* a variety of a color; the lightness or darkness of a color. □ *The artist painted the sky a light shade of blue.* **3.** *n.* a slight amount of a quality. □ *There was a shade of panic in David's actions.* **4.** *n.* a device that can be rolled down over a window so that light won't get in or so that people can't see in. (Short for **window shade**.) □ *I pulled the shades because I wanted to change my clothes.* **5.** *tv.* to prevent light from reaching an area; to make something darker or harder to see by blocking light. □ *John's large hat shaded his face.* **6.** *tv.* to make something darker by painting or drawing on it with a darker color. □ *The designer shaded the left side of the drawing with a pencil.*

**shading** ['ʃed ɪŋ] *n.* the use of darker colors in paintings and drawings to make shadows. (No plural form.) □ *Her expert shading made the picture come to life.*

**shadow** ['ʃæd o] **1.** *n.* the patch of shade created by someone or something blocking light. □ *Anne's house is in the shadow of a tall building.* **2.** *n.* a slight suggestion; a trace. (Fig. on ①.) □ *A shadow of uncertainty spread over the doomed project.*

**shady** ['ʃe di] **1.** *adj.* in the shade; blocked from direct exposure to light; shaded. (Comp: *shadier;* sup: *shadiest.*) □ *We sat in a shady spot in the park and talked.* **2.** *adj.* not honest; always making schemes and deceiving people. (Comp: *shadier;* sup: *shadiest.*) □ *The shady salesman left when he saw the police approach.*

**shaft** ['ʃæft] **1.** *n.* a rod or pole, such as part of an arrow. □ *The hunter held the arrow by its shaft and threw it.* **2.** *n.* a pole that is used as a handle, such as with the handle of an axe or a golf club.

S

□ *The shaft of the axe is made of wood, and the blade is made of metal.* **3.** *n.* a ray [of light]. □ *A shaft of light entered the dark room through the tiny window.* **4.** *n.* a long, narrow passage, often vertical. □ *An elevator travels up and down a shaft.*

**shaggy** ['ʃæg i] *adj.* covered with long, thick, messy hair; [of hair] long, thick, and messy. (Adv: *shaggily.* Comp: *shaggier;* sup: *shaggiest.*) □ *Mr. Smith ordered John to cut his shaggy hair.*

**shake** ['ʃek] **1.** *iv., irreg.* [for something large] to move up and down, back and forth, or side to side many times very quickly. (Pt: **shook**; pp: **shaken**.) □ *The walls shook when John jumped on the floor.* **2.** *iv., irreg.* [for someone] to move as in ① or seem less secure. □ *John shook with fear when he saw the monster.* **3.** *tv., irreg.* to cause someone or something to move up and down, back and forth, or side to side many times very quickly. □ *I shook the box to try to determine what was inside it.* **4. shake hands; shake** someone's **hand** *phr.* to take someone's hand and move it up and down to greet someone or mark an agreement with someone. □ *David shook my hand when he greeted me.* □ *Anne and John shook hands before their business appointment.*

**shaken** ['ʃek ən] **1.** pp of **shake**. **2.** *adj.* greatly upset; disturbed; bothered. □ *She was quite shaken and cried openly.*

**shaker** ['ʃek ɚ] *n.* a small container that has a few tiny holes on one end from which salt, pepper, and sometimes other spices are spread on food by shaking. □ *Can you pass the salt shaker?*

**shake-up** ['ʃek əp] *n.* a large change in the arrangement of an organization, including the movement, firing, or addition of people who have important jobs. □ *In the company shake-up, half of the employees were transferred.*

**shaky** ['ʃe ki] **1.** *adj.* shaking a small amount; not steady. (Comp: *shakier;* sup: *shakiest.*) □ *Aunt Jane has shaky handwriting because she is very weak.* **2.** *adj.* risky; not certain; not able to be relied on. (Comp: *shakier;* sup: *shakiest.*) □ *The bank declined to fund the shaky business deal.*

**shall** ['ʃæl] **1.** *aux.* <a form used with *I* and *we* to indicate something in the future.> (Formal. See also **will, should.**) □ *We shall go to New York next Saturday.* **2.** *aux.* <a form used with *you, he, she, it, they,* and names of people or things to indicate something one must do, a command, or a promise.> (Formal. See also **will** and **should**.) □ *You shall do your homework before you watch TV.* **3.** *aux.* <a verb form used with *I* and *we* in questions that ask the hearer or reader to decide something concerning the speaker or writer.> (Formal. See also **will** and **should**.) □ *Shall I go to the store now?*

**shallow** ['ʃæl o] **1.** *adj.* not deep; having only a small distance from the top of something to the bottom, especially used to describe water. (Adv: *shallowly.* Comp: *shallower;* sup: *shallowest.*) □ *The children went into the shallow end of the pool.* **2.** *adj.* not having deep, important thoughts. (Fig. on ①. Adv: *shallowly.* Comp: *shallower;* sup: *shallowest.*) □ *Mary was bored by her date, who was very shallow.*

S

**shame** ['ʃem] **1.** *n.* a bad feeling that someone has done something wrong or bad; a bad feeling of guilt. (No plural form.) □ *Have you no shame for all the bad things you've done?* **2.** *n.* an unfortunate situation. (No plural form.) □ *It's a shame that it rained during the picnic.* **3.** *n.* disgrace; loss of honor. (No plural form.) □ *The shame of the scandal caused the mayor to resign.* **4.** *tv.* to cause someone to feel ①. □ *Mary shamed her son in public.*

**shameful** ['ʃem fʊl] *adj.* causing or deserving shame or disgrace. (Adv: *shamefully.*) □ *John felt truly sorry for all of his shameful actions.*

**shameless** ['ʃem ləs] *adj.* without shame, especially when one should feel shame; not modest. (Adv: *shamelessly.*) □ *What a shameless person! Aren't you embarrassed?*

**shampoo** [ʃæm 'pu] **1.** *n.* a liquid soap used for washing hair. (Plural only when referring to different kinds, types, instances, or varieties.) □ *John rinsed the shampoo from his hair.* Ⓒ *I've tried a lot of shampoos, and this one is the best of all.* **2.** *n.* a washing of one's own or someone else's hair with ①. (Pl ends in *-s.*) □ *During her shampoo, Susan got some water in her ears.* **3.** *tv.* to wash someone's hair with ①. □ *Mary shampooed her hair while taking a shower.* **4.** *iv.* to wash [hair] with ①. □ *Anne shampoos every morning.*

**shape** ['ʃep] **1.** *n.* a form; a figure; a mass; an object. □ *The shape in the road ahead of me was a dead bird.* **2.** *n.* condition; a state of being—good or bad. (No plural form.) □ *The last time I saw my grandfather, he was in very bad shape.* **3.** *tv.* to cause something to have a certain form; to form something. □ *The sculptor shaped the clay into the form of a dog.* **4.** *iv.* to be able to be put in a certain form in some manner. □ *This soft clay shapes easily.* **5. in shape** *phr.* [of someone] in good physical condition. □ *I am not in shape, and I cannot run far without panting.* **6. take shape** *phr.* [for something, such as plans, writing, ideas, arguments, etc.] to become organized and specific. □ *My plans are beginning to take shape.*

**shapeless** ['ʃep ləs] *adj.* without a shape; having no definite form. (Adv: *shapelessly.*) □ *The scientist looked at the tiny shapeless creature under the microscope.*

**shapely** ['ʃep li] *adj.* having an attractive body; attractive in shape. (Especially used to describe women. Comp: *shapelier;* sup: *shapeliest.*) □ *A shapely dancer appeared onstage, and the audience fell silent.*

**share** ['ʃɛr] **1.** *n.* one person's part of something that belongs to more than one person; a portion. □ *I've certainly had my share of trouble for one evening!* **2.** *n.* a unit of stock; a unit into which the capital of a company or business is divided, and that is owned by a person or corporation. □ *Anne sold some shares of stock so she could buy a computer.* **3.** *tv.* to use something together with another person or other people; to own something together with another person or other people. □ *Jimmy, share your toys with Susie.* **4.** *tv.* to divide something between two or among three or more people so that each person has a portion of it. □ *Anne and John shared the responsibility of walking the dog.* **5.** *iv.* to use together with another person or other people; to own together with another person or other people. □ *Jimmy, you mustn't be so selfish. Learn to share.*

**shared** ['ʃɛrd] *adj.* belonging to two or more people; divided among two or more people. □ *Susie and Jimmy have the shared responsibility of washing the dishes.*

**shark** ['ʃɑrk] *n.* a large, dangerous fish with a pointed fin on its back and long, sharp teeth. □ *Some swimmers saw a shark and told everyone to leave the water.*

**sharp** ['ʃɑrp] **1.** *adj.* having an edge that cuts things easily or having a point that pierces things easily; not dull. (Comp: *sharper;* sup: *sharpest.*) □ *The sharp scissors cut the paper well.* **2.** *adj.* having a sudden change in direction; turning at a narrow angle. (Adv: *sharply.* Comp: *sharper;* sup: *sharpest.*) □ *At the edge of*

S

*the cliff, there's a sharp 600-foot drop.* **3.** *adj.* intelligent; smart; able to learn things quickly; aware. (Adv: *sharply.* Comp: *sharper;* sup: *sharpest.*) □ *A sharp manager runs our office efficiently.* **4.** *adj.* feeling like a sting, bite, or cut; causing a stinging, biting, or cutting feeling. (Adv: *sharply.* Comp: *sharper;* sup: *sharpest.*) □ *Bill felt a sharp pain when the nurse gave him a shot.* **5.** *adj.* distinct; clear; easily seen or heard. (Adv: *sharply.* Comp: *sharper;* sup: *sharpest.*) □ *The artist's lines were sharp and definite.* **6.** *adj.* [of speech or language] bitterly negative. (Adv: *sharply.* Comp: *sharper;* sup: *sharpest.*) □ *Mary's sharp sarcasm ridiculed John's lack of intelligence.* **7.** *adj.* slightly higher in tone. (Comp: *sharper;* sup: *sharpest.*) □ *The last note was a little sharp, and the singer corrected it and then stopped singing.* **8.** *adj.* excellent looking. (Adv: *sharply.* Comp: *sharper;* sup: *sharpest.*) □ *John bought a sharp new sports car.* **9.** *n.* a tone that is half a step higher than the next lowest natural tone. □ *There is not a single sharp in the whole piece of music.* **10.** *adv.* exactly at a stated time. □ *If you're not here at 4:20 sharp, I'm leaving.*

**sharpen** ['ʃɑr pən] *tv.* to cause something to become sharp; to cause something to become sharper. □ *Anne sharpened her pencil.*

**shatter** ['ʃæt ɚ] **1.** *iv.* to break into many tiny pieces. □ *The vase shattered when it fell off the table.* **2.** *tv.* to break something into many tiny pieces. □ *John shattered the vase when he threw it to the floor.*

**shave** ['ʃev] **1.** *tv., irreg.* to remove someone's or something's hair with a sharp blade; to scrape off hair by moving a razor over the skin. (Pt: *shaved;* pp: *shaved* or **shaven**.) □ *John shaves his beard with an electric razor.* **2.** *tv., irreg.* to cut a thin slice from something. □ *Anne shaved a slice of cheese from the big piece.* **3.** *iv., irreg.* to move a razor over one's skin to remove hair. □ *He shaves every other day.* **4.** *n.* an instance of removing hair from the body by using a razor. □ *A blunt razor blade gives a poor shave.*

**shaven** ['ʃev ən] a pp of **shave**.

**she** ['ʃi] **1.** *pron.* <the third-person feminine singular pronoun.> (Refers to female creatures. Used as the subject of a sentence or a clause. See also **her**, **herself**, and **hers**.) □ *I took my daughter to the doctor because she was sick.* **2.** *pron.* <the third-person feminine singular pronoun.> (Informal. Used to refer to certain objects, such as ships and cars.) □ *Ever since my car was wrecked, she just hasn't run quite right.* **3.** *n.* a female. □ *Is your dog a she or a he?*

**shear** ['ʃɪr] **1.** *tv., irreg.* to cut or remove something with ③ or scissors, especially wool from a sheep. (Pp: *sheared* or **shorn**.) □ *The barber sheared the soldier's hair.* **2.** *tv., irreg.* to trim a sheep totally, removing its wool. □ *After the sheep were sheared, they looked naked.* **3. shears** *n.* large scissors; a heavy pair of scissors used for cutting thick materials. (Treated as plural. Number is usually expressed with *pair(s) of shears.*) □ *I used garden shears to trim the bushes.*

**sheath** ['ʃiθ] *n., irreg.* a covering for the blade of a knife or sword. (Pl: ['ʃiðz].) □ *The knight pulled his sword from its sheath.*

S

**she'd** ['ʃid] **1.** *cont.* "she had," where **had** is an auxiliary. □ *She'd been sleeping for ten minutes when the phone rang.* **2.** *cont.* "she would." □ *Anne wondered if she'd arrive on time.*

**shed** ['ʃɛd] **1.** *n.* a small building, usually used for storage. □ *Mary keeps her gardening supplies in a small shed.* **2.** *iv., irreg.* to release or lose hair, or skin in the case of a reptile. (Pt/pp: *shed.*) □ *My dog always sheds in the spring.* **3.** *tv., irreg.* [for an animal] to lose skin or hair. □ *My dog shed its fur all over the furniture.* **4.** *tv., irreg.* to release a fluid, especially tears or blood. □ *The wounded soldier shed a lot of blood.* **5.** *tv., irreg.* to rid oneself of a burden or something embarrassing. (Fig. on ③.) □ *He wanted to shed all his problems and get on with his life.* **6.** *tv., irreg.* to remove clothing. □ *Mary shed her robe and stepped into the shower.*

**sheep** ['ʃip] *n., irreg.* an animal that grows wool on its body and is raised on farms for its wool and its meat. (Pl: *sheep.*) □ *Many sheep wandered about in the meadow.*

**sheepish** ['ʃip ɪʃ] *adj.* weak; timid; easily scared; shy; easily embarrassed. (Adv: *sheepishly.*) □ *The sheepish student was afraid to ask the professor a question.*

**sheer** ['ʃɪr] **1.** *adj.* complete; utter. (Comp: *sheerer;* sup: *sheerest.*) □ *The customer's sheer rudeness shocked the clerk.* **2.** *adj.* transparent; very thin; easy to see through. (Adv: *sheerly.* Comp: *sheerer;* sup: *sheerest.*) □ *John peered through the sheer curtain.* **3.** *adj.* straight up and down; vertical but not slanting or sloping. (Adv: *sheerly.* Comp: *sheerer;* sup: *sheerest.*) □ *The climbers slowly inched up the sheer slope.*

**sheet** ['ʃit] **1.** *n.* a large, thin piece of fabric that is used in pairs on beds. (People sleep between **sheets** ①.) □ *John tucked the edge of the bottom sheet under the mattress.* **2.** *n.* a thin, flat piece of something, such as paper, metal, glass, ice, etc., usually rectangular. □ *The children skated on a thick sheet of ice.*

**shelf** ['ʃɛlf] *n., irreg.* a horizontal, flat piece of wood, metal, or something similar that is put against or attached to a wall or is found in bookcases and other furniture. (Pl: **shelves**.) □ *Susan took a heavy book from the top shelf of the bookcase.*

**she'll** ['ʃil] *cont.* "she will." □ *She'll be finished with the report tomorrow.*

**shell** ['ʃɛl] **1.** *n.* the hard covering on the outside of seeds, nuts, eggs, and shellfish. □ *John removed the oyster from its shell.* **2.** *n.* a bullet. □ *The robber loaded some shells into his gun.* **3.** *tv.* to free something from ① [by removing ①]. □ *The bird shelled the seeds with its beak.* **4.** *tv.* to attack people or a place with shells ②. □ *The enemy shelled our camp, and several soldiers were killed.*

**shellfish** ['ʃɛl fɪʃ] **1.** *n., irreg.* an animal that lives in the water and has a shell, including clams, crabs, lobsters, and oysters. (Pl: *shellfish.*) □ *A lobster is a kind of shellfish.* **2.** *n.* the meat of ①. (No plural form.) □ *The soup is full of delicious shellfish.*

**shelter** ['ʃɛl tɚ] **1.** *n.* protection from weather, danger, or harm. (No plural form.) □ *The soldiers took shelter in a cavern.* **2.** *n.* a place or structure where one can find ①. □ *We stayed in the shelter all night, trying to keep warm.* **3.** *tv.* to protect someone or something from the weather, danger, or harm. □ *The mother bird sheltered her chicks from the cold.*

**sheltered** ['ʃɛl tɚd] *adj.* [of an area] protected, especially from the weather. □ *The campers spent the night in a sheltered place under the ledge.* □ *The deer grazed in a sheltered area near the brook.*

**shelve** ['ʃɛlv] **1.** *tv.* to place something on a shelf. □ *The clerk in the grocery store shelved the produce.* **2.** *tv.* to delay something until a later time. (Fig. on ①.) □ *The firm shelved its plans for the new product.*

**shelves** ['ʃɛlvz] pl of **shelf**.

**shelving** ['ʃɛl vɪŋ] *n.* shelves; a set of shelves. (No plural form.) □ *Because the shelving in the basement was metal, it rusted.*

S

**shepherd** ['ʃɛp ɚd] **1.** *n.* someone who raises and protects sheep. □ *The shepherds gathered each night to keep warm by the fire.* **2.** *tv.* to guide someone in the way that a shepherd leads sheep. (Fig. on ①.) □ *The tour guide shepherded the tourists through the castle.*

**sherbet** ['ʃɚ bət] *n.* a sweet, frozen dessert usually made of or flavored with fruit juice. (Plural only when referring to different kinds, types, instances, or varieties.) □ *John ate his sherbet too slowly, and it melted.* Ⓒ *Sherbets made with real fruit juices are the best.*

**sheriff** ['ʃɛr ɪf] *n.* the most important officer elected to enforce the law in a U.S. county. □ *The store owner told Sheriff Williams that his store had been robbed.*

**she's** ['ʃiz] **1.** *cont.* "she is." □ *Last year, Susie was 6, and now she's 7.* **2.** *cont.* "she has," where **has** is an auxiliary. □ *She's had more problems with her computer than I have had.*

**shield** ['ʃild] **1.** *n.* a cover for something (such as a part of a machine) that protects someone from being hurt. □ *This shield protects your eyes from damage.* **2.** *n.* a large piece of metal or wood carried in front of the body to protect it during fighting. □ *The guard protected his body with his shield.* **3.** *tv.* to protect someone or something from someone or something; to keep someone or something safe from someone or something. □ *Six guards shield the president when he is in public.*

**shift** ['ʃɪft] **1.** *n.* a change in policy, position, opinion, or behavior. □ *The poll measured slight shifts of public opinion.* **2.** *n.* a period during which a worker completes a day at work, such as day shift, night shift, or afternoon shift. (In a workplace that operates more than 8 hours per day.) □ *Bob works the day shift, from 8 to 5.* **3.** *tv.* to change the position of someone or something. □ *The driver shifted gears as the car went up the hill.* **4.** *iv.* to experience changes in behavior or opinion. □ *Voter opinion shifted dramatically after the election.*

**shimmer** ['ʃɪm ɚ] **1.** *iv.* to shine with small waves of light; to shine with reflected light that moves slightly. □ *The pool shimmered in the moonlight.* **2.** *n.* a gleam or glow that seems to move back and forth slightly. □ *The shimmer of moonlight on the lake was romantic.*

**shin** ['ʃɪn] *n.* the front of the leg between the knee and the ankle. □ *The young girl kicked the bully in the shin.*

**shine** ['ʃɑɪn] **1.** *iv., irreg.* to be bright with light; to reflect light. (Pt/pp: *shined* or **shone**.) □ *John likes to work outside when the sun shines.* **2.** *iv.* to do very well; to excel; to be excellent. (Fig. on ①.) □ *David really shined when it was his turn to cook.* **3.** *tv., irreg.* (Pt/pp: *shined* or **shone**.) to direct a beam or source of light in a certain direction. □ *The police shined a flashlight in my direction.* **4.** *tv.* to polish something; to cause something to become shiny. □ *John shined his shoes.* **5.** *n.* the brightness of a surface that has been polished. □ *Tom got a great shine on the car by polishing it for hours.*

**shingle** ['ʃɪŋ gəl] **1.** *n.* a thin panel of wood or another material used to cover a roof in overlapping rows. □ *The heavy winds blew shingles from the roof.* **2. shingles** *n.* a severe, painful disease of the nerves, causing blisters to form on the skin. (Treated as singular or plural, but not countable.) □ *If you have shingles, you should not scratch your skin.*

**shiny** ['ʃɑɪ ni] *adj.* bright; polished; reflecting a lot of light. (Adv: *shinily.* Comp: *shinier;* sup: *shiniest.*) □ *Johnny placed a shiny apple on his teacher's desk.*

**ship** ['ʃɪp] **1.** *n.* a large boat that travels on water and carries people and cargo.

S

☐ *The tourists traveled by ship from France to New York.* **2.** *tv.* to send something from one place to another by train, ①, or truck. ☐ *We shipped all of your order yesterday.*

**shipment** ['ʃɪp mənt] *n.* a load of goods and products ready to be shipped, being shipped, or just received. ☐ *The factory relied on timely shipments of parts from the warehouse.*

**shipping** ['ʃɪp ɪŋ] **1.** *n.* the activity or business of delivering products by ship, train, plane, or truck. (No plural form.) ☐ *John has worked in shipping for over ten years.* **2.** *n.* the cost of transporting something. (No plural form.) ☐ *They charged me $30.00 for shipping!* **3.** *adj.* <the adj. use of ①.> ☐ *The shipping clerk loaded the crates onto the truck.*

**shipwreck** ['ʃɪp rɛk] **1.** *n.* the destruction of a ship caused by running into something. ☐ *The shipwreck was caused by extremely high waves.* **2.** *n.* the remains of a ship that has undergone ①. ☐ *The scuba divers gathered around the shipwreck to watch the fish.* **3.** *tv.* to cause someone to be harmed or stranded owing to ①. ☐ *We feared the storm would shipwreck our crew and passengers.*

**shirt** ['ʃɚt] *n.* a piece of clothing worn above the waist, worn either next to the skin or over an undershirt, and sometimes worn beneath a sweater, jacket, vest, or coat. ☐ *Anne wore an old shirt while she painted the ceiling.*

**shit** ['ʃɪt] **1.** *n.* dung; feces. (All senses are taboo in polite company. Use only with caution. Colloquial. There are many expressions containing this word.) ☐ *Don't step in that shit there.* **2.** *n.* something poor in quality; junk. ☐ *What do you keep all this shit around here for?* **3.** *n.* nonsense; bullshit. ☐ *Don't give me that shit! I know you're lying.* **4.** *exclam.* a general expression of disgust. (Usually **Shit!** Potentially offensive. Use only with caution.) ☐ *Oh, shit! What a mess!*

**shiver** ['ʃɪv ɚ] **1.** *iv.* [for a living creature] to shake a little bit, especially because of cold, sickness, or fear. ☐ *Anne shivered terribly from the cold.* **2.** *n.* a slight shaking movement, especially because of cold, sickness, or fear. ☐ *Mary walked out into the cold air and felt a shiver.*

**shock** ['ʃɑk] **1.** *n.* a sudden surprise, especially one that is violent or disturbing. ☐ *The accident was a terrible shock to the families of the victims.* **2.** *n.* a weakened condition of the body caused by a violent or disturbing event. (No plural form.) ☐ *The people who barely escaped the fire were all in shock.* **3.** *n.* a strong, violent force, especially that caused by earthquakes or bombs. ☐ *The earthquake's first shock woke me.* **4.** *n.* the passing of electricity through someone's body. ☐ *I accidentally gave John a shock when I touched him lightly.* **5.** *tv.* to surprise someone, especially in a disturbing or violent way. ☐ *The news of Anne's accident shocked me.* **6.** *tv.* to offend someone; to disgust someone. ☐ *The vulgar joke shocked Tom's parents.* **7.** *tv.* to give someone or some creature ④. ☐ *The loose wire shocked Mary when it touched her.*

**shocking** ['ʃɑk ɪŋ] *adj.* causing surprise, especially in a disturbing or violent way; offensive; causing disgust. (Adv: *shockingly.*) ☐ *The shocking news made John weep.*

**shoddy** ['ʃɑd i] *adj.* done carelessly; poorly made or done. (Adv: *shoddily.* Comp: *shoddier;* sup: *shoddiest.*) ☐ *The house collapsed during the storm because of shoddy construction.*

**shoe** ['ʃu] **1.** *n.* an outer covering for one's foot, usually having a firm base, but less sturdy than a boot. ☐ *John bought a new pair of shoes for the party.* **2. fill** someone's **shoes** *phr.* to take the

S

place of some other person and do that person's work satisfactorily. ☐ *It'll be difficult to fill Jane's shoes. She did her job very well.*

**shoelace** ['ʃʊ les] *n.* a fabric band or string that is put through the holes on top of a shoe or boot and tied. ☐ *Anne tied her shoelaces into a bow.*

**shoestring** ['ʃu strɪŋ] **1.** *n.* a cord or string used in tightening the shoe to the foot. ☐ *Anne tied her shoestrings quickly.* **2. on a shoestring** *phr.* with a very small amount of money. ☐ *We lived on a shoestring for years before I got a good job.*

**shone** ['ʃon] a pt/pp of **shine**.

**shook** ['ʃʊk] pt of **shake**.

**shoot** ['ʃut] **1.** *tv., irreg.* to fire a gun or similar weapon. (Pt/pp: **shot**.) ☐ *The robber shot his gun into the air.* **2.** *tv., irreg.* [for a weapon] to send something, such as a bullet or arrow, with great force. ☐ *The hunter used a strong bow to shoot the arrow toward the target.* **3.** *tv., irreg.* to send something forward as though from a weapon; to thrust something forward. (Fig. on ②.) ☐ *The student shot a paper clip into the wastebasket.* **4.** *tv., irreg.* to strike someone or something with something, such as a bullet or an arrow, that has been sent from a weapon. ☐ *The police shot the criminal.* **5.** *iv., irreg.* to discharge [a weapon]. ☐ *The robber shot into the air.* **6.** *iv., irreg.* to move somewhere very quickly. ☐ *The raft shot down the river.* **7.** *iv., irreg.* to fire guns as a hobby, as for target practice. ☐ *John shoots for fun on the weekend.* **8.** *n.* a new bud or stem that sprouts from the ground or from an older part of a plant; a bit of new plant growth. ☐ *Many shoots sprang up from the potato.*

**shooting** ['ʃut ɪŋ] **1.** *n.* the sport and skill of hitting targets by firing a gun at them. (No plural form.) ☐ *Mary went to the range because she enjoys shooting.* **2.** *n.* an act of murder, attempted murder, or other harm using a gun. ☐ *The police were puzzled by the shooting at the university.*

**shop** ['ʃɑp] **1.** *n.* a small store, especially where a single class of products is sold. ☐ *At the flower shop, Anne bought a dozen roses.* **2.** *n.* a place where things are built or repaired. ☐ *When my TV was in the shop, I read a lot.* **3.** *iv.* to go to a store to buy things. ☐ *John loves to shop.* **4.** *tv.* to visit a particular store, mall, or area in order to buy things. ☐ *Anne shopped every store inside the mall.*

**shopkeeper** ['ʃɑp kip ɚ] *n.* someone who owns or manages a store. ☐ *The shopkeeper fired the dishonest cashier.*

**shoplift** ['ʃɑp lɪft] **1.** *tv.* to steal merchandise from a shop or store. ☐ *If you shoplift anything here, you will be arrested!* **2.** *iv.* to steal [something] as in ①. ☐ *If you shoplift here, you will end up in jail.*

**shoplifter** ['ʃɑp lɪft ɚ] *n.* someone who steals merchandise from a shop or store. ☐ *This store hired a security guard to prevent shoplifters from stealing jewelry.*

**shopping** ['ʃɑp ɪŋ] *n.* buying things; searching for the right thing to purchase. (No plural form.) ☐ *Grocery shopping is a chore for John.*

**shopworn** ['ʃɑp worn] *adj.* ruined or damaged from being on display in a store. ☐ *The shopkeeper gave the shopworn coat to one of the cashiers.*

S

**shore** ['ʃor] **1.** *n.* the land along the edge of a body of water. ☐ *The lifeguard stood on the shore, watching the swimmers.* **2. shore** something **up** *tv.* + *obj.* + *adv.* to support something that is weak; to prop something up. ☐ *John shored the sagging roof up with a beam.* 🅃 *John shored up the roof.*

**shoreline** ['ʃor laɪn] *n.* the land along the edge of a body of water, especially of an ocean, lake, or sea; the line where land meets water. □ *The house built too close to the shoreline slid into the sea.*

**shorn** ['ʃorn] a pp of **shear**.

**short** ['ʃort] **1.** *adj.* not tall; less than average height from top to bottom. (Comp: *shorter;* sup: *shortest.*) □ *Bill looks short because he stoops a little.* **2.** *adj.* not long; less than average length from side to side. (Comp: *shorter;* sup: *shortest.*) □ *The short ruler wasn't long enough to measure the plank.* **3.** *adj.* not long in time; less than average duration; happening only for a small amount of time; brief. (Comp: *shorter;* sup: *shortest.*) □ *Mary took a short time to finish eating.* **4.** *adj.* not having enough of something; lacking enough of something. (Comp: *shorter;* sup: *shortest.*) □ *I'm short of sugar, so I'll go buy some more.* **5.** *adv.* not close enough; not far enough; not enough. □ *The arrow fell short of the target.* **6.** *n.* a flaw in an electrical circuit that allows electricity to go where it should not go. (Short for **short circuit.**) □ *There is a short in the lamp, and I got a bad shock.* **7. shorts** *n.* a pair of pants whose legs end about at the knees. (Treated as plural. Number is expressed with *pair(s) of shorts.* Also countable.) □ *John made a pair of shorts by cutting off the legs of an old pair of jeans.* **8. shorts** *n.* underpants for men and boys. (Treated as plural. Number is expressed with *pair(s) of shorts.* Also countable.) □ *John's zipper was open, and I could see his shorts.*

S

**shortage** ['ʃor tɪdʒ] **1.** *n.* a lack; a state of not having enough of something. □ *Due to a shortage of funds, the library closed.* **2.** *n.* the amount by which something is short; the amount of something that is needed in order to have enough. □ *Federal funds made up the shortage in the library's budget.*

**shortchange** ['ʃort 'tʃendʒ] *tv.* to give less than is due someone; to give someone less **change** ③ than is due. □ *The dishonest cashier shortchanged the customer.*

**short circuit** ['ʃort 'sɚ kət] **1.** *n.* a fault in an electrical circuit where the circuit is completed before the electricity has traveled the entire path that it was meant to travel. (Can be shortened to **short.**) □ *John got a shock when he tried to repair the short circuit.* **2. short-circuit** *tv.* to cause ①. □ *Lightning short-circuited the electrical system.* **3. short-circuit** *iv.* [for an electrical circuit] to be completed before the electricity has traveled the entire path that it was meant to travel. □ *The overloaded electrical outlet short-circuited.*

**shortcoming** ['ʃort kəm ɪŋ] *n.* a fault; a flaw; a defect. □ *Sue is an excellent employee, despite her shortcoming of talking too much.*

**shortcut** ['ʃort kət] *n.* a path that is shorter, more direct, or quicker to travel than a different or more established route. □ *This path through the woods is a shortcut to the lake.*

**shorten** ['ʃort n] **1.** *iv.* to become shorter. □ *The days shortened as winter approached.* **2.** *tv.* to cause something to become shorter. □ *The principal shortened each class by five minutes.*

**shortening** ['ʃort nɪŋ] **1.** *n.* causing something to become shorter. (No plural form.) □ *Jane noticed the shortening of days as winter approached.* **2.** *n.* butter or some other kind of oily substance, used in frying and baking foods. (Plural only when referring to different kinds, types, instances, or varieties.) □ *The rich pastries contained lots of shortening.* Ⓒ *Shortenings made from vegetable oils are more healthful than those made from animal oils.*

**short-lived** ['ʃort 'lɪvd] *adj.* not lasting very long. □ *The short-lived television series was canceled after four shows.*

**shortsighted** ['ʃort 'sɑɪt ɪd] **1.** *adj.* not able to see things clearly in the distance; able to see some things that are near but not able to see things that are far away. (Adv: *shortsightedly.*) ☐ *The shortsighted woman couldn't read the sign in the distance.* **2.** *adj.* acting without considering what will happen in the future. (Fig. on ①. Adv: *shortsightedly.*) ☐ *The shortsighted manager never planned for the future.*

**short-staffed** ['ʃort 'stæft] *adj.* not having enough people to do a job properly; not having enough employees to run a business properly; needing more people in order to do a job properly. ☐ *The company was short-staffed because ten employees quit.*

**short-tempered** ['ʃort 'tɛm pɚd] *adj.* easily made angry. ☐ *The owner asked the short-tempered customer to leave the store.*

**short-term** ['ʃort 'tɚm] *adj.* only for a short period of time; not permanent; temporary. ☐ *The medicine had some unpleasant short-term effects.*

**shot** ['ʃɑt] **1.** pt/pp of **shoot**. **2.** *n.* the firing of a weapon; the shooting of a gun or other weapon. ☐ *The robber fired the first shot and killed the cop.* **3.** *n.* someone who shoots in a particular way, such as good or bad. ☐ *You're a bad shot, Tom. You never hit the target.* **4.** *n.* an injection of medicine, a vaccine, or a drug. ☐ *The doctor gave the baby a shot.* **5.** *n.* in a game, a ball or similar object that is aimed and sent toward a goal in order to score a point. ☐ *The shot fell wide of the goal.* **6.** *n.* a photograph or a length of film or video. ☐ *The last shot in the movie was a view from the bridge.*

**should** ['ʃʊd] **1. should [do something]** *aux.* **ought** ①. (Indicating that something must be done.) ☐ *We should arrive at the airport in an hour, or else we'll miss our flight.* **2. should [be something]** *aux.* **ought** ②. (Indicating that something is expected.) ☐ *It should be sunny tomorrow if the forecast is correct.*

**shoulder** ['ʃol dɚ] **1.** *n.* one of two parts of the body where an arm connects with the top of the chest below the neck. ☐ *The police officer grabbed the shoplifter's right shoulder.* **2.** *n.* the dirt or pavement along the side of a road. ☐ *The children rode their bicycles on the shoulder.* **3.** *tv.* to have responsibility for something; to take responsibility for something. ☐ *John shouldered the blame for David's problems.*

**shouldn't** ['ʃʊd nt] *cont.* "should not." ☐ *You shouldn't have done that.*

**should've** ['ʃʊd əv] *cont.* "should have," where **have** is an auxiliary. ☐ *I should've ordered the salad instead of the soup.*

**shout** ['ʃɑʊt] **1.** *iv.* to speak, laugh, or make spoken noises loudly. ☐ *The children shouted on the playground.* **2.** *tv.* to speak something loudly; to say something by shouting. (The object can be a clause with **that** ⑦.) ☐ *Dave shouted that he didn't care where we ate.* **3.** *n.* a loud utterance; a loud cry. ☐ *I heard the children's shouts from the other room.*

**shove** ['ʃʌv] **1.** *iv.* to push with force. ☐ *I shoved against the door, but it wouldn't budge.* **2.** *tv.* to push someone or something with force in some direction. ☐ *Mary shoved the door open.* **3.** *n.* a push made with force. ☐ *Jane gave Bill a shove, and he fell down.*

**shovel** ['ʃʌv əl] **1.** *n.* a tool—having a wide, flat blade attached to a handle—used to lift, move, or remove earth or other loose objects. ☐ *Jimmy put sand into his pail with a plastic shovel.* **2.** *iv.* to work by using ①; to move, lift, or remove [something] by using a ①. ☐ *John shoveled until all the snow was removed from the sidewalk.* **3.** *tv.* to move, lift, or remove something by using ①. ☐ *Mary shoveled snow from the driveway.* **4.** *tv.* to clear something

S

with ①. □ *Anne shoveled the sidewalk and then swept it.*

**show** ['ʃo] **1.** *tv., irreg.* to cause someone to see something; to put something in someone's sight. (Pt: *showed;* pp: **shown** or *showed.*) □ *Anne showed her new book to me.* **2.** *tv., irreg.* to reveal something; to let something be known. (The object can be a clause with **that** ⑦.) □ *John's actions show that he's being sincere.* **3.** *tv., irreg.* to lead someone; to guide someone to a place. □ *The guide showed the tourists around the castle.* **4.** *tv., irreg.* to prove something; to make something clear. (The object can be a clause with **that** ⑦.) □ *These results show that my theory is sound.* **5.** *tv., irreg.* to display or deliver a kind of treatment to someone. □ *John showed his guests complete respect.* **6.** *tv., irreg.* to reveal a condition or illness. □ *John's skin is showing signs of dryness.* **7.** *tv., irreg.* [for a movie theater] to present a movie. □ *The theater showed the new movie twice last night.* **8.** *iv., irreg.* [for a condition] to appear or be visible; to be noticeable. □ *Your slip is showing.* **9.** *iv., irreg.* [for a play or a film] to be **shown** ① or presented. □ *A classic play is showing at the theater tonight.* **10.** *n.* a movie, television program, or theater performance. □ *Would you like to go see a show tonight?* **11.** *n.* a grand spectacle; a noticeable display. □ *The Smiths' huge house is a vulgar show of wealth.* **12.** *n.* something that is put on display for the public. □ *Mary went to the auto show at the convention hall.* **13.** *n.* a display of something, such as raised hands, regard, praise, etc. □ *By a show of hands, who is available for the next meeting?*

**shower** ['ʃaʊ ɚ] **1.** *n.* a device [part of the plumbing] that sprays water onto someone who is bathing. □ *David turned off the shower and dried himself with a towel.* **2.** *n.* a bath using ①. □ *After his shower, John put on clean clothes.* **3.** *n.* the place or compartment where one does ②. □ *John cleaned the soap scum from the walls of the shower.* **4.** *n.* a brief fall of rain, snow, or other liquids in drops. □ *The roads became slippery because of the snow shower.* **5.** *n.* a party for a woman who is about to get married or have a baby. □ *Anne brought a gift to Susan's wedding shower.* **6.** *iv.* to rain; to fall like rain. □ *It showered all day yesterday.* **7.** *iv.* to wash under ①. □ *John showers in the morning after he wakes up.*

**showing** ['ʃo ɪŋ] **1.** *n.* a display of something. □ *There's a showing of Picasso's paintings at the art museum.* **2.** *n.* a display of one's success or lack of success. □ *The poor showing of the TV series disappointed the network.*

**shown** ['ʃon] a pp of **show**.

**showroom** ['ʃo rum] *n.* a room where products that are available for purchase are displayed. □ *Mary walked around the showroom, looking at new cars.*

**showy** ['ʃo i] *adj.* very noticeable; designed to get attention. (Adv: *showily.* Comp: *showier;* sup: *showiest.*) □ *I found the host's showy mannerisms to be annoying.*

**shrank** ['ʃræŋk] pt of **shrink**.

**shred** ['ʃrɛd] **1.** *n.* a very small piece of something; a scrap of something; a fragment. □ *John tore the worthless check to shreds.* **2.** *tv.* to rip or cut something into **shreds** ①; to make something into **shreds** ① by rubbing against a rough or sharp surface. □ *David shredded the papers with his hands.*

**shredded** ['ʃrɛd əd] *adj.* ripped or cut into shreds; made into shreds by rubbing against a rough or sharp object. □ *The pizza was topped with shredded cheese.*

**shrewd** ['ʃrud] *adj.* clever and intelligent; showing good judgment and common sense. (Adv: *shrewdly.* Comp: *shrewder;*

S

sup: *shrewdest.*) □ *The shrewd employee was soon promoted.*

**shrewdness** ['ʃrud nəs] *n.* the quality of being shrewd. (No plural form.) □ *Because of her shrewdness, Sally earned a lot of money.*

**shriek** ['ʃrik] *n.* a loud, shrill, high-pitched scream or sound. □ *The woman let out a shriek when the window broke.*

**shrill** ['ʃrɪl] *adj.* high-pitched and irritating; annoying or loud to the point of causing pain. (Adv: *shrilly.* Comp: *shriller;* sup: *shrillest.*) □ *The teacher's shrill voice gave me a headache.*

**shrimp** ['ʃrɪmp] **1.** *n., irreg.* a shellfish, about the size and shape of a finger, with a thin body, commonly eaten as food. (Pl: *shrimp* or *shrimps.*) □ *The waitress brought me a platter containing five large shrimp.* **2.** *adj.* <the adj. use of ①.> □ *Bill makes a wonderful shrimp dish that everyone likes.*

**shrink** ['ʃrɪŋk] **1.** *iv., irreg.* to become smaller in size. (Pt: **shrank**; pp: **shrunk** or **shrunken**. **Shrunk** is usually used with auxiliary verbs, and **shrunken** is usually used as an adjective.) □ *My wool sweater shrank when I washed it.* **2.** *tv., irreg.* to cause someone or something to become smaller in size. □ *The president tried to shrink the size of the deficit.*

**shrivel** ['ʃrɪv əl] **1.** *iv.* to become wrinkled while drying up; to wither. □ *The crops shriveled in the drought.* **2.** *tv.* to cause someone or something to wither. □ *The intense heat and lack of water shriveled the crops.*

**shrub** ['ʃrʌb] *n.* a plant similar to a very small tree that has many stems coming from the ground; a bush. □ *John trimmed the shrubs with clippers.*

**shrubbery** ['ʃrʌb (ə) ri] *n.* a group of shrubs; shrubs in general. (No plural form.) □ *Some shrubbery grew next to the pond in the park.*

**shrug** ['ʃrʌg] **1.** *n.* the lifting of one's shoulders to indicate doubt or a lack of caring or interest. □ *Anne's shrug indicated that she didn't care where we went.* **2.** *tv.* to lift one's shoulders as in ①. □ *Mary shrugged her shoulders when I asked her what we should do.* **3.** *iv.* to gesture with ①. □ *I asked Anne what she wanted to eat, and she shrugged.*

**shrunk** ['ʃrʌŋk] a pp of **shrink**.

**shrunken** ['ʃrʌŋ kən] a pp of **shrink**.

**shudder** ['ʃʌd ɚ] **1.** *iv.* to shake with fear, cold, or disgust. □ *John shuddered in fear when he saw the snake.* **2.** *n.* a brief, uncontrolled shaking of the body because of fear or disgust. □ *Bill felt a shudder when he saw the huge dog.*

**shuffle** ['ʃʌf əl] **1.** *iv.* to walk without picking up one's feet; to walk in a way that one's feet never leave the ground. □ *The old man shuffled toward his mailbox.* **2.** *iv.* to mix up [playing cards so that they are] in a different order. □ *Since John is the dealer, he will shuffle.* **3.** *tv.* to move one's feet without picking them up from the ground. □ *Anne shuffled her feet down the street.* **4.** *tv.* to mix up playing cards so that they are not in any specific order. □ *The dealer shuffled the cards and then dealt them.*

**shun** ['ʃʌn] *tv.* to avoid someone or something; to stay away from someone or something. □ *The arrogant students shunned the unpopular ones.*

**shut** ['ʃʌt] **1.** *tv., irreg.* to close something, such as a door, window, or drawer. (Pt/pp: *shut.*) □ *Bill shut his desk drawer and left his office.* **2.** *tv., irreg.* to close something, such as a door, an eye, or the mouth. □ *The students shut their mouths and stopped talking.* **3.** *iv., irreg.* to become closed. □ *My eyes shut, and I fell asleep.* **4. shut up** *iv., irreg. + adv.* to stop speaking. (Colloquial and rude when used as a command.) □ *I guess that I should shut up and listen.* **5.** *adj.* closed; moved into a

S

closed position. (Not prenominal.) □ *My eyes are shut.*

**shutdown** ['ʃʌt dɑʊn] *n.* an instance of closing a factory or other place of industry for a period of time. □ *Because of the factory shutdown, 2,000 employees were left without jobs.*

**shut-in** ['ʃʌt ɪn] *n.* someone who is not able or not allowed to go outside because of sickness. □ *The volunteers delivered food to shut-ins.*

**shutter** ['ʃʌt ɚ] **1.** *n.* one of a pair of doors or panels that can be closed over the outside of a window. □ *To prepare for the storm, we closed the shutters.* **2.** *n.* a device in a camera that opens quickly and shuts in front of the lens in order to allow the proper amount of light when someone takes a picture. □ *I heard the shutter click when I took a picture.*

**shuttle** ['ʃʌt əl] **1.** *n.* a bus or an airplane making regular trips back and forth between two places. □ *I took a shuttle from school to the train station.* **2. shuttle between** places *iv.* + *prep. phr.* to travel back and forth between two places. □ *John shuttled between his offices in New York and Miami.*

**shy** ['ʃɑɪ] **1.** *adj.* nervous around other people; not likely to talk around other people; timid; reserved. (Adv: *shyly.* Comp: *shier, shyer;* sup: *shiest, shyest.*) □ *The shy teenager was afraid to talk to other students.* **2.** *adj.* not quite reaching a stated amount; almost having enough of something, but not quite. (Not prenominal. Comp: *shier, shyer;* sup: *shiest, shyest.*) □ *I realized I was five dollars shy of the amount I needed.* **3. shy away from** someone or something *phr.* to avoid someone or something, especially because or as if one is ① or afraid. □ *The frightened mail carrier shied away from the growling dog.*

**shyness** ['ʃɑɪ nəs] *n.* the quality of being shy; the quality of being timid or nervous around other people. (No plural form.) □ *Because of John's shyness, he was afraid to speak to crowds.*

**sibling** ['sɪb lɪŋ] *n.* a brother or sister. □ *How many siblings do you have?*

**sick** ['sɪk] **1.** *adj.* not healthy; ill; having a disease. (Comp: *sicker;* sup: *sickest.*) □ *The sick clerk sneezed all morning long.* **2.** *adj.* having an upset stomach and feeling like one has to vomit. (Comp: *sicker;* sup: *sickest.*) □ *The smell of the rotten eggs made me sick.* **3. sick (and tired) of** someone or something *phr.* tired of someone or something, especially something that one must do again and again or someone or something that one must deal with repeatedly. □ *Mary was sick of being stuck in traffic.*

**sicken** ['sɪk ən] **1.** *tv.* to cause someone or some creature to become sick. □ *Anne was sickened by the bugs in the kitchen.* **2.** *tv.* to disgust someone. □ *These high taxes just sicken me.* **3.** *iv.* to become sick; to become ill. □ *The kittens sickened and died a short time after birth.* **4.** *iv.* to become disgusted [with something]. □ *We sickened of the high taxes and moved to another state.*

**sickening** ['sɪk (ə) nɪŋ] *adj.* causing disgust; disgusting; nauseating. (Adv: *sickeningly.*) □ *Anne left the sickening movie before it was over.*

**sickness** ['sɪk nəs] *n.* the condition of being sick; illness; disease. □ *John was hospitalized for one week for his sickness.*

**side** ['sɑɪd] **1.** *n.* one of the flat surfaces of an object shaped like a box, not including the top or the bottom; the vertical part of something; one of the edges of a flat object shaped like a box. □ *The side of the box had the word "fragile" stamped on it.* **2.** *n.* any of the flat surfaces of an object shaped like a box; any of the edges of a flat object shaped like a box. □ *A triangle has three sides.* **3.** *n.* either surface of something that is thin and flat. □ *John put butter on one side of the toast.* **4.** *n.* a particular surface of something. □ *The maid dusted the top side of the shelf.* **5.** *n.* the shore along either edge of a river. □ *Mary swam from one side of the river to the other.* **6.** *n.* a position or area that is to the right, left, or a certain direction from a central or reference point. □ *Mary sat on the right side of Susan.* **7.** *n.* the entire left or right part of a body. □ *The bullet lodged in the victim's side.* **8.** *n.* a group of people that opposes another group, including sports teams, countries at war, or groups involved with political or social causes. □ *The other side defeated our team 12–3.* **9.** *adj.* [of a location] at, toward, or beside something. □ *David placed his coffee mug on a side table.*

**sideline** ['saɪd laɪn] **1. sidelines** *n.* the line along the side of something, especially the line at the boundary of the playing area of a sport. (Treated as plural.) □ *The coach stood on the sidelines and watched the game.* **2.** *n.* an activity done in addition to one's primary interest or work. □ *Anne is a banker, but as a sideline, she paints portraits.* **3.** *tv.* to prevent a player from playing in a sporting event. □ *The star football player was sidelined by a knee injury.*

**sidestep** ['saɪd stɛp] **1.** *tv.* to avoid injury or a crash by stepping to the side. □ *The batter sidestepped the wild pitch.* **2.** *tv.* to avoid or evade something. (Fig. on ①.) □ *The politician sidestepped the question of his honesty.*

**side street** ['saɪd strit] *n.* a residential street that is not a main street. □ *The beautiful houses lined the quiet side street.*

**sideswipe** ['saɪd swaɪp] *tv.* to hit something along its side; to hit something with one's side. □ *The truck sideswiped my car and damaged the door badly.*

**sidetrack** ['saɪd træk] **1.** *tv.* to move a train from a main track to a minor one that runs parallel to the main track. □ *An engineer sidetracked the empty train.* **2.** *tv.* to cause someone to change from the main topic. (Fig. on ①.) □ *Anne's comment sidetracked the speaker.* **3.** *tv.* to cause the subject of a conversation or speech to shift away from the original subject. □ *Anne's question sidetracked the conversation.*

**sidewalk** ['saɪd wɔk] *n.* a paved path, usually along the side of a street, for people to walk on. □ *Mary cleared the snow from the sidewalk in front of her house.*

**sideways** ['saɪd wez] **1.** *adj.* to or from a side. □ *The football player executed a sideways move to the end zone.* **2.** *adv.* to, on, or from a side or both sides; positioned with the side or edge toward the front. □ *When they took our picture, we had to stand sideways so we would all fit into the photograph.*

**siege** ['sidʒ] *n.* the surrounding of a city, fort, or place by people who are trying to capture it; an attack. □ *The siege of the soldier's camp led to a violent battle.*

**sift** ['sɪft] **1.** *tv.* to separate small pieces from larger pieces by shaking the substance through a tool containing a screen. □ *The cook sifted the flour to remove the lumps.* **2. sift through** something *iv.* + *prep. phr.* to flow through something. □ *Sand sifted slowly through the hourglass.* **3. sift through** something *iv.* + *prep. phr.* to look among a group of things closely. □ *Jane sifted through the papers on her desk, looking for the important memo.*

**sigh** ['saɪ] **1.** *iv.* to breathe out slowly and noisily, especially to indicate that one is bored, relieved, sad, or tired. □ *After John's long lecture, Susan merely sighed.* **2.** *n.* the sound of breathing out as in ①. □ *When my lost dog was found, I let out a sigh of relief.*

**sight** ['saɪt] **1.** *n.* the ability to see; the power to see; vision. (No plural form.)

□ *The blind woman had lost her sight in a car accident.* **2.** *n.* something that is seen; something in one's range of vision; a view. □ *The sun setting over the lake was a beautiful sight.* **3.** *n.* something that is worth seeing. (Often plural.) □ *John went to New York City to see the sights.* **4.** *n.* something that looks funny or strange. (No plural form.) □ *John's weird clothing is quite a sight.* **5.** *tv.* to see someone or something for the first time, especially when one is looking for that person or thing. □ *When one of the sailors sighted land, he shouted.* **6. in sight** *phr.* able to be seen. □ *The locusts ate everything in sight.*

**sighted** ['sɑɪt ɪd] *adj.* [of someone] able to see; [of someone] not blind. □ *The sighted woman helped her blind husband across the street.*

**sightless** ['sɑɪt ləs] *adj.* unable to see; without sight; blind. (Adv: *sightlessly.*) □ *The sightless woman relied on her guide dog.*

**sightseeing** ['sɑɪt si ɪŋ] *n.* visiting famous or interesting places, especially when one is on vacation. (No plural form.) □ *When Mary was in Japan, she did a lot of sightseeing.*

**sign** ['sɑɪn] **1.** *n.* a mark that represents something; a mark that indicates something. □ *The plus sign "+" is used to indicate addition.* **2.** *n.* something that indicates something else. □ *Vomiting is a sign of many different health problems.* **3.** *n.* a flat object that has information printed on it, placed where everyone can see it. □ *A sign on the highway pointed to the exit to 55th Street.* **4.** *n.* a gesture used to communicate. □ *Mother made a sign for me to come to the door.* **5.** *tv.* to write one's name [somewhere]. □ *Please sign your name on the line.* **6.** *tv.* to mark or write on something with one's name. □ *John signed his contract, thus making it official.* **7.** *tv.* to communicate something by using **sign language.** □ *The deaf man signed his request to his friend.*

S

**signal** ['sɪg nəl] **1.** *n.* something that conveys a message by affecting one of the senses; a sound, light, movement, etc., that conveys a message. □ *I waited for the customs agent's signal to proceed.* **2.** *n.* the waves sent by a radio or television transmitter. □ *I adjusted the antenna so that the signal would come in better.* **3.** *tv.* to indicate something. (The object can be a clause with **that** ⑦.) □ *The peace treaty signaled the end of the war.*

**signature** ['sɪg nə tʃɚ] *n.* a person's name, handwritten by the person. □ *Jane wrote her signature on the bottom of the contract.*

**signed** ['sɑɪnd] *adj.* marked with someone's signature. □ *The author sold signed copies of her book.*

**significance** [sɪg 'nɪf ə kəns] *n.* importance; meaning. (No plural form.) □ *The science professor explained the significance of gravity.*

**significant** [sɪg 'nɪf ə kənt] *adj.* important; having meaning. (Adv: *significantly.*) □ *The jury listened to the witness's significant testimony.*

**signify** ['sɪg nə fɑɪ] *tv.* to mean something; to indicate something; to be a sign of something. (The object can be a clause with **that** ⑦.) □ *Dark clouds signify that it will rain soon.*

**sign language** ['sɑɪn læŋ gwɪdʒ] *n.* a visual form of communication where the hands assume specific positions that represent words or letters in the language. (No plural form.) □ *Many deaf people communicate with sign language.*

**silence** ['sɑɪ ləns] **1.** *n.* absolute quiet; the absence of all sound. (No plural form.) □ *The silence in the library was appreciated by the readers.* **2.** *n.* the absence of comments about something. (No plural form.) □ *The government* *insisted on the newspaper's silence about the war.* **3.** *tv.* to cause someone to be quiet; to cause someone to stop talking or to stop making noise. □ *The librarian silenced the loud students.*

**silent** ['sɑɪ lənt] **1.** *adj.* quiet; not speaking or making noise; done without making noise. (Adv: *silently.*) □ *The silent students studied all night long.* **2.** *adj.* not pronounced; not representing a sound. (Adv: *silently.*) □ *The* p *in* pneumonia *is silent.*

**silk** ['sɪlk] **1.** *n.* a smooth, fine thread that is created by a silkworm when making its cocoon. (No plural form.) □ *Sally touched the soft strand of silk made by the worm.* **2.** *n.* cloth woven from ①. (Plural only when referring to different kinds, types, instances, or varieties.) □ *Silk is a delicate, expensive material.* Ⓒ *Silks and satins are used in fine clothing.* **3.** *adj.* made of ②. □ *The silk shirt felt smooth against my skin.*

**silkworm** ['sɪlk wɚm] *n.* a creature that makes a cocoon of silk. □ *The silkworm is the larva of a type of moth.*

**silky** ['sɪl ki] *adj.* like silk; soft and smooth; [of cloth] soft and shimmering. (Adv: *silkily.* Comp: *silkier;* sup: *silkiest.*) □ *Anne wore a silky gold dress to the dance.*

**sill** ['sɪl] *n.* the bottom ledge of a window or door frame. (See also **window sill.**) □ *Bill tripped on the door sill as he entered the room.*

**silly** ['sɪl i] *adj.* foolish; not sensible. (Comp: *sillier;* sup: *silliest.*) □ *The professor ridiculed the student's silly idea.*

**silver** ['sɪl vɚ] **1.** *n.* a bright, white, valuable metal element, which in its pure form is soft and easily shaped. (No plural form.) □ *Silver is often mixed with other metals to make jewelry, coins, and other items.* **2.** *n.* coins, which are different from paper money. (From a time when major U.S. coins were made of ①. No plural form.) □ *John gave a handful of silver to the child who was collecting money for charity.* **3.** *adj.* made of ①. □ *Anne wore silver earrings to the party.*

**silverware** ['sɪl vɚ wɛr] **1.** *n.* eating or serving utensils that are made from or plated with silver. (No plural form.) □ *The maid polished the silverware after washing it.* **2.** *n.* knives, forks, and spoons made of steel, nickel, or metals other than silver. (No plural form.) □ *We took some old silverware to the picnic.*

**silvery** ['sɪl və ri] *adj.* looking like silver. □ *The chemist examined the silvery liquid.*

**similar** ['sɪm ə lɚ] *adj.* resembling something else, but not exactly the same. (Adv: *similarly.*) □ *Oranges and tangerines are similar.*

**similarity** [sɪm ə 'lɛr ɪ ti] *n.* a way or an aspect in which someone or something is like or resembles someone or something else. □ *The researcher noticed the similarities between the two viruses.*

**simmer** ['sɪm ɚ] **1.** *tv.* to boil something gently; to cook something at or just below its boiling point. □ *The cook simmered the stew for two hours.* **2.** *iv.* to boil gently; to cook at or just below the boiling point. □ *The soup is simmering on the stove.* **3.** *iv.* to be angry without letting other people know that one is angry. (Fig. on ②.) □ *My boss simmered for days before telling us what was wrong.* **4.** *iv.* [for a situation] to be currently somewhat calm but progressing toward violence. (Fig. on ①.) □ *Ethnic unrest had simmered for months before the war.*

**simple** ['sɪm pəl] **1.** *adj.* easy; not complicated; not complex. (Adv: *simply.* Comp: *simpler;* sup: *simplest.*) □ *The teacher taught simple math problems to the schoolchildren.* **2.** *adj.* plain; not complicated; not fancy. (Adv: *simply.* Comp: *simpler;* sup: *simplest.*) □ *John and Mary had a small, simple wedding.*

S

**simplicity** [sɪm 'plɪs ɪ ti] *n.* the quality of being simple or not complicated. (No plural form.) ☐ *The simplicity of the teacher's explanation pleased me.*

**simplify** ['sɪm plə fɑɪ] *tv.* to make something more simple; to make something easier to do or understand; to make something more clear. ☐ *The college simplified its complex entry requirements.*

**simplistic** [sɪm 'plɪs tɪk] *adj.* too simple; having been simplified too much. (Adv: *simplistically* [...ɪk li].) ☐ *The simplistic answer didn't explain all of the problems.*

**simply** ['sɪm pli] **1.** *adv.* easily; without difficulty. ☐ *The problem was solved quite simply.* **2.** *adv.* merely; only. ☐ *Johnny was not dying of the plague. He simply had a case of the flu.* **3.** *adv.* absolutely; completely; very. ☐ *The critic was simply thrilled with the new movie.*

**simulate** ['sɪm jə let] *tv.* to show the nature or effects of something, allowing the observer to learn about it without experiencing it. ☐ *The experiment simulated real weather conditions.*

**simulation** [sɪm jə 'le ʃən] **1.** *n.* a demonstration of the nature or effects of an event without anyone really experiencing it. ☐ *The computer's simulation of the crime helped the detective solve it.* **2.** *n.* something that has been simulated. ☐ *The computer simulation showed what I would look like in 30 years.*

**simultaneous** [sɑɪ məl 'te ni əs] *adj.* happening or existing at the same time. (Adv: *simultaneously.*) ☐ *The simultaneous responses from Anne and Mary show that they think alike.*

**sin** ['sɪn] **1.** *n.* evil; something that is wicked or wrong; an act that is in opposition to a religious or moral principle. (Plural only when referring to different kinds, types, instances, or varieties.) ☐ *Sin will be the downfall of wicked people.* Ⓒ *My sins are numerous, but I will behave properly in the future.* **2.** *iv.* to break a religious or moral principle. ☐ *John sinned, and then he prayed to be forgiven.*

**since** ['sɪns] **1.** *conj.* from a certain time in the past until now. ☐ *Mary has lived in Texas since she was born.* **2.** *conj.* because. ☐ *Since Mary was tired, she left the party.* **3.** *prep.* from a certain time in the past until now. ☐ *I have been awake since 6:00 A.M. this morning.* **4.** *adv.* from a certain time in the past until now. ☐ *Mary left town twenty years ago and hasn't been seen since.*

**sincere** [sɪn 'sɪr] *adj.* honest; real; genuine; true. (Adv: *sincerely.* Comp: *sincerer;* sup: *sincerest.*) ☐ *I was being sincere when I told you how I felt.*

**sincerely** [sɪn 'sɪr li] **1.** *adv.* honestly; really; genuinely; truly. ☐ *I sincerely wish the best for you in the future.* **2.** *adv.* <a word used as a polite way to finish a letter, before one's signature.> ☐ *The letter was signed, "Sincerely, Anne."*

**sincerity** [sɪn 'sɛr ɪ ti] *n.* the quality of being sincere; honesty. (No plural form.) ☐ *Because of John's sincerity, people don't believe that he would lie.*

**sinful** ['sɪn fʊl] **1.** *adj.* full of sin; having committed a sin. (Adv: *sinfully.*) ☐ *I don't feel sinful, but I am sure I have committed a few bad deeds.* **2.** *adj.* wicked; bad; evil; leading people into sin. (Adv: *sinfully.*) ☐ *The church members protested against the sinful movie.*

**sing** ['sɪŋ] **1.** *iv., irreg.* to make music with one's voice, uttering a melody with words. (Pt: **sang;** pp: **sung.**) ☐ *The performers will sing for the group after dinner.* **2.** *tv., irreg.* to make music as in ①. ☐ *John sings the tenor part in the choir.*

**singe** ['sɪndʒ] *tv.* to burn something slightly; to burn the edge or end of

S

something. □ *Mary singed her hair when she bent over the stove.*

**single** ['sɪŋ gəl] **1.** *adj.* one and only one. (Adv: *singly.*) □ *I placed a single slice of cheese on my hamburger.* **2.** *adj.* individual; meant for one thing or person. (Adv: *singly.*) □ *I rented a hotel room with a single bed.* **3.** *adj.* not married. (Adv: *singly.*) □ *The young man decided to stay single all his life.* **4.** *adj.* having only one part; not double; not multiple. (Adv: *singly.*) □ *My inexpensive bicycle only has a single gear.* **5.** *n.* something that is meant for one person. □ *The hotel guest asked the front-desk clerk for a single.* **6.** *n.* a $1 bill. □ *John paid for the $4 item with singles.* **7.** *n.* someone who is not married. □ *Dozens of singles were seated around the bar.*

**single-minded** ['sɪŋ gəl 'mɑɪn dɪd] *adj.* having only one purpose. (Adv: *single-mindedly.*) □ *The suspect was questioned repeatedly by the single-minded detective.*

**singular** ['sɪŋ gjə lɚ] **1.** *adj.* referring to only one person or thing; the opposite of plural. □ Mouse *is the singular form of* mice. □ *Although* data *is a plural noun, many people use it as a singular noun.* **2.** *adj.* unusual; exceptional; remarkable. (Adv: *singularly.*) □ *John developed a singular manner for dealing with angry people tactfully.* **3.** *n.* the form of a noun that refers to only one person or thing; the opposite of plural. □ Sheep *is a word that is the same in the singular as it is in the plural.* □ *The singular of* mice *is* mouse.

**sink** ['sɪŋk] **1.** *iv., irreg.* to go beneath a surface; to fall beneath a surface. (Pt: **sank** or **sunk**; pp: **sunk**.) □ *My shoes sank into the soft mud.* **2.** *iv., irreg.* to become smaller in number; to decrease. □ *I turn up the heat when the temperature sinks to 65 degrees.* **3.** *iv., irreg.* [for someone] to collapse or fall to the ground because of weakness, fear, respect, etc. □ *The sick man clutched his heart and sank to the floor.* **4.** *tv., irreg.* to cause something to go lower and lower beneath the surface of water or some other liquid. □ *The weight of all the children sank the raft.* **5.** *n.* a permanent basin, especially in a kitchen or bathroom, for washing dishes, one's hands or face, etc. □ *David's dirty dishes piled up in his kitchen sink.*

**sinking** ['sɪŋ kɪŋ] *adj.* going further downward into a liquid. □ *The captain abandoned the sinking ship.*

**sinner** ['sɪn ɚ] *n.* someone who sins. □ *The sinner prayed that God would forgive him.*

**sinus** ['sɑɪ nəs] **1.** *n.* one of a number of spaces inside the bones of the face that are connected to the outside air by way of the nose. □ *When John gets headaches, his sinuses throb with pain.* **2.** *adj.* <the adj. use of ①.> □ *I have a terrible sinus headache.*

**sip** ['sɪp] **1.** *tv.* to drink something a little bit at a time. □ *The campers sipped hot chocolate around the campfire.* **2.** *n.* a small drink of something; a little taste of something liquid. □ *Could I have a sip of your juice?*

**siphon** AND **syphon** ['sɑɪ fən] **1.** *n.* a tube that has one end in a container of liquid and, through gravity, pulls the liquid downward into another container placed at a lower level. □ *John drained the water from the container with a siphon.* **2. siphon** something **(off)** *tv. + obj. (+ adv.)* to remove liquid from a container by using ①. □ *She siphoned the gasoline from the tank.* [T] *The chemist siphoned off the oil at the top of the barrel.*

**sir** ['sɚ] *n.* <a word used to address a man politely.> □ *Excuse me, sir, you dropped your hat.*

**siren** ['sɑɪ rən] *n.* a device that makes a loud noise of warning, such as that

S

found on police cars, fire trucks, and ambulances. ☐ *The ambulance raced to the hospital with its siren blaring.*

**sissy** ['sɪs i] *n.* a weak and shy boy; a boy who behaves like a girl. (Derogatory.) ☐ *The bully called Jimmy a sissy and then pushed him into the mud.*

**sister** ['sɪs tɚ] **1.** *n.* a female sibling; a daughter of one's mother or father. ☐ *I have two sisters, who are both younger than I am.* **2.** *n.* a nun. (Also a term of address.) ☐ *Mary joined the convent because she wanted to become a sister.*

**sister-in-law** ['sɪs tɚ ɪn lɔ] *n., irreg.* the wife of one's brother or of one's brother-in-law; the sister of one's husband or one's wife. (Pl: **sisters-in-law.**) ☐ *My brother and sister-in-law visited me last night.*

**sisters-in-law** ['sɪs tɚz ɪn lɔ] pl of **sister-in-law.**

**sit** ['sɪt] **1.** *iv., irreg.* to be in a position where the upper part of the body is straight, and the buttocks are supported by a chair, a seat, the floor, or some other surface. (Pt/pp: **sat.**) ☐ *John sat in the comfortable chair.* **2. sit (down)** *iv., irreg. (+ adv.)* to move or bend so that one gets into a position as in ①. ☐ *Please sit down, won't you?* **3.** *iv., irreg.* [for something] to be in a certain position; to be in a place. ☐ *Our television set sits in the living room.* **4.** *iv., irreg.* [for an animal] to be positioned with the back end resting on a surface. ☐ *John ordered the dog to sit.* **5.** *tv., irreg.* to make someone **sit** ① in a location. ☐ *Tom's teacher sat him in the front row.*

**site** ['sɑɪt] *n.* a location where something is happening, was happening, has happened, or will happen. ☐ *The ambulance rushed to the accident site.*

**situate** ['sɪt ʃu et] *tv.* to place something; to have or make a place for something. ☐ *The king situated the castle at the top of the hill.*

**situation** [sɪt ʃu 'e ʃən] *n.* a condition; the circumstances of an event; the state of affairs. ☐ *The reporter commented on the tense situation with the hostages.*

**six** ['sɪks] 6. Go to **four** for senses and examples.

**six-pack** ['sɪks pæk] *n.* a package of six things, especially six cans of beer or soft drinks. ☐ *Anne brought a six-pack of soda to the party.*

**sixteen** ['sɪks 'tin] 16. Go to **four** for senses and examples.

**sixteenth** ['sɪks 'tinθ] 16th. Go to **fourth** for senses and examples.

**sixth** ['sɪksθ] 6th. Go to **fourth** for senses and examples.

**sixtieth** ['sɪks ti əθ] 60th. Go to **fourth** for senses and examples.

**sixty** ['sɪks ti] 60. Go to **forty** for senses and examples.

**sizable** ['sɑɪz ə bəl] *adj.* large; rather large; much. (Adv: *sizably.*) ☐ *I have a sizable amount of work to do before I leave the office.*

**size** ['sɑɪz] **1.** *n.* the degree to which someone or something is large or small. (No plural form.) ☐ *Considering David's small size, it's amazing that he's so strong.* **2.** *n.* one measurement in a series of measurements, used to describe the **size** ① of a product one wants, such as an article of clothing, a portion of food or drink, certain hardware, etc. ☐ *The soft drinks were available in small, medium, and large sizes.*

**sizzle** ['sɪz əl] **1.** *n.* the hissing noise made when frying fat or frying food in fat. (No plural form.) ☐ *I heard a sizzle when I placed the butter in the hot pan.* **2.** *iv.* [for fat or cooking oil] to make a hissing noise when it is fried; to sound like fat when it fries. ☐ *The meat sizzled in its own juices.*

**sizzling** ['sɪz lɪŋ] **1.** *adj.* frying; making the noise that fat does when it is heated.

S

☐ *The kitchen was filled with the smell of sizzling bacon.* **2.** *adj.* very hot. ☐ *The sizzling weather made everyone sweat.*

**skate** ['sket] **1.** *n.* an **ice skate**; a **roller skate**. ☐ *Mary put on her skates and rolled toward the rink.* **2.** *iv.* to move (over a surface) while wearing **skates** ①. ☐ *Jane skated across the ice.*

**skater** ['sket ɚ] *n.* someone who ice-skates or roller-skates. ☐ *A hockey player must be a good skater.*

**skeleton** ['skɛl ə tən] **1.** *n.* the bones of a person or an animal, usually connected in their proper arrangement. ☐ *The science museum displayed several dinosaur skeletons.* **2.** *n.* an outline; the basic structure that supports something. (Fig. on ①.) ☐ *This outline is just the basic skeleton of the book I'm writing.*

**skeptic** ['skɛp tɪk] *n.* someone who doubts faith, claims, theories, or facts; someone who questions the truth of something, especially religion. ☐ *The skeptic questioned the existence of God.*

**skeptical** ['skɛp tɪ kəl] *adj.* doubting; questioning; finding something hard to believe. (Adv: *skeptically* [...ɪk li].) ☐ *A skeptical jury doubted the witness's testimony.*

**skepticism** ['skɛp tə sɪz əm] *n.* doubt; the condition of being skeptical; skeptical attitude or behavior. (No plural form.) ☐ *The lawyer noted the jury's skepticism of the witness.*

**sketch** ['skɛtʃ] **1.** *n.* a simple drawing; a rough drawing that is quickly made. ☐ *The artist drew a sketch of the fountain.* **2.** *n.* a brief description; an outline. ☐ *Mary included a sketch of her story along with the manuscript.* **3.** *n.* a short skit; a very short play that is usually funny. ☐ *The critic noted that each sketch went on too long.* **4.** *tv.* to draw someone or something roughly and quickly; to make a quick drawing. ☐ *The artist sketched a picture of the fountain.* **5.** *iv.* to draw roughly and quickly. ☐ *The artist sketched on his notepad.*

**sketchy** ['skɛtʃ i] *adj.* not complete; without details. (Adv: *sketchily.* Comp: *sketchier;* sup: *sketchiest.*) ☐ *The reporter only had sketchy information about the bomb blast.*

**ski** ['ski] **1.** *n.* one of two long, narrow, thin strips of wood or plastic used to travel on the surface of snow or water. ☐ *Mary took a pair of skis with her on vacation.* **2.** *iv.* to move on the surface of snow or water on **skis** ①. ☐ *Anne skied down the slope.*

**skid** ['skɪd] **1.** *iv.* [for a wheel of a vehicle] to continue to move over a surface after the brakes have been applied. ☐ *The car skidded to a stop when I slammed on the brakes.* **2.** *iv.* to slip forward or sideways while moving. ☐ *The car skidded into the ditch.* **3.** *n.* a forward or sideways slipping movement as with ① or ②. ☐ *A sudden skid sent the car into the ditch.*

**skier** ['ski ɚ] *n.* someone who skis on water or snow. ☐ *The expert skier sped down the slope in under a minute.*

**skiing** ['ski ɪŋ] *n.* the sport or activity of moving over snow or water on skis. (No plural form.) ☐ *Anne went skiing in the mountains of Vermont.*

**skill** ['skɪl] *n.* the ability to do something well, especially because of talent, experience, or practice. ☐ *Anne has a natural skill for playing the piano.*

**skilled** ['skɪld] *adj.* having skill; experienced. ☐ *The skilled workers made a lot of money.*

**skillet** ['skɪl ət] *n.* a shallow pan used for frying foods. ☐ *John fried some fish in a skillet.*

**skillful** ['skɪl fʊl] *adj.* having skill; experienced; able to do something very well. (Adv: *skillfully.*) ☐ *Lisa is skillful at repairing lamps.*

**skim** ['skɪm] **1.** *tv.* to remove something from the surface of a liquid. □ *The cook skimmed the fat from the top of the gravy.* **2.** *tv.* to glide over the surface of something; to go over the surface of something quickly. □ *The plane skimmed the treetops before it crashed.* **3.** *tv.* to scan reading material; to read something quickly. □ *I skimmed the newspaper while eating breakfast.* **4. skim over** something *iv. + prep. phr.* to glide over the surface of something, without touching it. □ *The airplane skimmed over the runway and took off again.*

**skin** ['skɪn] **1.** *n.* the outer covering of humans and most animals; the outer covering of many fruits and vegetables. (Plural only when referring to different kinds, types, instances, or varieties.) □ *I peeled the brown skin from the potatoes.* Ⓒ *The cook peeled the skins from the potatoes.* **2.** *tv.* to remove the skin from something. □ *The hunter skinned the deer.*

**skinny** ['skɪn i] *adj.* very thin; without much fat. (Comp: *skinnier;* sup: *skinniest.*) □ *The skinny athlete could run very fast.*

**skip** ['skɪp] **1.** *iv.* to move so that one takes a step with one foot, hops on that foot, takes a step with the second foot, and then hops on the second foot, repeatedly. □ *The young children skipped through the park.* **2. skip past** someone or something**; skip over** someone or something *iv. + prep. phr.* to pass over someone or something. □ *I skipped past the boring stories in the textbook.* **3. skip about; skip around** *iv. + adv.* to move in a random order; to be random in doing things. □ *John skipped about when quizzing me on the vocabulary list.* **4.** *tv.* to pass someone or something over; to omit something. □ *The intelligent child skipped second grade.* **5.** *tv.* to avoid attending a school class and go someplace else. □ *David skipped math because he didn't like the teacher.*

**skirmish** ['skɚ mɪʃ] *n.* a small battle or argument. □ *Five soldiers were killed in the bloody skirmish.*

**skirt** ['skɚt] **1.** *n.* an item of women's clothing that wraps around the waist and hangs down, without separate sections for each leg. □ *Anne's skirt extended to just above her knees.* **2.** *tv.* to move along the edge of something; not to move through the center of something. □ *The police skirted the edge of the angry crowd.* **3.** *tv.* to evade an issue, topic, or question; to fail to address an issue, topic, or question. □ *The politician skirted all the questions about his dishonesty.*

**skit** ['skɪt] *n.* a short performance that is usually funny or that addresses a certain topic. □ *At the assembly, some students performed a skit about drug abuse.*

**skull** ['skʌl] *n.* the bone (or set of bones) of the head; the bone that protects the brain. □ *The scientist unearthed the skull of an ancient human.*

**skunk** ['skʌŋk] *n.* a small animal that has black fur with a white stripe down its back and a bushy tail, and that releases a very bad smell when attacked or frightened. □ *The skunk sprayed the dog that was chasing it.*

**sky** ['skɑɪ] *n.* the space above the earth; the air above the earth. (Sometimes plural.) □ *The airplane flew high in the sky.*

**skydive** ['skɑɪ dɑɪv] **1.** *iv.* to jump from an airplane, fall through the air, and then open a parachute. (Pt/pp: *skydived.*) □ *I'd like to skydive, but I'm too afraid.* **2.** *n.* an instance of jumping from an airplane as in ①. □ *The skydive was canceled because of high wind.*

**skylight** ['skɑɪ lɑɪt] *n.* a window in the roof or ceiling of a building. □ *We* *installed a skylight in our living-room ceiling.*

**skyscraper** ['skɑɪ skre pɚ] *n.* a very tall building. □ *You can see for miles from the top of the skyscraper.*

**slab** ['slæb] *n.* a thick slice of something; a thick, flat piece of something. □ *The butcher cut a thick slab of beef for me.*

**slack** ['slæk] **1.** *adj.* loose; not tight; not taut. (Adv: *slackly.* Comp: *slacker;* sup: *slackest.*) □ *We loosened all the ropes so that they were slack enough to allow us to untie the knots.* **2.** *adj.* not strict; relaxed. (Fig. on ①. Adv: *slackly.* Comp: *slacker;* sup: *slackest.*) □ *The teacher was very slack when it came to discipline.* **3.** *adj.* not active; not busy. (Adv: *slackly.* Comp: *slacker;* sup: *slackest.*) □ *John took his vacation while work was slack.* **4.** *n.* looseness; a part of something that is not pulled tight. □ *The climber took up the slack by coiling some of the rope.* **5. slacks** *n.* pants; trousers. (Treated as plural. Number is expressed with *pair(s) of slacks.* Also countable. Rarely singular.) □ *David ironed his slacks before wearing them.* **6. slack off** *iv.* + *adv.* to be lazy; to work only when absolutely necessary. □ *The worker slacked off by reading a newspaper on the job.*

**slacken** ['slæk ən] *iv.* to reduce, especially in speed or tightness; to become looser or slower. □ *The rope slackened as more of it became available.*

**slain** ['slen] pp of **slay**.

**slam** ['slæm] **1.** *tv.* to shut something noisily and with force. □ *Anne slammed the lid of the box shut.* **2. slam** someone or something **against** someone or something *tv.* + *obj.* + *prep. phr.* to shove someone or something against someone or something. □ *Anne slammed her fist against the table.* **3.** *tv.* to insult or criticize someone or something very strongly. (Informal.) □ *The critic slammed the boring play.* **4.** *iv.* [for something] to shut very noisily and with force. □ *The door slammed shut.* **5. slam into** someone or something *iv.* + *prep. phr.* to run into someone or something very forcefully; to crash into someone or something with great force. □ *The car slammed into a tree.* **6.** *n.* a loud and violent closing or crash. □ *Susan shut the door with a slam.*

**slander** ['slæn dɚ] **1.** *n.* a spoken lie that is meant to hurt someone's reputation; something false that is said in order to hurt someone's reputation. (No plural form.) □ *Mary ignored her enemy's slander against her.* **2.** *tv.* to damage someone's reputation by lying about that person. □ *Mr. Jones slandered the mayor when he claimed that the mayor had cheated on his taxes.*

**slanderous** ['slæn dɚ əs] *adj.* understood or intended to be slander. (Adv: *slanderously.*) □ *The politician was sued for his slanderous statements.*

**slang** ['slæŋ] **1.** *n.* words or expressions that are not expected in formal, educational, or business settings. (Not usually plural.) □ *The teenagers laughed at the adults who used slang incorrectly.* **2.** *adj.* <the adj. use of ①.> □ *Please avoid using slang words in writing.*

**slant** ['slænt] **1.** *n.* a slope; an angle. (No plural form.) □ *The slant of the hill was very steep.* **2.** *iv.* to slope; to angle; to move at an angle; to rise or fall while moving in a certain direction. □ *The cliffs slanted sharply up from the beach.* **3.** *tv.* to cause something to be angled; to cause something to move at an angle. □ *Mary slanted the antenna to improve the television picture.* **4.** *tv.* to express something in a way that favors one point of view. □ *The newspaper slanted its news coverage of the president.*

**slap** ['slæp] **1.** *tv.* to hit someone or something with one's open hand; to hit someone or something with something flat. □ *Bill slapped his brother's back as a greeting.* **2.** *tv.* to put something on a

S

surface carelessly and with force. □ *My boss slapped some papers onto my desk and told me to read them.* **3.** *n.* a hit with one's open hand or with something flat. □ *I killed a fly with a slap of a folded newspaper.* **4.** *n.* the noise made when someone or something is hit with someone's open hand or with something flat. □ *John's palm hit the table with a loud slap.*

**slash** ['slæʃ] **1.** *tv.* to cut something violently with a sharp object, using large, sweeping movements. □ *The cat slashed the couch with its claws.* **2.** *tv.* to reduce numbers or amounts greatly. □ *The president's policies slashed the crime rate.* **3.** *n.* a cut made by a violent movement as in ①; a gash. □ *The doctor stitched up the slash in the patient's skin.* **4.** *n.* the "/" symbol; the "\" symbol. □ *The "\" symbol is called a backslash as well as a slash.*

**slate** ['slet] **1.** *n.* a rock that splits easily into flat, thin layers. (No plural form.) □ *Old chalkboards were made of slate.* **2.** *n.* a group of candidates of the same political party in an election. □ *Mary voted for the entire Democratic slate.* **3.** *adj.* made of ①. □ *My kitchen has a slate floor.*

**slaughter** ['slɔ tɚ] **1.** *tv.* to kill and cut up an animal for food. □ *The farmer slaughtered the pig by slitting its throat.* **2.** *tv.* to kill living creatures ruthlessly. □ *The fur trappers slaughtered hundreds of rabbits.*

S

**slave** ['slev] *n.* someone who is owned by someone else; someone who is the property of someone else. □ *Slaves are forced to work against their will.*

**slavery** ['slev (ə) ri] *n.* the ownership of slaves. (No plural form.) □ *In 1865, slavery was ended in the various U.S. states that had permitted it.*

**slay** ['sle] *tv., irreg.* to kill someone or some animal; to murder someone. (Pt: **slew**; pp: **slain**.) □ *The bear was slain by the hunter.*

**slaying** ['sle ɪŋ] *n.* a murder; the killing of someone or some animal. □ *The slaying of the rich executive took place at his home.*

**sleazy** ['sli zi] *adj.* cheap and crude; of a bad reputation. (Adv: *sleazily.* Comp: *sleazier;* sup: *sleaziest.*) □ *We don't spend much time in the sleazy part of town.*

**sled** ['slɛd] **1.** *n.* a flat platform attached to long, thin blades that move easily over snow. □ *The children went down the snow-covered hill on a wooden sled.* **2.** *iv.* to ride somewhere on ①; to play with ①; to travel by ①. □ *The children sledded down the hill.*

**sleek** ['slik] **1.** *adj.* smooth and shiny. (Especially used to describe hair or fur—of people or animals—that is healthy or well cared for. Adv: *sleekly.* Comp: *sleeker;* sup: *sleekest.*) □ *Mary's hair is sleek and well groomed.* **2.** *adj.* having neat, smooth lines; stylish. (Adv: *sleekly.* Comp: *sleeker;* sup: *sleekest.*) □ *The elegant car was very sleek.*

**sleep** ['slip] **1.** *n.* the period of rest when the mind is not conscious; the period of rest when the body is not awake. (No plural form.) □ *Mary's sleep was interrupted by a loud noise.* **2.** *iv., irreg.* not to be awake; to rest the body and mind in an unconscious condition. (Pt/pp: **slept**.) □ *Anne slept peacefully in her new bed.* **3.** *tv., irreg.* to provide space for a certain number of people to **sleep** ②; to have enough space for a certain number of people to **sleep** ②. □ *Jane's new tent sleeps four.* **4. put** someone or something **to sleep** *phr.* to make someone or something **sleep** ②; to make someone or something unconscious. □ *This movie is so boring it's putting me to sleep!* **5. put** someone or something **to sleep** *phr.* to kill someone or something. (Euphemism.) □ *We had to put our dog to sleep.* **6. sleep in** *phr.* to oversleep; to **sleep** ② late in the morning. □ *Friday night I went to bed very late, so Saturday I slept in.*

**sleepless** ['slip ləs] *adj.* without sleep; unable to sleep. (Adv: *sleeplessly.*) □ *Jane spent a sleepless night tossing and turning in bed.*

**sleepwalk** ['slip wɔk] *iv.* to walk while sleeping. □ *Mary sleepwalked every night at camp.*

**sleepwalker** ['slip wɔk ɚ] *n.* someone who walks around while sleeping. □ *The sleepwalker went to the kitchen and drank a glass of water.*

**sleepy** ['slip i] *adj.* tired; drowsy; needing to sleep. (Adv: *sleepily.* Comp: *sleepier;* sup: *sleepiest.*) □ *Mary put her sleepy children to bed.*

**sleet** ['slit] **1.** *n.* partly frozen rain; partly frozen rain mixed with snow or hail. (No plural form.) □ *The cold, cold sleet slapped against my face.* **2.** *iv.* [for ①] to fall from the sky. □ *It's sleeting, so drive very carefully.*

**sleeve** ['sliv] *n.* the part of an item of clothing that covers the arm. □ *Be careful. You're dipping your sleeve into your food.*

**sleeveless** ['sliv ləs] *adj.* without sleeves. (Adv: *sleevelessly.*) □ *Bill wore a sleeveless shirt to the beach.*

**sleigh** ['sle] *n.* a large sled; a platform or carriage—usually pulled by horses or dogs—attached to long, metal blades for traveling over snow. □ *The visitors were taken to the castle by sleigh.*

**slender** ['slɛn dɚ] *adj.* slim; thin, in a pleasant or graceful way. (Adv: *slenderly.* Comp: *slenderer;* sup: *slenderest.*) □ *The slender ballet dancers glided across the stage.*

**slept** ['slɛpt] pt/pp of **sleep**.

**slew** ['slu] **1.** pt of **slay**. **2.** *n.* a large amount of something. (Informal.) □ *Anne won a slew of money in the lottery.*

**slice** ['slɑɪs] **1.** *n.* a thin, flat piece that is cut from something. □ *Mary put a slice of ham on her sandwich.* **2.** *n.* a part; a portion; a share. □ *Taxes take a large slice of my income.* **3.** *tv.* to cut a thin, flat piece from something; to cut something into thin, flat pieces. □ *John sliced the bread with a knife.*

**slick** ['slɪk] **1.** *adj.* wet and slippery; oily and slippery; icy and slippery. (Adv: *slickly.* Comp: *slicker;* sup: *slickest.*) □ *The roads are slick with ice tonight.* **2.** *adj.* clever; sly; shrewd. (Informal. Adv: *slickly.* Comp: *slicker;* sup: *slickest.*) □ *The slick criminal eluded the police.* **3.** *adj.* attractive or nicely designed, but without much content or meaning; shallow. (Adv: *slickly.* Comp: *slicker;* sup: *slickest.*) □ *Advertising is usually more slick than accurate.*

**slid** ['slɪd] pt/pp of **slide**.

**slide** ['slɑɪd] **1.** *iv., irreg.* to move or glide along a smooth surface; to move down a surface; to move without resistance. (Pt/pp: **slid**.) □ *Cars slide easily on ice.* **2.** *iv., irreg.* to move backward or forward on a groove or track. □ *The folding closet doors slid along a track.* **3.** *tv., irreg.* to move someone or something or glide someone or something along a smooth surface or on a track; to cause someone or something to move or glide along a smooth surface. □ *The children slid pennies across the floor.* **4.** *tv., irreg.* to move something quietly, especially without anyone else noticing. □ *The spy slid a message under the door.* **5.** *n.* a downward movement; a decline. □ *The stock market's slide caused many people to lose money.* **6.** *n.* a small, square frame with a picture on a piece of film in the center, the image of which can be projected onto a screen. □ *John showed us a lot of slides from his vacation.* **7.** *n.* a small, thin, rectangular piece of glass that small objects are placed on so that they can be examined under a

S

microscope. □ *The scientist examined the slide under a microscope.*

**slight** ['slɑɪt] **1.** *adj.* not very large; not very important. (Adv: *slightly.* Comp: *slighter;* sup: *slightest.*) □ *The pretty vase had a slight chip on its rim.* **2.** *adj.* frail; delicate; not strong. (Adv: *slightly.* Comp: *slighter;* sup: *slightest.*) □ *The slight lady had difficulty walking against the wind.* **3.** *tv.* to neglect mentioning someone or something; to insult a person by ignoring the person's presence or accomplishments. □ *The manager slighted his staff by not acknowledging their help.* **4.** *n.* the insult of treating someone as unimportant; the lack of attention paid to someone or something. □ *What Mary thought was a slight turned out to be an oversight.*

**slightly** ['slɑɪt li] *adv.* a little; to a small degree. □ *I like pizza slightly more than I like spaghetti.*

**slim** ['slɪm] **1.** *adj.* very thin; slender. (Adv: *slimly.* Comp: *slimmer;* sup: *slimmest.*) □ *John read the slim book in half an hour.* **2.** *adj.* small in amount or quality; slight. (Adv: *slimly.* Comp: *slimmer;* sup: *slimmest.*) □ *The chance that the limping horse would win the race was slim.*

**slime** ['slɑɪm] *n.* a soft, sticky, unpleasant fluid; filth. (No plural form.) □ *I cleaned the slime out from underneath my refrigerator.*

S

**slimy** ['slɑɪ mi] *adj.* covered with slime; like slime; filthy. (Adv: *slimily.* Comp: *slimier;* sup: *slimiest.*) □ *The green stuff growing on the inside of the aquarium felt slimy.*

**sling** ['slɪŋ] **1.** *tv., irreg.* to throw something with force; to hurl something; to fling something. (Pt/pp: **slung.**) □ *The pitcher slung the baseball toward the batter.* **2.** *tv., irreg.* to hang or suspend something from something or between two things. (Informal.) □ *David slung the wire between the two poles.* **3.** *n.* a strip of cloth that is used to support an injured arm by being looped around the neck. □ *Mary wore a sling while her broken arm healed.*

**slip** ['slɪp] **1.** *iv.* to fall accidentally while moving or being moved; to slide from a place or position. □ *Mary slipped on the curb and twisted her ankle.* **2.** *iv.* to move or happen quietly, quickly, smoothly, easily, secretly, or without being noticed. □ *The spy slipped into the castle.* **3.** *iv.* to grow worse; to lower; to diminish; to decline. □ *The president's approval ratings slipped during the war.* **4.** *n.* an accidental fall as in ①. □ *John's slip resulted in a broken leg.* **5.** *n.* a mistake; an error; something that was done wrong. □ *The accountant made a few slips when adding up the figures.*

**slipper** ['slɪp ɚ] *n.* a foot covering that one wears indoors and that can be taken on and off easily; a shoe made of light materials. □ *I took off my slippers and put on my shoes before going outside.*

**slippery** ['slɪp (ə) ri] **1.** *adj.* allowing things or people to slip. □ *Bill fell on the slippery ice.* **2.** *adj.* hard to catch or hold; likely to slip out of one's hands. □ *The slippery fish squirmed out of Anne's hands.*

**slit** ['slɪt] **1.** *n.* a straight, narrow cut or opening. □ *My skirt has a slit on one side.* **2.** *tv., irreg.* to cut or tear something in a straight line so that there is a narrow opening. (Pt/pp: *slit.*) □ *I slit the envelope and took out the letter.*

**sliver** ['slɪv ɚ] *n.* a small, thin, sharp piece or stick of something. □ *Slivers of glass from the broken window are all over the floor.*

**slogan** ['slo gən] *n.* a motto; a unique word or phrase used in advertising or politics. □ *The marketers developed a memorable slogan for the new product.*

**slope** ['slop] **1.** *n.* the slanted side of a mountain or hill. □ *The children sled-*

ded down the snowy slope. **2.** *n.* the amount that a line or surface **slopes** ③. (No plural form.) □ *The road on the mountain ran at a sharp slope.* **3.** *iv.* to lean, be set at, or be formed at an angle. □ *The roof sloped at a steep angle.* **4.** *tv.* to cause something to be at an angle; to cause something not to be level or straight up and down. □ *The artist sloped his drawing board appropriately.*

**sloping** ['slop ɪŋ] *adj.* at an angle; not flat or straight up and down. (Adv: *slopingly.*) □ *The worker fell off the sloping roof.*

**sloppy** ['slɑp i] **1.** *adj.* muddy; rainy; very wet as the result of bad weather. (Adv: *sloppily.* Comp: *sloppier;* sup: *sloppiest.*) □ *It's very sloppy out, so wear your boots.* **2.** *adj.* messy; not tidy; careless. (Adv: *sloppily.* Comp: *sloppier;* sup: *sloppiest.*) □ *The sloppy employee made a lot of mistakes.*

**slot** ['slɑt] **1.** *n.* a narrow opening in an object or machine. □ *Mary placed her credit card in the slot on the gas pump.* **2.** *n.* a place on a list or schedule. □ *The dentist has a slot open at 3:00 next Monday.* **3.** *tv.* to place someone or something on a list or schedule. □ *I've slotted a lunch date with you into my schedule for the 10th of August.*

**slouch** ['slɑʊtʃ] *iv.* to sit, stand, or move without holding one's body erect. □ *The instructor yelled at the dancers whenever they slouched.*

**slovenly** ['slʌv ən li] *adj.* [of someone] dirty or messy in appearance. □ *John is simply a very slovenly person.*

**slow** ['slo] **1.** *adj.* not fast; not quick; taking a long time; taking more time than average; moving with less speed than average. (Adv: *slowly. See also* **slow** ⑤. Comp: *slower;* sup: *slowest.*) □ *The slow turtle crossed the road.* **2.** *adj.* behind schedule; happening later than the time something is supposed to happen. (Comp: *slower;* sup: *slowest.*) □ *I'm late, so my watch must be slow.* **3.** *adj.* boring; dull; without much action or interest. (Comp: *slower;* sup: *slowest.*) □ *The audience yawned during the slow movie.* **4.** *adv.* at a **slow** ① pace. (Comp: *slower;* sup: *slowest.*) □ *This clock runs slow.* **5.** *iv.* to become ①; to become more ①; to move more ④. □ *People often slow as they become older.* **6.** *tv.* to cause something to become ①; to cause something to move more ④. □ *Jane slowed the car as she approached the intersection.*

**slow motion** ['slo 'mo ʃən] **1.** *n.* movement in a film or video image that appears slower than in real life. (No plural form.) □ *Slow motion made it possible to see the football play better.* **2. slow-motion** *adj.* moving slower than normally; moving at a speed slower than what is normal; happening at a slower speed, especially on film or video. □ *The slow-motion footage showed the impact of the accident.*

**slug** ['slʌg] **1.** *n.* a small, slimy creature, similar to a snail without a shell. □ *The slug left a slimy trail as it crawled across the pavement.* **2.** *n.* a hit or blow, especially with a closed fist. □ *John greeted his friend with a playful slug on the shoulder.* **3.** *tv.* to hit someone or something using one's closed fist. □ *The police officer slugged the thief in the alley.*

**sluggish** ['slʌg ɪʃ] *adj.* moving slowly or without energy; not very active. (Adv: *sluggishly.*) □ *The sluggish driver pulled into a rest stop for a nap.*

**slum** ['slʌm] *n.* a poor neighborhood where most of the people live in poverty. □ *The mayor vowed to rebuild the city's slums.*

**slumber** ['slʌm bɚ] **1.** *iv.* to sleep. □ *The prince killed the dragon as it slumbered in its cave.* **2.** *n.* sleep; deep rest. □ *My slumber was interrupted by the telephone.*

**slump** ['slʌmp] **1.** *n.* a financial collapse; a sudden fall or decline. □ *The new director helped the company out of its financial slump.* **2.** *iv.* to sink; to slouch. □ *The weary worker slumped in his chair.* **3.** *iv.* [for a value] to sink lower. (Fig. on ②.) □ *The price of gold slumped for the second day in a row.*

**slung** ['slʌŋ] pt/pp of **sling**.

**slur** ['slɚ] **1.** *tv.* to say something in a way that is not clear; to pronounce something in a way that is not clear. □ *Don't slur your words! Speak slowly and clearly.* **2.** *n.* an insult. □ *David apologized for his rude slur.*

**slush** ['slʌʃ] *n.* a mixture of snow and water; snow that has started to melt. (No plural form.) □ *My foot got wet when I stepped in a puddle of slush.*

**sly** ['slɑɪ] *adj.* sneaky; clever; able to do things secretly. (Adv: *slyly.* Comp: *slyer;* sup: *slyest.*) □ *John would make a good spy because he's very sly.*

**smack** ['smæk] *tv.* to hit someone or something, especially noisily; to strike someone or something noisily, as with an open hand or a flat object. □ *The door smacked me on the side of the head.*

**small** ['smɔl] **1.** *adj.* not large; less than average size or weight. (Comp: *smaller;* sup: *smallest.*) □ *Can that small child eat such a big piece of cake?* **2.** *adj.* little; slight; not a lot; having less than an average amount of something. (Comp: *smaller;* sup: *smallest.*) □ *I gave a small amount of change to the beggar.* **3.** *adj.* lowercase; not capital. □ *Several examples of small letters are* a, b, c, d, *and* e.

**small talk** ['smɔl tɔk] *n.* unimportant conversation; conversation about things that are not important. (No plural form.) □ *Weather is a common topic for small talk.*

**smart** ['smɑrt] **1.** *adj.* intelligent; not stupid; able to learn things quickly. (Comp: *smarter;* sup: *smartest.*) □ *The very smart child skipped fifth grade.* **2.** *adj.* showing current style; in style; in fashion; trendy. (Adv: *smartly.* Comp: *smarter;* sup: *smartest.*) □ *Mary wore smart shoes with her stylish clothes.* **3.** *iv.* to sting; to feel sharp pain; to cause sharp pain. □ *The bee sting smarted.*

**smash** ['smæʃ] **1.** *tv.* to break something into tiny pieces noisily or violently. □ *The vandal smashed the vase with a hammer.* **2.** *iv.* to break into tiny pieces noisily or violently. □ *The mirror smashed when I accidentally dropped it.*

**smear** ['smɪr] **1.** *tv.* to spread something on a surface, especially in a careless or messy fashion. □ *The child smeared paint everywhere.* **2.** *tv.* to ruin someone's reputation; to make someone look bad; to say bad things about someone. □ *The gossip columnist smeared the actor's reputation.* **3.** *n.* a stain; a mark made by wiping something on a surface. □ *Go wash that paint smear from your face.*

**smell** ['smɛl] **1.** *n.* odor; something in the air, sensed with one's nose. (Plural only when referring to different kinds, types, instances, or varieties.) □ *Smell and taste are closely related senses.* Ⓒ *There are bad smells in the basement.* **2.** *tv.* to sense something with the nose; to sense an odor or scent; to sense something that has an odor or scent. □ *John smelled the roses on the table.* **3.** *iv.* to have a certain quality of scent or odor. □ *These roses smell good.* **4.** *iv.* to stink; to have a bad smell. □ *A skunk's spray really smells!*

**smelly** ['smɛl i] *adj.* having a bad or strong odor. (Comp: *smellier;* sup: *smelliest.*) □ *Please wash your smelly shirt.*

**smile** ['smɑɪl] **1.** *n.* a facial expression where the ends of the mouth are turned up, indicating happiness, amusement, or a good mood. □ *David has a nice smile in this photograph.* **2.** *iv.* to have ①

S

on one's face; to look happy or pleased. □ *John smiled in response to my funny joke.*

**smiling** ['smɑɪl ɪŋ] *adj.* having a smile; happy; cheerful. (Adv: *smilingly.*) □ *A friendly photographer took a picture of the smiling children.*

**smock** ['smɑk] *n.* a light covering that one wears over one's clothes to protect one's clothes from becoming dirty while working, especially as worn by a doctor, nurse, painter, etc. □ *The painter's clothes were protected by a smock.*

**smog** ['smɔg] *n.* smoke and fog that are trapped in the air; a mixture of fumes and smoke that is trapped like fog over a place. (A combination of *smoke* and *fog.* No plural form.) □ *People with lung diseases should stay indoors when there's a lot of smog.*

**smoke** ['smok] **1.** *n.* a cloud of gas that can be seen in the air when something burns. (No plural form.) □ *Where there's smoke, there's fire.* **2.** *n.* an act or session of burning tobacco and inhaling the **smoke** ①. (Informal.) □ *The college students had a quick smoke between classes.* **3.** *iv.* to give off ①; to release ① into the air. □ *The overheated engine began to smoke.* **4.** *iv.* to inhale and then exhale ① from burning tobacco. □ *The teachers smoked between classes.* **5.** *tv.* to inhale ① of burning cigarettes, tobacco, etc., into the lungs. □ *You aren't allowed to smoke tobacco here.* **6.** *tv.* to preserve food by exposing it to ① from burning wood. □ *We smoked the fish we had caught.*

**smoking** ['smok ɪŋ] **1.** *adj.* giving off smoke. □ *David turned off the smoking toaster.* **2.** *adj.* <a word used to indicate that smoking is permitted.> □ *David took a smoking flight to Europe.*

**smoky** ['smok i] **1.** *adj.* [of air] full of smoke; tasting or smelling like smoke. (Comp: *smokier;* sup: *smokiest.*) □ *I began to cough in the smoky bar.* **2.** *adj.* giving off more smoke than normal or expected. (Adv: *smokily.* Comp: *smokier;* sup: *smokiest.*) □ *The campers sat far away from the smoky campfire.*

**smolder** ['smol dɚ] *iv.* [for wood or other fibers] to burn or give off smoke without having a flame. □ *The ashes from the fire smoldered for hours.*

**smoldering** ['smol dɚ ɪŋ] *adj.* burning or giving off smoke without having a flame. (Adv: *smolderingly.*) □ *The firefighters put water on the smoldering house.*

**smooth** ['smuð] **1.** *adj.* having an even surface; having a surface without bumps; not rough. (Adv: *smoothly.* Comp: *smoother;* sup: *smoothest.*) □ *The baby's skin is soft and smooth.* **2.** *adj.* gentle; not rough; calm; not harsh. (Adv: *smoothly.* Comp: *smoother;* sup: *smoothest.*) □ *We had a smooth flight across the Atlantic.* **3.** *adj.* without lumps; having an even texture. (Adv: *smoothly.* Comp: *smoother;* sup: *smoothest.*) □ *Bill stirred the paint until it was smooth.* **4.** *tv.* to cause something to become **smooth** ①; to cause something to become smoother. □ *Anne smoothed the coarse wood with sandpaper.*

**smother** ['smʌð ɚ] **1.** *iv.* to die because one cannot get enough oxygen, especially because something is covering one's mouth; to suffocate. □ *The victims had smothered from the smoke.* **2.** *tv.* to kill a living creature by preventing it from breathing. □ *The murderer smothered his victims with a pillow.* **3.** *tv.* to cover something with a thick layer of something. □ *John smothered his sandwich with mustard.*

**smudge** ['smʌdʒ] **1.** *n.* a dirty mark or stain; a smear. □ *John cleaned the smudge of dirt from his shoe.* **2.** *tv.* to dirty something with a mark. □ *I smudged my pants with the mustard that fell from my sandwich.*

**smug** ['smʌg] *adj.* confident and pleased with oneself and one's abilities; too satisfied with oneself. (Adv: *smugly.* Comp: *smugger;* sup: *smuggest.*) ☐ *The smug designer thought her designs were better than anyone else's.*

**smuggle** ['smʌg əl] *tv.* to bring something into or take something out of a country illegally. ☐ *The criminals smuggled drugs into the country.*

**smuggler** ['smʌg lɚ] *n.* a criminal who brings something into or takes things from a country illegally. ☐ *The drug smuggler was sentenced to life in prison.*

**smuggling** ['smʌg lɪŋ] *n.* the illegal business of bringing something into or taking things out of a country. (No plural form.) ☐ *The drug dealer was also arrested for smuggling.*

**snack** ['snæk] **1.** *n.* food that is eaten between meals; a small amount of food. ☐ *John gained weight because he ate too many snacks.* **2.** *iv.* to eat a small amount of food between meals. ☐ *I try to eat only healthy foods when I snack.*

**snag** ['snæg] **1.** *n.* a thread that is pulled out of place from a fabric. ☐ *Mary had a snag in her stockings.* **2.** *n.* something that gets in the way; something that causes a problem in a plan or procedure. ☐ *The project was delayed due to an unfortunate snag.* **3.** *tv.* to catch a piece of clothing or material by a thread. ☐ *A hook snagged Bob's sweater.*

S

**snail** ['snel] *n.* a small, soft creature that has no limbs, has two small feelers, and lives in a hard, round shell. ☐ *The snail left a slimy trail as it moved.*

**snake** ['snek] **1.** *n.* a long, thin reptile that has no limbs. ☐ *The snake coiled around the rat and squeezed it.* **2.** *iv.* to move in twists and turns; to curve like ①. ☐ *The river snaked toward the sea.* **3.** *tv.* to move something in twists and turns; to bend something into curves like the curves of ①. ☐ *Mary snaked the electrical cord around her furniture.*

**snap** ['snæp] **1.** *iv.* [for something] to make a sharp, popping sound, usually by breaking. ☐ *A branch snapped, making the deer run deep into the forest.* **2.** *iv.* [for something that is pulled tight or under pressure] to break suddenly. ☐ *The climber fell to his death when the rope snapped.* **3.** *tv.* to break something that is pulled tight or under pressure. ☐ *The car crash snapped John's leg.* **4.** *tv.* to take a picture with a camera. ☐ *John snapped a picture of his friends.* **5.** *tv.* to close a **snap** ⑧. ☐ *Anne snapped the snaps on her jeans.* **6.** *n.* the noise made when someone or something **snaps** as in ① or ②; a quick, sudden, popping sound. ☐ *The snap of the lid closing caught my attention.* **7.** *n.* a sudden breaking of something; the breaking of something that is pulled tight or under pressure. ☐ *I felt a snap and my pants came open.* **8.** *n.* a metal or plastic fastener that closes firmly when pressed. ☐ *The top snap of John's shirt popped open.*

**snapshot** ['snæp ʃɑt] *n.* a photograph; a picture taken with a camera. ☐ *John showed me snapshots of his vacation.*

**snare** ['snɛr] **1.** *tv.* to trap someone or something; to catch someone or something in a trap. ☐ *The hunter snared the fox.* **2.** *n.* a trap for catching animals. ☐ *The snare held the fox by its leg.*

**snarl** ['snɑrl] **1.** *iv.* to growl. ☐ *The angry dog snarled at the mail carrier.* **2.** *iv.* to become tangled. ☐ *My long hair snarled after I washed it.* **3.** *n.* an angry growl. ☐ *The dog's snarl scared the mail carrier.*

**snarling** ['snɑr lɪŋ] *adj.* growling angrily. ☐ *The snarling dog barked at the mail carrier.*

**snatch** ['snætʃ] *tv.* to grab someone or something suddenly; to steal something or kidnap someone. ☐ *The kidnapper snatched a four-year-old from the mall.*

**sneak** ['snik] **1.** *iv., irreg.* to move quietly and secretly; to move without being noticed. (Pt/pp: *sneaked* or **snuck.**) □ *The thief sneaked around the house.* **2.** *tv., irreg.* to obtain or take something, such as a taste, a look, a peek, a touch, etc., quietly and secretly. □ *The boys sneaked a look at the forbidden magazine.*

**sneaker** ['snik ɚ] *n.* one of a pair of gym shoes or tennis shoes; one of a pair of comfortable, casual canvas shoes with rubber soles. □ *Anne wore her sneakers to the gym.*

**sneaky** ['snik i] *adj.* doing something dishonest or wrong, quietly and secretly. (Adv: *sneakily.* Comp: *sneakier;* sup: *sneakiest.*) □ *The sneaky spy stole government secrets.*

**sneer** ['snɪr] **1.** *iv.* to show contempt by the look on one's face. □ *The actor sneered at the fan who asked for an autograph.* **2.** *n.* a look of contempt. □ *The actor looked at the fan with a sneer.*

**sneeze** ['sniz] **1.** *n.* a sudden and uncontrollable burst of air and mucus that is pushed out of the nose and mouth. □ *Mary's loud sneeze caught my attention.* **2.** *iv.* to make ①. □ *John sneezed into a tissue.*

**snicker** ['snɪk ɚ] **1.** *iv.* to laugh; to laugh at someone or something. □ *Mary snickered at the silly joke.* **2.** *n.* a laugh; a small laugh. □ *I responded to the joke with a snicker.*

**sniff** ['snɪf] **1.** *iv.* to breathe in through the nose in small, quick puffs that can be heard. □ *Mary sniffed a few times, and then she sneezed.* **2.** *iv.* to become aware of a smell by **sniffing** as in ①. □ *My dog sniffed at the base of the tree.* **3.** *n.* a small, quick breath made through the nose, made especially when smelling something. □ *I caught a sniff of onions and knew someone was cooking.*

**snip** ['snɪp] **1.** *tv.* to clip something; to cut something with scissors in short strokes; to cut something up into tiny pieces. □ *Mary snipped coupons from the newspaper.* **2.** *n.* a short cutting movement; a short stroke made with scissors. □ *Anne cut the string with a snip of her scissors.*

**snob** ['snɑb] *n.* someone who displays arrogance; someone who acts superior to others. □ *The snob ridiculed the way the others were dressed.*

**snobbish** ['snɑb ɪʃ] *adj.* arrogant; thinking that one is better than others. (Adv: *snobbishly.*) □ *The snobbish diner talked to the waiter as though he were stupid.*

**snoop** ['snup] *iv.* to sneak; to pry; to search through something without the owner's permission. □ *Mary snooped through Anne's desk for the confidential file.*

**snooze** ['snuz] **1.** *iv.* to sleep; to nap. □ *The bored students snoozed during the lecture.* **2.** *n.* sleep; a nap. (Informal.) □ *Mary took a quick snooze between classes.*

**snore** ['snor] *iv.* to breathe loudly while sleeping, especially to pass air through the nose so that it vibrates and makes a loud noise. □ *When John snored, I held his nose until he stopped.*

**snow** ['sno] **1.** *n.* water vapor that has frozen into small white flakes that fall from the sky. (No plural form.) □ *The main roads were closed because there was so much snow.* **2.** *n.* an instance of ① falling from the sky; a coating of ① on the ground. □ *After the snows of winter ended, it was spring.* **3.** *iv.* [for ①] to fall from the sky. □ *Because it had snowed, driving was rather dangerous.*

**snowball** ['sno bɔl] **1.** *n.* a ball of snowflakes that have been pressed together. □ *Anne knocked the hat off my head with a snowball.* **2.** *iv.* to grow at a rapidly increasing rate. (Fig. on ①.)

☐ *The sales of the new product snowballed rapidly, making it very profitable.*

**snowbank** ['sno bæŋk] *n.* a big, long mound of snow. ☐ *The wind swept the snow into large snowbanks.*

**snow blower** ['sno blo ɚ] *n.* a machine that clears snow from walks and pavements. ☐ *Mary cleared her driveway with a snow blower.*

**snowbound** ['sno bɑʊnd] *adj.* not able to leave home or travel because there is too much snow. ☐ *The snowbound campers stayed in their tent for a week.*

**snowdrift** ['sno drɪft] *n.* a ridge of snow shaped by wind blowing it along the ground. ☐ *The children hid among the large snowdrifts.*

**snowflake** ['sno flek] *n.* one individual piece of snow; a drop of water that freezes and falls from the sky as snow. ☐ *No two snowflakes are identical in shape.*

**snowman** ['sno mæn] *n., irreg.* a mass of snow that has been shaped like a person. (Pl: **snowmen.**) ☐ *I made a snowman, and my brother knocked it down.*

**snowmen** ['sno mɛn] pl of **snowman.**

**snowplow** ['sno plɑʊ] *n.* a tractor or other vehicle with a large scoop or blade in front to clear snow from roads, driveways, and other surfaces. ☐ *The snow moved by the snowplow covered my car.*

S

**snowstorm** ['sno storm] *n.* a storm with lots of snow; a blizzard. ☐ *Mary couldn't get home because she was caught in a snowstorm.*

**snuck** ['snʌk] a pt/pp of **sneak.**

**snug** ['snʌg] **1.** *adj.* warm; cozy; comfortable. (Adv: *snugly.* Comp: *snugger;* sup: *snuggest.*) ☐ *The children were snug in their beds on the cold night.* **2.** *adj.* too tight; fitting too closely. (Adv: *snugly.* Comp: *snugger;* sup: *snuggest.*) ☐ *Since I've gained weight, all of my clothes have become snug.*

**snuggle** ['snʌg əl] *iv.* to cuddle; to press against someone for warmth or to show affection. ☐ *It was so cold that we snuggled in bed for warmth.*

**so** ['so] **1.** *adv.* to a certain degree; to such a high degree; very. ☐ *John was so hungry that he ate a whole pizza.* **2.** *adv.* in such a way; in that way; in this way. ☐ *That won't work. You must do it so.* **3.** *adv.* also; too; as well. (Comes before the verbs, **be, do,** or **have.** In negative constructions, use **neither** or *not either.*) ☐ *Mary is cold, and so am I.* **4.** *conj.* in order that; with the result that. ☐ *Dave went to the lake so he could go swimming.* **5.** *conj.* therefore; hence; consequently. ☐ *Bill inherited a lot of money, so he quit his job.* **6.** *interj.* <a mild exclamation of surprise or indignation.> ☐ *So! Do you think you can fool me?* **7.** *adj.* true. ☐ *Please tell me that it is not so!*

**soak** ['sok] **1.** *iv.* to remain in [a container of] liquid for a period of time. ☐ *John soaked in the tub.* **2.** *tv.* to cause something to become or remain completely wet. ☐ *The rain soaked my clothes.* **3.** *n.* a period of time spent in [a container of] liquid. ☐ *These dirty clothes need a soak.*

**soap** ['sop] **1.** *n.* a substance that helps clean objects being washed. (Plural only when referring to different kinds, types, instances, or varieties.) ☐ *Mary squirted some liquid soap into the dishwater.* Ⓒ *Soaps having too strong a smell irritate my nose.* **2.** *tv.* to clean someone or something with ①; to cover someone or something with ① while washing. ☐ *Bill soaped himself and then washed off the lather.*

**soap opera** ['sop ɑp rə] *n.* a daily or weekly television drama that usually revolves around the lives and problems of people in a certain family, town, or place of work. ☐ *My friends and I watch our favorite soap opera every afternoon at 2:00.*

**soapy** ['so pi] *adj.* covered with soap. (Adv: *soapily.* Comp: *soapier;* sup: *soapiest.*) □ *John soaked the dirty dishes in hot, soapy water.*

**soar** ['sor] **1.** *iv.* to fly; to fly upward; to glide. □ *The kite soared over the trees.* **2.** *iv.* to increase suddenly and in a large amount; to go up suddenly and in a large amount. (Fig. on ①.) □ *The cost of gasoline soared during the oil crisis.*

**sob** ['sɑb] **1.** *iv.* to cry while breathing short, quick breaths. □ *I sobbed during the sad movie.* **2.** *n.* a short, quick sound made while one is crying. □ *I heard sobs coming from Jimmy's bedroom.*

**sober** ['sob ɚ] **1.** *adj.* not drunk; not having been drinking alcohol. (Adv: *soberly.* Comp: *soberer;* sup: *soberest.*) □ *You should never drive a car if you are not sober.* **2.** *adj.* very serious; with dignity. (Adv: *soberly.* Comp: *soberer;* sup: *soberest.*) □ *A sober and frowning judge ordered the courtroom to be quiet.*

**soccer** ['sɑk ɚ] *n.* a sport played by two teams of eleven people. (In Europe, soccer is called **football**. No plural form.) □ *John wanted to play soccer, but his school didn't have a team.*

**social** ['so ʃəl] **1.** *adj.* of or about friendship or interaction with other people. (Adv: *socially.*) □ *John attended a social function last weekend.* **2.** *adj.* living together or forming groups in an organized way. (Adv: *socially.*) □ *Since wolves travel in organized packs, they are considered to be social animals.*

**social security** ['so ʃəl sə 'kjɚ ə ti] **1.** *n.* a pension system operated by the government, making payments to people who have retired or to families of a worker who has died. (No plural form. Often capitalized.) □ *After John turned 65, he received social security.* **2.** *adj.* <the adj. use of ①.> □ *Anne receives social security payments each month.*

**society** [sə 'sɑɪ ə ti] **1.** *n.* all people; all humans. (No plural form.) □ *Society benefits greatly when the economy is strong.* **2.** *n.* all people in a certain culture during a certain period of time. □ *Anne studied the philosophy of Eastern societies.* **3.** *n.* an organization whose members have similar interests or goals; a club. □ *The esteemed professor was a member of many academic societies.* **4.** *n.* the upper-class people of a community; the community of people assumed to have good manners; people who are thought to be in a exclusive or desirable social class. (No plural form.) □ *That is not the proper way to behave in society.*

**sociology** [so si 'ɑl ə dʒi] *n.* the study of the functioning and organization of human society. (No plural form.) □ *Mary majored in sociology and wrote about family structure.*

**sock** ['sɑk] *n.* a knitted or woven fabric covering for the foot, usually worn inside a shoe. □ *The wool socks kept my feet warm.*

**socket** ['sɑk ət] *n.* one of a number of types of opening that something round fits into. □ *The blow knocked Bob's tooth right out of its socket.*

**sod** ['sɑd] *n.* turf; a piece of ground held together by the roots of grass. (No plural form.) □ *Workers replaced the dead grass with new sod.*

**soda** ['so də] **1.** *n.* a soft drink; a drink with lots of little bubbles, usually sweetly flavored. (Short for **soda pop**.) □ *I need a can of soda to give me some energy.* **2.** *n.* water containing lots of little bubbles, having little or no flavor. (Short for **soda water**.) □ *I usually have some soda water after I have eaten a big meal.*

**soda pop** ['so də pɑp] *n.* a **soft drink**; a bubbly drink that has no alcohol and is usually flavored and sweet. (Can be shortened to **soda** or **pop**.) □ *My* *brother drinks soda pop at almost every meal.* □ *I want to buy a few sodas at the store.*

**soda water** ['so də wɑ tə] *n.* water that has thousands of tiny bubbles in it, making it bubbly. (Can be shortened to **soda**.) □ *Soda water tickles my tongue.*

**sofa** ['so fə] *n.* a couch; a seat that is wide enough for more than one or two people. □ *I bought a matching sofa and chair for my living room.*

**soft** ['sɔft] **1.** *adj.* not hard; yielding to pressure; less hard than average. (Adv: *softly.* Comp: *softer;* sup: *softest.*) □ *Anne's head sank into the soft pillow.* **2.** *adj.* delicate; smooth; calm; not rough; not coarse; not harsh; gently affecting the senses. (Adv: *softly.* Comp: *softer;* sup: *softest.*) □ *The soft light masked the actress's wrinkles.* **3.** *adj.* not strong or strict; weak or lax. (Adv: *softly.* Comp: *softer;* sup: *softest.*) □ *Our mother was really soft when it came to handing out punishment.* **4.** *adj.* [of water] lacking certain minerals and able to make lather from soap easily. (Comp: *softer;* sup: *softest.*) □ *Soft water is usually better than hard water for washing clothes.* **5.** *adj.* [of a letter] pronounced like the *c* in *cent* rather than the *c* of *cold.* □ Genius *begins with a soft* g. □ *The* c *in the word* receive *is soft.* **6.** *adj.* quiet; not loud. (Adv: *softly.* See also **soft** ⑦. Comp: *softer;* sup: *softest.*) □ *Bill has a very soft voice.* **7.** *adv.* quietly; not as loudly. (Comp: *softer;* sup: *softest.*) □ *Don't speak so soft. I can't hear you.*

**softball** ['sɔft bɔl] **1.** *n.* a game that is similar to baseball but uses a bigger, softer ball. (No plural form.) □ *My sister taught her son to play softball.* **2.** *n.* a ball that is like a baseball but is bigger and somewhat softer. □ *The pitcher threw the softball to the catcher.* **3.** *adj.* <the adj. use of ①.> □ *Tom joined a softball team to get some exercise.*

**soft drink** ['sɔft drɪŋk] *n.* a carbonated drink without alcohol; **pop; soda; soda pop;** any refreshing drink that is a substitute for a drink containing alcohol. □ *The parents served soft drinks at their child's party.*

**software** ['sɔft wɛr] *n.* one or more computer programs meant to be used or stored on a computer. (No plural form.) □ *Susan updated the software on her computer.*

**soggy** ['sɔg i] *adj.* moist; wet; soaked. (Adv: *soggily.* Comp: *soggier;* sup: *soggiest.*) □ *I removed the soggy clothes from the broken washing machine.*

**soil** ['soɪl] **1.** *n.* the ground; the top layer of dirt that plants grow in. (Plural only when referring to different kinds, types, instances, or varieties.) □ *The rainstorm washed a lot of soil into the river.* Ⓒ *The soils in this area are excellent for farming.* **2.** *tv.* to make something dirty. □ *Anne soiled her shirt when she spilled coffee on it.*

**soiled** ['soɪld] *adj.* dirtied; made dirty. □ *John put the soiled clothes into the washing machine.*

**sold** ['sold] pt/pp of **sell.**

**soldier** ['sol dʒɚ] *n.* someone who serves or fights in an army, especially one who is not an officer. □ *The soldiers returning from the war were greeted with a parade.*

**sole** ['sol] **1.** *adj.* only; [the] only [one]. (Adv: *solely.*) □ *Mary is the sole owner of the huge office building.* **2.** *n.* the bottom surface of the foot; the bottom part of a shoe, boot, or other piece of footwear. □ *The sole of my shoe needs to be replaced.* **3.** *n., irreg.* a flat, edible fish. (Pl: *sole.*) □ *Where do people fish for sole?* **4.** *n.* the edible flesh of ③. (No plural form.) □ *Sole is good with lemon and butter.* **5.** *tv.* to put a new bottom part on a shoe or boot. □ *These boots were soled by a machine.*

**solid** ['sɑl ɪd] **1.** *n.* something that is hard and does not allow its shape to be changed easily; something that is not a liquid and not a gas. ☐ *Solids don't change their shape to fit their containers as liquids do.* **2. solids** *n.* food that is ③ and not liquid. (Treated as plural.) ☐ *The hospital patient was unable to eat solids after surgery.* **3.** *adj.* not liquid or gas; having a shape that does not change on its own to fit its container. (Adv: *solidly.*) ☐ *Ice is the solid form of water.* **4.** *adj.* not hollow; having an inside that is full of something. (Adv: *solidly.*) ☐ *This wooden cube is completely solid.* **5.** *adj.* [of a period of time] continuous and not interrupted. (Adv: *solidly.* Before or after a noun.) ☐ *The movie lasted for three solid hours.* **6.** *adj.* sturdy; well made; dependable; able to be relied on; strong; not likely to break, collapse, or fail. (Adv: *solidly.*) ☐ *The bridge was solid enough for heavy trucks to drive on.*

**solo** ['so lo] **1.** *n.* a musical piece performed by one person; a piece of music written primarily for one singer or one instrument. (Pl ends in *-s.*) ☐ *The soprano performed her solo quite well.* **2.** *adj.* done alone; done without help. ☐ *The spy undertook a dangerous solo mission.* **3.** *adv.* without help; alone. ☐ *Many of the people at the nightclub danced solo.* **4.** *iv.* to perform by oneself; to do something by oneself. ☐ *The pilot soloed for the first time after completing his training program.*

**solution** [sə 'lu ʃən] **1.** *n.* an answer to a problem or question; a way to fix a problem. ☐ *The solution to the math problem "What is 2 + 2?"* is 4. ☐ *Many social problems don't have easy solutions.* **2.** *n.* a liquid that has a solid or gas dissolved in it; a mixture of a liquid and a solid or gas that has been dissolved in it. ☐ *When the chemist added some powder, the solution turned cloudy.*

**solve** ['sɔlv] *tv.* to find the answer to a question or a problem. ☐ *The detective solved the terrible murder.*

**some** ['sʌm] **1.** *adj.* [of a person or creature] unnamed or unknown. ☐ *Some dog has been walking through my flower garden.* **2.** *adj.* a few; more than one, but not too many. (Use **any** in negative statements or questions.) ☐ *Anne bought some books at the bookstore.* **3.** *adj.* [of something] excellent, exciting, or extreme. (Informal. Always stressed.) ☐ *I had some headache last night.* **4.** *adv.* about; approximately. ☐ *The sculpture weighed some 500 pounds.* **5.** *n.* a number of people or things; a few people or things, but less than many. (No plural form.) ☐ *Some were upset by the violent movie.*

**somebody** ['sʌm bɑd i] **1.** *pron.* some person; someone; a certain unnamed person. (Compare this with **anybody.**) ☐ *Somebody called an ambulance right after the accident.* **2.** *n.* a famous or important person rather than just nobody. (Compare this with **anybody.**) ☐ *If you want to be somebody when you grow up, you should develop your talents now.*

**someday** ['sʌm de] *adv.* at some time in the future. ☐ *Anne thought she might someday travel to Japan.*

**somehow** ['sʌm haʊ] *adv.* in some way; in some manner; in a way that is not yet known. ☐ *Somehow, we must find a way to reduce crime.*

**someone** ['sʌm wən] *pron.* somebody; some person; a person; a certain unnamed person. (Compare this with **anyone.**) ☐ *Someone had vandalized the office building.*

**someplace** ['sʌm ples] *adv.* **somewhere;** at, in, or to some place. (Informal. **Somewhere** is preferred by some people. Compare this with **anyplace.**) ☐ *Do you want to go someplace for dinner?*

S

**something** ['sʌm θɪŋ] **1.** *pron.* some thing; a certain thing that is not known or named. (Compare this with **anything**.) □ *Anne told me something about the new worker, but I forgot what.* **2.** *n.* a thing that is more than nothing. (Compare this with **anything**. No plural form.) □ *I'm glad somebody finally did something about the broken lock on the door.* **3.** *adv.* somewhat; in some way. □ *These two vases looks something alike, but they are not exactly the same.* □ *This tastes something like chocolate, but it's probably not really chocolate.*

**sometime** ['sʌm tɑɪm] **1.** *adv.* at some point in time that is not known or not stated. □ *Could I make an appointment with you sometime soon?* **2. sometimes** *adv.* now and then; occasionally; from time to time. □ *Sometimes John just wants to be alone.*

**somewhat** ['sʌm ʍət] *adj.* rather; slightly; to some degree; kind of. □ *Mary was somewhat upset that John had lied to her.*

**somewhere** ['sʌm ʍɛr] *adv.* at, in, or to some place. (Compare this with **anywhere**.) □ *Would you go away and stand somewhere else?*

**son** ['sʌn] *n.* someone's male child; the male child of a parent. (Also used as a term of address by an older person to any boy or young man.) □ *Mary has two sons and one daughter.*

**song** ['sɔŋ] **1.** *n.* a story or words that are set to music; words that are sung. □ *This song is a poem that has been set to music.* **2.** *n.* singing; the art, practice, or action of singing. (No plural form.) □ *Members of the choir lifted up their voices in song.* **3.** *n.* the musical noise that birds make. □ *The bird watcher knew the different songs of different birds.*

**songbird** ['sɔŋ bɚd] *n.* any common bird with a characteristic song. □ *Keeping a songbird in a cage should be illegal!*

**soon** ['sun] *adv.* in a short period of time; before long; shortly. (Comp: *sooner;* sup: *soonest.*) □ *Mary arrived at the party soon after John.* □ *I hope we will eat soon!*

**soothe** ['suð] **1.** *tv.* to calm someone or something; to comfort someone or something; to ease pain or discomfort. □ *The cool lotion soothed my dry skin.* **2.** *iv.* to be a comfort; to be a relief. □ *Kind words can soothe when someone is upset.*

**soothing** ['suð ɪŋ] *adj.* comforting; calming; relieving. (Adv: *soothingly.*) □ *The soothing lotion felt good on my dry skin.*

**soprano** [sə 'præn o] **1.** *n.* someone, usually a woman, who sings the highest notes in a song. (Pl ends in *-s.*) □ *There are six sopranos in the choir.* **2. the soprano** *n.* the musical part written for ①; the notes usually sung by ①. (No plural form. Treated as singular.) □ *The soprano is really easy in this opera.* **3.** *adj.* <the adj. use of ①.> □ *The duet was written for soprano voices.*

**sorcerer** ['sors ə rɚ] *n.* a male magician who contacts evil spirits. □ *The old man was accused of being a sorcerer.*

**sorcery** ['sor sə ri] *n.* magic practiced with the help of evil spirits. (No plural form.) □ *The large book of sorcery contained secret spells.*

**sore** ['sor] **1.** *adj.* in a state of hurting; painful; aching. (Adv: *sorely.* Comp: *sorer;* sup: *sorest.*) □ *My feet were sore because I'd been walking all day.* **2.** *n.* a painful infection or injury on the skin. □ *I need some medicine for this sore.*

**sorrow** ['sɑr o] **1.** *n.* sadness; grief. □ *Four touching poems expressed the poet's sorrow.* **2.** *n.* a cause of sadness, grief, or misfortune. □ *My biggest sorrow in life was that I never finished school.*

**sorry** ['sɑr i] **1.** *adj.* expressing an apology. (Not prenominal. Comp: *sorrier;*

sup: *sorriest.)* ☐ *Anne said she was sorry about being a few minutes late.* **2.** *adj.* sad; feeling pity; wishing that something had happened differently. (Not prenominal. Comp: *sorrier;* sup: *sorriest.)* ☐ *We were sorry to hear that the athlete had broken his leg.* **3.** *adj.* regretful; wishing that one had acted differently. (Not prenominal. Comp: *sorrier;* sup: *sorriest.)* ☐ *If you don't obey me, you'll be sorry!* **4.** *adj.* not adequate or acceptable. (Only prenominal. Comp: *sorrier;* sup: *sorriest.)* ☐ *I cannot accept your sorry excuse.*

**sort** ['sort] **1.** *n.* a kind; a category; a group of similar persons, things, or qualities. ☐ *John likes movies of the violent sort.* **2.** *tv.* to put things in a particular order; to arrange things by category; to separate things by category. ☐ *The clerk sorted the invoices by their dates.*

**sought** ['sɔt] pt/pp of **seek.**

**soul** ['sol] **1.** *n.* the part of a human that is said to be separate from the body (and that some religions believe never dies); the part of the body that controls emotion and thought; the spirit. ☐ *Anne believes that her dead husband's soul is still with her.* **2.** *n.* a person; a human being. ☐ *The poor soul suffered in the cold weather.* **3.** *n.* the force or spirit that gives something depth or meaning. (Fig. on ①.) ☐ *The soul of her singing is in her energy and passion.*

**sound** ['sɑʊnd] **1.** *n.* a property of vibrating air that can stimulate the ears and be heard. (No plural form.) ☐ *Sound travels at about 1,100 feet per second.* **2.** *n.* a noise; vibrations that stimulate the ears. ☐ *Loud sounds frighten me.* **3.** *n.* a narrow channel of water that connects two larger bodies of water. ☐ *The sound froze during the harsh winter.* **4.** *tv.* to cause something to make a noise; to cause something to be heard. ☐ *The soldier sounded the bugle at 6:00 A.M.* **5.** *iv.* to make a characteristic noise. ☐ *The church bells sound every hour.* **6.** *iv.* to be heard in a certain way. ☐ *John's voice sounded funny because he had a cold.* **7.** *adj.* [of sleep] deep. (Adv: *soundly.)* ☐ *I need at least seven hours of sound sleep each night.* **8.** *adj.* healthy; not damaged or injured; in good condition. ☐ *Anne wrote her will while she was of sound mind and body.* **9.** *adj.* strong; sturdy; safe. (Adv: *soundly.* Comp: *sounder;* sup: *soundest.)* ☐ *Our house was still sound after the earthquake.* **10.** *adj.* sane; logical; reasonable; well reasoned; using good sense or judgment. (Adv: *soundly.* Comp: *sounder;* sup: *soundest.)* ☐ *Although your logic is sound, I still don't agree with you.*

**soup** ['sup] *n.* a liquid food that is made by boiling meat, fish, vegetables, or other foods. (Plural only when referring to different kinds, types, instances, or varieties.) ☐ *I ate a bowl of hot soup with my lunch.* Ⓒ *Some of the canned soups are too salty for me.*

**sour** ['sɑʊ ɚ] **1.** *adj.* tasting like an acid; having a taste like lemons; not sweet, salty, or bitter. (Adv: *sourly.* Comp: *sourer;* sup: *sourest.)* ☐ *I added some lime juice to my drink to make it sour.* **2.** *adj.* [of milk] spoiled. (Adv: *sourly.* Comp: *sourer;* sup: *sourest.)* ☐ *Is there any way we can use this sour milk?* **3.** *adj.* unpleasant; disagreeable. (Adv: *sourly.* Comp: *sourer;* sup: *sourest.)* ☐ *The sour clerk was very rude to the customer.* **4.** *iv.* [for milk] to become ②. ☐ *Let the milk sour before using it in the recipe.*

**source** ['sors] *n.* the origin of something; the place where something comes from. ☐ *The source of the river is a spring in the valley.*

**south** ['sɑʊθ] **1.** *n.* the direction to the right of someone or something facing east. (No plural form.) ☐ *The windows that face the south get a lot of sunlight.* **2.** *n.* the part of a region, country, or planet located toward ①, especially in the United States. (No plural form. Capitalized when referring to a region of the U.S.) □ *Mary once lived in the South and has a strong accent.* **3.** *adj.* to ①; toward ①; located in ②; facing ①. □ *Arizona is directly south of Utah.* **4.** *adj.* coming from ①, especially used to describe wind. □ *There were tornadoes where the warm south wind met the cool north wind.* **5.** *adv.* toward ①. □ *Jane drove south all the way to Florida.*

**southeast** [sɑʊθ 'ist] **1.** *n.* the direction halfway between south and east. (No plural form.) □ *Mississippi is to the southeast of Arkansas.* **2.** *n.* an area in the southeastern part of a region or country. (Capitalized when referring to a region of the U.S.) □ *London lies in England's southeast.* **3.** *adj.* located in the ②; toward ①; facing ①. □ *The furnace is in the southeast corner of the basement.* **4.** *adj.* from ①, especially describing wind. □ *The southeast breeze brought smells and sounds from the Atlantic Ocean.* **5.** *adv.* toward ①. □ *John drove southeast from Chicago to Indianapolis.*

**southeastern** [sɑʊθ 'is tɚn] *adj.* in the southeast; toward the southeast; facing the southeast. □ *The morning sunlight streamed through the southeastern windows.*

S

**southern** ['sʌð ɚn] **1.** *adj.* in the south; toward the south; facing south. □ *San Antonio is in the southern part of Texas.* **2.** *adj.* from the **south** ①, especially describing wind. □ *The spring day was warmed by southern winds.* **3.** *adj.* concerning the society and culture of the American South. □ *Mary's southern accent was obvious to the northerner.*

**southerner** ['sʌð ɚ nɚ] *n.* someone who lives in the south part of a country, especially someone from the southern United States. (Sometimes capitalized.) □ *The southerner decided to visit Chicago for the weekend.*

**south pole** ['sɑʊθ 'pol] **1.** *n.* the point in the Antarctic that is as far south as it is possible to go. □ *The south pole is exactly opposite the north pole.* **2. South Pole** *n.* the actual location of ①. □ *Absolutely no one lives near the South Pole.*

**southwest** [sɑʊθ 'wɛst] **1.** *n.* the direction halfway between south and west. (No plural form.) □ *The pilot flew the plane toward the southwest.* **2.** *n.* the southwestern part of a region of a country. (No plural form. Capitalized when referring to a region of the U.S.) □ *Susan attended school in the Southwest.* **3.** *adj.* located in ①; toward ①; facing ①. □ *Mary's office is in the southwest corner of the building.* **4.** *adj.* from ①, especially describing wind. □ *The southwest wind helped the eastbound flights.* **5.** *adv.* toward ①. □ *The pilot flew the plane southwest from Boston to New York City.*

**southwestern** [sɑʊθ 'wɛs tɚn] *adj.* in the southwest; toward the southwest; facing the southwest. □ *Robert was born in a city in southwestern Germany.*

**souvenir** [su və 'nɪr] *n.* something that reminds one of someplace, someone, or one's travels; a keepsake. □ *Many Germans kept a piece of the Berlin Wall as a souvenir.*

**sow 1.** ['so] *tv., irreg.* to scatter seed on the ground; to plant crops by scattering seed on the ground. (Pp: **sown** or *sowed.*) □ *The wheat was sown in April.* **2.** ['so] *iv., irreg.* to plant [crops] by scattering seed on the ground. □ *The gardener sowed in the spring.* **3.** ['sɑʊ] *n.* a female pig. □ *The farmer plans to slaughter the large sow.*

**sown** ['son] a pp of **sow.**

**space** ['spes] **1.** *n.* every location in existence in the universe. (No plural form.)

☐ *Some scientists believe that space is expanding.* **2.** *n.* **outer space**; every place past the air surrounding the earth. (No plural form.) ☐ *The astronaut viewed the earth from space.* **3.** *n.* a place or area that has length, width, or depth; a place where there is room for someone or something to be. (No plural form.) ☐ *My apartment has 800 square feet of space.* **4.** *n.* a blank line or empty box on a piece of paper where something is to be written. ☐ *Write your name in the first space.* **5.** *n.* an empty place between two words in a written or printed line. ☐ *Do I put a space or a hyphen between these two words?* **6.** *tv.* to place things with distance between them. ☐ *Space the lines of print on the poster four inches apart.*

**spacecraft** AND **spaceship** ['spes kræft, 'spes ʃɪp] *n., irreg.* a rocket or vehicle that travels in space. (Pl: *spacecraft* and *spaceships.*) ☐ *The astronauts landed the spaceship on the moon.*

**spade** ['sped] **1.** *n.* a tool, similar to a small shovel, used for digging. ☐ *Mary dug up the potatoes with a spade.* **2.** *n.* the black symbol (♠) found on playing cards; one of the four suits found on playing cards. ☐ *John played the king of spades.* **3.** *tv.* to dig something with ①. ☐ *John spaded the weeds from around the strawberry plants.*

**spaghetti** [spə 'gɛt i] *n.* long, thin, (often dried) sticks made of a flour and water mixture, which are boiled and then eaten as food; long sticks of pasta. (No plural form.) ☐ *Anne put some tomato sauce on her spaghetti.*

**spare** ['spɛr] **1.** *adj.* surplus; extra; free; not needed. ☐ *The manufacturer donated spare glasses to charity.* **2.** *adj.* extra; saved in case of emergency; reserved for emergency use; kept for emergency use. ☐ *Mary has a spare radio in her basement in case there is a tornado.* **3.** *n.* something that is extra and not immediately needed. ☐ *I often forget to carry my office key, so I keep a spare in my car.* **4.** *n.* an extra tire that is kept in a vehicle in case a tire loses its air. ☐ *John changed the flat tire, replacing it with the spare.* **5.** *tv.* not to permit someone to undergo punishment or execution. ☐ *The governor spared the criminal from execution.* **6.** *tv.* to be able to give time, money, or energy. ☐ *If you can spare a minute, I need to speak with you.*

**sparrow** ['spɛr o] *n.* a common, small, brown bird. ☐ *A sparrow has built a nest in a tree outside my window.*

**sparse** ['spɑrs] *adj.* scattered; not having many people or things in a certain area; not dense; having a very small amount of people or things in an area. (Adv: *sparsely.* Comp: *sparser;* sup: *sparsest.*) ☐ *The population is very sparse in that remote, mountainous area.*

**spat** ['spæt] **1.** a pt/pp of **spit**. **2.** *n.* an argument; a quarrel; a disagreement. ☐ *The little spat turned into a real fight.*

**speak** ['spik] **1.** *tv., irreg.* to say something; to utter something; to express one's thoughts in words. (Pt: **spoke**; pp: **spoken**.) ☐ *The shy student spoke his words softly.* **2.** *tv., irreg.* to use a language; to know how to talk in a language. ☐ *The new citizen learned to speak English by taking classes.* **3.** *iv., irreg.* to talk; to say words. ☐ *Please be quiet unless you are given permission to speak.*

**speaker** ['spik ɚ] **1.** *n.* someone who speaks; someone who makes speeches; someone who speaks a particular language. ☐ *My German class is taught by an authentic speaker of German.* **2. Speaker** *n.* the Speaker of the House; the presiding officer in the House of Representatives; the representative of the majority party who has the most seniority. ☐ *The Speaker was present for every session of Congress.*

S

**3.** *n.* a device that reproduces sound, as found in a stereo, television, computer, etc. □ *John balanced the sound between the two speakers.*

**special** ['spɛ ʃəl] **1.** *adj.* not ordinary; not regular; set apart from other things, especially for a particular purpose or reason. (Adv: *specially.*) □ *A child's birthday is a special day.* **2.** *n.* something that is set apart from other things, especially for a particular purpose or reason; a unique, **special** ① offering. □ *I looked at the restaurant's menu to see what the special of the day was.* **3.** *n.* the offering of something for sale at a **special** ① price. □ *I asked the butcher if there were any specials on meat today.*

**specific** [spə 'sɪf ɪk] **1.** *adj.* particular; certain; definite; precise; exact. (Adv: *specifically* [...ɪk li].) □ *The witness gave specific facts and figures.* **2. specifics** *n.* the details and facts of a matter. (Treated as singular.) □ *The newspaper printed the specifics of the new tax law.*

**spectacle** ['spɛk tə kəl] **1.** *n.* something to be viewed; something to be seen; a display; a scene. □ *The three brothers fighting made quite a spectacle.* **2. spectacles** *n.* eyeglasses. (Old-fashioned. Treated as plural. Number is expressed with *pair(s) of spectacales.*) □ *Grandpa can't see a thing without his spectacles.*

**spectator** ['spɛk te tɚ] *n.* someone who watches something but does not take part in it. □ *I was merely a spectator to John and Mary's argument.*

**speculation** [spɛk jə 'le ʃən] **1.** *n.* guessing; trying to determine something, especially without knowing all of the facts. (Plural only when referring to different kinds, types, instances, or varieties.) □ *Speculation is no substitute for facts.* Ⓒ *Your careless speculations ignore all the facts.* **2.** *n.* an investment in a risky business venture. □ *The banker lost thousands of dollars in risky speculations.*

**sped** ['spɛd] pt/pp of **speed**.

**speech** ['spitʃ] **1.** *n.* the production of words by talking. (No plural form.) □ *Dogs do not have the ability to create speech.* **2.** *n.* a lecture; a formal talk to a group of listeners. □ *The politician's speech was held in a large hall.*

**speed** ['spid] **1.** *iv., irreg.* to move fast; to go fast, especially to go faster than the legal limit. (Pt/pp: **sped**.) □ *The police give tickets to motorists who speed.* **2.** *tv., irreg.* to cause something to go or move fast; to cause something to go or move faster. □ *Susan sped her car down the freeway because she was late for work.* **3.** *n.* the rate at which someone or something moves or does something during a period of time. (Plural only when referring to different kinds, levels, degrees, or varieties.) □ *David's typing speed is sixty words per minute.* Ⓒ *This machine operates at two different speeds.* **4.** *n.* rapid movement; the quickness with which someone or something moves. (No plural form.) □ *Susan needed a secretary who could type with speed and accuracy.*

**speedboat** ['spid bot] *n.* a small boat that has a powerful engine that can be driven at high speeds, especially for pleasure on lakes and rivers. □ *The waves in the speedboat's wake were large.*

**speed limit** ['spid lɪm ət] *n.* the legal maximum speed that a vehicle is permitted to travel; the fastest speed that a driver can operate a vehicle under the law on a particular road. □ *Often, the speed limit is lower at night than during the day.*

**spell** ['spɛl] **1.** *tv., irreg.* to say or write the letters of a word in the right order. (Pt/pp: *spelled* or, less frequently, **spelt**.) □ *The teacher spelled the vocabulary words on the chalkboard.* **2.** *tv., irreg.* [for letters] to signify a word. □ W-o-r-d *spells* word. □ C-a-t *spells* cat. **3.** *iv., irreg.* to know how to say or write

S

the letters of many words; to be able to spell ① words. □ *The grammar school teacher taught children how to spell.*

**spelt** ['spɛlt] a pt/pp of **spell**.

**spend** ['spɛnd] **1.** *tv., irreg.* to pay an amount of money for something that one buys. (Pt/pp: **spent**.) □ *Bill was willing to spend up to $100 for a new watch.* **2.** *tv., irreg.* to pass time; to use time or energy; to consume energy. □ *Mary spends a lot of time helping others with their work.*

**spendthrift** ['spɛnd θrɪft] *n.* someone who wastes money; someone who spends too much money. □ *Look at the huge car Bill bought. He is such a spendthrift!*

**spent** ['spɛnt] pt/pp of **spend**.

**sphere** ['sfir] **1.** *n.* a perfectly round object; a globe; a ball. □ *Each bead of the necklace was a sphere of colored glass.* **2.** *n.* the area or domain where someone or something has an influence or an effect; the place or environment in which someone or something exists or acts. □ *The researcher's work was well-known in scientific spheres.*

**spherical** ['sfɛr ɪ kəl] *adj.* shaped like a sphere. (Adv: *spherically* [...ɪk li].) □ *The oranges were perfectly spherical and brightly colored.*

**spice** ['spɑɪs] **1.** *n.* an herb or other vegetable fiber or seed that tastes or smells unique and is used to give extra flavor to food. □ *Mary grew some spices in pots on her window sill.* **2.** *n.* something that adds excitement or flavor. (Fig. on ①. No plural form.) □ *The funny actor added some spice to the otherwise boring movie.* **3.** *tv.* to season or flavor food with ①. □ *The cook spiced the stew with curry powder.*

**spicy** ['spɑɪs i] **1.** *adj.* flavored with spices; seasoned with spices; having a sharp flavor. (Adv: *spicily.* Comp: *spicier;* sup: *spiciest.*) □ *Mary put some spicy tomato sauce on her hamburger.* **2.** *adj.* somewhat vulgar; slightly sexually oriented. (Adv: *spicily.* Comp: *spicier;* sup: *spiciest.*) □ *The spicy performance embarrassed the audience.*

**spider** ['spɑɪ dɚ] *n.* a small creature with eight legs whose body produces a silk thread that it uses to make a web, which is then used to trap insects, which it eats. □ *Several mosquitoes were trapped in a spider's web.*

**spike** ['spɑɪk] **1.** *n.* a large, thick, metal nail that comes to a sharp point. □ *I injured my hand on the large spike that was sticking through the board.* **2.** *n.* a pointed metal or plastic object on the bottom of a shoe that gives the wearer extra traction; also called a cleat. □ *The spikes on the golfer's shoes tap against the cement when he walks.* **3.** *n.* a sharp peak on a graph; an increase that can be represented as a peak on a graph. □ *After the war, there was a sharp spike in the number of births.*

**spill** ['spɪl] **1.** *tv., irreg.* to cause something, especially a liquid, to pour from a container by accident; to cause something, especially a liquid, to fall. (Pt/pp: *spilled* or, less frequently, **spilt**.) □ *John spilled a glass of milk during dinner.* **2.** *iv., irreg.* [for something, especially a liquid] to fall or be poured from a container by accident. □ *Oil spilled from the leaking pipe.* **3.** *n.* something, especially a liquid, that has fallen or poured from a container by accident. □ *The coffee spill stained my shirt.* **4.** *n.* a fall from something. □ *The bicyclist was injured in a bad spill.*

**spilt** ['spɪlt] a pt/pp of **spill**.

**spin** ['spɪn] **1.** *iv., irreg.* to turn around in circles quickly. (Pt/pp: **spun**. *Spinned* is often heard.) □ *The windmill spun when the wind blew.* **2.** *iv., irreg.* to rotate on an axis. □ *The tire spun on its axle.* **3.** *iv., irreg.* [for one's surroundings] to seem to revolve. □ *The injured*

S

*man thought the room was spinning.* **4.** *iv., irreg.* to pull and twist, making thread or yarn from wool, cotton, or other fibers. □ *She watched the children in the yard as she spun.* **5.** *tv., irreg.* to cause someone or something to turn around in circles quickly. □ *The amusement park ride spun the riders faster and faster.* **6.** *tv., irreg.* to pull and twist fibers into thread or yarn. □ *At the factory, cotton was spun into thread.* **7.** *tv., irreg.* [for a spider] to make a web. □ *A tiny spider worked all night to spin that web!* **8.** *tv., irreg.* to create a tale, story, or lie. □ *Mary loved to spin tales for her children.* **9.** *n.* a short trip in or on a vehicle. □ *Bill took a quick spin on his new motorcycle to try it out.*

**spinach** ['spɪn ɪtʃ] **1.** *n.* a leafy, green vegetable. (No plural form.) □ *I use spinach rather than lettuce in my salads.* **2.** *adj.* made of or with ①. □ *I really don't care for spinach pizza.*

**spine** ['spaɪn] **1.** *n.* the column of bones and the nerves within that are at the center of the back of humans and other animals. □ *The doctor examined the muscles and bones in John's spine.* **2.** *n.* any long, narrow, stiff thing that provides support, such as the side of a cover of a book where the pages are attached. (Fig. on ①.) □ *The spine of the book is held together with glue.* **3.** *n.* a stiff, pointed growth as found on certain plants and animals, providing protection. (See also porcupine.) □ *The cactus has many sharp spines.*

**spire** ['spaɪɚ] *n.* the top part of a steeple; the top part of a structure on top of a building that comes to a point. □ *The chapel's spire could be seen from three miles away.*

**spirit** ['spɪr ɪt] **1.** *n.* the part of a human that is separate from the body (and that some religions believe never dies); the part of the body that controls emotion and intellect; the soul. □ *Many Christians believe their spirits will go to heaven or hell.* **2.** *n.* a being that does not have a body; a ghost. □ *Evil spirits seemed to live in the old house.* **3.** *n.* the driving force of something; something that provides energy or force to something; zeal. (Fig. on ①. No plural form.) □ *Mary's energy is the basis of the true spirit of our team.* **4. spirits** *n.* strong alcoholic liquor. □ *The owner was fined for selling spirits to young people.*

**spit** ['spɪt] **1.** *iv., irreg.* to expel the natural fluid from one's mouth; to push fluid out of one's mouth. (Pt/pp: *spit* or spat.) □ *The soldier spat at his enemy.* **2.** *tv., irreg.* to expel something from one's mouth; to push something out of one's mouth. □ *John quickly spit the sour milk onto the floor.* **3.** *n.* fluid or mucus that comes from someone's mouth. (No plural form in this sense in standard English.) □ *Spit ran from the baby's mouth.* **4.** *n.* a thin rod with a sharp end that food is pushed onto so that it can be roasted over a fire. □ *We turned the spit over the fire to roast the meat evenly.*

**spite** ['spaɪt] **1.** *n.* a desire to annoy someone else or get revenge; malice. (No plural form.) □ *David's repeated acts of spite towards Anne frightened her.* **2. in spite of** someone or something *phr.* without regard to someone or something; even though another course had been prescribed; ignoring a warning. □ *In spite of the bad weather, I had fun on vacation.*

**splash** ['splæʃ] **1.** *iv.* [for liquid] to scatter in many drops; [for liquid] to fall and spread in waves. □ *Gasoline splashed from my car's tank when I put too much into it.* **2.** *tv.* to cause a liquid to scatter in many drops or waves. □ *The speeding car splashed water on the people waiting for the bus.* **3.** *n.* an instance of a liquid scattering as in ①, and the sound that goes with it. □ *I heard the splashes of the children playing in the pool.*

**splatter** ['splæt ɚ] **1.** *iv.* to splash, especially in a careless, clumsy, or messy way. □ *Mud had splattered all over Susan's clothes.* **2.** *tv.* to splash a liquid, especially in a careless, clumsy, or messy way. □ *Dave splattered gas onto the car while filling his tank.*

**splendid** ['splɛn dɪd] *adj.* excellent; very good; brilliant; wonderful; super. (Adv: *splendidly.*) □ *Our rooms at the expensive hotel were splendid.*

**splice** ['splɑɪs] **1.** *tv.* to fasten the ends of two pieces of something together by weaving, taping, or otherwise connecting them. □ *The sailor spliced the lines together.* **2.** *n.* a joint or connection that has been made by weaving, taping, or otherwise connecting the ends of two pieces of something. □ *The rope snapped because the splice was made wrong.*

**splint** ['splɪnt] *n.* a flat object that is secured to a person's finger, toe, or limb in order to give support or keep a broken bone in place. □ *I couldn't wear a shoe over the splint on my broken toe.*

**splinter** ['splɪn tɚ] **1.** *n.* a sliver; a thin, sharp broken-off piece of wood, glass, or some other material. □ *Be careful! There are splinters of glass all over the floor.* **2.** *adj.* [of a group of people] separated from a larger group of people. (Prenominal only.) □ *A splinter group of soldiers fought against the king's soldiers.* **3.** *iv.* to separate from a larger object or group; to break into smaller pieces or groups. □ *The rebel forces splintered into three armed groups.* **4.** *tv.* to break something into ①. □ *One blow of the hammer splintered the thin plastic.*

**split** ['splɪt] **1.** *tv., irreg.* to separate something into sections, layers, or groups; to divide something into sections, layers, or groups. (Pt/pp: *split.*) □ *The dealer split the cards into two piles.* **2.** *tv., irreg.* to cut something along its length. □ *Mary split the log with an axe.* **3.** *tv., irreg.* to share something among members of a group; to divide something among members of a group. □ *The students split the pizza among themselves.* **4.** *iv., irreg.* [for people or things] to separate into sections, layers, or groups. □ *Czechoslovakia split into two republics on January 1, 1993.* **5.** *iv., irreg.* [for something] to break or tear open along its length. □ *The ground split apart during the earthquake.* **6.** *n.* the crack, cut, or break made by breaking or cutting something, as in ②. □ *I avoided walking near the split in the ice.* **7.** *n.* a separation within a group. □ *The young minister's policies caused the split.* **8.** *adj.* separated; divided; cut from end to end. □ *The electrician repaired the split wire.*

**spoil** ['spoɪl] **1.** *iv.* to become rotten; to rot; to decay. □ *When milk spoils, it smells very bad.* **2.** *tv.* to ruin something; to destroy something; to make something so that it can no longer be used. □ *The warm temperatures spoiled the meat before we could cook it.* **3.** *tv.* to treat someone too well; to raise a child without discipline. □ *John's children are rude because he spoils them terribly.*

**spoke** ['spok] pt of **speak**.

**spoken** ['spok ən] pp of **speak**.

**sponge** ['spʌndʒ] **1.** *n.* any of a group of small animals that live in the water and attach themselves to underwater objects, forming a soft, flexible skeleton. □ *While scuba diving, we observed sponges growing on the coral.* **2.** *n.* the soft skeleton of ① used for cleaning or absorbing of liquids, or an artificial substance having the same qualities. □ *John wrung out the sponge in the sink.*

**sponsor** ['spɑn sɚ] **1.** *n.* someone or an organization that supports and guides another person or organization. □ *My baseball team is sponsored by our local hardware store.* **2.** *n.* someone who assumes responsibility for creating or developing something. □ *The woman who sponsored the petition spoke before the city council.* **3.** *n.* a business that advertises during a radio or television program. □ *Our program will continue after a message from our sponsors.* **4.** *tv.* to support someone or an organization, usually with money, often for the sake of publicity. □ *The radio program was sponsored by local businesses.*

**spool** ['spul] *n.* something that thread, film, wire, etc., can be wound around. □ *I need a spool of white thread for my sewing project.*

**spoon** ['spun] **1.** *n.* a utensil that is made of a small, shallow oval bowl at the end of a handle, used for serving food, stirring drinks, and eating liquids and soft foods. □ *Mary stirred her coffee with a spoon.* **2.** *tv.* to move something to a place with ①. □ *The nurse spooned the soup into the patient's mouth.*

**sport** ['sport] **1.** *n.* competition and physical activity as found in games and some outdoor activities. (No plural form.) □ *There is a lot of sport in fishing.* **2.** *n.* a particular game involving physical activity and competition. □ *John enjoys camping and most team sports.*

**sports car** ['sports kɑr] *n.* a kind of expensive, stylish, small car, which can go very fast. □ *The driver of the sports car was given a ticket for speeding.*

**sportsman** ['sports mən] *n., irreg.* a man who participates in sports events. (Pl: sportsmen.) □ *The coach was proud that his team consisted of well-trained sportsmen.*

**sportsmen** ['sports mən] pl of **sportsman**.

**sporty** ['spor ti] *adj.* stylish; in fashion. (Adv: *sportily.* Comp: *sportier;* sup: *sportiest.*) □ *Susan drives a sporty car.*

**spot** ['spɑt] **1.** *n.* a part (typically round) of a surface that is a different color from the rest of the surface in some way. □ *A leopard has dark spots on its fur.* **2.** *n.* a mark, as might be left by blood, paint, food, etc.; a dirty mark. □ *There were spots of blood on the murderer's hands.* **3.** *n.* a specific location; a place; a position. □ *There's an open spot on the doctor's schedule for next Tuesday.* **4.** *tv.* to recognize someone or something; to happen to see someone or something. □ *I spotted the president walking down Pennsylvania Avenue today.*

**spotless** ['spɑt ləs] *adj.* totally clean; without spots. (Adv: *spotlessly.*) □ *How do you keep your kitchen so spotless?*

**spouse** ['spɑʊs] *n.* a husband; a wife. □ *My spouse and I have been married for four years.*

**spout** ['spɑʊt] **1.** *n.* the opening of something from which a liquid comes out. □ *The gardener used a watering can with a long, narrow spout.* **2.** *tv.* to push out something, especially a liquid; to force a liquid out, especially through a narrow pipe or tube. □ *The beautiful fountain spouted streams of water.* **3.** *iv.* to flow into, out of, from, through, down, or onto someone or something. □ *Water spouted from the fountain onto my shirt.*

**sprain** ['spren] **1.** *tv.* to twist a joint in the body in a way that causes injury or pain. □ *Mary sprained her wrist while playing tennis.* **2.** *n.* a body joint that has been twisted in a way that causes injury or pain. □ *Susan put ice on her sprain.*

**sprang** ['spræŋ] pt of **spring**.

**spray** ['spre] **1.** *tv.* to direct a stream of small drops of liquid onto a surface. □ *John sprayed insect poison on the plants.* **2.** *tv.* to coat a surface with a stream of small drops of liquid. □ *John sprayed the plants with an insect poison.* **3.** *n.* liquid that is pushed through the air in small drops, especially under pressure. □ *The spray of perfume made me sneeze.*

**spread** ['sprɛd] **1.** *iv., irreg.* to move outward; to become longer, wider, or broader; to extend to a larger extent or to the largest extent possible; to expand. (Pt/pp: *spread.*) □ *The wine stain spread across the tablecloth.* **2.** *iv., irreg.* to be passed on to many people. □ *The gossip spread quickly throughout the department.* **3.** *tv., irreg.* to pass along something to many people. □ *John's sneeze spread the flu to all of his classmates.* **4.** *tv., irreg.* to stretch something out; to cause something to become longer, wider, or broader. □ *Mike spread the tablecloth on the table.* **5.** *tv., irreg.* to apply something onto something else by moving it around, making an even layer. □ *They are spreading gravel on our street now.*

**spree** ['spri] **1.** *n.* a session of wild drinking, spending, or partying. □ *I spent $1,000 while on a shopping spree at the mall.* **2.** *n.* a period of activity and action. □ *Our team went on a winning spree and won all its games this season.*

**spring** ['sprɪŋ] **1.** *n.* the season of the year between winter and summer. □ *I'm planning to visit Europe in the spring.* **2.** *n.* a natural source of water from the ground; a place where water comes out of the earth. □ *This bottled water comes from a spring in Wisconsin.* **3.** *n.* a metal coil; a metal object that is wound in the shape of a coil. □ *When you wind a watch, you tighten a spring inside it.* **4.** *iv., irreg.* to jump; to leap. (Pt: **sprang** or **sprung**; pp: **sprung**.) □ *Jimmy tried to spring over the rock.* **5.** *iv., irreg.* [for a **spring** ③] to fail and lose its elastic property. □ *The springs inside my mattress had sprung, so I threw it away.* **6.** *adj.* <the adj. use of ①.> □ *Anne planned to take four classes during the spring term.*

**sprout** ['spraʊt] **1.** *iv.* [for a plant] to bud; [for a plant] to start growing leaves, flowers, or buds; [for a plant] to grow from a seed. □ *The plants sprouted from the ground a week after I planted seeds.* **2.** *tv.* to grow something, such as a leaf or branch. □ *The tree sprouted new leaves even though it looked dead.* **3.** *n.* new growth; a new bud, leaf, flower, or stem. □ *The sudden cold snap froze the young sprouts.*

**spruce** ['sprus] **1.** *n.* a type of pine tree having short needles. □ *I cut down a spruce that was blocking the view from my porch.* **2.** *n.* the wood of ①. (No plural form.) □ *Spruce is sometimes used to make piano keys.* **3. spruce up** *iv. + adv.* to make oneself or a place neat or clean. □ *John went to the bathroom to spruce up before dinner.*

**sprung** ['sprʌŋ] pp of **spring**; a pt of **spring**.

**spun** ['spʌn] pt/pp of **spin**.

**spur** ['spɚ] **1.** *n.* a sharp object worn on the heel of a boot, used to make a horse that one is riding go faster. □ *Dave drove his spurs into the sides of his horse to make it go faster.* **2.** *n.* a highway or railroad track that branches from the main one. □ *The railroad ended service to towns on its secondary spurs.* **3.** *tv.* to poke a horse with ①. □ *The rider spurred the horse gently.*

**spy** ['spaɪ] **1.** *n.* someone whose job is to secretly watch other people, organizations, or governments in order to learn information. □ *The American spy obtained secret information about the foreign government.* **2.** *tv.* to see something; to discover something by sight; to see something for the first time. □ *The detective spied a piece of fabric on the floor near the corpse.*

**squad** ['skwɑd] *n.* a group of people who work together or who have been trained together for a job; a group of 11 soldiers and a leader who work together. □ *A police squad surrounded the robbers.*

**square** ['skwɛr] **1.** *n.* a shape made with four straight sides that are the same length and four right angles. □ *The worker installed squares of tile on the floor.* **2.** *n.* a four-sided area in a city surrounded by streets or buildings. □ *Mary took the subway from the town square to the suburbs.* **3.** *n.* an L-shaped or T-shaped tool, used for drawing and measuring right angles. □ *The carpenter drew a right angle on the board with a square.* **4.** *n.* a number that is the product of a number multiplied by itself. □ *64 is the square of 8 because 8 × 8 = 64.* □ *The area of any square shape is the square of the length of any one side of the shape.* **5.** *adj.* shaped like ①. (Adv: *squarely.*) □ *Mary's house was built on a square one-acre plot.* **6.** *adj.* forming a right angle; forming a 90-degree angle. (Adv: *squarely.*) □ *The bookshelf was square with the side of the bookcase.* **7.** *adj.* [of an area] roughly equal in size and shape to a **square** ① that has sides of the requested or demanded length. (Follows the measurement of length.) □ *A room that is ten feet square has an area of 100 square feet, because 10 × 10 is 100.* □ *The architect drew a shape that was two inches square.* **8.** *adj.* [of an area shaped like ①] having four sides of a certain length. (A square inch is the area measured by a square that is one inch long and one inch wide. Adv: *squarely.*) □ *A square mile is a measurement equal to the area of a square of land one mile long and one mile wide.* **9.** *adj.* having no debts; having settled all debts. □ *Are we square, or do I owe you more money?* **10.** *tv.* to multiply a number by itself. □ *If you square the length of one side of a square, you get its area.* **11.** *tv.* to make something ⑥. □ *The carpenter squared the shelf against the wall.*

**square meal** ['skwɛr 'mil] *n.* a meal that is complete and balanced. □ *The children's only square meals were at school. They ate snacks all the time and ate hardly any dinner at home.*

**squat** ['skwɑt] **1.** *iv.* to crouch; to rest, sitting with one's feet on the ground and one's legs bent under one's body. □ *John squatted as he picked up the papers that he'd dropped.* **2.** *adj.* shorter or thicker than normal or expected. (Adv: *squatly.* Comp: *squatter;* sup: *squattest.*) □ *The vase seemed squat and ugly when I placed it on the table.*

**squawk** ['skwɔk] **1.** *n.* a loud, harsh noise, especially one made by birds. □ *If I hear one more squawk from you kids, you're all going to bed.* **2.** *iv.* to make a loud, harsh noise. □ *The horrible singer didn't sing, but rather squawked.*

**squeak** ['skwik] **1.** *n.* a short, soft, high-pitched noise. □ *When I walk, my new shoes make squeaks.* **2.** *iv.* to make a short, soft, high-pitched noise. □ *The mouse squeaked loudly when Susan accidentally stepped on it.*

**squeal** ['skwil] **1.** *n.* a loud, shrill noise or cry. □ *The children made squeals of delight when I offered them cake.* **2.** *iv.* to make ①. □ *When the baby squealed, I picked her up from her crib.*

**squeeze** ['skwiz] **1.** *tv.* to press something with force. □ *Anne squeezed the trigger of the gun with her finger.* **2.** *tv.* to force the liquid from something by pressing it. □ *John squeezed every drop of water from the wet rag.*

**squint** ['skwɪnt] **1.** *tv.* to close one's eyes almost all the way when looking at someone or something. □ *I squinted my eyes so I could see well enough to find my glasses.* **2.** *iv.* to have one's eyes almost closed because the light is so bright. □ *Facing the sun, Mary squinted as she watched the tennis game.*

**squirm** ['skwɚm] *iv.* to move around uncomfortably; to writhe. □ *A dying squirrel squirmed on the road.*

**squirrel** ['skwɚ əl] *n.* a rodent that lives in trees and has a large, bushy tail. □ *The squirrels quickly ran up the tree.*

S

**squirt** ['skwɚt] **1.** *tv.* to force liquid through the air in a stream; to cause liquid to stream through the air. □ *Susan squirted some liquid soap on her hands.* **2.** *tv.* to hit someone or something with a stream of liquid. □ *David squirted his dirty car with water from the hose.* **3.** *n.* a short stream of liquid that is sent through the air. □ *Mary added a squirt of liquid soap to the dishwater.*

**stab** ['stæb] **1.** *tv.* to thrust a pointed object into someone or something. □ *Mary stabbed the slab of ham with her fork and put it on her plate.* **2.** *n.* a thrust of a pointed object. □ *The mugger made a stab at me, but he missed.* **3.** *n.* a sharp, painful feeling. □ *Tom felt the stab of the knife as it slipped and cut his thumb.*

**stabilize** ['steb ə lɑɪz] **1.** *tv.* to make something steady; to fix something in place; to keep something from moving or changing. □ *The soldiers stabilized the bridge before crossing it.* **2.** *iv.* to become steady; to be fixed in place. □ *The patient's heart rate stabilized after surgery.*

**stable** ['steb əl] **1.** *adj.* unlikely to fall, move, or shake; steady; firm. (Adv: *stably.*) □ *Don't lean on the table! It's not stable.* **2.** *adj.* not likely to change; constant; permanent. (Adv: *stably.*) □ *Mary is looking for stable employment because she wants a steady income.* **3.** *n.* a building where horses are kept. □ *Anne locked the stable after grooming the horses.*

**stack** ['stæk] **1.** *n.* an orderly pile of something; a neat pile of something. □ *I ordered a stack of blueberry pancakes.* **2.** *tv.* to place things in a neat, orderly pile; to arrange things into a neat, orderly pile. □ *My boss stacked a lot of work on my desk.*

**stadium** ['sted i əm] *n.* a playing field surrounded by rows of seats for spectators. □ *When the home team won, the fans in the stadium cheered.*

**staff** ['stæf] **1.** *n.* the workers who operate and manage an organization. (Plural but treated as singular.) □ *The office staff meets every Monday to discuss the week's work.* **2.** *n.* a large, heavy stick used for support; a large cane. □ *The shepherd put his weight on his staff as he walked.* **3.** *tv.* to provide something with enough workers so that a job can be done properly. □ *We staffed the project with volunteers.* **4.** *tv.* [for workers] to provide services to do a task. □ *We can't afford to staff the office properly.*

**stage** ['stedʒ] **1.** *n.* a period of development; one part of a process. □ *Tadpoles are frogs in an early stage of development.* **2.** *n.* the floor, usually raised, in a theater where performers perform. □ *The performers walked onto the stage, singing a song.* **3. the stage** *n.* theater; the business of producing and acting in live theater. (No plural form. Treated as singular.) □ *Susan was always fascinated by the stage.* **4.** *tv.* to produce a play at a theater; to put on a play. □ Romeo and Juliet *was staged by the high-school drama club.* **5.** *tv.* to plan and do something that attracts public attention. □ *The protesters staged a riot in front of city hall.*

**stain** ['sten] **1.** *tv.* to change or add to the color of something; to make something dirty by changing its color. □ *Muddy water from the storm stained my shoes and socks.* **2.** *tv.* to coat a wooden surface with a liquid that gives it a color. □ *John stained the bookshelf to make it darker.* **3.** *tv.* to color tissue or organisms so they can be observed or identified. □ *The technician stained the cells purple.* **4.** *iv.* [for a substance] to have the ability to change the color of something permanently. □ *Mustard stains, especially on light-colored material.* **5.** *n.* a mark, spot, or flaw. □ *I carefully removed the coffee stain from my tie.* **6.** *n.* a liquid that is used to give color to wood. (Plural only when referring to different kinds, types, instances, or varieties. See also **dye**.) ☐ *John put a layer of stain on the bookshelf.* Ⓒ *Lighter stains tend to reveal the wood grain better.*

**stair** ['stɛr] *n.* a step or series of steps that go from one level to another. (Usually plural.) ☐ *To get to the second floor, you have to take the stairs.*

**staircase** ['stɛr kes] *n.* a set of stairs that allows one to go from one level to another; a stairway. ☐ *The huge house had a long, curved staircase leading from the first floor to the second.*

**stairway** ['stɛr we] *n.* a set of stairs that allow one to go from one level to another; a staircase. ☐ *The stairway was carpeted to prevent people from slipping.*

**stake** ['stek] **1.** *n.* a pointed piece of wood or plastic that is driven into the ground. ☐ *I drove a stake in the ground to show where the tree should be planted.* **2. stakes** *n.* the amount of money bet in a game; the amount of risk involved in some activity. (Treated as plural, but not countable.) ☐ *John quit because the stakes were too high.*

**stale** ['stel] *adj.* no longer fresh. (Adv: *stalely.* Comp: *staler;* sup: *stalest.*) ☐ *The bread was stale and could not be served.*

**stalk** ['stɔk] **1.** *n.* the main stem of a plant, which is connected to the roots, and from which leaves grow. ☐ *After the corn was harvested, the farmer plowed the stalks into the ground.* **2.** *tv.* to pursue or approach an animal without being seen or heard. ☐ *The hunter stalked the deer through the forest.*

**stall** ['stɔl] **1.** *n.* a small, enclosed space. ☐ *The janitor cleaned the bathroom stalls twice a day.* **2.** *n.* a space within a barn for one animal, especially a horse. ☐ *Bill threw some fresh hay into the horse's stall.* **3.** *n.* a booth in a market, or in a building with an open wall in front, where products are sold. ☐ *Anne sold her own crafts at a stall at the fair.* **4.** *iv.* [for a vehicle] to stop because of engine trouble. ☐ *There was an accident when the truck stalled on the freeway.* **5.** *iv.* to hesitate so that one has more time; to evade something by taking extra time. ☐ *John stalled while he tried to think of an excuse.*

**stamp** ['stæmp] **1.** *n.* a square of paper issued by the government that must be attached to certain documents to make them official or to indicate that a fee or tax has been paid, especially as used for postage. ☐ *In the small country, every purchase I made required a tax stamp on the receipt.* **2.** *n.* a tool that prints a design (a picture or words) onto a surface. ☐ *The banker had a stamp that said "APPROVED."* **3.** *n.* the design that is printed onto a surface by ②. ☐ *The stamp's fresh ink smeared when I rubbed against it.* **4.** *tv.* to mark an object with ②, usually to make it official or to make an acknowledgment that a fee has been paid or that requirements have been met. ☐ *The city official stamped my building permit.* **5.** *tv.* to put a postage **stamp** ① on an envelope. ☐ *Bill stamped the company's mail with the correct postage.* **6.** *tv.* to hit something or make something flat by bringing down one's foot on it with force. ☐ *Mary stamped the can flat with her boot.* **7.** *iv.* to walk heavily somewhere; to walk with heavy steps. ☐ *Susan stamped loudly through the house in her heavy boots.*

**stampede** [stæm 'pid] **1.** *n.* a sudden rush of frightened horses or cattle. ☐ *The loud explosion caused the stampede of cattle.* **2.** *n.* a sudden rush of excited, angry, or impatient people. (Fig. on ①.) ☐ *Seven people were crushed in the stampede at the soccer stadium.* **3.** *iv.* to rush as part of a large crowd of people or creatures. ☐ *The crowd stampeded toward the fire exit.* **4.** *tv.* to cause ① or

S

②. ☐ *The sound of thunder stampeded the cattle.*

**stand** ['stænd] **1.** *iv., irreg.* to be in a normal or typical vertical position. (Pt/pp: **stood.**) ☐ *After the tornado, very few trees were still standing.* **2. stand (up)** *iv., irreg. (+ adv.)* to move to a position on one's feet where one is vertical. ☐ *Mary stood up and walked into the other room.* **3.** *iv., irreg.* to be a particular height when in a vertical position on one's feet. ☐ *Mary stands 5 feet 8 inches in her bare feet.* **4.** *iv., irreg.* to be in a particular location. ☐ *A police car stood right outside the bank.* **5.** *iv., irreg.* [for a law] to remain in force. ☐ *The popular law stood for many years.* **6.** *tv., irreg.* to move someone or something to a vertical position. ☐ *The nurse stood the patient next to his bed.* **7.** *tv., irreg.* to withstand something; to endure something; to put up with something. ☐ *John can stand a lot of abuse.* **8.** *n.* the position one takes on an issue. ☐ *The newspaper agreed with the president's stand on taxes.* **9.** *n.* a base, frame, or piece of furniture that supports something. ☐ *I placed the potted plant on a stand by the window.* **10.** *n.* the place where a witness sits in a court of law. (Short for **witness stand.**) ☐ *The witness was asked to take the stand, so she sat in the chair by the judge's desk.*

**standard** ['stæn dɚd] **1.** *n.* something against which something else is tested or measured; something that is the basis of comparison. ☐ *The food critic used her grandmother's cooking as the standard.* **2.** *n.* a degree of quality or excellence. ☐ *The employees who didn't meet company standards were fired.* **3.** *adj.* ordinary; conforming to a certain degree or amount; normal. (Adv: *standardly.*) ☐ *Mary bought a new car with standard features because she couldn't afford extra gadgets.* **4.** *adj.* correct and acceptable according to the formal rules of a language. (Adv: *standardly.*) ☐ *Lisa spoke the standard language at work and a regional dialect at home.*

**stank** ['stæŋk] a pt of **stink.**

**staple** ['step əl] **1.** *n.* a small, thin, U-shaped piece of wire that fastens papers together, or that fastens things to a surface. ☐ *David loaded the stapler with staples.* **2.** *n.* any one of the most basic foods. ☐ *We went to the store to buy staples for our camping trip.* **3.** *tv.* to fasten papers together or to attach something to something else with ①. ☐ *Please staple these papers.*

**stapler** ['step lɚ] *n.* a machine that drives staples through paper or into objects. ☐ *Every desk in the office has a stapler on it.*

**star** ['stɑr] **1.** *n.* a large object in space, such as the sun, that creates its own heat and light. ☐ *Alpha Centauri is the nearest star to Earth, besides our own sun.* **2.** *n.* a celebrity; a famous entertainer. ☐ *The sports star demanded special treatment at the hotel.* **3.** *n.* a figure that has five points that radiate from a center point. ☐ *The American flag has white stars against a blue background.* **4.** *n.* ③ used as a mark of a degree of quality. (The more stars, the better something is.) ☐ *The food critic gave the restaurant two stars because service was poor.* **5.** *tv.* [for a movie, play, or television show] to feature a particular performer. ☐ *Let's go see that movie that stars my favorite actress.* **6.** *iv.* [for a performer] to appear as a major performer in a movie, play, or television show. ☐ *Mary hoped to star in a successful movie someday.* **7.** *adj.* most outstanding; most excellent; best. ☐ *The editor sent the paper's star reporter to cover the trial.*

**starch** ['stɑrtʃ] **1.** *n.* a white food substance that is part of potatoes, rice, and other grains. (Plural only when referring to different kinds, types, instances, or varieties.) ☐ *Lisa eats a lot of foods that contain starch.* Ⓒ *Pasta, bread, and*

S

*rice are all considered starches.* **2.** *n.* a substance used to stiffen cloth. (Plural only when referring to different kinds, types, instances, or varieties. ② is added while clothes are being washed or sprayed on afterward.) □ *It has been years since it was necessary to use starch when washing clothes.* 🄲 *The different brands of spray-on starches are convenient but expensive.* **3.** *n.* a food that contains ①. □ *The nutritionist told me to eat fewer starches.* **4.** *tv.* to stiffen fabric or clothing by coating it with or soaking it in ②. □ *Bill starched his shirt before ironing it.*

**stare** ['stɛr] **1. stare (at** someone or something**)** *iv.* *(+ prep. phr.)* to look directly at someone or something with one's eyes wide open, as though in fear, shock, surprise, wonder, or stupidity. □ *I just stared when Bill said something very stupid.* **2.** *n.* a long, direct look at someone or something with one's eyes wide open. □ *The tourists ignored the stares of the local citizens.*

**start** ['stɑrt] **1.** *n.* the beginning point of something; the time or place where something begins. □ *Susan always drinks coffee at the start of her day.* **2.** *n.* a shock that may jerk or jolt the body. □ *The shocking news gave my heart a start.* **3.** *tv.* to begin a process; to begin doing something; to cause something to operate, work, or move. □ *Susan started the lawn mower and mowed the lawn.* **4.** *tv.* to originate something. □ *Who started this argument?* **5.** *iv.* to begin a movement; to begin a journey; to begin a process; to begin at the lower limit of something. □ *When should we start?* **6.** *iv.* to move or jerk suddenly, as though one were surprised or scared; to be startled. □ *The horse started when a gun was fired.*

**startle** ['stɑrt əl] *tv.* to cause someone to move or jump suddenly because of fear or surprise. □ *The loud noise startled John.*

**starvation** [stɑr 've ʃən] *n.* starving; suffering and possibly death caused by not having food. (No plural form.) □ *The tortured prisoners suffered from starvation.*

**starve** ['stɑrv] **1.** *iv.* to die because of a lack of food; to die because one does not or cannot eat. □ *Thousands of people starved during the war.* **2.** *tv.* to cause someone or some creature to die of hunger. □ *He refused to eat and starved himself to death as a protest.*

**starving** ['stɑr vɪŋ] *adj.* very hungry. □ *I'm starving. Let's go get some dinner.*

**stash** ['stæʃ] *tv.* to hide something somewhere secretly for future use. □ *Mary stashed some batteries in her tool box for emergencies.*

**state** ['stet] **1.** *n.* the condition that someone or something is in. □ *The president spoke about the state of the economy.* **2.** *n.* the government of a country. (No plural form.) □ *We believe in the separation of church and state.* **3.** *n.* a division of government within a country or a republic. □ *Both the U.S. and Mexico are divided into states.* **4.** *adj.* <the adj. use of ②.> □ *Tourists are not allowed to drink alcohol on state property.* **5.** *adj.* <the adj. use of ③.> □ *The mayor decided to run for a seat in the state senate.* **6.** *tv.* to express something; to say something. (The object can be a clause with **that** ⑦.) □ *Mary stated that her client had no opinion on the rumor.*

**statement** ['stet mənt] **1.** *n.* something that is said; something that is stated. □ *The newspaper corrected its false statements.* **2.** *n.* a list showing the status of an account during a period of time. □ *The accountant prepared the company's yearly financial statement.*

**stateroom** ['stet rum] *n.* a private cabin on a ship or train. □ *After dinner and dancing, Bob retired to his stateroom to sleep.*

**state trooper** ['stet 'tru pɚ] *n.* a state police officer. (Can be shortened to **trooper.**) □ *The state trooper rushed to the scene of the accident.*

**static** ['stæt ɪk] **1.** *n.* the buzzing noise made when a radio or television station is not tuned in properly or when there is electronic interference. (No plural form.) □ *I couldn't hear Bill on the phone because there was too much static.* **2.** *adj.* [of electricity] not flowing in an electrical current; tiny electric sparks as found indoors in cold, dry weather. □ *Bill gave me a shock of static electricity when he touched me.* **3.** *adj.* not changing; stable; steady. (Adv: *statically* [...ɪk li].) □ *Static air pressure indicates that the weather will not change soon.*

**station** ['ste ʃən] **1.** *n.* the building or platform where a train or bus stops to let people on and off. □ *If you're going to the museum, get off at the next station.* **2.** *n.* a building where workers in a particular service work. □ *The downtown electrical station was damaged in a fire.* **3.** *n.* the specific location where a worker is assigned to work. □ *My work station has a computer and a fax machine.* **4.** *n.* the building or offices from which a television or radio broadcast is transmitted. □ *I called the station to complain about today's news editorial.* **5.** *tv.* to place someone at a location for work; to assign someone to a location for work. □ *The firm stationed some of its employees downtown.*

**stationary** ['ste ʃə nɛr i] *adj.* remaining in place; not moving; standing still. (Compare this with **stationery.**) □ *I think your arm is broken. Try to keep it stationary until we get to the hospital.*

**stationery** ['ste ʃə nɛr i] *n.* writing paper; writing supplies, including paper, pen, ink, envelopes, etc. (No plural form. Compare this with **stationary.**) □ *Bob's stationery has his name printed on it in gold.*

**statue** ['stæ tʃu] *n.* a sculpture of someone or an animal, made of stone, clay, wood, plaster, etc. □ *There's a statue of the company's founder in the main lobby.*

**status** ['stæt əs] *n.* someone's position within society or business; rank. □ *The judge exploited his status to get special treatment.*

**status quo** ['stæt əs 'kwo] *n.* the way things are; the current state of affairs. (No plural form. Latin for "the state in which.") □ *The protesters intended to disrupt the status quo.*

**stay** ['ste] **1.** *iv.* to remain in a place or position; to continue to be in a place or position. □ *My keys stayed on the table until Anne moved them.* **2.** *iv.* to live in a place for a while, especially as a guest. □ *Where are you staying while you are in town?* **3.** *iv.* to continue being in a certain condition; to remain in a certain condition. □ *Mary stayed disappointed in me, and I couldn't regain her trust.* **4.** *n.* a visit; a period of time when one visits someplace or when one is a guest someplace; a period of time that one lives someplace. □ *I very much enjoyed my stay at your house.*

**steady** ['stɛd i] **1.** *adj.* not changing in condition, place, or position; firm. (Adv: *steadily.* Comp: *steadier;* sup: *steadiest.*) □ *The driver kept a steady grip on the steering wheel.* **2.** *adj.* moving at a smooth pace; not moving in jerks and bursts. (Adv: *steadily.* Comp: *steadier;* sup: *steadiest.*) □ *Traffic is moving in a steady flow on the highway.* **3.** *adj.* calm; not excited; not upset. (Adv: *steadily.* Comp: *steadier;* sup: *steadiest.*) □ *Despite the excitement, my nerves remained steady.* **4.** *tv.* to cause something to be stable and not changing. □ *I put some weight on the table to steady it while Dave was writing.*

**steak** ['stek] *n.* a slab of a particular meat or fish, eaten as food. (A **steak** is beef

S

unless stated otherwise.) □ *I ate a salmon steak at the restaurant.*

**steal** ['stil] **1.** *tv., irreg.* to take something that does not belong to one without paying for it or without permission. (Pt: **stole**; pp: **stolen**.) □ *My car was stolen last night from my driveway.* **2.** *tv., irreg.* [in baseball] to reach the next base before the pitcher throws the ball to the batter. □ *Bob stole second base but was put out at third.*

**steam** ['stim] **1.** *n.* the gas that water is changed into when it is boiled. (No plural form.) □ *Our apartment is heated with steam.* **2.** *adj.* powered by ①; containing or using ①. □ *A steam locomotive makes a loud noise.* **3.** *tv.* to cook something in ①. □ *Bill steamed the vegetables rather than boiling them.* **4.** *tv.* to subject someone or something to ① or very hot water vapor. □ *John steamed himself in the hot shower.* **5.** *iv.* to give off ①. □ *The kettle is steaming on the stove.* **6.** *iv.* [for food] to cook in ①. □ *The vegetables steamed for a minute, and then I turned off the heat.*

**steamer** ['stim ɚ] **1.** *n.* a ship that is powered by a steam engine. □ *The steamer sank when it crashed into an iceberg.* **2.** *n.* an enclosed pot or pan that uses steam to cook food. □ *Susan removed the carrots from the steamer.*

**steel** ['stil] **1.** *n.* a very hard substance made of iron, carbon, and other metals, used in constructing tools, machines, and buildings. (No plural form.) □ *Some kinds of steel will rust in the rain.* **2.** *adj.* made of ①. □ *The thick, steel vault door is impossible to open.*

**steep** ['stip] **1.** *adj.* slanted at a sharp angle that is almost straight up and down. (Adv: *steeply.* Comp: *steeper;* sup: *steepest.*) □ *We rode our bikes up the steep hill, and then we stopped to rest.* **2.** *iv.* [for something, such as tea] to soak in hot liquid for a period of time. □ *The tea bag steeped for three minutes before the tea was ready.* **3.** *tv.* to soak something in liquid; to immerse something. □ *You should have steeped the tea longer.*

**steeple** ['stip əl] *n.* a tower on the roof of a church or other building, especially a tower that ends in a point. □ *There is a tall steeple on the top of city hall.*

**steer** ['stɪr] **1.** *tv.* to cause something to go in a certain direction; to guide someone or something to go in a certain direction. □ *The pilot steered the boat away from the reef.* **2.** *tv.* to guide someone toward or away from a course of action. (Fig. on ①.) □ *Max steered Lisa toward a sensible decision.* **3.** *iv.* to aim in a certain direction. □ *The driver steered toward the highway exit.*

**steering wheel** ['stɪr ɪŋ wil] *n.* the wheel that a driver or pilot turns to control the direction of a vehicle. (Can be shortened to **wheel**.) □ *John suddenly turned the steering wheel to avoid an accident.*

**stem** ['stɛm] **1.** *n.* the main part of a plant above the ground, which is connected to the roots below the ground, and from which leaves or flowers grow. □ *I grabbed the weeds by their stems and pulled them from the ground.* **2.** *n.* the part of a word that suffixes and prefixes are added to. □ *In English, gerunds are formed by adding the suffix* -ing *to verb stems.*

**step** ['stɛp] **1.** *n.* the movement made by putting one foot in front of the other while walking. □ *The soldier walked with uniform steps.* **2.** *n.* the distance traveled by a single ①. □ *Each step brought Mary closer to where she wanted to be.* **3.** *n.* a flat surface that one places one's foot on when going up or down stairs or a ladder. □ *The wooden step creaked as I placed my foot on it.* **4.** *n.* an action in a series of actions in a particular order. □ *In the last step of the experiment, we analyzed the results.* **5.** *iv.* to

S

take a **step** ① in a certain direction. □ *Anne stepped to the right so that Susan could pass her.*

**stereo** ['stɛr i o] **1.** *adj.* [of sound or electronic equipment making sound] coming from two or more speakers in a way that gives realistic effect. □ *Mary bought a new stereo television set.* **2.** *n.* an electronic device that produces sound coming from two or more sources, providing realistic sound reproduction. (Pl ends in *-s.*) □ *Mary listened to her favorite record on the stereo.*

**stern** ['stɚn] **1.** *adj.* strict; rigid in discipline. (Adv: *sternly.* Comp: *sterner;* sup: *sternest.*) □ *The museum guard gave us a stern warning about not touching the paintings.* **2.** *n.* the rear part of a boat or ship. □ *Violent waves washed over the boat's stern.*

**stew** ['stu] **1.** *n.* a thick soup of vegetables and often meat cooked slowly in their own juices. (Plural only when referring to different kinds, types, instances, or varieties.) □ *This stew is thick with potatoes and carrots.* Ⓒ *I like meat stews of any kind.* **2.** *tv.* to cook something slowly in water and its own juices. □ *Mary stewed some vegetables and served them with rice.* **3.** *iv.* [for food] to cook slowly in water and juices. □ *The vegetables are stewing in the pot.*

**stick** ['stɪk] **1.** *n.* a small branch; a thin length of wood from a tree. □ *The children collected sticks and twigs for the fire.* **2.** *n.* a thin piece of wood used for a special purpose. □ *The camper hiked up the trail, using a walking stick.* **3.** *tv., irreg.* to attach something to something else with glue, tape, or something adhesive. (Pt/pp: **stuck.**) □ *Anne stuck a picture to the door of her office with tape.* **4.** *tv., irreg.* to put something in a position. (Informal.) □ *The librarian stuck the book on the shelf in its proper place.* **5.** *iv., irreg.* to remain attached to something with glue, tape, or something adhesive. □ *Some gum stuck to the bottom of my shoe.*

**sticky** ['stɪk i] **1.** *adj.* adhesive. (Comp: *stickier;* sup: *stickiest.*) □ *Some sticky glue has stuck to my fingers.* **2.** *adj.* hot and humid; causing one to sweat. (Comp: *stickier;* sup: *stickiest.*) □ *During the sticky weather, I used an air conditioner.* **3.** *adj.* awkward. (Comp: *stickier;* sup: *stickiest.*) □ *Bill had to make the sticky decision of whether to promote John or Anne.*

**stiff** ['stɪf] **1.** *adj.* rigid; not flexible; hard to bend. (Adv: *stiffly.* Comp: *stiffer;* sup: *stiffest.*) □ *My neck was stiff from driving all day long.* **2.** *adj.* firm; almost solid; not fluid. (Adv: *stiffly.* Comp: *stiffer;* sup: *stiffest.*) □ *As the wet cement became stiff, John wrote his name in it.* **3.** *adj.* harsh; severe. (Informal. Comp: *stiffer;* sup: *stiffest.*) □ *The judge issued the dangerous criminal a stiff sentence.* **4.** *adj.* very formal; not relaxed. (Adv: *stiffly.* Comp: *stiffer;* sup: *stiffest.*) □ *John is shy and seems stiff, but if you get to know him, he is a lot of fun.*

**stiffen** ['stɪf ən] *iv.* to become stiff. □ *Anne's muscles stiffened after she exercised for two hours.*

**still** ['stɪl] **1.** *adj.* not moving; at rest. (Comp: *stiller;* sup: *stillest.*) □ *The congregation could not remain still during the church service.* **2.** *adj.* quiet; not talking; not making noise. (Not prenominal.) □ *The teacher told the students to be still.* **3.** *adv.* at a time past what was expected. □ *Tom was still not home at 3:00 A.M.* **4.** *adv.* **even** ④; yet [more]. (Comes after the adjective. Used with comparisons to make them stronger.) □ *Jane drives fast, but Mary drives faster still.*

**stimulant** ['stɪm jə lənt] *n.* something, especially a drug or chemical, that keeps someone awake or causes someone to be more active. □ *John took a stimulant so he wouldn't fall asleep while driving.*

**stimulate** ['stɪm jə let] *tv.* to excite someone or something; to cause someone or something to be active or excited. □ *I stimulated the frog by touching it on the leg, and it jumped.*

**sting** ['stɪŋ] **1.** *tv., irreg.* to pierce the skin of someone or something with something sharp; [for a bee, wasp, hornet, etc.] to pierce the skin with a stinger and inject a substance that causes a burning pain. (Pt/pp: **stung**.) □ *The bee stung the boy who swatted at it.* **2.** *tv., irreg.* to cause someone to feel a tingling or burning pain. □ *The cigarette smoke stung my eyes.* **3.** *iv., irreg.* to be able to pierce skin as with ①. □ *An angry wasp can sting again and again.* **4.** *iv., irreg.* [for something] to hurt sharply. □ *When some acid dripped on my arm, it stung badly.* **5.** *n.* the piercing of the skin as with ① and the pain that accompanies it. □ *A bee's sting hurts quite a bit.* **6.** *n.* a tingling or burning pain. □ *The nurse soothed the sting with some medicine.*

**stinger** ['stɪŋ ɚ] *n.* the stinging organ of bees, hornets, and other animals that sting. □ *The stinger of a dead wasp is still dangerous.*

**stink** ['stɪŋk] **1.** *n.* a terrible smell; a very bad smell. □ *There's a horrible stink coming from the garbage can.* **2.** *iv., irreg.* to smell bad. (Pt: **stank** or **stunk**; pp: **stunk**.) □ *Those dirty clothes stink. Please wash them.*

**stir** ['stɚ] **1.** *tv.* to mix something with one's hand or with an object. □ *Bill stirred the batter with a large spoon.* **2.** *tv.* to excite someone or an emotion; to cause someone to feel emotion or passion. □ *The speaker stirred us with an emotional presentation.* **3.** *iv.* to change position; to move about. □ *The sleeping dog stirred in front of the fireplace.* **4.** *n.* an exciting event; something that disturbs the usual order of things. □ *The scandal created a stir at the office.*

**stitch** ['stɪtʃ] **1.** *n.* one movement of a threaded needle through an object while sewing. □ *Bill's cut required six stitches.* **2.** *n.* the thread that is seen after one movement of a threaded needle through an object while sewing. □ *The stitches were so small that I could hardly see them.* **3.** *n.* a small amount of clothing. (No plural form. Usually in negative constructions.) □ *She sleeps without a stitch on.* **4.** *n.* a sharp pain. □ *The stitch in Mary's neck made it hard for her to turn her head.* **5.** *tv.* to sew something; to sew things together. □ *The actors stitched their own costumes together.*

**stock** ['stɑk] **1.** *n.* a supply of something to be used or sold. (Plural only when referring to different kinds, types, instances, or varieties.) □ *The store's entire stock of winter clothes is on sale.* Ⓒ *Our stocks of the smaller sizes of shoes are getting low.* **2.** *n.* a heavy broth made by cooking meats, usually with vegetables, for a long time—used to prepare sauce or soup. (Plural only when referring to different kinds, types, instances, or varieties.) □ *The cook added some herbs to the beef stock.* Ⓒ *Meat stocks are easy to make.* **3.** *n.* the total assets of a company divided into equal shares that are usually bought and sold in a stock market. (No plural form.) □ *Lisa sold her stock in the troubled company.* **4.** *n.* [a group of] shares of ③ of a specific company. □ *Lisa bought two stocks in the steel industry.* **5.** *tv.* [for a store] to arrange to have ① of a product available for sale. □ *This sporting goods store stocks team uniforms.* **6.** *tv.* to furnish land with animals; to furnish water with fish. □ *One of the large lakes in the park was recently stocked with bass.* **7.** *adj.* [of a response that seems] trite, rehearsed, and not sincere. □ *The mayor's assistant gave the reporter a stock response.*

S

**stocking** ['stɑk ɪŋ] *n.* a long, knitted or woven sock. □ *Anne wore nylon stockings to the party.*

**stock market** ['stɑk mɑr kət] **1.** *n.* a market for the business of buying and selling stocks in general. □ *The retired teacher had made a fortune in the stock market.* **2.** *n.* some sort of measure of the general value of all the stocks at any one time. (Can be shortened to **market**.) □ *I hope the stock market will go down so I can afford to buy some shares.*

**stockpile** ['stɑk pɑɪl] **1.** *n.* a large amount of something that is stored for future use or in case of an emergency. □ *During the winter, we keep a stockpile of canned goods in the pantry.* **2.** *tv.* to store a large amount of something for future use or in case of an emergency. □ *David stockpiled weapons in case of an attack.*

**stole** ['stol] pt of **steal**.

**stolen** ['stol ən] **1.** pp of **steal**. **2.** *adj.* taken without the owner's permission or knowledge. □ *The police returned the stolen bicycle to its owner.*

**stomach** ['stʌm ək] **1.** *n.* the organ of the body in which food is digested. □ *Spicy food upsets my stomach.* **2.** *n.* the front of the body below the chest and above the waist. □ *Mary clasped her stomach because it hurt so much.*

**stone** ['ston] **1.** *n.* the hard material of which rocks are made. (Plural only when referring to different kinds, types, instances, or varieties.) □ *Bill's heavy paperweight is made of stone.* Ⓒ *Granite is one of the strongest stones known to exist.* **2.** *n.* a rock; a chunk of ①. □ *Max threw a stone at Bob.* **3.** *n.* a jewel; a gem. □ *A precious stone was stolen from the museum.* **4.** *n.* a small, hard object that forms in parts of the body, such as the kidney, that causes a lot of pain as it passes through the organ. □ *The doctor informed Anne that she had kidney stones.* **5.** *adj.* made of ①. □ *Bill built a stone patio in his backyard.* **6.** *tv.* to throw **stones** ② at someone or something, often as punishment or torment. □ *Two U.S. soldiers were stoned in Bosnia yesterday.*

**stood** ['stʊd] pt/pp of **stand**.

**stool** ['stul] **1.** *n.* a tall seat that usually has no support for one's back or arms. □ *The professor sat on a stool in front of the class and lectured.* **2.** *n.* feces; waste matter that is expelled from the body. (Plural only when referring to different kinds, types, instances, or varieties.) □ *I cleaned up my dog's stool from the sidewalk.* Ⓒ *Four stools a day is not normal for a healthy person.*

**stoop** ['stup] **1.** *n.* a small porch at the door of a house. □ *The mail carrier left a package for me on the stoop.* **2.** *n.* a bent posture, as if carrying a heavy weight on the shoulders. □ *A back brace helped correct Anne's stoop.* **3.** *iv.* to bend down; to bend forward; to hold one's head and shoulders downward in front of one's body. □ *Mary stooped so she wouldn't bump her head on the low ceiling.*

**stop** ['stɑp] **1.** *tv.* to end movement, progress, an activity, or an existence. □ *John stopped smoking because it was bad for his health.* **2.** *iv.* to move, progress, act, or function no longer; to cease. □ *I hope the rain stops soon.* **3.** *iv.* to stay for a period of time. □ *John stopped for a quick visit.* **4.** *n.* a short visit; a short stay. □ *Mary hadn't planned a stop at the store until she saw the word* SALE *in the window.* **5.** *n.* a place where a bus, train, or other vehicle **stops** ③ to let passengers get on and off the vehicle. □ *Someone announced each train stop as we approached it.* **6.** *n.* a consonant that is made by **stopping** ① the flow of the breath and suddenly releasing it. □ *In English, the stops are* [p, t, k, b, d, g]. □ *The word* wrap *ends with a stop.*

S

**stoplight** ['stɑp lɑɪt] *n.* a traffic signal that has colored lights that indicate whether drivers should stop or go. ☐ *The city installed a stoplight at the dangerous intersection.*

**stopover** ['stɑp ov ɚ] *n.* a place where one stops briefly during a journey, especially a stop at an airport between the city where one took off and the city that one is going to. ☐ *When Mary flew to Miami, she had a four-hour stopover in Atlanta.*

**stoppage** ['stɑp ɪdʒ] *n.* an organized strike; the organized stopping of work, such as during a disagreement between labor and management. ☐ *During the stoppage, the factory hired workers who did not belong to the union.*

**stopwatch** ['stɑp wɑtʃ] *n.* a watch that can be started or stopped at any moment, used to determine how long something lasts. ☐ *The coach timed the swimmers with a stopwatch.*

**storage** ['stor ɪdʒ] **1.** *n.* keeping or storing [things]. (No plural form.) ☐ *Our large apartment has plenty of room for storage.* **2. in storage** *phr.* in a place where things are stored or kept. ☐ *John's furniture is in storage while he is in the army.*

**store** ['stor] **1.** *n.* a shop where goods or products are sold. ☐ *At my favorite store, there is a sale on towels.* **2.** *n.* a supply of something. ☐ *John built up a store of office supplies in his desk.* **3.** *tv.* to keep something someplace so that it can be used later. ☐ *Mary stores bags of dog food in her garage.*

S

**storekeeper** ['stor kip ɚ] *n.* someone who owns or manages a store. ☐ *The thief threatened to kill the storekeeper.*

**storeroom** ['stor rum] *n.* a room where things are stored. ☐ *The shop's excess stock is kept in a large storeroom.*

**stork** ['stork] *n.* a large bird with a long, sharp beak and a long neck. ☐ *There are many types of storks found around the world.*

**storm** ['storm] **1.** *n.* a period of severe weather with very strong winds, heavy rain or snow, and sometimes thunder and lightning. ☐ *Many trees were uprooted in the violent storm.* **2.** *n.* a violent attack or burst of anger. (Fig. on ①.) ☐ *The reporter's rude remarks caused a storm of protest.* **3.** *tv.* to attack something with force. ☐ *The enemy army stormed the fort.* **4.** *iv.* [for the weather] to be severe, with strong winds, heavy rain or snow, and thunder and lightning. ☐ *Take your umbrella because it's going to storm today.*

**storm door** ['storm dor] *n.* a second door, outside the regular door, that keeps cold, wind, snow, or rain from entering. ☐ *Mary locked both the storm door and the inside door.*

**storm window** ['storm wɪn do] *n.* a second window placed outside a regular window, that keeps cold, wind, snow, or rain from entering a room or building. ☐ *John put up the storm windows in October when it became cold.*

**story** ['stor i] **1.** *n.* an account of something that has happened. ☐ *I read the story of President Roosevelt's life.* **2.** *n.* a tale; an account that is fiction, told or written for entertainment or amusement. ☐ *Bill is an author who writes fantastic adventure stories.* **3.** *n.* a lie. ☐ *Bill told his boss a story about being stuck in traffic.* **4.** *n.* a news report; an article of news. ☐ *The price of wheat is going up. For the story, here is our reporter.* **5.** *n.* one level of a building; one layer from floor to ceiling in a building. (The floor on ground level is the first story.) ☐ *My dentist's offices occupy the entire tenth story of this building.*

**stout** ['stɑʊt] *adj.* wide; fat; weighing too much. (Adv: *stoutly.* Comp: *stouter;* sup: *stoutest.*) ☐ *The doctor put the stout patient on a diet.*

**stove** ['stov] *n.* an appliance that usually contains an oven and has burners on the top, used for cooking. □ *Anne boiled some water on the stove for tea.*

**straight** ['stret] **1.** *adj.* not bent; not curved; direct; continuing in the same direction. (Adv: *straightly.* Comp: *straighter;* sup: *straightest.*) □ *John walked in a straight line to prove he wasn't drunk.* **2.** *adj.* honest; sincere; telling the truth. (Adv: *straightly.* Comp: *straighter;* sup: *straightest.*) □ *Tell the truth! Be straight with me!* **3.** *adj.* without an interruption; continuous. (Before or after a noun.) □ *I slept for two days straight when I was ill.* **4.** *adv.* [going] directly [to a place without making a detour]. □ *Mary went straight to bed when she got home.* **5.** *adv.* in a **straight** ① line; without turning. □ *John drove straight down Western Avenue from 47th Street to 35th Street.* **6.** *adv.* upright. □ *John sat straight in his chair.*

**strain** ['stren] **1.** *tv.* to stretch or pull something, especially as much as possible or in a way that causes injury. □ *Mary strained her eyes while reading in the dim light.* **2.** *tv.* to separate liquid from something solid by pouring it through a filter. □ *Jane strained the particles from the chemical solution.* **3.** *tv.* to place something under a burden; to place tension on something. (Fig. on ①.) □ *Constant arguing strained the couple's marriage.* **4.** *iv.* to stretch tightly; to work hard and hold a heavy load. □ *The rope strained, but did not break, as I lifted the climber to safety.* **5.** *iv.* to use a lot of effort to do something. □ *I strained to understand what my professor was talking about.* **6.** *n.* a burden or problem that causes someone distress. □ *Insurance costs are a big strain on our budget.* **7.** *n.* an injury to a muscle caused by stretching it or pulling it too hard. □ *John got a strain because he didn't stretch his muscles before running.* **8.** *n.* a variety of plant, bacterium, or virus. □ *This strain of wheat is only grown in Kansas.*

**strand** ['strænd] **1.** *n.* one thread of a rope; one wire of a cable; a thread; a fiber. □ *The weaker strands of the rope started to break.* **2.** *tv.* to cause someone or something to be stuck or held at a location. □ *The blizzard stranded the passengers at the airport.*

**strange** ['strendʒ] **1.** *adj.* unusual; odd; peculiar; not normal or usual. (Adv: *strangely.* Comp: *stranger;* sup: *strangest.*) □ *Mary woke up when she heard a strange noise in the house.* **2.** *adj.* not familiar; not usually experienced. (Adv: *strangely.* Comp: *stranger;* sup: *strangest.*) □ *Susan is always willing to try strange foods.*

**stranger** ['strendʒ ɚ] *n.* someone who is not known to someone else; someone who is not familiar to someone else. □ *Mary told her children to stay away from strangers.*

**strap** ['stræp] **1.** *n.* a strong, narrow strip of material used to secure something. □ *The large crate was secured with thick plastic straps.* **2.** *tv.* to secure someone or something with a strong, narrow strip of leather or other material. □ *The assistant strapped the violent patient to the bed.*

**straw** ['strɔ] **1.** *n.* dried stalks of the plant on which grain grows. □ *David pitched clean straw into the horse's stable.* **2.** *n.* a plastic or paper tube used for drinking a liquid by sucking. □ *I always ask for a straw when I order a drink at a restaurant.* **3.** *adj.* made of ①; containing ①. □ *Jane bought a straw purse at the market.*

**strawberry** ['strɔ bɛr i] **1.** *n.* a small, soft, red fruit that has tiny seeds on its surface. □ *John put some sliced strawberries on his cereal.* **2.** *adj.* made with or flavored with ①. □ *I put some* *whipped cream on my slice of strawberry pie.*

**stray** ['stre] **1.** *adj.* wandering. □ *Anne adopted the stray cat.* **2.** *adj.* occurring or arriving by chance. □ *Stray radio signals interfered with my cellular telephone.* **3.** *iv.* to wander; to become lost; to leave the main path or topic. □ *The lecturer strayed from the subject.* **4.** *n.* an animal that is lost; an animal that wanders around and has no home. □ *Bill fed a stray he found in his backyard.*

**streak** ['strik] **1.** *n.* a long, thin line or stripe. □ *A streak of lightning flashed across the sky.* **2.** *n.* a period of time during which something is constant; a period of time during which something is not interrupted. □ *David had an amazing streak of bad luck last month.* **3.** *tv.* to mark something with long, thin lines or stripes. □ *Rain streaked the dirty windows.* **4.** *iv.* to flow or race along in long, thin lines or stripes. □ *Tears streaked down the mourners' faces.* **5.** *iv.* to run or move somewhere very fast. □ *The rocket streaked through space, carrying its passengers to Mars.*

**stream** ['strim] **1.** *n.* a small river. □ *Bill waded across the stream to the other bank.* **2.** *n.* a steady flow of something, especially something liquid. □ *From the cracked glass, a stream of juice ran to the edge of the table.* **3.** *iv.* to flow somewhere steadily and in large amounts. □ *Blood streamed from the soldier's wounds.*

**streamer** ['strim ɚ] *n.* a very long, thin strip of paper or ribbon used as a decoration during a ceremony, parade, or celebration. □ *The people on the float threw streamers into the crowd.*

**street** ['strit] *n.* a road, usually one in a city or a town that has buildings or parks beside it. (Abbreviated *St.* in addresses.) □ *Look both ways before you cross the street.*

**streetlight** ['strit lɑɪt] *n.* a light, usually on a pole, that lights a street when it is dark outside. □ *New streetlights were installed to improve safety.*

**strength** ['strɛŋkθ] **1.** *n.* the quality of being strong. (No plural form.) □ *I have no strength in my left leg since the accident.* **2.** *n.* a virtue; a good feature of someone or something. (Fig. on ①.) □ *Good and fast work is one of John's strengths.*

**stress** ['strɛs] **1.** *n.* the pressure caused by something that is heavy; strain. (No plural form.) □ *Many heavy trucks put a lot of stress on the old bridge.* **2.** *n.* the mental pressure caused by something that is difficult or demanding; mental tension. (Fig. on ①.) □ *Stress at work caused John to quit.* **3.** *n.* emphasis placed on a syllable when speaking by saying it louder or in a different tone. (Plural only when referring to different kinds, types, instances, or varieties.) □ *The teacher placed extra stress on the final syllable in the word.* Ⓒ *There are two stresses in the compound* cottage cheese. **4.** *n.* emphasis. (No plural form.) □ *The teacher put too much stress on dates and not enough on concepts.* **5.** *tv.* to place ③ on a syllable when speaking. □ *In the word* caravan, *the first syllable is stressed.* □ *Lisa stressed the wrong syllable, and we misunderstood her.* **6.** *tv.* to place emphasis or focus on something. (The object can be a clause with **that** ⑦.) □ *The history teacher stressed dates too much and didn't teach the children about the causes of events.*

**stretch** ['strɛtʃ] **1.** *tv.* to extend something. □ *Anne stretched her arms wide and yawned.* **2. stretch (out)** *iv. (+ adv.)* to become wider; to become longer; to lengthen. □ *My pants stretched after I wore them for a few days.* **3. stretch (out)** *iv. (+ adv.)* [for something] to spread out over time or space. □ *The lecture seemed to stretch to fill an*

S

*hour and a half.* **4. stretch out** *iv. + adv.* to lie down on a bed and spread out to nap or sleep. □ *Dave stretched out and took a nap.* **5.** *iv.* to be elastic; to be able to be pulled without breaking. □ *The rubber band stretched to double its own length.* **6.** *n.* a continuous area of land. □ *The lifeguard protected a long stretch of beach.* **7.** *n.* a continuous period of time. □ *For a three-month stretch, Mary lived without a telephone.*

**stretcher** ['strɛtʃ ɚ] *n.* a device like a light bed or cot, used to carry someone who is sick or dead. □ *The injured player was carried from the field on a stretcher.*

**strict** ['strɪkt] **1.** *adj.* [of rules or discipline] severe, harsh, or demanding. (Adv: *strictly.* Comp: *stricter;* sup: *strictest.*) □ *The soldiers followed the strict military rules.* **2.** *adj.* absolute; exact. (Adv: *strictly.* Comp: *stricter;* sup: *strictest.*) □ *The judge gave a strict interpretation of the law.*

**strife** ['strɑɪf] *n.* fighting; a bitter struggle; a heated argument or battle. (No plural form.) □ *The proposed tax increase caused much strife in Congress.*

**strike** ['strɑɪk] **1.** *tv., irreg.* to hit someone or something; to hit something against something; to crash into something. (Pt/pp: **struck.**) □ *The car struck a tree when it drove off the road.* **2.** *tv., irreg.* to attack someone or something. □ *The government forces struck the militia's compound.* **3.** *tv., irreg.* to light a match; to cause something to burn with fire. □ *John struck three matches before he could light the fire.* **4.** *tv., irreg.* to discover something underneath the ground by digging or drilling. □ *The workers struck oil.* **5.** *iv., irreg.* [for a group of workers] to refuse to work until demands are met. □ *The teachers voted to strike until they had a contract.* **6.** *iv., irreg.* to attack. □ *The mayor's policies struck at the heart of the crime problem.* **7.** *iv., irreg.* to make contact; to have a negative effect [on someone or something]. □ *The terrible disease struck without warning.* **8.** *iv., irreg.* [for a clock] to make a sound like a bell to tell what time it is. □ *Shortly after the clock struck, I fell asleep.* **9.** *n.* the state that exists when workers refuse to work during a labor dispute. □ *The union settled the strike when the management offered a fair contract.* **10.** *n.* [in baseball] a penalty given to a player who swings the bat and misses the ball, who hits the ball foul, or who does not swing the bat when the umpire thinks that the ball went by the player in a way that the batter could have hit it. □ *Bob swung at and missed the ball, and the umpire yelled "Strike!"* **11.** *n.* [in bowling] an instance of knocking over all the pins at once. □ *The bowler needed a strike to win the game.*

**string** ['strɪŋ] **1.** *n.* a thin rope or a thick thread, especially used for tying something, binding something, or suspending something in the air. (No plural form.) □ *Where do you keep the string?* **2.** *n.* a length of ① or thread. □ *I need a few strings to tie up my packages.* **3.** *n.* a wire or cord that is stretched tight and is used to produce sound in certain musical instruments. □ *Pianos have wire strings.* **4.** *n.* a cord used to form the tightly pulled net found in a tennis racket and similar sports equipment. □ *The strings of the racket are made of nylon.* **5. strings** *n.* the musical instruments whose sounds are made by rubbing a bow across ③; the people who play the instruments having ③. (Treated as plural.) □ *This piece is written for strings.* **6.** *n.* a number of things or people in a row. □ *The manager interviewed a string of prospective employees.* **7.** *tv., irreg.* to put ③ or ④ on a guitar, violin, tennis racket, etc. (Pt/pp: **strung.**) □ *The tennis racket was strung with thin plastic strings.* **8.** *tv.,*

S

*irreg.* to place something on ②. □ *The jewelry maker strung beads to make a necklace.* **9.** *tv., irreg.* to stretch something that is like ① from one place to another. □ *Sally strung paper streamers over the doorway as a decoration.*

**strip** ['strɪp] **1.** *n.* a long, flat piece of something. □ *I used a strip of tape to stick the note to the wall.* **2.** *tv.* to undress someone; to remove someone's clothes; to remove something's covering. □ *Bob stripped himself for a shower.* **3.** *tv.* to make something empty or bare. □ *The maid stripped the bed.* **4.** *iv.* to take off one's clothes; to undress. □ *Max stripped and took a quick shower.*

**stripe** ['strɑɪp] **1.** *n.* a long band of color or texture; a wide line; a wide line of something that is different from what is around it. □ *The city worker painted yellow stripes down the middle of the road.* **2.** *tv.* to mark something with ①; to put ① on something. □ *The artist striped the canvas with lines of red chalk.*

**stroll** ['strol] **1.** *n.* a pleasant walk. □ *The busy executive relaxed by taking a stroll during lunch.* **2.** *iv.* to go for a pleasant walk. □ *Mary strolled for miles, enjoying the fresh air.*

**strong** ['strɔŋ] **1.** *adj.* having strength in the mind or body; having power in the mind or the body; using strength. (Adv: *strongly.* Comp: *stronger;* sup: *strongest.*) □ *The strong firefighter carried John down the ladder.* **2.** *adj.* able to last; able to withstand something; not easily broken; sturdy. (Adv: *strongly.* Comp: *stronger;* sup: *strongest.*) □ *These strong metal pipes can withstand great water pressure.* **3.** *adj.* [of a taste, smell, or color] intense. (Adv: *strongly.* Comp: *stronger;* sup: *strongest.*) □ *A strong taste of pepper ruined the flavor of the soup.* **4.** *adj.* having a certain number [of people]. (Follows a specific number.) □ *Our team of volunteers is 50 strong and still growing.*

**struck** ['strʌk] pt/pp of **strike**.

**structure** ['strʌk tʃɚ] **1.** *n.* the way that something is put together; the way that something is built; the way that something or some creature is arranged. (No plural form.) □ *The building's structure resembled that of an old castle.* **2.** *n.* a building. □ *Many tall structures blocked my view of the horizon.* **3.** *n.* something that is made from different parts. □ *The biologist examined the complex structure of the cell.* **4.** *tv.* to arrange something so that it has a certain form; to form something in a certain way; to make something from different parts. □ *The writer structured the novel around a southern family.*

**struggle** ['strʌg əl] **1.** *iv.* to work hard for or against something; to fight for or against something, using a lot of effort or energy. □ *When he was hit in the chest, Max struggled to breathe.* **2.** *n.* a hard fight for or against something; a difficult effort for or against something. □ *Quitting smoking was the biggest struggle of John's life.*

**strung** ['strʌŋ] pt/pp of **string**.

**strut** ['strʌt] *iv.* to walk somewhere arrogantly; to walk somewhere as though one were more important than one is. □ *The movie star strutted into the restaurant, demanding to be served immediately.*

**stub** ['stʌb] **1.** *tv.* to hurt a toe by hitting it against something. □ *John stubbed his toe on a log.* **2.** *n.* a short end of something that remains after the rest of it is taken or used. □ *The stub of Max's cigarette is still smoldering.*

**stubborn** ['stʌb ɚn] *adj.* not willing to do something that someone else wants; not yielding; not giving in. (Adv: *stubbornly.*) □ *The stubborn student would not obey the teacher.*

**stuck** ['stʌk] pt/pp of **stick**.

**student** ['stud nt] *n.* someone who studies or learns, especially at a school; a pupil. □ *The student asked the professor a question.*

**study** ['stʌd i] **1.** *tv.* to spend time learning information about something by reading, researching, observing, or experimenting. □ *The animal researcher studied advanced psychology.* **2.** *tv.* to examine something closely; to scrutinize something; to observe something closely. □ *The detective studied some hairs found at the scene of the crime.* **3.** *iv.* to be a student; to read, research, observe, or experiment in order to learn about something. □ *Bill works during the day and studies in the evening.* **4.** *n.* the work or effort involved in learning. (The same meaning in singular and plural, but not countable.) □ *A program in medicine involves years of hard study.* **5.** *n.* an examination of something, as with ②. □ *Mary is deeply involved in her study of the evidence.* **6.** *n.* a room where someone **studies** ③. □ *Bill closed the door to his study so he could concentrate.*

**stuff** ['stʌf] **1.** *n.* any substance that things are made of; the material that anything is made of. (No plural form.) □ *The stuff inside the walls began to rot.* **2.** *n.* things; unnamed objects; belongings; possessions. (No plural form.) □ *John bought a lot of stuff on sale at the store.* **3.** *tv.* to fill something with a substance; to pack something into a space or container until there is no room left. □ *I stuffed the bag with garbage and carried it out.* **4.** *tv.* to fill the inside of a dead animal with a material that preserves it and maintains its shape so that it can be displayed. □ *The hunter stuffed his kill and then displayed it in his house.*

**stumble** ['stʌm bəl] **1.** *iv.* to trip; to fall over something; to almost fall while one is moving; to walk in a clumsy way. □ *John stumbled and fell down the hill.* **2.** *iv.* to speak in a clumsy way; to make mistakes while speaking; to trip on one's words. (Fig. on ①.) □ *The nervous speaker stumbled over his words.*

**stump** ['stʌmp] **1.** *n.* the part of something that remains when the other part has been cut off, broken off, removed, or used. □ *They cut down all the trees and there was nothing left but stumps.* **2.** *tv.* to puzzle someone; to confuse someone. □ *The crime problem stumped even the mayor.*

**stun** ['stʌn] **1.** *tv.* to surprise someone completely; to amaze someone; to shock someone. □ *The magician stunned the audience with amazing tricks.* **2.** *tv.* to cause someone or something to become unconscious, by a blow or by electrical shock. □ *John was stunned when he touched the electrical fence.*

**stung** ['stʌŋ] pt/pp of **sting**.

**stunk** ['stʌŋk] a pt/pp of **stink**.

**stupid** ['stu pɪd] **1.** *adj.* not intelligent; not smart. (Adv: *stupidly.* Comp: *stupider;* sup: *stupidest.*) □ *The clerk is not stupid. He just made a simple mistake.* **2.** *adj.* silly; foolish. (Adv: *stupidly.* Comp: *stupider;* sup: *stupidest.*) □ *What a stupid question! Of course, I do!* **3.** *adj.* [of something] annoying; [of something] causing anger or irritation. (Comp: *stupider;* sup: *stupidest.*) □ *The stupid copy machine is broken again!*

**stupidity** [stu 'pɪd ɪ ti] **1.** *n.* a lack of intelligence. (No plural form.) □ *The new teacher was disturbed by the stupidity of her students.* **2.** *n.* the condition of being stupid, incorrect, or not appropriate. (No plural form.) □ *The stupidity of the novel amazed the reviewers.*

**sturdy** ['stɚ di] *adj.* strong; firm; not easily knocked over. (Adv: *sturdily.* Comp: *sturdier;* sup: *sturdiest.*) □ *Anne piled heavy weights on top of the sturdy table.*

**style** ['stɑɪl] **1.** *n.* a way in which something is made, designed, done, said, or written. □ *Business letters should be*

S

*written in a formal style.* **2.** *n.* a particular design or theme in clothing or products at a particular period of time. □ *The designer fashioned the actor's clothing in a 1920s style.* **3.** *n.* the manner in which someone behaves. □ *John's style of managing makes some workers uncomfortable.* **4.** *tv.* to design or form something in a certain way. □ *Jane styled the actor's hair before the show.*

**stylish** ['staɪ lɪʃ] *adj.* in the current fashion; in style; current; up-to-date. (Adv: *stylishly.*) □ *The popular students went only to the most stylish café.*

**sub** ['sʌb] **1.** *n.* a sealed boat that can remain still or travel under water. (Short for **submarine.**) □ *I toured a sub and decided that I could never live in such a small space.* **2.** *n.* someone or something serving in the place of someone or something else. (Short for **substitute.**) □ *Today, I am a sub for your regular teacher.*

**subdue** [səb 'du] **1.** *tv.* to bring someone or something under one's control. □ *The police subdued the excited suspect.* **2.** *tv.* to make someone or something less noticeable; to soften the strength or intensity of something. □ *The artist subdued the bright colors in her painting.*

**subject** ['sʌb dʒɪkt] **1.** *n.* a topic; something that is discussed, examined, or researched. □ *Lisa raised several subjects for discussion.* **2.** *n.* a course; something that is studied; a particular field of knowledge. □ *Anne's favorite subject in college is French.* **3.** *n.* someone used in an experiment. □ *The scientist examined the subjects' reactions to bright light.* **4.** *n.* someone who is ruled by a government or a ruler. □ *The loyal subject would not speak against the government.* **5.** *n.* a person, object, or scene that is painted or photographed. □ *Art students draw sketches of nude subjects.* **6.** *n.* the noun or noun phrase representing the person who performs the action in active sentences, or that is the receiver of an action in passive sentences. □ *The subject must agree with its verb.*

**subjective** [səb 'dʒɛk tɪv] *adj.* of or about what someone thinks about something instead of the actual facts. (Adv: *subjectively.*) □ *Mary would not be a good judge because she is too subjective.*

**subject matter** ['sʌb dʒɛk 'mæt ɚ] *n.* content; the subject that a piece of writing or speech deals with. □ *Most readers found the book's subject matter offensive.*

**sublime** [sə 'blaɪm] *adj.* supreme; wonderful; grand; inspiring. (Adv: *sublimely.*) □ *David spent a sublime weekend resting in Florida.*

**submarine** ['sʌb mə rin] **1.** *n.* a ship that can travel completely underwater, used especially in war and for research. (Can be shortened to **sub.**) □ *Submarines can fire missiles at targets on land.* **2.** *n.* a large sandwich; a sandwich made with two long pieces of bread. (Usually **sub.**) □ *I ordered a salami sub that was one foot long.*

**submerge** [səb 'mɚdʒ] **1.** *tv.* to put something under the surface of a liquid; to immerse something in water. □ *The coastal city was submerged by the flood.* **2.** *iv.* to go underwater; to go under the surface of liquid. □ *The scuba diver submerged and swam toward a coral reef.*

**submit** [səb 'mɪt] **1. submit** someone **to** something *tv.* + *obj.* + *prep. phr.* to make someone endure something. □ *I hate to submit you to so much pain, but these stitches will hurt.* **2. submit** something **to** someone or something *tv.* + *obj.* + *prep. phr.* to offer something to someone for review and analysis; to present something to someone for review and analysis. □ *David submitted his proposal to the company president.*

S

**subscription** [səb 'skrɪp ʃən] *n.* an order for a series of issues of a magazine or newspaper. □ *Anne renewed her subscription to her favorite magazine.*

**subsoil** ['sʌb soɪl] *n.* the layer of soil that lies below the surface of the earth. (No plural form.) □ *The farmer plowed the fertilizer into the subsoil.*

**substance** ['sʌb stəns] **1.** *n.* the material that something is made of; matter. □ *The doctor flushed the poisonous substance from the child's stomach.* **2.** *n.* the essence; the important part of something. (No plural form.) □ *Lisa's report detailed the substance of her findings.*

**substitute** ['sʌb stɪ tut] **1. substitute** someone or something **for** someone or something *tv. + obj. + prep. phr.* to replace someone or something with someone or something else; to exchange someone for someone else. □ *The softball coach substituted Jane for the injured pitcher.* **2.** *iv.* to be put in someone else's or something else's place as a replacement. □ *Bill's couch substitutes as his bed.* **3.** *n.* a replacement; someone or something that is put in someone else's or something else's place. (Can be shortened to sub.) □ *Use this one as a substitute for the real one.*

**substitution** [səb stɪ 'tu ʃən] **1.** *n.* the replacement of someone or something with someone or something else. (Plural only when referring to different kinds, types, instances, or varieties.) □ *The coach was criticized for the substitution of players he made late in the game.* Ⓒ *He made seven different substitutions in the game.* **2.** *n.* someone or something that has been substituted as in ①. □ *This is a very poor substitution for butter.*

**subtract** [səb 'trækt] **1.** *tv.* to take a part of something away; to take a quantity away from a quantity; to reduce something by a certain amount. (See also minus.) □ *Please remember to subtract the amount of the coupon.* **2.** *iv.* to lessen or reduce [something] as in ①. □ *The first-grade teacher taught the students to subtract.*

**subtraction** [səb 'træk ʃən] **1.** *n.* the reduction of something by a certain amount; the reduction of a quantity by a quantity. (Plural only when referring to different kinds, types, instances, or varieties.) □ *The subtraction of a number from a smaller number yields a negative number.* Ⓒ *I have to finish these subtractions, and then I will be finished.* **2.** *n.* an amount that is subtracted. □ *I made one small subtraction in my bank account to get it to balance.*

**suburb** ['sʌ bɚb] *adj.* a city, town, or village that is next to or near a large city. □ *Large cities are usually surrounded by many suburbs.*

**suburban** [sə 'bɚ bən] *adj.* of or about the suburbs. □ *Bill rode the train from a suburban station to the city.*

**subway** ['sʌb we] *n.* an underground electric train that provides transportation in large cities. □ *Anne saves money by taking the subway to work instead of driving.*

**succeed** [sək 'sid] **1.** *iv.* to be successful; to reach a goal. □ *Bill succeeded in losing ten pounds.* **2.** *tv.* to follow someone or something into a job or office. □ *Susan succeeded Dave as the head of the department.*

S

**success** [sək 'sɛs] **1.** *n.* accomplishment; achievement. (Plural only when referring to different kinds, types, instances, or varieties.) □ *Most people would prefer success rather than failure.* Ⓒ *The producer was honored for his numerous successes in the movie industry.* **2.** *n.* someone or something that is successful, especially someone or something that has become famous, important, or rich. □ *Through hard work, Susan became a success in her field.*

**successful** [sək 'sɛs fʊl] *adj.* showing evidence of having accomplished something or having reached high status. (Adv: *successfully.*) □ *Mary has a successful career in advertising.*

**such** ['sʌtʃ] **1.** *adj.* so great; so much. □ *There was such a noise from the explosion!* **2. as such** *phr.* considering the state something is in; as someone or something is. □ *You are new here, and as such, I will have to train you.* **3. such as** *phr.* for example. □ *I love to eat sweet foods, such as cookies, candy, and ice cream.*

**suck** ['sʌk] *tv.* to pull liquid into one's mouth by putting one's lips around something and drawing in; to pull something into one's mouth with one's lips. □ *Anne sucked the soda through a straw.*

**sudden** ['sʌd n] *adj.* unexpected; happening without warning. (Adv: *suddenly.*) □ *I was not prepared for the sudden rainstorm and got all wet.*

**suddenly** ['sʌd n li] *adv.* unexpectedly; without warning. □ *The fire alarm suddenly rang, startling me.*

**suds** ['sʌdz] *n.* bubbles formed by soap mixing with water; lather; froth. (Treated as plural, but not countable.) □ *The children played with the suds in the bathtub.*

S

**sue** ['su] **1.** *iv.* to start a lawsuit; to file a claim against someone or something in court. □ *The woman who fell at the store sued to cover hospital costs.* **2.** *tv.* to bring a lawsuit against someone or something; to file a claim against someone or something in court. □ *John sued the driver who had caused the car accident.*

**suffer** ['sʌf ɚ] **1.** *tv.* to experience physical or emotional pain because of illness or emotional loss. □ *Bill suffered a lot of pain before going to the doctor.* **2.** *iv.* to feel physical or emotional pain. □ *John suffered over the death of his parents.* **3.** *iv.* to worsen; to decline in quality. □ *The city schools have suffered under the current administration.*

**suffix** ['sʌf ɪks] *n.* a form added to the end of a word that changes or modifies the meaning or function of the word. □ *The most common plural suffix in English is spelled* -s. □ *The suffix* -ness *changes adjectives into nouns.*

**suffocate** ['sʌf ə ket] **1.** *tv.* to kill someone or a creature by preventing it from getting the oxygen that is needed. □ *The thick smoke suffocated the victims of the fire.* **2.** *iv.* to die because one is unable to get the oxygen that is needed. □ *Two people suffocated from the smoke in the building.*

**sugar** ['ʃʊg ɚ] **1.** *n.* a sweet substance, usually in crystal form, that is made from certain plants and used to sweeten food and drinks. (No plural form.) □ *The cakes were covered with powdered sugar.* **2.** *n.* a sweet substance that is found naturally in many foods. (Plural only when referring to different kinds, types, instances, or varieties.) □ *Many fruits contain sugar.* 🄲 *There are many chemically distinct sugars.*

**suggest** [səg 'dʒɛst] **1.** *tv.* to propose something that will be considered; to express something that one thinks should be considered; to offer something as an option. (The object can be a clause with **that** ⑦.) □ *"I suggest ordering the meatloaf," said the waiter.* **2.** *tv.* to bring something to one's mind; to cause something to be thought of in a certain way; to cause something to be a reminder to someone. (The object can be a clause with **that** ⑦.) □ *The rumbling in my stomach suggested that it was time for dinner.*

**suggestion** [səg 'dʒɛs tʃən] **1.** *n.* a hint; a trace; something that reminds someone of someone or something. (No plural form.) □ *I noticed a suggestion of anger in Susan's voice.* **2.** *n.* a proposal to be considered; an expression of something that one thinks should be considered; the offering of an option; something that is suggested. ☐ *The diner ordered one of the waitress's suggestions.*

**suicide** ['su ə saɪd] **1.** *n.* killing oneself on purpose. (No plural form.) ☐ *It was hard to tell whether the death was murder or suicide.* **2.** *n.* someone who has accomplished ①. ☐ *The coroner examined the suicide to determine the cause of death.*

**suit** ['sut] **1.** *n.* a set of formal clothes, consisting of a jacket, pants, and sometimes a vest, made from the same material. ☐ *Each piece of my suit is brown.* **2.** *n.* a set of things, such as clothing or armor, that are worn together. ☐ *Max put on his clown suit and entered the circus ring.* **3.** *n.* a statement of claims against someone or a business, brought to a court of law. (Short for **lawsuit**.) ☐ *Jane filed a number of suits after the accident.* **4.** *n.* one of the four different sets of cards found in a deck of playing cards. ☐ *A poker hand of cards of the same suit is called a flush.* **5.** *tv.* to meet the requirements of someone or something. ☐ *The new class suited Max perfectly.* **6.** *tv.* to look good with something; to look good on someone; to match someone. ☐ *Do these pants suit me?*

**suitable** ['su tə bəl] *adj.* right or proper for the situation. (Adv: *suitably.*) ☐ *Mary looked for a video that was suitable for young children.*

**suitcase** ['sut kes] *n.* a piece of luggage used for carrying clothing and personal items while traveling. ☐ *I packed my suitcase the evening before my trip.*

**sullen** ['sʌl ən] *adj.* being silent and looking angry and irritated because one is in a bad mood. (Adv: *sullenly.* Comp: *sullener;* sup: *sullenest.*) ☐ *The sullen waiter put the plates on our table and walked away.*

**sum** ['sʌm] **1.** *n.* the total of two or more amounts. ☐ *Can you figure out the sum of these numbers?* **2.** *n.* an amount of money. ☐ *Jane donated the sum of $500 to the charity.*

**summarize** ['sʌm ə raɪz] *tv.* to express the main ideas of something. ☐ *After Jane summarized her main points, she answered questions from the audience.*

**summary** ['sʌm ə ri] *n.* the main ideas of something; a short statement about the important points of a longer speech or text. ☐ *The author submitted a summary along with the complete manuscript.*

**summer** ['sʌm ɚ] **1.** *n.* one of the seasons of the year, after spring and before autumn. ☐ *Mary visited her grandparents during the summer.* **2.** *adj.* <the adj. use of ①.> ☐ *The student received extra help during summer school.*

**summertime** ['sʌm ɚ taɪm] *n.* summer; the season of summer. (No plural form.) ☐ *During the cold winter, Anne looked forward to summertime.*

**summit** ['sʌm ət] **1.** *n.* the highest point of something, especially a mountain. ☐ *The highest summit in the world is the top of Mt. Everest.* **2.** *n.* a meeting involving very important people, especially leaders of governments. (Fig. on ①.) ☐ *The president met with his staff at a secret summit.*

**sun** ['sʌn] **1.** *n.* a star; a star that gives light and warmth to a planet; a star that is orbited by a planet. ☐ *When the sun exploded, it destroyed the planets that orbited it.* **2. the sun** *n.* the star that gives light and warmth to Earth; the star that Earth orbits. (No plural form. Treated as singular.) ☐ *Earth is the third planet from the sun.* **3. the sun** *n.* sunlight; light and warmth that is radiated by ②. (No plural form. Treated as singular.) □ *Our kitten warmed itself in the sun.* **4.** *tv.* to expose oneself to ③; to "bathe" oneself in sunlight. (Takes a reflexive object.) □ *If you sun yourself too much, you will develop wrinkles.* **5.** *iv.* to absorb the rays of ②; to "bathe" in the light of ②. □ *Dozens of people sunned on the beach.*

**sunbeam** ['sʌn bim] *n.* a ray of sunlight; a beam of sunlight. □ *Early in the morning, I saw the first sunbeam peek over the horizon.*

**sunblock** ['sʌn blɑk] Go to **sunscreen**.

**sunburn** ['sʌn bɚn] **1.** *n.* redness and soreness of skin that has been exposed too long to sunlight. (Plural only when referring to different kinds, types, instances, or varieties.) □ *Jane prevented sunburn by wearing a good sunscreen.* Ⓒ *Don't get too many sunburns. They may cause skin cancer.* **2.** *iv.* [for one's skin] to acquire ①. □ *Anne sunburns easily because her skin is fair.*

**sundae** ['sʌn de] *n.* a dessert made with ice cream and flavored toppings. □ *Jane made a chocolate sundae with two scoops of vanilla ice cream.*

**Sunday** ['sʌn de] Go to **day**.

**sung** ['sʌŋ] pp of **sing**.

**sunglasses** ['sʌn glæs ɪz] *n.* glasses with dark lenses that are worn to block bright sunlight. (Treated as plural. Number is expressed with *pair(s) of sunglasses*.) □ *The actress concealed her identity by wearing sunglasses and a wig.*

**sunk** ['sʌŋk] a pt/pp of **sink**.

**sunlight** ['sʌn lɑɪt] *n.* the light that is given off by the sun. (No plural form.) □ *Car windshields are often tinted to reduce the glare of sunlight.*

**sunny** ['sʌn i] *adj.* with bright sunshine. (Comp: *sunnier;* sup: *sunniest.*) □ *Mary grows a lot of plants in her sunny bedroom.*

**sunrise** ['sʌn rɑɪz] *n.* the time of day when the sun appears to be moving above the horizon in the east. □ *Sunrise through the mist was beautiful.*

**sunscreen** AND **sunblock** ['sʌn skrin, 'sʌn blɑk] *n.* lotion or cream containing a chemical substance that helps prevent sun damage to the skin. (Plural only when referring to different kinds, types, instances, or varieties.) □ *To protect your skin from the sun, you should wear sunblock.* Ⓒ *I tried a variety of sunscreens and they all worked pretty well.*

**sunset** ['sʌn sɛt] *n.* the time of day when the sun appears to be moving below the horizon in the west. □ *The tourists were in awe of the beautiful sunset.*

**sunshine** ['sʌn ʃɑɪn] *n.* sunlight; light from the sun. (No plural form.) □ *I opened the curtains and let the sunshine into the room.*

**super** ['sup ɚ] **1.** *adj.* excellent; wonderful; great; marvelous; fabulous. □ *Mary told me about the super movie she'd seen last night.* **2.** *adj.* extra large. □ *After the first of the year, there were super savings throughout the mall.*

**superb** [sə 'pɚb] *adj.* very good; excellent; of the best quality. (Adv: *superbly.*) □ *The critic praised the superb movie highly.*

**superior** [sə 'pɪr i ɚ] **1.** *n.* someone who has a higher rank or position in relationship to someone else. □ *The soldier saluted his superior.* **2.** *adj.* very good; above average; better than something else. (Adv: *superiorly.*) □ *Mary spent the night in a superior room at the fancy hotel.*

**superiority** [sə pɪr i 'or ɪ ti] *n.* the condition of being superior to someone or something. (No plural form.) □ *The superiority of the fine meal impressed everyone at the table.*

**superlative** [sə 'pɚl ə tɪv] **1.** *n.* the form of an adjective or adverb, usually created with *most* or *-est*, that indicates the highest degree of the comparison of that adjective or adverb. □ *The superlative of "bad" is "worst."* □ *"Saddest" and "most sad" are both superlatives of "sad."* **2.** *adj.* best; having the highest quality. (Adv: *superlatively.*) □ *Anne wore a diamond of superlative quality.*

**supermarket** ['su pɚ mɑr kɪt] *n.* a large store that stocks several kinds of each item, allowing customers a wide choice. □ *Anne handed her coupons to the cashier at the supermarket.*

**supervise** ['su pɚ vɑɪz] *tv.* to direct a worker or a group of workers; to direct something; to oversee someone or something. □ *The architect also supervised the construction workers.*

**supervision** [su pɚ 'vɪ ʒən] *n.* paying attention to or watching over [someone or something]. (No plural form.) □ *Mature employees work well without supervision.*

**supper** ['sʌp ɚ] *n.* the meal eaten in the evening. □ *Bill ordered pizza for his supper.*

**suppertime** ['sʌp ɚ tɑɪm] *n.* the time when supper is eaten. (No plural form.) □ *My mother always called us to the dinner table at suppertime.*

**supply** [sə 'plɑɪ] **1.** *tv.* to give someone something that is needed or wanted; to give something to someone who needs or wants it. □ *The high school supplies each student with textbooks.* **2.** *n.* an amount of something that is available. (Sometimes plural.) □ *Today I purchased my monthly supply of medication.*

**support** [sə 'port] **1.** *tv.* to provide someone with money, shelter, clothing, and food. □ *The college student was supported by her scholarship.* **2.** *tv.* to bear the weight of something; to keep something vertical or in place so that it doesn't fall. □ *Three heavy wooden beams supported the ceiling.* **3.** *tv.* to give someone or something one's encouragement or favor; to show someone or something approval or favor. □ *Bill's friends supported his decision to find a new job.* **4.** *n.* providing someone with money, shelter, food, and clothing. (No plural form.) □ *Mary provided support for her ailing mother.* **5.** *n.* the strength and structure needed to bear the weight of someone or something. (No plural form.) □ *These shoes provide the support my feet need when I run.* **6.** *n.* something that carries the weight of something; a beam; a prop. □ *The steel supports were firmly welded into place.* **7.** *n.* encouragement. (No plural form.) □ *With Anne's support, Susan decided to look for a better job.*

**suppose** [sə 'poz] *tv.* to consider or imagine that something is or will be true. (The object is a clause with **that** ⑦.) □ *I suppose that you want me to leave, since everyone else has.*

**supreme** [sə 'prim] **1.** *adj.* having total authority; having total power; having the highest rank; being the most important. (Adv: *supremely.*) □ *The lawsuit was ruled on by the Supreme Court.* **2.** *adj.* of the highest degree of quality. (Adv: *supremely.*) □ *The very rich couple lived in supreme luxury.*

**sure** ['ʃʊr] **1.** *adj.* certain; confident or knowing that something is the case. (Adv: *surely.* Comp: *surer;* sup: *surest.*) □ *Our team is a sure win in tonight's game.* **2.** *adv.* certainly. (Informal.) □ *Your cat sure moves quickly!* **3.** *adv.* [in response to a yes-or-no question] yes. (Informal.) □ *"Will you help me move my furniture tomorrow?" "Sure."*

**surely** ['ʃʊr li] *adv.* certainly; without doubt; definitely. □ *Mary will surely come here before going to the party.*

**surf** ['sɚf] *n.* waves of water hitting the beach. (No plural form.) □ *John's sand castle was washed away by the surf.*

**surface** ['sɚ fəs] **1.** *n.* the outside of something; the outside layer of something. ☐ *David dusted the surface of the shelf.* **2.** *n.* the top of a liquid. ☐ *A fly floated on the surface of my soup.* **3.** *iv.* [for something underwater] to go up to or above the **surface** ② of the water. ☐ *The tiny fish surfaced to eat the fish food.*

**surge** ['sɚdʒ] **1.** *n.* a sudden, powerful burst of electricity. ☐ *A power surge tripped the circuit breaker.* **2.** *n.* a strong forward movement. ☐ *The surge of the crowd pushed me toward the fire exit.*

**surgeon** ['sɚ dʒən] *n.* a physician who performs surgery. ☐ *The nurse hands instruments to the surgeon.*

**surgery** ['sɚ dʒə ri] **1.** *n.* the science and practice of curing sickness and treating injury by performing a (cutting) **operation** ①. (No plural form.) ☐ *The doctors in the emergency room were trained in surgery.* **2.** *n.* using ① in treating illness and disease. ☐ *The use of clean equipment during surgery prevents infection.*

**surname** ['sɚ nem] *n.* the family name; [in the U.S.] the last name. (Compare this with **first name**.) ☐ *Please print your surname first, and your first name last.*

**surplus** ['sɚ pləs] **1.** *n.* an amount of something that is more than what is needed; an extra amount; an excess. ☐ *We have grown a surplus of wheat this season.* **2.** *adj.* <the adj. use of ①.> ☐ *The government gave surplus cheese to needy families.*

S

**surprise** [sɚ 'prɑɪz] **1.** *n.* something that is not expected; something that happens without warning. ☐ *The terrorist bombing was an unwelcome surprise.* **2.** *n.* the emotion that is caused by something unexpected happening. (No plural form.) ☐ *Mary screamed with surprise when we all shouted "Happy birthday!"* **3.** *tv.* to cause someone to feel ② by doing something or saying something unexpected. ☐ *The young politician surprised everyone by winning the election.* **4.** *tv.* to attack someone or something without warning. ☐ *The terrorists surprised the citizens with a late-night attack.* **5.** *adj.* unexpected; without warning. ☐ *The surprise attack killed dozens of innocent civilians.*

**surrender** [sə 'rɛn dɚ] **1.** *iv.* to give up, especially when one has lost a battle, argument, or fight; to yield to a force that one was fighting. ☐ *The soldiers surrendered because they were surrounded.* **2.** *tv.* to give someone or something up to someone; to yield someone or something to someone. ☐ *The drunken driver surrendered his license.* **3.** *n.* **surrendering** as in ①; giving up. (No plural form.) ☐ *The government demanded the terrorists' immediate surrender.*

**surround** [sə 'rɑʊnd] *tv.* to enclose someone or something on all sides; to be on all sides of someone or something. ☐ *Clear blue water surrounds the island.*

**survey 1.** ['sɚ ve] *n.* a set of questions used to collect people's opinions and evidence of their attitudes. ☐ *The government agency conducted a survey about public health.* **2.** ['sɚ ve] *n.* a document containing ①. ☐ *Please complete this survey when you have time.* **3.** ['sɚ ve] *n.* an examination or study of the condition, contents, or details of something. ☐ *A quick survey of the kitchen revealed a lack of drinking glasses.* **4.** ['sɚ ve] *n.* a description or analysis of a subject of study. ☐ *Lisa's grant application included an in-depth survey of her work.* **5.** ['sɚ ve] *n.* the measurement of land so that accurate maps can be made or so that the legal description of property boundaries is exact. ☐ *The real-estate agent checked the survey to see how far the property extended.* **6.** ['sɚ ve] *tv.* to collect people's opinions on an issue; to ask people for their opinions on an issue. □ *The researcher surveyed students about their drug use.* **7.** [sɚ 've] *tv.* to examine or study the condition, contents, or details of something. □ *The army general surveyed the losses on the battlefield.* **8.** [sɚ 've] *tv.* to measure part of the surface of the earth—or a similar area—exactly, so that accurate maps or legal descriptions can be made. □ *Satellites are now used to survey the earth.*

**survive** [sɚ 'vaɪv] **1.** *iv.* to remain alive even after a threat to one's life; to live a very long life. □ *Those who survived rebuilt the city.* **2.** *tv.* to endure someone or something and remain alive or functioning. □ *My car survived 15 years of hard service.* **3.** *tv.* to outlive someone; to live longer than someone. □ *David survived all of his brothers and sisters.*

**survivor** [sɚ 'vaɪv ɚ] *n.* someone who remains alive; someone who did not die while others died. □ *The firefighters pulled two survivors from the burning house.*

**suspect 1.** ['sʌs pɛkt] *n.* someone who is thought to have committed a crime. □ *The suspect was arrested and taken to the police station.* **2.** ['sʌs pɛkt] *adj.* causing questioning or doubt. (Adv: *suspectly.*) □ *Jane's testimony was suspect and drew the attention of the lawyer.* **3.** [sə 'spɛkt] *tv.* to consider something to be likely. (The object can be a clause with **that** ⑦.) □ *The general suspected that John was a traitor.*

**suspend** [sə 'spɛnd] **1.** *tv.* to hang something from something else; to cause something to hang down from something above it. □ *Bill suspended a string of lights from the ceiling.* **2.** *tv.* to delay something; to stop something for a period of time. □ *The police suspended the inquiry after three years.* **3.** *tv.* to prevent someone from working at a job, attending classes, etc., for a period of time, as a punishment. □ *The boss suspended the drunken worker without pay for a week.* **4.** *tv.* to cause something to float in the air or in liquid. □ *The scientist suspended the creatures in a liquid medium.*

**suspense** [sə 'spɛns] *n.* an anxious, scary, or uncertain feeling that is caused by not knowing what is going to happen next. (No plural form.) □ *The mysterious shooting left the audience in suspense until the final act of the play.*

**sustain** [sə 'sten] **1.** *tv.* to nourish and care for living plants and creatures. □ *Mary sustained her plants with plenty of water and sunshine.* **2.** *tv.* to keep something moving, going, or working; to prolong something. □ *Anne and Bill sustained their conversation for six hours.* **3.** *tv.* to suffer an injury; to have an injury. □ *He sustained a broken arm in the bus accident.*

**swallow** ['swɑl o] **1.** *tv.* to cause food or drink to go down one's throat and into the stomach. □ *Anne swallowed two vitamins with a glass of water.* **2.** *tv.* to believe something without question; to believe something that one is told, even if it is a lie; to accept something that one is told. (Fig. on ①. Informal.) □ *The jury swallowed the witness's testimony.* **3.** *iv.* to take [something] into the body by way of the throat. □ *When my throat was sore, it hurt to swallow.* **4.** *n.* the amount of something that can be taken into the mouth and sent down the throat. □ *Could I have a swallow of your drink?* **5.** *n.* a kind of small songbird. □ *Jane awoke at sunrise to the song of the swallows.*

**swam** ['swæm] pt of **swim**.

**swamp** ['swɑmp] **1.** *n.* an area of very wet, muddy ground, sometimes covered with water. □ *An alligator swam through the swamp.* **2.** *tv.* to flood something, especially a boat. □ *The heavy rains swamped the port city.*

**swan** ['swɑn] *n.* a large, white, bird that lives near the water and has a long, curving neck. ☐ *Many ducks, geese, and swans bred near the marsh.*

**swap** ['swɑp] **1. swap** someone or something **for** someone or something *tv. + obj. + prep. phr.* to exchange something for something else; to trade something for something else. ☐ *Bill swapped his desk for Mary's bookcase.* **2.** *iv.* to exchange; to trade. ☐ *I like the one you have. Do you want to swap?* **3.** *n.* an exchange; a trade. ☐ *Jane felt she got the better deal in the swap.*

**swarm** ['swɔrm] *n.* a large number of people or animals, especially bees or other insects, that move together in a densely packed group. ☐ *Swarms of people rushed toward the fire exit.*

**swat** ['swɑt] **1.** *tv.* to hit someone or something hard. ☐ *Jane swatted my hand when I tried to grab her cookie.* **2.** *n.* a hard hit; a sharp blow. ☐ *John gave me a swat when I took some of his pizza.*

**sway** ['swe] **1.** *iv.* to bend or swing back and forth; to bend to one side and then the other; to move back and forth. ☐ *The ship swayed from side to side on the rough seas.* **2.** *tv.* to cause someone or something to bend or move back and forth; to bend or move someone or something back and forth. ☐ *The violent sea swayed the ship from side to side.* **3.** *tv.* to change someone's opinion or judgment; to influence someone. (Fig. on ②.) ☐ *I have made my decision, and you cannot sway me.*

**swear** ['swɛr] **1.** *iv., irreg.* to curse; to say bad words angrily. (Pt: **swore**; pp: **sworn**.) ☐ *The angry manager swore and yelled.* **2. swear to** do something *iv., irreg. + inf.* to vow to do something; to make a pledge to do something. ☐ *The witness swore to tell the truth in court.* **3. swear** someone **in** *tv., irreg. + obj. + adv.* [for an officer of the court] to cause someone to pledge to tell the truth or perform the duties required by law; to cause someone to take an oath. ☐ *The Supreme Court justice swore the newly elected president in.* 🆃 *The justice swore in the new president.*

**sweat** ['swɛt] **1.** *n.* the moisture that comes out of the body through pores in the skin. (No plural form.) ☐ *After running 10 miles, Mary was covered with sweat.* **2.** *n.* hard work; labor; something that causes ①. (No plural form.) ☐ *A lot of sweat and planning went into this project.* **3.** *iv., irreg.* [for moisture] to come out of the body through pores in the skin. (Pt/pp: *sweat* or *sweated*.) ☐ *John sweated in the hot sun as he worked in his garden.* **4.** *iv.* to work very hard; to labor. ☐ *The architect sweated for days until the plans were finished.*

**sweater** ['swɛt ɚ] *n.* a warm piece of clothing worn above the waist, usually woven or knitted from wool or cotton. ☐ *Mary wore a sweater under her heavy coat because she was so cold.*

**sweatpants** ['swɛt pænts] *n.* warm pants, usually with a soft or fluffy inside layer. (Treated as plural. Number is expressed with *pair(s) of sweatpants*.) ☐ *Mary has a sweatshirt to match her sweatpants.*

**sweatshirt** ['swɛt ʃɚt] *n.* a warm, long-sleeved shirt, usually with a soft or fluffy inside layer. ☐ *The players wore matching sweatshirts while they practiced.*

**sweaty** ['swɛt i] **1.** *adj.* covered with sweat. (Adv: *sweatily*. Comp: *sweatier*; sup: *sweatiest*.) ☐ *The sweaty runners drank lemonade at the end of the race.* **2.** *adj.* causing sweat, especially because of hot, muggy weather or hard work. (Comp: *sweatier*; sup: *sweatiest*.) ☐ *John uses an air conditioner in sweaty weather.*

**sweep** ['swip] **1.** *tv., irreg.* to clean a floor by passing a broom over it; to

S

clean a surface by moving a broom or brush over it to push the dirt away. (Pt/pp: **swept.**) ☐ *John swept the floor and took out the garbage.* **2.** *iv., irreg.* to clean as in ①. ☐ *Bill swept and dusted after making a mess.* **3.** *n.* a smooth, flowing motion, especially in a curve; a swinging movement. ☐ *With each sweep of the searchlight, the guards could see the whole prison yard.*

**sweet** ['swit] **1.** *adj.* tasting like sugar; like sugar or honey. (Adv: *sweetly.* Comp: *sweeter;* sup: *sweetest.*) ☐ *John likes to eat sweet desserts.* **2.** *adj.* pleasant; pleasing; having personal charm. (Adv: *sweetly.* Comp: *sweeter;* sup: *sweetest.*) ☐ *Mary helped the sweet old lady across the street.* **3. sweets** *n.* candy; pieces of something made with sugar or honey. (Treated as plural.) ☐ *I'm going to the candy store to buy some sweets.*

**sweeten** ['swit n] *tv.* to cause something to become sweet; to add sugar to something. ☐ *Mary sweetened her coffee before drinking it.*

**sweet tooth** ['swit tuθ] *n.* a liking for candy, chocolate, or other sweet foods. (Always singular.) ☐ *Bill's sweet tooth is ruining his diet.*

**swell** ['swɛl] **1.** *iv., irreg.* to grow larger; to grow fuller; to rise or grow past the regular amount. (Pt: *swelled;* pp: *swelled* or **swollen.**) ☐ *The river swelled over its banks and flooded the town.* **2.** *iv., irreg.* to increase in size, amount, or intensity. ☐ *The music swelled grandly at the end of the symphony.* **3.** *tv., irreg.* to cause someone or something to grow larger or fuller; to increase something in size, amount, or intensity. ☐ *A new assignment swelled the amount of work Susan had to do.* **4.** *n.* the rise and fall of waves. ☐ *The motion of the ship—meeting one swell after another—made some passengers sick.* ☐ *The captain increased the boat's speed because of the swells.*

**swelter** ['swɛl tɚ] *iv.* to suffer in very hot weather. ☐ *The athletes sweltered because it was such a hot day.*

**swept** ['swɛpt] pt/pp of **sweep.**

**swift** ['swɪft] *adj.* rapid; quick; moving or passing fast. (Adv: *swiftly.* Comp: *swifter;* sup: *swiftest.*) ☐ *The swift current carried the raft down the stream.*

**swim** ['swɪm] **1.** *iv., irreg.* [for someone] to travel through water by moving arms and legs; [for an animal] to travel through water by moving paws, legs, fins, tail, etc. (Pt: **swam;** pp: **swum.**) ☐ *Bob watched the fish swim in his aquarium.* **2.** *iv., irreg.* [for something] to seem to spin or revolve, owing to one's illness or the loss of one's ability to properly perceive. ☐ *The room swam in front of the sick patient's eyes.* **3.** *n.* an instance of traveling through the water by moving one's arms and legs. ☐ *John took a refreshing swim after work.*

**swimming pool** ['swɪm ɪŋ 'pul] *n.* a container or tank that holds water for people to swim or play in. (Can be shortened to **pool.**) ☐ *Jimmy filled the plastic swimming pool with the garden hose.*

**swimsuit** ['swɪm sut] *n.* a piece of clothing worn for sunning or swimming; the clothing worn by someone who swims. ☐ *Bill got sand in his swimsuit when he lay on the beach.*

**swindle** ['swɪn dəl] **1.** *tv.* to cheat someone, especially to cheat someone out of money. ☐ *The treasurer swindled the company by stealing money.* **2.** *n.* cheating; cheating people out of their money. ☐ *No one discovered the company treasurer's elaborate swindle.*

**swing** ['swɪŋ] **1.** *tv., irreg.* to move something in a sweeping or curved pattern. (Pt/pp: **swung.**) ☐ *Dave angrily swung the door open.* **2.** *tv., irreg.* to move something in a sweeping or circular movement. ☐ *Sue will swing the rope in* *a circle above her head.* **3.** *iv., irreg.* to move in a sweeping or curved pattern. ☐ *The door swung open from the force of the wind.* **4.** *iv., irreg.* to move while hanging from a fixed point. ☐ *Mary's legs swung back and forth as she sat on the dock.* **5.** *iv., irreg.* to turn suddenly or quickly. ☐ *Public opinion quickly swung against the lying politician.* **6.** *iv., irreg.* to play on a **swing** ⑧; to move one's body through the air on a **swing** ⑧. ☐ *The children swung on the swings at the park.* **7.** *n.* a change; a variation. ☐ *The economist predicted a swing in the employment rate.* **8.** *n.* a seat that hangs on ropes or chains, which people, usually children, sit on and move back and forth. ☐ *Mary loves using the swing at the park.*

**switch** ['swɪtʃ] **1.** *n.* a lever that turns electricity on and off. ☐ *Jane turned the computer switch off.* **2.** *n.* a change from one thing to another. ☐ *Our manager approved the switch in the brand of paper we use.* **3.** *n.* a thin, flexible stick that is cut from a tree. ☐ *The farmer made a broom by tying many switches together.* **4. switch** something **on; switch** something **off** *tv. + obj. + adv.* to close or open an electric circuit; to turn something on or off. ☐ *Bill switched the lights off.* 🅃 *He switched off the lights.* **5.** *tv.* to change something; to swap or exchange things. ☐ *I switched pens when the one I was using ran out of ink.*

S

**switchboard** ['swɪtʃ bord] *n.* a control panel that an operator uses to connect telephone calls to the proper person. ☐ *The operator could listen to any call coming through the switchboard.*

**swollen** ['swol ən] **1.** pp of **swell**. **2.** *adj.* puffed up; having gotten bigger; growing in size. (Adv: *swollenly.*) ☐ *John put some ice on his swollen ankle.*

**sword** ['sord] *n.* a heavy metal weapon with a long, usually sharp blade attached to a handle. ☐ *The knight lifted the heavy sword and slew the wild beast.*

**swore** ['swor] pt of **swear**.

**sworn** ['sworn] pp of **swear**.

**swum** ['swʌm] pp of **swim**.

**swung** ['swʌŋ] pt/pp of **swing**.

**syllable** ['sɪl ə bəl] *n.* an uninterrupted segment of speech consisting of a vowel possibly with consonants on either side. ☐ *The words* cat, mat, red, *and* ant *are each a single syllable.* ☐ *The word* watermelon *has four syllables.*

**symbol** ['sɪm bəl] **1.** *n.* something that represents something else; something that stands for something else. ☐ *Married people wear wedding rings as a symbol of their endless love.* **2.** *n.* a letter, number, or shape that represents a quantity, chemical element, mathematical operation, or other function. ☐ *The* "+" sign is a symbol for addition. ☐ Au *is the chemical symbol for gold.*

**symmetry** ['sɪm ə tri] *n.* the arrangement of the opposite sides of something so that they look exactly alike. (No plural form.) ☐ *The symmetry of the building design was pleasing to the eye.*

**sympathy** ['sɪm pə θi] *n.* kind feelings for someone's problems and sorrows. ☐ *Anne expressed her sympathy for Jane's loss.*

**symphony** ['sɪm fə ni] *n.* a long piece of music written for an orchestra. ☐ *Mary listens to classical symphonies while she works.*

**symptom** ['sɪmp təm] *n.* a sign, feeling, or problem that is evidence of the existence of something, especially of an illness. ☐ *High unemployment is a symptom of a troubled economy.*

**synagogue** AND **synagog** ['sɪn ə gɑg] *n.* a building for worship in the Jewish religion. ☐ *The rabbi lived across the street from the synagogue.*

**synonym** ['sɪ nə nɪm] *n.* a word that has the same or almost the same meaning as another word. □ Sofa, couch, *and* davenport *are synonyms.* □ *You should replace the overused words in your paper with synonyms.*

**syphon** ['saɪ fən] Go to **siphon.**

**syringe** [sə 'rɪndʒ] *n.* a device from which liquids are pushed out or into which liquids are pulled, usually through a long, thin needle. □ *Dr. Smith needed a extra-large syringe to hold the full dose of medicine.*

**syrup** ['sɪr əp] *n.* a thick, sweet liquid eaten as food or used to deliver medication. (Plural only when referring to different kinds, types, instances, or varieties.) □ *Anne drank some cough syrup to soothe her sore throat.* 🄲 *Maple syrups from the Northeast are the best.*

**system** ['sɪs təm] **1.** *n.* a group of things that work together to form a network; a group of things arranged in a particular way that function as one thing. □ *Consultants were hired to help improve the city's subway system.* **2.** *n.* a method of arrangement; a plan. □ *Can you explain the accounting system used in your firm?*

**systematic** [sɪs tə 'mæt ɪk] *adj.* organized and structured; based on a system or plan. (Adv: *systematically* [...ɪk li].) □ *The tyrant ordered the systematic destruction of his enemies.*

S

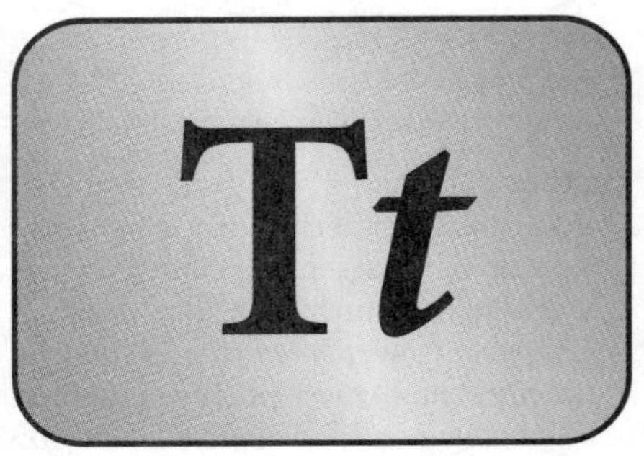

**table** ['teb əl] **1.** *n.* an item of furniture whose top is a raised, flat surface supported by legs. □ *The table was set with the best silver and china.* **2.** *n.* a chart of numbers, facts, or data presented in columns or rows. □ *The researcher formatted her data into a table.*

**tablecloth** ['teb əl klɔθ] *n.* a piece of fabric that covers the top of a table and hangs over the side, for decoration or protection of the table's surface. □ *Jane washed the tablecloth after the meal.*

**table of contents** ['teb əl əv 'kɑn tɛnts] *n.* a list at the beginning of a book, showing what is in the book and the page number of each part. □ *The table of contents listed the chapter titles and page numbers.*

**tablet** ['tæb lət] **1.** *n.* a pad of paper; blank sheets of paper that are bound together along the top or side. □ *The teacher instructed the students to take notes in their tablets.* **2.** *n.* a pill; a small, hard piece of medicine, drugs, or vitamins that a person swallows. □ *The doctor gave Bill some tablets to take for his allergies.*

**tack** ['tæk] *n.* a small, thin nail with a large head. (See also **thumbtack.**) □ *David repaired the door frame with a few tacks.*

**tackle** ['tæk əl] **1.** *tv.* to run after, dive onto, and throw a person to the ground, especially in playing football. □ *The police officer tackled the mugger.* **2.** *tv.* to undertake a duty or a problem; to start working on something difficult. (Fig. on ①.) □ *Susan tackled the problem and solved it easily.* **3.** *n.* equipment used for fishing. (No plural form.) □ *Tom left his tackle in the boat.*

**tact** ['tækt] *n.* the ability to deal with people without offending them. (No plural form.) □ *Mary lacks tact, so all of her requests seem rude.*

**tactful** ['tækt fʊl] *adj.* showing or having tact. (Adv: *tactfully.*) □ *If you want people to do as you say, try being more tactful.*

**tactic** ['tæk tɪk] *n.* a skillful way of doing something in order to reach a goal. (Often plural.) □ *The president's tactics were simply not honest.*

**tag** ['tæg] **1.** *n.* a small label that has information about the object that it is attached to. □ *Jane took the tag off the gift before she wrapped it.* **2.** *n.* a game in which a player runs around trying to touch someone else, who then runs to touch another person. (No plural form.) □ *Jimmy hated to play tag with the older, faster children.* **3.** *tv.* to put ① on something or some creature. □ *The scientist tagged the deer with a metal clip so the animal could be identified.* **4.** *tv.* to touch someone, especially in ②. □ *The slow runner couldn't tag any of the other players.*

**tail** ['tel] **1.** *n.* the part of an animal that hangs off from its back, as an extension of the spine. □ *The dog happily wagged its tail as its master approached.* **2.** *n.* the rear part of something; the last part of something. (Fig. on ①.) □ *The comet's tail stretched for thousands of miles.*

**tailor** ['te lɚ] **1.** *n.* someone who makes or repairs clothes. □ *The tailor put a new lining in my winter coat.* **2.** *tv.* to make or repair an item of clothing so that it fits a certain person. □ *The tailor tailored the jacket to fit me perfectly.*

**take** ['tek] **1.** *tv., irreg.* to get or obtain something by one's own action. (Pt: **took**; pp: **taken.**) □ *Bill took my coat instead of his own.* **2.** *tv., irreg.* to accept something that is offered. □ *The mayor took the man's hand and shook it with vigor.* **3.** *tv., irreg.* to capture something; to win something. □ *The football team took first place in the conference.* **4.** *tv., irreg.* to eat or swallow something, such as medicine. □ *I don't take many medicines.* **5.** *tv., irreg.* to use something on a regular basis; to require something as a habit. □ *Bill takes cream in his coffee.* **6.** *tv., irreg.* to transport someone or something somewhere. □ *A taxi took me from the museum to the bank.* **7.** *tv., irreg.* to use a form of public transportation. □ *We had to take a bus to the bank.* **8.** *tv., irreg.* to lead someone or something; to guide someone or something. □ *The guide took us on a hike in the forest.* **9.** *tv., irreg.* to record something; to make a picture with a camera. □ *A professional photographer took my picture for the newspaper.* □ *When I'm out, Bill always takes my telephone messages.* **10.** *tv., irreg.* to interpret something in a certain way. □ *Mary took my statement out of context, and now she is mad.* **11.** *tv., irreg.* to observe the measurement of something. □ *Bill took some measurements of the room so he could order carpet.* **12.** *tv., irreg.* to suffer something; to endure something; to accept something. □ *I couldn't take seeing the slaughter of the animals.* **13.** *tv., irreg.* to use up time; to consume time; to require that an amount of time be spent [doing something]. □ *That will take a lot of time.*

**take heed** ['tek 'hid] *phr.* to be careful; to take care and watch for danger. □ *Be careful when you walk on the ice. If you don't take heed, you will fall.*

**taken** ['tek ən] pp of take.

**takeoff** ['tek ɔf] *n.* [an airplane's] leaving the ground and flying. □ *During the takeoff, the passengers were seated.*

**tale** ['tel] **1.** *n.* a story. □ *Mary told Jane her unhappy tale.* **2.** *n.* a lie. □ *The girl's father warned her not to tell tales.*

**talent** ['tæl ənt] **1.** *n.* a special skill; a natural ability. □ *Mary has quite a talent for music.* **2.** *n.* people who have a special skill or a natural ability, especially singers or actors; people employed or seeking employment in the entertainment industry. (No plural form. Treated as singular.) □ *Good talent is hard to find unless you go through an agent.*

**talk** ['tɔk] **1.** *iv.* to communicate by speaking; to speak; to say words. □ *After I had jaw surgery, it was difficult for me to talk.* **2.** *iv.* to speak with someone; to have a conversation with someone. □ *Would you like to talk about your problems?* **3.** *n.* the production of words; speech. (No plural form.) □ *I hear lots of talk but see no action.* **4.** *n.* a conversation; a chat with someone. □ *Mary and I had a nice talk about politics.* **5.** *n.* a speech; a lecture. □ *John fell asleep during the long talk.* **6. talks** *n.* conversations held for the purpose of negotiating something. □ *The contract talks were successful, and the strike was ended.* **7.** *n.* gossip; rumors. (No plural form.) □ *Bob never listens to the office talk.*

**talk show** ['tɔk 'ʃo] **1.** *n.* a radio or television program devoted to conversation and opinion by different people. □ *Tom appeared on a talk show to discuss his new book.* **2. talk-show** *adj.* <the adj. use of ①.> □ *The talk-show host tried to keep the conversation orderly.*

**tall** ['tɔl] **1.** *adj.* great in height; of a greater height than average; not short. (Comp: *taller;* sup: *tallest.*) □ *Everyone in the Smith family is tall.* **2.** *adj.* extending a certain distance upward; reaching a certain distance above the ground.

T

(Comp: *taller;* sup: *tallest.*) □ *This tree is twenty feet tall.*

**tally** ['tæl i] **1.** *n.* a score; a mark used to keep track of the number of something being counted; the number of points or votes someone or something has received. □ *According to the tally, I'm ahead by 25 points.* **2. tally** something **(up)** *tv. + obj. (+ adv.)* to count the number of votes or points that someone or something has received. □ *When I tallied the points up, I realized David had won the match.* 🅃 *After the game was finished, I tallied up the score.* **3. tally (with** an amount**)** *iv. (+ prep. phr.)* [for an amount] to match another amount; [for two amounts] to be equal. □ *The accountant was glad that the two columns of figures tallied.*

**tame** ['tem] **1.** *adj.* not in a natural wild state; living with people; acting gentle rather than fierce. (Adv: *tamely.* Comp: *tamer;* sup: *tamest.*) □ *The monkeys born at the zoo are tame.* **2.** *adj.* not shocking; not wild; not exciting; dull. (Fig. on ①. Adv: *tamely.* Comp: *tamer;* sup: *tamest.*) □ *Some old movies that used to be very shocking now seem quite tame.*

**tan** ['tæn] **1.** *iv.* [especially of people with fair skin] to permit one's skin to darken by being outdoors in sunlight or by exposing oneself to artificial sunlight. □ *The teenagers tanned in the sun on the beach.* **2.** *tv.* to change the skin of an animal into leather by soaking it in a special chemical. □ *The hunter tanned the animal skin before selling it.* **3.** *n.* darkness of the skin from exposure to sunlight as in ①. □ *Mary always has a tan in the summertime.* **4.** *n.* a light brown color. □ *Tan is a light shade of brown.* **5.** *adj.* light brown in color. (Comp: *tanner;* sup: *tannest.*) □ *Mary rode the tan horse across the field.*

**tangent** ['tæn dʒənt] *n.* a line that touches a circle at only one point. □ *The rocket's new path was a tangent to its original orbit.*

**tangerine** [tæn dʒə 'rin] **1.** *n.* a small, orange citrus fruit; a kind of orange whose peel is easy to remove. □ *The fruit bowl is full of tangerines.* **2.** *adj.* <the adj. use of ①.> □ *I ate tangerine sherbet for dessert.*

**tangle** ['tæŋ gəl] **1.** *n.* a twisted clump of hair, string, chain, rope, limbs, etc. □ *The tangle in the necklace was hard to undo.* **2.** *n.* an argument; a disagreement. □ *A little tangle between Bob and Bill became a fight.* **3.** *iv.* [for strands] to become twisted together. □ *The strings tangled together as I pulled on them.* **4.** *tv.* to twist strands together; to snarl something. □ *The washing machine tangled my pantyhose.*

**tank** ['tæŋk] **1.** *n.* a container for storing air or liquid. (See also **fishtank**.) □ *The gas tank in the car leaked slowly.* **2.** *n.* a large vehicle, used by the military, that moves on heavy belts wrapped around a set of wheels. □ *The tank could travel over rough terrain.*

**tantrum** ['tæn trəm] *n.* a bad display of temper and emotion. (Short for **temper tantrum**.) □ *The baby threw a tantrum again today. She didn't want to eat her spinach.*

**tap** ['tæp] **1.** *n.* a slight pressure or a very light blow made by something. □ *A gentle tap on my shoulder caused me to turn to see who was there.* **2.** *n.* a device that controls the flow of a gas or a liquid from a pipe or a barrel; a faucet. □ *Please turn the tap all the way off.* **3.** *tv.* to touch someone or something gently a number of times, especially with the tip of one's finger. □ *Anne impatiently tapped the table with her middle finger.* **4.** *tv.* to cut something open so that liquid will flow out; to pierce something, such as a barrel, so that liquid will flow out. □ *I tapped the tree to get sap for syrup.*

T

**tape** ['tep] **1.** *n.* a paper or plastic strip with one side that is sticky, used to stick something to something else. (See also **adhesive tape**. Plural only when referring to different kinds, types, instances, or varieties.) □ *The poster was stuck to the wall with tape.* Ⓒ *Tapes of various kinds are available at the hardware store.* **2.** *n.* a magnetic strip of plastic onto which sound or images can be recorded. (No plural form.) □ *We did not have enough tape to record the entire concert.* **3.** *n.* a reel or cassette of ②; something recorded on a reel or cassette of ②. □ *We watched a tape of Anne's birthday party.* **4.** *tv.* to stick something to something else with ①; to seal something with ①. □ *Bill taped the note to the refrigerator.* **5.** *tv.* to fix something that is torn by placing ① over the tear. □ *Jimmy taped his ripped picture back together.* **6.** *tv.* to record sound onto ②; to record images onto ②. □ *Mary taped her favorite radio program on a new cassette.* **7.** *iv.* to make a sound or video recording; to record. □ *Jane will start singing once you begin taping.*

**tar** ['tɑr] **1.** *n.* a black substance similar to very thick oil, used to preserve or waterproof objects. (No plural form.) □ *The building's roof was covered with tar.* **2.** *tv.* to cover something with ①; to preserve or waterproof something with ①. □ *The worker tarred the holes in the roof to prevent leakage.*

**tardy** ['tɑr di] *adj.* late; not prompt; not on time. (Adv: *tardily.* Comp: *tardier;* sup: *tardiest.*) □ *My boss lectured on the consequences of being tardy.*

**target** ['tɑr gət] **1.** *n.* someone or something that someone tries to hit or shoot when using a weapon. □ *The shooting range has targets set up for practice.* **2.** *n.* someone who is ridiculed, blamed, or made fun of. (Fig. on ①.) □ *Bill was the target of blame for causing the accident.* **3.** *n.* a goal that one would like to reach; an aim. (Fig. on ①.) □ *Jane's target is to finish the project by Friday.* **4.** *tv.* to establish something as a goal. □ *The charity targeted a million dollars as its goal.* **5.** *tv.* to focus on someone, something, or some place; to give something, someone, or some place the greatest amount of thought or effort. □ *The principal targeted five problems that needed to be solved.*

**tariff** ['tɛr ɪf] **1.** *n.* a tax that a government charges on products entering or leaving a country. □ *The neighboring countries have tariffs on each other's goods.* **2.** *n.* the cost of a service, such as the service provided by a utility. □ *The residents protested the increased tariff on long-distance calls.*

**task** ['tæsk] *n.* a duty; an errand; a responsibility; a chore; an item of work that someone must do, especially a difficult one. □ *Mother gave Jimmy the task of vacuuming the house.*

**task force** ['tæsk fors] *n.* a group of people who are given a certain task, such as a military group that has a certain mission. □ *The report on poverty was submitted by the government task force.*

**taste** ['test] **1.** *n.* the ability to sense or experience sweetness, saltiness, bitterness, or sourness with one's tongue. (No plural form.) □ *Mary's allergies affect her sense of taste.* **2.** *n.* a particular flavor as experienced through ①. □ *The boy tried to describe the taste of an orange but could not.* **3.** *n.* a small sample of food or drink. □ *Mary asked for a taste of Bill's hamburger.* **4.** *n.* the quality of one's choice or selection in beauty, fashion, or art; the ability to judge what is suitable or fitting. (Plural only when referring to different kinds, types, instances, or varieties.) □ *My grandmother has very good taste in music. She loves opera.* Ⓒ *Tastes differ from person to person.* **5.** *tv.* to sense or experience flavor with one's tongue. □ *John tasted the salt on the potato chips.*

T

**6.** *tv.* to put something in one's mouth or on one's tongue so that one can know its flavor; to eat a very small amount of something so one can know its flavor. □ *I tasted a small piece of pie before taking a whole slice.* **7.** *tv.* to experience something for a short while. □ *My family tasted the good life on an expensive vacation.* **8.** *iv.* [for a food] to have a particular flavor. □ *A tangerine tastes a little like an orange.*

**tasteless** ['test ləs] **1.** *adj.* having no **taste** ②; having no flavor; bland. (Adv: *tastelessly.*) □ *Mary added lots of salt and pepper to the tasteless soup.* **2.** *adj.* showing poor **taste** ④; offensive; rude. (Adv: *tastelessly.*) □ *Mary regretted the tasteless comment the moment she said it.*

**tasty** ['tes ti] *adj.* full of flavor; delicious. (Adv: *tastily.* Comp: *tastier;* sup: *tastiest.*) □ *Anne's oatmeal cookies are always tasty.*

**taught** ['tɔt] pt/pp of **teach**.

**taunt** ['tɔnt] **1.** *tv.* to tease someone; to make fun of someone; to ridicule someone; to provoke someone by saying something unkind. □ *Mary's brother taunted her until she hit him.* **2.** *n.* an unkind remark that is made to tease or ridicule someone. □ *I was furious with John for directing taunts at me.*

**taut** ['tɔt] *adj.* pulled tight; having no slack; stretched. (Adv: *tautly.* Comp: *tauter;* sup: *tautest.*) □ *We were afraid that the taut rope would break.*

T

**tax** ['tæks] **1.** *n.* the money charged by a government to pay for the cost of the government and its services. □ *Taxes you pay provide police and fire protection.* **2.** *tv.* to make someone pay ①. □ *The government taxes its citizens' incomes.* **3.** *tv.* to charge ① on something; to burden something with ①. □ *The state taxes all money won at the racetrack.* **4.** *tv.* to burden someone or something; to place a strain on someone or something. (Fig. on ③.) □ *The screaming children taxed the teacher's patience.*

**tax bracket** ['tæks bræk ət] *n.* one of a series of federal income-tax rates and the levels of income associated with that rate. □ *The upper tax bracket gets taxed more than the lower ones.*

**taxi** ['tæk si] **1.** *n.* a **cab**, a **taxicab**. (Short for **taxicab**.) □ *You have to walk south a block to catch a taxi. They won't stop here.* **2.** *iv.* [for an airplane] to move on the ground. □ *After an hour's wait on the runway, the plane began to taxi.*

**taxicab** ['tæk si kæb] *n.* a car that, along with its driver, can be hired for short trips. (Can be shortened to **taxi** or **cab**.) □ *The taxicab pulled over to the curb to pick up the passengers.*

**tax return** ['tæks rɪ tɚn] *n.* a form, filled out by someone required to pay taxes, showing the amount of tax that is owed. □ *Mary filed her tax return on time this year.*

**tea** ['ti] **1.** *n.* the leaves of a bush grown in Asia which are dried and soaked in boiling water to make a refreshing drink. (Plural only when referring to different kinds, types, instances, or varieties.) □ *A local factory dries and processes tea.* Ⓒ *Teas from southeast Asia are favored by most countries.* **2.** *n.* a drink made from ①. (No plural form.) □ *Mary served tea and cookies to her guests.* **3.** *n.* a drink, like ②, made by soaking dried herbs or plants in boiling water. (No plural form.) □ *I drank some mint tea after dinner.*

**teach** ['titʃ] **1.** *tv., irreg.* to provide instruction in a particular subject. (Pt/pp: **taught**.) □ *The Smiths taught swimming to their children.* **2.** *tv., irreg.* to instruct someone in how to do something. □ *The Smiths taught their children how to swim.* **3.** *iv., irreg.* to work as a teacher. □ *It takes a lot of patience to teach.*

**teacher** ['titʃ ɚ] *n.* someone who teaches people something; someone who instructs people in some subject. □ *Mary asked her teacher for extra help.*

**team** ['tim] **1.** *n.* a group of players who form one side in a game or sport. □ *The coach spoke to the team in the locker room before the game.* **2.** *n.* a group of people who work together. □ *The construction team built the house in record time.* **3.** *n.* two or more animals that work together to pull a vehicle or farming equipment. □ *A team of mules pulled the miner's supplies.*

**teammate** ['tim met] *n.* a member of a team that one is a part of; another person on one's team. □ *The teammates supported each other in success and failure.*

**teamwork** ['tim wɚk] *n.* the action of working together as a team. (No plural form.) □ *Our side won the football game due to excellent teamwork.*

**teapot** ['ti pɑt] *n.* a container with a handle and a spout, used to hold and pour tea. □ *Mary poured each of us some tea from her new teapot.*

**tear 1.** ['tɪr] *n.* a drop of liquid that falls from one's eye when one cries. □ *Mary wiped the tears from her eyes during the sad movie.* **2.** ['tɛr] *n.* a rip; a place in a piece of cloth or paper that is ripped. □ *Mary taped the tear in the page.* **3.** ['tɛr] *tv., irreg.* to make a hole or a rip in something, especially by pulling it; to pull something into pieces. (Pt: **tore**; pp: **torn**.) □ *Mary took her skirt to the tailor because she had torn it.* **4.** ['tɛr] *iv., irreg.* to be ripped apart. □ *The paper tore when I grabbed it from David.* **5.** ['tɛr] *iv., irreg.* to move somewhere very quickly. □ *The sports car tore down the street and through the intersection.* **6.** ['tɪr] *iv.* to cry; to begin to cry; to have tears form in one's eyes. (Pt/pp: *teared* ['tird].) □ *The toddler's eyes began to tear, and he let out a wail.*

**teardrop** ['tɪr drɑp] *n.* one tear; one drop of liquid that falls from one's eye. □ *Mother brushed Jimmy's teardrops away.*

**tease** ['tiz] **1.** *tv.* to taunt someone; to make fun of someone. □ *Jane is always teasing Bill about his poor grades.* **2.** *tv.* to flirt with someone, especially with sexual hints. □ *Sally teased John to get him interested, but then refused to go out with him.* **3.** *tv.* to separate strands of hair; to comb strands of hair apart. □ *Mary teased her hair before going to the party.* **4.** *iv.* to taunt [someone or something]; to annoy on purpose. □ *Bill didn't stop teasing until Mary cried.* **5.** *n.* someone who **teases** someone else as in ②. □ *My dance partner was a tease, so I left the party alone.*

**technician** [tɛk 'nɪ ʃən] *n.* someone who works in the field of industrial or mechanical sciences; someone who works in a laboratory, performing tests. □ *The technicians tested the elevator after it was installed.*

**technique** [tɛk 'nik] **1.** *n.* a special method of doing something. □ *John explained his technique for frying shrimp.* **2.** *n.* the skill involved in creating or performing art; the way that art is performed, displayed, or exhibited—showing the artist's skill. (No plural form.) □ *The young violinist practiced her technique for hours every day.*

**technology** [tɛk 'nɑl ə dʒi] *n.* the science and study of mechanical and industrial sciences. (Plural only when referring to different kinds, types, instances, or varieties.) □ *John wants to attend a college that teaches technology.* Ⓒ *The spaceship was built using very advanced technologies.*

**teen** ['tin] **1.** *n.* a teenager. □ *The teens gathered at the park after school.* **2. teens** *n.* the numbers 13–19 or 10–19. (When referring to age, it refers to the period of someone's life from the age of 13 through the age of 19.) □ *Even*

T

*though Anne was in her teens, she worked 40 hours a week.* **3.** *adj.* <the adj. use of ①.> ☐ *Mary bought the teen magazine for her daughter.*

**teenage** ['tin edʒ] *adj.* of, for, or about teenagers; of the ages from 13 through 19. ☐ *These advertisements are aimed at teenage shoppers.*

**teenager** ['tin edʒ ɚ] *n.* someone whose age is between 13 and 19. ☐ *Those teenagers attend the local high school.*

**teeth** ['tiθ] pl of **tooth**.

**telegram** ['tɛl ə græm] *n.* a message sent by telegraph. ☐ *Grandma sent us a telegram announcing her arrival time.*

**telegraph** ['tɛl ə græf] **1.** *n.* a machine that sends messages in electrical code over electrical wires. ☐ *The widespread use of telephones replaced the telegraph.* **2.** *tv.* to send a message by using ①. ☐ *I telegraphed a message to my brother, inviting him to the wedding.* **3.** *tv.* to send [a message] to someone by ①. ☐ *We telegraphed all the winners, telling them of their good fortune.*

**telephone** ['tɛl ə fon] **1.** *n.* a device that transmits sound by converting it into electrical signals; a **phone**. ☐ *The telephone rang just as we were leaving the house.* **2.** *tv.* to call someone by using ①. ☐ *Please telephone me before you come over.* **3.** *iv.* to make a call with ①. ☐ *Someone always telephones when I'm taking a shower.*

**telephone call** ['tɛl ə fon 'kɔl] *n.* a message or a conversation using the telephone; an instance of someone contacting someone by telephone. (Can be shortened to **call**.) ☐ *Is there somewhere here where I can make a telephone call?*

**telescope** ['tɛl ə skop] **1.** *n.* a device that makes distant objects, especially objects that are in the sky, look larger so that one can see them better. ☐ *Through the telescope, I could see the mountains on the moon.* **2.** *iv.* to become shorter or longer by having one part slide over another as with ①. ☐ *The three-foot walking cane telescoped into a foot-long rod.* **3.** *tv.* to make something shorter or longer by sliding one part of it over another. ☐ *I telescoped my fishing rod so it would fit in my trunk.*

**television** ['tel ə vɪʒ ən] **1.** *n.* the transmission of an electronic signal containing sounds and images. (No plural form. Can be shortened to **TV**.) ☐ *Television is watched daily throughout much of the world.* **2.** *n.* the business of producing ① or the programs that are transmitted on ①. (No plural form. Can be shortened to **TV**.) ☐ *I spent three years as a radio announcer before I got into television.* **3.** *n.* an electronic device that converts electronic signals into sounds and images. (Short for **television set**.) ☐ *Please turn off the television and go to bed!* **4.** *adj.* <the adjective use of ① and ②.> ☐ *Will the conference be covered by a television broadcast or by radio?*

**television set** ['θel ə vɪʒ ən 'sɛt] *n.* an electronic device that turns a television signal into images and sound. (Can be shortened to **television, TV**.) ☐ *Television sets have gotten cheaper every year over the last decade.*

**tell** ['tɛl] **1.** *tv., irreg.* to express something in words. (Pt/pp: **told**.) ☐ *John told the truth.* **2.** *tv., irreg.* to inform someone [of something]. ☐ *No one told me. I figured it out myself.* **3.** *tv., irreg.* to signal information [to someone]. ☐ *My watch tells the date and the time.* **4.** *tv., irreg.* to reveal a secret. ☐ *Who told my secret?* **5.** *iv., irreg.* to reveal [a secret]. ☐ *After you promised to keep the secret, I can't believe that you told!* **6.** *iv., irreg.* to try to get someone in trouble by saying to someone in authority what that person did. ☐ *I'm telling on you!*

**teller** ['tɛl ɚ] *n.* someone who works at a bank, receiving and giving out money.

☐ *The robber asked the teller for all the money in her drawer.*

**temper** ['tɛm pɚ] **1.** *n.* mood; the condition of one's mind, especially in regard to anger. (No plural form.) ☐ *One never knows what kind of temper Max is in.* **2.** *n.* an angry mood; the potential of being angry. (No plural form.) ☐ *In a fit of temper, Jane threw the vase at the wall.* **3.** *tv.* to soften something; to lessen the force or impact of something; to make something more moderate. ☐ *Anne tempered her harsh words with a kind smile.*

**temperature** ['tɛm pɚ ə tʃɚ] **1.** *n.* the degree of how cold or hot something is. ☐ *What is the temperature outside?* **2.** *n.* the degree of the heat of one's blood, especially when it is above average; a fever. ☐ *The sick child had a high temperature.*

**temper tantrum** ['tɛm pɚ 'tæn trəm] *n.* a burst of anger; a display of temper like that of a child. (Can be shortened to tantrum.) ☐ *Jimmy had a temper tantrum because he was tired.*

**tempest** ['tɛmp əst] *n.* a violent storm. ☐ *A late summer tempest racked the Florida coast.*

**temple** ['tɛm pəl] **1.** *n.* a building used for worship and ceremonies. ☐ *We saw the paintings on the walls of the ancient temple.* **2.** *n.* a Jewish house of worship. ☐ *We entered the temple early and took seats near the front.* **3.** *n.* the flat part on the side of the head between the eye and the ear and above the cheekbone. ☐ *This cap is too tight on me. It hurts my temples.*

**temporary** ['tɛm pə rɛr i] *adj.* for a limited time; not permanent. (Adv: *temporarily* [tɛm pə 'rɛr ə li].) ☐ *The temporary worker was soon replaced by a permanent employee.*

**tempt** ['tɛmpt] *tv.* to arouse someone's desire; to make someone want something. ☐ *The chocolate cake tempted me.*

**temptation** [tɛmp 'te ʃən] **1.** *n.* desire; an instance of being tempted. (No plural form.) ☐ *Bill had to struggle against temptation when the salesclerk gave him too much money in change.* **2.** *n.* someone or something that tempts a person. ☐ *The candy store offers too many temptations, so I don't go there.*

**tempted** ['tɛmp tɪd] **tempted (to** do something**)** *adj.* *(+ inf.)* wanting to do something, especially something that one should not do. ☐ *I'm really tempted to go to the beach with you, but I ought to work today.*

**ten** ['tɛn] **1.** 10. Go to four for senses and examples. **2.** *n.* a $10 bill. ☐ *Bill's wallet was full of tens when he left home.*

**tend** ['tɛnd] **1.** *tv.* to take care of something. ☐ *Jane loves to tend her garden.* **2. tend to** someone or something *iv. + prep. phr.* to mind someone or something; to take care of someone or something. ☐ *Mary must tend to her sick mother.* **3. tend to** do something *iv. + inf.* to be likely to do something; to be inclined to do something. ☐ *I tend to sleep late on Sundays.*

**tendency** ['tɛn dən si] *n.* the likelihood that someone or something will do something naturally. ☐ *John told me about his tendency to eat when he's depressed.*

**tender** ['tɛn dɚ] **1.** *adj.* soft; not tough; easy to chew. (Adv: *tenderly.*) ☐ *The tender roast beef was easy to slice.* **2.** *adj.* sore; sore when touched; painful. (Adv: *tenderly.*) ☐ *Mary cried when the doctor touched the tender spot on her stomach.* **3.** *adj.* kind; gentle; showing love or affection. (Adv: *tenderly.*) ☐ *The young lovers were tender towards each other.* **4.** *tv.* to offer something formally or legally, such as to offer money in payment of a debt. ☐ *I tendered my*

T

*resignation in writing to the company president.*

**tennis** ['tɛn ɪs] *n.* a sport played by two people or two pairs of people who use rackets to hit a small ball from one side of the playing area, over a net, to the other side of the playing area. (No plural form.) ☐ *Bill and Sue play tennis every Saturday.*

**tense** ['tɛns] **1.** *adj.* taut; not loose; not relaxed. (Adv: *tensely.* Comp: *tenser;* sup: *tensest.*) ☐ *The strings on the violin became tense as I tuned it.* **2.** *adj.* nervous; not relaxed. (Adv: *tensely.* Comp: *tenser;* sup: *tensest.*) ☐ *The tense man paced up and down the halls.* **3.** *tv.* to tighten something, such as a muscle; to stiffen something; to make something taut. ☐ *Bob tensed his jaw muscles and parachuted from the plane.* **4.** *n.* a quality of a verb that indicates the time that the action or state it expresses takes place. ☐ *This sentence is written in the present tense.* ☐ *In English, verbs in the past tense often end in* -ed.

**tension** ['tɛn ʃən] **1.** *n.* the degree of tightness of something that is stretched. (Plural only when referring to different kinds, types, instances, or varieties.) ☐ *Because there was too much tension on the cable, it broke.* Ⓒ *Special instruments measured the different tensions on the ship's computer-controlled lines.* **2.** *n.* an anxious or nervous feeling; hidden anxiety and anger. ☐ *The extra work created a lot of tension at the office.*

T

**tent** ['tɛnt] *n.* a temporary shelter made of fabric supported by poles and ropes. ☐ *Bill purchased a waterproof tent for his camping trip.*

**tenth** ['tɛntθ] 10th. Go to **fourth** for senses and examples.

**term** ['tɚm] **1.** *n.* the length of time that something lasts; a particular period of time. ☐ *The chairman served a two-year term.* **2.** *n.* a division of a school year; a quarter or semester. ☐ *Students take new classes each term.* **3.** *n.* an expression used in a particular field; a word. ☐ *I looked up the scientific term in the dictionary.* **4. terms** *n.* requirements; details; provisions. ☐ *The editor objected to the terms of her employment.* **5. terms** *n.* charges; fees and requirements. ☐ *The lawyer's terms were too high, so I looked for another lawyer.*

**terminal** ['tɚ mə nəl] **1.** *adj.* happening at the end of something; at the end; last. (Adv: *terminally.*) ☐ *In the terminal session of the conference, the president concluded her remarks.* **2.** *adj.* resulting in death; causing death; not able to be cured. (Adv: *terminally.*) ☐ *Cancer is not always terminal.* **3.** *n.* a building that passengers enter and leave from, especially at an airport, bus station, or train station. ☐ *The taxi took the passenger directly to the terminal.* **4.** *n.* something that makes an electrical connection; the place where current enters or leaves a battery or a circuit. ☐ *John cleaned his car battery's terminals with a rag.* **5.** *n.* a computer device consisting of a keyboard and a screen that displays the messages sent to and from a computer. ☐ *I waited in the computer lab for the next available terminal.*

**termite** ['tɚ mɑɪt] *n.* an insect, similar to an ant, that eats a substance found in wood, causing great damage to wooden objects and structures. ☐ *The fallen tree was infested with termites.*

**terrace** ['tɛr əs] **1.** *n.* a flat area connected to or next to the side of a house or apartment; a balcony or patio. ☐ *The terrace was surrounded by a tiny wall.* **2.** *n.* a flat area of land that has been cut into the side of a hill or mountain. ☐ *The state workers cut a wide terrace into the hill for the new highway.*

**terrain** [tə 'ren] *n.* the physical features of an area of land. ☐ *This terrain does not allow easy hiking.*

**terrible** ['tɛr ə bəl] *adj.* awful; horrible; extremely bad. (Adv: *terribly.*) □ *Mary had a terrible headache and spent the day in bed.*

**terribly** ['tɛr ə bli] **1.** *adv.* badly; horribly; awfully. □ *This student writes terribly, so he is taking extra classes to learn to write better.* **2.** *adv.* very; extremely. □ *The last few minutes of the game were terribly exciting, and everyone shouted when our team won.*

**terrier** ['tɛr i ɚ] *n.* one of a group of breeds of small dogs, originally bred to be used in hunting. □ *The terrier followed the trail of the fox.*

**terrific** [tə 'rɪf ɪk] **1.** *adj.* great; wonderful; super; excellent. (Adv: *terrifically* [...ɪk li].) □ *Bill is a terrific manager.* **2.** *adj.* extreme[ly bad]. (Adv: *terrifically* [...ɪk li].) □ *Jane suffered a terrific loss in the stock market.*

**terrify** ['tɛr ə fɑɪ] *tv.* to scare someone or something greatly. □ *Insects terrify Mary, so she never gardens.*

**territory** ['tɛr ə tor i] **1.** *n.* land; area. (No plural form.) □ *How much territory is included in the national park?* **2.** *n.* an area of land controlled by a specific government, especially a government that is far away. □ *The island used to be a territory of that country, but now it is independent.* **3.** *n.* an area of land that is dominated by an animal or group of animals. □ *The deer marked its territory with its scent.*

**terror** ['tɛr ɚ] **1.** *n.* extreme fear. (Plural only when referring to different kinds, types, instances, or varieties.) □ *Jane awoke from her nightmare with a feeling of terror.* Ⓒ *You can't imagine the terrors I experience on that camping trip into bear country.* **2.** *n.* someone or something that causes extreme fear. □ *The new vaccine brought the terror of the disease under control.*

**terrorism** ['tɛr ɚ ɪz əm] *n.* the use of violence and terror to achieve political goals. (No plural form.) □ *The political group used terrorism to achieve its goals.*

**terrorist** ['tɛr ɚ ɪst] *n.* someone who practices terrorism. □ *The police arrested three terrorists involved in the attack.*

**test** ['tɛst] **1.** *n.* a series of questions or activities that determine someone's knowledge or skill; a school examination. □ *The test had one very long question and thirty short questions.* **2.** *n.* an experiment; an action that is done to see how something works. □ *Climbing the mountain was a test of courage for Bill.* **3.** *tv.* to determine someone's knowledge or skill by evaluating answers to questions or performance of activities. □ *Many colleges test students before accepting them.* **4.** *tv.* to subject something to ② in order to measure its condition or see how it works. □ *You should test the milk to see how hot it is before you give it to the baby.*

**testimony** ['tɛs tə mo ni] *n.* the statements of a witness, especially in a court of law. (Not usually plural. Treated as singular.) □ *The court recorder recorded everyone's testimony.*

**text** ['tɛkst] **1.** *n.* the main words in a book or article, not the pictures, tables, graphs, indexes, etc. (No plural form.) □ *The author improved the text with graphs and charts.* **2.** *n.* the words of a speech in written form. □ *The lecturer read from a prepared text.* **3.** *n.* a book used by students in school or college. (Short for **textbook**.) □ *How may texts are there for this course?*

**textbook** ['tɛkst bʊk] **1.** *n.* a book, designed for student use, that is used as a standard source of information about a specific subject. (Can be shortened to **text**.) □ *Mary studied her chemistry textbook the night before the test.* **2.** *adj.* [of possible examples] the best and most typical. □ *The lawyer's first case was a textbook example of mail fraud.*

**texture** ['tɛks tʃɚ] **1.** *n.* the evenness or smoothness—or unevenness or roughness—of something. □ *My oatmeal has a lumpy texture.* **2.** *n.* the appearance of having ①, such as with a design on paper or in art. □ *This thick paper has a texture that makes the printing on it hard to read.*

**than** ['ðæn] *conj.* as compared with someone or something; in comparison with someone or something. (Used before the second item of a comparison.) □ *Bill likes pizza more than chocolate.*

**thank** ['θæŋk] **1.** *tv.* to show someone gratitude by saying "thank you"; to express gratitude for something that has been given or done. □ *John thanked the police officer for saving his life.* **2. thanks** *interj.* <a polite expression that is used by the receiver of an action or gift, along with "yes" or "no" in response to a question, or to show gratitude.> (Less formal than **Thank you** as in ③.) □ *"Would you like a sandwich?" "Yes, thanks. I'm hungry."* □ *Thanks for helping me.* **3. Thank you.** *interj.* <a polite expression that is used by the receiver of an action or gift, along with "yes" or "no" in response to a question, or to show gratitude.> □ *"Would you like some coffee?" "Yes, thank you."* **4. thanks** *n.* gratitude. (Treated as plural, but not countable.) □ *We gave our thanks to God for the ample meal.* **5. thank-you** *n.* an expression of ④. □ *We sent out ten gifts, but have received only nine thank-yous.* **6. thank-you** *adj.* <the adj. use of ⑤.> □ *A bouquet of flowers makes a good thank-you gift.*

**thankful** ['θæŋk fʊl] *adj.* grateful; showing thanks; expressing thanks. (Adv: *thankfully.*) □ *The thankful student appreciated the scholarship.*

**Thanksgiving** [θæŋks 'gɪv ɪŋ] *n.* a holiday celebrated in North America as an expression of thanks. □ *In Canada, Thanksgiving is celebrated on the second Monday of October.* □ *My family had dinner at my grandmother's house on Thanksgiving, which is on the fourth Thursday in November in the U.S.*

**that** ['ðæt] **1.** *adj.* <a form referring to someone or something already mentioned or someone or something of which both the speaker and hearer are aware.> (Prenominal only. With plural nouns, use **those**.) □ *The dog dug up that plant you planted last week.* **2.** *adj.* <a form referring to someone or something further away or the furthest away from the speaker.> (Used in contrast with **this**. Prenominal only. With plural nouns, use **those**.) □ *This restaurant is too crowded. Let's go to that café over there.* **3.** *pron.* <a form standing for someone or something already referred to or someone or something of which both the speaker and hearer are aware.> (Pl: **those**.) □ *As the phone rang, John yelled, "Can someone get that?"* **4.** *pron.* <a form standing for someone or something that is further away or the furthest away from the speaker.> (Used in contrast with **this**. Pl: **those**.) □ *This is too small, but that is too big. Where can I find the right size?* **5.** *pron.* which. (Used to connect sentences, clauses, and phrases with noun phrases. Only used with *restrictive clauses.* See **which** for an explanation. Sometimes means "when" or "where" if it follows a noun phrase referring to a time or place.) □ *This is the toy that I bought for Jimmy.* **6.** *pron.* who; whom. (Used to connect sentences, phrases, or clauses with noun phrases. Only where **who** or **whom** would be appropriate. **Who** or **whom**, as appropriate, is preferred by many people.) □ *I apologized to the woman that I yelled at.* **7.** *pron.* <a form used to connect a verb with a sentence that is

the object of the verb.> (Only certain verbs use **that** ⑦ in this way. This **that** can be omitted.) □ *I promise that I will be there tomorrow.* **8.** *adv.* so; to such a degree. □ *You can stop laughing now. John's joke wasn't that funny.*

**that's** ['ðæts] **1.** *cont.* "that is." □ *Where is John? That's what I'd like to know.* **2.** *cont.* "that has," where **has** is an auxiliary. □ *That's happened twice this week!*

**thaw** ['θɔ] **1.** *iv.* [for ice] to melt; [for something frozen] to no longer be frozen; [for the weather] to be warm enough to melt ice or snow. □ *Last week it was so warm that the frozen pond thawed.* **2.** *iv.* to become less formal; to relax. (Fig. on ①.) □ *The relations between the countries thawed after the war.* **3.** *tv.* to melt something; to cause something to no longer be frozen. □ *We thawed the turkey by leaving it on the counter overnight.* **4.** *n.* a condition when the weather has become warm enough to melt ice or snow. □ *The ice on the frozen pond melted during the thaw.*

**the** [ðə, ði] **1.** *article* a certain one; certain ones. (The definite article. Used before nouns or noun phrases to show that a definite thing, person, or group of things or people is being referred to. Pronounced ['ði] when emphasized or before vowels.) □ *I bought the candle with the long wick.* **2.** *article* <a form showing a general category.> (Used before a noun that is used in a general sense.) □ *The moose lives for about 12 years.* **3.** *article* <a form indicating the special or specific one, the one that is being talked about.> (Used before some names and titles.) □ *The mountain climber got lost in the Himalayas.* **4.** *adv.* to a certain degree, especially in comparison with something else. □ *John invested his money foolishly, and now he's much the poorer for it.*

**theater** AND **theatre** ['θi ə tɚ] **1.** *n.* a building where movies are shown or where plays are performed. (The spelling *theatre* is used especially for buildings where plays are performed, and much less often for buildings where movies are shown.) □ *I will meet you at the theater about an hour before the play starts.* **2.** *n.* the business of producing plays for the stage; the study of drama, performance, and acting. (No plural form.) □ *Most of the people in theatre don't earn much money.*

**theft** ['θɛft] *n.* stealing; taking someone else's property without permission. (Plural only when referring to different kinds, types, instances, or varieties.) □ *Theft is increasing in the major cities.* Ⓒ *The recent thefts of lawn furniture in the neighborhood made us very uneasy.*

**their** ['ðɛɚ] **1.** *pron.* <the possessive form of **they**>; belonging to people, animals, or things that have already been mentioned. (Used as a modifier before a noun.) □ *Did you show the guests to their seats?* **2.** *pron.* <① standing for **his** ③>; belonging to a person who has already been mentioned. (Used to refer to a preceding noun or pronoun, the sexual reference of which is not important, indeterminate, undetermined, or irrelevant. Adopted as a replacement for **his** ③ by those who see **his** ③ as referring to males only. Objected to by some as an unnecessary violation of grammatical number when used for singular nouns.) □ *Each student took off their jacket.* **3. theirs** *pron.* <the possessive form of **they**>; belonging to people, animals, or things that have already been mentioned. (Do not use an apostrophe when writing **theirs**. Used in place of a noun.) □ *This cookie is mine. Theirs are on the counter.*

**them** ['ðɛm] **1.** *pron.* <the objective form of **they**.> (Used to refer to people, animals, and things, used after prepositions, and used as the object of verbs.)

☐ *I washed the dishes, and then I dried them.* **2.** *pron.* <a form standing for **him** ②, referring to a person already mentioned.> (Used to refer to a noun or pronoun, the sexual reference of which is not important, indeterminate, undetermined, or irrelevant. Adopted as a replacement for **him** ② by those who see **him** ② as referring to males only. Objected to by some as an unnecessary violation of grammatical number when used for singular nouns.) ☐ *If you do not know a person's name, you should ask them what it is.*

**theme** ['θim] **1.** *n.* a subject of a speech or a text; a topic. ☐ *The debate centered on the theme of eating less fat.* **2.** *n.* a melody that is used to identify a certain program, movie, character or emotion. ☐ *The tragic victim's theme was written in a minor key.* **3.** *n.* the main melody of a piece of music. ☐ *The theme was heard again and again throughout the opera.* **4.** *n.* a visual or decorative concept that connects several parts of something. ☐ *The restaurant was decorated around a southwestern theme.* **5.** *adj.* of or about a piece of music that is readily identified with someone or something. ☐ *Every time the murderer's theme music was played in the movie, we knew someone was going to die.*

**themselves** [ðɛm 'sɛlvz] **1.** *pron.* <the reflexive form of **they**, used after a verb or a preposition when the subject of the sentence refers to the same people, animals, or things that the pronoun refers to.> ☐ *My brothers shave themselves every morning.* **2.** *pron.* <the reflexive form of **they** used after **they** or a plural noun phrase as an intensifier.> ☐ *They themselves cleaned up the park.* **3. by themselves** *phr.* with help from no one else. ☐ *Mike and Max cannot lift the piano by themselves.* **4. by themselves** *phr.* with no one else present; alone. ☐ *They enjoy spending the evening at home by themselves.*

T

**then** ['ðɛn] **1.** *adv.* at that time. ☐ *In 1980, Anne, then only 12, learned to play the piano.* **2.** *adv.* next; following; after that. ☐ *Mary first told me the news, and then she told John.* **3.** *adv.* therefore; in that case; so. ☐ *If you like to cook, then you should make dinner.*

**theology** [θi 'ɑl ə dʒi] *n.* the study and science of religion. (Plural only when referring to different kinds, types, instances, or varieties.) ☐ *The expert in theology wrote a book comparing the world's major religions.* Ⓒ *Some religions recognize a variety of valid theologies.*

**theory** ['θɪr i] *n.* knowledge of a science or an art, as opposed to the actual practice of a science or an art; the principles on which a science or an art are based. (Plural only when referring to different kinds, types, instances, or varieties.) ☐ *Your skills are good, but your knowledge of theory is weak.* Ⓒ *The detective had a few theories about who stole my lawn furniture.*

**there** ['ðɛɚ] **1.** *adv.* to or toward that place; at that place; in that place; in that respect; at that point in time; at that point during a process. (Compare this with **they're** and **their**.) ☐ *I knew what the third step of the experiment was, but when I got there, I forgot it.* **2.** *adv.* <a form that begins a sentence or clause and is followed by a verb, which is then followed by the subject of the sentence.> (The verb is usually **be**—for example, *there is, there are*—but it can also be *go, come, stand, rest,* or another verb. In questions, the verb is placed before *there.*) ☐ *There was a lot of snow on the ground after the storm.* **3.** *pron.* a particular place or location. ☐ *Don't open that cabinet. I have a surprise for you in there.*

**there's** ['ðɛɚz] **1.** *cont.* "there has," where **has** is an auxiliary. ☐ *There's got to be a better explanation.* **2.** *cont.* "there is." □ *There's a package for you at the post office.*

**thermometer** [θɚ 'mɑm ə tɚ] *n.* a device that measures the temperature of someone or something. □ *The thermometer indicated that it was too warm in the house.*

**these** ['ðiz] pl of this.

**they** ['ðe] **1.** *pron.* <the third-person plural subject pronoun; the plural of **he, she,** or **it.**> □ *It is they who need help most that should receive it first.* **2.** *pron.* <the third-person plural subject pronoun used as a singular.> (Used to refer to a preceding noun or pronoun, the sexual reference of which is not important, indeterminate, undetermined, or irrelevant. Adopted as a replacement for **he** ② by those who see **he** ② as referring to males only. Objected to by some as an unnecessary violation of grammatical number when used for singular nouns.) □ *Each one was told that they should be here at noon.* **3.** *pron.* <a form used to mean people in general; a group of people.> □ *They call this a city, but to me it's just a small town.*

**they'd** ['ðed] **1.** *cont.* "they would." □ *If they'd come on time, they could leave on time.* **2.** *cont.* "they had," where **had** is an auxiliary. □ *They'd better arrive soon if they're going to be on time.*

**they'll** ['ðel] *cont.* "they will." □ *If John and Mary don't finish soon, they'll be in trouble.*

**they're** ['ðɛɚ] *cont.* "they are." (Compare this with **there, their.**) □ *They're trying to do the best they can.*

**they've** ['ðev] *cont.* "they have," where **have** is an auxiliary. □ *They've gone to the store, but they'll be back soon.*

**thick** ['θɪk] **1.** *adj.* not thin; having a greater than average distance between the two opposite sides; having a lot of space between the two opposite sides. (Adv: *thickly.* Comp: *thicker;* sup: *thickest.*) □ *Don't walk onto the ice unless you're sure that it's thick.* **2.** *adj.* measuring a certain distance between two opposite sides; having a certain depth or width. (Comp: *thicker.* No superlative.) □ *The strip of bacon was an eighth of an inch thick.* **3.** *adj.* dense; with very little space between things. (Adv: *thickly.* Comp: *thicker;* sup: *thickest.*) □ *It was difficult to move through the thick shrubbery.* **4.** *adj.* not pouring easily, like glue or molasses; being liquid but not flowing easily. (Adv: *thickly.* Comp: *thicker;* sup: *thickest.*) □ *The cook spread the thick sauce over the pizza dough.* **5.** *adj.* [of air] not clear; [of air] full of water vapor, smoke, or fog. (Comp: *thicker;* sup: *thickest.*) □ *The early morning sky was thick with fog.* **6.** *adj.* [of an accent or manner of speaking] showing where the speaker is from. □ *The Germans laughed because I spoke with a thick American accent.*

**thief** ['θif] *n., irreg.* someone who steals things. (Pl: **thieves.**) □ *My house was robbed by professional thieves.*

**thieves** ['θivz] pl of **thief.**

**thigh** ['θɑɪ] *n.* [in humans and many animals] the part of the leg between the hip and the knee. □ *Mary wears shorts that go down to her knees because she likes her thighs to be covered.*

**thin** ['θɪn] **1.** *adj.* not thick; having less than the average distance between the two opposite sides; having very little space between the two opposite sides. (Adv: *thinly.* Comp: *thinner;* sup: *thinnest.*) □ *Don't walk on the ice yet, because it's too thin to support you.* **2.** *adj.* not fat; slender; slim; not having much fat on one's body. (Adv: *thinly.* Comp: *thinner;* sup: *thinnest.*) □ *The thin student ate in moderation.* **3.** *adj.* not dense; spread out. (Adv: *thinly.* Comp: *thinner;* sup: *thinnest.*) □ *John usually wears a hat because his hair is thin.* **4.** *adj.* not thick; [of a liquid] containing a lot of water; flowing easily. (Adv: *thinly.* Comp: *thinner;* sup: *thinnest.*) □ *The sauce was too thin, and it had soaked into the pizza crust.* **5.** *tv.* to make something more **thin** ④ or runny. □ *You must thin this thick gravy.*

**thing** ['θɪŋ] **1.** *n.* any object; an object whose name is not known; an object whose name is not important. □ *Last night, I threw away some things from my refrigerator.* **2.** *n.* an event; an action; a deed; a statement; an idea. □ *I couldn't believe the offensive things coming from John's mouth.*

**think** ['θɪŋk] **1.** *iv., irreg.* to use one's mind; to have thoughts or opinions; to form ideas in the mind. (Pt/pp: **thought.**) □ *John thought for a while before replying.* **2.** *iv., irreg.* to be able to use one's mind; to have the ability to use one's mind. □ *Dogs don't think, but instead rely on instinct.* **3. think to** do something *iv., irreg. + inf.* to remember to do something; to get an idea about doing something. □ *Did you think to close the windows before you left the house?* **4.** *tv., irreg.* to have a certain belief or opinion; to believe something. (The object can be a clause with **that** ⑦.) □ *Jimmy thinks the moon is closer than it really is.*

**third** ['θɝd] 3rd. Go to **fourth** for senses and examples.

**thirdly** ['θɝd li] *adv.* in the third place; as a third point of discussion. □ *Thirdly, as if two reasons aren't enough, you should stop smoking because it smells.*

**thirst** ['θɝst] *n.* the feeling caused by having nothing to drink; the need to drink. (No plural form.) □ *The small sip of water didn't satisfy Mary's thirst.*

**thirsty** ['θɝs ti] *adj.* needing to drink; having had nothing to drink; having thirst. (Adv: *thirstily.* Comp: *thirstier;* sup: *thirstiest.*) □ *The thirsty students drank a gallon of tea.*

**thirteen** ['θɝt 'tin] 13. Go to **four** for senses and examples.

**thirteenth** ['θɝt 'tinθ] 13th. Go to **fourth** for senses and examples.

**thirtieth** ['θɝt i əθ] 30th. Go to **fourth** for senses and examples.

**thirty** ['θɝt i] 30. Go to **forty** for senses and examples.

**this** ['ðɪs] **1.** *adj.* <a form referring to a thing or person that has already been referred to or is obvious and present; a form referring to an object that one is pointing to or otherwise indicating.> (Prenominal only. Use **these** with plural nouns.) □ *This television program is really boring.* **2.** *adj.* <a form introducing a thing or person new to the conversation.> (Colloquial. Prenominal only. Use **these** with plural nouns.) □ *While I was driving today, suddenly there was this big log in the road!* **3.** *adj.* <a form referring to the thing, person, or point in time that is closer or the closest to the speaker.> (Used in contrast with **that.** Prenominal only. Use **these** with plural nouns.) □ *I don't like that painting over there. This one is much nicer.* **4.** *pron.* <a form standing for a thing or person that has already been mentioned or is obvious and present.> (Pl: **these.**) □ *"Could you buy me this?" Anne asked, pointing to a toy in a catalog.* **5.** *pron.* <a form standing for the thing, person, or point in time that is closer or the closest to the speaker.> (Used in contrast with **that.** Pl: **these.**) □ *I'll eat this, and you can eat that.* **6.** *adv.* to the indicated degree. □ *"I saw a dog today that was this big!" Tom said, spreading his arms wide.*

**thorn** ['θorn] *n.* a sharp, pointed growth on a plant. □ *The florist accidentally poked her finger with a thorn.*

**thorough** ['θɝ o] *adj.* complete; done with great attention and in great detail. (Adv: *thoroughly.*) □ *The maid did such* *a thorough job of cleaning our kitchen that it looked new.*

**those** ['ðoz] **1.** pl of that. **2. those [who do something]** *pron.* the people [who do something] □ *There are those who think my ideas are all wrong.* **3.** *adj.* <a form referring to people or things already mentioned or people or things of which both the speaker and hearer are aware.> (Prenominal only. With singular nouns, use **that**.) □ *The dog dug up those plants you planted last week.* **4.** *adj.* <a form referring to people or things further away or the furthest away from the speaker.> (Used in contrast with **these**. Prenominal only. With singular nouns, use **that**.) □ *These shops are too crowded. Let's go to those over there.*

**though** ['ðo] **1.** *conj.* in spite of something; in spite of the fact that; although. □ *Though it might rain, I want to go to the beach.* **2. as though** *conj.* as if. □ *This food tastes as though it were spoiled.* **3.** *adv.* however. □ *You could get two slices of pizza, though that wouldn't be fair.*

**thought** ['θɔt] **1.** pt/pp of **think**. **2.** *n.* thinking; attention; time taken to think about an idea. (No plural form.) □ *The mayor gave some thought to the citizens' request.* **3.** *n.* an idea; an opinion; something that one thinks. □ *I just had a thought that might interest you.*

**thousand** ['θɑʊ zənd] **1.** *n.* 1,000; the number between 999 and 1,001. (Additional numbers formed as with *two thousand, three thousand, four thousand,* etc.) □ *Five hundred plus fifteen hundred equals two thousand.* **2.** *n.* a group of 1,000 things or people. □ *This theater seats a thousand.*

**thousandth** ['θɑʊ zəndθ] 1,000th. Go to **fourth** for senses and examples.

**thread** ['θrɛd] **1.** *n.* fine string, made of twisted strands of cotton, silk, or other fiber, that is used to sew pieces of cloth together or is woven to make cloth. (Plural only when referring to different kinds, types, instances, or varieties.) □ *Jim cut off the extra thread with a pair of scissors.* 🄲 *The sewing store offers a wide variety of threads and needles.* **2.** *n.* a very thin strand of something; a length of ①. □ *The spider's web was woven with silky threads.* **3.** *n.* a theme or idea that links parts of an argument or a story. (Fig. on ②.) □ *The book's many threads were brought together in the last chapter.* **4.** *n.* the raised ridge that wraps around the length of a screw or a bolt. (Usually plural, but not countable.) □ *The nut turned around the threads of the bolt.* **5.** *tv.* to pass ① through something, usually a needle. □ *She threaded her needle and began to sew a patch on the jacket.* **6.** *tv.* to place something on ① or on string, wire, etc. □ *As a decoration, I threaded popcorn onto the string.*

**threat** ['θrɛt] **1.** *n.* a warning; a statement or action that indicates that someone is going to hurt or punish someone in a certain way. □ *The enemy made a threat to bomb the capital.* **2.** *n.* a sign of danger; a sign that something harmful or dangerous is going to happen. □ *The workers considered the appearance of robots to represent a threat to their jobs.*

**threaten** ['θrɛt n] **1.** *tv.* to express a threat against someone. (The object can be a clause with **that** ⑦.) □ *Bill threatened his neighbor with a loaded gun.* **2.** *iv.* + *inf.* [for something] to make a threat to do something. □ *The wind threatened to blow the tree down.* **3.** *iv.* to be a threat; to be an indication of danger. □ *When heavy rains threatened, we canceled our picnic.*

**three** ['θri] 3. Go to **four** for senses and examples.

**threw** ['θru] pt of **throw**.

**thrift** ['θrɪft] *n.* the careful use of money and things; the habit of not wasting money or things. (No plural form.)

☐ *Because of her thrift, Anne creates very little garbage.*

**thrill** ['θrɪl] **1.** *n.* an intense feeling of emotion, especially excitement, enjoyment, or fear. ☐ *Riding an old-fashioned train is a great thrill for me.* **2.** *tv.* to cause someone to feel full of emotion, especially excitement, enjoyment, or fear. ☐ *The skydive thrilled me more than anything else I've ever done.*

**thrive** ['θrɑɪv] **1.** *iv., irreg.* to grow and survive; to develop in a very healthy way. (Pt: **throve** or *thrived;* pp: **thriven** or *thrived.*) ☐ *My children thrived on my good cooking.* **2.** *iv., irreg.* to be successful; to become very rich. ☐ *The little café thrived because people loved the flavor of the coffee served there.*

**thriven** ['θrɪv ən] a pp of **thrive**.

**throat** ['θrot] **1.** *n.* the front of the neck. ☐ *The barber shaved John's beard from his throat and his cheeks.* **2.** *n.* the inside of the neck, where food and air pass. ☐ *I drank hot tea because my throat was sore.*

**throb** ['θrɑb] **1.** *iv.* to beat strongly and quickly, as with the beating of the heart or some other pulse. ☐ *Does your car's engine always throb like that, or is something wrong?* **2.** *iv.* to have a pain that occurs with each heartbeat. ☐ *When I have a headache, my head throbs with pain.* **3.** *n.* one beat in a series of strong, quick beats. ☐ *With each throb of one's heart, blood is pumped through the body.*

T

**throne** ['θron] **1.** *n.* the chair that a king, queen, ruler, or other important person sits on. ☐ *The royal throne was covered with jewels.* **2.** *n.* the position held by a king, queen, ruler, or other important person. ☐ *King Edward VIII left the British throne in 1936.*

**through** ['θru] **1.** *prep.* from the outside of one end of something, into it, to the other end of it, and out of the other side of it. ☐ *The jogger ran through the park.* **2.** *prep.* because of something; on account of something. ☐ *Anne got a promotion through her hard work.* **3.** *prep.* moving throughout or within something. ☐ *The excited dog tore through the house.* **4.** *prep.* during the entire time from beginning to end; during the entire way from start to finish. ☐ *Bill worked through the night to finish the project.* **5.** *adv.* in one side and out the other. ☐ *While I rested in the park, a pack of kids ran through.* **6.** *adv.* from beginning to end; from start to finish. ☐ *I read my contract through carefully.* **7.** *adj.* finished; done. ☐ *When Anne was through with the book, she let me borrow it.*

**throughout** [θru 'ɑʊt] *prep.* in every part of something; during every moment of something. ☐ *Someone in the audience was talking throughout the entire movie.*

**throve** ['θrov] a pt of **thrive**.

**throw** ['θro] **1.** *tv., irreg.* to send something through the air; to hurl something; to cause something to move through the air. (Pt: **threw**; pp: **thrown**.) ☐ *Please throw me those keys.* **2.** *tv., irreg.* to put someone or something someplace carelessly, with force, or in a hurry. ☐ *John threw himself onto the bed.* **3.** *tv., irreg.* [for an animal] to cause a rider to fall off. ☐ *The cowboy was thrown by the horse.* **4.** *tv., irreg.* to move a switch in order to start or stop the flow of electricity. ☐ *The worker threw the switch to stop the motor.* **5.** *tv., irreg.* to cause someone to be in a certain condition, especially a confused one. ☐ *When Anne changed her mind, it really threw me.* **6. throw** something **up** *tv., irreg.* + *obj.* + *adv.* to vomit something. ☐ *Poor Jane threw her dinner up.* 🅃 *She threw up her dinner.* **7. throw up** *iv., irreg.* + *adv.* to vomit. ☐ *The spoiled food made me throw up.*

**thrown** ['θron] pp of **throw**.

**thrust** ['θrʌst] **1.** *tv., irreg.* to push someone or something forward with force; to push someone or something in a certain direction with force. (Pt/pp: *thrust.*) □ *Anne thrust her dog through the door of the veterinarian's office.* **2.** *tv., irreg.* to drive a sharp object at or into someone or something. □ *The soldier thrust his knife at the enemy.* **3.** *iv., irreg.* to move forward with force; to lunge, especially with a sharp object. □ *The robber thrust at me with a large knife.* **4.** *n.* a forceful movement in a certain direction; a lunge; a stab. □ *With a powerful thrust of his foot, the policeman broke open the door.*

**thud** ['θʌd] *n.* the dull sound of something heavy falling onto or hitting something firm but unbreakable. □ *I heard a thud as my car ran into the tree.*

**thumb** ['θʌm] **1.** *n.* the first and shortest finger on the hand, separate from the other four, having two knuckles instead of three. □ *Anne used her thumb to tear into the peel of the orange.* **2.** *n.* the part of a glove or mitten that covers ①. □ *The thumb of my mitten has a large hole in it.*

**thumbnail** ['θʌm nel] **1.** *n.* the nail on one's thumb. □ *I cracked my thumbnail when I accidentally hit it with a hammer.* **2.** *adj.* small; short; brief; concise. (Prenominal only.) □ *The student wrote a thumbnail description of his project.*

**thumbtack** ['θʌm tæk] **1.** *n.* a tack with a large, flat head that is pressed with one's thumb to drive the pointed part into a surface. □ *John hung up the weekly schedule with a thumbtack.* **2.** *tv.* to attach something to a surface with ①. □ *I thumbtacked the schedule to the bulletin board.*

**thump** ['θʌmp] **1.** *n.* the sound made by hitting someone or something with something hard or against something hard. □ *The pumpkin made a thump when I threw it to the ground.* **2.** *tv.* to hit someone or something with something hard; to hit someone or something against something hard. □ *The old lady thumped the attacking dog with her cane.*

**thunder** ['θʌn dɚ] **1.** *n.* the loud noise that follows lightning. (No plural form.) □ *Thunder woke me up about midnight when it started to rain.* **2.** *n.* any loud noise or explosion that sounds like ①. □ *There was a thunder of applause when the jury announced its decision.* **3.** *iv.* [for weather conditions] to make ①. □ *It thundered for an hour, but our area didn't get any rain.* **4.** *iv.* to make a noise like ①; to walk or move, making noise like ①. □ *John thundered down the hallway in his heavy boots.*

**thundershower** ['θʌn dɚ ʃɑʊ ɚ] *n.* rain with thunder and lightning. □ *The forecaster predicted thundershowers for the weekend.*

**thunderstorm** ['θʌn dɚ storm] *n.* a storm with thunder and lightning. □ *I don't like to drive during violent thunderstorms.*

**Thursday** ['θɚʒ de] Go to **day**.

**thus** ['ðʌs] *adv.* therefore; for this reason; for these reasons; as a result. □ *The defendant was found not guilty, and thus he was freed.*

**tick** ['tɪk] **1.** *n.* the short, quiet sound made by a watch or a clock. □ *The ticks of the large, old clock were annoying.* **2.** *n.* a small, flat insect that attaches to the skin of animals and sucks their blood. □ *While we were camping, our tent was invaded by ticks.* **3.** *n.* a mark that is made when counting something or checking something. □ *There was a red tick by each spelling error in my essay.* **4.** *iv.* [for a clock, watch, or other timepiece] to make a short, quiet sound each second. □ *The package was ticking, so I was sure there was a timing device in it.*

**ticket** ['tɪk ɪt] **1.** *n.* a piece of paper that shows that its owner has paid for transportation or for entrance into a place. □ *An usher tore my ticket in half as I entered the theater.* **2.** *n.* a piece of paper that is given as a receipt when one leaves something at a repair shop, cleaners, or other business, so that one can get it back. □ *My ticket from the cleaners listed all the clothes I'd brought in.* **3.** *n.* a piece of paper that is given to someone who has broken a traffic law or parking law, requiring that person to pay a fine or appear in court. □ *When I returned to my car, there was a ticket on the windshield.*

**tickle** ['tɪk əl] **1.** *tv.* to touch a person's body in a way that causes him or her to laugh. □ *Mary tickled me until I was laughing very hard.* **2.** *tv.* to amuse someone. (Fig. on ①.) □ *Susan tickled me with her clever wit.* **3.** *iv.* to cause a feeling that causes someone to laugh. □ *Stop touching me like that! It tickles.* **4.** *n.* an itchy feeling; a feeling that one needs to scratch, cough, or sneeze. □ *The tickle in my throat was the first sign of a cold.*

**ticklish** ['tɪk lɪʃ] **1.** *adj.* sensitive to tickling; likely to laugh when tickled. (Adv: *ticklishly.*) □ *My ticklish friend screamed as I touched his skin with a feather.* **2.** *adj.* difficult; hard to answer; delicate; requiring careful thought or action. (Fig. on ①. Adv: *ticklishly.*) □ *You must handle this ticklish situation with a lot of tact.*

**tide** ['tɑɪd] *n.* the rise and fall of the ocean, caused by the pull of the sun and the moon. □ *As the tide came in, it destroyed the castle I had built of sand.*

**tidy** ['tɑɪ di] **1.** *adj.* very neat; orderly; not messy. (Adv: *tidily.* Comp: *tidier;* sup: *tidiest.*) □ *My boss likes to have a tidy desk.* **2.** *tv.* to make something ①. □ *The maid had tidied the hotel room while I was out.*

**tie** ['tɑɪ] **1.** *tv.* to form string, rope, cord, or thread into a knot or bow, often as a way to connect it to something or to join two pieces or ends together. (The present participle is *tying* for all senses of the verb.) □ *Mary tied a ribbon in her hair.* **2.** *tv.* to join someone in occupying the same position in a list that ranks a group of things; to have the same score as the opposite player or team. □ *By the end of the inning, our team tied the opponent 4–4.* **3. tie** something **(up)** *tv. + obj. (+ adv.)* to fasten something with string, rope, cord, or thread. □ *The postal clerk tied the parcel up with string.* **4.** *iv.* [for two teams] to have the same score; to occupy the same position as someone else in a list that ranks a group of things. □ *The two teams tied at 7–7.* □ *Two runners tied for first place.* **5.** *n.* a **necktie;** a strip of cloth that is looped around the neck and **tied** as in ① so there is a knot at the neck and the two ends hang down in front of one's shirt. □ *David spilled some coffee on his silk tie.* **6.** *n.* a result of a game where both teams or players have the same score; a ranking where two or more people or things have the same rank. □ *The game was still in a tie at midnight, so they just stopped playing.*

**tiger** ['tɑɪ gɚ] *n.* a large, fierce animal that is a member of the cat family and has orange or yellow fur with black stripes. □ *The tiger stalked its prey.*

**tight** ['tɑɪt] **1.** *adj.* not loose; having no extra room on the sides or around the edges; fitting closely. (Adv: *tightly.* Comp: *tighter;* sup: *tightest.*) □ *The tight shoes pinched Anne's feet.* **2.** *adj.* [of a schedule] having no extra time; having no appointments available. (Fig. on ①. Adv: *tightly.* Comp: *tighter;* sup: *tightest.*) □ *There is no room for lunch in my tight schedule.* **3.** *adj.* closely held; firmly fastened; fixed. (Adv: *tightly.* Comp: *tighter;* sup: *tightest.*) □ *The boss kept tight control of the budget.* **4.** *adj.*

stretched; taut. (Adv: *tightly.* Comp: *tighter;* sup: *tightest.*) ☐ *My tight muscles were very sore.* **5.** *adv.* in a **tight** ①-④ way; firmly; closely. (Comp: *tighter;* sup: *tightest.*) ☐ *The crack in the pipe was sealed tight.* **6. tights** *n.* a garment that is worn below the waist and fits closely against one's body, generally worn by women and dancers; pantyhose; nylons. (Treated as plural. Number is expressed with *pair(s) of tights.*) ☐ *The ballet dancers all wore white tights.*

**tighten** ['taɪt n] **1.** *tv.* to make something tight; to make something tighter. ☐ *Mary tightened her grip on Jimmy's arm.* **2.** *iv.* to become tight; to become tighter. ☐ *John's muscles tightened as he lifted the heavy crate.*

**tile** ['taɪl] **1.** *n.* baked clay or ceramic material formed into useful shapes for construction and decoration. (Plural only when referring to different kinds, types, instances, or varieties.) ☐ *The floor was made of tile.* Ⓒ *The strongest tiles are baked in an oven for a long time.* **2.** *n.* a thin, formed piece of ① used for covering floors, walls, roofs, and other surfaces in buildings and houses. ☐ *The janitor polished the tiles in the lobby.* **3.** *n.* a square of soft material that absorbs sound and provides decoration, used in the construction of ceilings. ☐ *John jumped up and touched the ceiling tiles.* **4.** *tv.* to cover a surface with ① or a similar substance. ☐ *I tiled my bathroom walls with expensive white marble.* **5.** *iv.* to work by covering surfaces with ①. ☐ *The architect hired four workers who knew how to tile.*

**till** ['tɪl] **1.** *tv.* to plow land; to prepare soil for planting. ☐ *The field had been tilled before the seeds were planted.* **2.** *n.* the drawer in a cash register or counter where money is kept in a place of business. ☐ *There was no slot for a $2 bill in my till.* **3.** *prep.* **until**; up to a certain time; during a period of time up to a certain time. ☐ *We stayed at her house till 5:00 A.M.* ☐ *Anne will be in Boston till Tuesday.* **4.** *conj.* **until**; up to a certain time. ☐ *We will be at the park till it gets dark.* **5.** *conj.* **until**; before. ☐ *I never went to France till I learned French.*

**tilt** ['tɪlt] **1.** *tv.* to turn something to its side; to slant something. ☐ *The earthquake tilted the house to one side.* **2.** *iv.* to be turned to the side; to be tipped; to slant; to slope. ☐ *The tree tilted toward the ground.*

**timber** ['tɪm bɚ] **1.** *n.* trees that are growing; a forest; woods. (No plural form.) ☐ *The farmer sold the timber growing behind the farm.* **2.** *n.* a thick length of wood. ☐ *The main beam is a very sturdy timber.*

**time** ['taɪm] **1.** *n.* every moment that ever was, is now, and ever will be; a continuous state of being from the past, through now, and into the future. (No plural form.) ☐ *Humans cannot reverse the flow of time.* **2.** *n.* a period of ①; a period of ① between two events. (No plural form.) ☐ *For a long time, John had wanted to be a doctor.* **3.** *n.* the amount of **time** ① that it takes to do something. (No plural form.) ☐ *How much time would it take to bake a cake?* **4.** *n.* an exact moment in the passage of ①; some moment in the passage of ①. ☐ *At what time is Mary's flight scheduled to arrive?* **5.** *n.* the appropriate moment, day, week, etc., to do something. (No plural form.) ☐ *It's time to change our way of doing business.* **6. times** *n.* periods of ① and the events that occurred during them. ☐ *I had a lot of good times in college.* **7.** *n.* an occasion of doing something; an instance of something being done. ☐ *"How many times have you seen this movie?" "I've seen it three times."* **8.** *tv.* to measure the existence of something that is happening; to measure how long or how fast it takes someone to do something. ☐ *The*

T

*coach timed the runner in the race.* **9.** *tv.* to determine the best ④ for doing something, and do it then. □ *The actor timed his entrance for the maximum comic effect.* **10.** *tv.* to set or arrange something so that it does something at a certain **time** ④. □ *Anne timed her arrival for 6:00 P.M.* **11. times** *prep.* multiplied by a number. (Represented by the symbol "×.") □ *Four times four is sixteen.*

**timepiece** ['tɑɪm pis] *n.* a device, especially a clock or a watch, that keeps track of time. □ *My grandfather gave me his antique timepiece.*

**timer** ['tɑɪm ɚ] *n.* someone or something that records time, especially a device that can be set to indicate when a certain amount of time has passed. □ *Microwave ovens always have timers.*

**timid** ['tɪm ɪd] *adj.* full of fear; easily scared. (Adv: *timidly.* Comp: *timider;* sup: *timidest.*) □ *The timid little mouse hid from the cat.*

**tin** ['tɪn] **1.** *n.* a metal that is mixed with other metals to make bronze and is used as a coating for steel so that it doesn't rust. (No plural form.) □ *The steel cans were coated with a layer of tin.* **2.** *n.* a can or a container made of ① or plated with ①, or a modern steel can containing no ①. (Usually limited to containers that hold cookies, crackers, and sardines. **Can** is used more frequently.) □ *Mary bought a tin of sardines.* **3.** *adj.* made of or coated with ①. □ *The soldier drank from a tin cup.*

**tinge** ['tɪndʒ] **1.** *n.* a very small amount of something, such as color or an emotion. □ *I felt a tinge of guilt for eating Mary's cookie.* **2.** *tv.* to add to or improve something with a small amount of something. □ *The routine news story was tinged with sensational details.*

**tingle** ['tɪŋ gəl] **1.** *n.* a light prickly or stinging feeling, as though one received a small shock or thrill. □ *The scary movie sent a tingle down my spine.* **2.** *iv.* to experience a light stinging feeling, as though one has received a small shock or thrill. □ *Lisa's foot tingled because she had been sitting on it.*

**tinkle** ['tɪŋ kəl] **1.** *n.* a short, quiet, high-pitched ring or clinking sound. □ *We heard the tinkle of glasses as Mother washed the dishes.* **2.** *iv.* to ring in a short, quiet, high-pitched way. □ *The charms on Mary's bracelet tinkle when she moves her arm.*

**tint** ['tɪnt] **1.** *n.* a color; a weakened shade of a color. □ *Mary wanted to paint her bathroom walls in a lighter tint.* **2.** *tv.* to color something slightly; to give a small amount of color to something; to dye hair with ①. □ *The hair stylist tinted my hair red.*

**tinted** ['tɪn təd] *adj.* slightly colored. □ *Mary's tinted hair is very attractive.*

**tiny** ['tɑɪ ni] *adj.* very small. (Adv: *tinily.* Comp: *tinier;* sup: *tiniest.*) □ *A tiny insect walked across the floor.*

**tip** ['tɪp] **1.** *n.* the very end part of an object; the top of an object. □ *I tapped the tip of the pencil against the desk.* **2.** *n.* money that is given to someone for a service. □ *I gave my barber a large tip.* **3.** *n.* a hint; a suggestion; a piece of advice. □ *The teacher read a list of tips on safe driving.* **4.** *tv.* to lean something to the side; to cause something to slant. □ *I tipped the barrel so the water would flow out.* **5.** *tv.* to give someone money for a service; to leave someone ②. □ *I tipped the porter for carrying my luggage.* **6.** *tv.* to give a certain sum or percentage of money in gratitude for service. □ *I always tip at least 15%.* **7.** *iv.* to lean to the side; to slant. □ *The floor of the porch tips to one side.* **8.** *iv.* to give people money for their services. □ *Waiters like customers who tip well.*

**tire** ['tɑɪɚ] **1.** *n.* a circular structure of rubber that surrounds a wheel and is filled with air. □ *That rubber plant recy-*

T

*cles old tires.* **2. tire of** someone or something *iv. + prep. phr.* to become impatient with someone or something. ☐ *I'm tired of your tardiness!* **3. tire (out)** *iv. (+ adv.)* to become weary or exhausted. ☐ *Bob tires easily because he has cancer.* **4. tire** someone **out** *tv. + obj. + adv.* to cause someone to become sleepy or weary. ☐ *The hard work tired her out.* [T] *The work tired out the whole crew.*

**tired** ['tɑɪɚd] **1.** *adj.* sleepy; wanting to sleep; exhausted. (Adv: *tiredly.*) ☐ *Because I was so tired, I fell asleep at work.* **2.** *adj.* impatient with someone or something; annoyed with someone or something. (Adv: *tiredly.*) ☐ *The teacher became tired of explaining the same things over and over.*

**tissue** ['tɪʃ ju] **1.** *n.* a very soft piece of paper that is used to wipe the skin or for blowing the nose. ☐ *Mary placed a box of tissues on her desk.* **2.** *n.* a part of a plant or an animal that is made of many cells having the same function; the group of cells in a plant or animal that form a particular organ. (Plural only when referring to different kinds, types, instances, or varieties.) ☐ *The surgeon cut through the tissue surrounding the bone.* [C] *Most organs are made of a variety of different tissues.*

**title** ['tɑɪt əl] **1.** *n.* the name of a book, movie, song, play, picture, or poem. ☐ *The title of the movie was changed twice during production.* **2.** *n.* a word, often abbreviated, that is placed before a person's name indicating rank, profession, or social position. ☐ *Which title do you prefer, "Ms." or "Mrs."?* **3.** *n.* the official name of a job or position. ☐ *Mary's business card listed her title—Associate Director of Marketing—as well as her name.* ☐ *What will John's new title be after his promotion?* **4.** *n.* an official document showing that someone owns something. (Compare this with **deed**.) ☐ *Anne keeps the title to her car in a safety-deposit box.* **5.** *tv.* to give something a **title** ①. ☐ *She titled her poem "Water Thoughts."*

**to** [tu, tə] **1.** *prep.* in the direction of someone or something; toward someone or something; in the direction of a place, position, or condition; toward and reaching a place to which one is going. ☐ *We went to New York City last year for a vacation.* **2.** *prep.* as far as some time, place, thing, or person; until; through. (Often indicated with a hyphen or short dash, as in "1997–1999.") ☐ *Cut the potatoes into strips that are 4 to 6 inches long.* **3.** *prep.* <a form that marks the indirect object of a verb, showing the action of a verb toward someone or something.> ☐ *David sent a letter to his parents.* **4.** *prep.* for each; in each; included in each. ☐ *There are 5,280 feet to a mile.* **5.** *prep.* as far as someone or something; against someone or something. ☐ *I pushed the sofa to the wall to make more space in the room.* **6.** *prep.* before a certain time. ☐ *It is five minutes to six o'clock.* **7.** <the marker of the infinitive form of verbs.> (This use of **to** is often considered to be a preposition, but it has none of the qualities of a preposition.) ☐ *You did it although I asked you not to!* **8.** *adv.* into a state of alertness and awareness. ☐ *The man was unconscious, so we threw cold water on his face to try to bring him to.*

**toad** ['tod] *n.* a small animal similar to a frog, but which lives mostly on land. ☐ *Toads cannot jump as far as frogs.*

**toast** ['tost] **1.** *n.* sliced bread that has been browned by heat. (No plural form. Number is expressed with *piece(s)* or *slice(s) of toast.*) ☐ *John ate only a piece of toast for breakfast.* **2.** *n.* a statement made before an invitation that everyone present take a drink in approval or agreement. ☐ *My brother offered a toast in honor of my wedding.* **3.** *tv.* to brown a slice of bread by heating it; to brown something by heating it. □ *David toasted his bread in the toaster.* **4.** *tv.* to warm something, especially marshmallows, over a fire. □ *Bob toasted his marshmallow until it burst into flame.* **5.** *tv.* to honor someone or something by taking a drink; to drink to the honor of someone or something. □ *We all toasted the birth of Anne's baby.*

**toaster** ['tos tɚ] *n.* an electrical appliance that toasts bread. □ *I removed the hot toast from the toaster.*

**tobacco** [tə 'bæk o] *n.* a plant whose leaves are dried to be smoked in cigars, cigarettes, or pipes or to be chewed. (Plural only when referring to different kinds, types, instances, or varieties.) □ *John rolled some tobacco in a paper and smoked it.* Ⓒ *The best tobaccos are grown in the South.*

**toboggan** [tə 'bɑg ən] **1.** *n.* a long sled without blades. □ *The toboggan overturned and threw Bob into a snowbank.* **2.** *iv.* to ride on ①; to go down hills on ①. □ *During the snowstorm, we tobogganed by the river.*

**today** [tə 'de] **1.** *n.* this day; the current day. □ *Until today, I had never been on an airplane.* **2.** *n.* in this period of time. □ *John plans only for today. Tomorrow, he says, will take care of itself.* **3.** *adv.* in the current age or general time period. □ *Today, polio is no longer a serious threat.* **4.** *adv.* on this day. □ *Has the mail come today?*

T

**toe** ['to] **1.** *n.* one of the finger-like projections on the front of the foot; one of the digits on one's foot. □ *My toes are cramped in these narrow shoes.* **2.** *n.* the part of a shoe, boot, sock, or other piece of footwear that covers or encloses one or more **toes** ①. □ *The toes of my shoes need to be polished.*

**toenail** ['to nel] *n.* the thin, hard plate that covers the front part of the end of the toe. □ *I cracked the toenail of my big toe when I bumped into the wall.*

**together** [tə 'gɛ ðɚ] **1.** *adv.* as one group of people or things. □ *Wales, England, and Scotland together are called Great Britain.* **2.** *adv.* at the same time; simultaneously. □ *All of the bank's alarms rang together during the robbery.*

**toil** ['tɔɪl] **1.** *n.* hard work; hard labor; work that requires a lot of physical energy or effort. (Plural only when referring to different kinds, types, instances, or varieties.) □ *All the toil made my hands blister.* Ⓒ *Your toils are wasted and your efforts are in vain.* **2.** *iv.* to work hard; to labor; to do work that requires a lot of physical energy or effort. □ *The workers toiled in the factory all day long.*

**toilet** ['tɔɪ lət] **1.** *n.* a bathroom; a room that has a ②; a restroom. □ *The door to the toilet was locked, so I had to wait.* **2.** *n.* a strong, ceramic bowl, connected to a drain and having a seat attached to it, into which one expels urine or feces. □ *David woke up in the middle of the night, needing to use the toilet.* **3. go to the toilet** *phr.* to use ② to expel feces or urine. □ *Excuse me, I have to go to the toilet.*

**toilet paper** ['tɔɪ lət pe pɚ] *n.* very thin, usually soft paper that is used to cleanse the affected areas of one's body after one has used the toilet. (No plural form.) □ *Mary buys the cheapest toilet paper that she can find.*

**token** ['tok ən] **1.** *n.* a sign of something; a reminder of something; visible proof of something; evidence of something. □ *I keep a special penny in my pocket as a token of luck.* **2.** *n.* a small piece of metal, similar to a coin, that is used instead of money. □ *The video game accepts tokens instead of quarters.* **3.** *adj.* only serving as a symbol of something; done solely for the way it will appear to others. □ *Mary deserved the job and had not been hired to be the token female.*

**told** ['told] pt/pp of **tell**.

**tolerant** ['tɑl ə rənt] *adj.* willing to allow others to do something or to live the way they want to. (Adv: *tolerantly.*) ☐ *The prejudiced man was not at all tolerant.*

**tolerate** ['tɑl ə ret] *tv.* to endure someone or something; to manage to accept someone or something. ☐ *Mary barely tolerated her horrible living conditions.*

**toll** ['tol] **1.** *n.* a fee paid for the privilege of doing something, especially traveling on certain routes. ☐ *You have to pay a toll to drive on some highways.* **2.** *n.* the extra charge for certain telephone calls that are not local. ☐ *Ask the operator if there is a toll for this call.* **3.** *iv.* [for a bell] to ring slowly and repeatedly. ☐ *The church bell tolls every morning at 6 A.M.* **4.** *tv.* to ring a bell slowly and repeatedly. ☐ *You toll the bell by pulling on the rope.*

**tomato** [tə 'me to] **1.** *n.* a roundish, soft, red fruit that grows on a vine and is eaten as food. (Pl ends in *-es.*) ☐ *I sliced up a tomato for my salad.* **2.** *adj.* made or flavored with ①. ☐ *Jane drank some tomato juice for breakfast.*

**tomb** ['tum] *n.* an enclosure in which someone is buried, especially a structure that is above ground level. ☐ *Friends of the family carried the coffin to the tomb.*

**tombstone** ['tum ston] *n.* a grave marker; a large slab of stone at a grave that shows who is buried at that place and when that person was alive. ☐ *Mr. Wilson's tombstone indicated that he had been born in 1930.*

**tomorrow** [tə 'mɑr o] **1.** *n.* the day after today. (Usually singular.) ☐ *You must finish this project by tomorrow.* **2.** *n.* the future. (No plural form.) ☐ *The science exhibit gave us a look at the world of tomorrow.* **3.** *adv.* during ①; at some time during ①. ☐ *What time do you have to be at work tomorrow?*

**ton** ['tʌn] *n.* a unit of measure of weight equal to 2,000 pounds. (Also called a *short ton;* used in the United States and Canada.) ☐ *The ton of paper was loaded onto the large truck.*

**tone** ['ton] **1.** *n.* a sound as it relates to its quality, intensity, or pitch. ☐ *The fire alarm emitted a shrill, loud tone.* **2.** *n.* a quality of one's voice that reveals one's feelings or attitude. ☐ *"Go away!" Jane said in an angry tone.* **3.** *n.* a style, character, or mood of an event or circumstance. ☐ *Our manager's warm welcome set the tone for the meeting.* **4.** *n.* firmness of the muscles. (No plural form.) ☐ *The advertiser wanted to hire a model with good body tone.*

**tongue** ['tʌŋ] **1.** *n.* the long, typically pink, movable organ in the mouth, used for tasting, managing food, and, in humans, speaking. ☐ *The kitten licked my hand with its tongue.* **2.** *n.* the ① of an animal, eaten as food. (No plural form.) ☐ *This sandwich is made from beef tongue.* **3.** *n.* a language. ☐ *This document is written in my native tongue.* **4.** *n.* the flap of material that is part of a shoe and fits under the laces. ☐ *Jane laid the tongue flat and laced the laces over it.* **5.** *n.* a flame; a pointed section of flame. ☐ *The yellow tongues of flame lighted the room.*

**tonic** ['tɑn ɪk] **1.** *n.* a remedy; something that is good for one's health; something that provides strength. ☐ *Jane made a tonic for her sick friend.* **2.** *n.* a kind of flavored soda water that is somewhat bitter. ☐ *Bill made a drink of gin and tonic for Bob.*

T

**tonight** [tə 'nɑɪt] **1.** *n.* this evening; this night. ☐ *Do you have any plans for tonight?* **2.** *adv.* during ①; at some time during ①. ☐ *I'd like to go out to a restaurant tonight.*

**tonsil** ['tɑn səl] *n.* one of two small organs in the very back of the mouth at the side of the throat. □ *The surgeon removed the sick child's tonsils.*

**too** ['tu] **1.** *adv.* as well; also; in addition. □ *I invited Bill to the party, and David, too.* **2.** *adv.* more than enough; more than is desired; beyond what is desired. □ *Your stereo is too loud.* **3.** *adv.* very; extremely. □ *Thank you. You are too kind, giving me this lovely gift.* **4.** *adv.* <a form used after **be, will, do, have, can, should, would,** and **could** to strengthen them in a response to a negative statement.> □ *"I am not responsible for this problem." "You are too!"*

**took** ['tʊk] pp of **take.**

**tool** ['tul] **1.** *n.* anything that helps someone work; an instrument that is used to help someone do work. □ *I brought some tools into the kitchen to fix the leaky faucet.* **2.** *n.* someone who is used by someone else, especially in an unfair way. (Fig. on ①.) □ *The citizens were tools of the corrupt government.*

**toolshed** ['tul ʃɛd] *n.* a small building where gardening tools are stored. □ *The Smiths stored their lawn mower in the toolshed.*

**toot** ['tut] **1.** *n.* a short blast of a horn or a whistle. □ *The toot of a car horn startled me.* **2.** *tv.* to cause a horn or whistle to make a short noise. □ *Bob tooted his horn, hoping Bill would hear him and come out.*

**tooth** ['tuθ] **1.** *n., irreg.* one of the hard, usually white, bony things in the mouth, used for biting and chewing while eating. (Pl: **teeth.**) □ *Susie wiggled her loose tooth with her fingers.* **2.** *n., irreg.* something shaped like ①, especially a small pointed object on a wheel that is part of a machine, the fingers of a rake, or the points along the length of a comb or saw. □ *Mary prefers to use a comb that has wide spaces between the teeth.*

**toothache** ['tuθ ek] *n.* a pain in or around a tooth. □ *Very cold liquids sometimes give me toothaches.*

**toothbrush** ['tuθ brəʃ] *n.* a small brush that is used for cleaning the teeth. □ *My dentist told me to brush my teeth with a toothbrush and toothpaste after every meal.*

**toothpaste** ['tuθ pest] *n.* a paste that is placed on a toothbrush and is used for cleaning the teeth. (Plural only when referring to different kinds, types, instances, or varieties.) □ *John removed the cap from the tube of toothpaste.* [C] *My dentist suggested that I try a variety of toothpastes until I found one that I liked.*

**toothpick** ['tuθ pɪk] *n.* a small, thin piece of wood that is used to remove pieces of food from between one's teeth. □ *There is a bowl of toothpicks on the counter at the restaurant.*

**top** ['tɑp] **1.** *n.* the highest part of something; the upper part of something; the peak of something; the upper surface of something. □ *Mary hid the candy on the top of the bookcase.* **2.** *n.* the highest position; the highest rank; the most successful position; the most important position. □ *When I have a complaint, I go straight to the top.* **3.** *n.* a cover; a cap; a lid. □ *Who left the top off the soda bottle?* **4.** *n.* a piece of clothing worn above the waist, especially on women. □ *Mary bought a vest to go with her top.* **5.** *adj.* on or at the highest part of something. □ *The top rung of the ladder is broken.* **6.** *adj.* first; best; most important. □ *Jane was the top performer at the competition.* **7.** *adj.* greatest; strongest; at the highest intensity. □ *John played the stereo at its top volume.* **8.** *tv.* to place something on the highest part of something; to place something on something else. □ *Mary topped the gift with a red bow.*

**topic** ['tap ɪk] *n.* the subject of something that is being written or talked about. □ *The essay's topic was stated in the opening paragraph.*

**torch** ['tortʃ] **1.** *n.* a large stick or club whose upper end is on fire. □ *The castle's hallways were lit by large torches.* **2.** *n.* a machine that makes a very hot flame, used to cut or join pieces of metal together by melting them. □ *The worker turned off the torch after cutting through the joint.* **3.** *tv.* to set something on fire; to destroy something with fire. □ *The criminals torched the stolen car so the police would not find it.*

**tore** ['tor] a pt of **tear**.

**torment 1.** ['tor mɛnt] *n.* a severe emotional or physical pain; agony. (Plural only when referring to different kinds, types, instances, or varieties.) □ *My broken foot gives me constant torment.* Ⓒ *The villagers suffered many torments under the evil ruler.* **2.** [tor 'mɛnt] *tv.* to cause someone severe pain or agony; to cause someone to suffer. □ *The murderer was tormented by guilt.*

**torn** ['torn] **1.** a pp of **tear**. **2.** *adj.* having a tear; ripped. □ *The tailor repaired my torn shirt.* □ *I taped the torn page back together.*

**tornado** [tor 'ne do] *n.* a violent wind that spins in circles very fast and can cause a great amount of damage. (Pl ends in *-s* or *-es*.) □ *There's a tornado coming! Get in the cellar!*

**torpedo** [tor 'pi do] **1.** *n.* an explosive device that is fired underwater from a submarine or ship toward another submarine or ship. (Pl ends in *-es*.) □ *The ship exploded when the torpedo hit it.* **2.** *tv.* to attack something with ①; to explode something by firing ① at it. □ *The ship was torpedoed by terrorists.*

**tortoise** ['tor təs] *n.* a turtle, especially one that only lives on land. □ *The tortoise pulled itself into its shell to protect itself.*

**torture** ['tor tʃɚ] **1.** *n.* the inflicting of pain in a cruel way. (No plural form.) □ *The hostages underwent torture while they were held captive.* **2.** *tv.* to cause someone to suffer pain in a cruel way. □ *The killer tortured the victims before shooting them.*

**toss** ['tɔs] **1.** *tv.* to throw something lightly or gently; to throw something carelessly. □ *Anne tossed the ball to John.* **2.** *tv.* to lift and throw something upward; to cause something to move as if it had been thrown. □ *Our ship was tossed by the rough waves.* **3.** *tv.* to flip a coin into the air in order to decide a choice based on whether the head or reverse of the coin appears when it falls; to roll dice. □ *Mary tossed the dice because it was her turn to play.* **4.** *iv.* to turn; to move restlessly. □ *I tossed and turned in bed all night, unable to fall asleep.* **5.** *iv.* to be thrown, especially by water; to be moved with force. □ *The boat tossed about in the heavy seas.* **6.** *n.* an instance of throwing something. □ *We decided the matter by the toss of a coin.*

**total** ['tot əl] **1.** *n.* the whole amount; the sum; the number obtained by adding other numbers together. □ *Your total includes tax.* **2.** *adj.* whole; complete; entire. (Adv: *totally.*) □ *The total effects of the storm won't be known for a few days.* **3.** *tv.* to calculate ①. □ *The students totaled the numbers in the left-hand column.* **4.** *tv.* to come to a certain amount; to reach a certain amount. □ *My income taxes last year totaled $5,000.*

**totally** ['tot ə li] *adv.* completely; entirely. □ *I'm totally exhausted. I need a nap.*

**tote** ['tot] *tv.* to carry something. □ *I had to tote my own golf clubs all day.*

**touch** ['tʌtʃ] **1.** *tv.* to place one's finger, hand, or some other body part on someone or something. □ *I touched the*

T

*button inside the elevator.* **2.** *tv.* to place one object against another; to place one object on another. □ *The blind man touched the edge of the sidewalk with his cane.* **3.** *tv.* to border something; to share a border with something. □ *Panama touches both the Atlantic Ocean and the Pacific Ocean.* **4.** *tv.* to make contact with something; to have no space between two or more objects. (No actual movement is involved.) □ *The edge of the carpet touches the wall on all four sides.* **5.** *tv.* to affect someone, especially in a sad way. □ *The young woman's story touched me deeply.* **6.** *tv.* to handle something; to use something. (Especially in negative constructions.) □ *Don't touch the paintings that hang on the walls of the museum.* **7.** *iv.* [for things or people] to make contact or be in contact. □ *The two lovers touched when they met.* **8.** *n.* an instance of placing of one's finger or hand on someone or something. □ *Jane responded to John's touch with a slap.* **9.** *n.* someone's handling or gentle pressure as sensed by the person being **touched** as in ①. (No plural form.) □ *The baby missed his mother's touch when she wasn't near him.* **10.** *n.* a detail that improves something or adds to something. □ *The vase of flowers on the dinner table was a nice touch.* **11.** *n.* a small amount of something; a little bit of something. □ *The cook put a touch of salt in the soup.* **12.** *n.* a special or unique skill or style; evidence of one's skill or style. □ *Even at her age, the veteran golfer had not lost her touch.*

T

**touchy** ['tʌtʃ i] *adj.* easily angered; easily upset; irritable; too sensitive. (Adv: *touchily.* Comp: *touchier;* sup: *touchiest.*) □ *I can't even joke with my touchy brother.*

**tough** ['tʌf] **1.** *adj.* not tender; difficult to chew. (Comp: *tougher;* sup: *toughest.*) □ *The overcooked chicken was very tough.* **2.** *adj.* hard to do; difficult; not easy. (Comp: *tougher;* sup: *toughest.*) □ *This math problem is really tough!* **3.** *adj.* strong and determined; not weak. (Adv: *toughly.* Comp: *tougher;* sup: *toughest.*) □ *The tough football player could lift 200 pounds over his head.* **4.** *adj.* stubborn; not likely to have a change of mind. (Adv: *toughly.* Comp: *tougher;* sup: *toughest.*) □ *The residents remained in tough opposition to the building project.* **5.** *adj.* rough; violent; dangerous. (Adv: *toughly.* Comp: *tougher;* sup: *toughest.*) □ *The criminal grew up in a tough neighborhood.* **6.** *adj.* unfortunate; unlucky. (Comp: *tougher;* sup: *toughest.*) □ *The unfortunate woman had a very tough life.* **7.** *n.* a criminal; someone who is violent or dangerous. □ *The toughs in the jail cell all glared at each other.*

**tour** ['tʊ ɚ] **1.** *n.* a trip in which several places of interest are visited; a trip in which one visits an interesting place. □ *When I was in Rome, I went on a guided tour of the city.* **2.** *tv.* to travel through a place; to move through a place for entertainment. □ *Jane toured all the castles in Belgium.* **3.** *tv.* [for a performance and its performers] to visit or travel to many places in order to be seen. □ *The jazz band toured small college towns.* **4.** *iv.* to travel around from place to place in order to be seen. □ *Mary saw that art exhibit the last time it toured.*

**tourism** ['tʊɚ ɪz əm] **1.** *n.* travel; visiting interesting places, especially for a vacation. (No plural form.) □ *Violence and unrest hurt tourism in several Caribbean islands.* **2.** *n.* the business of attracting and serving tourists. (No plural form.) □ *I work in tourism and get to visit exciting places for free.*

**tourist** ['tʊɚ ɪst] **1.** *n.* someone who travels for pleasure. □ *A tourist asked me how to get to the lake.* **2.** *adj.* <the adj. use of ①.> □ *Flights to Florida were heavily booked during tourist season.*

**tournament** ['tʊɚ nə mənt] *n.* a contest involving several people or teams who play several games in such a way that the winner of one game plays the winner of another game until there is only one champion remaining. □ *Our school was selected to participate in the basketball tournament.*

**tow** ['to] **1.** *tv.* to pull something with a rope or chain. □ *The truck towed a car that wouldn't run.* **2.** *n.* an instance of pulling something with a rope or chain. □ *The stranded motorist had to pay $100 for a tow during the storm.*

**toward(s)** ['tord(z)] **1.** *prep.* [facing] in a certain direction; facing someone. □ *I turned toward John when he called me.* **2.** *prep.* in relation to or about someone or something. □ *I have no ill will toward my neighbor.* **3.** *prep.* just before a certain time. □ *Toward noon, we ate lunch.* **4.** *prep.* as a payment to someone or something. □ *Your contribution will go toward building a new hospital.*

**towel** ['tɑʊ əl] *n.* a piece of cloth or paper that is used to take away moisture. □ *John dried the dishes with a clean towel.*

**tower** ['tɑʊ ɚ] *n.* a tall building or structure; a tall part of a building or structure. □ *The treasure was kept in the highest tower of the castle.*

**town** ['tɑʊn] **1.** *n.* an area where people live that is smaller than a city but larger than a village. □ *Anne lives in a small town south of Philadelphia.* **2.** *n.* the part of a city where the businesses, stores, and markets are found. (No plural form.) □ *The new suburban shopping mall caused many stores in town to close.* **3.** *n.* a city. □ *What's the largest town in Michigan?* **4.** *n.* all the people who live in a **town** ①. □ *Most of the town works at the local car factory.* **5.** *adj.* <the adj. use of ①.> □ *The vendor sold hot dogs in the town square.*

**toy** ['tɔɪ] **1.** *n.* something that is made to amuse a child. □ *Susie put her toys away when she was finished playing with them.* **2.** *adj.* made to be played with. □ *John tripped on his child's toy cars.*

**trace** ['tres] **1.** *n.* a very small amount of something. □ *I smelled a trace of perfume in the air.* **2.** *tv.* to draw or copy the outline of something by putting a thin piece of paper on top of it and then drawing over the lines one sees through the thin paper. □ *Mary traced the picture of the cow and then colored it with crayons.* **3.** *tv.* to follow the path of something's growth, development, or history. □ *These pictures trace the growth of my children.* **4.** *tv.* to seek the origin of something. □ *The police detective traced the annoying phone calls.*

**track** ['træk] **1.** *n.* the marks made by a vehicle, person, or animal traveling from place to place. □ *John didn't wipe his shoes clean, so he left tracks on the rug.* **2.** *n.* a pair of parallel metal rails that trains travel on. □ *No train was coming, so John drove across the track.* **3.** *n.* a trail; a path; a rough road. □ *Snow covered the only track to the remote village.* **4.** *n.* a circular pathway used for running or racing. □ *Each lap around this track is a quarter of a mile.* **5.** *n.* a group of sports activities including running, jumping, and other tests of individual endurance and strength. (No plural form.) □ *Training for track, John ran 10 miles every day.* **6.** *tv.* to follow the trail of a person or other creature. □ *The detective tracked the criminal across the country.*

**traction** ['træk ʃən] *n.* the grip of a wheel or shoe on a surface that allows the wheel or shoe to apply energy to the surface in order to move ahead. (No plural form.) □ *The jogger's shoes have excellent traction.*

**tractor** ['træk tɚ] *n.* a motor vehicle with large, thick tires, used for pulling farm equipment in fields. □ *The plow was pulled behind the tractor.*

**trade** ['tred] **1.** *n.* the business of buying and selling products. (No plural form.) □ *The nation practiced free trade with its neighboring countries.* **2.** *n.* a particular business. □ *What trade are you in?* **3.** *n.* a job that utilizes a skill. □ *The plumbing trade requires years of training.* **4.** *n.* the exchange of someone or something for someone or something else. □ *I regretted my trade of 4 rare stamps for 12 old maps.* **5.** *tv.* to exchange someone or something for someone or something else. □ *The baseball team traded a new pitcher for an old catcher.* **6.** *iv.* to exchange; to swap. □ *I traded with Bill because I liked his lunch better than mine.*

**trademark** ['tred mɑrk] **1.** *n.* a word, name, or symbol—used and owned by a manufacturer—that identifies a product. □ *The symbol for a trademark is ™.* **2.** *n.* a mark or feature that is associated with a certain person or thing. (Fig. on ①.) □ *My teacher's trademark is her colorful clothing.* **3.** *tv.* [for a manufacturer] to protect ① by registering it with the government. □ *You cannot trademark that symbol, because someone else already owns the rights to use it.*

**trader** ['tred ɚ] *n.* a merchant; someone who buys and sells things as a business. □ *The trader sold 10,000 shares of the troubled company.*

**tradition** [trə 'dɪ ʃən] *n.* the way that something has been done from generation to generation. (Plural only when referring to different kinds, types, instances, or varieties.) □ *My family carefully follows religious tradition for Passover.* Ⓒ *Our family's traditions have existed for decades.*

**traditional** [trə 'dɪʃ ə nəl] *adj.* relating to tradition. (Adv: *traditionally.*) □ *Each week, the tribe performed traditional religious ceremonies.*

**traffic** ['træf ɪk] **1.** *n.* vehicles and their movement—or slowness of movement—on land, on water, or in the air. (No plural form.) □ *I'm late because I was caught in traffic.* **2.** *n.* the process of buying and selling. (No plural form.) □ *The agent monitored the traffic of goods into the country.*

**traffic jam** ['træf ɪk dʒæm] *n.* a situation in which vehicles on roads have stopped or slowed down because there are too many of them. □ *I was an hour late because I was stuck in a traffic jam.*

**traffic light** ['træf ɪk lɑɪt] *n.* a signal, usually found at intersections, used to control traffic by a system of lights. (Can be shortened to **light**.) □ *The city installed a traffic light at the busy intersection.*

**tragedy** ['træ dʒə di] **1.** *n.* a serious play that has a sad ending. □ Hamlet *and* Othello *are two Shakespearean tragedies.* **2.** *n.* a disaster; a sad, unfortunate, or terrible event. □ *It was a tragedy that the visitors were attacked.*

**tragic** ['træ dʒɪk] **1.** *adj.* of or about serious plays with sad endings. (Adv: *tragically* [...ɪk li].) □ Romeo and Juliet *is the tragic tale of two young lovers.* **2.** *adj.* sad; terrible; unfortunate. (Adv: *tragically* [...ɪk li].) □ *The poor man's life came to a tragic end when he was hit by a bus.*

**trail** ['trel] **1.** *n.* the marks made by a vehicle, person, or animal as it travels from place to place; the scent left by a person or animal as it travels from place to place. (See also **track**.) □ *John left a trail on the clean floor with his muddy shoes.* **2.** *n.* a path through an area that a car cannot travel over; a path for walking, biking, etc. □ *The trail to the cottage is covered with snow.* **3.** *tv.* to follow someone or an animal by its scent, footprints, or other clues that it leaves behind. □ *The detective trailed the criminal across town.* **4.** *tv.* to leave something dirty on a surface by walking or dragging something across it. □ *The*

T

*dying man trailed blood across the floor as he stumbled.*

**train** ['tren] **1.** *n.* a line of railroad cars pulled by an engine. □ *Susan took a train to St. Louis.* **2.** *tv.* to teach someone a skill; to give someone the knowledge needed to do a job. □ *My father trained me in the proper way to use the lawn mower.* **3.** *iv.* to prepare [oneself] for a job, a contest, or a performance. □ *The football team trains every day for two hours.*

**traitor** ['tret ɚ] *n.* one who betrays one's country or leader. □ *The traitor will be executed at dawn.*

**tramp** ['træmp] **1.** *n.* someone who lives by begging; a male who lives on the streets and does not have a home. □ *Security guards removed the tramp from the private office building.* **2.** *n.* the sound of someone marching. (No plural form.) □ *The tramp of the soldier's boots alerted us to the danger.* **3.** *iv.* to walk heavily or steadily. □ *The hikers tramped through the newly fallen snow.*

**transaction** [træn 'zæk ʃən] *n.* a business deal; an agreement or negotiation that has been completed. □ *The illegal transaction was filmed on videotape.*

**transfer** ['træns fɚ] **1.** *n.* the movement of something from one place to another place. (No plural form.) □ *Jane's transfer of funds was carried out electronically.* **2.** *n.* a ticket that allows someone to get off one vehicle, usually a bus, and get on another one without paying a second fare. □ *I handed my transfer to the bus driver.* **3.** *iv.* to move from one vehicle to another; to get off one vehicle and get on another one. □ *Mary transferred at the station to a different train.* **4.** *iv.* to move from one site to another site. □ *The gifted student transferred away from the local school.* **5.** *tv.* to move something from one place to another place. □ *The broker transferred his investments out of the bond market.* **6.** *tv.* to cause someone to move from one job site to another job site. □ *Mary was transferred from Chicago and had to sell her house.*

**transform** [træns 'form] *tv.* to change something's or someone's shape, form, nature, or appearance. □ *Stage makeup transformed the actor from a man into a cat.*

**transfusion** [træns 'fju ʒən] *n.* the process of transferring blood from one person to another. □ *Anne had three transfusions before she started getting better.*

**transistor** [træn 'zɪs tɚ] *n.* a small electrical device that controls the flow of current in electronic circuits. □ *When the transistor failed, the radio stopped working.*

**transit** ['træn zɪt] **1.** *n.* transportation; movement of people or goods. (No plural form.) □ *John's transit to safety was dangerous and courageous.* **2. in transit** *phr.* while in the process of being transported. □ *The new stereo is now in transit from the manufacturer.*

**transitive verb** ['træn sə tɪv 'vɚb] *n.* a verb that is used with a **direct object**; a verb that requires a **direct object**. (Abbreviated *tv.* here.) □ *In the sentence* I rode the bike, rode *is a transitive verb.*

**translate** ['træn slet] **1.** *tv.* to change something written or spoken from one language to another. □ *The guard translated the sign into English for me.* **2.** *iv.* to change [something written or spoken in one language] to another language. □ *My friend translated while I gave my short speech.*

**translation** [trænz 'le ʃən] *n.* changing a message in one language into an equivalent message in another language; changing a sequence of symbols in one code into another code. (Plural only when referring to different kinds, types, instances, or varieties.) □ *We need someone who can supervise the translation of*

T

*this document.* Ⓒ *Hundreds of translations of the Bible have been prepared.*

**translator** ['trænz le tɚ] *n.* someone who translates sentences of one language into another. □ *I asked the translator to tell the guard that I was an American.*

**transmit** [trænz 'mɪt] *tv.* to send information by way of electricity or radio waves. □ *The radio station plans to transmit its broadcasts from a satellite.*

**transmitter** ['trænz mɪt ɚ] *n.* a piece of electronic equipment that transmits electromagnetic waves, as for radio or television. □ *The TV station went off the air when its transmitter was damaged.*

**transparent** [trænz 'pɛr ənt] **1.** *adj.* clear and able to be seen through. (Adv: *transparently.*) □ *The lenses of my glasses are made of transparent plastic.* **2.** *adj.* obvious; easily recognized; [of something meant to deceive] easy to figure out. (Fig. on ①. Adv: *transparently.*) □ *My reasons for leaving town were transparent to my friends.*

**transport** ['trænz port] **1.** *n.* carrying things or people from one place to another. (No plural form.) □ *All the transport of goods between states is regulated.* **2.** *tv.* to carry someone or something from one place to another. □ *The car parts were transported from the factory by train.*

**transportation** [trænz pɚ 'te ʃən] **1.** *n.* the system of moving people and goods from one place to another. (No plural form.) □ *My preferred mode of transportation is driving.* **2.** *n.* moving people or goods from one place to another. (No plural form.) □ *The transportation of lettuce requires refrigerated vehicles.*



**trap** ['træp] **1.** *n.* a device used to catch animals or people. □ *Mary baited the mouse trap with cheese.* **2.** *n.* a bend in a drain pipe in which water rests in order to prevent harmful gases from the sewer into a building. □ *Mary's ring fell down the sink, but she found it in the trap.* **3.** *tv.* to catch someone or something in ①. □ *Bob trapped the mouse in the garage and put it in the garbage.* **4.** *tv.* to prevent someone or something from escaping, leaving, or getting out. □ *An earthquake trapped the hikers inside the cave.*

**trapper** ['træp ɚ] *n.* someone who traps animals, skins them, and sells the pelts. □ *Some merchants from the east bought all the furs from the trappers.*

**trash** ['træʃ] **1.** *n.* things that are thrown away; rubbish; refuse. (No plural form.) □ *John took the trash out to the bin in the alley.* **2.** *tv.* to throw something away. (Slang.) □ *Who trashed my old sweatshirt? I wanted to keep it.*

**trauma** ['trɔ mə] **1.** *n.* an emotional shock; an emotional response to an emotional shock. □ *The trauma caused by the explosion haunted John for years.* **2.** *n.* an injury; a wound; damage to the body. □ *The surgeon repaired the trauma near the victim's eye.*

**travel** ['træv əl] **1.** *iv.* to visit [places other than where one lives]; to journey. □ *I have plans to travel to Asia next year.* **2.** *iv.* to move through space; to move across a distance. □ *The rocket traveled through space at a great speed.* **3.** *tv.* to move on a path or route as one **travels** ①. □ *I traveled the main highway from Des Moines to Chicago.* **4.** *tv.* to move over a specific distance as one **travels** ①. □ *Tom traveled 10 miles, and then his car ran out of gas.* **5.** *n.* going to and visiting places other than where one lives. (No plural form.) □ *I couldn't afford any travel while I was a student.* **6. travels** *n.* [someone's] journeys or visits to other places, especially over a long period of time. □ *I wrote a long letter to my parents about my travels during the summer.* **7.** *adj.* <the adj. use of

⑤.> □ *The travel guide listed the names of good hotels.*

**traveler** ['træv lɚ] *n.* someone who travels; someone who goes on trips or journeys. □ *The hotel near the train station lodges many travelers.*

**tray** ['tre] *n.* a flat panel with a slightly raised rim, used to carry things, especially food. □ *The waitress brought our food on a tray.*

**treasure** ['trɛ ʒɚ] **1.** *n.* valuable objects, especially ones that are stored; someone or something that is highly valued. □ *Mrs. Smith kept her art treasures locked in a vault.* **2.** *tv.* to value someone or something highly. □ *Mike treasured his new computer.*

**treasurer** ['trɛ ʒɚ ɚ] *n.* someone who is in charge of the money of an organization or unit of government. □ *The signature of the treasurer must appear on all company checks.*

**treasury** ['trɛ ʒə ri] **1.** *n.* the money that is owned by an organization or unit of government. □ *There is nothing left in the treasury, and the bank refuses to lend us any money.* **2.** *n.* the department of a government in charge of spending and saving public money. □ *The U.S. Treasury is in charge of issuing money.*

**treat** ['trit] **1.** *n.* a bit of tasty food, such as candy or ice cream. □ *Mother gave us all treats because we were quiet.* **2.** *n.* something that is pleasing. □ *It was a treat to go shopping with you.* **3. someone's treat** *n.* someone's act of kindness in paying for someone else's meal or entertainment. □ *Where would you like to eat? It's my treat.* **4.** *tv.* to handle or consider someone or something in a certain way. □ *Please stop treating me like a child!* **5.** *tv.* to try to cure something. □ *Mary treated her cold by drinking hot tea.*

**treatment** ['trit mənt] **1.** *n.* the way someone or something is dealt with. (No plural form.) □ *The enemy's treatment of the hostages was relatively good.* **2.** *n.* the method by which someone tries to cure someone. □ *Surgery is only one of the treatments for cancer.* **3.** *n.* the way in which a story or script is presented. □ *The director's treatment of the dead president's biography was criticized.*

**treaty** ['trit i] *n.* a formal agreement between two or more nations. □ *The small country broke the treaty four days after signing it.*

**tree** ['tri] **1.** *n.* a tall plant whose stem and branches are made of wood, and that often has leaves growing from the branches. □ *We cut down the dead tree in our front yard.* **2.** *n.* a diagram that represents the relationship between different levels or positions of power by expressing them as branches at different levels. □ *John's family tree goes back to the 18th century.*

**tree house** ['tri hɑʊs] *n., irreg.* a platform or structure built in a tree for children to play in. (Pl: [...hɑʊ zəz].) □ *From their tree house, Mary and John threw snowballs down at me.*

**treetop** ['tri tɑp] *n.* the top of a tree. □ *The kite soared above the treetops.*

**trek** ['trɛk] **1.** *n.* a long journey, often done walking. □ *I went on a long trek across the state.* **2.** *iv.* to travel on a long journey, often on foot. □ *John trekked across America.*

**tremendous** [trɪ 'mɛn dəs] **1.** *adj.* huge; enormous; very large; immense. (Adv: *tremendously.*) □ *John is unable to repay his tremendous debts.* **2.** *adj.* wonderful; excellent; superb. (Adv: *tremendously.*) □ *I always eat Thanksgiving dinner at John's house because he's a tremendous cook.*

**trial** ['trɑɪl] **1.** *n.* the examining of the evidence in a court of law by a judge or jury to settle a legal question, such as guilt or innocence. □ *The judge who*

T

*presided over my trial was completely fair.* **2.** *n.* an experiment; a test to see if something works; a test to see if something provides a benefit. □ *Susan explained the results of her experiment's first trial.* **3.** *n.* a difficult ordeal; a problem; a disease and the problems it causes. □ *Jane's unruly children were a daily trial.* **4.** *adj.* concerning the first test or an early attempt to get results. □ *The trial results looked very good to the scientist.* **5.** *adj.* <the adj. use of ①.> □ *The court recorder transcribed the trial proceedings.*

**triangle** ['trɑɪ æŋ gəl] **1.** *n.* a figure that has three sides and three angles. □ *I cut the square into two triangles.* **2.** *n.* a flat, three-sided object with three sides, used for drawing lines and angles. □ *These angles were drawn with the aid of a triangle.* **3.** *n.* a metal musical instrument in the shape of ①, that is struck with a small rod to make a ringing noise. □ *The conductor placed the triangle near the drummer.*

**tribe** ['trɑɪb] *n.* a group of people having the same customs, religion, language, and culture; a local division of a larger ethnic group. □ *The two tribes fought a huge battle every year at harvest time.*

**tribute** ['trɪb jut] *n.* a show of respect or honor. □ *Lisa's acceptance speech was a tribute to her parents.*

**trick** ['trɪk] **1.** *n.* something that is done to deceive someone. □ *Jimmy played a funny trick on his parents.* **2.** *adj.* made to be used in ①; intended to deceive. □ *Mary's trick cards are secretly marked on the back.* **3. play a trick on** someone *phr.* to do a **trick** ① that affects someone. □ *The little boys planned to play a trick on their teacher by turning up the heat in the classroom.*

**tricky** ['trɪk i] **1.** *adj.* difficult to do; puzzling; hard to deal with. (Adv: *trickily.* Comp: *trickier;* sup: *trickiest.*) □ *Assembling appliances can be tricky without a manual.* **2.** *adj.* full of tricks; clever and good at deceiving people. (Adv: *trickily.* Comp: *trickier;* sup: *trickiest.*) □ *I don't trust Jane because she is very tricky.*

**tricycle** ['trɑɪ sɪk əl] *n.* a small vehicle with three wheels, two in back and one in front, made for young children to ride on. □ *Jimmy keeps his tricycle in the garage.*

**trigger** ['trɪg ɚ] **1.** *n.* the small lever on a gun, used to fire the gun. □ *John pulled the trigger and shot the robber.* **2.** *n.* something that causes something else to happen. (Fig. on ①.) □ *John's movement was the trigger that set off the alarm.* **3.** *tv.* to cause something to happen; to cause something that starts a sequence of events. □ *The rise in interest rates was triggered by inflation.*

**trillion** ['trɪl jən] **1.** *n.* the number 1,000,000,000,000. (Additional numbers formed as with *two trillion, three trillion, four trillion,* etc.) □ *One million times one million is one trillion.* **2.** *n.* a group of 1,000,000,000,000 things or people. □ *There must have been over a trillion at the beach today!* **3.** *adj.* consisting of 1,000,000,000,000 things. □ *There must be a trillion water molecules in the ocean!*

**trillionth** ['trɪl jənθ] 1,000,000,000,000th. Go to **fourth** for senses and examples.

**trilogy** ['trɪl ə dʒi] *n.* a set of three books, plays, movies, etc., that share a common theme or characters and events. □ *The writer wrote a trilogy of horror stories.*

**trim** ['trɪm] **1.** *tv.* to make something neat by cutting; to cut something neatly. □ *The gardener trimmed the hedges.* **2.** *tv.* to reduce something; to decrease something. □ *The butcher trimmed the fat from the meat.* **3.** *tv.* to decorate something. □ *Mary trimmed the old dress with a silk sash.* **4.** *adj.* [of someone] thin and of the proper weight. (Adv: *trimly.* Comp: *trimmer;* sup: *trimmest.*)

☐ *Grandma is very trim for someone her age.* **5.** *n.* the wood around a door or window. ☐ *The trim around the door split when I pounded a nail into it.*

**trio** ['tri o] **1.** *n.* a group of three, especially a group of three performers. (Pl ends in *-s.*) ☐ *Anne and her two best friends are an accomplished trio.* **2.** *n.* a piece of music written for three instruments or three voices. (Pl ends in *-s.*) ☐ *The musician wrote a trio for three sopranos.*

**trip** ['trɪp] **1.** *n.* a journey between two places; a journey from one place to another. ☐ *Jane went on a business trip to Texas.* **2.** *iv.* to stumble; to fall over something; to hit one's foot against someone or something, causing a loss of balance. ☐ *There were toys all over the floor, causing Mary to trip.* **3.** *tv.* to cause someone to fall; to cause someone to stumble and lose balance. ☐ *The loose board tripped John when he walked past it.* **4.** *tv.* to release a lever or a switch, thus causing something to function. ☐ *Mary tripped the lever to reset the fuse.*

**tripod** ['traɪ pɑd] *n.* a support or stand that has three legs, especially one that supports a camera. ☐ *The small movie screen was attached to a metal tripod.*

**trite** ['traɪt] *adj.* [of an expression] shallow and simple-minded. (Adv: *tritely.* Comp: *triter;* sup: *tritest.*) ☐ *The speech was filled with trite arguments for new economic policies.*

**triumph** ['traɪ əmf] **1.** *n.* celebration; the glory of victory; a victory. (Plural only when referring to different kinds, types, instances, or varieties.) ☐ *In our moment of triumph, let's not forget those who made it all possible.* Ⓒ *Winning the game was one of the great triumphs for our team.* **2.** *iv.* to win; to be very successful. ☐ *We worked hard to win, and we triumphed.*

**trolley** ['trɑ li] *n.* a vehicle that is operated by electricity and runs along a track in the street. ☐ *Mary took a trolley from her apartment to work.*

**trombone** [trɑm 'bon] *n.* a brass musical instrument, played by blowing air into one end with tensed lips, while moving a long sliding part into different positions. ☐ *Eight people played trombones in the marching band.*

**troop** ['trup] **1.** *n.* a group of people or animals, especially a group of soldiers. ☐ *What troop are you in?* **2. troops** *n.* soldiers. (Treated as plural, but not countable.) ☐ *The general ordered the troops into battle.* **3.** *iv.* to walk or move as a group. ☐ *The soldiers trooped across the base.*

**trooper** ['trup ɚ] *n.* an officer in the state police, usually the highway patrol. (Short for **state trooper**.) ☐ *There is a trooper behind you flashing his red light. You had better pull over.*

**trophy** ['tro fi] **1.** *n.* something that is taken from a battle or a hunt as a symbol of one's success. ☐ *The soldiers kept trophies from the villages they captured.* **2.** *n.* a small statue or prize that is given to the winner of an event or contest. ☐ *My bowling team won the league trophy last night.*

**tropic** ['trɑp ɪk] **1.** *n.* one of two imaginary circles around the earth, 23.45 degrees north and south of the equator. ☐ *The tropic of Cancer is in the Northern Hemisphere.* **2. the tropics** *n.* the area between the two **tropics** ①; the areas of the earth near the equator. (Treated as singular or plural.) ☐ *The country of Indonesia is located in the tropics.* **3.** *adj.* **tropical**; hot and humid. ☐ *I fainted in the tropic heat.*

**tropical** ['trɑp ɪ kəl] *adj.* of or about the tropics; of or about the weather conditions of the tropics; found in the tropics. (Adv: *tropically* [...ɪk li].) ☐ *Most bananas are grown on tropical plantations.*

T

**trot** ['trɑt] **1.** *n.* the movement of a horse between a walk and a gallop; the movement of a human between a walk and a run. □ *My short morning trots through the park are healthful.* **2.** *iv.* to move faster than walking, but not as fast as running. □ *The horse trotted all the way back to the barn.*

**trouble** ['trʌb əl] **1.** *n.* worry; difficulty; anxiety. □ *Dave's boss causes him too much trouble at work.* **2.** *n.* annoyance; bother. □ *John's unruly children are real trouble for him.* **3.** *n.* a sickness; a health problem. □ *John takes medicine for his heart trouble.* **4.** *n.* someone or something that causes worry, difficulty, anxiety, irritation, bother, or problems. □ *Those kids are trouble, and I refuse to babysit them.* **5.** *tv.* to worry someone; to cause someone difficulty or anxiety. □ *The new budget troubled the office manager.* **6.** *tv.* to bother or delay someone with an inquiry. □ *The students troubled the teacher with silly questions.* **7.** *tv.* to cause someone to feel pain. □ *My sore feet trouble me a lot.*

**troublesome** ['trʌb əl səm] *adj.* causing trouble; causing problems. (Adv: *troublesomely.*) □ *I have a troublesome ache in my back.*

**trousers** ['trɑʊ zɚz] *n.* pants; a piece of clothing worn below the waist, having a separate tube, hole, or compartment for each leg and extending to the ankles. (Treated as plural. Number is expressed with *pair(s) of trousers.* Rarely singular.) □ *John bought a new pair of trousers for his friend's wedding.*

**trout** ['trɑʊt] **1.** *n., irreg.* a freshwater fish commonly eaten as food. (Pl: *trout.*) □ *The trout quickly swam away from my lure.* **2.** *n.* the flesh of ①, eaten as food. (No plural form.) □ *I would like some trout and boiled potatoes.*

**trowel** ['trɑʊ əl] **1.** *n.* a tool used to apply and smooth mortar or plaster. □ *The mason scooped up some mortar with his trowel and placed it on the top level of bricks.* **2.** *n.* a tool used in gardening for digging small holes and planting individual plants. □ *When I plant small plants, I use a trowel rather than a shovel.*

**truant** ['tru ənt] **1.** *adj.* absent from school without permission. (Adv: *truantly.*) □ *The parents of the truant students were called by the principal.* **2.** *n.* someone who is absent from school without permission. □ *The principal found some truants at the fast-food restaurant.*

**truce** ['trus] *n.* an agreement to stop fighting. □ *The rebels broke the truce by bombing the market square.*

**truck** ['trʌk] **1.** *n.* a large motor vehicle designed to carry objects or cargo rather than people. □ *The worker loaded the car parts onto the truck.* **2.** *adj.* <the adj. use of ①.> □ *John works at a truck factory.* **3.** *tv.* to transport something by ①. □ *The farmer trucked the crops to the market.*

**true** ['tru] **1.** *adj.* being a fact; actual; real; not false. (Adv: *truly.* Comp: *truer;* sup: *truest.*) □ *John's statement expressed a true proposition.* **2.** *adj.* sincere; genuine; not fake; not artificial. (Adv: *truly.* Comp: *truer;* sup: *truest.*) □ *David is a true friend of mine.* **3.** *adj.* properly fitted; at the proper angle. (Adv: *truly.* Comp: *truer;* sup: *truest.*) □ *The joint was not true and was finally knocked loose.*

**truly** ['tru li] *adv.* really; honestly; genuinely. □ *We truly hope you enjoy your stay in town.*

**trumpet** ['trʌmp ɪt] **1.** *n.* a brass musical instrument on which different notes are produced by blowing air into one end while pressing different combinations of three valves. □ *When I heard the trumpet blare, I knew the king had arrived.* **2.** *iv.* [for an elephant] to make a characteristic elephant noise. □ *The* *huge elephant ran toward the keeper and trumpeted loudly.*

**trunk** ['trʌŋk] **1.** *n.* the main stem of a tree. □ *I sawed through the trunk of the dead tree.* **2.** *n.* the body of a human without its head, arms, or legs. □ *The biology teacher showed a diagram of a human trunk, which is also called a torso.* **3.** *n.* a large, sturdy box for transporting or storing clothes or other objects. □ *I keep my sweaters in a large trunk during the summer.* **4.** *n.* the long, tube-shaped nose of an elephant. □ *The elephant picked up some hay with its trunk.* **5. trunks** *n.* a swimming suit for men. (Treated as plural. Number is expressed with *pair(s) of trunks.*) □ *Bill's trunks slipped down when he dove into the water.*

**trust** ['trʌst] **1.** *n.* a strong belief in the honesty of someone or something. (No plural form.) □ *Trust is important in a good relationship.* **2.** *tv.* to believe in the honesty of someone or something. □ *My parents trusted me to behave when they went out to dinner.* **3.** *tv.* to hope something. (The object is a clause with that ⑦.) □ *I trust that you're merely joking about my dinner.*

**truth** ['truθ] **1.** *n.* the quality of being true or a fact. (No plural form.) □ *Bill and Jane love to debate about truth and philosophy.* **2.** *n.* a fact; a true state. □ *There are a few basic truths that we all must remember.*

**truthful** ['truθ fʊl] **1.** *adj.* [of a statement] able to be proven as true. (Adv: *truthfully.*) □ *"Snow is white" is a truthful statement.* **2.** *adj.* regularly telling the truth; honest. (Adv: *truthfully.*) □ *The truthful man returned the extra change to the cashier.*

**try** ['trɑɪ] **1.** *iv.* to make an attempt. □ *Although Anne tried very hard, she couldn't do it.* **2. try to** do something *iv.* + *inf.* to attempt to do something. □ *Anne tried to run, but her feet hurt.* **3.** *tv.* to use something to see if one likes it; to test something to see if it works well. □ *You should try my new bicycle!* **4.** *tv.* [for a judge or jury] to hear a [legal] case in a court of law. □ *They will try Anne's case next week.* **5.** *tv.* [for a judge or jury] to subject an accused person to a trial in a court of law. □ *The jury that tried Anne had to spend a week in the courthouse.* **6.** *n.* an attempt; an effort to do something. □ *Mary didn't pass the French test until her third try.*

**T-shirt** ['ti ʃɚt] *n.* a light, cotton shirt with short sleeves and no collar. □ *I'm wearing a T-shirt under my sweater.*

**tub** ['tʌb] **1.** *n.* a large, round or oval container with a flat bottom. □ *The cook put the peeled potatoes in a large tub of water.* **2.** *n.* a bathtub. □ *The children played with plastic boats in the tub.*

**tuba** ['tub ə] *n.* a large brass instrument that makes very low notes. (**Tubas** are also sometimes made of lighter-weight material.) □ *The composer wrote the bass line for the tuba.*

**tube** ['tub] **1.** *n.* a hollow pipe used for holding or conveying something. □ *The painting was rolled up and placed in a cardboard tube.* **2.** *n.* a soft container that holds paste, such as toothpaste, icing, or medicine. □ *There's a tube of toothpaste in the drawer.*

**tuck** ['tʌk] **1. tuck** something **into** something *tv.* + *obj.* + *prep. phr.* to slip something flat and flexible into a space. □ *David tucked the money into his wallet.* **2. tuck** something **in** *tv.* + *obj.* + *adv.* to make something neater by slipping it into the place it belongs. □ *There is a sock sticking out of your suitcase. Tuck it in.* 🅃 *Please tuck in that sock!* **3.** *n.* a fold that is sewn shut to make an item of clothing shorter or fit tighter. □ *When Mary lost weight, she put some tucks in her pants.*

**Tuesday** ['tjuz de] Go to day.

T

**tug** ['tʌg] **1.** *n.* a hard pull; a yank. ☐ *I felt a tug on the back of my coat.* **2. tug at** someone or something; **tug on** someone or something *iv.* + *prep. phr.* to pull at someone or something with force. ☐ *I tugged at the door, but it was locked.*

**tulip** ['tu ləp] *n.* a flower with a bright, colorful, cup-shaped bloom. ☐ *Anne planted a row of tulips in front of the porch.*

**tumble** ['tʌm bəl] **1.** *n.* a fall. ☐ *Mary took a tumble when she slipped on the ice.* **2.** *iv.* to fall over; to fall accidentally; to fall helplessly. ☐ *I tripped on my shoelace and tumbled into a bush.*

**tummy** ['tʌm i] *n.* the stomach or belly. (Informal; used especially with children.) ☐ *Tom scratched the puppy's tummy.*

**tumor** ['tu mɚ] *n.* a group or cluster of diseased cells in a body that grow independently of the surrounding tissue or structure. ☐ *The doctor said that my tumor was not cancer.*

**tuna** ['tu nə] **1.** *n., irreg.* a large ocean fish, commonly used for food. (Pl: *tuna* or *tunas.*) ☐ *The boat held two huge tunas.* **2. tuna (fish)** *n.* the flesh of ①, eaten as food. (No plural form.) ☐ *Fresh tuna is very different from the canned tuna that is used in sandwiches.* **3. tuna(-fish)** *adj.* made with or flavored with ②. ☐ *John ate a tuna-fish sandwich for lunch.*

T

**tune** ['tun] **1.** *n.* a melody; a piece of music or a song. ☐ *Mary whistled a happy tune.* **2.** *tv.* to adjust a musical instrument so that its tones are at the proper intervals from each other. ☐ *Your piano needs to be tuned!* **3.** *tv.* to adjust something so that it works properly. ☐ *I tuned the television so that the picture was clearer.*

**tunnel** ['tʌn əl] **1.** *n.* a passage that is underground, underwater, or through a mountain. ☐ *A tunnel under the English Channel connects England with France.* **2.** *iv.* to make a passage that goes underground, underwater, or through a mountain. ☐ *The dog tunneled under the fence.*

**turbine** ['tɚ bɪn] *n.* a large engine or motor that is powered by pressure from wind, water, or some other liquid or gas. ☐ *We get our electricity from wind-powered turbines.*

**turd** ['tɚd] *n.* a lump of fecal material. (Potentially offensive. Use only with care. Colloquial.) ☐ *There are some little mouse turds in the kitchen.*

**turf** ['tɚf] **1.** *n.* the surface of soil with plants or grass growing on it. (No plural form.) ☐ *The farmer fertilized the turf with nutrients.* **2.** *n.* the area that is controlled by a person or group of people. (Usually singular.) ☐ *John accused me of making a sales call on his turf.*

**turkey** ['tɚ ki] **1.** *n.* a large fowl that is often raised for its meat. ☐ *Some turkeys weigh over 30 pounds.* **2.** *n.* the meat of ① used as food. (No plural form.) ☐ *Turkey is my favorite food at Thanksgiving dinner.* **3.** *adj.* made with ②. ☐ *We ate turkey stew for dinner.*

**turn** ['tɚn] **1.** *tv.* to move something around in a circle or an arc; to cause something to move in a circle or an arc. ☐ *I turned the bicycle's wheel to make sure it was securely attached.* **2.** *tv.* to aim a moving object or vehicle in a different direction. ☐ *David turned his car east on Maple Street.* **3.** *tv.* to change the position of something, such as an electrical switch lever or handle. ☐ *Please turn that switch to the "off" position.* **4.** *tv.* to reach a certain age. ☐ *We had a party for Mary because she turned 21 yesterday.* **5. turn into** something *iv.* + *prep. phr.* to change to a particular condition or state; to become something. ☐ *My happiness quickly turned into sadness.* **6.** *iv.* to go in a different direction; to change direction. ☐ *The bus turned east* *at Maple Street.* **7.** *iv.* to change position by moving in a circle or an arc; to change position to face a different direction. □ *The taxi driver turned to ask me a question.* **8.** *iv.* to change, especially in form, state, color, or quality; to become some form, state, color, or quality. □ *The sky turned red just before the sun set.* **9.** *n.* the movement of something that is going in a circle. □ *The wheel squeaked loudly with each turn.* **10.** *n.* a change in direction. □ *There is a turn in this road up ahead.* **11.** *n.* a change in a situation; a change in circumstances. □ *The reporter commented on the latest turn in the scandal.* **12.** *n.* a chance to do something, especially when two or more people alternate an action in cycles. □ *It's your turn to wash the dishes.*

**turtle** ['tɚt əl] *n.* a reptile with a round body that is protected by a thick, hard, rounded shell. □ *Turtles walk very slowly.*

**tusk** ['tʌsk] *n.* a very long, pointed tooth that projects from the face of some kinds of animals. □ *An elephant's tusks are made of ivory.*

**tutor** ['tut ɚ] **1.** *n.* someone who is employed as a private teacher; a teacher who gives private lessons. □ *Susie read aloud to her tutor.* **2.** *tv.* to teach someone privately. □ *Anne was tutored by professionals throughout high school.* **3.** *iv.* to work as ①. □ *I decided to tutor to supplement my income.*

**tuxedo** [tək 'si do] *n.* a man's outfit for very formal occasions, including a black jacket, a white shirt, a black bow tie, and pants. (Pl ends in *-s.*) □ *David wore a tuxedo to the formal event.*

**tv.** an abbreviation of **transitive verb**.

**TV** ['ti 'vi] an abbreviation of **television, television set**.

**tweed** ['twid] **1.** *n.* a rough wool fabric. □ *Tweed feels rough against the skin.* **2.** *adj.* made of ①. □ *David wore a tweed suit to the banquet.*

**twelfth** ['twɛlfθ] 12th. Go to **fourth** for senses and examples.

**twelve** ['twɛlv] 12. Go to **four** for senses and examples.

**twentieth** ['twɛn ti əθ] 20th. Go to **fourth** for senses and examples.

**twenty** ['twɛn ti] 20. Go to **forty** for senses and examples.

**twice** ['twɑɪs] **1.** *adv.* two times; on two occasions. □ *I told David twice to leave me alone.* **2.** *adv.* two times as much; double. □ *Tuition rates increased twice as much as I thought they would.*

**twig** ['twɪg] *n.* a small branch. □ *The bird made its nest from grass and twigs.*

**twilight** ['twɑɪ lɑɪt] **1.** *n.* the time of day after the sun sets and before the sky is completely dark. (No plural form.) □ *Anne didn't leave the office until twilight.* **2.** *n.* the dim light at ①. □ *I could not read in the fading twilight, so I turned on a lamp.*

**twin** ['twɪn] **1.** *n.* one of two children born at the same time from the same mother; one of two offspring born at the same time from the same mother. □ *Anne gave birth to a pair of twins.* **2.** *n.* one of two things that are part of a matched set. □ *That cup's twin was broken years ago when I dropped it.* **3.** *adj.* [of two offspring] born at the same time from the same mother. □ *The lion had twin cubs.* **4.** *adj.* forming a pair of two things that are similar or matching. □ *I chose twin lamps so I could put one on each side of the sofa.*

**twine** ['twɑɪn] *n.* strong string made of two or more strands that are twisted together. (Plural only when referring to different kinds, types, instances, or varieties.) □ *I tied the mattress to the roof of my car with heavy twine.* 🄲 *Twines made of natural fibers are cheaper than synthetic twines.*

T

**twirl** ['twɚl] **1.** *tv.* to spin something; to move something in circles. □ *I twirled the rope over my head like a cowboy.* **2.** *iv.* to spin; to turn in circles. □ *The skater twirled in the air.* **3.** *n.* a spin; a circular movement. □ *The dancers' repeated twirls were very energetic.*

**twist** ['twɪst] **1.** *tv.* to turn something; to rotate something in an arc. □ *Anne twisted the screw into place.* **2.** *tv.* to injure a body part by turning it sharply. □ *Susan twisted her back when she picked up the box.* **3.** *tv.* to bend and turn part of something to change its shape. □ *Years of hard work had twisted the tailor's hands.* **4.** *iv.* to curve; to bend; to change shape or direction; to turn one part of a length of something while keeping another part in place. □ *The snake twisted and turned when I stepped on it.* **5.** *n.* a curve; a state resulting when one part of a length has been turned while another part stays in one space. □ *A twist in the hose kept the water from flowing.* **6.** *n.* the movement of twisting as in ①. □ *One twist and I had opened the jar of pickles!*

**two** ['tu] 2. Go to **four** for senses and examples.

**type** ['tɑɪp] **1.** *n.* a kind, sort, or category; a group of related things or people. □ *Mary wanted to buy the type of candles that her sister owned.* **2.** *n.* a block of wood or metal, with the raised shape of a letter or number on it, used in printing. (No plural form.) □ *Jane arranged the type for the headline.* **3.** *n.* a style or **type** ① of print, especially the shape or darkness that printed letters have. (No plural form.) □ *The first word of the paragraph was set in bold type.* **4.** *tv.* to write something using a keyboard. □ *Bill typed his paper on a typewriter because his computer was broken.* **5.** *iv.* to use a keyboard. □ *I typed as fast as I could.*

**typewriter** ['tɑɪp rɑɪ tɚ] *n.* a machine for printing letters onto paper. □ *I found my old typewriter when my computer broke.*

**typical** ['tɪp ɪ kəl] *adj.* average; usual; ordinary; regular; having the main qualities of a type of something. (Adv: *typically* [...ɪk li].) □ *In 1992, the life expectancy of a typical American woman was 72.*

**typo** ['tɑɪp o] *n.* an error made in printing or typing. (Pl ends in -*s*. Short for *typographical error*.) □ *The professor circled all of my typos with red ink.*

**tyranny** ['tɪr ə ni] *n.* the cruel and unfair use of government power. (No plural form.) □ *The refugees fled to America to escape tyranny.*

**tyrant** ['tɑɪ rənt] *n.* a ruler who is cruel and unfair. □ *The rebels who overthrew the tyrant were loved by the people.*

T

**ugly** [ˈʌg li] **1.** *adj.* not pleasant to look at; not attractive. (Comp: *uglier;* sup: *ugliest.*) □ *David sometimes felt he was very ugly.* **2.** *adj.* not pleasant; menacing. (Comp: *uglier;* sup: *ugliest.*) □ *The argument soon became an ugly fight.*

**ultimate** [ˈʌl tə mət] **1.** *adj.* final. (Adv: *ultimately.*) □ *The ultimate decision in hiring is made by the company president.* **2. the ultimate** *n.* the best thing or person; the most superior thing or person. (Informal. No plural form. Treated as singular.) □ *I love Tom because he's just the ultimate!*

**ultimately** [ˈʌl tə mət li] *adv.* in the end; at the final decision about an issue. □ *We will need a new car, ultimately.*

**umbrella** [əm ˈbrɛl ə] *n.* a dome-shaped wire frame connected to a handle and covered with waterproof fabric. □ *The strong wind blew the umbrella from David's hands.*

**umpire** [ˈʌm pɑɪɚ] **1.** *n.* a referee; someone who enforces the rules of certain sports; someone who judges the plays in certain sports. □ *An umpire stood along the third-base line, watching the players.* **2.** *iv.* to act as ①. □ *David umpires on the weekends.* **3.** *tv.* to referee a game; to judge the plays in certain sports. □ *Anne will umpire today's softball game.*

**unable** [ən ˈe bəl] **unable to do something** *adj.* + *inf.* not able to do something; not having the ability to do something. □ *I regret that I was unable to attend the party.*

**unafraid** [ən ə ˈfred] *adj.* not afraid; brave; without fear. □ *Jimmy is unafraid of the dark.*

**unanimous** [ju ˈnæn ə məs] *adj.* in complete agreement; agreed to by everyone; with everyone saying "yes." (Adv: *unanimously.*) □ *My friends and I made a unanimous decision to order pizza.*

**unarmed** [ən ˈɑrmd] *adj.* not armed; not carrying any weapons; without any weapons. □ *The unarmed man could not defend himself against the attack.*

**unassisted** [ən ə ˈsɪs tɪd] *adj.* without assistance; without help. □ *Even an unassisted child can build this simple toy.*

**unbelievable** [ən bə ˈliv ə bəl] *adj.* extreme and not able to be believed. (Adv: *unbelievably.*) □ *David spends an unbelievable amount of time watching television.*

**unbiased** [ən ˈbɑɪ əst] *adj.* not biased; fair; not favoring one side over another. (Adv: *unbiasedly.*) □ *The unbiased mediator helped solve the contract dispute.*

**unbreakable** [ən ˈbrek ə bəl] *adj.* not able to be broken. (Adv: *unbreakably.*) □ *The construction worker carried his lunch in an unbreakable container.*

**uncertain** [ən ˈsɚt n] **1.** *adj.* [of a decision] able to change or be changed; not sure. (Adv: *uncertainly.*) □ *I was uncertain about how much medicine to take, so I called my doctor for advice.* **2.** *adj.* not known for sure; not yet decided. □ *The exact date of our wedding is uncertain.* **3.** *adj.* changeable; not reliable. (Adv: *uncertainly.*) □ *The uncertain weather kept us guessing about whether or not it would rain.*

**uncle** [ˈʌŋ kəl] *n.* the brother of one's father or mother; the husband of one's aunt. (Also a term of address.) □ *I asked my Uncle John what my mom was like when she was a girl.*

U

**unclear** [ən 'klɪr] *adj.* not clear; not understood well. (Adv: *unclearly.*) □ *John's confusing directions are unclear to me.*

**uncomfortable** [ən 'kʌmf tə bəl] **1.** *adj.* not comfortable; feeling uneasy. (Adv: *uncomfortably.*) □ *John is uncomfortable speaking in front of a large group of people.* **2.** *adj.* causing discomfort. (Adv: *uncomfortably.*) □ *Jane returned the uncomfortable furniture to the store.*

**unconscious** [ən 'kɑn ʃəs] **1.** *adj.* not conscious; no longer conscious. (Adv: *unconsciously.*) □ *The drunken man slumped unconscious on the park bench.* **2.** *adj.* done without thinking. (Adv: *unconsciously.*) □ *Susan's unconscious glance in the direction of the door indicated that she was expecting someone.* **3.** *n.* the part of one's mind of which one is not aware. (No plural form.) □ *The doctor used hypnotism to reveal the man's unconscious.*

**undecided** [ən dɪ 'sɑɪd ɪd] **1.** *adj.* unsure of how one will decide; not having made a decision. (Adv: *undecidedly.*) □ *The undecided customer did not buy anything.* **2.** *adj.* [of a matter that has] not yet been determined. (Adv: *undecidedly.*) □ *Bob left the undecided matters for his boss to answer.*

**under** ['ʌn dɚ] **1.** *prep.* in or at a place below someone or something; in or at a place beneath someone or something; to or into a place below someone or something; to or into a place beneath someone or something. □ *Bill reached under the desk to pick up his pen.* **2.** *prep.* less than something. □ *When it's under 32 degrees Fahrenheit, water freezes.* **3.** *prep.* affected by the control or influence of someone or something; ranked beneath someone or something. □ *John is under a vice president who reports directly to the president.* **4.** *adv.* below; below the surface; beneath. □ *The ship started to sink, and then went under.*

**underclothes** ['ʌn dɚ klo(ð)z] *n.* underwear; underpants and undershirts; the clothing worn next to the skin, usually under other pieces of clothing. (Treated as plural, but not countable.) □ *Bill sat around the house in his underclothes on hot days.*

**underclothing** ['ʌn dɚ klo ðɪŋ] *n.* underwear; underclothes. (No plural form. Treated as singular.) □ *Mary packed enough underclothing for the seven-day trip.*

**undergo** [ən dɚ 'go] *tv., irreg.* to experience something, especially something that is difficult. (Pt: **underwent;** pp: **undergone.**) □ *Mary told of the ordeal she underwent during the robbery.*

**undergone** [ən dɚ 'gɔn] pp of **undergo.**

**undergraduate** [ən dɚ 'græ dʒu ət] **1.** *n.* a college student who has not yet received a bachelor's degree. □ *When Anne was an undergraduate, she declared chemistry as her major.* **2.** *adj.* <the adj. use of ①.> □ *Susan is an undergraduate counselor at the local college.*

**underline** ['ʌn dɚ lɑɪn] **1.** *tv.* to draw a line under a word to give the word emphasis; to emphasize a word by drawing a line under it. □ *David underlined some words on the poster for emphasis.* **2.** *n.* a line that is drawn under a word to give the word emphasis. □ *Mary erased the underline beneath the verb in the sentence.*

**underneath** [ən dɚ 'niθ] **1.** *prep.* beneath someone or something; below someone or something; under someone or something. □ *Bill stored empty boxes underneath the basement stairs.* **2.** *adv.* under someone or something that is on top; under someone or something. □ *John jumped from the bridge to the river underneath.*

**underpaid** [ən dɚ 'ped] *adj.* not paid as well as one should be; not given enough

U

money for one's work. □ *The busy secretary felt underpaid and not appreciated.*

**underpants** ['ʌn dɚ pænts] *n.* an article of clothing worn next to the skin below the waist, usually under other clothing. (Treated as plural. Number is expressed with *pair(s) of underpants.* Also countable.) □ *Bob always wears underpants and an undershirt under his clothes.* Ⓒ *He packed five underpants and four undershirts.*

**undershirt** ['ʌn dɚ ʃɚt] *n.* a piece of clothing worn above the waist next to the skin, usually under other clothing. □ *On warm days, I wear an undershirt with nothing over it.*

**undershorts** ['ʌn dɚ ʃorts] *n.* underpants; a piece of clothing worn below the waist next to the skin, usually under other clothing. (Treated as plural. Number is expressed with *pair(s) of undershorts.*) □ *Bill answered the door in his undershorts and shocked the visitor.*

**underside** ['ʌn dɚ saɪd] *n.* the surface of the bottom part of someone or something. □ *The underside of the car was covered with mud.*

**understand** [ən dɚ 'stænd] **1.** *iv., irreg.* to know; to be aware of the meaning of something; to know about something; to be familiar with something. (Pt/pp: **understood**.) □ *I want to be left alone. Do you understand?* **2.** *tv., irreg.* to know something; to know the meaning of something. □ *I understand your concern about the situation.* **3.** *tv., irreg.* to assume something; to believe something. (The object is a clause with **that** ⑦.) □ *We understood that you would be on an earlier plane.*

**understanding** [ən dɚ 'stænd ɪŋ] **1.** *n.* the ability to understand. (No plural form.) □ *Alcoholism had affected the student's understanding.* **2.** *n.* an informal agreement. □ *The two former enemies reached an understanding and shook hands.* **3.** *adj.* able to understand; sympathetic. □ *I appreciated my manager's understanding view of my personal problems.*

**understood** [ən dɚ 'stʊd] pt/pp of **understand**.

**undertaker** ['ʌn dɚ te kɚ] *n.* someone who arranges funerals. □ *The undertaker came to the house to take away the body of Aunt Jane.*

**underwater** [ən dɚ 'wɑ tɚ] **1.** *adj.* under the surface of water. □ *The diver explored the underwater cave.* **2.** *adj.* made for use under the water. □ *The underwater camera took magnificent photos of sea life.* **3.** *adv.* under the surface of water. □ *Some birds can dive underwater to catch fish.*

**underwear** ['ʌn dɚ wɛr] *n.* underclothing, especially underpants; clothing worn next to the skin, usually under other clothing. (No plural form. When this refers to underpants, number is expressed with *pair(s) of underwear.*) □ *The actors wore their own underwear under their costumes.*

**underweight** ['ʌn dɚ wet] *adj.* not weighing as much as one should; weighing too little. □ *The underweight athlete was not allowed to wrestle in the match.*

**underwent** [ən dɚ 'wɛnt] pt of **undergo**.

**underworld** ['ʌn dɚ wɚld] *n.* the world of crime; criminals and their society. □ *The reporter wrote about the underworld of organized crime.*

**undid** [ən 'dɪd] pt of **undo**.

**undo** [ən 'du] **1.** *tv., irreg.* to cancel the effects of something; to cause something to be as though something had never been done. (Pt: **undid**; pp: **undone**.) □ *This software allows you to undo changes that were accidentally made.* **2.** *tv., irreg.* to untie something;

to unfasten something. □ *Bob couldn't undo the zipper because it was stuck.*

**undoing** [ən 'du ɪŋ] *n.* something that causes failure or ruin. (No plural form.) □ *The rainstorm was the undoing of the outdoor wedding.*

**undone** [ən 'dʌn] pp of undo.

**undress** [ən 'drɛs] **1.** *tv.* to remove someone's clothes. □ *John undressed himself and took a shower.* **2.** *iv.* to take off one's own clothes. □ *Bill was caught in the rain, so he undressed when he got home.*

**unduly** [ən 'du li] *adv.* in an excessive way; in an excessively negative way. □ *Bill was unduly criticized for being late.*

**unearth** [ən 'ɚθ] **1.** *tv.* to remove something from the ground; to dig something from the earth. □ *The gardener unearthed some potatoes.* **2.** *tv.* to discover and reveal something; to disclose something; to expose something. (Fig. on ①.) □ *The newspaper reporter unearthed the lawyer's dark secret.*

**uneasy** [ən 'i zi] *adj.* upset; anxious; not comfortable; worried. (Adv: *uneasily.*) □ *The strange man on the bus made Bill uneasy.*

**uneducated** [ən 'ɛdʒ ə ket ɪd] *adj.* not educated; not having attended school; not having been taught. □ *Jane taught the uneducated immigrants how to read.*

**unequal** [ən 'i kwəl] *adj.* not equal in size, amount, degree, importance, or worth. (Adv: *unequally.*) □ *The children complained that their portions of food were unequal.*

U

**uneven** [ən 'i vən] **1.** *adj.* [of a surface] not even; not smooth; rough; bumpy. (Adv: *unevenly.*) □ *The uneven road damaged the car's tires.* **2.** *adj.* [of a process or flow] not constant; varying; irregular. (Adv: *unevenly.*) □ *The radio signal was uneven. It came in better on clear days.* **3.** *adj.* not equal; unequal. (Adv: *unevenly.*) □ *The boards are uneven in length. This one is an inch longer than that one.*

**unexpected** [ən ɛk 'spɛk tɪd] *adj.* not expected; surprising; [of something that happens] not known about before it happens. (Adv: *unexpectedly.*) □ *The unexpected news that Anne was moving surprised me.*

**unfair** [ən 'fɛr] *adj.* not fair; unjust; not right; not equal. (Adv: *unfairly.*) □ *The loser challenged the unfair election.*

**unfasten** [ən 'fæ sən] **1.** *tv.* to open something by removing a fastener; to make something loose by adjusting a fastener. □ *Mary unfastened the buckles on her boots.* **2.** *iv.* to become loose or open. □ *A stage actor's clothing must unfasten easily for quick costume changes.*

**unfold** [ən 'fold] **1.** *tv.* to spread something out; to open something that is folded. □ *Anne unfolded her napkin and set it on her lap.* **2.** *iv.* to develop; to become known; to be revealed. □ *The movie bored me because the plot unfolded too slowly.*

**unforeseen** [ən for 'sin] *adj.* not anticipated; not foreseen; not known in advance. □ *The computer program failed because of unforeseen difficulties.*

**unforgettable** [ən for 'gɛt ə bəl] *adj.* unable to be forgotten; always remembered. (Adv: *unforgettably.*) □ *My rough airplane flight through the storm was quite unforgettable.*

**unfortunate** [ən 'for tʃə nət] *adj.* not fortunate; not lucky. (Adv: *unfortunately.*) □ *The unfortunate victim died in the car crash.*

**unfriendly** [ən 'frɛnd li] *adj.* not friendly; hostile. (Comp: *unfriendlier;* sup: *unfriendliest.*) □ *The unfriendly clerk did not return my greeting.*

**unguarded** [ən 'gɑr dɪd] **1.** *adj.* not guarded; not protected; open to attack.

□ *The thief stole the unguarded jewelry.* **2.** *adj.* careless, especially in trying to keep secrets. (Adv: *unguardedly.*) □ *I overheard Mary's unguarded whisper.*

**unhappy** [ən 'hæp i] *adj.* sad; not happy; not pleased. (Adv: *unhappily.* Comp: *unhappier;* sup: *unhappiest.*) □ *The manager was very unhappy with Bill's poor work habits.*

**unhealthy** [ən 'hɛl θi] **1.** *adj.* bad for one's health. (Adv: *unhealthily.* Comp: *unhealthier;* sup: *unhealthiest.*) □ *John eats too many unhealthy foods.* **2.** *adj.* sick; having bad health. (Adv: *unhealthily.* Comp: *unhealthier;* sup: *unhealthiest.*) □ *The doctor tried to treat the unhealthy patient.*

**unicorn** ['ju nə korn] *n.* a mythical creature resembling a horse with a single horn on its brow. □ *The unicorn's horn magically cured the sick knight.*

**uniform** ['ju nə form] **1.** *n.* the clothes that are worn by all the members of a certain group. □ *The children found it hard to keep their school uniforms clean.* **2.** *adj.* identical; alike; not varying; having no variation. (Adv: *uniformly.*) □ *Most mornings, all the cars are moving at a uniform rate of speed.*

**unify** ['ju nə fɑɪ] **1.** *tv.* to unite something or a group; to bring many parts together to make one whole thing. □ *The religious leader sought to unify a number of similar faiths.* **2.** *iv.* to become united; to be brought together to make one whole thing. □ *Dozens of rebels unified behind one leader.*

**unimportant** [ən ɪm 'port nt] *adj.* not important; not significant. (Adv: *unimportantly.*) □ *David spent a few dollars on some unimportant items at the store.*

**union** ['jun jən] **1.** *n.* the joining together of two or more things. □ *The union of the two companies resulted in a powerful corporation.* **2.** *n.* the bond between two or more things that are joined together. □ *The union among the related agencies began to weaken.* **3.** *n.* an organization whose members work together in support of a common interest, especially an organization of workers in a particular trade. □ *My mail is delivered by members of the American Postal Workers Union.* **4.** *adj.* <the adj. use of ③.> □ *The union workers approved the proposed contract.*

**unique** [ju 'nik] *adj.* unlike anything else; having no equal; being the only one of its kind. (No comparative or superlative. Adv: *uniquely.*) □ *The letter was written in Anne's unique style.*

**unison** ['ju nə sən] **1. in unison** *phr.* [of musical notes, instruments, or voices] having the same pitch. □ *The twins sang in unison.* **2. in unison** *phr.* acting as one; together and at the same time. □ *John and his wife responded to my question in unison.*

**unit** ['ju nɪt] **1.** *n.* a single thing or person; one part of a group of things or people. □ *This school requires 180 units of coursework for graduation.* **2.** *n.* a group of things thought of as being one thing. □ *Our company's sales unit is made up of fifty salespeople and five district managers.* **3.** *n.* an amount of a standard measurement. □ *A pound is a standard unit for measuring weight.* **4.** *n.* an apartment within an apartment building. □ *Mary rents a two-bedroom unit on the 12th floor of this building.*

**unite** [ju 'nɑɪt] **1.** *tv.* to join two or more things together; to bring two or more things together. □ *The bride and groom were united in marriage.* **2.** *iv.* to join together; to come together. □ *The two schools united to form one large one.*

**united** [ju 'nɑɪt ɪd] *adj.* brought together; joined together, especially because of a common purpose. (Adv: *unitedly.*) □ *The angry students presented a united front to the school administration.*

U

**unity** ['ju nə ti] *n.* the condition of being together; the condition of being united. (No plural form.) □ *All the rebel groups sought unity with each other.*

**universal** [ju nə 'vɚ səl] **1.** *adj.* shared by every member of a group; of or about everyone; understood by everyone. (Adv: *universally.*) □ *The desire to be loved is universal.* **2.** *n.* a concept that is ①. □ *A universal similar to the golden rule exists in almost every religion.*

**universe** ['ju nə vɚs] *n.* everything that exists in space; all of space and everything that exists in it. □ *Our solar system is just one very small part of the universe.*

**university** [ju nə 'vɚ sə ti] *n.* a school for higher education, usually consisting of one or more colleges for undergraduates and usually one or more schools for graduate students. □ *More than 8,000 students attend the local university.*

**unjust** [ən 'dʒʌst] *adj.* not just; not fair; not right. (Adv: *unjustly.*) □ *The defendant appealed the unjust ruling.*

**unkind** [ən 'kaɪnd] *adj.* not kind; mean; without concern for others. (Adv: *unkindly.* Comp: *unkinder;* sup: *unkindest.*) □ *Bill apologized for his unkind behavior.*

**unknown** [ən 'non] **1.** *adj.* not known; not familiar. □ *The actual number of stars in the universe is unknown.* **2.** *adj.* not famous; not recognized. □ *The independent film featured unknown actors.* **3.** *n.* someone who is not (widely) known; something that is not known. □ *The experienced politician was beaten by an unknown.*

U

**unlawful** [ən 'lɔ fʊl] *adj.* not legal; illegal; against the law. (Adv: *unlawfully.*) □ *Smoking in public buildings is unlawful in some cities.*

**unless** [ən 'lɛs] *conj.* except under the circumstances that something specific happens. (Followed by a clause.) □ *I'm going to quit my job unless you give me a raise.*

**unlike** [ən 'laɪk] **1.** *adj.* not like someone or something else; not equal; not similar; different. (Prenominal only.) □ *The twins look alike, but they have unlike personalities.* **2.** *prep.* not similar to someone or something; different from someone or something. □ *Unlike her tall sisters, Sue is of average height.* **3.** *prep.* not characteristic or typical of someone or something. □ *This wild behavior is quite unlike Bob. He's usually a very quiet person.*

**unlikely** [ən 'laɪk li] *adj.* not probable; not likely; likely to fail; not likely to succeed. □ *Who is the candidate who is unlikely to lose?*

**unlimited** [ən 'lɪm ə tɪd] *adj.* not limited; without limits; not restricted. (Adv: *unlimitedly.*) □ *I wished the newlyweds unlimited happiness.*

**unlock** [ən 'lɑk] *tv.* to open a lock. □ *Susan unlocked the safe and removed her valuables.*

**unlucky** [ən 'lʌk i] **1.** *adj.* not lucky; not having good luck; unfortunate. (Adv: *unluckily.* Comp: *unluckier;* sup: *unluckiest.*) □ *The unlucky gambler lost $1,000.* **2.** *adj.* causing bad luck; causing misfortune. (Adv: *unluckily.* Comp: *unluckier;* sup: *unluckiest.*) □ *Some actors consider it unlucky to whistle before appearing on stage.*

**unmentionable** [ən 'mɛn ʃə nə bəl] *adj.* not able to be mentioned; not to be mentioned, especially because it would not be polite to do so. (Adv: *unmentionably.*) □ *David just got kicked in an unmentionable place.*

**unpack** [ən 'pæk] **1.** *tv.* to remove objects that have been packed; to remove objects that are in a box or suitcase. □ *Anne unpacked the glasses from the crate.* **2.** *iv.* to remove objects that have been packed. □ *Bill unpacked as soon as he arrived at the hotel.*

**unpleasant** [ən 'plɛz ənt] *adj.* not pleasant; not pleasing; not nice; not enjoyable. (Adv: *unpleasantly.*) □ *My vacation was unpleasant because the weather was bad.*

**unpopular** [ən 'pɑp jə lɚ] *adj.* not popular; not preferred by many people. (Adv: *unpopularly.*) □ *The unpopular television show was soon canceled.*

**unreal** [ən 'ril] *adj.* not real; incredible; unbelievable. □ *Everything seemed unreal to Bill, as though he were dreaming.*

**unrealistic** [ən ri ə 'lɪs tɪk] **1.** *adj.* not seeming real; seeming fake; not realistic. (Adv: *unrealistically* [...ɪk li].) □ *Jane's unrealistic wig did not look at all like real hair.* **2.** *adj.* not practical. (Adv: *unrealistically* [...ɪk li].) □ *My boss expects me to finish an unrealistic amount of work before I leave today.*

**unreasonable** [ən 'ri zə nə bəl] **1.** *adj.* not reasonable; not sensible; not rational. (Adv: *unreasonably.*) □ *The unreasonable clerk refused to accept my $20 bill.* **2.** *adj.* too much; excessive. (Adv: *unreasonably.*) □ *I waited an unreasonable amount of time for the delayed flight.*

**unrest** [ən 'rɛst] **1.** *n.* a feeling of not being satisfied; a troubled or uneasy feeling. (No plural form.) □ *Susan suffered considerable unrest when I told her the disturbing news.* **2.** *n.* rebellion. (No plural form.) □ *The tyrant's actions caused unrest among the people.*

**unruly** [ən 'ru li] **1.** *adj.* badly behaved; not obedient; not paying attention to authority. □ *The unruly students were sent to the principal's office.* **2.** *adj.* [of hair] not orderly; [of hair] hard to control. □ *John brushed his unruly hair out of his eyes.*

**unsatisfactory** [ən sæt ɪs 'fæk tə ri] *adj.* not satisfactory; not good enough; not adequate. (Adv: *unsatisfactorily.*) □ *This food is unsatisfactory. Please return it to the kitchen.*

**unscientific** [ən saɪ ən 'tɪf ɪk] *adj.* not scientific; not using principles of science. (Adv: *unscientifically* [...ɪk li].) □ *Your experiment was unscientific, so I cannot believe your conclusions.*

**unscrew** [ən 'skru] **1.** *tv.* to remove something, such as a screw or a lid, by turning it. □ *Anne unscrewed the cap on the tube of toothpaste.* **2.** *iv.* [for a screw, lid, bolt, etc.] to rotate and become loose. □ *The safety lid unscrews only if you push down on it.*

**unstable** [ən 'ste bəl] **1.** *adj.* not secure; not having proper balance. (Adv: *unstably.*) □ *The unstable chair fell over when I tried to sit down.* **2.** *adj.* not steady; likely to change. (Adv: *unstably.*) □ *The unstable stock market made the investor very nervous.* **3.** *adj.* [of someone] mentally disturbed or troubled. (Adv: *unstably.*) □ *Whoever committed this crime was very unstable!*

**unsteady** [ən 'stɛd i] **1.** *adj.* shaky; not secure. (Adv: *unsteadily.*) □ *When I leaned on the unsteady desk, it collapsed.* **2.** *adj.* not dependable; likely to change. (Adv: *unsteadily.*) □ *The unsteady growth rate of sales meant that some employees were fired.*

**unsure** [ən 'ʃʊr] *adj.* not sure; not certain. (Adv: *unsurely.*) □ *The driver was unsure whether to turn right or left.*

U

**untidy** [ən 'taɪ di] *adj.* not tidy; not clean; messy. (Adv: *untidily.* Comp: *untidier;* sup: *untidiest.*) □ *John hired someone to clean his untidy apartment.*

**untie** [ən 'taɪ] **1.** *tv.* to loosen something that is tied; to undo something that is tied. (The present participle is *untying* in both senses of the verb.) □ *Anne untied the string that was around the* *package.* **2.** *iv.* to become **untied** as in ①. □ *The knot untied because it was loose.*

**until** [ən 'tɪl] **1.** *prep.* up to a certain time; during a period of time up to a certain time; continuing during a period of time, and then stopping at a certain time. (See also **till.**) □ *These items will be on sale until next week.* **2.** *conj.* up to a time when something happens; up to a time when a certain condition is met. (Followed by a clause.) □ *I had fun on my vacation until I became sick.* **3.** *conj.* before. (Used with a negative construction in the main clause.) □ *John couldn't see well until he got glasses.*

**unto** [ən tu] *prep.* to someone or something. (Formal or old.) □ *Splendid gifts were brought unto the queen.*

**untold** [ən 'told] **1.** *adj.* not told; not expressed; not revealed. □ *The reporter tried to uncover the untold story about the scandal.* **2.** *adj.* countless; too great to be counted. □ *The pirates buried untold treasures on several islands.*

**untrue** [ən 'tru] **1.** *adj.* not true; false; not correct. (Adv: *untruly.*) □ *That Chicago is the capital of Illinois is untrue. Springfield is the capital.* **2. untrue (to someone or something)** *adj. (+ prep. phr.)* not loyal to someone or something; not faithful to someone or something. □ *Bill was untrue to the principles he once lived by.*

**unusual** [ən 'ju ʒu əl] *adj.* not usual; strange; different; not ordinary. (Adv: *unusually.*) □ *My car's engine made an unusual noise, so I pulled off the road.*

**unwanted** [ən 'wɑn tɪd] *adj.* not wanted. (Adv: *unwantedly.*) □ *I throw out the unwanted catalogs that I receive in the mail.*

**unwelcome** [ən 'wɛl kəm] *adj.* not welcome; not wanted. (Adv: *unwelcomely.*) □ *I would not invite the unwelcome guest into my house.*

**unwholesome** [ən 'hol səm] *adj.* not good for one's morals or one's health. (Adv: *unwholesomely.*) □ *I stopped eating unwholesome foods and soon started feeling better.*

**unwind** [ən 'wɑɪnd] **1.** *tv., irreg.* to remove something that is wound around an object. (Pt/pp: **unwound.**) □ *The police unwound the rope that bound the hostage to the chair.* **2.** *iv., irreg.* to relax. □ *Anne likes to unwind by riding her bike along the lake.* **3.** *iv., irreg.* [for something] to become loose and to pull away from an object that it is wound around. □ *The bandage unwound from my ankle by itself.*

**unwise** [ən 'wɑɪz] *adj.* not wise; foolish; silly. (Adv: *unwisely.*) □ *The unwise driver sped on the icy roads.*

**unwound** [ən 'wɑʊnd] pt/pp of **unwind.**

**up** [ʌp] **1.** *adv.* from a lower level toward a higher level. □ *The price of gas went up last week.* **2.** *adv.* toward the north; northward; in the north. □ *My friends drove up from the south last week.* **3.** *adv.* into a vertical or almost vertical position; in a vertical or almost vertical position. □ *Mary stood up from her chair and looked out the window.* **4.** *adv.* completely; totally. (Used especially with verbs such as *eat, drink, use,* and *finish.*) □ *The hungry man ate up everything on his plate.* **5.** *adv.* tightly; into a tight condition; firmly. (Used especially with verbs such as *roll, curl, fold,* and *wind.*) □ *The garden hose is rolled up on its stand.* **6.** *adv.* together; into a condition in which things are together. (Used especially with verbs such as *add, total, count, link, connect,* and *gather.*) □ *The computer totaled up the figures in the column.* **7.** *adj.* over; finished. (Not prenominal.) □ *When the prisoner's term was up, he returned home.* □ *My time is up. I'm leaving.* **8.** *prep.* on or along something to a higher level or position. □ *I walked up the stairs slowly.*

**update** ['ʌp det] **1.** *n.* something that has new information, especially a news report that has more information about something. □ *The latest weather update said a tornado was heading our way.* **2.** *tv.* to make something more modern; to make something up-to-date. □ *The office manager updated the office equipment.* **3.** *tv.* to provide the latest information; to inform someone of the latest news. □ *Mary updated me about John's medical information.*

**updated** [əp 'det ɪd] *adj.* made modern; changed or made to be modern or current. □ *The actors performed an updated version of* Romeo and Juliet. □ *The updated equipment was much easier to use.*

**upkeep** ['ʌp kip] **1.** *n.* maintenance; the work required to maintain something. (No plural form.) □ *The upkeep of the large yard is very time-consuming.* **2.** *n.* the cost of ①. (No plural form.) □ *How much is the upkeep for this old building?*

**upon** [ə 'pɔn] **1.** *prep.* on the surface of someone or something. □ *The snow fell upon the ground.* **2.** *prep.* at the instant of doing something; on the occasion of something happening; immediately or very soon after something has happened. □ *Upon returning home, I realized I had been robbed.*

**upper** ['ʌp ɚ] *adj.* the higher of two things; closer to the top of something than to the bottom. □ *Mary placed the dangerous poison on an upper shelf.*

**uppercase** ['ʌp ɚ 'kes] *adj.* [of a letter or letters] in the larger size as with *B* in *Bill;* majuscule. (Compare this with **lowercase.**) □ *The* T *that starts this sentence is uppercase.* □ *Use all uppercase letters for the headline.*

**uproar** ['ʌp ror] *n.* a loud, noisy, confused activity. □ *The crowd was in an uproar when gunshots were fired.*

**uproot** [əp 'rut] **1.** *tv.* to pull up a plant, including its roots. □ *You have to uproot all the weeds. Don't just break them off.* **2.** *tv.* to cause someone to move from where one lives. (Fig. on ①.) □ *We were uprooted from our homes by the flood.*

**upset 1.** [əp 'sɛt] *adj.* worried about something. □ *Mary was upset because we were going to be late.* **2.** [əp 'sɛt] *adj.* [of someone's stomach] feeling bad or sick. □ *Bill's stomach gets upset when he eats spicy food.* **3.** [əp 'sɛt] *tv., irreg.* to knock something over; to tip something over; to turn something over. (Pt/pp: *upset.*) □ *I upset my glass of milk when I gestured wildly.* **4.** [əp 'sɛt] *tv., irreg.* to defeat someone or something that was expected to win. □ *The last-place team upset the highest-ranked team.* **5.** [əp 'sɛt] *tv., irreg.* to disturb someone; to bother someone; to make someone worried. □ *I upset my parents when I didn't come home on time.* **6.** [əp 'sɛt] *tv., irreg.* to make someone's stomach feel bad. □ *Coffee upsets Anne's stomach.* **7.** ['əp sɛt] *n.* a surprise victory; the defeat of someone or something by someone or something that was not expected to win. □ *The last-place team won the game against the first-place team, and everyone was amazed by the upset.*

**upside down** ['ʌp saɪd 'daʊn] *adj.* having the top part at the bottom; having the wrong end or side up. (Hyphenated before a nominal.) □ *The pen wouldn't write because it was upside down.*

**upstairs 1.** ['ʌp 'stɛrz] *adj.* located on an upper floor; located on a higher floor. □ *Mary waved to me from an upstairs window.* **2.** [əp 'stɛrz] *adv.* on or toward the next floor of a building; on or toward an upper floor of a building. □ *I ran upstairs to find out why the baby was crying.* **3.** ['ʌp 'stɛrz] *n.* the top floor of a building; the upper floor of a building. (Treated as singular.) □ *John* *heard a strange noise coming from upstairs.*

**upstream** ['ʌp 'strim] *adv.* against the current of a river. □ *John paddled the canoe upstream.*

**up-to-date** ['ʌp tə 'det] *adj.* current; including or based on the latest facts or information. □ *Where can I find an up-to-date map that includes the most current names for these countries?*

**upward** ['ʌp wɚd] **1. upward(s)** *adv.* to or toward a higher position; to or toward a higher level; to or toward the top part of something. □ *The excellent worker rose upward in the company ranks.* **2.** *adj.* moving **upward** ①; climbing; rising; advancing. (Adv: *upwardly.*) □ *The chart is showing an upward movement of sales and profits.*

**uranium** [jə 'ren i əm] *n.* a chemical element used mainly as fuel for nuclear reactors. (No plural form.) □ *The terrorists smuggled uranium out of Russia.* □ *Uranium's atomic symbol is U, and its atomic number is 92.*

**urban** ['ɚ bən] *adj.* of or about a city or cities in general; not suburban or rural. □ *The magazine had a special report about urban crime.*

**urge** ['ɚdʒ] **1.** *n.* a strong feeling, desire, or need to do something. □ *I had an urge to hit the rude cab driver.* **2. urge someone to do something** *tv. + obj. + inf.* to try to persuade someone to do something; to beg someone to do something. □ *Anne urged Susan to seek help for her emotional problems.* **3.** *tv.* to force or encourage someone or something to go forward. (The object can be a clause with **that** ⑦.) □ *The leader urged the troops onward through the swamp.*

**urgent** ['ɚ dʒənt] *adj.* very important; [of something] needing attention before anything else. (Adv: *urgently.*) □ *It is urgent that you speak with me right now.*

**urinate** ['jʊr ə net] *iv.* to cause or allow urine to flow from the body. □ *David went into the bathroom so he could urinate.*

**urine** ['jʊr ɪn] *n.* a liquid waste product removed by the kidneys and discharged from the body. (No plural form in this sense except in reference to urine samples for medical tests.) □ *My doctor ran tests on the sample of urine I provided.*

**urn** ['ɚn] **1.** *n.* a large vase or pot, often used for plants or for ashes from a dead person's remains. □ *We keep John's remains in an urn next to the bookcase.* **2.** *n.* a large container for holding hot liquids, especially coffee. □ *Don't touch the urn! It's filled with hot coffee.*

**us** ['ʌs] *pron.* <the objective form of **we**, referring to a group of people including the speaker or writer.> □ *We asked the teacher to help us.*

**U.S.** Go to **U.S.A.**

**U.S.A.** AND **U.S.** ['ju 'ɛs ('e)] the United States (of America). □ *English spoken in the U.S.A. is different from that spoken in England.*

**usage** ['ju sɪdʒ] *n.* the way words in a language typically occur in speech. (No plural form.) □ *Anne uses a dictionary to find the correct usage of words.*

**use 1.** ['jus] *n.* consuming or operating something; the intended function of something; the purpose of something, especially the purpose of meeting people's needs. (Plural only when referring to different kinds, types, instances, or varieties.) □ *The television set undergoes a lot of use in our house.* Ⓒ *I just found another use for my dictionary—as a doorstop.* **2.** ['juz] *tv.* to employ someone or something for a certain purpose; to put something into service. □ *The researcher used five students in the scientific experiment.* **3.** ['juz] *tv.* to treat someone badly or to one's own advantage. □ *Anne used her coworkers to get* *ahead in the business.* **4. use** something **up** ['juz...] *tv.* + *obj.* + *adv.* to consume all of something. □ *Jimmy used all the milk up.* 🅃 *He used up the milk.*

**used 1.** ['juzd] *adj.* already owned; not new; secondhand. □ *David bought a used desk from an antique shop.* **2. used to** do something ['jus tə...] *phr.* did something in the past as a matter of habit or custom. □ *I used to eat lots of pastry, but I began to gain too much weight.* **3. [be] used to someone or something** [...'jus tə...] *phr.* [to be] familiar and comfortable with someone or something. □ *I am used to the doctor I have, and I don't want to change.* **4. [be] used to doing something** [...'jus tə...] *phr.* [to be] accustomed to doing something; [to be] comfortable with doing something because it is familiar. □ *I am used to walking to work. I have done it for years.*

**useful** ['jus fʊl] *adj.* helpful; able to be used. (Adv: *usefully.*) □ *Your advice has been very useful. Thank you.*

**useless** ['jus ləs] *adj.* not helpful; not able to be used; having no effect; having no purpose. (Adv: *uselessly.*) □ *A car is useless if you can't afford to buy gasoline for it.*

**usher** ['ʌʃ ɚ] **1.** *n.* someone who shows people to their seats in a church, auditorium, theater, or other place where people gather. □ *The usher tore my theater ticket in half and handed me the stub.* **2.** *tv.* to guide someone to a seat; to escort someone to a seat. □ *The groom's friends ushered the wedding guests to their seats.*

**usual** ['ju ʒu wəl] *adj.* ordinary; typical; customary; common; regular. (Adv: *usually.*) □ *An accident blocked my usual route to work.*

**utensil** [ju 'tɛn səl] *n.* a tool that helps someone do something, especially a tool that helps someone cook or eat. □ *Metal utensils will scratch the coating on this frying pan.* □ *A fork is a type of eating utensil.*

**utility** [ju 'tɪl ə ti] **1.** *n.* a service providing products such as electricity, water, gas, and waste removal to homes and businesses. □ *The cost of utilities is included in my monthly rent.* **2.** *n.* a company that provides a public service. □ *The utility announced that it will raise its rates this fall.* **3.** *adj.* having a basic function; providing for basic service. (Prenominal only.) □ *The soldiers drove the utility vehicle across the field.*

**utilize** ['jut ə laɪz] *tv.* to use something practically; to make use of something; to employ something for a purpose. □ *John utilized the knife blade as a screwdriver.*

**utter** ['ʌt ɚ] **1.** *tv.* to say something; to express something aloud. □ *Not a word was uttered during the thrilling movie.* **2.** *adj.* complete; total. (Adv: *utterly.*) □ *The student held authority figures in utter contempt.*

**utterance** ['ʌt ə rəns] *n.* speaking; uttering words. (Plural only when referring to different kinds, types, instances, or varieties.) □ *The teacher was shocked at the utterance of such a crude word by the young student.* 🄲 *Bill accented the important words in his utterances by saying them louder.*

U

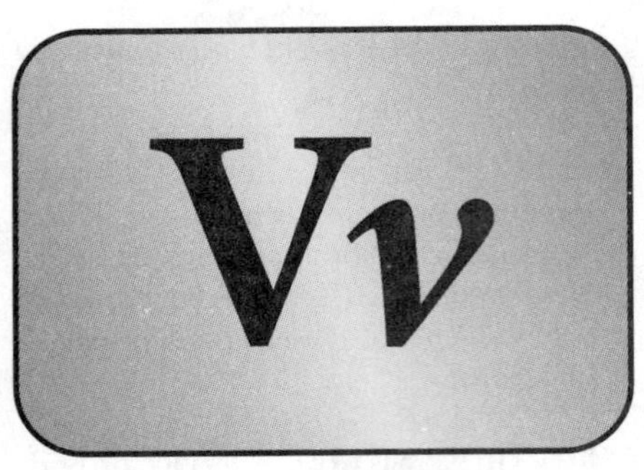

**vacancy** ['ve kən si] **1.** *n.* a job or position that is not filled; an opening in employment; a job opening. □ *Bill's retirement left a vacancy in the production division.* **2.** *n.* an empty room or building that is available for rent. □ *Mary asked the hotel clerk if there were any vacancies.*

**vacant** ['ve kənt] **1.** *adj.* not occupied; not being used; empty; not filled. □ *Jane parked her car in the vacant lot.* **2.** *adj.* [of a look on someone's face] blank, showing no thought or intelligence. (Fig. on ①. Adv: *vacantly.*) □ *The stranger's vacant stare made me nervous.*

**vacation** [ve 'ke ʃən] *n.* time when one does not have to work or go to school. (Plural only when referring to different kinds, types, instances, or varieties.) □ *Each employee is allowed two weeks of vacation each year.* Ⓒ *John showed us all the boring pictures from his recent vacations.*

**vaccination** [væk sə 'ne ʃən] *n.* the use of a vaccine to protect people against disease. (Plural only when referring to different kinds, types, instances, or varieties.) □ *Vaccination is a good way to prevent measles.* Ⓒ *The doctor gave the vaccinations by injection.*

V

**vaccine** [væk 'sin] *n.* a substance that is given to people in order to protect them from a certain disease. □ *The scientist was awarded a prize for a life-saving vaccine.*

**vacuum** ['væk jum] **1.** *n.* a space that is completely empty and does not have any air in it. □ *Most of outer space is a huge vacuum.* **2.** *n.* a machine used to suck up dirt from carpets and other floor coverings. (Short for **vacuum cleaner.**) □ *Please run the vacuum before the guests get here.* **3.** *adj.* creating or causing ①. □ *The air was drained from the area with a vacuum pump.* **4.** *tv.* to clean a surface by sucking up dirt with ②. □ *Anne vacuumed the living-room carpet.* **5.** *iv.* to clean by sucking up dirt with ②. □ *John vacuumed before his guests arrived.*

**vacuum cleaner** ['væk jum klin ɚ] *n.* a machine that cleans carpets or other materials by creating a partial **vacuum** that sucks up dirt. (Can be shortened to **vacuum.**) □ *The vacuum cleaner is stored in the hallway closet.*

**vague** ['veg] **1.** *adj.* not precise; not exact. (Adv: *vaguely.* Comp: *vaguer;* sup: *vaguest.*) □ *Tom evaded Jane's question by giving her a vague answer.* **2.** *adj.* having no expression on one's face. (Fig. on ①. Adv: *vaguely.* Comp: *vaguer;* sup: *vaguest.*) □ *Bob's vague expression masked the stress I knew he was under.*

**vain** ['ven] **1.** *adj.* having too much pride about how one looks or about what one has done. (Adv: *vainly.* Comp: *vainer;* sup: *vainest.*) □ *The vain man spent a lot of money on the latest fashions.* **2. in vain** *phr.* futile(ly); without having the result one wanted. □ *I tried in vain to convince my teacher to change my grade.*

**valiant** ['væl jənt] *adj.* very brave; very courageous; heroic. (Adv: *valiantly.*) □ *The doctors made a valiant effort to save the man's life.*

**valid** ['væl ɪd] **1.** *adj.* effective; legally usable or acceptable. (Adv: *validly.*) □ *This coupon is valid until the end of the month.* **2.** *adj.* true; able to be defended or proved; based on facts. (Adv: *validly.*)

☐ *The data in your report seems to be valid to me.*

**valley** ['væl i] *n.* a low area of land between two high areas of land; a low area of land that is drained by a large river and the smaller rivers that flow into the larger river. ☐ *Much of the Mississippi Valley was explored in the early 19th century.*

**valor** ['væl ɚ] *n.* courage. (No plural form.) ☐ *The soldier was decorated for his valor in battle.*

**valuable** ['væl jə bəl] **1.** *adj.* worth a lot of money; having a great value. (Adv: *valuably.*) ☐ *Anne wore a valuable diamond ring to the party.* **2.** *adj.* helpful; useful; important. (Adv: *valuably.*) ☐ *The firefighter taught the children valuable safety tips.* **3. valuables** *n.* items that are ①. (No singular.) ☐ *Susan insured her precious valuables.*

**value** ['væl ju] **1.** *n.* the amount of money that something is worth. (No plural form.) ☐ *The value of the painting increased when the artist became famous.* **2.** *n.* something that is actually worth more than one paid for it; a bargain. ☐ *These shoes are a good value. I bought them on sale for half the regular price.* **3.** *n.* something of great use; benefit. (No plural form.) ☐ *The first-aid kit was of great value on our hiking trip.* **4.** *n.* an amount that is represented by a sign, symbol, or variable. ☐ *The math students determined the values of the variables in the equations.* **5.** *tv.* to believe that something is worth a certain amount of money. ☐ *I valued the watch at $100, but the buyer would only pay $80 for it.* **6.** *tv.* to think someone or something is valuable; to regard someone or something as useful or worthy; to regard someone or something highly. ☐ *Mary values her medical skills.*

**van** ['væn] *n.* a covered motor vehicle that has a large amount of space behind the driver's seat for carrying large objects or extra people. ☐ *Bill borrowed my van to move some furniture.*

**vandal** ['væn dəl] *n.* someone who damages other people's property or public property on purpose. ☐ *The police caught the vandal who broke the school windows.*

**vandalize** ['væn də lɑɪz] *tv.* to damage other people's property or public property on purpose. ☐ *The youths who vandalized the school were caught and punished.*

**vanilla** [və 'nɪl ə] **1.** *n.* a flavoring made from the bean of a certain tropical plant. (No plural form.) ☐ *I added a teaspoon of vanilla to the pancake batter.* **2.** *adj.* flavored with ①; tasting like ①. ☐ *I love chocolate syrup on vanilla ice cream.*

**vanish** ['væn ɪʃ] *iv.* to disappear; to be seen no longer. ☐ *The spy vanished from his hotel room without a trace.*

**vanity** ['væn ə ti] **1.** *n.* the condition of being vain; the condition of having too much pride about how one looks or what one has done. (No plural form.) ☐ *Anne's vanity would not allow her to cut off her long hair.* **2.** *n.* a flat surface on top of a cabinet with drawers, especially such a unit in bathrooms, with a sink included in the top surface. ☐ *Jane chose the vanity to match the marble tile on the walls.*

**vapor** ['ve pɚ] *n.* a liquid or solid in the form of a gas. ☐ *Steam, fog, and mist are water vapors.*

**variant** ['vɛr i ənt] **1.** *adj.* different; a particular difference as compared with something standard or the norm. ☐ *The researcher analyzed the variant data from his experiments.* **2.** *n.* a different form of something, especially a different way of spelling a word. ☐ Colour *is the British spelling variant of* color.

**variation** [vɛr i 'e ʃən] *n.* (minor) differences; a minor difference. (Plural only when referring to different kinds, types, instances, or varieties.) ☐ *Accepting variation in language is difficult for some people.* Ⓒ *The surface is very smooth with no variations.*

**variety** [və 'rɑɪ ə ti] *n.* differences of choice; diversity. (Plural only when referring to different kinds, types, instances, or varieties.) ☐ *Variety adds interest to living.* Ⓒ *The electronics department has three varieties of radios.*

**various** ['vɛr i əs] *adj.* different; several; several kinds of something; many kinds of something. (Adv: *variously.*) ☐ *The editor had various problems with the reporter's article.*

**varnish** ['vɑr nɪʃ] **1.** *n.* a clear liquid that is painted onto the surface of objects made from wood to protect the wood and give it a hard, shiny appearance. (Plural only when referring to different kinds, types, instances, or varieties.) ☐ *Please don't walk on the porch while the varnish is still wet.* Ⓒ *The newer varnishes last much longer than the older varieties.* **2.** *tv.* to paint a surface with ①. ☐ *Mary will varnish the antique desk.*

**vary** ['vɛr i] **1.** *iv.* to change; to be different; to appear or be used in different forms. ☐ *My work schedule varies depending on what time of year it is.* **2.** *tv.* to change something; to cause something to be different; to make something different. ☐ *Bill varied his writing style because he thought it was boring.*

**vase** ['ves] *n.* a decorative container, often used for holding flowers. ☐ *Mary put the yellow roses in a crystal vase.*

**vast** ['væst] *adj.* very large in size or amount; of an immense size or amount. (Adv: *vastly.* Comp: *vaster;* sup: *vastest.*) ☐ *The movie star got a vast amount of fan mail every week.*

**vastly** ['væst li] *adv.* in a way that is very large in size or amount. ☐ *Mary's singing ability improved vastly after she took lessons.*

**vat** ['væt] *n.* a large container, used for storing liquid, especially liquor while it is being made. ☐ *The factory workers carefully covered the vat of paint.*

**vault** ['vɔlt] **1.** *n.* a secure, locked room where valuable things are kept and protected. ☐ *The bank keeps its money in a steel vault.* **2.** *n.* a leap; a jump made with the help of a pole or one's hands. ☐ *John cleared the puddle in a single vault.* **3.** *tv.* to jump a certain distance. ☐ *The athlete vaulted exactly fifteen feet.*

**veal** ['vil] *n.* the meat of a young cow used as food. (No plural form.) ☐ *John ate roast veal with mashed potatoes.*

**vegetable** ['vɛdʒ tə bəl] **1.** *n.* a plant that is eaten as food; a part of a plant that is eaten as food. ☐ *A carrot is an orange vegetable.* **2.** *adj.* made with or including ①. ☐ *I ordered some vegetable soup at the restaurant.*

**vegetarian** [vɛdʒ ɪ 'tɛr i ən] **1.** *n.* someone who does not eat the flesh of animals. ☐ *Vegetarians get their protein from rice and beans.* **2.** *adj.* [of food] made without the flesh of a once-living creature. ☐ *Anne ate a vegetarian pizza for lunch.* **3.** *adj.* serving or eating food other than animal tissue. ☐ *My vegetarian guests couldn't eat the hamburgers I'd made.*

**vegetation** [vɛdʒ ɪ 'te ʃən] *n.* plant life; plants in general. (No plural form. Treated as singular.) ☐ *Thick vegetation grows in tropical jungles.*

**vehicle** ['vi ɪ kəl] *n.* a machine that is used to carry people or things, especially on the ground on roads, including cars, buses, trucks, vans, motorcycles, bicycles, sleds, sleighs, and carriages. (But not trains or airplanes.)

□ *Twenty vehicles were involved in the crash on the highway.*

**vehicular** [vɪ 'hɪk jə lɚ] *adj.* of or about vehicles. (Adv: *vehicularly.*) □ *The automobile engineer studied vehicular accidents.*

**veil** ['vel] *n.* a piece of cloth used to hide something. □ *The widow wore a black veil to conceal her sorrow.*

**vein** ['ven] **1.** *n.* a vessel that carries blood from parts of the body back to the heart. □ *His veins are clogged with fatty deposits.* **2.** *n.* a line that forms part of the framework of a leaf or the wing of an insect. □ *John tore the leaf along one of its veins.* **3.** *n.* a layer of coal or a metal within a mass of rock. □ *The miner struck a rich vein of gold.*

**velocity** [və 'lɑs ə ti] *n.* speed, especially the speed of an object moving in a specific direction. (Plural only when referring to different kinds, types, instances, or varieties.) □ *At the current velocity, this plane will land in London in one hour.* Ⓒ *Different size bullets travel at different velocities.*

**velvet** ['vɛl vɪt] **1.** *n.* a soft fabric whose threads are short and close together and stick up on one side of the fabric. (Plural only when referring to different kinds, types, instances, or varieties.) □ *The smooth velvet felt nice against my skin.* Ⓒ *The thicker velvets are more expensive.* **2.** *adj.* made of ①. □ *Mary wore an elegant black velvet dress to the opera.*

**venom** ['vɛn əm] **1.** *n.* the poison in the bite or sting of a snake, spider, and other similar creatures. (No plural form.) □ *The snake's deadly venom killed the careless hiker.* **2.** *n.* extreme hatred. (Fig. on ①. No plural form.) □ *John's criticism of Jane was filled with venom.*

**venomous** ['vɛn ə məs] **1.** *adj.* full of venom; containing venom. (Adv: *venomously.*) □ *A venomous snake crawled across my toes, terrifying me.* **2.** *adj.* full of extreme hatred. (Fig. on ①. Adv: *venomously.*) □ *The politician's venomous speech disturbed many voters.*

**vent** ['vɛnt] **1.** *n.* an opening to a passage through which air or other gases can move. □ *Cool air came through the ceiling vent in the office.* **2.** *tv.* to express one's feelings; to make one's feelings known. □ *Jane vented her anger in a destructive manner.*

**ventilate** ['vɛn tɪ let] *tv.* to bring fresh air into a room or an enclosed space; to expose something or someplace to fresh air. □ *This fan can ventilate 500 square feet of space.*

**ventilator** ['vɛn tɪ le tɚ] **1.** *n.* a fan that moves air into or out of a room or enclosed space. □ *Bill turned on the ventilator because the room was stuffy.* **2.** *n.* a device that supplies air or oxygen to someone who cannot breathe without help. □ *John, who had inhaled smoke during the fire, required a ventilator.*

**venture** ['vɛn tʃɚ] **1.** *n.* a risky thing to do; especially an action taken in business where one risks one's money in order to gain more money. □ *John's venture into business wasn't very successful.* **2.** *tv.* to risk something; to expose something to danger; to place something in danger. □ *Mary ventured her paycheck on the bet.* **3.** *iv.* to go into a place that could be dangerous. □ *The young children ventured into the abandoned building.*

**verb** ['vɚb] *n.* a word that describes what someone or something is or does; a word that expresses being, action, or occurrence. □ *The past tense of many English verbs is formed by adding* -ed *or* -d.

**verbal** ['vɚb əl] **1.** *adj.* expressed in words; oral; spoken, not written. (Adv: *verbally.*) □ *Anne gave a quick verbal report at the meeting.* **2.** *adj.* of or about a verb; formed from a verb. (Adv: *verbally.*) □ *The progressive verbal suffix is "-ing" in English.* □ *Past participles can be thought of as verbal adjectives.*

**verbal auxiliary** ['vɚb əl ɔg 'zɪl jə ri] Go to **auxiliary verb.**

**verse** ['vɚs] **1.** *n.* poetry; language as it is used in poetry. (No plural form.) □ *Many of Shakespeare's plays are written in verse.* **2.** *n.* a group of lines in a poem or song. □ *Mary knows all four verses of the song.* **3.** *n.* a portion of a chapter of a book of the Bible. □ *The shortest Bible verse is only two words long.*

**version** ['vɚ ʒən] **1.** *n.* one person's account or description of something that happened. □ *Bob gave his version of the accident in a statement to the police.* **2.** *n.* a form of something that is different from another form of it, such as being in a different language or medium. □ *The class read the English versions of famous Russian poems.*

**vertical** ['vɚ tɪ kəl] *adj.* straight up and down. (Adv: *vertically* [...ɪk li].) □ *The carpenter made sure the wall was vertical.*

**very** ['vɛr i] **1.** *adv.* especially; quite; extremely; greatly; to a large degree. (Used to strengthen the meaning of an adjective or another adverb. *Very* is not used with the comparative forms, but is used with superlative forms, with *the,* to strengthen meaning.) □ *Jane and Bill were very, very happy to win the prize.* □ *He did the very best that he could.* **2.** *adj.* same; actual; identical. (Prenominal only.) □ *This less expensive ring is the very one I saw in the jeweler's shop.* **3.** *adj.* mere; simple. (Prenominal only.) □ *The very thought of eating liver makes me sick.*

**vessel** ['vɛs əl] **1.** *n.* a container used to hold liquids. □ *Soup was served from a large, silver vessel.* **2.** *n.* a large ship or boat. □ *The captain ordered the crew to board the vessel.*

**vest** ['vɛst] *n.* a piece of clothing that has no sleeves and is worn above the waist on top of a shirt and usually under a suit coat or jacket. □ *Susan wore a brightly colored vest over her blouse.*

**vet** ['vɛt] **1.** *n.* someone who has served in the military, especially during a war. (Short for **veteran.**) □ *My uncle is a vet. He was in the Korean War.* **2.** *n.* a doctor who treats only animals. (Short for **veterinarian.**) □ *I had to take our two cats to the vet for their shots.*

**veteran** ['vɛt (ə) rən] **1.** *n.* someone who has served in the military, especially during a war. (Can be shortened to **vet.**) □ *The local veterans of foreign wars meet in this hall every Friday.* **2.** *n.* someone who has a lot of experience with something. (Fig. on ①.) □ *Veterans of the fire department hold a reunion once a year.* **3.** *adj.* experienced; having a lot of experience with something. □ *Susan is a veteran writer of mystery books.*

**veterinarian** [vɛt (ə) rə 'nɛr i ən] *n.* a doctor who treats only animals. (Can be shortened to **vet.**) □ *We called a veterinarian to help us with our sick horse.*

**veto** ['vi to] **1.** *n.* an instance of using one's authority to stop a proposed bill from becoming law. (Pl ends in *-es.*) □ *The Senate voted to override the veto.* **2.** *tv.* to stop a bill from becoming law; not to allow something to happen. □ *The president vetoed the budget proposed by Congress.*

**vibrate** ['vɑɪ bret] **1.** *iv.* to move back and forth very quickly; to shake; to quiver. □ *The guitar string continued to vibrate after I plucked it.* **2.** *tv.* to move something back and forth very quickly; to shake something. □ *What is vibrating the floor? Is it an earthquake?*

**vibration** [vɑɪ 'bre ʃən] *n.* the motions of moving back and forth very quickly.

V

□ *The vibrations from a large truck set off my car alarm.*

**vice** ['vɑɪs] *n.* a bad or immoral habit. □ *David tried to quit the vice of smoking cigarettes.*

**vice president** ['vɑɪs 'prɛz ə dənt] *n.* someone who is at a rank just lower than president. □ *Anne has been promoted to senior vice president at the bank.*

**vicinity** [vɪ 'sɪn ə ti] *n.* a neighborhood; the location around someone or something; the surrounding area. □ *The storm hit the downtown area but passed over the nearby vicinities.*

**vicious** ['vɪʃ əs] **1.** *adj.* fierce; cruel; likely to cause pain; dangerous. (Adv: *viciously.*) □ *Keep that vicious dog away from me!* **2.** *adj.* evil; cruel. (Adv: *viciously.*) □ *Bob spread a vicious rumor about John at the office.*

**victim** ['vɪk təm] *n.* someone or an animal that dies, suffers, or loses something because of someone else's actions, a sickness, an accident, or a natural disaster. □ *The flood victims were given emergency funds.*

**victimize** ['vɪk tə mɑɪz] *tv.* to cause someone to be a victim; to cause someone to suffer. □ *The police officers victimized the poor suspect.*

**victor** ['vɪk tɚ] *n.* a winner; someone who wins a fight, game, contest, race, etc. □ *Olympic victors are awarded medals.*

**victory** ['vɪk tə ri] *n.* winning; achieving success: the success of defeating an enemy or opponent. (Plural only when referring to different kinds, types, instances, or varieties.) □ *Victory is very satisfying.* Ⓒ *The citizens celebrated the army's victories by having a parade.*

**video** ['vɪd i o] **1.** *n.* moving visible images, such as what is recorded on videotape; the visible part of a television program; the display seen on a computer monitor. (No plural form.) □ *The video is poor, but the audio is good.* **2.** *n.* a movie that is available on videotape; motion or action that is recorded on videotape. (Pl ends in *-s.*) □ *Bill rented some videos to watch after dinner.* **3.** *n.* a short film or taped version of a song. (Pl ends in *-s.*) □ *Dave watches music videos on cable television.* **4.** *adj.* <the adj. use of ①.> □ *I bought a video camera so I could record Anne's wedding.*

**videocassette** ['vɪd i o kə 'sɛt] *n.* a device that holds videotape, which is put into a video camera or a videocassette recorder to record and play back images. □ *You should rewind videocassettes after watching them.*

**videotape** ['vɪd i o tep] **1.** *n.* a length of plastic tape on which images can be recorded and played back. (No plural form.) □ *The film editor spliced two pieces of videotape together.* **2.** *n.* a reel or cassette of ①; a copy of a movie or a television show that is recorded on ①. □ *Anne rented a videotape of her favorite movie and watched it at home.*

**view** ['vju] **1.** *n.* the way something looks from a place; a scene. □ *The view from my hotel window was beautiful.* **2.** *n.* an opinion; the way someone thinks about something. □ *In my view, the mayor should do more to prevent crime.* **3.** *tv.* to examine someone or something; to look at someone or something closely. □ *Mary viewed a robin in its nest, feeding its young.*

**viewpoint** ['vju pɔɪnt] *n.* an opinion; the way someone thinks about something. □ *Susan compared her viewpoint on gun control with mine.*

**vigil** ['vɪdʒ əl] *n.* an act or instance of staying awake during the night to watch something, to pray, or to take care of someone who is sick. □ *The family kept a vigil all night after the child was injured.*

V

**vigilant** [ˈvɪdʒ ə lənt] *adj.* on guard; watchful; watching over someone or something. (Adv: *vigilantly.*) □ *The vigilant guards protected the museum all day long.*

**vigor** [ˈvɪg ɚ] *n.* strength; energy; **drive** ⑥. (No plural form.) □ *A cup of coffee renewed the worker's vigor.*

**vile** [ˈvɑɪl] **1.** *adj.* very bad; very unpleasant; disgusting. (Adv: *vilely.* Comp: *viler;* sup: *vilest.*) □ *I spat the vile food out of my mouth.* **2.** *adj.* evil; wicked; immoral. (Adv: *vilely.* Comp: *viler;* sup: *vilest.*) □ *The vile murderer tortured his victims.*

**village** [ˈvɪl ɪdʒ] **1.** *n.* a small town; a group of houses and businesses in the country or suburbs. □ *I grew up in a small village of 500 people.* **2.** *n.* all the people who live in a particular **village** ①. □ *The village objected to the way tax money was spent.* **3.** *adj.* <the adj. use of ①.> □ *I visited the mayor at the village hall.*

**villager** [ˈvɪl ɪdʒ ɚ] *n.* someone who lives in a village. □ *Many of the villagers go to the town hall on Friday night.*

**villain** [ˈvɪl ən] *n.* someone who is wicked or evil, especially someone who is the bad person in a story or movie. □ *The evil villain was very mean to everyone in the village.*

**vine** [ˈvɑɪn] *n.* a plant that has long, thin stems that crawl along the ground or the sides of an object. □ *The farmer removed a large pumpkin from its vine.*

**vinegar** [ˈvɪn ɪ gɚ] *n.* a sour liquid made from wine or apple juice, used to flavor or preserve food. (No plural form.) □ *I put vinegar and oil on my salad.*

**vinyl** [ˈvɑɪ nəl] **1.** *n.* a common plastic. (No plural form.) □ *Our kitchen floor is covered with vinyl.* **2.** *adj.* made of ①. □ *Mary bought a vinyl purse because it is easy to clean.*

**viola** [vi ˈo lə] *n.* a stringed musical instrument that is similar to, but larger than, a violin. □ *David practices the viola for hours at a time.*

**violence** [ˈvɑɪ ə ləns] *n.* rough force; actions that hurt or damage people or things. (No plural form. Number is expressed with *act(s) of violence.*) □ *The mayor was dismayed by all of the violence in the city.*

**violent** [ˈvɑɪ ə lənt] **1.** *adj.* using rough force that can hurt or damage people or things. (Adv: *violently.*) □ *The violent winds tore down many power lines.* **2.** *adj.* showing violence. (Adv: *violently.*) □ *I wouldn't let my children watch violent movies.*

**violet** [ˈvɑɪ ə lɪt] *n.* a small plant that has dark purple flowers with a delicate smell. □ *Mary stopped to smell the violets growing in the park.*

**violin** [vɑɪ ə ˈlɪn] *n.* a four-stringed musical instrument played with a bow. □ *There are six violins in our orchestra.*

**violinist** [vɑɪ ə ˈlɪn ɪst] *n.* someone who plays a violin. □ *The concert violinist practiced for eight hours every day.*

**viper** [ˈvɑɪ pɚ] *n.* a venomous snake, especially one with fangs. □ *The deadly viper sank its fangs into its prey.*

**virtual** [ˈvɚ tʃu əl] **1.** *adj.* having an effect as though someone or something were the real thing or person. (Adv: *virtually.*) □ *The real-estate agent said the condo was located in a virtual paradise.* **2.** *adj.* of or about interaction on the Internet; of or about interaction with other people through computers. (Adv: *virtually.*) □ *A virtual business is one that exists on the Internet.*

**virtue** [ˈvɚ tʃu] **1.** *n.* goodness, especially in behavior or morals. (No plural form.) □ *What I lack in virtue, I make up for in good intentions.* **2.** *n.* a good moral behavior or trait; a trait that is valued by society. □ *Faith, hope, and* *charity are all virtues.* **3.** *n.* an advantage; a benefit. □ *My job isn't perfect, but it has many virtues.*

**virus** ['vɑɪ rəs] *n.* a living thing so small it can only be seen under a microscope. (Viruses cause infections and diseases in humans, animals, and plants, including chicken pox, rabies, and the common cold.) □ *The deadly virus was spread through casual contact.*

**visa** ['vi zə] *n.* an official stamp, signature, or attachment put in a passport, which allows its owner to enter a certain country. □ *Mary went to the American embassy to renew her visa while abroad.*

**vise** [vɑɪs] *n.* a machine made of metal jaws that can be pushed tightly together, used for clamping something tightly so that it doesn't move while someone works on it. □ *John clamped the rod in the vise while he sanded it.*

**visible** ['vɪz ə bəl] *adj.* able to be seen; not hidden. (Adv: *visibly.*) □ *Employees must wear their badges so they are visible.*

**vision** ['vɪ ʒən] **1.** *n.* the ability to see; the power of sight. (No plural form.) □ *Surgery restored the blind woman's vision.* **2.** *n.* something that is seen or experienced in a dream, in one's imagination, or in one's memory. □ *Alone in the old house, Bill thought he saw a ghostly vision.* **3.** *n.* insight; the ability to understand what something means and how it will affect the future. (No plural form.) □ *Because of the owner's vision, the company remained quite competitive.*

**visit** ['vɪz ɪt] **1.** *tv.* to go to a person or a place for a period of time; to be with a person as a visitor; to be at a place as a visitor. □ *John visited Europe for three weeks last summer.* **2.** *tv.* to examine or inspect something as part of one's job. □ *The company owner visited each branch once a month.* **3.** *iv.* to be someone's guest; to stay at someone's house or at a place as a guest or tourist. □ *We aren't living with my parents. We're just visiting.* **4.** *n.* an act or instance of someone going or coming to a place for a period of time in order to see someone or something, experience something, or talk with someone. □ *John decided that his cousin in the hospital needed a visit.*

**visitor** ['vɪz ɪ tɚ] *n.* someone who visits someone or some place as a guest or tourist. □ *Bill offered his visitors something to drink.*

**visual** ['vɪ ʒu əl] *adj.* of or about vision or seeing. (Adv: *visually.*) □ *Special glasses corrected David's visual problem.*

**vital** ['vɑɪt əl] **1.** *adj.* very important; absolutely necessary; essential. (Adv: *vitally.*) □ *Secrecy is vital for national security.* **2.** *adj.* of or about life; necessary for life. □ *The heart and brain are vital organs.* **3.** *adj.* active; full of life. (Adv: *vitally.*) □ *John was quite a vital individual before his illness.*

**vitamin** ['vɑɪ tə mɪn] *n.* a chemical compound that is important for a person's health and cannot be made by the body. □ *Citrus fruit is rich in vitamin C.*

**vivid** ['vɪv ɪd] **1.** *adj.* clear; distinct. (Adv: *vividly.*) □ *Mary remembered her vivid dream.* **2.** *adj.* strongly or brightly colored; deeply colored. (Adv: *vividly.*) □ *David's tie was a vivid green.*

**vocabulary** [vo 'kæb jə lɛr i] **1.** *n.* the words that someone knows; the words that are port of someone's language. (No plural form.) □ *Mary studied the dictionary to improve her vocabulary.* **2.** *n.* the words used in a certain business, profession, or activity. (No plural form.) □ *The medical vocabulary confused the patient.* **3.** *n.* a list of words with a brief meaning, like those found in foreign-language dictionaries; a glossary of words and their meanings. □

*The German textbook included an 800-word vocabulary.* **4.** *n.* all the words of a language. (No plural form.) □ *Much of the vocabulary of English consists of technical and scientific terms.*

**vocation** [vo 'ke ʃən] *n.* an occupation; a trade; a profession; one's calling. □ *What vocation are you training for?*

**voice** ['vɔɪs] **1.** *n.* the sounds made by a person who is speaking or singing; the sound made when speaking or singing. □ *Anne trained her voice to sing opera.* **2.** *n.* a medium or channel for representing someone's opinions. □ *I will serve as your voice in the planning meetings.* **3.** *n.* <a grammar term that describes the relation of the subject of a sentence to the verb.> □ *I wrote this sentence in the active voice.* □ *This sentence was written in the passive voice.* **4.** *tv.* to express an opinion by speaking. □ *Mary voiced a complaint about the rude clerk.* **5.** *tv.* [in phonetics] to give a certain quality to a sound by vibrating the vocal folds and making the sound of the **voice** ①. □ *In English, you must always voice nasal consonants.*

**void** ['vɔɪd] **1.** *adj.* not binding according to the law; having no legal authority; having no legal effect; no longer valid. □ *The judged ruled John's contract to be void.* **2.** *tv.* to cause a law to stop being a law. □ *The Supreme Court voided the law.* **3.** *n.* an area that is empty; an empty space; a gap. □ *Most of the universe is a large void.*

**volcano** [vɑl 'ke no] *n.* a mountain with an opening at the top or on the sides from which steam, gas, molten rock, and ash sometimes are ejected by pressure or force from inside the earth. (Pl ends in *-s* or *-es.*) □ *The majority of the world's volcanoes surround the Pacific Ocean.*

**volleyball** ['vɑl i bɔl] **1.** *n.* a sport where two teams on opposite sides of a net try to hit a large, light ball back and forth over the net without letting the ball touch the ground. (No plural form.) □ *Anne played volleyball each year while in college.* **2.** *n.* the ball used to play ①. □ *Jane smacked the volleyball over the net.*

**volt** ['volt] *n.* a unit of measurement of electrical force. □ *Five thousand volts of electricity surged through the wire.*

**voltage** ['vol tɪdʒ] *n.* an amount of an electrical force, measured in volts. □ *The voltage in the electric fence was low enough that it would only stun, not kill, anyone who touched it.*

**volume** ['vɑl jəm] **1.** *n.* a book, especially one book in a series of books. □ *One volume of the nature series was devoted to birds.* **2.** *n.* the loudness of sound. (Plural only when referring to different kinds, types, instances, or varieties.) □ *The music is too loud. Please reduce the volume.* Ⓒ *I tried listening to the song at different volumes, but it was distorted at all of them.* **3.** *n.* an amount of something. □ *A large volume of oil washed up on shore from the spill.* **4.** *n.* the expression of space in three dimensions, determined by multiplying an object's length, width, and depth. □ *The math student calculated the volume of the cube.*

**voluntary** ['vɑl ən tɛr i] **1.** *adj.* [done] by one's own choice. (Adv: *voluntarily* [vɑl ən 'tɛr ə li].) □ *Employees could make voluntary contributions to several charities.* **2.** *adj.* supported by volunteers or gifts. □ *Voluntary helpers deliver meals to sick people at home.*

**volunteer** [vɑl ən 'tɪr] **1.** *n.* someone who does work for free; someone who agrees to take on a job or task. □ *Mary is a volunteer at the local day-care center.* **2.** *tv.* to offer one's time, help, or energy at no cost; to give one's services for free. □ *John volunteered his time to help organize the party.* **3.** *tv.* to say something without being forced to talk; to say something by one's own choice.

V

□ *John volunteered his comments when he felt they were appropriate.* **4.** *adj.* <the adj. use of ①.> □ *The volunteer soldier served for four years.*

**vomit** ['vɑm ɪt] **1.** *tv.* to throw food up after one has eaten it; to bring something up from the stomach. □ *The man vomited the bad food he'd just eaten.* **2.** *iv.* to throw [something] up from the stomach through the mouth. □ *The drunken student vomited into a trash can.* **3.** *n.* something that has been thrown up from the stomach through the mouth. (No plural form.) □ *The dormitory bathroom smelled of vomit.*

**vote** ['vot] **1.** *n.* a formal or legal expression of one's opinion on an issue, especially on political issues. □ *Jane cast her vote for the youngest candidate.* **2. the vote** *n.* the right to **vote** ④. (No plural form. Treated as singular.) □ *We fought long and hard to pass a law that would give us the vote.* **3.** *n.* the **votes** ①, viewed collectively, of a large number of people who share a certain characteristic or background. (No plural form. Treated as singular.) □ *The president received 75% of the Hispanic vote.* **4.** *iv.* to express one's opinion on an issue by raising one's hand or marking one's choice on a ballot. □ *Anne has voted since she turned 18.*

**voter** ['vot ɚ] *n.* someone who has the right to vote in an election. □ *The candidate met with many voters before the election.*

**vow** ['vɑʊ] **1.** *n.* an oath; a solemn promise. □ *I made a vow to never reveal Jane's secret.* **2.** *tv.* to make ①; to swear that one will do something. (The object can be a clause with **that** ⑦.) □ *Jimmy vowed that he would improve his grades next semester.*

**vowel** ['vɑʊ əl] **1.** *n.* a speech sound that is made without completely closing any parts of the mouth while air passes through it. □ *The word* sweet *has only one sound that is a vowel, and it is* [i]. □ *The vowel* [e] *can be represented in writing by* ai, ay, *and* eigh. **2.** *n.* a letter of the alphabet that represents a speech sound that is not a **consonant**; [in English] the letters *a, e, i, o,* and *u.* □ *The word* sweet *contains two vowels.* □ *There are two vowels in the word* fought, *but only one vowel sound.* **3.** *adj.* <the adj. use of ①.> □ *The letter* e *stands for a vowel sound.* □ *We are studying vowel production in speech class.*

**voyage** ['voɪ ədʒ] *n.* a journey, especially one made over water, through the air, or in space; a journey made on a ship, airplane, or spacecraft. □ *We were excited about our upcoming voyage to Europe by ship.*

**vulture** ['vʌl tʃɚ] *n.* a large bird that lives on the meat of dead animals. □ *Vultures circled over the dying animal.*

V

**waddle** ['wɑd l] *iv.* to walk with slow, short steps while moving the body from side to side, as a duck walks. □ *The overweight man waddled across the street.*

**wade** ['wed] **1.** *iv.* to walk through shallow water or mud. □ *After the rainstorm we had to wade through the mud to get to the car.* **2.** *tv.* to cross a shallow body of water by walking through it. □ *The children waded the length of the shallow pond.*

**waffle** ['wɑf əl] **1.** *n.* a thick round or square pancake with depressed squares that form a grid. □ *My mother makes waffles for breakfast on Sundays.* **2.** *iv.* to change one's mind on an issue many times. □ *The president kept waffling about the important issues.*

**wag** ['wæg] **1.** *tv.* to move something up and down or from side to side many times. □ *Susan wagged her finger at her son as she scolded him.* **2.** *iv.* to move up and down or from side to side many times. □ *The tree's branches wagged in the strong wind.*

**wage** ['wedʒ] **1.** *tv.* to begin and continue a war, battle, or struggle against someone or something. □ *The citizens waged a battle with the state over the proposed highway.* **2.** *n.* payment for work, especially when a certain amount is paid for each hour worked. (Often plural with the same meaning. Compare with **salary**.) □ *Susan gets paid a good wage for her work.*

**wager** ['we dʒɚ] **1.** *n.* a bet. □ *John lost the wager that he had made on the horse race.* **2.** *tv.* to risk an amount of money on the outcome of an event. □ *I wagered $10 that my school's team would win the game.* **3.** *tv.* to bet that something will happen; to bet that something is or will be the case. (The object is a clause with **that** ⑦.) □ *Bill wagered that I couldn't beat him in a game of tennis.*

**wagon** ['wæg ən] **1.** *n.* a strong four-wheeled vehicle with a flat bottom that is pulled by horses, mules, or oxen. □ *Four horses pulled the farmer's wagon into town.* **2.** *n.* a small, light four-wheeled cart with a flat bottom that is pulled as a children's toy. □ *Jimmy filled his wagon with toys.*

**wail** ['wel] **1.** *n.* a long, loud cry, especially one of pain or sadness. □ *The mourners let out a loud wail of grief.* **2.** *iv.* to cry out with a long, loud sound because of pain or sadness. □ *The dead man's family wailed at his funeral.* **3.** *tv.* to utter something with a long, loud cry of pain or sadness. (The object can be a clause with **that** ⑦.) □ *Jimmy wailed that his head hurt.*

**waist** ['west] **1.** *n.* the part of the body below the bottom of the ribs and above the hips. □ *Anne measured her waist before buying new pants.* **2.** *n.* the part of a piece of clothing that covers ①; the part of a piece of clothing that hangs from ①. □ *A belt fits through loops sewn around the waist of the pants.*

**waistline** ['west lɑɪn] *n.* an imaginary line around the body at the smallest part of one's waist, usually where the top hem of a pair of pants or a skirt rests on the body. □ *Some models have quite a small waistline.*

**wait** ['wet] **1.** *iv.* to stay in a place until someone or something else arrives or returns; to stay in a place until something happens. □ *Anne waited in the doorway until it stopped raining.* **2. wait**

**for** someone or something**; wait on** someone or something *iv.* + *prep. phr.* to anticipate the arrival of someone or something. □ *Bill isn't ready, but we can't wait on him any longer. Let's go without him.* **3. wait on** someone *iv.* + *prep. phr.* to serve someone as a waiter or waitress or as a clerk behind a counter. □ *While the clerk was waiting on me, another customer rudely interrupted.* **4.** *n.* a period of time that one **waits for** someone or something as in ②. □ *There was a short wait before the play while the people found their seats.*

**waiter** ['we tɚ] *n.* a man who serves customers at a restaurant. □ *John did not leave the rude waiter a tip.*

**waitress** ['we trɪs] *n.* a woman who serves customers at a restaurant. □ *The waitress asked us if we'd like to order dessert.*

**waive** ['wev] **1.** *tv.* to give up something, especially a right or a privilege. □ *Since John doesn't have a car, he waived his right to claim a parking space.* **2.** *tv.* to allow someone not to have to do something that is usually required; to excuse someone from fulfilling a requirement. □ *Tax payments are usually waived for charities.*

**wake** ['wek] **1. wake (up)** *iv., irreg.* (+ *adv.*) to stop sleeping. (Pt: *waked* or **woke**; pp: *waked* or **woken**.) □ *Susan woke up at sunrise.* **2. wake** someone or some creature **(up)** *tv., irreg.* + *obj.* (+ *adv.*) to cause someone or some creature to stop sleeping. □ *Barking dogs woke me up at 3:00 A.M.* **3.** *n.* a gathering, shortly before a funeral, of friends and relatives of someone who has recently died. □ *Mary said a prayer at her best friend's wake.* **4.** *n.* the path on the surface of a body of water caused by a boat or ship traveling through it. □ *The motorboat's rough wake upset my rowboat.*

**waken** ['wek ən] **1.** *iv.* to wake from sleep; to stop sleeping. □ *John wakened to the sound of his neighbor's loud radio.* **2.** *tv.* to wake someone or something from sleep. □ *Jane wakened Susan from her nap.*

**walk** ['wɔk] **1.** *iv.* to move on foot at a normal speed and in a way that only one foot at a time is on the ground. □ *John walked down the hallway.* **2.** *iv.* [for a baseball player who is batting] to go to first base after the pitcher has thrown four **balls** ③. □ *Bill walked, so the player on first base moved to second base.* **3.** *tv.* to move in, on, or through a space as in ①. □ *I walked the path that others had taken through the meadow.* **4.** *tv.* to exercise an animal, usually a dog, by taking it for ⑦. □ *David walked his dog in the park.* **5.** *tv.* [for a baseball pitcher] to throw four **balls** ③ to a player who is batting, which allows the player to go to first base. □ *The powerful batter was walked by the pitcher on purpose.* **6.** *tv.* to go with someone to a certain place. □ *The security guard walks students home from the library at night.* **7.** *n.* an act of **walking** as in ①, especially as exercise or for pleasure; a journey on foot. □ *My dog enjoys his daily walks outside.* **8.** *n.* a path; a place where one can **walk** ①. □ *Mary ran down the walk near the hotel and crossed the street in a hurry.*

**wall** ['wɔl] **1.** *n.* the side of a room from the floor to the ceiling; the side of a building from the ground to the roof. □ *John crashed his car through the wall of his garage.* **2.** *n.* a large, flat side of anything; anything that looks like ①. □ *The old fence has become a wall of ivy over the years.* **3.** *n.* a thin tissue that encloses a part of the body of a human, plant, or animal. □ *The chemical passed rapidly through the cell wall.*

**wallet** ['wɑl ət] *n.* a small, flat case that is used for carrying money, identification,

W

credit cards, etc. (Often made of leather.) □ *Jane put the money in her wallet.*

**wallpaper** ['wɔl pe pɚ] **1.** *n.* paper, usually with a design on it, that is used to cover and decorate walls. (No plural form.) □ *Without thinking, Bob placed new wallpaper over the old, peeling layer.* **2.** *tv.* to cover a wall with ①. □ *Anne wallpapered the living room with a bright print.* **3.** *iv.* to apply ① to a wall; to put up ①. □ *Mary decided to wallpaper instead of paint.*

**walnut** ['wɔl nət] **1.** *n.* the tree that produces a delicious, edible nut. □ *Squirrels climb on the branches of the walnuts in our front yard.* **2.** *n.* the nut of ①; the nut of ① and its shell. □ *A squirrel sat under the tree, eating a walnut.* **3.** *n.* wood from ①. (Plural only when referring to different kinds, types, instances, or varieties.) □ *I painted the pine and coated the expensive walnut with a layer of varnish.* Ⓒ *The denser and harder walnuts have a more interesting grain.* **4.** *adj.* made from ③. □ *David polished the walnut bookshelves.*

**waltz** ['wɔlts] **1.** *n.* a dance, with three beats to every measure of music, in which couples turn in a circle as they dance around the dance floor. □ *The dance instructors performed a waltz for the class.* **2.** *n.* music that has three beats to every measure and is written for ① or suitable for ①. □ *The orchestra played a lively waltz.* **3.** *iv.* to dance ①. □ *I learned how to waltz when I took dance lessons.*

**wander** ['wɑn dɚ] *iv.* to travel in no specific direction without a specific location in mind; to roam somewhere. □ *Anne wandered around the large park.*

**wane** ['wen] **1.** *iv.* to become less important, less strong, less intense, or smaller. □ *The politician's popularity waned as a result of the scandal.* **2.** *iv.* [for the moon] to gradually appear to be smaller after a full moon. (Compare with **wax** ④.) □ *The moon had visibly waned within a few days of the full moon.*

**want** ['wɑnt] **1.** *tv.* to desire to have someone or something. □ *Jimmy wants a new toy.* **2. want to** do something *iv.* + *inf.* to desire to do something; to wish to do something. □ *We want to go to Europe for a vacation.* **3.** *n.* a desire; a need; something that someone would like to have. □ *Aunt Sally asked the children what their wants were.* **4.** *n.* a lack. (No plural form.) □ *The beggar died for want of shelter and food.*

**war** ['wor] *n.* fighting or conflict between two or more nations, especially involving a military force of one country attacking another country. (Plural only when referring to different kinds, types, instances, or varieties.) □ *When John was 19, he joined the army and went to war.* Ⓒ *Parents have declared a war on drunk driving in our neighborhood.*

**ward** ['word] **1.** *n.* someone, especially a child, who is under the protection of the state, the government, a judge, or someone chosen by a court. □ *The judge ruled that the orphans should become wards of the state.* **2.** *n.* a political division of a city, especially one that is represented by someone in a city council. □ *This city is divided into 50 wards.* **3.** *n.* a section of a hospital, usually containing the beds for patients having similar medical conditions. □ *I was put into a ward on the third floor of the hospital.*

**warden** ['word n] *n.* someone who is in charge of a prison or jail. (See also **game warden**.) □ *The prison warden was unable to quell the riot.*

**wardrobe** ['wor drob] **1.** *n.* a collection of clothes. □ *Bill's wardrobe includes five different suits.* **2.** *n.* a piece of furniture that looks like a large box with a door, and is used to store clothing. □ *Bill keeps his ties inside the oak wardrobe.*

**warehouse** ['wɛr hɑʊs] **1.** *n., irreg.* a place where large amounts of goods are stored before they are sold or used. (Pl: [...hɑʊ zəz].) □ *The manager took an inventory of the goods in the warehouse.* **2.** *tv.* to store something in ①. □ *The surplus inventory was warehoused in a large building.*

**warm** ['worm] **1.** *adj.* somewhat hot; not too hot but not cold. (Adv: *warmly.* Comp: *warmer;* sup: *warmest.*) □ *I like my coffee to be hot, not just warm.* **2.** *adj.* capable of retaining heat. (Adv: *warmly.* Comp: *warmer;* sup: *warmest.*) □ *During the winter, John wears warm sweaters to work.* **3.** *adj.* pleasant; friendly; indicating that one is pleasant or friendly. (Adv: *warmly.* Comp: *warmer;* sup: *warmest.*) □ *The guests received a warm reception at the banquet.* **4. warm (up)** *iv. (+ adv.)* to become ①. □ *The soup is warming on the stove.* **5. warm up** *iv. + adv.* to exercise and move one's body to prepare one's muscles for athletic activities. □ *If you don't warm up, you risk injuring yourself.* **6. warm** someone or something **(up)** *tv. + obj. (+ adv.)* to cause someone or something to become ①. □ *John warmed the soup on the stove.*

**warmth** ['wormθ] **1.** *n.* a small amount of heat. (No plural form.) □ *The warmth of the spring weather was a relief after the cold winter.* **2.** *n.* kindness; pleasantness; friendliness. (No plural form.) □ *Anne appreciated the warmth of her new neighbors.*

**warn** ['worn] **1.** *tv.* to alert someone to danger; to inform someone about something dangerous or risky. □ *The spy warned the general of the enemy's plans.* **2.** *tv.* to tell someone not to do something, implying that punishment will follow repeated violations. □ *The police officer warned me not to speed again.*

**warning** ['wor nɪŋ] *n.* a statement, sign, or threat of danger; something that warns. □ *My boss issued a verbal warning when I was late for work.*

**warranty** ['wɑr ən ti] *n.* an official guarantee; a written promise from a manufacturer that something will function in the way that it is supposed to. □ *John's new car has a limited warranty for parts and service.*

**warrior** ['wor jɚ] *n.* someone who is trained to fight; a soldier; a fighter. □ *The warriors fought on the field.*

**warship** ['wɚ ʃɪp] *n.* a ship equipped with weapons for making war. □ *Two warships cruised into the enemy's harbor.*

**wart** ['wort] *n.* a hard, ugly bump that swells from the skin, especially on the face, neck, and hands. □ *A small wart developed on the end of John's nose.*

**wary** ['wɛr i] *adj.* aware; on guard against harm or danger; careful. (Adv: *warily.* Comp: *warier;* sup: *wariest.*) □ *I'm wary of dogs, because when I was a child a dog bit me.*

**was** ['wʌz, 'wɑz, wəz] *iv.* <a pt of **be** used with the first and third persons singular.> □ *The house was red before they painted it white.*

**wash** ['wɑʃ] **1.** *tv.* to clean someone or something with water or some other liquid. □ *John always washes the dishes after dinner.* **2.** *tv.* to remove dirt through the use of water or some other liquid. □ *The butcher washed the blood from the knife.* **3.** *tv.* [for water] to carry or move something. □ *The current washed the raft down the river.* **4.** *iv.* to clean [oneself or some part of oneself] with water or some other liquid. □ *Bob washed behind his ears.* **5.** *iv.* to be carried or moved by water. □ *The trash washed downstream.* **6.** *n.* laundry; clothes that need to be, are being, or have been **washed** as in ①; clothes that are **washed** ① together at one time. (No plural form.) □ *Dave hung the wash out to dry on the clothesline.* **7.** *n.* an act

W

or instance of cleaning or being cleaned as in ①, ②, or ④. □ *I gave my car a wash because I'd been driving on muddy roads.*

**washcloth** ['wɑʃ klɔθ] *n., irreg.* a small cloth used for washing one's body, especially the face. (Pl: ['wɑʃ klɔðz].) □ *Who left the wet washcloth in the bathtub?*

**washer** ['wɑʃ ɚ] **1.** *n.* a washing machine; a machine that washes clothing. □ *The new parents bought a washer to clean all the diapers they would have to use.* **2.** *n.* a small, flat circle of metal or rubber, with a hole in the center, that is put under the head of a bolt or screw or between a nut and a bolt to make a tighter seal. □ *The metal washer protected the wood from the head of the screw.*

**washroom** ['wɑʃ rum] *n.* a bathroom; a restroom; a room with a toilet. □ *When you're done in the washroom, turn out the light!*

**wasn't** ['wʌz ənt] *cont.* "was not." □ *John wasn't at the party last night, was he?*

**wasp** ['wɑsp] *n.* a large stinging insect that is similar to a bee but is able to sting again and again. □ *John angered the wasps by throwing rocks at their hive.*

**waste** ['west] **1.** *tv.* to use something foolishly or wrongly; to use too much of something. □ *Anne wasted her time trying to convince John that she was right.* **2.** *n.* garbage; trash; something that is not used and is thrown away. (No plural form.) □ *The company illegally burned its waste.* **3.** *n.* a poor or foolish use of something; the failure to use all of the parts of something that are able to be used. (No plural form.) □ *This watch was a waste of money because it doesn't work.* **4.** *n.* material that is sent out from the body; urine and feces. (Sometimes plural with the same meaning, but not countable.) □ *It's necessary to flush one's waste down the toilet.*

**wastebasket** ['west bæs kɪt] *n.* a container that is used to hold trash. □ *The janitor emptied all the wastebaskets in the office.*

**wastepaper** ['west pe pɚ] *n.* paper that is not needed and is thrown away or reused. (No plural form.) □ *John threw the wastepaper in the trash.*

**wastepaper basket** ['west pe pɚ 'bæs kət] *n.* a container for receiving wastepaper. □ *You should empty the wastepaper basket into the large container outside.*

**watch** ['wɑtʃ] **1.** *tv.* to observe something as it happens; to pay someone or something attention; to look at someone or something to see what happens. □ *David watched the parade from his apartment window.* **2.** *tv.* to guard someone or something; to protect someone or something. □ *Shepherds watched the flocks of sheep.* **3.** *iv.* to pay attention to someone or something; to look at someone or something carefully and attentively. □ *The audience watched closely as the magician performed the trick.* **4.** *n.* a device, typically worn on one's wrist, that displays the time. □ *What time does your watch say?*

**water** ['wɔt ɚ] **1.** *n.* the liquid that forms oceans, lakes, and rivers; the liquid that falls from the sky as rain and is drunk by humans and animals. (No plural form.) □ *John swallowed some water when he was swimming.* **2.** *n.* the surface of a body of ①. (No plural form.) □ *The calm water reflected my image.* **3. waters** *n.* vast amounts of ① as found in rivers, oceans, or large lakes. □ *The lake's waters provided swimming and boating.* **4.** *tv.* to provide a plant with ①; to put ① on the soil around a plant. □ *John watered the tomato plants with a garden hose.* **5.** *iv.* [for one's eyes] to fill with tears. □ *My eyes water a lot*

W

*when I slice onions.* **6.** *iv.* [for one's mouth] to fill with moisture, especially when one is about to eat or is thinking about eating food. □ *The children's mouths watered when they saw the delicious cake.*

**waterfall** ['wɔt ɚ fɔl] *n.* a flow of water off the side of a mountain, rock, or dam. □ *We hiked three miles through the forest to see the waterfall.*

**waterproof** ['wɔt ɚ pruf] **1.** *adj.* not allowing water to pass through; able to keep water inside or outside; not leaking water. □ *John's waterproof boots keep his feet dry.* **2.** *tv.* to cause something to resist water as in ①. □ *The wooden deck was waterproofed to protect it from the rain.*

**watertight** ['wɔt ɚ tɑɪt] **1.** *adj.* not allowing water to pass through; able to keep water inside or outside; not leaking water. □ *The watertight seal kept moisture from getting into the container.* **2.** *adj.* perfect; [of an agreement or argument] having no mistakes or defects. (Fig. on ①.) □ *She was forced to keep her end of the agreement because she signed a watertight contract.*

**wave** ['wev] **1.** *n.* a moving ridge of water made by wind or the movement of something through water. □ *The raft bobbed on the waves.* **2.** *n.* a ridge in the surface of something. □ *The wind created small waves in the sand.* **3.** *n.* a movement of the hand as in ⑥. □ *The traffic cop's wave indicated that I should turn right.* **4.** *n.* an increase in crime, heat, or cold. □ *The crops withered during the intense heat wave.* **5.** *tv.* to move something, especially one's hand, when greeting someone, trying to get someone's attention, or calling attention to oneself. □ *Anne waved her hands wildly so that we would see her.* **6.** *iv.* to greet someone, to get someone's attention, or to call attention to oneself by moving one's hand. □ *Mary was waving from her window.* **7.** *iv.* to move up and down or back and forth in the air. □ *The kite waved as it hung from the tree.*

**wax** ['wæks] **1.** *n.* an oily or fatty substance that melts easily when it is warmed but hardens when it is cool, used to make candles, floor polish, and other substances. (Plural only when referring to different kinds, types, instances, or varieties.) □ *The floor shined with its new coat of wax.* 🄲 *Modern waxes stand up well to heavy traffic.* **2.** *n.* an oily substance that is produced in the ears. (No plural form.) □ *John's hearing problem was caused by too much wax in his ears.* **3.** *tv.* to coat or polish a floor with ①. □ *Anne just waxed the floor, so it's very slippery.* **4.** *iv.* [for the moon] to gradually appear to be brighter and fuller before a full moon. (Compare with **wane**.) □ *The moon waxes before it becomes full and bright. Then it wanes.*

**way** ['we] **1.** *n.* a manner; the manner in which something is done; a method. □ *The teacher showed the students a new way to do division.* **2.** *n.* a habit; a custom; a regular manner in which something is done. (Usually plural.) □ *I grew up on a farm, and city ways seem strange to me.* **3.** *n.* the route to a certain place. (No plural form.) □ *The way to the stadium was blocked by an accident.* **4. one's way** *n.* one's desire; one's wish. (No plural form.) □ *Jimmy cried until he got his way.* **5.** *adv.* far; far away in time or space. □ *I'm way behind in my work.*

**we** ['wi] **1.** *pron.* <the first-person plural subjective pronoun, referring to the speaker or writer—"I"—together with at least one other person.> □ *I spoke for my friends when I said we were ready to order.* **2.** *pron.* <a special use of ① as a first-person singular subjective pronoun, meaning "I, the speaker or writer."> (Used by writers and sometimes by royalty.) □ *"We are not* *amused!" said the queen, speaking only for herself.* **3.** *pron.* everyone; all humans. □ *We must eat to live.*

**weak** ['wik] **1.** *adj.* lacking power or strength; not strong or powerful. (Adv: *weakly.* Comp: *weaker;* sup: *weakest.*) □ *The ballplayer became weak suddenly and collapsed on the field.* **2.** *adj.* lacking strong morals; lacking a moral character. (Adv: *weakly.* Comp: *weaker;* sup: *weakest.*) □ *Bill was very weak against the temptation to cheat.* **3.** *adj.* having too much water; diluted. (Adv: *weakly.* Comp: *weaker;* sup: *weakest.*) □ *This tea is far too weak for me. Please let it steep longer.*

**weaken** ['wik ən] **1.** *iv.* to become weak. □ *The batteries in the flashlight had weakened over time.* **2.** *tv.* to cause someone or something to become weak. □ *The army weakened the prime minister's power.*

**wealth** ['wɛlθ] *n.* riches; a large amount of money or property. (No plural form.) □ *The successful inventor donated part of his wealth to charity.*

**wealthy** ['wɛl θi] **1.** *adj.* rich; having a large amount of money or property. (Adv: *wealthily.* Comp: *wealthier;* sup: *wealthiest.*) □ *Bill's wealthy parents paid his college expenses.* **2. the wealthy** *n.* people who are ①. (No plural form. Treated as plural, but not countable.) □ *The wealthy are able to afford the best of medical care.*

**wean** ['win] *tv.* to cause a child or young animal to begin to eat food other than milk from the mother. □ *The farmer weaned the calves as they got older.*

**weapon** ['wɛp ən] *n.* any object or machine used to hurt someone, to kill someone, or to defend oneself during a fight or an attack. □ *No weapons are permitted on the school grounds.*

**wear** ['wɛr] **1.** *tv., irreg.* to have something on the body, including clothes, glasses, jewelry, perfume, makeup, and similar things. (Pt: **wore;** pp: **worn.**) □ *Anne wore the necklace that I had given her.* **2.** *tv., irreg.* to have something on or related to the body kept or held in a particular way. □ *The cashiers were all instructed to wear a smile.* **3.** *tv., irreg.* to damage something gradually because of continued use. □ *Over the centuries, the river wore the rocks down.* **4.** *iv., irreg.* to damage or worsen gradually. □ *The soil wore away with each rainstorm.* **5.** *n.* gradual damage that is caused because of continued use. (No plural form.) □ *Heavy wear on the car lessened its resale value.* **6.** *n.* clothing, especially a collection of clothing available for sale at a store. (Used in combinations such as *resort wear, business wear,* etc. No plural form. Treated as singular.) □ *The advertisement featured a new line of casual wear.*

**weary** ['wɪr i] **1.** *adj.* tired; exhausted; fatigued. (Adv: *wearily.* Comp: *wearier;* sup: *weariest.*) □ *The weary driver fell asleep at the wheel and crashed into a tree.* **2.** *iv.* to become tired, exhausted, or fatigued. □ *The man wearied after driving for 18 hours.*

**weather** ['wɛð ɚ] **1.** *n.* the condition of the outside air, including the temperature, the amount of moisture in the air, and the presence or absence of rain, snow, wind, clouds, and sunshine. (No plural form.) □ *I use an air conditioner when the weather is hot.* **2.** *tv.* to withstand something (especially bad **weather** ①) without damage. □ *The plane easily weathered the rough journey.* **3.** *tv.* [for kinds of ①] to damage something. □ *The sun weathered the paint on the barn.* **4.** *iv.* to change because of exposure to ①. □ *Even well-built buildings weather over the course of time.*

**weave** ['wiv] **1.** *tv., irreg.* to make something by crossing threads or strips of material from side to side so that they go over and under threads or strips of material that are stretched up and down. (Pt: **wove**; pp: **woven**.) □ *I wove a small basket to carry flowers in.* **2.** *tv., irreg.* to cross threads or strips of material from side to side so that they go over and under threads or strips of material that are stretched up and down. □ *The machine wove wool thread into a bolt of material.* **3.** *tv., irreg.* to make something by combining different things into a whole. (Fig. on ①.) □ *The suspect wove a web of lies when questioned by the police.* **4.** *iv., irreg.* to move so that one is always changing direction. (Pt: sometimes *weaved.*) □ *The police officer stopped the driver who kept weaving between lanes.*

**web** ['wɛb] **1.** *n.* a net of thin, silky threads made by spiders in order to trap other insects for food. □ *The corners of the room were covered with spider webs.* **2.** *n.* a network; a detailed arrangement of things that cross and connect each other. (Fig. on ①.) □ *The detective was fooled by the suspect's web of lies.* **3.** *n.* the piece of thin skin between the toes of ducks and other animals that live in or near the water. □ *The webs of ducks' feet help them swim.* **4. the Web** *n.* the **World Wide Web**; a branch of the computer Internet. □ *Do you have any favorite locations on the Web?*

**we'd** ['wid] **1.** *cont.* "we had," where **had** is an auxiliary. □ *If we'd had more time, we could have gone to the party.* **2.** *cont.* "we would." □ *We'd like to order our food now, please.*

**wed** ['wɛd] **1.** *tv., irreg.* to marry someone; to take someone as a husband or wife. (Pt/pp: *wedded* or *wed.*) □ *Mary wedded her high-school sweetheart.* **2.** *tv., irreg.* to cause two people to become married by performing a marriage ceremony. □ *A judge wed Jane and Bob in a simple ceremony.* **3.** *iv., irreg.* to become married. □ *After the couple wed, they took a trip to Hawaii.*

**wedding** ['wɛd ɪŋ] **1.** *n.* the ceremony where two people become married to each other; a marriage ceremony. □ *Hundreds of people attended the couple's wedding.* **2.** *n.* a merger or formation of a close association. (Fig. on ①.) □ *Your theory is nothing more than the wedding of two simple ideas.*

**wedge** ['wɛdʒ] **1.** *n.* a piece of wood, metal, or other material that is thick at one end and narrows to an edge at the other end. □ *Anne kept the door open by putting a rubber wedge under it.* **2.** *n.* any object shaped like ①. □ *Tom placed a wedge of lime in my drink.* **3.** *tv.* to stick someone or something in a tight space between two things or people, especially so that nothing or no one can move. □ *Susan wedged her car between two parked cars.*

**Wednesday** ['wɛnz de] Go to **day**.

**weed** ['wid] **1.** *n.* a rough plant that grows in a place where it is not wanted. □ *The farmer killed the weeds with poison.* **2.** *tv.* to remove ① from an area of ground, such as a lawn or garden. □ *John weeded the flower patch with a spade.* **3.** *tv.* to remove a specific kind of ①. □ *Jane weeded the crab grass from the yard.* **4.** *iv.* to clean or improve [a garden or lawn] by removing ①. □ *Mary weeds every week, but the weeds keep growing back.*

**week** ['wik] **1.** *n.* a period of seven days. (See a list of days of the week at **day**.) □ *Mary will go to Florida a week from Wednesday.* **2.** *n.* a period of seven days beginning on a Sunday and ending on a Saturday. (According to the calendar.) □ *John is going to visit during the third week of April.* **3.** *n.* the five or six days during which most workers work, especially Monday through Friday. □ *Jane spent the week analyzing last month's budget report.*

**weekday** ['wik de] **1.** *n.* Monday, Tuesday, Wednesday, Thursday, or Friday. □ *Every weekday, I awake at 7:00 A.M. and get ready for work.* □ *My dentist is only available on weekdays.* **2.** *adj.* happening on ①; of ①. (Prenominal only.) □ *The train that goes downtown is very crowded on weekday mornings.*

**weekend** ['wik ɛnd] **1.** *n.* the period of time from Friday evening to Sunday night. □ *We're going to have a party next weekend.* **2.** *adj.* happening at some time between Friday evening and Sunday night. (Prenominal only.) □ *The student works weekend shifts at the restaurant.*

**weep** ['wip] **1.** *iv., irreg.* to cry. (Pt/pp: **wept**.) □ *The audience wept during the sad movie.* **2.** *tv., irreg.* to shed tears; to cry and make tears. □ *The hostages' families wept tears of joy upon their release.*

**weigh** ['we] **1.** *tv.* to use a scale to determine the weight of someone or something. □ *The doctor weighed the infant.* **2.** *tv.* to think carefully and compare different options or alternatives when making a choice or decision. □ *The voter weighed the strengths and weaknesses of each candidate.* **3.** *iv.* to have a certain weight. □ *The huge chair weighs 135 pounds.* **4.** *iv.* to have a particular kind of influence on someone or something. □ *Guilt weighed mightily on the sinner's conscience.*

**weight** ['wet] **1.** *n.* the degree of heaviness of someone or something or how heavy someone or something is, as measured according to a specific system. (No plural form.) □ *Bill went on a diet to lose weight.* **2.** *n.* a heavy object, used for exercising. □ *John wore weights around his ankles while he jogged.* **3.** *n.* a heavy object, especially one that keeps something in place, holds something down, or balances something. □ *The worker added a few weights to the pulleys.* **4.** *n.* a mental burden; something that occupies one's thoughts. (No plural form.) □ *The weight of my responsibility was very stressful.*

**weird** ['wɪrd] *adj.* very strange; very odd; very unusual. (Adv: *weirdly.* Comp: *weirder;* sup: *weirdest.*) □ *I called the police when I heard some weird noises in the alley.*

**welcome** ['wɛl kəm] **1.** *tv.* to greet someone in a friendly way. □ *John welcomed his guests with open arms.* **2.** *tv.* to be happy to receive or experience something. (Fig. on ①.) □ *The teachers welcomed the adoption of a dress code.* **3.** *n.* the act of greeting or receiving someone or something with pleasure. □ *The speaker received a warm welcome of applause.* **4.** *adj.* accepted with pleasure; wanted. □ *I accepted the welcome promotion at work.*

**welfare** ['wɛl fɛr] **1.** *n.* a state of having good health, comfort, and enough money to live satisfactorily. (No plural form.) □ *Who looks out for the welfare of the poor?* **2.** *n.* money provided by the government for poor people to live on; the system of providing money for poor people to live on. (No plural form.) □ *The agency helped people find jobs and leave welfare.*

**we'll** ['wil] *cont.* "we will." □ *We'll be arriving at the restaurant around eight o'clock.*

**well** ['wɛl] **1.** *adv., irreg.* in a good way. (Comp: **better**; sup: **best**.) □ *Bob plays chess very well for someone who has just learned.* **2.** *adv.* enough; sufficiently; to a good degree. □ *Your plan is well thought out.* **3.** *adv.* completely; thoroughly; fully. □ *Please wash your hands very well before cooking dinner.* **4. well-** *adv.* <**well** ①–③ used in compounds.> □ *The well-respected woman was chosen to lead the organization.* **5.** *adj., irreg.* healthy; in good health. (Comp: **better**.) □ *Are you feeling well? You look* *rather tired.* **6.** *n.* a deep hole that is dug in the ground to reach water, gas, or oil. ☐ *Bill lowered the bucket into the well.* **7. as well as** *phr.* in addition to [someone or something]. ☐ *I'm studying biology and chemistry, as well as history.*

**well-fed** ['wɛl 'fɛd] *adj.* eating enough good food to be healthy. (Usually with hyphens only before a nominal.) ☐ *The well-fed puppy grew quickly.*

**well-known** ['wɛl 'non] *adj.* known by many people; [of people] famous. (Usually with hyphens only before a nominal.) ☐ *The well-known actress disguised her identity when she appeared in public.*

**well-liked** ['wɛl 'lɑɪkt] *adj.* popular; liked by many people. (Usually with hyphens only before a nominal.) ☐ *The well-liked student won the office of class president.*

**well-made** ['wɛl 'med] *adj.* properly constructed; sturdy; made with skill. (Usually with hyphens only before a nominal.) ☐ *This well-made building has stood for centuries.*

**well-off** ['wɛl 'ɔf] *adj., irreg.* rich; wealthy; prosperous. (Comp: *better-off.*) ☐ *Anne is so well-off that she owns three homes.*

**went** ['wɛnt] pt of **go**.

**wept** ['wɛpt] pt/pp of **weep**.

**we're** ['wɪr] *cont.* "we are." ☐ *When we're inside the store, I want you to behave.*

**were** ['wɚ] **1.** *iv.* <pt of **be** used with plural forms and **you** singular.> (Reduced to *'re* in contractions.) ☐ *You were very annoying last night.* **2.** *iv.* <the form of **be** used with all nouns and pronouns to indicate something that is contrary to fact.> ☐ *If he were here, he would help us.*

**weren't** ['wɚnt] *cont.* "were not." ☐ *You weren't at the party, were you?*

**west** ['wɛst] **1.** *n.* the direction to the left of someone or something facing north; the direction in which the sun sets. (No plural form.) ☐ *Mary lives to the west of Clark Street.* **2.** *n.* the western part of a region or country. (No plural form. Capitalized when referring to a region of the U.S.) ☐ *David vacationed in the west of France.* **3. the West** *n.* Western Europe, North America, and South America, as contrasted especially with East Asia and sometimes other parts of Asia. (No plural form. Often capitalized.) ☐ *After years of living in Tokyo, Bill returned to the West.* **4. the West** *n.* the part of Europe that was not under the influence of the former Soviet Union or ruled under a political and economic system similar to that in the former Soviet Union. (No plural form.) ☐ *Many formerly communist countries embraced the West after the Soviet Union fell.* **5.** *adj.* to ①; on the side that is toward ①; facing ①. (Not prenominal.) ☐ *Bill painted the west side of his house green.* **6.** *adj.* from ①. (Especially used to describe wind. Not prenominal.) ☐ *The plane was flying against a strong west wind.* **7.** *adv.* toward ①; into the western part of something. ☐ *Turn west at the stop sign.*

**western** ['wɛs tɚn] **1.** *adj.* in the west; toward the west; facing the west. ☐ *The candidate campaigned heavily in the western states.* **2.** *adj.* from the west. (Especially used to describe wind.) ☐ *The plane flying from Chicago to New York was pushed along by western winds.* **3.** *n.* a movie, book, or television show about the development of the **western** ① United States during the 1800s. (Sometimes capitalized.) ☐ *Bill went to see a Western about a rancher trying to protect his cattle from outlaws.*



**wet** ['wɛt] **1.** *adj.* not dry; covered with or soaked with liquid. (Adv: *wetly.* Comp: *wetter;* sup: *wettest.*) ☐ *I dried my wet hair with a towel.* **2.** *adj.* [of weather] rainy. (Adv: *wetly.* Comp: *wetter;* sup: *wettest.*) ☐ *My clothes are* *always damp because of the wet weather.* **3.** *adj.* allowing liquor to be sold [legally]. □ *Wet states allow liquor to be sold to adults. Dry states do not.* **4.** *tv., irreg.* to make someone or something ①; to cause someone or something to be ①. (Pt/pp: *wet, wetted.*) □ *Anne wetted the flap and sealed the envelope.* **5.** *tv., irreg.* to urinate on oneself, on something, or in one's own clothes. (Pt/pp: usually *wet.*) □ *The little boy wet his bed.*

**wetness** ['wɛt nəs] *n.* moisture; liquid that can be felt or seen. (No plural form.) □ *The warm wetness of humid air is very uncomfortable.*

**we've** ['wiv] *cont.* "we have," where **have** is an auxiliary. □ *Do you think we've gotten lost?*

**whale** ['ʍel] *n.* a very large mammal that lives in the ocean and breathes through an opening on top of its head. □ *The fat of whales is called blubber.*

**wharf** ['worf] *n., irreg.* a platform where ships can dock in order to load or unload people or cargo; a pier. (Pl: **wharves.**) □ *The part of town near the wharf is dangerous at night.*

**wharves** ['worvz] pl of **wharf.**

**what** ['ʍʌt] **1.** *interrog.* <a form used as the subject or object of a sentence or clause when asking questions to get more information about someone or something.> □ *What did he say to you?* **2.** *interrog.* <a form used before nominals when asking questions to get more information about that noun or nominal.> □ *What suit did John wear?* **3.** *pron.* that which; the thing that; the things that. □ *Do what you want while I'm at the store.* **4.** *interj.* <a form showing great surprise.> □ *"Bill was fired today." "What? Are you kidding?"*

**whatever** [ʍət 'ɛv ɚ] **1.** *pron.* anything that; everything that. □ *I'll eat whatever you decide to order.* **2.** *pron.* no matter what. □ *Whatever you tell me, I promise not to laugh.* **3.** *interrog.* <an emphatic form of **what** ①, similar to *What possibly?*> □ *Whatever did Bill do that made you so mad?* **4.** *adj.* any; no matter what. □ *Whatever food you eat, eat it in moderation.*

**what's** ['ʍʌts] **1.** *cont.* "what is." □ *What's going on in here?* **2.** *cont.* "what has," where **has** is an auxiliary. □ *What's Jimmy done today?*

**wheat** ['ʍit] **1.** *n.* a kind of cereal plant grown for its seeds. (No plural form.) □ *The farmer planted wheat in all his fields.* **2.** *n.* the seed of ①, ground to make flour. (No plural form. Number is expressed with *grain(s) of wheat.*) □ *Wheat is carried to the mill in trucks or in barges on the river.* **3.** *adj.* made from ②. □ *Would you like wheat toast or rye toast?*

**wheel** ['ʍil] **1.** *n.* a sturdy circular object that turns around a central point and is connected to an axle. □ *The wheel is bent and won't roll straight.* **2.** *n.* the round object used to steer a vehicle. (Short for **steering wheel.**) □ *I held onto the wheel tightly while we traveled over the rough road.*

**wheelbarrow** ['ʍil bɛr o] *n.* an open container attached to a frame with one wheel in front. □ *The gardener dug up weeds and threw them in the wheelbarrow.*

**wheelchair** ['ʍil tʃɛr] *n.* a chair that has wheels instead of legs, usually two large wheels in back and two small ones in front, for people who are unable to walk. □ *John had to use a wheelchair after he broke his leg.*

**when** ['ʍɛn] **1.** *interrog.* at what time? □ *When was World War II fought?* **2.** *conj.* at the time that; at that certain time. □ *Let's go see a movie when I'm finished with my homework.* **3.** *conj.* considering [the fact that]; as. □ *What am I sup-*

*posed to think when you won't return my calls?*

**whenever** [ʍɛn 'ɛv ɚ] **1.** *conj.* at any time; at whatever time. □ *I'm ready to go whenever you are.* **2.** *conj.* every time; each time. □ *Whenever it rains, I stay indoors.* **3.** *interrog.* when?; at what time? (Used for emphasis.) □ *Whenever will you stop smoking?*

**where** ['ʍɛr] **1.** *interrog.* in what place?; at what place?; in which location? □ *Where is the post office?* **2.** *conj.* in that place; at that place; in that location. □ *John led the police to the place where he'd seen the body.* **3.** *conj.* in the case; such that; wherever. □ *Where X + 3 = 5, X = 2.*

**whereas** [ʍɛr 'æz] **1.** *conj.* but; however; on the other hand; on the contrary. □ *Bill doesn't like large crowds, whereas John does.* **2.** *conj.* since; because. (Used to introduce legal documents.) □ *Whereas my client has met the stated requirements, action is now called for.*

**where's** ['ʍɛrz] **1.** *cont.* "where has," where **has** is an auxiliary. □ *Where's the cat gone to?* **2.** *cont.* "where is." □ *Where's the nearest bank?*

**whether** ['ʍɛð ɚ] **1.** *conj.* <a form used with some kinds of questions when more than one answer is possible>; if. □ *I wonder whether Susan can help us with this problem.* **2. whether or not** *phr.* either if something is the case or if something is not the case; one way or the other. □ *I'm going to the mall whether you come with me or not.*

**which** ['ʍɪtʃ] **1.** *interrog.* <a form used in questions to ask about or distinguish among specific things or people>; what [one or ones]? (Used before a noun.) □ *Which students passed the test?* **2.** *interrog.* <a form used in questions to ask about or distinguish among specific things or people>; what one or ones? (Treated as singular or plural.) □ *Of all the places you have traveled, which was the most exciting?* **3.** *adj.* <a form used to distinguish among things or people already mentioned or known from the context>; what [one or ones]; the [one or ones]. (Prenominal only.) □ *I don't know which flavor of ice cream to choose.* **4.** *pron.* <a form used to show the differences among things or people already mentioned or known from the context>; what one or ones; the one or ones. (Treated as singular or plural.) □ *There are so many flavors of ice cream. I don't know which to choose.* **5.** *pron.* <a form used after a word, phrase, or clause and serving to introduce *extra, incidental,* or *descriptive* information about the word, phrase, or clause rather than information needed to identify it>; the one or ones that. (Treated as singular or plural. The phrase or clause that begins with **which** is set off by commas. This is called a *nonrestrictive clause.*) □ *I give you a package, and I say, "Please put this package, which is very valuable, on my desk." You already know what package I mean, but I am telling you something extra about it.* □ *I have been speaking about a wall, and it happens to face west. I say, "The wall, which faces west, has begun to crack." The direction that it faces is extra or incidental information.* **6.** *pron.* <a form used after a word or a phrase and serving to introduce *special, contrastive,* or *distinctive* information about the word or phrase>; the one or ones that. (Treated as singular or plural. The phrase or clause that begins with **which** does not have commas around it, because the phrase is needed to permit the hearer or reader to correctly identify the object or person referred to. This is called a *restrictive clause.* Some people do not accept this sense of **which** and require **that** ⑤ instead.) □ *There are two cars in front of the house—one on the street and one in the driveway—so I say, "The car which is sitting*



W

*in the driveway belongs to my father." You needed to know the location before you could identify the car that I meant.* □ *There are two walls visible, and I am talking about only one of them. I say, "The wall which faces west has begun to crack." I have identified the relevant wall by saying where it faces.*

**while** ['ʍaɪl] **1.** *conj.* during that time; during a certain time that; at the same time as that. □ *While the teacher was talking, some students were misbehaving badly.* **2.** *conj.* and, in contrast; although; on the other hand; and; whereas. □ *I don't like tomatoes, while Mary loves them.* **3.** *n.* a length of time. (No plural form.) □ *We were stuck in the elevator for just a short while.*

**whim** ['ʍɪm] *n.* a sudden wish to do something, especially an unreasonable wish. □ *John's whim to take a vacation surprised me.*

**whimper** ['ʍɪm pɚ] **1.** *n.* a small, quiet moan or cry, especially from someone or something that is afraid. □ *I could hear the baby's whimper from the next room.* **2.** *iv.* to moan quietly, as though one were afraid. □ *The dog whimpered when I put him outside.* **3.** *tv.* to say something while whimpering, as in ②. (The object can be a clause with **that** ⑦.) □ *Mary whimpered an apology.*

**whine** ['ʍaɪn] **1.** *n.* a cry made with the mouth not open very much; a soft, high-pitched cry. □ *The baby's soft whine kept us awake all night.* **2.** *iv.* to complain in a sad, annoying, childish voice. □ *John whines whenever he doesn't get to do what he wants.* **3.** *tv.* to make a complaint in a sad, annoying, childish voice. (The object can be a clause with **that** ⑦.) □ *Bill whined that he hadn't been able to get the seat by the window.*

**whip** ['ʍɪp] **1.** *n.* a long strip of leather, usually attached to a handle, used for hitting people or animals. □ *The cowboy bought a long, slender whip at the leather shop.* **2.** *n.* a member of a political party who organizes and manages members of the party serving in a legislative body. □ *The majority whip persuaded everyone in his party to vote for the measure.* **3.** *tv.* to hit or strike someone or an animal with ①. □ *The criminals were whipped as a punishment.* **4.** *tv.* to beat eggs or cream until the mixture bubbles into a froth. □ *The cream has to be whipped for just a few minutes.* **5.** *tv.* to beat an opponent in a contest or game by a wide margin. (Fig. on ③.) □ *The home team whipped the visiting team by a score of 10–2.*

**whisk** ['ʍɪsk] **1.** *n.* a wire tool for beating eggs, cream, and other mixtures. □ *I washed the whisk and placed it with the other utensils.* **2.** *tv.* to beat eggs, cream, and other mixtures into a froth. □ *The cook whisked the batter until it was smooth.*

**whisker** ['ʍɪs kɚ] *n.* a hair that grows from near the mouth of a cat and certain other animals; a hair that is part of a beard. □ *Bill trimmed his whiskers with a razor.*

**whiskey** ['ʍɪs ki] **1.** *n.* a strong alcohol for drinking made from corn, rye, or other grains. (Plural only when referring to different kinds, types, instances, or varieties.) □ *Bill kept a bottle of whiskey in the cupboard.* Ⓒ *Jed prefers Scotch whiskeys over bourbons.* **2.** *n.* a glass of ①; a drink of ①. □ *Anne asked for a whiskey with ice.*

**whisper** ['ʍɪs pɚ] **1.** *tv.* to say something with the breath only, not using the full voice. (The object can be a clause with **that** ⑦.) □ *Anne whispered that she had to leave the room.* **2.** *iv.* to speak as in ①. □ *You should whisper when you're in the library.* **3.** *n.* speaking done with the breath only, not using the voice. □ *The librarian spoke in a whisper.*

W

**whistle** ['ʍɪs əl] **1.** *n.* a small metal or plastic instrument that makes a shrill, high-pitched sound when one blows air into it. □ *The football referees blew their whistles when a foul was made.* **2.** *n.* a shrill, high-pitched sound made by passing air through a small opening between one's lips or through ①. □ *The police officer's whistle indicated danger nearby.* **3.** *tv.* to make a melody with a shrill, high-pitched sound made by passing air through one's lips. □ *The children whistled the simple tune.* **4.** *iv.* to make a shrill, high-pitched sound by passing air through ① or through one's lips. □ *The train whistled as it approached the station.*

**white** ['ʍɑɪt] **1.** *adj.* having the color of salt or milk. (Adv: *whitely*. Comp: *whiter;* sup: *whitest.*) □ *The surrendering soldiers waved a white flag.* **2.** *adj.* pale. (Comp: *whiter;* sup: *whitest.*) □ *The frightened man turned white with fear.* **3.** *adj.* [of people, usually of European descent or their skin] light-colored. (See also **Caucasian**. Comp: *whiter;* sup: *whitest.*) □ *The white landlord happily rented to persons of any race.* **4.** *n.* the color of salt or milk. (Plural only when referring to different kinds, types, instances, or varieties.) □ *I decorated the bathroom in white and light blue.* Ⓒ *I had no idea there were so many whites! Some seem almost blue or gray.* **5.** *n.* someone who has light-colored skin, usually persons of European descent. □ *Five whites were arrested during the riot.* **6.** *n.* the clear part of an egg, which turns **white** ① when it is cooked. □ *The cook separated the white of the egg from the yolk.*

**white elephant** ['ʍɑɪt 'ɛl ə fənt] *n.* something that is useless and is either a nuisance or expensive to keep up. □ *Those antique vases Aunt Mary gave me are white elephants. They're ugly and take ages to clean.*

**whiten** ['ʍɑɪt n] **1.** *tv.* to cause something to become white; to make something white. □ *I use a special toothpaste to whiten my teeth.* **2.** *iv.* to turn pale. □ *Tom's skin whitened while he was away from the sun in the hospital for three months.*

**whittle** ['ʍɪt əl] **1.** *tv.* to cut pieces of wood away a little bit at a time with a knife; to shave off small strips from a piece of wood. □ *David whittled a branch while he sat on the porch waiting for John.* **2.** *tv.* to carve an object from wood, cutting away small pieces. □ *Jane used a small knife to whittle a peg of the proper size.*

**whiz** ['ʍɪz] **1.** *iv.* [for something] to move very quickly through the air while making a sound as it passes by someone or something. □ *A bullet whizzed by the police officer's shoulder.* **2.** *n.* an expert; someone who is very skilled at something; someone who can do something quickly and very well. (Fig. on ①.) □ *I asked Mary for help because she's a whiz at biology.*

**who** ['hu] **1.** *interrog.* what or which person or people? (The possessive form is **whose**. The objective form is **whom**.) □ *Who is the person sitting next to Jane?* **2.** *pron.* a person or the people mentioned. (Standard English requires **whom** instead of **who** as the object of a verb or preposition. **Who** can be used in *restrictive* and *nonrestrictive clauses.* See the comments at **which**.) □ *My father, who is a lawyer, gave me some good legal advice.*

**who'd** ['hud] **1.** *cont.* "who had," where **had** is an auxiliary. □ *Jane, who'd been working for twelve hours, was very tired.* **2.** *cont.* "who would." □ *Who'd have believed that computers could do so much?*

**whoever** [hu 'ɛv ɚ] **1.** *pron.* anyone; any person who. □ *Whoever comes to the conference must pay a $10 fee.*

**2.** *interrog.* who? □ *Whoever has heard of such a ridiculous idea?*

**whole** ['hol] **1.** *adj.* made of the entire amount; consisting of all parts; not divided; not separated; complete. (Adv: *wholly.*) □ *Mary did the whole job herself.* **2.** *adj.* having the feeling of good health, in the mind or body. □ *The doctor helped Anne feel whole once more.* **3.** *adj.* not expressed as a fraction or a decimal number. □ *Please round your answer to the nearest whole number.* **4.** *n.* something that is complete; something that has all of its parts; the entire amount. □ *If you look at the problem as a whole, the answer becomes clearer.*

**wholesale** ['hol sel] **1.** *adj.* [of products] sold in large numbers to people who will sell the products one at a time to customers. □ *The wholesale merchandise was sold in packages of 48.* **2.** *adj.* done on a large scale; in large amounts. (Fig. on ①.) □ *The wholesale destruction of the town by the flood left many people without homes.* **3.** *adv.* in large quantities at **wholesale** ① prices. □ *Merchants always buy goods wholesale.*

**wholesaler** ['hol sel ɚ] *n.* someone who buys products from a manufacturer and sells them to store owners. □ *I buy my clothing directly from a wholesaler.*

**who'll** ['hul] *cont.* "who will." □ *Do we know who'll be coming to fix the plumbing?*

**whom** ['hum] *pron.* <the objective form of **who**.> (Not common in informal English. **Whom** can be used in *restrictive* and *nonrestrictive clauses.* See the comments at **which.**) □ *I gave it to Lisa, whom I saw yesterday.*

**who's** ['huz] **1.** *cont.* "who has," where **has** is an auxiliary. □ *I wonder who's been sitting in my chair while I've been gone.* **2.** *cont.* "who is." □ *Who's standing next to Susan?*

**whose** ['huz] **1.** *pron.* <the possessive form of **who** and **which**>; of whom or of which. (**Whose** can be used in *restrictive* and *nonrestrictive clauses.* See the comments at **which.**) □ *John, whose mother owns a bakery, said he would bring us a box of cookies.* **2.** *interrog.* <a form used in questions to determine the identity of the person who owns, possesses, or is associated with something>; of or belonging to whom? □ *Whose books are on the kitchen table?*

**why 1.** ['ʍaɪ] *interrog.* for what reason? □ *Why does it get cold in the winter?* **2.** ['ʍaɪ] *conj.* the reason that; the reason for which. □ *Anne explained why she was upset with me.* **3.** ['waɪ] *interj.* <a form used to express surprise, dismay, disgust, or some other emotion.> □ *Bill failed the test? That's impossible! Why, Bill is the best student in the class.*

**wicked** ['wɪk əd] *adj.* evil; very bad; vile. (Adv: *wickedly.*) □ *The wicked owner treated the employees badly.*

**wide** ['waɪd] **1.** *adj.* not narrow; broad. (Adv: *widely.* Comp: *wider;* sup: *widest.*) □ *The wide truck could not fit into the narrow garage.* **2.** *adj.* being a certain distance from side to side; measured from side to side. (Follows the measurement of width. Comp: *wider.*) □ *The bookcase is three feet wide and six feet high.* **3.** *adj.* large in size, range, or scope. (Adv: *widely.* Comp: *wider;* sup: *widest.*) □ *Mary discussed a wide variety of issues with her professor.* **4.** *adv.* as far as possible; to the greatest amount or extent. □ *Please open the door wide.*

**widow** ['wɪd o] *n.* a woman whose husband has died, and who has not married again. □ *The widow vowed never to marry again.*

**widower** ['wɪd o ɚ] *n.* a man whose wife has died, and who has not married again. □ *The widower vowed never to marry again.*

**width** ['wɪdθ] *n.* distance, from side to side. (No plural form.) □ *The Amazon River has great width but little depth.*

**wield** ['wild] **1.** *tv.* to hold and use something, especially a weapon. □ *The carpenter wielded the hammer with skill and strength.* **2.** *tv.* to have and use power, especially as though it were a weapon. (Fig. on ①.) □ *The mayor wielded absolute control over the city council.*

**wiener** ['win ɚ] *n.* a beef or pork sausage, often eaten on a long bun. □ *The campers roasted some wieners over the fire.*

**wife** ['wɑɪf] *n., irreg.* the woman a man is married to. (Pl: **wives.**) □ *Please inform your wife that she's invited to the party, too.*

**wig** ['wɪg] *n.* a head covering simulating one's own hair; a head covering made of real or artificial hair. □ *The cancer patient wore a wig after his hair fell out.*

**wiggle** ['wɪg əl] **1.** *iv.* to move back and forth in quick, little movements. □ *The worm I used for bait wiggled as I put it on the hook.* **2.** *tv.* to cause something to move back and forth in quick, little movements. □ *The rabbit wiggled its nose.*

**wild** ['wɑɪld] **1.** *adj.* growing or living in nature; not tame; not grown or kept by a human. (Comp: *wilder;* sup: *wildest.*) □ *A wild lion was captured and sent to a zoo.* **2.** *adj.* not in control; out of control; lacking control; reckless. (Adv: *wildly.* Comp: *wilder;* sup: *wildest.*) □ *Wild prisoners staged a riot.*

**wilderness** ['wɪl dɚ nəs] *n.* a large area of land with no human residents. (No plural form. Number is expressed with *wilderness area(s).*) □ *Much of the natural wilderness is federally protected land.*

**wildflower** ['wɑɪld flɑʊ ɚ] *n.* a flower that is not grown by a person; a flower that grows in nature. □ *The abandoned field was full of wildflowers.*

**wild-goose chase** ['wɑɪld 'gus tʃes] *n.* a worthless hunt or **chase** ①; a futile pursuit. □ *John was angry because he was sent out on a wild-goose chase.*

**will** ['wɪl] **1.** *interrog.* <a form used with a verb to indicate politeness by turning a command into a question.> (See also **would** ③.) □ *Will you please speak more quietly?* **2.** *aux.* <a form used with a verb to indicate the future tense.> (See also **shall.** See **would** ① for the past tense form. Reduced to *'ll* in contractions.) □ *I will see you at the party next week.* **3.** *aux.* <a form used with a verb to command someone to do something.> □ *You will go to the store and get some milk!* **4.** *aux.* can; be able to. □ *This computer will organize your work for you.* **5.** *aux.* <a form used to express something that is always true or something that always happens.> □ *John will go on vacation twice a year.* **6.** *n.* the power one has in one's mind to do what one wants to do; an intention to do something. □ *The patient with cancer lost his will to live.* **7.** *n.* a legal document that details how one's assets will be distributed after one's death. □ *Many greedy relatives contested the dead millionaire's will.*

**willow** ['wɪl o] **1.** *n.* a tree that has many long, thin, drooping branches with long, thin leaves. □ *I sat in the shade under the large willow.* **2.** *n.* wood from ①. (No plural form.) □ *Willow is not strong enough to be used in construction.* **3.** *adj.* made of or from ①. □ *This basket is woven from willow branches.*

**willpower** ['wɪl pɑʊ ɚ] *n.* the ability to control one's will. (No plural form.) □ *I lacked the willpower to stay on my diet.*

**wilt** ['wɪlt] **1.** *iv.* to wither; [for the leaves or branches of a plant] to lose their strength and sag downward. □ *My flowers wilted because I forgot to water* *them.* **2.** *iv.* [for someone] to lose energy. (Fig. on ①.) □ *The horses wilted under the hot sun.* **3.** *tv.* to cause something to wither or sag as in ①. □ *Tom wilted some lettuce for his special salad.*

**win** ['wɪn] **1.** *tv., irreg.* to receive or achieve first place in a contest or competition. (Pt/pp: **won**.) □ *The fastest runner wins the gold medal.* **2.** *tv., irreg.* to achieve or earn something through hard work or effort. □ *Women in America won the right to vote in 1920.* **3.** *iv., irreg.* to be in first place in a contest or competition; to be the best in a contest. □ *I was surprised when the horse with the weak leg won.* **4.** *n.* a victory; a triumph. □ *The athlete needed a win to remain in the competition.*

**wind 1.** ['wɪnd] *n.* the movement of air; moving air. (Plural with the same meaning, but not countable.) □ *The wind blew the hat from my head.* **2.** ['wɪnd] *n.* breath or the ability to breathe. (No plural form.) □ *Toward the end of the race, the runner lost her wind.* **3.** ['wɪnd] *tv.* to cause someone to be out of breath; to cause someone to have a hard time breathing. □ *Running up the stairs winded Anne.* **4.** ['waɪnd] *tv., irreg.* to tighten the spring of a device such as a watch or a clock. (Pt/pp: **wound**.) □ *Bill wound the music box, and it played a tune.* **5.** ['waɪnd] *iv., irreg.* to move in one direction and then another; to move in twists and turns. □ *The path winds through the mountains.*

**winded** ['wɪn dɪd] *adj.* out of breath; gasping for breath. □ *After running for a mile, he was totally winded.*

**window** ['wɪn do] **1.** *n.* an opening in a wall or door, usually covered with a sheet of glass, that allows light into a place. □ *Mary looked out the window to the street below.* **2.** *n.* the sheet of glass that covers an opening in a wall or door. □ *A vandal broke my car window and stole my car radio.* **3.** *n.* an opening or opportunity to do something. (Fig. on ①.) □ *We have a brief window between appointments, when we can meet with the president.*

**windowpane** ['wɪn do pen] *n.* the sheet of glass that covers an opening in a wall or door. □ *The thief entered the house by breaking the windowpane in the front door.*

**window shade** ['wɪn do 'ʃed] *n.* a sheet of fabric designed to cover a window to keep the sun out and to prevent people from seeing in. (Can be shortened to **shade**.) □ *The window shade keeps a lot of the sun's heat out.*

**window sill** ['wɪn do sɪl] *n.* the flat ledge next to the place that the edge of a window touches when it is closed. □ *The cat slept on the window sill.*

**windpipe** ['wɪnd pɑɪp] *n.* the tube in the body that allows air to travel between the mouth and the lungs. □ *Some water went down Mary's windpipe when she was swimming, and she started coughing.*

**windshield** ['wɪnd ʃild] *n.* the large, curved piece of glass in the front of a car, truck, or bus. □ *I cleared the snow and ice from my windshield.*

**windy** ['wɪn di] *adj.* having a lot of wind; with a lot of wind. (Comp: *windier;* sup: *windiest.*) □ *I closed the window because it was too windy in the room.*

**wine** ['wɑɪn] **1.** *n.* a drink that contains alcohol and is made from fruit juice, especially the juice of grapes. (Plural only when referring to different kinds, types, instances, or varieties. If the fruit or plant is not stated, it is almost always grape.) □ *Our server poured wine in each glass.* Ⓒ *The wines grown in California are recognized as being among the best in the world.* **2. wines** *n.* different kinds or types of ①. □ *We only drink white wines.*

**wing** ['wɪŋ] **1.** *n.* one of the upper limbs of a bird, or a flying mammal, used for

W

flight. □ *The artist painted a bird with large, white, feathery wings.* **2.** *n.* an extension on the side of an insect's body, used for flight. □ *Dragonflies have two pairs of wings.* **3.** *n.* a structure on an airplane that stands out from its body, which allows the airplane to stay in the air during flight. □ *There's an emergency exit over each wing of the plane.* **4.** *n.* a part of a building that is built out from the central or main part of the building. □ *A new wing was added to the school.* **5.** *tv.* to shoot a bird in the **wing** ① without killing it. □ *The injured duck had been winged by a hunter's bullet.*

**wink** ['wɪŋk] **1.** *iv.* to shut and open one eye quickly, especially either as a signal or to show amusement or interest. (Compare with **blink.**) □ *Mary ignored the stranger who winked at her on the street.* **2.** *n.* an act of shutting and opening one eye quickly, especially either as a signal or to show amusement or interest. □ *Lisa gave me a friendly wink when she got out of the car.*

**winner** ['wɪn ɚ] *n.* someone or something that wins. □ *The winner of the race received a prize.*

**winter** ['wɪn tɚ] **1.** *n.* one of the four seasons of the year; the season between fall and spring. □ *Some wild animals rest and sleep during the winter.* **2.** *adj.* concerning or associated with ①. □ *David went to Florida for the winter holidays.* **3.** *iv.* to live in a certain place during ①. □ *My aunt and uncle winter in Arizona.*

**wipe** ['wɑɪp] **1.** *tv.* to rub the surface of someone or something with something in order to clean or dry it. □ *Bill wiped his hands with a towel.* **2.** *tv.* to remove something liquid from a surface, using something absorbent. □ *David wiped the puddle on the floor with an absorbent mop.*

**wire** ['wɑɪɚ] **1.** *n.* a thin metal strand; a thread of metal, especially one used to transmit electricity. (No plural form.) □ *If the wires in the building become too hot, they can start a fire.* **2.** *n.* a length or segment of ①. □ *Many colored wires can be seen inside my computer.* **3.** *n.* a message that is sent by telegram. □ *The wire informed me that my brother was coming to visit me.* **4.** *tv.* to send a message or money by telegraph. (The object can be a clause with **that** ⑦.) □ *I wired a message of congratulations to Susan.* **5.** *tv.* to install ① in a building for electricity; to install or adjust any kind of ①. □ *The alarm was wired to sound if anyone entered the room.* **6.** *tv.* to fasten or secure something with ①. □ *We wired the pieces together to hold them until they could be repaired properly.* **7.** *tv.* to install hidden microphones in a place so that one can record what is said there. □ *Don't discuss our secret plans on that phone. I think it's wired.*

**wisdom** ['wɪz dəm] *n.* intelligence, especially intelligence that is a result of experience; the knowledge required to make good decisions; the quality of being wise. (No plural form.) □ *Lisa is widely respected for her wisdom.*

**wise** ['wɑɪz] *adj.* able to make good decisions; showing good judgment; intelligent. (Adv: *wisely.* Comp: *wiser;* sup: *wisest.*) □ *Your decision to finish school is wise.*

**wish** ['wɪʃ] **1.** *n.* a desire for something; a longing for something. □ *My wish is to travel around the world.* **2.** *tv.* to express ①; to hope that something happens. (The object is a clause with **that** ⑦.) □ *Mary wished that she had more free time.* **3. wish to** do something *iv.* + *inf.* to have a desire to do something. □ *I wish to leave school early today.*

**wit** ['wɪt] **1.** *n.* the ability to understand ideas quickly and make intelligent, clever, and funny comments about them. (No plural form.) □ *I like talking with Anne because of her clever wit.*

W

**2.** *n.* someone who has the ability to understand ideas quickly and make intelligent, clever, and funny comments about them. □ *Bob, you are such a wit! Always joking.* **3. one's wits** *n.* one's intelligence; one's control of one's thinking, understanding, temper, and actions. □ *She acts like she lost her wits most of the time!*

**witch** ['wɪtʃ] **1.** *n.* someone, usually a woman, who has or claims to have magical powers or who practices a pagan religion. □ *The witch handed the queen a magic charm.* **2.** *n.* a mean or ugly woman. (Derogatory.) □ *The old witch at the end of the street yells at her neighbors.*

**with** ['wɪθ] **1.** *prep.* among someone or something; including someone or something; in the company of someone or something; in addition to someone or something. □ *I love to eat mashed potatoes with gravy.* **2.** *prep.* by means of something; by using something. □ *We viewed the huge star with a telescope.* **3.** *prep.* showing a quality or characteristic; showing a state or emotion. □ *The soldier's eyes widened with fear.*

**wither** ['wɪð ɚ] **1.** *iv.* to shrivel; to wilt; [for a plant] to turn brown, sag, and dry out. □ *I forgot to water my plant, and it withered.* **2.** *tv.* to cause a plant to shrivel, droop, or wilt; to cause a plant to turn brown and dry out. □ *The hot sun has withered my flower garden.*

**withheld** [wɪθ 'hɛld] pt/pp of **withhold.**

**withhold** [wɪθ 'hold] *tv., irreg.* to hold or keep something back [from someone or something]. (Pt/pp: **withheld.**) □ *The audience members withheld their questions until the speech was over.*

**within** [wɪθ 'ɪn] **1.** *prep.* inside someone or something; in or into the inside part of someone or something. □ *News of the change had come from within the organization.* **2.** *prep.* not beyond a specific boundary; between certain limits. □ *The bullet had come within three inches of striking me.* **3.** *adv.* into the inside of someone or something. □ *Don't look to others as the cause of your problems. Look within.*

**without** [wɪθ 'ɑʊt] **1.** *prep.* not including someone or something; lacking someone or something. □ *I'd like to have a cheese sandwich without lettuce.* **2.** *prep.* by avoiding doing something; by not doing something; while avoiding doing something; while not doing something. (Takes the *-ing* form of a verb.) □ *I drove for 10 hours without stopping.*

**withstand** [wɪθ 'stænd] *tv., irreg.* to resist someone or something; to oppose someone or something; not to yield to someone or something. (Pt/pp: **withstood.**) □ *The coastal town withstood the storm's force.*

**withstood** [wɪθ 'stʊd] pt/pp of **withstand.**

**witness** ['wɪt nəs] **1.** *n.* someone who sees something happen; someone who is in the same place where something happens; a spectator. □ *In court, the witness described the murder in detail.* **2.** *n.* someone who sees the signing of a legal document. □ *John and Anne served as witnesses to the signing of the contract.* **3.** *tv.* to see something happen; to be in the same place where something happens. □ *I witnessed the protest last night.* **4.** *tv.* to sign a legal document as a way of swearing that one has watched another person, who is directly affected by the document, sign it, and thus that the other person's signature is real. □ *The lawyer witnessed my signature.*

**witness stand** ['wɪt nəs 'stænd] *n.* the place where someone gives testimony under oath in court. (Can be shortened to **stand.**) □ *You are under oath to tell the truth while you are on the witness stand.*

**wives** ['waɪvz] pl of **wife.**

**wizard** ['wɪz ɚd] **1.** *n.* someone, usually a male, who has or claims to have magical powers. □ *The wizard chanted a magic spell.* **2.** *n.* an expert; someone who is very skilled at something. (Fig. on ①.) □ *When it comes to calculus, Bill is a real wizard.*

**woke** ['wok] a pt of **wake.**

**woken** ['wok ən] a pp of **wake.**

**wolf** ['wʊlf] *n., irreg.* a wild animal related to the dog that eats meat and travels in groups. (Pl: **wolves.**) □ *The wolf caught and killed one of the shepherd's sheep.*

**wolves** ['wʊlvz] pl of **wolf.**

**woman** ['wʊm ən] **1.** *n., irreg.* an adult female person; an adult female human being. (Pl: **women.**) □ *Sally Ride was the first American woman in space.* **2.** *adj.* <the adj. use of ①.> (In some contexts.) □ *A woman racing driver won the race.*

**womb** ['wum] *n.* the organ in women and some female animals where the developing baby is protected and fed until birth. □ *Jane's baby shifted in her womb.*

**women** ['wɪm ən] pl of **woman.**

**won** ['wʌn] pt/pp of **win.**

**wonder** ['wʌn dɚ] **1.** *n.* someone or something that is amazing, surprising, or like a miracle. □ *Mount Everest is one of the natural wonders of the world.* **2.** *tv.* to wish to know something; to want to know something. □ *Susan wondered what time it was.* **3.** *adj.* very good, helpful, or of great benefit. □ *The man claimed that certain wonder foods could help prevent cancer.*

**wonderful** ['wʌn dɚ fʊl] *adj.* very good; amazing; remarkable; marvelous. (Adv: *wonderfully.*) □ *John was rewarded for the wonderful job he did.*

**wonderland** ['wʌn dɚ lænd] *n.* an area or place that is wonderful. □ *The amusement park is a wonderland for children.*

**won't** ['wont] *cont.* "will not." □ *If you don't eat your peas, you won't get any dessert.*

**woo** ['wu] **1.** *tv.* to court someone with the intention of marriage. □ *David wooed Susan by writing romantic poetry for her.* **2.** *tv.* to encourage someone or a group to cooperate, join something, or buy something. □ *The salesclerk wooed customers with a tempting sales pitch.*

**wood** ['wʊd] **1.** *n.* the hard substance that trees make as they grow. (Plural only when referring to different kinds, types, instances, or varieties.) □ *The sturdy beam was made of solid wood.* Ⓒ *The harder woods make good flooring.* **2.** *n.* a kind or type of ①. □ *For the front of the cabinet, the carpenter chose a wood that would match the furniture in the room.* **3.** *n.* a small forest; an area where there are many trees. (Usually plural, but not countable. The meaning is the same for the singular and the plural.) □ *Many foxes live in the woods.* **4.** *adj.* made of ①; **wooden.** □ *I painted the wood door to protect it from the weather.* **5.** *adj.* <the adj. use of ①.> □ *The playground was covered with soft wood chips.*

**woodchuck** ['wʊd tʃək] *n.* a large, burrowing rodent with brown fur that lives in the United States and Canada. □ *The dog chased the woodchuck through the forest.*

**wooden** ['wʊd n] **1.** *adj.* made of wood. □ *The wooden staircase made noises as I walked up it.* **2.** *adj.* stiff; not easily moved; not moving easily; not flexible. (Fig. on ①. Adv: *woodenly.*) □ *The reviewer criticized the actor's wooden expressions.*

**woodland** ['wʊd lænd] *n.* an area of land that is covered with trees. (Singular or plural with the same meaning, but not countable.) ☐ *The developer destroyed some woodlands to make a shopping mall.*

**woodpecker** ['wʊd pɛk ɚ] *n.* a bird that has a long, sharp beak for piercing holes in trees and a long tongue to catch insects inside the tree. ☐ *The woodpecker ate beetles living inside the tree trunk.*

**woodwind** ['wʊd wɪnd] *n.* a group of musical instruments, many of which are made of wood or used to be made of wood, and many of which are played by blowing air across a reed. ☐ *Although a flute does not have a reed, it is still one of the woodwinds.*

**woodwork** ['wʊd wɚk] *n.* something that is made of wood, especially the trim on the inside of a house or building. (No plural form.) ☐ *The woodwork around the door frame was very fancy.*

**woody** ['wʊd i] **1.** *adj.* covered with woods; covered with trees. (Comp: *woodier;* sup: *woodiest.*) ☐ *The hikers walked up the woody hillside.* **2.** *adj.* [of a plant] containing wood. (Comp: *woodier;* sup: *woodiest.*) ☐ *Please trim all those woody shrubs away from the sidewalk.*

**wool** ['wʊl] **1.** *n.* the soft, curly hair of sheep and goats. (Plural only when referring to different kinds, types, instances, or varieties.) ☐ *Anne sheared the wool off all our sheep.* 🄲 *Wools from the colder climates are sturdier.* **2.** *n.* thread, yarn, or fabric, made from ①. (No plural form.) ☐ *I knitted Fred a sweater out of wool.* **3.** *adj.* made from ②. ☐ *The wool socks kept my feet warm and dry.*

W

**woolen** ['wʊl ən] *adj.* made of wool. ☐ *My new woolen mittens really keep my hands warm.*

**word** ['wɚd] **1.** *n.* a speech sound or group of speech sounds that has a particular meaning; a written symbol or a group of written symbols that represent a speech sound or group of speech sounds that has a particular meaning. ☐ *The German word for "three" is* drei. ☐ *I looked up the meaning of the unusual word in the dictionary.* **2. one's word** *n.* someone's promise; someone's pledge. (No plural form.) ☐ *The general kept his word that he would return.* **3. the word** *n.* an order; a command. (No plural form. Treated as singular.) ☐ *When I give you the word, start the engine.* **4. the word** *n.* news; information. (No plural form. Treated as singular.) ☐ *What's the word about your test results?* **5.** *tv.* to express something by choosing **words** ① carefully. ☐ *Unfortunately, Bill worded his comments in an offensive way.*

**wordy** ['wɚd i] *adj.* having too many words; using more words than necessary to express something. (Adv: *wordily.* Comp: *wordier;* sup: *wordiest.*) ☐ *The wordy speech was rather boring.*

**wore** ['wor] pt of **wear**.

**work** ['wɚk] **1.** *n.* an activity that requires effort. (No plural form.) ☐ *The whole project is a lot of work.* **2.** *n.* the effort required to do an activity. (No plural form.) ☐ *That job requires a lot of work!* **3.** *n.* something that is a result of effort or energy; a piece of music or art. ☐ *Anne was proud of her works of art.* **4.** *n.* a job; an occupation; a career; what one does for a living; what a person does to make money. (No plural form.) ☐ *Her work is preparing other people's tax forms.* **5.** *n.* the place where one's job is located; the job site. (No plural form.) ☐ *Yesterday I left my car at work and took the train home.* **6.** *iv.* to be employed; to have a job; to labor; to earn money at a job. ☐ *David works at a law firm downtown.* **7.** *iv.* to function properly; to operate properly. ☐ *The television is working again because I fixed it.* **8. work out** *iv.* + *adv.* to exercise; to lift weights and do exercises to build the body. ☐ *Lisa doesn't have time to work out.* **9.** *tv.* to cause something to function as intended. ☐ *Bill doesn't know how to work his computer.* **10.** *tv.* to cause someone or something to operate or function; to cause someone or something to be active; to cause something to use energy. ☐ *Dave really worked the car's engine when he drove up the hill.* **11.** *tv.* to plow or farm land. ☐ *I worked the soil with a plow.*

**workbook** ['wɚk bʊk] *n.* a textbook for students, often including pages that assignments can be written on. ☐ *At the start of the school year, each student was given a workbook.*

**worker** ['wɚk ɚ] *n.* someone who works; someone who is employed. ☐ *The workers were very unhappy with the new management.*

**workout** ['wɚk ɑʊt] *n.* a period of physical exercise. ☐ *After John's workout, he relaxed in the shower.*

**world** ['wɚld] **1.** *n.* the planet Earth. ☐ *The traveler had been to almost every country in the world.* **2.** *n.* the people who live on the planet Earth; the human race. ☐ *The world awaited the end of the terrible war.* **3.** *n.* a planet other than Earth, especially as the source of other life forms. ☐ *People from a distant world landed in the farmer's cornfield and asked the farmer for directions.* **4.** *n.* a certain part of ①. ☐ *North and South America are sometimes referred to as the New World.* **5.** *n.* an area of human activity, thought, or interest. ☐ *In the world of baseball, Babe Ruth is a familiar name.*

**worldwide** ['wɚld 'wɑɪd] *adj.* found or occurring throughout the world; involving everyone in the world. ☐ *The local battle grew into a worldwide war.*

**World Wide Web** ['wɚld 'wɑɪd 'wɛb] *n.* an international network of data storage, transfer, and its visual display, designed to be accessed through a computer connection. (Abbreviated *WWW* and the **Web**.) ☐ *I checked the World Wide Web for information on books.*

**worm** ['wɚm] *n.* any of numerous small, soft, tube-shaped animals having no legs or head, including some that crawl underground and others that live as parasites in animals or people. ☐ *Mary baited her fishing hook with a worm.*

**worn** ['worn] **1.** pp of **wear**. **2.** *adj.* reduced in value or usefulness owing to wear. ☐ *The worn carpet had faded from exposure to sunlight.*

**worn-out** ['worn 'ɑʊt] **1.** *adj.* completely reduced in value or usefulness because of wear. ☐ *I replaced my car's worn-out motor.* **2.** *adj.* very tired; exhausted. ☐ *After a hard day at work, Mary was completely worn-out.*

**worry** ['wɚ i] **1.** *n.* a feeling of anxiety; a fear of trouble. (Plural only when referring to different kinds, types, or varieties.) ☐ *Worry kept Anne awake at night.* Ⓒ *Money worries are what bother me the most.* **2.** *n.* someone or something that causes ①. ☐ *Low approval ratings were a worry to the politician.* **3.** *tv.* to be anxious that something bad might happen; to suspect, regrettably, that something bad might happen. (The object is a clause with **that** ⑦.) ☐ *John worried that he wouldn't get to work on time.* **4.** *tv.* to cause someone to feel anxiety or to fear trouble. ☐ *Max and his problems really worried Bill.*

**worse** ['wɚs] **1.** *adj.* more bad; less good; inferior. (The comparative form of **bad**.) ☐ *John's sore throat is worse than it was yesterday.* **2.** *adv.* in a **worse** ① way. (The comparative form of *badly*.) ☐ *I scored worse on the test than everyone else did.*

**worsen** ['wɚs ən] **1.** *tv.* to make something worse. □ *Bad acting worsened an already dull play.* **2.** *iv.* to become worse. □ *The horrible movie worsened with each passing minute.* **3.** *iv.* to become more sick. □ *John's sore throat worsened throughout the week.*

**worship** ['wɚ ʃɪp] **1.** *tv.* to honor someone or something greatly; to adore someone or something. (Pt/pp: *worshiped.* Present participle: *worshiping.*) □ *Anne worships her grandparents.* **2.** *iv.* to attend a church service. (Pt/pp: *worshiped.* Present participle: *worshiping.*) □ *Tom worships at the temple.* **3.** *n.* what is done at a church service; the praise and honor of a spirit, ancestor, god, object, or person. (No plural form.) □ *Some kinds of worship require peace and quiet.*

**worst** ['wɚst] **1.** *adj.* most bad; least good; most inferior. (The superlative of **bad**.) □ *Our team has the worst record in the whole league.* **2. the worst** *n.* [among three or more] someone or something that is the most bad or least good. (Treated as singular or plural, but not countable.) □ *Of all the excuses I've ever heard, that is the worst.*

**worth** ['wɚθ] **1.** *n.* the value of something; the amount of money that something could sell for. (No plural form.) □ *I calculated the worth of all my assets.* **2.** *n.* the importance of someone or something; the degree to which something is able to be used. (No plural form.) □ *The firm paid me far less than my worth.* **3.** *n.* the amount of something that can be bought for a specific amount of money. (No plural form.) □ *Could I have three dollars' worth of sliced ham?*

**worthless** ['wɚθ ləs] *adj.* having no value or importance; useless. (Adv: *worthlessly.*) □ *I threw away the worthless plastic jewelry.*

**worthy** ['wɚ ði] *adj.* deserving one's time, energy, or attention; deserving; useful; having value or importance. (Adv: *worthily.* Comp: *worthier;* sup: *worthiest.*) □ *I would praise him, but he is not worthy.*

**would** ['wʊd] **1.** *aux.* <a form used as the past tense of **will** to express the future from a time in the past, especially in indirect quotes or in constructions where other past tense verbs are used.> (Contraction: *-'d.*) □ *Mary said she would have gone to the party if she had known about it.* **2.** *aux.* <a form used to express something that happened many times in the past.> (Contraction: *-'d.*) □ *I would often play in the sandbox when I was young.* **3.** *aux.* <a form used instead of **will** to make commands more polite by turning them into questions.> (Contraction: *-'d.* See also **will** ①; using *would* is usually more polite than using *will.*) □ *Would you mind being quiet while I'm talking?*

**wouldn't** ['wʊd nt] *cont.* "would not." □ *John wouldn't have gone to the party if he had known that I would be there, too.*

**would've** ['wʊd əv] *cont.* "would have," where **have** is an auxiliary. □ *I would've phrased your request more politely.*

**wound 1.** ['waʊnd] pt/pp of **wind** ④ and ⑤. **2.** ['wund] *n.* an injury where the skin is torn or punctured. □ *The nurse cleaned the soldier's wounds.* **3.** ['wund] *n.* an injury to one's feelings. (Fig. on ②.) □ *I feared that my emotional wounds would never heal.* **4.** ['wund] *tv.* to injure someone; to cause someone to have ②. □ *Five people were wounded in the car accident.*

**wove** ['wov] pt of **weave**.

**woven** ['wo vən] pp of **weave**.

**wrap** ['ræp] **1. wrap** someone or something **(up)** *tv.* + *obj.* (+ *adv.*) to enclose someone or something in a cover. □ *Anne wrapped the present in colorful paper.*

**2. wrap** something **up** *tv.* + *obj.* + *adv.* to bring something to an end; to conclude something. □ *John wrapped the production report up with some good news.* 🅃 *He wrapped up the report, and we all went home.*

**wrath** ['ræθ] *n.* severe anger, especially from someone with a lot of power. (No plural form.) □ *The sinners feared the wrath of God.*

**wreak** ['rik] *tv.* to cause damage or harm to someone or something. □ *The gangster wreaked revenge on his brother's murderer.*

**wreath** ['riθ] *n., irreg.* a decoration of flowers and leaves arranged in a certain shape, especially a circle. (Pl: ['riθs] or ['riðz].) □ *A mourner put a wreath of flowers near the coffin.*

**wreathe** ['rið] *tv.* to make a circle around something. □ *A circle of flowers wreathed the tree.*

**wreck** ['rɛk] **1.** *n.* a serious accident, especially where something is destroyed. □ *Many people died in the wreck.* **2.** *n.* a ruined vehicle that remains after a serious accident. □ *The police carefully pulled the injured man out of the wreck.* **3.** *n.* someone or something that is a mess. (Fig. on ②.) □ *I feel like a wreck because I drank too much last night.* **4.** *tv.* to destroy something. □ *The scandal wrecked the politician's chances of being elected.*

**wreckage** ['rɛk ɪdʒ] *n.* whatever remains after a serious accident or disaster. (No plural form. Treated as singular.) □ *The rescue workers examined the plane wreckage.*

**wrench** ['rɛntʃ] **1.** *n.* a tool that turns nuts, bolts, pipes, and other objects that are rotated into or out of position. □ *I tightened the wrench around the nut.* **2.** *tv.* to twist or pull something with force. □ *Anne wrenched the stubborn lid from the jar.* **3.** *tv.* to injure a part of the body by twisting it or pulling it. □ *David wrenched his ankle when he fell off his skis.*

**wrestle** ['rɛs əl] **1.** *tv.* to force someone or something loose, down, away, etc., with force. □ *Anne wrestled the knife from the criminal.* **2.** *iv.* to participate in the sport of wrestling. □ *My brother wrestled when he was in high school.*

**wrinkle** ['rɪŋ kəl] **1.** *n.* a crease; a small fold or line, such as in clothing that has not been ironed or on the skin of an old person. □ *I used an iron to remove the wrinkles from my cotton shirt.* **2.** *iv.* to become creased; to get small lines in one's skin or on the surface of something. □ *John's face has wrinkled from excessive exposure to the sun.* **3.** *tv.* to cause someone's skin or the surface of something to have **wrinkles** ①; to cause creases, folds, or lines to form on the surface of someone or something. □ *John wrinkled his pants by sleeping in them.*

**wrist** ['rɪst] *n.* the part of the body where the hand joins the lower part of the arm. □ *I wear a bracelet around my wrist.*

**write** ['rɑɪt] **1.** *tv., irreg.* to make words or symbols on a surface with a pen, pencil, chalk, etc. (Pt: **wrote**; pp: **written**.) □ *Mary wrote a 4 on the check.* **2.** *tv., irreg.* to put thoughts or ideas into writing; to organize words or symbols into meaningful prose. □ *Susan wrote her term paper on a computer.* **3. write** something **down** *tv., irreg.* + *obj.* + *adv.* to **write** ① information onto something, such as paper. □ *I know I wrote her address down and put it in my desk.* 🅃 *I wrote down her address and put it somewhere.* **4.** *iv., irreg.* to mark on a surface with a pen, pencil, chalk, etc., as with ②. □ *The young children wrote on the walls with crayons.* **5.** *iv., irreg.* to work by creating the content for books, articles, movies, plays, or other texts; to be an author; to be a writer. □ *Jane writes now, but she used to be an editor.* **6.** *iv., irreg.* to prepare and send a letter or note to someone. □ *Bill wrote to me, asking if he could borrow $100.*

**writer** ['raɪt ɚ] *n.* an author who writes for a living; someone who has written something. □ *Who is the writer of this report?*

**writhe** ['raɪð] *iv.* to twist and turn (as though) in pain. □ *Bill writhed in pain after he had been struck.*

**writing** ['raɪt ɪŋ] **1.** *n.* making sentences, words, or letters with a pen, a pencil, chalk, or other writing instrument. (No plural form.) □ *I hurt my wrist, and that makes writing difficult.* **2.** sentences, words, or letters made with a pen, a pencil, chalk, or other writing instrument. (No plural form.) □ *I saw that the piece of paper had writing on it.* **3.** *n.* something that is written; a book, poem, or other document. (Sometimes plural with the same meaning.) □ *Susan bought a book of her favorite author's early writing.*

**written** ['rɪt n] **1.** pp of **write**. **2.** *adj.* placed in writing; printed or spelled out in writing. □ *She asked the plumber for a written estimate of the repair bill.* □ *Jane quit her job after receiving a written contract for a better one.*

**wrong** ['rɔŋ] **1.** *adj.* not correct; not true; mistaken; in error. (Adv: *wrongly.*) □ *You're driving the wrong way down a one-way street!* **2.** *adj.* bad; evil; illegal; immoral; not lawful. (Adv: *wrongly.*) □ *Harming animals is wrong.* **3.** *adj.* not desired; not wanted; incorrect. (Adv: *wrongly.*) □ *I almost got on the wrong train this morning!* **4.** *adj.* out of order; not working properly; faulty. □ *What is wrong with the elevator?* **5.** *adv.* in the **wrong** ③ way. □ *She sang the note wrong, and it sounded very bad.* **6.** *n.* a bad, illegal, improper, or immoral action. □ *This is a wrong that I cannot forgive you for.* **7.** *tv.* to treat someone badly or unfairly. □ *John wronged me when he spread gossip about me.*

**wrote** ['rot] pt of **write**.

W

**Xerox™** ['zɪr ɑks] *n.* a copy of a document, made on a copier manufactured by Xerox™. (A protected trade name for a process used to make copies of documents.) □ *Please make a Xerox of this for me.*

**X-ray** ['ɛks re] **1.** *n.* a ray of energy that can pass through solid or nearly solid matter, such as the body. (Used especially to take pictures of the insides of people or objects.) □ *A lot of exposure to X-rays is very dangerous.* **2.** *n.* a picture of the inside of a person or an object, made by passing ① through the person or object onto film. □ *The emergency-room doctor looked at the X-ray of Jane's foot.* **3.** *tv.* to take a picture of the inside of a person or an object using ①. □ *The technician X-rayed Jane's foot.*

**xylophone** ['zɑɪ lə fon] *n.* a musical instrument made of a series of wooden bars of different sizes, each of which makes a different note when struck with a small wooden hammer. □ *Mary plays the xylophone in the orchestra.*

**yacht** ['jɑt] **1.** *n.* a large boat or ship used for pleasure or racing. (Powered by sails, engines, or both.) □ *I will never be wealthy enough to own a yacht.* **2.** *iv.* to travel somewhere on water in ①. □ *The Smiths yacht to their private island each spring.*

**yam** ['jæm] **1.** *n.* a vegetable similar to the potato, grown in tropical areas. □ *On the tropical island, the people ate mostly yams and rice.* **2.** *n.* a sweet potato, which is orange and does not taste like a potato. □ *We always have yams with our Thanksgiving dinner.*

**yank** ['jæŋk] **1.** *tv.* to pull someone or something quickly, with force. □ *Jane yanked the door open and left the room angrily.* **2. yank on** something *iv. + prep. phr.* to pull or jerk something, with force. □ *Susie yanked on the rope too hard and broke it.* **3.** *n.* a quick pull; a sharp tug. □ *I gave the stuck door a yank, and it opened.*

**yard** ['jɑrd] **1.** *n.* a unit of measurement of length equal to 36 inches, 3 feet, or 91.44 centimeters. □ *The tailor bought three yards of fabric.* **2.** *n.* the land that surrounds a house or other dwelling. □ *The dog is out in the yard.*

**yardstick** ['jɑrd stɪk] **1.** *n.* a ruler that is 36 inches—that is, one yard—long. □ *Dave measured the couch with a yardstick before buying it.* **2.** *n.* something that other things are compared with; a standard. (Fig. on ①.) □ *I use my mother's cooking as a yardstick to judge all others'.*

**yarn** ['jɑrn] **1.** *n.* thick, soft thread that is used for things like knitting or weaving. (Number is expressed with *ball(s)* or *skein(s) of yarn.)* □ *Mary knitted a sweater with cotton yarn.* **2.** *n.* a tale; a story that is not completely true. □ *Max told Mary a yarn about his past.*

**yawn** ['jɔn] **1.** *iv.* to stretch one's mouth open and breathe in and out slowly and deeply, especially when one is tired or bored. □ *The student yawned during the boring lecture.* **2.** *iv.* [for something like a hole] to have a very wide opening. (Fig. on ①.) □ *A gaping hole yawned in the road ahead of us, and we had to stop the car quickly.* **3.** *n.* an act of opening one's mouth, as in ①. □ *The cat opened its mouth with a big yawn.*

**year** ['jɪr] **1.** *n.* 12 months; 365 or 366 days; the time it takes for Earth to revolve around the sun. □ *A year has passed since I've seen my parents.* **2.** *n.* ① or part of ① spent doing a certain activity. □ *The school year lasts from September through May.* **3.** *n.* a particular level of study in a school, college, or university. □ *Most of my friends are in the same year in school as I am.*

**yearly** ['jɪr li] **1.** *adj.* happening once a year; occurring each year; happening every year. □ *Jane makes a yearly visit to her mother in January.* **2.** *adv.* once a year; each year; every year. □ *John sees his doctor yearly.*

**yeast** ['jist] *n.* a very small plant that causes bread to rise and is also used to make alcohol. (Plural only when referring to different kinds, types, instances, or varieties.) □ *Yeast is an important ingredient of bread.* Ⓒ *Not all yeasts are suitable for making bread.*

**yell** ['jɛl] **1.** *tv.* to say something loudly; to scream something; to shout something. □ *Jane yelled the message to me* *from across the house.* **2.** *iv.* to speak loudly; to scream; to shout. □ *We try not to yell at our children.* **3.** *n.* a loud cry; a shout. □ *Mary thought she heard a yell from downstairs.*

**yellow** ['jɛl o] **1.** *n.* the color of a ripe lemon or of the yolk of an egg. (Plural only when referring to different kinds, types, instances, or varieties.) □ *The lemons growing on the trees made a bright display of yellow and green.* Ⓒ *Bright yellows and fresh, clean greens will make this drab old kitchen really sparkle!* **2.** *adj.* <the adj. use of ①.> (Comp: *yellower;* sup: *yellowest.*) □ *This flower has a yellow center and white petals.* **3.** *adj.* timid; scared to do something. (Informal. Comp: *yellower;* sup: *yellowest.*) □ *Bill was too yellow to stand up to the bully.*

**yelp** ['jɛlp] **1.** *n.* a short, high-pitched bark; a short, high-pitched shout of pain or emotion. □ *The puppy gave a yelp when I stepped on its tail.* **2.** *iv.* to make ①. □ *The puppy yelped in pain when its tail got closed in the door.*

**yen** ['jɛn] **1.** *n.* a strong desire; a strong feeling of wanting something. (No plural form.) □ *Jane has a yen to go climbing in the Rockies.* **2.** *n., irreg.* the basic unit of money in Japan. (Also ¥. Pl: *yen.*) □ *I exchanged my dollars for yen when I traveled to Tokyo.*

**yes** ['jɛs] **1.** *n.* a statement showing that someone agrees with something or gives permission to do something. □ *The boss gave me a yes. We can do it.* **2.** *n.* an act of voting showing that one agrees with the proposal. □ *There were four yeses and two nos.* **3.** *adv.* <a word showing approval, consent, or willingness.> □ *Yes, I will.* **4.** *adv.* <a word emphasizing a positive statement, especially when denying a negative one.> □ *"I will not eat my peas." "Yes, you will."*

**yesterday** ['jɛs tɚ de] **1.** *n.* the day before today. □ *Yesterday was my birthday, so that's why I wasn't at work.* **2.** *adv.* on the day before today. □ *I sent the package yesterday. It should be there tomorrow.*

**yet** ['jɛt] **1.** *adv.* up to a certain point in time; by a certain point in time; as of a certain point in time. □ *Our guests have not arrived yet.* **2.** *adv.* eventually, even with barriers and delays. □ *I will conquer this problem yet!* **3.** *adv.* still; even; even more. □ *The doorbell rang yet again.* **4.** *adv.* and in spite of that; however; nevertheless. □ *Mary is friendly and yet very shy.* **5.** *conj.* but; however; nevertheless; although. □ *I'm glad you got the promotion, yet I wish it had been me.*

**yield** ['jild] **1.** *iv.* to bend, break, or move out of the way because of someone or something that is stronger or more powerful. □ *The sign yielded in the wind and fell over.* **2.** *iv.* to surrender to someone or something, especially someone or something that is stronger or more powerful; to submit to someone or something. □ *Mary finally yielded and gave her children more candy.* **3.** *iv.* to allow other traffic or people to have the right of way; to allow another vehicle or person to move first. □ *The van yielded to the car at the stop sign.* **4.** *tv.* [for plants or animals] to supply or produce something such as food. □ *The damaged crops yielded very little.* **5. yield** something **to** someone *tv. + obj. + prep. phr.* to surrender or give up something to someone. □ *The dying leader yielded his power to his assistant.* **6.** *n.* the amount of something that is produced. □ *The field's high yield made the farmer rich.*

**yoke** ['jok] **1.** *n.* a frame of wood that fits around the necks of animals so they can pull something heavy that is attached to it. (Compare this with **yolk**.) □ *The oxen wore a yoke, which was attached to the plow.* **2.** *tv.* to put ① on oxen or other strong animals. ☐ *Max yoked the mules and began to plow.*

**yolk** ['jok] **1.** *n.* the round, yellow part inside an egg. (Compare this with **yoke**.) ☐ *The chef broke open an egg and carefully separated the yolk from the white of the egg.* **2.** *n.* the substance of ①. (No plural form. Compare this with **yoke**.) ☐ *Egg yolk contains a lot of fat and vitamins.*

**yonder** ['jɑn dɚ] *adv.* over there. ☐ *My aunt lives yonder, past the bridge.*

**you** ['ju] *pron.* <the second-person pronoun, singular and plural.> ☐ *I gave you the letter yesterday, and you gave it to Jane.*

**you'd** ['jud] **1.** *cont.* "you would." ☐ *If you'd move over, I would sit down.* **2.** *cont.* "you had," where **had** is an auxiliary. ☐ *I called you, but you'd already gone out.*

**you'll** ['jul] *cont.* "you will." ☐ *You'll be finished with school before you know it!*

**young** ['jʌŋ] **1.** *adj.* in the early part of life; not old; having been alive for a short period of time as compared with an average age. (Comp: *younger;* sup: *youngest.*) ☐ *The young student was eager to experience the world.* **2.** *adj.* new; in an early stage of development; recently formed or started. (Comp: *younger;* sup: *youngest.*) ☐ *The historian spoke of the time when the country was young.* **3.** *n.* the offspring of an animal or a human. (No plural form. Treated as plural. Countable, but not usually used for one offspring.) ☐ *Some wild animals abandon their young.*

**young lady** ['jʌŋ 'led i] *n.* a young girl of any age; a female who is young, relative to the speaker. (Also a term of address.) ☐ *How are you, young lady?*

**young man** ['jʌŋ 'mæn] *n.* a boy of any age; a male who is young, relative to the speaker. (Also a term of address.) ☐ *Thank you, young man, for opening the door for me.*

**youngster** ['jʌŋ stɚ] *n.* a young person; a child. ☐ *All the youngsters gathered around Grandpa for a story.*

**young woman** ['jʌŋ 'wʊm ən] *n.* a young adult female human; a female who is young, relative to the speaker. ☐ *Ask the young woman at the desk what office you should go to.*

**your** ['jʊɚ] *pron.* <the possessive form of **you**, the second-person singular and plural pronoun>; belonging to the person(s) being spoken or written to. (Used as a modifier before a noun.) ☐ *This is your shirt. Please put it on.*

**you're** ['jʊɚ] *cont.* "you are." ☐ *You're late again.*

**yours** ['jʊɚz] *pron.* <the possessive form of **you**, the second-person singular and plural pronoun>; the one or ones belonging to the person(s) being spoken or written to. (Used in place of a noun.) ☐ *I have my sandwich. Where is yours?*

**yourself** [jʊɚ 'sɛlf] **1.** *pron.* <the reflexive form of the singular of **you**.> ☐ *Be careful with those scissors! You'll cut yourself!* **2.** *pron.* <a strong form of **you** [singular].> ☐ *You yourself must be there to accept the gift.* **3. by yourself** *phr.* with the help of no one else. ☐ *Bill, can you lift this by yourself?* **4. by yourself** *phr.* with no one else present; alone. ☐ *Don't sit at home by yourself. Come to the movie with me.*

**yourselves** [jʊɚ 'sɛlvz] **1.** *pron.* <the reflexive form of the plural of **you**.> ☐ *I can't help all of you. You'll have to fend for yourselves.* **2.** *pron.* <a strong form of **you** [plural].> ☐ *All of you listening to me here, you yourselves must make the decision, and it should be the right one.* **3. by yourselves** *phr.* with the help of no one else. ☐ *Can you do this by yourselves?* **4. by yourselves** *phr.* with no one else present; alone. □ *Don't sit home by yourselves. Come to the party.*

**youth** ['juθ] **1.** *n.* the quality of being young. (No plural form.) □ *The older woman wished she still had her youth.* **2.** *n.* the period of time when one is a child or teenager. (No plural form.) □ *Bill spent his youth in a home for orphans.* **3.** *n.* children or teenagers, as a group. (No plural form. Treated as plural, but not countable.) □ *Tom worked with poor youth in the city.* **4.** *n.* someone who is young, especially a male; a child or teenager. □ *The policeman caught the two youths who stole the bicycle.*

**you've** ['juv] *cont.* "you have," where **have** is an auxiliary. □ *Let me know when you've finished with the computer.*

**yummy** ['jʌm i] *adj.* having a good taste; delicious. (Comp: *yummier;* sup: *yummiest.*) □ *Bill served us some yummy cookies.*

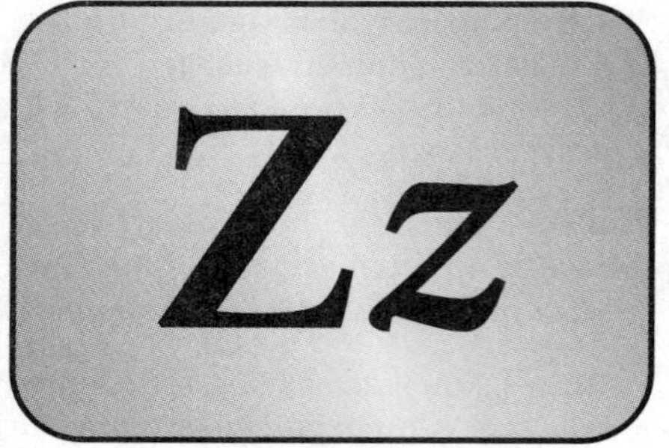


**zeal** ['zil] *n.* a strong passion for a belief or cause; excitement. (No plural form.) □ *The preacher always preached with great zeal.*

**zebra** ['zi brə] *n., irreg.* a horse-like mammal that has a whitish hide with dark brown or black stripes. (Pl: *zebra* or *zebras.*) □ *Zebras live on the plains of Africa.*

**zenith** ['zi nɪθ] **at the zenith of something** *phr.* at the highest point of something; at the peak of something. □ *At the zenith of his career, the teacher died suddenly.*

**zephyr** ['zɛf ɚ] *n.* a gentle wind; a breeze. □ *A zephyr rustled the tall grass by the shore.*

**zero** ['zi ro] **1.** *n.* the number 0; 0. (Pl ends in *-s* or *-es.*) □ *Six plus zero is six.* **2.** *n.* nothing. (No plural form.) □ *I did absolutely zero at work today.*

**zest** ['zɛst] *n.* enjoyment, especially for life; excitement. (No plural form.) □ *The hikers had a zest for adventure.*

**zinc** ['zɪŋk] *n.* a metal and an element. (No plural form.) □ *Zinc is a metal that is used in making brass.* □ *Zinc's atomic number is 30, and its atomic symbol is Zn.*

**zip** ['zɪp] **1.** *tv.* to open or close something, using a zipper. □ *Mary zipped Jimmy's coat.* **2.** *iv.* to move somewhere very quickly. □ *The kitten zipped across the room.* **3.** *n.* energy; vigor. (No plural form.) □ *Mary had lots of zip after her nap.*

**zip code** ['zɪp kod] *n.* one of the five-digit or nine-digit numbers that is part of the United States Postal Service's postal coding system. (An acronym for *Zone Improvement Plan.* Often written *ZIP code.*) □ *You must include the ZIP code in the address.*

**zipper** ['zɪp ɚ] **1.** *n.* a fastener made of two strips of tiny teeth that lock together when a sliding piece is moved over them. □ *The zipper on Mike's pants jammed.* **2.** *tv.* to zip something; to open or close something using ①. □ *Mary zippered Jimmy's coat for him.*

**zone** ['zon] **1.** *n.* an area, especially one that is different in some way from nearby areas. □ *The factory was built in a manufacturing zone.* **2.** *tv.* to divide a city into different areas limited only to certain uses; to limit an area to certain uses. □ *This neighborhood has not been zoned for industry.*

**zoo** ['zu] *n.* a place or park where wild animals are kept so that they can be seen by people. □ *Jimmy's parents took him to the zoo to see the elephants.*

**zookeeper** ['zu kip ɚ] *n.* someone who takes care of animals at a zoo. □ *The city zoo employs dozens of zookeepers.*